CHEMICAL ANALYSIS

other volumes in preparation

CHEMICAL ANALYSIS

A SERIES OF MONOGRAPHS ON
ANALYTICAL CHEMISTRY AND ITS APPLICATIONS

Volume 22

INTERSCIENCE PUBLISHERS

A division of John Wiley & Sons, New York/London/Sydney

The Analytical Toxicology
of
Industrial Inorganic Poisons

MORRIS B. JACOBS, Ph.D.

late Professor of Occupational Medicine
School of Public Health and Administrative Medicine
Columbia University, New York City

1967

INTERSCIENCE PUBLISHERS

a division of John Wiley & Sons, New York/London/Sydney

Library of Congress Catalog Card Number 66-28539

PRINTED IN THE UNITED STATES OF AMERICA

PREFACE

Twelve years have passed since the publication of the second edition of *The Analytical Chemistry of Industrial Poisons, Hazards, and Solvents* and over twenty since the first edition of that book. In this period of time *Analytical Chemistry of Industrial Poisons* has been accepted virtually throughout the world as the standard text for chemical analytical methods in the field of industrial hygiene. This acceptance has been a source of great pride to the author.

With the passage of years new problems have arisen and new methods have appeared so that it has become necessary to make a complete revision of the second edition. The revision, indeed, has been so complete as to become an entirely new book, now entitled *The Analytical Toxicology of Industrial Inorganic Poisons*. Some of the material of the first and second editions of *Analytical Chemistry of Industrial Poisons* has been deleted. Indeed, the author was tempted to delete much more but the temptation was resisted because of the need to include in some book the historical background of the methods used in industrial hygiene. It would be a mistake, however, to assume that the older methods are of little value merely because they are old or that newer methods are better merely because they are new. A well established method has the advantage that the analyst knows the manipulative steps and the possible sources of error well.

This book differs from *Analytical Chemistry of Industrial Poisons* not only in the incorporation of methods for new industrial poisons and new methods for some well known industrial poisons but also by the addition of new chapters on (*1*) methods for evaluating the absorption of industrial poisons, that is, methods for the determination of such substances in the blood and urine, (*2*) radioactive nuclides, and (*3*) tube detectors. The chapter on war gases that was present in the first edition of *Analytical Chemistry of Industrial Poisons* and deleted from the second edition has been revised and expanded in the light of more recent knowledge.

As in prior editions the author has tried to give adequate acknowledgement.

Morris B. Jacobs

Jericho, Long Island

v

Note

My father, Dr. Morris B. Jacobs, died suddenly on July 12, 1965. Unfortunately he had not completed the preface and it is therefore impossible to thank specifically the many people who were generous with help and information. To those I offer my sincere apologies and hope that adequate acknowledgment is included either in the text or in the references.

Special thanks must be given to Mr. Moe Braverman who helped me to write Chapter XIX, and to Mr. Roger Jacobs who searched the literature to provide missing references and methods. Mrs. Margaret Jacobs also provided valuable assistance by her patient searching among her husband's papers for necessary material. The bulk of the book was completed by Dr. Jacobs before his death, including the compilation of most of the material for Chapter XIX. Completion of that chapter, with the index and some purely mechanical work on the references and illustrations for other chapters, are my sole contribution to this volume.

ROBERTA LEAH GELLIS

Roslyn Heights, Long Island
Jan. 1967

Definitions of Terms and Explanatory Notes

1. The term *water* used in the methods means distilled water.

2. The terms *alcohol* and *ether* refer respectively to 95% ethyl alcohol and to ethyl ether.

3. The following reagents, unless otherwise specified or qualified in the text, have the approximate strength stated and conform in purity with the requirements of the United States Pharmacopoeia.

sulfuric acid	specific gravity 1.84
hydrochloric acid	specific gravity 1.184
nitric acid	specific gravity 1.42
fuming nitric acid	specific gravity 1.50
glacial acetic acid	specific gravity 1.048 (25°C)
hydrobromic acid	specific gravity 1.38
phosphoric acid	85% strength by weight
ammonium hydroxide	specific gravity 0.90

4. All other reagents and test solutions, unless otherwise described in the text, conform to the specifications of the United States Pharmacopoeia or of the American Chemical Society. When the anhydrous salt is intended to be used, it is so stated; otherwise, the salt referred to is the crystallized product.

5. In the expressions (1:2), (5:4), etc., used in connection with the name of a reagent, the first numeral indicates the volume of the reagent used, and the second numeral indicates the volume of water. For example, hydrochloric acid (1:2) means a reagent prepared by mixing one volume of hydrochloric acid with two volumes of water. When one of the reagents is a solid, the expression means parts by weight, the first numeral representing the weight of the solid reagent and the second numeral the weight of water in similar units.

6. In making up solutions of definite percentage, it is understood that x g of substance is dissolved in water or other solvent and made up to 100 ml. Although not theoretically correct, this procedure will not result in any appreciable error in any of the methods given in this book.

7. All calculations are based on the table of international atomic weights.

8. The following abbreviations are used and have the indicated meaning:

C	Centigrade degrees	$m\mu$	millimicron
cfm	cubic feet per minute	μ	micron
emf	electromotive force	μg	microgram
F	Fahrenheit degrees	N	normal, with reference to solutions
g	gram		
lb	pound	ppm	parts per million
lpm	liters per minute	rem	roentgen equivalent man
mg	milligram	rpm	revolutions per minute
mg/liter	milligrams per liter	sp gr	specific gravity
ml	milliliter	STP	standard temperature and pressure
mm	millimeter		
mm^3	cubic millimeters		

The abbreviations of periodicals, bulletins, circulars, leaflets, etc., referred to in the footnotes follow, in general, the system of *Chemical Abstracts*.

9. In the use of the expression "parts per million of X," it is understood that the expression means volumes of X per million volumes of air. The author has tried to differentiate when this expression is used with reference to a solution, by the statement "parts of X per million of solution."

The proper way to proceed is to read the method at least twice to completion. On the third reading the reagents are prepared. Then if the determination has never been performed by the analyst before, known control and blank samples are used. Only after some experience with known samples has been obtained should the test samples be analyzed.

CONTENTS

CHAPTER I

INDUSTRIAL HYGIENE AND INDUSTRIAL POISONS

A. Introduction

The expanded use of chemicals in industry, in commerce, and in the home over the past six decades has made the study of these chemicals and their effects on our health of current and continuing importance. One need only think of the greatly increased use of household chemicals, food additives, plastics, synthetic organic chemicals, organic solvents, diluents and plasticizers, insecticides, fungicides, germicides, rodenticides, blowing agents, plating solutions, and radioactive isotopes to realize how widely chemicals are used and how closely they affect us at work, in commerce, at home, and indeed even at play.

The World War of 1914–1918 very likely was the greatest single factor in the introduction of care in the manufacture of organic chemicals, for it drew an impressive picture of the dangers of gases and vapors. The war certainly stressed the need for protection against these hazards. The huge increase in the production of organic chemicals to meet the needs of war for explosives, chemical agents, and other war matériel made it necessary to learn how to protect both workers and soldiers using or subjected to this matériel. The precautionary measures developed as a result of World War I received even greater emphasis in World War II, particularly in measures which had to be devised to protect workers engaged in the manufacture of fissionable material and other war matériel such as poison gas and bacterial toxins.

The prevention, control, and regulation of industrial poisoning lie in the hands of the physician, the industrial hygiene engineer, the chemist, and, more recently, the health physicist. The earliest and unquestionably the most important progress in recognizing, treating, and remedying industrial hazards was made by the medical profession. In more recent years the role of the industrial hygiene engineer and the chemist has become relatively more important.

Over 40 years of industrial hygiene experience have emphasized the work of the chemist and industrial hygiene engineer in the prevention of industrial poisoning, the protection of the worker, and the control of the industrial environment. Such prevention, protection, and control depends upon the chemical analyses performed to give an evaluation of (1) the concentration of a poisonous or noxious substance in the working atmosphere and therefore the exposure level, (2) the amount of poisonous or harmful material absorbed by the worker, (3) the efficiency of control devices, and (4) the adequacy of placement of control devices.

In addition, analyses must also be performed in industry-wide surveys, in investigations of complaints, and in research work such as the evaluation of a potential hazard of a new substance or of a well-known substance used in a new manner. The latter may imply the development of new methods of analysis.

The chemist supplies the necessary analytical devices and methods. His results indicate how much of a toxic, noxious, or hazardous material is present. The ability to estimate quantitatively the amount of a toxic or otherwise hazardous material is a most important factor in the lessening of any menace to the health of employees. Based upon these quantitative analytical results, the corrections and improvements needed to alleviate a hazardous condition can be made. The knowledge of the amount and location of contamination is of inestimable value in designing the means of prevention and elimination of the poison. In testing the air of a large garage, it was found that 10 ft away from the exhaust of a running car, there were 1000 parts of carbon monoxide per million parts of air present (0.1% by volume), whereas 30 ft away from the same car it was impossible to get a positive test for this poisonous gas (1). The prevention of hazard in such an instance and in analogous cases needs special design and treatment that can more readily be obtained with the aid of the analysis made by the chemist.

Where new materials or substances are developed or where well-known substances are used for new procedures, the chemist can devise methods for the estimation of these substances, taking into consideration the methods of use. A veritable host of new materials is being developed.

B. Industrial Hygiene

Industrial hygiene is an applied science, as distinguished from the theoretical sciences such as mathematics or physics. It is defined (2) as the art and science of the preservation and improvement of the health and comfort of workers. More broadly, "industrial hygiene is that science and art devoted to the recognition, evaluation and control of those environmental factors or stresses, arising in or from the work place, which may cause sickness, impaired health and well being, or significant discomfort and inefficiency among workers or among the citizens of the community" (3). It therefore involves primarily a program of health conservation and accident and occupational-disease prevention. Such a program necessarily extends beyond prevention of accidents and occupational diseases; it includes also the broad subject of the health of the worker. It is obvious that some of the problems arise from the nature of the industrial environment itself—namely, the control of poisons, dusts, excessive temperatures and humidities, defective lighting, noise, overcrowding, and general plant sanitation. The problems also involve such factors as hours of work, fatigue, communicable diseases in the factory, mental health, and personal hygiene. An industrial hygiene program thus necessitates the cooperation of a number of professional personnel including the physician, engineer, chemist, physicist, statistician, nurse, and dentist. Its aim is to protect and improve the health of workers. As an applied science, it has a number of major subdivisions, among which may be mentioned:

Industrial Medicine, which includes medical care, prevention of industrial illness, hospitalization, and medical aspects of compensation.

Industrial Mental Hygiene, which includes behavior of workers and the mental state and health of workers.

Industrial Management, which includes hours of labor, rest periods, adequate food, supervision, and the general economic relationships of laborers and their health.

Industrial Sanitation, which includes environment of the worker, buildings, machinery, air conditioners, ventilation, exhaust, and, in general, all engineering aspects.

Industrial Toxicology, which includes detection and estimation of hazards; prevention, diminution, and elimination of hazards, toxicants, etc. (Industrial toxicology may be more broadly defined as that section of industrial hygiene that deals with diseases attributable to exposure in the course of work to materials or substances the harmfulness of which is due to their chemical nature.)

Our main study will be with the one secton of industrial toxicology that deals with the detection, estimation, and determination of industrial poisons and other harmful industrial substances.

There has been substantial progress in the field of industrial hygiene over the past five decades, but it must be understood that the rate of development of industrial products has been so rapid that the direct and indirect effects of these products on the health of the worker and also on the health of the user and on the general environment have not been evaluated adequately (4). Indeed, when one looks at the problem from this point of view, industrial toxicology is only one phase of the general field of environmental health.

The definition of an industrial hygienist and the scope and functions of industrial hygiene have been stated by the American Industrial Hygiene Association with the aid of a committee consisting of Radcliffe, Clayton, Fredrick, Nelson, and Wheeler (3) as follows:

Industrial Hygienist

An Industrial Hygienist is a person having a college or university degree or degrees in engineering, chemistry, physics, or medicine or related biological sciences who, by virtue of special studies and training, has acquired competence in Industrial Hygiene. Such special studies and training must have been sufficient in all of the above cognate sciences to provide the abilities: (1) to recognize the environmental factors and stresses associated with work and work operations and to understand their effect on man and his well being; (2) to evaluate, on the basis of experience and with the aid of quantitative measurement techniques, the magnitude of these stresses in terms of ability to impair man's health and well being; and (3) to prescribe methods to eliminate, control or reduce such stresses when necessary to alleviate their effects.

Scope of Industrial Hygiene

Industrial Hygiene primarily involves: (1) the recognition of environmental factors and stresses associated with work and work operations, and the understanding of their effects on man and his well being in the work place and the community; (2) the evaluation, through training and experience, and with the aid of quantitative measurement techniques, of the magnitude of these factors and stresses in terms of ability to impair man's health and well being; and (3) the prescription of methods to control or reduce such factors and stresses when necessary to alleviate their effects.

Recognition of environmental factors and stresses which influence health requires a familiarity with work operations and processes. The categories of stresses most frequently of interest are: (1) chemical, in the form of liquid, dust, fume, mist, vapor or gas; (2) physical energy, such as electromagnetic and ionizing radiations, noise and vibration, and extremes of temperature and pressure; (3) biological, such as insects and mites, molds, yeasts and fungi, bacteria, and viruses; (*4*) ergonomic, such as body position in relation to task, monotony, boredom, repetitive motion, worry, work pressure and fatigue. The effect of these four areas of stress on man's health and well-being must be recognized. It is important to know whether such stresses are immediately dangerous to life and health, whether they produce an acceleration of the aging process or whether they will cause only significant discomfort and inefficiency.

Evaluation of the magnitude of the environmental factors or stresses arising in or from the work place is essential in order to predict the probable effect on health and well being. The Industrial Hygienist, by virtue of training and experience, and aided by quantitative measurement of the chemical, physical energy, biological or ergonomic stresses can render an expert opinion as to the healthfulness of the environment, either for short periods or for a lifetime of exposure.

Prescription of corrective procedures, when necessary to protect health, is based on past experience, knowledge and the quantitative data available. Among control measures most frequently used are: (*1*) isolation of a process or work operation to reduce the number of persons exposed; (*2*) substitution of a less harmful material for one which is more dangerous to health; (*3*) alteration of a process to minimize human contact; (*4*) ventilation and air cleaning to provide an atmosphere safe for human occupancy; (*5*) reduction of exposure to radiant energy by shielding, increasing distance and limiting time; (*6*) wet methods to reduce emission of dust to the atmosphere such as in mining and quarrying; (*7*) good housekeeping, including cleanliness of the work place, proper waste disposal, adequate washing, toilet and restroom facilities, healthful drinking water and eating facilities, and control of insects and rodents; (*8*) personal protective devices, such as special clothing and eye and respiratory protective equipment.

The terms *worker*, *workplace* and *community* as used in this discussion, are hereby defined. A worker is a person engaged in any occupation or vocation. A workplace is any building, structure, excavation, site, device or area in which work is done. A community is the environs of one or more workplaces.

Function of the Industrial Hygienist

Within his sphere of responsibility, the Industrial Hygienist will:

1. Direct the Industrial Hygiene program.
2. Examine the work environment and environs:
    a. Study work operations and processes and obtain full details of the nature of the work, materials and equipment used, products and by-products, number and sex of employees, and hours of work.
    b. Make appropriate measurements to determine the magnitude of exposure or nuisance to workers and the public. In doing so, he will:
       (1) select or devise methods and instruments suitable for such measurements;
       (2) personally or through others under his direct supervision conduct such measurements; and
       (3) study and test material associated with the work operation.

c. Study and test biological materials, such as blood and urine, by chemical and physical means, when such examination will aid in determining the extent of exposure.

3. Interpret results of the examination of the work environment and environs in terms of ability to impair health, nature of health impairment, workers' efficiency and community nuisance and/or damage, and present specific conclusions to appropriate interested parties such as management and health officials.

4. Make specific decisions as to the need for, or effectiveness of, control measures, and when necessary, advise as to the procedures which will be suitable and effective for both the environment and environs.

5. Prepare rules, regulations, standards and procedures for the healthful conduct of work and the prevention of nuisance in the community.

6. Present expert testimony before courts of law, hearing boards, workmen's compensation commissions, regulatory agencies and legally appointed investigative bodies covering all matters pertaining to Industrial Hygiene as described in this document.

7. Prepare appropriate text for labels and precautionary information for materials and products to be used by workers and the public.

8. Conduct programs for the education of workers and the public in the prevention of occupational disease and community nuisance.

9. Conduct epidemiologic studies among workers and industries to discover possibilities of the presence of occupational disease, and establish or improve threshold limit values or standards as guides for the maintenance of health and efficiency.

10. Conduct research to advance knowledge concerning the effects of occupation upon health and means of preventing occupational health impairment, community air pollution, noise, nuisance and related problems.

C. Historical Background

Poisons have been known and used from time immemorial. The Bible and ancient myths make reference to them. However, poisoning attributable to occupation was not so clearly defined in the minds of ancient and medieval men. Hippocrates (ca. 460–357 B.C.) described lead poisoning as an occupational disease only in the smelting of metals. Hippocrates, however, not only noted lead poisoning but also recorded occupational diseases involving other metal workers, fullers (cleaners and dyers), tailors, horsemen, farm hands, and fishermen.

From the time of Hippocrates virtually up to the time of Ramazzini (1633–1711, born in Capri, died in Padua), a period of approximately two millenia, there are only sporadic references to be found in the literature to industrial poisoning. Most of such citations refer to poisoning in miners, but there were some observers who noted other causes of occupational poisoning. Lucretius (ca. 98–55 B.C.), the Roman author, points out in his well-known work *De Rerum Natura* (On the Nature of Things) that the longevity of miners was markedly reduced. Vitruvius Pollio (70–16 B.C.), a Roman architect, engineer, and author, observed that lead poisoning resulted from drinking water that had been collected from lead-covered roofs, transferred to lead storage cisterns, then fed to the public through lead pipes. Pliny the Elder (23–79 A.D.), the famous Roman scholar, describes in *Historiae Naturalis*, Lib. XXXIII, c. 5 (Natural History, Book 33, Chap. 5) a mask comprising a bladder that was tied over the mouth to prevent the inhalation of poisonous dusts and vapors. Martial (ca. 40–102 A.D.), the Roman epigrammatist, in the 57th epigram of his 12th book noted the effects of poisoning from sulfur with the statement: ". . . the blear-eyed huckster of matches."

Galen (ca. 120–200 A.D.), the Greek physician, considered the most illustrious physician after Hippocrates, wrote more about occupational hazards than anyone living before him with the exception of Hippocrates. He described the illness resulting from the fumes of liquid vitriol among other diseases affecting workers.

The poisonous qualities of sulfide ores and carbon monoxide were known to the Greeks and Romans. During the Dark Ages, virtually no references are found to occupational illnesses. Avicenna (980–1036), the Arabian writer of the 11th century, recognized the poisonous properties of arsenic trioxide. In somewhat later medieval times, it was known that arsenic and lead compounds were toxic.

The first printed book on specific industrial poisons, *Von den gifftigen Besen Tempffen und Reüchen der Metal* (On the Poisonous and Noxious Vapors and Fumes of Metals), was written by Ulrich Ellenbog of Feldkirch, Swabia, ca. 1473 although it was not published until about 1524. This book discussed the hazards of lead and mercury.

Paracelsus (ca. 1493–1541), the well-known physician and chemist, who founded the science of iatrochemistry, wrote a book entitled *Von der Bergsucht und anderen Bergkrankheiten der Bergleute* (Concerning Phthisis and other Diseases of Miners) in the period 1531–1534, but it was not published until 1567—some 20 years after he died. It contained the most complete description of such diseases written up to that time.

Georgius Agricola (1494–1555) was a physician and chemist-metallurgist. In his noted book *De Re Metallica* (On Metallic Things) he wrote about poisoning attributable to metals. He mentions a region in the Carpathian mountains where women lost so many husbands from poisoning they were able to marry seven times. The diseases of miners were also discussed in German translations of his Latin writings: *Zwölf Büchern vom Berg- und Hüttenwesen* (Twelve Books on Mining and Smelting) published shortly after his death in 1556. Agricola latinized his name of George Bauer. He was a contemporary of Paracelsus.

Martinus Pansa, a pupil of Agricola, wrote a book the contents of which are readily gathered from the title: *Consilium peripneumoniacum oder Ein getreuer Rath in der beschwerlichen Berg- und Lungensucht, darinnen verfasst was die fürnehmsten Uhrsachen seyn derley Beschwerungen, beydes des giftigen, die vom Bergwerk entsteht so wohl der gemeinen, die von den Flüssen berührt: zuvor aber wie der Mensch mit der kleinen Welt und mit dem Bergwerk Artlich zu vergleichen und wie beyderley suchten zu vertreiben seyn:* Gedruckt zu Leipzig bei Lorenz Kober in Verlegung Thomae Schürers Buchhändlers, in Jahre 1614 (Advice concerning pneumonia or a true Counsel about the troublesome Phthisis and Consumption, wherein is written what the principal Causes are of that kind of Troubles, both the Poisons which arise from the Mine: as well as the common type which derive from the Fusion: above all how the Man with the small World and with the Mine Types compare and how both Diseases can be driven away. Published by Thomae Schürers Publishers, Leipzig bei Lorenz Kober, 1614).

Fallopius Gabriello (1523–1562), an Italian anatomist, noted poisoning in mercury miners in *De Metallis et Fossilibus* (On Metals and Fossils). Jean Fernel discussed mercury poisoning in 1557.

Jan Baptiste Van Helmont (1577–1644), a Belgian physician and chemist (who introduced the word *gas*), thought that the symptoms of miners' diseases were caused by a metallic gas. He wrote *Tractatus De Asthmata Ac Tussi* (Treatise on Asthma and Coughs). Van Helmont was seriously poisoned by coal gas and probably, like Paracelsus, succumbed to the poisons with which he worked.

Samuel Stockhausen, a physician of the Lüneberg mines in Germany, wrote *Tractatus de lithargyri fumo noxio morbifico ejusque metallico frequentiori morbo vulgo die Hüttenkatze cum appendice de montano asthmate, metallicis famililari, vulgo die Bergsucht* (Treatise on the noxious sickening smoke of litharge and other frequent metal diseases commonly called the "Hüttenkatze" with an appendix on mine asthma and familiar metal diseases, commonly the Phthisis). This was published at Goslar in the Harz Mountains in 1656, and it contained as an appendix *Die Bergsucht und anderen Bergkrankheiten* of Paracelsus. This book differentiated the relative toxicities of lead, mercury, arsenic, and cobalt from that of other metals.

One should mention that Antonio Gallonio (who died in 1605), writing under the name of Gallonius, points out in *De Martyrum Cruciatibus* (Crucified Martyrs) that one of the tortures imposed on the early Christians was to sentence them to work in the mines.

An excellent review of the history of the period from Hippocra'es to Ramazzini, with respect to occupational diseases in general as contrasted with industrial poisoning specifically, is given by Goldwater (5). To commemorate the 50th year of service of the Division of Occupational Health of the Public Health Service, the U.S. Department of Health, Education and Welfare issued a pamphlet on historic events in occupational medicine (6).

In the 17th century, Ramazzini, regarded as the "father of industrial hygiene," wrote his famous book *De Morbis Artificum Diatriba* (On Diseases of Tradesmen) (7). The first edition appeared in 1700 and was mainly concerned with dust and metal fumes. The second edition was published in 1717 and contained in addition many occupational illnesses, including chemical poisoning. This book was so important that it was repeatedly translated. Among the more important translations were those of Fourcroy and Ackermann. A. F. Fourcroy (1755–1809), a French chemist wrote *Essai sur les maladies des artisans traduit du Latin de Ramazzini* (Essay on the diseases of artisans, translated from the Latin of Ramazzini), Paris 1777. In addition to the translation, Fourcroy detailed rules for the prevention of occupational poisoning, particularly for those workers doing gilding by use of gold amalgam. An even more comprehensive translation of Ramazzini's book was that of Johann Christian Gottlieb Ackermann: *B. Ramazzini's Abhandlung von den Krankheiten der Künstler und der Handwerker*, neu bearbeitet und vermehrt (B. Ramazzini's Treatise on the Illnesses of Artists and Artisans, reedited and enlarged), Stendal, 1780. This book was about three times as large as the original. Ackermann described gases in mines, such as carbon monoxide and methane, and also described the dangers of dust. He suggested that smelting be carried out in windy places and not in valleys. A review of the period after Ramazzini is given by Teleky (8).

Though a few books were written and some physicians and chemists (Paracelsus, Van Helmont, Agricola, Pansa, and Fourcroy were chemists) were aware of the problem of industrial poisons, actually there was little known, done, or thought with respect to industrial hygiene until recent times (9). The development of industrial hygiene in modern times has been, in a sense, international. Representative of this point of view are the publications of a Frenchman, a Briton, an American, and a German.

Patissier, a Frenchman, reedited Ramazzini's book in 1822 and gave advice on the prevention of occupational poisoning.

Charles Turner Thackrah, a British physician, was one of the earliest observers and commentators on industrial hazards and hygiene. He wrote a short but significant book, published in 1831, entitled *The Effects of the Principal Arts, Trades, and Professions, and of Civic States and Habits of Living on Health and Longevity, with a Particular Reference to the Trades and Manufactures of Leeds, and Suggestions for the Removal of Many of the Agents Which Produce Disease and Shorten the Duration of Life* (10).

In the United States, as early as 1837, B. W. McCready wrote *On the Influence of Trades, Professions, and Occupations in the United States in the Production of Disease* (republished by Johns Hopkins University, Baltimore, in 1943), stressing the influence of industrial activity on disease.

One can mention here that early notice of lead poisoning in America is to be found in Dr. Thomas Cadwalader's *Essay on the West-India Dry-Gripes* published in Philadelphia in 1745. It contained information on the treatment of lead poisoning attributable to distilling rum through lead pipes. Incidentally, this pamphlet was the first medical publication in Philadelphia.

In Germany, A. C. L. Halfort wrote *Entstehung, Verlauf und Behandlung der Krankheiten der Künstler und Handwerker* (Origin, Course, and Treatment of Diseases of Artists and Artisans), Berlin, 1845. In this work, Halfort recommended the replacement of white lead by zinc white.

Had the countries mentioned listened to these pioneers for the betterment of working conditions, the cause of safe and adequate industrial care would have been advanced at least 50 years. It was not until much later that interest in this major problem was again aroused. Dr. Thackrah unfortunately died young and many of his ideas died with him.

A direct result of the expansion caused by the industrial revolution in England was the appalling sanitary conditions described in a report to Parliament in 1842. Edwin Chadwick (11) pioneered in eliminating these evils.

Herman Eulenberg wrote a text on the noxious and poisonous gases in 1865 (*Lehre von den Schaedlichen und giftigen Gasen*, Braunschweig bei Vieweg) and later followed this with a more general text on industrial hygiene (*Handbuch der Gewerbe-Hygiene auf experimentelles Grundlage*, Verlag von August Hirschwald, 1876).

In the past the United States lagged behind other nations in its interest in industrial hygiene, but interest was aroused in the second decade of the 20th century and now probably exceeds that of any other country. Although the first state in the United States to pass any industrial hygiene legislation was Massachusetts in 1852, governmental regulation of industrial hazards may be said to have begun with the passage of the Esch Law in 1912. This law prevented the use of white phosphorus (yellow phosphorus) in matches by placing a prohibitive tax on its use for this purpose. This substance was the cause of the horrible phossy jaw of match workers.

In the United States Government three agencies have been active in the field of industrial hygiene: (*1*) the Public Health Service (presently an arm of the Department of Health, Education and Welfare) started a Division of Industrial Hygiene and Sanitation in 1915; (*2*) the Department of Labor, which was the successor of the Bureau of Labor (1885), was organized in 1913 and had as one of its objectives the collection and distribution of information concerning industrial hygiene; and (*3*) the Bureau of Mines, which was organized in 1910 and has as one of its objectives the protection of mine workers.

The development of industrial hygiene and toxicology has been profoundly influenced by certain scientific organizations. As early as 1914, the Industrial Hygiene Section of the American Public Health Association was organized. In 1916, the American Association of Industrial Physicians and Surgeons was started; in 1938, the American Conference of Governmental Industrial Hygienists; in 1939, the

American Industrial Hygiene Association; and in 1946, the American Academy of Occupational Medicine. Each of these organizations helped to develop the field of industrial hygiene in the United States.

More specifically, the journals and proceedings published by these organizations and others were important in the development of methods in the analytical chemistry of industrial hygiene. Among the more important of these publications were the *United States Public Health Reports, Public Health Service Bulletins, United States Bureau of Mines Reports of Investigations* and *Information Circulars Journal of Public Health, American Industrial Hygine Quarterly* and its successor *American Industrial Hygiene Association Journal, Journal of Industrial Hygiene* (started in 1919) and its successors, *Journal of Industrial Hygiene and Toxicology, Journal of Occupational Medicine, A.M.A. Archives of Industrial Health, Archives of Environmental Health,* and also *Analytical Chemistry* and *The Analyst.*

As mentioned, interest in industrial poisoning was international in the first half of the 19th century. The principal international organizations of the 20th century are the International Labor Organization (ILO) and the World Health Organization (WHO). The ILO was created in 1919 under the terms of the Treaty of Versailles and initially was supported financially by the League of Nations. Both the ILO and WHO are agencies of the United Nations presently. The ILO works principally through governmental labor agencies and the WHO through governmental health departments and ministries. The international aspects of occupational health have been discussed by Goldwater (12).

Interest in industrial hygiene in Latin America was awakened in the 1940's and stimulated and maintained over the succeeding 20 years by John Bloomfield aided by his book, *Introducción a la Higiene Industrial,* published in 1959.

D. Governmental Aspects

That industrial hygiene and the prevention of industrial poisoning in the United States became a recognized major problem is clear from the following quotation from an address given in 1936 by Dr. R. R. Sayers (13), then Chief of the U.S. Bureau of Mines, on "Industrial Hygiene Activities in the United States."

The United States Census for 1930 shows that, at that time, there were approximately 49 million persons gainfully employed in the United States. Of this number, manufacturing, mechanical and mineral industries accounted for nearly 15 million workers. If the term "Industrial Hygiene" means the protection of the health of the worker, it is at once apparent that it is a major problem in public health.

More important than specific occupational diseases associated with the industrial environment is the fact that the incidence of other diseases as tuberculosis, pneumonia and degenerative conditions are greater among the industrial workers than the general population. It has also been shown that the life expectancy of the industrial worker is less than that of the non-industrial worker.

In recent years large industrial establishments have contributed much toward the protection of the health of their workers. However, as nearly 90 per cent of the plants in the United States employ less than 100 persons, many establishments are not prepared to handle effectively the problem of industrial hygiene alone. It would seem, therefore, that the protection of the health of our workers is indeed an important health function and one which can be handled best through a governmental agency, such as a State or local department of health cooperating with the employers and workers.

Responsibility for safeguarding the health of industrial workers rests chiefly with State and local governments. The Federal Government's agencies concerned with industrial hygiene are engaged in collection and dissemination of information, conducting field studies, laboratory research, and protection of the health of the Federal employees.

In 1965 there were over 17 million persons employed in the manufacturing, mechanical, and mineral industries (14). Approximately 2000 plants had 1000 or more employees; some 3000 more plants had less than 1000 but more than 500; thus, these 5000 plants employed nearly 50% of all such workers. Hosey, Keenan, and Yaffe (15) estimated that only 10% of such firms had industrial hygiene programs and that, of the other 8 million persons employed in over 260,000 plants in such industries, very few had industrial hygiene supervision.

One must also remember that some 50 million persons are employed in commerce, transportation, trade, and agriculture and that many of these workers are also exposed to occupational poisoning and other occupational illnesses. With few changes, Sayers's statement is applicable to conditions in 1965. Industrial poisoning is still a major problem.

In the Department of Health, Education and Welfare, the Occupational Health Program conducts the industrial hygiene work of the Public Health Service.   Hosey et al. have listed the major functions of this program:

(1) Studies health hazards on the site and in the laboratory.

(2) Provides technical and consultative assistance to state and local health departments.

(3) Encourages development of preventive health services for employees.

(4) Publishes reports on occupational health problems.

(5) Provides specialized training of state, local, and industrial health personnel.

(6) Cooperates with other governmental agencies concerned with or interested in the health, safety, and welfare of workers.

Governmental industrial hygiene control is, as mentioned, a responsibility of state and local governments.   Existing state agencies offer some or all of the following services (15):

(1) Engineering, laboratory, medical, and nursing consultation on industrial health problems.

(2) Investigation of occupational disease cases reported by physicians.

(3) Assistance in planning or expansion of plant medical and nursing services.

(4) Surveys and detailed studies of workplaces for conditions or processes which may be harmful to health.

(5) Maintenance of a laboratory for analysis of environmental and biological samples and development of methods.

(6) Reports of investigations made, including recommendations for the control of hazards found.

(7) Follow-up services to determine the effectiveness of controls installed.

(8) Examination of plans prepared by industry for the control of hazards.

(9) Educational and informational material on industrial health subjects.

An added factor in the furtherance of industrial health activities is the provision in the federal Wage and Hour Act of 1938 which forbids the employment of children under 16 or the employment of boys or girls under 18 at hazardous or unhealthful work.   This latter provision of the act necessitates determination of whether an occupation is or is not hazardous or unhealthful.   The extension of

Social Security legislation and the participation of the Federal Government in industrial enterprises during World War II, the Korean War, and the postwar period were additional factors in the development of governmental influence on industrial hygiene.

E. Role of the Chemist

While all this has been realized by public-spirited citizens and conscientious civil workers and much work has already been done, even more work for protection needs to be accomplished before one can feel that the problem has been adequately attacked. In this, the chemist should play a most important role. Chemists and chemical engineers should be part of the personnel of every industrial hygiene division, be it of a large industrial establishment, of a medical unit, or of a governmental arm. The plant chemist could well employ part of his time in work that would lead to the diminution and elimination of hazards.

The employer should realize that adequate industrial hygiene—the prevention, diminution, and elimination of industrial hazards and industrial poisoning—is of direct financial importance to him. He gains because better work is obtained as the prevalence of fatigue is diminished. Less time is lost due to illness. Expenses caused by the need of medical care and hospitalization are reduced. The reduction in compensation losses alone is enormous. Sappington (16) noted that of the closed cases in the state of Wisconsin for 1936, 71 cases dealing with "noxious dust," accounted for only 6.6% of the total number of cases of occupational disease disability indemnified during that year. However, the payment of compensation for these cases was $119,737.00, or 54% of the total indemnity paid to the entire group. Compensation payments for occupational illness still comprise a substantial percentage of all such payments.

Not only industry and commerce but also every taxpayer, citizen, and consumer is affected by proper industrial hygiene, for in the last analysis the cost of every item and the governmental budget itself reflects the cost of compensation and the cost of care of the ill and the disabled. Not only does the individual worker gain from the adequate control of hazards and baneful substances but industry and commerce also profit.

The industrial hygiene chemist can aid in the diminution, elimination, prevention, and cure of hazards and poisoning by being able to detect industrial poisons in concentrations far below any quantity that that can cause an injurious or toxic effect. The ability to do this implies, in general, the ability to keep such concentrations down to harmless levels.

The role of the industrial hygiene chemist or industrial toxicologist may be differentiated from that of the medical and forensic toxicologist. Toxicology is that department of pathology or medicine which deals with the nature and effects of poisons. The function of the toxicologist is to analyze, detect, and estimate poisons in order to evaluate their forensic and medical importance. His work is generally limited to a particular victim or patient. A large part of the interest of forensic toxicologist lies in the estimation of alkaloidal, drug, and food poisons and in detecting deliberate poisonings of a homicidal or suicidal nature or poisonings of an accidental or undetermined origin. The function of the industrial hygiene chemist and toxicologist is to detect and estimate poisonous, hazardous, and baneful materials used in industry and commerce. The chemical analyses of the hygiene chemist are used by the physician as an aid in diagnosis and proper therapy.

The importance of the chemist employed for the purpose of the elimination of industrial hazards has another aspect not readily seen. Often the true hazard is not recognized until complete analysis has been made.

In the middle of the 20th century the differentiation between the industrial hygiene chemist working specifically in research on industrial poisons and poisoning and the medical toxicologist became less sharp and the term *industrial toxicologist* became common for such personnel.

F. Scope of Analytical Chemistry as Applied to Industrial Poisons

Whereas many other types of chemical analysis are fairly well delimited—as, for example, inorganic analysis, gas and air analysis, and analysis of metals and alloys—industrial hygiene chemistry covers a wider field. Hazards in industry cover the vast field of chemistry itself, for there are life and fire hazards in every branch of chemistry. Inorganic compounds and mixtures such as rocks, ores, and minerals; organic compounds such as benzene, aniline, and their derivatives; gases such as carbon monoxide, hydrogen sulfide, and methane; and metals such as lead, mercury, arsenic, chromium, and their compounds are all important chemical industrial poisons within the purview of the industrial hygiene chemist.

Not all industrial hazards are poisons in the strict sense of the word. Thus, methane is a hazard because it may be present in sufficient quantity to be either an asphyxiant or a fire hazard. Industrial solvents such as the chlorinated hydrocarbons may not be fire hazards but they can be life hazards. In addition, the industrial hygiene chemist or toxicologist is often called upon to evaluate the potential hazard of known chemicals receiving greater utilization and new chemicals for which extensive use may be found in the future.

Harmful substances are not limited to a small number of industries. Thus, for example, lead is a hazard in over 150 industries, arsenic is a hazard in at least 50 industries, and benzene is a hazard in about 50 industries. The use of industrial solvents is steadily increasing. One may readily see that methods for a definite chemical hazard may be used in a large number of industries with only a few modifications, involving sampling and the like, which are necessary because of the manufacturing process used in the particular industry. Wet-test analyses of solvents have been detailed by Jacobs and Scheflan (17).

The number of occupational disease hazards encountered in an industry may be small, but many industries have a large number of industrial disease hazards. The one industry of tanning has as many as 42 occupational disease exposures (18), many of which are of a chemical nature and among which may be mentioned exposure to hydrogen sulfide, hydrogen cyanide, and arsenic, mercury, and chromium compounds.

G. Industrial Hazards and Poisons

Broadly speaking, the term occupational diseases includes a great variety of conditions arising from the use of harmful substances in connection with various trades and industries, and from exposure to unusual physical conditions, such as excessive heat, prolonged dampness, compressed air, radioactive air, repeated motion, pressure shock, and the like. These causes may conveniently be grouped as follows:

(1) Mechanical
(2) Thermal
(3) Chemical
(4) Photic and radioactive
(5) Electrical
(6) Bacterial and parasitic (anthrax, glanders, etc.)
(7) Atmospheric (air compression, etc.)

or more succinctly classified as physical, chemical, and biologic. We are concerned in this text with the chemical and toxicologic aspects.

Other terms used synonymously with occupational diseases are industrial diseases, diseases of dangerous trades, diseases of environment, maladies of professions, diseases of hazardous occupations, etc. (19–21). The associated diseases, especially those of the respiratory system, such as tuberculosis, pneumonia, chronic bronchitis, and pleurisy, are also included by some authorities; while not due primarily to the occupational hazard, they are sometimes the result of that hazard.

An industrial exposure is not necessarily an occupational disease hazard. The amount, kind, and length of exposure are the determining factors in most cases.

1. DEFINITION OF INDUSTRIAL DISEASE

Sappington (16) defined an industrial disease as one which occurs with characteristic frequency and regularity in occupations where there is a specific hazard as the cause that operates to produce effects in the human body recognized clinically by the medical profession as pathological changes and effects produced by the specific occupational hazard involved.

In this book we cannot be concerned with the conditions of exposure to excessive heat, prolonged dampness, compressed air, infective material such as hides, rags, or wool, or electrical causes, for these conditions are only indirectly concerned with analytical chemistry as applied to industrial hazards. Organic poisons, which are certainly the concern of the analytical chemist, are also excluded from this volume due to size considerations. However, a companion volume on organic industrial poisons by another author is planned.

2. DEFINITION OF INDUSTRIAL POISON

Dr. Thomas M. Legge, a British authority on industrial hygiene, defined an industrial poison (22) not only as a substance which acts chemically and effects transient or permanent injury to the tissues, organs, or functions of the body but also as one that is employed, produced, or somehow occasioned in an industrial occupation and that is brought about (in the absence of sufficient precaution) inadvertently and consequently against the will of the person poisoned.

As a more general definition of a poison, we may use that of Sollmann (23,24): A poison is any substance, which, acting directly through its inherent chemical properties and by its ordinary action, is capable of destroying life or of seriously endangering health when it is applied to the body, externally or in moderate doses (to 50 g) internally.

McNally (25) defines a poison as a substance that, introduced into or upon the body and absorbed into the blood stream, and acting chemically, is capable of seriously affecting health or destroying life.

It is clear from these definitions and that of Sappington's of an industrial disease that an industrial poison is one which produces its harmful effects as a result of repeated exposures or long exposure to even small concentrations of a substance that is not harmful in those small concentrations taken as one dose or inhaled for a short time.

3. CLASSIFICATION OF INDUSTRIAL POISONS

Classification of industrial poisons may be attempted by dividing them into their physical states, viz., gases, liquids, and solids. In order to see how these physical states apply, we must realize that these are the three states in which chemical industrial poisons and hazards may be taken into the body, namely: as gases or vapors, as liquids, and as solid substances or dust.

There are, moreover, three main channels through which these baneful materials can enter the human system and they are:

(1) Breathing into the respiratory tract, as dust, fumes, vapors, mists, or gases.
(2) Swallowing with saliva, water, or food into the digestive tract.
(3) Absorption through the skin.

An example of (1) is the breathing of dust in mine drilling or quarrying, or the breathing of benzene during the use of rubber cement. An example of (2) is the sucking of brushes dipped in radioactive paint. An example of (3) is the absorption of hydrogen cyanide gas or mercury through the skin.

While the above-mentioned means of entrance may be considered the normal modes of entrance into the system, it is necessary to include a fourth type, accidental entrance of industrial poisons. This type includes a miscellaneous grouping such as absorption through cuts into the flesh or irritation of the skin and entrance through the ears and eyes.

The toxicologist classifies poisons into four main groups: metallic poisons, volatile poisons, alkaloidal poisons, and nonalkaloidal poisons. He does so mainly because in many instances he may not know what the poison is and so must isolate and classify it before identification. The industrial hygiene chemist in most instances knows the identity of the hazard and is mainly interested in how much of the baneful substance is present, and where it may be located.

For purposes of clarity and for the purposes this book is designed to serve, harmful substances, industrial poisons, and hazards may better be classified as inorganic or organic chemical substances. These two basic groups may be further subdivided for analytical purposes—the former into metallic and nonmetallic substances and the latter into the main organic chemical groups. The methods of analysis of these substances consequently will fall into one or another of these group types of analysis.

4. Effects of Industrial Poisons

The effect produced in and on the human body by specific industrial poisons will be discussed in the sections devoted to the methods for the analysis of that harmful substance. The damage arising from the inhalation, swallowing, or absorption of an industrial poison may be either local or remote, and depends upon whether the material is a protoplasmic poison, whether it is caustic in reaction, or whether it is absorbed into the blood stream and carried to other centers that in turn are affected (24). Systemic, remote, or indirect effects are produced when the chemical agent is absorbed, i.e., when it has been taken into the blood stream and subsequently carried to all parts of the body. The absorption can be through the lungs, the gastrointestinal tract, or the skin. Some substances affect many parts of the body as, for instance, arsenic which, when absorbed, can cause disturbances in the nervous system, blood, kidneys, liver, and skin. Other substances like benzene appear to affect only one organ, in this instance, the blood-forming bone marrow. These aspects of industrial toxicology have been discussed by Goldwater (26).

The effects of industrial hazards and their causes (27) may be summarized as follows:

(1) Irritation of the mucous membranes—chlorine, nitrous fumes, sulfur dioxide, formaldehyde, and others.

(2) Alteration of the components of the blood—this effect is peculiarly the property of nitro and amino derivatives of benzene, arsine, and carbon monoxide. Greenburg, Goldwater and their co-workers (28) state that the glycols belong to this group.

(3) Action on the brain and nervous system—carbon disulfide and unsaturated carbon compounds.

(4) Remote action on the metabolism, by action on organs and tissues—lead, phosphorus, tetrachloroethane, benzene, toluene, and their nitro derivatives.

(5) Action on the respiratory tract, such as action on the lungs—silica and asbestos dust.

Chemists are interested in the effects and symptoms of industrial poisoning because they are in immediate contact and control where poisonings of this nature are liable to occur. A physician is unlikely to see a case until it is too late to remedy or alter the industrial condition (29).

Sayers, DallaValle, and Yant (30) summarize more fully the effects of industrial poisons on the body.

a. Action of Air-Borne Contaminants

The actions of such substances upon the body differ widely, but in general they may have the following effects:

(1) They may cause skin irritation, or dermatosis, or affect the mucous membranes of the respiratory tract and eyes. This is true of acid vapors and certain caustic compounds easily distributed into the air.

(2) They may enter the lungs or be absorbed by the blood stream and produce systemic poisoning. Such substances as benzene vapors and lead fumes or dust are typical examples. Substances in this group may have their action on the blood, on the nervous system, or on the

other body tissues, and may produce deleterious effects when the exposure is severe or prolonged.

(*3*) They may produce asphyxia directly or indirectly, as in the case of excessive amounts of hydrogen cyanide, hydrogen sulfide, or carbon monoxide. The action of these gases is varied. They may affect the respiratory center or the nerve endings in the lungs, causing a cessation of breathing, or, as in the case of carbon monoxide, combine with the hemoglobin of the blood so that oxygen cannot be furnished the tissues.

(*4*) They may, as in the case of certain dusts such as silica, granite, and asbestos, cause a fibrosis of the lung tissue which predisposes to tuberculosis.

(*5*) They may exhibit a combination of the above effects. Some substances, such as nitrobenzene, not only cause a dermatosis when in contact with the skin but also may act as systemic poisons.

(*6*) They may produce no demonstrable effects on prolonged exposure. This is particularly true of cotton and some wood dusts.

b. Skin Affections

Industrial skin affections, according to available statistics, account for the largest number of occupational disease claims of any one group of causes (31). Occupational dermatergoses have been classified by White (32,33), Schwartz (34), and Schwartz, Tulipan, and Birmingham (35).

c. Acute and Chronic Poisoning

Industrial poisoning is of two main types: acute and chronic. The first is induced by large or relatively massive doses of a poisonous or baneful substance, while chronic poisoning is the result of repeated small doses. Thus, for instance, acute poisoning from carbon tetrachloride vapors does not result until an exposure to a concentration of 1000–1500 ppm for 30 min occurs. A concentration below this amount is, however, by no means a safe level. Continuous exposure to concentrations only slightly higher than 100 ppm will cause serious physiological disturbances (30). The threshold limit value for carbon tetrachloride in 1965 was 25 ppm.

Though the effects of acute poisoning are more readily apparent, the deep-seated effects of slow and chronic poisoning are often much more damaging. The chances of recovery from acute poisoning, if it is not lethal, are greater than from chronic poisoning.

From the viewpoint of the industrial hygiene chemist, the conditions causing chronic poisoning are far more significant than those causing acute poisoning. Acute poisoning is more often likely to be accidental or deliberate in nature and thus falls within the scope of the medical or forensic toxicologist, whereas chronic poisoning is generally the result of some industrial or manufacturing condition and therefore is distinctly a problem for the industrial toxicologist and industrial hygiene chemist.

d. Effective Dosage

Poisoning is due not only to the concentration of a given substance and the length of exposure to that substance but also to a number of other factors. These have been listed by Goldwater (26) as:

(1) Concentration
(2) Length of exposure
(3) State of dispersion (size of particle or physical state, such as solid, colloid or aerosol, liquid, gas)
(4) Affinity for human tissue
(5) Solubility in human tissue fluids
(6) Sensitivity of human tissues or organs.

e. Individual Susceptibility

Under like conditions of exposure to toxic substances, there is a variation in the effects produced on human beings and animals. Indeed, the variation may range from severe damage or even death to mild intoxication to no signs or actual poisoning at all. The reasons for such variation are not fully understood. In some instances a relationship can be established, as, for example, in individuals who have had tuberculosis and are particularly susceptible to silicosis.

f. Rate of Breathing

The rate of breathing is an important factor in the effective toxicity of a given material. Under conditions where rapid breathing occurs, poisoning may result when with ordinary breathing no poisoning would occur. It can be seen from Table I-1 that under intense exer-

tion or very hard working conditions twice the amount of air is
breathed as when ordinary work is performed and five times as much
air is breathed as when walking.   Persons using air-supplying masks
have succumbed because of failure to consider the rate of breathing
when establishing the time period for which the mask remains
effective.

TABLE I-1
Volumes of Air Breathed

Position or action	Liters per minute		
	Henderson and Haggard[a]	Ferguson[b]	Jennings[c]
Lying down	6	6	—
Sitting	7	7	6–7
Standing	8	—	8
Walking, 2 mph	14	—	—
Walking	—	20	—
Walking, 4 mph	28	—	—
Walking to running	—	—	14–40
Slow run	43	—	—
Working	—	48	—
Hard work	—	72	—
Intense exertion	65–100	—	60–100

[a] Henderson, Y., and H. W. Haggard, *Noxious Gases*, 2nd ed., Reinhold, New York, 1943.

[b] Ferguson, C., personal communication, 1956.

[c] Jennings, B. H., *Hazardous Vapors and Dust in Industry*, Ventilating and Air Conditioning Contractors Assoc., Chicago, 1957.

g. Threshold Limit Values

As will be discussed in the Appendix in some detail, the concept of
threshold limit values, i.e., the concentration of a given substance
or material to which a worker can be exposed for 8 hr per day,
5 days a week with safety, has been thoroughly embedded in industrial hygiene thought and control over the past 30 years.   Modifications of this concept have appeared which are of great significance
in analytical industrial toxicology.   One of these is that of the Daily
Weighted Average exposure over a 3-month period in which time
of exposure to a concentration for each operation in a given process
must be taken into consideration.   In such a system it is necessary

TABLE I-2

Daily Weighted Average for the Period October through December, 1960[a]

(Operation: Reduction furnace operator; 2 men/shift; 3 shifts/day; 6 men/day)

Operation or operating area	Time per operator, min	Operations per shift	Time per shift, (min) (T)	Number of samples	Concentration (C), µg Be/m³ Low	High	Av.	Conc. × total time, (T × C)
GA Reduction furnace area	369	1	369	29	0.2	5.5	0.8	295.2
GA Shoe change room	6	1	6	13	0.2	44.1	10.8	64.8
GA Locker room	12	1	12	5	0.3	2.7	1.8	21.6
GA Cafeteria	30	1	30	5	0.1	4.9	1.7	51.0
GA General plant	30	1	30	27	0.2	3.0	0.8	24.0
BZ Charge furnace	3.5	3	10.5	7	1.1	12.1	4.0	42.0
BZ Change drums in charge cart	1.5	3	4.5	8	0.7	58.3	17.9	80.6
BZ Probe melt	0.5	15	7.5	7	0.3	9.6	5.1	38.3
BZ Pour furnace	2	3	6	9	1.0	5.9	3.0	18.0
BZ Put melt into transfer pot cart	0.5	3	1.5	9	2.0	15.9	6.7	10.1
BZ Dump melt into crusher elevator	3	3	9	6	0.8	4.9	2.5	22.5
BZ Chip and rake dross	4	3	12	8	2.0	6.7	3.2	38.4
			$\Sigma T = 498$					$\Sigma(T \times C) = 706.5$

$$\frac{(T \times C)}{T} = 1.4 \ \mu g \ Be/m^3$$

[a] Data obtained by the Brush Beryllium Company, Elmore, Ohio.

to make analyses at every step of the process.   An excellent example in the manufacture of beryllium has been given by Hiser, Donaldson, and Schwenzfeir (36) and may be quoted:

About 1946, berylliosis was recognized as an occupational disease. Since the Atomic Commission and its contractors were the principals involved at this time in working with beryllium, the Advisory Committee of the Atomic Energy Commission in 1949 set up recommended limits for the control of air-borne beryllium. The recommendations were, that for in-plant exposures, no person should be exposed for any one day to an average concentration of more than 2 micrograms beryllium per cubic meter, and that no instantaneous exposures should exceed 25 micrograms per cubic meter. It is apparent that in applying these limits recommended by the Atomic Energy Commission Advisory Committee to a beryllium production facility considerable interpretation was necessary. In 1956 when the Atomic Energy Commission issued invitations to bid for the construction of two beryllium facilities, this interpretation was formalized and incorporated as Appendix D in the Health and Safety section in the contract between Brush Beryllium Company and the Atomic Energy Commission.

The most significant difference from the original Atomic Energy Commission Advisory Committee recommendation is that, instead of limiting each employee to an exposure of 2 micrograms beryllium per cubic meter for each day, the period of averaged exposure was extended to three months. Hence, the concept of the Daily Weighted Average over a three month period was adopted. This means, that though inevitable accidents in processing would throw an operator over the 2 micrograms beryllium per cubic meter limit for some days, they could be balanced by days of normal operation. Also, realizing that accidents or malfunctioning of equipment would result in instantaneous exposures over 25 micrograms beryllium per cubic meter, respirator protection was permitted for exposures from 25 micrograms beryllium per cubic meter up to 100 micrograms beryllium per cubic meter. Operations over 100 micrograms per cubic meter are shut down until alterations can be made to bring them under control. However, in any case where operations must be run and exposures are over 100 micrograms per cubic meter, fresh air masks are worn.

In order to maintain a plant under Atomic Energy Commission control, it is necessary to sample each operation at such intervals as necessary to know the degree of contamination in the plant and to amass enough data to calculate the Daily Weighted Average on each operator over a three-month period. Both the operator's general environment and his environment while performing operational functions must be measured for air-borne beryllium. These data go into his Daily Weighted Average by applying a time versus exposure study through his average work day over a three-month period.

The data obtained in a typical study are shown in Table I-2, taken from the above reference.

H. Air Pollution

Much of the analytical chemistry of industrial poisons deals with the estimation of substances in air, for although there are three or four channels through which chemical poisons can enter the body, the chief portals of entry are the respiratory tract and the skin. The swallowing of industrial poisons can almost be prevented at will. Absorption through the skin, except where it is a matter of contact with a chemical agent, is again a question of the chemical contaminant being in the air. Accidental entrance cannot be considered. Hence, methods for the estimation of contaminants in the surrounding air will form a most important part of this book. There is, however, an essential difference between industrial poison air analysis and customary gas analysis. In the usual type of air or gas analysis, the analyst is concerned with the per cent composition of the air or gas as a whole. In the analytical chemistry of industrial hazards, the analyst is interested in the contaminants and noxious materials in the air, not in the actual composition of the air. Since these occupational poisons are usually only a very small portion of the composition of the air to be analyzed, the ordinary methods of air analysis are not applicable.

Because these methods do deal with air, they are not at all limited to factory, shop, garage, mine, or quarry, but are equally applicable to the study of air pollution and air sanitation. The sampling instruments and methods used are in many instances identical. Indeed, the American Public Health Association delegated its Committee on Ventilation and Atmospheric Pollution to a subsection of the major division of Occupational Health.

The field of air pollution control is closely allied with industrial hygiene control. Some industrial hygiene chemists have decided to devote their careers to this growing field. The developments in the analytical chemistry of air pollution have been so numerous that three books (37–39) appeared within about a year.

Many of the methods and techniques described and detailed in this book are applicable to air pollutant analysis, but one important distinction should be borne in mind. Most industrial poison analyses are in the realm of microchemistry; most air pollutant analyses are in the field of ultramicrochemistry. Other distinctions have been made by Jacobs (37).

I. Error and Accuracy

The subject of error and accuracy presents a somewhat different aspect in the field of industrial poisons. Purists in analytical chemistry might be horrified by the latitude permitted in some types of industrial hygiene analysis. It is indeed true that every measurement entails some error. Hence, to work far outside the limits of that error is to involve useless labor with no gain in accuracy. The accuracy of the final result is quantitatively governed by the accuracy of the least accurate measurement.

In the field of analytical chemistry as applied to occupational poisons, we encounter substances which are toxic in minute quantities. Our methods must, naturally, be sufficiently accurate and sensitive to enable us to detect and estimate these minute quantities. The methods must be more than sufficiently sensitive to detect the toxic threshold of a noxious material. Once, however, the threshold of toxic concentration is reached and passed, it really matters little how accurate the analysis is. In such cases, the method must be accurate enough to warn of the danger and to disclose the degree of danger. Thus, for example, Lehmann (40,41) found that 0.015 g/liter (4700 ppm) of benzene produces listlessness and confusion after half an hour, and that 0.02–0.03 g/liter (6260–9390 ppm) for a few hours may cause loss of consciousness. For the purposes of accuracy as far as the analysis of benzene in this instance is concerned, it is not significant whether 90 or 100 ppm of benzene is present in the air, but whether there are 50, 100, 200, 300, 500, 1000, etc. ppm present. We are more interested in the relative amount of benzene vapor in the air, expressed in round numbers, than in the precise amount present. Furthermore, when one considers that, under plant conditions, particularly in the summer season when windows are open and natural ventilation is good, the benzene vapor concentration in workrooms is subject to large and almost continuous variations, errors of as much as 10% are not of serious consequence.

Practically speaking, the same conditions hold for the accuracy to be expected in all analyses. To be valuable in the field of the analytical chemistry of industrial hazards a method must be sufficiently accurate to *detect* and thus to warn of danger and to disclose the *degree* of hazard. Tables 3 through 7 (Appendix) give information on limits of toxicity and the toxic threshold of a number of industrial hazards.

Effort to obtain accuracy greater than that which is necessary to give the needed and useful information is impractical.

Throughout the text more than one procedure is often detailed for any particular determination. This is done intentionally, for the analyst is wont to find one method preferable to another. Furthermore, in the opinion of the author, check results obtained by different methods are more indicative of the true estimation than check results obtained by the same method. References to still other methods are given in the bibliography appended to each chapter.

There is, however, one other aspect of industrial hygiene analysis that King (42) stresses. Most of the toxicological thought of industrial hygiene chemistry has been oriented toward continuous exposure during the working day. In aviation there exists the possibility of exposures to very high concentrations for a relatively short time. There are few data that have been gathered from this point of view, that is, data concerning adequate tolerances for short time–high concentration exposures. It will be found that some of the methods in this text are designed for the purpose of obtaining such information.

The more important industrial hazards, from the point of view of number of workers injured and number of industries in which they are hazards, are treated more fully than those which do not have the same importance. Among these might be mentioned carbon monoxide, lead, arsenic, mercury, radioactive materials, free silica, and dust.

A survey made by the U.S. Public Health Service (43) showed that approximately 1,500,000 workers in the United States are exposed to carbon monoxide; 800,000 persons handle lead and its compounds; 34,000 are exposed to arsenic and its compounds; nearly 33,000 handle mercury and mercury products; somewhat more than 1,000,000 persons are exposed to the inhalation of silica dust and 1,500,000 more are exposed to silicate dust; and more than 750,000 workers are exposed to organic solvents, while some 30,000 may inhale benzene vapors. These few figures, more of which may be obtained in the references cited, indicate the vastness of the industrial hygiene problem.

References

1. Sayers, R. R., and S. Davenport, *U.S. Public Health Serv. Bull. 195* (1937).
2. *Ind. Hyg. Newsletter*, **1**, No. 4, 13 (1947).
3. *Am. Ind. Hyg. Assoc. J.*, **20**, 428 (1959).
4. Burney, L. E., in *Rept. on Environmental Health Problems,*" Hearings before The Committee on Appropriations House of Representatives," 86th Congress, 2nd Session, Govt. Printing Office, Washington, D. C. 1960
5. Goldwater, L. J., *Ann. Med. History (New Series)*, **8**, 27 (1936).
6. Felton, J. S., J. P. Newman, and D. L. Read, "Man, Medicine, and Work— Historic Events in Occupational Medicine," *Public Health Serv. Publ. 1044*, Govt. Printing Office, Washington, D.C., 1965.
7. Goodman, H., *Diseases of Tradesmen by Bernadino Ramazzini*, Medical Lay Press, New York, 1933.
8. Teleky, L., *History of Factory and Mine Hygiene*, Columbia Univ. Press, New York, 1948.
9. Legge, T. M., *J. Ind. Hyg.*, **1**, 475 (1919–20).
10. Legge, T. M., *J. Ind. Hyg.*, **1**, 578 (1919–20).
11. Legge, R. T., *Am. Ind. Hyg. Assoc. J.*, **7**, 5 (1946).
12. Goldwater, L. J., *J. Lancet*, **78**, No. 6, 251 (1958).
13. Sayers, R. R., and J. J. Bloomfield, "Industrial Hygiene Activities in the United States", *Public Health Serv. Publ.*, 1936.
14. *Statistical Abstract of the United States*, Govt. Printing Office, Washington, D.C., 1965.
15. "The Industrial Environment . . . Its Evaluation and Control," *Public Health Service Publ. 614* (1958).
16. Sappington, C. O., *Medicolegal Phases of Occupational Diseases*, Industrial Health, Chicago, 1939.
17. Jacobs, M. B., and L. Scheflan, *The Chemical Analysis of Industrial Solvents*, Interscience, New York, 1953.
18. Minster, D. K., *J. Ind. Hyg.*, **7**, 299 (1925).
19. Graham-Rogers, C. T., *Industrial Diseases Rapid Reference Manual*, N.Y. State Dept. Labor (1925).
20. Dublin, L. I., and R. J. Vane, *U.S. Bur. Labor Statistics, Bull. 582* (1933).
21. Gafafer, W. M., Ed., "Occupational Diseases," *Public Health Serv. Publ. 1097*, Govt. Printing Office, Washington, D.C., 1964.
22. Legge, T. M., *J. Ind. Hyg.*, **2**, 121 (1920).
23. Sollmann, T., *A Manual of Pharmacology*, Saunders, Philadelphia, 1944.
24. Sayers, R. R., *U.S. Public Health Rept.*, **53**, 217 (1938).
25. McNally, W. D., *Toxicology*, Industrial Medicine, Chicago, 1937.
26. Goldwater, L. J., in *Dangerous Properties of Industrial Materials*, 2nd ed., N. J. Sax, Ed., Reinhold, New York, 1927.
27. Legge, T. M., *J. Ind. Hyg.*, **2**, 293 (1921).
28. Greenburg, L., M. R. Mayers, L. Goldwater, W. J. Burke, and S. Moskowitz, *J. Ind. Hyg. Toxicol.*, **20**, 134 (1938); *N.Y. State Ind. Bull.* **17**, 269 (1938).
29. Henderson, Y., and H. W. Haggard, *Noxious Gases*, Reinhold, New York, 1927.

30. Sayers, R. R., J. M. DallaValle, and W. P. Yant, *Ind. Eng. Chem.*, **26**, 1251 (1934).
31. Sappington, C. O., *Medicolegal Phases of Occupational Diseases*, Industrial Health, Chicago, 1939.
32. White, R. P., *J. Ind. Hyg.*, **8**, 367 (1926).
33. White, R. P., *Dermatergoses*, Lewis, London, 1934.
34. Schwartz, L., *U.S. Public Serv. Bull. 215* (1934); *229* (1936); *249* (1939).
35. Schwartz, L., *Occupational Diseases of the Skin*, P. Hoeber, London, 1946.
36. Hiser, R. A., H. M. Donaldson, and C. W. Schwenzfeir, *A Rapid Analytical Method for the Determination of Beryllium in Air Samples*, The Brush Beryllium Company, Elmore, Ohio.
37. Jacobs, M. J., *The Chemical Analysis of Air Pollutants*, Interscience, New York, 1960.
38. *Air Pollution Manual . . . Part I Evaluation*, Am. Ind. Hyg. Assoc., Detroit, 1960.
39. *Laboratory Methods*, Air Pollution Control, Dist. Co. of Los Angeles, Calif., 1958.
40. Lehmann, K. B., *Arch. Hyg.*, **75**, 1 (1911–12).
41. Greenburg, L., *U.S. Public Health Serv. Reprint 1096* (1926).
42. King, B. G., Greater New York Safety Council Convention, New York, 1949.
43. Bloomfield, J. J., V. M. Trasko, R. R. Sayers, R. T. Page, and M. F. Peyton, *U.S. Public Health Service Bull. 259* (1940).

General References

Bloomfield, J. J., V. M. Trasko, R. R. Sayers, R. T. Page, and M. F. Peyton, "A Preliminary Survey of the Industrial Hygiene Problem in the United States," *U.S. Public Health Serv. Bull. 259* (1940).
Dublin, L. I., and R. J. Vane, "Occupation Hazards and Diagnostic Signs," *U.S. Dept. Labor, Div. Labor Standards, Bull. 41* (1943).
Elkins, H. B., *The Chemistry of Industrial Toxicology*, 2nd ed., Wiley, New York, 1959.
Eulenberg, H., *Handbuch der Gewerbe-Hygiene auf experimentelles Grundlage*, Hirschwald, Berlin, 1876.
Flury, F., and F. Zernick, *Schaedliche Gase*, Springer, Berlin, 1931.
Gafafer, W. M., *Manual of Industrial Hygiene*, Saunders, Philadelphia, 1943.
Goodman, H., *Diseases of Tradesman by Bernadino Ramazzini*, Medical Lay Press, New York, 1933.
Graham-Rogers, C. T., *Industrial Diseases Rapid Reference Manual*, N.Y. State Dept. Labor, 1925.
Hamilton, A., *Exploring the Dangerous Trades*, Little, Brown, Boston, 1943.
Hamilton, A., *Industrial Poisons in the United States*, Macmillan, New York, 1925.
Hamilton, A., *Industrial Toxicology*, Harper, New York, 1934.
Henderson, Y., and H. W. Haggard, *Noxious Gases*, Reinhold, New York, 1943.
Hunter, D., *Diseases of Occupation*, Little, Brown, Boston, 1955.
International Labor Office, *Occupation and Health*, Vol. 1, 1930; Vol. 2, 1934; Supplements 1938, 1939, 1940, 1944.

Lanza, A. J., and J. A. Goldberg, *Industrial Hygiene*, Oxford, New York, 1939.

McNally, W. D., *Medical Jurisprudence and Toxicology*, Philadelphia, 1939.

McNally, W. D., *Toxicology*, Industrial Medicine, Chicago, 1937.

Occupational Health Program, "The Industrial Environment. . .Its Evaluation and Control," *Public Health Service Publ. 614* (1958).

Patty, F. A., Ed., *Industrial Hygiene and Toxicology*, 2 vols., Interscience, New York, 1960, 1962.

Sappington, C. O., *Essentials of Industrial Health*, Lippincott, Philadelphia, 1943.

Sappington, C. O., *Medicolegal Phases of Occupational Diseases*, Industrial Health, Chicago, 1939.

Sayers, R. R., and J. J. Bloomfield, "Industrial Hygiene Activities in the United States," *U.S. Public Health Serv. Publ.*, 1936.

Schwartz, L., "Skin Hazards in American Industry," *U.S. Public Health Serv. Bull. 215* (1934); *229* (1936); *249* (1939).

Shaw, N., and J. S. Owens, *The Smoke Problem of Great Cities*, Constable, London, 1925.

Sollmann, T., *Manual of Pharmacology*, Saunders, Philadelphia, 1944.

White, R. P., *Dermatergoses*, Lewis, London, 1934.

CHAPTER II

SAMPLING

A. Precision of Sampling

In order to make a correct analysis, a proper, representative, and adequate sample of the material to be analyzed must be obtained. Very likely there are as many incorrect determinations resulting from improper sampling as from the combined errors of manipulation, measurement, and calculation. An improper sample makes subsequent analysis practically worthless. No analysis can be better than the sample nor can the chemist improve the quality of the sample. Sampling is as important in the field of the analytical chemistry of industrial hazards as it is in other fields. This importance is never to be underestimated for often comfort, illness, and even life itself depend upon an accurate estimation of the noxious components of a sample presumed to be accurately obtained.

Sampling of industrial poisons is often beset with more and greater difficulties than the sampling of other materials. Thus, it becomes a serious problem to sample the air that a workman breathes at the point that he breathes it for a partial or entire working period. Various attempts have been made to overcome this difficulty. These will be discussed in the text. At times, it is important to sample in relatively inaccessible places, such as the blisters of a ship, a manhole, a sewer, or a mine. One can readily see the numerous difficulties involved.

This chapter will be concerned principally with the general methods of sampling of air and gases. The devices and methods for sampling of dust and dust-borne contaminants will be described and detailed in Chapter V. The methods of sampling for a specific substance will be given in connection with the discussion of the analytical methods for that substance. The sampling aspects of direct-reading instruments, indicators, detectors, and field test equipment will be considered in Chapter XVIII.

The material to be sampled may be the noxious substance itself or it may be a mixture of which the poison is a component. In any event it will be, as explained in Chapter I, either solid, liquid, or gaseous. The times that it is necessary to sample solids or liquids are reserved, in the main, to obtain samples which will yield information concerning the composition of the material the workmen handle. If it is merely desired to obtain some idea of the constituents or components qualitatively, rather than to make a precise determination of the exact per cent composition, then it may be sufficient to scrape the settled dust off a rafter or beam of a shop or out of a ventilation duct or flue, to take a random sample of raw material or finished product from a warehouse, or to take some portion of a plating bath or a sample from a collector bin. The sample so obtained is then subjected to analysis by the usual gravimetric, titrimetric, colorimetric, etc. methods.

Where it is necessary to obtain the exact per cent composition of raw materials, settled dust, or other solid or liquid material, sampling should be performed by the standard customary methods. For instance, for bags or boxes of ground raw materials or finished products or substances in a collector bin, a sampling tube, trier, or scoop may be used. Liquid substances, which form a most important group of industrial hazards, may be sampled with a thief or ladle. Products in smaller subdivisions, such as cans of paint, may be sampled by taking sufficient cans to make a representative sample from a given lot number. The sampling of gaseous materials will be discussed fully in subsequent sections. A method for sampling rock in a quarry is described in Section C of Chapter VII.

B. Sampling Criteria

In taking an air sample, three kinds of action are required: (*1*) drawing or aspirating the air, (*2*) measuring the volume of air drawn, and (*3*) trapping the toxic substance to be determined. The means of carrying out these three actions vary from those as simple as using a bottle filled with water and subsequently emptying it to using very expensive recording monitors. Thus, the three actions can be combined into one, for instance, when a liquid-displacement gas collector of known volume is used (see Sections E-2 and F-3 of this chapter) or the three actions can be performed with such a common combination as using a pump to draw the air (see Section E-1), a rotameter (see Chapter III, Section A-4-d) to measure the volume of air drawn, and an impinger (see Chapter V, Section C-7-c) containing an absorbing solution to trap the toxic material.

Keenan (1) has pointed out that sampling methods for gases and vapors should meet the following requirements:

(*1*) Provide an acceptable efficiency of collection for the substance or substances involved.

(*2*) Maintain this efficiency at a rate of air flow which can provide sufficient sample for the analytical procedure in a reasonable period of time.

(*3*) Retain the collected gas or vapor in a form which is transportable to the analytical site.

(*4*) Yield the sample in a form suitable for the analytical method.

(*5*) Require minimal manipulation in the field.

(*6*) Avoid the use of corrosive or otherwise hazardous sampling media whenever possible.

1. Sampling Time

The length of sampling is governed by the need to collect sufficient contaminant for analysis. This, in turn, depends upon the sensitivity of the analytical method to be used, the assumed concentration of the contaminant in the air being sampled, the time sequence of manufacturing or other operations, and where applicable, the threshold limit value.

With some knowledge of these factors, the minimum length of sampling time can be computed by the analyst (see Chapter III, Section C-8). For many types of analysis, particularly for continuous operations, a sampling time is given in the details of the method in this book.

Hosey and Keenan (2) cite an example of the influence of an operating cycle on the length of sampling time. The operation of drawing molten zinc from smelter retorts into a ladle and then pouring the metal into molds to form pigs takes about 25 min. The next drawing of molten zinc from the same retort is performed 6 hr later. In this instance, samples should be collected for entire length of drawing time, i.e., for the 25 min, each time the molten zinc is drawn. In the furnace breakdown operations, some of the manipulative cycles last for only 3–5 min. Here it is best to collect a sample for a total of 25–30 min over 5 to 6 cycles. A number of samples of the general air in the vicinity of these operations should also be collected at different times during the shifts. With these and breathing zone samples taken during the drawing and breakdown operations, the weighted exposure of the worker can be calculated (see Chapter III, Section C-7). Jacobs (3) discusses sampling time in relation to sampling in stacks and ducts.

2. Number of Samples

The number of samples to be collected depends on the information sought. With respect to obtaining information concerning a given working environment, it has been recommended that samples be collected in at least three general sampling locations (4) in order to get a fairly complete sample of the worker's environment. These are:

(1) In the immediate vicinity of the workers in a particular environment.

(2) Near the source of the contaminant entering the general atmosphere.

(3) From the general workroom atmosphere.

It is not always possible to obtain all of these types of samples. It is important to bear in mind the type of sample obtained and not to generalize or average results indiscriminately. Only similar types of samples may be justifiably compared.

If a survey is being made, then it may be necessary to obtain daily, weekly, and monthly samples in order to find out whether or not there are diurnal and seasonal variations. For instance, in some plants which are not air conditioned, windows and doors are kept open in the summer and are kept closed in the winter. This will make a difference in the natural ventilation and, in consequence, will tend to increase the exposure of workers during the times the natural ventilation is reduced. To get the average yearly exposure, in this case, it will be necessary to average the seasonal variations.

If the pollutant is being generated at a relatively constant rate, it is customary to take 3–5 samples during different operating and weather conditions to get sufficient data for calculating the exposure. The complexity of the problem of choosing the number of samples is emphasized by the example of Flinn (5), who collected 25 samples for dust count in order to evaluate the weighted daily exposure of a coal mine undercutter. Thus, three samples were taken during the miner's trips into and out of the mine, four when setting up, repairing, and changing the teeth of the undercutter, 15 during undercutting and shearing, and three when loading and moving the undercutter.

A number of samples have to be taken to test the efficiency of a given protective or abatement device. If it is a protective device like a hood, then the air should be sampled before the protective device is put into operation and again after it is put into operation. If the protective device can be operated at different speeds or capacities, then samples should be collected at each significant speed or capacity change. In the case of testing the efficiency of an abatement device, such as a filter, scrubber, cyclone, electrostatic precipitator, etc., samples must be taken of the entering air or gas stream and of the effluent air or gas stream at low load, usual load, and overload to be able to calculate the true efficiency of the device.

The number of samples to be collected is, then, a matter of judgment of the industrial hygienist using the general suggestions given in this section as a guide.

3. Sampling Rates

The sampling rate for a given piece of sampling equipment is usually specified in the methods detailed in this text. Usually, sampling is performed at the same flow rate as the velocity of the air or gas stream being sampled, i.e., the sampling is done isokinetically. Isokinetic methods of sampling are discussed by Watson (6). Actually, it is not necessary to sample isokinetically when sampling for gases, vapors, and dusts made up of particles smaller than 5–10 μ.

C. Basic Methods of Air and Gas Sampling

The proper sampling of air for the examination of noxious substances, dust, etc., presents greater difficulties than does the sampling of solids and liquids. It is often necessary not only to obtain a sample of air but also to obtain it in a particular spot at a particular time. It may be necessary to take a sample right near a worker's nose or mouth, or near or within an exhaust duct. You may recall the example given in Chapter I concerning the variation in concentration of carbon monoxide from the exhaust of an automobile near the exhaust and at a distance of 30 ft. The same sampling problem exists for many industrial poisons.

In general, samples must be taken with a particular purpose in mind. Not only is the position at which the sample is taken of importance—whether it is to represent the locale of the worker, the average workroom atmosphere, or the source of the contaminant—but the time of exposure of the worker also must be considered.

For the purposes of the analytical chemistry of industrial hazards, there are two basic methods of sampling air and gases. The first method is to obtain a definite volume of air within a gas collector, at a known pressure and temperature, in a manner entirely analogous to the sampling of gases (7). Then this sample is analyzed in the field or is taken to the laboratory to be analyzed.

The second basic method is to pass a known volume of air or gas through an absorbing medium or solution or equivalent device. The noxious material or contaminant is thus absorbed or adsorbed, and the absorbing or adsorbing medium or agent is subsequently subjected to analysis either in the field or preferably in the laboratory. Where the gross components of a gas or of air are to be estimated, the first basic method may be used; where a small or minute amount of a contaminant is to be estimated, the second basic sampling method is preferred.

Where a definite volume of gas is required or desired as the sample to be analyzed, there are two possible types of sample that may be taken. These are known as "instantaneous" (also known as "grab," "spot," and "snap") samples and "continuous" or "integrated" samples. Instantaneous samples are those taken at a particular time and place within an interval of a few seconds to a minute or two, and they represent the composition of the air or gas at that time and location. They are taken most often with evacuated bottles or gas collectors, although they may be taken with liquid-displacement devices or with a spring or hand-operated pump.

Continuous samples are taken where a comparatively large volume of gas must be sampled or where the composition of the air being sampled is not uniform. In the former case, it is necessary to pass the air or gas through some absorbing agent in order to trap the contaminant to be estimated. In the latter instance, a sample taken continuously for a given period of time will give the average composition, as explained in the section describing gas- or liquid-displacement collectors for continuous sampling (Section D-4). It may be preferable, if the composition of the gas or air is not uniform, to take several grab samples at different times and locations rather than to take one continuous sample.

Grab sampling has limitations: (1) The sensitivity of the method used must be adequate for the sample and, since the volume of the sample taken seldom exceeds 1 liter, the method must be sensitive enough to be able to determine an amount of pollutant of the order of the threshold limit value in a volume of 1 liter. (2) It is necessary to take a series of grab samples to evaluate the exposure of a worker and this, in turn, requires the use of a large quantity of sampling equipment and, at times, analytical equipment. An advantage of grab sampling is that it does tell the concentration of the pollutant at the time the sample is taken. It must be stressed that a single or grab sample gives information only for conditions at the time of sampling and the results cannot be extrapolated to other situations.

Integrated, composite random, or continuous samples give a better measure of the average exposure of a worker than grab samples. On the other hand, more elaborate sampling apparatus is needed and, in addition, peak concentrations may be missed. The latter disadvantage can sometimes be overcome by the use of monitors which sample continuously but also analyze continuously and record the results. Thus, the peak results are recorded. (See the method for sulfur dioxide in Chapter XII, Section B-2h.) Continuous sampling gives more and better information and often permits extrapolation of results.

Where one of the noxious components to be estimated is a highly reactive substance, as, for instance, sulfur dioxide, hydrogen sulfide, or nitrogen tetroxide, and the atmosphere is sampled by means of a gas collector, it is preferable to make the analysis directly in the field, for by the time the gas collector gets to the laboratory, the noxious component may have reacted completely with the container itself. A moderately accurate field test is better than a totally inaccurate laboratory analysis.

The devices and methods used in the sampling of dust and dust-borne contaminants will be described and detailed in Chapters V and VI.

D. Gas-Sample Containers and Collectors

In order to obtain a sample of gas or air by either of these basic methods, the air containing the contaminant must be placed in a sample container or collector or must be, as was previously explained, passed through some absorbing medium by some device. Sample collectors and containers may be classified as follows:

(1)   Vacuum tubes
(2)   Vacuum bottles
(3)   Gas- or liquid-displacement tubes
(4)   Gas- or liquid-displacement tubes for continuous sampling
(5)   Metal containers
(6)   Glass bottles
(7)   Plastic containers
(8)   Syringes
(9)   Traps, bubblers, and absorbers.

Each of these types of gas collectors lends itself to some special means of sampling.

1. VACUUM TUBES

Vacuum tubes (Fig. II-1) are strong glass bulbs from which 99.97% or more of the air has been removed by a vacuum pump and the necks of which have been hermetically sealed by heating and drawing during the final stage of evacuation. For the analysis of the gross components of air or mine gases, vacuum bulbs with a capacity of 250–300 ml are sufficient. For the analysis of air or gases in which low-concentration ingredients are being estimated, for instance, in the determination of carbon monoxide, larger bulbs of about 1000-ml capacity may be used. The glass must be sufficiently strong to withstand the atmospheric pressure of 13–14 psi, for the internal pressure of the vacuum tube is practically zero.

In use, the ampoule-like drawn-out end is scratched and broken. The air rushes in to fill the vacuum until the internal pressure equals the external pressure. Then the broken end is sealed with a ball of wax or with a wax-filled cartridge, shown in Figure II-28. The bulb may now be shipped to a laboratory for analysis. For practical considerations vacuum tubes are used almost exclusively for grab samples.

These sample containers were recommended by the U. S. Bureau of Mines for all samples of mine air taken for shipment to its gas laboratory at the Pittsburgh Experiment Station. They have the advantage of being very simple to use, as neither pumps nor evacuating devices are needed at the point of sampling. No manometer need be attached, for the pressure of the sample is taken as the barometric reading. Because of its simplicity of use, field men and workmen may

Breaking scratch

Wax-filled cartridge

250–300-ml Capacity

Fig. II-1. Vacuum-tube sample collector.

be trained to do the sampling.   Its disadvantage lies in the fact that the tube must be reevacuated, redrawn, and resealed to be used again.

2. Vacuum Bottles

Generally, bottles or flasks with strong walls are used.   They are fitted with a two-hole rubber stopper as in Figure II-2.   One hole is equipped with a thermometer and the other contains a T tube fitted with two stopcocks and attached to a manometer.   The bottle is evacuated by opening stopcock A by means of some evacuating device such as a suction pump.   Then stopcock A is closed and stopcock B is opened.   The pressure registered by the manometer and the temperature shown by the thermometer are recorded.   Stopcock B is then closed.   The tube arm with stopcock A is connected with the source to be sampled and then it is opened.   When equilibrium has been established, stopcock A is closed and stopcock B is again opened.   The pressure indicated by the manometer and the temperature indicated by the thermometer are again noted.   The amount of gas or air taken into the bottle may then be computed as directed in Chapter III, Section C-7.   The bottle may then be quickly sealed with rubber stoppers, Bakelite screw caps, etc., or if the analysis is to be made near the

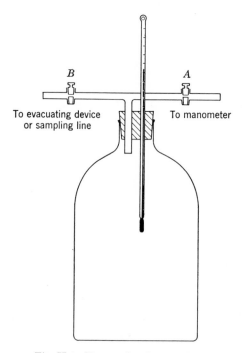

Fig. II-2. Vacuum-bottle sampling.

point of sampling, the stopcocks may merely be closed and the manometer disconnected. Collector tubes may be handled in an entirely analogous manner.

Alternative vacuum bottle collectors are illustrated in Figures II-3 and II-4. These collectors, sometimes called Shepherd bottles, have been designed for sampling atmospheres containing contaminants that are not readily trapped in absorbing solutions or on adsorbents. The bottles are evacuated and then are sealed by giving the cap a half turn. To take the sample the cap is turned to the open position at the spot to be sampled. After being filled with the air sample, reagents such as 10 ml of dilute sulfuric acid and a few drops of hydrogen peroxide may be added in a nitrogen oxide determination or 10 ml of nitrating acid in the case of a benzene determination.

The Shepherd bottle has great versatility. It can be used as a "universal" sampling flask. Thus, it can be used for sampling (1) by evacuating it, (2) by aspirating after inserting a glass tube, (3) by

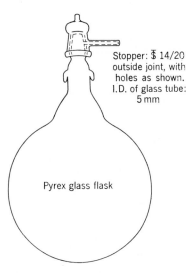

Stopper: ⑤ 14/20
outside joint, with
holes as shown.
I.D. of glass tube:
5 mm

Pyrex glass flask

Fig. II-3. Vacuum-bottle collector, rotating-cap type (500-ml-capacity flask must be able to stand high vacuum).

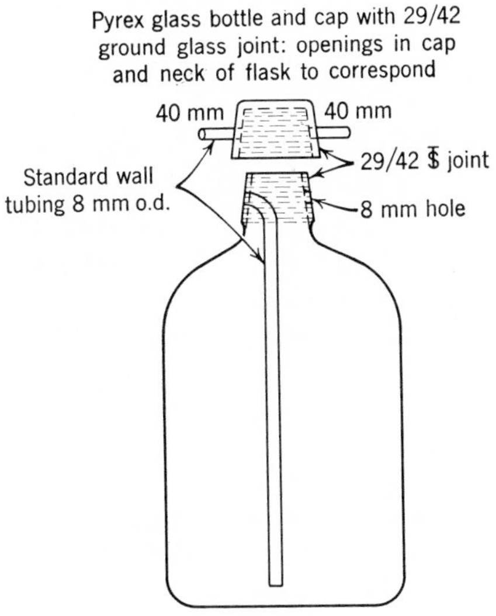

Pyrex glass bottle and cap with 29/42
ground glass joint: openings in cap
and neck of flask to correspond

40 mm   40 mm

Standard wall
tubing 8 mm o.d.

29/42 ⑤ joint

8 mm hole

Fig. II-4. Gas-sampling bottle, standard 500-ml rotating-cap type.

displacing a liquid, and (4) as a bubbler using an adapter head.   The flask may subsequently be used for operations such as boiling or distillation, and as originally designed may be attached to a Shepherd gas buret with sufficient sample for triplicate determinations.

3. Gas- or Liquid-Displacement Collectors

These gas collectors are of various designs, some of which are shown in Figure II-5.   They are adequate if analysis is to be made shortly after sampling or within a few days of sampling.   The simplest of these devices is a glass bulb of about 250-ml capacity with two end tubes suitable for closing with heavy rubber tubing and screw clamps. Short pieces of glass rod or glass plugs may be used instead of the screw clamps, but they must make a tight fit with the rubber tubing and they should be pushed up to make a flush contact with the end of the tube of the sampling collector.

Better than the container just described is the gas collector fitted with stopcocks instead of the tubes to be sealed with rubber tubing and screw clamps.   These are furnished by many firms handling chemical laboratory equipment.   Those in which the stopcocks are joined very close to the body of the bulb, so that there is practically no stem between the body and the stopcock, are considerably less apt to be broken.

A variation of this type of gas collector is the separatory funnel.

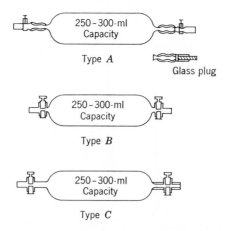

Fig. II-5. Gas-sample collectors, gas- or liquid-displacement type.

Various chemists have used small and large separatory funnels as gas-displacement collectors (8,9).

Another type of gas- or liquid-displacement gas collector is the one (Fig. II-6) equipped with two three-way stopcocks and two tubulatures at each end. These tubulatures may be of different bores to suit the flow of gas through the upper stopcock and the flow of liquid through the lower stopcock. By means of the extra tube, this type of collector permits the flushing of the sampling line either with the

Fig. II-6. Gas collector.

material to be sampled itself or with a confining fluid at the time of drawing the sample. This type also provides for the displacement of air from the tubing which connects the leveling bulb of an analytical device or measuring device to the collector.

4. Gas- or Liquid-Displacement Collectors for Continuous Sampling

These gas collectors are very similar to those described in the previous section. They are fitted with stopcocks of the two-, three-way type (Fig. II-7). However, they are generally equipped with an inner tube and the rate at which the sample is to be taken can be controlled by the distance between the end of the inner tube and the end of the tube tap (10). The bore of the tube taps may also be used to regulate the flow, as may the length of the tube. If necessary, an extra piece of tubing may be sealed on in order to increase the length of the exit tube.

The inner tube prevents sucking back or backward diffusion of the sampled gas. However, the rate of sampling may be controlled by using a sample collector without the internal tube by arranging the exit tap of the gas collector so that it will dip into a vessel of such a shape that the rate of outflow decreases as the pressure of the gas increases (11). In another device the sample of gas is drawn into the collector by a filter pump at a rate controlled by a counterpoise (12).

Fig. II-7. Inner-tube sampling collector. (Courtesy Will Scientific, Inc.)

5. METAL GAS COLLECTORS

Metal gas collectors (Fig. II-8) are analogous to the gas- or liquid-displacement collectors described in the preceding paragraphs. They have the advantage that they are practically nonbreakable and are readily available from laboratory equipment concerns. On the other hand, this type of container is likely to rust or react with the oxygen in the collector. They cannot be used for sampling air or gases containing hydrogen sulfide, sulfur dioxide, or nitrogen tetroxide, as these gases will react with the metal container. If this type of gas sample collector is used, the analysis should be made as soon as possible after sampling. If it is necessary to delay the analysis, the stopcocks should be sealed with paraffin or sealing wax after the sample has been taken. This should be done by dipping the taps of the gas collector into molten paraffin or wax several times very

Fig. II-8. Metal gas collectors.   (Courtesy Will Scientific, Inc.)

rapidly so that successive thin layers of wax are formed as a coating. These successive thin layers are a more effective seal than one thick coat.

6. Glass Bottles

Ordinary glass bottles may also be used as gas collectors.   However, if vacuum sampling is to be done they must be of strong glass.   Bottles used for the bottling of magnesium citrate [the druggists' citrate of magnesia bottles (Fig. II-9)] are adequate.   The rubber washers must be in good condition.   One to 2 ml of mercury may be added at

Fig. II-9. Magnesia-bottle collector.   (Courtesy Will Scientific, Inc.)

times to act as a seal after the bottle is inverted and prevent the collected gas from coming in contact with the rubber gasket. If the analysis is not to be made shortly after sampling, it is best to seal the top of the bottle in the manner described for sealing the stopcocks of metal gas collectors. If ordinary bottles are used (they should be used only in an emergency), the cork or rubber stopper should be cut off a little below the neck of the bottle and the recess should then be filled with the molten paraffin or sealing wax.

The procedure used in sampling will be described in the following sections for, with the exception of vacuum-type and liquid-displacement gas collectors, it is necessary to use some means to get the gas into the collector.

Traps, bubblers, absorbers, adsorbers, etc. are discussed in Chapter IV.

7. Plastic Containers

Usually, known volume containers are of small volume, of the order of 250 ml to 2 liters. Several cubic feet of air can be sampled by means of multilayer plastic containers, such as polyethylene bags. Only a few inches of water pressure are required to fill the bag. After returning to the laboratory, successive portions of the sample can be removed without dilution with air or displacement by a liquid (13). Another instance involving the use of a plastic container is given in Section G-1-c of this chapter.

Such polyethylene bags are relatively inert chemically and do not react with formaldehyde or with sulfur dioxide, but they cannot be used for the sampling of aerosols because they generate electrostatic charges that cause aerosols to migrate to the walls of the container.

Welch and Terry (14) used Mylar bags that could contain as much as 7 cu ft (200 liters) of air to prepare test samples for an autometer. In 1965, such plastic sampling bags were commercially available and some were equipped with shipping containers so that they could be shipped from the sampling point to the testing laboratory. Others were used for shipping test mixtures for the calibration of automatic testing instruments.

E. Aspirating Devices

In most cases, except where a positive pressure of gas or air is obtainable, it is necessary to use some method or device to pass the air or gas being sampled into the sampling collector or bottle. This is generally done by the principle of aspiration. Aspiration is the action of drawing a gas or a vapor from or through a vessel. An aspirator is an apparatus for drawing a gas or vapor through a tube.

There are three main types of aspirators: "dry," "wet," and ejector. Distinction between the dry type and wet type depends upon whether or not liquid comes directly in contact with the air being sampled. In a sense the ejector type is also a dry-type aspirator, but there is sufficient difference in use to place it in a different category. The devices within each type may be classified as follows:

Dry Type
    Aspirator bulb
    Hand bellows pump
    Hand and foot pumps
    Electric pumps
Wet Type
    Aspirator bottles
    Liquid-displacement gas collectors
Ejector Type
    Water aspirator (so-called filter pump)
    Compressed air ejectors
    Compressed gas ejectors

1. Dry Type

a. Aspirator Bulb

Aspirator bulbs are rubber bulbs which have two valves (Fig. II-10). When the bulb is squeezed, the air or gas is expelled through valve A while valve B is closed. On the release of the pressure, valve A closes while valve B opens, admitting more gas or air. These bulbs ordinarily have a capacity of about 40–60 ml. In general, it will

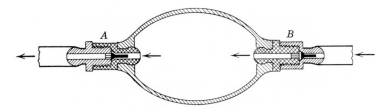

Fig. II-10. Rubber-bulb hand aspirator.

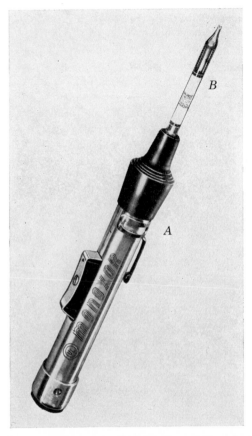

Fig. II-11. Monoxor carbon monoxide detector: (*A*) aspirator pump with connector for holding detector tube; (*B*) replaceable detector tube contains yellow colored chemical which turns brownish-gray when CO passes through tube. (Courtesy Bacharach Industrial Instrument Co.)

take about 50 compressions of the rubber aspirator bulb to replace the air in a 250-ml sample collector.

Aspirator bulbs are simple to use and carry. They can be used almost anywhere. However, the rubber ages so that these bulbs become less efficient with use. The valves leak at times because dirt accumulates and lodges in the valve seat. Sometimes this can be remedied by removing the dust and wetting the valve seat. The

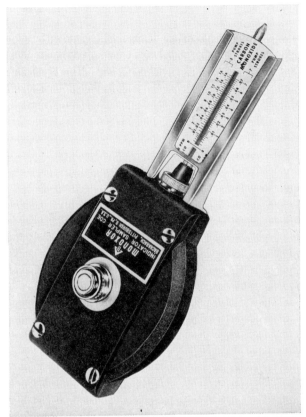

Fig. II-12. Monoxor carbon monoxide indicator (range: 10–2000 ppm CO or 0.001–0.2% CO).   The indicator directly indicates per cent carbon monoxide in the air sample tested by measurement of CO stain in the indicating tube. (Courtesy Bacharach Industrial Instrument Co.)

greatest disadvantage of these bulbs is that the use of them is extremely tedious and fatiguing.

Variations of the aspirator bulb have been developed.   One device is shaped like a cylinder and is equipped with a push button arrangement for compressing the aspirator (Fig. II-11) which on expansion draws in about 16 ml of air.   Another device has the shape shown in Figure II-12.   This aspirator also has a push button arrangement and a capacity of 16 ml.   Both are designed for use with carbon monoxide detector tubes.

b.   Hand Bellows Pump

Hand bellows pumps have been adapted for use in the sampling
of air.   They can be operated by one hand in a fashion similar to an
aspirator bulb.   The Draegerwerk design permits 100 ml to be drawn
in with each stroke and this volume is then passed through a detector
tube at a reproducible rate.   (See Chapter XVIII.)

c.   Hand Pump

The British Department of Scientific and Industrial Research has
adopted as the official sampling device a hand exhausting pump with a
barrel of approximately 1.25-in. bore and a capacity of 126 ml.   To
the inlet end of the pump is screwed a spigot with an external screw
$\frac{7}{16}$ in., outside diameter 0.437 in., having 14 threads per inch according to the American National coarse thread dimensions system.

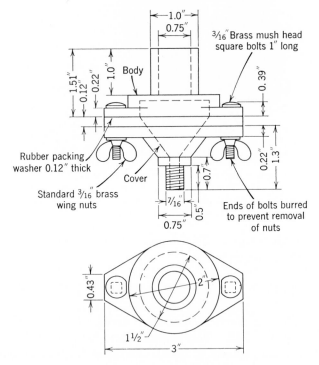

Fig. II-13. Test-paper holder.

To this is screwed a special holder (Fig. II-13) containing a test paper, or the sampling train is attached if an absorber is used. On the upward stroke, the air to be sampled is drawn through the test paper or test solution and is expelled on the downward stroke by a system of valves analogous to the bulb aspirator. The strokes should be slow and steady and a counter may be attached so that the number of strokes made can be read from the counter.

Other hand pumps are described by Viles (15), Haldane (16), Lee (17), and Silverman (18). The pump designed by Lee can also be

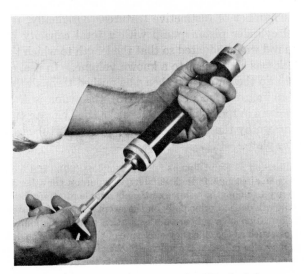

Fig. II-14. MSA hand pump for 500 ml of air.

used for a gas sampler, for when it is clean, dry, and airtight, it will store dry air approximately 24 hr without measurable change in carbon dioxide or oxygen percentage. The Aitken nuclei counter (Chapter V, Section C-1) and the Owens jet dust counter (Chapter V, Section C-7-b) are also equipped with hand pumps. The pump used for the filter-paper method of Brown is described on page 192.

A hand pump (Fig. II-14) that permits drawing 500 ml at one stroke of the piston is sold by Mine Safety Appliances Company. It is equipped with a head to hold filter papers that can be used for direct testing for instance, for lead and for chromates, or for measuring radioactivity.

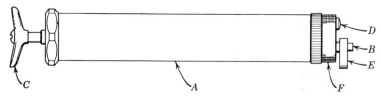

Fig. II-15. Precision metal hand pump: *A*, cylinder; *B*, gas inlet; *C*, handle of piston; *D*, release valve; *E*, tube cutter; *F*, orifice plate.

Kitagawa (19) developed a hand pump for use with detector tubes that has a number of distinctive features. Originally, it consisted of a metal cylinder piston pump with a total capacity of 100 ml. The piston rod was graduated so that the length to which the rod was pushed back was equivalent to a known volume. In use, the sample was drawn into the pump and then was pushed through the detector tube. In an improved model (Fig. II-15), the piston is drawn out to create a vacuum in the cylinder and is locked. The rate at which the sample is drawn by the vacuum through a detector tube is controlled by an orifice plate.

The Calibration of Hand Pumps for Air Sampling (20). If a hand pump is used to take an air sample for industrial hygiene purposes or other air analyses, it is necessary to know the volume of the air sample at atmospheric pressure. This volume will depend principally on the swept volume of a piston pump, or on the deformation of a rubber-bulb aspiration at compression, and also on other factors, such as the efficiency of closure of the valves. The dead space in the pump may also influence the volume of the air sample if the elastic nature of the air-exit valve during compression permits the development of a significant pressure in the dead space; if the swept volume of the pump is V and the dead space v, and p is the excess pressure in the dead space above atmospheric pressure P, then the per cent error in assuming that the volume of the air sample is equal to V is $100vp/VP$. In addition, if the pump is connected to a bubbler containing a head of liquid equal to h, expressed in the same units as p and P, or if the air-inlet valve requires a pressure difference h before opening, then the per cent error attributable to this is $100h/P$; the total possible error is therefore $100(vp + hV)/VP$. With aging of the pump, the magnitude of this error may alter, because of a change in the elasticity of the valve.

The apparatus shown in Figure II-16, which may be constructed from ordinary laboratory glassware, has been used by Gage (20) for several years to check the efficiency of hand pumps, as it gives a direct reading of the volume of the air sample at atmospheric pressure taken under actual conditions of use. For measuring air volumes of about 120 ml, the glass tube, *A*, should be about 40 cm long and 3 cm in diameter. Its lower end is fitted with a rubber stopper through which passes a glass tube, *B*, rising to a height of about 25 cm within *A*, and a drain stopcock, C. The lower end of tube B is connected by means of rubber tubing to the outlet of a water aspirator, E, the neck of which is closed by a stopper fitted with a water-leveling tube, F. The pump to be tested is connected by means of rubber tubing to a glass tube, D, which passes through a rubber stopper in the upper end of tube A. If the pump is to be used with a liquid bubbler, it is preferable to connect it to the apparatus through the bubbler, charged with an appropriate amount of the liquid.

In operation, the stopcock of the aspirator is opened and water is allowed to flow into B with D open to the atmosphere. The relative heights of the aspirator and of tube B are then adjusted so that the water level is just at the top of

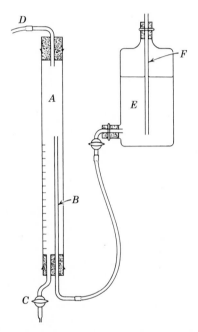

Fig. II-16. Apparatus for hand pump calibration (20).

B, but does not overflow. Stopcock C is opened to drain tube A, and then closed. The pump to be tested is attached at D and operated at the required sampling rate. Water from the aspirator enters A to replace the air withdrawn by the pump, and the pressure in A does not depart appreciably from atmospheric pressure unless the pumping rate is extremely fast.

The volume of water in A gives a measure of the volume of air sampled by the pump at atmospheric pressure; this volume may be determined by draining off the water into a graduated cylinder. Alternatively, tube A may be calibrated to give a direct reading of the volume.

d. Midget-Impinger Pump

The midget-impinger pump (21) (Chapter V, Section C-7-d) is a hand-operated device which has four cylinders set radially at 90° intervals around a single-throw crank (Fig. II-17). The cylinders and crankcase are formed from an integral aluminum casting. The bore is $1\frac{1}{4}$ in. and the stroke is 1 in., equivalent to a total displacement of 4.9 cu in. per revolution. The pistons are made of brass and are attached to a mother bearing on the crank. Rotation of the mother bearing about the crank is prevented by attaching one connecting rod rigidly to it. In each cylinder head there is an intake and exhaust

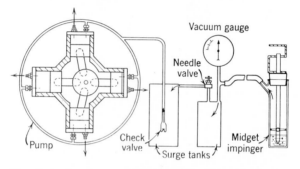

Fig. II-17. Pump for midget-impinger sampling apparatus.

valve of the ball-check type with springs. The intake valves connect to a collector ring attached to a check valve in a surge tank. This is connected in turn to the needle valve of a second surge tank. These tanks serve to make the rate of flow uniform by eliminating the variations arising from uneven cranking and from the separate impulses of the four cylinders. With 60 turns per minute of the crank, a flow of 0.1 cu ft of air through an impinger with a 1-mm orifice can be obtained. The vacuum at this rate of flow is equivalent to 12 in. of water. Sampling instruments using this pump are commercially available.

e. Foot Pumps

Where the use of an aspirator bulb or even a hand pump would be extremely laborious, as in the sampling of mine gas, sewer gas, etc., from an inaccessible place, and where there is no water or other type of power easily available, a double-acting foot pump may be used to purge the long sampling extension line.   The principle of operation is the same as that of the aspirator bulb, i.e., compression drives the gas out of the pump through one valve and release of the pressure admits the gas through another valve in the pump.   These pumps may not be as free from air leakage as desired, especially when sampling by forcing the gas into the collector.   In such a case, the foot pump should be used to purge the extension line and the aspirator bulb should be used to fill the gas collector and thus complete the sampling.

f. Electric Pumps

Over the past two decades there has been a marked increase in the kinds of electrically driven vacuum pumps suitable for industrial hygiene sampling that are commercially available (Fig. II–18).   The tendency has been to use "oilless" direct-drive carbon vane pumps like the Gast pump and small diaphragm pumps rather than pumps requiring oil and a belt.   The larger pumps should be as light in weight as possible and capable of drawing 1 cfm, which is a common sampling rate.   The smaller pumps should have a capacity of at least 0.1 cfm.   Motor pumps for air sampling have been developed that

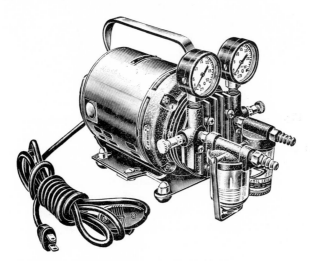

Fig. II-18. Motor-driven pump. (Courtesy Fisher Scientific Co.)

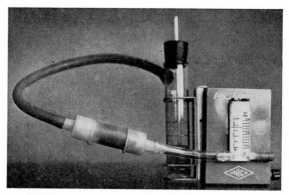

Fig. II-19. Mighty-Mite miniature air sampler. (Photo by R. Jacobs)

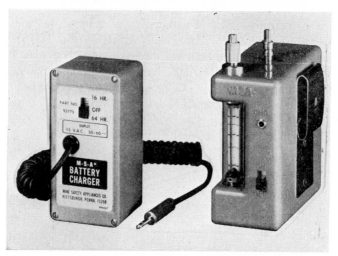

Fig. II-20. Monitaire. (Courtesy Mine Safety Appliances Co.)

can run continuously with recording monitors or sequence samplers for as long as a year. Wheeled carriers are available for heavier pumps. A number of battery-operated pumps are available. Examples of air samplers with this type of pump are the Mighty-Mite (21a) (Fig. II-19) and the Monitaire (21b) (Fig. II-20), which has a miniaturized self-powered vacuum source consisting of a diaphragm pump and battery unit. These are especially useful in the field where no electric power is available. Such sampling pumps are more compact than a midget-impinger pump, are easier to use, and do not weigh very much. Those equipped with wet batteries must be recharged when they run down and those using dry cells must have their batteries replaced or, if they are rechargeable, charged. Some electric pumps are made that can operate on the power of an automobile battery. (See Chapter V for high-volume samplers.)

g.   Motor Vehicle Vacuum Line

In this connection one can mention the use of the suction line of the windshield wipers of a motor vehicle as a source of vacuum for drawing air samples. A tee can be placed in the line with a shutoff valve and the sampling train can be connected when desired. Such a system has the disadvantage that the engine of the vehicle must be operating to supply the power.

2.   WET TYPE

a.   Aspirator Bottles

Where a dry-type aspirator is not available or for other reasons cannot be used, a simple type of wet-form aspirator can be arranged by the use of two large bottles or small carboys. The bottles should be of at least 5-liter capacity and at least one of the bottles should be calibrated and graduated so that the volume of gas aspirated can be ascertained. Bottle or aspirator A (Fig. II-21), which is the one that should be graduated, is filled with water or other suitable liquid such as salt water or water saturated with the gas to be sampled, up to the uppermost graduation. It is connected to the other bottle and to the sampling extension line by means of two glass tubes and a two-hole rubber or other suitable stopper, with one or two screw clamps or stopcocks, as desired. The long glass tube, which should reach the lowest graduation mark, is connected by tubing to the aspirator B. The short glass tube, which should be above the level of the liquid in aspirator A, is connected to the sampling line. By permitting the water or other liquid to flow from A to B, air or gas is drawn into A. The rate of flow, hence the time of sampling, can be regulated by a screw clamp or glass stopcock inserted in the tubing line. The volume drawn in is known from the calibration of A. The air or gas sampled in this way can be drawn into a gas collector which is inserted somewhere in the line between the sampling point and the short tube of the aspirator bottle *A* or through an absorption device as shown in Figure II-21, or the aspirator bottle may serve as the gas collector itself. This setup can be simplified by the

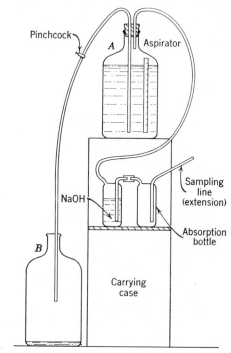

Fig. II-21. Sampling with aspirator bottles.

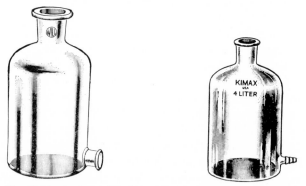

Fig. II-22. Aspirator bottles. (Courtesy Will Scientific, Inc.)

use of aspirator bottles which have exit openings at the bottom of the bottle. With such devices the liquid no longer needs to be siphoned over (Fig. II-22).

Metal aspirators of this form can also be used if they are provided with a glass gauge so that the liquid contents can be ascertained by inspection of the gauge. They are, however, not recommended for sampling of corrosive gases or air which contains contaminants that are likely to react with the metal container, unless the absorption apparatus or gas collector is in the line before the aspirator.

b. Liquid-Displacement Gas Collectors

Actually, liquid-displacement gas collectors are also self-aspirating devices, for as the liquid is withdrawn or as it is permitted to flow out, the gas or air to be sampled is drawn into the collector. The use of collectors that have entrance and exit taps is clear. Bottles used as gas collectors must be arranged as is aspirator A (in Fig. II-21) if they are to act as aspirators. If water is the aspirating liquid, it can generally be discarded. With this type of gas collector or self-aspirator, the rate of sampling can be controlled by the rate of egress of the liquid being displaced.

An aspirating unit made from two 5-gal gasoline cans is described by Silverman and Wardlow (22).

3. EJECTOR TYPE

As mentioned in the instance of pumps there has been considerable development in the use of ejectors for industrial hygiene sampling, particularly the development of compressed gas devices.

a. Water Aspirator or Filter Pump

Very likely the simplest device to use for the aspiration of gases is the water aspirator, or common laboratory filter pump (Fig. II-23). Almost any one of these devices is adequate. Where a faucet is available to which an internal or external nipple can be attached, a water aspirator can also be attached. Pressure tubing, wired if necessary, can be used to connect the faucet and pump when metal nipples are not available or cannot be used. After attaching the water pump, the suction end is attached to the sampling collector and flowmeter, the water is turned on, and the sample is taken. Water

Fig. II-23. Filter pump. (Courtesy Will Scientific, Inc.)

ejectors placed in water lines as permanent installations can be used instead of filter pumps.

b.   Compressed Air Ejectors

The principle of operation of compressed air ejectors is shown in Figure II-24.   Commercial types are available.   Actually, the principle of operation is the same as that of the water filter pump.   If compressed air is available at a plant, the use of such an ejector is advantageous since it can be operated under conditions that avoid the use of electricity.   A compressed air ejector is described in Chapter III, Section A-4-d.

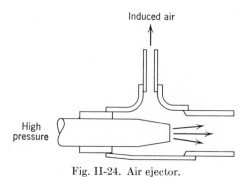

Fig. II-24. Air ejector.

c. Compressed Gas Ejectors

One of the disadvantages of the ejectors mentioned in the preceding paragraphs is lack of portability. A small, lightweight ejector pump operated by the vaporization and expansion of Freon 12R from a disposable container through a microaspirator can develop sufficient vacuum to draw air to be sampled through a collection device. Figure II-25 shows the arrangement of a commercial unit known as the Uni-Jet air sampler used with a midget impinger (see Chapter V, Section C–7-d) and a small rotameter. The entire assembly weighs only 2 lb and can be attached to the side or back of a worker so that it can be used to take samples as the worker performs his duties. Figure II-26 is a section view of the microaspirator. Dichlorodifluoromethane (Freon 12R) entering the nozzle cavity P under pressure is released through the orifice in the lower tip of the nozzle N in the form of a jet which on expansion through the throat T entrains the air in the venturi section between N and T. The removal of air from this cavity creates the vacuum that is used as the power source by connection through a side channel V bored through the aspirator body opposite to the nozzle orifice. Thus, the principle used here is the same as that of the other type of ejectors.

Fig. II-25. Uni-Jet air sampler. (Photo by R. Jacobs)

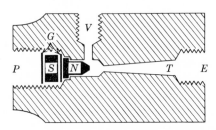

Fig. II-26. Section view of Uni-Jet aspirator (not to scale): *S*, orifice plate; *N*, nozzle; *T*, throat; *G*, gaskets (O rings); *P*, $\frac{7}{16}$ × 20 SAE thread—pressure; *V*, $\frac{1}{8}$ in. pipe thread—vacuum; *E*, $\frac{1}{8}$ in. pipe thread—exhaust.

When operating against low sampling flow resistance, 0.18 cu ft of dichlorodifluoromethane (at atmospheric pressure) will aspirate 1 cu ft of air, or on a weight basis 1 lb of dichlorodifluoromethane will aspirate up to 17 cu ft of air at less than 2 in. of water pressure drop. Generally, 1 lb of this propellant will pump from 6–15 cu ft of air over a total sampling time of 4 hr.

As the propellant evaporates, the static vacuum drops with time of use. Hence, the sample rate is dependent on the dichlorodifluoromethane gas pressure at the aspirator jet. This pressure can be controlled by orifices inserted between the nozzle and the propellant supply valve. A set of four such orifices (6, 8, 10, and 12 thousandths of an inch) can be used to control sampling rates over the range of 2–10 cfh. The volume of air sampled can be read from the time the jet is operated and the ambient temperature by use of a temperature-compensated calibration chart (23) that is supplied with the commercial device. Other types of calibration charts can also be used (24).

Instead of using such calibration charts, the low-pressure drop rotameter mentioned can be used, but it is necessary to remember that the rate deviations must be kept within 5% and the time elapsed must be determined with the aid of a stopwatch. From the time and the rate of flow, the volume of air sampled can be calculated.

A constant sampling rate can be achieved by various methods such as (*1*) keeping the propellant container in a constant-temperature bath, (*2*) chilling the container so that the dichlorodifluoromethane temperature is between 32 and 37°F (0–3°C), or (*3*) using a large enough dichlorodifluoromethane reservoir so that the heat required to vaporize the propellant for aspiration does not cool the liquid dichlorodifluoromethane more than 5°F. In another development Linch, Charsa, and Wetherhold (25) invert the propellant container and allow the liquid dichlorodifluoromethane to escape through a refrigerator-type valve at a uniform rate. The liquid, in turn, evaporates uniformly at ambient temperature and draws the air sample at a constant flow rate.

Among the advantages of this type of ejector is that it can be used safely in explosion hazard areas because of the absence of moving parts, electric circuits, or the accumulation of static charges. Because it requires little attention except to start the flow of the compressed gas, multistation surveys can be performed easily if calibration charts or constant-flow methods are used. Atmospheres containing toxic concentrations can be sampled even in inaccessible places.

The use of this microaspirator is not limited to employing a propellant such as compressed dichlorodifluoromethane, for, if portability is not a controlling factor, compressed nitrogen or compressed air can also be used. Again, if portability is not a factor, larger tanks of dichlorodifluoromethane can be employed as the propellant and thus longer periods of sampling can be carried out.

F. Sequence and Multiple Samplers

Among the more commonly used instruments for automatically collecting samples are the sequence samplers, a number of different devices being available.

1. AUTOMATIC IMPINGERS

The Wilson automatic impinger (26) is a device that can be used for automatic sampling over a 24-hr period, the sample collected being dependent upon the absorbing reagent. It has been used for collecting samples for the determination of sulfur dioxide by the peroxide method (see Chapter XII, Section B-2-b), for ammonia by nesslerization (see Chapter XIV, Section B-2-b), for oxidants by the Smith and Diamond method (see Chapter XV, Section B-2-b), and for more general sampling for the determination of gaseous and particulate matter in the air. These have been discussed in detail by Jacobs (27).

The instrument is shown diagrammatically in Figure II-27. The absorbent solution is placed in the reservoir which is inverted over the

leveling funnel.　When the three-way stopcock has been rotated by
the synchronous motor of the hour clock so that it is connected to the
reservoir, absorbing solution will flow from the reservoir to the impinger up to a level equivalent to that of the leveling funnel.　The
three-way stopcock continuing its rotation will shut off the flow from
the reservoir and the cam rotated by the same motor engages a microswitch which turns on the vacuum pump drawing air through the

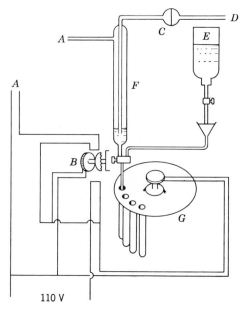

Fig. II-27. Wilson automatic sequence sampler for nitrogen dioxide (26): *A*, to
pump; *B*, hour clock; *C*, dust filter; *D*, to sampling point; *E*, reservoir; *F*, fritted
bubbler; *G*, 24-hr clock.

absorbing liquid.　At the end of the selected sampling period, usually
of the order of 40 min, the cam disengages the microswitch turning
off the pump, while the rotating three-way stopcock is now open to the
discharge port at the bottom of the impinger.　In this interval, one
of the collecting tubes held by the turntable is brought into position
by the synchronous motor of the 24-hr clock and the collected sample
is emptied into the collecting tube.　The turntable is equipped to

carry 24 tubes so that the cycle can be repeated 24 times. By arranging the flow from the reservoir over a 10-min period, the sampling period for 40 min, and the discharge period for 10 min, 24 samples can be collected in a period of 24 hr.

By use of a solenoid valve instead of a three-way stopcock, the period of filling the impinger can be reduced to 1 min, and the discharge time can be reduced to 1 min, thus increasing the sampling time to 58 min out of every hour.

The samples collected in this manner can then be analyzed in the field or can be brought back to the laboratory for analysis. It is clear that this type of sampling gives an integrated sample for the period in which the sampling was conducted. When a 40-min sampling period is used, the 20 min missed in the sampling time out of every hour may be significant. This possibility of missing a significant emission is reduced by use of the solenoid valves. In any event, however, peak concentrations, except on an hourly basis, cannot be obtained by such sequence samplers.

Jacobs and Hochheiser (28) modified this type of automatic impinger.

Cholak and co-workers (29) used a sequence sampler consisting of a pump, 12 scrubbing devices, and a clock mechanism that opened each scrubbing flask to the atmosphere in regular turn.

A different type of sequence sampler is described by Gelman (30). In this device, which can be used with midget impingers, bubblers, or filter papers, 12 consecutive samples may be collected. A bellows pump is used for the midget impingers and a rotary vacuum pump for filter samples. Other types of sequence samplers are commercially available.

2. SEQUENCE ABSORBERS

Jacobs and Hochheiser (28) modified the Wilson sequence sampler by replacing the modified macroimpinger with a gas disperser of coarse fritted glass in a bubbler of equivalent dimensions to the impinger. A filter paper trap 11 in. in diameter was placed in the line to retain particulate matter, and a flowmeter capable of registering 1.3 lpm was also used. This modified sequence sampler was used for the collection of samples for the ultramicrodetermination of nitrogen oxides in air (27).

3. MULTIPLE GAS SAMPLER

The National Air Sampling Network of the Community Air Pollution Program, USPHS, developed a multiple gas sampler (31,32) which could be placed at various stations throughout the country in a fashion analogous to their particulate matter sampling program.

This sampler was designed to permit the concurrent sampling of five different gases. The collection system, consisting of five bubblers, is mounted in a wooden box $11\frac{1}{2} \times 10\frac{1}{2} \times 8$ in. The air to be sampled is first filtered through a membrane filter to remove particulate matter and is then passed through a manifold to the bubblers which contain absorbing or reacting solutions for the particular gaseous pollutants to be determined. The effluent air stream is filtered through glass wool to remove any absorption solution droplets and is passed through critical capillary orifices to the exhaust manifold. A constant air flow of 100 ml/min is maintained through each bubbler by means of these critical orifices. A constant temperature of 100°F is maintained in the box by the use of two heaters controlled by a thermostat. A diaphragm pump is used to draw the air at the specified rate. It uses 1.35 A and 110 V ac. The diaphragm has a life of about 300 hr.

The sampler is designed to permit sampling for 24-hr periods so that it can be used in conjunction with high-volume samplers.

G. Sampling Procedure

Before a sample is taken, it is necessary to note the condition of the air or gas being sampled—whether the air is moving appreciably, whether the air is stratified and heterogeneous, or whether the air is still, i.e., air movement less than 25 fpm. A different method of sampling procedure is to be followed in each case. If there is a good air current and there is reason to believe that the air is fairly uniform, and it is desired to take a sample at a given point, only one sample need be taken as representative. If doubt exists, it is best to take more than one sample, following the recommendations given on page 38. If the air is still or is moving only slowly or if there is contamination at a given point—for instance, where a volatile solvent is evaporating or in a mine where there are gaseous products of explosions— the air in such instances is very likely to be stratified and nonhomogeneous. In this case, it is necessary either to take a sample at the given point, which represents the composition only at that point, or to take several samples. In the instance in which several samples are to be taken, the method of dividing a cross section into imaginary rectangles may be used. Take a cross section of a room, mine passage, or other air passage and divide it by eye into equal rectangles. Then take a sample of gas from the center of each rectangle. This procedure is really a modification of the method of sampling by quartering as applied to gases (33,34).

It has been made clear from the description of gas-sample collectors and aspirating devices that these devices fall into six sampling groups.

(1) Vacuum displacement
(2) Air displacement
(3) Liquid displacement
(4) Inflation
(5) Absorption or adsorption in or on some medium
(6) Condensation, freezing, etc.

1. VACUUM DISPLACEMENT

a.   Vacuum Gas Collector

When a gas collector having a very high sealed-in vacuum is employed in order to take the sample, it is common procedure to select a straight-section of the air course, if there is appreciable air movement of at least 100 fpm. If a nick has not been made in the neck of the vacuum tube, make one with a sharp file or other means at an appropriate point to facilitate breaking. Stand facing the air current with the vacuum tube at arm's length. Break the sealed tip by holding the shoulder of the tube in one hand, while the sealed tip is bent and broken by the other hand with some adequate device, such as a $\frac{1}{4}$- $\times$ 3-in. pipe nipple or a small piece of hardwood with a hole slightly larger than the capillary neck, a pair of pliers, the head of a cabinet-lock key, an old-fashioned clock-winding key, or some similar device. The tube should not be struck against a wall or rock, the roof, ribs, and timbering of a mine, or a bench in a shop: first, if it is broken at any of those points, the sample will be of that point; second, the tube neck may be broken in such a spot that it will be practically impossible to seal it after the sample has been taken; or third, the tube may be shattered completely and so be entirely useless. When the tip of the tube is broken as has been described, the inward rush of air produces a

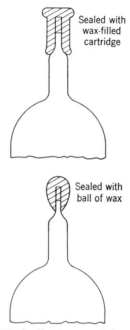

Sealed with
wax-filled
cartridge

Sealed with
ball of wax

Fig. II-28. Sealing vacuum-tube collectors.

hissing noise. When the hiss ceases, the tube may be assumed to be full. Hold the tube in place for about 5 sec after the hissing ceases to be certain sampling is completed. Care must be taken that the break is clean so that no glass particles or obstruction prevents the air from rushing into the tube. If such an obstruction exists, it must be removed.

After sampling has been finished, place the tube in a suitable position and seal it with wax (35) by working the metallic cartridge containing the wax over the tip of the collector tube with a twisting motion so that the wax is forced into the capillary opening but not with so much force that it enters into the sample container. Make a tight joint around the shoulder of the tube with the wax which protrudes from the cartridge (Fig. II-28). If a piece of wax is used instead of the cartridge, work it around into a ball after forcing it into the capillary tip. The proper type of wax should be prepared at the laboratory by heating two parts beeswax with one part Venice, or larch, turpentine. Venice, or larch, turpentine is the type obtained from the European larch. During summer months or for the sampling of gases in warm places, the proportion of beeswax should be increased by 20%. Melt the wax and pour it into empty cartridges—.38 caliber, short, brass cartridge shells—or cut it into pieces of adequate size to give a good ball seal. Do not melt the wax when using it for sealing, because the combustible vapors formed will spoil the subsequent analysis. Do not use chewing gum, paraffin wax, or tar, as these substances do not form a proper seal with the glass.

When the vacuum tube is used to sample gas or air in an inaccessible place, such as the blister or hold of a ship, a tank car, behind a fire or gas seal in a mine, or a sewer or manhole, the following procedure may be used. An extension line or tube, preferably of glass or metal that will not be attacked by or react with the components of the gas or air being sampled, to which is attached an end of rubber tubing of an adequate coupling device, is placed, pushed, or dropped, as the case may be, to the point to be sampled. When sampling at the point at which a workman breathes, the extension line must be fixed at that point by some device. If the workman moves in a limited area, arrangement must be made to have the connecting line move with him. The length and volume of the extension line should be known. It should then be purged with one of the aspirator devices previously described. At least 10–15 times the volume of the gas to be sampled should be used in the purging process. After purging, close the rubber end of the tube with a pinch clamp or with some stopcock arrangement or use the T-tube method illustrated in Fig. II-36. As quickly as possible fit the line tightly over the neck of the vacuum tube. Break the tip by grasping and bending as shown in Fig. II-29. Wait one-half minute for the tube to fill. Remove from the extension line and seal as described previously.

An alternative device has been described by Fene (36). It employs a common snap-type mousetrap to break the neck of a vacuum tube at the place where it is desired to collect the sample. A mousetrap is mounted on one end of a block of wood $11\frac{3}{4} \times 3 \times \frac{3}{4}$ in. in such manner that a lead weight attached to the trigger will spring the trap when the device is given a sharp jerk. A vacuum tube is placed on the other end of the block and held in place by a strong rubber band. A strip of corrugated rubber is placed on each side of the grooved block to prevent the tube from slipping when the sample is taken. An adjustable shoulder provided with a rubber cap is placed so that the

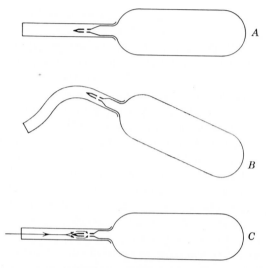

Fig. II-29. Method for filling vacuum containers through extension hose leading to inaccessible places.

(*A*) After purging hose, tightly insert shoulder of container.

(*B*) Break tip by grasping tip in one hand, the container in the other, and bend hose.

(*C*) Allow gas to flow past loosely fitting end of broken tip into container.

neck of the vacuum tube will rest on it. The shoulder is made adjustable to accommodate various sizes of tubes and to keep the neck of the tube from breaking too far back from the point. A metal handle is fastened to one end of the block, with a hole in the end through which the brass wire used for lowering the device is tied. The device is enclosed by a strong wire-gauze covering, hinged on one side and so arranged that it can be locked shut on the other side. This covering prevents breaking of the tube while it is being lowered or raised in a shaft or other place. Brass wire of not less than 22 gauge should be used for lowering the device. A drawing of the device is shown in Figure II-30.

In collecting air samples in shafts, sewers, gas wells, or empty oil tanks, a vacuum tube is adjusted so that the spring of the trap will hit the neck of the tube about halfway between the file mark and the tip of the tube. The trap is set, making certain that the lead weight is extended downward as far as possible. The device is lowered in a ver-

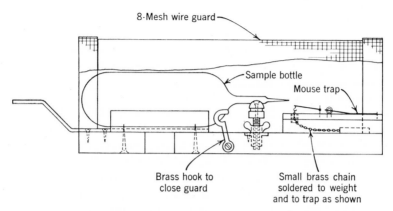

Fig. II-30. Sampling device for collecting gas samples in inaccessible places (36).

tical position to the point where the sample is to be collected, and the lowering wire is given a sharp jerk, which will cause the trap to spring and break the neck of the tube.   The device is pulled quickly to the surface and a seal placed on the opening in the neck of the tube. Under ordinary atmospheric pressure, none of the sample will be displaced in the tube while it is being raised to the surface.   Samples have been collected with this device in shafts at depths of 450 ft and through a 6-in. vent pipe in a concrete seal over an air shaft. The device permits collection of samples at any desired place in a shaft or well.

In collecting samples from behind seals in mines, it is necessary to provide the seal with a pipe large enough to permit passage of the sampling device.   With the cover removed, the device can be passed through a 3-in. pipe.   To collect a sample of air from behind a seal, the device should be fastened securely to a pole or rod and pushed through the pipe, making sure that the lead weight connected to the trigger of the trap is extended as far as it will go.   A sharp jerk forward will cause the trap to spring and break the neck of the tube.

b.   Continuous Sampling Device

When gas flows through a fixed orifice inserted in a tube, its velocity increases with the pressure drop across the orifice until the ratio of upstream to downstream pressure is about 2:1.   When this ratio is reached, the gas passes through the orifice at the velocity of sound, and further increase in pressure drop has no effect on gas velocity, which is now independent of both upstream and downstream pressures (37). The ambient volume flow rate is also constant and the mass flow rate is proportional to the upstream density.

If a flask is evacuated and ambient gas is permitted to enter through a small orifice inserted in an inlet tube, the ambient volume flow rate remains fixed, regardless of ambient pressure, until the internal pressure reaches half ambient. If the flow is allowed to continue beyond this point, it falls gradually off until pressure equilibrium is reached. By proper choice of flask volume and orifice area, the period of constant flow may be varied within wide limits. If two stopcocks and a pressure gauge are fitted to the flask, the result is an acoustic flow device that can be used to sample ambient air at a constant rate over any desired period of time.

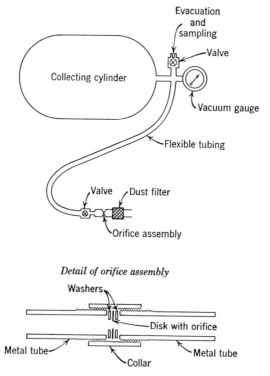

Fig. II-31. Diagram of fixed-orifice-type continuous gas-sampling device.

The apparatus is detailed in Figure II-31. The collecting flask must be able to withstand a vacuum and have a convenient size and weight. U. S. Army-type low-pressure aviation oxygen cylinders were found satisfactory. Orifices 50–165 μ in diameter permit flows of 25–250 ml/min. These are most convenient in practice. Such orifices can be made easily by drilling disks of metal foil or by piercing such disks with a sharp needle. The disks may be cemented between washers and mounted as indicated in Figure II-31. The flows indicated are small and it is therefore important to use care in sealing all joints to avoid residual leakage. The internal pressure is best measured with an accurate absolute pressure gauge. A differential-pressure or vacuum gauge will also serve, but it is then necessary to determine the ambient pressure for each reading. A filter is desirable where dust or smoke particles may clog the orifice; however, it should introduce only a very small pressure drop. The dead space between the intake nozzle and the control stopcock should be small enough to introduce very little time lag in the gas collection. The inlet tube may be rubber pressure tubing, $\frac{1}{8}$ to $\frac{1}{4}$-in. diameter and 5–10 ft long, which will generally be long enough to permit the flask to be put in a convenient place.

Sampling Procedure. Before use, the apparatus must be evacuated to a pressure low enough to keep the constant-flow period within proper limits. Under ordinary conditions a water-sealed pump or an aspirator is satisfactory; however, a high-vacuum pump can be used also. After the apparatus has been evacuated, the valves are closed and the flask is set up for the test with the intake nozzle placed so as to sample at a desired point. As the orifice valve is opened, the internal pressure and time are recorded. At the end of the collection period, as the valve is closed, the internal pressure and time are recorded again, and the device is ready to have a sample taken for analysis. Since the flask is still half evacuated, it is good practice to fill it with clean air up to ambient pressure, particularly when time will elapse before an analysis is made. This procedure minimizes the effect of residual leaks but a correction factor must be applied to the analytical results.

Analytical Procedure. Connect a clean gas sampling tube to a leveling bulb with about 2 ft of rubber tubing and fill the system with water. Connect the inlet of the gas sampling tube to the outlet nipple of the collecting flask with a short piece of rubber tubing fitting the glass as near to the metal as possible. With the stopcocks open, lower the leveling bulb until about 30 ml. of water is displaced by gas from the flask. By proper manipulation of the stopcocks, close off the flask and open the sampling tube to the outside. Raise the leveling bulb to displace the gas from the sampling tube with water. This process serves to flush out dead-space air and should be repeated once or twice. Finally, take the gas into the sampling tube, fill it completely, and retain it for analysis.

The use of a water-sealed collecting system requires that the gas in the collecting flask be diluted to ambient pressure with clean air, that is, air free from carbon monoxide, mercury, organic solvents, etc. The volume of the sampling tube must be large enough to hold the amount of gas required for analysis, but should be small compared with the volume of the collecting flask. For example, with a 16-liter collecting flask and a 200-ml sampling tube, two partial flush-outs and one filling of the sampling tube remove less than 300 ml from the flask, which is 2% of its volume. Thus, a suction of 15 mm Hg, or about 7 in. w.g., is required. The entire sampling process may be performed, if necessary, three times with the 2-ft tube from the sampling tube to the collecting flask. Analyses for specific compounds may be performed as described in the text.

Calculations. The time average partial pressure $\bar{p}$ of the gas under study may be calculated from the concentration C, in the flask, using the formula

$$\bar{p} = \frac{V}{ut} p_3 C$$

where V = volume of the flask, including the inlet tube and pressure gauge; u = ambient volume flow rate; p_3 = pressure in the flask; t = duration of the collection period.

If the sample is diluted to atmospheric pressure, p_3 is simply the barometer reading. This formula is strictly valid only when the ambient temperature is constant throughout the test run. The error introduced by a temperature variation of 60°C, in 1 hr, is only 5%; hence, in practice this formula may be used for a wide variety of field conditions.

c.   Vacuum Bottle

The method of sampling with vacuum bottles evacuated at or near the point of sampling has been described in connection with the de-

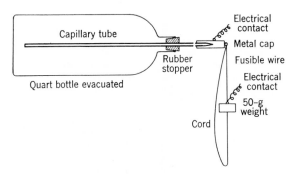

Fig. II-32. Vacuum sampling bottle for sampling in inaccessible places.

scription of the bottle itself (Section D-2). Inaccessible places may be sampled, as explained in the previous paragraph, with the use of an extension line connected to the arm having stopcock A in Figure II-2. The volume sampled must be computed, for the residual pressure generally is sufficiently great to introduce a volume error if not corrected by calculation.

Illustrative of the use of evacuated bottles in sampling at a distance is the electrical method for sampling for hydrocyanic acid used as a fumigant in ships (38).

A Winchester quart bottle closed with a rubber stopper is evacuated through a capillary tube, which is then sealed hermetically. It is placed horizontally in a wicker frame and a weight is attached to the end of the capillary tube by a cord about 2 ft in length, and also by a short piece of fusible wire as shown in Figure II-32. The electric wires are connected with the two ends of the fuse wire so as to form a closed circuit which can be operated from a distance. On passing a current sufficiently strong to fuse the wire, the weight is released, which on falling to the full length of the cord causes the fracture of the capillary, and thus permits the surrounding air to enter into the bottle. The vacuum sampling containers can be set before the fumigation begins. Sampling can then take place when desired and the samples collected after the hold is clear of gas.

A simpler method that does not require the use of electricity, which is not always available, is the following (38).

A Winchester quart bottle, fitted with a ground glass stopper with a sealed-in capillary tube reaching almost to the bottom of the bottle, is evacuated through its side arm and sealed hermetically as shown in Figure II-33. The part of the capillary above the side arm ends in a stout glass ring to which may be attached a thin cord or wire. At point A the capillary tube is nicked with a file so that on pulling the cord the capillary will break readily at that point. The evacuated

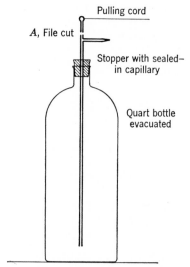

Fig. II-33. Vacuum sampling bottle for sampling in inaccessible places.

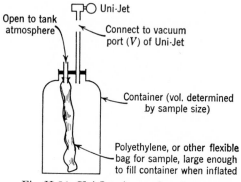

Fig. II-34. Uni-Jet air sample collector.

bottles are placed in position before fumigation and are tied to stanchions or other supports. Cords or wires are attached to the rings and are led out to the deck or dock side through keyholes, hatch covers, small openings, etc., so as to give a direct right-angle pull on the capillary tube. The samples may then be collected after the hold, compartment, or room is free of gas.

In both instances, a reagent with which the contaminant will react may be placed in the vacuum bottle before evacuation. In the case of hydrocyanic acid, 50 ml of 0.04N sodium hydroxide solution is used.

A variation of the vacuum bottle method of sampling by vacuum displacement is one in which the vacuum is prepared in the field by use of a compressed gas ejector. A polyethylene or other plastic flexible bag is attached to the intake port of a rigid sampling container as shown in Figure II-34 and the air in the container is evacuated by aspiration with the compressed gas. This procedure eliminates the need for preparation and transportation of the vacuum container.

2. AIR DISPLACEMENT

Where sampling by air displacement (7) is desired, the methods illustrated in Fig. II-35 may be used. The rubber aspirator symbolizes the position of the aspirating devices that may be used. It is necessary to purge the entire line and the gas collector itself with at least ten times the capacity of both the gas collector and extension line, when they are used to get at an inaccessible place. Thus, for example, it will require 50 squeezes of the ordinary 50-ml rubber bulb aspirator to take a 250-ml sample. The tube or bottle should be held in place after the required amount of purging and sampling has been completed until the gas collector has been sealed and the aspirating device removed. Where sampling by gas displacement from inaccessible places is necessary, the position of the gas collector, aspirator,

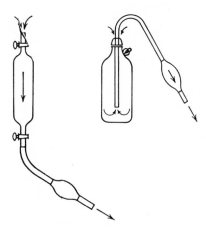

Fig. II-35. Sampling by gas displacement. The atmosphere sampled should be discharged outside sampling zone (7).

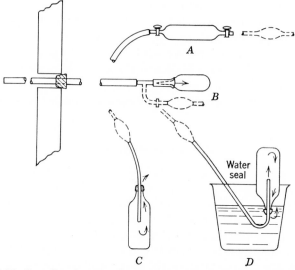

Fig. II-36. Sampling by gas displacement from inaccessible places (7).

and extension line should be as is indicated in Figure II-36. Purging and sampling then proceed as described.

As noted in the preceding paragraph, it has been known for many years, on an empirical basis, that a gas collector should be purged with at least ten times its volume to make certain that all, or virtually all, of the initial air has been flushed out by air to be sampled. Silver (39), in studying constant-flow gas chambers (see Chapter III, Section C-7), has shown that the time required to raise the concentration of the pollutant in the chamber (in this instance the sampling flask) to 99% of its concentration in the air being sampled, i.e., the entering air can be calculated by the following expression:

$$t = 4.6052a/b$$

where t = time in minutes, a = volume of flask in liters, and b = air flow in liters per minute.

3. LIQUID DISPLACEMENT

As was explained in the section on aspirators, liquid-displacement gas collectors are actually self-aspirators. The procedure of sampling where the place of sampling is accessible is very simple and convenient.

The liquid in the gas collector is run out by draining or pouring within the zone of the gas to be sampled and then the container is closed and sealed. The liquid to be used depends on the type of sample. Water, water saturated with the gas or gases to be tested, salt solutions, and mercury are the ordinary liquids used. Solubility errors may be minimized or eliminated by use of gas–salt solutions or mercury. Where the solubility of a gas is very small, this precaution is unnecessary. When mercury is used, it should, of course, be poured into another container and not be permitted to escape on the ground or floor.

Sampling by liquid displacement from places that are not within easy reach, and therefore require an extension sampling line, is performed in an entirely analogous manner to the procedure previously described. The extension line must first be purged of the ordinary air it contains with ten times its volume of the air to be sampled by means of some independent aspirating device. Then the extension sampling line is attached to the liquid displacement gas collector and the liquid is permitted to drain or pour out as illustrated in Figure II-37. Capillary extension tubes may be attached to the exit tube of the gas collector to prevent back flow of air, or tubes with an internal extension tube may be used for the same purpose. Gas collector tubes with three-way stopcocks and extra tubulatures at the entrance tap simplify the purging procedure, for the use of T tubes is no longer necessary. The extension line may be purged through the side tubulature. The rate of sampling when using liquid-displacement gas collectors is controlled by the rate of exit flow of draining or pouring.

4. INFLATION

Multilayer plastic bags and other types of plastic containers can be inflated with the air, gas, or effluent to be sampled by means of a pump. Such containers are commercially available (40). It is interesting to note that the use of inflatable containers for sampling extends back to the 18th century—to the very origins of air and gas analysis, that is, to Priestley, who used inflatable bladders.

5. ABSORPTION AND ADSORPTION

The most useful method of sampling when large volumes of gas have to be handled in order to obtain the necessary amount for adequate

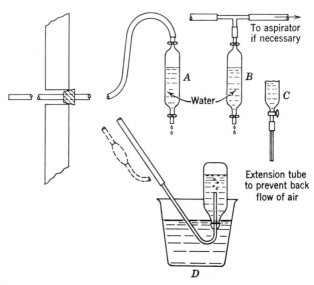

Fig. II-37. Sampling by water displacement from inaccessible places (7).

analysis of a component present in minute quantity is that of absorption or adsorption of the component to be estimated by some agent. Some absorbers, traps, bubblers, absorbents, and adsorbents will be discussed in Chapter IV. An absorber containing the absorbing medium is placed in the sampling line after that line has been purged with the air to be sampled. Then a sufficient quantity of the air being sampled is aspirated at a rate sufficiently rapid to pass through enough air to give an adequate estimation, but this flow must not be so rapid that the ingredient to be determined fails to be absorbed. A flowmeter of some type or other gas-measurement device must also be in the line so that the amount of gas sampled will be known. If necessary, other absorbers must be in the line. Thus, after using a very strong acid-absorbing medium, it is necessary to place an absorber containing sodium hydroxide or other alkali to neutralize any acid that may be carried over during the aspiration process. (See Fig. II-21.)

In general, when homogeneous solutions are obtained by use of an absorber as a result of the reaction or solution of the component being estimated with or in the absorbent, rinsings should not be combined with the sampling fluid. The volume of the absorbent recovered should be noted. This practice avoids unnecessary dilution of the sample.

6.   OTHER SAMPLING PROCEDURES

If a gas under positive pressure is to be sampled, as is the case with gas cylinders or in a main provided with outlet cocks, the gas collector must be attached by some short extension line to the cylinder or to the outlet taps of the main.   After purging the sampling line with the gas to be examined by permitting four or five volumes of that gas to pass through the connecting tube and some side arm or through the collector itself, if the gas displacement method is being used, the gas collector is permitted to be filled under the outward pressure of the gas itself, and the cocks are closed and then sealed.

Syringes such as Luer syringes have been used for sampling—principally for field determinations.   Illustrative of such procedures are those of Patty and Petty, and Jacobs and Brody for nitrogen dioxide–nitrogen tetroxide mixtures detailed in Chapter XIV, those for the determination of oxygen (41), and those for the estimation of carbon monoxide (42,43).

Brief mention should be made of the sampling of hot gases, occluded gases, and gases under reduced pressure.   When hot gases have to be sampled, glass, heat resistant glass, quartz, porcelain, and metal connecting tubes must be employed according to the temperature of the gas.   Porcelain tubes should be preheated and metal tubes should be cooled by a condenser jacket.

When occluded gases or gases under reduced pressure are desired for analysis, they must be swept out into the sampling vessel by some means, they must be pumped out by the use of a Toepler pump (11) or its equivalent, or they must be obtained by aspiration.

If a gas is to be sampled in a flue or large pipe where the composition varies considerably between the sides and center of the flue, an extension tube, passing through the pipe from one side to the other cross-sectionally, having openings at different points along its length or a length-long slit, comparable to the slot in a sampling tube, may be used to obtain a sample, or a number of samples can be taken at different points.

It is well to remember that very likely the safest procedure from the point of view of accuracy is to take duplicate samples for any point sample, if at all possible.

Sampling methods for the determination of air pollutants have been discussed in considerable detail by Jacobs (44).

7. SAMPLING SOLIDS AND LIQUIDS

Various implements have been developed to assist in the proper sampling of solid and liquid substances.   The more important of these are the sampling tube, the trier, the scoop, and the thief.   The *sampling tube* (Fig. II-38) is an instrument designed for the sampling of powders.   It is generally a brass tube, 2–3 ft long and ½–1 in. wide, with a conical sharp tip at one end and a handle at the other. The tube has a slot which extends almost the entire length of the sampling device from the tip to the handle.   Some of these instru-

Fig. II-38. Sampling tube.   (Courtesy Eimer and Amend)

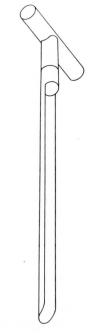

Fig. II-39. Sampling trier.

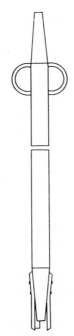

Fig. II-40. Oil thief.

ments consist of two brass telescopic tubes having slots which may be opened and closed by rotation of the inner tube. The outer tube is equipped, as was described above, with a conical tip and handle. The sharp tip enables the instrument to penetrate the material being sampled.

The *sampling trier* (Fig. II-39) is a very long gouge. It has about the same dimensions as the sampling tube. The tip and edges of the trier are sharpened so that, after insertion into the material to be sampled, turning the trier will cut a core of the material. The general method of use of either the trier or sampling tube is to insert the instrument practically its full length into the material being sampled from a point near a top edge or corner, through the center, to a point diagonally opposite the point of entry. Usually, two or more cores are withdrawn from points equidistant from the first.

The *thief* is an instrument which is used for sampling liquids. It is a tube, generally about 2 or 3 ft long, which has holes in a cap at the bottom end. The tube is inserted into the liquid and when the solvent has risen to the same level as the surrounding liquid, the tube is closed by pushing the cap against the bottom of the container. The thief is then withdrawn and the sample is transferred to a sample bottle. A variation of this type of thief is the oil thief (Fig. II-40), which is a copper tube about 3 ft long and $1\frac{1}{4}$ in. in diameter, with cone shaped ends having an opening $\frac{3}{8}$ in. in diameter. Three legs are placed on the lower end to hold the opening $\frac{1}{8}$ in. from the bottom of the drum. Two rings, soldered to opposite sides at the upper end, permit holding the thief with two fingers, leaving the thumb free to close the upper opening and thus withdraw the sample. Sampling methods for liquids have been discussed in detail by Jacobs and Scheflan (45).

The U. S. Bureau of Mines (46,47) uses the "scoop and brush" method of collecting settled dust samples. A metal scoop, 6 in. wide, a 3-in. paint brush, a sizing screen, and a piece of oilcloth comprise the outfit.

After the sample has been withdrawn or taken with one of these instruments (or even by simpler methods, such as by the use of a ladle or dipper in the case of liquids or by a shovel in the case of solids), it must be transferred to a proper sample bottle, jar, or container. If the liquid is a solvent, care must be taken not to place it in a container which has some part soluble in the solvent. Thus, if benzene is being sampled, the sample should not be placed in a rubber stoppered container or one which has a rubber gasket.

All containers should be properly labeled, giving the date of sampling, the time, if necessary, the place, and the type of sample. The container should be sealed in such a way that the contents cannot be tampered with nor the contents leak or spill. Metal sampling instruments should not be used with corrosive materials unless adequately protected.

8. SAMPLING DATA

In order to correlate the analysis of a sample of air or gas with the sampling, certain pertinent data must be known. These data may be listed as follows:

(1) Identification Purposes
  (a) Sample number
  (b) Sample type

(c)   Date, time, place, and locality
(d)   Name of inspector or collector
(e)   Method of sampling

(2)   Computation Purposes

(a)   Pressure

Barometer reading and all other pressures needed, such as residual and final pressures in vacuum bottle sampling, or outward or negative pressure in a mine fire seal

(b)   Temperature

Wet bulb⎱
Dry bulb⎰ if necessary

(c)   Humidity
(d)   Velocity
(e)   Quantity

With the data of group (2), the gas calculations given for the measurement of quantity in gases, Chapter III, Section C, may be performed.

References

1. Keenan, R. G., in "The Industrial Environment. . .Its Evaluation and Control," *Public Health Service Publ. 614* (1958).
2. Hosey, A. D., and R. G. Keenan, in "The Industrial Environment. . .Its Evaluation and Control," *Public Health Service Publ. 614* (1958).
3. Jacobs, M. B., *The Chemical Analysis of Air Pollutants*, Interscience, New York, 1960.
4. Report of Subcommittee on Chemical Methods in Air Analysis, Sampling and Sampling Devices, *Am. Public Health Assoc. Yearbook 1939–40*, p. 92.
5. Flinn, R. H., *Public Health Bull. 270* (1941).
6. Watson, H. H., *Am. Med. Hyg. Assoc. Quarterly*, **15**, 21 (1954).
7. Yant, W. P., and L. B. Berger, *U.S. Bur. Mines Miners' Circ. 34* (1936).
8. Siegel, J., and W. J. Burke, *N.Y. State Ind. Bull.*, **18**, 17 (1939).
9. McNally, W. D., *Toxicology*, Industrial Medicine, Chicago, 1937.
10. Huntly, G. N., *J. Soc. Chem. Ind.*, **29**, 312 (1910).
11. Lunge, G., and H. R. Ambler, *Technical Gas Analysis*, Van Nostrand, New York, 1934.
12. Gray, T., *J. Soc. Chem. Ind.*, **29**, 312 (1910).
13. Magill, P. L., in *Air Pollution Abatement Manual*, Mfg. Chemists' Assoc., Washington, D. C., 1952, Chap. 6.
14. Welch, A. F., and J. P. Terry, *Am. Ind. Hyg. Assoc. J.*, **21**, 316 (Aug. 1960).
15. Viles, F. J., *J. Ind. Hyg. Toxicol.*, **22**, 188 (1940).

16. Haldane, J. S., and J. I. Graham, *Methods of Air Analysis*, Griffin, London, 1935.
17. Lee, R. C., *Ind. Eng. Chem. Anal. Ed.*, **5**, 354 (1933).
18. Silverman, L., and J. F. Ege, Jr., *J. Ind. Hyg. Toxicol.*, **26**, 316 (1944).
19. Kitagawa, T., "Rapid Measurement of Toxic Gases and Vapors," 13th Intern. Congr. Occupational Health, New York City, July 25–29, 1960.
20. Gage, J. C., *Analyst*, **84**, 519 (1959).
21. Littlefield, J. B., and H. H. Schrenk, *U.S. Bur. Mines Rept. Invest. 3387* (1938).
21a. Union Industrial Equipment Co., 150 Cove Street, Fall River, Mass.
21b. Mine Safety Appliances Co., 201 North Braddock Ave., Pittsburgh, Pa.
22. Silverman, L., and W. B. Wardlow, *Ind. Eng. Chem. Anal. Ed.*, **12**, 682 (1940).
23. Charsa, R. C., and A. L. Linch, *Am. Ind. Hyg. Assoc. Quarterly*, **18**, No. 2, 135 (June 1957).
24. Dowling, T., R. B. Davis, R. C. Charsa, and A. L. Linch, *Am. Ind. Hyg. Assoc. J.*, **19**, 239 (1958).
25. Linch, A. L., R. C. Charsa, and J. M. Wetherhold, "The "Uni-Jet" Air Sampler—Operating Characteristics and Applications," Paper 34-4, 8th Intern. Congr. Occupational Health, New York City, July 1960.
26. Wilson, W. L., "An Automatic Impinger for Air Sampling," Air Pollution Control Assoc. Meeting, Chattanooga, Tenn., May 1954.
27. Jacobs, M. B., *The Chemical Analysis of Air Pollutants*, Interscience, New York, 1960, Chap. 17.
28. Jacobs, M. B., and S. Hochheiser, *Anal. Chem.*, **30**, 426 (1958).
29. Cholak, J., L. J. Schafer, D. Yeager, and W. J. Younker, *Arch. Ind. Health*, **15**, 198 (1957).
30. Gelman Instrument Co., Ann Arbor, Mich.
31. Perry, W. H., and E. C. Tabor, *Arch. Environ. Health*, **4**, 44 (1962).
32. Tabor, E. C., and C. C. Golden, *J. Air Pollution Control Assoc.*, **15**, 7 (1965).
33. Jacobs, M. B., *Chemical Analysis of Foods and Food Products*, 3rd ed., Van Nostrand, Princeton, N. J., 1958.
34. Welcher, F. J., *Standard Methods of Chemical Analysis*, 6th ed., Van Nostrand, Princeton, N. J., 1963.
35. Burrell, G. A., F. M. Seibert, and G. W. Jones, *U.S. Bur. Mines Bull. 197* (1926).
36. Fene, W. J., *U.S. Bur. Mines Inform. Circ. 7122* (1940).
37. Goldman, D. E., and J. A. Mathis, Naval Med. Research Inst., Res. Project X-417, Rept. 4 (1945).
38. Stock, P. G., and G. W. Monier-Williams, *Rept. Public Health Med. Subjects, 19*, Ministry of Health, London, 1923.
39. Silver, S. D., *J. Lab. Clin. Med.*, **31**, 1153 (1946).
40. Vilutis and Company, Chicago, Illinois 60628.
41. Henderson, Y., and L. A. Greenberg, *J. Am. Med. Assoc.*, **96**, 1474 (1931).
42. Setterlind, A. N., *Ind. Hyg. Newsletter*, **8**, No. 2, 7 (1948).
43. Setterlind, A. N., *Ind. Hyg. Quarterly*, **9**, 35 (1948).
44. Jacobs, M. B., *The Chemical Analysis of Air Pollutants*, Interscience, New York, 1960, Chap. 1.

45. Jacobs, M. B., and L. Scheflan, *Chemical Analysis of Industrial Solvents*, Interscience, New York, 1953.
46. Owings, C. W., *U.S. Bur. Mines Inform. Circ. 6129* (1929).
47. Owings, C. W., W. A. Selvig, and H. P. Greenwald, *U.S. Bur. Mines Inform. Circ. 7113* (1940).

General References

Burrell, G. A., F. M. Seibert, and G. W. Jones, "Sampling and Examination of Mine Gases and Natural Gas," *U.S. Bur. Mines Bull. 197* (1926).

Haldane, J. S., and J. I. Graham, *Methods of Air Analysis*, Griffin, London, 1935.

Jacobs, M. B., *The Chemical Analysis of Air Pollutants*, Interscience, New York, 1960.

Jacobs, M. B., *Chemical Analysis of Foods and Food Products*, 3rd ed., Van Nostrand, New York, 1958.

Lunge, B., and H. R. Ambler, *Technical Gas Analysis*, Van Nostrand, New York, 1934.

Owings, C. W., "Sampling Dust in Rock-Dusted Mines," *U.S. Bur. Mines Inform. Circ. 6129* (1929).

Silverman, L., *Industrial Air Sampling and Analysis*, Ind. Hyg. Foundation, Pittsburgh, 1947.

Welcher, F. J., *Standard Methods of Chemical Analysis*, 6th ed., Van Nostrand, New York, 1963.

Yant, W. P., and L. B. Berger, "Sampling Mine Gases," *U.S. Bur. Mines Inform. Circ. 34* (1936).

CHAPTER III

MEASUREMENT OF GAS VOLUME, VELOCITY, AND QUANTITY

When relatively large volumes of air or gas are to be analyzed for a given contaminant, they are generally passed through some absorbing medium or adsorbent. In order to compute the concentration of the pollutant, it is necessary to measure the volume of air being sampled. Not only does the volume of air used in the sampling need to be known, but often the industrial hygiene chemist must know the rate of flow of air and gases being eliminated by means of ducts, vents, stacks, and the like. It is also of interest to know the velocity of air in the workroom itself as a measure of its ventilation. Therefore, instruments used for the measurement of volume and of flow rate and velocity will be described.

A. Air and Gas Measurement Devices

1. Classification

The various measuring devices used to measure the quantity of air or gas sampled or flowing fall into three main categories. In the first group are those instruments which measure all the air or gas that passes by volumetric means. In the second group are those devices which measure the velocity of the air or gas stream. With these instruments the velocity of a portion of the air passing the instrument is measured. In the third group are those that meter the flow rate of the air or gas. With these instruments, usually all of the air or gas flowing passes through the device. They can be classified as follows:

1. Total Volume Instruments
   (a) Wet meter
   (b) Dry meter
   (c) Rotary gas meter
2. Velocity Instruments
   (a) Anemometers
      (1) Rotating vane anemometers
      (2) Swinging vane anemometer

(*b*) Pressure Variation Instruments
  (*1*) Standard pitot
  (*2*) Spec'al pitot
  (*3*) Airfoil pitometer
  (*4*) Pitot–venturi
  (*5*) Air-speed nozzle
(*c*) Temperature Variation Instruments
  (*1*) Thermometer anemometer
  (*2*) Thermocouple anemometer
  (*3*) Thomas electric gas meter
  (*4*) Kata thermometer
3. Gas Flow Meters
  (*a*) Orifice meters
  (*b*) Capillary flowmeters
  (*c*) Venturi meter
  (*d*) Rotameters

Caplan (1) classified air measurement devices into two categories, combining the first and the third groups above as one category which he termed *air flow meters* with the second category comprising air velocity instruments.   Olive (2) classified the devices used to measure fluid flow into three main divisions as volumetric devices equivalent to group *1* above: variable head meters such as group *2* but including orifice meters and venturi meters, as well as pitot tubes; and a third group of variable-area meters into which he placed the rotameters.

2. Total Gas Volume Instruments

a. Wet Meter

The wet meter (Fig. III-1) is the principal instrument for measuring total gas volume.   It is an apparatus generally made of brass tinned to withstand corrosion.   It consists of a cylindrical case which contains a rotor drum suspended in a liquid, on a horizontal axis. This drum is divided by metal vanes into four spiral compartments of exactly equal volume.   The gas is led in from a cock through an opening near the axis in each chamber and emerges from an opening near the periphery of the drum.   The liquid used is water or glycerol, the height of which is measured by means of a glass gauge attached to the case.   The liquid is usually set at half height but may be adjusted, if desired, to some other height.   The pressure of the incoming gas causes the drum to rotate.   An indicator hand is attached to the drum, which registers the volume passed on a dial as the drum rotates.

Each revolution of the drum corresponds to the passage of a definite volume of gas so that the dial may be read directly in units of volume. Some instruments are constructed so that the indicator makes a complete revolution for $\frac{1}{10}$ cu ft. Wet meters must be equipped with

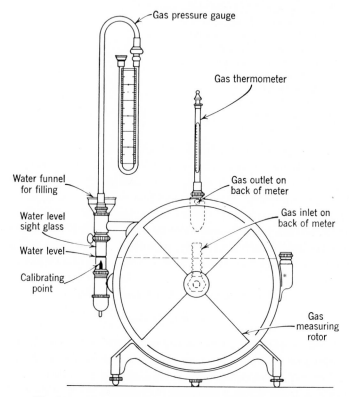

Fig. III-1. Wet gas meter.   (Courtesy Emil Greiner Co.)

spirit levels and leveling screws so that the case may be set evenly to allow the drum to rotate freely. They must also be fitted with a thermometer and pressure manometer so that the measured gas volume may be reduced to standard temperature and pressure if necessary. A modification of this type of instrument is one in which the rotor drum is suspended inside a case, the upper part of which is made of glass so that the rotating drum is visible.

Wet-test meters cannot be operated at too rapid or even too slow rates of gas flow because of the characteristics of their design.   If the flow is too rapid, the water or other liquid will surge within the meter.   If the flow is too slow, pulsations may occur because of the time lag between the filling and rotation of the compartments in the drum.   The manometer is designed to indicate pressures of just a few inches of water and must never be filled with mercury.

The wet meter is used in industrial hygiene work principally for the calibration of other air- and gas-flow measuring instruments.   For optimum results, it is well to remember that the wet-test meter is designed to operate at nearly atmospheric pressure.   It is best to choose a meter of suitable capacity so that it will work within the limits recommended by the manufacturer.   For industrial hygiene work, it is desirable to have one meter whose dial indicates 0.1 cu ft or 3 liters per revolution, one meter reading 1 liter per revolution, and one meter reading 1 cu ft per revolution.

b. Dry Meters

Dry meters are meters of the positive-displacement type.   The entering gas or air stream moves diaphragms or bellows.   The movement of the diaphragms operates a crank that transfers the motion to a rotating indicating hand on a scale.   These instruments are used mainly for measuring rapid and large volumes of gas.   They are also used to calibrate flowmeters.   They are not often used in industrial hygiene analysis.   Neither the wet type nor the dry type of meter can be used with corrosive or acid gases.   For such gases a simple meter made of glass, containing a liquid which siphons over each time the apparatus is filled to a definite volume, may be used (3).

c. Rotary Gas Meters

Rotary gas meters are meters with lobed rotors.   Two lobed impellers rotate in a close-fitting chamber without contact with the chamber or each other by the action of timing gears.   They are not used to any extent in industrial hygiene work because they are heavy and large.   Thus, even small units weigh about 200 lb.   However, they are used in process industries generally as permanent installations for metering large volumes of gas of the order of 500 to 1 million cfh with an accuracy within 2%.

3. Gas-Velocity Measurement Instruments

The flow of a fluid, especially of a gas, is difficult to measure. Gas-velocity measuring devices measure variations in a physical property such as a change in pressure head, in temperature, or in another property caused by the velocity of an air or gas stream. With such instruments only a portion of the fluid passes through or over the instrument. From the change in physical property, the quantity passing a given section of a conduit can be computed and expressed as liters of air per minute (lpm) or as cubic feet of gas per hour (cfh), and analogous expressions of fluid flow such as gallons of water per minute, pounds of steam per minute, etc. The gas flowmeter, orifice meter, and pitot tube are among the more common devices used in industrial hygiene work that belong to this group.

a. Anemometers

Rotating Vane Anemometer. One of the simplest of the velocity-type instruments to use is the rotating vane anemometer (4) (Fig. III-2). It comprises a set of fan blades connected through a gear train to indicating dials. These instruments are somewhat expensive, if carefully made, and require frequent adjustment. The anemometer is held in the air stream so that the air flow rotates its blades, or the gas is directed so that it hits and rotates the blades of the instrument. The rotation of the vane is registered on a calibrated tachometer. The instrument must be used with a stop watch for the dial reading gives the result in linear feet of air travel.

A common type of anemometer (5) consists of a metal cylindrical frame about 3 or 4 in. in diameter and 1.5 or 1.75 in. wide, with a base or legs on the bottom so that the instrument will not roll when set down. Sometimes the device is equipped with a small metal loop which serves as a hand hold. Attached to a light axle that has a relatively frictionless bearing are a number of arms to which are attached blades. The blades, arms, and axle are known as the vane, one revolution of which corresponds to an air velocity of 1 fpm. Either at the center of the device attached to its frame by arms or supported on separate legs is the calibrated tachometer, consisting of a number of dials with pointers. On the large dial comprising the face is a circle with 100 divisions, each division representing one revolution of the vane. Thus, one complete revolution of the pointer is

Fig. III-2. Anemometers.   (Courtesy Taylor Instrument Companies.)

equivalent to 100 ft.   Within the large dial are a number of smaller
ones that indicate hundreds, thousands, and tens of thousands of feet,
respectively, depending on the number of dials.   A catch or lever is
provided which permits the vane to be engaged or disengaged at will.
Some devices are equipped with a lever that resets all the dials to zero.

To use the anemometer it should be placed or held so that air will
flow through the anemometer from the back or sides opposite the
dials.   As Grove points out, when it is used in a mine, the anemometer should be held at arm's length, as nearly perpendicular as possible to the air current.   It should be moved regularly and slowly,
up, down, and across the airway, so as to obtain an average reading
of the air velocity.   This is necessary because the velocity of air in a
mine is generally greater at the center of a passage than near the
bottom, sides, or top.   If it is desirable to obtain readings that can be
compared, it is preferable to post the anemometer in the same spot
at stated periods.

To take a reading, place the anemometer as described, push the
lever to the "on" position, and note the exact time.   At the end
of a known time interval, say one or more minutes, push the lever to
the "off" position, stopping the dial pointers, and read the velocity.
This will be in linear feet per minute.   To obtain the amount of air

passing the reading position, it is necessary to make a calculation by multiplying the linear velocity by the area at the point at which the reading was made. Thus, if the area-way is 12 ft wide and 7 ft high, corresponding to a cross section of 84 sq ft and the linear velocity is 200 fpm, there will be a flow of 16,800 cfm. Average anemometer readings will give average flow rates.

These devices will not function well if the velocity of the air is under 30 fpm. Readings will not be accurate if the velocity is under 80–100 fpm. The range can be extended to 10,000 fpm by using more than one anemometer.

Since the sensing area of the rotating vane anemometer is relatively large because the diameter of the fan blades is 3–4 in., it cannot be used for obtaining point velocities or narrow slot-type hood velocities.

Fixed Vane Anemometer. A variation of the rotating vane anemometer is the static vane anemometer. The air stream passing across the fan blades causes a torque that is registered on a dial calibrated in terms of linear feet of flow. When used with a stopwatch, the linear feet per minute can be obtained and the quantity of air flow can be computed as detailed in the preceding section.

Direct Reading Anemometer. A direct reading anemometer provides an instantaneous direct reading of air velocity in feet per minute or miles per hour without timing or reference to charts in the range of 0–3000 fpm or 0–35 mph. It is used for measuring air current velocities in laboratory fume hoods, ventilating shafts, wind tunnels, and analogous air streams. It is also used for measuring surface winds.

Readings are taken by holding the instrument aloft into the air stream so that the air blows directly against its circular face. The velocity is determined by the pressure which the air stream exerts on a multiblade rotor mounted in the instrument housing. The rotation of the rotor is controlled by a calibrated spring and one revolution of the rotor is equivalent to the maximum air velocity for which the anemometer is calibrated. The reading can be retained by the instrument by a scale lock, and in this way readings can be made under optimum conditions. The instrument is also equipped with a zero adjustment.

Swinging Vane Anemometer. The swinging vane anemometer, one commercial model of which is known as the Velometer (6) is an instantaneous direct-reading air-velocity instrument that can obtain spot velocities over a very small area in ranges from 20 to 2500 fpm and 3 in. static or total pressure. Special arrangements of this instrument can measure up to 25,000 fpm and 20 in. pressure.

The impact or pressure of the air entering the meter, with or without the aid of jets of different types and shapes, actuates a vane mounted on a jeweled movement. A pointer is attached to the vane.

This meter indicates air velocities directly on a scale in feet per minute without the necessity of timing or the use of mathematical calculations. It can be used for measurement of air flow in ducts, grilles, flues, etc., and to locate leaks and drafts.

Since this is a velocity instrument, the volume of air flow must be computed. The total cubic feet of air per minute (cfm) is equal to the product of the average velocity reading in feet per minute and the total free area in square feet.

The Velometer is equipped with special pitot tubes but these require a larger opening in a conduit than the customary pitot tubes (see Section A-3-b of this chapter). Swinging vane anemometers can also be adapted for the measurement of static pressure.

Since air passes through the swinging vane anemometer, the condensation of water, the collection of dust, and corrosive gases may affect it adversely. Some models of this instrument are equipped with dust filters. These may become a source of error if their resistance increases markedly because of clogging with dust. To avoid this error, the filter should be checked against a new filter from time to time.

The swinging vane anemometer should be calibrated periodically. The jets and connecting tubes are calibrated for a specific instrument and therefore should not be used with other instruments. Even the same instrument should be recalibrated if different lengths of sampling line, such as rubber tubing, are used.

b. Pressure Variation Instruments

The principal instrument used to determine the quantity of air or a gas by measuring its velocity of flow as evidenced by a variation in pressure head is the pitot tube and its modifications.

Standard Pitot Tube. To measure the flow of large volumes of gas, a pitot tube may be employed. The pitot tube (7) consists of two independent tubes, one of which is bent at right angles to the other in the simplest construction (Fig. III-3). A more accurate device is one

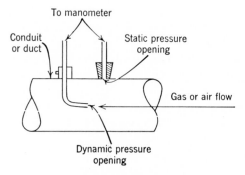

Fig. III-3. Simple pitot tube.

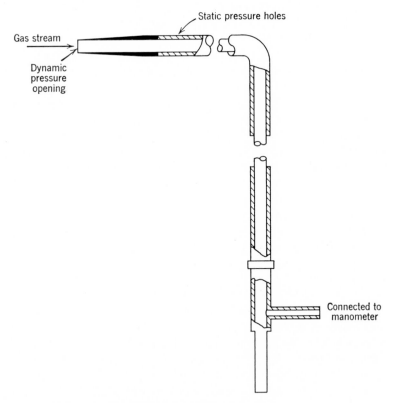

Fig. III-4. Concentric pitot tube.

in which these tubes are joined concentrically and arranged to form an inverted L, which still permits them to act independently (Fig. III-4). When either of these instruments is inserted into a gas stream, the tube facing the direction of flow measures the total pressure within the gas stream, consisting of a dynamic or kinetic pressure and a static pressure, while the tube perpendicular to the gas stream, or the tube with the static holes, measures the static pressure alone. The dynamic pressure is that pressure attributable to the impact of the moving gas. The static pressure is the pressure attributable to the presence of the gas itself. By connecting the two tubes of the simple pitot or the terminal arms of the L to a manometer, the difference in pressure may be noted. This difference in pressures is a measure of the speed with which the gas or air is traveling. The device measures this speed accurately only when the tube is properly pointed upstream.

This is not absolutely critical, for if the alignment of the pitot is within 5° of the actual flow direction the readings obtained will be substantially correct. For field use, the relative insensitivity of the pitot tube is an advantage, but this factor limits the usefulness for determining exact direction of flow.

The location and size of the static holes in a pitot are critical, but the shape and size of the dynamic port are noncritical. Most "standard" commercial pitots do not require the use of a correction factor in the computation of air or gas velocities. A properly constructed standard pitot tube requires no calibration. For large conduits jointed pitot tubes may be used.

Generally, inclined draft gauges are used for measuring the difference in the pressure in the arms of a pitot. A vertical U-tube manometer may be used if the velocity pressure head is more than 0.5 in. w.g. It must be remembered, however, that an error in reading of 0.1 in. will represent approximately a 10% error in the flow rate. The customary draft gauges may not be sensitive enough when the flow rate is of a low order, below 600–1000 fpm. Under such conditions which occur in the flow of flue gases, such as in domestic or residential incinerators, micromanometers or microdraft gauges must be used. These devices have a workable range of 0.001–6 in. of water column. For the lower pressure differences the scale can be read in a slant position. For higher pressure differences, the scale can be placed vertically.

If the total pressure is denoted by h_w the dynamic pressure by h_k, and the static pressure by h_s, then the pressure exerted at the opening pointed upstream is

$$h_w = h_k \pm h_s \tag{1}$$

depending upon whether there is a positive or negative pressure.

Fundamental hydrodynamic theory shows that in a stream of a moving fluid the pressure is greatest in the wide portions of the stream where the velocity is least, and is least in the narrow portions of the stream where the velocity is greatest. This relationship between pressure and velocity may be expressed by the equation for velocity of flow and the height of the water above an exit orifice as

$$v = (2gh_w)^{\frac{1}{2}} \tag{2}$$

or

$$h_w = v^2/2g \tag{3}$$

where v = velocity in feet per second, h_w = height of water level above exit orifice, that is, velocity head; and g = gravity constant = 32.2. The same relationship holds for air pressures and air velocities or for gas pressures and gas velocities, i.e., the pressure created by a column of air of height h_a is proportional to the square of the air velocity, and

$$h_a = v^2/2g \tag{4}$$

Because air and gas pressures are measured by water manometers or other types of manometer in which the pressures are expressed in inches of water, it is best to convert feet of air into inches of water.

$$h_a \times \text{density of air} = h_w \times \text{density of water} \tag{5}$$

$$h_a = \frac{\text{density of water}}{\text{density of air}} \times h_w \tag{6}$$

If the density of air is taken as 0.0749 lb/cu ft and water as 62.4 lb/cu ft at 70°F, then, by substitution,

$$h_a = \frac{62.4}{0.0749} \times h_w = 833 h_w \tag{7}$$

Thus, the height of a column of air at 70°F equivalent to 1 in. of water is 833 in., or 69.4 ft, of air.   By substituting this value and the value of the gravity constant in Eq. 4, we get

$$69.4h_w = v^2/64.4 \tag{8}$$

Expressing the velocity of the air in feet per minute, we get

$$v = 4009(h_w)^{\frac{1}{2}} \tag{9}$$

To obtain the volume of air flow from the pitot reading, the velocity must be related to the cross-sectional area of the duct.   If Q represents the volume of air flowing in cubic feet per minute at an average velocity equal to v and A is the cross-sectional area of the duct in square feet,

$$Q = Av = 4009A\,(h_w)^{\frac{1}{2}} \tag{10}$$

It is common in industrial hygiene, air pollution control, and ventilation work to round off the factor 4009 to 4000 or 4010.   It is also necessary at times to correct for the density of the air or effluent gas stream.   Expression 10 then becomes

$$v = 4000(h_w)^{\frac{1}{2}} \times (0.075/d)^{\frac{1}{2}} \tag{11}$$

in which d is the density of the air being sampled and 0.075 is taken as the weight of a cubic foot of air at 70°F.   The term $(0.075/d)^{\frac{1}{2}}$ is known as the correction factor.   Other corrections are considered in Section C of this chapter.

Caplan (1) has outlined the procedure for determining air volume with a pitot as follows:

(1)   Determine the measured velocity pressure at the proper traverse points.

(2)   Convert the velocity pressure readings to velocity.

(3)   Average the velocity values (not the velocity pressure values).

(4)   Determine the density of the air from the preceding equations.

(5)   Determine the correction factor CF from Figure III-5.

(6)   Multiply the average velocity by CF to obtain the true velocity.

(7)   The true velocity in feet per minute multiplied by the cross-section area of the duct in square feet will give the actual flow in cubic

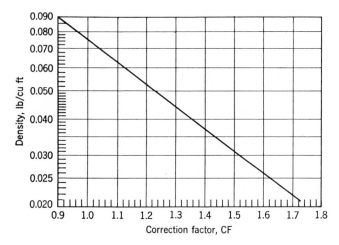

Fig. III-5. Density correction factor for velocity head meters (1).

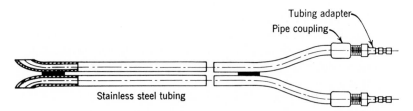

Fig. III-6. Stauscheibe pitot tube. (Courtesy Western Precipitation Corp., Los Angeles, Calif.)

feet per minute at the temperature and pressure and humidity of the gas.

(8) If flow in standard cubic feet per minute (scfm) is required, the gas laws as explained in succeeding sections must be applied.

Special Pitot Tube. If the gas or air stream whose velocity is being measured is very dusty or wet, the "standard" or L-shaped pitot cannot be used satisfactorily and the "special" or Stauscheibe tube (Fig. III-6), in which two tubes are also used, one facing the gas stream and the other facing away from the gas stream, must be employed. If the special or Stauscheibe tube is used to measure the computation. It is also necessary in this case to calibrate the special pitot tube, taking into consideration the density of the gas to be measured.

Airfoil Pitometer. The ordinary pitot is relatively insensitive to the direction of flow. A modification of the pitot developed by First and Silverman (8) termed the *airfoil pitometer* permits determination of the direction of airflow to within less than 1°.

Pitot-Venturi. Instead of using a micromanometer, it is possible to obtain a greater differential pressure for a given air velocity with a device, described by Stoll (9), which combines the principles of the pitot and the venturi (see Section A-4-a, this chapter). With this instrument, manometer readings ranging from five times the differential for moderate air velocities of the order of 1500 fpm to ten times the differential for flows of 5000 fpm as compared with the standard pitot can be obtained.

Air Speed Nozzle. The air speed nozzle is another device which enables one to obtain manometer differentials greater than with the standard or special pitot. Thus, at 600 fpm the differential is 0.15 in. w.g. and at 4000 fpm the differential is 6.7 in. w.g.

c. Temperature Variation Instruments

A group of instruments depending on the change in temperature caused by a flow of air across the instrument in which the cooling is proportional to the flow can be utilized to measure the velocity of the air flow, from which the quantity of the air flow can be computed.

Thermometer Anemometer. The thermometer anemometer (10) is an instrument capable of accurately measuring velocities of 10–6000 fpm. It consists of an ordinary glass thermometer with an electric coil surrounding its bulb. Small dry cells furnish the heating current and the voltage is regulated by means of a rheostat. This auxiliary equipment is assembled in a small box. The equipment is commercially available.

The principle of operation depends upon the fact that the heated bulb cools off when exposed to air currents and the extent of cooling, as indicated by the difference of temperature between heated and unheated thermometers, varies with the air velocity. Readings are taken of the temperatures of heated and unheated thermometers and of the voltage used. The velocity is read from a table or chart or it may be computed from an equation. By varying the voltage, any velocity within the range can be measured with accuracy. It can be used almost anywhere— in the open air or inside pipes—for measuring velocity or quantity of air flow. It is particularly useful for measuring air movement in rooms or in front of exhaust hoods that cannot be conveniently or accurately measured by other methods.

Thermocouple Anemometer.   The thermocouple, thermopile, or hot wire anemometer is an instrument in which a thermocouple is

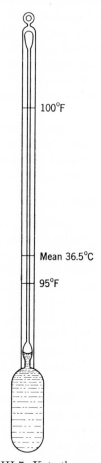

Fig. III-7. Kata thermometer.

heated by alternating current.   The cooling effect of the air flow is measured as the direct current output of the thermocouple by a millivoltmeter.   The range of flow rate is from 50 ml/min to 10 lpm.   Such devices are of limited value in very dusty gas flows.

Thomas Electric Gas Meters.   The Thomas electric gas meter (11) depends on the principle that, if the specific heat of a gas is known, the amount of heat put into that gas by a coil—sufficient to maintain a given difference in temperature between two thermometers, one before and one after the coil—is a measure of the volume of gas flowing.

Kata Thermometer.   An instrument that can be used to measure air velocities, but which is based on an entirely different principle from those already discussed, is the kata thermometer (12–18).   This type of thermometer is generally called the kata.   It was originally devised by Hill as a means of studying ventilation for body comfort; it was designed to simulate a human body and thus correlate the effects of temperature, relative humidity, and relative air movement.   It is really an adaptation of the wet- and dry-bulb thermometer.   It is so sensitive to air and gas movements that it can be used for velocity measurements.

The dry kata (Fig. III-7) is an alcohol thermometer with a very large bulb and a stem which is about 20 cm long.   The stem has two main graduations, at 95 and 100°F.   The alcohol is colored red for ease of vision.   The reading of the dry kata gives the loss of heat due to convection, conduction, and radiation.   This reading can be related to air movement (17).

To measure air velocity when the temperature is below 95°F, the kata is dipped into water at about 180°F until the meniscus of the red-colored alcohol rises halfway into the safety bulb at the top of the thermometer.   Then the bulb of the thermometer is rapidly and thoroughly dried and is held at the point where the velocity of air is to be measured.   The time, T, in seconds necessary for the alcohol to drop between the 100 and 95°F markings is noted.   This procedure should be repeated two or three times and the average time of temperature decrease observed and computed to avoid error.   This time, T, divided into the factor number K, calibrated and given for each kata instrument, gives the cooling power, H, in millicalories per square centimeter per second.   That is

$$H = K/T \tag{12}$$

If the temperature is above 100°F, in order to measure air velocity the kata must first be cooled below 95°F by dipping the bulb into cold water.   The bulb is then quickly and thoroughly dried and the time for the temperature to rise from 95 to 100°F is noted.   The heating power, H, is calculated using the same Formula 12 but H is now considered negative.

The kata is not very accurate in the 85–100°F range, because these temperatures are near its cooling range and air movements have little effect.   A special high-temperature kata, the blue kata, has been developed to overcome this defect.

TABLE III-I
Characteristics of Air Velocity Instruments (23)

Instrument	Velocity range, fpm	Portability	Directional?	Calibration requirement	Ruggedness	Sensing area size	Range temp. and pressure	Dust and fume difficulty	Radiation error	General usefulness[a]	Remarks
Standard pitot	600 up	Fair	Yes	None	Good	Small area but long	Wide	Some	None	Good	
Double pitot	400? up	Fair	Yes	Once	Good	Small	Wide	Small	None	Special	
Airfoil pitometer	600 up	Fair	Highly	Once	Good	Small	Wide	Some	None	Special	Directional to 1°
Pitot-venturi	600? up	Poor	Yes	Once	Good	Large	Wide	Yes	None	Special	Magnified VP
Air speed nozzle	600? up	Poor	Yes	Once	Good	Large	Wide	Yes	None	Special	Magnified VP
Rotating vane anemometer	30–10,000	Good	Yes	Occasional	Poor	Large	Narrow	Yes	None	Fair	
Swing vane anemometer	30–10,000	Good	Yes	Occasional	Fair	Large; small for fittings	Medium	Yes	None	Good	Use filters for dust
Heated thermometer anemometer	10–6000	Good	No	Once	Poor	Small	Narrow	Yes	Yes	Limited	Best for low-velocity room air
Heated thermocouple anemometer	10–6000	Good	Either	Occasional	Fair	Small	Medium	Yes	Slight	Good	
Kata thermometer	50–500	Good	No	Once	Poor	Large	Narrow	Yes	Yes	Limited	

[a] Author's opinion; and pertaining only to industrial hygiene.

Table III-1 provides a summary of the characteristics of air velocity instruments.

4. Gas Flow Meters

a. Venturi Meter

Another device used for the measurement of large volumes of gas flow is the venturi meter (7).   There are many variations of this instrument.   They are all based on the principle, as is the pitot tube, that the pressure and velocity head of a fluid are interchangeable.

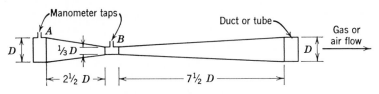

Fig. III-8. Venturi meter.

In the case of the venturi meter this principle is reduced to the fact that the pressure of a gas on either side of a constriction in a pipe through which it is flowing is dependent upon the rate of flow.   The rate of flow is increased by inserting in the pipe or conduit a fitting which converges to a minimum.   The standardized venturi meter consists of a converging and diverging duct connected by a narrow collar, as illustrated in Figure III-8.

The diameter of the converging duct tapers down to one-third of its original diameter at the minimum section in a distance of $2^{1}/_{2}$ diameters.   The meter then diverges to its original diameter in a distance of $7^{1}/_{2}$ diameters.   The length of the diverging taper minimizes loss attributable to the reduction in air velocity and eddying.   The ratio dimensions of the standardized venturi meter are given in Figure III-8.

The meter is tapped just before it begins to converge and at the minimum diameter.   The taps are connected to a manometer.   The difference in pressure created by the interchangeability of the velocity and static heads at A and B may be noted.   It may be shown that the volume of air handled, Q, may be expressed by the formula

$$Q = \frac{21.2 d_A{}^2 h^{\frac{1}{2}}}{(d_A{}^4/d_B{}^4 - 1)^{\frac{1}{2}}} \tag{13}$$

where d_A = diameter of main in inches, d_B = diameter of minimum collar in inches, and h = the difference in pressures.

The venturi meter is used mainly for the continuous measurement of large volumes of air flow or fluid flow in pipes and ducts. The manometers used in conjunction with the meter are often recording instruments. Venturi meters, as such, are not often used for the determination of the quantity of gas or air flow in sampling.

b. Orifice Meter

The orifice meter is a device that has at some point a standard capillary aperture. These orifices may be sharp-edged or bell-shaped. The tube with its capillary opening is connected to a manometer of some type. As the gas passes through the orifice, there is a difference in pressure created on one side of the orifice by the flow of gas with respect to the other side of the opening. This differential head is proportional to the square of the flow. The diminution in pressure between the downstream side and the upstream side of the orifice is registered by the connected manometer. The gauge may be graduated to read liters per minute directly, as in the gas flowmeter, or it may be graduated merely to read centimeters and millimeters. The corresponding volume may be read from a prepared graph. The graph is prepared from a formula

$$Q = \frac{13.4 d_A{}^2 h^{\frac{1}{2}}}{(d_A{}^4/d_B{}^4 - 1)^{\frac{1}{2}}} \tag{14}$$

where d_A = diameter of tube in inches, d_B = diameter of orifice in inches, and the other symbols have the meaning previously indicated. The similarity to the formula for the measurement of volume of flow is clear. The energy losses are larger in the case of the orifice meter and therefore a greater correction must be made. The proportionality factor has a value of 0.60. An orifice meter having a hollow interchangeable stopper which is provided with four orifices of approximately $\frac{1}{4}$, $\frac{1}{2}$, 1, and 2 mm diameter is commercially available.

Orifice meters are widely used for estimating gas volumes in industrial hygiene work. For dust determinations, these meters must be placed in the line after the absorbing, impinging, or collecting device rather than before the device, for the orifice may become obstructed by impinged dust and consequently failed to give a proper flow reading.

Critical Orifice. A sampler can be operated at virtually constant rate by use of a critical orifice. The operation of such a "critical" orifice depends on the fact that the flow of air through an orifice will increase as the downstream pressure is decreased until the air is flowing through the orifice at sonic velocity. There will be no additional increase in flow with decrease in the downstream pressure. The critical flow point for air occurs when the downstream pressure is 53% of the upstream pressure. Thus, the air flow will be independent of the downstream pressure as long as the downstream pressure is less than 53% of the upstream pressure. The expression for calculation of the flow rate through a critical orifice is

$$v = 0.533 A p_1 \times T^{\frac{1}{2}}$$

where v = flow rate of air in pounds per second, A = area of orifice in square inches, p_1 = upstream pressure in pounds per square inch, and T = temperature in degrees Rankine.

Air flow through a critical orifice is directly proportional to the upstream pressure and inversely proportional to the absolute temperature. Consequently, where the resistance upstream increases, for example, in a filter sampling system using a critical orifice when the filter becomes clogged, the flow through the orifice may decrease. The amount of decrease is dependent on how great the buildup of dust is on the filter and what the consequent increase in resistance is. The error attributable to temperature change can be corrected by applying a correction factor.

Sets of critical orifices are commercially available.

Vacuum Gauges. Often pumps used for sampling with impingers (see Chapter V, Section C-7) are fitted with vacuum gauges, the impinger jet nozzle serving as the resistance. The macroimpinger is made with an orifice that is 2.3 mm in diameter. With this jet opening, a vacuum of 3 in. Hg will indicate a flow rate of 1 cfm. The midget impinger is made with an orifice that is 1 mm in diameter. With this jet opening, a vacuum of 12 in. w.g. will indicate a flow rate of 0.1 cfm. Since it is difficult to make such impingers with exactly these orifices, it is best to calibrate each impinger. It is necessary, however, to calibrate the vacuum gauge first to see that its scale reading is correct and then to calibrate the impingers with the gauge in the line.

c.   Gas Flowmeter

The gas flowmeter (Fig. III-9) is an instrument that is based on the same principle as the venturi meter.   The constriction employed in the tube or conduit is a capillary tube.   Some of these instruments consist of a tube A which can be connected to a tube B by replaceable capillary tubes (Fig. III-9).   On either side of the capillary tube there

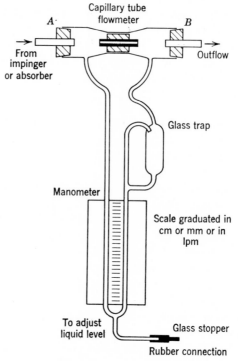

Fig. III-9. Gas flowmeter.

are taps in the tubes A and B, which can be connected to a manometer. The difference in pressure created on the upstream and downstream ends of the capillary is registered by the manometer, which may be graduated to read liters per minute.   The gas flowmeter may be calibrated against a direct-reading instrument such as a dry meter. Some instruments are equipped with a graph reading difference in height in arms of manometer against volume of gas passed.   This in-

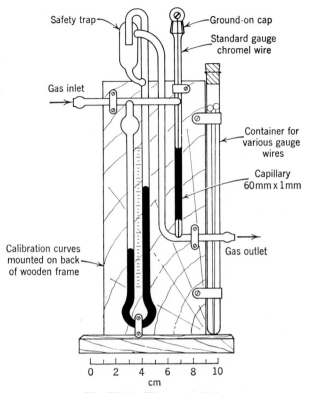

Fig. III-10. Flowmeter (20).

strument is fairly inexpensive, is one of the simplest to use, and is probably used more than any other device for measuring flow of gas in the field of industrial hygiene chemistry.   If used for dust determinations, it should, as with the orifice meter, be placed after the absorber in the sampling line.

Flowmeter with Variable Orifices.   The conventional capillary flowmeter (20) is limited to a relatively narrow range of gas flows, depending upon the diameter and length of the capillary tube used.   In many laboratories it is customary to use flowmeters provided with interchangeable capillaries, each of which may be attached to the flowmeter by means of one or two interchangeable ground connections.

In the type of flowmeter shown in Figure III-10, the vertical capillary tube is designed for the maximum gas flow expected.

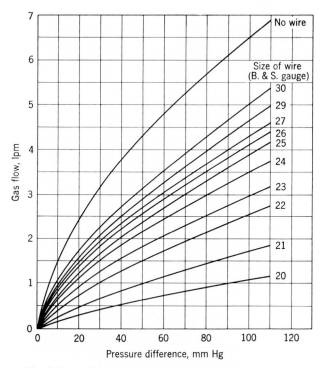

Fig. III-11. Calibration curves for Bruun flowmeter (20).

TABLE III-2

Relation between Gas Flow and Pressure Difference for Various Wire Sizes (20)

B. and S. wire in 60 × 1.1-mm glass capillary, gauge	Approximate gas flow, lpm		
	10 mm Hg	60 mm Hg	100 mm Hg
20	0.2	0.7	1.1
21	0.3	1.2	1.7
22	0.4	1.7	2.6
23	0.5	2.1	3.0
24	0.6	2.4	3.5
25	0.7	2.7	3.9
26	0.8	2.9	4.2
27	0.9	3.1	4.3
29	1.0	3.3	4.7
30	1.1	3.6	5.0
None	1.5	4.8	6.5

Wherever the flowmeter is to be used accurately for lower gas rates, the bore is decreased by inserting a corrosion-resistant alloy gauge wire such as chrome-nickel, Chromel, etc. into the entire length of the capillary.   By using wires of different sizes, a flowmeter having a capillary 60 mm. long and 1.1 mm in diameter can be used for accurate measurements of gas flow covering the complete range between 0.2 and 7.0 lpm.   The calibration curves are shown in Figure III-11.   The approximate ranges of gas flows to which each wire is applicable when used in the capillary tube of the same dimensions is given in Table III-2.   This type of flowmeter can be readily cleaned by removing the gauge wire.

Capometer.   The capometer (21) is an apparatus, used in Germany, which consists of a series of capillary tubes of different bores.   The capillaries are independently connected to a manometer by means of stopcocks, and the difference in pressure due to the flow through any one capillary is noted by the manometer.   The capometer is really a type of gas flowmeter that has a fixed set instead of having replaceable capillaries.

d. Constant Flowmeter

Hatch, Warren, and Drinker describe an ejector device that can be utilized as a constant flowmeter (19).   Many industrial establishments have compressed air available.   When compressed air is obtainable, the energy provided may be converted into suction as is the flow of water through a filter pump.   This device uses about 50 cu ft of free air when functioning and a constant rate is obtained with it regardless of the variation in air pressure, so long as this pressure is between the limits of 30 and 75 psi.   For an indicating device, a simple pressure gauge connected to the compressed-air supply is employed (Fig. III-12).

The constant flow in this meter is due to the fact that the pressure drop across the orifice ($p_1 - p_2$) is greater than the critical pressure, which for air is $0.53p$ (p_1 is the upstream and p_2 is the downstream pressure).   Under this condition, the flow depends upon p_1 only, and since this remains constant, within the barometric-pressure range, the rate of air flow has a constant value.   With a barometric pressure equal to 30 in. Hg and the pressure loss through an impinger device equal to 2.9 in., $p_1 = 27.1$ in.   To meet such a requirement $p_1 - p_2$ must be equal to or greater than 14.5 in. (that, is, it must be equal to or

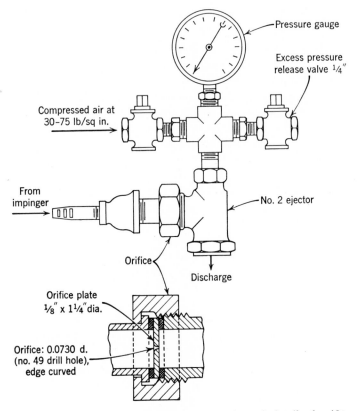

Fig. III-12. Compressed-air ejector flowmeter unit and detail of orifice and mounting (19).

greater than $0.53p$), and p_2 (absolute) must be less than 12.6 in. Hg, that is, -17.4 in. Hg gauge pressure.   A suction in excess of this value is obtained with the aid of a No. 2 Hancock ejector when the pressure in the air line is between 30 and 75 lb.   The orifice as designed by Hatch, Warren, and Drinker yields rates of flow of 28–29 lpm, which is equivalent to about 1 cfm.   The maximum variation is 3.5%.

e. Rotameter

The rotameter, which is the instrument of choice for measurement of air flow in industrial work, is a variable area device.   It comprises

Fig. III-13. Rotameter.

a uniformly tapered tube (Fig. III-13) of glass or plastic which can be
leveled plumb, containing a float or a bob made of various materials,
such as metal, glass, clay, talc, etc.   The upward flow of gas or air
causes the float to seek an equilibrium position proportional to the
flow rate.   At this point the upward push of the flow of air or gas is
counterbalanced by the downward pull of gravity.   The rotameter is
designed to give a linear response because the taper of the tube is adjusted so that equal increases in flow rates will produce equal incre-

TABLE III-3

Characteristics of Air Flowmeters (23)

Meter type	Capacity range, cfm	Portability	Calibration requirement	Restriction on piping location	Foul gas difficulty	Pressure loss	General usefulness[a]
Orifice	Wide[d]	[b]	None	Yes	Low	High	Good
Flow nozzle	Wide[d]	[b]	None	Yes	Low	Moderate	Fair
Venturi	Wide[d]	[b]	None	Yes	Low	Low	Good
Wet gas meter	0.05–20[e]	Fair	Once	No	Yes	0.3 in. w.g.	Fair
Dry gas meter	0.10–30[e]	Fair	Occasional	No	Yes	0.5 in. w.g.	Fair
Rotameter	5 cc/m to 27 cfm[c]	Good	Once	No	Some	Moderate	Good
Rotary gas meter	10 up	Heavy	Once	No	Some	Moderate–high	Limited

[a] Author's opinion only; and pertaining only to use in industrial hygiene.

[b] Meters of this class are usually designed for a specific installation and have no portability requirement. In small sizes, as for sampling equipment, they are quite portable.

[c] Laboratory styles only. Commercial installations may be much larger.

[d] No upper limit. Lower limit imposed only by construction difficulties, and standard proportions are not used. Such meters require calibration.

TABLE III-4

Comparison of Devices Used in the Measurement of Air Flow (7)

Device	Method of use	Range of air velocities or volumes which can be measured	Calculations based on	Accuracy obtainable	Skill required
Pitot tube	Used for measuring velocity head in ducts. Is pointed against direction of air flow.	200 ft/min. Upper limit not determined.	Formula: $v = 4009(\bar{h}_w)^{\frac{1}{2}}$ (ft/min).	Depends on sensitivity of the manometer used.	Some. Location of tube is important.
Special pitot	Used for measuring point velocities and velocity of air in ducts. Requires special mounting.	100 ft/min. Upper limit not determined.	Formula or curve. Device requires calibration against a standard pitot.	Depends on sensitivity of the manometer used.	Considerable. The device is sensitive to direction of flow and requires careful mounting.
Anemometer	A vane instrument actuating a tachometer arrangement.	200–5000	Requires stopwatch timing. Device is direct reading, giving linear feet of air travel.	Requires a correction curve for high and low air velocities.	No skill required.
Kata thermometer	Bulb must be dried, and time of fluid fall or rise between 2 markings and air temperature are correlated with velocity.	15–500	Requires a chart.	With careful use, the device is very accurate.	Radiant energy sources must be avoided.
Venturi	Fixed convergent and divergent tubes forming part of the duct system.	Can be built to handle any volume of air flow.	Formula: $$Q = \frac{21.2 d_A^2 h^{\frac{1}{2}}}{[d_A^4/d_B^4 - 1]^{\frac{1}{2}}}$$ d_A = diam. of main, in. d_B = diam. of throat, in.	Device is very accurate for volume determinations (0.5–5% error).	No skill required. Manometer scale can be made to read volumes directly.
Orifice	Orifice plate is fixed between two flanges in duct system.	Can be made to handle any volume of air flow.	Formula. $$Q = \frac{13.4 d_A^2 h^{\frac{1}{2}}}{[d_A^4/d_B^4 - 1]^{\frac{1}{2}}}$$ d_A = diam. of main, in. d_B = diam. of orifice, in.	Device is very accurate when carefully calibrated.	No skill required. Manometer scale can be made to read volumes directly.

ments in height. For this reason ordinary graph paper can be used to plot the calibration readings of a rotameter.

Some rotameters have interchangeable floats so that a range of flow rates can be measured. Calibrated rotameters are commercially available. Some have two bobs, one with a higher specific gravity than the other. The two bobs and calibration charts supplied with the instrument serve as checks on the flow rate. The theoretical aspects of rotameter flow rates have been discussed by Whitwell and Plumb (22). Relatively inexpensive calibrated plastic rotameters are commercially available and cover a range of flow from less than 5.0 to 37,000 ml/min.

Table III-3 provides a summary of the characteristics of air flow-meters, and Table III-4 gives a comparison of the properties of some of the devices used for the measurement of air flow.

B. Calibration of Air- and Gas-Measurement Devices

In order to be certain that the volume of air sampled is correct, it is necessary to calibrate the instruments used to measure that volume. Some instruments are sold that have been calibrated by the vendor, but even in such instances it is wise to run a check calibration.

1. PRIMARY STANDARDS

There are two principal primary standards. These are aspirator or mariotte bottles (see Chapter II, Section E-2-a) and spirometers or gasometers. Wet-test meters (see Chapter III, Section A-2-a) are often used as primary standards, but these should first be checked against a calibrated aspirator bottle. Occasionally, syringes and pumps of known volume are used as primary standards.

a. Aspirator or Mariotte Bottles

These have been described in Chapter II. For use as primary standards for air measurement devices, they must themselves be calibrated. For example, fit a 20-liter or 5-gal glass bottle or carboy with a siphon and then transfer distilled water at a known temperature liter by liter to the carboy. Mark the height of each liter with a piece of masking or adhesive tape. A similar method of calibrating a mariotte or aspirator bottle can be followed.

b. Spirometers

Another device that can be used for calibrating air measurement devices is the spirometer or gasometer. This device consists of a counterbalanced bell floating in water to which is attached an indicator. Because of the counterweight, the only resistance to movement of the bell is due to the buoyancy. By balancing the bell and counterweight at the center of its travel, the resistance, which will be small, will be positive above the balance point and negative below it. As air is drawn out of or into the apparatus, the bell falls or rises and the indicator falls or rises correspondingly.

The change in volume can be represented by

$$V = A\Delta h$$

where V = volume, A = the area of a cross section of the bell, and Δh = change in the height of the bell.

For low flow rates, of the order of 1–2 lpm, clinical spirometers which are commercially available may be used. Larger spirometers can be constructed for larger flow rates.

c. Wet and Dry Meters

For flow rates ranging up to 1 cfm, i.e., 28.3 lpm, wet-test meters are suitable. For higher flow rates, the method for calibrating high-volume samplers using gas meters may be employed.

2. SECONDARY STANDARDS

Secondary standards for air-measurement instruments are devices that have been calibrated accurately against some primary standard. The principal type of secondary standard is the calibrated rotameter. Such secondary standards should be used for no other purpose. Tebbins and Keagy (24) give an example of using a calibrated venturi for the calibration of a high-volume sampler.

a. Calibration Methods

Flowmeters and Orifice Meters. Connect the flowmeter and sampling apparatus in series with the calibrated air-measurement instrument. Start the flow of air by starting the flow of water from the aspirator bottle or mariotte bottle and simultaneously start a stopwatch. Repeat the entire procedure to obtain the time to aspirate known volumes of air through the flowmeter. Record the volumes and times of flow. Average replicate determinations. The manometer readings or pressure head differentials vary exponentially with increase in air flow; hence, plot the data, volumes of air versus time, on log-log paper to obtain a straight-line relationship.

An analogous procedure can be used with a calibrated wet-test meter or rotameter. In such instances, however, a pump or ejector must also be in series to draw the air.

It is best to calibrate a flowmeter with the sampling device with which it is to be used, and it is also best to attach the calibration chart to the instrument. The flowmeter can be marked with an equivalent flow scale as well as in inches of water if only one leg of the manometer is read as is the usual practice.

It is important to allow adequate time for flow if a wet-test meter or spirometer is used. The flow should be regulated so as to be as uniform as possible and sufficient data—that is, points for the curve—should be obtained so that a good curve can be drawn. From time to time the device should be recalibrated.

C.   Measurement of Quantity in Gases

It is well known that the volume of a gas alone gives no true measure of the quantity of matter present. In order to obtain the real quantity of gaseous matter present from the volumes obtained by the use of meters or of velocity instruments, the fundamental laws of gases must be applied. We have learned that the concentration of a sample of gas is proportional to the pressure it exerts. The fundamental considerations in the measurement of gases are the laws of Boyle and Charles.

1. Boyle's Law

The law of Boyle states that the volume occupied by the same sample of any gas at constant temperature is inversely proportional to the pressure. Mathematically stated,

$$p \propto 1/V \tag{15}$$

Introducing a proportionality factor K, we have

$$p = K/V \quad \text{or} \quad pV = K \tag{16}$$

If, now, we were to change the pressure we should, according to this law and the above relationships, obtain the expression

$$p_1V_1 = K \tag{17}$$

Dividing Eq. 16 through by Eq. 17, we get

$$pV = p_1V_1 \tag{18}$$

or

$$V = p_1V_1/p \tag{19}$$

This expression enables us to calculate a volume of gas knowing the original volume, the original pressure, and the changed pressure, provided the temperature remains constant.

2. LAW OF CHARLES

The law of Charles gives the relationship between volume and temperature. This law states that the volume of a given sample of gas is directly proportional to the absolute temperature, the pressure remaining constant. Mathematically stated,

$$V \propto T \tag{20}$$

and introducing a proportionality factor

$$V = K'T \tag{21}$$

If, now, we change the temperature, we should, according to this law and the above relationship, obtain the expression

$$V_1 = K'T_1 \tag{22}$$

Dividing Eq. 21 through by Eq. 22, we get

$$V/V_1 = T/T_1 \tag{23}$$

or

$$V = V_1T/T_1 \tag{24}$$

3. COMBINED LAW

If the pressure and the temperature of a gaseous material change simultaneously, the volume is related to these changes by an expression known as the combined, law, or the Boyle-Charles law. It can be seen by relating Eqs. 15 and 20 that

$$V \propto 1/p \text{ and } T \tag{25}$$

Multiplying the factors and introducing a proportionality factor, we get the expression

$$V = kT/p \quad \text{or} \quad pV = kT \tag{26}$$

or

$$pV/T = k \tag{27}$$

If, now, the temperature and pressure of this gaseous system are changed, we get the expression

$$p_1V_1/T_1 = k \tag{28}$$

and dividing Eq. 27 through by Eq. 28, we get the well-known mathematical expression for the combined law:

$$pV/T = p_1V_1/T_1 \tag{29}$$

which for the purpose of calculating a volume from known data is generally expressed as

$$V = V_1 \times (p_1/p) \times (T/T_1) \tag{30}$$

4. Ideal Gas Law

If expression 25 is used for 1 mole of a gaseous substance, under "ideal" conditions, then the molar gas constant R may be substituted for k, and we get

$$pV = nRT$$

It must be understood that R must be in the same units as those used to represent the pressure volume relationship. The values for R are given in Table 14; Appendix.

Another form of this expression is

$$pV = wRT$$

where w equals the weight of the gas and the other symbols have the meaning previously assigned, but in consistent units. More generally, the expression can be written

$$pV = (W/M)RT$$

where W is the weight of the gas and M is the molecular weight of the gas.

5. Standard Temperature and Pressure

Some standard reference has to be accepted, if the measurement of gas volumes is to have meaning. This standard is known as the volume of a gas at "Standard Temperature and Pressure," (STP). The standard temperature is $0°C$ and the standard pressure is defined as the pressure of 760 mm of mercury at $0°C$. Hence, to refer any volume of a gas to STP, noting that the absolute zero of temperature is equal to $-273°C$, or conversely that $0°C$ is equivalent to $273°K$, by substitution in Eq. 27 we obtain

$$V_{STP} = V_1 \times (p/760) \times [273/(273 + t°C)] \qquad (31)$$

$$V_{STP} = V_1 \times (p/760) \times [492/(460 + t°F)] \qquad (32)$$

In industrial hygiene and air pollution control work it is common to use gauges and manometers calibrated in inches rather than in millimeters. Expressions 31 and 32 then become

$$V_{STP} = V_1 \times (p/29.92) \times [273/(273 + t°C)] \qquad (31a)$$

and

$$V_{STP} = V_1 \times (p/29.92) \times [492/(460 + t°F)] \qquad (32b)$$

Since few of these gauges can be read accurately or are accurate to $1/100$ of an inch, it is common practice to round off the pressure in inches to the value 30.

6. Dalton's Law

In sampling and in analyses made with gases or air for industrial poisons, we know we are dealing with mixtures. There is another law which expresses the relationships of a mixture of gases. It is known as Dalton's law. This principle states that the pressure contributed by each component of a gaseous mixture is proportional to its concentration in that mixture and consequently the total pressure of gas or atmosphere is the sum of the pressures of its components, that is

$$pV = V(p_1 + p_2 + p_3) \qquad (33)$$

There are two very important uses of this law in the field of industrial hazards. These are the corrections to be applied in the measurement of gas volume for the presence of water vapor and for the presence of residual gas in a partially evacuated vacuum gas collector.

In the case of measuring a volume of gas, say air, which is saturated with water vapor or which contains a known amount of water vapor, the actual volume of the gas is the volume measured, less the portion of the volume attributable to the water vapor. Expressed with respect to Dalton's law, the total pressure exhibited and measured is equivalent to the partial pressure of the gas and the partial pressure of the water vapor. That is, the pressure of the gas is equal to the total pressure less the partial pressure of the water vapor. The partial pressure of water, generally termed the *aqueous tension*, is known for a given temperature and may be obtained from the usual sources. By substitution of this value in Eq. 31, or Eq. 32, we get

$$V_{STP} = V_1 \times [(p - p_w)/760] \times [273/(273 + t°C)] \qquad (34)$$

$$V_{STP} = V_1 \times [(p - p_w)/760] \times [492/(460 + t°F)] \qquad (35)$$

in which p_w is the partial pressure of the water vapor.

As noted above, if the gauges and manometers being used are calibrated in inches rather than in millimeters, then the following expressions can be used:

$$V_{STP} = V_1 \times [(p - p_w)/29.92] \times [273/(273 + t°C)] \qquad (34a)$$

$$V_{STP} = V_1 \times [(p - p_w)/29.92] \times [492/(460 + t°F)] \qquad (35a)$$

$$V_{ISC} = V_1 \times [(p - p_w)/(30 - 0.51)] \times [520/(460 + t°F)] \qquad (35b)$$

where V_{ISC} is the volume at industrial standard conditions, 30 insaturated with water at 60°F.

7. CALCULATIONS

For specimen examples of the reduction of gases to standard temperature and pressure and for the corrections to be applied because of the presence of water vapor, the reader is referred to any text on the analysis of gases or on general chemistry.

On occasion it is necessary to sample with a bottle or other vessel which has only been partially evacuated. The following equations may be used to calculate the volume of gas or air sampled.

Let V_0 = effective volume of the bottle used for sampling (this is equivalent to the actual volume of the bottle less the volume of any absorbing or oxidizing solution if any is used); b = barometric pressure; and p_1 = partial pressure or residual pressure after evacuation.

Then, after permitting the bottle to take the sample by coming to atmospheric pressure and the same temperature as before, we have by Dalton's law that

$$b - p_1 = p_0$$

in which p_0 is the partial pressure attributable to the entering gas. Reducing the volume of the entering gas, V_2, to that occupied at barometric, pressure, we have

$$V_2 b = V_0 p_0$$

and

$$V_2 = V_0 p_0 / b$$

and by substitution

$$V_2 = V_0(b - p_1)/b \tag{36}$$

Thus, if the volume of the bottle, V_0, equals 5000 ml, the barometric pressure, b, equals 750 mm Hg and the residual pressure, p_1, equals 50 mm Hg then by substitution

$$V_2 = 5000(750 - 50)/750 = 4666.7 \text{ ml}$$

This volume is uncorrected for water vapor and is not reduced to standard conditions.

If a partially evacuated flask is used for sampling and after sampling the pressure and temperature of the sampled gas is taken, the expression

$$V_s = V_0 \left(1 - T_s p_1 / T_1 p_s\right)$$

in which V_s = volume of the gas collected, T_s = absolute temperature in °K of the sample, T_1 = temperature of flask in °K when residual pressure was measured, p_s = pressure of sample, and p_1 = residual pressure after evacuation of flask.

In Chapter II, Section G-2, it was noted that in order to make certain that all of the original air in an air-displacement collector is displaced by the air to be sampled, it was necessary to introduce at least ten changes of the air being sampled.   In effect, the sample container may be considered a small dynamic gassing chamber.   Silver (25) has considered the theoretical aspects of constant-flow gassing chambers.   These are chambers in which air is drawn at a fixed rate.   Here the nominal concentration in milligrams per liter is equal to the agent flow in milligrams per liter divided by the air flow in liters per minute. In such a system

$$C = (W/V_1)[1 - \exp(V_1t/V_0)] \tag{37}$$

where C = concentration of the substance to be determined in milligrams per liter at time t, W = milligrams of substance introduced per minute, V_0 = volume of flask, and V_1 = volume of air passing through flask each minute.   The percentage of the final concentration, W/V_1, obtained in time t is

$$\text{Percentage} = 100[1 - \exp(V_1t/V_0)] \tag{38}$$

Expression 36 implies that the concentration rises rapidly at first, then slowly approaches a constant value at infinite time.   For practical purposes it can be considered that the sampling can end at 99% of the theoretical value.   By substitution in Eq. 37

$$99 = 100[1 - \exp (V_1t/V_0)]$$

$$99 = 100 - 100 \exp (V_1t/V_0)$$

$$\exp (V_1t/V_0) = \frac{100 - 99}{100} = 0.01$$

changing to logs

$$-V_1t/V_0 = \ln 0.01 = -4.6052$$

$$t_{99} = 4.6052(V_0/V_1)$$

or, more generally, for any percentage x of the theoretical concentration, the time t will be

$$t_x = k(V_0/V_1)$$

where k is a constant.

The constants for various percentages of the theoretical value have been computed by Silver and are given in the following table.

x	k
99	4.065
95	2.996
90	2.303
85	1.897
80	1.609

a. Weighted Daily Exposure

It is important to be able to calculate the weighted exposure of a worker in order to evaluate his "true" exposure and thus compare it with the maximum allowable concentration or threshold value (see Appendix, Table 3). This is based in large measure on an averaging expression using the principle of $C \times t$ or concentration multiplied by the time exposed. Then

$$WE = (C_1 t_1 + C_2 t_2 + C_3 t_3 \ldots + C_n t_n)/t$$

where WE = weighted daily exposure; C_1, C_2, C_3, ... C_n = concentrations of substance at each part of cycle; t = total time of working day; and t_1, t_2, t_3, ... t_n = times of exposure corresponding to concentrations of substance at each part of cycle.

Hosey and Keenan (26) give a typical example:

Assume that a degreaser operator spends 4 hr per day cleaning parts and the average concentration of trichloroethylene vapor is 250 ppm at this operation (Task A). Also assume that 3 hr each day are spent at odd jobs in that vicinity where the average vapor concentration is 25 ppm (Task B) and the last hour of work each day is spent removing parts from a heat treating furnace (Task C), located in another area of the plant, where a concentration of 200 ppm of carbon monoxide occurs when the furnace door is open. This worker's weighted daily exposure to trichloroethylene is calculated as follows:

$$\frac{250 \text{ ppm} \times 4 \text{ hr (Task A)} + 25 \text{ ppm} \times 3 \text{ hr (Task B)}}{8} = 134+ \text{ ppm}$$

threshold limit value which is below the (TLV) of 200 ppm. This same worker's exposure to carbon monoxide would be:

$$\frac{200 \text{ ppm} \times 1 \text{ (Task C)}}{8} = 25 \text{ ppm CO}$$

which is also well below the TLV. It must be borne in mind, however, that even short exposures to high concentrations of many toxic materials can cause systemic injury or even death.

A final word of caution is indicated at this point. Assume, after the study is complete, that the calculated weighted exposure for a group of workmen to lead fumes was found to be 0.17 mg/m³ (and this value was based on a number of samples). One would not ordinarily recommend costly local exhaust systems to reduce the exposure to 0.15 mg/m³ (the TLV) or lower. Instead, a return visit should be made to the plant, and if the results of the second study were essentially the same as before, recommendations would be made to observe these workmen clinically at 4- to 6-month intervals for evidence of lead absorption. If blood and urine values were above normal levels, then control measures would be indicated. On the other hand, if weighted exposures were 0.25 to 0.30 mg/m³ during the first study, control measures would have been recommended immediately and without hesitation. In other words, a few milligrams or parts per million below the TLV's does not necessarily mean the environment is safe nor would a dangerous situation exist if the TLV's are exceeded slightly. A great deal of judgment is necessary in determining the exact cutoff point above which control measures should be instituted. It must be emphasized again that the TLV's are designed to serve as guides only; such factors as individual susceptibility and synergism must also be taken into consideration. For instance, there is evidence that alcohol increases an individual's susceptibility to chlorinated hydrocarbons; therefore, if a degreaser operator is known to be an habitual drinker, his TLV for trichloroethylene should be considerably below the recommended value of 200 ppm.

8. Gas Concentrations and Conversion Formulas

There are a number of different systems of expressing concentrations of substances in air. In industrial hygiene chemistry the usual expressions are: parts of the contaminant per million of air; milligrams of the contaminant per liter of air; milligrams of the pollutant per cubic meter of air; per cent volume of the contaminant in air; milligrams of the contaminant per cubic meter of air (this is used mainly in expressing the concentrations of solids in air). All of these expressions are interchangeable. Thus

$$\frac{ppm}{10,000} = \% \text{ by volume}$$

or

$$1\% = 10,000 \text{ ppm}$$

In order to convert milligrams per liter or any other weight per unit volume ratio to a volume per volume ratio, such as parts of vapor per million of air, use must be made of the gram-molecular volume relationship, namely, that the volume occupied by a gram-molecular weight of a gas at standard temperature and pressure (0°C and 760 mm pressure), is equal to 22.4 liters, or 24.45 liters at 25°C (a convenient value for the temperature at which most industrial hygiene sampling is performed) and 760 mm pressure.   Thus

$$\text{ppm} = \frac{24{,}450 \times \text{mg}}{M} \tag{39}$$

where M is the molecular weight of the substance and the other symbols have the meanings previously assigned.   Suppose in a determination it was found that 1 mg/liter of carbon disulfide was present and it was desired to convert this to parts of carbon disulfide per million of air, then by substitution in the above formula

$$\text{ppm} = \frac{24{,}450 \times 1}{76.12} = 321.2 \text{ ppm}$$

Or suppose the result had been calculated on the basis of parts per million and it was desired to convert to milligrams per liter, then

$$\text{mg} = \frac{\text{ppm} \times M}{24{,}450} \tag{40}$$

If 1 ppm was found, this is converted by substitution

$$\text{mg} = \frac{1 \times 76.12}{24{,}450} = 0.00311 \text{ mg/liter}$$

For any multiple of 1 ppm or 1 mg/liter, the result is obtained by simple multiplication.   By use of Appendix Table 1, which converts 1 mg/liter into parts per million, and 1 ppm into milligrams per liter, these calculations are greatly simplified.

To convert from milligrams per cubic meter to parts per million, use Eq. 39 but divide the right-hand side of the equation by 1000.

The expression cubic millimeters per cubic meter is also used occasionally; this is equivalent to parts per billion.

In order to obtain the quantity of a contaminant in an atmosphere that has been sampled by passing it through an absorbent, the analysis is made to find out the per cent of the contaminant in the aliquot part of the absorbing solution taken for analysis.   From this result, the total quantity of toxic or hazardous material in the entire volume of the absorbing solution is calculated.   From this value and the known volume of the air or atmosphere sampled, the amount of contaminant per unit of air or atmosphere can be computed.

Some factors for conversion of some units are the following:

(1) mg/liter $\times$ 28.32 = mg/cu ft
(2) mg/liter $\times$ 1000 = mg/m³
(3) mg/cu ft $\times$ 35.314 = mg/m³
(4) mg/m³ $\times$ 0.02832 = mg/cu ft

A useful approximate conversion is 1mg/m³ $\approx$ 1 oz/1000 cu ft.

A convenient method of computation when the samplinig rate is 0.1 cfm, i.e., 2832 ml/min is based on the relationship that

1 ml. 0.01N reagent $\approx$

  0.2445 ml of monovalent gas at 25°C and 760 mm

Then

$$\frac{0.2445 \times 1,000,000 \times \text{ml reagent}}{2832 \times \text{min}} =$$

  ppm for gases of 1 hydrogen equivalent

which becomes

$$\frac{86 \times \text{ml reagent}}{\text{min}} = \text{ppm for gases of 1 hydrogen equivalent}$$

This becomes

$$\frac{43 \times \text{ml reagent}}{\text{min}} = \text{ppm for gases of 2 hydrogen equivalents}$$

These formulas have been used successfully for computing the concentration of the common acid gases and ammonia.

References

1. Caplan, K. J., *Chem. Eng. Progr.*, **50**, 409 (1954).
2. Olive, T. R., *Chem. Eng.*, Part 2 (May 1952).
3. Beckett, E. G., *J. Soc. Chem. Ind.*, **36**, 52 (1917).
4. Ower, E., *Measurement of Air Flow*, Chapman and Hall, London, 1933.
5. Grove, G. W., *U.S. Bur. Mines Inform. Circ. 7037* (1938).
6. Alnor Velometer, Illinois Testing Laboratories, Inc., Chicago, Illinois.
7. Bloomfield, J. J., and J. M. DallaValle, *U.S. Public Health Service Bull. 217* (1938).
8. First, M. W., and L. Silverman, *Ind. Eng. Chem.*, **42**, 301 (Feb. 1950).

9. Stoll, H. W., *Trans. Am. Soc. Mech. Engrs.*, **73**, 963 (Oct. 1951).
10. Yaglou, C. P., *J. Ind. Hyg. Toxicol.*, **20**, 497 (1938).
11. Lunge, G., and C. A. Keane, *Technical Methods of Chemical Analysis*, Van Nostrand, New York, 1924.
12. Hill, L., Med. Research Council, Special Rept. Series 32, London.
13. Hill, L., *Sunshine and Open Air*, Arnold, London, 1924.
14. Hill, L., and A. Campbell, *Health and Environment*, Arnold, London, 1925.
15. Angus, T. C., *J. Ind. Hyg.*, **6**, 20 (1924).
16. Hill, L., T. C. Angus, and E. M. Newbold, *J. Ind. Hyg.*, **10**, 391 (1928).
17. Kerr, J., *The Air We Breathe*, Faber & Gwyer, London, 1926.
18. Yaglou, C. P., and K. Dokoff, *J. Ind. Hyg.*, **11**, 278 (1929).
19. Hatch, T., H. Warren and P. Drinker, *J. Ind. Hyg.*, **14**, 301 (1932).
20. Bruun, J. R., *Ind. Eng. Chem. Anal. Ed.*, **11**, 655 (1939).
21. Flury, F., and F. Zernik, *Schaedliche Gase*, Springer, Berlin, 1931.
22. Whitwell, J. C., and D. S. Plumb, *Ind. Eng. Chem.*, **31**, 451 (1939).
23. Caplan, K. J., *Heating Ventilating*, **51**, No. 11, 100 (Nov. 1954).
24. Tebbens, B. D., and D. M. Keagy, *Am. Ind. Hyg. Assoc. Quarterly*, **17**, No. 3, **327** (1956).
25. Silver, S. D., *J. Lab. Clin. Med.*, **31**, 1153 (1946).
26. Hosey, A. D., and R. G. Keenan, "The Industrial Environment. . .Its Evaluation and Control," Public Health Service Publ., Govt. Printing Office, Washington, D.C., 1958.

General References

Bloomfield, J. J., and J. M. DallaValle, "The Determination of Dust," *U.S. Public Health Service, Bull. 217* (1938).
Chem. Met. Eng., "Process Industries—Flow Sheets and Data Book," p. 141, "Charts for Gas Flow Measurement."
DallaValle, J. M., *The Industrial Environment and Its Control*, Pitman, New York, 1948.
DallaValle, J. M., "Principles of Exhaust Hood Design," *U.S. Public Health Service* (1939).
Eason, A. B., *The Flow and Measurement of Air and Gases*, Griffin, London, 1919.
Fieldner, A. C., S. H. Katz, S. P. Kinney, and Y. Henderson, "Gas Masks for Gases Met in Fighting Fires," *U.S. Bur. Mines Tech. Paper 248* (1921).
Flury, F., and F. Zernik, *Schaedliche Gase*, Springer, Berlin, 1931.
Furman, N. H., *Scott's Standard Methods of Chemical Analysis*, Vol. II, Van Nostrand, New York, 1939.
Ower, E., *Measurement of Air Flow*, Chapman & Hall, London, 1933.
"Symposium on Fluid Flow," *Ind. Eng. Chem.*, **31**, 407–482 (1939).

CHAPTER IV

ABSORBERS, ABSORBENTS, AND ADSORBENTS

In most instances when studies, investigations, and analyses are made in the field of industrial hazards, the substance to be estimated is present in such small quantities that a large volume of air must be sampled in order to obtain a sufficient amount of the substance to ascertain its concentration with any degree of accuracy. There are a great many devices designed to give maximum absorption or adsorption when dusts, smokes, fumes, mists, or gaseous contaminants are passed into them. The absorbing fluid wets, dissolves, or reacts with the contaminant and thus retains the contaminant. The adsorbing material adsorbs the contaminant on its surfaces. It is important to have a proper evaluation of the efficiency not only of the absorber itself but also of the absorbing fluid.

A. Absorbers

The laws governing the absorption of gases in liquids are the laws governing heterogeneous equilibria and reaction velocity in heterogeneous systems. In the simplest case, where a gas dissolves in the absorbing medium and does not react with it, Henry's law applies: the concentrations of any single molecular species in two phases at equilibrium bear a constant ratio to each other. However, in those systems in which the gas or other substance absorbed forms a different molecular species in or reacts with the absorbing medium, Henry's law must be modified by combination with the mass law or by taking into account the association or dissociation of the substance absorbed.

In many instances these considerations are merely theoretical, for instance, in the absorption of hydrogen chloride by water, because the partial pressure of hydrogen chloride in aqueous solutions containing up to 250 g/liter is practically negligible. However, in other instances the partial pressure of the gas to be absorbed in the atmosphere above the absorbing fluid cannot be neglected. By the use of multiple absorbers, the partial pressure of the gas in the air stream can be reduced to a negligible amount.

In general, when absorption in a reacting medium is used, the rate of sampling should be slow enough to permit the reaction of the substance being trapped with the trapping reagent to go to completion in the time it takes to traverse the sampling vessel. There must also be an excess of the reagent used in the trapping solution. This excess can be computed in a manner analogous to the calculations given in Chapter III, Section C.

It is important to choose the proper absorbing medium. For example, Nordlander (1) points out that where aqua regia is used as the absorbent for mercury vapòr, errors may result because a white coat of mercuric chloride forms around a drop of mercury and protects it from further solution. Nitric acid alone is a better absorbent.

Solubility and insolubility of a contaminant are not the only criteria for choosing an absorbing medium. Thus, a long sampling time may lead to erroneous results where the contaminant may be oxidized by the aeration stream, as in the case of low concentrations of formaldehyde.

1. Efficiency

The efficiency of an absorber, absorbent, adsorbent, etc. may be defined as the ratio of contaminant trapped by the device or substance to the total amount of contaminant present in the air stream (2). The percentage efficiency is equal to the parts per million of contaminant in the entering gas minus the parts per million of the contaminant in the effluent gas divided by the parts per million of contaminant in the entering gas multiplied by 100:

$$\% \text{ efficiency} = \frac{\text{ppm entering gas} - \text{ppm effluent gas}}{\text{ppm entering gas}} \times 100$$

Efficiency depends on a number of factors, such as the design of the absorber device, the rate of flow of the sampling stream, the absorbing solution, absorbent or adsorbent used, the temperature, and other factors. Increasing the number of absorbers increases the efficiency of absorption. The theoretical aspects of absorption in nonreacting media are discussed by Elkins and his co-workers (3). The velocity of reaction at a gas–liquid interface is discussed by Taylor (4).

Elkins, Hobby, and Fuller (3) have pointed out that when an absorbing solvent is used to trap a substance with which it does not react, for example, water for trapping butyl alcohol, the absorption is not complete because the vapor pressure of the substance being trapped is reduced by the solvent effect of the trapping solution.

The efficiency of such absorptions can be calculated. With a perfect absorbing solution in which complete equilibrium of distribution can be achieved between the absorbing solvent and the incoming carrier air, the rate of absorption of the vapor is given by the expression

$$dC/dV = p - kC$$

where C = vapor concentration in absorbing solution, V = ratio of air volume to liquid volume, p = vapor concentration in air (equivalent to its partial pressure), and k = a constant. Integrating this expression for a given volume of sampled air we get

$$C = (p/k)(1 - e^{-kV})$$

and the efficiency of absorption

$$C/pV = (1/kV)(1 - e^{-kV})$$

Thus, the efficiency of absorption is dependent on the ratio of the volumes of air sampled to the volume of absorbing solution and the constant k, not upon the original concentration of the vapor in the air nor on the concentration in the absorbing solvent.

Elkins (5) has shown that the value of the constant k is dependent on the solubility of the vapor being trapped in the absorbing solvent and its volatility. Its value for a given substance can be estimated by aspirating a measured volume of air through a known dilute solution of that substance and then determining the residual concentration. From this value the loss attributable to aeration can be calculated. From these data k can be computed for

$$\ln C_0/C = kV$$

or

$$\log C_0/C = 0.43kV$$

where C_0 is the initial concentration and C is the final concentration of the substance in the dilute solution being aerated.

To obtain an efficiency of 95% in sampling with a trapping solution for a given substance, the volume of air sampled should not exceed that volume which causes a loss of more than 10% on aspiration through a known concentration in the absorbing solvent.

The efficiency of an absorber or sampling device should be tested before it is adopted for field use. This may be done in a number of ways:

(1) By the use of a gas-tight compartment, chamber, or tank into which it is possible to introduce known concentrations of a vapor, or a cylinder filled with a synthetic gas mixture for reference.

(2) By the comparison of the results obtained with a device under test with those of a device known to be accurate.

(3) By the introduction of a known quantity of material into the sampling train. Typical of such methods is that of Jacobs, Braverman, and Hochheiser (6) in the development of a test for sulfides in air.

(4) By noting the amount of material trapped in a second unit of the absorption train when a single absorber is being tested. This method sometimes leads to erroneous results. Paluch (7) found that a second impinger only collected a small part of the sulfur dioxide and hydrogen sulfide which passed through the first impinger without being trapped. Littlefield and co-workers (8) found more lead fume trapped in a second impinger than in the first impinger of a sampling train.

(5) In addition, to test the efficiency at different sampling rates, two absorbers of the same type may be tested in parallel, the rate of flow through one of them having been adjusted to be faster than the rate of flow through the other.

There are two general methods of preparing known concentrations of substances: *static* and *dynamic*. Static methods of preparing known concentrations are those in which a known amount of the agent or material being tested is introduced into a known volume of air, the known volume being a small or large test chamber. Thus, static systems are batch methods of preparing test concentrations. Such systems have been discussed by Sayres and co-workers (9), Setterlind (10), and Stead and Taylor (11). The disadvantages of static systems have been emphasized by Scherberger and co-workers (12).

Dynamic methods of preparing known concentrations are those in which the desired concentration of the substance being tested is achieved by feeding the test substance at a known rate into an air stream moving at a known rate into the test chamber. Dynamic systems are dilution methods in which known amounts of a test substance are injected into a moving air stream in known periods of time. Dynamic or constant-flow methods of concentration control have been discussed by Irish and Adams (13), Silver (14), Silverman and co-workers (15), Amdur, Schulz, and Drinker (16), Lewis and Koepf (17), Charnley (18), Sunderman and co-workers (19), Urban (20), and Scherberger and co-workers (12).

It is beyond the scope of this text to discuss the methods of uniform concentration control. A number of such methods are detailed in the references cited for dynamic methods of preparing known concentrations given in the preceding paragraph. Some methods utilize timing devices (12,13,21,22) to deliver the test material. Other methods depend upon observation of the flow rates of both the carrier air and the diluting air.

The method of choice for the delivery of known volumes of liquid to be vaporized at known rates of flow is the use of a syringe of known volume, the plunger of which is driven by a clock mechanism of some type. For example, Sunderman et al. (19) used a Luer syringe powered by a Flexo-Action synchronous motor (23), Amdur and co-workers (16) used a syringe driven by an electric clock motor, and Carpenter and co-workers used a syringe actuated by a Monodrum (24) which is a single-drum kymograph. Saltzman (25) has discussed in detail the use of motor driven syringes for the micrometering of gases.

2. TRAPPING DEVICES

It is necessary to choose the absorption device used for a particular purpose with care because the accuracy of the test may depend upon the absorption or adsorption device used. The devices may, for the sake of convenience, be placed into three main groups:

(a) U-tubes and bulbs in which the contaminant is trapped by an adsorbent or absorbent, generally of a solid nature, such as activated charcoal, silica gel, Ascarite, soda lime, Dehydrite, impregnated porous materials, or glass wool or cotton wet with some active reagent. The devices may be simple U-tubes or bulbs or even more elaborate devices with interchangeable glass ground connections and stoppers.

(b) Devices which depend upon the washing of the incoming gas

stream to absorb the contaminant.   This group may be subdivided
into four subgroups:

(1) The simple gas-wash bottles or absorbers, in which the length
     of travel is equivalent to the height or length of the absorbing
     liquid in the device.
(2) The spiral devices, in which the length of travel is many times
     greater than the height or length of the apparatus.
(3) Devices equipped with some dispersion mechanism, such as a
     fritted-glass plate or an Aloxite distributor.   These devices are
     often termed *bubblers*.
(4) Devices that increase the length of travel by increasing the
     direct path traversed.   These types are in reality multiple
     simple absorbers combined into one apparatus.
(c) Devices which increase the path by means of baffles and so are,
in reality, scrubbing rather than merely washing devices.

One cannot state dogmatically that any one particular type of absorber is preferred for industrial hygiene work because each absorber
has some particular feature which lends itself to best advantage in a
given method.   There are some absorbers that lend themselves to
more general use than others.   In the following description of the
more common types of absorbers that are employed in the chemical
determination of contaminants in air, the particular advantage of each
will be mentioned.   Such characteristics as ease of washing, ease of
recovery of the absorbed material, durability, adaptability, and expense are all to be considered in the selection of adequate absorbers.

a. U-Tubes and Bulbs

U-tubes or, at times, bulbs and simple tubes are used principally
when it is desired to weigh the material absorbed or adsorbed or when
it is necessary to liberate the trapped material for further analytical
treatment.   They are also generally used when the contaminant to
be sampled is trapped by freezing, as these devices lend themselves
more readily to immersion in a freezing bath.   A typical illustration of
this use is a method for the determination of benzene.   In this
method the benzene is trapped by freezing in a U-tube packed with
solid carbon dioxide, then is volatilized and refrozen in a test vessel.
As examples of the use of U-tubes that are weighed before and after
sampling, see the general methods for the determination of solvent

vapors as detailed in Chapter XII of Jacobs, *The Analytical Chemistry of Industrial Poisons, Hazards, and Solvents* (26), and the procedure for *p*-dichlorobenzene on page 596 of that volume.

One can include in this group the many combustion absorption bulbs designed for holding solid absorbents, such as Ascarite (27,28), a special sodium hydroxide–asbestos absorbent mixture; Dehydrite, magnesium perchlorate trihydrate, $MgClO_4 \cdot 3H_2O$ (29,30); Anhydrone, anhydrous magnesium perchlorate; Desicchlora, anhydrous barium perchlorate; soda lime, a mixture of calcium oxide and sodium hydroxide, the sodium hydroxide content ranging from 5 to 20%, etc. These devices are used in the trains designed for the determination of carbon in steel and in organic chemicals. They can also be used for other trapping purposes. Among these may be mentioned the absorption bulbs of Turner (31), Midvale, Fleming, Vanier, and others. Illustrations of these devices can be found in almost any laboratory equipment catalog.

b. Washing Devices

Washing Bottles and Bulbs. There are many different types of these gas-washing devices. In the simple type the gas is permitted to enter at some point and it can find its way out only by traversing the length of the absorbing liquid. In these types the length of travel of the gas bubble is practically equivalent to the height or length of the

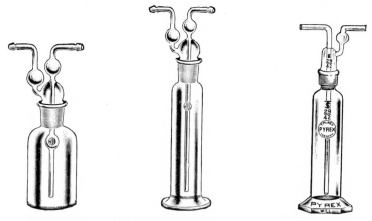

Fig. IV-1. Drechsel high- and low-form gas washing bottles.

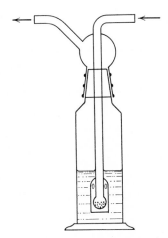

Fig. IV-2. Petticoat bubbler.

absorbing liquid.   Among those that may be taken as representative of this group are the Drechsel (Fig. IV-1) and Allihn types. Some others are the Drehschmidt petticoat inner-tube absorbing cylinder, the Fieldner (2) petticoat type, Petri tubes (32), and Habermann, Muencke, Bunsen, etc. absorption gas-washing bottles.

These devices are not particularly efficient absorbers and generally must be connected in multiples for maximum efficiency.   They do, however, have certain advantages over other, more efficient absorbers.   Thus, in those instances in which a precipitate is to be recovered —for example, the formation of diphenylurea from aniline and phosgene in the test for phosgene (Chapter XVI, Section A-5-b), detailed on page 390 of reference 26— the Drehschmidt petticoat and Drechsel types are preferred, for they can be washed out readily and the precipitate cannot lodge in inaccessible places.   They also can be cleaned more readily than other types and can be used as direct titration vessels.

Included among the simple absorbing devices is the impinger, described in detail in Chapter V.   It differs somewhat in principle, however, in that the forward motion of a particle is momentarily arrested by impingement against a baffle, thus assisting the washing action.

Spiral and Helical Devices.   The spiral absorption devices, in which the length of travel is considerably greater than the height or

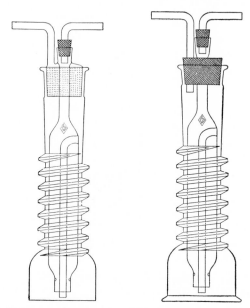

Fig. IV-3. Spiral gas washing bottles.   (Courtesy Chicago Apparatus Corp.)

Fig. IV-4. Milligan gas-washing bottles.   (Courtesy Fisher Scientific Co.)

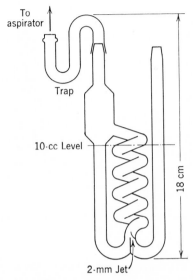

Fig. IV-5. Bubbler used for the absorption of benzene vapors in nitration acid.

length of the absorbing liquid itself, are among the most efficient absorbers of the single type.   In such equipment the gas is forced to travel in a helical path either in a tube or because of a helical baffle arrangement, so that the gas is in a washing fluid for from 5 to 10 times the length of travel of the simple washing type.   The stream of gas bubbles forces some of the liquid up the incline, which in turn rotates the gas bubbles as they themselves travel up the helical path. This gives an added washing effect.   Some of these devices are illustrated in Figures IV-3 and IV-4.

Rhodes and Rakestraw (33), testing the efficiency of gas-washing bottles, found that the Friedrichs (34,35) spiral gas-washing bottle was the most efficient for the absorption of carbon dioxide by a sodium hydroxide solution.   A spiral type of absorber that was efficient for the absorption of carbon dioxide and contained only a relatively small volume of alkaline absorbing medium (30 ml) as compared with the Friedrichs and Milligan gas-washing bottles is described by Martin and Green (36).

Other spiral-type gas-washing bottles are those of Pearce and Roberson (37), Corson (38), Weaver and Edwards (39), and Keller (40). Smyth (41) describes one which is designed to hold only a small volume of nitrating acid for trapping benzene (Fig. IV-5).

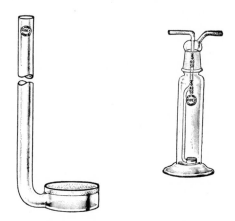

Fig. IV-6. Fritted-glass-disk bubblers. (Courtesy Corning Glass Works.)

Dispersers and Bubblers. It has been shown, however, that besides the length of travel in which a gas and liquid are in contact with each other, the size of the gas bubbles distributed within the liquid absorbing medium is also of decided importance (42,43). The size of the entrance orifice of a single tube may be used to regulate the size of the entering bubble, but such a constriction may impede the flow of the gas stream. In order to achieve adequate dispersion without diminishing efficiency or increasing flow resistance to a considerable extent, use may be made of sintered- or fritted-glass disks and thimbles. One of the most important applications of glass filters is in securing intimate contact between gaseous and liquid phases. The early bibliography of this subject has been reviewed by Prausnitz (44).

Fritted-glass disks are made of ground and sifted glass powder sintered in suitable molds, without any binder, into porous plates, etc., which may subsequently be fused into any desired shape of solid glass of the same coefficient of expansion. By choosing a particular type of glass, any quality of chemical or temperature resistance may be obtained. Ordinary soft glass, or Pyrex, or even fused quartz may be used and joined to glass of a different composition by the use of special joining glasses. Figure IV-6 shows an absorber and tube fitted with fritted disks. Other devices are illustrated by Prausnitz (44). Indeed, almost any washing bottle, such as the Drechsel or

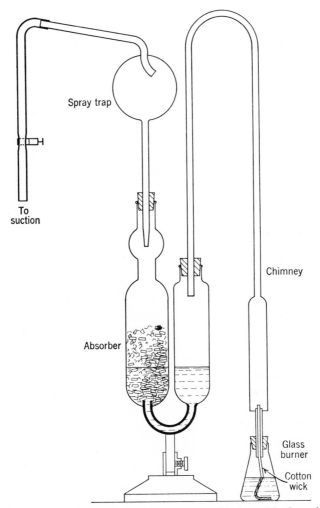

Fig. IV-7. Sulfur lamp for determination of chlorinated hydrocarbons.

Petri types, may be equipped with such sintered-glass distributors and thereby have its efficiency greatly improved.

The absorption section of the sulfur lamp (Fig. IV-7) when equipped with a coarse frit instead of with glass beads or short rods, can be used as a fritted bubbler. Such sections are commercially available.

The size of the bubbles is a function not only of the diameter of the orifice from which it emerges but also of the surface tension of the liquid surrounding the disperser (45). Thomas (46) developed a continuous carbon dioxide recorder that had an absorber with a fritted porous plate in which dispersion of gas bubbles was obtained not only by the use of the porous plate but also by the addition of a higher alcohol, like butyl alcohol, which acted as a surface-tension depressant and thus reduced the size of the entering bubbles. The butyl alcohol also produced a froth, which served to increase the time of contact of the gas with the liquid. This made an apparent increase in the volume of the absorbing liquid of 2 or 3 times for the tiny bubbles had to circulate and recirculate within the froth before they were able to emerge.

Fritted-glass-disk bubblers in various porosities are commercially available. Directions for the preparation of fritted disks, particularly for specialized uses, may be found in the literature (47–50). For most industrial hygiene work the porosity designated as coarse is preferred. The customary rate of sampling is 0.5–1 lpm. Too fine a porosity increases the need for greater power to drive the air stream through the device. This in turn requires bulkier apparatus.

Crabtree and Kemp (51) and subsequently Wadelin (52) used a round-bottomed flask with a spray jet (Fig. XV-2, Chapter XV, Section B-2-c) in order to distribute the incoming air stream rapidly, finely, and uniformly.

The midget impinger (Chapter V, Section C-7-d) has been modified to make it a fritted-disk bubbler (Fig. IV-8). By means of these modifications it can be used for the collection of vapors with a small volume of aqueous and nonaqueous reagents, at a sampling rate of 1–3 lpm.

Apparatus of New York State Industrial Hygiene Laboratory (53). The New York State Division of Industrial Hygiene laboratory decided to standardize their absorbers by using the following types for most of their sampling requiring absorption. One device consists of a 250-ml glass-stoppered Drechsel wash bottle with standard taper ground-glass connections at the entrance and exit tubes, equipped with glass hooks sealed at the connections as an aid in keeping joints tight when several bottles are used in series. A sintered-glass disk with No. 1 porosity (German designation), which corresponds very closely to porosity B of disks manufactured in the United

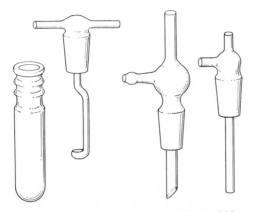

Fig. IV-8. Midget all-glass fritted-disk bubbler.

Fig. IV-9. Aloxite gas distributors.   (Courtesy Fisher Scientific Co.)

States, is fused to the end of the gas-entrance tube near the bottom of the bottle.   About 100 ml of absorbing fluid is used in each bottle. Two or more of these devices can be connected in series without the use of any rubber because of the standard taper connections.   This apparatus is used for those estimations in which contact between the air to be analyzed, or the medium used for absorption, and rubber, metal, or cementing materials is to be avoided.

For use with small volumes of liquids, a smaller all-glass absorber is made of one piece, about 7 in. high with a 1-in. diameter.   The ground-glass joints at the ends of the gas-entrance and gas-exit tubes are of standard taper but of smaller dimensions than those on the larger all-glass apparatus.   Because the sintered-glass disk is smaller in diameter in this device, it is best to reduce the rate of gas flow through this absorber to about two-thirds the rate through the larger apparatus.   From 10 to 15 ml of absorbing liquid are sufficient for this type.

Another type consists of a glass vial about 4.5 in. high with a 1.75-in. outside diameter.   This vial is fitted with a two-hole rubber stopper.   An Aloxite stone (Fig. IV-9) is attached to the gas-entrance tube by means of cement or by a rubber connection fitted to the metal nipple with which some of these stones are supplied.   The Aloxite stone acts as the gas distributor.   About 35 ml of absorbing liquid are used in each vial and as many vials as necessary are connected in series.   This type of apparatus is relatively inexpensive and has the additional advantage of flexibility between absorbers.   It may be used in many instances, but not where the presence of metal, rubber, or cementing material will interfere with the analysis.

The Drechsel washing bottle described above may be fitted with an Aloxite stone with the aid of cement instead of being equipped with a fritted-glass distributor.   Errors resulting from rubber connections in gas-washing bottles not equipped with standard taper connections may be eliminated or minimized by carefully squaring the ends of the absorbers and arranging glass-to-glass connections held in place with rubber tubing as described in Chapter II (Fig. II-5).   In these instances the cementing material must then be selected so that it will cause no interference with the absorption and analysis.   Litharge and glycerol, magnesium oxychloride, and Bakelite resin are a few of the cements which may be employed for this purpose.   This apparatus is less expensive and has most of the advantages of the all-glass apparatus.

In using these pieces of equipment for the absorption of gases from industrial air, it has been found necessary to use only two absorbers in series when the air is run through at a rate of 30 lph.   The length of time required for sampling depends on the concentration of contaminants encountered and on the precision and accuracy of the chemical analytical method.   The usual sampling time varies from 20 min to 2 hr.   With the all-glass apparatus, an all-glass flowmeter with a standard taper connection to fit those of the washing bottles may be used on the downstream side of the sampling train; any flowmeter connected with rubber tubing may be used on the upstream side.   In the latter case the flowmeter must be calibrated to read in terms of flow of air at atmospheric pressure, although at that point the gas passing through the flowmeter is at a pressure somewhat below atmospheric.   The drop in pressure through each sintered-glass disk is about 1 in. Hg when the rate of air flow is 30 lph.   The absorption devices using Aloxite stones are used with a flowmeter on the downstream side.   The drop in pressure across each stone is about 3 in. with an air flow of 30 lph.

The Laboratory of the Division of Industrial Hygiene of New York State used the all-glass device for the estimation of hydrogen sulfide, carbon disulfide, both gases simultaneously, acid vapors and mist, and ammonia.   The apparatus containing an Aloxite-stone gas disperser is used for the estimation in air of methyl alcohol, other alcohols, formaldehyde, and other aldehydes and phenols.

Harrold Mist and Gas Collector.   One of the disadvantages of fritted-disk bubblers as a means of sampling gases and vapors is the channeling of the air stream through a relatively small number of pores in the fritted disk, with subsequent decrease in the efficiency of absorption.   Harrold (54) overcomes this by using the method of the common impinger (Chapter V, Section C-7-c) to baffle the air flow and thus distribute it evenly, with the aid of a small plenum chamber, through the fritted disk.   With this device efficiencies of over 95% were obtained in the collection of sulfur dioxide, sulfur trioxide, carbon dioxide, hydrogen sulfide, and hydrogen chloride and over 97% in the collection of hydrochloric acid and chromic acid mists.

Multifold Absorbers.   The length of travel of a gas through an absorbing solution may be increased in ways other than by spiraling the path.   One of the older forms is Lunge's or Meyer's 10-bulb absorption tube.   Another is the bulb tube designed by Thomas (46) and fitted with a fritted disk.   Still another arrangement is a multiple absorber that can be filled and emptied as a single unit (3).   These devices are in reality multiple absorbers built into one unit instead of being attached mechanically and then separated for filling, rinsing, washing, etc.   They have the advantage that they are more efficient than a single absorber, for the most efficient way to absorb vapors in nonreacting liquids is to use a number of absorbers in series.

The well-known potash bulbs, illustrations of which can be seen in most laboratory equipment catalogs, are also types of devices which are multifold absorbers.

Lift-Pump Gas Absorber.   As has been stated before, intimate contact of a gas with the absorbing liquid is one of the important prerequisites of satisfactory absorption of a contaminant.   The principle of the air-lift pump was used by Nichols (55) in designing a device to absorb sulfur dioxide from air.   Greater contact with an iodine-absorbing solution was achieved by causing turbulence in an inner tube of the apparatus.

c. Scrubbing Devices

These absorption devices increase the path of travel of the gas stream by means of baffles and so exert a scrubbing effect rather than merely a washing effect, as the incoming gas stream is completely broken up in finding its way out of the devious path set up by the baffles.   Such devices generally consist of a glass tube filled with glass beads wet with the absorbing medium.   The incoming gas stream is admitted in such a manner that it can only find its way out by passing through the maze presented by the glass beads or short glass rods. These designs are very often used where only a very small amount of absorbing solution is permissible or desired.   Among the devices in this group that may be mentioned is the one Shaw (56) used for the determination of nitric oxide in coke-oven gas; the absorber for

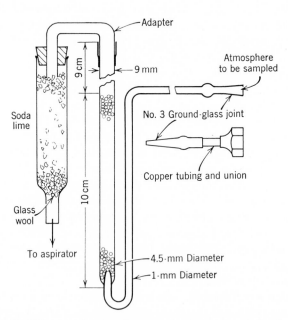

Fig. IV-10. Bubbler for nitrating benzene or toluene vapor–air mixtures (21).

the microdetermination of benzene (57) and toluene (21) (Fig. IV-10);
the absorber used in the sulfur lamp-apparatus method for the determination of chlorinated hydrocarbons (Fig. IV-7); absorbers used in
combustion methods for the determination of chlorinated hydrocarbons (58,59) (Fig. IV-11); that of Barrett (60) for the estimation
of trichloroethylene (Fig. IV-12); and that of Petersen and Radke (61)
for the determination of acrylonitrile (Fig. IV-13).

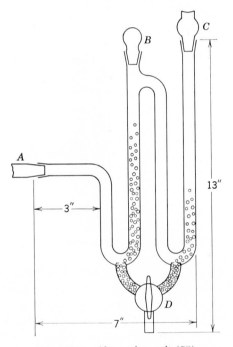

Fig. IV-11. Absorption unit (58).

The siphon section of a Soxhlet extractor filled with glass beads,
which is placed in the sampling train so that the gas being tested passes
through the siphon tube before reaching the beads, can also be used
as a scrubbing device.   Still another variation of these devices may
be made from a tube similar to an Ostwald viscosimeter or one of its
modifications, the wide section of which is filled with glass beads.
The device is placed in the sampling line so that the incoming atmosphere passes through the capillary section first.

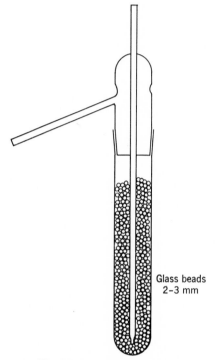

Fig. IV-12. Absorption tube.

In a sense, the addition of a surface-tension depressant or foaming agent to an absorbing solution in a gas-washing bottle or in an impinger serves to convert the device to a scrubbing trap because the interfaces and surfaces of the foam serve to provide for more intimate contact between the absorbing solution and the contaminant to be trapped.   Illustrative of this type of scrubbing action are the method of Thomas (46), already mentioned, and that of Jacobs and Hochheiser (62) for the determination of nitrogen dioxide.

Venturi Scrubber.   A completely different means of obtaining a scrubbing action is that of the venturi scrubber.   This apparatus is designed to trap a pollutant in a minimum volume of water by recirculating the water from the bottom of a cyclonic separator back into the system through the spray jet of a venturi throat.   The Stanford Research Institute (63) developed a laboratory model venturi scrubber (Fig. IV-14) made of nonreactive Lucite plastic so that

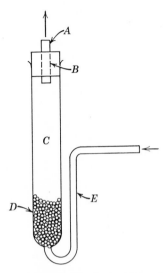

Fig. IV-13. Absorption trap (61): (A) glass outlet tube; (B) one-hole rubber stopper; (C) 0.25-in. test tube; (D) glass beads; (E) glass inlet tube.

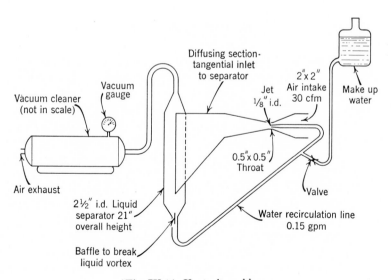

Fig. IV-14. Venturi scrubber.

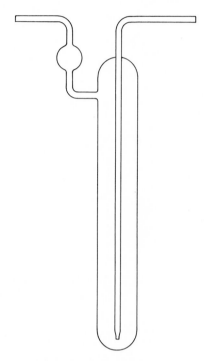

Fig. IV-15. Freezing trap.

the spray and the separatory action could be watched.   The size of
the model was kept small so that it could be operated by a tank-type
vacuum cleaner.   The venturi, made with a square cross section,
had a 2 × 2-in. intake and a 0.5 × 0.5-in. throat so that a gas velocity of 250–300 fps could be obtained.   The cyclone separator had a
2.5-in. internal diameter and was 21 in. long.   For this model, 150
ml of water was used and it was found that the integrated recircu-
lation volume should be of the order of 10–15 gal of water per 1000 cu
ft of air for optimum results.   In order to make up evaporation losses,
the original volume of water was maintained constant by use of a reservoir.   The flow was maintained at a constant rate by adjusting controls so that the reading on a gauge was constant.

With this type of apparatus it was possible to wash 10,000 cu ft of
air in from 5 to 6 hr.   At least 80% of concentrations less than 1 ppm
of sulfuric acid mist of the size order of 0.5–0.7 μ could be recovered.

3. Freezing Traps

In addition to the use of U-tubes and bulbs as freezing traps, there are devices which are specially designed for this purpose. One of these devices is illustrated in Fig. IV-15. It fits readily into a dewar flask or thermos bottle and so can easily be immersed in a fluid freezing mixture.

Carbon monoxide, mercury, benzene, p-dichlorobenzene, and refrigerants and solvents, in general, may be estimated by freezing methods.

In using a freezing trap either for the collection of the vapor or for estimation by weighing, one must consider the possible formation

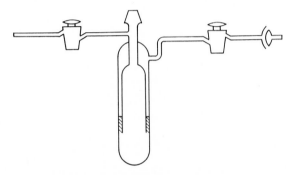

Fig. IV-16. Shepherd freeze-out trap.

of a fine mist, which will pass out of the tube without condensing, and the possible freezing of water vapor, which will cause a clumping within the collecting tube and thus completely obstruct the flow of air. Thus, bromine cannot be efficiently trapped using a 16-mm U-tube in a Dry Ice–methanol freezing mixture (64).

Shepherd (65) developed a freeze-out trap (Fig. IV-16) which had a wide mouth entrance tube and a glass-wool barrier. The purpose of the wide mouth is to prevent clogging of the mouth by condensation and freezing of water; the purpose of the barrier is to prevent any mist from being carried out of the trap. Jacobs (66) developed a freeze-out trap with a detachable bottom section (Fig. IV-17) which was designed to assist in weighing the material recovered by condensation methods. A tare weight of the detachable section is taken before sampling. After sampling and subsequent manipulative steps,

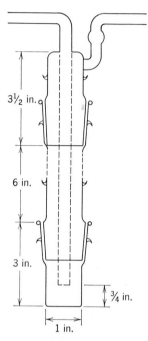

Fig. IV-17. Jacobs' freeze-out trap.

the bottom section is reweighed to get the weight of the trapped material.

4. Heated Traps

Heated trapping devices are generally quartz, heat-resistant glass, or metal tubes which are heated and in which some contaminant of the air stream is deposited because of decomposition. Examples are the deposition of an arsenic or antimony mirror in a heat-resistant glass tube by heating a stream of gas containing arsine or stibine. Another is the decomposition of iron pentacarbonyl and nickel tetracarbonyl by heat with the deposition of the iron or nickel in the heated tube. Generally, a silica or heat-resistant glass tube is used at a red-heat temperature for this purpose. Chlorinated hydrocarbons are also decomposed by passing them through heated tubes, but in this instance there is no deposition in the tube and so it does not act as a trap. The chlorides formed must be caught by some other means.

5. Classification of Absorbers Used for Gases and Vapors

This classification generally follows the recommendations of the American Public Health Association (7).

(*1*) The following gases and vapors are readily soluble in the absorbing agent commonly employed (Table IV-1) and can be absorbed with success in fritted-glass bubblers, and possibly in the impinger:

Acetic acid	Hydrochloric acid
Acetone	Hydrofluoric acid
Ammonia	Hydrogen cyanide
Amyl acetate	Methyl alcohol
Butyl acetate	Nitric acid
Carbon disulfide	Sulfur dioxide
Formaldehyde	

(*2*) The following gases are less soluble and more care must be taken or absorption will not be sufficiently complete.   One or more fritted-glass bubblers in series are recommended.

Acrolein	Iodine
Aniline	Ozone
Arsine	Phenol
Bromine	Phosgene
Carbon dioxide	Phosphine
Chlorine	Phosphorus chlorides
Diethyl ether	Sulfur monochloride
Hydrogen sulfide	

(*3*) This group of gases and vapors requires special absorbers or sampling devices:

(*a*) Benzene, toluene, and xylene—absorb in nitrating acid in fritted-glass Petri tube at 0.25 lpm, or in glass-bead column at 0.05 lpm.

(*b*) Nitrogen dioxide—use several fritted bubblers in series, condense with liquid nitrogen, or collect in sampling bottles.

(*c*) Nitric oxide and carbon monoxide—collect in sampling bottles or tubes.

(*d*) Halogenated hydrocarbons—pass through combustion apparatus and collect acid halides and free halogen in any suitable absorber, or absorb in amyl acetate using fritted bubblers.

TABLE IV-1

Gases Determined by Various Absorbing Devices (7)

Device	Air flow	Gas	Absorbing reagent	Efficiency,[a] %
Impinger	1 cfm	Sulfur dioxide	NaOH	80–90 A
		Sulfur dioxide	NaOH	Not checked
		Sulfur dioxide	I_2	90 B
		Acetic acid	NaOH	95 A
		Ammonia	H_2SO_4	95 A
		Ammonia	H_2SO_4	Not checked
		Hydrochloric acid	Na_2CO_3	Not checked
		Nitric acid	Na_2CO_3	Not checked
		Chloronaphthalene	Amyl acetate	ca. 90 B
		Ozone	KI	95 B
		Nitrogen dioxide	KI	95 B
		Nitrogen dioxide	NaOH	80 B
		Nitrogen dioxide	NaOH	ca. 30 A
		Nitrogen dioxide	Na_2CO_3	Not checked
		Mercury	I_2	90 B
		Hydrogen sulfide	I_2	50 A
	$\frac{1}{2}$	Phenol	NaOH	90 A
	1	Formaldehyde	NaOH	90 A
	1 cfm	Hydrogen chloride	NaOH	80 A
Two impingers (in series)	5 lpm	Hydrogen chloride	NaOH	ca. 90 A
Single fritted bubbler		Sulfur dioxide	NaOH	95 A
		Hydrogen sulfide	I_2	95 A
	4	Sulfur chloride	NaOH	95 A
	10	Chloronaphthalene	Amyl acetate	90 B
	2	Carbon disulfide	Alcoholic KOH	95 B

	1	Carbon dioxide	Dilute Ba(OH)₂	60-80 B
		Hydrochloric acid, chlorine	NaAsO₂	95 A
	1	Bromine	KOH	—
	1	Bromine	KI	95 B
	1	Nitrogen dioxide	NaOH, H₂O₂	90 A
	1	Nitrogen dioxide	H₂SO₄, H₂O₂	90 A
	3–14	Hydrogen chloride	NaOH	ca. 95 A
Two fritted bubblers (in series)	1 lpm	Sulfur dioxide	I₂	—
	5	Hydrochloric acid	NaOH	95 B
	5	Phosgene	NaOH	95 B
	5	Nitrogen dioxide	NaOH	50–70 A
	5	Nitrogen dioxide	H₂SO₄, H₂O₂	50–70 A
	5	Nitrogen dioxide	Na₂O₂	50–70 A
Three fritted bubblers (in series)	0.5 lpm	Phosphine	KBr, Br₂	—
	0.5	Phosgene	Aniline solution	—
	0.5	Ether	H₂SO₄, K₂Cr₂O₇	—
Nichols absorber	1 cfm	Sulfur dioxide	I₂	—
		Chlorine	KI	95
Semifritted Petri tube	0.25 lpm	Benzene	Nitrating acid	95 A
Glass-bead column	0.05 lpm	Benzene	Nitrating acid	95 A
		Hydrochloric acid, chlorine	NaAsO₂	—
	1	Hydrogen cyanide	Na₂CO₃	—
Multiple absorber	1 lpm	Carbon tetrachloride	Amyl acetate	90 A
10-bulb Meyer tube	0.2 lpm	Ozone	KI	95 A
Liquid-nitrogen trap	0.2 lpm	Nitrogen dioxide	—	95 A

ᵃ A indicates determined on known concentration of substance.   B indicates calculated from amount found in second absorber.

The absorber of choice is generally given in the methods detailed in this text. Sometimes it is better to use a simple absorber or an impinger rather than a fritted bubbler. For example, very low concentrations of sulfur dioxide may be missed with a fritted bubbler possibly because of oxidation of the sulfurous acid formed to sulfuric acid and the retention of the latter in the frit. In such instances an impinger makes a better absorption vessel.

B. Adsorption

Adsorption is the phenomenon of the condensation on the surfaces of solids, or more generally solids and liquids, of a layer of a gas or vapor, liquid, or solid which comes into contact with that solid. Thus, there is a higher concentration of the condensed component at the surface of the solid or liquid. The term *adsorption* should be distinguished from the term *absorption* which implies a uniform penetration of a component into a system.

The factors that govern the amount of substance adsorbed are the area of the solid adsorbent, the pressure or concentration of the gas or vapor, the temperature of the system, and the characteristics of the adsorbing agent and the substance adsorbed. It is beyond the scope of this text to discuss the theoretical aspects of adsorption. The reader is referred to general texts such as that by Glasstone and Lewis (67). More specific treatment as applied to industrial hygiene and air pollution control is given by Sleik and Turk (68).

The adsorbing properties of silica gel and other precipitated hydrous oxides and hydroxides, charcoal and activated carbon, dehydrated zeolites, and many other porous and even nonporous materials have been studied. The principal adsorbing media used in industrial hygiene chemistry are activated carbon and silica gel. Some impregnated carbons and porous materials are also used. Scheflan and Jacobs (69) present a discussion of the use of adsorbents in solvent recovery which is pertinent to the use of adsorbents in analytical chemistry as applied to industrial hygiene.

The efficiency of the various adsorbents varies widely both among themselves and for the materials adsorbed. One should note that even a good adsorbing agent will not adsorb everything even if its capacity is undiminished. Thus, true gases like hydrogen, nitrogen, oxygen, carbon monoxide, helium, argon, and methane, which have boiling points below −150°C and critical temperatures far below −60°C, are practically nonadsorbable at ordinary temperatures. Indeed, gases like ammonia, ethylene, formaldehyde, hydrogen chloride, and hydrogen sulfide—i.e., gases which contain less than three atoms excluding their hydrogen content, that boil in the range −100–0°C, and have critical temperatures in the range of 0–150°C—are also virtually unadsorbable. Toxic smokes like diphenylaminechloroarsine will go through the activated charcoal in a gas mask and also in an analytical determination. Special filters must be used to trap such smokes. Substances like phosgene, which hydrolyze readily, may not be adsorbed except on anhydrous activated charcoal.

1. Activated Charcoal

Activated charcoal, also known as decolorizing charcoal, is a type generally made from vegetable matter specially treated to render it highly adsorbent toward gases, vapors, and coloring matters. The USP product is in the form of a fine black powder, which is odorless and tasteless and contains 5–15% moisture and 2–3% ash. The form used for the adsorption of gases and vapors is generally composed of granules of 8–14 mesh. A very active form of charcoal is made from coconut shells, peach pits, and other shells and pits. Processes have been developed for the production of very highly activated charcoal from sawdust, coal, and hardwood charcoal (70). Large quantities of activated charcoal are used commercially for the recovery of solvent vapors, gasoline from natural gas, and light oils from manufactured gas, and for the removal of odors from air, the purification of carbon dioxide gas, etc.

2. Silica Gel

Silica gel is a precipitated silicic acid in the form of lustrous granules, specially prepared and adapted for the adsorption of various vapors. It can be used for the adsorption of water and can be regenerated when used for this purpose by heating in a stream of air at a temperature of 110–150°C. Two tubes containing silica gel as the adsorbent are generally used because it is less efficient than activated charcoal. However, silica gel has the advantage in that its weight upon equilibration remains constant to a greater degree than activated charcoal (71).

When comparing the adsorption properties of silica gel and activated carbon Turk (72) pointed out that activated carbon is nonpolar and, because it has relatively little affinity for water, will adsorb organic compounds in preference to water. Silica gel, on the other hand, is polar and will adsorb water and may reject an organic compound. However, it can discriminate more selectively than activated carbon in adsorption effects and thus may be used for the fractionation of organic solvents.

3. Chemisorption

In certain instances it is difficult to distinguish between adsorption and absorption effects. Consequently, the more general term *sorption* is used. In those instances in which the sorbate, i.e., the adsorbed or absorbed substance, enters into a reaction with the sorbent, i.e., the adsorbent or absorbent, the chemical reaction is termed *chemisorption* and the process *activated adsorption*. These terms also include those instances in which two or more sorbates react because of their close proximity in the sorbed state, although the term *surface catalysis* is also used for this type of reaction.

Chemisorption may be used to trap gases which cannot be sampled readily by adsorption or absorption. For instance, ethylene, which cannot be adsorbed or absorbed easily, can be trapped by use of activated carbon impregnated with bromine (73). In this instance of chemisorption, the ethylene and bromine react to form ethylene dibromide which is retained by the adsorbent.

Impregnated porous materials can be called absorbents as well as adsorbents (lines in these instances cannot be drawn sharply). Asbestos impregnated with sodium hydroxide is used for trapping carbon dioxide. Asbestos upon which has been precipitated silver oxide is used for the absorption of hydrogen sulfide. Other instances are the use of porous stones prepared with manganese dioxide from potassium permanganate precipitation for the adsorption of sulfur dioxide and the trapping of carbon disulfide on stone soaked in sodium ethylate.

4. Adsorption Value

The adsorption value of any material may be considered under two heads: activity and capacity (71). Either may be tested by standard tube tests.

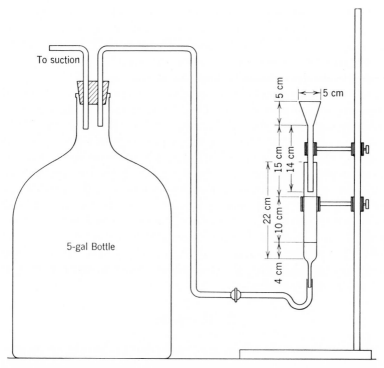

Fig. IV-18. Apparatus for filling absorption tubes (inside dimensions).

The adsorbent under test is filled into a sample tube of specified diameter (2 cm) to a depth of 10 cm by a standard method for filling tubes as described below; a standard concentration, usually 1000 or 10,000 ppm of a contaminant in air of a definite humidity (usually 50%), is passed through the adsorbent at a rate of 500 ml/cm^2/min. The concentration of the entering contaminant in the air is determined by analysis.   The length of time is noted from the instant the gas–air mixture is started through the adsorbent to the time the gas or other contaminant or some toxic or irritating reaction product of the gas begins to come through the adsorbent as determined by some quali- tative test.   Quantitative samples of the outflowing gas are then taken at known intervals and from the amount of gas found in the effluent sample, the per cent efficiency of the adsorbent at the corre- sponding time is calculated from the formula given on page 133.

Standard Method of Filling Tubes. The adsorption tube and funnel (Fig. IV-18) are supported in a vertical position with the funnel stem "centered" in the tube. The distance from the apex of the funnel to the upper layer of adsorbent when the adsorption tube is filled to the desired height should be 15 cm.

Pour the entire sample of adsorbent on a large sheet of rubberized fabric and mix thoroughly by rolling the sample. This may be done by lifting opposite corners of the fabric alternately. Smooth out the sample on the fabric and take portions with a spoon at regular intervals of space over the entire surface of the sample to insure having a representative portion for the test. Pour the adsorbent from the spoon a few grains at a time so that no grains have a free fall through the orifice of the funnel. The time for filling a 2-cm tube to a height of 10 cm should be not less than 1.5 min. The tube should not be tapped at any time. Connect the tube to a strong source of suction and draw air through it at least 5 times to remove dust. In removing dust from the adsorbent, the stopcock is turned on quickly for 1 or 2 sec and quickly closed.

C. Absorption

The choice of an absorbing agent is governed primarily by the ease with which the absorbed contaminant can be estimated. Another important factor is, of course, the efficiency with which the absorbent acts. Some mention of solid absorbents was made in a prior section of this chapter.

In the analysis of the gross components of air, mine gas, or fuels such as natural gas and producer gas, there are only a few well-known components of these gas mixtures and for their absorption only a few absorbents are used. For complete details concerning the analysis of gas, the reader is referred to the bibliography at the end of Chapter XVII.

The principal absorbing solutions used in the analysis of gross components of gas mixtures are sulfuric acid, potassium hydroxide, silver nitrate, pyrogallol, cuprous chloride, acid ferrous sulfate, nitric acid, and bromine.

In the analysis of industrial hazards the number of substances used as absorbents is very much greater. Each determination described in the text notes the absorbent to use and the concentration that will give a relatively high efficiency. Table IV-1 lists the device, absorbing reagent, and the efficiency of absorption for some of the gases and vapors commonly sampled. The rated efficiency of the devices mentioned in Table IV-1 has been questioned by some investigators.

References

1. Nordlander, B. W., *Ind. Eng. Chem.*, **19**, 522 (1927).
2. Fieldner, A. C., C. G. Oberfell, M. C. Teague, and J. N. Lawrence, *Ind. Eng. Chem.*, **11**, 519 (1919).
3. Elkins, H. B., A. K. Hobby, and J. E. Fuller, *J. Ind. Hyg. Toxicol.*, **19**, 474 (1937).
4. Taylor, H. S., *Treatise on Physical Chemistry*, Van Nostrand, New York, 1931.
5. Elkins, H. B., *The Chemistry of Industrial Toxicology*, 2nd ed., Wiley, New York, 1959.
6. Jacobs, M. B., M. M. Braverman, and S. Hochheiser, *Anal. Chem.*, **29**, 1349 (1957).
7. *Am. Pub. Health Assoc. Yearbook* **1939–40**, p. 92.
8. Littlefield, J. B., F. L. Feicht, and H. H. Schrenk, *U.S. Bur. Mines Rept. Invest. 3401* (1938).
9. Sayers, R. R., W. P. Yant, C. P. Waite, and F. A. Patty, *Public Health Rept.*, **45**, 224 (1930).
10. Setterlind, A. N., *Am. Ind. Hyg. Assoc. Quarterly*, **14**, 113 (1953).
11. Stead, F. M., and G. J. Taylor, *J. Ind. Hyg. Toxicol.*, **29**, 408 (1947).
12. Scherberger, R. F., G. P. Happ, F. A. Miller, and D. W. Fassett, *Am. Ind. Hyg. Assoc. J.*, **19**, 494 (1958).
13. Irish, D. D., and E. M. Adams, *Ind. Med. Ind. Hyg. Section*, **9**, 1 (1940).
14. Silver, S. D., *J. Lab. Clin. Med.*, **31**, 1153 (1946).
15. Silverman, L., *Rev. Sci. Instr.*, **11**, 346 (1940); Silverman, L., J. L. Whittenberger, and J. Muller, *J. Ind. Hyg. Toxicol.*, **31**, 74 (1949).
16. Amdur, M. O., R. Z. Schulz, and P. Drinker, *A.M.A. Arch. Ind. Hyg. Occupational Med.* **5**, 318 (1952).
17. Lewis, R. A., and G. F. Koepf, *Science*, **98**, 407 (1941).
18. Charnley, A., *J. Sci. Instr.*, **31**, 145 (1954).
19. Sunderman, F. W., J. F. Kincaid, W. Kooch, and E. A. Birmelin, *Am. J. Clin. Pathol.*, **26**, 1211 (1956).
20. Urban, E. C. J., *A.M.A. Arch. Ind. Hyg. Occupational Med.* **9**, 62 (1954).
21. Yant, W. P., S. J. Pearce, and H. H. Schrenk, *U.S. Bur. Mines Rept. Invest. 3323* (1936).
22. Carpenter, C. P., H. F. Smyth, Jr., and U. C. Pozzani, *J. Ind. Hyg. Toxicol.*, **31**, 343 (1949).
23. Inerkle-Korff Gear Co., Chicago, Illinois.
24. Gorell and Gorell, Haworth, N. J.
25. Saltzman, B. E., *Am. Ind. Hyg. Assoc. Quarterly*, **16**, 121 (1955).
26. Jacobs, M. B., *The Analytical Chemistry of Poisons, Hazards, and Solvents*, 2nd ed., Interscience, New York, 1949.

27. Stetser, J. B., and R. H. Norton, *Iron Age*, **102**, 443 (1918).
28. Buck, J. S., *Ind. Eng. Chem.*, **18**, 1321 (1926).
29. Smith, G. F., M. Brown, and J. F. Ross, *Ind. Eng. Chem.*, **16**, 20 (1924).
30. Willard, H. H., and G. F. Smith, *J. Am. Chem. Soc.*, **44**, 2255 (1922).
31. Turner, W. D., *Ind. Eng. Chem. Anal. Ed.*, **3**, 63 (1931).
32. Zhitkova, A. S., S. I. Kaplun, and J. B. Ficklen, *Poisonous Gases*, Service to Industry, Hartford, 1936.
33. Rhodes, F. H., and D. R. Rakesaw, *Ind. Eng. Chem. Anal. Ed.*, **3**, 143 (1931).
34. Friedrichs, J., *Angew. Chem.*, **32**, 252 (1919).
35. Friedrichs, F., *Chem. Fabrik.*, **4**, 203 (1931).
36. Martin, W., and J. R. Green, *Ind. Eng. Chem. Anal. Ed.*, **5**, 114 (1933).
37. Pearce, P. H., and E. C. Roberson, *Chem. Ind. (London)*, **55**, 543 (1936).
38. Corson, B. B., *Ind. Eng. Chem. Anal. Ed.*, **10**, 646 (1938).
39. Weaver, E. R., and J. D. Edwards, *Ind. Eng. Chem.*, **7**, 534 (1915).
40. Keller, K., *Chemiker-Ztg.*, **47**, 506 (1923).
41. Smyth, H. F., *J. Ind. Hyg.*, **11**, 338 (1929).
42. Sieverts, A., and S. Halberstadt, *Chem. Fabrik.*, **3**, 201 (1930).
43. Halberstadt, S., *Ind. Eng. Chem. Anal. Ed.*, **4**, 425 (1932).
44. Prausnitz, P. A., *Ind. Eng. Chem. Anal. Ed.*, **4**, 430 (1932).
45. Ralston, O. C., and C. G. Maier, *U.S. Bur. Mines Bull. 260* (1927).
46. Thomas, M. D., *Ind. Eng. Chem. Anal. Ed.*, **5**, 193 (1933).
47. Kirk, P. L., R. Craig, and R. S. Rosenfels, *Ind. Eng. Chem. Anal. Ed.*, **6**, 154 (1934).
48. Bruce, W. F., and H. E. Bent, *J. Am. Chem. Soc.*, **53**, 990 (1931).
49. Stone, H. W., and L. C. Weiss, *Ind. Eng. Chem. Anal. Ed.*, **11**, 220 (1939).
50. Cool, R. D., and J. D. Graham, *Ind. Eng. Chem. Anal. Ed.*, **6**, 579 (1934).
51. Crabtree, J., and A. R. Kemp, *Ind. Eng. Chem.*, **38**, 278 (1946); *Anal. Chem.*, **18**, 769 (1946).
52. Wadelin, C. W., *Anal. Chem.*, **29**, 441 (1957).
53. Moskowitz, S., J. Siegel, and W. J. Burke, *N.Y. State Ind. Bull. 19*, 33 (1940).
54. Harrold, G. C., Production Equipment Co., Detroit 2, Mich.
55. Nichols, N. S., *U.S. Public Health Rept.*, **53**, 538 (1938).
56. Shaw, J. A., *Ind. Eng. Chem. Anal. Ed.*, **6**, 479 (1934).
57. Schrenk, H. H., S. J. Pearce, and W. P. Yant, *U.S. Bur. Mines Rept. Invest. 3287* (1935).
58. Tebbens, B. D., *J. Ind. Hyg. Toxicol.*, **19**, 204 (1937).
59. Drinker, C. K., M. F. Warren, and G. A. Bennett, *J. Ind. Hyg. Toxicol.*, **19**, 283 (1937).
60. Barrett, H. M., *J. Ind. Hyg. Toxicol.*, **18**, 341 (1936).
61. Petersen, G. W., and H. H. Radke, *Ind. Eng. Chem. Anal. Ed.*, **16**, 63 (1944).
62. Jacobs, M. B., and S. Hochheiser, *Anal. Chem.*, **30**, 426 (1958).
63. "The Smog Problem in Los Angeles County," Stanford Research Inst. 2nd Interim Rept., Western Oil Gas Assoc., Los Angeles, 1949.
64. Goldman, F. H., and J. M. DallaValle, *U.S. Public Health Rept.*, **54**, 1728 (1939).
65. Shepherd, M., U. S. Bur. Std. Res. Rept. to Los Angeles Co. Air Pollution Control District, Jan. 12, 1951.

66. Jacobs, M. B., *The Chemical Analysis of Air Pollutants*, Interscience, New York, 1960, p. 333.
67. Glasstone, S., and D. Lewis, *Elements of Physical Chemistry*, 2nd ed., Van Nostrand, Princeton, 1960.
68. Sleik, H., and A. Turk, *Air ConservationE ngineering*, 2nd ed., Connor Engineering Co., Danbury, Conn., 1953.
69. Scheflan, L., and M. B. Jacobs, *Handbook of Solvents*, Van Nostrand, New York, 1953.
70. Ray, A. B., *Ind. Eng. Chem.*, **32**, 1166 (1940).
71. Moskowitz, S., and W. J. Burke, *N.Y. State Ind. Bull.*, **17**, 168 (1938).
72. Turk, A., *Ann. N.Y. Acad. Sci.*, **58**, 193 (1954).
73. Turk, A., "Desorption Products from Activated Carbon," 3rd Air Pollution Seminar, New Orleans, 1960, Public Health Service (1960).

General References

Burke, W. J., S. Moskowitz, J. Siegel, B. H. Dolin, and C. B. Ford, "Industrial Air Analysis," *N.Y. State Dept. Labor, Div. Ind. Hyg.* (1942).
Elkins, H. B., A. K. Hobby, and J. E. Fuller, *J. Ind. Hyg. Toxicol.*, **19**, 474 (1947).
Fieldner, A. C., C. G. Oberfell, M. C. Teague, and J. N. Lawrence, *Ind. Eng. Chem.*, **11**, 519 (1919).
Prausnitz, P. A., *Ind. Eng. Chem. Anal. Ed.*, **4**, 430 (1932).
"Report of Sub-Committee on Chemical Methods in Air Analysis. Sampling and Sampling Devices," *Am. Public Health Assoc. Yearbook 1939–40*, 92.
Zhitkova, A. S., S. I. Kaplun, and J. B. Ficklen, *Poisonous Gases*, Service to Industry, Hartford, 1936.

CHAPTER V

CHARACTERISTICS AND SAMPLING OF DUST

With the exception of the large and miscellaneous group of chemicals causing dermatitis, dust is the most important cause of occupational illness. More workmen are incapacitated for performing their jobs because of exposure to dust than for any other cause with the exception of industrial dermatoses. This incapacitation results from damage to which the respiratory tract, in particular, and the body, in general, are subjected by inhalation of dust. Such respiratory illnesses are known as *pneumoconioses*.

The term *pneumoconiosis* is considered to be a generic term (1) applied to any type of dust deposited in the lungs, regardless of the physiological effects. Hence, in some pneumoconioses severe incapacitation and even death may result whereas in others the effects may be benign.

It must be stressed that greater knowledge of pneumoconioses indicates that silica and asbestos are not the only materials that cause disabling illness. In Table V-1, a summary of both disabling and benign types of pneumoconiosis is tabulated. Pneumonitis is a type of pneumonia caused by the inhalation of dusts, principally metallic dusts like those of beryllium, cadmium, manganese, and vanadium.

One must remember that dusts can cause more generalized and systemic illness. Among the more important classified with inorganic compounds, in addition to those mentioned in Table V-1, are dusts of arsenic, lead, phosphorus, manganese, zinc, hexavalent chromium compounds, fluorides, and silicofluorides, and among the more important organic chemical dusts are *p*-nitroaniline, dinitrobenzenes, chloronitrobenzenes, picric acid, nitronaphthaline, *p*-phenylenediamine, and tar dust.

There can be no question that the diminution of the dust hazard in all trades will result in a corresponding diminution of morbidity and mortality from tuberculosis and other respiratory diseases.

TABLE V-1

Pneumoconioses[a]

Disease or effect	Type of dust
Major	
Silicosis, nodular	Crystalline SiO_2
Silicosis, nonnodular	
Silica pneumonitis	Ultramicroscopic crystalline SiO_2
Diatomite pneumoconiosis	Calcined diatomite, crystalline SiO_2
Shaver's disease	SiO_2 in fume form
Asbestosis	$3MgO \cdot 2SiO_2 \cdot 2H_2O$ (a silicate)
Talcosis	$3MgO \cdot 4SiO_2 \cdot H_2O$ (a silicate)
Coal miners' pneumoconiosis	Coal dust (principally C)
Berylliosis	Beryllium and beryllium compounds.
Minor	
Anthracosis	Carbon dust
Diatomaceous earth pneumoconiosis	Amorphous SiO_2
Silicatosis	
Mica, silica-free	Complex silicates with SiO_2 bound in
Clays	the molecule
Feldspars	
Vegetable dust pneumoconioses	
Mill fever	Different types of organic dusts
Byssinosis	Cotton
Bagossosis	Moldy sugar cane, bagasse dust
Farmer's lung	Moldy hay, straw, etc.
Grain asthma	Grain
Tamarin asthma	Tamarind seed
Weaver's cough	Moldy cotton yarn
Benign	
Baritosis	Silica-free barium sulfate, $BaSO_4$, and silica-free barium oxide, BaO
Siderosis	Silica-free ferric oxide, Fe_2O_3
Stannosis	Silica-free stannic oxide, SnO_2
Titanosis	Silica-free titanium dioxide, TiO_2
Graphosis	Silica-free carbon, C
Chalicosis	Silica-free calcium-bearing compounds and materials like limestone, marble, and cement

[a] After R. T. Johnstone and S. E. Miller, *Occupational Diseases and Industrial Medicine*, W. B. Saunders Co., Philadelphia, 1960, p. 200.

A. Definition of Dusts, Fumes, Smokes, Mists and Fogs, and Vapors

Particles dispersed in the atmosphere of both the outside and the workshop may be classified into a number of groups based on particle size, degree of dispersion, and whether they are either accidentally present in the atmosphere because of some mechanical or chemical process of dispersion or they are normally present. The particles normally present in the atmosphere are due to the action of the winds, rain, tides, variations in weather, volcanoes, meteoric dust, and the decomposition of vegetable and animal matter. The particles accidentally present in the atmosphere are those which have come about through the development of civilization. Every fire, whether for the production of heat or of power, every grinding or rubbing action, and generally all mechanical friction in industrial and constructional activity creates dust. For the purposes of the study of industrial dusts and air pollution, atmospheric components other than the normal gaseous components can be classified as particulate and nonparticulate matter. The particulate matter consists of *dusts, fumes, smokes, mists, and fogs*. The nonparticulate matter consists of *vapors* and *gases*. Tables 8–13, Appendix, list common particulate and nonparticulate air contaminants.

1. DUSTS

Dusts may be defined as *aerosols* of a particular type, i.e., they are disperse systems in which air is the continuous phase, or dispersion medium, and some solid material is the dispersed phase, or dispersoid. Dusts are sometimes called colloidal systems, but such a definition is too strict for, in the main, dusts are not true colloidal systems even though they are disperse systems. They settle out, whereas a true colloid will not settle.

Broadly speaking, atmospheric dusts are dispersions of solid materials in air. The particles of which they are composed vary in size from the submicroscopic to the visible. Drinker and Thomson (2) define dusts as particles or aggregates of particles, 150 to 1 μ in diameter, that are thrown into the air by mechanical agencies during the processes of grinding, crushing, blasting, drilling, and other industrial and constructional processes.

For the industrial hazard aspect, dusts may be considered as particles or aggregates of particles suspended in the atmosphere, of some size that is capable of being inhaled (3). This restricts the particle size to the range of 0.5–10 μ.

Harrington (4) points out, however, that asbestos fibers 200 μ in length have been found in the lungs of men and must have had a detrimental effect. It is probable that dust particles even of larger size do have harmful effects in that they clog the air passages leading to the lungs, which might ordinarily trap more harmful particles thus permitted to pass into the lungs.

De Mello (5) gives an even broader definition of dust as a generic name for all solid particles of any size, nature, or origin suspended or capable of being suspended in the air.

The particle size of true colloidal systems is arbitrarily set as that of particles having diameters between 0.001 and 1 μ. Those disperse systems having particles smaller in size are generally considered true solutions and those having particle sizes larger than 1 μ are generally considered ordinary matter. Thus, we see that only in the lower limits of particle size do dusts fall within the definition of colloidal systems.

2. Fumes

Fumes are colloidal systems which are formed from chemical reactions or by processes like combustion, distillation, sublimation, calcination, and condensation. The particle size varies from 0.2 to 1 μ. Examples of fumes are the disperse systems formed from burning zinc or magnesium with the formation of zinc and magnesium oxides; the formation in air of ammonium chloride from the reaction of ammonia and hydrogen chloride; the reaction and condensation of water with titanium tetrachloride and burning phosphorus.

3. Smokes

Smokes are complex colloidal systems that are generally formed by the incomplete combustion of carbonaceous and other material. Particles of a smoke are generally less than 0.3–0.5 μ in diameter. Drinker and Hatch (6) use the word with particular reference to the disperse systems that are organic in origin, such as the smoke from burning tobacco, wood, oil, coal, etc. Necessarily, as is clear from the chemical warfare point of view, a prerequisite of smoke is that it have a definite degree of optical density.

4. Mists and Fogs

Mists and fogs are disperse systems in which the particle size varies greatly. They are akin to fumes rather than to smokes. They carry the implication of a liquid rather than that of a solid dispersed in the atmosphere. They are generally formed by the condensation of water vapor on nuclei such as submicroscopic particles of dust or gaseous ions, or by the atomization of liquids.

5. Vapors

Vapors are gaseous bodies which are formed from liquids by increase of temperature but which readily resume their fluid form because of decrease in temperature (7). Obviously, as true vapors they form true solutions with the atmosphere. Our interest in them lies in the fact that, while they do form true solutions with air in their vapor state, as soon as they regain their liquid state they form mists, fogs, and fumes.

B. Classification and Physiological Action of Dusts

It is possible, as has been explained, to classify dusts according to particle size and according to origin, and to place them in two main groups according to physiological action, namely, those which cause respiratory disorders and those which cause systemic poisoning. It is of value, however, to classify dusts with respect to physiological action on a broader basis. Thus, Oliver (8,9) divided dusts into those which have a mechanical and irritant action and those of the chemical and toxic, or caustic, types.

Thompson (10) divided the physiological action of dust on human beings into four types:

(1) Mechanical obstruction of air passages.
(2) Laceration of mucous membranes.
(3) Conveyance of toxic material into the system.
(4) Conveyance of germs into the system.

Actually, dusts cannot be placed into groups which show a specific type of physiological action because no dust is composed of a single variety of material.

The physiological response to dusts is grouped as follows by Drinker (11):

(*1*) Specific lung diseases such as silicosis and asbestosis.

(*2*) Toxic systemic effects caused, for example, by breathing of such toxic dusts as lead, cadmium, and radium.

(*3*) Metal-fume fever, which follows the inhalation of finely divided particles such as zinc oxide.

(*4*) Allergic manifestations that result from breathing dusts such as pollen and certain types of pulverized wood and flour.

The physical, chemical, and physiological actions of dusts may also be grouped as in the following classification (12):

(*1*) Cutting dusts—these are in the main composed of minute crystalline or amorphous particles which have sharp cutting edges such as sand, stone, lime, steel, asbestos, glass, minerals, etc.

(*2*) Irritant dusts—this group is composed of vegetable and animal matter such as wood, ivory, and hair, and fibers such as wool, silk, cotton (13), flax, hemp, and the fabrics and cordage made from them.

(*3*) Inorganic poisons and compounds of mercury, copper, arsenic, lead, and even soluble compounds such as the sulfates of iron, copper, and sodium.

(*4*) Organic poisons such as tobacco and, in general, organic compounds and drugs.

(*5*) Obstructive and irritating dusts such as soot, coal, flour, and starch.

It is readily seen that this classification also falls into the grouping of physical action (mechanical and irritating), (*1*), (*2*), and (*5*), and chemical action, (*3*) and (*4*). It must be borne in mind, however, that dusts act both physically and chemically on the body to some degree.

A more comprehensive classification of dusts according to physical, chemical, and physiological effects is that of Sayers (14).

A. Organic dusts

Organic dusts are those which contain carbon, and are originally supposed to have come from organized substances derived from animal or plant life. Thousands of organic substances are made synthetically by chemical processes, such as dyestuffs, explosives, drugs, and similar substances.

(1) Nonliving organic dusts

    (a) Toxic and/or irritant dusts—all organic dusts which produce untoward symptoms, either systemic or local. Those producing local symptoms are usually described as irritant; those producing general or systemic symptoms are termed toxic. A dust may be both toxic and irritant. Among the chief offenders are p-nitraniline, the dinitrobenzenes, the chlorodinitrobenzenes, picric acid, nitronaphthalene, p-phenylenediamine, and trinitrotoluene. Many organic substances and dusts cause dermatitis.

    (b) Allergic dusts—many apparently innocuous substances may produce reactions in persons of peculiar personal susceptibility. The term *allergy* is used to describe this condition of hypersensitiveness, or susceptibility, and allergic phenomena most frequently manifest themselves in skin reactions. They may cause acute reactions elsewhere in the body; thus, when the respiratory tract is involved, diseases such as hay fever or asthma may result. Substance like pollens from plants, horsehair, furs, feathers, and the like may cause these illnesses. Some persons are also allergic to hexamethylenetetramine and formaldehyde. Impregnated woods from abroad may also cause illness.

(2) Living organic dusts

    (a) Bacteria—most important is anthrax bacillus. Other illnesses traced to infected dusts are tetanus, diphtheria, tuberculosis, smallpox, typhoid, and others.

    (b) Fungi (15)—dusts containing the mycelia and spores of parasitic fungi give rise to annoyance and discomfort. (Some cause serious illness.)

B. *Inorganic dusts*

(1) Toxic and/or irritant dusts—toxic dusts are those which are inherently toxic when inhaled, ingested, or otherwise absorbed. Among those which produce systemic poisoning, some of which are also irritant, are the dusts from heavy metals and their salts, such as lead, mercury, arsenic, cadmium, zinc, and similar metals. Irritant dusts are injurious by reason of their strong irritative or corrosive properties. As a rule, inhaled irritant substances immediately cause a reaction in the upper respiratory tract of such severity that they are prevented from reaching the lungs, although they may cause lung damage by extension of inflammation if the mucous membrane is corroded. Lime, calcium oxide, and the dichromates are examples of irritant dusts. An inorganic dust may possess both toxic and irritant properties, and the poisoning produced may be the combined effect of more than one mode of entrance into the body. Lead oxide, carbonate, and chromate are the most widely prevalent directly poisonous dusts. Alkalies and metallic oxides are common causes of dermatoses.

(2) Fibrosis-producing dusts—the most important are the inorganic, slightly soluble dusts which cause fibrous changes in the lung tissues, some of which are serious and some of which cause little or no disability. Examples of siliceous dusts are granite, quartz, sand, pumice, slate, and similar sub-

stances. Asbestos causes an allied disease. Other fibrosis-producing dusts have been listed in Table V-1.

(*3*) Nonfibrosis-producing dusts—these are inert, i.e., they do not cause fibrous tissue to be produced. Included among them are alundum, corundum, emery, limestone, magnesite, marble, plaster of Paris, gypsum, and polisher's rouge.

1. Characteristics of Dust

There are three important characteristics of dust that control its action as an industrial hazard. They are particle size and frequency, quantity, and chemical action. It is known that particle size and frequency of distribution play an important part because it has been shown that in normal atmospheres, 97% of outdoor dust particles are less than 1 μ in diameter. Practically no dust particles larger than 1.5 μ are to be found in uncontaminated outside air. On the other hand, practically all dust particles in an industrial establishment are larger than 1 μ Table VI-1 and Figure VI-8 show the difference between the size frequency of outdoor dust and industrial dust. About 60% of the particles have a diameter between 1 and 3 μ.

It has been shown that silicosis develops more rapidly the more intensive the exposure to dust. Thus, we need methods to determine the amount of dust in the air of an industrial establishment. Insofar as the chemical composition of dusts is concerned, they will be treated as air contaminants in subsequent chapters of the book. Chapters V and VI will be concerned with the methods for the determination of the quantity of dust and the estimation of particle size and frequency.

C. Dust-Sampling Apparatus and Methods of Sampling

There are a number of methods and types of equipment used for the sampling of dust by means of which determinations of particle size and frequency can be made. These methods enable us to estimate the quantity of dust by (*1*) counting of dew drops which have condensed around particles of dust, (*2*) weighing the particles, (*3*) estimation of the intensity of some physical property, generally photometric methods, (*4*) rapid centrifugal methods, (*5*) electrostatic methods, and (*6*) counting the number of particles after impingement or absorption. Each of these methods has advantages and disadvantages. Those most important will be described.

The methods used to sample dusts so that these means of estimation can be used fall into groups classified according to the physical principle utilized by the sampling instrument (16).   The more important methods used for sampling dust of both indoor and outdoor atmospheres are condensation, sedimentation and deposition, absorption, electrostatic precipitation, thermal precipitation, filtration, and impingement.   These methods are by no means mutually self-exclusive, as many instruments use more than one physical principle.

The methods of choice, particularly for dust counting, are those which depend on the principles of filtration, thermal precipitation, and impingement or impaction.   However, in order to give a relatively complete discussion of this subject, which is not done elsewhere, devices and procedures using other principles will be described.

Dust studies concerning air pollution may be made with the same instruments as are used for indoor dust determinations, but some devices and methods have been particularly developed for outdoor dust determinations.   These are discussed in detail by Jacobs (17).

1. CONDENSATION

As early as 1890, Aitken (18) devised an apparatus making use of the fact noticed by Coulier (19), in 1875, that dust in air could be rendered visible by reducing the pressure within a containing vessel, causing the moisture present in the air to condense on the dust particles.   Since that time, Aitken (20) and others have modified his original apparatus.   The new forms still depend for their operation upon the facts that when air containing condensation nuclei becomes saturated by having its pressure suddenly reduced, a condensation of water vapor takes place upon the nuclei, and the droplets formed by this condensation settle rapidly.   By means of a simple microscope, built into the instrument the number that settle on a glass plate is easily read.   From this number and the dimensions of the instrument the number of condensation nuclei in a cubic centimeter of air can be calculated (21).

The instrument consists of an air chamber, the walls of which are covered with moistened blotting paper, a calibrated pump for the taking in, expulsion, or the sudden expansion of a given volume of air, a glass plate ruled in millimeter squares, a simple microscope with dark-field illumination, and the necessary stopcocks for taking in or expelling air from the chamber.   The air chamber is 1 cm deep and has a capacity of about 7 ml.   The total capacity of the pump is about one-fifth of that of the air chamber.   When determining the number of nuclei in a given sample of air, the expansion of the air in the chamber should be repeated from 2 to 10 times, until no droplets are formed in the chamber upon successive expansions.   The sum of all the droplets formed on successive expansions is taken as the number of condensation nuclei present in the air.

The number of condensation nuclei present in the air is much greater than that of the dust particles.   Ives (21) and co-workers found that the average number of dust particles present in a milliliter of air in the winter time was 815, whereas the average number of condensation nuclei in a milliliter of air was 207,000.   Condensation nuclei may be solid, liquid, or even gaseous particles such as gaseous ions, upon which water vapor condenses when the air becomes saturated or approaches saturation.

It is evident then that insofar as actual dust determinations are concerned, the Aitken instrument and its modifications are inadequate because condensation occurs not only on dust particles but also on other condensation nuclei, such as large molecular aggregates and gaseous ions.   On the other hand, no instrument will give information as to the number of condensation nuclei in an atmosphere as will a condensation counter.

Thus, Fawcett and Gardner (22) also use the ability of particles to act as condensation nuclei as a measure of their number and size. In this variation of the nuclei counter developed by Aitken, a long brass tube is used to hold a wet blotter which keeps the interior at 100% humidity and by accessories at higher humidities.   A light source is placed at one end of the tube and a photoelectric cell and meter at the other end.   The light cut off by the formation of the fog, caused by condensation of water on the particles in the tube as a result of the sudden expansion of a plunger, is a measure of the number of condensation nuclei present.

2. SEDIMENTATION AND CENTRIFUGAL DEPOSITION METHODS

Sedimentation methods of dust sampling are of little value as a means of measuring the number of dust particles that a sample of air contains, unless special devices such as the Green (23) cell are used.

On the other hand, sedimentation methods are very useful for collecting samples of settled dust.

The dust caught on a plate by sedimentation is some function of the dust in the air but the exact mathematical relationship is not known. Green (23) uses a cell of known capacity provided with a rapid means of closing so that the air under examination can be sampled quickly. There is a ½-in. cover slip on the bottom plate, upon which the dust in the cell settles. The cell is moved through the

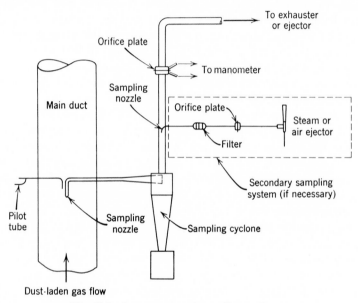

Fig. V-1. Arrangement of sampling cyclone.

air until it is purged. The ends are closed quickly and the cell is placed in a vertical position for 3 hr to permit the dust to settle. Temperature and vibration must be controlled.

Davies (24) improved the sampling cell by using thick metal to make the walls of the cell, thus cutting down convection. The advantages and disadvantages of this method are discussed by Green and Lane (25). The principal advantage of the settlement dust counter is that the particles are not altered physically during the collection step and are seen on the slide in virtually the same condition in which they existed in the air.

a. Cyclone

The cyclone sampler (Fig. V-1) is a device in which centrifugal force is used to collect the sample.   Gases carrying the dust are drawn into the device and the dust particles, under the influence of the centrifugal force induced by the direction of flow, move to the walls of the cyclone where they collect and subsequently fall to the bottom of the device into some type of collector.   Such devices are poor collectors of particles less than 5 μ in diameter; hence, they have severe limitations for industrial hygiene work.

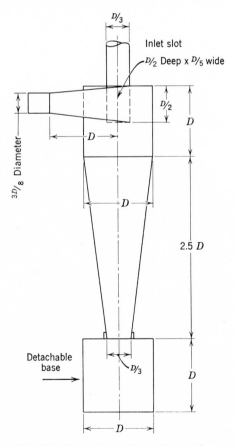

Fig. V-2. Proportions of sampling cyclones.

High-efficiency cyclones can be used to collect large quantities of dust, such as that from a stack or duct, without marked increase in resistance. The general proportions of sampling cyclones are shown in Figure V-2. The diameters usually range from 1 to 8 in.

An adequate cyclone will trap about 95% of the particulate matter in a gas stream so that it may be used without an accessory filter for approximate or routine determinations, but if the dust is very fine, the cyclone should be followed by a more efficient trapping device, such as a filter.

Centrifugal methods have been developed for the determination of particle size. These are discussed briefly in Chapter VI, Section C.

b. Labyrinth

Cylindrical or other shape labyrinth dust collectors are devices used for collecting larger samples of dust over longer periods of time. This period may extend from 1 to 8 weeks. The purpose of the long sampling time is to obtain sufficient samples of dust to make a complete analysis. The device described by Matthews (26) consists of 32 copper plates held together by a long brass tube and kept in place at right angles by short, equal lengths of brass tube. The baffle assembly is wrapped with an overlapping sheet of celluloid, held in place by a spiral winding of woolen yarn. Then the entire assembly is placed in a copper casing. The dusty air is drawn through by suction and the dust deposits on the plates of the baffle arrangements. Particles of a size larger than a given diameter may be excluded by means of an elutriator.

The efficiency of the labyrinth varies with the rate of flow and the type of dust. Most of the sample is collected in the first few sections of the labyrinth. The chief advantage of the labyrinth is that it enables one to obtain a large sample of uncontaminated dust that requires no further treatment. A further advantage is that the labyrinth sample is graded in particle size according to the different sections. The particle size falls off, so that in the last sections all the particles are 5 μ and under. These are the particles considered to be most dangerous to the lungs. The efficiency of the labyrinth is high for a dust like flint and low for a dust like asbestos.

c. Collection of Outdoor Dust

This phase of sampling dust by deposition is described in considerable detail by Jacobs (27) who gives many references to literature on the subject.   Consequently, the collection of outdoor dust as it is applied to air pollution will not be considered here.

3. Absorption Methods

In general, absorption methods of dust collection consist of passing a known amount of air through some absorber in such a manner that the air will bubble through the absorbing medium, which is usually water.   The water will wet the dust and bring it into suspension and the dust-free air will then pass through.   Many of these apparatuses have been devised since a fair estimate of both weight and count of dust can be obtained with them.

a. Palmer Device (28)

This apparatus (Fig. V-3) consists of a pear-shaped glass bulb at the base of which is a U-tube water trap.   Air is drawn through the

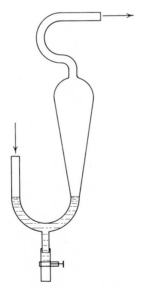

Fig. V-3. Palmer apparatus (28).

trap in such a manner that the water it contains is thrown up into the pear-shaped bulb section in the form of a spray.   This spray is again trapped by an S-shaped exit tube.   The spray washes the dust from the incoming air stream.

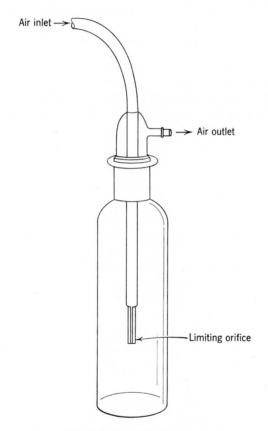

Air inlet →

→ Air outlet

Limiting orifice

Fig. V-4. Liquid impinger.

These absorption or washing methods, as they are termed by Greenburg (16), have pronounced drawbacks: first, absorption may be far from complete and, second, many particles, particularly those of small diameter, may not be wetted and therefore will pass out unabsorbed.   The use of the Palmer device has been replaced by impingement instruments which also use the absorption principle.

b. Bacterial Sampling by Absorption

It is beyond the scope of this text to discuss bacterial samplers in detail. This subject has been considered by Wells (29), Albrecht (30), and by the Safety Division of the Army Chemical Corps.

Modifications of the impinger (see Section C-7-(a–d) of this chapter), which is also an absorption device, were developed by Rosebury (31), Druett and May (32), Henderson (33), and the Safety Division of the Army Chemical Corps. The latter device is shown in Figure V-4. This sampler has a curved (90°) air inlet tube which excludes most of the particles larger than 15–17 μ in size by deposition on the glass walls.

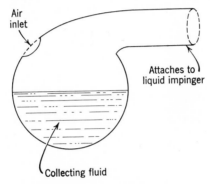

Fig. V-5. Preimpinger (34).

The limited orifice is placed at the tip of the inlet tube and is calibrated for a sampling rate of 13 lpm. Samplers of this type are generally characterized by a particle retention efficiency of nearly 99.9%. For a flow rate of 13 lpm, this limiting orifice provides a linear air flow of 20,000 cm/sec. Such high-velocity liquid impinger absorbers can be made selective with respect to particle size by use of the preimpinger devised by May and Druett (34), shown in Figure V-5. When this is attached to the absorber, most particles greater than 5 μ in diameter are retained in the 4 ml of sampling fluid it contains.

c. Rapid Method

Most absorption methods use water as the absorbing medium, an aliquot portion of which is then evaporated in a tared dish, dried, and weighed, or the dust particles of which are counted microscopically.

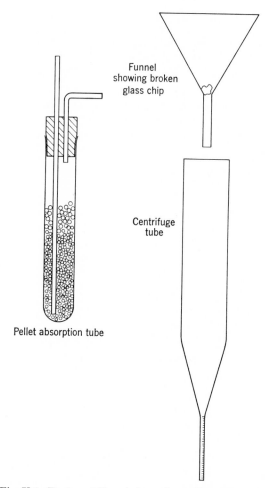

Fig. V-6. Dust centrifuge tube and sampling apparatus.

Naeslund (35) used a different absorbing medium.   He developed a rapid method using olive oil.

With the aid of a water-driven pump, or other suitable suction pump such as the vacuum pump from a vacuum tank of an auto or of a vacuum cleaner, aspirate air through a glass tube down into the bottom of a suitable shape such as a small absorbing test tube.   Fill the tube half or two-thirds full with glass pellets, 3–4 mm in diameter, and place on top of these a number of larger pellets to keep the small ones from being lifted by the passing air.   Coat the tube, together with the glass pellets, with a thin layer of olive oil by pouring the oil into the tube containing the pellets so that all of the pellets are oiled. Drain off the excess oil by turning the tube upside down for a while on filter paper. Aspirate air at a comparatively high speed of 3–5 m³/hr. The actual flow should be measured with a gas flowmeter of some type. From 10 to 30 m³ of air should be tested in streets and living quarters. One to 10 m³ are sufficient in dusty factories and work shops.

After the sampling is finished, fill the test tube with ether and shake. Remove the suction lead tube and pour the ether and pellets into a small funnel with an uneven piece of broken glass (as shown in Fig. V-6) or some other device to keep the pellets but not the dust from passing through. Catch the ether in a centrifuge tube to the bottom of which is attached a thick-walled capillary tube of 1-mm inside diameter and 2 cm or more in length. Wash the tube, pellets, and funnel 4 or 5 times more with small portions of ether. Centrifuge and if necessary use a wooden pin to press down the dust so there will be an even line of demarcation. As a contrast use 2 or 3 mg of red lead as the bottom layer (see Section C-6-k of this chapter). Read, if necessary, with the aid of a magnifying glass. Compare the height of the column obtained with known quantities of known dust.

This rapid method cannot give any estimate of the count of dust particles. However, where a rapid method is desired to give some measure of total dust in an atmosphere, it will serve. It has the advantage that it does trap most of the dust and that the reagents used, olive oil and ether, can be prepared practically dust free.

4. Electrostatic Precipitation

Dust particles in the air can be caused to flocculate and thus precipitate by means of a high electric potential. The flocculation and precipitation are caused (1) in part, by electrostatic attraction and (2) mainly by ionic bombardment of the electric wind created by the corona discharge (36). Devices using the principle of electrostatic flocculation for dust sampling are commercially available.

Drinker (37) describes a comparatively simple apparatus that can be made from easily obtainable equipment. The larger model consists of a tube in which is centered a gold-plated drill-steel wire, which serves as one electrode. In the small apparatus, gold or platinum wire serves as one electrode. The other, outer electrode is made either of metal netting, metal foil, or copper wire wrapped spirally along the tube. Such wrappings must be pulled tight by hand and may be kept in place by friction tape. Celluloid foil or filter paper placed inside the tube is used as the collecting medium. The precipitating electrode must be kept well up the tube to insure efficient collection on

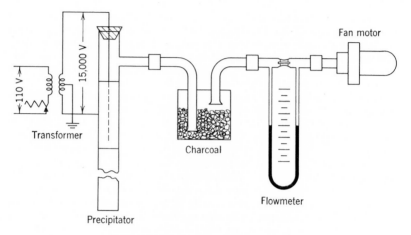

Fig. V-7. Electrical precipitator assembly.

the celluloid foil or filter paper. The observance of this precaution precludes dust from being caught on the glass tube itself.

In operation, a sufficient volume of air (measured with a flow-meter), drawn by means of a compressed-air ejector or hand-size vacuum cleaner fan, is passed through the precipitating tube at about 50 lpm until a visible deposit of dust is obtained. The foil or filter paper containing the dust deposit is then removed from the tube and placed in a receptacle for transmittal to the laboratory.

Since gases of a toxic nature may be produced in the operation of this type of precipitating device, and because these gases react with the rubber stoppers and tubing of the apparatus, it is necessary to insert an absorbing vessel containing activated charcoal in the setup to absorb the noxious gases formed.

Electrolytic flocculation is particularly suited for the precipitation of smokes and fumes. It is not used as much for dusts because there are simpler apparatuses operating on different principles with an equal efficiency for dusts. The greatest disadvantages of the electrostatic precipitator are that it needs electric power, which is not always available, that noxious gases may be formed and must therefore be guarded against, and that the equipment is fairly complicated.

An electrostatic dust-weight sampler is described by Barnes and Penney (38,39). A sample of dusty air is trapped in a cylinder and deposited electrostatically over its inside surface. A microscope

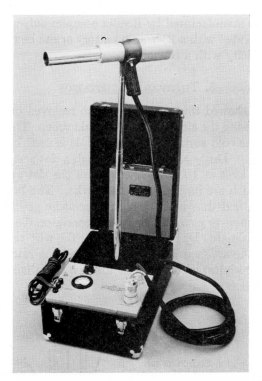

Fig. V-8. Electrostatic dust and fume sampler, including sampling tube kit.
(Courtesy Mine Safety Appliances Co.)

slide placed in one side of the cylinder receives its proportionate share
of the total dust, the dust particles being, in general uniformly distributed over the slide.   This slide can be removed, covered with a
rectangular cover slip, and examined microscopically.   Lea (40) has
described a portable electrostatic precipitator.   Wilner (41) devised
a small laboratory type of electrostatic precipitator.

Lauterbach et al. (42) used electrostatic precipitation methods to
investigate the inhalation of radioactive materials.   They employed
aluminum collecting tubes.   The efficiency of collection was 99.98%,
with concentrations ranging from 0.1 to 7.7 mg/m^3 and particle sizes
ranging from 0.2 to 0.7 μ.

A number of electrostatic precipitators for industrial hygiene work
are commercially available; the MSA device is shown in Figure V-8.

An instrument manufactured by Bendix occupies only about ¼ cu ft and can be operated with a 12-V auto battery or can be run on 115-V, 60-cycle electricity with a converter.

5. THERMAL PRECIPITATION

Aitken (43) showed that smoke could be removed quantitatively from air by passing the air through a hot-cold tube. The smoke precipitated on the cold surface. This principle is used by Green and Watson (44,45). Dusty air is drawn through a slot across which is a nichrome wire kept at 100°C. The walls of the slot are formed by cover slips, which are backed by brass blocks. The brass conducts the heat away and thus maintains a temperature gradient between the wire and the cover glasses. The dust deposits on the cover glasses and may be estimated by counting. When the wire temperature is 100°C above the ambient air temperature and the rate of flow is 7 ml/min, the precipitation of particles under 5 μ in diameter is practically complete.

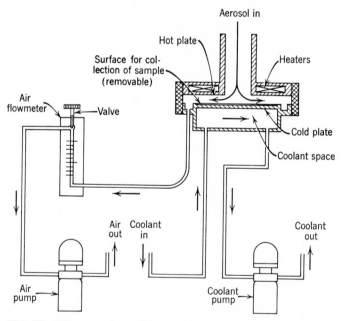

Fig. V-9. The Thermopositor. (Courtesy American Instrument Co., Inc.)

In England, as Green and Lane (25) point out, the thermal precipitator has become the standard instrument for environmental sampling. A self-contained model has been developed by the British National Coal Board for use in sampling in gassy mines. There has been some use made of this instrument in the United States, particularly as a reference instrument.

The thermal precipitator has also been used for the determination of mass concentration of dust. Kethley, Gordon, and Orr (46) describe a parallel plate device in which a hot plate is used to maintain a temperature gradient over a cold plate on which the particles deposit. Wright (47) made an analogous sampling instrument in which the gap between the hot plate and a cold aluminum plate is 0.015 in. At flow rates of 100 ml/min, precipitation of dust is virtually complete. The aluminum plate can be removed and weighed.

In a commercial instrument known as the Thermopositor (Fig. V-9) the air enters a plenum between closely approximated hot and cold plates. The rate of flow is controlled by a flowmeter and valve. All of the particles in the aerosol deposit on the cold surface which may be filter paper, a glass slide, plastic, aluminum foil, coated electron microscope screens, or other material that will lie flat. The intensity of the heat and the flow rate can be regulated in such a manner that all of the dust will deposit before it reaches the outside edge of the collection material. This is demonstrated by the presence of a clear margin around the outside edge. The use of this type of thermal precipitator in air pollution studies has been discussed by Gordon and Orr (48) and the use of this instrument for the sampling of air-borne microorganisms is detailed by Orr, Gordon, and Kordecki (49).

6. FILTRATION

There are many methods which use the principle of filtration as a means of collecting dust and fume samples. Many depend upon sucking the dust or fume through a weighed insoluble material such as filter paper, absorbent cotton, filter bags, cotton cloth, a Gooch crucible with an asbestos mat, a paper thimble, an alundum thimble, etc. The dust or fume is then estimated gravimetrically with these media or the depth of a stain is compared. Others depend on filtration of the atmosphere to be tested through a soluble material such as sugar, salicylic acid, naphthalene, anthracene, etc., which is subsequently dissolved in water, alcohol, ether, or another appropriate dust-free solvent, or is sublimed, and the dust is then estimated either by counting or refiltering through a tared device and finally weighing the collected dust. Among the more important of the first group were the Owens (50) automatic air filter, which is used to study outdoor atmospheric pollution; the koniogravimeter, a device used in Russia; the paper thimble; the Brown filter-paper method; the Silverman filter-paper method; and the bag test. The most important of the second group was the sugar-tube method. Filtering methods are among the most efficient for the collection and sampling of fumes.

In more recent years, filtration methods have been exploited considerably in industrial hygiene work. Thus, the filtration method of choice (1) for the counting of dust particles and measurements of their size has been the membrane filter method, (2) for total suspended particulate matter has been the use of glass filter webs and special filter papers, (3) for dust loading in stacks has been the thimble or equivalent device, and (4) for determination of a specific metal has been ashless filter paper. Filtration methods as used in air pollution control analyses have been discussed in detail by Jacobs (51). (See Chapter XI for the use of filters in the measurement of radioactivity.)

a. Membrane Filters

Membrane filters, also known as molecular filters and ultrafilters, were used over 60 years ago in bacteriological and immunological work. Those made of collodion, a solution of pyroxylin, consisting principally of cellulose tetranitrate, $[C_{12}H_{16}O_6(NO_3)_4]_n$, in 3 parts ethyl ether and 1 part ethyl alcohol, were among the earliest types. They were prepared with the aid of a porous support, usually in the laboratory, when required. A different type was prepared by dissolving the pyroxylin in glacial acetic acid. After the membranes were formed, they were used for filtration, dialysis, isolation of viruses, and related purposes. In 1931, Elford (52,53) prepared analogous membranes incorporating amyl alcohol in the alcohol–ether solution of the collodion; the pore size was controlled by the use of graded amounts of acetic acid and water. These filters were known as Gradocol membranes. Others describing ultrafilters were Jander and Zakowski (54), Burstein (55), and Grabar (56).

It was pointed out by Jacobs (57) in 1949 in the second edition of *The Analytical Chemistry of Industrial Poisons, Hazards, and Solvents,* that nitrocellulose was used for dust evaluation by Fritzsche as long ago as 1898 and the use of collodion for this purpose was patented by Hahn in 1907.

Under the sponsorship of the Army Chemical Corps, membrane or molecular filters of controlled pore size were developed on a commercial scale.   In 1947, Goetz (58) described in a report not generally available, materials, techniques, and testing methods for the sanitation, i.e., bacterial decontamination, of small-scale water supplies in the field used in Germany during and after World War II which included some information on membrane filters.   Subsequently, in 1951, Goetz and Tsuneishi (59) showed how molecular filters could be applied to the bacteriological assay of water and about the same time the use of such membranes in sanitary bacteriology was discussed by Clark and co-workers (60).   In 1953 Goetz (61) described further work in this field including the use of membranes in air analysis.   First and Silverman (62) discussed the use of such filters for air sampling and mentioned that Resnick (63) had used such filters for the gravimetric determination of dust in air.   A bibliography concerning membrane filters which includes specific uses in air analysis has been prepared by the Millipore Filter Corporation (64).   Because of the ease of use both in the field and the laboratory there has been extensive commercial exploitation of such filters and they are available from several firms.

Molecular filters are thin membranes 150 μ in thickness which have 80–85% voids and approximately 1×10^8 pore openings per square centimeter.   Those with a mean pore size of 0.8 μ have been shown to be of greatest value to the industrial hygienist.   Particles drawn against the membrane may penetrate to a depth of 15–20 μ.   Such filters retain dust particles by both a sieving action and electrostatic attaction.   Because of the latter action, particles much smaller than the pore size can be retained by the filter.   Thus, particles as small as 0.1 μ can be trapped readily and it has been shown that metal fume with particle sizes down to 0.01–0.02 μ are trapped by the electrostatic charge.   The characteristics of membrane filters with respect to their application to industrial hygiene and analytical toxicology have been described by Gelman (65) and are listed in Table V-2.

TABLE V-2
Characteristics of Membrane Filters

Type	Av. pore size, μ	Flow at 15″ Hg, liter air/min/ cm²	Smallest size particles completely retained, μ	Recommended uses	Ash, mg/cm²
AM-1	7.5	75	1.0	Pollen sampling, cement, process dust	0.011
AM-3	2.0		0.5	Radioactive debris	
AM-4	0.85	15	0.3	General air pollution sampling	0.006
AM-5	0.7	10	0.3	Radioactive aerosols, critical air sampling	
AM-7	0.4	5	0.1	Experimental sampling, airborne microorganism	0.005
AM-8	0.25	10	0.5	Research	0.005
Green	0.4	5	0.1	Quartz sampling, reflectance examination	
Black	0.75	10	0.3	UV examination of dusts	

Membrane filters have an additional advantage. They can serve both as insoluble and soluble media for subsequent dust counting. Thus, by dissolving the membrane in acetone and suspending the dust particles in a known volume of the solvent, the methods described in Section C-6-1 of this chapter can be applied.

If membrane filters are to be used for the gravimetric determination of dust, one must specify glycerol-free types because normally glycerol is incorporated in order to make the filter more flexible. During the drying step of a gravimetric determination, the glycerol will volatilize and introduce an error.

b. Glass Filter Webs

The glass filter web developed by Arthur D. Little, Inc., for the Atomic Energy Commission is a felt-like material composed of a combination of glass fibers of mixed sizes with a small amount of an organic binder and dispersing agent. This type of filter was developed to achieve nearly absolute removal of air-borne radioactive particulate matter in atomic energy installations. It fills a need for a high-temperature, chemically resistant filter medium. Eighty per cent by weight of the fiber composition is composed of glass fibers 3 μ in diameter and the remainder consists of fibers 0.5 μ in diameter. The binder, which is an acrylic resin, and the dispersing agent are required in order that the webs be manufactured by paper machines and for filter construction. This organic material may be removed by heating the webs in air to 400°C. The tensile strength of this type of filter is lowered by the removal of the binder and dispersing agent, but the filtering performance is not affected to any appreciable extent.

Initially, when these glass filter webs were made available on a commercial scale, just these two types were marketed. Subsequently, additional types of glass fiber webs were made available. Each firm handling these filters has its own code designations. Representative of these are the designations of the Gelman Instrument Company.

Type E is the glass filter web containing a small amount of organic binder. It is efficient for air sampling and will retain 99.6% of particles larger than 0.25 μ; its filtering efficiency is 98% for particles as small as 0.05 μ. It can withstand temperatures up to 480°C (900°F).

Type A is the type of glass filter web that contains no organic binder. It can be used for the sampling of organic aerosols and for chromatographic and electrophoretic analysis. It does not absorb protein material and can be sprayed with sulfuric acid for identification purposes in chromatographic types of analysis. It, too, can withstand temperatures up to 480°C.

Type G is a glass web with very low pressure drop. It is reinforced with gauze in order to achieve maximum air flow.

Type H is a very high-efficiency filter designed for filtration and sampling. The penetration of the particles trapped is approximately half that of the type E and A glass webs.

Type M is a glass web designed for good efficiency at moderate pressure drop. It is recommended for the collection of particles larger than 1 μ in diameter.

The principal analytical use of these filters has been in air pollution investigations. The methods employed and a bibliography are given by Jacobs (66). Types E and A and analogous types can be used for determining the mass concentration of dust or total suspended particulate matter, but the binder-free type is preferred for samples which are to be analyzed chemically.

Initially, as used by the National Air Sampling Network of the Air Pollution Division of the U. S. Public Health Service and by others, there was relatively wide variation in the trace element content of these filters, but in recent years such glass filter webs have been manufactured to fit rigid, uniform specifications.

There are severe limitations in using glass filter webs for subsequent chemical and spectrographic analysis after sampling. The large amount of ash left with all types gives the analyst considerable difficulty. In addition, the very large blank for certain elements makes some analyses worthless.

c. Polystyrene Filters

There has been an interesting increase in the types of filter material available for analytical toxicology and industrial hygiene chemistry.

In addition to those mentioned in preceding sections and those which will be discussed in detail in subsequent sections, there is available a mat-like filter manufactured from filaments of polystyrene with fiber diameters as small as 0.3 μ. This type of material, one brand of which is known as Microsorban, has a high efficiency with little pressure drop for the collection of particles, even under heavy loading. Consequently, relatively large quantities of dust can be collected at a constant sampling rate by using a simple pump. However, these filters can only be used at temperatures as high as 90°C (200°F).

The filter is soluble in organic solvents and thus can be separated from the collected dust for centrifugal and sedimentation types of analysis. These filters can also be easily ashed.

d. Filter Paper

By use of lintless, hardened filter paper of high wet strength (67) for fine precipitates, dust can be trapped and subsequently resuspended for estimation. Results obtained by this method are said to be comparable to those obtained by impingement methods. A comprehensive review of filter paper methods is given by Brown. This method lends itself to direct counting of the dust as in the impinger method (see Chapter VI, Section A-1), to estimation by light transmission methods, or to an evaluation of the amount of dust by length of time of return of the pump handle. The efficiency of this method is greater than that of the impinger for the collection of metal fumes such as those of cadmium, lead, mercury, and zinc and for collecting fine particles of dust.

The filter-paper sampler consists of a hand-operated, single-action pump capable of drawing 283 ml (0.01 cu ft) of air per stroke through filter paper and a paper holder.   The pump is equipped with a ball-type check valve, which prevents air from being pushed back through the filter paper on the return stroke, and with a counter for counting the strokes.   The plunger has a leather cup-type gasket.   By means of an adjustable stop on the pump rod, the volumes of air drawn in per stroke can be regulated.   Ten strokes per minute with a pump of

Fig. V-10. Aerosol universal filter holder. (Courtesy Millipore Filter Corp.)

the volume stated will sample 0.1 cfm, which is equivalent to the sampling rate of the midget impinger.

The filter paper holder (Fig. V-10) consists of two flat metal surfaces. Whatman No. 50 5.5-cm filter paper is placed in a case equipped with removable covers in the laboratory to avoid soiling the paper.   In use the cover of the case is removed and the case is screwed on to the pump. The second cover is removed and the light transmission is taken if desired.   In sampling, the pump is drawn out smartly, held for several seconds to make certain that all the air passes through the filter paper and equilibrates the air pressure, and then returned for the next stroke.   Light transmission can be taken again after sampling is complete.

To count the dust, remove the filter paper from the holder in the laboratory and shake in a dust-free liquid. The estimation can then be made as in the case of impinger sampling (see page 229ff).

Silverman and Ege (68) constructed a field filter-paper sampling device for sampling lead fume from a hand vacuum blower, a filter paper holder, and a U-tube manometer. Air flow was controlled by means of a pinch clamp on the blower discharge. The holder, of brass tubing and sheet brass, is made to press-fit the blower. It is fitted with a heavy wire-mesh grille to support the filter paper and with six bolts on which the cover, also equipped with a wire guard, can be clamped by means of six wing nuts. This arrangement enables one to change easily the 125-mm Whatman No. 44 or 42 filter paper used for sampling. Single filter papers had a mean collection efficiency of 86.7% at sampling rates of 27.7–48.9 lpm, while double filter papers had a mean collection efficiency of 98% at flow rates of 3.5–29.0 lpm.

Bayrer and Hough (69) modified the aforementioned device by the use of two funnels clamped together, as in an original design of Silverman and Ege, but they connected the collecting head to the suction device by tubing so that the head could be held in the sampling zone.

The amount of lead caught on such filter papers can be determined by direct weighing if the papers are equilibrated (70,71), or by ashing and weighing, or by methods detailed in Chapter VIII, Section D.

Another device using filter paper for the rapid sampling of large volumes of air of the order of 55–65 cfm is described by Silverman and Williams (72).

In the 1950s and 60s, considerable use of Whatman No. 41 filter paper was made for air sampling, especially for the analysis of trace amounts of metallic contaminants. Whatman No. 41 and equivalent filter papers are acid-washed, low-ash cellulose papers. They can be used for sampling up to temperatures of 149°C (300°F). They are, however, adversely affected by high humidity.

Mention may be made here of the use of Whatman No. 4, particularly in the form of tape, in automatic filter paper samplers.

Other types of filter paper are used in the closely allied field of air pollution work and may find some utilization in industrial hygiene sampling. Three different types were initially used with high-volume air samplers. One was an accordion-pleated circular type of filter paper. Such a filter paper presented a large surface and enabled air to be sampled at rates of 65 cfm. The disadvantage of such filter papers is that they have such high and variable blanks for trace materials that their subsequent use for determinations other than suspended particulate matter is inadvisable.

A second type of filter is matted material. Here the flow rates are relatively high but, in this instance also, the large and variable blanks make the paper unsuitable for subsequent analysis other than total suspended particulate matter.

A third type of filter paper used is equivalent to Whatman No. 1 or Whatman No. 4. The volume of air which can be passed through such filters is materially reduced and thus the length of time that sampling can be continued is also materially reduced. An additional marked disadvantage is that these are not quantitative filter papers and therefore do not lend themselves to analysis for micro work.

Schleicher and Schuell acid-washed FF2W filter paper may be used for such purposes because its blanks are relatively uniform. The initial flow of air through these filter papers is of the order of 70 cfm. This flow, however, drops relatively rapidly to about 20 cfm. in about 4 hr. For this reason it is best to sample with these filter papers for only 1–2 hr periods.

There has been some use made of an asbestos–vegetable filter paper, known as HV-70, in industrial hygiene analyses. This type of filter is treated with a silicone to make it water repellent, thus making it suitable for use under conditions of high humidity.

e. Automatic Filter Samplers

Automatic filter tape samplers are widely used for suspended particulate matter evaluation by determination of "smoke shade," particularly in air pollution control investigations. There has been an increasing use of these instruments for industrial hygiene work also. In general, a dust spot or trace is produced and the amount of dust is determined by measuring the decrease in light transmission or reflectance. The details of such measurements have been given by Jacobs (66) and need not be repeated here.

A number of automatic filter paper samplers have been developed. The Hemeon (AISI) automatic smoke filter (73) and the Von Brand filter paper recorder (74) are among the more commonly used instruments. The Chaney auto sampler (75) is described in the literature. Each of these devices has its advantages.

The Chaney (Hall) instrument takes parallel samples by filtration of the air through a prepared Gooch crucible, thus permitting subsequent analysis of the material caught in the crucible.

The high-volume sampler and the Hall device permit the analyst to make full-scale chemical analyses of the deposited material. In general, this cannot be done with the other devices at the present time. However, the stains produced on these filter paper samplers give a measure of the pollution that is relatively simple to interpret.

By impregnation of the filter paper, many of these devices can be used for the automatic recording or estimation of specific polutants such as hydrogen sulfide.

Nader (76) developed a high-flowrate sampler for the determination of smoke shade. The filter medium is the WS microweb membrane filter (77), that is, a nylon thread-reinforced membrane filter. The total air flowrate through a filter area of 2 cm² can be varied from 5 to 32 lpm. A special spiral-loading cartridge is used for storing the tape so that the sample spots remain intact and undisturbed. The smoke shade can be evaluated by transmission or reflectance measurements. Nader suggested that the mass loading of particulate matter on the tape could be determined by a beta-gauge technique measuring the beta radioactivity able to pass through the tape and that other accessory equipment could be developed for particle size determination, microchemical analyses, and x-ray diffraction analyses.

f. Owens Automatic Air Filter

The Owens automatic air filter (21) is a device which is used widely in Great Britain for making a continuous automatic record of the pollution in the air. It is a prototype of the automatic samplers mentioned in the preceding paragraphs. In this instrument a known volume of air drawn by means of a siphon is filtered through the outer portion of a disk of white filter paper with a 7-in. diameter, and the impurity present in the air is measured by the depth of shade produced on the filter paper. Two liters of air are filtered, at regular intervals of time, through a round spot of ⅛-in. diameter. The filtering through each spot takes approximately 4 min, and from 4 to 6 spots are recorded in an hour. The disk is rotated by clockwork and makes a complete revolution in 24 hr. Since the instrument is in operation continuously during any period, a record of the variation in pollution is obtainable for that period. The degree of pollution, represented by the grayness of a spot, is determined by comparing its grayness with that of a standard scale of shades.

The standard scale of shades consists of a row of ten rectangles each $\frac{1}{2}$ in. square, varying in grayness from a very light gray, marked "1," to a very dark gray, marked "20." The ten shades are numbered 1, 2, 3, 4, 6, 8, 10, 12, 15, and 20, respectively. They are made by applying a standard wash of lampblack to white paper as many times as the number of the shade. The density of each shade is therefore a multiple of unit shade. Each shade has a hole $\frac{1}{8}$-in. in diameter punched in its center, and a spot on the disk is compared with a standard shade by inserting it under the hole. In comparing spots on the disk with the standard shades, it is sometimes difficult to obtain an exact match. Ives and co-workers (21) used the number that most nearly matched the sample spot, for example, calling a shade lying between 0 and 0.5, 0.

The Owens automatic air filter measures dust by the degree of blackness of a stain. Where the air pollution is caused by dust which is not black, the method fails unless different standards are prepared.

g. Koniogravimeter

The koniogravimeter (78), a device which was used in Russia, was designed to be worn by a workman, if desired. It consisted of a special set of tubes. These tubes were so arranged that they could be loaded with a filtering tube which could subsequently be dried and weighed. They were adjusted to nosepieces so that they could be worn by a worker as he performed his duties or by an investigator where the sampling of dust was to be done. They could also be attached to a vacuum pump. The gain in weight shown by the tared filtering tube showed the amount of dust inhaled by a workman in a given time.

h. Paper Thimble

A standardized method of using the paper thimble for the sampling of dust is the method of Trostel and Frevert (79). These investigators used Whatman extraction thimbles, 33 $\times$ 94 mm, containing a small amount of cotton wool (125 mg), well fluffed out, for the purpose of supporting the dust and preventing the clogging of the pores of the thimble. The thimble is put into a brass cell to hold it in place as shown in Figure V-11.

The dusty atmosphere is drawn through the thimble by means of suction applied through the arm in the brass cell. The dust is caught

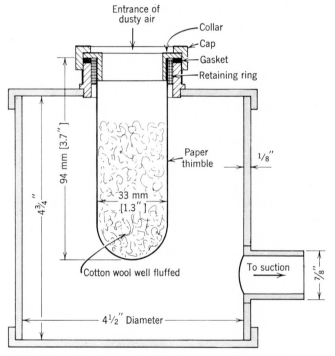

Fig. V-11. Details of paper thimble and suction capsule (79).

by the fluffed absorbent cotton and the thimble itself. The suction device used should be capable of sampling at the rate of about 2 cfm and the amount of air sampled should be measured by some type of flowmeter.

The thimbles must be tared before being used. All the thimbles should be given a preliminary drying treatment by heating in a constant temperature oven at 90–95°C for 3–7 days. Then the drying may be completed by heating in a vacuum oven for 7 hr at 90°C, after which the thimbles are weighed as described below. A check weight should be obtained on the thimbles by exposing them to room air overnight and then redrying them in the vacuum oven at 90°C for 7 hr. The drying may also be completed by continuing the heating in the constant temperature oven at 90–95°C for 2 days more, which is generally sufficient to bring them to constant weight. The same drying procedure used in obtaining the tare weight is used in obtaining the dry-dust weight after sampling.

The thimbles are dried in weighing bottles and permitted to cool in desiccators. A counterpoise weighing bottle should be used in order to compensate for possible moisture condensation on the comparatively large surface of the weighing bottle. The difference in weight between the weighing bottle and the thimble before and after sampling represents the dry weight of the collected dust. This weight divided by the volume of air sampled, which is obtained by the use of the flowmeter, yields the weight of dust per unit volume, as, for instance, milligrams per cubic meter.

The paper thimble has a very high sampling efficiency. It samples large volumes rapidly and is very simple to use. It is particularly useful in the sampling of radioactive dusts. On the other hand, samples of dust collected by the paper thimble method do not lend themselves to estimation by count.

i. Resistance Pressure

The method which measures resistance pressure is really a filter device variation. The amount of material on the filter is estimated indirectly by the increased resistance to air flow as the filter becomes clogged.

The apparatus known as the Anderson and Armspach dust determinator (16) consists of a holder in which a piece of filter paper or other porous fabric is clamped. Air is drawn through the paper at a constant rate and the difference of pressure between the two sides of the paper is determined by means of a manometer, which is connected to the holder on each side of the paper. The gauge reading indicates the difference of pressure existing between the two sides of the filter. As the paper clogs, more pressure is required to keep the air passing through at the same rate, and the manometer reading thus increases. For hygienic purposes this device is of little value for, although some correlation can be obtained between the amount of dust and the increase in pressure, neither the actual weight of the dust nor the count can be obtained.

j. Bag Test

The bag test (80) is used for estimating "dust loading" in flues. It is especially convenient when large volumes of gas containing heavy dust loadings are to be estimated. The method consists of diverting a known volume of gas from the main gas stream and then passing this gas through a number, usually three, of dried and weighed heavy Canton flannel or unbleached muslin bags. The bags are dried and weighed after sampling and thus the amount of dust retained by the bags is ascertained. Pitot tube and temperature readings must be made at frequent intervals in order to obtain the volume of gas tested. The method is useful mainly for industrial and technical, rather than for investigational, purposes.

The Aerotec flue-gas sampler (81) and similar devices are also bag-test instruments.

k. Sugar Tube

The sugar-tube method (82,83) of sampling consists of filtering 15 cu ft of air through pure granulated sugar, which retains the dust. The sugar is then dissolved in dust-free water, leaving the insoluble dust particles in suspension. An aliquot portion of the solution is placed in a Sedgwick-Rafter cell, such as that used for counting blood corpuscles, and is examined under a microscope at $110\times$. The dust particles are counted, and from this result the number of dust particles per milliliter of air is computed. The method was originally developed by Frankland (84) in 1886 for the quantitative estimation of microorganisms in the atmosphere.

Rapid Method. A rapid modification of the sugar-tube method has been devised by McNair and Hirst (85). The dust is collected by aspirating a measured volume of the air to be examined, 5–10 cu ft usually being sufficient, through a Gooch crucible (Fig. V-12) with small holes, packed with 5 g of clean powdered sugar.

The prepared Gooch crucible is fitted to an ordinary adapter and filter flask. The air is drawn through the packing of sugar. On completion of the sampling, the sugar is dissolved in water and the sugar solution together with the occluded dust, which is now in suspension, is washed into a centrifuge tube (Fig. V-6). The centrifuge tube is about 18 cm long and 2 cm in diameter. To the bottom of the centrifuge tube, 3 cm of thick-walled tubing of 1-mm bore is attached. In order to facilitate the measurement of the dust, about 0.1 g of red lead is suspended in alcohol and is centrifuged in the tube prior to centrifuging the sample. This

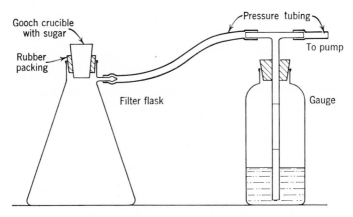

Fig. V-12. Apparatus for rapid sugar-tube method.

procedure eliminates inaccuracies of the tube end and provides a horizontal, conspicuously colored surface from which to measure the height of the dust column. After pouring off the alcohol, the sugar solution is transferred to the tube and centrifuged for 2 min at 2000 rpm. The height of the column is then measured on the graduated scale of the capillary section of the tube or is ascertained by means of a traveling microscope. The tubes should be calibrated by weighing out quantitatively 1–5 mg of the particular dust being tested and then centrifuging from similar sugar solutions. The relationship is not a linear one.

The greatest disadvantage of the sugar-tube method is the difficulty of obtaining dust-free sugar, or even uniformly dusted sugar so that a correction may be applied. Nevertheless, the method is simple and will serve in many instances to give an adequate measure of dust contamination in the atmosphere.

l. Salicylic Acid Filter

Another type of filter using a porous pad is described by Matthews (26,45,86). This filter is primarily intended to obtain samples of the order of 20–500 mg for quantitative analysis. The samples are collected in a relatively short time, say 1–6 hr, so that working conditions, temperature, humidity, etc., are fairly constant. The differences in the composition of the dust attributable to these factors can be determined if necessary. This type of filter is designed to give almost complete retention of the dust, so that the mass concentration of dusts may be determined.

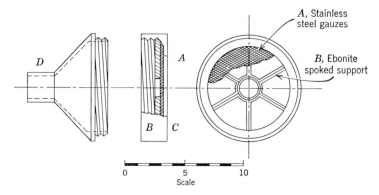

Fig. V-13. Salicylic acid filter holder.

Reagent-quality salicylic acid is sieved through a 40-mesh sieve, crystals of 40-mesh size being used. Finer crystals are more resistant to flow and coarser crystals are not so retentive of dust. The crystals are packed on stainless-steel gauzes (A, Fig. V-13). There are three stainless-steel gauzes—two coarse-mesh gauzes with a fine-mesh gauze in between. The coarse-mesh gauzes give the arrangement rigidity. These meshes are screwed into position in the holder by means of a spoked support (B) made of ebonite. The holder itself is also made of ebonite.

A filter cell, 7 cm in diameter, requires 10 g of salicylic acid to give a pad thickness of about 4 mm. This thickness is sufficient to provide good retention without obstructing the flow. As sampling is continued, the filter clogs with the dust it retains, thus cutting the flow to a negligible amount. Hence, it can be used to obtain only small samples.

For transportation the prepared cell is covered with a flat cellophane lid and may then be handled freely. Before the dust is sampled, the crystals are shaken back over the whole surface and gently pressed into position again. The cell is fitted to its support horizontally, the cellophane is removed, and the suction started. The greater the suction, the more efficient is the filter. When the suction is on, the filters are very stable and sampling may be carried out in any position.

When sampling is completed, the pads are covered with cellophane and the whole filter is returned to the laboratory. The entire salicylic acid pad, together with the dust, is transferred to a centrifuge tube, a 50-ml tube for 10 g of salicylic acid, and the salicylic acid is removed by treatment with absolute alcohol. The dust is then air-dried and is in a suitable condition for chemical analysis or petrographic examination (see Chapter VII, Section D).

Other variations of methods in which the dust is trapped in or on a material that can subsequently be volatilized or dissolved are the use of volatile materials like benzoic acid, anthracene, and naphthalene (87), or the use of nitrocellulose (88) or collodion (89) in special solvents.

The use of the latter materials in analytical toxicology is discussed in detail in Section C-6-a of this chapter. Membrane filters and polystyrene filters can also be dissolved and used in the manner described.

m. Miscellaneous Devices

Harrold (90) and co-workers devised a packed-tube collector for their studies of the toxicity of lead chromate. This collector was designed to be worn by a person on the job. It consisted of a tight-fitting face piece to which was sealed a rubber tube holding a glass tube 4–5 in. long and of 0.5-in. diameter, and having three constrictions. The glass tube was packed with successive layers of glass wool, sodium bicarbonate, 3 in. of glass beads wet with 2 ml of nitric acid (1:1), and another layer of glass wool. The nitric acid served to trap the lead and the bicarbonate was used to neutralize any acid vapors given off by the acid layer. This collection tube proved to be superior to the electrical precipitator. It has a resistance of 80 mm at 32 lpm and 40 mm at 14 lpm. The contents of the tube can be analyzed in conventional ways.

Using a glass tube 30 cm × 38 mm packed with dry Pyrex glass wool, Keenan and Fairhall (91) found that lead fume was quantitatively retained.

A device used by Dudley for trapping selenium-bearing dusts is described in Chapter X, Section F-2, Fig. X-1.

7. IMPINGEMENT AND IMPACTION

Many of the most successful instruments used in the determination of dust in industrial hygiene studies are those based on the principle of impingement. In these devices, the dust-laden air is drawn or driven at a high velocity against a prepared surface and is thus trapped on the prepared surface itself, or is absorbed by some medium such as water. Of these types of instruments, the konimeter, the Owens jet dust counter, the cascade impactor, and the Greenburg-Smith impinger and its modifications are the most important. The theoretical aspects of impingement and impaction have been considered by Davies, Aylward, and Leacey (92).

a. Konimeter

The konimeter originally developed by R. N. Kotzé is a hand-size instrument (3,93,94). It consists essentially of a valveless cylindrical suction pump with a piston of the leather-cup type and a brass dial (Fig. V-14). The piston of the pump is actuated by a spring that insures uniform operation. It draws into the cylinder 2.5, 5.0, or 10 ml of air at a high velocity through a nozzle which is about 0.6 mm in diameter. The nozzle is held about 0.5–0.6 mm above a glass plate which is coated with a thin layer of petrolatum, glycerine jelly, mineral oil, or other adhesive film. A 250-mesh screen protects the nozzle from being clogged by large particles. The glass plate, cemented in a metal rim, is held by the brass dial chamber and may be revolved so that a fresh surface may be exposed to each sample. The dial is divided into 30 sectors, each one of which is numbered to record each sample taken. At most only 26 samples are taken, leaving at least 4 blank, usually 1, 10, 20, and 30.

The Bureau of Mines (95) which used the konimeter as an adjunct of the impinger, described methods for checking the volume of air sampled by means of a microburet.

To prepare the konimeter for use, check to see that the plunger moves smoothly and that the screen and nozzle are clear. Clean the disk, using mild soap and water, by scrubbing with a camel's-hair brush or with the fingers. Rinse thoroughly, dry, polish with clean linen, and brush in one direction with a camel's-hair brush. If the humidity is low and dust and lint are held on the glass by static charges, breathe lightly on the disk to assist in removing these particles.

Apply an adhesive film to the sample side of the glass plate. The Bureau of Mines (95) recommended a mixture made from 1 oz of glycerine jelly used for microscope work and 1 oz of glycerol with 10–20

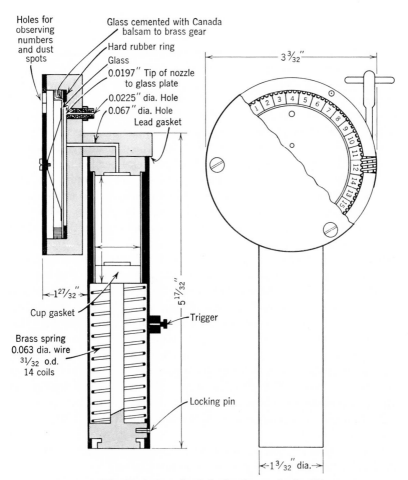

Fig. V-14. Details of the konimeter device (3).

drops of water. Use less water in hot weather than in cold weather. Heat the components in a bottle held in hot but not boiling water until the jelly melts and mixes completely with the water and glycerol. Allow the mixture to cool and set to a soft jelly.

Prepare sample disks in an atmosphere as free from dust as possible. Hold the sampling side of the plate down while the adhesive is applied to avoid deposition of atmospheric dust. Use the index finger to apply the jelly to the sample disk. Wash the hands thoroughly in warm water, hold the index finger and thumb in cold water to close the pores, dry with linen cloth, and brush to remove lint.   Hold a piece of jelly of about $\frac{1}{16}$-in. diameter between the thumb and finger until it softens, and spread on the sample disk with the index finger, turning the disk with a sweeping circular motion.   Do not rub the jelly between the fingers, as small bubbles that form in the jelly cannot be removed and may be confused with dust particles.   Breathe gently on the disk until the jelly has taken up enough moisture to spread and thus remove the streaks left by the finger ridges.   Examine the disk under the microscope, and if there are more than 8–10 particles per field, clean and prepare the disk over again.   Place the disk on the konimeter with the adhesive side toward the orifice, or in a special metal carrying box, adhesive side down, if it is to be used at a later time.   Place the threaded rim over the disk on the konimeter and turn until the rubber gasket makes good contact.

To obtain a sample of dust, push the piston inward until it is caught and held in place at the 2.5-, 5.0-, or 10-ml mark by a locking pin. Hold the orifice at the back of the konimeter at the sampling point and procure a sample by pressing the trigger, which releases the spring. Air rushes in through the nozzle at a high velocity, impinging its dust content in the glycerine jelly or petrolatum film on the glass plate and forming a dust spot about 1 mm in diameter.   To obtain another sample, turn the pinion to bring the next sector into position and cock the piston again.   Examine the dust spot under a microscope at $200 \times$ and count the visible particles, as described in Section A-3 of this chapter.   The results are expressed as number of particles per milliliter of air (83).

Some konimeters are equipped with a small microscope so that the dust samples obtained may be counted directly (96).

The konimeter is one of the simplest and most compact of dust sampling instruments.   It has the advantage that it can be used very effectively to obtain grab samples and that 26 samples can be obtained on one plate.   The other 4 sectors are used for blank determinations.   Because of its ability to take grab samples, fluctuations in dust content can easily be sampled.   It works best in atmospheres of low or medium dust content.   Its disadvantages are that it has a low sampling efficiency in very dusty atmospheres, that it takes only an instantaneous sample of 2.5, 5.0, or 10 ml, and that the dust can be evaluated only in number of particles.   The konimeter is well adapted to taking samples of oil- or fat-bearing dust particles such as the dust in a fur-felting industry (97).

Minnesota Dust Counter. The Minnesota dust counter (98) is a device related to the konimeter in that the adhesive-impingement principle is used. It has, however, a moving slide upon which 5–6 samples may be taken and a fixed orifice. A hand pump is used to give the vacuum required for the air sample.

b. Owens Jet Dust Counter

The Owens jet dust counter (3,21,99) is a device that depends upon the combined principles of impingement and condensation. A high-velocity jet of air is caused to strike a microscope cover glass; this high velocity brings about a fall of pressure in the jet, accompanying which, and resulting from it, is a corresponding fall of temperature.

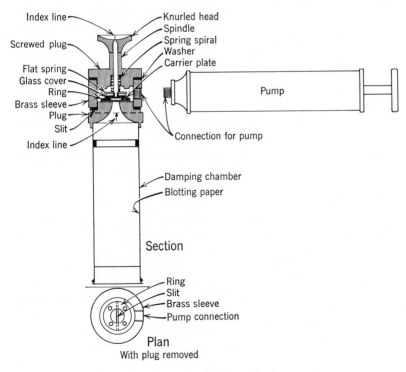

Fig. V-15. Details of the Owens jet dust counter.

This in turn causes a condensation of the moisture in the air upon the dust particles, which are thus projected wet against the cover glass, and, as the water evaporates, are left behind adhering to the glass.

The Owens jet dust counter consists of a damping chamber communicating through a narrow slit with an air pump, operated at right angles to the chamber (Fig. V-15). The air pump has a capacity of 50 ml. The damping chamber is lined with moist blotting paper. The capacity of the damping chamber is two or three times that of the pump. When the dust in the air is to be sampled, the damping chamber is unscrewed from the instrument, passed through the air to be sampled, and replaced, the plunger of the pump being left pushed in.

A cover glass is then placed behind the slit and the pump plunger is pulled out smartly so as to draw one or more volumes of air through the slit. The rapid expansion of the air drawn through the slit lowers its temperature, the air becomes supersaturated, and water condenses on the dust particles in the air. When the pump plunger is pulled out, the air passes at high velocity through the narrow slit and impinges upon the cover glass. The air is deflected, but the particles of water containing the dust strike the cover glass and adhere to it. The water subsequently evaporates, as the velocity falls off and the pressure and temperature again rise, and the dust particles are left on the cover glass. The narrow slit is 1 cm long and the cover glass is placed at about 1 mm from it. This leaves a sample of dust in the shape of a fine ribbon about 1 cm long and about 0.2–0.4 mm wide.

The cover slide may then be cemented to a microscope slide and may subsequently be examined under the microscope with an oil-immersion objective having a magnification of approximately 1000×.

The Owens jet dust counter is a light instrument and is simple to use. It is particularly useful in air pollution studies of smoke contamination. Its disadvantages are that it can only be used for the counting of dust particles; it cannot be used for the sampling of industrial dust of high concentrations, for in this case the dust record is so thick that it cannot be counted; and it is only capable of obtaining instantaneous samples. A modification of this instrument as describe by Hatch and Thompson (100) is designed so that eight slides can be used.

The Bausch and Lomb (101) dust counter is in principle an Owens jet dust counter with several modifications.

c. Impinger (3,102–106)

The Greenburg-Smith impinger is the standard instrument in the United States for the collection of dusts (107,108). It is also widely used for the collection of fumes and mists. Its efficiency for certain types of fumes, such as lead (109) and mercury, is low and variable, but nevertheless agrees reasonably well with that of the electrical precipitator.

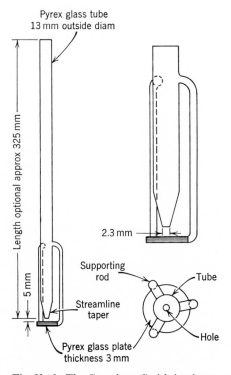

Fig. V-16. The Greenburg-Smith impinger.

The Greenburg-Smith impinger is a device through which air is sampled at a high velocity. The air is impinged at this high velocity against a glass plate which is immersed in an absorption medium. The dust particles are momentarily arrested by the impinging process, are wetted by the water or the absorption liquid, and thus are trapped. The Greenburg-Smith impinger also acts as an absorber

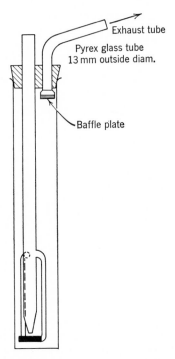

Fig. V-17. Impinger tube and collection tube assembled.

and traps any gases or liquids which are soluble in water or in the other absorption mediums used.

The impinger tube (Fig. V-16) is made entirely of glass. It consists of a piece of Pyrex glass tubing 13 mm in outside diameter, about 32 cm long, having a tip drawn to a 2.3-mm orifice. At the end of the tube, attached to it by three supporting arms, is a circular plate of glass, 25 mm in diameter and set in place at exactly 5 mm from the orifice of the tube. The impinger tube may be set in a cylinder (Fig. V-17) or a 500-ml wide-mouth flask. Sufficient liquid must be in the vessel to cover the impinger plate to a depth of approximately 3 cm. In large tubes or cylinder-type vessels, 100 ml are generally sufficient. In the 500-ml wide-mouth flasks, 225–250 ml of the absorbing liquid are necessary. During winter or when cold air is being sampled, it may be necessary to heat the liquid in the impinger flask in order to keep it from freezing. Ives (21) and co-workers used an electric lamp in a box, keeping the impinger flask in the box.   Other solvents such as ethyl, *n*-propyl, or isopropyl alcohol can be used for the same purpose.   These solvents also reduce the risk of solubility of the dust in water.

The Greenburg-Smith impinger apparatus needs some device to draw the air in with sufficient velocity to impinge against the plate. Electric suction, compressed-air suction, and hand-driven suction devices are all used in connection with the impinger.   Sufficient suction must be developed to give a sampling rate of 1 cfm.   With a standard orifice immersed, as mentioned, to a depth of 3 cm, this flow rate will be obtained at 3 in. Hg negative pressure.   Greater speeds than that are likely to disturb the trapping liquid so violently as to expel it from the flask.   A gas-measuring device of some type may also be in the line and should be calibrated so that one may control the rate and quantity of air sampled; however, the standard orifice is an excellent metering nozzle and by using an air-bleeding device and a vacuum gauge to maintain the negative pressure, the air-flow rate of 1 cfm can be maintained.   The standard orifice can also serve as a critical orifice, as at any suction pressure the maximum air-flow rate obtainable is 1 cfm.

Modified Impinger.   A more compact and convenient impinger flask and nozzle have been developed by Hatch, Warren, and Drinker (110).   The modified impinger (Fig. V-18) does away with the glass impinging plate and utilizes the bottom of the trapping flask for this purpose.   The suction connection is combined with the inlet tube, thus simplifying the device still further.   The essential parts of this modification are a straight piece of Pyrex tubing, 15 mm in outside diameter and approximately 275 mm in length.   The tube is drawn down in streamlined form at its lower end to a tip with a 2.3-mm orifice.   In sampling this orifice is kept approximately 5 mm from the bottom of the flask, a guide line on the flask indicating this distance.   The flask is a cylinder 50 mm in diameter and 210 mm in height.   It requires a fluid volume of only 75 ml to give the proper depth of immersion to the nozzle.   An entrainment trap in the form of a rubber ring prevents the possibe loss of the liquid, and possibly dust, with the outgoing air.

The cylinder-type impinger flasks may be placed in a leather holster, which may be suspended from the shoulders of a worker and strapped to his chest (104,111).   This enables an investigator to take

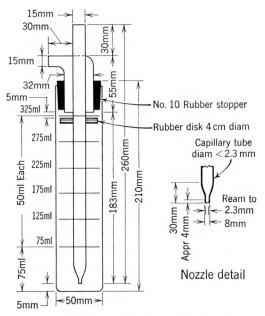

Fig. V-18. Modified impinger.

a sample of air very close to the locations or positions that a worker occupies during his work.

All-Glass Impinger. An impinger has been constructed which embodies the best features of the Greenburg-Smith and Hatch impingers. This is an all-glass Pyrex impinger (112) (Fig. V-19). It consists of a flat-bottomed cylindrical flask, with three graduations, 100 ml, 250 ml, and 500 ml. These graduations permit dilutions of samples to be made easily in the flask itself without the necessity of transferring to larger containers, as is usually the case. The tops of all flasks are ground uniformly for ℥ 45/50 glass stoppers. The nozzles are equipped with fixed disks, but with much shorter supporting arms. This tends to cut down breakage, which formerly was a serious drawback to the all-glass Greenburg-Smith type of nozzle. The combination suction connection and inlet tube used on the Hatch impinger is retained, but the former now has been carefully ground so as to be interchangeable with all flasks.

This impinger is a rigid unit. There is little opportunity for the fixed disk or the supporting rods to break. The all-glass construction also makes it possible to use the device for sampling those gases,

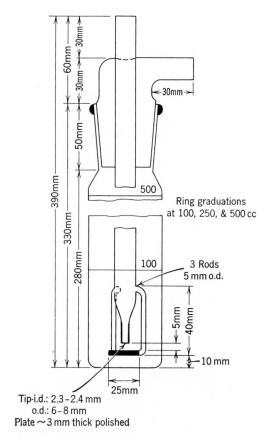

Fig. V-19. All-glass impinger.

liquids, etc. which attack rubber.   In addition, the complete nozzle can be immersed in caustic solutions for cleaning.

The Greenburg-Smith impinger and its modifications have many advantages.   One of great importance is that it has been standardized and used by the U.S. Public Health Service.   It not only acts as a dust sampling device but also as an absorber.   It is, however, a fragile instrument, it needs a strong source of power, it can rarely be used by one person alone, and it is at times exceedingly cumbersome. The other instruments described of a simpler nature can very often give equally valuable information.   Table V-3 gives a comparison of some of the instruments described.

TABLE V-3

Summary of Characteristics of Certain Dust-Sampling Instruments

Instrument	Principle of operation	Efficiency against industrial dusts, %	Applica- tion	Method of quantifi- cation	Skill in quantifi- cation	Sampling skill	Volume of sample	Advantages of instrument	Disadvantages of instrument
					Characteristics				
Impinger	Impinge- ment	98+	General	Count, gravi- metric, chemical	Consider- able	Some	Any amount: rate 1 cfm	1. High sampling efficiency in either low or high dust con- centrations 2. Sample can be estimated by counting, weighing, or chemical analy- sis 3. Can be used as absorber	1. Requires power for operation 2. Low efficiency, for certain fumes 3. Particles shattered
Electrical precipi- tator	Electrical precipi- tation	100	"	"	"	Consider- able	Any amount: rate 10–50 lpm	1. High sampling efficiency in either low or high dust con- centrations 2. Sample can be estimated by counting, weighing, or chemical analysis 3. Large samples obtained rapidly 4. Very useful for fumes	1. Requires elec- tric power for operation 2. Some danger from high voltages 3. Particles ag- glomerated

Paper thimble	Filtration	100	Gravimetric, chemical	Some	Very little	Any amount: rate 1–2 cfm	1. High sampling efficiency 2. Samples large volumes rapidly 3. Laboratory technique requires only drying and weighing for most dusts 4. Samples may be kept indefinitely without deterioration	1. Samples cannot be counted 2. Drying of thimbles is a very slow process
Membrane filter	Filtration	100	"	Count, optical measurements, some chemical centrifugal methods, bacteriologic particle size	Considerable	Very little	Any amount	1. High efficiency 2. Sample can be estimated by counting, weighing, optical measurements; chemical analysis; suitable for radiochemical determinations 3. Can be dissolved 4. Particles in original condition	1. Requires power or hand pump 2. Most types of filter cannot be used for gravimetric determinations
Thermal precipitator	Thermal precipitation	100	"	Count, gravimetric, some chemical, bacteriologic particle size	Considerable	Some	7–100 ml/min	1. High efficiency 2. Sample can be estimated by count and weight 3. Particles in original condition	1. Unwanted segregation of particles

(continued)

TABLE V-3 (*continued*)

Instrument	Principle of operation	Efficiency against industrial dusts, %	Application	Method of quantification	Skill in quantification	Sampling skill	Volume of sample	Advantages of instrument	Disadvantages of instrument
					Characteristics				
Filter paper	Filtration	50-99+	Total suspended particulate matter	Gravimetric, chemical, optical measurements	Some to considerable	Little	Any amount: order of cfm	1. Sample can be used for trace metal determination, radioactivity, smoke shade	1. Efficiency depends on type of paper
Glass filter web	Filtration	99+	Total suspended particulate matter	Gravimetric, some chemical and optical measurements	Some to considerable	Little	Any amount: order of cfm	1. Sampling can be continued for long periods, order of hours 2. Large samples can be collected 3. High sampling efficiency 4. Suitable for extraction of organic compounds 5. Can be used for radiochemical determinations	1. High ash interferes with chemical analysis 2. Variable trace element content makes evaluation of blank difficult 3. Loss of fibers causes gravimetric errors 4. Organic binder interferes sometimes
Cascade impacter	Impaction	99+	General	Particle size	Considerable	Little	Order of lpm	1. Separation of particles according to sizes 2. Particles shattered	1. Separation of particles prevents total count 2. Particles shattered

			Count	Some	Very little	Volume	Advantages	Disadvantages
Owens jet dust counter	Jet condensation	99+	Outdoor dust and for particle-size studies	Count	Some	Very little	50–1000 ml	1. Light, simple, and quick to operate 2. High efficiency for atmospheric smoke 3. No power needed for operation 4. Laboratory technique requires only a microscope	1. Dust cannot be weighed or analyzed chemically 2. Obtains only "grab" samples due to small sampling volume 3. Impractical in high dust concentrations 4. Selective action; efficient only for dusts 2 μ or less
Konimeter	"	99+	For concentrations less than 18 million particles per cubic foot	"	"	"	10 ml	1. Light, simple, and quick to operate 2. Efficiency high for moderate concentrations 3. No power needed for operation 4. Laboratory technique requires only a microscope	1. Dust cannot be weighed or analyzed chemically 2. Obtains only "grab" samples 3. Not practical in high dust concentrations; limited to 15 or 18 million particles, or less, per cubic foot

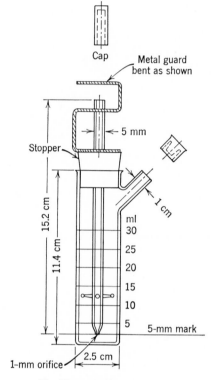

Fig. V-20. Midget impinger.

d. Midget Impinger

The midget impinger (113–115) developed by the U. S. Bureau of Mines, is a hand-cranked sampling instrument which samples at low rates of flow.   It is an efficient collecting device for toxic dusts but because of its low sampling rate, of the order of 3 lpm, the accuracy of analyses may be less than with the large impinger.   On the other hand, it can be used far more easily than the large impinger where electricity or other means of driving the air through the large impinger is not available.   Its efficiency for sampling fumes is low and therefore it should not be used for this purpose.   The usual sampling rate for the midget impinger is 0.1 cfm.

The midget impinger flask (Fig. V-20) is a flat-bottomed tube, about 11 cm long and 2.5 cm in diameter, with a side arm 1 cm in diameter

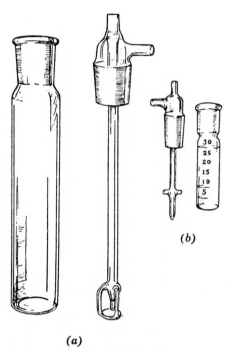

(b)

(a)

Fig. V-21.(a) All-glass impinger to show relative size of (b) midget impinger.

tilted upward at an angle of 45° to facilitate emptying, dilution, and cleaning. The flask is graduated at 5-ml intervals from 5 to 30 ml and a mark at 5 mm serves as a guide for setting the nozzle of the intake tube at the proper distance. The four projections at the lower end of the intake tube serve to hold it centrally in the flask. The orifice of the intake tube must be carefully adjusted to 1 mm. Generally 10 ml of sampling fluid is used. Solvents analogous to those employed in the regular impinger are used for the midget impinger.

All-glass midget impingers (116) are available and these are particularly useful when a collection fluid other than water is being used (Fig. V-21). If rubber-stoppered impingers are used with nonaqueous collection media, then the samples should be transferred to all-glass containers as soon as possible.

The pump specially designed for this impinger has been described in Chapter II, Section E-1-d. The pump and impinger flasks are set in a case which can be supported by an operator by means of a

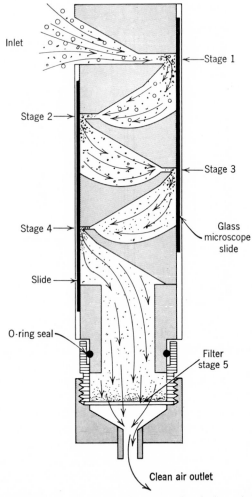

Fig. V-22a. Cascade impactor.   Pictorial cross-sectional view of the instrument
    while sampling.   The particle size is grossly exaggerated.

shoulder strap.   The flask is connected to the suction pump by
¼-in. tubing and may be placed in a small holster to be held at the
sampling point.   The apparatus is commercially available.

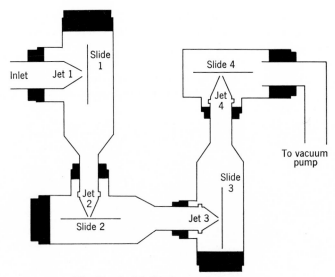

Fig. V-22b. Modified cascade impactor.

Special Impinger. Another modification of the Greenburg-Smith impinger is the portable motor-driven impinger unit devised by Smith and Friis (117). The trapping vessel is so designed as to act as an absorber. It was used particularly for sulfur dioxide estimations.

e. Cascade Impactor

The cascade impactor (118,119) is a device designed for the measurement of the particle size and concentration of airborne solid or liquid particles. This instrument consists of a series of four jets arranged perpendicularly to four glass slides at a distance of 1 mm from each slide (Fig. V-22a). The opening of each jet is made successively smaller so that when air or a gas is drawn through the device, the linear velocity increases as the gas emerges from each jet and thus particles of progressively smaller size are impacted on each succeeding slide. The size distribution can be obtained by microscopic count and by weighing the material deposited on each slide.

The device made by Sonkin (Fig. V-22b) consisted of 4 separate glass sections fitted together with rubber stoppers. The slides were held in place by indentations in the glass.

The dimensions of the jets, the air speed through the jet at flow rates of 16.5–17.5 lpm, and the approximate range of droplet size is given in Table V-4.

May (120) improved his impactor by use of movable slides. Lippmann (121) reviewed the use of the cascade impactor for particle-size determination and subsequently developed the field instru-

Fig. V-23. Field-type cascade impactor.

ment (122) which is shown in Figure V-23. The over-all dimensions of the device are $1\frac{3}{8} \times 1\frac{1}{2} \times 6$ in.; this includes a $1\frac{1}{8}$-in.-diameter filter holder and slide movement mechanism. The impaction surfaces are standard 1×3-in. microscope slides coated with a layer of silicone grease to act as the adhesive. The silicone serves two purposes: to collect the particles efficiently and to seal the slide to the body of the impactor, thus preventing air leakage. The entire device weighs 10 oz. The instrument is available commercially.

TABLE V-4
Jet Dimensions, Air Speed, and Droplet Size Obtained with Cascade Impactor
(119)

Jet number	Dimensions of jet, cm	Air speed through jet, mph	Approximate range of particle size, μ
Cascade impactor[a]			
1	1.9 × (0.6–0.7)	5	200–10
2	1.4 × 0.16	30	20–3
3	1.4 × 0.10	50	7–1
4	1.4 × 0.06	80	3–0.7
Modified cascade impactor[b]			
1	1.1 × 0.1	~60	0.7
2	0.9 × 0.08	~90	1.5–0.25
3	0.7 × 0.05	~180	1.1–0.15
4	0.7 × 0.02	<700	0.7–<0.1

[a] Air speed at flow rate of 17.5 lpm.

[b] Measurements for jet dimensions and air speed of modified cascade impactor are approximate.   Air speed at flow rate of 16.5 lpm.

References

1. Kleinfield, M., and C. P. Giel, *J. Chronic Diseases*, **9,** 117 (1959).
2. Drinker, P., and R. M. Thomson, *J. Ind. Hyg.*, **7,** 261 (1925).
3. Bloomfield, J. J., and J. M. DallaValle, *U.S. Public Health Service Bull. 217* (1938).
4. Harrington, D., *U.S. Bur. Mines Inform. Circ. 7072* (1939).
5. De Mello, J. B., *J. Ind. Hyg. Toxicol.*, **28,** 162 (1946).
6. Drinker, P., and T. Hatch, *Industrial Dust*, McGraw-Hill, New York, 1936.
7. Flury, F., and F. Zernik, *Schaedliche Gase*, Springer, Berlin, 1931.
8. Goldberg, R. W., *Occupational Diseases*, Columbia Univ. Press, New York, 1931.
9. Oliver, T., *Diseases of Occupation*, Dutton, New York, 1916.
10. Thompson, W. G., *Occupational Diseases*, Appleton, New York, 1914.
11. Drinker, P., *J. Ind. Hyg. Toxicol.*, **18,** 524 (1936).
12. *N.Y. State Special Bull. 90* (1918).
13. Caminita, B. H., W. F. Baum, P. A. Neal, and R. Schneiter, *U.S. Public Health Service Bull. 297* (1947).
14. Sayers, R. R., *U.S. Public Health Rept.*, **53,** 217 (1938).
15. Smith, A. R., *N.Y. State Ind. Bull.*, **18,** 15 (1939).
16. Greenburg, L., *U.S. Public Health Rept.*, **40,** 765 (1925).
17. Jacobs, M. B., *The Chemical Analysis of Air Pollutants*, Interscience, New York 1960.

18. Aitken, J., *Proc. Roy. Soc. (London)*, **18**, 39 (1890–91).
19. Coulier, M., *J. Pharm.*, **22**, 165 (1875).
20. Aitken, J., *Collected Scientific Papers*, University Press, Cambridge, 1923.
21. Ives, J. E., R. H. Britten, D. W. Armstrong, W. A. Gill, and F. H. Goldman, *U.S. Public Health Service Bull. 224* (1936).
22. *General Electric Rev.*, **60**, No. 4, 22 (1957); Fawcett, H. H., and G. Gardner, Am. Chem. Soc. Meeting, Chicago, 1958.
23. Green, H. L., *J. Ind. Hyg.*, **16**, 29 (1934).
24. Davies, C. N., *Proc. Roy. Soc. (London)*, **B133**, 282 (1946).
25. Green, H. L., and W. R. Lane, *Particulate Clouds: Dusts, Smokes and Mists*, Van Nostrand, New York, 1957.
26. Matthews, J. W., *Analyst*, **63**, 467 (1938).
27. Jacobs, M. B., *The Chemical Analysis of Air Pollutants*, Interscience, New York, 1960, Chaps. 1, 3, and 4.
28. Palmer, G. T., *Am. J. Pub. Health*, **6**, 54 (1916).
29. Wells, W. F., *Airborne Contagion and Air Hygiene*, Harvard Univ. Press, Cambridge, Mass., 1955.
30. Albrecht, J., *Z. Aerosol-Forsch. Therap.*, **4**, 3 (1955).
31. Rosebury, T., *Experimental Air-Borne Infection*, Williams & Wilkins, Baltimore, 1947.
32. Druett, H. A., and K. R. May, *J. Hyg.*, **50**, 69 (1952).
33. Henderson, D. W., *J. Hyg.*, **50**, 52 (1952).
34. May, K. R., and H. A. Druett, *Brit. J. Ind. Med.*, **10**, 142 (1953).
35. Naeslund, C., *J. Ind. Hyg.*, **14**, 113 (1932).
36. Drinker, P., and T. Hatch, *Industrial Dust*, McGraw-Hill, New York, 1936.
37. Drinker, P., *J. Ind. Hyg.*, **14**, 364 (1932).
38. Barnes, E. C., *Am. J. Public Health*, **26**, 274 (1936).
39. Barnes, E. C., and G. W. Penney, *J. Ind. Hyg. Toxicol.*, **20**, 259 (1938).
40. Lea, W. L., *J. Ind. Hyg. Toxicol.*, **25**, 152 (1943).
41. Wilner, T., *Am. Ind. Hyg. Assoc. Quarterly*, **12**, 115 (1951).
42. Lauterbach, K. E., T. T. Mercer, A. D. Hayes, and P. E. Morrow, *A.M.A. Arch. Ind. Hyg.*, **9**, 69 (1954).
43. Aitken, J., *Collected Scientific Papers*, University Press, Cambridge, 1923.
44. Green, H. L., and H. H. Watson, *Med. Council Privy Council Special Reprint 199*, London (1935).
45. Watson, H. H., *J. Chem. Met. Mining Soc. S. Africa*, **37**, 166 (1936); *Analyst*, **62**, 232 (1937).
46. Kethley, T., M. T. Gordon, and C. Orr, *Science*, **116**, 358 (1952).
47. Wright, B. M., *Science*, **119**, 195 (1953).
48. Gordon, M. T., and C. Orr, "Thermal Precipitation in Air Pollution Studies," Air Pollution Control Assoc. Meeting, Chattanooga, May 1954.
49. Orr, C., M. T. Gordon, and M. C. Kordecki, *Appl. Microbiol.*, **4**, 116 (1956).
50. Shaw, N., and J. S. Owens, *The Smoke Problem of Great Cities*, Constable, London, 1925.
51. Jacobs, M. B., *The Chemical Analysis of Air Pollutants*, Interscience, New York, 1960, Chaps. 1, 4, and 5.
52. Elford, W. J., *J. Pathol. Bacteriol.*, **34**, 505 (1931).

53. Elford, W. J., *Proc. Roy. Soc. (London)*, **B112**, 384 (1933).
54. Jander, G., and J. Zakowski, *Membranfilter, Cella und Ultrafeinfilter*, Akademische Verlag, Leipzig, 1929.
55. Burstein, E., See Fraser, *A.M.A. Arch. Hyg. Occupational Med.*, **8**, 412 (1953).
56. Grabar, P., *L'Ultrafilteration Fractionnée*, Hermann Paris, 1943.
57. Jacobs, M. B., *Analytical Chemistry of Industrial Poisons, Hazards, and Solvents*, 2nd ed., Interscience, New York, 1949, p. 124.
58. Goetz, A., *Fial Final Rept. 1312*, Joint Intelligence Objectives Agency, U. S. Dept. Commerce, 1947.
59. Goetz, A., and N. Tsuneishi, *J. Am. Water Works Assoc.*, **43**, 943 (1951).
60. Clark, H. F., E. E. Geldreich, H. L. Jeter, and P. W. Kabler, *Public Health Rept.*, **66**, 951 (1951).
61. Goetz, A., *Am. J. Public Health*, **43**, 150 (1953).
62. First, M. W., and L. Silverman, *A.M.A. Arch. Ind. Hyg. Occupational Med.*, **7**, 1 (1953).
63. Resnik, J. B., *Gigiena i Sanit.*, 28–31 (Oct. 1951).
64. Millipore Filter Corp., Bedford, Mass.; Gelman Instrument Co., Chelsea, Mich.; Schleicher and Schnell, Keene, N. H.
65. Gelman, C., *Air Eng.*, **1**, No. 4, 25 (July 1959).
66. Jacobs, M. B., *The Chemical Analysis of Air Pollutants*, Interscience, New York, 1960, Chaps. 5, 6, 7, and 13.
67. Brown, C. E., *U.S. Bur. Mines Rept. Invest. 3788* (1944).
68. Silverman, L., and J. F. Ege, Jr., *J. Ind. Hyg. Toxicol.*, **25**, 185 (1943).
69. Bayrer, O. D., and W. A. Hough, *J. Ind. Hyg. Toxicol.*, **27**, 89 (1945).
70. Katz, S. H., and G. W. Smith, *U.S. Bur. Mines Rept. Invest. 2378* (1922).
71. Yant, W. P., E. Levy, R. R. Sayers, C. E. Brown, C. E. Traubert. H. W. Frevert, and K. L. Marshall, *U.S. Bur. Mines Rept. Invest. 3585* (1941).
72. Silverman, L., and C. R. Williams, *J. Ind. Hyg. Toxicol.*, **28**, 21 (1946).
73. Hemeon, W. C. L., "Determination of Haze and Smoke by Filter Paper Samplers," Air Pollution Control Assoc. Meeting, Pittsburgh, May 1954.
74. Von Brand Filtering Recorders, Hopewell Junction, N. Y.
75. Clayton, G. D., *Determination of Atmospheric Contaminants*, Am. Gas Assoc., New York, 1955.
76. Nader, J. S., "A Versatile, High Flowrate Tape Sampler," Air Pollution Control Assoc. Meeting, Philadelphia, May 1958.
77. Millipore Filter Corp., Bedford Mass.
78. Burstein, A. I., *J. Ind. Hyg.*, **10**, 279 (1928); **12**, 24 (1930).
79. Trostel, L. J., and H. W. Frevert, *Ind. Eng. Chem.*, **15**, 232 (1923).
80. Bubar, H., *Dust Problems*, Dust Recovery, New York, 1930.
81. Jacobs, M. B., *The Chemical Analysis of Air Pollutants*, Interscience, New York, 1960, Ch. VII, pp. 155–57.
82. Fieldner, A. C., S. H. Katz, and E. S. Longfellow, *U.S. Bur. Mines Tech. Paper 278* (1921).
83. Katz, S. H., G. W. Smith, and W. M. Meyers, *J. Ind. Hyg.*, **8**, 300 (1926).
84. Frankland, P. F., *Phil. Trans. Roy. Soc.*, **A178**, 113 (1886).
85. McNair, L. C., and J. F. Hirst, *J. Ind. Hyg.*, **11**, 336 (1929).

86. Briscoe, H. V. A., J. W. Matthews, P. F. Holt, and P. M. Sanderson, *Trans. Inst. Mining Met.*, **46**, 145 (1936).

87. Matthews, J. W., and H. V. A. Briscoe, *Trans. Inst. Mining Met.*, **44**, 11 (1934).

88. Fritzsche, P., *Z. Anal. Chem.*, **37**, 92 (1898).

89. Hahn, M., Ger. Pat. 201,789 (1907).

90. Harrold, G. C., S. F. Meek, G. R. Collins, and T. F. Markall, *J. Ind. Hyg. Toxicol.*, **26**, 47 (1944).

91. Keenan, R. G., and L. T. Fairhall, *J. Ind. Hyg. Toxicol.*, **26**, 241 (1944).

92. Davies, C. N., M. Aylward, and D. Leacey, *A.M.A. Arch. Ind. Hyg. Occupational Med.*, **4**, 354 (1951).

93. Innes, J., *J. Chem. Met. Mining Soc. S. Africa*, **19**, 132 (1919).

94. Thomson, R. M., *J. Ind. Hyg.*, **7**, 385 (1925).

95. Littlefield, J. B., C. E. Brown, and H. H. Schrenk, *U.S. Bur. Mines Inform. Circ. 6993* (1938).

96. Haldane, J. S., and J. I. Graham, *Methods of Air Analysis*, Griffin, London, 1935.

97. Sayers, R. R., P. A. Neal, R. R. Jones, J. J. Bloomfield, J. M. DallaValle, and T. I. Edwards, *U.S. Public Health Service Bull. 234* (1937).

98. Rowley, F. B., and R. C. Jordan, *J. Ind. Hyg. Toxicol.*, **25**, 293 (1943).

99. Owens, J. S., *J. Ind. Hyg.*, **4**, 522 (1923).

100. Hatch, T., and E. W. Thompson, *J. Ind. Hyg.*, **16**, 93 (1934).

101. Gurney, S. W., C. R. Williams, and R. R. Meigs, *J. Ind. Hyg. Toxicol.*, **20**, 24 (138).

102. Greenburg, L., and G. W. Smith, *U.S. Bur. Mines Rept. Invest. 2392* (1922).

103. Katz, S. H., G. W. Smith, W. M. Meyers, L. J. Trostel, M. Ingels, and L. Greenburg, *U.S. Public Health Service Bull. 144* (1925).

104. Greenburg, L., and J. J. Bloomfield, *U.S. Public Health Service Reprint 1528* (1935).

105. Brown, C. E., and H. H. Schrenk, *U.S. Bur. Mines Inform. Circ. 7026* (1938).

106. Bloomfield, J. J., *Am. Public Health Assoc. Yearbook 1935–36*, p. 86.

107. *Am. Public Health Assoc. Yearbook 1939–40*, p. 92.

108. *Ind. Hyg. Newsletter*, **7**, No. 5, 15 (1947).

109. Littlefield, J. B., F. L. Feicht, and H. H. Schrenk, *U.S. Bur. Mines Rept. Invest. 3401* (1938).

110. Hatch, T., H. Warren, and P. Drinker, *J. Ind. Hyg.*, **14**, 301 (1932).

111. Badham, C., H. E. G. Rayner, and H. D. Broose, *Rept. Director-General Public Health, New South Wales*, Serial No. 12 (1927).

112. DallaValle, J. M., *U.S. Public Health Service Reprint 1848* (1937).

113. Littlefield, J. B., F. L. Feicht, and H. H. Schrenk, *U.S. Bur. Mines Rept. Invest. 3360* (1937).

114. Littlefield, J. B., and H. H. Schrenk, *U.S. Bur. Mines Rept. Invest. 3387* (1938).

115. Schrenk, H. H., and F. L. Feicht, *U.S. Bur. Mines Inform. Circ. 7076* (1939).

116. Engineering Unit, Div. Ind. Hyg., U.S. Public Health Service, *Ind. Eng. Chem. Anal. Ed.*, **16**, 346 (1944).

117. Smith, R. B., and B. S. T. Friis, *J. Ind. Hyg.*, **13**, 338 (1931).

118. May, K. R., *J. Sci. Instr.*, **22,** 187 (1945).
119. Sonkin, L. S., *J. Ind. Hyg. Toxicol.*, **28,** 269 (1946).
120. May, K. R., *A.M.A. Arch. Ind. Health*, **13,** 481 (1956).
121. Lippmann, M., *Am. Ind. Hyg. Assoc. J.*, **20,** 406 (1959).
122. Lippmann, M., *Am. Ind. Hyg. Assoc. J.*, **22,** 348 (1961).

CHAPTER VI

METHODS OF DUST EVALUATION

Methods for the evaluation of dust fall into a number of major categories: those in which (*1*) the number of particles is estimated, (*2*) the size and frequency or size distribution are determined, (*3*) a measure of the weight or mass is obtained, and (*4*) the blackness or opacity of a deposit is measured.

A. Counting of Dust Particles

It was explained in a previous section that one of the methods used for the estimation of dust particles is the counting of the particles and the subsequent correlation of the count with the volume of air sampled. Dust counts have a threefold application: (*1*) They are an index of the dustiness of a working atmosphere. (*2*) They help to determine the effectiveness of dust-removal equipment. (*3*) They can be used in conjunction with medical data to determine the threshold or safe limit of exposure to a specific dust. Dust counts are a quantitative measure of a working environment. Coupled with a knowledge of the safe or threshold limits (Tables 6 and 7, Appendix), they may be used to tell whether the atmospheric conditions found are inimical to the health of workers. DallaValle (1) recommends that dust counts be expressed as being greater or less than a maximum tolerance, such as the threshold limit, without any reference to the actual counts themselves.

In the preceding chapter, methods for the collection of dust samples have been detailed. The methods employed in counting these different types of samples are also varied. For instance, in using samples collected by the macro or the midget impinger, a direct count using an ordinary microbiological microscope provided with a 10× objective and a 7.5 or 10× ocular is the general practice whereas membrane-filter samples are often counted with a 97× objective. Owens jet dust counter and similar dust counter samples must be counted with an oil-immersion or 97× objective. Many more particles of smaller size will be seen and counted with the oil-immersion lenses than with the 10× objectives used for the impinger samples. Consequently, the size distribution will be markedly different in these methods and the average size of the particles counted in the oil-immersion method will be smaller than the average size of those counted with the 10× objectives.

Indeed, the counting of particles is reminiscent of the well-known quip paraphrasing Swift's *On Poetry—A Rhapsody* (1733):

> Little fleas have lesser fleas
> Upon their backs to bite 'em
> And lesser fleas have smaller fleas
> And so *ad infinitum*.

So too, in the counting of particles, an increase in the power of the objective increases the number of particles of smaller size that can be seen. Methods range from using a 10× objective, as mentioned, of the light microscope through the oil-immersion 97× objective of the light microscope to the very high magnification of the electron microscope. Actually all of these have been used to count and, in particular, measure the size of particles collected on membrane filters (2). If valid comparisons of counts are to be made, they must be made only on samples in which the objective magnification is essentially the same or on samples in which methods have been used about which the correlation of count is known.

1. Impinger Samples

An estimate in an aliquot portion of a water or other solvent suspension can be made by counting the dust particles with the aid of a microscope where (1) the dust particles are caught in a medium such as water, ethyl alcohol, *n*-propyl alcohol, or isopropyl alcohol, as, for example, in the Greenburg-Smith impinger, which is the method approved by the U. S. Public Health Service; (2) the dust is absorbed or filtered out by sugar or some other solid, which can subsequently be dissolved and the dust suspended in water, for example, in the sugar-tube method; (3) the dust can be shaken from a lintless hardened filter paper of high wet strength and suspended in a dust-free liquid; or (4) the dust is trapped on a filter such as a membrane filter or polystyrene filter that can be dissolved in a dust-free liquid.

Greenburg and Bloomfield (3) recommended the following procedure. As soon as practicable and preferably before 24 hr have elapsed be-

Fig. VI-1. Sedgewick-Rafter cell. (Courtesy Will Scientific Inc.)

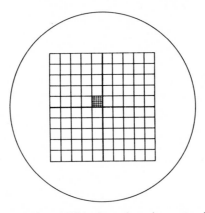

Fig. VI-2. Ruling of Whipple ocular micrometer disk.

cause dust particles are slightly soluble in water, remove and carefully wash the stopper of the flask in which the sampling was done.
Add the washings to the contents of the flask. Filter the entire
sample into a volumetric flask through a screen of approximately
325-mesh fineness. This will eliminate all particles over 40 μ,
for only smaller ones will go through the filter. If the dust suspension in the volumetric flask is too dense, it should be transferred to
a larger volumetric flask and diluted further, or an aliquot should be
removed and diluted to a known volume. The dilution should be
continued until the number of particles counted in each microscope
field is about 50–75. Agitate the contents of the volumetric flask
so that a uniform suspension is obtained. Remove two 1-ml aliquots
with a 1-ml pipet and just fill two Sedgwick-Rafter counting cells
(Fig. VI-1).

A Whipple ocular micrometer disk (Fig. VI-2) or a modification
(Fig. VI-4) should be used as the eyepiece. This disk has a large
square engraved on it, covering a large part of the field, and this

square is divided into 100 medium-sized squares. One of these is in turn further subdivided into 25 small squares. Using an ordinary microscope provided with a suitable eyepiece (7.5 or 10✕) and objective (16 mm or 10✕) and fitted with an Abbe condenser, the proper tube length of the microscope is determined by calibration with a stage micrometer, so that the side of the large square of the eyepiece covers 1000 μ (1 mm). The large square of the eyepiece ruling, therefore, encloses the dust in an area of 1 mm²; and since the cell is 1 mm deep, all the dust suspended in 1 mm³ of the water is under the ruled field. This examination is accomplished by raising and lowering the lens system so as to focus throughout the entire depth of the cell. As a source of illumination, an ordinary small electric microscope lamp may be used.

The dust is permitted to settle for 20 min before counting is done if water is used and for 25–30 min with other solvents. In general, only particles less than 10 μ in diameter are counted for the reasons previously given. The inclusion of particles larger than 10 μ makes very little difference in the total count. The average diameter of a particle for the purpose of this exclusion is judged by inspection. In practice it is necessary to count the dust in only one-quarter of each ruled field, the entire field having been examined for uniformity. Such counts on 5 fields, so dispersed as to be representative, are made on each of the two Sedgwick-Rafter cells. These 10 counts are averaged, but this average is not to be taken as the final count until a corresponding control count has been subtracted. In all cases a sampling flask that has been handled in the plant, but through which no air has been aspirated, is used as the control for the particular series of samples taken in that plant on that particular day, and counts are made on this control fluid in the same manner as on the fluid through which the air sample has been impinged. The control sample takes into consideration any dust which may be present in the eyepiece micrometer, in the lenses of the microscope, in the Sedgwick-Rafter counting cell, and in the sampling liquid itself. From the average gross count obtained on the impinger sample, the average control count is to be subtracted to give the average net count per one-quarter microscopic field.

The average net count per one-quarter microscopic field is multiplied by 4 to yield the average count in the total field. Since the Sedgwick-Rafter cell is 1 mm deep, this figure represents the number of particles in 1 mm³ of the diluted sample. This value is multiplied by 1000 to give the count per milliliter of sample and again by the total number of milliliters of liquid to which the original sample was diluted. This product is divided by the number of cubic feet of air sampled.

To summarize, the number of particles per cubic foot of air equals the average net count per one-quarter field multiplied by a factor, where the factor equals

$$\frac{4 \times 1000 \times \text{total volume of diluted sample in ml}}{\text{Volume of air sampled in cubic feet}}$$

The average dust exposure of a worker is ascertained by multiplying the average dust concentration obtained in the count in each activity by the time spent in the atmosphere (1).

In addition to the light-field technique detailed above, particles can be counted by a special dark-field procedure using a microscope (4) fitted with a dark-field condenser, painted with a black spot in the middle of the underside of the bottom lens of the condenser, a 16-mm (0.25 numerical aperture) objective, and a 30× compensated eyepiece containing a micrometer outlining an area of 0.01 mm². More particles can be seen by the dark-field procedure than by the light-field method.

The limit of visibility (5) for counting dust in impinger and filter-paper samples by the light-field method has been found by Brown and Feicht (6) to be of the order of 0.9 μ for a microscope equipped with an objective having a numerical aperture of 0.30 and 1 μ for a microscope equipped with an objective having a numerical aperture of 0.25. Not all particles down to this size are included in a count because some of them fail to settle. In the dark-field method, using an objective with a numerical aperture of 0.30, the limit of visibility appears to be 0.4 μ; hence, more particles can be counted by the dark-field procedure than by the light-field method. Counting may also be performed by means of a microprojector (see Section B-2-b of this chapter).

First and Silverman (7) pointed out that when using a midget impinger and a Neubauer counting cell, each particle counted under the microscope usually represented 2.5×10^6 particles in the original sample. For a 10-min sample taken at a rate of 0.1 cfm, each particle represented one-half of the threshold limit for silica dust. Consequently, they implied that membrane filter determinations of dust counts were to be preferred.

a. Modified Counting Cells

In addition to the Sedgwick-Rafter cell other counting cells are available (8).   Hatch and Pool (9) describe a one-piece cell (Fig. VI-3), which has a depth of 0.25 mm.   Its main advantage lies in its one-piece rugged construction.   It takes less time for the dust to settle in this cell since it is one-fourth as deep as the Sedgwick-Rafter cell.

Williams (10) uses a Spencer "Bright-Line" hemacytometer. The cover glass is placed on glass supports, which are raised from the body of the slide as in the Hatch cell, but the clearance is only 0.1 mm.   Because of this depth, this cell requires practically no waiting time at all before making the counts (11).

The Dunn (12) counting cell is made of Pyrex glass.   It consists of two parts, one of which is a glass plate 1 mm thick, ground on both surfaces, with a central hole of such a diameter that the cell will hold approximately 0.25 ml.   An optical flat, polished slide completes the arrangement.

Couchman and Schulze (13) describe a circular glass-disk counting cell.   The disk is held between two threaded circular metal frames.

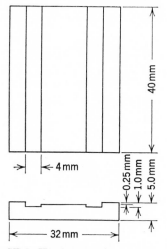

Fig. VI-3. Hatch one-piece counting cell.

The upper frame has a central circular opening 35.6 mm in diameter and is machined to 1 mm thickness. The accuracy of the cell is dependent upon the latter dimension. The other dimensions need only be approximate. Its greatest advantage lies in the replaceability of the glass disk. It is also easy to clean.

Double circular cells, one a two-hole, two-piece cell having circular brass rings cemented to a microscope slide and the other a three-piece cell having two circular holes in a microscope slide, have been suggested by Brown (8). These cells have the advantage that both of the cell parts can be filled (preferably not with the same pipetful of sample liquid), counted, and washed at the same time.

b. Modified Ocular Micrometer for Dust Counting

In making plankton counts, it is customary to count the whole field covered by the Whipple micrometer disk. In making dust counts, on the other hand, it is the practice to count the dust in only one-quarter of each ruled field. Only one of the three quadrants which do not contain the finely subdivided square is counted; the remaining three are unused and are therefore unnecessary. To facilitate the counting of dust samples, a micrometer (14) similar to that shown in Figure IV-4 may be used. The ruled grid corresponding to one quadrant of the Whipple grid is located in the center of the visible field. The grid consists of an etched square of 3.5-mm side measurement, divided into 25 small squares. Results obtained

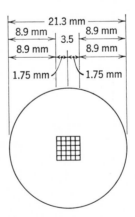

Fig. VI-4. Modified ocular micrometer.

with this micrometer disk are identical with results obtained when counting one-fourth of the Whipple field. Calculations are made in a manner entirely analogous to that detailed for the Whipple disk.

c. ACGIH Method

It must be remembered that the threshold limits for dusts set by the American Conference of Governmental Industrial Hygienists are based on the standardized technique adopted by that organization in 1942. If such standards are to be used as guides, then the method of count and sampling should follow this technique or some other method having a reasonable correlation with the ACGIH method. (See the discussion in Section E of this chapter on comparison of methods.)

The ACGIH method is used for the determination of the atmospheric concentration of insoluble inorganic dusts such as those associated with the production of lung fibrosis, the particle sizes of which are generally below 10 μ and not below 0.5 μ.

Sampling Instrument. The sampling instrument is the U. S. Public Health Service macro (Greenburg-Smith) impinger, an acceptable modification, or a standard midget impinger. The macro impinger should operate at a rate of 1.0 cfm at 3 in. Hg negative pressure and the midget impinger at a rate of 0.1 cfm at 12 in. water negative pressure.

Any type of suction apparatus may be employed which is capable of maintaining the rate of flow within $\pm 3\%$ of the rated capacity, i.e., within 1.0 cfm for the macro and 0.1 cfm for the midget impinger, and which is equipped with a calibrated flowmeter and indicating gauge. The use of a constant-flow orifice is recommended by the ACGIH with the compressed air ejector and an automatic negative pressure regulator with the motor or hand-driven pump. If an indirect-indicating gauge is used, it should be checked against a U-tube flowmeter or dry meter at regular intervals.

Sampling. Use distilled water with or without ethyl or isopropyl alcohol as the collecting liquid. The collecting liquid and the liquid used for the subsequent washing and diluting steps should not contain more than six countable particles in a 0.25-mm^2 counting area in the counting cell. A blank count must be made for each series of samples.

All the glassware must be thoroughly cleaned and then protected against contamination by dust in the field. One impinger flask should be used to carry the blank and should be handled in the same manner as the impingers for collecting the test samples except that no air is drawn through it.

The number and spacing of the samples at a given operation, the location of the sampling points, and the length of each sampling period should be selected in such a manner as to yield a sample representative of the exposure throughout an operation cycle; a sample should also be taken to indicate the peak concentration. At least two samples should be taken at each sampling point.

In addition to the samples that are collected in the breathing zone of the exposed workers, samples should be taken to determine the dust concentration in the general workroom atmosphere and, in special studies, to determine the sources of the dust dispersion or distribution.

Microscope and Apparatus. The microscope used should be a conventional biological instrument or its equivalent, preferably equipped so that the length of the tube can be adjusted. It should also be equipped with an Abbe condenser with an iris diaphragm, a 16-mm objective, and a 7.5 or 10X ocular.

The microscope tube length should be adjusted so that the counting area corresponds to 0.25 mm² in the counting cell, or, in the case of a fixed tube length, the ruled area should be equivalent to 0.25 mm² ±3%.

The illumination should be provided by means of a 15-W substage lamp placed directly under the condenser, or by a 75-W microscope lamp placed 10 in. from the plane mirror. A "daylight" filter should be used.

The counting area should be defined by an ocular grid or by rulings on the counting cell. It should have an area equivalent to 0.25 mm² in the counting cell and should be divided into 25 subsquares.

A standard counting cell with a liquid depth of 1.0 mm should be employed. Counting cells less than 1.0 mm in depth may be used but the liquid depth should be reported with the dust concentration obtained with this type of cell.

The counting area defined by an ocular grid should be accurately measured by means of a stage micrometer and should be recorded with the dust concentration data.

The cells must be cleaned before use and the efficiency of cleaning should be checked by examination under the microscope before being filled with the test or blank solution.

Sample Dilution.   Make the sample up to a known volume, after washing and removing the impinger nozzle.   The dilution should be adjusted in such a manner that the test specimen used contains at least 4 times the number of particles in the blank and less than 150 particles in any 0.25-mm^2 counting area.   If the initial dilution has to be diluted additionally to reduce the field count to the specified number, the dilution should be made in steps not exceeding 1:10. Mix the suspension by vigorous agitation before removing the aliquot to be diluted.   This aliquot should be not less than 10% of the total volume of the suspension to be diluted, except that the minimum volume used should not be less than 5 ml.   The need for large dilutions can be avoided by selecting a proper sampling time in relation to the dust concentration expected.

Preparation of Sample.   Shake the suspension to be counted vigorously and transfer an aliquot immediately to the cell by means of a pipet.   Take care to prevent the inclusion of bubbles of air.   Fill one or more cells with portions of each sample.   Allow the cell contents to settle before counting for at least 30 min for the 1.0-mm cell and for proportionately less time for the cells of lesser depth.   Make up one cell from the blank flask for every series of samples.   Do not fill the cells in advance of the time required for settling before counting.

Counting Procedure.   Count in a darkened room, using the artificial illumination detailed on the microscope apparatus in this section.   Center the light and mirror so that no shift of position of the particles is seen when focusing up and down.   Adjust the condenser and diaphragm to give an even, moderate illumination.   Each observer must determine and use the optimum lighting for his own eyes.

Examine the field of the microscope before counting and, if required, clean the ocular grid to remove any dust particles that may be present.   Make the count in a plane just above the surface of the cell rather than throughout the depth of the liquid.   The microscope may be focused up and down by means of the fine adjustment in order to bring individual particles into focus.   Before making the count, also examine the cell contents carefully throughout the entire depth to make certain that all of the countable particles have settled.

Count five fields 0.25 mm^2 in area, one in the central part and four toward the edges of the cell.   It is not necessary to make any distinction between the number of particles above and below 10 μ in size except in the case of abnormal samples.

Calculation.   Express the concentration of dust in millions of particles per cubic foot of air (MPPCF), and report only to two significant figures.   Compute the number as follows:

$$\mathrm{MPPCF} = \frac{(N_s - N_b) \times CF \times V_w}{V_a}$$

where

N_s = mean count per field for the sample for 5 or more fields
N_b = mean count per field for the blank for 5 or more fields
CF = cell factor

$$= \frac{1000}{\text{(area of counting field in mm}^2) \times \text{(depth of cell in mm)}}$$

V_w = total water volume (equivalent total, when aliquot diluted, i.e., initial sample volume $\times$ dilution factor)
V_a = air volume sample in cubic feet

2. MEMBRANE FILTER SAMPLES

There are several variations used for counting membrane filter samples.   First and Silverman (7), using a light-field technique, suggest putting the membrane filter with the dust side down on a clean microscope slide, adding a few drops of oil to the upper side, and counting immediately.   In their dark-field technique, they suggest using black membrane filters which are subsequently examined with a surface-illuminated microscope objective.   With this type of microscope the light intercepted by the dust particles is reflected and thus the particles are seen as bright spots against the black background.

Paulus et al. (15) also place the filter membrane dust side down on a slide, add a drop of immersion oil of refractive index 1.5, and count as in the light-field technique.   They recommend subtracting a count made on a blank membrane filter.

Whitby et al. (16) used Hydrosol-type Millipore filters because of their lack of grain under the microscope.   Sampling time was adjusted to give a final optical density of 0.03.   A 0.5-in. square is cut out of the filter and is placed face down on a cover glass and, after wetting with immersion oil, the cover slip is placed on a slide, care being taken to prevent any relative motion between the filter and the cover slip.   In effect, the dust particles are now face up.

Counting is performed with the aid of a Porton graticule in a microscope equipped with a 97× objective, 1.25 numerical aperture, a 10× ocular, and a blue diffusing filter below the substage condenser.   A multistage count, in the manner of Work (17) is made. Approximately 1000 particles in at least 50 fields are counted.

To avoid movement of the particles to the periphery of the filter and to count in a manner that would correlate fairly well with impinger samples, the following technique may be used

Procedure.   Place the membrane filter dust side up on a clean microscope slide.   Place thickened collodion or Duco cement on the membrane and then put a clean cover glass on top of the cement. Examine the slide, fixed in this manner, with a conventional microbiological microscope employing a 16-mm objective and the customary 7.5 or 10× ocular.   As in the ACGIH method, a 0.25-mm² field should not contain more than 150 particles.   Subtract a blank membrane dust count using a membrane and slide prepared in an identical manner.

If the dust concentrations are higher than this value per field, dissolve the filter in acetone.   Make up to a known volume with this solvent.   Place an aliquot in a Dunn cell and count in the manner described in the ACGIH method detailed in Section A-1-c of this chapter.

For counting outdoor and residential dust samples and samples in which the size of the dust particles is mainly below 1 μ, the low magnification used in the method detailed in the preceding section is inadequate for it does not give sufficient differentiation, and higher magnification techniques must be employed.   Jacobs (18) details methods for the counting of membrane filter samples of outdoor dust in air pollution studies and Jacobs, Manoharan, and Goldwater (19) discuss the use of membrane filter counting methods in the counting of "domestic" atmospheric dust.

3. Counting Konimeter Samples

The konimeter glass plate upon which the samples are impinged is particularly adapted for microscope counting.   The glass plate with its numbered samples is adjusted on the microscope stand with

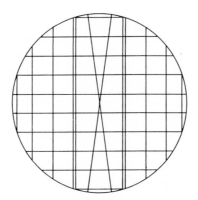

Fig. VI-5. Konimeter ocular micrometer.

the aid of a special holder having a pinion similar to that on the konimeter. This device enables one to bring the various dust spots into view much more simply than can be done with the naked eye, for once one spot is located, the others may readily be turned into position. The microscope is provided with an ocular and objective so adjusted as to give approximately a 200-diameter magnification. An 8-mm or 20✕ objective and a 10✕ ocular have been found to give this result. A 10✕ (16-mm) objective with a compensated 20✕ eyepiece is also used (20). A micrometer screen placed in the ocular is so designed as to have two cross lines which outline 9° sectors (Fig. VI-5) or 18° sectors. It is necessary for the microscopist to project imaginary lines to the center of the sectors, for these do not actually extend that far. If such lines were drawn to the center, they would obscure that portion of the spot having the most particles.

Before the actual counting of the dust particles is begun, a blank determination is run on unused portions of the glass plate. Usually four sectors are averaged for the blank determination. This blank determination is necessary in order to obtain a count of the dust impurities in the petrolatum or glycerine jelly. It is subtracted from the sample counts. The petrolatum used in practice has a refractive index of 1.48, enabling most dusts that occur in industry to be readily visible.

The dust spots are adjusted under the microscope so that the ocular sectors divide them symmetrically. All the particles in one sector are then counted; by rotating the eyepiece other portions of the spot are brought into the sector. Counting four such sectors on one spot has been found to give a representative result. Subtracting the blank and then multiplying by 10 will give the dust count in the entire spot. This factor is used because four 9° sectors have been counted, which gives a total of 36°. Ten times 36° equals 360°, or, in other words, the dust count for the entire spot. If the konimeter samples exactly 10 ml of air per stroke, then it is unnecessary to multiply by the factor 10 in order to obtain the number of dust particles per milliliter, as the tens cancel out. The following formula can be used to calculate the number of particles per milliliter:

$$\frac{\text{no. particles in four } 9° \text{ sectors, or } 36° \times 10}{\text{ml sampled per konimeter stroke}} = \text{no. particles per ml}$$

If 18° sectors are used, generally two sectors are counted and the calculations are made as above. For more accurate work four 18° sectors are counted, but in this instance the factor 10 must be replaced by 5.

To obtain the number of particles per cubic foot in millions, multiply the result by 28,320 and divide by 1 million.

The konimeter was used widely in several countries of the British Commonwealth, namely, in Canada, the Union of South Africa, and Australia. In these countries, it was common to use heat-resistant glass sampling disks, which can be ignited and acid washed before being counted. Thus, for instance, with mineral oil as the adhesive film, the plate was heated to a dull cherry red in a muffle oven, cooled, washed with a few drops of 50% hydrochloric acid and subsequently with water and alcohol, and warmed to remove the alcohol. The dust sample was then counted with dark-field illumination and a magnification of 150 diameters (see also page 278).

4. OWENS JET DUST COUNTER SAMPLES

It was pointed out that dust particles impinged on slides with the Owens jet dust counter were examined under an oil-immersion objective. The ribbon of dust produced by this sampling instrument may be located with the aid of a 16-mm objective and dark-ground illumination. Dark-ground illumination may be readily obtained by inserting a suitable stop under the substage condenser. Counts

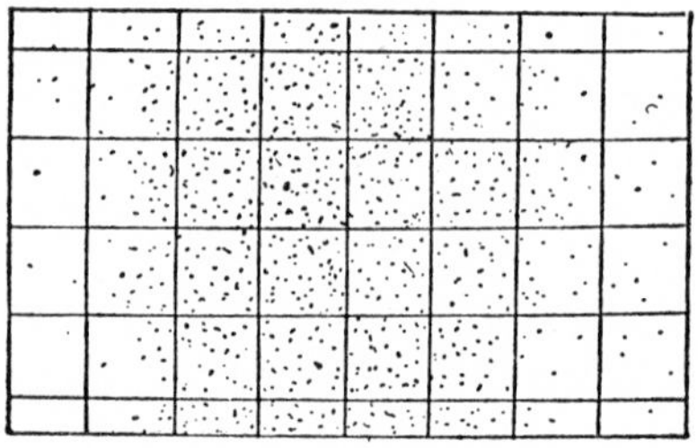

Fig. VI-6. Typical Owens dust record and ruled ocular disk (3).

of the particles are generally made using a $\frac{1}{12}$-in. oil-immersion objective. In order to facilitate counting, the eyepiece is provided with a net-ruled micrometer of 1-mm squares (Fig. VI-6). With the aid of this eyepiece micrometer, a count of the number of particles in a strip one square wide is made across the entire record at one or two places and an average is taken. This figure multiplied into a factor, depending on the magnification used, will give the number of dust particles on the record. To determine the factor it is first necessary to ascertain the number of strips in the length of the sample ribbon. This may be done by low magnification. For example, with a $\frac{2}{3}$-in. objective, 50 strips in the length of the ribbon are found. Then, the $\frac{1}{12}$-in. objective, which is found to magnify 10 times as much as the $\frac{2}{3}$-in. objective, will have 500 strips. Assuming that 300 particles are found in a strip across the ribbon using a $\frac{1}{12}$-in. objective and that the volume of air sampled was 50 ml, then the number of particles per milliliter will be

$$\frac{300 \times 500}{50} = 3000$$

If S represents the number of strips found in the record, N the number of particles per strip, and V the number of milliliters drawn through the jet in making the record, then

$$\frac{N \times S}{V} = \text{no. particles per ml}$$

Actually, the dust record made by the Owens jet dust counter is not a ribbon of equal width throughout its entire length, for it has knob-like ends. Therefore, the count as described above is not exactly correct. Kagan and Broumstein (21) use a graphic method

Fig. VI-7. Shape of Owens dust record (greatly magnified).

of distribution triangles.   For most practical purposes the counting method described above serves adequately.

5. Electronic Counting

Particles in aerosols may be counted electronically by an experimental device described by Guyton (22).   In this instrument a vacuum sucks the air through a jet at high speed so that particles in the air stream are impacted against a wire or metal plate.   The impact of impingement produces an electrical impulse that can be amplified and recorded either on a counter or an oscilloscope.   This electrical pulse appears to be generated electrostatically between the particle and the pickup wire or between the particle and the turbulent air in the nozzle.   With a jet aperture of 0.8 mm in diameter, a jet taper of 45°, and a wire 0.4 mm in diameter almost in contact with the orifice, 61% of the particles are counted.   There is no additional change in air flow when the pressure difference between the two ends of the pickup is increased beyond the critical value of 360 mm Hg. By holding the vacuum line pressure below the critical value, equivalent to a critical flow of 5.75 lpm, it is not necessary to record the flow.   The air flows from the jet at about 345 m/sec, approximately the speed of sound.

When a metal plate is used, it is held at 1 mm from the opening of the jet.   With the plate all particles above a certain size are counted. The pulse duration is a limiting factor in the efficiency of the device. Water particles do not record readily unless the pickup wire is charged. The particle size recorded is of the order of 2.5 μ and above, but smaller particles may be counted by altering the design of the machine. The device may possibly be constructed to count concentrations of particles from a few particles to several million per liter.

Gucker and a number of co-workers (23–25) developed a series of instruments for the automatic counting of air-borne particles which depend upon the pickup of light scattered by an individual particle by a photoelectric cell.   This pulse is amplified and counted by a scaler.   The first instruments were only able to count particles with a minimum size of 1 μ, but by use of stops to eliminate extraneous light and by collecting and focusing the light scattered by the particles being counted on a photomultiplier cell a considerable reduction in the size necessary to actuate the instrument was achieved.

Peterson (26) also developed a differential photometer in which the optical system elaborated by LaMer and Sinclair (27) was employed. Here dark-field illumination was used to light up the particles which scattered this light onto a photomultiplier.

Another instrument that depends on the scattering of light is the Sinclair-Phoenix forward-scattering aerosol and smoke photometer (29,30). In the optical projection system of this instrument, a diaphragm stop defines a cone of darkness which fills the aperture of a light-collecting lens. This lens is free to collect all the light that is scattered by particles passing a converging cone of light. The instrument is calibrated by using a dioctyl phthalate oil fog of 0.3-μ droplet diameter. The instrument has difficulty handling large numbers of particles.

Additional developments in the use of light-scattering instruments for the measurement and count of atmospheric particles have been discussed by Nader, Ortman, and Massey (28).

In the "Aerosoloscope" (31), the air being analyzed is diluted to a point where the particles it contains may be examined individually by a photoelectric tube as they go through an observation zone. Light scattered by a particle is analyzed by an optical system capable of transforming the light flash from a particle into an electric pulse. The pulses produced by the particles are counted and registered at high speed in a series of 12 channels representing size classes. The application of this instrument in industrial hygiene work is greater than in air pollution since it counts and measures particles in the range of 1–64 μ which represent only a small fraction of the normal outside atmospheric particles.

Fawcett and Gardner (32,33) use the ability of particles to act as condensation nuclei, as mentioned in Chapter V, Section C-1, as a measure of their number and size. In this variation of the nuclei counter developed by Aitken in 1890, a long brass tube is used to hold a wet blotter which keeps the interior at 100% humidity and by accessories at higher humidities. A light source is placed at one end of the tube and a photoelectric cell and meter at the other end. The light cut off by the formation of the fog, caused by condensation of water on the particles in the tube by the sudden expansion of a plunger, is a measure of the number of condensation nuclei present.

6. Gold-Leaf Dust Indicator

The gold-leaf electroscope dust indicator is based on the principle that dust can be charged electrically by means of an electrified plate. The air stream carrying the charged dust particles is drawn through an electroscope, the rate of discharge being proportional to the number of dust particles. Thus, the number of dust particles can be estimated from the time necessary to collapse the leaves of the electroscope.

7. Comparison of Dust Counting Techniques

Comparisons of various methods of sampling and types of dust counting have been made. For instance, First and Silverman (7) compared the counting of membrane filter dust samples with those of the midget impinger and with those obtained with a Bausch & Lomb dust counter. They found good correlation. Davies, Aylward, and Leacey (34) studied the efficiency of the Owens jet dust counter, the British konimeter, the Kotzé konimeter, the Bausch & Lomb dust counter, and the cascade impactor against the thermal precipitator as the standard instrument. They found that they obtained the best results with each instrument by using glycerine jelly as an adhesive. The results were 0.78, 0.68, 1.24, 1.06, and 1.38 MPPCF, respectively.

Paulus et al. (15) found good agreement between direct count of membrane filter samples taken at the midpoint of sampling periods with the midget impinger. The latter samples were counted by the ACGIH standard technique. Kruse and Bianconi (35) found in 53 comparative tests that the dust concentration determined by the molecular filter method agreed closely with that determined by the thermal precipitator but was, on the average, one-third of that determined by the midget impinger and one-half that determined by the Bausch & Lomb dust counter. Lippmann (36) claimed excellent agreement between samples collected by his variation of the cascade impactor and membrane filter samples.

Baier and Diakun (37) compared dust counts in a study of dust in coal mines and found the counts on samples obtained by the midget impinger powered by a manual pump assembly, the midget impinger powered by a Freon ejector assembly, the membrane filter, and the thermal precipitator were in fairly good agreement when a large number of samples were collected. The mean dust counts were in MPPCF 6.91, 7.91, 7.43, and 6.66, respectively.

The work of First and Silverman, Paulus et al., Baier and Diakus, and Lippmann give evidence of fair correlation between and among different methods of sampling and counting of particles. The work of Davies and co-workers and Kruse and Bianconi indicates that the correlation between some of the methods of sampling and counting is poor. Jacobs (38) has pointed out how dependent the count is upon the method of sampling and the method of counting. It is best, because of these variations, to report the method of sampling and the method of counting along with the result so that a better comparison of the result can be made.

B. Measurement of Size of Dust Particles

Because dust particles have, in general, been crushed or ground, they seldom have definite geometrical shape. Therefore, they really do not have what is commonly understood to be a diameter. By an arbitrary convention, the "size" of a dust particle is assumed to be the distance between the extreme points of the particle when measured in a horizontal direction (39).

The membrane filter and thermal precipitator are used extensively as the sampling instruments for the measurement of the size of dust particles because they obtain samples of dust from an atmosphere in a more or less unaltered condition. Formerly, the Owens jet dust counter and filter paper methods were used for this purpose. Greenburg-Smith impinger samples may also be used for this purpose; however, some question exists as to whether the particles are shattered in this method of sampling (40–42).

Measurements of the size of particles can be made by means of a filar micrometer ocular, using a $1000\times$ oil-immersion objective. With this magnification particles as small as 0.5 μ can be measured, while smaller particles can be distinguished and recorded. The filar micrometer eyepiece is calibrated so that one division on the micrometer represents a known length on the stage of the microscope. After the microscope is focused upon a representative section of the sample, the horizontal diameters of 200 particles are measured with the filar micrometer by moving the cross hair across the field from left to right and measuring the first 200 particles encountered.   This is done in several representative fields.   The sizes of the particles are recorded in terms of divisions of the filar micrometer and may later be converted into microns by means of a calibration factor. Only one dimension of the particles need be measured, since the particles lie in the field at random and at times it is impossible to rotate the stage of the microscope.   However, because a large number of particles can be measured, if desired, the results are the same as if the average of the length and breadth are determined for each particle.   Details are given in Section B-1-b of this chapter.

By means of a filargraph (43), the measurement of particle size can be made mechanically and a permanent inked record permits simple particle-size grouping.

The size of dust particles may also be obtained by the use of photomicrographs.   In order to obtain good results, the particles must be in one plane, have no Brownian movement, and be well dispersed.   Since industrial dusts are seldom uniform in size, the first requirement cannot be filled.   Bloomfield and DallaValle hold that there is not much to be gained by use of photomicrographs over the simpler and less expensive filar micrometer method.   There is unquestionably a more permanent record obtained by the use of the photographic method and there is the further advantage that it is less strenuous and less fatiguing to the analyst.

Possibly the most common method of sizing particles by direct microscopic count is the use of sizing graticules (see Section B-1-a of this chapter).

Other methods for sizing particles and separating particles into size groups have been mentioned. such as those using the cascade impactor (Chapter V, Section C-7-e), centrifugal force, electronic and photometric measurements (Section G of this chapter), and the electron microscope (44).   Some of these will be discussed in greater detail in subsequent sections.

1. Size Frequency

The frequency with which any particle size occurs is the number of times that a particular particle size occurs in a given count. This can be expressed as a per cent, if that number is divided by the total number of particles measured.   Such frequencies can be studied

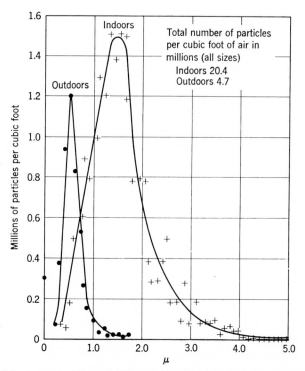

Fig. VI-8. Amount of dust of different sizes found in the general atmosphere of granite-cutting plants in comparison with that outdoors in the vicinity of these plants (45).

either graphically or tabularly, as shown in Figure VI-8 and in Table VI-1. Thus, percentage number can be plotted against size.

The importance of size frequency can be gleaned from the fact that many investigators have shown that most of the dust particles recovered from both human and experimental animal silicotic lungs were between 1 and 3 μ in size. It has already been pointed out that the significant sizes of hazardous industrial dusts fall within the range of 0.5–10 μ (45).

Nevertheless, it should not be inferred that particles above or below this range in size cannot cause illness. Thus, it is known that in asbestosis the harmful particles may be as long as 200 μ and it has been shown that with heavier dusts such as uranium oxide particles sizes of less than 0.5 μ are important physiologically.

TABLE VI-1

Size-Frequency Distribution of Various Industrial Dusts as Compared with Outdoor Dust (45)

Kind of dust	Number of samples	Me-dian	Average frequency in % — Size group in μ											
			0 to 0.49	0.5 to 0.99	1.0 to 1.49	1.5 to 1.99	2.0 to 2.49	2.5 to 2.99	3.0 to 3.49	3.5 to 3.99	4.0 to 4.49	4.5 to 4.99	5.0 to 5.49	5.5 to 5.99
Outdoor dust	179	0.5	56.0	41.0	2.5	0.5	—	—	—	—	—	—	—	—
Sandblasting	9	1.4	1.4	19.7	34.7	20.3	12.6	5.2	2.8	1.6	1.1	0.2	0.2	0.2
Granite cutting	4	1.4	2.0	19.0	33.6	24.5	10.4	4.6	3.1	0.6	0.9	0.3	1.0	—
Traprock milling														
Crusher	1	1.4	0	13.0	39.0	33.0	10.5	2.5	2.0	—	—	—	—	—
Screen house	1	1.3	2.0	31.5	33.0	16.0	10.0	4.5	2.5	0.5	—	—	—	—
Disk crusher	1	0.9	10.0	48.0	31.0	6.0	3.0	1.0	1.0	—	—	—	—	—
Foundry parting compound	2	1.4	0.5	22.0	42.0	17.3	9.2	5.0	1.5	2.0	0.5	—	—	—
General foundry air	1	1.2	0	26.0	48.0	17.0	8.0	1.0	—	—	—	—	—	—
Talc milling	1	1.5	0	16.0	32.0	20.0	13.0	7.0	5.0	2.0	2.0	2.0	0	1.0
Slate milling	1	1.7	1.0	13.0	29.0	17.0	14.0	14.0	6.0	4.0	1.0	1.0	1.0	—
Marble cutting	1	1.5	0	12.0	37.0	21.0	11.0	3.0	3.0	—	1.0	2.0	2.0	1.0
Soapstone dust	2	2.4	1.2	16.0	19.0	13.0	11.0	6.0	6.5	4.5	5.5	3.3	2.5	11.5
Aluminum dust	1	2.2	3.0	8.0	20.5	14.0	11.5	9.0	6.5	3.0	3.5	4.0	7.0	10.0
Bronze dust	1	1.5	1.0	12.0	33.5	25.0	21.0	6.0	1.5	—	—	—	—	—

a. Particle-Size Measurement with Graticules

A number of scales on glass or other transparent material for the measurement of objects has been developed for use in optical instruments. These are known as graticules or reticules. They are placed in the focal plane of the ocular of microscopes. They have geometric figures of various sizes which enable the observer to compare these with the particles on the slide. If only approximations are desired, such sizing can be done very rapidly. One of the

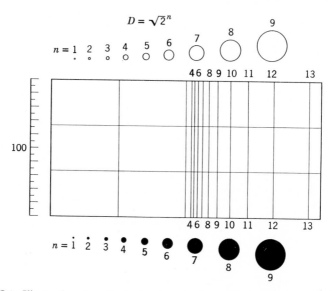

Fig. VI-9. Illustration of graticule showing eyepiece with rectangular grid divided by vertical lines arranged in logarithmic scale.

first of these was that devised by Patterson and Cawood (46) which consisted of a rectangle subdivided into nine equal, smaller rectangles. In addition, there were nine circles of increasing size and nine circular spots also of increasing size and of the same dimensions as the circles above and below the rectangle. Fairs (47) suggested that the diameters of the circles and spots increase by a factor $\sqrt{2}$ to assist in the subsequent statistical evaluation. May (48) improved these graticules by converting the rectangle with smaller rectangles to a rectangle divided by vertical lines arranged in a logarithmic scale as shown in

Figure VI-9.   The relationship of the diameter d of the circles and the spots is

$$d = \sqrt{2^N}$$

in which N represents the number of the circle or spot.   The large rectangle is $200d$ units in length and $100d$ units in width when N is equal to 1.   The numerical value of d will be the same for any given value of N but the dimensional measure of d will be dependent upon the optical system used.   It is therefore necessary to determine the linear dimensions of numerical values by calibration of the graticule with each optical system used.   This is done by use of a stage micrometer in a manner analogous to determining the dimensions of the squares in the Whipple disk.

Watson (49) developed a graticule suitable for the measurement of thermal precipitator samples and Hamilton et al. (50) discussed the factors to be considered in the design of such graticules.

All of these graticules, as well as ocular micrometers with simple rulings which can be of known dimensions or which can be calibrated against a stage micrometer, are available commercially.

In use, the graticule is calibrated, for instance, as detailed by Jacobs, Manoharan, and Goldwater (19), and the count is then made as in the filar micrometer method.   Sometimes, however, the size is taken to be that of the circle closest in size and this is different than the conventional method of taking the projection to the horizontal as the diameter of the particle.

b. Measurement with the Filar Micrometer

The filar micrometer is an ocular eyepiece which consists essentially of a scale and cross hair, either of which is made to traverse the field by means of a screw provided with a micrometer thread. The amount of the movement is indicated by the revolution of a graduated drum attached to the screw head.   It can be attached very simply to either the ordinary microscope or the polarizing microscope.   It is calibrated by means of a stage micrometer.   In this way the value of a division on the filar drum is obtained in terms of microns.   The calibration can be made on a microscope with any fixed tube length and objective, but it should be remembered that when either the tube length or objective is changed, the filar micrometer must be recalibrated.

In actual practice it is usually simpler to work in terms of filar division units rather than in actual microns. These units can be converted to microns after making all the necessary calculations. For example, if one filar drum unit equals 1.3 μ and the average size of a particular fraction happens to be 10 drum units, then the size in microns will be 10 $\times$ 1.3 or 13 μ.

Measurements. All the particles in a field are measured and counted. The diameter of the particle measured is its maximum projection on a given straight line which is used as a base line for all measurements. At least 200 particles are measured.

As an example, let us assume a distribution in a given sample to be such that the range for the most part is between 0 and 10 μ. A table is now set up (see table below) arbitrarily grouping the particles under certain convenient size ranges. All the particles from 0.5 to 1.9 μ, inclusive, are in one group. Those from 2.0 to 3.9 μ, inclusive, are in another group, etc. These groupings are chosen according to the size range of the material under consideration. If all the particles were ten times as large, the convenient groupings might be 10–19 μ, 20–29 μ, etc.

Size, μ	No. of particles
0.5–1.9	60
2.0–3.9	56
4.0–5.9	34
6.0–7.9	18
8.0–9.9	10
10.0 and over	22

From the above table a new table (see table below) is made up. All the particles up to the various sizes, 2, 4, 6, 8, and 10 μ, are grouped together and the percentage of such particles under the stated size is calculated.

Size, μ	Particles	Per cent less than stated size
0.5–1.9	60	30
0.5–3.9	116	58
0.5–5.9	150	75
0.5–7.9	168	84
0.5–9.9	178	89
All	200	100

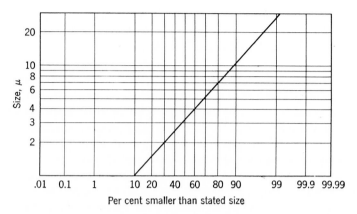

Fig. VI-10. Particle-size distribution curve.

The data given above are plotted as in Figure VI-10 on logarithmic probability paper. The size in microns is plotted against the percentage of particles less than the stated size. If enough particles have been counted and the size distribution is random, then the curve obtained is a straight line. From such a particle-size distribution curve, the number of particles in any particular size range can be read off very easily.

From the curve the median size, Mg (50% size) can be read off. In this example it is 3.2 μ. The standard geometric deviation, σg, can now be obtained by computing the ratios:

$$\sigma g = (84.13\% \text{ size})/(50\% \text{ size}) = 8.0/3.2 = 2.5, \qquad (1)$$

or

$$\sigma g = (50\% \text{ size})/(15.87\% \text{ size}) = 3.2/1.3 = 2.5 \qquad (2)$$

Either ratio, if the data plot is a straight line on a logarithmic-probability grid, will give the same value of σg.

The values of Mg and σg are characteristics of the size distribution of the particles. They define the particle size in greater detail than is possible by means of the average diameter alone. Moreover, the average diameter D can be obtained from Mg and σg by using the equation

$$\log D^3 = \log^3 Mg + 10.3617 \log^2 \sigma g \qquad (3)$$

What is more important, however, is the fact that the percentage of particles below or above a certain given size or within certain size limits can be determined directly from the curve.

2. MICROPROJECTOR

A microprojector for the determination of particle-size distribution and number concentration of atmospheric dust is described by Brown and Yant (51–53). The theory and practice of microprojection are described in detail in a number of texts (54–56). This procedure has been used and found to be satisfactory for measuring the particle-size distribution of subsieve-size substances, such as pigments and powders (57,58) which are of the same size range as atmospheric dust. The U. S. Bureau of Mines has used the microprojector and found it to be satisfactory for (1) the determination of the number concentration of atmospheric dust in samples collected by the Owens jet dust counter; (2) particle-size distribution in samples of atmospheric dust collected by the Owens jet dust counter and by the electric precipitator; (3) particle-size distribution of dusts, blood cells, bacteria, and pollen; and (4) it may also be used for counting impinger samples.

The microprojector used by the U. S. Bureau of Mines is shown diagrammatically in Figure VI-11. It consists of an arc lamp (A), a condensing lens (B) for concentrating the light from the arc lamp, a water cell (C) for filtering heat from the light before it enters the microscope (D), a light shield (E) for shutting off all light except that which strikes the screen, and a screen (F) onto which the images are projected. The screen, which is 50 cm square, consists of a piece of ordinary blue tracing cloth lacquered on both sides and ruled into centimeter squares. The horizontal 10-cm strip across the center of the screen is ruled further into ½-cm squares. Most observations are made in this strip. From a position in back of the screen the observer can examine the images directly in front of him without casting shadows on the screen. Remote controls are necessary to permit the observer at the screen to focus the microscope and to operate the mechanical stage. Microprojectors are commercially available.

Particle-size distribution is determined by comparing the size of the images with that of the ruled or known areas on the screen (59). The number concentration of uniformly distributed samples of

Fig. VI-11. Microprojector (51).

dust from measured volumes of air is determined by counting the number of particles in known areas.   The two determinations usually are made simultaneously on such samples, since the estimation of size involves counting the number of particles.   The dust images on the screen are magnified approximately 4000 diameters.

Jacobs and co-workers (60) devised the following simple, direct, and uniform method for the counting of dust and the measurement of the particle size of dust.   It depends on passing a known volume of air through a membrane filter, placing this filter on a slide, adding a drop of cedar oil, and counting and measuring the particles with the aid of a microprojector.   It has been found to be the most satisfactory with respect to (1) reproducibility of results, (2) ability to count those particles most significant in atmospheric pollution studies, and (3) diminution of eyestrain.

Sampling.   A total of 2.47 cu ft of air is aspirated in an interval of 7 min through a 1-in. membrane filter paper (17 mm in effective diameter) held in an aerosol microanalysis holder (61), using the 10-lpm orifice.   This volume of air is the most satisfactory for dust counts in the range of 0–25 MPPCF.

Counting.   The filter paper on which the sample was collected is placed on a microscope slide (25 × 75 mm, 0.038 mm thickness).   A drop of cedar oil or Shillaber's nondrying immersion oil is placed on the paper and a microscope slide cover glass is set over it.   The slide prepared in this fashion is placed in the Mine Safety Appliances Company Microprojector (Fig VI-12) and a dust count is made at a magnification of approximately 4500.   A 45× objective with a numerical aperture of 0.85 and a 30× ocular are used.   The count is continued until sufficient fields are counted to give approximately 500 particles.   Each field of the screen is equivalent to an area of 0.0024 mm^2.

Particle-Size Measurement.   The size distribution of the various particles is determined during the dust count by use of the calibrated boxes on the screen.   These are 11, 2, 1, and 0.4 μ in length.

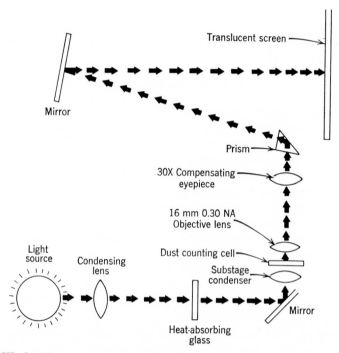

Fig. VI-12. Schematic diagram of Dust-Vue microprojector. (Courtesy Mine Safety Appliances Co.)

Calculation.   The dust count is calculated by means of the formula

MPPCF = (total count × effective area)/
(cu ft of air sampled × no. of fields × 0.0024 × 10⁶)

Calibration of Microprojector.   The screen of the microprojector is calibrated using a stage micrometer having divisions which are 0.01 mm apart.   Actual dimensions on the stage micrometer are indicated as five boxes of the projection screen.   This is equivalent to a distance of 0.055 mm.   The total magnification is therefore the width of the screen divided by the apparent size of the micrometer scale, that is, 250 mm divided by 0.055 mm, which equals 4545.

C. Centrifugal Methods

Centrifugal methods for the determination of size frequency fall into two categories: those in which the particles are trapped and separated as they move with the gas stream around or along the device, and those in which the particles are trapped first, as by filtration, and are subsequently segregated by subjection to centrifugal force for sedimentation.

1. SEPARATION DEVICES

Sawyer and Walton (62) developed a size-separating sampling device for air-borne particulate matter which they named the "Conifuge." This instrument is a conical centrifuge device consisting of an inner solid cone rotated on the same axis as an outer cone in which particles under centrifugal force move at speeds that are proportional to but exceed their settling velocities attributable to gravity. By means of this instrument, the particles can be deposited in a size spectrum-like arrangement because the larger particles deposit near the apex of the outer cone and the smaller ones near the base.

Yaffe, Hosey, and Chambers (63) discuss the use of an instrument in which air is forced through a spiral track depositing the dust it carries in a size-separated manner. This was useful for sizes greater than or equal to 1 μ. Schwendemann (64) managed to separate particles according to size in the range of particles greater than or equal to 0.8 μ in a helix with strong radial electric-field gradients.

Goetz (65) and subsequently Goetz and Stevenson (66) developed an Aerosol Spectrometer for the analysis of size-frequency and mass distribution of air-borne particles in the submicron range. This instrument is based on the principle of exposing a continuous laminar flow of aerosol in a helical channel to a strong centrifugal acceleration of the order of 5–30,000 $\times$ g. With this device particles can be quantitatively separated and classified according to size down to 0.2 μ.

2. CENTRIFUGAL SEDIMENTATION

In the second group mentioned that of the use of centrifugal force for size classification by sedimentation is the method of Whitby (67). In a sense this method is closely related to that of Naeslund (68) described in Chapter V, Section C-3-c. Briefly, the membrane filter is dissolved in a solvent in which the dust is not soluble, the dust is resuspended, and then it is sedimented in a special centrifuge.

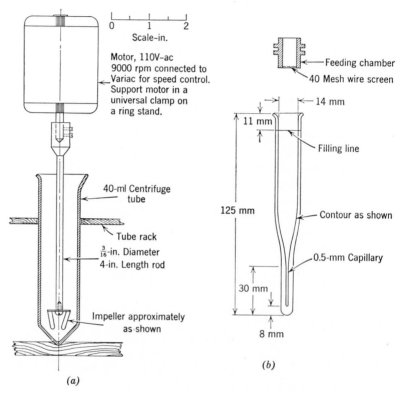

Fig. VI-13. (a) Cone tip centrifuge tube (40 ml) and special stirrer for dissolving membrane filters and dispersing dust (67). (b) Feeding chamber and special centrifuge tube.

Procedure.   Place the membrane filter sample into a 40-ml cone tip centrifuge tube (Fig. VI-13a) with about 35 ml of acetone and stir it vigorously for several minutes with the stirrer shown in Figure VI-13a. Centrifuge this suspension in an ordinary centrifuge at 3000–3500 rpm for 1 hr to precipitate all particles above approximately 0.1 μ. Siphon off the supernatant acetone solution and resuspend the sediment without drying by stirring for several minutes in about 1 ml of a mixture of 15% naphtha and 85% acetone.

It may be practical when it is desired not to dissolve the filter, particularly with many mineral dusts, to wash the dust from the filter by placing it, with the dust load inward, into a 40-ml centrifuge tube with the appropriate liquid and then brushing off the dust. The sample may subsequently be concentrated and resuspended as described.

Transfer the suspension of particles with the aid of an eye dropper to the feeding chamber (Fig. VI-13b) and then place the feeding chamber in the tube and release the suspension in such a manner so that the suspension floats as a sharp layer on the sedimentation liquid.

Read the height of the sediment in the capillary, first after sedimentation is permitted to proceed under gravity alone for from 4 to 10 min—depending upon a time schedule previously calculated from Stokes' law for the sizes involved—and then repeatedly after centrifuging in a special centrifuge for known times and speeds, removing the tube for reading at each given time–speed interval. Centrifuges designed specially for this type of centrifugal sedimentation analysis are commercially available.

D. Measurement by Elutriation

In the preceding sections the measurement of the particle size of air-borne dust has been detailed. On occasion it is necessary for the analyst to measure the size of subsieve particles of collected dust, fly ash, powders, and other samples. A relatively simple sedimentation method has been adopted by the Western Precipitation Corporation for this purpose. In this method, the particles to be measured are permitted to settle in a still liquid of known density and viscosity through a selected distance for a predetermined time. Knowing the density and viscosity of the liquid and the density of the dust being analyzed, the end velocity of the largest particle in the fraction settling can be calculated from Stokes' law:

$$v = 2gr^2(d_1 - d_2)60/9\eta$$

expressed in centimeters per minute, where v = velocity of the particle in cm/min, g = the gravity constant, 980 cm/sec/sec, r = radius of particle in cm, d_1 = density of particle, d_2 = density of fluid, and η = viscosity of fluid in poises. It must be remembered that Stokes' law applies to spherical particles so that the results obtained by this method mean that the sample contains a given fraction of particles falling in a time equivalent to spherical particles of a given diameter. By this method we can determine the weight of fractions

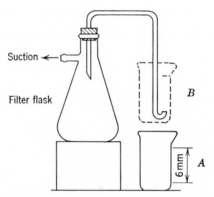

Fig. VI-14. Elutriation apparatus: (*A*) stirring and settling position; (*B*) decantation position.

of a sample in the size range of 0–44 μ, the latter being equivalent to the sieve opening of a 325-mesh sieve.

Apparatus. The elutriation or sedimentation apparatus consists of a 300-ml tall-form beaker, a siphon tube, and a suction flask arranged as shown in Figure VI-14. Mark off a 6-cm height on the beaker with a piece of masking tape, starting the lower mark at the entrance port of the siphon tube. This arrangement is used for particles in the range of 0–20 μ. For particles in the 20–44-μ range substitute a 250-ml cylinder on which marks can be set off at least 20 cm apart.

Calculation of End Velocity. Use a sedimentation liquid of known density and viscosity. Determine or obtain the density of the test sample. Use Stokes' formula for the calculation.

Western Precipitation Corporation gives the following example for a cement dust with a density of 3.01, using a kerosine settling medium with a density of 0.79 and a viscosity of 0.0107 poise. A 10-μ particle having a radius of 0.0005 cm will have a velocity of fall of

$$v = [2 \times 980 \times (0.0005)^2 \times (3.01 - 0.79) \times 60]/(9 \times 0.0107)$$
$$= 0.0653/0.0963$$
$$= 0.6778 \text{ cm/min}$$

The settling time for the 6-cm height will be

$$\text{settling time} = 6/0.6778 = 8.86 \text{ min} = 8 \text{ min } 52 \text{ sec}$$

Procedure. Place a 0.5-g sample into the beaker and add sufficient kerosine to bring it up to the upper mark. Stir thoroughly to suspend the particles, adding a wetting agent if necessary. Make certain all agglomerates are dispersed. Stop stirring, start the timer, and at the end of the calculated time raise the beaker from A to B (Figure VI-14) and connect the siphon tube to the suction flask. Draw off all of the liquid to the lower mark and then filter through a tared Gooch crucible. Refill the beaker to the upper mark with kerosine. Repeat all the elutriation steps of settling, timing, and decanting and then filter through the same tared Gooch. Repeat the elutriation process until the amount of particles under 10 μ is negligible. This may require from 15 to 25 decantations. Dry the Gooch crucible. Place in a desiccator and weigh when cool. The weight of collected material represents the weight of the 0–10-μ fraction.

Calculate the end velocity of a 20-μ particle and repeat the elutriation for this fraction. Calculate the end velocities of 30- and 44-μ particles and repeat using the 250-ml cylinders and a height of 20 cm. Check all fractions with a microscope to see that they conform to the designated fraction.

E. Comparison of Size-Measurement Methods

A number of the references cited in Section A of this chapter also deal with size measurement and size distribution. In particular, Whitby et al. (69) and Davies and co-workers (34) have done considerable work in comparing various methods. Differences in results in size distribution arise not only from differences in the methods used for sampling and for sizing but also from differences in the conventions used in measuring the so-called "diameters." Green and Lane (70) tabulate the mathematical definitions of the various diameters used for describing the size of particles.

In the United States in industrial hygiene work, it has become conventional to take as the "diameter" of a particle the distance between the extreme points of the dust particle when measured in a horizontal direction, as shown in Figure VI-15. This convention has been adopted because dust particles seldom have a definite geometric shape. Consequently, they do not have what is commonly termed a diameter so that an arbitrary size has to be assigned.

Other conventions, however, are used. Hence, results obtained using different conventions may not be comparable. For instance,

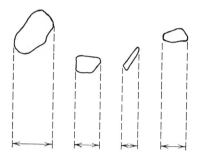

Fig. VI-15. Maximum projection of a particle referred to a straight line.

Davies, Aylward, and Leacey (34) in sizing take the diameter of a particle to be the diameter of the circle having an area equal to the particle seen under the microscope. The comparison circles are those of a May's graticule or similar graticule. The imaginary circle of the particle, in this method, is compared with those on the graticule and is assigned to the size defined by the circle equal to or larger than itself and by the next circle smaller than itself. The cumulative distribution is worked out and the curve plotted on logarithmic-probability paper.

It is best, as in counting particles, to report size-distribution and size-frequency measurements with a notation giving the methods of sampling, counting, and means of determining the size.

F. Gravimetric Dust Analysis

The gravimetric method of dust analysis has been described in some detail with respect to the thimble-filtration method. Other filtration methods of a similar type lend themselves to the same method of estimation. Dust samples obtained by the sugar-tube method, or an absorption method such as the Greenburg-Smith impinger, can also be estimated gravimetrically. The weight of the dust sampled by the impinger may be determined by evaporating an aliquot of the mixture prepared for the microscope count in a tared dish. The dish is then dried in a constant-temperature oven at 100–105°C, placed in a desiccator, allowed to cool, and weighed. The gain in weight is considered the weight of the dust. This is corrected by running a control on the water used, in a similar dish and through the same treatment for the same length of time.

Alternatively, a Gooch crucible prepared with a mat of asbestos sufficiently thick to retain all the dust may be used.   An aliquot of the prepared sample solution mixture is filtered through the Gooch crucible, which is placed in an oven at 105°C for 4 hr, removed to a desiccator to cool, and weighed.

Total combustible matter can be obtained in both instances, provided the dish is of heat-resistant material, by igniting the dish or crucible, cooling, and weighing.   The loss in weight is generally considered organic material.   The residue is considered the inorganic portion of the dust.

Methods for the gravimetric estimation of sootfall have been detailed by Jacobs (71).

Polystyrene mat-type filters lend themselves to gravimetric determination of dust.   They can be dried, weighed, used for obtaining the sample, and redried and reweighed to get the weight of the collected dust.

Whatman No. 41 filters can only be used for approximate gravimetric determinations.   Glass fiber webs are used widely for gravimetric determinations, especially for total suspended particulate matter, but the weighings in such estimations are usually performed to the nearest 10 mg on a trip scale (almost essential with large 8 × 10-in. sheets) and it is doubtful if they are correct to such a weight. There is always the chance that glass fibers will split off and be lost. Membrane filters may be made with glycerol to make them pliable. Such types of molecular filters cannot be used for gravimetric determinations.

G. Light Transmission and Reflection

The amount of light transmitted through a gaseous or liquid medium containing dispersed opaque particulate matter may be expected to follow the Beer-Lambert law (72).   Various photoelectric instruments have been devised for such measurements, particularly for testing air filters (73) and as smoke detectors (74–76).   Such methods have also been used for estimating the amount of dust (77–79).

Brown (4) applied such methods to the preliminary estimation of the amount of dust collected by the filter-paper method.   The light-transmission equipment consisted of a light source like a flash light, a glass window for the paper holder, and a light meter.   The light transmission is measured before and after sampling the dust. A calibration curve can be prepared and the amount of dust may be calculated.

The use of light transmission for the evaluation of smoke shade spots produced with an automatic tape sampler has been discussed by Hemeon, Haines, and Ide (80). Gruber and Alpaugh (81), using the same sampling instrument, have evaluated the blackness of the deposits by means of reflection. The use of these methods in air pollution work has been detailed by Jacobs (82). Whitby, Algren, and Jordan (16) used photometric evaluation of dust spots collected on membrane filters in combination with their centrifugal sedimentation method for measurement of the size distribution and concentration of air-borne dust. Katz and Sanderson (83) have reviewed the literature in this field through 1958 and include a mathematical treatment attempting to relate the absorbance to mass concentration, carbon content of the deposit, and the number and size distribution of the collected particles.

References

1. DallaValle, J. M., *U.S. Public Health Service Reprint 2038* (1939).
2. Jacobs, M. B., *The Chemical Analysis of Air Pollutants*, Interscience, New York, 1960, pp. 71–75.
3. Bloomfield, J. J., and J. M. DallaValle, *U.S. Public Health Service Bull. 217* (1938).
4. Brown, C. E., *U.S. Bur. Mines Rept. Invest. 3788* (1944).
5. Chamot, E. M., and C. W. Mason, *Handbook of Chemical Microscopy*, Wiley, New York, 1938.
6. Brown, C. E., and F. L. Feicht, *U.S. Bur. Mines Rept. Invest. 3821* (1945).
7. First, M. W., and L. Silverman, Trans. 5th Annual Meeting Am. Conf. Governmental Ind. Hygienists (1942).
8. Brown, C. E., R. L. Beatty, and T. B. Kirby, *U.S. Bur. Mines Inform. Circ. 7331* (1945).
9. Hatch, T., and C. L. Pool, *J. Ind. Hyg.*, **16**, 177 (1934).
10. Williams, C. R., *J. Ind. Hyg. Toxicol.*, **19**, 226 (1937).
11. Annetts, M., and J. D. Leitch, *J. Ind. Hyg. Toxicol.*, **18**, 98 (1936).
12. Dunn, K. L., *J. Ind. Hyg. Toxicol.*, **21**, 202 (1939).
13. Couchman, C. E., and W. H. Schulze, *U.S. Public Health Rept.*, **53**, 348 (1938).
14. Page, R. T., *U.S. Public Health Rept.*, **52**, 1315 (1937).
15. Paulus, H. J., N. A. Talvitie, D. A. Fraser, and R. G. Keenan, *Am. Ind. Hyg. Assoc. Quarterly*, **18**, 267 (1957).

16. Whitby, K. T., A. B. Algren, and R. C. Jordan, *ASHAE Trans.*, **61**, 463 (1955).
17. Work, P. T., *Am. Soc. Testing Mater. Proc.*, **28**, Part II, 771 (1928).
18. Jacobs, M. B., *The Chemical Analysis of Air Pollutants*, Interscience, New York, 1960, p. 72.
19. Jacobs, M. B., A. Manoharan, and L. J. Goldwater, *Intern. J. Air Water Pollution*, **6**, 205 (1962).
20. Littlefield, J. B., C. E. Brown, and H. H. Schrenk, *U.S. Bur. Mines Inform. Circ. 6993* (1938).
21. Kagan, M., and W. Broumstein, *J. Ind. Hyg.*, **13**, 10 (1931).
22. Guyton, A. C., *J. Ind. Hyg. Toxicol.*, **28**, 133 (1946).
23. Gucker, F. T., C. T. O'Konski, H. B. Pickard, and J. N. Pitts, *J. Am. Chem. Soc.*, **69**, 2422 (1947).
24. Gucker, F. T., and C. T. O'Konski, *J. Colloid Sci.*, **4**, 541 (1949).
25. Gucker, F. T., and D. G. Rose, *Brit. J. Appl. Phys.*, **5**, Suppl. 3, S 138 (1954).
26. Peterson, A. H., in *Air Pollution*, L. C. McCabe, Ed., McGraw-Hill, New York, 1952, p. 620.
27. LaMer, V. K., and D. Sinclair, *OSRD Rept. 1857* (1943); U.S. Dept. Commerce Office of Publications Board Rept. 944.
28. Nader, J. S., C. Ortman, and M. T. Massey, *Am. Ind. Hyg. Assoc. J.*, **22**, 42 (1961).
29. Sinclair, D., *Air Repair*, **3**, 51 (1953).
30. Müller, R. H., *Anal. Chem.*, **26**, No. 8, 33A (1954).
31. Alexander, N. E., *Air Eng.*, **1**, No. 4, 43 (1959).
32. *General Electric Rev.*, **60**, No. 4, 22 (1957).
33. Fawcett, H. H., and G. Gardner, Am. Chem. Soc. Meeting, Chicago, 1958.
34. Davies, C. N., M. Aylward, and D. Leacey, *A.M.A. Arch. Ind. Hyg. Occupational Med.*, **4**, 354 (1951).
35. Kruse, C. W., and W. O. Bianconi, *Tenn. Ind. Hyg. News*, **16**, No. 2, 7 (Apr. 1959).
36. Lippmann, M., *Am. Ind. Hyg. Assoc. J.*, **20**, 406 (1959); **22**, 348 (1961).
37. Baier, E. J., and R. Diakun, *J. Occupational Med.*, **3**, No. 11, 507 (1961).
38. Jacobs, M. B., *The Chemical Analysis of Air Pollutants*, Interscience, New York, 1960, Chap. 4.
39. Drinker, P., and T. Hatch, *Industrial Dust*, McGraw-Hill, New York, 1936.
40. Ficklen, J. B., and L. L. Goolden, *Science*, **85**, 587 (1937).
41. Anderson, E. L., *J. Ind. Hyg. Toxicol.*, **21**, 39 (1939).
42. Silverman, L., and W. Franklin, *J. Ind. Hyg. Toxicol.*, **24**, 80 (1942).
43. Palmes, E. D., *J. Ind. Hyg. Toxicol.*, **26**, 64 (1944).
44. Fraser, D. A., *A.M.A. Arch. Ind. Hyg. Occupational Med.*, **8**, 412 (1953).
45. Bloomfield, J. J., *U.S. Public Health Rept.*, **48**, 961 (1933).
46. Patterson, H. S., and W. Cawood, *Trans. Faraday Soc.*, **32**, 1084 (1936).
47. Fairs, G. L., *Chem. Ind. (London)*, **62**, 374 (1943).
48. May, K. R., *J. Sci. Instr.*, **22**, 187 (1945).
49. Watson, H. H., *Brit. J. Ind. Med.*, **9**, 80 (1952).
50. Hamilton, R. J., J. F. Holdsworth, and W. H. Walton, *Brit. J. Appl. Phys.*, **5**, Suppl. 3, S 101 (1954).

51. Brown, C. E., and W. P. Yant, *U.S. Bur. Mines Rept. Invest. 3289* (1935).
52. Brown, C. E., L. A. H. Baum, W. P. Yant, and H. H. Schrenk, *U.S. Bur. Mines Rept. Invest. 3373* (1938).
53. Brown, C. E., and H. H. Schrenk, *U.S. Bur. Mines Inform. Circ. 7026* (1938).
54. Chamot, E. M., and C. W. Mason, *Handbook of Chemical Microscopy*, Wiley, New York, 1938.
55. Gage, S. H., and H. P. Gage, *Optic Projection*, Comstock, Ithaca, 1914.
56. Drinker, P., R. M. Thomson, and J. L. Finn, *J. Ind. Hyg.*, **7**, 567 (1925).
57. Dunn, E. J., *Ind. Eng. Chem. Anal. Ed.*, **2**, 59 (1930).
58. *Proc. Am. Soc. Testing Mater.* **30**, Part 1, 919 (1930).
59. Green, H. L., *J. Ind. Hyg.*, **16**, 29 (1934).
60. Jacobs, M. B., M. M. Braverman, C. Theophil, and S. Hochheiser, *Am. J. Public Health*, **47**, 1430 (1957).
61. Millipore Filter Corp., Bedford, Mass.
62. Sawyer, K. F., and W. H. Walton, *J. Sci. Instr.*, **27**, 272 (1950).
63. Yaffe, C. D., A. D. Hosey, and J. T. Chambers, Jr., *A.M.A. Arch. Ind. Hyg. Occupational Med.*, **5**, 62 (1950).
64. Schwendemann, K., *Ber. Schwebstofftechn. Arbeitsstagung Mainz*, **1954**, 63.
65. Goetz, A., *Rev. Geofis. Pura Appl.*, Proc. 2nd Intern. Symposium Condensation Nucli Basel-Locarno, 1956, **36**, 49 (1957).
66. Goetz, A., and H. J. R. Stevenson, "The Aerosol Spectrometer, An Instrument for the Measurement of Size—Frequency and Mass Distribution of Air-Borne Particulate Matter in the Submicron Range," 1957.
67. Whitby, K. T., *ASHAE Trans.*, **61**, 33449 (1955).
68. Naeslund, C., *J. Ind. Hyg.*, **14**, 113 (1932).
69. Whitby, K. T., A. B. Algren, and J. C. Annis, *ASTM Special Tech. Publ. No. 234* (1958).
70. Green, H. L., and W. R. Lane, *Particulate Clouds: Dusts, Smokes, and Mists*, Van Nostrand, New York, 1957.
71. Jacobs, M. B., *The Chemical Analysis of Air Pollutants*, Interscience, New York, 1960, Chap. 3.
72. Simson, A. W., L. C. Kron, C. H. Watson, and H. Raymond, *Rev. Sci. Instr.*, **2**, 67 (1931).
73. Rowley, F. B., and R. C. Jordan, *Heating Piping Air Conditioning*, **15**, 487 (1943).
74. Reynolds, S. R., *Elec. J. (London)*, **23**, 135 (1926).
75. Sawford, F., *Mech. Eng.*, **49**, 999 (1927).
76. Hill, A. S. G., *Trans. Faraday Soc.*, **32**, 1125 (1936).
77. Cadden, J. F., and E. T. Roetman, *West Virginia State Dept. Health Bur. Ind. Hyg. Rept.* (1939).
78. Davis, D. H., and G. R. Gardner, *Trans. Am. Inst. Mining Met. Eng.*, **149**, 193 (1942).
79. Pool, C. L., J. Wuraftic, and R. J. Kelly, *Ind. Med. Ind. Hyg. Section 2*, 39 (1941).
80. Hemeon, W. C. L., G. F. Haines, Jr., and H. M. Ide, *Air Repair*, **3**, No. 1, 22 (1953).
81. Gruber, C. W., and E. L. Alpaugh, *Air Repair*, **4**, No. 3, 143 (1954).

82. Jacobs, M. B., *The Chemical Analysis of Air Pollutants*, Interscience, New York, 1960, Chap. 6.
83. Katz, M., and H. P. Sanderson, *ASTM Special Tech. Publ. No. 250* (1958).

General References

Blacktin, S. C., *Dust*, Chapman, London, 1934.

Bloomfield, J. J., "Dust Procedures in Air Analysis. The Sampling and Analysis of Industrial Dusts," *Am. Public Health Assoc. Yearbook 1935–36*, 86.

Bloomfield, J. J., and J. M. Dalla Valle, "Determination of Industrial Dust," *U.S. Public Health Service Bull. 217* (1938).

DallaValle, J. M., *Micromeritics*, Pitman, New York, 1948.

DallaValle, J. M., "The Significance of Dust Counts," *U.S. Public Health Service Reprint 2083* (1939).

Drinker, P., and T. Hatch, *Industrial Dust*, McGraw-Hill, New York, 1936.

Drinker, P., R. M. Thomson, and J. L. Finn, "Photometric Methods for Studying and Estimating Dusts, Fumes and Smokes," *J. Ind. Hyg.*, **7**, 567 (1925).

Flury, F., and F. Zernik, *Schaedliche Gase*, Springer, Berlin, 1931.

Gibb, T. R. P., *Optical Methods of Chemical Analysis*, McGraw-Hill, New York, 1942.

Goldberg, R. W., *Occupational Diseases*, Columbia Univ. Press, New York, 1931.

Greenburg, L., "A Review of the Methods Used for Sampling Aerial Dust," *U.S. Public Health Rept.*, **40**, 765 (1925).

Haldane, J. S., and J. I. Graham, *Methods of Air Analysis*, Griffin, London, 1935.

Ives, J. E., R. H. Britten, D. W. Armstrong, W. A. Gill, and F. H. Goldman, "Atmospheric Pollution of American Cities for the Years 1931–1933," *U.S. Public Health Service Bull. 224* (1936).

Oliver, T., *Diseases of Occupation*, 3rd ed., Dutton, New York, 1916.

Sayers, R. R., "Harmful Industrial Dusts," *U.S. Public Health Rept.*, **53**, 217 (1938).

Schrenk, H. H., "Rapid Methods for the Estimation of Air Dustiness," *Am. J. Public Health*, **30**, 1183 (1940).

Shaw, N., and J. S. Owens, *The Smoke Problem of Great Cities*, Constable, London, 1925.

CHAPTER VII

THE CHEMICAL AND MICROSCOPIC
ESTIMATION OF SILICA

Previous sections have stressed the importance of dusts containing silica as the cause of fibrosis of the lungs. This has been shown to be the cause by many investigators. While most authorities agree that silicosis is a disease caused by breathing air containing free silica, characterized anatomically by generalized fibrotic changes (1), other investigators point out that some silicates were as likely to cause silicosis (2,3) as free silica. They have isolated the mineral sericite (muscovite), a hydrated potassium aluminum silicate, from silicotic lungs. These investigators contend that certain mineral silicates are as soluble in the lungs as free silica minerals (4).

Silica is the name given to the chemical compound silicon dioxide, SiO_2. Its most common natural pure crystalline form is quartz. Its most common form, not necessarily pure, is sand, which is quartz that has been crushed by the movement of water. Quartz itself occurs in different crystalline forms, such as tridymite and cristobalite, each of which has a number of crystalline forms. In comparison with quartz, the other crystalline forms of silica are rare.

Silica also occurs naturally in amorphous forms, among the more important of which are chalcedony, carnelian, chrysoprase, and onyx. These forms also are rare in comparison with quartz and seldom, if ever, become an industrial hazard.

A. Nomenclature

In many types of chemical analysis, it is customary to obtain a measure of the silicon present by estimating total silica. This type of analysis, however, fails to distinguish between silicates, on the one hand, and free silica, on the other.

A long-established convention has led to the reporting of chemical analyses of rocks and minerals in terms of certain chemical compounds, as, for example, oxides, rather than in terms of chemical elements. This convention has arisen because in many instances, such as silicon, no purpose would be served by isolating the element itself. Hence, the analysis is reported in the form that it is made. For instance, the chemical analysis of an average granite is reported as containing 70% silica. About 30% or roughly one-third of this granite consists of quartz, whereas the other two-thirds of the granite is made up chiefly of minerals that are complex salts of silicon-bearing acids. These acids are known as *silicic acids* and the salts of these acids are termed *silicates.* The remainder of the material reported as silica in this analysis comes from the silicate minerals of the granite, chiefly feldspar and mica.

This system of reporting rock and mineral analyses, as well as other analyses, in terms of oxides necessitates the use of the expressions *free silica* and *combined silica* to distinguish between the silica that makes up quartz or the other forms of minerals composed of silica alone, and the silica that is combined with other elements in the various silicate minerals. Thus, in the aforementioned sample of granite which contained 70% silica, the total silica is composed of 30% free silica plus 40% combined silica. Quartz and other forms of the chemical compound SiO_2 are termed *free silica;* that contained in feldspar and other silicates is known as *combined silica.*

As the relative danger of silicosis (5) to workers in certain dusty trades—among which may be mentioned rock drilling, granite cutting, foundries, and the manufacture of scouring powder—is determined chiefly by the amount of free silica present in the dust in the form of quartz rather than by the silica that is in chemical combination, it is necessary to use a method which will enable one to estimate how much of the dust of a given sample consists of quartz.

B.   Free-Silica Standards

The dust hazard is regulated in certain states by code. These permissible dust concentrations are tabulated in Table 7, Appendix. Thus, in New York State it is regulated, in so far as rock drilling is concerned, by Industrial Code No. 33 and certain rules promulgated by the Industrial Commissioner. According to the terms of this code, all rock formations are divided into two classes depending on their free-silica content, as follows:

Class 1—rock formations containing uniformly less than 10% by weight free silica.

Class 2—rock formations containing 10% or more by weight free silica and those formations having a variable and unpredictable content of free silica.

Under this classification the code allows dust concentrations up to and including 100 MPPCF of air for drilling operations in Class 1 rock, whereas the maximum permissible dust concentration for drilling in Class 2 is fixed at 10 MPPCF of air. It is clear that in the enforcement of such a code the problem of determining a dust classification of rock is very important.

C. Sampling in Quarries

Some quarries are many acres in area and have working faces as high as 200 ft. Often there are several formations of different kinds of rock occurring at various depths or at different sections of the quarry. A representative sample (6) cannot be obtained under such conditions merely by sampling the rock at one point. Therefore, in order to obtain samples that are representative of the quarry as a whole, the specimens should be taken from the large storage piles of quarried stone that has been through the crushing process. These piles often represent the accumulation of several months of operation and contain well-mixed stone from all parts of the quarry. Sampling of these piles may be done with the aid of a clam-shell bucket or bucket loader. Take grab samples at random from the pile and from its interior with the bucket and deposit these grab samples together in a separate pile. After a representative sample has been taken, it should be thoroughly mixed by raising and dropping the stone by means of the bucket. Because the sample pile taken in the manner described usually amounts to from 1 to 2 tons, it is necessary to quarter it until a final sample of about 35 lb is obtained.

In a few of the largest crushed-stone quarries the sampling procedure is simplified considerably because the crushed stone is stored in large concrete silos that are filled and unloaded via a conveyor system. Here conveyor belts lead from under the bins to the wharfage or railroad siding, where scows or freight cars receive the stone for shipping. To obtain a good sample of the quarry's production here, it is only necessary to open the discharge gate in the storage bin selected and run about a ton of stone onto the conveyor. Handfuls or scoopfuls of rock can then be selected at random from the belt until a 35-lb composite sample is obtained.

D. Petrographic Analysis

The methods for the estimation of free silica in a dust fall into three main groups of analysis: petrographic (7,8), chemical, and physical-chemical methods such as spectrographic and x-ray analysis.

A petrographic analysis is one in which the identity of a material is established by a study of its structure, texture, color, refractive index, other optical properties, etc. In the case of rock analysis, this can be done with the aid of a petrographic or polarizing microscope. This type of microscope has, in addition to its usual equipment, three other pieces of apparatus. It needs a polarizer or a Nicol prism in order to polarize the light; an analyzer, which is another prism needed to examine the light after it has passed through the polarizer and the thin section of rock which is being examined; and a rotating stage, which revolves about an axis in the line of sight of the microscope. A petrographic microscope has been described by Faust (9).

In the petrographic method a thin section or rock specimen is examined. Therefore, it cannot be used as such on collected dust. However, if some of the material worked upon is available, then the petrographic method may be applied to that. A section approximately 0.03 mm thick should be cut from the material to be examined. This is mounted in Canada balsam on a glass slide. Powdered specimens may also be examined in this way, but the grains of powder must be about 0.06 mm in size. Particles less than 10 μ in size cannot be accurately identified with a polarizing microscope. Various oils are used in which to immerse the grains, depending upon their refractive indices. By means of the Rosiwal method a quantitative estimate of the amount of quartz in a mineral can be made. This is done by measuring the linear intercepts of a given mineral along numerous parallel lines, the percentage of quartz being determined by the ratio between the sum of all of the intercepts of quartz and the length of the measured traverse. It can be shown mathematically that the linear intercepts are proportional to volumes. The measurement is carried out by the use of a screw-micrometer ocular or a mechanical stage.

1. Petrographic Estimation of Quartz

The percentage of quartz and material having approximately the same refractive index as quartz in a specimen of dust whose origin is not definitely known, as, for instance, open-air dust (10), may be determined by immersing a specimen in an oil of known refractive index and observing the sample under dark-field illumination. When the source of the dust is known, as, for instance, in samples taken in a tunnel or mine, then oils of various refractive indices are used.

Atmospheric dust samples may be collected by the methods detailed in Chapter V. Those that are collected on micro cover glasses may be used directly; those collected on celluloid or metal foil, as in the case of the electric precipitator, should be transferred by scraping off a representative sample of the dust and placing it on a microscope slide; those collected by the impinger, using alcohol as the collection medium, are centrifuged in order to transfer the dust to a micro slide.

Preparation of Sample. Support a dark-field type, No. 1 thickness, 9-mm-diameter cover slide in a glass tube 17 mm in diameter and 12 cm long so that it rests flat on a bottom stopper. Add a 5-ml aliquot of a well-shaken dust sample from the impinger, stopper the upper end of the tube, and centrifuge at 3000–3500 rpm for 15 min. Remove the top stopper, loosen the bottom stopper so that the alcohol can drain away, and slowly turn the tube to a horizontal position by the time all of the alcohol has drained off. Remove the bottom stopper, holding it so that the cover slide is in a vertical position held in place by the alcohol. This action assists in complete drainage of the alcohol. Remove the cover slide from the stopper with a forceps, place on filter paper to dry, and then place in an inverted position on a slide for examination.

Procedure. Set a microscope for dark-field illumination. Run a drop of a mixture of mineral oil and α-chloronaphthalene with an index of refraction of 1.56 around the dust sample, between the cover glass and the slide. Another mixture that may be used is mineral oil and α-bromonaphthalene. The liquids like xylidine, bromobenzene, and tri-o-cresyl phosphate, which also have a refractive index in the neighborhood of 1.56, may also be used. Estimate the percentage of quartz and minerals with a similar refractive index to the nearest 10% by number, basing this estimate on the fact that quartz and the minerals of similar refractive index appear as faint blue to gray particles without a halo, while transparent particles of different indices show brighter colors with a halo, and opaque particles show a peculiar shade of bright orange. Since the density of quartz is 2.65 and the density of most of the common minerals ranges from 2.5 to 3.0, the value obtained may be accepted as the percentage by weight.

As Foster and Schrenk (10) note, this method fails to distinguish between quartz particles and those of similar refractive index. Any mineral with an index in the range 1.53–1.59 may be confused with quartz; for this reason the material identified as quartz by this method may be quartz, may be a mixture of quartz and other minerals, or may actually contain no quartz at all. However, in practical work, the feldspars will be the ones usually found. Other common minerals which may not be possible to distinguish from quartz by the procedure outlined are anhydrite, chlorite, halite, kaolinite, some of the micas, serpentine, and talc. While Larsen and Berman (11) list some 240 minerals with the intermediate refractive index (beta) in the range 1.53–1.59, the majority of the minerals with refractive indices similar to that of quartz are rare so that significant amounts will ordinarily not be found in dust. Thus, though this method does not identify quartz as such in a dust, it is useful in setting a maximum limit for the amount of quartz possibly present, giving, in effect, high values but not low values for the quartz content. If no quartz is found by the procedure detailed above, less than 1% quartz is present.

The method may be modified to make estimates of quartz in dusts whose approximate composition is known by immersing samples of the dust under separate cover glasses in oils of different refractive indices, such as 1.53, 1.545, 1.56, and 1.70, and noting the disappearance of certain particles. Thus, quartz will apparently disappear in an oil with a refractive index of 1.545, albite will apparently disappear in an oil with a refractive index of 1.53, hornblende and pyroxene will appear faint in an oil of refractive index of 1.70, and analogous conditions can be arranged for other minerals.

2. Modified Petrographic Immersion Method

Ross and Sehl (7) have modified the petrographic method. In their modified petrographic immersion method, separate amounts of powdered mineral or dust are made with fennel-seed oil and mononitrobenzene and then are examined with an ordinary microscope equipped with a Whipple disk (Fig. VI-2). The method depends on the principle known as the method of central illumination (11,12) in which a nonopaque body or material is identified by its optical behavior in an immersion medium having an index of refraction different from the material being examined.

The quartz or free silica commonly encountered has a definite index of refraction, 1.544. Certain minerals have higher and others have lower indices of refraction. If dust, consisting of quartz and minerals of lower and higher refractive indices than quartz, is immersed in fennel-seed oil, which has a refractive index of 1.540, a microscope objective focused correctly and then raised above this point of good focus makes several particles appear lighter than the surrounding medium while the remainder appear darker. The bright or transparent particles will consist of quartz plus particles which have a higher refractive index than quartz. Similarly, if another portion of the same dust is immersed in mononitrobenzene, which has a refractive index of 1.55, some of the particles appear brighter than the surrounding medium when the objective is raised slightly above the point of good focus. In this instance, however, the bright or transparent particles are only those which have a higher refractive index than quartz. Therefore, if the percentage of transparent particles in the fennel-seed oil is placed equal to A and the percentage of transparent particles in mononitrobenzene is placed equal to B, then

$$A - B = \%\ \text{quartz or free silica}$$

Preparation of Sample. Care should be exercised in the selection and preparation of the sample. Only a very small amount of powder need be examined. It should be uniform and representative. Rock specimens are crushed, quartered, and ground in an agate mortar to pass a 150-mesh screen. Samples of dust taken from rafters, beams, ledges, and the like generally need not be ground, for they are usually of the correct size.

Preparation of Slides. Place a very small amount of ground mineral or dust, approximately 10 mg, in a 50-ml beaker, add 5 ml of fennel-seed oil, and swirl to obtain a suspension of the mineral particles in the oil. Make a similar suspension of the ground mineral or dust in mononitrobenzene. Use a pipet or a medicine dropper to transfer a sufficient amount of oil–mineral suspension to a Sedgwick-Rafter cell. A cover slip, similar to that used in counting dust particles (as explained in Chapter VI), should be employed to cover the cell. Thus, two slides are prepared, one containing the pulverized mineral or dust specimen in fennel-seed oil, and the other, a similar sample, in mononitrobenzene. The oil should be the purest obtainable. The mononitrobenzene should be redistilled. A new sample of

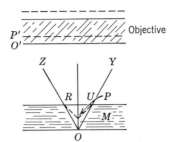

Fig. VII-1. Use of Sedgwick-Rafter cell.

oil should be checked with a pure, ground-quartz specimen to verify the refractive index of the oil.   Sunlight affects mononitrobenzene and it should therefore be protected against direct rays of light.

In order to prevent errors, it is good practice to use separate beakers, pipets, and cells for fennel-seed oil and for mononitrobenzene.

Apparatus.   An ordinary microscope, meeting the U.S. Public Health Service specifications, as described in Chapter VI, Section A-1, may be used for this method.   Ross and Sehl (7) used a microscope with a 7.5✕ eyepiece and a 16-mm objective.   They suggest a higher powered microscope for very fine dusts.   The eyepiece, as explained, must be provided with a Whipple disk (Fig. VI-2).   As a means of illumination, an ordinary small electric microscope lamp is used.

Procedure.   After the Sedgwick-Rafter cell has been filled and a cover slip placed over it, care having been exercised to exclude all air bubbles, it is permitted to stand for 30 min to allow the dust to settle. After this time has elapsed, place the cell under the microscope and raise or lower the objective until a point is reached where the dust particles are visible.   It is not necessary to focus through the entire depth of the liquid, because nearly all the particles will have settled to almost a single plane within the 30 min.   A sufficient amount of sample should be taken to show about 2000 particles on the entire Whipple disk field.

In Figure VII-1, O represents the definite position of the objective in the case of a particle in focus when nothing but air separates the particle from the objective.   If a transparent plate M of any medium is placed over the particle, between it and the objective, it is necessary to raise the objective somewhat to bring the object back into focus. This is due to the fact that all rays from O are refracted away from the normal on emerging from the transparent plate (Fig. VII-1) by the two rays ORZ and OUY. In order to bring the particle back into focus, it will then be necessary to raise the objective through the distance OP or $O'P'$.

Since nearly all the particles of minerals or dusts are thinner on the edge than in the center, when they are immersed in liquids they act as imperfect lenses to refract the light, provided they differ in index of refraction from the liquid. If the particle has a higher index than the liquid, it tends to bring light to the focus above the fragment. Therefore, a slight raising of the objective from good focus on the particle causes brightness or transparency within the area of the particle. As the microscope tube is raised higher above focus, this bright area contracts and becomes brighter or more transparent. If the tube is lowered below focus, the particle appears darker than the rest of the field and a highly illuminated halo may surround it. As the tube is lowered, this halo moves outward from the particle. If the mineral has a lower index of refraction than the liquid, it brings light to a focus before the particle. Therefore, a slight lowering of the objective from good focus on the particle causes brightness or transparency within the fragment, and conversely a slight raising above good focus causes the particle to darken.

In order to obtain quantitative results, it is necessary not only to count the number of particles but also to apportion to each particle its due weight, depending upon its size. Ross and Sehl (7) divided the particles into two unit sizes, the first including those particles having an area of less than one-tenth the area of the smallest division on the Whipple disk. These units were given a weight of 1. The second grouping included all the larger particles, which were divided into 10-units, each 10-unit being given a weight of 10. A particle having an area of one-tenth of the smallest division on the Whipple disk was called one 10-unit. The entire area of the smallest division on the Whipple disk was given a weight of 100, or ten 10-units. A particle having one-half the area of the smallest square on the disk was given a weight of 50, or five 10-units. It is simpler and more rapid if the larger particles are counted first in units of ten, then the 1-unit particles are counted. The weight of transparent particles may be computed in the following manner:

$$\text{no. of transparent 10-size units} \times 10 = A$$
$$\text{no. of transparent 1-size particles} \times 1 = B$$
$$A + B = \text{weight of transparent particles}$$

The objective is then lowered until all the particles are in good focus and the procedure outlined above is followed, this time counting and weighting all particles, both light and dark, in order to determine the particle weight.

$$\text{total no. of 10-size units} \times 10 = C$$
$$\text{total no. of 1-size particles} \times 1 = D$$
$$C + D = \text{total weight of all particles}$$

Then

$$(A + B)/(C + D) = \% \text{ transparent particles}$$

This procedure is followed with both the fennel-seed oil cell and the mononitrobenzene cell. In fennel-seed oil, the transparent particles represent quartz and also those minerals having a higher index of refraction than quartz. The transparent particles in mononitrobenzene represent only minerals having a higher index of refraction than quartz. It is clear then that per cent transparent particles in fennel-seed oil minus per cent transparent particles in mononitrobenzene equals per cent free silica.

A modified petrographic method to obtain the silica content of dust is used by Franks and Tressidder (13). Samples obtained by the use of the Kotzé konimeter are used. The glass plate containing the samples is treated with hydrogen chloride vapor and heat. This treatment removes all but the siliceous material from the dust spots. They are then examined with a dark-field microscope. The size, nature, and quantity of the siliceous material affect the quantity of light given off with a dark-field microscope. They found a rough parallelism between the photometric value and the silica content of the dust spots.

While the petrographic method is preferable when the amount of quartz is to be compared with the amounts of such materials as pumice, shale, clay, etc., it is insufficiently quantitative nor can it be applied to fine dust particles. It is very useful as a guide along with chemical analysis. The Ross and Sehl method, while rapid and of undoubted value, does not attempt to distinguish the other materials present. It has the error of including other minerals whose refractive indices fall between 1.54 and 1.55, although these are seldom present. Furthermore, it is only reasonably accurate.

3. Dispersion Staining Method (Dark-Field Modification)

Crossmon (14) developed a method for the determination of free silica by dispersion staining. If the difference in refractive index between free silica particles and their immersion liquid is small, certain portions of their dispersion curves will approach coincidence, and light of the corresponding wavelengths will be transmitted straight through or slightly refracted obliquely to the optic axis of the microscope and thus will not enter the objective. The remaining light for which the free silica and immersion liquid differ to a greater extent in index is refracted and reflected into the objective. The free silica is seen as colored because of the subtraction of the wave lengths passing straight through or slightly refracted from the white light.

Preparation of Index Liquids. Prepare the index liquids by mixing proper proportions of diethylene glycol monobutyl ether (butyl Carbitol), refractive index 1.429 at 25°C, with cinnamaldehyde, refractive index 1.619 at 25°C. These proportions can be computed by use of the equation

$$V_1n_1 + V_2n_2 = V_xn_x$$

where V = the volume of the respective liquid, n = the refractive index of the respective liquid, and V_xn_x = the volume and index desired. Thus, a 10-ml volume of refractive index 1.544 would require 3.95 ml of diethylene glycol monobutyl ether of the stated refractive index plus 6.05 ml of the cinnamaldehyde. This is computed as follows:

$$V_1(1.429) + V_2(1.619) = 10(1.544)$$
$$V_1(1.429) + V_2(1.429) = 10(1.429)$$
$$0.190V_2 = 1.15$$
$$V_2 = 6.05 \text{ ml}$$
$$V_1 = 3.95 \text{ ml}$$

In the same manner, it can be computed that 10 ml of liquid with a 1.553 index of refraction can be made by mixing 6.53 ml of cinnamaldehyde and 3.47 ml of diethylene glycol monobutyl ether. The actual refractive index of the mixture should be checked with a refractometer, and adjustment of the refractive index can be made by adding the ether if the index is high or cinnamaldehyde if the index is low. The indices should be checked from time to time and readjusted, if necessary.

Microscope Apparatus. Crossmon (14) used a microscope with an achromatic condenser having a numerical index of 0.59. He made this by removing the top element of the standard 1.40 numerical aperture (N.A.) condenser.

For examination of the standard particles a 20× (10.25 mm) objective, N.A. 0.40, with antireflection coated lenses may be used. This objective is generally used in the metallographic microscope with a 215-mm tube length rather than in the customary microbiological microscope with a 160-mm tube length; however, this difference in tube length is not considered important when applied to observation of dispersion colors. A dark-field stop having a diameter of exactly 17 mm is placed in the slotted ring below the 0.59 N.A. condenser. This size stop can be made by cutting a circle of the correct size out of black cardboard, metal, or black plastic and cementing it to the center of the customary 16-mm stop.

For examination of the smaller particles, a 43× (4 mm), 0.65 N.A. or a 45× (4 mm), 0.85 N.A. objective is used. In this instance antireflection coated lenses are not necessary, but they give better results. The numerical aperture of these objectives should be reduced by inserting a funnel stop, of 1.092-in. overall length and 0.116 aperture, screwed into the objective. The stop designed for reducing the aperture of the 97× (1.8 mm) objective can be used for this purpose. If this proves to be too long for the 43 or 45× objective, cut off 2 mm from the aperture end and cement the aperture to the shortened tube. The dark-field stop used is the customary 16-mm stop. A 15-mm stop can also be employed. This gives a lighter background and slightly increased dispersion color brilliance.

A research microscope illuminator having a focusable condenser iris diaphragm and a 108-W, 6-V ribbon-filament bulb is suggested as a light source. A "daylight" filter ground on one side can be used in the lamp filter rack when employing the 10.25-mm objective but should not be used with the 4-mm objective since its use appreciably decreases the brilliance of the dispersion colors in the case of small particle size. In operation, the microscope illuminator without filter is focused on the plano side of the mirror and the microscope is focused on the specimen. The substage iris diaphragm of the microscope and the lamp diaphragm are partially closed so as to reduce appreciably the amount of light. The substage condenser is then racked up or down, as necessary, to focus in the center of the field the image of the lamp iris diaphragm in the plane of the object.   The back lens of the objective will now be filled with light of even intensity and an image of the lamp diaphragm can be found in the field of view whenever this diaphragm is sufficiently closed.   The correct-size, dark-field stop can now be inserted, centered in the slotted ring below the condenser, and the substage iris diaphragm opened to full aperture. The preparation should now be observed through the eyepiece and, while viewing, the condenser should be slightly raised or lowered, as necessary, to result in the strongest coloration of the free silica particles.   The illuminator diaphragm should now be adjusted to increase further the coloration.   This is very important as it prevents internal reflections which often cause a haze over the field.   The accuracy of the dark-field method can be greatly increased by the additional use of polarized light.   This form of illumination is most easily obtained by placing a cap analyzer over the eyepiece of the microscope.

Wash the microscope slides and cover slips with soap and water. Rinse them thoroughly with distilled water and dry with lens paper.

Preparation of Sample.   Samples collected on cover glasses may be examined without additional preparation.   Scrape off a representative portion of samples collected on celluloid or metal foil and place on a microscope slide.   Centrifuge the impinger samples collected in alcohol so that the dust is deposited on a microscope cover glass. Place two representative samples of the dust on a clean slide.   Put a drop or two of the 1.544-index-of-refraction liquid on one specimen and apply a cover glass.   Put a drop or two of the 1.553 liquid on the second specimen and cover with a slip.

Foster (15) suggested the use of a wetting agent like a zinc naphthenate (Nuodex zinc 12%) in the index liquids.   A sufficient amount of the wetting agent is added to give a 0.25% solution.   Since this material has a different index of refraction, it is necessary to adjust the index liquids with the aid of a refractometer.   In this variation, twice as much test specimen as would be used directly on a slide is placed into a small boron carbide mortar.   Two drops of the modified-index liquid are added and a pestle is turned in the mortar 200 times to form a suspension by grinding.   The pestle is used to put two drops of the suspension on a slide which is then covered with a slip.   This step is repeated with the second index liquid.

Scheinbaum (16) prepared air-borne dust samples, which had been collected in midget-impinger flasks containing isopropyl alcohol for microscopy, by evaporating them completely on thin glass slides. In this variation styrene monomer or a mixture of ethyl cinnamate and ethylene glycol monobutyl ether with a refractive index of 1.552 was used. Samples obtained on membrane filters were examined directly by immersion in ethyl cinnamate and ethylene glycol monobutyl ether made up to a refractive index of 1.507.

Procedure. The method of counting detailed in the Ross and Sehl method given in Section D-2 of this chapter may be followed.

Free silica particles immersed in the 1.544-index liquid appear blue with a small amount of red. With small particles the amount of red is decreased. In the 1.533 liquid, these particles appear colored a pure blue.

By use of the cap analyzer over the eyepiece, particles in the 1.544-index liquid oriented for the 1.544 index are colored blue with a few large particles colored red; particles oriented for the 1.553 index are colored red although large particles may show only a small amount of red.

Particles identified as free silica are those that shift in color from predominantly blue to predominantly red or the reverse on rotating the cap analyzer 90°. Free silica particles in a 1.553 liquid oriented for that index and examined with polarized light appear colored a dark blue (in the case of large particles a small amount of red is evident); particles oriented for the 1.544 index are light blue. As in the case of the 1.544-index liquid, a shift in color from dark to light blue or the reverse can be obtained by rotating the cap analyzer 90°.

E. Fusion Method

Quartz is relatively refractory as compared with many of the minerals with which it is associated, for it has a melting point of the order of 1700°C. Methods based on this property of quartz have been devised for its estimation by McIntyre and Bozsin (17) and Salazar and Silverman (18).

In the latter method dust, passed through an impinger section, is heated and fused by passage through the air–acetylene flame of a blast burner. The air/fuel ratio is 8.6:1, corresponding to an air flow of 50.9 lpm and an acetylene flow of 5.9 lpm. The heated dust is collected by electrostatic precipitation and is caught in a Vycor crucible, from which it is transferred to a microscope slide and examined under high dry or oil magnification.

Use samples of air-borne dust, rafter dust, or specimens which have been ground so that particles of the size of 10 μ can be obtained.

Procedure. Weigh 1–2 g of the sample, transfer to a beaker, and add a 0.05% aqueous solution of Triton K-12 or an analogous wetting agent. Place on a hot plate and add sufficient water to wet the sample completely and remove all air. Add an equal volume of concentrated hydrochloric acid, cover the beaker with a watch glass, and heat to boiling. Cool, dilute with 1–3 volumes of water, depending upon whether or not a gel has formed, filter through an ashless filter paper, and wash three times with hot water. Transfer the filter paper and contents to a tared crucible, ignite, cool, and weigh to determine the amount of insoluble material.

Grind the residue again, if necessary, to break up any aggregates and transfer to the flask of the fusion apparatus. Light the main burner and the ring burners, adjusting the flame of the former so that it is long, bright, and yellowish white, and so that there is no appreciable air gap between the small canopy and the top of the steel tube. Adjust the flame gradually by means of the flowmeters until the flows mentioned above are obtained. Move the crucible used to catch the precipitate into place and connect the transformer to a current source. Open one bypass slowly to avoid overloading the chamber and precipitator, while gradually closing the second bypass valve. Collect an amount sufficient for several glass slides, disconnect the current, and shut off the air and acetylene. Transfer the treated sample from the crucible to the slides with the aid of a camel's-hair brush or razor blade. Estimate the amount of silica by a direct count of the fused and unfused particles.

Refractory materials—i.e., materials having melting points considerably higher than that of quartz, like Carborundum, chromite, corundum, diasporite, spinel, and zircon—interfere, since such materials would also give unfused particles. Andalusite, dumortierite, cyanite, mullite, and sillimanite may also interfere.

F. Chemical Methods

The amount of free silica in a material can be obtained by the method of ultimate analysis, i.e., an analysis in which every element is determined and its proportion in compounds computed. This method is time consuming, laborious, and of no more value in many instances than the methods of proximate analysis in which a certain type of constituent, as, for instance, total silica, is determined. The chemical methods used for the estimation of free silica in the presence of silicate depend on the greater solubility of silicates in hydrofluosilicic acid, fluoboric acid, or pyrophosphoric acid as compared with the solubility of quartz in these acids. The essential prerequisite for a reagent that can be used for the determination of free silica in the presence of silicate is that its action on silica be slight and its action on silicates be rapid. Chemical methods are often used on the rock sample itself, rather than on the dust obtained from that rock.

1. KNOPF HYDROFLUOSILICIC ACID METHOD

The Knopf (5) method is a series of acid digestions in which the carbonates of the dust are decomposed by hydrochloric acid, the silicates are decomposed by cold hydrofluosilicic acid, H_2SiF_6, and the silica is decomposed by hydrofluoric acid, H_2F_2.

Preparation of Sample. If nonpulverized rock is being examined, grind the material to pass a 150-mesh sieve. This treatment will insure a certain uniformity in size and will aid the action of the hydrofluosilicic acid. Dust ordinarily does not need to be ground.

Procedure. Weigh 0.5 g of the properly prepared sample into a tared, ignited platinum dish. If the preliminary petrographic examination shows the presence of any organic material, the dish should be placed in a muffle oven at white heat for 30 min to burn off the organic matter. Dusts that contain much oil should be defatted with petroleum ether, filtered, and the filter and residue returned to the platinum dish, which should then be ignited as described above. Cool.

If the preliminary examination shows the presence of carbonates, add hydrochloric acid to the dish and heat gently. After the action has ceased, filter on ashless filter paper, wash well with water, return the filter and the residue to the platinum dish, dry, and then ignite again. Allow to cool.

Add hydrofluosilicic acid in moderate excess to the residue in the platinum dish. If the composition of the dust shows no carbonates to be present, the hydrochloric acid treatment is not necessary and the hydrofluosilicic acid may be added directly after the sample is weighed, if no organic matter is present, or after the first ignition and cooling, if organic matter is present. Cover the crucible or dish and set it away in a place where the temperature is reasonably constant and not above room temperature. Care must be exercised not to raise the temperature during the hydrofluosilicic acid treatment, because hydrofluosilicic acid decomposes on heating into silicon tetrafluoride, SiF_4, and hydrofluoric acid, H_2F_2. The hydrofluoric acid will, of course, attack any silica that may be present. Permit the dish to remain with the hydrofluosilicic acid acting on the silicates present for 24, 48, or even 72 hr, depending on the amount and difficulty with which the silicates present dissolve.

Decant the contents of the dish carefully onto an ashless filter paper and wash the crucible thoroughly, the washings being passed through the filter paper. Wash the residue until the wash water gives no precipitate in a clear mixture of dilute potassium chloride and 95% alcohol. Return the filter and its residue to the platinum dish or crucible, dry, ignite, cool, and weigh. The loss in weight is noted and is calculated as silicate. The hydrofluosilicic acid treatment is continued until the weight of the residue remains relatively unchanged.

Treat the residue unchanged by the hydrofluosilicic acid with 2–3 ml of 48% hydrofluoric acid. Free silica volatilizes completely with hydrofluoric acid. Repeat the hydrofluoric acid treatment, if necessary. Ignite, cool, and weigh. The loss in weight may be calculated as free silica.

Hydrofluosilicic acid does have some solvent action on free silica even at low temperatures. The more insoluble the silicates present, the greater length of time will be necessary for them to be dissolved and therefore the greater the amount of free silica dissolved also. Knopf (5) however, has shown that the rate of loss in weight, i.e., the rate of solubility of free silica in hydrofluosilicic acid, is relatively constant. Therefore, a correction factor or equation can be used to correct for the amount of free silica dissolved by the hydrofluosilicic acid during the time it was in contact with the free silica (see page 287). Knopf found an average of 0.7% per day as the rate of loss in original weight of the silica. By using this factor of error, it is possible to compute at the end of an analysis the maximum possible loss in weight of quartz originally present and thus obtain a maximum figure for quartz.

Moke (19–21) found that the action of hydrofluosilicic acid against pure quartz increases with decreasing particle size. Thus, the smaller the particles being treated by this method the greater is the solubility of silica and therefore the greater the error involved. To minimize this error, grind the rock to pass a 150-mesh sieve but not so fine as to pass a 200-mesh sieve or screen. Analyze only the portion whose particle size falls between 150- and 200-mesh fineness.

2. Fluoboric Acid Method

Line and Aradine (22) point out that there is a comparatively large correction factor to be applied in the Knopf method. They suggest the use of fluoboric acid as the silicate solvent. In their method, the silicates are decomposed by fluoboric acid, which attacks free silica much less than does hydrofluosilicic acid. Thus, at room temperature, quartz lost only 0.3% per day in fluoboric acid, as compared with a loss of 0.7% per day for hydrofluosilicic acid; the silicates generally dissolved more readily in fluoboric than in hydrofluosilicic acid. Moreover, fluoboric acid does not decompose as readily as hydrofluosilicic acid does at higher temperatures, its solvent action is greater, and therefore the time of solution is greatly reduced.

Preparation of Fluoboric Acid. Dissolve 32 g of purified boric acid in 75 ml of pure 48% hydrofluoric acid. Pour the hydrofluoric acid into a 125-ml platinum dish and cool in an ice bath. Keeping the dish in the ice bath, add the boric acid in small amounts, allowing each portion to dissolve before more is added. In this way the solution does not become overheated. When all the boric acid has been added, even though the last portion added may not dissolve while the solution is cold, concentrate the solution to about 50 ml on a steam bath. Cool to 0–5°C and filter. The resulting acid is a slightly yellow, fuming, syrupy liquid that should have a specific gravity of about 1.45 and should analyze about 40–45% HBF_4 by the Lange (23) method. It should give no test for fluoride with calcium chloride or lead nitrate solutions. It must be stored in wax or rubber bottles, but the filtration may be made with glass apparatus.

Apparatus. For maintaining the crucibles at a constant temperature for long periods, a large vacuum desiccator may be placed in an electric oven, the heating unit of which is controlled by a thermostat.

An outlet tube is connected to a suction pump and a constant current of warm air is drawn through the desiccator to remove the fumes. The inlet tube may be arranged so that a thermometer can be inserted into the desiccator to check the temperature at which the digestion is taking place without disturbing the apparatus.

Procedure. Weigh into a platinum crucible or dish 0.15–0.2 g of the sample that has been ground to pass a 100-mesh sieve. Add 5 ml of fluoboric acid, 1 ml of phosphoric acid, sp gr 1.39, and 2 ml of $2M$ ferric chloride. Heat the crucible at 50°C for 48 hr, adding more ferric chloride if the yellow color of the solution fades. Transfer the residue to an ashless filter, wash four times with N hydrochloric acid, and five times with hot water. Unless the residue is negligible at this point, place paper and residue in the crucible and destroy the paper by heating the crucible only to dull redness. Repeat this treatment for 48 hr longer. Filter, wash, and determine the weight of the residue. Unless solution has been complete, repeat this treatment for 48-hr periods until a loss of only 1–2 mg is found. This indicates complete solution of the silicate.

Some siliceous materials may be decomposed in less than 48 hr, in which case the treatment with fluoboric acid should be stopped as soon as complete decomposition is apparent. Experience with known materials and dusts will give this information. In other instances, even 8 or 12 days may not effect complete decomposition.

Treat the residue insoluble in fluoboric acid with 2–3 ml of 48% hydrofluoric acid, and repeat until constant weight is obtained after ignition. The loss in weight corresponds to the free silica content of the residue. This value must be corrected for the amount of free silica dissolved during the time required to decompose the silicate. The correction factor is 0.34% per day.

When the residue is practically pure silica, the treatment with hydrofluoric acid will give the correct value for quartz; if undecomposed silicates remain, the loss with hydrofluoric acid will be too high, owing to attack of the silicates.

The increased solubility of the free silica in the fluoboric acid at higher temperatures is undoubtedly due to hydrofluoric acid. Line and Aradine (22) suggest that if the fluoride ion is removed from solution, i.e., if its so-called ionization is depressed, it will have less effect on the free silica. They achieve this result by the addition of ferric chloride and phosphoric acid. The ferric ion most probably forms the complex ion $FeF_6{}^{3-}$, or a ferric fluoborate, and the phosphoric acid reacts to form monofluorophosphoric acid:

$$2H_3PO_4 + H_2F_2 \rightleftharpoons 2H_2PO_3F + 2H_2O$$

Both of these reagents do have the effect of reducing the solubility of free silica in fluoboric acid at higher temperatures. The color of the ferric ion has the additional advantage of indicating its absence as the color of the solution fades.

Calculation of Free Silica. Both the Knopf method and the fluoboric acid method of Line and Aradine for the estimation of free silica in the presence of silicates employ a correction factor to account for the solubility of free silica in the solvents used. In the Knopf method this solubility averages 0.7% of the amount of free silica per day. In the fluoboric acid method this correction factor is 0.34% per day.

In order to compute the milligrams of quartz or free silica originally present from the milligrams of free silica found in the residue, Kaplan and Fales (24) make use of the compound-interest law, also called the law of organic growth or the snowball law, which may be expressed for rates of decrease by the differential equation

$$dy/dx = -ky$$

This expression is the first derivative of the exponential equation

$$y = y_0 e^{-kx}$$

This may be expressed in the logarithmic form

$$\log y = \log y_0 - kx \log e$$

Applied to the solution of computing the amount of free silica originally present from the amount of free silica in the residue, the symbols of this equation have the following meaning:

y = mg of free silica in residue
y_0 = mg of free silica originally present
k = rate of loss, equivalent to 0.7% per day in the Knopf method and 0.34% per day in the fluoboric acid method
x = time of action in days
$\log e$ = 0.43429

For example, if in a determination of quartz in the presence of refractory silicates by the Knopf method, 500 mg of dust required 10 days of treatment with hydrofluosilicic acid, leaving a residue corresponding to 50 mg of quartz, then the amount of quartz originally present in the original sample of dust may be calculated as follows:

$$\log y_0 = \log y + kx \log e$$
$$= \log 50 + (0.007 \times 10 \times 0.43429)$$
$$= 1.72937$$
$$y_0 = 53.63 \text{ mg}$$

The portion analyzed contained 53.63 mg of free silica or quartz present, originally. This corresponds to 10.7% quartz in the portion of dust taken for analysis.

Where the error in estimating free silica is very large due to improper sampling or other reasons, calculation by use of this formula is unwarranted.

3. Pyrophosphoric Acid Method

The chemical method for free silica most commonly used in industrial hygiene analysis over the past decade has been the pyrophosphoric acid method described by Talvitie (25), or variations of this method. Hot pyrophosphoric acid dissolves silicates and metallic oxides, forming water-soluble complexes with both acidic and basic constituents. Pyrophosphoric acid has little solvent action on the quartz fraction. The pyrophosphoric acid is formed and simultaneously the silicates and oxides are dissolved by heating the sample with 85% phosphoric acid (orthophosphoric acid) for an empirically determined time at a given temperature. The quartz is separated from the test solution by diluting the syrupy pyrophosphoric acid with water, filtering, and igniting the residue. It is then weighed and its purity evaluated by volatilization with hydrofluoric acid.

Two variations of this method will be detailed: one in which a petrographic examination is also made and the other in which the solution step is so controlled that correction factors can be applied. The first modification is a variation described by Landry (26).

a. Landry's Modification of the Talvitie Method

This method, which requires the simplest of laboratory equipment, is applicable to the rapid determination of quartz in a wide variety of rocks, ores, clays, and industrial dusts in the presence of silicates. Fluoboric acid is used to avoid clogging of the filter paper by traces of gelatinous silicic acid formed during the procedure, but difficulty from precipitation of dissolved silica is unlikely since its deposition in even small amounts also clogs the filter paper and prevents continuation of the analysis.

Before volatilization by hydrofluoric acid of the quartz from the phosphoric acid residue (and after separation from the dissolved silicate material by filtration), a small amount is removed for petrographic examination to verify the presence of silicon dioxide and/or the efficiency of the phosphoric acid treatment—the petrographic examination is based on the Becke line and birefringence which are the two major optical properties of interest in the respirable dust size, according to Williams (27).

Nagelschmidt (28) has shown by interlaboratory tests that the best results obtained by chemical (or x-ray) procedures for the determination of quartz in respirable sizes showed a variation of $\pm 7\%$ which is considerably higher than Landry's evaluation data for Talvitie's method. That gave a standard deviation of 1.8% for material ground to pass 200 mesh. Unless the sample can be elutriated to a given size range, it is probably better to use only broad correction factors for the quartz dissolution error and the unattached silicates remaining in the phosphoric acid residue. The reported data, based on duplicate samples, should preferably include the standard deviation for this procedure as determined by the laboratory involved.

Apparatus. *Heater.* The recommended source of heat is a 550-W Type RH Precision heater mounted on a continuous, mechanical, swirling device known as the Yankee Rotator. A 0.25-in. Transite or asbestos board with a hole slightly larger than the bottom of the Phillips flask serves as a retainer for it. As a preliminary adjustment, the rheostat should be set to apply 150 V across the heating element with a 220-V source of electricity and eventually adjusted to a temperature that will cause phosphoric acid to dissolve completely oligoclase, orthoclase, or talc in 14 min.

An alternative heating device is a Lindberg hot plate whose top has been removed to expose the Nichrome heating element set at a temperature to obtain a standardized optimum time of solution for the minerals mentioned above.

Funnel (see Fig. VII-2).

Phillips Flasks. 250 ml in pairs selected to match by weight.

Reagents. *Fluoboric Acid.* Pour with continuous stirring (while wearing a plastic safety visor) 100 g of 48% hydrofluoric acid into a mixture of 56 g of boric acid crystals in 100 ml of distilled water contained in a Bakelite vessel (or plastic beaker made from an empty hydrofluoric acid bottle) immersed in ice water. The resulting exothermic reaction will cause all the boric acid to dissolve. The fluoboric acid is transferred to an empty, dry plastic bottle with a safety

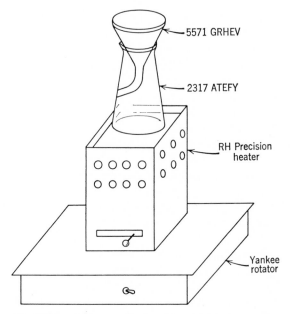

Fig. VII-2. Apparatus for Landry's modification (26).

spout (such as a hydrofluoric acid bottle) while still quite warm since the excess will recrystallize out upon cooling to room temperature. A correction factor should be determined for each new batch of fluoboric acid that is prepared.

Hydrochloric Acid, conc., C.P.

Hydrofluoric Acid, 48%, C.P.

Nitric Acid, conc., C.P.

Paper Pulp.

Phosphoric Acid, 85%, C.P.

Quartz, 200 Mesh. Selected, clear crystals of quartz are washed with concentrated hydrochloric acid, well rinsed with distilled water, dried, and ground to pass through 200 mesh.

Canada Balsam.

Procedure. *Preparation of Sample.* Settled Dust. A 2.0-g sample obtained by quartering a 25.0-g portion is sieved through a 200-mesh screen, and the retained material is weighed to determine the per cent passing through, which should be greater than 90% for a typical settled dust. This type of sample should never be ground.

Minerals. A sufficient amount of representative material is ground and quartered to produce 2.0 g of 200-mesh mineral.

Chemical. Weigh at least duplicate (and preferably triplicate) 0.500-g portions (M) of the 200-mesh material on a watch glass and transfer to individual 250-ml Phillips flasks, using 25 ml of 85% orthophosphoric acid to rinse down the sides of each container. Swirl the flask vigorously to disperse the mineral completely throughout the acid, cover with the funnel, place the flask directly on the element of the rotating Precision heater (or Lindberg hot plate) which has been allowed to preheat for 45 min, and simultaneously begin to time with a stopwatch. When a hot plate is used and the boiling subsides, swirl the flask for 3 sec at 1-min intervals (but *without removing it from the surface of the hot plate*) to prevent superheating by maintaining the sample distributed in the phosphoric acid.

At the end of 14 min, remove the flask from the heater, swirl it for 1 min to dissolve any gelatinous silicic acid which has formed on the sides of the flask at the acid level. Then transfer the flask to a cool surface and immediately remove the funnel with care, simultaneously allowing any adhering liquid to run down the sides of the flask. After cooling to room temperature, add 125 ml of 60–70°C distilled water to wash down the sides of the flask, and immediately swirl vigorously to dissolve completely the syrupy phosphoric acid. Then wash down the upper part of the flask with 10 ml of fluoboric acid and finally rinse with 25 ml of distilled water. Allow the solution to stand undisturbed for an hour.

Filter the solution through a No. 42 Whatman filter paper lined with a small amount of paper pulp. Using a policeman and wash bottle containing cold 1:9 hydrochloric acid, transfer the residue quantitatively to the filter paper which should be washed thoroughly and successively with cold, then hot 1:9 hydrochloric acid, followed by several washes with distilled water.

Place the filter paper in a tared platinum crucible, ignite at low heat to char the paper, and finally heat at 950°C for 15 min. Cool in a desiccator and weigh to obtain the weight of the phosphoric acid residue (R_0). These data should be tabulated, along with the weight of the residue after removing a small amount of it for petrographic analysis (R_p). A portion of the residue can conveniently be kept in a small gelatin capsule.

Moisten the remaining residue with a few drops of 1:1 sulfuric acid, add approximately 5 ml of 48% hydrofluoric acid, and heat on a water bath to volatilize the quartz and hydrofluoric acid. Evaporate off the sulfuric acid by imbedding the crucible in a sand bath and gently heating it until sulfur trioxide fumes are no longer liberated. Repeat the volatilization procedure, carefully remove any particles of sand adhering to the crucible, ignite at 950°C for 5 min, cool, and weigh to obtain the quantity of nonvolatile bases remaining (B). Correct this value for the amount of original residue removed for petrographic examination by multiplication with the ratio R_0/R_p to obtain B_r and subtract from the phosphoric acid residue data (R_0) to get C, the quartz content.

Calculate the percentage of quartz from the formula:

$$C/M \times f_c \times 100 = \% \text{ quartz}$$

where f_c is a correction factor for each batch of fluoboric acid.

Correction Factor, f_c. Using pure 200-mesh quartz, determine duplicate samples, according to the procedure outlined, each time a new batch of fluoboric acid is prepared, and calculate the factor as follows:

$$f_c = \frac{\text{weight of quartz}}{\text{phosphoric acid residue} - \text{hydrofluoric acid residue}} = \frac{M_c}{R_c - B_c}$$

Petrographic Examination. This evaluation is based on the fact that of the common minerals, whose dissolution times in phosphoric acid have been studied by Talvitie (25), only the common silicates such as albite, oligoclase, and orthoclase have both a birefringence and indices of refraction similar to quartz, which results in a potential major source of interference from the viewpoint of petrographic identification. Fortunately, the latter two are completely dissolved within the time of treatment specified and the use of Canada balsam as a mounting medium permits an estimation of the amount of albite present, since this mineral is practically invisible in that medium due to similarities in their respective refractive indices but will reappear as colored particles when the 550 retardation plate is inserted in the corresponding slot of the petrographic microscope.

Other minerals that are quite resistant to the phosphoric acid treatment, which include andalusite, corundum, cyanite, topaz, and beryl, also have a low birefringence, but their indices of refraction are generally very high except beryl; the remainder, tourmaline, sillimanite, pyrophyllite, and spodumene, have high birefringences and high indices of refraction which, in both cases, permit differentiation from the quartz, as follows:

Using the tip of wooden match stick sharpened to a fine point remove a small amount of the phosphoric acid residues stored in the gelatin capsule and transfer the mineral to a drop of Canada balsam located on a microscope slide. Disperse the particles thoroughly throughout the balsam by stirring with the match tip, and place the slide on a preheated Lindberg hot plate to cook the balsam until its surface is free of air bubbles, at which time remove the slide immediately from the hot plate and cover with a cover glass. Any bubbles trapped in this operation can usually be forced out by slight additional heating with the gentle application of pressure using the match tip. Cool the slide to room temperature and study it under the petrographic microscope.

As the first step, observe various fields under crossed Nicol prisms while using the 550 retardation plate at low magnification (10×) to obtain a differential count of the number of particles having a low birefringence (i.e., having a greenish-blue color that changes to orange-yellow upon rotating the stage 90°, or vice versa) in respect to the total number present in a given field. These data, after deducting the quantity of albite (or similar minerals) present, will give a rough estimate of the percentage of quartz to be expected for comparison with the corrected chemical results. Repeat the petrographic examination of the various fields at higher magnification (45×), identify the particles showing low birefringence as quartz according to their Becke-line characteristics, and enumerate by count (or area, if desired, utilizing a filar micrometer).

With experience, the Becke-line data—which is the halo surrounding the imbedded particles that moves towards the substance with the higher refractive index upon raising the focus—can be obtained without removing the 550 retardation plate for greater facility of operation. Using cooked Canada balsam, the quartz (with low birefringence) has indices of refraction slightly higher than the medium and the halo will move into the crystals. In all these examinations, a slide similarly prepared from pure quartz carried through the complete chemical procedure should be observed for comparative purposes.

The principal objective of such petrographic data is to confirm the presence of quartz in the phosphoric acid residue and ascertain the occurrence of resistant, high-index-of-refraction material like beryl, pyrophyllite, sillimanite, spodumene, and tourmaline to explain a high-index-of-refraction residue from the hydrofluoric acid treatment. Naturally, the source of the original material will give a clue to the potential presence of such minerals.

Precision. The data obtained in determining the various correction factors, f_c, can be plotted as a control chart.

In addition, prepare 200-mesh synthetic mineral samples of known quartz content in the presence of interfering minerals such as the ones mentioned above, in the three ranges of interest—below 5%, between 5% and 50%, and greater than 50% quartz—and determine in replicate according to the technique outlined to obtain the standard deviation for this procedure; these data should be reported with all analytical results. Normally, this value should be in the vicinity of 1.8% for these synthetic mineral samples, and approaching 0.3% for pure quartz.

Sampling Procedure. Take the settled dust sample at the breathing level in the zone of operation in an amount exceeding 25 g if possible.

Precautions and Notes. Pretreat samples containing amorphous silica, cristobalite, diatomaceous earth or trydimite as follows: gently boil a 1.00-g sample for 30 min with 50 ml of 10% sodium hydroxide, using a 250-ml Phillips flask. Dilute with 75 ml of distilled water, heat again to incipient boiling, allow the residue to settle for 15 min, and decant the supernatant liquid while still hot through No. 42 Whatman filter paper containing a small amount of paper pulp. Add 75 ml of water and repeat the process of washing by heating, settling, decantation, and filtration. The combined filtrate may then be subjected to rational analysis (Section F-4 of this chapter) according to the technique of Goldman (32) to determine the soluble silica content.

Ash the filter paper and transfer the filtration residue obtained, if any, to the 250 ml Phillips flask (containing the sodium hydroxide insoluble residue) by rinsing out the platinum crucible with small portions of 85% phosphoric acid until 25 ml have been added to the flask. Continue the analysis as indicated under Procedure, Chemical and Petrographic.

A sample of pure quartz should be carried through the complete procedure to obtain the corresponding solubility correction factor.

Frothing of the phosphoric acid will occur if an appreciable amount of organic material is present. This may be removed in the absence of alkalies or carbonates, by ignition of a 2.00-g sample in a porcelain crucible at a temperature not to exceed 700°C. If the latter constituents are present, the weighed sample should be treated with dilute hydrochloric acid, and the residue filtered and then washed with 1:9 hydrochloric acid (to avoid conversion of any quartz present to more soluble forms) prior to ignition. Carbon or graphite do not have to be removed.

Generally, it is best to eliminate sulfides by heating a 0.5-g sample in a Phillips flask with 10 ml of freshly prepared aqua regia for approximately 30 min. After careful dilution with 50 ml of water, allow the residue to settle and decant the major portion of the supernatant liquid through No. 42 Whatman filter paper (which is saved for filtering the same sample after treatment with phosphoric acid, etc.) containing paper pulp. Add phosphoric acid and continue procedure as outlined under Procedure, Chemical and Petrographic.

Since threshold limits are stated in terms of ranges, i.e., below 5%, between 5% and 50%, or above 50% quartz, it is evident that analytical results should be reported only to the nearest per cent, but they should include the standard deviation.

Unless the silicates originally present in the mineral sample producing the hydrofluoric acid insoluble bases can be completely identified, it is not recommended that an arbitrary conversion factor be utilized to apply a correction for this residue—this is based on the assumption that no correction is always preferable to a doubtful one.

Although it is recognized that 200-mesh material includes an appreciable quantity of particles larger than those of known etiological interest and may not be truly representative of the per cent composition of the respirable dust according to Hatch and Moke (19) the Talvitie method is recommended for use until more information becomes available or new techniques are developed.

b. Jephcott and Wall Method

Jephcott and Wall (29) developed a variation of the pyrophosphoric acid method for the determination of silica which depends upon control of the particle size and the time of heating to obtain uniform results.

Preliminary Treatment of Samples. Grind samples of a particle size greater than 74 μ to pass through a 200-mesh sieve before analysis. If sulfide minerals are present, digest the sample in a few milliliters of warm aqua regia and evaporate on a hot plate. Transfer the residue to a 100-ml platinum dish with dilute hydrochloric acid and again evaporate to dryness. Treat the sample as described below except add the phosphoric acid, after cooling to 100°C, to the residue in the platinum dish.

Procedure. Put 30 ml of 85% orthophosphoric acid into a 100-ml platinum evaporating dish and heat slowly with constant stirring to 220°C (the excess water is driven off at about 180°C and on further heating an anhydrous mixture of phosphoric acids is obtained). Cool to about 100°C and add 0.25 g of the sample. Hold the mixture at this temperature until any foaming subsides. Reheat the mixture and maintain with constant stirring at a temperature between 230 and 240°C for 5 or 15 min, depending on the nature of the sample.

A 5-min heating interval is sufficient for mixtures such as foundry sands or ceramic clays. A 5-min heating interval can also be used with silicates decomposed with more difficulty, but only if the particle size of the sample is known to be less than 5 μ.

Cool for 2 or 3 min and pour the mixture slowly into a 400-ml beaker containing 125 ml of water. Rinse out the platinum dish with water, stir the mixture in the beaker, and allow the undissolved particles to set. When very fine particles are present, add some macerated filter paper and a few drops of hydrochloric acid. Allow the mixture to stand overnight before filtering. Filter the mixture through Whatman No. 44 filter paper, using double papers if necessary, to obtain a clear solution. Refilter opalescent filtrates through the same filter paper. Wash the precipitate several times with hot dilute hydrochloric acid. Ignite in a tared platinum crucible, cool, and weigh.

If the particle size of the larger quartz grains is unknown, determine particle size at this time. Do this by dispersing a very small amount of the quartz in water, evaporating a drop of the suspension on a microscope slide, and measuring the size of the larger particles with the aid of a graticule or filar micrometer.

Moisten the precipitate in the crucible with a few drops of con-

centrated sulfuric acid and add cautiously 5 ml of 48% hydrofluoric acid. Allow to stand for 15 min, warm on a hot plate, and
keep at 50–60°C until a clear solution is obtained. This may take
from a few minutes to a few hours, depending upon the particle size
of the quartz. Evaporate the solution to dryness. Bring the crucible
to a red heat, cool, and weigh. Record the weight of the residue.
Subtract this weight directly from the weight of the quartz precipitate.
Generally the residue is small, except with dusts containing materials
such as quartz with imbedded impurities, talc, graphite, or artificial
abrasives.

Calculation. Calculate the quartz content of the sample as follows:

$$\% \text{ quartz} = \frac{P - R}{S} \times C \times 100$$

where P = weight of precipitate after treatment with phosphoric
acid, R = weight of residue after final treatment with hydrofluoric
and sulfuric acids, C = correction factor for the dissolution of quartz
(Table VII-1), and S = weight of sample.

TABLE VII-1

Correction Factor for Loss of Quartz in Analyses of
Quartz–Silicate Mixtures

Particle size of quartz, μ	Heating interval, 5 min	Heating interval, 15 min
44–74	1.01	1.01
20–44	1.01	1.01
10–20	1.01	1.01
5–10	1.02	1.02
2–5	1.02	1.04
1–5	1.03	1.07
1–2	1.09	1.14
Less than 1	1.13	1.23

4. RATIONAL ANALYSIS

a. Shaw's Modification of Selvig's Method (30,31)

The principle for the rational analysis of materials for the determination of quartz is the attempt to remove from the sample all
minerals except the quartz. The various minerals present are de-

composed by suitable treatment with acids such as sulfuric and hydro-chloric, and the products of decomposition are removed by solution in water and Lunge solution, which consists of 100 g of crystallized sodium carbonate and 10 g of sodium hydroxide dissolved in water and diluted to 1 liter. The decomposition of these minerals is seldom complete, with the result that the residue obtained after such treatment contains not only the quartz but also varying quantities of undecomposed silicates. A correction is usually made for the presence of these undecomposed minerals by assuming them to be orthoclase, the amount being calculated from the alumina present in the residue. In the case of shales and coal-measure rocks (32), the error introduced is negligible.

Procedure. Grind 5 g of the sample to pass a 60-mesh sieve. Mix with 300 ml of dilute hydrochloric acid, 2.5% by volume, and heat to boiling in a deep porcelain dish of 1300-ml capacity. Allow the dish to stand for 2 hr or until the material has settled, and siphon off the clear liquid. It is advisable to have a tap or pinch clamp in the siphon tube to reduce the rate of flow toward the end of the operation; if the siphon is clamped so that the end of the short limb is adjustable in the liquid, it will be found possible to remove practically the whole of the solution without disturbing the solid material. Stir the residue with 100 ml of water, add 100 ml of sulfuric acid (1:1), and boil the mixture. Stir frequently and boil until acid fumes are freely evolved. The temperature of the solution should not rise above 200°C. It is best to use a thermometer in order to keep a check on the temperature. The total time of the evaporation should be approximately 45–60 min. Allow the dish to cool for 30 min and dilute its contents with 1 liter of water. Stir well and allow to settle. Siphon off the clear solution. Treat the residue with 100 ml of water and 100 ml of sulfuric acid (1:1) and evaporate once more. After dilution, settling, and siphoning off the solution again, neutralize with Lunge solution. If the amount of acid liquid remaining in the dish is large, i.e., of the order of 20 ml or more, use 50% sodium hydroxide solution for the neutralization in order to prevent excessive dilution of the Lunge solution in the following operation.

Add 300 ml of Lunge solution and heat the liquid to boiling with frequent stirring. Allow the mixture to stand for 2 hr, siphon off the supernatant liquid, and boil the residue for 5 min with 500 ml of concentrated hydrochloric acid. Dilute to 1 liter and allow to settle.

Siphon off the acid solution, neutralize the remaining acid with Lunge solution or with 50% sodium hydroxide solution, add 150 ml of Lunge solution, and heat the mixture to boiling. Allow to stand for 2 hr. Siphon off the Lunge solution and boil the residue for 5 min with 200 ml of concentrated hydrochloric acid. Add 200 ml of water and filter the mixture through Whatman No. 40 filter paper. Transfer the residue to the filter, wash twice with hydrochloric acid (1:3), then with water until the washings are free from chlorides, and, finally, ignite to constant weight in a tared platinum crucible. To the ignited residue add 5 ml of water, 5–10 drops of concentrated sulfuric acid, and 15 ml of hydrofluoric acid. Evaporate the resultant mixture on a hot plate until sulfuric acid fumes are evolved. Repeat the evaporation with 2 further quantities of hydrofluoric acid, continuing the heating during the final evaporation until sulfuric acid fumes are *freely* evolved, to insure complete removal of fluorine, which would interfere with the determination of alumina in the residue.

Extract the contents of the crucible with water and filter the solution. Determine alumina in the usual way by precipitating with ammonia, using methyl red as an indicator to avoid excess (33). The weight of alumina, multiplied by 5.41, gives the equivalent weight of potash feldspar, and this, subtracted from the weight of the ignited residue previously determined, gives the amount of quartz or free silica in the sample.

This method of rational analysis when applied to coal-measure rocks and shales tends to give low results, but the method can, in general, be relied upon to give results accurate within 2% for these rocks.

5. Flotation Methods for Quartz

Quartz may be separated from other minerals which differ from it in specific gravity by flotation (34), using various liquids of known specific gravity. Bromoform is one of the liquids commonly used. Others (35) have used a mixture of acetylene tetrabromide, i.e., tetrabromoethane, and ethylene bromide. The dust is treated with sulfuric acid, dried, and then centrifuged in this mixture, whose specific gravity approaches that of quartz, 2.65. By centrifuging at great speed, 10,000 rpm, it is possible to remove everything under a specific gravity of 2.63. The remaining particles are examined for quartz.

6. Micro Method for Silica in Dust (3,36)

Place 5–10 mg of dust in a tared platinum crucible of 2–3-ml capacity. Determine the loss on heating at 100°C and the loss on ignition. Fuse the dust with 3–4 times its weight of sodium carbonate. Take up the melt in 1 ml of water and neutralize without danger of squirting by exposing it to the acid vapor from a small dish of hydrochloric acid warmed slightly on the top of an air oven run at 100°C. Support the crucible in a small triangle resting on the dish of acid and cover both with a large crystallizing dish or a small bell jar. Render the silica insoluble by evaporation 3 times with hydrochloric acid, followed each time by drying for 20 min at 105°C. Take up the residue in water containing about 0.25 ml of hydrochloric acid and filter through a King (37) filter stick into a glass micro beaker for other determinations such as iron or aluminum, if desired.

Ignite the insoluble matter, cool, and weigh. Volatilize the silica by treatment with hydrofluoric acid and evaporate in the presence of water containing dilute sulfuric acid. Finally, ignite the crucible for 2 min and reweigh. Nitric acid may also be used for the dehydration of the silica.

a. King Filter Stick

The filter stick of Emich (38,39) and other microanalysis has been modified by King (37) to make it suitable for silica determinations.

A thick-walled capillary tube, of about 0.5-cm diameter and with a bore of about 1 mm, is pulled out slightly at one end and cut off smoothly at the other end at a length of about 10 cm. A piece of ordinary glass tubing of 5- or 6-cm length is selected to fit snugly around the first tube. The glass tubes are held telescoped together by a piece of rubber tubing fitted around the inner tube 3 or 4 cm below the pull-out end and over the end of the outer tube. The inner tube can now be pushed back and forth within the outer tube while they remain held together by the rubber collar. The inner tube is so adjusted that its broad end is about 2 mm within the opening of the outer tube. In the shallow cavity thus formed is in-

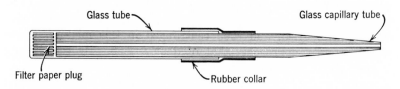

Fig. VII-3. King filter stick (37).

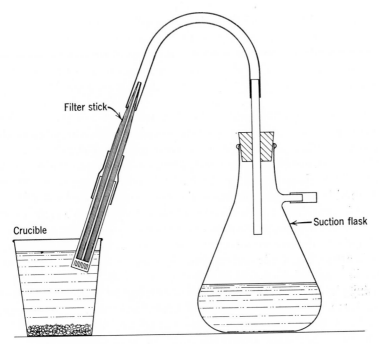

Fig. VII-4. Filtration operation with King filter stick.

serted a roll of ashless filter paper, made by rolling up two or three strips of paper about 7 cm long, or a disk of filter paper fiber, which can be made very conveniently by cutting out a circle from a Fisher's ashless filter-paper "accelerator" with a cork borer of the correct diameter. Fisher's "accelerators" are small squares of pressed filter-paper fiber of approximately 1-mm thickness. When shaken with water these disintegrate and form a uniform suspension of paper fiber. Any crevices in the filter-paper roll or at the edge of the disk can be filled by sucking in a little filter-paper fiber suspended in water.

After filtering the supernatant solution and washings in the silica determinations through the filter stick, the plug of filter paper is pushed out into the crucible by moving down the inner tube through the rubber collar of the filter stick. Any particles of silica adhering to the glass are washed down into the crucible with the aid of a wash bottle.

7. INTERPRETATION OF SILICA RESULTS

Care should be taken in calculating the quartz content of a material from its chemical analysis. Calculations based on formulas for certain minerals as given in texts on mineralogy should seldom be made (32), because such formulas are empirical and may refer only to a particular sample from some definite locality or they may refer to an ideal formula for the pure mineral.   It is best to analyze the particular mineral from which the dust arises and then apply the results of the analysis for the required calculations.   Even this should be done with caution.

The hydrofluosilicic acid method is inaccurate (7) for such materials as shale, clay, pumice, etc., when compared with the petrographic method.   The method should be used only on 150-mesh material. Garnet, sillimanite, zircon, beryl, forstirite, and dumortierite are not completely decomposed by the fluoboric acid method (22).   Shaw's method is applicable only for coal-measure rocks and shales (30).

It is clear from a consideration of these methods that they are not completely adequate for dust determinations, since the median size of industrial dust samples runs below 10 μ.   For rafter samples, it is about 7 μ, while quartz ground to pass a 200-mesh sieve has a median size of 65 μ.   It is therefore necessary to run controls on quartz having the same particle-size distribution as the sample to be analyzed in order to determine whether the correction for the solubility of the quartz will be small enough to insure reasonable accuracy.

Petrographic analysis should always be made and a complete chemical analysis is also valuable, as the total silica content alone gives the upper limit for the amount of free silica present.   With judgment, a certain minimum amount of silica necessary for combination with the other elements may be calculated.

By judicious sampling it is possible to overcome many of the difficulties inherent in the analysis of dusts for free silica.   The more information the analyst can obtain concerning the sample, the easier it is for him to make a satisfactory analysis.   Goldman (32) recommends the accompanying form, which is designed to provide such information.

Supplementing the actual dust sample, samples of all the materials from which the dust may presumably have arisen should be obtained. Such materials will usually prove amenable to analysis, whereas the dust itself may not.   In many cases it happens that the dust sample has practically the same chemical composition as the parent material. In any case excess sampling is not of great moment, but the lack of a particular sample may make itself keenly felt.

DUST SAMPLE SUBMITTED FOR ANALYSIS

Sample number.......... Industry .... Location ....

Where was sample collected?........(Name of factory, quarry, mine, etc.)

What process was carried on where this sample was collected?...........

Method used for collecting sample....................................

From what material did this dust presumably arise?...................
     (Samples of coarse material should be submitted, together with any
     available analytical data)

IF SAMPLE IS OF MINERAL ORIGIN
     Name of principal mineral ....
     Location of deposit..
     Name of deposit (vein, dike, bed, etc.).......................
     Size of deposit..
     Associated gangue materials................................
     Geological description of area.............................

ADDITIONAL INFORMATION

Date.............Collected by...........Submitted by...........

---

8. ESTIMATION OF DISSOLVED SILICA

Solutions containing dissolved silica react with acid solutions of
ammonium molybdate to form colored silicomolybdates (40). A
bibliography of the literature on the colorimetric determination of
silica is given by Schwartz (41).

Reagents. *Sodium Hydroxide–Borate Buffer Solution.* Solution A.
Dissolve 12.4 g of boric acid in water, add 100 ml of N sodium hydroxide solution, and dilute to 1 liter.

Solution B. Prepare a 0.1N solution of sodium hydroxide. Add
6 parts of solution A to 4 parts of solution B to prepare the buffer
solution. Keep in a hard rubber bottle.

Standard Picric Acid Solution. Dissolve 102.4 mg of pure picric
acid in water and make up to 100 ml. Diluting 1 part of this stock
solution to 100 parts with water yields a solution 50 ml of which has
the same quality and intensity of color as that developed in a solution
containing 1 mg of silica when treated with 2 ml of 10% ammonium
molybdate solution and 4 drops of sulfuric acid and then made up to
50 ml. Two ml of ammonium molybdate solution is sufficient for 3.5
mg of silica, but not more.

Potassium Chromate Standard.   Dissolve 0.63 g of potassium chromate in water and dilute to 1 liter.   One ml of this solution diluted with 50 ml of a 1% solution of sodium tetraborate, $Na_2B_4O_7 \cdot 10H_2O$, or other appropriate buffer and enough water to make a total of 100 ml is equivalent to 1 ppm of silica.   Aliquots of this solution ranging from 0.0 to 15.0 ml when diluted with 25 ml of a 1% borax solution and sufficient water to make 55 ml are equivalent to 2 ppm of silica per milliliter (42).

Procedure (41).   To 110 ml of the test solution add 50 ml of sodium hydroxide–borate buffer solution, 2 ml of $1M$ calcium chloride solution, and stir vigorously.   A flocculent precipitate of calcium phosphate forms, which settles rapidly.   Allow the solution to stand for 2 hr with occasional stirring, and then filter.   To 50 ml of the filtrate add 2 ml of 10% ammonium molybdate solution (100 g of ammonium molybdate, $(NH_4)_6Mo_7O_{24} \cdot 4H_2O$, dissolved in water and made to a liter).   Add 1 ml of hydrochloric acid (3:2).   Allow the solution to stand for 10–15 min and compare with an appropriate potassium chromate or picric acid standard.   Subtract the buffer blank from the observed reading and multiply the result by the dilution factor 1.54.

G. Physical-Chemical Methods

Both the petrographic and the chemical methods for the estimation of free silica in dusts and rock have their limitations, as has been discussed.   Bale and Fray (43), Clark and Reynolds (44), and Ballard and Schrenk (45) have described x-ray diffraction methods for the quantitative analysis of dusts.

Hull (46) pointed out a number of facts concerning the diffraction of x-rays by powdered crystalline materials.   Of these the most important is that each crystalline chemical compound, when pulverized and placed in a monochromatic beam of x-rays, gives rise to a *diffraction pattern*, which may be registered photographically and which is unique for that compound.   The same compound always gives rise to the same diffraction pattern, which is different from the pattern obtainable from any other compound or from an allotropic modification of the same compound.   For a mixture of crystalline materials each substance present gives its own pattern, regardless of the presence of the other components, and the resultant pattern is the sum of the patterns of all the component compounds.   By proper resolution of such a complex pattern into its constituent parts, it is found that x-ray diffraction is a most powerful method of qualitative analysis in that it shows not only the elements present but also their true state of chemical combination.

If the sample is not received as a powder, it is thoroughly ground, a small portion is shaped into a wedge, and it is set in the camera, which has a strip of film placed flush against its cylindrical wall. A narrow beam of x-rays emerging from a small window is directed against the sample. The rays diffracted by the sample impinge on the film to yield a picture of lines varying in intensity, which is

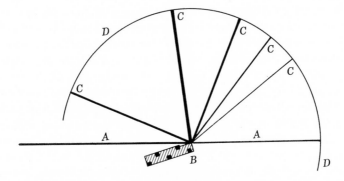

Fig. VII-5. Diagram of x-ray diffraction camera (47): (*A*) x-ray beam; (*B*) specimen; (*C*) diffracted x-ray beam; (*D*) photographic film.

characteristic for different substances, as mentioned previously. The density of these lines may be measured by the use of a microphotometer and recorded.

Clark and Reynolds (47) developed a method which is a modification of the "internal-standard" method of ultraviolet spectroscopy applied to the Hull method of x-ray diffraction by a crystalline powder. A pure crystalline powder, known not to be present in the mixture being examined, is added to the unknown in a definite ratio and the x-ray diffraction pattern registered by a suitable apparatus. The ratio of the density of a line of the substance sought to that of a nearby line of the added standard is determined photometrically. The ratio thus obtained is proportional to the line intensity of the substance sought, which in turn is proportional to the amount of substance in the mixture. By reference to a curve prepared empirically by using mixtures of known composition, the percentage of the component sought is obtainable.

For the registration of the diffraction pattern, a circular reflection type camera, shown diagrammatically in Figure VII-5, may be used. The samples of natural ores and mine dusts or other dusts should first be ground to pass a 200-mesh sieve and then should be ground further by a steel-ball mill, using ball bearings in a cylindrical steel case of such size that samples 1 g in size can be handled without appreciable loss. Twenty-four hours of grinding is necessary to reduce quartz that has already passed a 200-mesh screen to a powder of the required fineness.

The extra grinding insures a homogeneous sample. It is very important to make the specimen homogeneous because the amount of sample actually bathed by the x-ray is somewhat less than 1 mg.

Procedure. Press the specimen being examined into the shape of a wedge and mount it so that the tip of the wedge falls at the center of the camera. Bathe the tip of the wedge by the lower half of the main x-ray beam, which is defined with the aid of a series of lead pinholes 0.075 cm (0.030 in.) in diameter. Register the resulting diffraction pattern on a photographic film held tightly against the outside of a machined circle of which the tip of the wedge is the geometric center. It may be observed that in certain directions from the wedge there is a focusing effect which causes a narrowing of the diffraction lines in those directions. By taking advantage of this, a high degree of resolution can be obtained in any desired portion of the pattern, together with a rather uniform background blackening in the region particularly to be investigated.

The type of camera to be used in this work should have an arrangement so that the wedge-shaped sample may be revolved about its tip. This permits the side of the wedge next to the x-ray tube to be inclined at any angle to the incident beam of x-rays so that the maximum effect of the focusing may be realized. Results may be duplicated exactly because the shape of the specimen is always the same, it can be set at the same angle to the beam every time, and all parts of the camera are permanently fixed with respect to each other and may be locked into position on the instrument table so that conditions surrounding the registration of the diffraction pattern may be maintained at maximum constancy.

The sample may be irradiated with a Philips Metalix fine-structure research x-ray tube with copper anode, mounted in a Hayes x-ray spectrograph, operating at 30 kV and 25 mA. The exposure time is varied from 1 to 6 hr, depending upon the concentration range of the specimen being examined, those samples having the lowest percentages of the substance sought requiring the longer exposures. The amount of the substance being estimated is then obtained by having the principal lines of the diffraction pattern photometered and compared with the standard or reference. The ratios thus obtained are proportional to the relative intensities of the line, and hence to the concentration of the substance sought in the specimen.

Bale and Fray (48) use a somewhat different technique. The dust is finely ground and is placed in a capillary glass tube. The properly filtered K radiation of a molybdenum-target x-ray tube is used to produce a nearly monochromatic beam, which is passed through the contents of the capillary tube. This procedure produces diffractive effects that are identified on a film as bands of different intensity and density, separated by areas of comparatively clear film. Comparison is made with known spectra. The quantitative estimation may be made by comparing the relative film densities of selected strong bands of the substance in a mixed sample with that of a known mixed control of the same substances.

Ballard and Schrenk (45,49) revised the internal-standard method by use of two internal standards yielding five lines (two for calcium fluoride and three for nickel oxide) for comparison with four lines of quartz. By use of the five lines of the two internal standards, it was usually possible to have one or more free from interference with other diffraction lines. A microphotometer record of the diffraction pattern was used to obtain the heights, i.e., the relative intensities, of the quartz lines compared to the standard lines.

For further information concerning chemical analysis by x-ray diffraction, the reader is referred to the work of Hanawalt, Rinn, and Frevel (50), the American Society for Testing and Materials (51), Clark (52), Davey (53,54), and Frevel (55).

The quartz or free-silica content of dusts may be estimated by petrographic, fusion, chemical, physical chemical, or a combination of petrographic and chemical methods. Each method has its advantages and disadvantages. The petrographic method can best be applied to thin sections of the raw material. X-ray diffraction methods must be applied to very finely ground powders. X-ray methods require rather expensive apparatus. The combination of the petrographic and chemical methods provides good information and serves as a check upon the progress of the chemical method.

It is well to recall that danger from free silica, with subsequent production of fibrosis and silicosis, is by no means limited to rock drilling, quarrying, or even foundries. Silica occurs not only in minerals but is also present in vegetable and animal matter. The straw from bamboo and from the grains that are used to make cereals contains fairly large quantities of silica. The common horsetail weed has a large siliceous skeleton. The feathers of birds contain silica and it also occurs in animal remains such as kieselguhr, which consists of the siliceous skeletons of extinct diatoms and is almost pure silica. All of these products are used in industry and hence all of them may provide a silica hazard.

H. Asbestos

Asbestos is the class name for several different fibrous minerals, but commercial asbestos (56–58) is mainly the fibrous form of serpentine known as chrysotile. One of the most important industrial uses of this substance is in the manufacture of fire-resistant textiles. Chrysotile is a hydrous magnesium silicate, $3MgO \cdot 2SiO_2 \cdot 2H_2O$, or $Mg_3Si_2H_4O_9$, containing 44.1% silica, 43.0% magnesia, and 12.9% water. Other types of asbestos often contain silicates of iron, calcium, and aluminum, as well as magnesium (59).

Asbestos dust can be trapped with an impinger dust-sampling apparatus, using 25% aqueous ethyl alcohol as the collecting medium. This solution prevents flocculation of the dust particles without causing excess evaporation in either the sampling flasks or counting cells. Samples may be counted by the light-field technique detailed on page 229ff, using the modified ocular micrometer disk (Fig. VI-4). The dust in 20–30 cu ft of air should be sampled.

The safe threshold value for asbestos dust exposure is considered 5 MPPCF (58). Values are given in Table 7, Appendix.

References

1. Sayers, R. R., and R. R. Jones, *U.S. Public Health Rept.*, **53**, 1453 (1938).
2. Jones, W., *J. Chem. Met. Mining Soc. S. Africa*, **34**, 99 (1933).
3. Matthews, J. W., *Analyst*, **63**, 467 (1938).
4. Jones, W., *Analyst*, **59**, 456 (1934).

5. Knopf, A., *U.S. Public Health Rept.*, **48**, 183 (1933).
6. Greenburg, L., C. B. Ford, W. J. Burke, and B. H. Dolin, *N.Y. State Ind. Bull.*, **17**, 575 (1938).
7. Ross, H. L., and F. W. Sehl, *Ind. Eng. Chem. Anal. Ed.*, **7**, 30 (1935).
8. Faust, G. T., and A. Gabriel, *U.S. Bur. Mines Inform. Circ. 7129* (1940).
9. Faust, G. T., *U.S. Bur. Mines Rept. Invest. 3503* (1940).
10. Foster, W. D., and H. H. Schrenk, *U.S. Bur. Mines Rept. Invest. 3368* (1938)
11. Larsen, E. S., and H. Berman, *U.S. Geol. Survey Bull. 848* (1934).
12. Larsen, E. S., *U.S. Geol. Survey Bull. 679* (1921).
13. Franks, W. R., and L. C. Tressidder, *Mining Mag. (London)*, **51**, 265 (1934)
14. Crossmon, G., *Am. Ind. Hyg. Assoc. Quarterly*, **12**, 117 (1951).
15. Foster, W. D., *U.S. Bur. Mines Rept. Invest. 4573* (1949).
16. Scheinbaum, M., *Am. Ind. Hyg. Assoc. J.*, **22**, 313 (Aug. 1961).
17. McIntyre, C. H., and M. Bozsin, *Ind. Eng. Chem. Anal. Ed.*, **12**, 326 (1940).
18. Salazar, A., and L. Silverman, *J. Ind. Hyg. Toxicol.*, **25**, 139 (1943).
19. Hatch, T., and C. B. Moke, *J. Ind. Hyg. Toxicol.*, **18**, 91 (1936).
20. Moke, C. B., *J. Ind. Hyg. Toxicol.*, **18**, 299 (1936).
21. Travers, M. W., *Chem. Ind. (London)*, **58**, 226 (1939).
22. Line, W. R., and P. W. Aradine, *Ind. Eng. Chem. Anal. Ed.*, **9**, 60 (1937).
23. Lange, W., *Chem. Ber.*, **59**, 2110 (1926).
24. Kaplan, E., and W. T. Fales, *Ind. Eng. Chem. Anal. Ed.*, **10**, 388 (1938).
25. Talvitie, N. A., *Anal. Chem.*, **23**, 623 (1951).
26. Landry, A. S., Institute of Occupational Health, Servicio Cooperative Inter-Americano de Salud Publica, Los Amopolas 350, San Eugenio, Lince, Lima, Peru.
27. Williams, C. R., *J. Ind. Hyg. Toxicol.*, **19**, 44 (1937).
28. Nagelschmidt, G., *Analyst*, **81**, 210 (1956).
29. Jephcott, C. M., and H. F. V. Wall, *A. M. A. Arch. Ind. Health*, **11**, 300 (1954).
30. Shaw, A., *Analyst*, **59**, 446 (1934).
31. Selvig, W. A., *Carnegie Inst. Technol., Mining Met. Invest. Bull. 21* (1925).
32. Goldman, F. H., *U.S. Public Health Rept.*, **52**, 1702 (1937).
33. Hillebrand, W. F., and G. E. F. Lundell, *Applied Inorganic Analysis*, Wiley, New York, 1929.
34. Goldman, F. H., *U.S. Public Health Rept.*, **52**, 1709 (1937).
35. Sartorius, F., and K. W. Joetten, *Arch. Hyg. Bakteriol.* **115**, 135 (1935).
36. Thurnwald, H., and A. A. Benedetti-Pichler, *Mikrochemie*, **11**, 200 (1932).
37. King, E. J., *Analyst*, **58**, 325 (1933).
38. Emich, F., *Lehrbuch der Mikrochemie*, Bergmann, Munich, 1926.
39. Benedetti-Pichler, A. A., *Z. Anal. Chem.*, **64**, 409 (1924).
40. King, E. J., *J. Biol. Chem.*, **80**, 25 (1928).
41. Schwartz, M. C., *Ind. Eng. Chem. Anal. Ed.*, **6**, 364 (1934); **14**, 893 (1942).
42. Swank, H. W., and M. G. Mellon, *Ind. Eng. Chem. Anal. Ed.*, **6**, 348 (1934).
43. Bale, W. F., and W. W. Fray, *J. Ind. Hyg.*, **17**, 30 (1935).
44. Clark, G. L., and D. H. Reynolds, *Ind. Eng. Chem. Anal. Ed.*, **8**, 36 (1936).
45. Ballard, J. W., and H. H. Schrenk, *U.S. Bur. Mines Rept. Invest. 3888* (1946)
46. Hull, A. W., *J. Am. Chem. Soc.*, **41**, 1168 (1919).

47. Clark, G. L., and D. H. Reynolds, *Univ. Toronto Studies Geol. Ser.*, **38,** 13 (1935).
48. Bale, W. F., and W. W. Fray, *J. Ind. Hyg.*, **17,** 30 (1935).
49. Ballard, J. W., H. I. Oshray, and H. H. Schrenk, *U.S. Bur. Mines Rept. Invest. 3520* (1940).
50. Hanawalt, J. D., H. W. Rinn, and L. K. Frevel, *Ind. Eng. Chem. Anal. Ed.*, **10,** 457 (1938).
51. Am. Soc. Testing Materials, Symposium on Radiography and X-Ray Diffraction Methods (1937).
52. Clark, G. R., *Applied X-Rays*, McGraw-Hill, New York, 1932.
53. Davey, W. P., *Study of Crystal Structure and Its Applications*, McGraw-Hill New York, 1934.
54. Davey, W. P., *J. Appl. Phys.*, **10,** 820 (1939).
55. Frevel, L. K., *Ind. Eng. Chem. Anal. Ed.*, **16,** 209 (1944).
56. Page, R. T., and J. J. Bloomfield, *U.S. Public Health Rept.*, **52,** 1713 (1937).
57. Ries, H., and T. L. Watson, *Engineering Geology*, Wiley, New York, 1937.
58. Sayers, R. R., and W. C. Dreessen, *Am. J. Public Health*, **29,** 205 (1939).
59. Fulton, W. B., A. Dooley, J. L. Matthews, and R. L. Houtz, *Pennsylvania Dept. Labor Ind. Special Bull. 42* (1935).

CHAPTER VIII

LEAD

From the broad point of view, almost every metal or metallic compound encountered in manufacture and industry presents some type of industrial hazard. From the more realistic point of view, the important metallic industrial hazards are lead, mercury, arsenic, beryllium, chromium, cadmium, antimony, and their compounds. Of lesser importance, although not necessarily any less hazardous, may be mentioned manganese, vanadium, tellurium, thallium, selenium, nickel, zinc, copper, tin, and their compounds. As a general rule it may be stated that all of these metals are much more hazardous in their compounds than the metal itself, except in the case of fumes, and that the more soluble the compound, the more poisonous it is likely to be. For example, men are often badly poisoned when mining carbonate or oxide ores of lead, whereas lead poisoning is rare among men mining only lead sulfide (galena) (1).

The damage produced by inhalation is much more severe than that produced by swallowing. Lead poisoning is rated as 10 times more liable to occur from breathing lead dust than from swallowing it. This is probably due to the fact that the liver filters out swallowed substances like lead and removes them from the blood before harm can be done. If they are breathed, they are taken up by the blood stream, pumped all over the body, and thus make themselves felt more readily than would otherwise be possible (2).

Plumbism was known in Biblical times. Hippocrates (about 460–357 B.C.) described the illness as a result of working in the smelting of lead ores and other metal ores. The alchemists and early metallurgists were well aware of it. Ramazzini describes the symptoms of lead encephalopathy in his book, *Diseases of Tradesmen*, in 1700. The history of lead poisoning is discussed by Teleky (3). A general discussion is given by Cantarow and Trumper (4).

While deaths from plumbism have practically disappeared from industry (5) and cases of acute lead poisoning are far less frequent than they were a decade ago, there are still large numbers of cases of lead poisoning of the subacute and chronic types. The prevention of lead poisoning is largely a matter of adequate sanitary engineering and medical discipline. It rests essentially upon the elimination of lead-bearing fumes, discipline as to cleanliness, and medical supervision of exposed workers (6,7).

Kehoe (8) has discussed the criteria one can use for evaluating plumbism. Goldwater, Jacobs, and Ladd were engaged in a study of normal values of lead in blood and urine in the period 1961–1964.

A. Lead Compounds in Industry

Among the more important lead compounds to which workers are exposed are lead fume and dust in the melting of lead; lead carbonate, lead sulfate, red lead, and lead chromate in the pigment industry; lead arsenate dust in the manufacture and use of insecticides; lead silicate in the pottery industry; litharge, red lead, and lead peroxide in the storage-battery industry; and the sulfide, carbonate, and oxide of lead in the mining and milling of lead ore (9).   Other lead compounds met in industry are lead suboxide, lead sesquioxide, basic lead carbonate, lead acetate, lead chloride, lead nitrate, tetraethyllead and tetramethyllead.

These compounds generally enter the body by way of the respiratory tract and the gastrointestinal tract. The portal of entry of lead into the system in industrial exposure chiefly associated with lead poisoning is now generally conceded to be the respiratory tract rather than the alimentary tract (10). However, it is to be noted that tetraethyllead is a lipoid solvent and therefore can be absorbed through the skin. Furthermore, when tetraethyllead is exposed to sunlight or is allowed to evaporate, it decomposes and forms as one of its decomposition products triethyllead, which is a poisonous compound.

B. Toxicity of Lead Compounds

The importance of the lead hazard from an economic point of view may be shown by the time spent on compensation in a certain plant. In the mixing department of a storage-battery plant the compensation cases rose to the level of 33% in the third month of exposure to lead (11).

The toxicity of lead compounds is influenced by a number of factors, among which may be mentioned solubility in body fluids, length of time in contact with body fluids, quantity ingested, inhaled, or absorbed, and the quantity present in the circulation at a given time. Lead is thought to be toxic only when present in the systemic circulation. Thus, it can be stored by the body and only becomes a danger when it is returned to circulation in greater amounts than the body can safely eliminate (5).

1. Solubility of Lead Compounds

One of the significant factors of lead poisoning is the failure to realize that a lead compound that is insoluble in water may not necessarily be insoluble in the fluids of the body. This can be seen readily from Table VIII-1.

TABLE VIII-1
Solubility of Lead Compounds

Compound	In serum at 25°C, mg/liter	In water, mg/liter
Lead monoxide, PbO (litharge)	1152.0	17.1
Lead	578.0	—
Lead sulfate, $PbSO_4$	43.7	44.0
Lead carbonate, $PbCO_3$	33.3	1.7
Lead chromate, $PbCrO_4$		0.01

Lead peroxide is slightly soluble in sulfuric acid and is insoluble in water (6,12). Its solubility in blood serum has not been studied.

2. Relative Toxicity of Lead Compounds

Fairhall and Sayers (13), using the storage of lead in bone tissue as an index of the extent to which the system of guinea pigs was flooded with lead in a given space of time and considering the relationship of other factors indicating possible damage, arrange the toxicities of various lead compounds into two groups, those more toxic and those less toxic. This arrangement is shown in Table VIII-2.

TABLE VIII-2
Relative Toxicity of Lead and Its Compounds

Order of toxicity	Method of introduction		
	Injection	Ingestion	Inhalation
Most toxic	Lead arsenate	Lead arsenate	Lead carbonate
		Lead carbonate	Lead monoxide
		Lead monoxide	
		Lead sulfate	
Of similar but lower degree of toxicity	Metallic lead	Metallic lead	Metallic lead[a]
	Lead carbonate	Lead chromate	Lead arsenate[a]
	Lead chromate	Red lead	Lead chromate
	Lead monoxide	Lead dioxide	Red lead
	Red lead	Lead phosphate	Lead dioxide
	Lead dioxide	Lead sulfide	Lead phosphate
	Lead phosphate		Lead silicate
	Lead sulfate		Lead sulfide
	Lead sulfide		

[a] Inconclusive.

3. LEAD STANDARDS

Legge (14) stated that 2 mg of lead per day is the lowest dose that, when inhaled as dust fumes, may in the course of years set up lead poisoning. Oliver (15) concluded that 1 mg of ingested or inhaled lead causes plumbism. Greenburg (15) and co-workers found that employees exposed to an average amount of 0.009 mg of lead per cubic foot of air not present evidences of chronic lead poisoning when the duration of exposure is $1\frac{1}{2}$ years or less but when the duration at such an occupation is $2\frac{1}{2}$ years or more, evidences of chronic lead poisoning are present. Based on Legge's figures for the amount of air respired in a working day of 8 hr, air analyses in the casting shop of a lead-battery plant indicate that inhalation of 1.45 mg of lead per day produces lead poisoning within $2\frac{1}{2}$ years.

The generally accepted standard for the lead concentration in a permissible working atmosphere is 0.2 mg/m^3, as shown in Table 3, Appendix. A study of the toxicity of lead chromate led Harrold (16) and co-workers to conclude that in the case of insoluble compounds like lead chromate the level of lead allowable in the atmosphere should be raised. From his investigation Kehoe (17) concluded that the daily ingestion of slightly more than 2 mg of lead, for a period of more than 1 year, failed to result in any demonstrable effect upon the health or well-being of a healthy adult, but it induced a level of lead elimination higher than that caused by the ingestion of 1 mg daily and a slightly greater rate of lead retention in the tissues.

The U. S. Food and Drug Administration of the Federal Security Agency, taking into consideration the changed views on the toxicity of ingested lead, has raised the tolerance on lead spray residue from the 3.58 ppm (0.025 grain/lb) to 7.15 ppm (0.05 grain/lb) (18).

The minimal amounts of lead normally present in the atmosphere of industrial establishments are 0.10 mg per 10 m^3, generally, and 0.13 mg per 10 m^3 in auto-repair shops. At congested street intersections the corresponding concentration is 0.09 mg per 10 m^3 (19).

The reduction in the number of cases of "painter's colic" is due to the virtual elimination of on-the-job mixing of lead-bearing paints and the substitution of titanium dioxide, magnesium silicate, lithopone (a mixture of zinc sulfide and barium sulfate with some zinc oxide) for all or a substantial portion of the lead white formerly used. Indeed, the use of lead-bearing paint for children's furniture has been forbidden by law in some communities, and the use of lead pigments in most indoor paints has been markedly reduced. The development of good non-leaded outdoor paints of reasonable longevity will assist in reducing this hazard also.

The toxicology of lead has been discussed in considerable detail by Kehoe (8).

C. Field Test and Detection

Lead may be detected by the standard tests of qualitative analysis. For the purposes of analytical toxicology and particularly industrial hygiene chemistry, the following field test and a microscopic test will be useful.

1. TETRAHYDROXYQUINONE FIELD TEST

Tetrahydroxyquinone solution forms a pink complex with compounds of lead such as lead sulfide, arsenate, carbonate, nitrate, chlorate, chromate, and other lead compounds (20). The intensity of the stain has been found to be proportional to the concentration of lead.

Reagents. *Tetrahydroxyquinone Solution.* Dissolve 0.3 g of disodium tetrahydroxyquinone in 0.5 ml of water and slowly add 1 ml of acetone. This should yield a clear orange-colored solution. Prepare the solution just prior to use in the field. Store in a bottle equipped with a dropper which delivers 0.02 ml per drop.

Buffer Solution. This solution has a pH of 2.8. Dissolve 19.0 g of sodium acid tartrate, $NaHC_4H_4O_6 \cdot H_2O$, plus 15 g of tartaric acid, $HOOC(CHOH)_4COOH$, in 100 ml of water. This buffer solution may be stored.

Color Standards. Quino (21) developed a series of color standards by taking atmospheric samples close to a source of lead fumes at different intervals of time. He developed colors on filter paper by adding to the collection surface 2 drops of tetrahydroxyquinone solution followed by 2 drops of the buffer solution. The gradations of color obtained were placed into groups according to the intensity of the stain and six filters of the same stain intensity were assigned to a single group. Five filters from each group were analzyed chemically to obtain the actual concentration. Quino chose four color standards corresponding to 0.10, 0.20, 0.30, and 0.40 mg of lead per cubic meter of air.

For convenience in making comparisons, the four color standards may be arranged in a radial pattern of a circular disk which is provided with a central aperture. Each unknown sample may be placed in turn under the aperture in such a manner that it can be compared visually with the surrounding standards.

The standards are stable for about six months. Artificial standards may be constructed and a field comparator may be made.

Procedure. Place 2.5-cm-diameter Whatman No. 42 filter paper in a suitable holder so that an effective diameter of 2.0 cm is exposed. Draw air at a rate of 4–5 lpm through the filter paper with the aid of a Uni-Jet air sampler or other sampling device for 10 min. Remove the filter from the holder and add 2 drops of tetrahydroxyquinone solution to the center of the paper. Wait 20 sec. Add 2 drops of buffer solution and compare the stain with the standards. Run a blank with each set of tests to make certain there has been no inadvertent contamination.

2. QUALITATIVE TEST

The microscopic test based on the identification of potassium copper lead hexanitrite (22–24) is often used as a qualitative means of ascertaining if lead is present. The lead is precipitated as sulfide in the presence of ammonium sulfate and copper acetate, the copper acting as a collector. After careful washing of the filtered precipitate, the lead sulfide is dissolved in a few drops of concentrated nitric acid. A drop of this solution is evaporated to dryness on a microscope slide. Minute quantities of sodium acetate, acetic acid, and a small crystal of potassium nitrite are added. Lead, if present, crystallizes out as characteristic brown squares and cubes of potassium copper lead hexanitrite, $K_2CuPb(NO_2)_6$.

D. Determination of Lead

The literature contains numerous methods for the detection and estimation of lead. With the realization of the danger from continual inhalation, ingestion, and absorption of even small amounts of lead has come the development of methods by which one can estimate extremely small quantities of lead, that is, of the order of 1 μg, with great accuracy. Not all of the methods can conveniently be detailed here and consequently only the various types of chemical methods will be described. A comprehensive review of the preferred methods for the determination of lead in air and in biological materials has been prepared by the Subcommittee on Determination of Lead in Air of the Committee on Chemical Procedures of the Industrial Hygiene Section (Occupational Health Section) of the American Public Health Association (25). Another review is given by Jacobs (26). The preferred physical method is the spectrographic method. This has been given in detail in the APHA booklet.

The choice of a procedure for the estimation of lead is dependent on a number of factors, the principal ones being the equipment available, the order of the quantity of lead being estimated, and the preference of the analyst. The methods generally used can be classified as follows:

Large and Medium Quantities of Lead:

(1) Precipitation and estimation as lead sulfide.

Medium and Small Quantities of Lead:

(2) Precipitation of lead as sulfide, then as chromate, and estimation with s-diphenylcarbazide or by iodide–thiosulfate titration.

Minute Quantities of Lead:

(3) Extraction with dithizone and colorimetric, photometric or indirect estimation by titration of the dithizone that combines with lead.

These methods are the most widely used and the titration method is particularly suitable when photometric and colorimetric equipment are not available. Such methods for the determination of lead in urine and blood are given in Chapter XIX Section B-1.

(4) Coprecipitation of lead and copper, separation of lead by electrolysis as peroxide and estimation by iodometric titration.

(5) A combination of the dithizone and electrolytic methods.

Polarographic methods for the estimation of lead are described by Kolthoff and Lingane (27), Feicht, Schrenk, and Brown (28), and Goldman and May (29).

In making analyses for microquantities of lead it is essential that all the equipment, glassware, and reagents be as free from lead as possible. This reduces possible sources of contamination and minimizes the blank. The water used in the analyses must be distilled water, preferably redistilled or treated so as to be lead-free. The glassware should be Pyrex or a similar type glass. New silica dishes should be ignited and treated with hot hydrochloric acid before use. Reagents such as hydrochloric acid, nitric acid, ammonium hydroxide, and chloroform should be redistilled and stored in Pyrex glassware. Filter papers should be soaked overnight in nitric acid (1:1000) and then washed free of lead and acid, using large volumes of water with the aid of a Büchner funnel and suction. The papers may be dried in a vacuum desiccator over sulfuric acid to avoid the brittleness induced by drying in an oven. It is good practice in the dithizone method to give the glassware used an additional washing with a mixture of 50 ml of nitric acid (1:1000), 10 ml of ammonia–cyanide mixture, and a few milliliters of dithizone in chloroform solution. Then rinse thoroughly with lead-free water. In other methods, in addition to the usual treatment with cleaning solution, washing, etc., the glassware should be rinsed thoroughly with tap water, distilled water, and lead-free water.

1. SAMPLING

If a sample under examination is in solid form, it should be pulverized to pass through a 100-mesh sieve. A representative specimen, containing not more than 0.2 mg of lead, should then be taken for analysis if one of the methods designed for smaller quantities of lead is used.

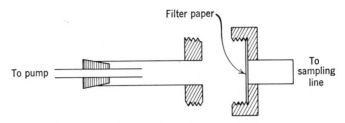

Fig. VIII-1. Filter device for lead fumes and dust.

Lead fumes and lead dust in the atmosphere of the workshop may be sampled as described in Chapters II, IV, and V. The macro or Greenburg-Smith impinger gives excellent results with lead dusts (15,30). Nitric acid (1:99) may be used as the collection medium. Electric precipitators are preferable for the collection of fumes. Filtration devices are also used for fumes and dusts. Fairhall and Sayers (13) used the filtering device shown in Figure VIII-1. The filter-paper devices of Brown, Silverman and Ege, and Bayrer and Hough have been previously described (see pages 192–194). A relatively large selection of holders for filter papers, membrane filters, glass fiber webs, and other filter media are commercially available.

When the electric precipitator is used for the collection of fumes, a convenient procedure is sampling for $23\frac{1}{2}$ min at a rate of 3 cfm. This is equivalent to a total sample of 2 m^3, which makes the calculations of results simpler.

The Greenburg-Smith impinger has a varying efficiency in the collection of lead fumes, which depends on the sampling flow rate. Thus, at sampling rates of 28.3 lpm the efficiency of a single large impinger ranged from 21 to 53%, and for two impingers in series from 55 to 60%. The efficiency of a single midget impinger ranged from 13 to 21% (31). It was shown by Keenan and Fairhall (32) that the efficiency of the large impinger could be brought to nearly 100% by increasing the sampling flow rate to 1.5 cfm, thus insuring impingement of the fume particles against the plate.

Sampling may also be performed by passing air at a rate of 200–300 ml/min through two absorbers in series containing 10% nitric acid.

The general procedure, using the all-glass Greenburg-Smith impinger, is to trap the lead dust in 250 ml of lead-free water. Some lead compounds require collection in a dilute nitric acid solution. In this case, 10 ml of nitric acid, sp gr 1.42, in 250 ml of water is adequate. If modified impingers of this type that require less absorbing solution are used, the amount of acid added should be known, for it is important if the dithizone method is to be used. Since the sampling rate with the Greenburg-Smith impinger is generally kept slightly below 1 cfm, in order to obtain a sample of 1 m³, from 30 to 40 min should be allotted for the sampling. It may be necessary to sample as much as 60–90 cu ft or as little as 10 cu ft, depending, of course, entirely on the lead content of the air being sampled. The samples should be taken at positions which make them representative of the general conditions of the workroom or of the air breathed by the worker. If the dithizone method is to be used, the sample should not exceed 0.1 mg of lead.

Preparation of Sample. If the electric precipitator has been used for sampling, close one end of the precipitator tube with a tight-fitting Davel rubber cap (25). Add 50 ml of nitric acid (1:19) and rub the sides with a rubber policeman. Transfer the acid to a Pyrex beaker, add an additional 50 ml of nitric acid (1:19), and after scrubbing the tube transfer to the beaker. Rinse the tube with water, adding the rinsings to the acid wash, and evaporate to a small volume. Store in a glass-stoppered Pyrex cylinder if analysis is not to be performed immediately.

The absorber liquid used in impingers or absorbers should be evaporated to a small volume after the addition of acid. If lead sulfate is present, ammonium acetate should be added to aid in dissolving this compound. Nitric acid should not be used if alcohol is the absorbing liquid. Add either sulfuric acid or hydrochloric acid in place of the nitric acid.

Digest factory and street dusts with nitric acid (1:4) and leach with hot 25% ammonium acetate solution. Filter off the extracts and use the combined filtrate for the analysis.

2. Lead Sulfide Method

The following method based on the precipitation of lead as the sulfide is a comparatively simple method and is easily adaptable to all types of sampling. It is limited, however, to those instances where most of the other metals of the insoluble sulfide group are absent or are present in negligible amounts and where lead is present in more than minute amounts. If the lead-bearing dust is caught on filters, papers, or cellulose materials, place these lead-bearing substances in a silica dish and ash at 550°C. Dissolve the ash in 10 ml of water and 1 ml of nitric acid. Filter, add a drop of phosphoric acid, and make the colorless filtrate alkaline with ammonium hydroxide solution. The phosphate precipitate will contain practically all of the lead and the copper, if any is present, will remain in the filtrate as the complex ammonia compound. Filter, wash well and dissolve the precipitate in 5 ml of dilute acetic acid. Make up to 50 ml in a Nessler tube. Add 5 ml of hydrogen sulfide solution and match the color with that of standard lead solutions treated in the same way. The lead sulfide precipitate may be stabilized by the use of solutions of gum arabic or ghatti by adding 1 ml of a 5% solution of gum ghatti or arabic to the solution in the Nessler tube before it is made to volume. The standards are treated in the same manner. The quantity of lead present is taken to be that of the closest standard.

3. DIPHENYLCARBAZIDE METHOD

In this method (33–37), which is used for medium quantities of lead, the lead sample is ashed, if necessary. The ash is dissolved and the lead is precipitated as the sulfide. If further separation is necessary, the sulfides are dissolved, separated in the usual manner, and the lead reprecipitated as the sulfide. The lead sulfide is redissolved and precipitated as the chromate. This precipitate is dissolved in turn in hydrochloric acid and the amount of lead present is ascertained by iodometric estimation with the addition of potassium iodide and titration with standard sodium thiosulfate solution, or it may be determined colorimetrically with s-diphenylcarbazide.

Procedure. Add 50 ml of nitric acid (1:1) to the sample of lead dust collected with the aid of a macro impinger or other impinger, or dissolve the lead specimen in the nitric acid. Evaporate the mixture to dryness on a hot plate. Care should be taken to avoid spattering. Digest the residue with 5 ml of hydrochloric acid. Again evaporate the mixture to a volume of about 2 ml and dilute to 100 ml with water. In cases where the original residue is small, the dilution at this point is halved. Neutralize the solution with 25% sodium hydroxide solution until it is just alkaline to 4 drops of methyl orange indicator solution (0.5 g in 100 ml water), then add hydrochloric acid (1:2) until the faintest pink appears. Cool. Precipitate by passing in hydrogen sulfide gas for 1 hr. Allow to stand overnight. Filter on a 12.5-cm Whatman No. 40 filter paper. Wash with freshly prepared hydrogen sulfide water to which has been added 0.1% of its volume of hydrochloric acid. Wash the precipitate off the paper, using hot nitric acid (1:1), into the beaker in which the sulfide precipitation was made. Wash well with hot water. Wash down the sides of the beaker and the inside and outside of the hydrogen sulfide delivery tube, using hot nitric acid (1:1) followed by hot water. Remove the gassing tube. Evaporate the solution to a small volume on a hot plate and transfer to a 100-ml beaker. Add 1 ml of sulfuric acid (sp gr 1.84) and evaporate to sulfur trioxide fumes. Cool. Take up in 30 ml of a mixture of 10 ml of 95% ethyl alcohol and 20 ml of water. Allow to stand overnight.

Filter on a 7-cm hard filter paper such as Munktell No. 1 F. Wash the beaker and the paper thoroughly, using a solution containing 1 ml of sulfuric acid (sp gr 1.84), 10 ml of 95% alcohol, and 20 ml of water. Dissolve the precipitate off the paper into a 600-ml beaker, using 10 ml of hot 10% ammonium acetate solution, followed by hot water. It is well to wash the beaker first and decant the solution through the filter. Dilute the filtrate to 300 ml, using cold water, add 2 drops of nitric acid (sp gr 1.42). Neutralize after adding 4 drops of methyl red (1 g in 100 ml of 50% ethyl alcohol) by adding 25% sodium hydroxide solution to alkalinity, then hydrochloric acid (1:2) to a faint pink color. Add 1 ml of hydrochloric acid in excess. Cool, precipitate the lead by passing hydrogen sulfide gas through the solution for 1 hr, and allow to stand overnight.

Filter as described above. Dissolve the sulfides (38) from the paper with hot nitric acid (1:1), catching the solution and the washings in the beaker in which the sulfide precipitation was made. Wash the paper thoroughly with hot water and wash the sides of the beaker and the inside and outside of the hydrogen sulfide delivery tube with hot nitric acid (1:1) followed by hot water. Remove the gas-delivery tube. Evaporate the solution to a small volume, 1–2 ml, and transfer it to a 150-ml beaker. Dilute to 80 ml with cold water. Neutralize, after adding 4 drops of an aqueous solution of phenolphthalein (½ g in 100 ml of 1% sodium hydroxide solution) using 25% sodium hydroxide solution free from iron and aluminum. Make the solution alkaline. Add an excess of 5 drops of 25% sodium hydroxide. Acidify with 5% acetic acid till the pink color just disappears, and add 2 ml. of 5% acetic acid in excess.

Bring the solution to a boil and precipitate the lead as chromate by adding 1 ml of a 1% potassium chromate solution. Place on a steam bath for 1 hr and allow to stand at 60°C overnight. Filter on a Munktell No. 1 F filter paper. Wash the beaker and paper carefully and thoroughly with hot water to remove all possible traces of soluble chromate. Dissolve the precipitate from the paper into a 250-ml volumetric flask containing 100 ml of water, using 15 ml of cold hydrochloric acid (1:2), followed by cold water. Wash the beaker and rod and decant through the paper.

a. Colorimetric Estimation with s-Diphenylcarbazide

In a 250-ml volumetric flask prepare a standard containing sufficient potassium dichromate solution to be equivalent to 0.30 mg of lead, precipitated as lead chromate. Add 100 ml of water and 15 ml of cold hydrochloric acid (1:2). To each of the samples and the standard, add 2 ml of a 1% solution of s-diphenylcarbazide in glacial acetic acid. Make to volume and mix thoroughly. Estimate the lead in the samples by comparing the intensity of the pink colors, using a colorimeter.

An alternative method of preparing the lead standard to be used for matching against the unknown is the following (38): Dissolve 0.142 g of potassium dichromate in water and make up to 1 liter. One ml of this solution is equivalent to 0.2 mg of lead. Take 5 ml of this solution, add 2 ml of s-diphenylcarbazide, and make up to 1 liter. One ml of this solution is equivalent to 0.001 mg of lead.

b. Titrimetric Procedure

The use of s-diphenylcarbazide should be limited to the lower concentrations of lead. For larger amounts of lead, of the order of 10 mg, the titration method of Fairhall (Section D-3 above) may be used, starting at the point of dissolving the precipitated lead chromate in hydrochloric acid, in which the lead chromate dissolves readily. The lead may be estimated by adding an excess of potassium iodine and titrating the iodine liberated by the action of the chromic acid with $0.005N$ sodium thiosulfate solution with the aid of a microburet.

The following reactions proceed:

$$Pb(NO_3)_2 + K_2CrO_4 \rightarrow PbCrO_4 + 2KNO_3$$

$$2PbCrO_4 + 16HCl + 6KI \rightarrow 2PbCl_2 + 2CrCl_3 + 6KCl + 3I_2 + 8H_2O$$

$$6Na_2S_2O_3 + 3I_2 \rightarrow 6NaI + 3Na_2S_4O_6$$

It is clear that 3 moles of thiosulfate are equivalent to 1 mole of lead chromate, in other words, 1 ml of $0.005N$ sodium thiosulfate is equivalent to 0.345 mg of lead.

4. Dithizone Methods

With the introduction by Fischer (39) of the dithizone method for the determination of lead, numerous variations of this method, among which may be mentioned the colorimetric, mixed color, and photometric modifications, have appeared (25,40–52). With these methods, very small quantities of lead can be detected. They are based on the formation of a red precipitate of a lead–dithizone complex, which is soluble in chloroform or carbon tetrachloride when an ammoniacal cyanide solution of dithizone is added to a solution containing lead.

Dithizone is the short name for diphenylthiocarbazone. It is the type of reagent which is best used for estimation of low concentrations. It forms green solutions in chloroform. The lead complex has a red color and is soluble in chloroform but is practically insoluble in dilute ammonia, whereas dithizone itself is soluble in this solvent. The

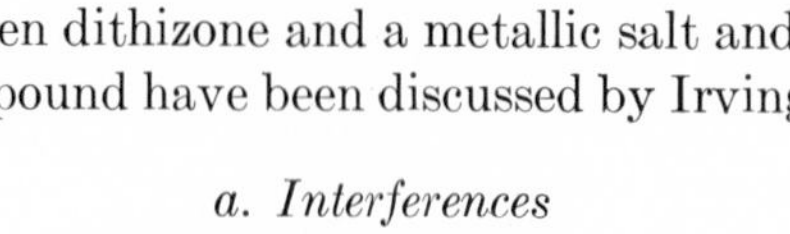

Diphenylthiocarbazone

various methods for the isolation and subsequent determination of lead depend upon these factors. The nature of the reaction that takes place between dithizone and a metallic salt and the structure of the resulting compound have been discussed by Irving (53).

a. Interferences

Dithizone is not a specific reagent for lead, for it will form colored compounds with many other metals. Even in the presence of excess potassium cyanide, stannous tin, bismuth, and thallium interfere.

Bismuth is eliminated as an interference by an extra dithizone extraction (44) from the lead solution before its final estimation by extracting a nitric acid solution of the two metals, which has been adjusted to a pH of 3.5, with a chloroform solution of dithizone. Table VIII-3 shows the pH at which dithizone will extract different metal ions.

TABLE VIII-3

Separations with Dithizone in Chloroform (54)

pH of aqueous solution	Metal ions extracted
Less than 2	Noble metals plus Hg
2–3	Cu, Bi, Sn^{2+}
4–7	Zn, Cd, Pb, Tl, and all the above
7–10	All the above. Washing with 0.04 ammonia solution removes Sn^{2+}. Addition of KCN leaves only Pb, Tl, or Bi, if not previously removed.

Both thallous thallium and stannous tin are converted to the thallic and stannic states during the evaporation step in the preparation of the sample by oxidation with nitric acid. This minimizes the possibility of their extraction by dithizone.

If interferences, such as tin, bismuth, or thallium, are likely to be present, it may be better to use the Wichmann-Clifford electrolytic method (Section D-5 below) rather than any of the dithizone methods, especially if medium concentrations of lead are present.

b. Purification

Some commercial diphenylthiocarbazone must be purified before use. Dissolve about 1 g of the commercial reagent in 50–75 ml of chloroform and filter if insoluble material remains. Shake out in a Jacobs-Singer separatory flask (Fig. VIII-2), an apparatus designed to permit multiple extractions with a solvent of lighter specific gravity without disturbing the solvent layer of higher specific gravity, with four 100-ml portions of metal-free, redistilled ammonium hydroxide solution (1:99). Dithizone passes into the aqueous layer to give an orange solution. Filter the aqueous extracts into a large separatory funnel through a pledget of cotton inserted in the stem of a funnel. Acidify slightly with dilute hydrochloric acid and extract the precipitated dithizone with two or three 20-ml portions of chloroform. Combine the extracts in a Jacobs-Singer separatory flask and wash two or three times with water. Pour off into a beaker and evaporate the chloroform with gentle heat on the steam bath, avoiding spattering as the solution goes to dryness. Remove the last traces of moisture by heating for 1 hr at not over 50°C *in vacuo*. Store the dry reagent

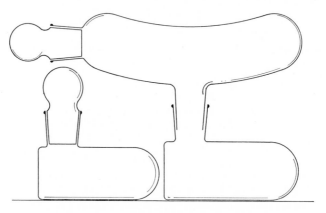

Fig. VIII-2. Jacobs-Singer separatory flask.

in the dark in a tightly stoppered bottle. Make up the reagent solutions for extraction to contain approximately 100, 50, and 10 mg/liter in redistilled chloroform. A stock solution of dithizone in chloroform containing 1 mg/ml will keep a long time and is convenient for use in making dilutions.

c. *Mixed-Color Photometric Method*

In this method (55) lead is extracted with an excess of dithizone in chloroform solution but the excess is allowed to partition between the aqueous and chloroform phases and thus modify the color of the extract according to the relative amounts of lead and dithizone. Because, according to this proportion, a series of colors from red to green could be arranged with intermediate crimsons, purples, and blues, Clifford and Wichmann (45) termed this procedure the *mixed-color method*. If the extraction is made under definite conditions of volume and strength of dithizone solution and volume and strength and pH of aqueous fraction, the mixed color obtained is definite, reproducible, and, provided excess dithizone is present, depends only upon the amount of lead present.

The transmission spectra of the two components in the dithizone extract, namely, lead dithizonate and free dithizone, show a marked difference in their ability to absorb light of a wave length of 510 mμ, for the red-lead complex absorbs strongly and the free dithizone transmits freely. Consequently, when the absorption of light of this wave length by the individuals of a standard color series, measured through suitable cell length, is determined photometrically, a practically linear relation is observed between the amounts of lead and the absorption coefficient.

The method as detailed and the Bambach-Burkey modification (50, Section D-4-d below) provide for the elimination of interferences particularly of bismuth and thallium.

Preparation of Reagents. *Ammonia–Cyanide Solution.* Add 75 ml of concentrated ammonium hydroxide solution, sp gr 0.9, to 100 ml of 10% potassium cyanide solution and make up to 500 ml with distilled water.

Standard Dithizone Solution. Dissolve 0.125 g of purified dithizone (see page 325) in chloroform in a 250-ml volumetric flask and complete to volume with chloroform. Each milliliter is equivalent to 0.5 mg of dithizone. The standard solutions listed in Table VIII-4 may be prepared from this solution.

Standard Lead Solutions. Solution A. Weigh out accurately 1.5984 g of recrystallized lead nitrate, $Pb(NO_3)_2$, and transfer to a 1-liter volumetric flask. Add 10 ml of concentrated nitric acid and a few milliliters of redistilled water to dissolve the salt. Make to volume with water and mix. This solution contains 1 mg of lead per ml. It is stable and should be used as the standard lead stock solution. It should be discarded if any cloud or sediment appears.

Solution B. Dilute 100 ml of solution A to 1 liter with water and then dilute 50 ml of this to 500 ml with nitric acid (1:1000). One ml of this solution contains 0.01 mg of lead. This solution may be used for standardizing the dithizone in the 0–100 and 0–200-μg lead ranges.

Solution C. Dilute 50 ml of solution B to 500 ml with nitric acid (1:1000). This solution may be used for standardizing the dithizone for the 0–5, 0–10, 0–20, and 0–50-μg lead ranges.

Prepare solutions B and C as needed.

Standardization of Dithizone Solutions.   The appropriate volumes and concentrations of solutions specified for the various ranges of lead content and the cell length are given in Table VIII-4.

Transfer with the aid of pipets the required volumes of standard lead solution, 1 ml of which equals some simple fraction or multiple of 1 μg of lead, to a series of separatory funnels.   Add sufficient nitric acid (1:1000) to bring the volume to 50 ml.   For so-called zero lead, use 50 ml of nitric acid (1:1000).   Saturate each mixture with 2 ml of chloroform by shaking.   Allow to stand for a few minutes, swirling the funnel to carry down any globules of chloroform clinging to the side, and draw off the chloroform layer completely, being careful

TABLE VIII-4

Dithizone Concentrations and Cell Lengths for Various Lead Ranges

Lead ranges, μg	Dithizone concentration, mg/liter	Volume, ml	Cell length, in.
0–5	4	5	2
0–10	4	10	2
0–20	8	10	1
0–50	8	25	1
0–100	10	30	$1/2$
0–200	20	30	$1/2$

not to draw off any of the aqueous layer.   Remove any chloroform in the stem with a pledget of cotton, or use filter paper.   Add 10 ml of the ammonia–cyanide mixture and mix.   Immediately add the appropriate volume of dithizone solution as given in Table VIII-4 and shake for 1 min.   Allow to stand for 2 min and then filter the chloroform extract through lead-free filter paper (see page 318) inserted gently into the neck of a dry 50-ml Pyrex Florence or similar flask in order to avoid loss of chloroform by evaporation.   Rinse the proper absorption cell with a small volume of the dithizone extract and then fill the cell almost to the top of the vent with the extract. Set the cell in the trough of the photometer.   Take the average of 5 or 10 readings, which seldom vary more than 2 mm.   Plot scale readings against micrograms of lead on a large-scale graph.

Procedure (56).   Prepare the sample as previously directed or, if organic matter is present, evaporate to dryness on a steam bath or hot plate. Transfer the dish to an electric muffle oven and gradually raise the temperature to 500°C. Ash overnight at this temperature. Remove the dish, cool, wash down the sides with 2 ml of concentrated nitric acid, and evaporate to dryness as before. Replace in the muffle furnace and heat for about 30 min or until a white ash is obtained. Remove the dish, cool, add 10 ml of concentrated hydrochloric acid, and evaporate to dryness on a steam bath or hot plate. Add another 10-ml portion of concentrated hydrochloric acid and again evaporate to dryness. Remove the dish and, while it is still hot, add 2 ml of hydrochloric acid and about 20 ml of hot water to dissolve the ash completely. Transfer to a 250-ml separatory funnel. Add 10 ml of 50% citric acid solution to the dish, add a small quantity of hot water, swirl gently, and add to the separatory funnel. Rinse the dish three times with hot water and add the washings to the funnel. Mix the contents of the separatory funnel and add 2–3 drops of metacresol purple indicator solution. Adjust the pH to 8.5 with concentrated ammonium hydroxide with the aid of a buret and cool. Generally 7–8 ml is needed. Add 5 ml of 10% potassium cyanide solution to the dish, rinse into the separatory funnel with water, and mix. The total volume should be about 100–125 ml. Add 5-ml portions of the dithizone solution (20 mg dithizone per liter of chloroform), shaking between additions until the chloroform extract assumes a purple color. Allow to stand for a few minutes and swirl to shake down the chloroform globules. Draw off the chloroform phase into a 125-ml separatory funnel containing 50 ml of nitric acid (1:1000) but permit a drop or two of chloroform to remain in the first funnel. Repeat the extraction of the aqueous phase with 20 ml of the dithizone solution and combine the chloroform extracts. Shake for 1 min to strip the lead from the dithizone complex. Discard all but 2–3 ml of the dithizone solution, dilute with 2–3 ml of chloroform and shake for 2 min. If the dithizone retains its original green color, bismuth is absent. A trace of bismuth will give the dithizone solution a dirty purple or iridescent blue color; a larger amount of this metal yields a yellowish brown. If bismuth is present, extract repeatedly with excess dithizone, shaking for 2 min between extractions until the dithizone retains its original color. Discard the dithizone layer and wash the aqueous portion with successive 2–3-ml portions of chloroform until free from dithizone. Shake down globules of chloroform and allow to stand for a few minutes. Draw off the chloroform layer completely, being careful not to draw off any of the aqueous layer.

Add 10 m of the ammonia–cyanide mixture and mix. Add the appropriate volume of standardized dithizone solution (see Table VIII-4) and shake for 1 min. Allow to stand for 2 min and filter through specially prepared filter papers inserted directly into the neck of a 50-ml Pyrex Florence or similar flask. The lead-free filter papers are prepared by soaking overnight in nitric acid (1:100) and then washing with large volumes of water with the aid of a Büchner funnel until free of acid. Rinse out the proper cell with a small amount of the filtered extract and fill it almost to the top. Determine the absorption coefficient, using the standardized dithizone with the same cell used in making the standard curve, and read the amount of lead from the curve.

Simple color matching may be made without the use of a photometer by making a series of 10 standards as detailed on page 327, but drawing off the dithizone layers into a series of tubes, vials, or Nessler tube. The unknown is treated in a similar way and drawn off into a similar tube or vial. View longitudinally for ranges up to 20 μg in the flat-bottomed vials and transversely for higher ranges in Nessler tubes. If the range is exceeded, use a smaller aliquot, or reextract with nitric acid reagent and make standards covering a higher range.

d. Bambach–Burkey Modification (50)

Preparation of Reagents *Ammonium Citrate Solution.* Dissolve 400 g of citric acid in water and add sufficient ammonium hydroxide solution to make the solution alkaline to phenol red. Dilute the solution to 1 liter with water and extract with successive portions of a chloroform solution of dithizone until the dithizone solution retains its original green color. Remove the excess dithizone by repeated washes with chloroform. Sodium citrate may be used in place of the citric acid and ammonium hydroxide. It should be purified in the same way.

Hydroxylamine Hydrochloride Solution. Dissolve 20 g of hydroxylamine hydrochloride, $NH_2OH \cdot HCl$, in sufficient water to make 65 ml of solution. Add a few drops of metacresol purple indicator solution. Add concentrated ammonium hydroxide solution until a yellow color is obtained. Add sufficient 4% aqueous sodium diethyldithiocarbamate solution to combine with all the lead and most of the other metals present and leave an excess of reagent. Extract the excess and the metallorganic complexes with chloroform. Test for complete removal by shaking a portion of the chloroform extract with a dilute aqueous solution of a copper salt. Add distilled hydrochloric acid until the indicator turns pink, and complete the volume to 100 ml with water.

Potassium Cyanide Solution. Dissolve 50 g of potassium cyanide in sufficient water to make 100 ml. Extract repeatedly with a chloroform solution of dithizone until all the lead has been removed. Excess dithizone in the aqueous layer can be removed by successive washes with chloroform. Dilute with water to give a 10% solution.

Dithizone Extraction Solution. Shake 1 liter of chloroform with 100 ml of water containing about 0.5 g of hydroxylamine hydrochloride, which has been made alkaline to phenol red with ammonium hydroxide. Drain off the chloroform and dissolve 30 mg of dithizone in it. Add 5 ml of alcohol to this solution if it is to be kept for several days. Shake the quantity of dithizone that is to be used with 100 ml of hydrochloric acid (1:100) just before use.

Standard Dithizone Solutions. Prepare chloroform as directed in the preceding paragraph. Filter the chloroform through dry filter paper into a Pyrex bottle equipped with a glass stopper and shield from light with wrapping paper or a wooden box. Dissolve dithizone in the following ratios in the chloroform: 5 mg/liter for the 0–10-μg range of lead; 10 mg/liter for the 0–50-μg range; and 20 ml/liter for the 0–100-μg range. Add 5 ml of absolute alcohol per liter and hold in a refrigerator.

Buffer Solution. Transfer 9.1 ml of reagent nitric acid to a 1-liter volumetric flask and dilute to about 500 ml with water. Add bromophenol blue indicator and adjust the pH to 3.4 with ammonium hydroxide solution. Add 50 ml of double-strength Clark and Lubs potassium acid phthalate–hydrochloric acid buffer (pH 3.4) prepared by diluting 50 ml of 0.2M potassium acid phthalate and 9.95 ml of 0.2M hydrochloric acid to 100 ml, and dilute the entire mixture to 1 liter.

Procedure. Transfer 15 ml of ammonium citrate solution to a separatory funnel. Add the proper aliquot of the sample being analyzed and 1 ml of hydroxylamine hydrochloride solution, mix, and make the mixture alkaline to phenol red with ammonium hydroxide solution. Add 5 ml of potassium cyanide solution.

Start the extraction of lead with 5 ml of dithizone extraction solution and note the color to assist in choosing the proper standard dithizone solution to be used later. Less than 10 μg of lead is indicated by a greenish-blue color. Add another 5-ml portion of dithizone extraction solution. Shake, allow to separate, and again note the color to ascertain whether the quantity of lead is greater than 50 or 100 μg. Drain off the dithizone and continue the extraction with successive 5-ml portions of dithizone solution, noting the color in each instance before draining, until all of the lead is extracted. Wash the combined dithizone extracts with 50 ml of water, and wash the water with 5 ml of chloroform. This wash should be green in color; if it is not, the presence of more lead or of zinc is indicated. Add a drop of potassium cyanide solution and shake the funnel again. If the chloroform layer does not become green, the water should be washed at least once with dithizone extraction solution. Add all chloroform washings to the dithizone extract and discard the aqueous layer. Strip the lead from the dithizone extract by shaking with 50 ml of buffer solution (pH 3.4); if the dithizone solution does not return to its original color, bismuth is present. Drain the dithizone solution from the separatory funnel. If more than 100 μg of lead is indicated, discard an aliquot portion of the buffer solution, sufficient to bring the quantity within the 100-μg range, and make up to 50 ml again with buffer solution. If bismuth is indicated, shake the buffer solution with one 5-ml portion of dithizone solution. Drain, add 5 ml of chloroform, and shake. Allow to stand until the supernatant drop of chloroform evaporates and draw off as much chloroform as possible without permitting any of the aqueous phase to enter the bore of the stopcock.

Estimation of Lead. Do not allow direct sunlight to strike the solutions. Add the proper standard dithizone solution, described above, to the separatory funnel containing the lead in the buffer solution, using 10 ml of the 0–10-μg solution and 25 ml of the other solutions. Add 7 ml of ammonia–cyanide mixture and shake immediately for 1 min. Do not release the pressure that is developed through the stopcock, but permit the gases to escape through the stopper. Flush the stem of the separatory funnel with 2 ml of the 0–10-μg standard and with 10 ml of the other standards and dry the stem. Rinse the photometer cells twice with the test solution, but since the 0–10-µg cell will hold the entire 8 ml remaining of the test solution, these cells should be cleaned and dried with acetone after each determination. Use a 5-cm (2-in.) cell for the 0–10-µg solution; a 1.25-cm (0.5-in.) cell for the 100-µg solution; and a 2.5-cm (1 in.) cell for the 0–50-µg solution. Read in a photometer and refer to a calibration curve prepared as directed below.

Prepare a fresh lead standard by taking an aliquot of the lead standard solutions prepared as directed above and adjust the pH to 3.4 by addition of dilute ammonium hydroxide. Add the proper amount of 3.4-pH buffer and dilute the mixture to a known volume. Add measured quantities of this prepared standard lead solution to separatory funnels, adjust the volume to 50 ml with additional buffer solution, and add the dithizone solution to be standardized. Read in a photometer as described on page 328 and prepare a calibration curve.

Echegaray and Quiñones (57) detail a modification of this method which was proposed by Landry.

e. USPHS Variation

The USPHS variation of the mixed-color dithizone method for the determination of lead as described by Keenan and co-workers (58) has been developed over a period of 25 years. It is a double extraction variation that is applicable only in the absence of bismuth.

Apparatus. Beckman Model DU and B spectrophotometers and the Bausch & Lomb Spectronic 20 are recommended for this variation. Matched 22 × 175-mm test tubes are used with the Beckman DU fitted with a tube holder which does not interfere with the use of the standard cells. The same tubes may be employed in a Beckman Model B equipped with an adaptor. For the B&L instrument, their ¾-in. tube may be used.

Glassware. Only borosilicate glassware should be used for each step of the procedure. Phillips beakers of 250-ml capacity are suitable for the ashing step. Lead-free white petrolatum may be used as stopcock grease but Teflon plugs may also be employed.

Glassware Cleaning. The ashing beakers are soaked in a detergent solution such as that containing Alconox or Duponol immediately after an ashing step has been completed. This helps to prevent any material from drying on the surface. Then the beakers are rinsed

8–10 times with hot water and stored in a closed cabinet until they are used again.

Immediately before an analysis, the Phillips beakers are rinsed with a saturated solution of sodium dichromate in concentrated sulfuric acid. A 1–2-ml portion of the cleaning solution is permitted to remain in the beaker. From 5 to 10 ml of warm tap water is added and is allowed to cover all of the inner surfaces. This mixture is rinsed away with 3–4 portions of cold tap water. One portion of nitric acid (1:1) is used to wash the beaker; then it is rinsed 3 or 4 times each with tap water, distilled, and double-distilled water. The beakers are set upright and covered with a large piece of filter paper. The same washing procedure may be used for the volumetric flasks except that less than 1 ml of the dichromate cleaning solution is retained in the flask.

Separatory funnels should be rinsed immediatey after use. In those instances in which high lead values are encountered, the funnels should be rinsed first with the nitric acid (1:1) (this should be discarded) and afterwards four times with tap water. If required, the funnels should be regreased with the petrolatum before use. They are then rinsed just before use with small portions of nitric acid (1:1) and four times each with tap water and distilled water, draining the rinsings through the stopcock each time with two or three turns

Immediately after use, the spectrophotometer tubes should be rinsed with tap and distilled water four times each and then dried in an upright position in an oven thermostatically controlled at 105°C before being stored. From time to time, they should be cleaned with dichromate cleaning solution.

Preparation of Reagents. *Concentrated Nitric Acid.* ACS reagent grade nitric acid (69.0% minimum, sp gr 1.42) is redistilled in an all-glass still. An electric heating jacket should be used around the boiling flask to prevent breakage and a boiling rod should be inserted in the flask to prevent bumping. The first 50 ml of distillate are discarded. A small automatic buret may be used to dispense the acid, but no grease should be used on the stopcock. The discarded distillate and the residue in the still may be employed for washing the glassware.

Nitric Acid (1:99). Ten ml of the redistilled, concentrated acid is diluted to 1 liter with double-distilled water.

Concentrated Ammonium Hydroxide Solution. Three liters of ACS reagent grade concentrated ammonium hydroxide solution (28.0% minimum, sp gr 0.8957 at 60°F) are distilled from an all-glass still into 1.5 liters of double-distilled water, which is contained in a 2-liter reagent bottle and chilled in an ice bath. The distillation is continued until the bottle is filled to the previously marked 2-liter level. The condenser tube is deeply submerged in the receiver, but is withdrawn before discontinuing the heat to avoid siphoning back of the distillate.

The ammonium hydroxide reagent may also be prepared from a tank of ammonia gas by using a small wash bottle to scrub the gas and a sintered glass delivery tube that extends to the bottom of a reagent bottle. The ammonia is run into double-distilled water until the solution reaches the required specific gravity.

Chloroform. Only chloroform that passes the ACS test for use in dithizone procedures and is sold in glass containers should be employed. It should be tested to make certain that it is suitable for use in the preparation of dithizone solutions. A very small amount of dithizone is added to a quantity of chloroform in a test tube, shaken gently, and stoppered with a cork. The faint green color should last for a day.

Dithizone Extraction Solution. Sixteen mg of diphenylthiocarbazone (Eastman Kodak Co. No. 3092 or an equivalent grade) are dissolved in 1 liter of chloroform. The solution is stored in an amber bottle in a refrigerator.

Standard Dithizone Solution. Eight mg of reagent grade diphenylthiocarbazone is dissolved in 1 liter of chloroform. It is stored in an amber bottle in the refrigerator, but it must be allowed to warm to room temperature before it is used, otherwise a volume error will be introduced. It is aged for at least 1 day and is standardized as detailed in the procedure. It should be restandardized at regular intervals.

Sodium Citrate Solution. Sufficient distilled water is used to dissolve 125 g of crystalline sodium citrate salt, $2Na_3C_6H_5O_7 \cdot 11H_2O$, to yield about 500 ml of solution. The pH is adjusted to 9–10, using both sufficient phenol red indicator solution to give a strong red color and fresh pHydrion paper to check the pH. The reagent solution is transferred to a large separatory funnel and is extracted with a dithizone solution containing 100 mg/liter and toward the end of the extraction with the dithizone extraction solution (16 mg/liter) until a green color is obtained with this extractant. A small volume of lead-free citric acid solution is added until an orange color, i.e., a pH of 7, is obtained and the excess of dithizone is extracted by repeated washing with chloroform until a colorless wash is obtained. The last traces of chloroform must be removed.

Hydroxylamine Hydrochloride Solution. Twenty g of hydroxyl-amine hydrochloride, $NH_2OH \cdot HCl$, are dissolved in sufficient water to make 65 ml of solution and this is treated as described in the Bambach-Burkey modification of the mixed-color method (Section D-4-d of this chapter).

Potassium Cyanide Solution. Sufficient distilled water is added to 50 g of potassium cyanide to make a sludge. This mixture is transferred to a separatory funnel marked at 100 ml. A small amount of water is added to the original beaker and the remainder of the cyanide is dissolved by warming. This solution is added to the separatory funnel, but a volume of 100 ml should not be exceeded. This is a virtually saturated solution of potassium cyanide. Any lead present is extracted by repeated shakings with dithizone extraction solution. Although a part of the dithizone is dissolved by the aqueous phase, a sufficient amount remains dissolved in the chloroform so that the green color can serve as an indicator of the removal of the lead. The dithizone in the aqueous phase is then removed by repeated extractions with chloroform. The concentrated solution of potassium cyanide is diluted with double-distilled water to 500 ml. It is best to perform the lead extraction before dilution because the diluted solution has a less favorable pH. Keenan and co-workers (58) found that if these directions for the preparation of the potassium cyanide solution are followed, it will be unnecessary to filter the solution. Jacobs (59) stored the solution in an amber bottle and kept it in a dark closet. If the solution becomes discolored, it is best to discard it and make a fresh solution. It should be unnecessary to stress that great care must be exercised in the use of all cyanide solutions.

Ammonium Hydroxide–Cyanide Mixture. The ammonium hydroxide–potassium cyanide extraction solution is prepared by mixing 200 ml of the purified potassium cyanide reagent solution with 150 ml of the distilled ammonium hydroxide reagent solution and diluting to 1 liter with double-distilled water. The 150-ml volume is based on an ammonium hydroxide solution containing 28.4% ammonia with a specific gravity of 0.9. If the specific gravity is not 0.9, it is necessary to use an equivalent volume as calculated from a table of specific gravities and percentages of ammonia.

Standard Lead Solutions. The stock standard lead solution is prepared by dissolving 1.5984 g of pure, reagent grade lead nitrate in 1 liter of nitric acid (1:99). This solution contains 1 mg of lead per ml. Exactly 20 ml of this stock solution is transferred by pipet to a 500-ml volumetric flask and is diluted to the mark with nitric acid (1:99). This diluted stock standard solution contains 40 μg of lead per milliliter. The working standard solution is prepared immediately before it is used by transferring by pipet 5 ml of the dilute standard solution to a 100-ml volumetric flask and completing to volume with nitric acid (1:99).

Ash-Aid Solution. An acid ash-aid solution is made by dissolving 25 g of potassium sulfate in enough redistilled, concentrated nitric acid to make 100 ml.

Phenol Red Indicator Solution. A 0.1% aqueous solution is prepared.

White Petrolatum. Only white petrolatum sold in glass jars should be used. In order to check its suitability as a grease for stopcocks of funnels to be used in the determination of lead, a tipful of the petrolatum is placed in a beaker and a few milliliters of the standard dithizone solution is added. If the dithizone solution loses its color after mixing and standing for a few minutes, the petrolatum is not suitable for use.

Double-Distilled Water. One crystal each of potassium permanganate and barium hydroxide are added to distilled water in an all-glass still and the water is distilled again. The double-distilled water should be used for the preparation of the reagents.

Preparation of Sample. Samples collected in electrostatic precipitator tubes are washed out with redistilled ethyl alcohol with the aid of a policeman made from a rubber disc cut to fit the precipitator tube like a piston. The sample is transferred through a short stem funnel to a 250-ml Phillips beaker and is evaporated just to dryness. The ethyl alcohol helps to remove any greasy deposits. Hot 1–5% nitric acid may also be used for the transfer of the sample.

Membrane-filter samples and impinger samples are also transferred to Phillips beakers. In such samples, it is best to add 2 ml of the ash-aid solution in order to prevent the loss of lead by glazing the surface of the beaker during the ashing step.

After adding 2 ml of concentrated nitric acid, the mixture is evaporated to dryness on a hot plate kept at 130°C. The Phillips beaker should be covered with a lead-free watchglass. The beaker is removed from the hot plate, allowed to cool, and an additional 2 ml of nitric acid is added. The acid is evaporated off on the hot plate just to dryness and is then transferred to a hot plate at 400°C and kept there only long enough to blacken the residue, after which the beaker is removed and allowed to cool. Follow the successive steps of addition of acid—using less acid as the digestion proceeds down to 0.5 ml—evaporation to dryness, baking the residue, and cooling, until the residue remains a pale yellow on heating on the 400°C hot plate for 5 min.

The ash is dissolved in 2 ml of concentrated nitric acid and distilled water, transferred quantitatively to a 100-ml volumetric flask, and made to the mark with double-distilled water. An appropriate aliquot is transferred by pipet to a separatory funnel containing 5 ml of water and enough additional water is added to make the total volume 25 ml.

Procedure. Cool to room temperature, add 1 ml of hydroxylamine hydrochloride solution, 4 ml of sodium citrate solution, 1 drop of phenol red indicator solution, and titrate to a deep red color with concentrated ammonium hydroxide solution. Add a few drops of ammonium hydroxide solution in excess and check the pH with pHydrion test paper.

Add 5 ml of potassium cyanide solution and mix. Add 5 ml of dithizone extraction solution and shake for 2 min, releasing the initial pressure by opening the stopcock for a moment while the funnel is in an inverted position. Replace the separatory funnel in its holder and allow the phases to separate. Draw off the dithizone extraction layer into a second funnel containing exactly 30 ml of nitric acid (1:99).

Add a second 5-ml portion of dithizone extraction solution to the first funnel and shake out again. Allow the phases to separate and add the second extract to the first extract in the second funnel Continue the extraction with additional 5-ml portions of dithizone extraction solution, adding each new extract to the second funnel until the extraction reagent remains green. An approximation of the amount of lead present can be made on the assumption that each cherry-red 5-ml extract contains 20 μg of lead.

Shake the second funnel for 2 min to extract the lead from the chloroform layer into the aqueous layer. Allow the phases to separate and discard the chloroform layer. Shake the nitric acid solution with 5 ml of chloroform and allow to separate. Drain off the chloroform as completely as possible without permitting any of the aqueous layer to drain. Evaporate off the last drop of chloroform clinging to the top surface.

Add 6.0 ml of the ammonium hydroxide–cyanide solution, add exactly 15.0 ml of the standard dithizone solution, and shake for 2 min. Allow the layers to separate, drain off the chloroform phase, which contains the lead dithizonate, into a dry test tube, and cork the tube at once. Decant this chloroform solution into a dry photometer tube, making certain not to carry over any water, and, if necessary, decant into another photometer tube to free the solution from water.

Set the spectrophotometer at a wavelength of 510 mμ and then set the photometer at zero absorbance, using a zero lead standard. Read the absorbances of the samples, the reagent blank, and the standards.

Calculate the lead content of each by multiplying the absorbance by the standardization factor, which is the slope of the standardization graph in micrograms of lead per unit of absorbance. Subtract the blank value from the gross lead content of each sample to obtain the net amount of lead expressed in micrograms.

Standards. At the same time the lead is transferred from the initial shake out to the nitric acid (1:99), place 30 ml of nitric acid (1:99) in a separatory funnel, and use this as the zero standard. To set up the other standards, transfer 5-ml portions of nitric acid (1:99) to each of four separatory funnels, add in order 2.5, 5.0, 7.5, and 12.5 ml of the dilute standard lead solution containing 2 μg of lead per ml, and then add sufficient nitric acid (1:99) to each funnel to make the total volume 30 ml. Add 5 ml of reagent chloroform to each of the funnels containing the standards, shake, and allow to settle. Draw off the chloroform as before without loss of the aqueous phase and continue with the method after adding 6.0 ml of ammonium hydroxide–cyanide solution, exactly 15.0 ml of standard dithizone solution, and shaking for 2 min.

f. One-Color Extraction Method

In this method (60) the lead is extracted with a small excess of dithizone in chloroform solution and the excess dithizone is removed from the combined extracts by washing with dilute ammonia–potassium cyanide solution. The amount of lead in the extract is then estimated colorimetrically by a comparison of the red color of the lead–dithizone complex. A variation of this method was used by Jacobs and Herndon (59) for the determination of lead in urine and blood (see Chapter XIX, Section B-1-a).

Preparation of Reagents. Prepare a 5% solution of ammonium citrate from citric acid by the addition of ammonium hydroxide until just alkaline to litmus paper.

Lead Extractive Solution. Mix 15 ml of 10% potassium cyanide solution, 10 g of potassium cyanide dissolved in water and made up to 100 ml, and 20 ml of ammonium citrate solution with 53 ml of concentrated ammonium hydroxide solution (sp gr 0.9) and then add 450 ml of water. This solution is used to neutralize the excess nitric acid and provide the proper pH of from 9.5 to 10.

Dithizone Extractive Solution. Dilute 5 ml of 10% potassium cyanide solution and 15 ml of concentrated ammonium hydroxide to 500 ml with water.

Standard Lead Solution. Dissolve 1.5984 g of recrystallized lead nitrate in 0.1% nitric acid and make up to 1 liter with this solvent. One ml of this solution contains 1 mg of lead. Dilute 10 ml of this solution to 1 liter. One ml of this dilution equals 0.01 mg of lead.

Procedure. Collect the sample in a macro impinger either with 10 ml of nitric acid or in water as has been previously explained on page 319. If collected in water, add the same quantity, i.e., exactly 10 ml of concentrated nitric acid, or the additional amount of acid if a lesser quantity was used in the collector, after collection. Boil the sample in the original sampling vessel until the volume is less than 90 ml. After cooling, transfer to a 100-ml volumetric flask. Wash the sampling flask with two 5-ml portions of water and add this water to the volumetric flask. Then dilute to the mark with water. Remove a 5-ml aliquot containing approximately 0.5 ml of concentrated nitric acid. It is important to add exactly 10 ml of nitric acid and no more. Too little acid will cause the destruction of the dithizone reagent. Too great an amount will lower the pH below 9.7, which is the alkalinity to which the lead extractive solution has been adjusted. This was shown to be the optimum pH by Clifford and Wichmann (45). The reagents have been adjusted to care for all the commonly interfering metallic ions; nevertheless, the procedure must be closely followed.

Place 15 ml of the lead extractive solution containing the potassium cyanide, ammonium citrate, ammonium hydroxide, and water into a Squibb or pear-shaped separatory funnel. Add the 5-ml aliquot of the unknown with the aid of a standard pipet. Add dithizone solution, 25 mg of dithizone per liter of chloroform, from a semimicro buret in 0.3-ml portions, shaking the separatory funnel after each addition until a slight purple tinge is noticed in the chloroform layer. This purple tinge shows that uncombined dithizone is now present. The dithizone in the chloroform layer turns a bright cherry red when shaken with solutions containing lead. Add chloroform from a buret in sufficient amounts so that the total of dithizone–chloroform solution and chloroform is equal to exactly 10 ml. Shake for not over 10 sec. Allow the layers to separate. Drain the chloroform layer into another Squibb separatory funnel containing 20 ml of the dithizone extractive solution, consisting of potassium cyanide and ammonium hydroxide. Shake the chloroform layer with the 20 ml of dithizone extractive solution if too great an excess of dithizone has been added. Repeat if necessary to remove the excess dithizone. It has been shown that two extractions are usually sufficient to remove any excess. The color of the resulting chloroform solution is a bright, clear cherry red. The drop at the top of the aqueous layer may be brought down to the rest of the chloroform by repeatedly tapping and shaking with a slight rocking motion. Transfer the chloroform layer into a test tube or comparator tube, first wiping the inside of the stem of the separatory funnel with a cotton swab or pipe cleaner to remove moisture. The test tube or comparator tube should then be stoppered.

Three standard solutions containing 0.005, 0.01, and 0.015 mg of lead, respectively, are made at the same time that the unknown is prepared for analysis. These standards, after the lead extraction and the removal of excess dithizone, are placed in tubes similar to those used for the unknown. By placing the unknown sample between the two standards that are nearest the unknown in shade, and holding it up in front of a standard source of white light, one is able to determine the lead content within 0.001 mg. This does not hold when more than 0.1 mg of lead is present in the sample taken for analysis. Best results are obtained when the aliquot taken contains less than 0.04 mg of lead.

To prepare the 0.005-mg standard, add 5 ml of the dilute lead nitrate standard solution to 40 ml of water and 5 ml of concentrated nitric acid. Then, after this solution has been thoroughly mixed, take a 5-ml aliquot and treat it exactly as has been described for the unknown. Use proportionately larger amounts of the dilute lead standard solution for the other standard comparison solutions.

To make up standards for comparison containing 0.045 mg or more of lead, use the concentrated lead nitrate solution containing 1.0 mg of lead per ml. Thus, for making an 0.07-mg standard, add 0.7 ml of the concentrated lead nitrate standard solution to 5 ml of nitric acid and dilute to 50 ml with water. Take 5 ml of this as an aliquot for analysis. The resultant pH is between 9.5 and 10 under conditions as stated.

When large amounts of iron (61) are present in samples analyzed for lead by the colorimetric dithizone method, fading will occur unless a small amount of hydroxylamine hydrochloride is present as an inhibitor.

Add 2–4 drops of a saturated aqueous solution of hydroxylamine hydrochloride to each sample and standard prior to the addition of dithizone. When 200–300 times as much iron as lead is present, extract the lead with an excess quantity of very strong dithizone solution (approximately 100 mg/liter) and then strip the excess with the dithizone extractive solution. The final color is developed after adding 2 drops of hydroxylamine hydrochloride to the solution, which is brought to a pH of 9.5–10.0 by the addition of a known quantity of standard dithizone solution, as in the procedure above.

g. Titrimetric Method

In this method (62,63) the lead is separated from a given solution by means of dithizone and the resulting lead–dithizone complex is then isolated. The latter is freed of lead by washing with acid. The chloroform solution of dithizone remaining is mixed with some dilute cyanide solution, which removes most of the dithizone from the chloroform, imparting a brown color to the aqueous layer. A lead solution is added from a buret to this mixture until all the dithizone has been reconverted to lead dithizonate, as indicated by (1) the disappearance of the brown color in the aqueous layer and (2) the absence of a red color when the aqueous layer is mixed with chloroform and additional lead solution. As the final titration is carried out directly with a known standard lead solution, it eliminates the necessity for special precautions in the handling of the dithizone.

Preparation of Reagents. *Dithizone Solution.* Dissolve 40 mg of dithizone in 400 ml of chloroform and filter into a 500-ml Pyrex separatory funnel. Add 50 ml of water containing 2 ml of 25% hydroxylamine hydrochloride solution and shake. Keep in a cool dark place and withdraw the chloroform solution as needed. The acid aqueous layer not only prevents the oxidation of the dithizone but also extracts any lead that might be present.

Potassium Cyanide Solution, 0.5%. Prepare when needed by diluting 25 ml of a freshly prepared 10% solution of potassium cyanide to 500 ml with water. It is important that this solution be lead free. To insure this, place 100 ml of 10% potassium cyanide solution into a separatory funnel and extract with 2 ml of chloroform containing 2 drops of dithizone solution. If a pink color appears in the chloroform layer, withdraw it and repeat the extraction until the chloroform layer is colorless. The slight excess of dithizone which remains in the 10% potassium cyanide solution is insignificant because the amounts which remain after dilution to form the 0.5% solution of potassium cyanide are not detectable.

Standard Lead Solution. Dissolve 1.5984 g of recrystallized lead nitrate with the aid of 1 ml of nitric acid in a volumetric flask and dilute to 100 ml. This solution, which contains 10 mg of lead per milliliter, is stable. By diluting 10 ml of this solution to 100 ml and then in turn diluting 10 ml of the latter to 1 liter, a solution containing 0.01 mg of lead per milliliter is prepared.

Sodium Citrate, 20%. To 800 ml of this solution add 8 ml of 10% potassium cyanide and extract in a 1-liter separatory funnel with 15-ml portions of dithizone solution until the citrate mixture is free of lead. Wash twice with 25-ml portions of chloroform, acidify with 4 ml of 20% hydrochloric acid, and complete the extraction of the excess dithizone with 20-ml portions of chloroform.

Procedure. Wash the sample of dust collected from the air or the ash from other type collections into a 250- or 400-ml Pyrex beaker with the aid of about 10 ml of hot concentrated nitric acid. Evaporate the contents of the beaker just to dryness. Place 15 ml of hydrochloric acid (1:1) in the beaker and heat to boiling.   Wash the mixture into a 100-ml volumetric flask with small portions of hot water.   Wash the beaker with a mixture consisting of 10 ml of 20% sodium citrate solution and 3 ml of ammonium hydroxide solution (1:1).   Warm and transfer to the volumetric flask.   Wash with 2 or 3 small portions of hot water and add the washings to the contents of the flask.   Cool to room temperature, and add 1 ml of 25% hydroxylamine hydrochloride solution and 2 drops of phenol red.   Adjust the pH of the solution to 8.0 by the addition of ammonium hydroxide solution (1:1). Cool the solution again to room temperature and make up to volume. After thorough mixing, proper aliquots may be removed and transferred by means of pipets to separatory funnels for analysis.   Dilute to 75 ml.

If the lead-bearing material contains organic matter, place the specimen in a silica evaporating dish, evaporate to dryness, if necessary, dry, and ignite in a muffle oven at about 475°C.   Remove the dish from the muffle and if a clean ash is not obtained, add 2 ml of nitric acid, evaporate to dryness, and ignite again in the muffle. Place the dish on a hot plate, carefully add 15 ml of 20% hydrochloric acid (1:1), and heat until the ash is dissolved.   Wash the contents into a 125-ml separatory funnel with about 20 ml of hot water.   Add 10 ml of 20% sodium citrate solution and 3 ml of ammonium hydroxide to the silica dish, mix, and transfer to the separatory funnel with enough water to make a total volume of about 75 ml.   Cool, add 1 ml of 25% hydroxylamine hydrochloride solution, 1 drop of phenol red, and bring to pH 8.0 with ammonium hydroxide delivered from a Pyrex buret.   Cool.

Add 0.5 ml of 10% potassium cyanide solution drop by drop, shaking between additions, and immediately extract with 0.5 ml of dithizone solution and 4 ml of chloroform.   If, after shaking, the chloroform layer does not contain a noticeable excess of uncombined dithizone, add 0.5-ml portions of dithizone solution, shaking between additions until the green excess becomes evident.   Transfer the chloroform phase to another separatory funnel and repeat the extraction of the aqueous phase twice with 0.2-ml portions of dithizone in 2 ml of chloroform.   To the combined chloroform solutions add an amount of 0.5% potassium cyanide equal to 1.5 times the volume of the chloroform solution and shake for 10 sec.   Transfer the chloroform layer to another separatory funnel and wash the aqueous cyanide solution with 1 ml of chloroform. Combine the chloroform solutions and again extract with 1.5 volumes of 0.5% potassium cyanide solution. The extraction with cyanide removes the uncombined dithizone unless a very large excess has been used, in which case the extraction with 0.5% potassium cyanide solution is continued until the absence of color in the aqueous phase indicates that the dithizone excess has been removed.

Remove any lead which may have dissolved in the aqueous layer by extraction with 2 ml of chloroform. Separate the lead from the red dithizone complex by shaking for 15 sec with 2 volumes of 1.0% hydrochloric acid. Withdraw the green chloroform layer and then extract the acid aqueous solution with 1 ml of chloroform to recover the last traces of dithizone. Combine the chloroform fractions.

Add to the dithizone solution 0.5 of its volume of 0.5% potassium cyanide and shake. Most of the dithizone goes into the aqueous layer, giving that mixture a brown color. Add the standard lead solution (0.01 mg/ml) from a buret a drop at a time, shaking between additions until only a very faint color remains in the aqueous layer. This is evidence that practically all of the dithizone has combined with lead and gone into the chloroform phase. Discard the red chloroform layer and wash the aqueous layer with chloroform, 2 ml at a time, until the chloroform layer remains colorless after shaking. Add 1 or 2 drops of the lead solution and shake for 5 sec. Draw off the pink chloroform solution and continue the extraction with 2-ml portions of chloroform plus 1 or 2 drops of lead solution until further addition of lead gives no pink color to the chloroform solution after shaking. The end point is a slight pink in the chloroform solution; extraction with 1 drop more results in a colorless solution. In order to facilitate the titration, a solution of the lead–dithizone complex containing a small amount of the order of 1 or 2 drops of the lead solution in 2 ml of chloroform is kept for comparison. When the color obtained after an addition of lead solution is less than that given by 1 drop of the lead solution, the end point has been attained. It is suggested that the analyst unaccustomed to this analysis add 2 drops (equivalent to about 0.0006 mg) at a time until his eyes become accustomed to the change.

For ease of manipulation, the aliquot taken for analysis should contain less than 0.050 mg of lead. A rough estimate of the quantity of lead in the aliquot can be made by observing the volume of dithizone solution used to produce an excess. One ml of dithizone solution will combine with approximately 0.040 mg of lead.

The number of milliliters of standard lead solution used in the titration multiplied by 0.01 gives the quantity of lead in milligrams in the aliquot taken for analysis.

5. WICHMANN-CLIFFORD METHOD

This method (64,65) is based on the electrolytic separation of lead as the peroxide and its titration by iodometric means. The lead is deposited on the anodic, positive pole, by the use of a low electric current. Tin, antimony, bismuth, and manganese interfere with the deposition and must, therefore, be removed. Samples are ashed, if necessary, and precipitated with hydrogen sulfide, using copper as a collector for the lead. The sulfides are filtered, washed with hot polysulfide solution, and finally with sodium sulfate solution. The lead and copper sulfides remaining are then dissolved in hot nitric acid, neutralized with ammonium hydroxide, and made up to 2% acid with nitric acid. Potassium dichromate solution is added, the solution heated and electrolyzed, and the lead deposited as the peroxide, PbO_2. It is then washed thoroughly and removed from the anode with a sodium acetate acidic solution. Potassium iodide is added and the liberated iodine titrated with $0.001N$ sodium thiosulfate solution, using starch as an indicator.

6. COMBINATION METHOD

As an illustration of a method combining the information of the preceding methods, namely, dithizone extraction, electrolytic deposition of lead peroxide, and iodometric estimation, the following method is appended (66).

Prepare an acid solution of the lead specimen by one of the methods previously detailed. Add to an aliquot in a separatory funnel 20 ml of citric acid solution (20 g of citric acid dissolved in water and made up to 100 ml) and 8 g of sodium hexametaphosphate. Make this solution just alkaline with ammonium hydroxide, and add 10 ml of potassium cyanide solution (10 g of KCN dissolved in water and made up to 100 ml). Extract with small portions of dithizone solution (50 mg of dithizone in 100 ml of chloroform) until the color of one portion remains unchanged. Drain the successive chloroform extracts into a smaller separatory funnel containing 20 ml of ammonium hydroxide (1 : 99), and shake as a means of washing the chloroform. When the extraction is complete, drain the combined portions of dithizone–chloroform solution, containing the lead, into a 150-ml beaker and evaporate to dryness over a steam bath. After the chloroform has been completely evaporated, add 2 ml of concentrated nitric acid, place a watch glass over the beaker, and boil until the gases evolved are colorless. Dilute to about 100 ml, heat to 75–80°C, add 2 ml of potassium dichromate solution, and electrolyze, maintaining the stated temperature as directed in the preceding method. Dissolve the lead peroxide in a mixture of 2 ml of potassium iodide (2 g of KI dissolved in water and made up to 100 ml) and 4 ml of acid sodium acetate solution (consisting of 20 ml of saturated sodium acetate solution, 10 ml of glacial acetic acid, and 70 ml of water). Titrate with approximately $0.001N$ sodium thiosulfate solution that has been previously standardized against a known amount of lead, as described in the foregoing. The very dilute thiosulfate solution may be protected from decomposition for several weeks by adding 1% amyl alcohol to the boiled water with which it is prepared.

7. Spectrographic Method

In the APHA booklet on lead (25), Cholak has detailed methods for the determination of lead spectrographically.

A grating spectrometer is commercially available for monitoring lead in air (67). The air is sampled by filtration, using a special filter and portable air sampler. The filter sample is taken to the laboratory where it is inserted in the instrument. The device uses two photomultiplier tubes to monitor a lead line. It has a sensitivity of about 3 μg of lead per cubic meter.

References

1. Sayers, R. R., *U.S. Bur. Mines Rept. Invest. 2660* (1924).
2. Drinker, P., *Ind. Med.*, **4**, 253 (1935).
3. Teleky, L., *Ind. Med. Ind. Hyg. Section*, **9**, 17 (1940).
4. Cantarow, A., and M. Trumper, *Lead Poisoning*, Williams & Wilkins, Baltimore, 1944.
5. Mayers, M. R., and M. M. McMahon, *N.Y. State Dept. Labor Special Bull. 195* (1938).
6. Aub, J. C., L. T. Fairhall, A. Minot, and P. Reznikoff, *Medicine*, **4**, 1 (1925).
7. Drinker, P., *J. Ind. Hyg.*, **7**, 531 (1925).

8. Kehoe, R. A., "The Metabolism of Lead in Man in Health and Disease (the Harben Lectures, 1960)," *J. Royal Inst. Public Health Hygiene* (1961).

9. Fairhall, L. T., R. R. Sayers, and J. W. Miller, *U.S. Public Health Service Bull. 253* (1940).

10. Flinn, F. B., *J. Ind. Hyg.*, **8,** 51 (1926).

11. *U.S. Public Health Rept.*, **48,** 1043 (1933).

12. Russell, A. E., R. R. Jones, J. J. Bloomfield, R. H. Britten, and L. R. Thompson, *U.S. Public Health Service Bull. 205* (1933).

13. Fairhall, L. T., and R. R. Sayers, *U.S. Public Health Service Bull. 253* (1940).

14. Legge, T. M., and K. W. Goadby, *Bleivergiftung und Bleiaufnahme*, Springer, Berlin, 1921.

15. Greenburg, L., A. A. Schaye, and H. Shlionsky, *U.S. Public Health Service Reprint 1299* (1929).

16. Harrold, G. C., S. F. Meek, G. R. Collins, and T. F. Markell, *J. Ind. Hyg. Toxicol.*, **26,** 47 (1944).

17. Kehoe, R. A., J. Cholak, D. M. Hubbard, K. Bambach, R. R. McNary, and R. V. Story, *Experimental Studies on the Ingestion of Lead Compounds*, Kettering Laboratory of Applied Physiology, University of Cincinnati, 1940.

18. Federal Security Agency, Social Security Board, Washington, D. C., August 10, 1940.

19. Bloomfield, J. J., and H. S. Isbell, *J. Ind. Hyg.*, **15,** 144 (1933).

20. Henderson, S. R., and L. J. Snyder, *Anal. Chem.*, **33,** 1172 (1961).

21. Quino, E. A., *Am. Ind. Hyg. Assoc. J.*, **20,** No. 2, 134 (1959).

22. Harwood, R. U., and D. Brophy, *J. Ind. Hyg.*, **16,** 25 (1934).

23. Behrens, H., and P. D. C. Kley, *Mikrochemische Analyse*, Voss, Leipzig, 1915.

24. Zhitkova, A. S., S. I. Kaplun, and J. B. Ficklen, *Poisonous Gases*, Service to Industry, Hartford, 1936.

25. Sayers, R. R., J. Cholak, R. A. Kehoe, F. H. Goldman, and M. B. Jacobs, *Methods for Determining Lead in Air and in Biological Materials*, Am. Public Health Assoc., New York, 1955.

26. Jacobs, M. B., in *Lead Poisoning*, A. Cantarow and M. Trumper, Eds., Williams & Wilkins, Baltimore, 1944.

27. Kolthoff, I. M., and J. J. Lingane, *Polarography*, Interscience, New York, 1941.

28. Feicht, F. L., H. H. Schrenk, and C. E. Brown, *U.S. Bur. Mines Rept. Invest. 3639* (1942).

29. Goldman, F. H., and I. May, *Ind. Hyg. Quarterly*, **7,** No. 3, 21 (1946).

30. Katz, S. H., E. G. Meiter, and F. W. Gibson, *U.S. Public Health Service Bull. 177* (1928).

31. Littlefield, J. B., F. L. Feicht, and H. H. Schrenk, *U.S. Bur. Mines Rept. Invest. 3401* (1938).

32. Keenan, R. G., and L. T. Fairhall, *J. Ind. Hyg. Toxicol.*, **26,** 241 (1944).

33. Fairhall, L. T., *J. Ind. Hyg.*, **4,** 9 (1922–23).

34. Kehoe, R. A., G. Edgar, F. Thamann, and L. Sanders, *J. Am. Med. Assoc.*, **87,** 2081 (1926).

35. Kehoe, R. A., F. Thamann, and J. Cholak, *J. Ind. Hyg.*, **15,** 257 (1933).

36. Letonoff, T. V., and J. G. Reinhold, *Ind. Eng. Chem. Anal Ed.*, **12,** 280 (1940).

37. Bloomfield, J. J., and J. M. DallaValle, *U.S. Public Health Service Bull. 217* (1935).
38. Krans, E. W., and J. B. Ficklen, *J. Ind. Hyg.*, **13**, 140 (1931).
39. Fischer, H., *Angew. Chem.*, **42**, 1025 (1929).
40. Wichmann, H. J., C. W. Murray, M. Harris, P. A. Clifford, J. H. Loughrey, and F. A. Vorhes, *J. Assoc. Offic. Agr. Chemists*, **17**, 108 (1934).
41. Vorhes, F. A., and P. A. Clifford, *J. Assoc. Offic. Agr. Chemists*, **17**, 130 (1934).
42. Winter, O. B., H. M. Robinson, F. W. Lamb, and E. J. Miller, *Ind. Eng. Chem. Anal. Ed.*, **7**, 265 (1935).
43. Wilkins, E. S., C. E. Willoughby, and E. O. Kraemer, *Ind. Eng. Chem. Anal. Ed.*, **7**, 33 (1935).
44. Willoughby, C. E., E. S. Wilkins, and E. O. Kraemer, *Ind. Eng. Chem. Anal. Ed.*, **7**, 285 (1935).
45. Clifford, P. A., and H. J. Wichmann, *J. Assoc. Offic. Agr. Chemists*, **19**, 130 (1936).
46. Cholak, J., D. M. Hubbard, R. R. McNary, and R. V. Story, *Ind. Eng. Chem. Anal. Ed.*, **9**, 488 (1937).
47. Hubbard, D. M., *Ind. Eng. Chem. Anal. Ed.*, **9**, 493 (1937).
48. Fischer, H., and G. Leopoldi, *Z. Anal. Chem.*, **119**, 161 (1940).
49. Bambach, K., *Ind. Eng. Chem. Anal. Ed.*, **11**, 400 (1939); **12**, 63 (1940).
50. Bambach, K., and R. E. Burkey, *Ind. Eng. Chem. Anal. Ed.*, **14**, 904 (1942).
51. Schultz, J., and M. A. Goldberg, *Ind. Eng. Chem. Anal. Ed.*, **15**, 555 (1943).
52. Gómez, E. N., *Rev. Sanidad Asistencia Social (Venezuela)*, **11**, 477 (1946).
53. Irving, H. M. N. H., "The Structure of Dithizone and Its Metal Complexes," paper presented at Meeting of Society for Analytical Chemistry, London, Nov. 7, 1956.
54. Hibbard, P. L., *Ind. Eng. Chem. Anal. Ed.*, **9**, 127 (1957).
55. Jacobs, M. B., in *Lead Poisoning*, A. Cantarow and M. Trumper, Eds., Williams & Wilkins, Baltimore, 1944.
56. Gant, V. A., *Lead Poisoning*, Industrial Health, Chicago, 1939.
57. Echegaray, R. M., and H. Quiñones S., *Salud Ocupacional (Peru)*, **5**, No. 3, 32 (1960).
58. Keenan, R. G., *Am. Ind. Hyg. Assoc. J.*, **24**, 481 (1963).
59. Jacobs, M. B., and J. Herndon, *Am. Ind. Hyg. Assoc. J.*, **22**, 372 (1961).
60. Harrold, G. C., S. F. Meek, and F. R. Holden, *J. Ind. Hyg.*, **18**, 725 (1936).
61. Harrold, G. C., S. F. Meek, and F. R. Holden, *J. Ind. Hyg. Toxicol.*, **20**, 589 (1938).
62. Horwitt, M. K., and G. R. Cowgill, *J. Biol. Chem.*, **119**, 553 (1937).
63. Moskowitz, S., and W. J. Burke, *N.Y. State Ind. Bull.*, **17**, 492 (1938); *J. Ind. Hyg. Toxicol.*, **20**, 457 (1938).
64. Wichmann, H. J., and P. A. Clifford, *J. Assoc. Offic. Agr. Chemists*, **17**, 123 (1934).
65. Jacobs, M. B., *Chemical Analysis of Foods and Food Products*, Van Nostrand, New York, 1945.
66. Cassil, C. C., and C. M. Smith, *Am. J. Public Health*, **26**, 902 (1936).
67. National Spectrographic Labs., Inc., Cleveland 3, Ohio.

CHAPTER IX

MERCURY AND ARSENIC

A. Mercury

1. MERCURIALISM

Mercurialism is an illness that was known in early and medieval history, since quicksilver was used by goldsmiths. Mercury was one of the few metals well characterized by the alchemists and, indeed, was representative of metals as a class to them. With increase in the use of mercury in many industrial processes, such as the mercury boiler and catalytic applications, has also come the possible increase in the hazard of mercury poisoning. The large expansion in the use of organic mercurials for agricultural and commercial purposes such as fungicides, bacteriocides and bacteriostats, seed dressings, etc. has markedly increased the danger of mercury poisoning not only in industry but also in the office and home.

2. VAPOR PRESSURE OF MERCURY

It is often not realized that mercury has a definite measurable vapor pressure at normal temperatures, which increases markedly with increase in temperature. This is illustrated by the following table.

TABLE IX-1
Vapor Pressure of Mercury (1)

Temperature, °C	Vapor pressure, mm Hg	Theoretical concentration of mercury in the air	
		mg/liter	ppm
20	0.0013	0.0152	1.84
30	0.0029	0.0339	4.10
40	0.0060	0.0700	8.5
60	0.0300	0.3500	42.5
100	0.28	3.26	396.0
200	18.3	213.0	25,800.0
300	246.0	2879.0	348,000.0

3. Industrial Exposure

Because of its volatility there is considerable mercury vapor in the air wherever mercury is worked, for instance, in the manufacture of thermometers, barometers, switches, batteries, mercury-vapor and neon lamps, teeth fillings, pharmaceuticals (such as mercurial ointments), dyestuffs, and synthetic chemicals, among many other uses. Mercury hazards are present in treating seeds with mercurial fungicides such as ethyl mercury phosphate and ethyl mercury chloride (2). There is danger in the use of mercury in instruments in laboratories such as in the use of Van Slyke gasometric devices, polarographs, manometers and pressure gauges, and, in general, instruments in which mercury is used.

Formerly, one of the greatest sources of mercury poisoning in the manufacture of felt hats was in the "carrotting" of furs with "secret formulas" containing mercuric nitrate as a component. Fur cutters and felt-hat workers contracted mercury poisoning because this process contaminated the air in which they worked with mercury vapor and mercury-bearing dust. The fine hairs of the fur of rabbits, hares, and other animals used in making felt are smooth and straight. By treating them with acid nitrate of mercury, they are made limp and twisted, which aids in the felting process. The use of secret formulas was begun about the middle of the 17th century in France and spread to other countries with the dispersion of the Huguenots. The process is termed carrotting because of the yellow color produced on the felt. The French formulas also include arsenic trioxide, white arsenic, and mercuric chloride.

Lloyd and Gardner (3) found by analysis that carrotted rabbit fur contained 0.09–0.17% mercury and that vapors escaping from the planker's acid vat contained 0.0012% mercury. A fringed cloth tied around the hood of the vat was found to contain 0.01% mercury. In this instance, it is clear that mercury was deposited upon the cloth only by evaporation.

While the literature on mercurialism among fur-felt hatters contains many statements concerning the severity of the hazard among carrotters, it was shown by the study of the U. S. Public Health Service (4) that the workers who come in contact with the felt after carrotting are in greater danger. This study also shows that the greatest part of the mercury hazard in this trade is from mercury vapor rather than mercury-impregnated dust.

4. Toxicity and Physiological Response

The inhalation of relatively large concentrations of mercury vapor, for instance, in the case of a mercury-boiler leak (5), is accompanied by the warning effect of a brassy taste in the mouth and discomfort in the throat. Longer exposure to amounts not capable of being tasted or smelled causes severe headache and, if exposure is continued, distress in the alimentary canal with either looseness or constipation.

Koelsch and Ilzhöfer (6) assert that from 0.4 to 1 mg of mercury taken daily for a month will produce poisoning.

Turner (7) concluded that daily exposure to an atmosphere containing as little as 0.02 mg of mercury per cubic foot of air, with a consequent absorption of from 0.771 to 1.2585 mg daily, results in signs and symptoms of mercury poisoning in 2–3 months.

Nordlander (8) disputed this contention on the basis that Turner's analytical results were low and that therefore the amount of mercury inhaled actually must have been greater. He concluded that it requires greater amounts of inhaled mercury before poisoning takes effect.

Investigators of the U. S. Public Health Service (4) were inclined to agree with Nordlander. They found that from their data it was not possible at that time to define a reasonably safe maximum concentration of mercury in the workroom atmosphere. Symptoms of chronic mercurialism developed among individuals working in atmospheric concentrations ranging from 0.6 to 7.2 mg of mercury per 10 m³ of air. The severity of chronic mercurialism and the percentage of persons affected increased with the degree of exposure to mercury. The incidence of chronic mercurialism increases rapidly with increasing mercury concentration after the concentration exceeds 2.0 mg/10 m³.

One very interesting point observed by these investigators was that the small "back-shop" type of plants, even with their extremely unsanitary conditions, had relatively small amounts of mercury vapor and dust in the air as compared with larger plants. They explained this by the fact that the small plants do not allow stock to accumulate but work intermittently as orders are received. For this reason, very little mercury is handled from day to day and practically no treated furs are allowed to accumulate in the factories. On the other hand, in the larger plants considerable quantities of mercury are being used and hundreds of thousands of treated skins and vast quantities of treated fur are continually present in the factory. These treated skins give off mercury vapor continually.

Other investigators insist that minute. amounts are dangerous. Stock and Cucuel (9) believe that it is injurious to health to breathe continuously any air containing a few thousandths of a milligram of mercury per cubic meter of air, as did Turner. Goodman (10) proposed an approximate safe concentration of 0.25 mg/m^3 of air but agreed with a subsequent recommended toxic limit (11) of 0.1 mg/m^3.

The question should certainly be resolved in the favor of those investigators who believe that lower limits of mercury are dangerous, for keeping the amounts of mercury down to those limits unquestionably will diminish the possibility of mercury poisoning.

Goldwater, Jacobs, and Ladd (12) reviewed the literature and their own work covering a span of years in order to evaluate the threshold limit values for inorganic and organic mercury compounds and made the following comments:

On the basis of information now available it cannot be stated with any degree of certainty that a correlation exists between blood and urine levels of mercury on a group basis. It can be stated quite definitely, however, that in any individual case there is unlikely to be any close correlation. Toxicologically, there are differences between the behavior of organic and inorganic mercury compounds. It is not unreasonable to assume that there might also be metabolic differences.

5. Sampling of Mercury

Mercury vapor in the air may be detected directly by means of photoelectric detectors or by the selenium sulfide detector. Detector tubes are also available. Mercury-bearing dust may be sampled by the use of impinger devices. However, mercury-bearing fur dust is also fat bearing and consequently difficult to wet and retain in an impinger. In such instances it is better to use 25% ethyl alcohol–water mixtures as the collecting medium. Nordlander (8) points out that where aqua regia is used as the absorbent for mercury vapor, errors may be introduced because a white coat of mercuric chloride forms around a drop of mercury, protecting it from further solution. Even nitric acid alone as the absorbent is better.

One means of trapping mercury vapor is the use of traps immersed in freezing mixtures such as liquid air, liquid nitrogen, or a mixture of solid carbon dioxide and ether (9,13,14).

The atmosphere to be sampled may contain the mercury as mercury vapor and mercury liquid aerosol, as inorganic compounds, and as organic mercury compounds. Iodine in potassium iodide solution, as detailed in the method in Section A-6-d of this chapter, is an efficient trapping solution for all of these forms. It has the disadvantage that one cannot differentiate the forms in which mercury is in the working atmosphere.

6. DETECTION AND DETERMINATION OF MERCURY

a. Photometric Detection and Measurement

Photometric devices for the determination of mercury vapor in air have been in use for many years but, despite the ease of their use, they have serious limitations that have caused them to be criticized severely. One of the principal difficulties has been that it has apparently not been possible to adjust the zero reading and set the span of the instrument within the work area with grille-type instruments and with some open-cell-type devices because of the difficulty of getting a mercury-free air zone near such mercury-bearing work areas. Another serious limitation has been the difficulty of providing an adequate source of electricity where no line current is available. Procedures (15) for overcoming these limitations with only slight modification of commercial instruments and devices are described in this section.

The strong absorption of ultraviolet light of 2537 Å by mercury is a well-known phenomenon. Woodson (16) invented an instrument for the direct measurement of mercury vapor in air and subsequently this system was incorporated into an instrument by a commercial firm. Although the balanced ultraviolet photometric instrument devised by Hanson (17) was primarily designed for the determination of perchloroethylene and trichloroethylene, it is to be noted that the sensitivities per scale division of mercury, tetraethyllead, perchloroethylene, and trichloroethylene were in the ratio of 0.0001, 0.13, 0.5, and 10, expressed as parts per million. In other words, the amounts in parts per million of the above-mentioned substances necessary to move the indicator of the instrument an equal number of scale divisions were mercury 1, tetraethyllead 1300, perchloroethylene 5000, and trichloroethylene 100,000.

Another balanced photocell system for determining mercury in air by estimation of the decrease in ultraviolet light reaching the test photocell, which is attributable to the absorption of the ultraviolet light by a cell containing air with a concentration of mercury, was described by van Suchtelen, Warmoltz, and Wiggerink (18).

Fig. IX-1. Beckman mercury vapor meter modified by replacement of grille by optical cell. (Courtesy Beckman Instruments, Inc.)

Kruger used a balanced ultraviolet photometric instrument for the determination of mercury vapor in air. Modifications of this instrument are presently being marketed by Beckman Instruments Company (Fig. IX-1). This instrument (19) may be briefly described as follows:

The Beckman Model K23 grille-type mercury is a small, portable instrument designed for use in the determination of mercury vapor concentration in an open atmosphere. It is an ultraviolet light photometer consisting of a mercury vapor lamp, two phototubes, and an amplifier, all contained in a single housing (19). The ultraviolet light generated by the lamp travels to both a nearby reference phototube and a more distant operating phototube. A photoelectric balance is established between the two phototubes in an atmosphere free of mercury. When the instrument is now brought into an atmosphere containing mercury vapor, the photoelectric balance is upset. The resulting change in photoelectric equilibrium is sensed, amplified, and indicated on a meter. It can be calculated that the minimum scale reading of 0.005 mg/m^3 is equivalent to 0.7 nanogram of mercury vapor in the column of air being sensed. Thus, absolute concentrations as low as 0.1–0.2 nanogram can be approximated.

Other photoelectric instruments have been described by Ipatov and Pakhornov (20) and by Trog (21) who modified Hanson's design (17). McMurray and Redmond (22) describe a battery-operated ultraviolet photoelectric mercury vapor meter for use in mines, but this is a very heavy instrument because of the weight of the batteries, even though it is described as portable.

It is necessary to mention the use of ultraviolet photometric instruments to determine mercury in biologic materials. Such methods have been detailed by Ballard and Thornton (23), Monkman et al. (24), Lindström (25), and subsequently Freyschuss et al. (26), Yamaguchi (27) and Jacobs et al. (28). Mansell and Hunemorder (29) converted a Beckman DU spectrophotometer to an ultraviolet photometer for the determination of mercury. Hemeon and Haines (30) trapped the mercury on Whatman No. 4 paper impregnated with potassium iodide and then volatilized the mercury and measured it with a General Electric vapor detector and a recorder.

By simple modifications, both the cell-type and grille-type instruments can be adapted for use in plants and mines.

Apparatus. *Mercury Vapor Meter.* Beckman Model K23 equipped with an optical cell assembly. The cell assembly consists of an aluminum or stainless-steel cell with inlet and outlet ports, fused-quartz end windows, and mounting brackets. In addition, for this modification the ports are closed with rubber tubing and pinch clamps or stopcocks.

Activated Carbon Adsorber. Commercially available from Union Industrial Equipment Corporation.

Mercury Vapor Trap Train. Prepare a trap for the elimination of mercury vapor by adding 10 ml of 0.25% iodine in 3% potassium iodide solution to an all-glass midget impinger. Connect this impinger to another containing 10 ml of 10% potassium iodide solution and to a third dry impinger.

Vacuum Pump. Dyna-Pump, 115 V, 60 cycles, 45 W, capable of sampling at 3 lpm.

Rotameter. Fischer & Porter Flowrator Tube No. OIN-150A.

Converter. Torado 50134, 12 V dc input to operate 110-V appliance.

Battery Eliminator and Charger. Eico Model 1050 operating from 105–125 V ac line to give 0–8 V or 0–16 V adjustable to 6 or 12 V.

Batteries. Two 6-V motorcycle batteries, highest ampere-hour rating or equivalent.

Procedure. *Closed Cell without Absorber.* Set up a train consisting of the pump, cell of the mercury vapor meter, and rotameter connected with rubber or Tygon tubing in an area free of mercury vapor, for example, in an office or a laboratory known to be virtually mercury free. Turn on the pump motor and adjust the flow to draw 3 lpm through the optical cell. Turn on the mercury vapor meter and allow it to stand for the warm-up period of 5 min if it has been in regular operation and 20 min if it has not been in operation. Check the zero and the span (balancing of the phototubes) of the instrument in the manner given by the instruction manual (19) while continuing to draw air through the cell. Disconnect the pump and the rotameter and immediately seal off the cell by placing tight rubber caps or rubber tubing closed by pinch or screw clamps on inlet and outlet. Check the instrument once more to make certain that the zero and balance have not changed appreciably. Turn the instrument off. It is now ready for use in the field.

Transport the instrument and apparatus to the location where the mercury is to be measured. Plug it in, turn it on, and allow it to warm up. Check and adjust the zero and span, assuming that the cell contains air without mercury. Remove the rubber stoppers, connect the pump and rotameter to the cell and a probe to the cell, and, after allowing a few minutes for equilibration, read the mercury concentration. Move the train and the instrument, if possible, without disconnecting the electric current. If it is necessary to do this, it is preferable to use the variation below.

Closed Cell with Absorber. Set up a train consisting of the pump, cell of mercury vapor meter, a two-way stopcock, one arm of which is connected to the mercury trap train, which in turn is connected to the rotameter and the probe, and the other arm of which is free to the air through the sampling probe. Initially, the zero can be established as described above. The zero can also be established by turning the stopcock so that the air enters the cell through the absorber.

Transport the apparatus to the location to be tested, turn on the mercury vapor meter, and check the zero and balance span again. Take the stoppers off the cell, attach the pump and the rest of the apparatus, adjust the stopcock so that the arm without the absorber is connected directly to the sampling probe, and turn on the pump. Adjust the flow rate to 3 lpm. Allow a few minutes for equilibration and read the concentration of mercury on the meter.

Transport the apparatus to the second location. Turn on the meter, turn the stopcock so that the air is drawn through the mercury vapor absorber, and turn on the pump. Allow the mercury-free air to be drawn through the cell until a zero reading is obtained. Check the span and zero, adjusting with the flowing mercury-free air. Turn the stopcock to the arm leading directly to the mercury-laden air, adjust the flowrate to 3 lpm, and read the mercury concentration.

Repeat these steps for the third and other test locations.

Procedure for Mines. Check the field instrument that is the grille type in a place equipped with 110 V ac and set the zero and span. If only a 220-V line is available, use a transformer to obtain 110 V.

Transport the field instrument, the converter, and the batteries to the mine sampling location. This, in general, will have to be done by a team using sling carriers or equivalent devices. At the mine location connect the batteries in series, and attach the converter and then the meter. Turn on the converter and the vapor meter. Allow the instrument to warm up for 5 min and take the reading. Using the available length of line, test the air at several spots at the work location and, if possible, in a corridor.

Disconnect the apparatus, replace in carriers, and proceed to the second work location.

b. Tape Samplers

Tape samplers such as the AISI (30a) or Gelman Tape Sampler (30b) may be used with impregnated tapes to trap the mercury vapor or filter out mercury-bearing dusts and aerosols. Such tape samplers may be used to sample the air in a plant automatically. Subsequently, the tapes may be analyzed for mercury by the methods described in this chapter.

c. Selenium Sulfide Detector

This method is based on the reaction between active selenium sulfide and mercury vapor (31,32). The selenium sulfide is applied as a coating to paper and the coated paper is blackened on exposure to air containing mercury vapor, the degree of blackening being a function of time of exposure, concentration of mercury vapor, and other factors which can be definitely controlled. At a velocity of 1 m/sec of the impinging air and at a reaction temperature of 70°C, a concentration of mercury in the air as low as 1 in 4 million parts by volume can easily be detected after a 4-min exposure.

Preparation of Active Selenium Sulfide. Saturate a solution of aluminum chloride, containing about 100 mg of aluminum per liter, with hydrogen sulfide at room temperature, preferably in a flask that is partly closed in order to retain an atmosphere of hydrogen sulfide above the liquid and thus promote its absorption by the solution during the reaction. Vigorous stirring is also useful for the same purpose. While continuing the current of hydrogen sulfide, add normal selenious acid solution slowly, delivering it below the surface of the reaction mixture in the flask. A yellow precipitate separates out readily. A moderate temporary excess of the acid will form a sol which quickly clears up if the addition is stopped for the time, but too much will give trouble. The operation should be carefully watched to keep the hydrogen sulfide in excess.

Filter, wash, and dry the precipitate. It is a fine yellow powder, and can be dried on the steam bath without turning red. Short exposure to strong sunlight causes it to turn slightly reddish, but it goes back to yellow in darkness. Long exposure gives a permanent red to reddish violet. On rubbing it becomes strongly electrified and it is probable that this electrification has some connection with the tenacity with which it adheres to paper. When kept in the dark, no decrease in sensitivity to mercury vapor with age has been detected.

The selenium sulfide is applied to paper by dipping a pad of cotton wool into the powder and rubbing lightly over the surface of the paper until a uniform film, judging by the color, is formed. The operation is easy if conditions are right. Among the most important of these conditions is the character of the paper. It should be smooth and dense, but not so highly glazed that adhesion and distribution of the powder are poor. The paper used by Nordlander (31) is "Warren's Cumberland Coated Paper, 70 lbs." A successful result is characterized by a surface of even light yellow and of a durability approaching that of a dyed surface. The powder can also be applied to other carriers, such as wood, finely ground or etched glass, celluloid, and certain metals like lead, to produce a surface sensitive to mercury vapor.

Procedure. A portable apparatus has been developed by the General Electric Co. The air or gas to be analyzed is blown into the apparatus by means of a small blower, the velocity of the air current being measured through a tap by a pressure gauge, which serves as a flowmeter. By turning an opening ring, the incoming air current may be bled off, making possible an adjustment of velocity. The air then passes over an electric heater to attain the proper temperature and into another tube, which ends in a nozzle. The selenium sulfide sensitized paper is exposed to the air containing the mercury vapor opposite the nozzle. After impinging against the paper, the air is turned back into the annular space between the nozzle and the housing of the apparatus and is discharged through holes. In this space the outgoing air passes over an adjustable thermoregulator, which controls the heating current around the incoming air.

The relation of time of exposure to the degree of blackening furnishes a very simple way of making a color scale from which, by comparison with the results from a test with a gas of unknown mercury vapor content, almost any concentration can be estimated. A series of prints is made up at an arbitrarily chosen concentration by varying the times of exposure. One can thus get the densities of the prints to increase in any convenient way, preferably in arithmetical progression. This series is naturally limited to the densities that can readily be differentiated by the eye, but the range of concentrations can be indefinitely extended simply by changing the time of exposure. It is evident that by then applying the above relation, the scale so produced can be calibrated and used to determine any concentration of mercury vapor. In case of low mercury concentrations, it is necessary to increase the time of exposure, but with high mercury concentrations the reverse procedure should be adopted. In this way a scale has been made up which can, by changing the time of exposure in geometrical progression from 8 min to 1 min, be used to measure any concentration between 1:8,000,000 and around 1:15,000, the latter corresponding to the saturation of air with mercury at the standard reaction temperature of 70°C.

d. Iodine–Potassium Iodide Method

In the I_2–KI methods, the mercury in the air is absorbed in a solution of iodine in potassium iodide in absorbers. The unknown is added to a mixture of copper sulfate and sodium sulfide in colorimeter tubes. The color produced is compared with that produced by standards made with mercuric chloride.

Sampling Apparatus. Uni-Jet constant-rate Freon-powered sampler; midget impingers, preferably all-glass. (This apparatus can be obtained from Union Industrial Equipment Corp., Fall River, Mass.) An equivalent small electric line or battery-powered vacuum pump sampling at a rate of 2.7–3.0 lpm may be used. It is necessary to insert an activated carbon adsorber after the impinger to protect the sampler or pump from the vapors of iodine or aerosol of iodine in potassium iodide.

Reagents. *Sampling Absorption Solution.* Dissolve 30 g of potassium iodide in 30 ml of water. Dissolve 2.5 g of iodine in this concentrated potassium iodide solution. Transfer to a 1-liter volumetric flask, wash the beaker in which the iodine was dissolved thoroughly with water, add the washings to the flask, and make to volume.

Standard Mercury Solution. Dissolve 0.135 g of mercuric chloride, $HgCl_2$, in 1 liter of sampling solution. This solution contains 0.1 mg of mercury per ml. Dilute this stock standard mercury solution to 2 μg of mercury per ml with additional sampling solution.

Copper Sulfate Solution. Dissolve 10 g of $CuSO_4 \cdot 5H_2O$ in water and dilute to 100 ml.

Sodium Sulfite Solution. Dissolve 38.82 g of anhydrous sodium sulfite, Na_2SO_3, in water and dilute to 200 ml.

Sampling. Place 10 ml of sampling solution into a midget impinger and connect to the Uni-Jet sampler. Open the escape valve for the Freon. Note the time and the rate of sampling. It is essential to watch the rotameter for the Freon may be exhausted (only 3 or 4 samples can be taken with a 1-lb can at the rate specified) or the orifice for the escape of the liquid Freon may become plugged. Continue sampling for 30 min or other suitable time.

Shut the escape valve for the Freon. Note the total time elapsed and the final sampling rate. Transfer the absorbing solution to a small glass-stoppered erlenmeyer flask or equivalent bottle and wash the impinger with two 5-ml portions of the sampling absorption solution. (This step may be omitted if the analysis is to be performed on the premises.)

Procedure. Transfer with the aid of pipets 0, 1, 2, 3, 4, and 5 ml of the standard mercury solution containing 2 μg of mercury per ml to Nessler tubes (50 ml or 100 ml) and, also with the aid of pipets, 5, 4, 3, 2, 1, and 0 ml of the sampling absorption solution. This gives a set of standards containing in 5 ml of total solution, 0, 2, 4, 6, 8, and 10 μg of mercury.

Determine the total volume of the sample. Make a preliminary test to ascertain the range of mercury concentration. Dilute the sample or an aliquot of the sample to a known volume with additional sampling absorption solution to place the mercury concentration within the optimum range.

Transfer a 5-ml aliquot of the sample or transfer 1, 2, 3, or 4 ml of the test solution, depending upon the concentration, to a 50-ml Nessler tube and dilute to 5 ml with the sampling absorption solution. Add 1 ml of copper sulfate solution and swirl. Add 2 ml of 3N sodium sulfite solution and swirl or shake, continuing this action for 0.5 min. Permit the precipitate to settle. This is white if mercury is absent and pink orange if mercury is present. Treat the standards in a similar way. Shake the unknown and the standards at the same time to resuspend the precipitates and compare them.

Calculation. Multiply the rate of air sampling in liters per minute by the number of minutes of sampling time. Let this equal V. Compute the number of micrograms of mercury found in 1 ml of the aliquot used and multiply by the total volume of sampling absorption solution. Let this equal C. Then

$$C/V = \text{concentration of Hg/m}^3$$

For example, if the rate was 3 lpm for 30 min, then the total volume sampled is 90 liters. If the aliquot of the total absorption solution volume used was 2 ml, this test sample contained 2 μg of Hg, and the total volume of absorption solution was 20 ml (10 ml of original sampling solution plus two 5-ml portions used for washing), then the total amount of Hg trapped was 20 μg. Here $C = 20$ and $V = 90$; therefore, the Hg was 0.22 mg/m^3.

e. Dithizone Methods

Dithizone, diphenylthiocarbazone, may also be used for the estimation of mercury. This method is based on the following principles. When a dilute acid solution containing mercury and other metals is shaken with a chloroform or carbon tetrachloride solution of dithizone, the normal green color of dithizone solution changes to a bright orange-yellow color attributable to the formation of a soluble organic mercury complex, which approaches two molecules of dithizone to one atom of mercury. (One mg of mercury reacts with 2.6 mg of dithizone.) The yellow color persists as long as the mercury is in excess. When sufficient dithizone is added to react with all the mercury present, any excess reagent turns the solution green or red or reddish violet, depending upon whether traces of copper are present in the mixture. The fact that mercury under proper conditions will react with dithizone first is the basis of a determination of mercury by titration. High concentrations of copper must be removed before titration of the mercury. This may be done by the addition of potassium iodide, for in the presence of iodide the copper is extracted with dithizone whereas mercury remains in the aqueous solution. Mercury cannot be extracted or titrated with dithizone in acid solution when iodides are present, but it can be extracted in ammoniacal solution. It can also be extracted from an acid solution containing iodides by the use of sodium diethyldithiocarbamate and chloroform as the extractant.

Procedure. Collect and trap the mercury-bearing dust (33) by means of a macro impinger device or some other adequate dust collector. If an impinger is employed, use water as the collecting medium; if the dust is oil or fat bearing, use water and alcohol.

Digest the sample of collected dust and the washings under an efficient reflux condenser with about 25 ml of concentrated nitric acid, 2 ml of concentrated sulfuric acid, and sufficient potassium permanganate until the organic matter is completely destroyed. Use an air condenser above the reflux condenser to prevent loss of mercury. Add more permanganate and nitric acid if necessary. Remove the excess permanganate and the manganese dioxide by the dropwise addition of 30% hydrogen peroxide. Expel the dissolved oxygen by boiling. Cool, add about 0.5 g of hydroxylamine hydrochloride, and extract the solution by shaking with successive portions of a chloroform solution of dithizone, containing 25 mg/liter, until it is present in excess, i.e., the green color of the dithizone predominates over the yellow of the mercury complex.

Treat the chloroform extract with 50 ml of water at 50–60°C, 2 ml of 5% potassium permanganate solution, and 2 ml of sulfuric acid (1:1). The mercury passes into the aqueous layer. Withdraw the chloroform layer and discard. To the aqueous solution add sufficient 10% sodium or potassium nitrite solution to react with the excess permanganate. Destroy the remaining free nitrous acid by the addition of about 0.5 g of hydroxylamine hydrochloride and heat just to boiling.

If large amounts of copper are present, the mercury may be inactivated by the addition of iodide ion. On reextracting with dithizone, the copper is removed and the mercury is left in the aqueous solution. After the excess iodide is destroyed or the solution made ammoniacal, the mercury may be estimated by the titration procedure described below. Small amounts of copper will not interfere with the analysis for mercury since only a small percentage of the copper present will be extracted with dithizone from a solution at a pH 2, which is sufficiently acid to permit complete extraction of the mercury present (34).

Titrate the cool solution in a separatory funnel with a carbon tetrachloride solution of dithizone containing about 1.25 mg of dithizone per liter. Add small portions of this solution until it is present in excess. Use standard mercuric nitrate solution, containing exactly 10 mg of mercury per liter, for back-titration of the excess. Determine the exact strength of the dithizone solution each time it is used by treating a solution containing 0.1 mg of mercury as mercuric nitrate in the same manner as described for a test sample. All the reagents used must be as pure as it is possible to procure them, and blank determinations on water alone must be performed to determine the mercury content of the water and the reagents used in the analytical procedure. Subtract the mercury found in the blank from that found in the test sample to ascertain the quantity actually present in the material analyzed.

A number of variations of the dithizone method are used relatively widely for the determination of mercury. The variation of Jacobs and Singerman (35) is detailed in Section B-2-b of Chapter XIX. An alternative means of eliminating the interference of copper is that of Winkler (36).

f. Electrolytic Method

Mercury vapor can be estimated conveniently by the selenium sulfide detector, but this detector is inapplicable for the estimation of mercury compounds or mercury-bearing dust. The electrolytic method as modified by Stock and Cucuel (9) and by Fraser (14) can be used for all types of air samples contaminated by mercury. In principle the contaminated air is trapped by passing it through a tube chilled by liquid air, liquid nitrogen, or a mixture of solid carbon dioxide and ether. The deposited mercury is then dissolved in chlorine water and may subsequently be estimated by one of two methods, namely, electrolytic deposition alone or a combination of electrolytic deposition and micrometric measurement. Micrometric estimation consists of isolating the mercury as the metal and measuring the diameter of the drop produced by means of a microscope.

Mercury-bearing dust may be sampled with a macro impinger. However, since most of this type of dust is also oil bearing, the dust is trapped in water and alcohol. Then the organic material must be destroyed (37).

Transfer the sample to a 500-ml kjeldahl flask and boil off the alcohol very rapidly for 5–10 min. Cool, add 10 ml of concentrated sulfuric acid and then 4 g of potassium permanganate. Wash down the neck of the flask with water. Allow the sample to digest at a temperature just below boiling for 2 hr. Decolorize with oxalic acid, for which 3 g is generally required, warming if necessary. If the reaction mixture is not cold, add the oxalic acid in small amounts during this step. Transfer the solution to a 250-ml wide-mouth glass-stoppered centrifuge bottle, add 1 ml of 0.5% copper sulfate solution, and then pass in hydrogen sulfide for about ½ hr. Stopper the flask and permit the precipitate to settle overnight. Wash by centrifuging. Pass chlorine gas into the centrifuge bottle containing the washed mercury and copper sulfides after the addition of 5 ml of water. Solution is generally effected in 15 min. Aspirate air through the flask to remove the excess chlorine.

Transfer this solution to a 50-ml beaker. Add 2 ml of a saturated solution of oxalic acid and 5 ml of a saturated ammonium oxalate solution. Plate out the mercury, using a pure gold cathode, 1 × 3 cm and 1/4 mm thick. Keep the voltage at about 1.3–1.5 V. At this voltage, 18–24 hr are required for complete deposition. The gold electrode can be easily made in the laboratory.   Cut a piece of gold foil to the specified dimensions and weld it to a platinum wire by heating the wire and foil in position on an anvil with a Bunsen flame, finally tapping gently with a small hammer.   Care must be taken not to melt the gold by excessive heating.   Wash the electrode upon which both copper and mercury have deposited with water, alcohol, and ether, successively, dry in a desiccator, and weigh on a micro balance.

After weighing, place the electrode in a Pyrex combustion tube, pass through a stream of hydrogen, heat the tube carefully, and drive off the mercury.   Cool in a desiccator and weigh again on a micro balance.   The difference in weight represents mercury.   Never dry the original mercury deposit in an oven.

If the original sample consists of mercury vapor trapped in a U-tube immersed in a freezing mixture and no organic matter is present, the analysis may be begun from the point of passing in the chlorine gas in order to dissolve the mercury.   In other words, the acid digestion and copper coprecipitation of sulfide may be eliminated.

g. Sulfide Method

Minot (38) used the sulfide method to estimate the quantity of mercury present in hatters' felt.   The felt is first oxidized by the use of nitric acid and potassium permanganate.   It is then precipitated as the sulfide.   The sulfide is purified by solution in sodium hydroxide and after reprecipitation as the sulfide it is estimated gravimetrically.

Procedure.   Treat 10 g of the fur with 100 ml of concentrated nitric acid.   Allow to stand overnight.   In the morning add 100 ml of water, boil gently, and add small amounts of potassium permanganate. Continue the addition of permanganate until all organic matter is destroyed, which is shown by an excess of undissolved manganese dioxide precipitate or by a permanganate color after the solution has been boiled several minutes.   Reduce the excess permanganate by boiling the solution with 0.5 g of oxalic acid.   The solution should now be clear and light straw-colored.   Almost neutralize by the addition of sodium carbonate in small amounts.   With the solution still acid, precipitate the mercury with hydrogen sulfide.   Precipitation in nitric acid solution separates mercury from the other heavy metals.   Filter the mixture.   Wash the precipitate with hot water and dissolve in aqua regia.   Repeatedly wash the filter paper with boiling water.

Filter, neutralize the filtrate with sodium hydroxide, and precipitate the mercury with ammonium sulfide. Add sodium hydroxide until the solution appears lighter colored. Then add still more sodium hydroxide while boiling until the mixture forms a clear solution. The mercuric sulfide is thus converted to the soluble sodium sulfo compound, $Hg(SNa)_2$. From this solution, mercury is reprecipitated as sulfide in a filtrable form by excess solid ammonium nitrate. Boil with sodium sulfide to remove excess ammonia and to convert any sulfur present to sodium thiosulfate. Allow to stand overnight and filter on a tared Gooch crucible. Dry at 110–120°C, cool in a desiccator, and weigh. The weight is taken as mercuric sulfide, from which the weight of mercury is obtained by multiplication by the proper factor.

The following reactions take place in the method.

$$HgS + 2NaOH + (NH_4)_2S \rightarrow Hg(SNa)_2 + 2NH_4OH$$

$$Hg(SNa)_2 + 2NH_4NO_3 \rightarrow 2NaNO_3 + (NH_4)_2S + HgS$$

h. Other Methods

Other methods for the determination of mercury are those of Pyankoff (39) and Moldavsky (40), which are based on the formation of mercuric iodide and mercuric bromide.

In the Pyankoff (39) method, air is aspirated through a U-tube containing crystals of iodine in the curve. After sampling is completed, the tube is immersed in a water bath at about 70°C to warm and air is drawn through to remove the excess iodine. The mercuric iodide crystals which remain in the tube are dissolved in alcohol (the heating aids the solution of yellow mercurous iodide, if formed) and the solutions are transferred to Nessler tubes or other colorimetric tubes. A series of standards is prepared within the range expected and to each tube is added 0.5 ml of hydrogen sulfide water. The brown colors developed are compared. Alternatively, the mercury salts may be dissolved in ether, transferred to a tared dish, dried, and weighed.

In the Moldavsky (40,41) method, the mercury in the air is absorbed by the use of gaseous bromine. The mercuric bromide solution is transferred to a beaker, chlorine water is added, and the solution is evaporated in a vacuum desiccator over sodium hydroxide. A drop each of sodium acetate and of alcoholic diphenylcarbazone solution is added.   The color thus produced is compared with a series of standards.

Radioactive mercury has been applied as a tracer for the measurement of mercury vapor in air (42).   Using radioactive mercury of atomic weight 197 with a half life of 25 hr, an average concentration of 0.01 mg of mercury per cubic meter of air was found to be present in a particular industrial operation suspected of causing chronic mercurialism.   This technique is said to be capable of detecting 10^{-8} g of mercury.

B. ARSENIC

1. Arsenic Poisoning

Mention poison to a layman and likely as not he will think of arsenic.   With growth in the use of arsenic as a benefactor of mankind— for example, its use in arsenicals and in fungicides, herbicides, insecticides, and drugs—have also come the dangers associated with arsenic as a poison.   Our present-day civilization almost cannot continue without the use of these materials and therefore attempts must be made to keep the presence of arsenic at a minimum.   The hazards associated with the use of arsenic in industry are many.   One particular hazard, in reality not attributable to the use of arsenic compounds as such, but owing to the fact that the arsenic is present as a contaminant, is the danger of the formation of arsine (arseniuretted hydrogen) whenever hydrogen is being evolved in any step of an industrial process.   Another danger is the possible hazard from arsenic-contaminated organic chemicals manufactured from arsenic-contaminated sulfuric or nitric acids, which are often used in making organic chemicals.   Smelting of arsenical ores, manufacture of paints, dyes, insecticides, fungicides, drugs, and felt hats, and curing hides are among the varied industries in which arsenic is a hazard.   A dangerous arsenic chemical is arsenious chloride (arsenic trichloride), which can cause death through inhalation or even by direct application to the skin (43).

2. Actual Role of Arsenic as an Industrial Hazard

One of the difficulties associated with industrial poisoning resulting from arsenic is the actual role that the industrial hazard plays. Cannon (44) says that the effects of arsenic as observed in the majority of cases of chronic arsenic poisoning are not due to the arsenic derived from any single source, but from the combined effects of arsenic taken in from a multiplicity of sources, and in a great variety of forms. It is virtually impossible under present living conditions to remove a person from all contacts with arsenic.

One of the great sources of arsenic intake is the arsenic present in foods. Some of this is so-called natural arsenic, i.e., the arsenic found in marine food products such as fish or lobster. Arsenic in foods is also due to the addition of insecticides and fungicides to fruits and vegetables. In order to keep the possibility of poisoning from this source to a minimum, there is a U. S. Government tolerance of 0.01 grain per lb, or 1.4 ppm, of arsenic in foodstuffs. This has been increased to 0.025 grain per lb (3.58 ppm) for spray residue (45).

The maximum allowable concentration suggested by the American Standards Association as an American War Standard (46) was 1.5 mg of arsenic, calculated as arsenic, per 10 m³ of air. Governmental hygienists (47) suggests 0.5 mg/m³. Higher concentrations are recommended by others (48,49).

The above-mentioned discussion holds true for arsenic compounds but not for gaseous arsenic compounds. The type of poisoning caused by arsine is entirely typical for it is one of the very few hemolytic poisons encountered in industry (50).

Because of its historic position as a poison, arsenic was one of the first elements for which methods to detect minute quantities were developed. One need but mention the names of Berzelius and Marsh to recall the qualitative and quantitative arsenic mirror tests developed.

3. Sampling of Arsenic

Arsenic compounds fall into three main groups: solid or liquid inorganic arsenic compounds, and volatile compounds of both groups. Arsenic-bearing dust and spray of the first two groups may be trapped by means of impinging devices, filtering devices, or bubblers containing absorbing agents such as sodium hydroxide and bromine in potassium bromide or bromine water. The electrostatic precipitator is recommended for the sampling of arsenical fumes. Volatile arsenic compounds should be trapped by adsorption on silica gel or by absorption in silver nitrate solution or some volatile solvents in bubblers. The vapors of volatile arsines can be recovered (51) by distillation from the silica gel into an oxidizing mixture of sodium peroxide and sodium carbonate. Care must be taken whenever the possibility of forming arsenious chloride exists that an oxidizing medium be present so that no arsenic may be lost.

4. ACID DIGESTION

Because arsenic-bearing compounds are often organic compounds, some description of the customary methods for the destruction of organic matter is appropriate at this point. There are two general methods for the destruction of interfering organic matter. The first is called the "wet-ash," or acid-digestion, method and the second is ordinary ashing by means of heat with or without the aid of an ash-aid mixture or of an alkaline fixative for volatile metals, such as arsenic, antimony, mercury, or tin. Acid digestion is preferred for these metals except in the instance of antimony.

Transfer the sample or an appropriate aliquot or portion containing the arsenic to a 300-ml Pyrex kjeldahl flask. If the sample is a liquid and an oxidizing medium is present so that no arsenic will be lost on evaporation, the sample may be concentrated by evaporation. Add 25 ml of concentrated nitric acid and then carefully add 5 ml of concentrated sulfuric acid. Heat cautiously so that no excessive foaming takes place. Add nitric acid in small portions until all the organic matter is destroyed. This point is reached when no further darkening of the solution occurs on continued heating after the production of a clear solution and copious fumes of sulfur trioxide. Cool. Add 20 ml of water and 5 ml of a saturated solution of ammonium oxalate to aid in the expulsion of nitrogen fumes. Evaporate again until the appearance of sulfur trioxide fumes. Cool, dilute with water, transfer to a 500-ml or 1-liter volumetric flask, and make to volume. Use aliquot portions for analysis as needed.

Wet ashing by means of nitric acid and potassium permanganate and by means of sulfuric acid and potassium permanganate has been described in connection with the methods for the estimation of mercury. In recent years, methods of ashing by means of nitric and perchloric acids (52–54) have been developed in order to overcome the difficulties presented by volatile substances, those having an appreciable vapor pressure at the boiling temperature of a mixture of nitric and sulfuric acids, or those which produce an insoluble precipitate in those acids. The author finds it difficult to recommend these procedures, for ashing with perchloric acid is extremely dangerous and serious explosions have occurred during its use.   All the details may be found in the literature.

5. DETECTION AND DETERMINATION OF ARSENIC

a. Reinsch Test

The Reinsch test is a simple though not very sensitive one.   It is based on the deposition of arsenic from solution as a copper arsenide. The test may very often be applied directly without previous destruction of organic matter.   Place 200 ml of the suspected arsenic-bearing material, if trapped in water by an impinger or a bubbler device, in a casserole, and acidify with 1 ml of arsenic-free hydrochloric acid. Evaporate to one-half its volume.   Add 15 ml more of hydrochloric acid and also a piece of pure burnished copper foil.   Keep the liquid simmering for an hour and replenish the water lost by evaporation from time to time.   If at the end of this time the copper foil remains bright, arsenic is not present in greater quantity than traces.   If the copper has a black or brown deposit, remove it and wash well with water, alcohol, and ether, and dry.   Place the foil in a subliming tube and heat over a low flame.   If a sublimate is present, examine it under a microscope.   Arsenic forms tetrahedral crystals while mercury forms globules.   Antimony, silver, and bismuth will also give a deposit on the copper foil but will not sublime with the application of heat.

b. Gutzeit Method

The Gutzeit method is based on the liberation of arsine under carefully controlled conditions from an arsenic solution.   The arsine subsequently reduces mercuric bromide on a prepared strip of paper with the production of stains.   The stain, if the method is followed in detail, is proportional to the amount of arsenic present.

Prepare a generator (Fig. IX-2) as follows: Use a 2-oz wide-mouth bottle.   Equip the bottle by means of a perforated stopper with a glass tube 1 cm in diameter and 6–7 cm long with an additional constricted end to facilitate connection.   Place a small wad of glass wool in the constricted bottom end of the tube and add 3.5–4 g of 30-mesh clean sand.   Moisten the sand with 10% lead acetate solution and remove the excess by light suction.   The lead acetate is used to remove any hydrogen sulfide that might be generated along with the arsine and thus vitiate results if permitted to reduce the mercuric bromide. Connect the tube by means of a rubber stopper with a narrow glass tube 2.6–2.7 mm in internal diameter and 10–12 cm long, and place in this tube a strip of mercuric bromide paper. These strips may be made by cutting paper similar to Whatman No. 40 filter paper into strips exactly 2.5 mm wide and about 12 cm long. Commercial strips are available. Soak the strips for 1 hr or longer in a fresh 3–6% solution of mercuric bromide in 95% alcohol. Dry and use within 2 days. For approximately quantitative work, these strips may be stored in a well-stoppered blackened tube.

Fig. IX-2. Gutzeit generator.

Instead of preparing strips each time a determination is to be made, Goldstone (55) suggests that a sheet of 32 strips be cut into 9-cm lengths, which may be suspended permanently in the alcoholic mercuric bromide solution stored in a 10-ml glass-stoppered cylinder. Withdraw the strips as required, press immediately between filter paper, and permit the strips to dry in air for 0.5 hr before use.

Determine the acid in an aliquot of the solution prepared from the wet ash as described above. Place aliquots, not to exceed 30 ml, depending on the amount of arsenic trioxide, 0.01–0.03 mg, in the Gutzeit generator. If the aliquot contains only hydrochloric acid, add sufficient hydrochloric acid to make a total volume of 5 ml. If it contains sulfuric acid, add sufficient arsenic-free 25% sodium hydroxide to exactly neutralize it and add 5 ml of hydrochloric acid;

or add sufficient hydrochloric acid to the sulfuric acid in the aliquot to make a total volume of 5 ml. Cool, if necessary, and add 5 ml of potassium iodide solution (15 g of potassium iodide dissolved in water and made up to 100 ml) and 4 drops of stannous chloride solution (40 g of arsenic-free stannous chloride, $SnCl_2 \cdot 2H_2O$, in hydrochloric acid made up to 100 ml with hydrochloric acid). Add a piece of activated zinc (prepared by placing the zinc in contact with hydrochloric acid (1:3), to which has been added 2 ml of the stannous chloride reagent and allowing the action to proceed for 15 minutes) 10–15 g in weight or 2–5 g of granulated zinc, center the strip of mercuric bromide paper in its tube, and set the tubes in position.

Immerse the apparatus in a water bath kept at 20–25°C to within 1 in. of the top of the narrow tube and allow the evolution of the arsine to proceed for 1 hr or $1\frac{1}{2}$ hr. Remove the strip and average the length of the stains on both sides in millimeters. Locate the length of the unknown on a standard graph and read off on the abscissa the quantity of arsenic present. The graph may be made by running known quantities of arsenic by the above method, using length of stain as ordinates and milligrams of arsenic trioxide as abscissas. Many authorities advise against the use of a standard graph on the ground that one cannot be prepared. They advise the running of a series of controls with every unknown determination.

All the reagents used in this determination should be arsenic free. However, as a precaution, it is best to run blanks on the reagents. In some cases the test may be made without previous destruction of organic material, but the results obtained are probably only approximate. An aliquot containing 0.02–0.025 mg of arsenic trioxide is considered optimum for reading the stain.

Clarke (56) says that general experience has made it plain that not one of the various modifications of the Gutzeit method can be used by the average analyst with the assurance or even probability that his results will be accurate unless he attains considerable experience in its use.

Goldstone Modification

The Gutzeit method for arsenic is an empirical one. It requires strict adherence to all details. To overcome one source of error, namely, the uneven evolution of hydrogen, Goldstone (55) suggested the use of short zinc rods treated so that a constant surface area would be exposed and thus a relatively even evolution of hydrogen would result.

Preparation of Zinc Rods.   Clamp a 15 × 125-mm Pyrex test tube on a stand in a vertical position, place a 6-in. stick of arsenic-free zinc into the tube, and heat carefully with a bunsen burner until the zinc melts and fills the entire tube.   As an alternative procedure, melt the zinc in a beaker and pour the molten metal into a preheated Pyrex tube.   Tap the tube to dislodge any air pockets that may have formed and allow the mass to solidify gradually, playing the flame on the upper portion in order to make this section solidify last.   This precaution prevents the formation of a hollow core attributable to the contraction of the metal as it solidifies and insures a solid, uniform cylinder of zinc metal.   Allow to cool and remove the cylinder by breaking the test tube.   Cut the cylinder into lengths slightly less than the diameter of the generating bottle with the aid of a hack saw, grind the ends smooth with an emery wheel, and coat with the wax composition, described below.   Lengths of 1.5 in. are suitable and generally last for 15 determinations before they become too short.

Rub some magnesium carbonate into gum arabic paste, coat the plane ends of the short rods with the paste, and allow to dry.   Dip one end of the short rods into a beaker of molten wax prepared from 3 parts of paraffin and 1 part of Acrowax C, withdraw, allow to harden, and repeat the operation on the other end of the rod, covering the entire surface with a layer of wax about $\frac{1}{16}$ in. thick.   It may be necessary to repeat the coating in order to get it sufficiently thick.   Scrape the plane ends free of the wax and soak in water to remove the paste coating.   Activate the uncoated ends of the rods with stannous chloride, as directed above, and store under water acidified with a drop of concentrated hydrochloric acid.   Since after each arsenic determination the plane surfaces remain activated, the initial activation is the only one necessary.   As the zinc is dissolved during a series of determinations, the protruding collar of wax should be scraped off.

c. Jacobs Molybdenum Blue Method

The molybdenum blue method (57–68) for the estimation of arsenic is one of the most sensitive methods that can be used for this purpose. Phosphorus reacts with ammonium molybdate to form a complex molybdiphosphate.   This may subsequently be reduced with the formation of a complex molybdenum compound strongly colored blue,

Arsenic undergoes an entirely analogous reaction with the formation of an intensely colored blue complex. This reaction of arsenic and its use in methods for the estimation of arsenic have been discussed by a number of investigators.

The arsenic is put into solution by methods previously detailed. It is evolved as arsine, which is trapped and oxidized by bromine water or by sodium hypobromite solution. Ammonium molybdate is added, and the color of molybdenum blue is developed by the use of hydrazine sulfate, $N_2H_4 \cdot H_2SO_4$.

Reagents. *Ammonium Oxalate Solution.* Prepare an aqueous saturated solution of ammonium oxalate, $(NH_4)_2C_2O_4 \cdot H_2O$.

Potassium Iodide Solution. Dissolve 15 g of potassium iodide in water and make up to a volume of 100 ml.

Stannous Chloride Solution. Dissolve 40 g of arsenic-free stannous chloride, $SnCl_2 \cdot 2H_2O$, in concentrated hydrochloric acid and make up to 100 ml with this reagent.

Lead Acetate Solution. Dissolve 10 g of lead acetate, $Pb(OOCCH_3)_2 \cdot 3H_2O$, in water and make up to a volume of 100 ml.

Sodium Hypobromite Solution. Add 3 ml of half-saturated bromine water to 1 ml of 0.5N sodium hydroxide solution. This reagent must be made up immediately prior to use.

Ammonium Molybdate Solution. Dissolve 25 g of ammonium molybdate, $(NH_4)_6Mo_7O_{24} \cdot 4H_2O$, in 300 ml of water. Dilute 75 ml of concentrated sulfuric acid to 200 ml with water by adding the acid carefully to the water and add the diluted acid to the ammonium molybdate solution.

Hydrazine Sulfate Solution. Prepare a half-saturated solution of hydrazine sulfate, $N_2H_4 \cdot H_2SO_4$, by diluting a saturated solution of hydrazine sulfate in water with an equal volume of water.

All these reagents must be as free of arsenic as possible. It is best to purchase reagents specially prepared for arsenic determinations.

Procedure. Place the sample into a 300-ml kjeldahl flask and add 20 ml of nitric acid and 5 ml of sulfuric acid. Heat until dense fumes of sulfur trioxide are produced. If necessary, add small amounts of nitric acid to clear the residue. When the digestion is complete, add 5 ml of a saturated solution of ammonium oxalate and again heat until fumes are given off. Cool and transfer to a Gutzeit generator bottle (Fig. IX-3). Wash the kjeldahl flask 5 times with 5-ml portions of water and add these washings to the generator. Add 5 ml of 15%

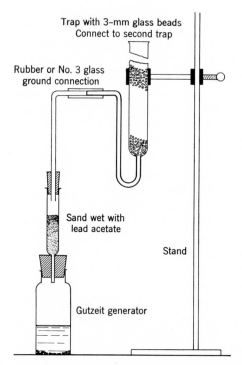

Fig. IX-3. Apparatus for Jacobs' molybdenum blue method.

potassium iodide solution, 4 drops of stannous chloride solution, and allow to stand for 20 min so that reduction will be complete. Add a piece of $\frac{1}{4}$-in. diameter zinc rod, about 1 in. in length, and connect the rest of the Gutzeit generator, i.e., the hydrogen sulfide absorber and the tube leading to the arsine absorber. This is a trap which consists of a vapor trap with a detachable spiral of glass around the inlet tube. Add 3 ml of sodium hypobromite solution to the absorber tube and after connecting the apparatus, put the generator in an ice bath. Allow the generation to proceed for 1 hr. Transfer the sodium hypobromite solution to a 1-in. Bausch & Lomb colorimeter tube. Wash the absorber 5 times with 2 ml of water and add these washings to the colorimeter tube. Add 10 ml of $1N$ acid and stir; add 1 ml of ammonium molybdate reagent and shake. Add 1 ml of the half-saturated hydrazine sulfate solution and swirl, make to a volume of 25 ml, and allow to stand for 0.5 hr for full development of the blue color. Read in a Bausch & Lomb colorimeter in which the visual range lamp has been replaced and the red filter has been inserted at 830 mμ or compare with standards or a standard treated in a similar way at the same time.

Preparation of Standards. Prepare the standards or standard from the diluted stock standard arsenious oxide solution (page 381). Add 3 ml of sodium hypobromite solution to the aliquot or aliquots selected, dilute to 10 ml with water, add exactly 10 ml of $1N$ or 5 ml of $2N$ sulfuric acid, and stir. Add 1 ml of the molybdate reagent, stir, add 1 ml of half-saturated hydrazine sulfate solution, and stir. Make up to the same volume as the test solution. A standard curve for the photometric determination may be constructed by running known concentrations of arsenic through the entire procedure. Run a blank on all the reagents as a check.

If a final volume of 25 ml is to be used in making the comparisons, use exactly 5 ml of $2N$ sulfuric acid, in order to have the proper acidity for the development of the molybdenum blue color. If less than this quantity of acid is used, the blank may itself be reduced. If more than this quantity of acid is used, the development of the blue complex will be delayed.

The method may be used directly for the determination of arsine in industrial air by trapping in hypobromite solution, provided no phosphates or phosphorus compounds are present along with the arsine.

d. Diethyldithiocarbamate Method

In 1952, with the introduction of the use of silver diethyldithiocarbamate in pyridine by Vasak and Sedivec (69) as the absorbing agent for arsine with the production of a red color, many analysts have abandoned the use of the Gutzeit method and the variations of the molybdenum blue method. In Jacobs' laboratory, there has been serious objection, particularly on the part of female chemists, to the use of the diethyldithiocarbamate method because it involves the use of pyridine outside a hood. The stench of the pyridine and the difficulty of removing the odor from one's hands and clothing is serious. Since a principal objective of the industrial hygienist is to improve working conditions, the author cannot recommend its use.

The diethyldithiocarbamate method is detailed here since it is widely used, but the claims (70,71) that it is better and more sensitive than the Jacobs (72) variation of the molybdenum blue method are not factual.

Reagents. *Silver Diethyldithiocarbamate Solution.* Silver diethyldithiocarbamate $(C_2H_4)_2NCSSAg$, is available commercially; therefore, there is no need for the tedious preparation from sodium diethyldithiocarbamate and silver nitrate. Weigh accurately 0.5 g of the dry salt and dissolve in anhydrous pyridine, reagent grade. Transfer to a 100-ml volumetric flask and make up to volume with pyridine.

The other reagents used in this method are described in the preceding Section B-5-c, on the Jacobs molybdenum blue method.

Procedure. If necessary, perform an acid digestion as detailed under Procedure, Section B-5-c of this chapter.

Transfer the digest or the test solution to a Gutzeit generator bottle and proceed in the same manner as detailed for the Gutzeit method and the Jacobs molybdenum blue method, but place 3 ml of the pyridine solution of silver diethyldithiocarbamate in the special absorber with the spiral baffle instead of the sodium hypobromite solution. Continue with the elaboration of the arsine for 30 min. Transfer the absorbing solution to a Bausch & Lomb cuvette and read in a B & L Spectronic 20 or an equivalent instrument at 540 mμ, using a blank carried through the method to adjust the zero. Read the micrograms of arsenic from a calibration curve made with standards treated in the same manner as the test solution and calculate the concentration of arsenic from the original volume of the test sample and the volume of air sampled.

Monitoring Variation

A continuous arsenic monitor has been developed which is based on the reaction between arsine and a pyridine solution of silver diethyldithiocarbamate and also upon the reaction of various arsenic compounds and atomic hydrogen to form arsine.

In this device (73), air is drawn into a hydrogen generator by means of a small air pump, as shown in Figure IX-4. Any arsine that is formed is drawn into a detector cell containing the diethyldithiocarbamate. In the presence of arsine, the solution changes in color from pale yellow to various shades of red, depending upon the concentration of arsine. The cell is monitored by use of a simple colorimeter. If, at the end of a predetermined time, the threshold limit of

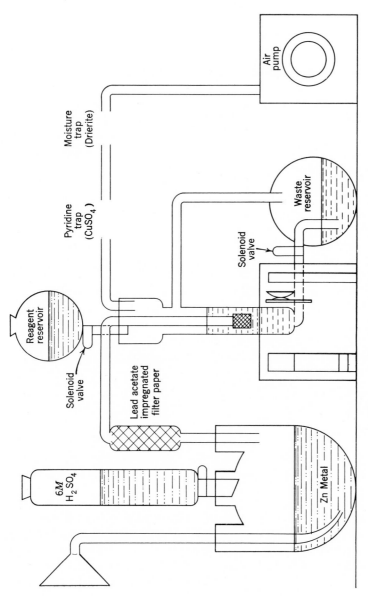

Fig. IX-4.   Device for monitoring arsenic continuously.

arsenic is not indicated, the solution is changed automatically.   The monitoring cycle is then repeated.

e. Bromate Method

The bromate method (74) for the determination of arsenic is applicable when the amount of arsenic trioxide to be estimated is of the order of 0.35 mg.   The method is based on placing the arsenic into solution by means of the wet method, or acid digestion.   Then the arsenic is distilled as arsenious chloride, $AsCl_3$, along with hydrogen chloride.   The distillate is titrated with standard bromate solution using methyl orange as indicator.

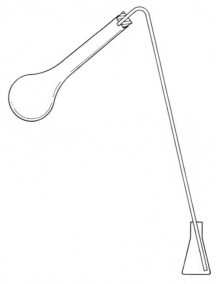

Fig. IX-5.   Distillation apparatus for determination of arsenic by the bromate method.

Apparatus.   The distillation apparatus (Fig. IX-5) consists of an 800-ml kjeldahl flask, a tube, and a 300-ml wide-mouth flask.   To make the tube, bend a 10–15-mm glass tube to an acute angle of about 70°.   Draw the longer arm, which is about 15–20 in. long, down to an orifice of about 3 mm.   Fit the shorter arm, which is about 4 in. long, with a rubber stopper, which has previously been boiled in 10% sodium hydroxide solution for about 15 min, and then in hydrochloric acid for 15 min in order to remove most of the sulfur compounds which might be distilled and react with the bromate solution.

Preparation of Reagents. *Standard Potassium Bromate Solution.* Dissolve 0.1823 g of potassium bromate, $KBrO_3$, in water and dilute to 1 liter. One ml of this solution is equivalent to 0.324 mg of arsenic trioxide, As_2O_3. Standardize by titration against standard arsenious oxide solution, making the titration at about 90°C and in the presence of about 100 ml of water and 25 ml of hydrochloric acid, in order to simulate the conditions under which the unknown samples will be titrated. One ml of the bromate solution should be equivalent to 1 ml of the arsenious oxide solution.

Standard Arsenious Oxide Solution. Dissolve 0.3241 g of arsenic trioxide, As_2O_3, in 25 ml of 10% sodium hydroxide solution, make slightly acid with sulfuric acid (1:6), and dilute with water to 1 liter.

Hydrazine Sulfate–Sodium Bromide Solution. Dissolve 20 g of hydrazine sulfate and 20 g of sodium bromide in 1 liter of hydrochloric acid (1:4).

Procedure. Proceed with the wet-ash digestion, using exactly 20 or 25 ml of concentrated sulfuric acid at the beginning of the digestion. After the digestion is complete, add 50 ml of water and 25 ml of saturated ammonium oxalate solution containing 50 g of urea per liter, and boil until white sulfur trioxide fumes extend up into the neck of the flask to decompose oxalates and urea completely.

Add 25 ml of water and cool to room temperature. Place 100 ml of water into the 300-ml wide-mouth flask. Add to the mixture in the kjeldahl flask 20 g of sodium chloride, not iodized, and 25 ml of the hydrazine sulfate–sodium bromide solution. Connect the distilling apparatus. Heat the kjeldahl flask over a small well-protected flame and catch the distillate in the water in the wide-mouth flask. The heating generates hydrogen chloride gas, which carries over the arsenious chloride with it. The absorption of the evolved hydrogen chloride gas by the water causes a rise in temperature, by means of which rise the progress of the distillation can be followed. Adjust the flame so that the temperature of the distillate solution will rise to 90°C in 9–11 min, and then discontinue the distillation. The residual mixture in the kjeldahl flask should not be less than 55 ml. If the distillation proceeds further or a larger quantity of sulfuric acid than that specified is used in the digestion, sulfur dioxide may be distilled. This is titrated as arsenious oxide.

Titrate the distillate at once with the bromate solution, using 3 drops of methyl orange indicator. Single drops of indicator, but not exceeding 3, may be added during titration as the red color fades. Toward the end of the titration add the bromate solution very slowly and with constant agitation to prevent local excess. The end point is reached when a single drop of the bromate just destroys the final tinge of red color. To determine when this point has been reached, use a similar wide-mouth flask of clear water for comparison. The end point must not be exceeded, as the action of the indicator is not reversible and back titrations are not reliable. At the proper end point, the red color produced by 2 additional drops of methyl orange indicator should persist for at least 1 min. Correct the results for the volume of bromate used in a blank determination using 5 g of pure sucrose and the same quantities of reagents, as well as the same distillation procedure. The blank titration should not exceed 0.7 ml of bromate solution and variations in the blank should not exceed 0.1 ml when chemicals from the same lot are used. If doubt arises, run a Gutzeit determination on an aliquot.

f. Other Methods

Iodometric Method

Cassil and Wichmann (75) describe a rapid volumetric method for the determination of arsenic in microgram quantities. An acid digestion is performed on the material. Then the arsenic is evolved in a special generator as arsine, which is trapped in a mercuric chloride solution contained in a special tube made of methyl methacrylate resin. The liberated arsine is absorbed quantitatively by the mercuric chloride solution, forming mercury arsenides. The arsenides are oxidized by the excess mercuric chloride with the formation of mercurous chloride and arsenious acid. The arsenious acid may then be oxidized to arsenic acid with $0.001N$ iodine solution.

Chlorometric Method

Arsenic may also be determined by chlorometry, using the method of Goldstone and Jacobs (76) as detailed in Chapter X, Section C-1-c for the estimation of antimony.

6. Arsine

Arsine—arseniuretted hydrogen, hydrogen arsenide, arsenic trihydride, AsH_3—occurs in potentially dangerous concentrations in many industries, among which may be mentioned the manufacture of zinc chloride and sulfate, the smelting of arsenical and arsenic-bearing ores, the manufacture of enamel ware, dyestuffs and dyestuff intermediates, electroplating and galvanizing works, and the production of hydrochloric and sulfuric acids. In general, wherever hydrogen is evolved, there is also the possibility of evolution of arsine.

Several deaths and injuries occurred in 1949 from arsine, apparently resulting from the presence of an aluminum arsenide in some metal dross where aluminum was used in the drossing process (77).

Arsine is a colorless gas with an extremely offensive odor resembling that of garlic. It is 2.7 times as heavy as air. It is somewhat soluble in water but is insoluble in ether and alcohol. It decomposes with heat and is inflammable.

a. Physiological Response

Arsine is a nerve and blood poison. There is generally some delay, sometimes a day or so, before the onset of symptoms. These are at first usually indefinite. There is a general feeling of malaise, difficulty in breathing, severe headache, giddiness, fainting fits, nausea, vomiting, and gastric disturbances (78,79). In more severe cases the vomiting may be more pronounced, the mucous membranes may have a bluish discoloration, and the urine is dark or bloodstained. After a day or two there is severe anemia and jaundice.

A concentration of 500 ppm is lethal for a man after exposure of a few minutes. A concentration of 250 ppm, equivalent to 0.75 mg/liter, is dangerous to life in an exposure of 30 min. Concentrations of 6.25–15.5 ppm, i.e., 0.02–0.05 mg/liter, are dangerous after exposure for 30–60 min. The maximum concentration tolerated for several hours without serious symptoms is 3.1 ppm (1). Sayers (79) gives a concentration of 10 ppm as the concentration that can be tolerated for several hours without serious symptoms. Table 4, Appendix, gives the maximum allowable concentrations suggested by several authorities. There are no recorded figures as to the limits of concentration that may be regarded as harmless for continuous daily exposure, but there is evidence that repeated exposures to very low concentrations may have cumulative effects resulting in severe poisoning (78). The threshold limit submitted by the Committee on Threshold Limits and accepted by the American Conference of Governmental Industrial Hygienists is 0.05 ppm (see Table 3, Appendix).

b. Detection

The official British method for the detection of arsine in air uses a mercuric chloride test paper. Although silver nitrate test paper is about 20 times as sensitive as mercuric chloride paper, it has the following drawbacks: the stains vary in color from yellow to black, depending on the drying temperature; they continue to darken rapidly so that matching is difficult; and the papers do not keep well.

In the British (78) standard test, the test papers are prepared by immersing the strips of filter paper in 5% mercuric chloride solution, drying them, and cutting off and discarding the ends.

The atmosphere under examination is drawn by means of a hand pump described in Chapter II, Section E-1-b and c, through the test paper, and the resulting stain, if any is produced, is compared within 5 min with the standard stains issued with the leaflet. The concentration of arsine is then found by reference to the color chart, which shows the intensities of stains corresponding with 10–50 strokes of the pump. In this way concentrations of arsine down to 4 ppm, i.e., 0.013 mg/liter, can be detected. The atmosphere to be tested is passed through lead acetate paper to absorb any traces of hydrogen sulfide before coming in contact with the mercuric chloride paper.

Alternatively, mercuric bromide test paper prepared as directed in the Gutzeit method may be used. The depth and intensity of the stain are indicative of the amount of arsine.

c. Determination

Arsine may be estimated quantitatively by absorption in potassium iodide solution acidified with sulfuric acid with subsequent titration of the liberated iodine. It may be determined by absorption in silver nitrate solution with subsequent titration of the resulting arsenious acid. It may be trapped in nitric acid, bromine, or other oxidizing medium and then estimated by one of the methods detailed in the preceding sections. Alternatively, arsine may be trapped in sodium hypobromite solution and then the arsenic may be estimated by the molybdenum blue method or the diethyldithiocarbamate method.

References

1. Flury, F., and F. Zernik, *Schaedliche Gase*, Springer, Berlin, 1931.
2. Schulte, H. F., *J. Ind. Hyg. Toxicol.*, **28**, 159 (1946).
3. Lloyd, L. L., and W. Gardner, *J. Soc. Chem. Ind.*, **31**, 1109 (1922).
4. Sayers, R. R., P. A. Neal, R. R. Jones, J. J. Bloomfield, J. M. DallaValle, and T. I. Edwards, *U.S. Public Health Service Bull. 234* (1937).
5. *Chem. Met. Eng.*, "Process Industries —Flow Sheets and Data Book," p. 133.
6. Koelsch, F. F., and H. Ilzhöfer, *Zenter. Gewerbehyg. Unfallverhut.*, **7**, 11, 17, 42 (1919); *J. Ind. Hyg.*, **2**, 135 (1920).
7. Turner, J. A., *U.S. Public Health Rept.*, **39**, 329 (1924).
8. Nordlander, B. W., *Ind. Eng. Chem.*, **19**, 522 (1927).
9. Stock, A., and F. Cucuel, *Chem. Ber.*, **67B**, 122 (1934).
10. Goodman, C., *Rev. Sci. Instr.*, **9**, 233 (1938).
11. Shepherd, M., S. Schukmann, R. H. Flinn, J. W. Hough, and P. A. Neal, *J. Res. Natl. Bur. Std. (Res. Paper 383)*, **26**, 357 (1951).
12. Goldwater, L. J., M. B. Jacobs, and A. C. Ladd, *Arch. Environ. Health*, **5**, 537 (1962).
13. Stock, A., and R. Heller, *Angew. Chem.*, **39**, 466 (1926).
14. Fraser, A. M., *J. Ind. Hyg.*, **16**, 67 (1934).
15. Jacobs, M. B., and R. Jacobs, *Am. Ind. Hyg. Assoc. J.*, **26**, 261 (1965).
16. Woodson, T. T., *Rev. Sci. Instr.*, **10**, 308 (1939); U.S. Pat. 2,227,117 (Dec. 31, 1940).
17. Hanson, V. F., *Ind. Eng. Chem. Anal. Ed.*, **13**, 119 (1941).
18. H. Van Suchtelen, N. Warmoltz, and G. L. Wiggerink, *Philips Tech. Rev.*, **11**, 91 (1949); *A.M.A. Arch. Ind. Hyg. Occupational Med.*, **3**, 432 (1951).
19. Mercury Vapor Meter K23, K24, Beckman Instruments Co., Fullerton, Calif.
20. Ipatov, V. A., and L. P. Pakhornov, *Pribory i Tekhn. Eksperim.*, **2**, 91 (1958); *Chem. Abstr.*, **53**, 7679c (1959).
21. Trog, D. J., *Anal. Chem.*, **27**, 1217 (1955).
22. McMurray, C. S., and J. W. Redmond, "Portable Mercury Vapor Detector," *U.S. At. Energy Comm. Rept. Y-1188* (1958).
23. Ballard, A. E., and C. W. D. Thornton, *Ind. Eng. Chem. Anal. Ed.*, **13**, 893 (1941); A. E. Ballard, D. W. Stewart, W. O. Kamm and C. W. Zuehlke, *Anal. Chem.*, **26**, 921 (1954).
24. Monkman, L. J., P. A. Maffett, and T. F. Doherty, *Am. Ind. Hyg. Assoc. Quarterly*, **17**, 418 (1956).
25. Lindström, O., *Anal. Chem.*, **31**, 461 (1959).
26. Freyschuss, S., O. Lindström, K. D. Lundgren, and A. Swensson, *Svensk Papperstid.*, **61**, 568 (1958); *Chem. Abstr.*, **53**, 18481c (1959).
27. Yamaguchi, S., *M. D. J. (Philippines)*, **8**, 558 (1959).
28. Jacobs, M. B., S. Yamaguchi, L. J. Goldwater, and H. Gilbert, *Am. Ind. Hyg. Assoc. J.*, **21**, 475 (1960); **22**, 276 (1961).
29. Mansell, R. E., and E. J. Hunemorder, *Anal. Chem.*, **35**, 1981 (1963).
30. Hemeon, W. C. L., and G. F. Haines, Jr., *Am. Ind. Hyg. Assoc. J.*, **22**, 75 (1961).

30a. American Iron and Steel Institute, 150 E. 42nd St., New York, N. Y.

30b. Gelman Instrument Company, Ann Arbor, Michigan.

31. Nordlander, B. W., *Ind. Eng. Chem.*, **19**, 518 (1927).

32. Biggs, L. R., *J. Ind. Hyg. Toxicol.*, **20**, 161 (1938).

33. Burke, W. J., S. Moskowitz, and B. H. Dolin, *N.Y. State Ind. Bull.*, **18**, 235 (1939).

34. Wichmann, H. J., *Ind. Eng. Chem. Anal. Ed.*, **11**, 66 (1939).

35. Jacobs, M. B., and A. Singerman, *J. Lab. Clin. Med.*, **59**, No. 5, 871 (1962).

36. Winkler, W. O., *J. Assoc. Official Agr. Chemists*, **18**, 638 (1935).

37. Goldman, F. H., *U.S. Public Health Service Reprint 1804* (1937).

38. Minot, A. S., *J. Ind. Hyg.*, **4**, 253 (1922–23).

39. Pyankoff, V. A., *J. Appl. Chem. USSR*, **9**, 580 (1936); *Chem. Abstr.*, **30**, 7488 (1936).

40. Moldavsky, L. R., *Zh. Prikl. Khim.*, **3**, 955 (1930); *Chem. Abstr.*, **25**, 1179 (1931).

41. Zhitkova, A. S., S. I. Kaplun, and J. B. Ficklen, *Poisonou Gases*, Service to Industry, Hartford, 1936.

42. Goodman, C., J. W. Irvine, and C. F. Horan, *J. Ind. Hyg. Toxicol.*, **25**, 275 (1943).

43. Delépine, S., *J. Ind. Hyg.*, **4**, 346 (1922–23).

44. Cannon, A. B., *N.Y. State J. Med.*, **36**, 219 (1936).

45. Federal Security Agency, Social Security Board, Washington, D. C., Aug. 10, 1940.

46. American Standards Association, Z37.9-1943.

47. Threshold limit value adopted at meeting of American Conference of Governmental Industrial Hygienists, April 1964.

48. Cook, W. A., *Ind. Med.*, **14**, 936 (1945).

49. Watrous, R. M., and M. B. McCaughey, *Ind. Med.*, **14**, 639 (1945).

50. Guelman, I., *J. Ind. Hyg.*, **7**, 6 (1925).

51. Jurecek, M., *Collection Czech. Chem. Commun.*, **6**, 468 (1934); *Chem. Abstr.*, **29**, 705 (1935).

52. Gieseking, J. E., S. H. Snider, and C. Getz, *Ind. Eng. Chem. Anal. Ed.*, **7**, 185 (1935).

53. Gerritz, H. W., *Ind. Eng. Chem. Anal. Ed.*, **7**, 167 (1935).

54. Jacobs, M. B., *Chemical Analysis of Foods and Food Products*, 3rd ed., Van Nostrand, New York, 1958.

55. Goldstone, N. I., *Ind. Eng. Chem. Anal. Ed.*, **18**, 797 (1946).

56. Clarke, J. O., *J. Assoc. Official Agr. Chemists*, **11**, 438 (1938).

57. Deniges, G., *Compt. Rend.*, **171**, 802 (1920).

58. Atkins, W. R. G., and E. G. Wilson, *Biochem. J.*, **20**, 1225 (1926).

59. Maechling, E. H., and F. B. Flinn, *J. Lab. Clin. Med.*, **15**, 779 (1930).

60. Deemer, R. B., and J. A. Schricker, *J. Assoc. Official Agr. Chemists*, **16**, 226 (1933).

61. Zinzadze, C., *Ind. Eng. Chem. Anal. Ed.*, **7**, 227, 230 (1935).

62. Snell, F. D., and C. T. Snell, *Colorimetric Methods of Analysis*, Van Nostrand, New York, 1936.

63. Chaney, A. L., and H. J. Magnuson, *Ind. Eng. Chem. Anal. Ed.*, **12,** 691 (1940).
64. Jacobs, M. B., and J. Nagler, *Ind. Eng. Chem. Anal. Ed.*, **14,** 442 (1942).
65. Ruchoft, C. C., O. R. Placak, and S. Schott, *U.S. Public Health Service Reprint 2527* (1943).
66. Boltz, D. F., and M. G. Mellon, *Ind. Eng. Chem. Anal. Ed.*, **19,** 873 (1947).
67. Kingsley, G. R., and R. R. Schaffert, *Anal. Chem.*, **23,** 914 (1951).
68. Jacobs, M. B., *Chemical Analysis of Poisons, Hazards, and Solvents*, 2nd ed., Interscience, New York, 1949.
69. Vasak, V., and V. Sedivec, *Chem. Listy*, **46,** 341 (1952); *Chem. Abstr.*, **47,** 67a (1953).
70. Quispe P., Luis, *Salud Ocupational (Peru)*, **6,** No. 1, 3 (1961).
71. Teichman, T., L. Dubois, and J. L. Monkman, "The Determination of Arsenic in Biologic Materials," 3rd Intern. Meeting Forensic Toxicol., London, 1963.
72. Jacobs, M. B., "Microdetermination of Arsenic," Am. Ind. Hyg. Assoc. Meeting, Philadelphia, 1964.
73. Brau, M. J., personal communication.
74. *Methods Assoc. Offic. Agr. Chemists*, 11th ed., 1965.
75. Cassil, C. C., and H. J. Wichmann, *J. Assoc. Offic. Agr. Chemists*, **22,** 436 (1939).
76. Goldstone, N. I., and M. B. Jacobs, *Ind. Eng. Chem. Anal. Ed.*, **16,** 206 (1944).
77. Harger, R. N., personal communication, 1949.
78. *Dept. Sci. Ind. Research Brit. Leaflet 9* (1940); *Analyst*, **65,** 354 (1940).
79. Sayers, R. R., *International Critical Tables*, Vol. II, McGraw-Hill, New York 1927.

CHAPTER X

OTHER HARMFUL METALS

Increase in occupational diseases in more recent years has been associated to a large extent with changes in the methods of industry. The application of chemistry to industrial processes has been the means of introducing certain new hazards to health, since in many instances the chemicals involved in the new processes are of such a nature as to constitute a source of injury unless precautionary measures are exercised (1). Two well-known examples are the electrodeposition of chromium and the use of benzene as a solvent.

The metals discussed in the previous chapter are not only serious hazards but also extensive hazards in that they are industrial poisons in many different trades. The metals discussed in this chapter are not used as extensively in trade as are those of the previous chapter. Some of them are true poisons, such as antimony, chromium, cadmium, manganese, and selenium. Others have a deleterious effect because of their state of subdivision when inhaled, for instance, zinc and magnesium oxides. The metals zinc, magnesium, and nickel have not been shown to be poisonous as such. Nevertheless, they may form poisonous compounds, for example, zinc chloride, which is caustic, and nickel carbonyl, which is extremely poisonous.

The utilization of such metals as beryllium and cobalt and their compounds for newer purposes, such as the use of beryllium for the preparation of alloys and cobalt carbonyl as a catalyst in the manufacture of motor fuels, are accompanied by hazards not heretofore encountered.

A. Beryllium

The relatively great increase in the use of beryllium and beryllium salts during World War II, particularly for the preparation of fluorescent powders and fluorescent lamps, focused attention on illness attributable to the metal and such compounds. Since then, beryllium,

388

because of its physical and chemical properties—low density, rigidity, good thermal conductivity, high melting point, capability of being used as a neutron moderator, and resistance to corrosion and oxidation—has been used increasingly in industry and in the nuclear energy field. Most of the beryllium is used to manufacture alloys, principally copper alloys as a hardening agent and for nonsparking tools. There are a number of other metals with which it is alloyed, such as zinc and nickel, for the special properties it contributes.

The principal source of illness and poisoning from beryllium is exposure during milling and manufacturing. The fumes and dusts of beryllium metal, beryllium oxide, beryllium hydroxide, beryllium fluoride, and beryllium sulfate have been implicated in causing illness. Indeed, poisoning from beryllium is of a most insidious character and it is recognized not only as an industrial hazard but also as an air pollution problem. The toxicity of, poisoning by, and illness attributable to beryllium and its compounds were reviewed at a symposium (2). Beryllium disease is characterized by weight loss, dyspnea, cough, chest pains, fatigue, and general weakness. In the period of 1952–1958, some 606 cases of beryllium disease were compiled in a beryllium registry (3).

As pointed out by Hiser, Donaldson, and Schwenzfeier (4), beryllium disease was recognized as an occupational disease about 1946 and since the Atomic Energy Commission and its contractors were those principally handling beryllium, an Advisory Committee of the Atomic Energy Commission set up recommended limits for the control of air-borne beryllium in 1949. The recommendations were (1) for in-plant exposures no worker should be exposed for any one day to an average concentration exceeding 2 μg of beryllium per m^3 of air and (2) no instantaneous exposure should be greater than 25 μg of beryllium per m^3 of air. In 1956, recognizing the difficulties in keeping such criteria, The Atomic Energy Commission Advisory Committee recommended that the rule be interpreted so that the average daily exposure over a 3-month period did not exceed 2 μg/m^3 instead of limiting this value to a daily basis. This is in effect a daily weighted average over a 3-month period. In addition, instantaneous exposures in the range of 25–100 μg/m^3 were permitted if workers were protected by respirators. The recommended outside air concentration of beryllium in the vicinity of a beryllium plant should not exceed 0.01 μg/m^3.

1. DETERMINATION

The analysis of beryllium has been reviewed by Cholak (5). The major methods for the detection and determination of beryllium fall into three principal categories: spectrographic, fluorimetric, and colorimetric. Some analysts believe the method of choice to be the spectrographic method but, of course, this entails the use of expensive equipment. Others prefer the colorimetric and fluorimetric methods.

a. Spectrographic Determination

Cholak and Hubbard (6) and Fitzgerald (7) have detailed spectrographic methods using a direct current arc and the 2348.6 Å line. Smith and Fredrick (8) used a rotating electrode and an alternating current spark. A spectrographic monitor for beryllium oxide is commercially available. The instrument is automatic and can give results every 75 sec (9). The air to be sampled is drawn through a filter tape at a fixed sampling rate for a given period of time, in this instance 60 sec. The tape is advanced by a synchronous motor to the analytical portion of the apparatus in which it is burned and an electrical spark excitation is applied. The light emitted is directed into a spectrograph where a 1P28 photomultiplier tube converts the energy of the 3131.1 Å line to an electrical signal. This signal is then integrated for a 30-sec period of excitation by an integrating electrometer-amplifier. The instrument is also equipped with a visual and audible alarm so that if the concentration exceeds the 2 $\mu g/m^3$ mentioned in a previous paragraph, the alarm is sounded. The alarm must be reset manually.

A less expensive instrument is also available. Filter samples are obtained in the field, transported to the laboratory, and fed into the instrument for analysis.

b. Colorimetric Determination

Colorimetric methods have the advantage of economy, simplicity, and wide range. They are sufficiently sensitive and can be performed by taking samples at many locations in a plant.

Zenia Method

When an alkaline solution of 4-(p-nitrophenylazo)orcinol, known as Zenia, is added to an alkaline solution of a beryllium compound, a red-brown lake is formed (4). The absorption of light by these colored solutions does not follow the Beer-Lambert law strictly. However, calibration curves can be made which are adequate for quantitative determinations by empirical adjustment of the alkalinity, presence of foreign ions, temperature, and reagent dye strength. The pH adjustment is critical and is controlled by use of a buffer. The interference of iron and some heavy metals can be controlled by use of a chelating agent. Copper and zinc can be complexed by use of cyanide. Some magnesium can be complexed by use of a chelating agent but it is best if it is absent. Chlorides, too, should be absent.

Sampling. Since best results with this method are obtained with samples containing from 5 to 45 μg of beryllium, it is necessary to use a high-volume sampler in order to get sufficient sample in the short space of time available during certain operational steps. Whatman No. 41 paper with a diameter to fit the head of a high-volume sampler capable of drawing 0.5 m^3 of air per min is adequate. For sampling the general workroom air, any sampler capable of operating for a sufficient period of time to get the required amount of sample for the analysis is adequate.

Apparatus. Any spectrophotometer capable of measuring light absorption at 500 mμ or a Klett-Summerson color-m meter, using the green filter No. 54, may be employed.

Reagents. *Zenia Solution.* Dissolve 0.25 g. of 4-(p-nitrophenyl-azo)orcinol in 1 liter of 0.1N sodium hydroxide solution and stir in the dark for at least 5 hr with the aid of a magnetic stirrer or an equivalent device. Filter with the aid of vacuum. Allow the solution to stand for 8 hr in the dark and refilter to obtain a more constant standard curve. Since the reagent is not uniform, it is necessary to make a new standard curve for each lot of reagent purchased. The chemical is available from Eastman Kodak Company.

Buffer Solution. Dissolve 31.5 g of citric acid, 18.5 g of boric acid, and 78 g of sodium hydroxide in water. Transfer to a 1-liter volumetric flask and make up to volume with water.

Chelating Reagent. Dilute 1 volume of Versene T, a mixture of the tetrasodium salt of ethylenediaminetetraacetic acid and triethanolamine (Dow Chemical Co.), containing 55% solids with 1 volume of water.

Standard Beryllium Solutions. Dissolve sufficient powdered beryllium of known assay in a small volume of sulfuric acid (1:1) to yield a solution containing 100 μg/ml. It is generally necessary to boil the mixture gently to get all of the beryllium into solution after the initial reaction between the beryllium and the acids subsides. Take aliquots equivalent to the standards required to plot a curve of spectrophotometer absorption readings or Klett-Summerson readings against micrograms of beryllium.

Procedure. Remove the filter paper sample from its cellophane wrapper and place it in a platinum dish. Wet the sample with sulfuric acid (1:1) with the aid of a dropping bottle. Evaporate the contents on a hot plate to sulfur trioxide fumes. Place the dish on a gas burner and increase the heat slowly until the sample is completely ashed. Cool the dish, wet the contents with nitric acid, place on a cooler portion of the hot plate to evaporate the acid, and repeat the ignition step. Cool the dish again, add 10 drops of hydrofluoric acid, and swirl the dish to dissolve the ash. Evaporate again to dryness at low heat. It is essential not to permit the temperature of the surface of the hot plate to exceed 90°C (200°F). Dissolve the residue in the dish with a few milliliters of cold water and add 1 drop of Versene T reagent. Test the mixture with litmus. If it is not alkaline, adjust the alkalinity with a few drops of 1N sodium hydroxide solution. If copper is present, as will be indicated by a blue color, or the presence of zinc is suspected, add potassium cyanide solution until the color disappears. Add 1.0 ml of buffer solution and transfer to a cuvette, making certain to allow sufficient volume for the addition of 1 ml of Zenia reagent. Add the Zenia reagent and make up to 10 ml with water. Mix, centrifuge for 10 min, place the cuvette in the colorimeter, and read against a reagent blank containing the same volume of Zenia reagent, buffer, and Versene T used to set the zero.

Read the concentration of beryllium from the standard graph prepared by use of the standard beryllium solution and the same concentration of reagents. A zero should be run with each group of samples; it is also preferable to run known controls to check the standard curve. Aliquots should be run on samples containing over 45 μg.

Quinizarin Method

The amount of beryllium in dust may be estimated by its reaction with an anthraquinone derivative, 1,4-dihydroxyanthraquinone-2-sulfonic acid (quinizarin-2-sulfonic acid), to give a red color, which is proportional to the amount of beryllium present when buffered at pH 7.0 with ammonium acetate.

Dilute weakly acid solution of beryllium dust to a convenient volume. Remove phosphates, if present, by use of zirconium nitrate solution and remove the excess of zirconium by use of selenious acid. Adjust the hydrogen ion concentration of the filtrate to pH 3.5. To a 1-ml aliquot of test solution add 5 ml of 5% ammonium acetate solution and 0.2 ml of a 0.5% aqueous solution of 1,4-dihydroxy-anthraquinone-2-sulfonic acid. Allow to stand 5 min and compare in a visual colorimeter against the closest match of a set of standards containing from 0 to 10 μg of beryllium treated the same way.

c. Fluorimetric Determination

A fluorimetric method based on the fluorescence of a tetrahydroxy-flavanol, morin, with beryllium in an alkaline test solution is a very sensitive test for beryllium. Few substances interfere if rigorously controlled analytical conditions are observed. This method is satisfactory for beryllium concentrations in the range of 0.05–3 μg.

Sampling. Collect air samples by filtration through Whatman No. 41 filter paper, $1\frac{1}{8}$ in. in diameter.

Apparatus. A Klett fluorimeter with No. 5850 lamp filter, No. 3385 photocell filter, and a cylindrical cuvette or equivalent instrument may be employed.

Reagents. *Digestion Mixture.* Add 200 ml of concentrated sulfuric acid and 200 ml of 70% perchloric acid, sp gr 1.6, to 600 ml of concentrated nitric acid and mix.

1N Sodium Hydroxide Solution (approx.). Transfer 40 g of sodium hydroxide pellets, analytical reagent grade, to a 1-liter volumetric flask and add 500 ml of water. Stir continuously but do not stopper and when the sodium hydroxide has dissolved, cool under running water, if necessary, and mix. Make up to volume with water.

0.1N Sodium Hydroxide Solution (approx.). Dilute 100 ml of the 1N sodium hydroxide solution to 1 liter with water.

0.1N Sulfuric Acid (approx.). Add 3.6 ml of concentrated sulfuric acid to approximately 500 ml of water in a 1-liter volumetric flask. Mix, cool, and dilute to volume with water.

Saturated Sodium Pyrophosphate Solution. Dissolve 25 g of sodium pyrophosphate, $Na_4P_2O_7$, analytical reagent grade, in 250 ml of water and mix.

Morin Stock Solution. Add about 2 g of 5,7,2′,4′-tetrahydroxy-flavanol or 3,5,7,2′,4′-pentahydroxyflavone, $C_{15}H_{10}O_7 \cdot 2H_2O$ (morin), to 25 ml of 95% ethyl alcohol. Stir with the aid of a magnetic stirrer for several hours and store in a refrigerator. This saturated stock solution is stable for about 3 months when kept in a refrigerator. The reagent can be purchased from L. Light and Co., Ltd., Colnbrook, Bucks, England.

Dilute Morin Solution. Transfer, with the aid of a pipet, 1 ml of the supernatant liquid of the morin stock solution to a 100-ml volumetric flask and dilute to volume with 95% ethyl alcohol. This working solution must be prepared fresh each day as required.

Beryllium Standard Solutions. Stock Solution. Dissolve 19.638 g of beryllium sulfate, $BeSO_4 \cdot 4H_2O$, analytical reagent grade, in $0.1N$ sulfuric acid. Transfer to a 1-liter volumetric flask and make up to volume with the same strength acid. This stock solution contains 1 mg of beryllium per ml.

Dilute Beryllium Standard Solution. Dilute 1 ml of the beryllium stock standard solution to 100 ml with $0.1N$ sulfuric acid. This standard solution is equivalent to 10 $\mu g/ml$.

Working Beryllium Standard Solution. Dilute 1 ml of the dilute beryllium standard solution containing 10 $\mu g/ml$ to 100 ml with $0.1N$ sulfuric acid to obtain a standard solution containing 0.1 $\mu g/ml$.

Procedure. Soak the Whatman No. 41 filter-paper sample for 1 hr in a small beaker with 10–15 ml of $0.1N$ sulfuric acid. Transfer the acid solution to a 50-ml volumetric flask. Repeat the soaking a second time with an additional 10–15 ml of the acid, allow to leach for 1 hr, and again transfer the acid to the 50–ml volumetric flask. Neutralize the acid solution with an equal volume of $0.1N$ sodium hydroxide solution and check with litmus paper.

Prepare a blank and a set of standards by adding 0, 0.5, 1.0, 1.5, and 2.0 ml of the working beryllium standard solution to 50–ml volumetric flasks to obtain standards containing 0.05, 0.1, 0.15, and 0.2 μg of beryllium. More concentrated standards may be set up if desired. Carry a blank and standards through the entire determination with the samples.

Add 2 ml of saturated sodium pyrophosphate solution to each sample, the blank, and standards to chelate any calcium that might be present for calcium gives some fluorescence with morin in an alkaline solution. Add 5 ml of $1N$ sodium hydroxide solution to each flask. If insoluble metallic hydroxides are formed or suspected, or if loose fibers from the filter paper are present, transfer the test solution to a centrifuge tube and centrifuge for 20 min at 2000 rpm. Decant the supernatant liquid into the original 50-ml volumetric flask and complete to volume with water. This makes the final dilution a 0.1N sodium hydroxide solution.

Add the morin solution according to an exact time schedule for the intensity of the fluorescence decreases with time. The total elapsed time between the addition of the morin reagent and the fluorimeter readings should equal 2 min.

Add 1 ml of morin reagent to the volumetric flask to be read. Mix the solution. Rinse the cuvette 5 times with the sample being read and fill to the 10-ml mark. Wipe the sides and bottom of the cell with lens paper, insert the cell into the cuvette holder, and open the shutter. These manipulations should take 1 min. Allow the cuvette to remain in the fluorimeter for 1 min to adjust its temperature to that of the instrument and read.

Turn on the transformer and main switch of the fluorimeter and allow the lamp to warm up for 30 min before readings are taken.

Follow the instructions of your fluorimeter. In the case of the Klett instrument, set the zero at the center of the scale with the regulator on the top of the galvanometer or by sliding the glass scale. Set the slit width at 6 units. Fill the cuvette with the blank test solution and place it in the cuvette holder. Open the shutter by pulling out the small knob on the left side of the instrument and allow the blank to warm for 1 min as mentioned above. Set the potentiometer at 50. Move the galvanometer sensitivity switch to position H and set the zero of the galvanometer as above. Close the shutter, return the sensitivity switch to midposition, and remove the cuvette. Read the samples as directed in the procedure, using the 2-min period, including inserting the cuvette and opening the shutter. Move the galvanometer sensitivity switch in position H and move the potentiometer dial to zero or the galvanometer. Record the potentiometer reading.

A standard curve must be prepared for each set of analyses. Plot the standard curve using potentiometer reading against concentrations of the standard solutions on linear graph paper. Read the concentrations of the unknowns from the standard curve. Calculate the concentration in micrograms per cubic meter of air.

Calculation.   The following equation may be used for the calculation:

$$\frac{\mu g \; Be}{m^3 \; air \; sampled} = \mu g \; Be/m^3$$

B. Chromium

It has generally been recognized that the spray of chromic acid produced during the process of plating is injurious to workers.   Practically all of the chromium-plating baths now used have chromic acid as their principal component, which may be present in concentrations from 200 to 500 g/liter (27–67 oz/gal).   In addition, there are present small amounts of some other anion such as sulfate, introduced either as the sulfate of a salt or as sulfuric acid.   Variable amounts of trivalent chromium and trivalent iron, which is derived from the iron tanks or anodes, are also likely to be present in used baths, either in true or in colloidal solution.   Lead anodes are generally employed, which produce at least small amounts of lead chromate and peroxide upon their surfaces and possibly in suspension in the baths.   Oxygen is evolved on the insoluble anodes and considerable hydrogen is liberated on the cathodes.   These gases tend to carry a fine mist or spray of the liquid present in the tank into the surrounding air.   The injurious component is deemed to be the chromic acid.

Injuries from chromates have been known for over 100 years. They occur, generally, in the form of ulcers known as "chrome holes."

The manufacture of chromate from chromite ores presents a serious industrial hazard.   The incidence of cancer in the air passages of the lungs of such workers was found to have increased to some 30 times that of other chemical workers (10).   Continuous daily exposure to concentrations of chromic acid greater than 1 mg/10 m³ is likely to cause definite injury to the nasal tissue of workers (11).   This concentration is the recommended maximum allowable concentration. Contact with abrasions in the skin is also dangerous.   Chromates also cause severe kidney damage and intestinal inflammation.   Chromium may also be a hazard in welding operations.

Dermatitis in cement finishers has been attributed to hypersensitivity to the water-soluble chromate compounds in the cement (12). The significance of the soluble chromium-compound content in

titrimetric reagent is the apparent difficulty of preparing such solutions. It may be prepared in the following simple manner.

Preparation of Standard Sodium Hypochlorite Solution. Transfer 8.0 ml of a commercial preparation of sodium hypochlorite solution containing 5% available chlorine to a glass-stoppered brown-glass bottle, and dilute with water to about 2 liters. If necessary, add sufficient sodium hydroxide (1 g) to raise the pH to about 12.5, the optimum pH for stability. To ascertain if the proper pH has been reached, the customary colorimetric methods for the determination of pH in the range 12–14 may be used. Obtain the titer of the solution by titration against a primary standard of sodium arsenite made as follows:

Weigh 0.2473 g of arsenious oxide (arsenic trioxide, As_2O_3, National Bureau of Standards) and dissolve in 25 ml of 10% sodium hydroxide solution. Transfer to a 1-liter volumetric flask, make slightly acid with sulfuric acid (1:6), and dilute with water to 1 liter. This solution is $0.005N$.

The solution of sodium hypochlorite made as directed above is generally somewhat stronger than $0.005N$. Its exact titer can be determined by titration against the standard arsenite solution. Its normality may be adjusted to exactly $0.005N$ by the usual procedure.

Titrimetric Procedure. Transfer a known aliquot of standard arsenite solution to a 125-ml erlenmeyer flask or a 150-ml beaker: a 4-ml aliquot if a microburet is to be used for the standard hypochlorite solution and a 5-ml aliquot if a semimicroburet is to be used. A standard solution of tartar emetic [potassium antimonyl tartrate, $2K(SbO)C_4H_4O_6H_2O$] containing 1 mg of antimony per 10 ml of solution may also be used. Add 5 ml of concentrated hydrochloric acid and adjust the volume of the solution to 35–40 ml by adding distilled water. Fill a micro- or semimicroburet with the standard hypochlorite solution. Add 1 drop of 0.05% methyl orange indicator solution to the test solution and titrate directly with the sodium hypochlorite solution. Add another drop of methyl orange indicator solution near the end point and continue the titration until the color of the methyl orange is destroyed. Make a blank titration using exactly the same volume of hydrochloric acid, water, and 2 drops of methyl orange indicator solution, replacing the volume of arsenite or antimony test solution by additional distilled water. The blank should run about 0.12–0.14 ml.

Antimony solutions prepared from samples treated as described in previous paragraphs, particularly on page 404, may be estimated titrimetrically as detailed above.

Several precautions, however, must be observed in using sodium hypochlorite solution as a titrimetric reagent. It must be preserved in brown glass-stoppered bottles. It may be kept at room temperature without deterioration over considerable periods of time. Keeping the solution at lower temperatures is perhaps preferable.

The optimum conditions for the titrations are a volume of at least 35–40 ml with an acid concentration equivalent to 5 ml of concentrated hydrochloric acid.

d. Rhodamine B Method

In this method all the antimony in the intermediate or unreactive state (see page 403) is either oxidized to the pentavalent state by use of perchloric acid at the end of the digestion, or is reduced to trivalent antimony by sulfur dioxide following the destruction of organic matter by the acid digestion and subsequently oxidized to the pentavalent state by ceric sulfate in the presence of hydrochloric acid. A lake is prepared using Rhodamine B; this lake is extracted by a suitable solvent, and the color is estimated colorimetrically or photometrically (30–33). If perchloric acid is used in the digestion (34), it is not necessary to use the sulfur dioxide reduction or the ceric sulfate oxidation.

Procedure. Add 2 drops of 60% perchloric acid to the water-white acid digest and heat until fumes of sulfur trioxide are evolved. If charring or yellowing occurs, it is necessary to add additional perchloric acid but not over a total of 0.5 ml when 10 ml of 18N sulfuric acid is used initially. Cool, add 3 ml of water, and heat until fumes are evolved. Cool again and place in a cold-water bath. Add 5 ml of 6N hydrochloric acid.

Benzene Extraction. Add 8 ml of 3N phosphoric acid, 70 ml of concentrated acid diluted to 1 liter, and 5 ml of 0.02% Rhodamine B solution (0.20 g of the dye dissolved in water and diluted to 1 liter). Shake the flask and cool again if necessary. The benzene extraction must now be performed without delay. Transfer to a separatory funnel. Rinse the digestion flask with 10 ml of benzene and transfer the benzene to the separatory funnel. Shake 150–200 times, draw off the lower aqueous layer, and transfer the benzene phase to a tube.

Allow to stand and settle.   The color is stable at this point.   Transfer 6–8 ml to a cuvette and read at 565 mμ or use a green filter.

Isopropyl Ether Extraction.   After the addition of the hydrochloric acid add 13 ml of water and transfer to a separatory funnel.   Add 15 ml of isopropyl ether to the digestion flask, rinse, and transfer to the separatory funnel.   Shake about 100 times.   Discard the aqueous layer.   Add 5 ml of 0.02% Rhodamine B solution.   Shake again 150 times and, after settling, discard the aqueous layer.   Transfer the ether layer to a tube.   Read immediately at 545 mμ or use a green filter.

Standard Solutions.   Weigh accurately 0.1000 g of chemically pure antimony and add 25 ml of concentrated sulfuric acid.   Heat until the metal dissolves.   Cool and dilute to 1 liter.   It is stable and contains 100 μg of antimony per ml.   It can be diluted to give working standards.

In preparing a standard curve, add known amounts of antimony up to 40 μg to 5 ml of sulfuric acid.   Make an acid digestion with nitric acid.   Treat with perchloric acid as detailed and then proceed with the remainder of the analysis.

2. Stibine

Stibine, antimony hydride (SbH_3), is a colorless, poisonous gas having an unpleasant odor.   It weighs about 5.3 g/liter.   In the liquid state, it boils at $-17°C$.   About 20 ml of the gas is soluble in 100 ml of cold water and much less is soluble in hot water.

Stibine is a powerful hemolytic agent (35) and its order of toxicity is similar to that of arsine (36).   Cats and dogs are readily affected, for a single exposure to concentrations of the order of 40–45 ppm for 1 hr is dangerous.   The recommended maximum allowable concentration is 0.1 ppm.

The toxicology of the volatile hydrides as a group has been discussed by Webster (35).

a. Detection and Determination

Stibine may be detected in a manner analogous to arsine by thermal decomposition.   Webster and Fairhall (37) used filter paper impregnated with silver nitrate for the detection and semiquantitative determination of stibine.

Dip strips of Whatman No. 1 filter paper, 1 × 7 cm, into a 1% solution of silver nitrate, allow to drain, and wave in the atmosphere for 1 minute. A brown coloration is produced, the intensity of which is proportional to the amount of gas present. Compare with standards made previously. Other hydrides such as hydrogen sulfide, arsine, hydrogen selenide, etc., and phosphorus will affect such papers. They are not stable to light.

To prepare standards, expose strips of bromide enlarging paper to light for varying lengths of time, develop, and tone in a copper bath. Match these strips with the stain produced by exposing silver nitrate papers to known concentrations of stibine, and make a color chart.

Rhodamine B Method

By use of a modification of the Rhodamine B method (37) stibine may be estimated. The gas is trapped in mercuric chloride solution, trivalent antimony is oxidized to pentavalent antimony by ceric sulfate in the presence of hydrochloric acid, excess ceric sulfate is removed by hydroxylamine hydrochloride, and the remainder of the method follows lines previously detailed.

Procedure. Trap the gas by passing it through a bubbler containing 20 ml of mercuric chloride solution, prepared by dissolving 60 g of mercuric chloride, $HgCl_2$, in $6N$ hydrochloric acid and diluting to 1 liter with the same acid. Transfer the trapping solution to a dry, 50-ml glass-stoppered graduated cylinder. Rinse the bubbler, both inside and out, and then the tube with 9 ml of $6N$ hydrochloric acid and add the washings to the cylinder. Allow to drain and complete the volume to 30 ml. Transfer 15.0 ml of the acid with a pipet and a safety pipetter to a 125-ml conical beaker. Add 0.5 ml of $0.1N$ ceric sulfate solution, prepared by dissolving 33 g of anhydrous ceric sulfate, $Ce(HSO_4)_4$, in 3% sulfuric acid and diluting to 1 liter. Set a timer for 1 min and mix. At the end of this time blow clean air into the beaker for 5–10 sec to remove free chlorine. Add 3 drops of 1% hydroxylamine hydrochloride solution, prepared by dissolving 1 g of hydroxylamine hydrochloride, $NH_2OH \cdot HCl$, in water and diluting to 100 ml, and mix. Add 5 ml of $6N$ hydrochloric acid, mix, and blow out the air of the beaker with clean air to remove the last traces of chlorine. Add immediately 1 ml of 0.2% Rhodamine B solution, filtering the reagent before use, mix, and transfer to a 60-ml separatory funnel. Add 25 ml of benzene, using 2 ml to rinse out the beaker, and shake for 1 min. Draw off the aqueous layer and a portion of the benzene layer. Transfer the remainder to centrifuge tubes. Centrifuge, stoppering the tubes to prevent evaporation and using pins to prevent the corks from being drawn into the tubes. Transfer to a cuvette and read the density of the color at 565 mμ.

D. Cadmium

It has been shown that cadmium is a poison entirely analogous to arsenic and mercury. It does not have a noxious effect merely because of the state of subdivision of the cadmium compounds inhaled. Cadmium melts at 320.9°C, a few degrees lower than lead. Its major use is in cadmium electroplating.

As a result of increased use of cadmium for industrial purposes the industrial hygienist has been presented with another problem. Among the industrial processes in which cadmium poisoning may occur are the smelting of cadmium ores, working up of residues, production of cadmium compounds, spraying of cadmium-bearing paints and pigments, welding alloys, flanging operations on cadmium-plated pipe, cadmium-plating processes—particularly of marine hardware and other fittings which were formerly zinc-coated—and melting the metal (38).

In industry, cadmium poisoning usually occurs from the accidental absorption of cadmium fumes or dusts through the respiratory system (39). It seldom occurs by ingestion.

The generally accepted maximum safe permissible working concentration of cadmium fume and dust is 0.1 mg/m³ as shown in Table 6, Appendix.

1. DETECTION AND DETERMINATION

a. Sulfide Method

A method for the detection and estimation of cadmium in air is based on the separation of cadmium from other metals as the sulfide, with its subsequent estimation by the amount of yellow color produced in a solution containing cadmium when viewed under a mercury-arc lamp. In concentrations of less than 0.1 mg of cadmium in 50 ml of solution, differences in the yellow color of cadmium sulfide are indistinguishable in ordinary light, while under the quartz mercury-vapor lamp the yellow color is perceptible in concentrations as low as 0.01 mg/50 ml of solution.

Cadmium dust may be trapped by means of an impinger in water, or the dust and fumes may be collected electrostatically or by filtration. Because cadmium and its salts are relatively volatile, cadmium-bearing materials are best ashed by the wet-ash method. If ignition is used, an ash aid must also be used.

Add sufficient nitric acid to the cellulosic materials or other organic material to cover them and heat gently. After the solid material has dissolved, add 10 ml of concentrated sulfuric acid and add, when necessary, small amounts of nitric acid until oxidation is complete. The method described for arsenic (Chapter IX, Section B-4) may also be used. Dilute to 75 ml and add the equivalent of 0.5 mg of copper and 2 g of sodium citrate. The copper is added to act as an entrainer or collector. Neutralize the acid solution for the first precipitation with ammonium hydroxide and adjust the concentration of hydrogen ion to pH 3 by means of the indicators thymol blue (thymolsulfonphthalein) and bromophenol blue (tetrabromophenolsulfonphthalein). Saturate with hydrogen sulfide solution for 5–10 min, add 1 drop of 5% aluminum chloride solution, and allow the solution to stand for 6–12 hr. Filter, dissolve the precipitate in nitric acid and hydrochloric acid, and carefully evaporate to dryness. Repeat the precipitation as sulfide twice more, omitting the addition of sodium citrate the last time and adjusting the pH to 2 by means of dilute potassium hydroxide. Carefully evaporate the final solution of chloride to dryness, dissolve it in water, and make up to a convenient exact volume in a volumetric flask. Transfer an aliquot portion of this prepared solution to a Nessler tube for the final reading. To each tube add 5 drops of 10% potassium cyanide, water and 5 ml of hydrogen sulfide water; make to volume. Mix thoroughly and compare under a flood of ultraviolet light with standards similarly prepared. The solution should exhibit a bright, clear yellow color under the mercury arc. Dark or turbid solutions may indicate incomplete removal of iron.

For larger quantities of cadmium, the following method may be used: Neutralize the wet-ash solution, make slightly acid—sufficient to hold all the zinc in solution—and pass in hydrogen sulfide. Yellow cadmium sulfide is precipitated. If copper is present, it may be separated as follows: Redissolve the sulfides in either sulfuric or hydrochloric acid. Add an excess of sulfurous acid to make certain that no oxidizing medium exists and then add N ammonium thiocyanate solution. Copper precipitates as the dimeric cuprous thiocyanate, $Cu_2(SCN)_2$. Filter; wash with cold water. Collect the filtrate and the washings. Precipitate the cadmium in the filtrate with hydrogen sulfide and estimate in a manner similar to lead by comparing with standard cadmium sulfide precipitates in Nessler tubes. This method has a large error, at times, since cadmium sulfide is often contaminated with a basic salt in the hydrogen sulfide precipitation.

In the presence of copper, 1-(2-quinolyl)-4-allylthiosemicarbazide (40) may be used as a precipitant for cadmium. One ml of a saturated 50% alcohol solution of this reagent with 10 ml of solution gives a precipitate with 1 ppm of cadmium in the presence of potassium iodide. Zinc, nickel, cobalt, sulfate, and ammonia interfere. The metals may be eliminated by the usual sulfide separation, the sulfates with barium and the ammonia by evaporation.

b. Dithizone Method

A number of variations of the dithizone method have been developed for the determination of cadmium. One of these variations has been detailed by Sandell (41) and another by Butts, Gahler, and Mellon (42) which is designed to eliminate copper and iron by use of cupferron and a number of other cations, including zinc, by extraction of a brucine–cadmium iodide complex with chloroform. Saltzman (43) developed a dithizone variation in which extractions are made from a strongly alkaline solution using a small amount of cyanide as a suppressing agent and tartaric acid as the stripping medium.

Apparatus. *Spectrophotometer.* A Beckman Model DU with a light path of 2.02 cm, wavelength 518 mμ, and matched tubes 22 $\times$ 175 mm or an equivalent instrument may be used. A shaking machine for separatory funnels capable of making 3 strokes per sec with a 1.5-in. amplitude will be found useful.

Glassware. Because of the strong alkali employed in this variation, it is necessary to regrease the stopcocks of the separatory funnels after each use. The funnels are cleaned by rinsing with hydrochloric acid (1:1) and the funnels are freed of the acid fumes by filling them completely with water; then they are washed as usual with tap and distilled water.

Reagents. *Sodium Hydroxide Solution.* Dissolve 400 g of reagent grade sodium hydroxide in distilled water and make to a volume of 1 liter. This solution should be stored in an adequate polyethylene bottle.

Sodium Hydroxide 40%–Potassium Cyanide 1% Solution. Prepare the solution as in the preceding paragraph, but dissolve 10 g of potassium cyanide in the sodium hydroxide solution before making to volume. Store in an adequate polyethylene bottle in the dark. Prepare a new solution after a period of 1 month.

Hydroxylamine Hydrochloride Solution. Dissolve 20 g of hydroxylamine hydrochloride and make up to 100 ml with distilled water.

Potassium Sodium Tartrate Solution. Dissolve 25 g of Rochelle salt, $KNaC_4H_4O_6 \cdot 4H_2O$, in water and make up to 100 ml.

Chloroform. Use reagent grade chloroform specified for use in dithizone determinations.

Dithizone Extraction Solution. Dissolve 80 mg of diphenylthiocarbazone in chloroform and make up to 1 liter with this solvent. Store in an amber bottle in a refrigerator. Allow to age for 1 day before use. Use the cold solution.

Standard Dithizone Solution. Dissolve 8 mg of diphenylthiocarbazone in chloroform and make up to 1 liter with this solvent. Store in an amber bottle in the refrigerator. Allow the solution to age for at least 1 day before use. It must be allowed to come to room temperature at the time of analysis.

Tartaric Acid Solution. Dissolve 20 g of tartaric acid in water and make to 1 liter. Store the solution in the refrigerator and use the cold solution.

Cobalt Wash Solution. This solution is used for the thallium separation when this step is required. Dissolve 0.10 g of crystallized cobalt sulfate, $CoSO_4 \cdot 7H_2O$, and 5 g of Rochelle salt in water. Dissolve 40 g of sodium bicarbonate, $NaHCO_3$, in water. Add the bicarbonate solution to the cobalt sulfate–Rochelle salt solution and make up to 1 liter with water. Discard after a few weeks.

Standard Cadmium Solutions. Stock Solution. Dissolve 0.010 g of pure cadmium metal in nitric acid (1:99) and complete to 1 liter with this acid. This solution contains 10 μg of cadmium per ml.

Working Solution. Transfer 10 ml of the standard stock cadmium solution with the aid of a volumetric pipet to a 100-ml volumetric flask and make to volume with nitric acid (1:99). This is a standard solution containing 1 μg/ml.

Preparation of Sample. Transfer filter and precipitator samples to 250-ml Phillips beakers and ash by dissolving the samples in small amounts of nitric acid, successively bringing down almost to dryness, adding another small volume of nitric acid, and continuing this treatment until no further change takes place. This can be done by using a low-heat hot plate and another hot plate at 400°C.

Procedure. It is preferable to take an aliquot containing not more than 10 μg of cadmium. This will avoid subsequent aliquoting. If more than 0.5 ml of nitric acid is present in the test specimen, dilute, add thymol blue indicator solution, and titrate to a yellow color with sodium hydroxide solution. Transfer to a separatory funnel, adjust the volume to 25 ml, and add the following reagents in the order given, mixing after each addition. Add 1 ml of Rochelle salt solution, 5 ml of 40% sodium hydroxide–1% potassium cyanide solution, and 1 ml of hydroxylamine hydrochloride solution. Add 15 ml of dithizone extraction solution, shake for 1 min, and drain the chloroform phase into a second funnel containing 25 ml of cold tartaric acid solution. Add 10 ml of chloroform to the first funnel, shake this for 1 min, and drain the chloroform layer into the second funnel also. Be careful to avoid permitting any of the aqueous layer to enter the second funnel. Vent all vapors and gases through the mouth of the funnel and not through the stopcock. Do not permit the chloroform to remain in contact with the strong alkali solution for longer than the 1 min of shaking and the time necessary to drain the phase. At this point, one can tell if too concentrated a test specimen has been taken for analysis because there will be no orange color of excess dithizone.

Shake the second funnel containing the chloroform layers and the tartaric acid solution for 2 min, allow to separate, and discard the chloroform layer. Add 5 ml of chloroform, shake again for 1 min, and discard the chloroform layer. This time draw off the chloroform layer as closely as possible and evaporate the floating drop of chloroform by use of a current of air. Add 0.25 ml of hydroxylamine hydrochloride solution and then with the aid of a pipet and a safety pipetter add 15 ml of standard dithizone solution. Add 5 ml of 40% sodium hydroxide–1% potassium cyanide solution and shake at once for 1 min. Put a pledget of absorbent cotton into the stem of the funnel and filter at once into a dry cuvette. Read the optical density at 518 mμ, using water as the reference. If any of the aqueous solution has passed into the cuvette, transfer to another dry cuvette and read. It is best to use covered or stoppered cuvettes and to keep them out of direct sunlight.

An estimate of the concentration can be made on the difference in intensity of the pink color produced at the first extract and the pink color of the chloroform-wash extract. Most of the cadmium is present in the first extract whereas the interfering metals give nearly the same color in both extracts. After shaking with the tartaric acid, the pink cadmium complex changes to green immediately. The colors of most of the interferences, except that of lead, do not change.

Standard Curve. Arrange a series of separatory funnels containing known amounts of cadmium up to 10 μg and add sufficient tartaric acid solution to yield a total volume of 25 ml. Follow the method as detailed after the tartaric acid stripping step, starting with the addition of 5 ml of chloroform.

Separation of Thallium. As mentioned, a special variation must be used for elimination of interference from thallium. This is rarely necessary, but occasions arise when this procedure must be employed.

Combine the chloroform phases from the first extraction of cadmium in a separatory funnel containing 25 ml of cobalt wash solution. Shake for 2 min. Drain into the funnel containing 25 ml of tartaric acid solution. Add 5 ml of standard dithizone solution to the funnel with the cobalt wash solution and shake for 2 min. Draw off the chloroform phase into the funnel with the tartaric acid. Continue with the analysis as detailed in the above procedure, beginning with the second paragraph.

Calculation. Obtain the amount of cadmium in the test specimen from the standard curve, calculate the amount in the original ash solution, and determine the air concentration from the volume of air sampled.

E. Manganese

Manganese poisoning due to manganese-bearing dusts and compounds is comparatively rare. However, serious and even fatal poisonings have occurred through its use in industry. Among its many and growing uses are the manufacture of manganese steels and alloys, its use in the prevention of blowholes in castings, in the neutralization or decolorization of iron color in glass, as an aid in the liberation of chlorine, in the lacquer, paint, varnish, and enamel industry as a dryer, and as manganese dioxide in the so-called "dry" cell or battery.   It is also a hazard where manganese ores are crushed. There is generally a manganese hazard in welding operations, since many welding rods contain manganese.

1. Physiological Response

Manganese causes systemic poisoning and attacks the neuromuscular system.   It is not in the metal-fume fever group.   The disease is characterized by muscular stiffness and incoordination, which progresses until disability results.   It is usually first apparent as disturbances in gait and difficulty in stepping backward without falling down, speech disturbances including stuttering and running together of words, muscular twitchings or tremors, and occasionally a masked facial expression.   There may be complaints of extreme drowsiness, weakness, or lassitude, muscular twitchings and cramps, and difficulty in walking and talking.   Later, many other parts of the body may be affected and a crippling disability results.   Longevity is not affected.

In a study of chronic manganese poisoning in an ore-crushing mill (44), it was found that none of 9 men exposed to less than 30 mg of manganese per cubic meter had the disease, although only 2 of these 9 had been employed for more than 3 years; on the other hand, 5 of 6 men exposed for more than 3 years to atmospheric concentrations of manganese exceeding 90 mg/m³ were found to have the disease. Tests made by these investigators in a modern mill showed that workers' exposure could be reduced to at most 6 mg/m³ by the use of enclosed machinery, mechanical conveyors, and exhaust ventilation.

The maximum permissible concentration of manganese dust and fumes in the working atmosphere recommended by the American Standards Association (45) is 60 mg/10 m³ of air.

2. Determination

The dusts and fumes of materials containing manganese may be collected by the methods previously described for the collection of other dusts and fumes, the impinger and precipitator being more commonly used.

a. Willard-Greathouse Periodate Method

The periodate method (46–48) is suitable for estimating quantities of manganese of less than 1 mg. After removal of chlorides, manganous salts are oxidized to permanganate by means of periodate and the color produced is compared with that of standards. The periodate method is preferred to the persulfate method described in the next section.

Preparation of Standard. *Standard Manganous Sulfate Solution.* Dissolve 0.1438 g of potassium permanganate in water containing 2–3 ml of 2N sulfuric acid. Reduce by the addition of 0.4 g of sodium bisulfite. Boil off the excess sulfur dioxide, cool, transfer to a 1-liter volumetric flask, and make to volume. One ml is equivalent to 0.05 mg of manganese.

Sulfuric Acid Reagent. Add 120 ml of concentrated sulfuric acid to 1500 ml of water. Dilute to 2 liters. Add 2.4 g of sodium periodate (sodium paraperiodate, $Na_2H_3IO_6$), heat to boiling, and place in a boiling-water bath for 30 min. This gives a 6% by volume solution of sulfuric acid.

Color Standard. Oxidize exactly 20 ml of the standard manganous sulfate solution to which are added 1.2 ml of concentrated sulfuric acid and 30 ml of 6% sulfuric acid, with 0.3 g of periodate in the usual way. Cool, transfer to a 1-liter volumetric flask, and make up to volume with the 6% sulfuric acid reagent. One ml of this solution is equivalent to 0.001 mg of manganese.

Procedure. If necessary, ash the sample or a portion of it in a silica dish. Take up in hydrochloric acid and evaporate to dryness. Evaporate liquid samples to dryness with concentrated hydrochloric acid. Add a few milliliters of sulfuric acid (1:2) and 3–4 drops of concentrated nitric acid. Evaporate carefully to dryness on a water bath and sand bath, finishing the evaporation by gentle ignition with a bunsen flame. Add 2–2.5 ml of sulfuric acid (1:2) and a little water, and evaporate to white fumes of sulfur trioxide, thus removing all traces of chlorides. Cool, dilute, and filter into a 50-ml flask for oxidation. Add to the solution 1 or 2 small pieces of pumice stone, previously purified by boiling with 5% sulfuric acid, and a little periodate. Evaporate down to about 10 ml, so that the concentration of sulfuric acid will be equivalent to a 5–6% solution.

Add 0.3 g of sodium periodate or potassium periodate and insert a loosely fitting pear-shaped glass stopper or similar arrangement in the neck of the flask.   Heat to boiling, immerse in a boiling water bath, and heat for 30 min.   Cool and transfer to colorimeter tubes.   Depending on the depth of color, use 10-, 22.5-, 50-, or 100-ml tubes, and dilute to the mark accordingly.   If diluted with water before matching, the solution should be boiled in the water bath for 15 min longer.

Photometric Variation

Manganese can be oxidized to permanganate by periodate and can be determined photometrically by measuring the absorbance at 526 mμ against water as the reference.   The minimum amount detectable with a 1-cm cell is of the order of 30 μg.   With a 5-cm cell, 5 μg can be detected.   Thus, the use of large-volume colorimeter tubes such as the Nessler tubes detailed in the preceding variation may be preferable to the use of a spectrophotometer

Procedure.   Transfer an aliquot of the sample containing not more than 50 μg of manganese to a 20-ml beaker.   Evaporate to dryness on a hot plate kept at low heat.   Cool, add 3 ml of phosphoric acid, and dissolve the residue by warming.   Cool, add with a pipet 3 ml of water, warm once more, and transfer the test solution to a glass-stoppered test tube with a 10-ml volume graduation.   Wash the beaker with two 1.5-ml portions of water and add these to the calibrated test tube.   Add 0.5 g of potassium periodate and add sufficient water to bring the level of the solution just above the 10-ml mark. Place the test tube into a boiling water bath, adjust the stopper so that it will fit loosely, and heat the test mixture for 30 min.   Cool, complete to volume with water, stopper, and mix.   Read in a spectrophotometer at 526 mμ against water as a reference.   Carry out a blank with all the reagents.

Standard Curve.   Transfer known amounts of manganese, using the standard manganous sulfate solution to make the proper dilutions, in the range of 0–50 μg with pipets to 10-ml glass-stoppered test tubes. Add 3 ml of phosphoric acid to each tube and continue with the method from the point of addition of the periodate.   Read the absorbances and construct a curve.

b. Persulfate Method

In this method the manganous sulfate is oxidized to permanganate by means of ammonium persulfate (ammonium peroxydisulfate) (48–50).

Samples containing much chloride and organic matter are best freed of chloride and the organic matter in the manner described under the periodate method. Samples containing little chloride or organic matter may be treated as follows: Take an aliquot containing not more than 0.2 mg of manganese. Add 2 ml of nitric acid and adjust to a 50-ml volume. Precipitate any chloride by the addition of silver nitrate solution, containing 20 g of silver nitrate, $AgNO_3$, in 1 liter of water, and add at least 1 ml in excess. Add about 0.5 g of ammonium persulfate crystals and warm the solution until the maximum permanganate color is developed. This usually takes about 10 min. At the same time prepare standards by diluting portions of 0.2, 0.4, 0.6 ml, etc., of the standard manganous sulfate solution to about 50 ml, and treat them exactly as the sample was treated. Transfer the sample and the standards to 50-ml Nessler tubes and compare the colors immediately.

To prepare the standard manganous sulfate solution for this method, dissolve 0.2873 g of potassium permanganate in about 100 ml of distilled water. Acidify the solution with sulfuric acid and heat to boiling. Add slowly a sufficient quantity of dilute solution of oxalic acid to discharge the color. Cool and dilute to 1 liter. One ml of this solution contains 0.1 mg of manganese.

F. Selenium

One of the major uses of selenium compounds is in the glass industry, where they are used to color glass a deep red and to neutralize iron color. The use of selenium in industry is growing. Among these uses may be mentioned rectifiers, red and yellow glazes, paint and ink pigments, production and coloring of plastics, alloying of machinable stainless steels, alloying of free-machining copper-base alloys, rubber accelerators and antioxidants, fireproofing of electric cable, photoelectric cells and apparatus, and in chemicals (51). Danger of exposure to selenium is not limited to those industries where it or its compounds are used as a raw material, for selenium is also a hazard where it occurs as an impurity or contaminant, as in the manufacture of chamber sulfuric acid from seleniferous iron pyrites or in the electrolytic refining of copper where it is found in the anode sludge. Some of the industries in which selenium may be a hazard are listed in Table X-1.

TABLE X-1
Industries and Their Possible Selenium Hazards (51)

Industry	Source of hazard	Type of hazard
Primary industries:		
Copper	Ore concentrate and flue dusts, sludges	Se, SeO_2, and mixed dusts
Lead and zinc	Ore concentrate and flue dusts, sludges	Se, SeO_2, and mixed dusts
Pyrites roasting	Roasting towers, sludges	Mixed dusts, Se
Lime and cement (certain areas)	Dust, kiln gases	Mixed dusts, SeO_2
Secondary industries:		
Glass, ceramics	Melting pots and furnaces	Fumes of Se, SeO_2
Rubber	Vulcanizing and curing processes	Organic vapors, H_2Se
Steel and brass	Alloy furnaces	Dusts, Se, SeO_2. Fumes
Paint and ink pigments	Pigment compounding and mixing	H_2Se, SeO_2, soluble dusts
Plastics	Mixers, presses	Organic vapors
Photoelectric	Melting and casting operations	Vapors, Se, SeO_2
Chemicals	Mixing, melts, synthesis	Se, SeO_2, H_2Se, organic vapors

1. Physiological Response and Toxicity

Selenium is closely allied to sulfur and tellurium in its chemical properties. It follows arsenic in the periodic system of the elements and also resembles that element in some of its chemical and physical properties. One marked characteristic that they have in common is that they are both semimetallic. In its physiological action on the human system, it also resembles arsenic. It forms a poisonous compound with hydrogen—hydrogen selenide, which is a colorless, inflammable gas with an intensely offensive odor similar to that of rotten horse-radish. The subject of selenium-bearing soils has been given a great deal of study by the U.S. Bureau of Chemistry and Soils (52). It has been shown that 4 ppm is an outside tolerance limit in foodstuffs, and that 3 ppm is a safer tolerance (53). There can be little question that seleniferous materials are poisonous.

The acute effects of ingestion of soluble selenium compounds may be summarized as consisting of progressive anemia, loss of weight, abdominal pains, and early cellular destruction in the liver, with later pathological changes throughout the organism. The ingestion of small quantities of selenium compounds over a long period results in retrograde changes in the liver and kidneys, accompanied by general debility. The acute and subacute effects resulting from single exposures of guinea pigs to hydrogen selenide are primarily an early severe fatty metamorphosis of the liver and late hypertrophy of the spleen.

The symptoms of men poisoned by selenium while employed at copper refineries extracting or purifying selenium are given by Hamilton (54) and Dudley (55) as pallor, gastrointestinal disturbances, garlicky odor of breath and perspiration, irritation of nose and throat (rose cold), coating of tongue, metallic taste in mouth, and nervousness. The excretion of selenium in the urine is conclusive evidence that workers are absorbing selenium.

The recommended threshold limit concentration for selenium compounds, calculated as selenium, is 0.1 mg/m³ of air.

Selenium oxychloride, $SeOCl_2$, is toxic and extremely vesicant. As little as 0.01 ml applied to the skin of rabbits will cause death within 24 hr (51). The toxic action of this compound is in part attributable to the selenium absorbed, as evidenced by the presence of the element in the blood and liver of animals treated in this way.

Selenium oxychloride produces third-degree burns when applied to the skin of man. The burn is painful and slow to heal. If selenium oxychloride, which is a strong chlorinating and oxidizing agent, is used, it is best to have large quantities of water available for immediate use, for rapid flushing with water will hydrolyze it and thus prevent burns.

2. Sampling

Vapors and gaseous components of plant atmospheres and contaminations in laboratory workrooms may be sampled quantitatively (51,57) by means of the apparatus outlined in Figure X-1. The sampling arrangement for absorbing gases or vapors consists first of a sintered-glass plate, overlaid by a fine, dried asbestos mat A, which is designed to screen out all solid particles or droplets that might enter the bubblers. After passing this screen the air-gas mixture is bubbled successively through two bubblers B, each containing a mixture of 50 ml of 40–48% hydrobromic acid, with free bromine 10% by weight. The oxidizing power of this solution is utilized to oxidize the selenium, so that it can be dissolved by the acid medium. After passing through the bubblers, the air stream moves into an absorption tube D containing some suitable material, such as coarse granular soda lime or activated charcoal or calcium hydroxide, to remove hydrogen bromide and bromine vapors. The aspirator bottle E contains water. As this water issues from the outlet at the bottom of the bottle, air is drawn into the bottle through the bubbler train. Since the volume of water displaced by the air can be read, it is possible to ascertain the amount of selenium contained in this volume of air by an analysis of the bubbler solutions. A sample of 10 liters will prove sufficient in gas–air mixtures with selenium concentrations of more than 0.01 mg of selenium per liter. For smaller concentrations, 20 liters or more of

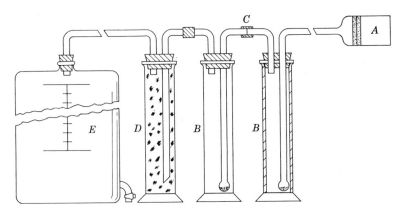

Fig. X-1. Selenium sampling apparatus (51).

the atmosphere must be sampled. Two bubblers have been found sufficient to trap all the selenium in atmospheres with concentrations ranging from 0.005 to 0.30 mg of selenium per liter. The maximum rate of sampling used with uniform success was 2 lpm.

The aspirator bottle should be of sufficient capacity so that water to the height of 5–8 in. remains in the bottle after 10 or 20 liters have been withdrawn. This layer of water is necessary to overcome the resistance of the bubbler train caused by the hydrostatic pressure of the hydrobromic acid in the bubblers. By controlling the rate of outflow of the water from the sampling bottle by means of the outlet stopcock, it is possible to obtain a relatively constant sampling rate. With decrease in the height of the water in the sampling bottle, the rate of sampling tends to decrease.   Suitable manipulation will overcome this difficulty.

For trapping selenium-bearing dusts, the filter methods described in Chapter V may be used.   The filter shown in Figure X-1 is also suitable for certain dusts.   This filter consists of a tube in which is sealed a sintered-glass plate, approximately 1.5 in. in diameter. This porous plate is overlaid by a smooth, fine, dried asbestos mat. The mat may be easily washed off and reformed from prepared Gooch asbestos suspensions.   By drying the mat at 105°C for 1 hr, very little resistance will be built up in the suction lines.   Such a mat will screen out the more commonly encountered dust as well as fog particles.

The filter, prepared as above, may be acid-washed, dried, and weighed.   The dusty air may be drawn through the filter, which is again dried and weighed.   The weight of dust particles per unit volume of air may be calculated if the volume of air sampled is known.

Fumes of selenium compounds also selenium-bearing dusts may be sampled with the aid of an electrostatic precipitator.

3. DETERMINATION

a. Precipitation Methods

Combine the contents of the bubblers and precipitate the selenium (51,57) directly with sulfur dioxide or solid sodium sulfite.   After the bromine is completely discharged, add 1 or 2 g of solid hydroxylamine hydrochloride.   Heat the mixture on a steam bath for 30 min and allow to settle overnight.   Filter the resulting precipitate on asbestos, redissolve with 40% hydrobromic acid containing 0.5% free bromine, and reprecipitate as above, using filtered, saturated aqueous solutions of the reagents.   If sufficient selenium is present, the second precipitate may be weighed on a tared Gooch crucible, after drying 1 hr at 105°C.

If the total amount of selenium in the combined hydrobromic acid bubbler solutions is less than 1 mg, partially remove the free bromine with solid sodium sulfite.   Sufficient bromine should remain to impart a deep yellow color to the solution.   Then proceed with the distillation method as described on page 425, estimating the selenium colorimetrically (59,60).

If the total amount of selenium in the bubbler solutions ranges between 1 and 5 mg, it may be made up to standard volume of 100 ml on dissolving the first precipitate with hydrobromic acid and bromine. A suitable aliquot may be taken and made up to 25 ml, the colorimetric estimation being carried out with this fraction. In practice the colorimetric estimation has been found to be most accurate when the amount of selenium is between 0.05 and 0.50 mg of selenium per 25 ml of the sample solution. The concentration of hydrogen bromide must be kept between 25 and 30%, since at this acid concentration the precipitate appears with readiness and in a form most easily matched in color. Hydrobromic acid of 25–30% concentration has been found to be most advantageous for the precipitation of selenium from hydrobromic acid solutions. As a rough approximation, when precipitating selenium from 48% hydrobromic acid solutions, add aqueous solutions of reagents or water to increase the volume one-third to obtain the 25–30% mixture.

In practice, the above method for the absorption of gaseous selenium products has been found applicable to a variety of gases, namely, hydrogen selenide, selenium dioxide, ethyl selenide, and methyl selenide, as well as various mixtures of unknown volatile selenium compounds produced on putrefaction of organic materials (51).

Distillation Method (61)

The following method is based on the fact that selenium may be separated from all other elements except arsenic and germanium by distillation with concentrated hydrobromic acid. The selenium must be in, or converted into, the hexavalent condition before distillation in order to insure its distillation with the acid will be complete. In most cases the conversion may be accomplished by the use of bromine. The excess bromine distils at a low temperature and the hydrobromic acid then reduces the selenium to the tetravalent condition. In this form it readily distils along with the hydrobromic acid. The selenium is subsequently estimated in the distillate by reduction with hydroxylamine hydrochloride and sulfur dioxide.

Transfer the hydrobromic acid–bromine mixture from the bubblers to the distillation apparatus (Fig. X-2). Triturate the seleniferous dust with 100 ml of concentrated hydrobromic acid and transfer to the distillation apparatus. The apparatus consists of a Pyrex 500-ml round-bottom flask fitted with a ground-glass stopper into which has been sealed a thistle tube with a stem long enough to reach within 5

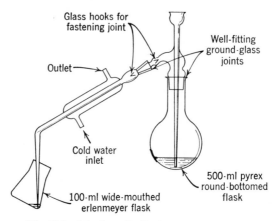

Fig. X-2. Selenium distillation apparatus (61).

mm of the bottom of the flask. The ground-glass stopper also has a side arm with a ground-glass end fitted to a condenser whose end is drawn out into a long adapter, bent and with a capillary tip so that it may fit easily into a 100-ml wide-mouth flask, which acts as the receiver.

. Connect the distillation apparatus described with the adapter just below the surface of 2–3 ml of bromine water in the receiver flask and apply heat gradually. One or 2 g of bromine should distill over in the first few milliliters of distillate. If insufficient bromine has been added to produce this quantity of bromine, more must be added through the thistle tube. A somewhat greater excess of bromine does no harm, but too great an excess is to be avoided because of the formation of too much sulfuric acid later. Collect 30–50 ml of the distillate by increasing the heat. Make a second or even third distillation, with intervening additions of hydrobromic acid and bromine through the thistle tube, unless it is certain from experience that all the selenium is in the first distillate. Remove the distillate and pass in sulfur dioxide until the yellow color due to bromine is discharged. Add 0.25–0.5 g of hydroxylamine hydrochloride, stopper the flask loosely, put it on the steam bath for 1 hr, and allow to stand overnight at room temperature. If selenium is present, it will appear as a characteristic pink or red precipitate. If much selenium is present, it will shortly turn black.

Collect the precipitated selenium on an asbestos mat in a Gooch crucible, and wash slightly with hydrobromic acid containing a little hydroxylamine hydrochloride. Dissolve the selenium on the pad by passing through 10–15 ml of a solution of 1 ml of bromine in 10 ml of hydrobromic acid in small quantities and wash into a 25-ml measuring flask if the quantity is small and is to be estimated colorimetrically. If it is over 0.5 mg, filter into a small beaker, precipitate as before, gather on an asbestos mat as before, and wash with hydrobromic acid containing a little hydroxylamine hydrochloride and then with water. Prepare a tare in the same way. Dry at 90°C for 1 hr, place in a vacuum desiccator, and exhaust the air while the crucibles are still hot. Cool for 1/2 hr. Allow air to enter the desiccator, cool an additional 1/2 hr, and weigh against the tare. Check the weight by drying again.

Colorimetric Estimation

If the quantity is small and is to be estimated colorimetrically, add 1 ml of a solution containing 5% gum arabic and precipitate the selenium by sulfur dioxide and hydroxylamine hydrochloride. Prepare comparison solutions containing known quantities of selenium in exactly the same manner and allow them to stand overnight. Shake the standards and test solution and compare the depth of color in Nessler tubes. This comparison is best carried out in sunlight. It is difficult to match solutions containing more than 0.5 mg of selenium in 25 ml. The color comparison is most satisfactory when 0.01–0.1 mg is present.

As a variation of the above colorimetric method, the following procedure may be employed for the determination of selenium dioxide in air. Trap the air by passing it through an absorber containing 25 ml of water. Transfer the solution to a 50-ml volumetric flask. Add sufficient hydrochloric acid, sp gr 1.19, to make the acidity equal to 1:4, and complete to volume. Transfer a known aliquot, 20–25 ml, to a Nessler tube, add 1 ml of a 5% solution of gum arabic or gum ghatti solution and 1 ml of 10% stannous chloride solution, and estimate the amount of selenium dioxide by comparison with standard solutions treated similarly (62).

Titrimetric Method

Transfer the liquid from the absorber to a flask, add approximately 0.1 g of sodium bicarbonate, 1 ml of starch solution, and $0.0025N$

iodine solution from a buret until a blue color is obtained.   Decolorize the solution with 1–2 drops of $0.0025N$ sodium thiosulfate solution. Add 6–10 ml of $0.0025N$ sodium thiosulfate solution, acidify the mixture with 10 ml of sulfuric acid (1:5), shake, and titrate immediately with $0.0025N$ iodine solution.   Determine the amount of selenium dioxide from the difference between the number of milliliters of iodine solution required for the thiosulfate and that required for the titration. One ml of $0.0025N$ iodine solution is equivalent to 0.0695 mg of selenium dioxide.

b. Diaminobenzidine Micro Method

An important improvement in the analysis of selenium by micromethods was the development of the diaminobenzidine method by Hoste and Gillis (63) and subsequently by Cheng (64).   Further improvements, particularly by Strenge (65), Taussky et al. (66), and Cummins and co-workers (67), were made to apply the method to biologic materials.

Rapid Variation

In a rapid variation (67), the organic material is destroyed by a special digestion mixture designed to avoid loss of selenium by volatilization, the selenium is reduced to the elemental state by ascorbic acid, is subsequently put into solution with hydrobromic acid–bromine reagent, and is determined colorimetrically as the 3,3′-diaminobenzidine monoselenium complex (68).

Reagents.   Add slowly and cautiously 150 ml of concentrated sulfuric acid to a solution of 10 g of sodium molybdate in 150 ml of water. Cool the mixture and add 200 ml of 70–72% perchloric acid.   Prepare the reagent in a hood and carry out all digestions in a hood designed for perchloric acid digestions.

Bromine–Hydrobromic Acid Solution.   Place 60 ml of 48% hydrobromic acid into a beaker in a hood.   Add 0.9 ml of bromine and mix. Dilute the mixture to 200 ml with water.

Diaminobenzidine Reagent.   Weigh out 0.5 g of 3,3′-diaminobenzidine tetrachloride, $(NH_2)_2C_6H_3 \cdot C_6H_3(NH_2)_2 \cdot 4HCl$, dissolve in water, and make up to 100 ml.   This reagent must be prepared just before use.

Standard Selenium Solutions.   Stock Standard.   Dissolve 0.352 g of dried reagent grade selenium dioxide, SeO_2, in water, add 20 ml of hydrobromic acid, and dilute to 250 ml.

Dilute Standard Solution. Transfer 1 ml of the stock standard solution with a pipet to a 1-liter volumetric flask and dilute to volume. This standard should be prepared just before use.

Procedure. Transfer an amount of dust sample or an aliquot of bubbler or impinger samples containing not more than 8 μg of selenium to a microkjeldahl flask and add 10 ml of digestion mixture. Heat the microkjeldahl flask with a low flame and swirl constantly. Use boiling chips, if necessary, to avoid bumping. If considerable organic matter is present, the reaction will be vigorous in about 5–10 min. If the solution is not clear after boiling and any carbonaceous material remains, add an additional 2–3 ml of digestion mixture. The digestion should be complete in 15–20 min.

Cool the contents of the microkjeldahl flask and wash down the sides of the flask. Add 5 ml of concentrated hydrochloric acid, 2 g of ascorbic acid, and mix. If selenium is present, a green color is produced. Allow the mixture to stand for 45 min to permit the selenium to precipitate completely.

Filter the precipitated selenium through a fine-porosity fritted-glass filter with the aid of suction. Wash down the sides of the filter to free it of traces of ascorbic acid. Transfer the fritted filter to another filter flask and add 1.0 ml of the bromine–hydrobromic acid solution to dissolve the elemental selenium. Make certain that the bromine–hydrobromic acid wets the entire fritted filter by tilting and revolving it before suction is applied. After an interval of 3 min, turn on the suction, and wash the solution into the filter flask with water.

Transfer the test solution to a beaker and adjust the volume, including the washings, to 20–25 ml. Add 3 drops of 5% aqueous phenol solution to destroy the bromine. Add 5 ml of $2.5M$ formic acid and 2 to 3 drops of metacresol purple indicator solution. Add $7M$ ammonium hydroxide solution carefully to pH 2.8, which is obtained when the indicator changes to a yellow color. Add 2 ml of 0.5% diaminobenzidine solution, mix, and place in a dark cabinet for 1 hr. At the end of this period, add sufficient $7M$ ammonium hydroxide solution to obtain a pH of 7.3, at which value the indicator just turns purple.

Transfer the test solution quantitatively to a 125-ml separatory funnel, rinsing the beaker with a few milliliters of water. Add, with a volumetric pipet, 2 ml of toluene, and extract the complex selenol by shaking vigorously for 1 min. Allow the phases to separate clearly, which generally requires 3 or 4 min, and draw off the aqueous phase. Pour the toluene phase through the mouth of the separatory funnel into a centrifuge tube and centrifuge for a few minutes to free it of water. Transfer the toluene solution to a 1-cm plunger cell of an Evelyn colorimeter with a microattachment or use an equivalent colorimeter and read the absorbance at 420 mμ. Since the microcolorimeter has a small aperture, it is necessary to adjust the readings for 50% transmittance instead of the customary 100% transmittance.

Run a blank, by adding 3 to 4 drops of bromine–hydrobromic acid to 20 ml of water and then continuing with the procedure as detailed.

Standard Curve. With the aid of pipets, transfer 0, 2, 4, 6, and 8 ml of the standard solution to beakers containing 20 ml of water. Add 3 to 4 drops of the bromine–hydrobromic acid to each standard and continue with the method as detailed in the procedure.

Zinc Dithiol Variation

If necessary, the sample is wet-ashed with nitric and sulfuric acids with a small amount of mercuric oxide and then is distilled with bromine–hydrobromic acid as detailed in a preceding section of this chapter. Zinc dithiol (68,69) is used to complex the selenium in the distillate and this complex is extracted into ethylene chloride. The solvent is evaporated off and the residue is wet-ashed again (to free it of any extraneous fluorescence). The selenious acid produced is reacted with 3,3'-diaminobenzidine to form the selenol which is estimated either colorimetrically or fluorimetrically.

4. HYDROGEN SELENIDE

A soda lime tube may be used with success in sampling atmospheres for hydrogen selenide content. The tube is of simple construction, being made from a 6 × ¾-in. Pyrex tube test by sealing a glass tube in the closed end. At sampling rates of 4 lpm or less, these tubes, when charged with fresh, dry soda lime, are satisfactory at all concentrations below 0.10 mg of selenium per liter of air. The selenium is recovered from the soda lime tube by distillation with hydrobromic acid as described. The selenium so distilled may be weighed or estimated colorimetrically.

G. Tellurium

Tellurium is related chemically to selenium and sulfur but it resembles arsenic in its physiological action. Its principal use in industry is in the coloring of glass, in rubber compounding, in stainless steel, and in chilled iron. However, it may be a hazard wherever tellurium-bearing ores are worked, as in the electrolytic refining of lead (70). Hydrogen telluride is a hemolytic agent. The most pronounced physiological effects of the inhalation of tellurium-bearing fumes and dusts are dry mouth, metallic taste, inhibition of sweat, languor, somnolence, loss of appetite, salivation, nausea, vomiting, garlic odor of the breath, and constipation.

The recommended maximum allowable workroom concentration for tellurium fumes (71) is less than $0.1–1$ mg/10 m^3. The accepted value is the latter.

1. DETECTION AND DETERMINATION

Tellurium compounds can be trapped in water or in hydrochloric acid. If water is used, add hydrochloric acid and then pass in sulfur dioxide gas. Tellurium is precipitated. Selenium will also precipitate, as previously described, but may be separated from tellurium by the distillation method given on page 425.

If sufficient tellurium is present, it may be estimated gravimetrically by precipitation with sulfur dioxide and hydrazine sulfate.

Prepare the test solution so that it is about $3N$ with respect to hydrochloric acid, $1:3$. Heat to boiling, then add 15 ml of a saturated solution of sulfur dioxide, 10 ml of a 15% solution of hydrazine hydrochloride or sulfate, and then 25 ml more of saturated sulfur dioxide solution. Boil till the precipitate settles, which takes about 5 min. Filter through a tared, prepared Gooch crucible. Wash quickly with hot water until free of chlorides then with alcohol, and dry in a thermostatically controlled oven at 105°C.

Tellurium in the form of tellurates or telluric acid may be estimated titrimetrically by boiling with hydrochloric acid. Chlorine is evolved as shown by the following formula:

$$K_2TeO_4 + 4HCl \rightarrow 2KCl + H_2TeO_3 + H_2O + Cl_2$$

The chlorine is trapped in an efficient bubbler containing potassium iodide solution. The liberated iodine is then titrated with $0.1N$ or other appropriate standard sodium thiosulfate solution. One ml of 0.1N thiosulfate solution is equivalent to 0.006375 g of tellurium.

Methods of analysis for tellurium are also discussed by Steinberg (71) and co-workers. A method for the rapid estimation of tellurium has been described by Nelson and Swingle (72).

H. Vanadium

Exposure to vanadium occurs principally in three fields: the working of its ores, the manufacture of vanadium steels, and as a mordant in dyeing. Fairhall (73) states that there is no question that vanadium conpounds are toxic, for even such materials as the crude ore dust cause striking toxic effects.

The principal early symptoms produced by vanadium poisoning are anemia, coughing, emaciation, irritation of the mucous membranes, and gastrointestinal disturbances (74). Later symptoms include nervous disorders and vertigo. Lung damage, pneumoconiosis, and systemic intoxication have been shown to result from vanadium poisoning.

In a study of vanadium poisoning in rats (75) it was found that there was no apparent cumulative effect but that there was an immediate nervous reaction.

1.   DETECTION AND DETERMINATION

Vanadium fumes and dusts may be trapped in nitric or sulfuric acids, since most vanadium minerals yield readily to acid treatment.

Vanadium, freed from molybdenum, titanium, cerium, and other interfering metals, may be detected by the use of hydrogen peroxide, with the production of a red brown color. Dilute the sulfuric acid solution so that it is about 1:4. Transfer to a volumetric flask. Add 1–2 ml of 30% hydrogen peroxide. Make to volume with sulfuric acid (1:4) and compare with standards similarly treated. The colorimetric peroxide method is used mainly for the detection and confirmation of the presence of vanadium.

Vanadium may be estimated by preliminary reduction to the tetravalent state with sulfur dioxide, expulsion of the sulfur dioxide with carbon dioxide, and subsequent titration with hot standard potassium permanganate solution.

If nitric acid was used to trap the sample, evaporate to dryness.

Take up again in sulfuric acid. Evaporate carefully at a low temperature to sulfur trioxide fumes. Do not fume for longer than 10 min. There is no loss of vanadium even when baked at 175°C or when heated at this temperature with sulfuric acid (76).

Dilute the solution so that there are about 2 parts of acid to 98 of water. Heat to boiling and add concentrated potassium permanganate solution till the mixture is pink. Reduce the vanadium by passing in sulfur dioxide gas, preferably from a cylinder of the gas, for 5–10 min. Pass in carbon dioxide gas free from oxygen and hydrogen sulfide to free the reaction mixture from sulfur dioxide. This may be tested by passing the effluent gas through very dilute potassium permanganate solution. Cool the mixture to 60–80°C and titrate with standard 0.1N potassium permanganate solution. One ml of 0.1N potassium permanganate solution is equivalent to 0.0051 g of vanadium.

For the separation of vanadium from other interfering metals, consult one of the texts on inorganic analysis listed in the general references at the end of the chapter.

I. Thallium

Industrial exposure to thallium occurs in the manufacture of thallium compounds used in rat and vermin poisons, luminous paint, window glass, and in some industries where it is a contaminant, as in the flue dust of sulfuric acid works. Thallium compounds have been used unwisely as depilatories. It resembles lead in its toxic properties and is a cumulative poison. The principal symptoms exhibited in thallium poisoning are loss of hair, cramps, pains in the limbs with paralysis, diarrhea, nephritis, cardiac degeneration, and death.

1. DETECTION AND DETERMINATION

Thallium may be detected spectroscopically by the green color it gives to the flame. It can be precipitated from sodium carbonate solution, in the presence of potassium cyanide, by ammonium sulfide. The precipitated thallous sulfide is soluble in hot 10% sulfuric acid and may be reprecipitated as the chloride (thallous chloride, TlCl), as thallous iodide in solutions neutralized with sodium carbonate, and as thallous chromate, Tl_2CrO_4, from neutral solutions.

Small amounts of thallium may be estimated by a method similar to that used for copper by the liberation of iodine from thallic chloride, $TlCl_3$, by the addition of potassium iodide with the formation of thallous iodide, TlI, and free iodine which is subsequently titrated by standard sodium thiosulfate solution. A variation depending on an ether extraction is detailed below.

Thallium may also be estimated titrimetrically by oxidation from the thallous to the thallic state in hydrochloric acid solution by the use of standard potassium permanganate or bromate (77,78).

a.   Extraction–Titration Method

Destroy organic matter with concentrated hydrochloric acid and potassium chlorate, or with $4N$ hydrochloric acid and potassium chlorate, using $0.1N$ potassium permanganate solution as a catalyst, or with nitric and sulfuric acids in the usual manner (79,80). In the latter instance it is necessary to add some free chlorine, for instance, by use of a heated solution of potassium chlorate in $4N$ hydrochloric acid.

Transfer the sample containing free chlorine to a Jacobs-Singer separatory flask. Check the reaction with starch-iodide paper. Add an equal volume of ether. Shake vigorously, allow the layers to separate, and draw off the ether layer into a separatory funnel. Add 1–2 ml of sulfur dioxide water to the ether layer and shake vigorously, until the aqueous layer no longer reacts with starch-iodide paper. Adjust the volume of the aqueous layer to about 5 ml and draw off into an evaporating dish. Shake out the ether layer with 2 ml of water and add this washing to the evaporating dish. Repeat the extraction of the sample an additional 2 times with ether. Extract the second and third ether extractions successively with sulfur dioxide water and water. Add each aqueous extract and wash to the evaporating dish, making a total of 6 additions.

Evaporate the combined aqueous sulfur dioxide extracts on a steam bath in a hood. Transfer, with the aid of a glass rod and a few drops of nitric acid, to a 50 × 18-mm Pyrex glass tube, add 0.2 ml of concentrated sulfuric acid, and digest in the customary manner. Wash the evaporating dish with drops of nitric acid, adding the washings to the digestion tube. The digestion may be considered complete when the sulfuric acid remains colorless or a light yellow.

Add 0.8 ml of water, mix, cool, and filter with suction through a micro filter of sintered glass into a precipitation tube 40 × 10 mm. Adjust the volume to 1.8 ml, add 0.1 ml of a freshly prepared saturated solution of sodium sulfite, $Na_2SO_3 \cdot 7H_2O$, and mix with a glass rod. Add 0.2 ml of 10% potassium iodide solution and mix. An orange-yellow precipitate indicates thallium. Rinse off the rod and allow the covered tube to stand for 12–18 hr in the dark. Centrifuge at 1500 rpm for 5 min, pour off the supernatant liquid with the aid of a glass rod, and wash the precipitate with 2 ml of 50% alcohol, stirring the precipitate with the rod, which is rinsed off with a few drops of alcohol. Centrifuge and decant. Wash again with 2 ml of 90% alcohol. At this point the precipitate may be estimated gravimetrically by the usual micro gravimetric methods, the factor Tl/TlI being 0.6160.

Titrimetric Procedure. Dry the tube. In the range of 10–250 µg of thallium add 0.1 ml of glacial acetic acid and a small drop of bromine. Shake for a moment every 5 min until no solid particles are visible and allow to stand an additional 15 min. Transfer the contents of the tube to a 25-ml flask with not more than 2 ml of water. Heat until the mixture is light yellow, allow to cool, add 2M sodium formate solution (prepared by dissolving 24.2 g of sodium formate, $HCOONa \cdot 3H_2O$, in water and diluting to 100 ml) until the solution is colorless, and then add an excess of 0.2 ml. Mix carefully and moisten the walls of the flask. Allow to stand 5 min. Add 2 ml of 30% sodium chloride solution, 1 drop of 10% potassium iodide solution, 0.2 ml of 4N sulfuric acid, and 5 drops of 0.2% starch-indicator solution. Titrate with 0.01N sodium thiosulfate solution.

Comparison solutions of thallium must be standardized because many salts are of dubious purity. Dissolve 131 mg of thallous carbonate, Tl_2CO_3, or an equivalent amount of another salt in water and dilute to 100 ml. This is approximately 1 mg of thallium per milliliter. Transfer 1 ml of this solution to a 100-ml flask, add 10 ml of water, 0.3 ml of glacial acetic acid, and sufficient bromine water to give a yellow color and 2 drops in excess. Allow to stand for 15 min, and remove the excess bromine with 2M sodium formate solution. Allow to stand an additional 5 min. Add 20 ml of 30% sodium chloride solution, 0.5 ml of 10% potassium iodide solution, 1 ml of 4N sulfuric acid solution, and 2 ml of 0.2% starch-indicator solution, and titrate with $0.01N$ sodium thiosulfate solution. One ml of the latter is equivalent to 1.022 mg of thallium.

Lead, mercury, copper, arsenic, antimony, bismuth, and iron do not interfere in this method.

b. Jacobs Triphenylmethane Dye Method

Thallium in small and minute concentrations has been determined colorimetrically by means of dithizone, p-phenetidine, aminopyrine, and more recently by use of triphenylmethane dyes. Other methods for this range of thallium concentrations involve polarographic, chromatographic, radioactivity, fluorimetric with Rhodamine B, and complex ion procedures.

The methyl violet variation of the triphenylmethane dye method for thallium, particularly the variation of Campbell, Milligan, and Lindsey (81), appeared to the author to be the most suitable. It would be out of place here to review the literature of the analytical chemistry of thallium in depth but since there is no general review of the literature of the method using methyl violet and triphenylmethane dyes in general, it is of interest to mention that since the introduction of the method by Gurev (82) and Shemeleva and Petrashen (83) in 1955, over 16 references as quoted by Jacobs (84) to the use of the variations of this method appeared by 1962.

In this method, the thallium is freed from organic matter by means of wet ashing, is oxidized to the thallic state, and is subsequently estimated colorimetrically by a methyl violet variation of the triphenylmethane method.

Reagents. *Sulfuric Acid, concentrated.* ACS Reagent grade, 95% minimum, sp gr 1.84.

Sulfuric Acid, 0.5N. Prepare in the customary manner.

Nitric Acid, concentrated. ACS Reagent grade, 69.0% minimum, sp gr 1.42.

Hydrobromic Acid, fuming. Reagent grade, 49%. This reagent may contain free bromine.

Hydrobromic Acid, dilute. Prepare a diluted (1:10) solution of hydrobromic acid just prior to use.

Bromine Water, saturated. Add sufficient reagent grade bromine to saturate a given volume of distilled water. Make certain that some liquid bromine is always present in the reagent bottle and stir vigorously for a short time, about 0.5 hr before using.

Methyl Violet. Prepare a 0.1% stock solution by dissolving 0.1 g of the pH reagent grade methyl violet in 100 ml of distilled water. Immediately before using, mix 5 ml of this stock with 1 ml of 0.5N sulfuric acid and 4 ml of distilled water.

Amyl Acetate. Fisher Scientific Company amyl acetate purified solvent (A-718).

Standard Thallium Solution. Weigh out accurately 0.3258 g of thallous nitrate, TlNO$_3$, purified, and transfer to a 250-ml volumetric flask. Dissolve in 0.5N sulfuric acid and make up to volume with this reagent. This solution contains 1 mg of thallium per ml. Prepare by dilution a solution containing 1 μg of thallium per milliliter.

Standard Curve. Transfer to five 100-ml kjeldahl flasks, 0, 1, 2, 4, and 10 ml, respectively, of the 1-μg/ml standard thallium solution and add sufficient 0.5N sulfuric acid to bring the total volume to 10 ml. Add 5 ml of a digestion mixture consisting of 1 volume of concentrated sulfuric acid and 9 volumes of concentrated nitric acid. Place the kjeldahl flasks on a micro combustion heater apparatus or over adequate burners and boil off the aqueous portion. Continue heating until fumes of sulfur trioxide are formed, but stop the heating as soon as the fumes are well up in the neck of the kjeldahl flasks. Continue with the method as detailed in the procedure.

Procedure. Transfer 50 ml of the well-mixed sample to a 300-ml kjeldahl flask; add 2 ml of concentrated sulfuric acid and 20 ml of concentrated nitric acid. Boil to sulfur trioxide fumes. Add concentrated nitric acid in 3-ml portions, bringing down to sulfur trioxide fumes again, and repeat the addition and evaporation of the concentrated nitric acid until the mixture no longer turns black or dark. This may require from 1 to 6 additions. Cool, dilute with 20 ml of water, add 1 ml of fuming hydrobromic acid, and boil to fumes. Cool, dilute with 20 ml of water, and add 1 ml of 1:10 hydrobromic acid and 1 ml of saturated bromine water. (If desired, check for an excess of bromine with an indicator such as methyl red indicator solution. The indicator is destroyed if an excess is present.) Boil briskly for 3 min. Cool and transfer to a separatory funnel. Wash 3 times with 20 ml of water, adding the washings to the separator. Make certain the total volume is at least 75–80 ml to bring the solution to be extracted to the proper pH. Add 10 ml of amyl acetate and 1 ml of methyl violet reagent; shake for 15 sec immediately after this addition. After settling shake again for 45 sec, allow to separate, discard the water layer, transfer to centrifuge tubes, and centrifuge or dry with powdered anhydrous sodium sulfate; read in $\frac{3}{4}$-in. tubes at a 585 mμ in a Bausch & Lomb colorimeter. In a series of determinations immediately after the addition of amyl acetate and methyl violet reagent, shake for 15 sec, allow to settle while making the additions of these reagents to the other members of the series, and, after all the additions have been made, then go back and shake each separatory funnel for an additional 45 sec.

J. Zinc

Zinc is not a poison in the usual sense of the word. Pure zinc, in contrast to metals such as lead, arsenic, antimony, and cadmium, has virtually no poisonous qualities even if ingested in relatively large amounts. However, there are indications (85) that continuous ingestion of soluble zinc compounds, for instance, swallowing zinc-bearing dusts with the saliva, may cause chronic gastritis with emesis. Certain zinc compounds are caustic. The one most commonly met in industry is, as was mentioned, zinc chloride. This is used as a flux in soldering, and if spattered may cause bad burns. Zinc sulfate is also caustic, while zinc chromate may cause dermatitis. Other zinc compounds are harmful because of their state of subdivision. This is the greatest single hazard to workers in zinc and zinc products.

1. METAL-FUME FEVER

It was formerly thought that zinc metal was the cause of brass-founders' ague, spelter shakes, and brass chills. The term *metal-fume fever* is now used to cover such affections (86). It has been shown that the chill and fever thought to be produced by zinc oxide alone can also occur when oxides of other metals or finely divided powders of other metals are inhaled. Thus, it has been demonstrated that zinc stearate, copper oxide (87,88), and magnesium oxide can also give rise to this type of illness. Koelsch (89) concluded that metal-fume fever may occur from the inhalation of all heavy metals. Drinker (88,90) and co-workers found that 45 mg of zinc oxide, measured as zinc, per cubic meter of air could be inhaled for 20 min without causing symptoms. They found that in a metallurgical plant, 14 mg/m^3 produced no reaction in 8 hr. The recommended maximum allowable concentration for zinc oxide fumes is 15 mg/m³ of air.

2. SAMPLING

Zinc-bearing dust-laden air may be sampled by means of the macro impinger, as described for the sampling of lead dust. Otherwise the fumes may be flocculated in an electrical precipitator. An alternative method is to pass air through a trap containing cotton moistened with nitric acid.

Evaporate, dry, and char the sample or an aliquot. Then ash in an electric muffle oven at 450°C or low red heat. Extract the ash with hydrochloric acid (1:1). Filter. If a clean ash has not been obtained, it may be necessary to reash the filter paper and residue in the original dish and then reextract with hydrochloric acid (1:1).

3. DETERMINATION

a. Ferrocyanide Method

Small quantities of zinc may be estimated by the use of the ferrocyanide method (91,92). The zinc is freed from iron by the use of cupferron or phosphate. It is precipitated as the sulfide with the addition of copper, if necessary, to act as a collector. The sulfides are redissolved and the zinc is separated from the copper by the usual sulfide separation. Zinc is then converted to the chloride and estimated with ferrocyanide, either by titration using uranium acetate as an external indicator, or nephelometrically.

Preparation of Reagents. *Potassium Ferrocyanide Solution.* Dissolve 3.464 g of recrystallized potassium ferrocyanide, $K_4Fe(CN)_6 \cdot 3H_2O$, in water and dilute to 1 liter. Allow to stand for a day or two and filter from any residue. This solution may be standardized by running a titration against known amounts of standardized zinc chloride solution as described in the method. One ml of this solution is equivalent to 1 mg of zinc.

Standard Zinc Chloride Solution. Dissolve 1.2446 g of ignited zinc oxide in a slight excess of hydrochloric acid (1:1). Dilute to 1 liter with water. One ml is equivalent to 1 mg of zinc.

Uranium Acetate Solution. Dissolve 40 g of uranium acetate [uranyl acetate, $UO_2(C_2H_3O_2)_2 \cdot 2H_2O$] in 800–900 ml of water. Allow to stand for several days. Filter from any residue into a volumetric flask and dilute to 1 liter.

Procedure. Adjust the volume of the prepared hydrochloric acid solution of zinc to about 75 ml containing 10–15 ml of hydrochloric acid (1:1). To precipitate iron, add to the cold solution an excess of an aqueous solution of cupferron (ammonium nitrosophenylhydroxylamine). The iron is completely precipitated when white crystals of the cupferron are noticed on further addition of the reagent. If a colloid forms, shake and stir until it is flocculated. Filter. Partly neutralize with sodium hydroxide solution and add ammonium acetate until the free hydrochloric acid is replaced by acetic acid, as is shown by using methyl orange as indicator. Add 0.5 mg of copper as copper nitrate to act as a collector and saturate with hydrogen sulfide. Filter. Wash the precipitate with water and finally with hot alcohol. Dissolve the precipitate from the filter with alternate washings of concentrated nitric acid and hot water, catching the filtrate in the original sulfide precipitation vessel, until completely dissolved. Evaporate to dryness. Add 1 ml of sulfuric acid (1:2) and 2 ml of nitric acid. Heat in a hood until all traces of organic material have been oxidized and the excess sulfuric acid has been driven off. Dissolve the residue in 5 ml of hydrochloric acid (1:1) and 20 ml of water. Heat to boiling and titrate with the standard potassium ferrocyanide solution, using a spot plate and uranium acetate as an external indicator.

Nephelometric Method (93–96)

As an alternative method the following may be used. Iron is not precipitated but is held in solution by sodium citrate. The mixed sulfides of copper and zinc are precipitated as before, but the ionic strength of the salts in the final solution is adjusted so that the sensitivity of the reaction with ferrocyanide is increased.

Adjust the volume of the prepared hydrochloric acid solution of the zinc to about 75 ml, add 5 g of sodium citrate, 2 mg of copper as copper sulfate, and a drop of thymol blue indicator. Add dilute potassium hydroxide solution until the solution becomes yellow and then add a drop of bromophenol blue. If the solution is bluish at this point, add dilute acid until the yellow color is just restored. Saturate the cold solution with hydrogen sulfide, filter, and wash well to free from iron salts. Dissolve the combined sulfides in nitric acid and hydrochloric acid, dissolve the residue in hydrochloric acid, and adjust the pH of the solution as described above, omitting the use of sodium citrate. This makes the color changes sharper because of the absence of the citrate buffer. Saturate the cold solution with hydrogen sulfide. Filter and wash well. Dissolve the sulfides in 5 ml of hydrochloric acid (1:1) and 20 ml of water. Slowly saturate the cold solution with hydrogen sulfide and filter. Copper alone is precipitated and the zinc is in the filtrate. Evaporate the filtrate to dryness and dissolve the residue in 4–5 drops of hydrochloric acid (1:1) and a little water. If necessary, warm slightly before the addition of water. Transfer to a 25-ml volumetric flask and make to volume. To an appropriate aliquot, usually 5 or 10 ml of this solution, add 10 ml of $0.1341N$ potassium hydroxide, standardized against potassium hydrogen phthalate. Carefully neutralize the excess potassium hydroxide with $0.1N$ hydrochloric acid, using phenolphthalein as indicator, and then add exactly 1 ml of acid in excess. Transfer to a 50-ml Nessler tube. Dilute with water to 45 ml, add 1 ml of 2% potassium ferrocyanide solution, mix thoroughly, and make to volume. The solution is $0.002N$ with respect to acid, and $0.0268M$ with respect to potassium chloride. The nephelometric standards in Nessler tubes should be prepared in exactly the same way in order to insure that the ionic strength is the same in the standards and in the unknown. The most suitable range for comparison is that of standards containing 0.20–0.25 mg/50 ml matched against solutions of the unknown of nearly the same opacity. The standards for comparison should vary from 0.25 to 0.50 mg of zinc in steps of 0.05 mg. They may be prepared from ignited zinc oxide as directed in a preceding paragraph.

b. Dithizone Method

The dithizone method (97,98) provides a fairly rapid means of estimating zinc. After trapping the zinc-bearing dust by means of an impinger, the zinc may be brought into solution as described for lead on page 343. The solution is made alkaline with ammonia, a chloroform solution of dithizone is added, the mixture is shaken, and then permitted to stand and separate. If zinc is present, it combines with the dithizone in chloroform and colors it red. The intensity of the color is proportional to the amount of zinc, which should be kept within the range of 0.001–0.010 mg. In the method detailed below, the zinc is extracted with the lead, the total amount of dithizone is estimated titrimetrically, and the amount of zinc is calculated by subtracting the volume used in the lead determination.

Reagents. The reagents are prepared as directed in the method for lead, page 343.

Procedure. Transfer an aliquot of the solution prepared as directed on page 343, containing less than 25 μg of zinc or the equivalent of zinc and lead, to a 125-ml separatory funnel. Do not add potassium cyanide solution. However, if copper is present, it will be extracted along with the zinc and lead, and consequently the method should be modified as detailed below.

Add 5 ml of chloroform and small portions of dithizone. Shake and continue the addition of dithizone until it is present in excess. Draw off the chloroform layer and wash the aqueous phase with a small portion of chloroform containing a few drops of dithizone solution. Combine the chloroform layers.

Wash the chloroform layer at least twice with 3 volumes of dilute ammonium hydroxide solution in each washing. To break the emulsion that may form with the first washing, draw off the clear portion of the chloroform, as formed on standing. Add 1 ml of chloroform and invert the separatory funnel several times gently. Again draw off the clear chloroform layer as it forms. After the major portion of chloroform has been withdrawn, add an additional 1–2 ml and repeat as above. Avoid too many washings, since some free dithizone will distribute itself between the aqueous and chloroform phases. The chloroform extract should be bright red and should have no free dithizone. The last wash of ammonia water should be colorless.

Shake the chloroform layer with 2 volumes of 1% hydrochloric acid vigorously in order to break the zinc and lead complexes. Draw off the dithizone solution, add half its volume of 0.5% potassium cyanide solution, and titrate with the same standard lead solution as used for the determination of lead (pp. 343–344) in exactly the same way. Subtract the volume of standard lead solution equivalent to the amount of lead found in an equal aliquot as that taken for the zinc determination from the volume found above, representing both zinc and lead. Multiply this difference by 3.15 to give the quantity of zinc in micrograms present in the aliquot taken for analysis.

Blank analyses should be run using the water and reagents used in the analysis, and the result should be subtracted from the results obtained in the regular analysis to get the corrected results.

Copper Interference. To remove copper, which will be an interference in the lead and zinc determination, since copper will also be extracted by dithizone in the absence of cyanide, the test solution must be treated with successive acid and alkaline washes.

Shake the chloroform extract with twice its volume of 1% hydrochloric acid. Repeat the acid extraction. If copper is to be estimated (page 447), retain the chloroform layer; otherwise it may be discarded. Adjust the pH to 8 with ammonium hydroxide solution (1:1), using phenol red as the indicator. Reextract the zinc, lead, and any residual copper with an excess of dithizone solution and repeat the acid extraction. Adjust the pH to 8, extract again with excess dithizone solution, and wash out the excess dithizone with dilute ammonium hydroxide solution. Decompose the zinc and lead complexes with hydrochloric acid, and titrate the liberated dithizone with standard lead solution in the presence of potassium cyanide.

c. Sulfide Method

The foregoing methods have been detailed for the estimation of small quantities of zinc. Larger quantities of zinc may be estimated by the sulfide method (99). In this procedure the zinc is separated from the other metals by first precipitating the metals having sulfides insoluble in relatively high acid concentration, the zinc remaining in the filtrate, and then determining the zinc by precipitating it as zinc sulfide in a buffered faintly acid solution, thus separating the metal from those other metals whose sulfides are soluble in faintly acid solution.

Procedure. Often this determination is made after estimation of copper. Boil the filtrate from the copper separation to expel the hydrogen sulfide and reduce the volume to 250 ml. Add a drop of methyl orange indicator, 5 g of ammonium chloride, and make alkaline with ammonium hydroxide. Add hydrochloric acid (1:9) dropwise to faintly acid reaction, add 10–15 ml of sodium or ammonium acetate (50 g of salt made up to 100 ml with water), and pass in hydrogen sulfide until precipitation is complete. Allow the precipitate to settle, filter, and wash twice with hydrogen sulfide water. Dissolve the precipitate on the filter with a little hydrochloric acid (1:3), wash the filter with water, boil the filtrate and washings to expel hydrogen sulfide, and cool. Add a distinct excess of bromine water. Add 5 g of ammonium chloride and then ammonium hydroxide until the bromine color disappears. Add hydrochloric acid (1:3) dropwise until the bromine just reappears. Then add 10–15 ml of sodium or ammonium acetate solution and 0.5 ml of ferric chloride solution (10 g of $FeCl_3 \cdot 6H_2O$ in 100 ml of water) or enough to precipitate the phosphates. Boil until all the iron is precipitated. Filter while hot and wash the precipitate with water containing a little sodium acetate. Pass hydrogen sulfide into the combined filtrate and washings until all the zinc sulfide, which should be pure white, is precipitated. Filter through a weighed, prepared Gooch crucible and wash with hydrogen sulfide–ammonium nitrate water. Dry the crucible, ignite at a bright red heat, cool, and weigh as zinc oxide, ZnO. Calculate the weight of metallic zinc, using the factor 0.8034.

Zinc sulfide sometimes forms colloidal precipitates that will not flocculate and consequently pass through the filter. Caldwell and Moyer (100) recommend the addition of a solution of gelatin, containing from 0.5 to 2 mg of gelatin of very low ash content. The gelatin solution will produce instantaneous and complete flocculation of as much as 0.3 g of zinc sulfide in 300 ml of solution.

K. Copper

Poisoning from copper fumes is undoubtedly rare because of the high boiling point of copper (melting point, 1083°C, and boiling point, 2310°C). It has been previously mentioned that copper oxide may be a cause of metal-fume fever, although in this instance most cases are most probably due to zinc fumes rather than to copper when these metals occur together as in brass and the so-called commercial bronze, or red brass. There are some authorities who maintain that chronic copper poisoning is associated with a definite disease (101,102). The views on copper as a poison have undergone changes and it is now accepted that minute amounts of the metal are necessary for proper human metabolism. Undoubtedly, larger amounts of copper have a deleterious effect, nor can inhaled copper compounds be considered in the same light as ingested copper.

1. DETERMINATION

Copper-bearing dusts may be trapped by methods previously detailed. Ignition ashing is suitable, when needed, if copper is to be estimated alone. However, if other metals, much more volatile, are to be determined and ashing is necessary, the wet-ash method is preferred.

a. Iodide–Thiosulfate Method

In the methods detailed, the copper is separated from other metals by means of a sulfide precipitation and it is subsequently estimated by the iodine liberated in the cupric–cuprous iodide reaction.

Prepare an acid solution of the copper-bearing material and pass in hydrogen sulfide for 15 or 20 min. Filter the precipitate through quantitative filter paper. Wash. Place the filter paper plus the precipitate directly into a 100-ml flask—a squat flask with a wide mouth, customarily called a "fat" flask, is preferable—and add 3–4 ml of concentrated sulfuric acid and 6 ml of concentrated nitric acid. Place glass hooks on the flask and cover with a watch glass. If the resultant mixture is dark, add nitric acid until it is clear. Evaporate to 1 or 2 ml, cool, and add 30 ml of water and an excess of bromine water. Place the flask on the steam bath until the solution is colorless; then cool and add ammonium hydroxide. In case iron or other metal yielding an insoluble hydroxide is present, filter and then evaporate off the ammonium hydroxide. A rough estimate of the amount of copper can be obtained from the blue color and the volume, at this point. Make acid with acetic acid and titrate with 0.01N sodium thiosulfate solution in the presence of about 5 g of potassium iodide and 1–2 ml of 1% starch solution.

As an alternative method (103) dissolve the ash in hydrochloric acid, neutralize with ammonium hydroxide, add 5 ml of sulfuric acid, dilute to 200 ml, and boil for 1 min. Cautiously add 10 ml of a hot, saturated solution of sodium thiosulfate and continue boiling for 5 min. Filter the precipitate, wash 6 times with hot water, and reserve the filter if desired for a zinc determination. Fold the filter paper, place in a crucible, and ignite in a muffle at 500°C. Treat the residue with 1 ml of nitric acid (2:5) and dry on the steam bath. Add 20 ml of water and an excess of ammonium hydroxide and heat until the copper salts dissolve. Transfer to a 100-ml flask.

Make acid to litmus with acetic acid (1:1) and add 1 ml in excess. Boil for 1 min and cool to room temperature. Add 2 g of potassium iodide, dissolved in enough water to make the final solution 50 ml and titrate the free iodine with 0.01 or 0.005N sodium thiosulfate solution until the end point is nearly reached. Add 2 ml of 1% starch solution and continue titrating until the color is discharged.

b. Potassium Ethyl Xanthate Method

Very small amounts of copper may be estimated colorimetrically by either the potassium ethyl xanthate method or the sodium diethyldithiocarbamate method. Separate the copper from other metals as the sulfide. Dissolve in a drop of nitric acid, if possible, otherwise keep the nitric acid down to a minimum. Transfer to a 50-ml volumetric flask and make to volume. Transfer a 5-ml aliquot to a Nessler tube containing 10 ml of a freshly prepared 0.1% solution of potassium ethyl xanthate. Dilute to 25 ml and mix. Place 10 ml of the ethyl xanthate reagent into another Nessler tube. Dilute to 15 ml. Add from a 10-ml semimicroburet, a drop at a time, while continually stirring, a standard copper solution containing 0.1 mg of copper per milliliter. To prepare this standard, dissolve 0.3928 g of copper sulfate, $CuSO_4 \cdot 5H_2O$, in water, transfer to a 1-liter volumetric flask, make to volume, and mix. Continue the addition and stirring until the color in the tube containing the standard copper solution apparently matches the color of the unknown. Adjust the volume to 25 ml and the color to match the test solution as closely as possible. Compute the quantity of copper from the volume of standard copper solution used.

c. Sodium Diethyldithiocarbamate Method (104,105)

After the copper has been separated as the sulfide, dissolve in a minimum amount of nitric acid. Evaporate almost to dryness to drive off excess acid if necessary. Dissolve in water, transfer to a volumetric flask, and make to volume. Take a 50-ml aliquot, add 5 ml of ammonium hydroxide solution (1:5), and filter if a precipitate forms. Transfer to a Nessler tube and add 5 ml of a 0.1% solution of sodium diethyldithiocarbamate (1 g of sodium diethyldithiocarbamate, $N(C_2H_5)_2 \cdot CS_2Na$, dissolved in water and diluted to 1 liter). Compare the color produced within 1 hr with that of standards treated the same way. The standards may be prepared by diluting 25 ml of the 0.1 mg of copper per milliliter standard of the potassium ethyl xanthate method to 250 ml. This yields a solution containing 0.01 mg of copper per milliliter. Convenient standards contain from 0.005 to 0.05 mg of copper.

d. Dithizone Method

Copper may often be present along with lead and zinc, particularly in soldering operations that involve the heating of copper or copper alloys. It may be estimated in such mixtures by the dithizone method (106).

Wash the initial extract of lead, zinc, and copper dithizonates (see page 443) with dilute ammonium hydroxide solution to remove the excess free dithizone. Treat with 1% hydrochloric acid and retain the aqueous layer for the estimation of zinc and lead. Shake the chloroform solution with half its volume of 0.5% potassium cyanide solution and titrate with the standard lead solution (pp. 343–344). The presence of potassium cyanide makes it unnecessary to decompose the copper–dithizone complex by acid since this is done by the cyanide. The difference between the volume of lead solution used in this titration and that used for the titration of zinc and lead together, multiplied by 3.07, equals the quantity of copper, in micrograms, present in the aliquot taken for the analysis.

L. Tin

Very few industrial illnesses are directly traceable to tin. It has been shown that tin tetrachloride is irritating and has caused illness. This compound is used in the weighting of silk and as a mordant for dyeing. It is produced when so-called tin plate, scrap tin-plated metal, is detinned with chlorine. Pedley (107) quotes the U.S. Bureau of Mines in saying that 8.5 ppm in air caused coughing and that 1 ppm, 1 mg/liter, caused death of mice in 10 min. However, Pedley himself found that guinea pigs could tolerate as much as 3 ppm for months with no apparent ill effect. Organic compounds of tin such as tin tetramethyl have been found to produce illness (108). Tin has a comparatively low melting point, 231.9°C, but it has a high boiling point, 2270°C. The high boiling point tends to minimize danger from fumes.

1. Determination

Tin-bearing dust may be sampled as previously detailed. A method for its separation as the sulfide and its subsequent estimation by titration with standard iodine solution has been indicated in Section X-C on antimony.

a. Sulfide Method

Tin may be precipitated as stannous sulfide and separated from sulfides insoluble in polysulfide by solution in polysulfide and filtration. The tin is then reprecipitated as the sulfide and estimated as the oxide after roasting.

If an acid digestion has been made, which is the preferable procedure if ashing is required when tin is being determined because of the volatility of tin tetrachloride, add 200 ml of water to the digested sample and transfer to a 600-ml beaker. Rinse the kjeldahl flask with three portions of boiling water, making a total volume of approximately 400 ml. If the tin has been brought into solution without the need of an acid digestion, dilute to approximately the same volume. Cool, and add ammonium hydroxide until just alkaline, then add 5 ml of hydrochloric acid or 5 ml of sulfuric acid (1:3) for each 100 ml of solution. Place the beaker, covered, on a hot plate. Heat to about 95°C and pass in a slow stream of hydrogen sulfide for 1 hr. Digest at 95°C for another hour and allow to stand for ½ hr longer. Filter, and wash the precipitate of stannous sulfide alternately with 3 portions each of wash solution and hot water. The wash solution consists of 100 ml of saturated ammonium acetate solution, 50 ml of glacial acetic acid, and 850 ml of water. Transfer the filter and precipitate to a 50-ml beaker, add 10–20 ml of ammonium polysulfide, heat to boiling, and filter. Repeat the digestion with ammonium polysulfide and the filtration twice, and then wash the filter with hot water. Acidify the combined filtrate and washings with acetic acid (1:9), digest on a hot plate for 1 hr, allow to stand overnight, and filter through a double 11-cm quantitative filter. Wash alternately with two portions each of the wash solution and hot water, and dry thoroughly in a weighed porcelain crucible. Ignite over a bunsen flame, very gently at first to burn off the filter paper and to convert the sulfide to oxide, then partly cover the crucible and heat strongly over a large meker burner. Weigh as stannic oxide, SnO_2, and calculate to metallic tin by using the factor 0.7877.

b. *Thioglycolic Acid Method*

In this method (109) the tin is separated as stannous sulfide, it is redissolved in sodium hydroxide solution, and after being made acid with hydrochloric acid, the color obtained with a reagent containing thioglycolic acid is compared against standards.

Convert the tin to stannous sulfide as described above and filter. Digest the paper and precipitate with 10 ml of 10% sodium hydroxide solution on the steam bath for at least 10 min. Filter and wash well. Make the solution just acid by adding concentrated hydrochloric acid, add 2 drops of thioglycolic acid, and dilute to 100 ml with water. Take an aliquot of 5 ml in a boiling tube with 5 ml of water; add 0.5 ml of concentrated hydrochloric acid and 0.5 ml of a reagent containing 0.1 g of dithiol and 0.25 ml of thioglycolic acid dissolved in 50 ml of 1% sodium hydroxide solution. Immerse in a bath of boiling water for 30 sec, allow to stand for 1 min, and compare with standards treated similarly.

The reagent is best kept in an atmosphere of hydrogen but should be rejected as soon as a white precipitate of disulfide appears. It seldom keeps longer than two weeks.

Tin may also be estimated colorimetrically by dissolving the purified stannous sulfide in 2.5 ml of hydrochloric acid. Place this solution in a test tube fitted with a cork and delivery tube. Add a small piece of zinc; when it is dissolved, pass in carbon dioxide to replace the air and add 2 ml of 0.2% dinitrodiphenylaminesulfoxide in $0.1N$ sodium hydroxide solution. Boil the mixture for a few minutes and dilute to 100 ml. Add a few drops of ferric chloric solution. The violet color so obtained may be matched against standard solutions of tin treated the same way.

M. Nickel

Nickel is an industrial hazard from three main sources: nickel plating and nickel salts such as nickel sulfate, nickel dust in grinding, and nickel carbonyl. Metallic nickel has been shown not to be poisonous as an inherent property (110). Nickel carbonyl, on the other hand, is an extremely poisonous compound. Amor (111) states that it is relatively at least five times as toxic as carbon monoxide. It has been shown that a concentration of 0.018% by volume of nickel carbonyl would kill a full-grown healthy rabbit after 1 hr of exposure (112). Metallic nickel, in an extremely fine state of subdivision, may also give rise to fever.

1. DETERMINATION

a. Potassium Dithiooxalate Method

Very small amounts of nickel may be determined by use of this method (113–116). The nickel is separated from iron and, if necessary, from cobalt. Its concentration is then determined by the formation of magenta-colored nickel dithiooxalate.

Samples may be collected by one of the many methods previously detailed. If necessary, evaporate, dry, and char the specimen in a porcelain dish. Ash at low red heat, being careful not to fuse the ash. Cool; add 15 ml of hydrochloric acid (1:1) and sufficient water, if necessary, to cover the residue. Cover the dish with a watch glass and heat to boiling. Filter, and extract two more times with hot water. If a clean ash has not been obtained, return the filter paper and its residue to the original ashing dish, dry, and reash in a muffle. Extract as directed above. Combine all the filtrate extracts and washings, and neutralize the hydrochloric acid with ammonium hydroxide, using methyl orange as indicator. Add a few drops of hydrochloric acid until the solution is just acid. Saturate the cold solution with hydrogen sulfide and allow to stand overnight. Filter and wash the precipitate with hydrogen sulfide water. Combine the filtrate and washings, which contain the nickel, and boil until free of hydrogen sulfide. Add bromine water to oxidize iron to the ferric state.

If cobalt is present, proceed as directed below. If cobalt is absent, it is necessary to free the solution only of iron, which interferes with the determination. To the cold, slightly acid solution, add 10 ml of 50% ammonium acetate solution and 0.5 ml of glacial acetic acid. Under these conditions, iron is precipitated in the cold. Warming should be avoided to prevent reduction of iron to the ferrous state. Filter the cold solution through quantitative filter paper into a volumetric flask. Dilute to a known volume, depending upon the nickel concentration. Transfer 50 ml of this solution to a Nessler tube and add a small amount of potassium dithiooxalate. If nickel is present, a clear magenta color develops at once. If nickel is absent, no color will develop except a slight yellow.

Procedure in the Presence of Cobalt. If cobalt is present, it must be separated from the nickel. To do this both calcium and magnesium are precipitated as oxalate and phosphate, respectively. Then nickel is isolated with α-benzil dioxime and subsequently can be estimated as detailed above.

To the nickel solution, add 10 ml of 20% sodium citrate solution to prevent precipitation of iron. Add saturated ammonium oxalate solution to precipitate calcium. When precipitation is complete, add dilute ammonium hydroxide solution slowly to precipitate ammonium magnesium phosphate in the same solution. Filter. Dissolve the precipitates in hydrochloric acid and then reprecipitate calcium and magnesium as oxalate and phosphate, as above. Filter and combine this filtrate with the main filtrate. This step recovers any nickel occluded on the calcium and magnesium precipitates. To the alkaline filtrate add an excess of α-benzil dioxime, filter the nickel precipitate, dissolve in aqua regia, and evaporate the acid solution to dryness in a porcelain dish. Dissolve in a few drops of dilute hydrochloric acid and make to volume in a volumetric flask. Determine nickel colorimetrically with potassium dithiooxalate.

Standards containing from 0.005 to 0.05 mg of nickel can be prepared by dissolving a weighed portion of nickel dimethylglyoxime, which contains 20.32% nickel, in aqua regia, evaporating, redissolving in hydrochloric acid, evaporating again, redissolving in hydrochloric acid, and making up to a known volume. To prepare standards make further dilutions. Higher concentrations of nickel can be matched in a colorimeter.

b. Dimethylglyoxime Method

Larger quantities of nickel can be estimated by the dimethylglyoxime or α-benzil dioxime methods. The analytical chemistry of the dioximes particularly as applied to nickel has been discussed by Diehl (117) and by Prodinger (118).

Prepare an acid solution of the nickel salt. Filter, if necessary, and evaporate in a porcelain dish on a water bath. Dissolve the residue in 50 ml of hot absolute alcohol, rendered just alkaline with ammonium hydroxide, and add 50 ml of a hot saturated solution of dimethylglyoxime or α-benzil dioxime.   Heat the mixture for a few minutes on the bath and filter through a tared Gooch crucible, wash with hot alcohol, dry at 100°C, cool, and weigh.

If α-benzil dioxime is used, then the weight of precipitate multiplied by the factor 0.1093 equals the weight of nickel.   If dimethylglyoxime is used, then the weight of precipitate multiplied by the factor 0.2032 equals the weight of nickel.

2. Nickel Carbonyl

Nickel carbonyl, $Ni(CO)_4$, is a clear, straw-colored liquid which boils at 43°C.   It can be decomposed by heating to 150°C, at which temperature it breaks up into nickel and carbon monoxide.   This is the basis for the Mond process of obtaining pure nickel.

Nickel carbonyl is a highly poisonous substance.   The recommended maximum allowable concentration is 1 ppm.   The concentration may be estimated by passing a known volume of air containing gaseous nickel carbonyl through a silica or heat-resistant glass tube heated to red heat.   The nickel deposits on the walls of the tube in the form of a mirror.   The nickel may then be dissolved in sulfuric acid and determined by one of the methods outlined above. Nickel carbonyl may also be trapped in a bubbler containing aqua regia or sulfuric acid, after which the acid solution may be analyzed by an appropriate method.

N. Cobalt

The toxicology of cobalt from an industrial-hygiene point of view has been reviewed by Fairhall (119).   The use of cobalt industrially has increased within the past decade, principally in sellite-, carbide-, and Alnico-type alloys.   It is also used as a bonding material in the preparation of tungsten carbide.   While the toxicity of cobalt by mouth is low—indeed it has been shown that cobalt is a micronutrient, particularly for sheep and cattle—cobalt salts have been shown to cause polycythemia in animals, and powdered cobalt produces dermatitis (120).

Cobalt carbonyls are used as catalysts in the manufacture of motor fuels.   The presence of these compounds in air may be detected by passing a known volume of air through a silica or heat-resistant glass tube heated to red heat.   The cobalt deposits on the walls of the tube and may then be determined as detailed in the nitroso R salt method below. Most probably absorbers containing aqua regia or sulfuric acid can also be used to trap the cobalt carbonyl.

1. DETERMINATION

A method for the determination of cobalt in atmospheric dust samples of special steels, alloys, ores, and minerals has been developed by Keenan and Flick (121). The samples are collected by means of an electrostatic precipitator, the dust collected is weighed, fused, and an aliquot is analyzed by the nitroso R salt method.

a. Nitroso R Salt Method

Preliminary Treatment. Collect the dust by means of a dc electrostatic precipitator using aluminum collecting electrodes. Upon receipt of the electrodes in the laboratory, remove the metal or Bakelite caps, wipe the outer surfaces of the electrodes, clean with alcohol on a gauze pad, dry by wiping with a clean pad of dry gauze, and weigh after a 15-min waiting period for equilibrium to take place.

Transfer the samples from the electrodes to Pyrex test tubes, using a minimum amount of 30% alcohol—usually 10–20 ml is adequate—with the aid of a rubber policeman. Dry the inner surface of the electrode by forcing through a dry pad of gauze, clean the outer surfaces again as before, and weigh after a 15-min waiting period. The weight of the sample is the difference between the weighings.

Evaporate the samples to dryness in an oven at 105°C and thus concentrate each sample at the bottom of the test tube.

Fusion Treatment. Carbides such as those obtained from samples of cemented tungsten carbide may be decomposed by fusion with potassium peroxydisulfate to give a clean white or yellowish white melt in 3–4 min by heating with a meker burner.

Heat the samples with a meker burner to remove any free carbon. Cool, add a sufficient amount of potassium peroxydisulfate, $K_2S_2O_8$, and heat gently at first and then more strongly, while rotating the tube at an angle to permit the molten peroxydisulfate to come in contact with and to decompose the carbides.

By this treatment cobalt, nickel, and titanium are converted to their sulfates; tungsten is converted to potassium tungstate; and tantalum and columbium to the oxides or tantalates and columbates.

Allow to cool, and dissolve the melt in hot water. Add 5 ml of 6N hydrochloric acid and dilute to 25 ml with water. If the samples are heavy, dilute to 50 or 100 ml. Tungstic acid and hydrolyzed titanium salts may precipitate during the dilution, but cobalt remains in solution in the 1.2N hydrochloric acid.

Standard Cobalt Solution. Dissolve 0.0249 g of cobalt oxalate, CoC_2O_4, in 10 ml of 6N hydrochloric acid and dilute to 1000 ml with water. Transfer 100 ml of this solution to a liter volumetric flask, add 10 ml of 6N hydrochloric acid, and dilute to volume. One ml of this standard solution is equivalent to 0.001 mg of cobalt.

Procedure. Transfer a suitable aliquot portion of the prepared sample after thorough mixing of the insoluble residue of tungstic acid, if any is present, to a beaker. Filter, if necessary, and wash 3 times with water. Evaporate the filtrate almost to dryness, add 2 ml of concentrated nitric acid, and evaporate to dryness. Dissolve the sample by boiling in 10 ml of water and 2 ml of 6N hydrochloric acid. Neutralize the sample with 20% sodium hydroxide solution, using phenolphthalein as an indicator. Add 2 ml of Spekker acid (prepared from 150 ml of phosphoric acid, sp gr 1.75, and 150 ml of sulfuric acid, sp gr 1.84, diluted to 1 liter with water), 10 ml of 0.1% aqueous solution of nitroso R salt, and 10 ml of 50% sodium acetate trihydrate (w/v solution). Bring the mixture to a vigorous boil, add 5 ml of concentrated nitric acid, and boil the mixture for 1–2 min. Cool, dilute to 100 ml with water, and obtain the optical density difference between the test solution and a reagent blank balanced at zero on a Coleman Universal spectrophotometer at 510 mμ. Estimate the amount of cobalt from a standard-curve graph of optical density against concentration, prepared from a series of 0–0.500-mg cobalt standards carried through the same procedure.

O. Iron

1. Iron Carbonyls

Carbon monoxide forms volatile compounds with iron such as iron tetracarbonyl, $Fe(CO)_4$, and iron pentacarbonyl, $Fe(CO)_5$, when passed over iron, especially finely divided iron, at 40–80°C. They may be formed by the passage of illuminating gas through iron pipes. These compounds are only slightly less toxic than nickel carbonyl (111).

These compounds may be trapped and decomposed by heat in silica or heat-resistant glass tubes in a manner entirely analogous to nickel carbonyl (122–124). The iron deposited in the tubes may then be estimated by one of the usual methods.

If iron carbonyl can be obtained as an ether extract, it may be detected by dissolving 1 drop of the residue in methyl alcohol. Add perhydrol and 10% sodium hydroxide solution. Dissolve the ferric hydroxide formed in hydrochloric acid and add 2 ml of 10% potassium thiocyanate solution. If iron carbonyl is present, a red color is produced.

2. Iron Oxides

Iron oxide fume is generated in welding operations (125,126). It has been shown that continued exposure to concentrations above 30 mg/m³ may cause a chronic bronchitis. The recommended maximum allowable concentration is 15 mg/m³ of air.

Iron oxide fume may be sampled by means of the electric precipitator, although at times an impinger containing water has been used (127).

The iron in iron oxide fume is present principally in the ferric form. It may thus be estimated by titration with ceric sulfate, since

$$Ce^{4+} + Fe^{2+} \rightarrow Fe^{3+} + Ce^{3+}$$

Dissolve the fume in 15 ml of hydrochloric acid (2:1) and reduce the iron to the ferrous state by use of $0.5N$ stannous chloride solution in the usual way. Cool, dilute, and oxidize any excess stannous chloride by the addition of saturated mercuric chloride solution. Titrate with standard ceric sulfate solution, prepared by dissolving an accurately weighed amount of anhydrous ceric sulfate, $Ce(SO_4)_2$ (formula weight, 332.25), equivalent to the normality required in 500 ml of 1 or $2N$ sulfuric acid and diluting to 1 liter with water. Erioglaucin, eriogreen, o-phenanthroline–ferrous complex, and other substances may be used as the indicator.

P. Barium

Barium salts are used in substantial amounts in about 20 industries, among which may be mentioned the manufacture of dyes, paints, chemicals, insecticides, linoleum, explosives, and incendiary bombs.

The soluble salts of barium are poisonous when ingested. Barium salts may cause dermatitis and loss of hair, as well as gastric symptoms, for these have been reported in industrial poisonings. The recommended maximum allowable concentration is 0.5 mg/m³.

1. Determination

The customary method for estimation of barium is precipitation as barium sulfate. Yagoda has developed a method for the estimation of barium (128) in atmospheric dusts that depends upon the fact that when barium sulfate is precipitated from solutions containing potassium permanganate, a marked pink color is imparted to the precipitate. In addition Yagoda uses his system of confined spot tests (129) and a special sampling bottle.

Sampling. Add 10 ml of 5% nitric acid to 30-ml Pyrex bottles (Fig. X-3) equipped with inverted ⚶ 19/22 stoppers and bubbling tubes. Adjust the bubbling tube when ready to sample and pass 30–45 liters of air through at a rate not exceeding 3 lpm. Wash down any dust collected on the bubbling tube with 1–3 ml of 5% nitric acid, running the acid through the funnel-shaped opening of the tube. Close the bottle with the cap and fasten with broad rubber bands.

Preparation of Sample. Transfer the sample to a No. 9 Coors low-form porcelain crucible and evaporate almost to dryness on a steam bath. Rinse the sampling bottle with 1–2 ml of concentrated nitric

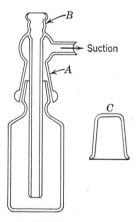

Fig. X-3. Sampling bottle: (A) bubbling tube with ⚶ 19/22 inverted stopper;
(B) entrance for sampled air; (C) ⚶ 19/22 cap.

acid and transfer the rinse to the crucible. Add 1 drop of 20% potassium nitrate solution and evaporate to dryness. Treat the residue with 1 ml of an ash aid consisting of 0.5% magnesium oxide dissolved in concentrated nitric acid and evaporate to dryness. Heat the dry crucible over a small flame until the evolution of nitrogen oxide stops. When cool the residue should be white; if not, add 0.5 ml of nitric acid, evaporate to dryness again, and reignite.

Dissolve the residue in a few drops of nitric acid and evaporate again almost to dryness on a steam bath. Add 1 ml of 10% potassium carbonate solution and evaporate to dryness. Digest the residue on the steam bath with 5 ml of water until all the caked matter is in suspension. Filter the precipitated magnesium carbonate carrying the trace of coprecipitated barium carbonate into a 3-ml sintered-glass filter funnel of porosity M by use of an eyedropper pipet with a rubber nipple of 0.2–0.3-ml displacement. Wash the crucible with several 1-ml portions of water until the wash water is free of alkali, using phenolphthalein solution as indicator. This washing is made more efficacious by repeatedly sucking the wash water into the tube and ejecting it against the walls of the crucible before transferring it to the funnel.

Add 0.5 ml of 5% nitric acid to the washed crucible, warm on the steam bath, and transfer to the filter containing the bulk of the carbonates. Support a 2-ml precipitation tube, requiring a No. 9 ground-glass stopper, beneath the stem of the funnel and after the magnesium carbonate is completely dissolved apply suction. Wash the crucible and funnel with several 0.3-ml portions of water until the 2-ml mark is almost reached. Cool to room temperature and adjust the volume carefully to 2 ml.

Reagents. *Primary Standard.* Dissolve 89.0 mg of barium chloride, $BaCl_2 \cdot 2H_2O$, in water and dilute to 1 liter. This solution contains 50 μg of barium per milliliter.

Recrystallized Potassium Permanganate. Dissolve 20 g of potassium permanganate, $KMnO_4$, in 100 ml of water, bring to boiling, and allow to simmer for 10 min. Filter the hot solution through a sintered-glass funnel of porosity M to remove hydrated manganese oxides and cool the filtrate rapidly by rotating the flask under a stream of tap water. When cold, filter off the crystals on a sintered-glass funnel, drain by suction, and dry the crystals in an oven at 105°C. Hold in a glass-stoppered bottle.

Potassium Sulfate. Grind fine crystals of potassium sulfate, K_2SO_4, to pass through an 80-mesh sieve. Separate the 80–100 mesh fraction by rejecting the fines passing through a 100-mesh sieve.

Precipitating Reagent. Mix equal parts by weight of recrystallized potassium permanganate and the 80–100 mesh potassium sulfate.

Reducing Solution. Dissolve 15 g of tartaric acid in 30 ml of water, cool, and add slowly with intermittent cooling 10 ml of concentrated sulfuric acid. Dilute to 50 ml and transfer to a dropping bottle. Note the number of drops equivalent to 0.3 ml of solution. The reduction of the permanganate is not instantaneous. The reaction starts about 1 min after the addition of the reducing solution and is completed about 3 min after the initial evolution of carbon dioxide.

Precipitation. Add 100 mg of the powdered potassium permanganate–potassium sulfate mixture to the test solution prepared as above, stopper the tube, and mix by inverting slowly for a period of 1 min. At the end of a 2-hr digestion period at room temperature, decolorize the permanganate by the addition of 0.3 ml of reducing solution. Prepare a series of standards containing 150, 75, 70, 25, 10, and 5 μg of barium by transfer of suitable aliquots of the primary standard to precipitation tubes and dilute to the 2-ml mark. Treat as above.

Filter the pink mixed crystals on C.S.S. No. 598 confined-spot-test papers, wash with water, and dry at room temperature. Compare with the standards in a field of uniform illumination. Small quantities are compared best under reflected light and larger quantities by transmitted light. The latter is done by immersing the papers in a petri dish containing carbon tetrachloride.

The intensity of the mixed barium crystals is reduced by calcium and strontium ions. When the lead/barium ratio exceeds 1:2, lead must be separated before the barium is estimated. Large amounts of trivalent iron interfere.

Q. Alkalies

Alkalies which have a significance in industrial hygiene are calcium hydroxide and oxide, barium hydroxide and oxide, sodium and potassium hydroxide, and sodium carbonate. These substances may cause dermatitis and conjunctivitis. Sodium and potassium hydroxides are extremely caustic and may cause severe and even fatal burns. Barium is also poisonous.

The alkalinity of the dust caused by these substances or, in general, of alkali-bearing dusts, fumes, and mists can be estimated by trapping the dust fume or mist in a known volume of standard acid, usually $0.02N$, and then determining the excess acid by back-titration with standard alkali solution. Sometimes water is used as the trapping medium and at times the pH of this is obtained. These may be sufficient for industrial-hygiene purposes. If further information is desirable, calcium may be determined as the oxalate, barium as the sulfate, sodium as the magnesium or zinc uranyl acetate complex, and potassium as potassium cobaltinitrite. For the details of these methods, the reader is referred to some of the texts listed at the end of the chapter.

R. Platinum

Exposure to complex platinum salts has been shown to cause symptoms (130) such as wheezing, coughing, running of the nose, tightness of the chest, shortness of breath, and cyanosis. This indicates that such atmospheres should be carefully controlled.

Traces of platinum in the air may be estimated spectrographically (131).

S. Palladium

Palladium and palladium salts are used chiefly in the electrical industry and in dentistry. The toxicology of palladium and methods of analysis have been reviewed by Meek, Harrold, and McCord (132).

T. Indium

Investigations of the toxicity of indium have shown that it possesses potentially highly toxic properties (133). Silver ornaments plated or diffused with indium appeared to have no irritant action. A method for the determination of indium in food and feces is described by Harrold, Meek, Whitman, and McCord (134).

References

1. Bloomfield, J. J., and W. Blum, *U.S. Public Health Rept.*, **43**, 2330 (1928).
2. "Beryllium Disease and Its Control," Conference held at Massachusetts Inst. Technol., Oct. 1958, *A.M.A. Arch. Ind. Health*, **19**, 91 (1959).
3. Peyton, M. F., and J. Worcester, *A.M.A. Arch. Ind. Health*, **19**, 94 (1959).
4. Hiser, R. A., H. M. Donaldson, and C. W. Schwenzfeier, *Am. Ind. Hyg. Assoc. J.*, **24**, 280 (1961).
5. Cholak, J., *A.M.A. Arch. Ind. Health*, **19**, 205 (1959).

6. Cholak, J., and D. M. Hubbard, *Anal. Chem.*, **20**, 73 (1948).
7. Fitzgerald, J. J., *A.M.A. Arch. Ind. Health*, **15**, 68 (1957).
8. Smith, R. G., and W. G. Fredrick, *Anal. Chem.*, **24**, 406 (1952).
9. Stross, W., and G. H. Osborn, *J. Soc. Chem. Ind.*, **63**, 249 (1944).
10. Gafafer, W. M., *U.S. Public Health Service Publ. 192* (1953).
11. Sayers, R. R., J. M. DallaValle, and W. P. Yant, *Ind. Eng. Chem.*, **26**, 1251 (1934).
12. Denton, C. R., R. G. Keenan, and D. J. Birmingham, *J. Invest. Derm.*, **23**, 189 (1954).
13. Bloomfield, J. J., and W. Blum, *U.S. Public Health Service Reprint 1245* (1928).
14. Vogel, F., *Z. Anal. Chem.*, **2**, 390 (1863).
15. Akatsuka, K., and L. T. Fairhall, *J. Ind. Hyg.*, **16**, 1 (1934).
16. Saltzman, B. E., *Anal. Chem.*, **24**, 1016 (1952).
17. Urone, P. F., M. L. Druschel, and H. K. Anders, *Anal. Chem.*, **22**, 472 (1950).
18. Quinby, R. S., *J. Ind. Hyg.*, **8**, 103 (1926).
19. Fairhall, L. T., and F. Hyslop, *U.S. Public Health Rept. Supplement 195* (1947).
20. Hillebrand, W. F., and G. E. F. Lundell, *Applied Inorganic Analysis*, Wiley, New York, 1929.
21. Goldstone, N. I., personal communication of unpublished work to the author, 1940.
22. Jacobs, M. B., unpublished work, 1940.
23. Maren, T. H., *Bull. Johns Hopkins Hosp.*, **77**, 338 (1945); *Anal. Chem.*, **19**, 487 (1947).
24. Conrad, C. P., *Chem. News*, **40**, 197 (1879).
25. Mellor, J. W., *A Comprehensive Treatise on Inorganic and Theoretical Chemistry*, Vol. IX, Longmans, Green, London, 1929.
26. Bamford, F., *Analyst*, **59**, 101 (1934).
27a. Sen, B. H., *Anal. Chim. Acta*, **24**, 386 (1961).
27b. Korenman, I. M., and G. A. Shatalina, *Tr. Khim. i Khim. Tekhnol.*, **1**, 352 (1958).
28. Anderson, C. W., *Ind. Eng. Chem. Anal. Ed.*, **11**, 224 (1939).
29. Goldstone, N. I., and M. B. Jacobs, *Ind. Eng. Chem. Anal. Ed.*, **16**, 206 (1944).
30. Fredrick, W. G., *Ind. Eng. Chem. Anal. Ed.*, **13**, 992 (1941).
31. Maren, T. H., *Bull. Johns Hopkins Hosp.*, **77**, 338 (1945).
32. Maren, T. H., *Anal. Chem.*, **19**, 487 (1947).
33. Webster, S. H., and L. T. Fairhall, *J. Ind. Hyg. Toxicol.*, **27**, 183 (1945).
34. Freedman, L. D., *Anal. Chem.*, **19**, 502 (1947).
35. Webster, S. H., *J. Ind. Hyg. Toxicol.*, **28**, 167 (1946).
36. Stock, A., and O. Guttman, *Chem. Ber.*, **37**, 885 (1904).
37. Webster, S. H., and L. T. Fairhall, *J. Ind. Hyg. Toxicol.*, **27**, 183 (1945).
38. Prodan, L., *J. Ind. Hyg.*, **14**, 132, 174 (1932).
39. Spolyar, L. W., J. F. Keppler, and H. G. Porter, *J. Ind. Hyg. Toxicol.*, **26**, 232 (1944).

40. Scott, A. W., and E. G. Adams, *J. Am. Chem. Soc.*, **57**, 2541 (1935).
41. Sandell, E. B., *Ind. Eng. Chem. Anal. Ed.*, **11**, 364 (1939).
42. Butts, P. G., A. R. Gahler, and M. G. Mellon, *Sewage Ind. Wastes*, **22**, 1543 (1950).
43. Saltzman, B. E., *Anal. Chem.*, **25**, 493 (1953).
44. Flinn, R. H., P. A. Neal, W. H. Reinhart, J. M. DallaValle, W. B. Fulton, and A. E. Dooley, *U.S. Public Health Service Bull. 247* (1940).
45. *Am. Standards* Z37.6-1942.
46. Willard, H. H., and L. H. Greathouse, *J. Am. Chem. Soc.*, **39**, 2366 (1917).
47. Richards, M. B., *Analyst*, **55**, 554 (1930).
48. *Standard Methods for the Examination of Water and Wastewater*, 11th ed., Am. Public Health Assoc., New York, 1960.
49. Marshall, H., *Chem. News*, **83**, 76 (1901).
50. Wester, D. H., *Rev. Trav. Chim.*, **39**, 414 (1920).
51. Dudley, H. C., *U.S. Public Health Service Reprint 1910* (1938).
52. Byers, H. G., *U.S. Dept. Agr. Tech. Bull. 530* (1936).
53. Munsell, H. E., G. M. DeVaney, and M. H. Kennedy, *U.S. Dept. Agr. Tech. Bull. 534* (1936).
54. Hamilton, A., *Industrial Toxicology*, Harper, New York, 1934.
55. Dudley, H. C., *Am. J. Hyg.*, **23**, 181 (1936).
57. Dudley, H. C., *Am. J. Hyg.*, **24**, 227 (1936).
59. Dudley, H. C., and H. G. Byers, *Ind. Eng. Chem. Anal. Ed.*, **7**, 3 (1934).
60. Dudley, H. C., *Am. J. Hyg.*, **23**, 169 (1936).
61. Robinson, W. O., H. C. Dudley, K. T. Williams, and H. G. Byers, *Ind. Eng. Chem. Anal. Ed.*, **6**, 274 (1934).
62. Chernyi, M. E., *Tr. i Materialy Inst. Eksperim. Med. Acad. Nauk Sverdlov.*, **1940**, No. 4, 175; *Ref. Zh. Khim.*, **4**, No. 5, 67 (1941); *Chem. Abstr.*, **37**, 5935 (1943).
63. Hoste, J., and J. Gillis, *Anal. Chim. Acta*, **12**, 158 (1955).
64. Cheng, K. L., *Anal. Chem.*, **28**, 1738 (1956).
65. Strenge, K., *Arch. Gewerbepathol. Gewerbehyg.*, **16**, 588 (1958).
66. Taussky, H., J. V. Comunale, A. Washington, and A. T. Milhorat, *Federation Proc.*, **20**, No. 1 (1961).
67. Cummins, L. M., J. L. Martin, G. W. Maag, and D. D. Maag, *Anal. Chem.*, **36**, 382 (1964).
68. Parker, C. A., and L. G. Harvey, *Analyst*, **86**, 54 (1961).
69. Watkinson, J. H., *Anal. Chem.*, **32**, 981 (1960).
70. Shie, M. D., and F. E. Deeds, *U.S. Public Health Rept.*, **35**, 939 (1920).
71. Steinberg, H. H., S. C. Massari, A. C. Miner, and R. Rink, *J. Ind. Hyg. Toxicol.*, **24**, 183 (1942).
72. Nelson, K. W., and D. M. Swingle, "Rapid Estimation of Selenium and Tellurium in Urine," Am. Ind. Hyg. Conf. Philadelphia, April 29, 1964; American Smelting and Refining Co., Salt Lake City, Utah.
73. Fairhall, L. T., *Ind. Hyg. Newsletter*, **7**, No. 1, 6 (1947).
74. Underhill, F. P., *Toxicology*, Blakiston, Philadelphia, 1928.
75. Danial, E. P., and R. D. Lillie, *U.S. Public Health Rept.*, **53**, 765 (1938).

76. Hillebrand, W. F., and G. E. F. Lundell, *Applied Inorganic Analysis*, Wiley, New York, 1929.
77. Marshall, H., *J. Soc. Chem. Ind.*, **19**, 994 (1900).
78. Zintl, E., and G. Rienaecker, *Z. Anorg. Allgem. Chem.*, **153**, 276 (1926).
79. Noyes, A. A., W. C. Bray, and E. B. Spear, *J. Am. Chem. Soc.*, **30**, 516, 559 (1908).
80. Reith, J. F., and K. W. Gerritsma, *Rec. Trav. Chim.*, **65**, 770 (1946).
81. Campbell, E. E., M. F. Milligan, and J. A. Lindsey, *Am. Ind. Hyg. Assoc. J.*, **20**, 23 (1959).
82. Gurev, S. D., *Nauchn. Tr. Gos. Nauchn. Issled. Inst., Tsvetnykh Metal., 1955*, No. 10, 371; *Ref. Zh. Khim.* 1956; Abstr. No. 4155; *Chem. Abstr.*, **52**, 970d (1958); *Anal. Abstr.*, **3**, 3301 (1956).
83. Shemeleva, G. C., and V. I. Petrashen, *Trudy Novocherk. Politekhn. Inst.*, **31**, 87 (1955); *Ref. Zh. Khim., 1957*, Abstr. No. 27164; *Chem. Abstr.*, **53**, 8937d (1959).
84. Jacobs, M. B., *Am. Ind. Hyg. Assoc. J.*, **23**, 411 (1962).
85. Hegsted, D. M., J. M. McKibben, and C. K. Drinker, *U.S. Public Health Rept. Supplement 179* (1945).
86. Hamilton, A., *Industrial Toxicology*, Harper, New York, 1934.
87. Sturgis, C. C., P. Drinker, and R. M. Thomson, *J. Ind. Hyg.*, **9**, 88 (1927).
88. Drinker, P., R. M. Thomson, and J. L. Finn, *J. Ind. Hyg.*, **9**, 98, 187, 331 (1927).
89. Koelsch, F., *J. Ind. Hyg.*, **5**, 87 (1923–24).
90. Drinker, C. K., and L. T. Fairhall, *U.S. Public Health Rept.*, **48**, 955 (1933).
91. Fairhall, L. T., *J. Ind. Hyg.*, **8**, 165 (1926).
92. Drinker, K. R., J. W. Fehnel, and M. Marsh, *J. Biol. Chem.*, **72**, 375 (1927).
93. Fairhall, L. T., and J. R. Richardson, *J. Am. Chem. Soc.*, **52**, 938 (1930).
94. Bartow, E., and O. M. Weigle, *Ind. Eng. Chem.*, **24**, 463 (1932).
95. *Standard Methods of Water Analysis*, 8th ed., Am. Public Health Assoc., New York, 1936.
96. Ouzdina, I. L., and N. F. Blajek, *Chim. Ind. (Paris)*, **37**, 1096 (1936).
97. Hibbard, P. L., *Ind. Eng. Chem. Anal. Ed.*, **9**, 127 (1937).
98. Moskowitz, S., and W. J. Burke, *N.Y. State Ind. Bull.*, **17**, 492 (1938).
99. *Methods Assoc. Official Agr. Chemists*, 6th ed., 1945.
100. Caldwell, J. R., and H. V. Moyer, *J. Am. Chem. Soc.*, **57**, 2372 (1935).
101. Mallory, F. B., *Am. J. Pathol.*, **1**, 117 (1925).
102. Mallory, F. B., *Arch. Internal Med.*, **37**, 336 (1926).
103. *Methods Assoc. Official Agr. Chemists*, 6th ed., 1945.
104. Callan, T., and J. A. R. Henderson, *Analyst*, **54**, 650 (1929).
105. Haddock, L. A., and N. Evers, *Analyst*, **57**, 495 (1932).
106. Burke, W. J., S. Moskowitz, J. Siegel, B. H. Dolin, and C. B. Ford, *Industrial Air Analysis*, Division of Industrial Hygiene, N.Y. State Dept. Labor, New York, 1943.
107. Pedley, F. G., *J. Ind. Hyg.*, **9**, 43 (1927).
108. Seifter, J., *J. Pharmacol.*, **66**, 32 (1939).
109. DeGiacomi, R., *Analyst*, **65**, 216 (1940).

110. Drinker, K. R., L. T. Fairhall, G. B. Ray, and C. K. Drinker, *J. Ind. Hyg.*, **6**, 307 (1924).

111. Amor, A. J., *J. Ind. Hyg.*, **14**, 216 (1932).

112. Armit, H. W., *J. Hyg.*, **7**, 525 (1907); **8**, 565 (1908).

113. Jones, H. O., and H. S. Tasker, *J. Chem. Soc.*, **95**, 1905 (1909).

114. Fairhall, L. T., *J. Ind. Hyg.*, **8**, 528 (1926).

115. Drinker, K. R., L. T. Fairhall, G. B. Ray, and C. K. Drinker, *J. Ind. Hyg.*, **6**, 346 (1924).

116. Yoe, J. H., and F. H. Wirsing, *J. Am. Chem. Soc.*, **54**, 1866 (1932).

117. Diehl, H. C., *The Applications of the Dioximes to Analytical Chemistry*, Iowa State College, Ames, 1940.

118. Prodinger, W., *Organic Reagents Used in Quantitative Inorganic Analysis*, Elsevier, New York, 1940.

119. Fairhall, L. T., *Ind. Hyg. Newsletter*, **6**, No. 10, 6 (1946).

120. Schwartz, L., S. M. Peck, K. E. Blair, and K. E. Markuson, *J. Allergy*, **16**, 51 (1945).

121. Keenan, R. G., and B. M. Flick, *Anal. Chem.*, **20**, 1238 (1948); R. S. Young, E. T. Pinkney, and R. Dick, *Ind. Eng. Chem. Anal. Ed.*, **18**, 474 (1946).

122. Roscoe, H. E., and H. E. Scudder, *Proc. Chem. Soc.*, **7**, 126 (1891).

123. Griffith, R. H., and G. C. Holliday, *J. Soc. Chem. Ind.*, **47**, 311 (1928).

124. Lunge, G., and H. R. Ambler, *Technical Gas Analysis*, Van Nostrand, New York, 1934.

125. Noyes, A. M., A. Tienson, G. W. Daubenspeck, L. Kirschner, and R. Rink, *Illinois State Dept. Labor Tech. Paper 4* (1944).

126. Drinker, P., and A. G. Cranch, *U.S. Dept. Labor, Div. Labor Standards, Special Bull. 5* (1942).

127. Harrold, G. C., S. F. Meek, and C. P. McCord, *J. Ind. Hyg. Toxicol.*, **22**, 347 (1940).

128. Yagoda, H., *J. Ind. Hyg. Toxicol.*, **26**, 224 (1944).

129. Yagoda, H., *Ind. Eng. Chem. Anal. Ed.*, **9**, 79 (1937).

130. Hunter, D., R. Milton, and K. M. A. Perry, *Brit. J. Ind. Med.*, **2**, 92 (1945).

131. Fothergill, S. J. R., D. F. Withers, and F. S. Clements, *Brit. J. Ind. Med.*, **2**, 99 (1945).

132. Meek, S. F., G. C. Harrold, and C. P. McCord, *Ind. Med.*, July, 1943.

133. McCord, C. P., S. F. Meek, C. G. Harrold, and C. E. Heussner, *J. Ind. Hyg. Toxicol.*, **24**, 243 (1942).

134. Harrold, G. C., S. F. Meek, N. Whitman, and C. P. McCord, *J. Hyg. Toxicol.*, **25**, 233 (1943).

General References

Bloomfield, J. J., and W. Blum, "Health Hazards in Chromium Plating," *U.S. Public Health Service Reprint 1245* (1928).

Cook, W. A., "Chemical Procedures in Air Analysis. Methods for the Determination of Poisonous Atmospheric Contaminants," *Am. Public Health Assoc. Yearbook 1935–36*, p. 80.

Diehl, H. C., *The Applications of the Dioximes to Analytical Chemistry*, Iowa State College, Ames, 1940.

Dudley, H. C., "Selenium as a Potential Industrial Hazard," *U.S. Public Service Reprint 1910* (1938).

Flinn, R. H., P. A. Neal, W. H. Reinhard, J. M. DallaValle, W. B. Fulton, and A. E. Dooley, "Chronic Manganese Poisoning in an Ore-Crushing Mill," *U.S. Public Health Service Bull. 247* (1940).

Furman, N. H., *Scott's Standard Methods of Chemical Analysis*, Van Nostrand, New York, 1939.

Hamilton, A., *Industrial Toxicology*, Harper, New York, 1934.

Hillebrand, W. F., and G. E. F. Lundell, *Applied Inorganic Analysis*, Wiley, New York, 1929.

Lanza, A. J., and J. A. Goldberg, *Industrial Hygiene*, Oxford, New York, 1939.

Methods Assoc. Official Agr. Chemists, 10th ed., 1962.

Moore, R. B., S. C. Lind, J. W. Marden, J. P. Bonardi, L. W. Davis, and J. E. Conley, "Analytical Methods for Certain Metals, Including Cerium, Thorium, Molybdenum, Tungsten, Radium, Uranium, Vanadium, Titanium, and Zirconium," *U.S. Bur. Mines Bull. 212* (1923).

Noyes, A. M., A. Tienson, G. W. Daubenspeck, L. Kirschner, and R. Rink, "Industrial Survey of Arc Welding Operations," *Illinois State Dept. Labor Tech. Paper 4* (1944).

Patty, F. A., Ed., *Industrial Hygiene and Toxicology*, 2nd ed., Interscience, New York, 1962.

Prodinger, W., *Organic Reagents Used in Quantitative Inorganic Analysis*, Elsevier, New York, 1940.

Standard Methods of Water Analysis, 11th ed., Am. Public Health Assoc., New York, 1960.

Steward, C. P., and A. Stolman, *Toxicology, Mechanisms and Analytical Methods*, Academic Press, New York, 1961.

Underhill, F. P., *Toxicology*, Blakiston, Philadelphia, 1928.

CHAPTER XI

RADIOCHEMICAL DETERMINATIONS

The development of nuclear energy and its utilization for industrial purposes has presented industrial hygienists with a problem of the first magnitude. It is beyond the scope of this text to discuss the problem adequately. Methods involving radiochemical treatment will, however, be considered. The control of radioactivity hazards is discussed by Sullivan (1) and by Morgan (2). These hazards arise from exposure to fast and thermal neutrons, gamma rays, x-rays, beta rays, alpha rays and emitters of alpha rays, and radioactive fission products. The hazards, particularly in the last instance, can be considered as (1) external radiation effects; (2) internal effects in the lungs and gastrointestinal tract following inhalation and ingestion; and (3) effects produced after absorption by the body tissues of radioactive material present in the blood stream as a result of prior inhalation, ingestion, penetration through the skin, or injection through cuts and wounds of such radioactive material.

Before the development of nuclear energy, exposure of industrial workers to radioactive substances occurred chiefly in the luminous paint industry. Luminous paint is made from zinc sulfide crystals which have been made radioactive by the addition of radium compounds. Sometimes mesothorium is added when a cheaper paint is desired, although this substitution is diminishing. The dry materials are mixed with oil and a thinner, sometimes with shellac or varnish, or with an adhesive such as gum arabic and water. Other radioactive material has been made available for this purpose. Luminous paint is used for watch and clock dials, gauge and other indicating dials on airplanes and automobiles, on scientific instrument panels, for glass drops on lamp indicators, and for house and Pullman-berth numbers and the like (3,4). Thorium compounds are radioactive and several instances of illness have been described as arising from this source (5).

Physicians, dentists, and technicians using radioactive materials for fluoroscopy and radiography are also exposed, but it has been suggested that the term radium poisoning should be limited to those conditions in which radium, mesothorium, or other radioactive substances are ingested, inhaled, or have been injected, and should not include untoward results from exposure to external radiation. This is a debatable definition.

Since the explosion of the first "atomic" bomb on July 16, 1945, at Alamogordo, New Mexico, and the subsequent use of plutonium, uranium-235, and "hydrogen" or thermonuclear bombs as weapons and test weapons, there has been intense interest in the possibility of damage to health that can be attributed to the intake of radioactive material, principally from radioactive fallout.

It was on March 1, 1954, that a combination fission–thermonuclear bomb was exploded at Bikini in the Pacific Ocean. In this type of weapon an atomic plutonium or uranium-235 fission-type bomb is used to trigger a thermonuclear or hydrogen bomb and fast neutrons from the latter cause the uranium casing to undergo fission. Such a bomb is in the megaton (approximately equivalent to 15 million tons of TNT in this instance) range and huge quantities of radioactive materials are produced.

The Japanese tuna-fishing sampan, *Daigo Fukuryu Maru* (Lucky Dragon No. 5) was unlucky enough to be showered by the radioactive fallout from the aforementioned bomb. As a result of this exposure, 1 crewman died and some 20 other crewmen were hospitalized for over one year. The fish catch was found to be contaminated and had to be destroyed.

It would, however, be a mistake to assume that the danger from radioactive fallout is only caused by or may only be caused by the testing of atomic and thermonuclear weapons. There has been some development of energy production from nuclear sources and this development will increase markedly in the future. Such industrial applications of nuclear materials inevitably bring with them the danger of air contamination and radioactive fallout. The classic example of such fallout from an industrial source is the "atomic mishap" at the Windscale Plutonium Plant in England on October 10, 1957. In this accident, an overheated reactor, in a plant presumably shut down for repair, sprayed an area of over 200 square miles with radioactive iodine-131. In this instance, since radioactive iodine-131 is short lived, and steps were taken to minimize the danger, it was fortunate that no harm resulted. It is clear, however, that methods must be available to evaluate such danger.

TABLE XI-1

Generally Useful Samples for Evaluation of Environmental Contamination (6)

Environment	Radionuclides apparently of greatest interest	Remarks
Air	Any that are disseminated	See Table XI-4 for list in order of importance
Drinking water	Any that are disseminated	See Table XI-5 for list in order of importance
Soils	^{89}Sr, ^{90}Sr, ^{226}Ra	
Vegetation	^{131}I, ^{89}Sr, ^{90}Sr, ^{137}Cs, ^{226}Ra, ^{140}Ba	
Milk	^{89}Sr, ^{90}Sr, ^{137}Cs, ^{131}I, ^{140}Ba, ^{226}Ra	
Other dairy products	^{89}Sr, ^{90}Sr, ^{137}Cs, ^{226}Ra	Only for external contamination of product
Meat	^{137}Cs	
Thyroid glands	^{131}I	
Animal bone	^{89}Sr, ^{90}Sr, ^{226}Ra	
Terrestrial water	Any that are disseminated	See Table XI-5 for list in order of importance
Aquatic food	^{89}Sr, ^{90}Sr, ^{137}Cs, ^{60}Co, ^{106}Ru, ^{65}Zn, ^{55}Fe, ^{59}Fe, ^{141}Ce, ^{144}Ce	Attention must be given to concentration of specific radionuclides by various tissues and organisms

TABLE XI-2

Maximum Permissible Exposure to Radiation (7)

Type of radiation	Mr/day	Mrep/day	Mrem/day
X-ray	100	100	100
Gamma	100	100	100
Beta	—	100	100
Fast neutron	—	20	100
Thermal neutron	—	50	100
Alpha[a]	—	10	100

[a] This alpha-tolerance level is considered only from the standpoint of internal irradiation effects.

The International Commission on Radiological Protection (6) has compiled a table of generally useful samples for evaluation of environmental contamination (Table XI-1).

The first symptoms are generally skin disorders, burns, ulceration of the skin, trouble with the teeth, and the like. Later symptoms are

TABLE XI-3
Maximum Permissible Exposure to Radiation (8)

Material or radiation	Radiant energy	Material or radiation	Radiant energy
Gamma (roentgen/day)	0.1	Thoron (curies/m³)	10^{-8}
Radon (curies/m³)	10^{-8}	X-ray (roentgen/day)	0.1

TABLE XI-4
Maximum Permissible Concentration in Air for Occupational Exposure (8)

Radionuclide	$\mu c/cm^3$ air	Types of radiation emitted
^{239}Pu (sol. or insol.)	2×10^{-12}	α, γ
^{227}Ac + daughters	4×10^{-12}	α, β^-, γ
^{226}Ra + 55% of daughters	8×10^{-12}	α, β^-, γ
Natural Th (sol. or insol.)	3×10^{-11}	α, β^-, γ
Natural U (sol. or insol.)	3×10^{-11}	α, β^-, γ
^{233}U (sol. or insol.)	3×10^{-11}	α, γ
^{241}Am	4×10^{-11}	α, γ
^{210}Pb + daughters	8×10^{-11}	α, β^-, γ
^{210}Po (insol.)	10^{-10}	α, γ
$^{90}Sr-^{90}Y$	2×10^{-10}	β^-
^{242}Cm	2×10^{-10}	α
^{210}Po (sol.)	5×10^{-10}	α, γ
^{211}At	5×10^{-10}	K, α
^{154}Eu	2×10^{-9}	β^-, γ
$^{144}Ce-^{144}Pr$	2×10^{-9}	β^-, γ
^{151}Sm	3×10^{-9}	β^-
^{131}I	6×10^{-9}	β^-, γ
^{45}Ca	8×10^{-9}	β^-
^{91}Y	9×10^{-9}	β^-
^{89}Sr	2×10^{-8}	β^-
$^{106}Ru-^{106}Rh$	2×10^{-8}	β^-, γ
$^{140}Ba-^{140}La$	2×10^{-8}	β^-, γ
$^{95}Zr-^{95}Nb$	8×10^{-8}	β^-, γ
^{32}P	10^{-7}	β^-
^3H	10^{-5}	β^-

blood disorders with severe anemia, lung disorders, and bone disorders such as necrosis and suppuration of the bones, especially the jaw bone.

The tolerance recommended for total or limited body exposure is 0.1 rem for a 24-hr period. The roentgen equivalent man, or rem, is defined as that quantity of radiation which, when absorbed by man, produces an effect equivalent to the absorption by man of 1 roentgen of x- or gamma radiation. Sullivan points out that it is undesirable to work in radiation fields of greater than 1 roentgen/hr, which gives an exposure time limit of 6 min.

TABLE XI-5

Maximum Permissible Concentration in Water for Occupational Exposure (8)

Radionuclide	$\mu c/cm^3$ water	Types of radiation emitted
^{226}Ra + 55% daughters	4×10^{-8}	α, β^-, γ
Natural Th	5×10^{-7}	α, β^-, γ
^{90}Sr–^{90}Y	8×10^{-7}	β^-
^{210}Pb + daughters	2×10^{-6}	α, β^-, γ
Natural U (sol.)	2×10^{-6}	α, β^-, γ
^{242}Cm	2×10^{-6}	α
^{210}Po	3×10^{-6}	α, γ
^{211}At	3×10^{-6}	K, α
^{227}Ac + daughters	3×10^{-6}	α, β^-, γ
^{233}U (sol.)	3×10^{-6}	α, γ
^{239}Pu (sol.)	3×10^{-6}	α, γ
^{241}Am	3×10^{-6}	α, γ
^{131}I	6×10^{-5}	β^-, γ
^{89}Sr	7×10^{-5}	β^-
^{45}Ca	10^{-4}	β^-
^{106}Ru–^{106}Rh	10^{-4}	β^-, γ
^{32}P	2×10^{-4}	β^-
^{91}Y	3×10^{-4}	β^-
^{140}Ba–^{140}La	3×10^{-4}	β^-, γ
^{154}Eu	4×10^{-4}	β^-, γ
^{95}Zr–^{95}Nb	6×10^{-4}	β^-, γ
^{144}Ce–^{144}Pr	8×10^{-3}	β^-, γ
^{151}Sm	8×10^{-3}	β^-
^{3}H	0.2	β^-

Since fast neutrons are about five times as damaging as x- or gamma rays, the tolerance set at the Clinton National Laboratory for this type of radiation was 20 mrep. The roentgen equivalent physical, or rep, is the intensity of radiation such that it may be absorbed at the rate of 83 ergs per gram of tissue. An rep becomes a roentgen if the radiation is x or gamma and the absorption takes place in air. The tolerance or maximum permissible exposure to radiation adopted at the Clinton National Laboratory is tabulated in Table XI-2 and that of the Governmental Hygienists in Table XI-3.

One can classify the major sources of radioactive contamination in the 1960s as (1) ore production and processing, (2) nuclear fuel production, (3) nuclear reactor installation, (4) nuclear fuel reprocessing plants, (5) radioactive wastes disposal, (6) hospitals (and as mentioned in the prior paragraph), (7) laboratories utilizing radioisotopes, (8) industrial applications, (9) military and defense utilization, (10) fallout, and (11) natural background exposure.

The maximum permissible body burdens and maximum permissible concentration of radionuclides in air and water or food for occupational exposure have been discussed in detail in the report of the International Commission on Radiological Protection (ICRP) (6) and have been tabulated by the National Committee on Radiation Protection (NCRP). It is unnecessary to repeat these recommendations in full here. The basic standards will, however, be quoted and Tables XI-4 and XI-5 contain data concerning the MPCs of the more important radionuclides.

A. Basic Standards of Maximum Permissible Radiation Exposure (10)

The NCRP has formulated the four following basic rules and recommendations concerning exposure to ionizing radiation.

1. BASIC RULES

a. Accumulated Dose (Radiation Workers)

External Exposure to Critical Organs: Whole Body, Head and Trunk, Active Blood-Forming Organs, Eyes, or Gonads. The maximum permissible dose (MPD) to the most critical organs, accumulated at any age, shall not exceed 5 rem multiplied by the number of years beyond age 18, and the dose in any 13 consecutive weeks shall not exceed 3 rem.

Thus, the accumulated MPR = $(N - 18) \times 5$ rem where N is the age in years and is greater than 18.

COMMENT: This applies to radiation of sufficient penetrating power to affect a significant fraction of the critical tissue.

External Exposure to Other Organs. Skin of Whole Body.
MPD = 10 $(N - 18)$ rems, and the dose in any 13 consecutive weeks shall not exceed 6 rem.

COMMENT: This rule applies to radiation of low penetrating power.

Hands and Forearms, Feet and Ankles. MPD = 75 rem/year, and the dose in any 13 consecutive weeks shall not exceed 25 rem.

Internal Exposures. The permissible levels from internal emitters will be consistent as far as possible with the age-proration and dose principles above. Control of the internal dose will be achieved by limiting the body burden of radioisotopes. This will generally be accomplished by control of the average concentration of radioactive materials in the air, water, or food taken into the body. Since it would be impractical to set different MPC values for air, water and food for radiation workers as a function of age, the MPC values are selected in such a manner that they conform to the above-stated limits when applied to the most restrictive case, viz., they are set to be applicable to radiation workers of age 18. Thus, the values are conservative and are applicable to radiation workers of any age (assuming there is no occupational exposure to radiation permitted at age less than 18).

The maximum permissible average concentrations of radionuclides in air and water are determined from biological data whenever such data are available, or are calculated on the basis of an averaged annual dose of 15 rem for most individual organs of the body, 30 rem when the critical organ is the thyroid or skin, and 5 rem when the gonads or the whole body is the critical organ. For bone seekers the maximum permissible limit is based on the distribution of the deposit, the relative biological effectiveness (RBE), and a comparison of the energy release in the bone with the energy release delivered by a maximum permissible body burden of 0.1 μg of ^{226}Ra plus daughters.

b. Emergency Dose (Radiation Workers)

An accidental or emergency dose of 25 rem to the whole body or a major portion thereof, occurring only once in the lifetime of the person need not be included in the determination of the radiation exposure status of that person.

c. Medical Dose (Radiation Workers)

Radiation exposures resulting from necessary medical and dental procedures need not be included in the determination of the radiation exposure status of the person concerned.

d. Dose to Persons In the Neighborhood of Controlled Areas

The radiation or radioactive material outside a controlled area, attributable to normal operations within the controlled area, shall be such that it is improbable that any individual will receive a dose of more than 0.5 rem in any 1 year from external radiation.

The maximum permissible average body burden of radionuclides in persons outside of the controlled area and attributable to the operations within the controlled area shall not exceed one-tenth of that for radiation workers, based on continuous occupational exposure for a 168-hr week. This will generally entail control of the average concentrations in air or water at the point of intake, or of the rate of intake to the body in foodstuffs, to levels not exceeding one-tenth of the maximum permissible concentrations allowed in air, water, and foodstuffs for continuous occupational exposure. The body burden and concentrations of radionuclides may be averaged over periods up to 1 year.

The maximum permissible dose and the maximum permissible concentrations of radionuclides as recommended above are primarily for the purpose of keeping the average dose to the whole population as low as reasonably possible, and not because of the likelihood of specific injury to the individual.

2. Detection of Exposure

The monitoring of personnel, plant, equipment, and air so that exposure to dangerous concentrations of radioactive material is prevented is a difficult problem. The principal devices for the evaluation of radioactive hazards are electroscopes and Geiger-Müller counters. The latter consist of vacuum tubes in the form of an envelope containing copper or other metal cylinders charged negatively through which positively charged wires are stretched. The tubes contain neon, argon, helium, or krypton and ethyl ether or ethyl alcohol at very low pressure, the latter making the tube self-quenching. Energy of high radiation such as those mentioned in the previous discussion can penetrate the thin-wall glass window or envelope of such counters and can ionize or charge the neutral gas molecules. Sometimes thin windows of Lindemann glass, mica, or beryllium form one end of the envelope. The positive particles move toward the metal wall and the electrons move toward the charged wire, creating a pulse of electricity. This is amplified and each pulse may be counted. The intensity of radiation is measured by counting the pulses or by meter deflection. Morgan (11) does not recommend the use of Geiger-Müller counters for quantitative health-physics measurements.

One type of device using the ionization method (12) for measurement of individual exposure consists of a cylindrical ionization chamber about the size of a fountain pen, adequately insulated. In use, it is inserted in the bushing of the case of a string electrometer. In this way the central electrode of the ionization chamber is brought into contact with the rod extending from the insulated fiber of the electrometer. The central rod of the chamber and the fiber of the electrometer are brought to a definite voltage by an energy source inside the case through a contact key, and the corresponding reading of the electrometer serves as the zero of the instrument for dosage measurements.

The ionization chamber is now removed and can be carried by the individual while working. The ionization chamber is again connected to the electrometer at the end of the day and the deflection of the electrometer is noted. With a calibrated instrument, a direct reading of the exposure dose in roentgens can be obtained. The assumption made concerning this reading is that the decrease in voltage of the central electrode of the ionization chamber is entirely due to the ionization of the air in the chamber curing the exposure period.

Alternative means of monitoring exposures to radioactive hazards are available. These are film badges containing films, sensitive to gamma, beta, and x-rays, sealed in a waterproof cover with a lead cross fastened to the outside of the badge (13). The less penetrating beta rays will darken the film not protected by the lead, while the penetrating x- and gamma rays will interact with the lead, giving secondary radiations which will in turn affect the film underneath. After 1 or 2 weeks the density of the film is determined optically and compared with standard films so that the total ionizing radiation received by the wearer in that period can be estimated. Each lot of film must be calibrated.

Diamonds are highly sensitive to gamma rays and may be used to detect this type of radiation in the same way as a Geiger-Müller counter. When a diamond is placed in a strong electric field, it can initiate sharp electrical pulses when gamma radiation is absorbed (14).

Bloomfield and Knowles (15) sampled atmospheric dust with the paper thimble. Single-thickness Whatman extraction paper thimbles, 100 × 25 mm, containing well-fluffed cotton wool to reduce clogging are suitable. The thimble is placed in an appropriate holder at the worker's breathing level, usually less than 1 ft from the face, and air is passed through the thimble at a rate of 2 cfm, measured by a calibrated orifice meter or other device. Air samples of various sizes, from 60 to 200 cu ft, should be taken at representative positions. The settled dust should also be sampled because it gives off emanations and radiation. At the Clinton National Laboratory, electrical precipitators were used for collecting suspended radioactive products from the air. A cylindrical aluminum foil was used to collect the dust and its activity was measured by alpha, beta, and gamma counters.

The thimbles or dust are ashed and the ash is fused with potassium acid sulfate, $KHSO_4$, and then analyzed electroscopically according to the method of Barker (16), or as described by Roberts (17).

Ives, Knowles, and Britten (18,19) used a Wulf electroscope for gamma-ray determinations and estimated thoron and radon with the Lind electroscope. Morgan (2) considers the fiber electroscope of the Landsverk-Wollan or Lauritsen types to be a most reliable survey instrument.

To measure alpha-particle active dust such as that emitted by uranium, plutonium, and radium, Carmichael and Tunnicliffe (20) suggest the use of a filter apparatus or a precipitator. The latter gives more consistent results and higher counts. Six hours are permitted to elapse after the collection of the samples in order to permit the natural alpha-particle activity of atmospheric dust to decay. Then the counts are made with a special counter (21) of the methane proportional type which only counts alpha particles even in the presence of strong beta-particle activity.

Neutrons, in contradistinction to alpha particles, protons, and beta particles, carry no electrical charge, hence, they do not ionize atoms directly as do charged particles. For this reason their concentration cannot be measured as are charged particles or x- or gamma rays. They do produce, however, secondary effects and consequently some measure of individual exposure can be obtained by an evaluation of these secondary effects. These are conditioned by the type of neutron and neutrons are classified for this purpose into two groups, fast neutrons and slow neutrons.

By making the walls of the ionization chamber, described above, of a material containing hydrogen atoms, such as Bakelite, the concentration of fast neutrons, can be estimated, for though the fast neutrons have no charge, on collision with hydrogen atoms they give up much of their energy to the hydrogen atoms producing protons. The number of protons produced can then be measured.

Slow neutrons are very quickly absorbed by matter, resulting in production of new types of atoms with subsequent liberation of gamma and beta rays. When they impinge on the body, the radiations produced, principally gamma rays, can be measured by a device for evaluating gamma rays held close to the body.

For additional information on the estimation of exposure to radioactive material, the reader is referred to Curtiss (22) and to the symposium on nucleonics and analytical chemistry (23) sponsored by the Division of Analytical and Micro Chemistry of the American Chemical Society, in 1948.

B. Radiotoxicity

It has been stressed by Kahn and Goldin (24) and by many others that the mere determination of the amount of radioactivity of a material is not an adequate measure of the possible damage that such a material can cause or the hazard that may be expected. Such possible damage can only be evaluated on the basis of the biochemical and physical properties of the radionuclides present in the material. The dose rate to an organ from the inhalation or the ingestion of such a radioactive material depends on the amount inhaled or ingested, the fraction reaching the organ in question, the effective energy, the effective half-life, the time of exposure, and the mass of the critical organ, as discussed in detail in *Handbook 69* of the National Bureau of Standards (10). Slack and Way (25) discuss in detail the radiations of 18 of the most frequently used radioisotopes.

One can, for instance, calculate the dose rate to bone from the continuous ingestion over a long period of three different radionuclides like strontium-90, phosphorus-32, and molybdenum-99. The ingestion of these three isotopes, for example, from radioactive fallout on water, for a 40-yr period at a level of 100 $\mu\mu c$/ml (10^{-4} μc/ml) or 1000 times the maximum permissible concentration for isotopes of unknown composition, would reach the respective bone dose rates of 11 rem per week for strontium-90, 0.0333 rem per week for phosphorus-32, and 0.000002 rem per week for molybdenum-99. For comparison, it can be noted that the occupational permissible dose is 0.1 rem per week. These values indicate that strontium-90 is about 300 times as toxic as phosphorus-32 and some 5 million times as toxic as molybdenum-99. Kahn and Goldin (24) point out that while these values would be modified if exposure to the intestinal tract were also considered, they serve to illustrate the difference in dosage resulting from the inhalation or ingestion of equal quantities of activity of different nuclides.

The measurement of gross activity alone is not adequate for the evaluation of a radioactivity problem. It is necessary to know what particular kinds of radioactivity are present. The determination of strontium-90 in a mixture of the aforementioned three radionuclides would be of greater value than a determination of the gross activity.

The significance of a radionuclide is due not only to its relative radiotoxicity but also to its concentration. Among the more abundant radioisotopes and consequently the more likely to be present in appreciable concentrations in fallout and rainout are the major fission products and heavy elements resulting from the operation of nuclear reactors, the naturally occurring radioactive elements and their compounds, and some radionuclides made in quantity because of their usefulness. Some of the important radioisotopes are given in Table IX-6. The relative importance of such nuclides depends upon their low maximum allowable concentration or conversely their high toxicity or their high abundance or both. In Table XI-6, it is shown that the toxicity of these radioisotopes varies over a wide range. Thus, the maximum permissible concentrations range from 40 $\mu\mu c$/kg for radium-226 to 2 million $\mu\mu c$/kg for cesium-137 and niobium-95, respectively.

Kahn and Goldin (24) suggested that a term, pMPC, representing the comparative toxicity be used in addition to the conventional maximum permissible concentration. This term, pMPC, is analogous to pH, for it is defined as the negative logarithm of the concentration, expressed in microcuries per gram or microcuries per milliliter. Thus, it can be employed as a convenient unit for it has the advantages of

TABLE XI-6
Some Hazardous Radionuclides (24)

Nuclide	Origin	MPC in water[a]		pMPC$_w$
		μc/ml	$\mu\mu$c/liter	
^{226}Ra	Natural	4×10^{-8}	40	7.4
Unknown	—	1×10^{-7}	100	7.0
^{90}Sr	Fission product	8×10^{-7}	800	6.1
^{210}Po	Natural	3×10^{-6}(g)	3,000(g)	5.5
^{233}U	Irradiation	3×10^{-6}(g)	3,000(g)	5.5
^{239}Pu	Irradiation	3×10^{-6}(g)	3,000(g)	5.5
^{241}Am	Irradiation	3×10^{-6}(g)	3,000(g)	5.5
^{131}I	Fission product	6×10^{-5}	60,000	4.2
^{89}Sr	Fission product	7×10^{-5}	70,000	4.2
^{45}Ca	Irradiation	1×10^{-4}	100,000	4.0
^{106}Ru	Fission product	1×10^{-4}(g)	100,000(g)	4.0
^{144}Ce	Fission product	1×10^{-4}(g)	100,000(g)	4.0
^{32}P	Irradiation	2×10^{-4}	200,000	3.7
^{60}Co	Irradiation	4×10^{-4}	400,000	3.4
^{95}Nb	Fission product	2×10^{-3}	2,000,000	2.7
^{137}Cs	Fission product	2×10^{-3}	2,000,000	2.7

[a] MPC values marked (g) are for damage to the intestinal tract and are one-day values from K. Z. Morgan and M. R. Ford, *Nucleonics*, **12**, No. 6, 32 (1954); other values from the Report of Sub-Committee II, ICRP (Recommendations of the Committee on Radiation Protection (ICRP), Supplement 6, British Institute of Radiology, London, 1955, p. 23.

eliminating the exponential notation and of using a larger, rather than a smaller, number for a radioisotope of greater toxicity.

Attention was called by Shipman, Simone, and Weiss (26) to the possibility that manganese-54 might be a dangerous nuclide for it has a relatively long half-life of 291 days.

C. Counting

As will be stressed in the section on identification in this chapter, the characterization of a specific radionuclide may depend on the type of radiation, namely, alpha, beta, or gamma or the energy of the disintegration (see Table XI-7). Counting procedures depend on such characteristics also. The disintegration of radioactive nuclides yields alpha or beta particles which may or may not be accompanied by the emission of gamma rays. These emissions are detected by

TABLE XI-7
Characteristics of Radiations

Radiation	Type	Charge	Typical energy range	Path length[a]		Primary mechanism of energy loss	General comments
				Air	Solid		
Alpha	Particles	2+	5–9 MeV	3–5 cm	25–40 μ	Ionization, excitation	Identical to ionized He nuclei, arise from nucleus
Beta	Particle	—	0–4 MeV	0–10 m	0–1 mm	Ionization, excitation	Identical to electron, arise from nucleus
Neutron	Particle	None	0–10 MeV	0–100 m	0–cm	Elastic collision with nuclei	Arise from nuclear bombardment
X-ray	Electromagnetic radiation	None	eV–100 keV	μ–10 m	cm	Photoelectric effect	Photons arising from atomic electron transitions
Gamma ray	Electromagnetic radiation	None	10 keV–3 MeV	cm–100 m	mm–10 cm	Photoelectric effect, Compton effect, pair production	Photons arising from nuclear transitions

[a] Exponential attenuation in the case of electromagnetic radiation.

TABLE XI-8
Characteristics of Detectors

	Ionization chamber	Proportional counter	Geiger-Müller counter	Scintillator photomultiplier
Sensitive medium	Gas	Gas	Gas	Solid
Detector multiplication	1	10^2–10^4	10^7	10^7
Output signal, V	10^{-6}–10^{-3}	10^{-4}–10	0.1–10.0	10^{-2}–10.0
Resolving time, min	10^{-6}–10^{-3}	10^{-6}	10^{-4}–10^{-3}	10^{-9}–10^{-6}
Efficiency				
Electron	Low	High	High	Medium
X	Low	Medium	Medium	High
Gamma	Low	Low	Low	Very high
Electronic gain required	Very high	High	Low	Medium

instruments and it is the function of such instruments to do this as efficiently as possible.

While usually any detector instrument will have some sensitivity to all the different types of radiation, there is no single type of instrument that will be satisfactory for all detection work. It is preferable to use a specific type of instrument for a specific type of radiation. Consequently, the instrument selected will depend on the characteristics of the radiation emitted by the material being analyzed. In Table XI-8 the properties of the principal types of detection instruments are tabulated. These depend mainly on gas counting, such as internal proportional counters and Geiger-Müller counters, or on scintillation counting.

The actual method of counting used, however, will depend in large measure on the instrumentation available. Consequently, the analyst must obtain the details of the procedures of counting recommended by the manufacturer of the particular equipment purchased. To give a general picture of such procedures the counting methods suggested by the Sanitary Engineering Center of the United States Public Health Service will be detailed (27).

Most counters work on the principle of collecting the electrons that are produced by the passage of alpha or beta particles through a counter gas. These electrons are drawn to a thin wire maintained at a high positive voltage. The USPHS suggests the use of an internal proportional counter because it has been found capable of counting either alpha or beta activity with a high efficiency. Such counters will detect either alpha or alpha plus beta particles, depending upon the operating voltage.

1. INTERNAL PROPORTIONAL COUNTER

The internal proportional counter comprises a methane–argon flow type of counting chamber, a preamplifier, an electronic scaler, register, timer, counting gas, and a power supply assembly. Setter, Goldin, and Nader (28) describe such an arrangement. A cross section of the counting chamber is given in Fig. XI-1. The chamber consists of a center wire assembly in a hemisphere-and-piston arrangement.

By proper adjustment of the operating voltage both alpha and beta emissions can be counted. At the low voltage appropriate for alpha

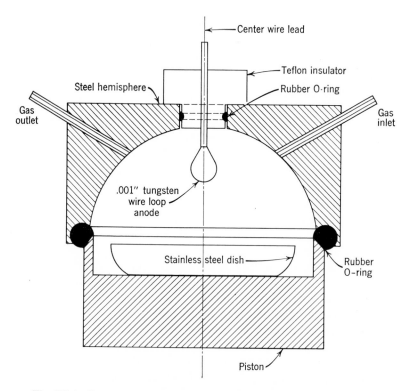

Fig. XI-1. Cross section of internal proportional counter chamber (28).

counting, beta particles are not detected because the counting gas is not ionized sufficiently to induce a response in the preamplifier. When the voltage is set at a higher value to count the beta emissions, then both beta and alpha particles are counted for both can activate the preamplifier.

Operating Voltage Plateau. It is necessary to count at a voltage where the rate does not change substantially for a small change in voltage. To find this plateau, make a series of determinations using an alpha source of counting rates at voltages above and below the approximate alpha operating voltage stated by the manufacturer of the instrument and graph the results. There should be a region extending over a range of 150 V in which the counting rate is relatively independent of the voltage. Select the alpha counting operating voltage at approximately the midpoint of this range.

Make an analogous series of measurements using a beta particle source. Determine the beta voltage plateau and select the midpoint of this range as the operating voltage.

Background. To make certain that the instrument is working properly, it is necessary to check two or three times a day by counting an alpha or a beta source with a known counting rate for a total of at least 10,000 counts. The known counting rate must be determined by counting the source for a total of not less than 40,000 counts. The standard source, actually a secondary standard, for alpha counting calibration is uranium oxide plated on stainless steel. An analogous standard source is used for the calibration of beta counting except that the uranium oxide plated on stainless steel is covered with aluminum foil, weighing 8 mg/cm² (0.001 in. thick) which completely masks alpha activity.

The counting rate determined in this manner should check the known rate within 3%. If it does not do so, check the operating voltage and make a redetermination of the voltage plateau. If such reevaluation still does not correct the discrepancy, the instrument must be serviced.

Measure the alpha and beta background by determining the counting rate at an appropriate voltage using a clean, empty, similar counting dish in the chamber. Do this two or three times a day; obtain the average background counting rate by calculation. The total background counting time should equal the longest counting time used for any sample.

The alpha radiation background is generally less than 0.5 count per minute (cpm) if the counting chamber has not become contaminated. With the voltage used for counting beta activity, the background is 50–60 cpm, attributable to gamma and cosmic radiation. If background counts are made with blank dishes three times a day for two 8- and one 16-min intervals, following calibration with a standard, the total 32-min counting period will yield an alpha-background value reliable to ±5%.

A high background count may be attributed to contamination of the counting chamber. Counting that is erratic may be attributed to high-voltage discharge from dust or excessive roughness of the electrode. Check the preamplifier tubes, condensers and resistors, and the scaler tubes and circuitry in the order mentioned for trouble shooting.

Calibration. No instrument can detect all of the radioactive disintegrations occurring in a sample. For this reason it is necessary to correct the observed counting rate of any sample. The factors involved in this loss of counting efficiency are (1) the geometry of the counting chamber, (2) backscatter, (3) absorption, and (4) self-absorption. These factors are relatively constant for any given instrument, radionuclide, and method of preparing the sample. If the nature of the radioisotope is not known, the factors cannot be determined accurately. In the USPHS method (27) the corrections used are based on the assumption that alpha activity is due to natural uranium and the beta activity to mixed fission products, that is, to fallout.

Geometry. Not all of the radiation given off by a sample is sent in the direction of the detecting unit. This factor (G) is a measure of the fraction of the emitted radiation that reaches the detector. For internal proportional counters and for a small sample in the center of a counting dish, this factor is considered to be 0.5. This factor has been shown to be experimentally adequate for a sample spread uniformly over a 2-in. counting dish, hence, $G = 0.5$.

Backscatter. The reflection of beta and alpha particles into the counter from the sample dish is known as backscatter (B). For alpha particles there is very little backscatter. The amount is seldom more than 2%; hence, for alpha particles $B = 1.00$–1.02. The factor for the backscatter of beta particles is dependent upon the energy of the radiation and the effective atomic number of the sample dish and its support. Nader, Hagee, and Setter (29) have shown that 1-year-old mixed fission products in aluminum dishes mounted in a brass chamber have a backscatter factor of 1.31.

Absorption. The stoppage of particles by a window or wall of the detector when the sample is outside the detector is termed absorption. This does not occur in internal proportional counters.

Self-Absorption. In principle, this factor is the same as that of absorption but it happens in the sample, itself. Thus, some of the particles formed in the disintegrations are absorbed before they can get out of the sample into the counting gas and consequently are not counted. The transmission factor (T) of radiation through a sample is dependent upon the quantity and chemical composition of the ash, the type of radiation, and the energy of the radiation.

Alpha particles have a very low order of penetrating power and the alpha activity of natural uranium, which has an energy of 4.2 and 4.76 MeV, is markedly reduced by a sample thickness of a few milligrams per square centimeter. Indeed a sheet of paper will stop such alpha particles. Samples of thickness less than 4 mg/cm^2 should be used when determining the alpha count of ash of unknown activity.

While the loss by self-absorption of beta particles is less than that of alpha particles, beta particles of low energy are lost by self-absorption.

The factors to be used in calculating the counting efficiency (E) from the equation

$$E = GBT$$

are given in Table XI-9.

Calibrating Standard. In the USPHS method, it is pointed out that the overall efficiency of counting may be determined, without any knowledge of the efficiency factors discussed above, by adding a known amount of radioactive material to a series of counting dishes and then measuring the counting rate. It is necessary to run a series of determinations in which different weights of ash are used because the self-absorption varies with the thickness of the samples.

Standard solutions of various radioisotopes that can be used for calibrating standards can be obtained from the National Bureau of Standards. Thallium-204 is used most frequently as the standard for mixed fission products and is suggested for the beta determination. Uranium salts are suggested as the standard for alpha determinations. One mg of natural uranium emits 1520 alpha particles per minute.

TABLE XI-9
Counting Efficiency Factors (27)

	Alpha	Beta
G	0.50	0.50
B	1.02	1.36[a]
T (sample thickness), mg/cm²		
1.00	0.0	0.0
0.90	0.8	1.4
0.80	1.6	3.9
0.70	2.4	6.6
0.60	3.2	13.5
0.50	4.0[b]	

[a] Stainless-steel dish.

[b] For alpha thickness above 4.0 mg/cm², divide 2 by the thickness in milligrams per square centimeter. Thus, for example, for 10 mg/cm², $T = 0.2$ and for 16 mg/cm², $T = 0.12$.

Prepare several nonradioactive samples of different weights up to 300 mg by processing variable volumes of tap water in tared counting dishes. If the solids content of the water is too low to give this amount of ash, add a sufficient amount of fine calcium carbonate to obtain the amounts desired. Add to each dish an identical aliquot of uranium salt or thallium-204 compound containing about 1000 cpm for the alpha or beta calibration, respectively. Add water, disperse the radioactive substances uniformly, dry, weigh, and count. Divide the net counting rate for each sample to obtain the counting efficiency. Plot a curve of counting efficiency against weight of sample ash as a calibration graph.

Counting Procedure. Count the samples by placing them in the counting chamber at the appropriate operating voltage, flushing the chamber to replace the air with the counting gas, and record the counts over a specified time. Count each sample for two 16-min periods, preceding each counting period by a 30–60-sec flushing of the counting chamber with the counting gas. If the two measurements do not agree, it is probable that the counting gas was not properly flushed out and a third count should be made immediately using the same time period.

For this practical time period of counting, the minimum detectable alpha and beta activities are, according to Goldin, Nader, and Setter (30), 0.5 and 4 cpm, respectively. When it is desired to obtain greater precision of counting, increase the counting time. When samples of moderate or high activity are being counted the counting time may be reduced.

Calculations. The net sample counting rate in counts per minute (cpm) for alpha activity is given by the expression

$$(NR)_\alpha = R_\alpha - B_\alpha$$

in which $(NR)_\alpha$ = net sample alpha counting rate, cpm, R_α = observed sample alpha counting rate, cpm, B_α = background alpha counting rate, cpm, and the net sample counting rate for beta activity is given by the expression

$$(NR)_\beta = R_\beta - B_\beta - (NR)_\alpha$$

in which $(NR)_\beta$ = net sample beta counting rate, cpm, R_β = observed sample beta counting rate, cpm, B_β = background beta counting rate, cpm.

The alpha activity can be calculated by use of the expression

$$A_\alpha = (NR)_\alpha/2.2VE_\alpha$$

in which A_α = alpha activity in $\mu\mu c$/liter, V = volume of the original sample in liters, and E = efficiency of alpha counting, counts per minute per disintegrations per minute.

The counting error in alpha activity can be calculated, based on the variability, as discussed in the succeeding section, by the expression

$$(CE)_\alpha = (1.96/2.2VE_\alpha)/(R_\alpha/T_\alpha + B_\alpha/t_\alpha)^{1/2}$$

in which T = alpha counting time in minutes, t = background alpha counting time in minutes, and the other terms have the meanings previously assigned.

The beta activity can be calculated by use of the expression

$$A_\beta = (NR)_\beta/2.2VE_\beta$$

in which A_β = beta activity in $\mu\mu c$/liter; E_β = efficiency of beta counting, counts per minute per disintegrations per minute.

The counting error in beta activity can be calculated based on the variability as discussed in the succeeding section, by the expression

$$(CE)_\beta = (1.96/2.2VE_\beta)[(H_\beta/T_\beta) + (B_\beta/t_\beta) + (R_\alpha/T_\alpha) + (B_\alpha/t_\alpha)]^{1/2}$$

in which T_β = beta counting time in minutes, t_β = background beta counting time in minutes, and the other terms have the meaning previously assigned.

The USPHS suggests the following data be reported: the sample identification number; the sample collection station and date) sample type, such as rainwater, sootfall, etc.; the volume in liters or the weight processed in grams; the method of preparation of sample, that is whether oven-dried ashed in a muffle, wet ashed, etc.; the alpha activity plus or minus the counting error in micromicrocuries per liter; the beta activity plus or minus the counting error in micromicrocuries per liter; the percentage of total solids; the percentage of ash; and the radioisotopes used as the calibration standards.

Analogous calculations can be made on a weight basis by substituting g, the weight of the original sample in grams, for the term, V. The results can then be given in micromicrocuries per gram.

Variability. Radioactive disintegrations occur in a random manner. For this reason, the counting rate of any sample will vary about a mean value. This has been discussed by Goldin, Nader, and Setter (30). It can be shown that the standard deviation of certain quantities is given by the following:

Quantity	Standard deviation of quantity
Number of counts, N	$N^{1/2}$
Counting rate, R, measured in time, T, that is: $R = N/T$	$(R/T)^{1/2}$
Sum or difference of counting rates: $R_1 \pm R_2$	$[(R_1/T_1) \pm (R_2/T_2)]^{1/2}$

An especially important instance of the last form is that concerned with the counting detailed in the preceeding section in which a net counting rate is calculated by subtracting the background counting rate from the observed counting rate when the latter comprises the sample plus the background counting rate.

As noted, determinations will be more accurate as the counting time is increased; consequently, the longest counting time practical for the analyses involved should be used. In the method above, a counting time of 16 min was suggested. Other suggested minimum counting times are 30 min or a total of 2500 counts above the background, whichever is less. By using two equal counting periods as detailed in the counting procedure, a check of the observed counting rate is obtained.

Confidence Level. If the standard deviation is multiplied by a constant, one can obtain limits of error. In the following tabulation, the confidence level is given for each constant.

Confidence level, %	Constant
50	0.67
68	1.0
90	1.64
95	1.96

It is stressed in the USPHS method that the method is not one of great accuracy. It is questionable that great accuracy is required in such instances for there may well be a thousandfold difference in the significance of the pollution depending upon the particular radioisotopes present, as was discussed in the section on radiotoxicity.

A major source of inaccuracy in this method is the self-absorption factor, discussed before. The uncertainty in the evaluation of this factor may lead to an error of the order of 20–25% in the beta assay of samples containing 100 mg of ash, with an even larger error in the alpha assay. If there is sufficient activity to warrant making a determination of greater accuracy, then a smaller sample of the order of 25 mg should be counted. The self-absorption error in consequence will be reduced, but there is a residual error of about 15% in the beta assay which can be attributed largely to uncertainty in the backscatter factor and to nonuniform deposition of the sample. This error cannot be materially reduced without additional knowledge of the energy of the radiation.

As mentioned, alpha particles cause an error in the beta counting for the alpha plateau extends into the beta region; consequently, more than one count is recorded at the beta voltage for each alpha count. The amount of this depends on the sample thickness, the uniformity of deposition, the energy of the radiation, and possibly on other factors. If the alpha count is considerably lower than the beta count because either the alpha activity itself is low or the alpha self-absorption losses are high, this error will be small. Since alpha particles are of greater significance from the point of view of pollution, if the alpha count is of the same order of magnitude as the beta count, the resulting error in the beta count is not too important.

2. GEIGER-MÜLLER COUNTER METHOD

In general, the method detailed for the internal proportional counter can be applied to radioactivity counting with a Geiger-Müller tube and scaler but with some changes, depending on the instrument. Thus, most end-window Geiger-Müller tubes are designed to be used with samples that are 1 in. in diameter. The standards used for calibration must be of the same dimensions.

The detector of a Geiger-Müller counting unit comprises a tube having a very thin end window with a weight of less than 2 mg/cm² so that some beta particles and gamma rays can penetrate readily. This tube is encased in a lead shield approximately 1–2 in. thick to reduce the background effect. Because the Geiger-Müller type produces a pulse of sufficient energy, no amplifier is necessary and the tube can be used to actuate a scaler directly. It is, however, an "all-or-nothing" instrument in that the radioactive particles and gamma rays must have sufficient energy, otherwise no pulse is produced.

Instruments of the Geiger-Müller type have the advantage of simplicity since they do not require an amplifier and no difficulties attributable to the electrical or chemical nature of the sample are encountered because the sample is placed externally to the counter.

They have certain marked disadvantages. First, they have virtually no sensitivity for alpha particles; second, their sensitivity for beta particles is about 10–20% of that of the internal proportional counter; and third, this sensitivity is even less for beta particles of low energy. The latter disadvantages are only slightly offset by the lower background count. Great care must be exercised in establishing the voltage plateau, otherwise the Geiger-Müller tube may be ruined. Such counters have their greatest value in the determination of higher levels of radioactivity.

As representative of such instruments the operation of a Baird-Atomic, Model 1081 scaler, with an Anton "pancake" Geiger-Müller tube and lead shield can be described.

Starting Instrument. With high voltage switch at "off" position, and the coarse and fine voltage controls turned completely counterclockwise, with the 60-cycle switch at "off" and the "count" switch at "off," turn the power switch on.

60-Cycle Test. Set the timer and counter at zero, the automatic control at $10\times$ and the scale selector at 256 (this arrangement sets the scaler to turn off automatically when a count of 2560 is reached), throw the 60-cycle switch to "on" and allow the machine to operate until 10 is reached on the counter, at which time the counting will stop. Repeat for different total counts or run manually for 1 min.

Thus, with the instrument set as noted, the timer will reach 0.71 min when it stops, hence

$$2560/0.71 = 3600 \text{ cpm}$$

This checks the operation of the instrument for a 60-cycle current should give 3600 impulses or counts per minute. If the instrument is set at $10\times$, a scale selector setting of 1024 will stop the instrument when a count of 10240 is reached. The time will be 2.84 min, hence

$$10240/2.84 = 3610 \text{ cpm}$$

as an alternative check of the instrument.

Voltage Plateau. The voltage range in which large changes in voltage will give small changes in counts per minute must be determined. With the particular Anton tube used, a voltage of 1000 must not be exceeded.

Set the 60-cycle switch to "off," turn the count indicator to "off," reset the counter and timer, turn the fine and coarse high voltage controls completely counterclockwise, and turn the voltage switch to "on." Wait until the indicator light turns bright red and turn the coarse knob control until the voltage reaches 500.

Place a 0.1-μc standard 1 in. away from the end window of the Geiger-Müller type and take counts at 50-V intervals from 500–950 V. Set the automatic control at $10\times$ and the scale selector at 16 so that the instrument will stop automatically at a count of 160 per min. With such settings assume the following readings were obtained:

Voltage	Time, min	Cpm
500	0.0	—
550	0.0	—
600	0.0	—
650	0.0	—
700	5	32
750	0.71	220
800	0.50	320
850	0.46	350
900	0.43	370
950	0.43	370

Thus, the plateau is in the 900–950-V range. Actual counting can be performed in the manner previously detailed; that is, obtain the background count, the sample count, the background count, the check sample count, etc.

Background Count. Set the voltage at 900; set all the switches at "off" and all counters at zero. Set up the Geiger tube and lead shield exactly as they are to be used subsequently for the sample. Determine the time for 160 counts. For instance, if this takes 6.07 min, then the counts per minute are 26. Use a clean filter paper of the same type as that to be used for the sample for the background count.

Radioactivity Count. Make a similar count using the filter paper sample. Repeat the background count. Repeat the sample count. Repeat the background count. Average the background counts and the sample counts. Subtract the background average count from the sample average count.

Calculation. The 0.1-μc standard will give a count of 10,000 per min. Assume that a fast-flow filter paper sample gave a reading of 1.16 min for a 160 count. This is equivalent to 138 cpm. Assume additionally that the background count was 32. Then the actual count was $138 - 32 = 106$ cpm.

To express this count in microcuries, it is necessary to multiply the count by the factor 1×10^{-5} obtained from the value of the standard and the counts per minute:

$$0.1/10,000 = \text{cpm} \times 10^{-5}$$

Hence, our sample has a radioactivity of $106 \times 10^{-5} = 1.06 \times 10^{-3}$. If we assume additionally that 90 m³ of air were sampled, then

$$(1.06 \times 10^{-3})/90 = 1.18 \times 10^{-4}\ \mu\text{c/m}^3$$

that is, the sample of air contained $1.18 \times 10^{-5}\ \mu\text{c/m}^3$.

3. SCINTILLATION COUNTER

There are various types of scintillation counters as there are other radioactivity measuring instruments. Usually this type of apparatus comprises a photomultiplier tube equipped with a sensitive phosphor and its circuit enclosed in a light-tight housing. Because the output pulses are too weak to actuate a conventional scaler, it is necessary to use an amplifier. In addition, some method of mounting the samples must be provided so that sample positions can be duplicated. It is customary with this type of instrument to have a more accurate voltage regulator than with Geiger-Müller types of apparatus.

With the scintillation type of instrument it is essential to determine the voltage plateau in order to avoid placing excessive voltage on the photomultiplier tubes. It is best to operate in a voltage range some 50–75 V above the lower end of the voltage plateau. Care must also be exercised not to expose the photomultiplier tubes to light when the high voltage is on.

Scintillation counters are also used as gamma-ray spectrometers and such instruments can be used to evaluate a radioisotope like iodine-131. A Geiger-Müller counter cannot be used for this purpose because it is an "all-or-nothing" instrument and the radiation must be sufficiently strong to activate the detector.

By replacing the sensitive phosphor with anthracene crystals or organic plastic scintillators, such type of counters can be used for the determination of beta rays.

Scintillation counters have a number of advantages. Thus, they may be used at times for direct counting of the sample whether liquid or solid but their counting efficiency appears to be somewhat lower than that of the internal proportional counters.

D. Gross Radioactivity

The analysis of radioactivity of the air and the particulate matter carried by the air can be placed into a number of principal categories, namely: (1) the suspended particulate matter, (2) the air-borne dust from an industrial operation, (3) the "immediate" or short-term fallout (24-hr periods or less), (4) the dustfall collected in the usual monthly manner, and (5) rainout.   Methods for the determination of radioactivity of each of these groups will be described.   It is beyond the scope of this book to consider the contamination of foods and food products by radioactive material and the methods for the detection and determination of such radioactivity.   This has been treated in detail by Jacobs (31).

In Chapters V and VI the sampling of air for suspended particulate matter was considered in detail and the methods for the collection of dustfall and its analysis were detailed. Where necessary, the procedures for the other types of sampling will be included in this chapter.

It is necessary to take into consideration the process by means of which the air is contaminated. Often such air contamination occurs only intermittently and unexpectedly during a short time period so that it is necessary to sample continuously and perferably by means of an instrument capable of showing both the peak concentration and an integrated concentration.

In some types of processing, a fairly wide range of particle size may result in a sample of millions of particles per cubic foot. It is entirely possible in such an instance that a very small number of particles may carry the bulk of the radioactivity. It is necessary in such instances to sample a large volume of the air being tested.

1. SUSPENDED PARTICULATE MATTER

There are a number of different methods for the sampling of air for suspended particulate matter for the purpose of determining radioactivity. These include the use of fluted filters, glass filter webs (both of which have already been discussed in considerable detail in Chapter V), membrane filters, and fast-flow filter papers.

a. Fluted Filters

List (32) mentions, in a study on the transport of atomic debris in the atmosphere, the use of modified tank-type vacuum cleaners (high-volume samplers) which draw air through a 4-in. diameter dust filter at a rate of 35 cfm for 24 hr. The filters subsequently were ashed and treated in the manner detailed in the AEC sticky paper method described by Jacobs (9) in Chapter 13 of *The Chemical Analysis of Air Pollutants*. List stressed that there was no observable difference in the radioactivity collected by filtration on rainy days as compared with days on which there was no precipitation.

b. Glass Filter Web

The methods of sampling have been detailed in Chapter V, Section C-6-b. The scheme of analysis of the National Air Sampling Network of the U. S. Public Health Service and that of the New York State Air Pollution Control Board includes the determination of the radioactivity trapped by the glass filter web. This is a sheet 8 × 10 in., from which in the initial schemes 2-in. circles were cut to be used for counting, by means of an internal proportional counter. This instrument has been modified to accept the entire sheet so that the gross alpha and beta activity can be determined without destruction of the sheet. The actual dimensions are, however, 7 × 9 in., for the 0.5-in. borders of the sheet, which collect no material because they are protected by the frame, are cut off. Roughly 200 m³ are sampled in a 24-hr period.

The gross beta activity was determined upon receipt of the samples but not before two days after collection. This fitted in with the scheme for the collection of samples since they were collected in various areas and mailed first class to Cincinnati. The samples were usually recounted for decay after 4–6 days. From these two determinations, the volume of air sampled, and the weight of dust collected, the gross beta activity in micromicrocuries per cubic meter on the date of sample collection and the decay rate expressed as the half-life beginning from the date of the first count can be computed.

Samples having a half-life of less than 10 days were corrected for decay to the date of sample collection by extrapolating a plot of the decay results on log-log paper for an assumed date of bomb debris formation providing the decay slope was between 1.1 and 1.2. It has been shown that log-log plots of decay data of high level fresh bomb debris usually follow the theoretical negative exponential decay rate of 1.2 rather closely while those of low level or 10 or more day old activity have decay slopes less than 1.2 but rarely less than 1.0.

Instrument. The instrument used by the Sanitary Engineering Center consists of a thin-window large-area proportional gas flow counting chamber, Nuclear Measurements Corporation (Indianapolis, Indiana) Model PCC-12, having a thin, 0.9 mg/cm², metal-coated plastic window (Mylar). The chamber-preamplifier unit is connected to a conventional scaler (in this instance a Nuclear-Chicago Model No. 181A Decade) and timer (Nuclear-Chicago Dual timer Model T1). The piston of the counter chamber was replaced with a steel plate covered with aluminum foil for ease of decontamination. The resultant shelf on which the samples were placed was 5 mm below the thin window.

Counting Procedure. Preflush the counting chamber at a high rate with P-10 gas for about 1 hr. Proper flushing is ascertained by counting the background and a secondary standard to find out whether these have changed from the counting of the day before. Low background or standard counts, as mentioned, indicate insufficient flushing and high background or standard counts indicate contamination. Repeat the check at midday and at the end of the work day.

Counting Intervals. Count the samples for two 2-min intervals at the first count, after the 2-day period, and again after 4–7 days. If the rate of decay is relatively low indicating fission products formed at least 10 days or more before the first count, plot the data on semilog paper and extrapolate back to the time of sample collection. If a rapid rate of decay is observed, plot the results on log-log paper in such a fashion that the Hunter and Ballou decay factor of -1.2 or somewhat less is obtained and extrapolate the results to the time of collection.

Calibration Technique. The Sanitary Engineering Center obtains an initial calibration of the counter efficiency. It will be recalled that such calibrations depend on the factors of geometry, backscatter, absorption, and self-absorption. Since the dust of a sample is deposited on an area 7 × 9 in. or 63 sq in. when it is placed under a window having a diameter of 7.5 in. with an equivalent area of 44.19 sq in., only a portion of the sample area is observed with an efficiency that varies, depending on the counting chamber geometry. In order to evaluate the effective area of the counter, a point source of activity was counted in various positions from the center outward to beyond the diameter of the window. From these data the "effective area" of counting was computed by Simpson's rule and was found to be 66% of the sample area. Second, a source was counted in an internal proportional counter of known efficiency and the same source was counted under the thin window counter. The ratio of the latter count to the former count was 0.86. It had also been found that the efficiency of the internal proportional counter was 65.5% based on a geometry factor of 0.5 and a backscatter factor of 1.32 for thallium-204 and a self-absorption factor of 1.0 for zero sample thickness. The filter absorption factor was 1.09.

The self-absorption factor varies with the amount of sample solids and is taken as 1.0 for zero thickness, 1.2 for 600 mg of suspended particulate matter, and 1.4 for 1 g of dust. For routine tests of the activity a convention was adopted to assume a self-absorption factor of 1.1 for samples containing less than 601 mg and a factor of 1.3 for samples containing from 601 mg to 1 g of suspended particulate matter.

Calculation. To compute the radioactivity, obtain the average gross counts per minute from the results of the 2-min counts and subtract the background counts per minute from the average counts per minute of the sample to get the net counts per minute. Correct for counting efficiency and filter absorption by use of the expression

$$\text{dpm} = \text{net cpm} \times (1/0.563) \times (1/0.665) \times (1/0.903)$$

where $1/0.563 = $ correction for efficiency $= (1/0.86) \times (1/0.655)$, $1/0.665 = $ effective counting area, and $1/0.903 = $ filter absorption factor. Hence

$$\text{dpm} = 2.92 \times \text{net cpm}$$

To convert disintegrations per minute to micromicrocuries

$$\text{dpm}/2.22 = \text{total } \mu\mu\text{c}$$

To express the radioactivity in terms of volume of air sampled

$$\mu\mu\text{c}/V = \mu\mu\text{c}/\text{m}^3 \text{ (uncorrected)}$$

when V is the volume of air sampled in cubic meters.

To correct for self-absorption of sample

$$\mu\mu\text{c}/\text{m}^3 \text{ (uncorrected)} \times F_s = \mu\mu\text{c}/\text{m}^3 \text{ (corrected)}$$

where F_s is the filter absorption factor.

To find the average half-life of the radionuclides in the sample, plot on semilog paper the net counts per minute against the counting dates, plotting the counts on the log scale and the days between the two counts on the linear scale. Draw a straight line through the two points. Find the point on the line where the net counts per minute are one-half that found when the sample was first counted. Drop a vertical line to the base. The number of days from the date of the first count to this point is the average half-life of the radionuclides present in the sample.

To find the radioactivity on the date of sample collection for samples having an apparent half-life of less than 10 days, extrapolate a plot of the decay results on log-log paper to correct for the decay to the date of collection. This extrapolation is based on the assumption that the Way-Wigner expression

$$A T^k = \text{constant}$$

is valid and an assumed date of bomb debris formation which provides values for k between 1.1 and 1.2. If the half-life is greater than 10 days, the results of the two counts are plotted on semilog paper and the activity of the sample is determined by extrapolating back to the date of collection.

Log-log graphs of decay data of high level bomb debris generally follow the theoretical negative exponential decay rate of 1.2 but low level or 10 or more day old activity have decay slopes of less than 1.2 and rarely less than 1.0.

Standards. The standards of the Sanitary Engineering Center consists of extended sources (2 in. in diameter) of radium plated on stainless steel and covered with 7 mg/cm² aluminum foil. Standard solutions of thallium-204 obtained from the National Bureau of Standards and deposited on dishes are also used. These standards are used to determine the counting efficiency of the internal proportional counters and the thin-window counter.

The secondary standard used for determining the plateau and for making daily calibrations is a sample of uranium oxide plated on a 2-in. diameter, stainless-steel disk covered with 7 mg/cm² aluminum foil to shield out the alpha activity. Such calibrations are made three times a day so that one can be assured that the instrument is working properly. The standard has an activity of 10,400 cpm including a background count of 500 cpm.

Reliability Estimate. The estimate of the reliability of the data is variable for it depends on many factors, such as the accuracy of the volume of air filtered, the filter characteristics, the age of the bomb debris when first counted, the number of days from collection to the date of first count, and the counting error which is a function of the counting rate. For fresh bomb debris less than 5 days old with a relatively high counting rate it is possible that the extrapolated value could be off by a factor of 2 because fractional parts of a day are not considered. For activity having an age of 10 or more days, the determination should be within 10% of the correct value, provided reliance can be placed on the volume of air sampled and uniform characteristics of the filter. For low activity in the order of 1000 cpm per sample, the raw counting error at the 95% confidence level may be estimated to be

$$1.96/2 \times (1500 + 500)^{\frac{1}{2}} = 44 \text{ cpm}$$

or 4.4%, whereas the error of a sample counting 500 cpm or equal to the background would be

$$1.96/2 \times (1000 + 500)^{1/2} = 38 \text{ cpm}$$

or 7.6%.

c. Membrane Filter

The use of fluted filters has the disadvantages of high and variable blanks for trace materials. Consequently, other methods have been adopted for such sampling as described in Chapter 5 of Jacobs (9), *The Chemical Analysis of Air Pollutants*. The Radiological Health Program of the Sanitary Engineering Center, U. S. Public Health Service, adapted a membrane filter method for the sampling of airborne particulate matter for radioactivity determinations (33).

Procedure. Set up a sampling probe on a roof with the customary precautions about walls and parapets and connect this to a membrane-filter holder with a flow-meter in the line. Insert a membrane filter (type AA) of known size and filter the air at about 20 lpm through it for 24 hr or 72 hr. Measure the flow rate at the beginning and at the end of the sampling period and obtain the average sampling rate and thus the total volume of air sampled. Compute the total volume sampled.

Remove the filter and insert it immediately on the pedestal of a zinc sulfide scintillation counter and count for two 1-min intervals. This activity is due in large measure to the alpha daughter products of radon which exhibit a composite half-life of 31–33 min. This activity has accumulated in the last 2 hr of the sampling period. The thoron daughter products which have a composite half-life of 11.6 hr are included in this measurement. Consequently, by counting the alpha activity immediately, after 5 and 6 hr, and again after several days one can differentiate between long-lived alpha activity having substantially no decay, thoron daughter activity, and radon daughter activity. A scintillation counter in use at the Sanitary Engineering Center had an efficiency of 41.3%.

One can also use an internal proportional counter for such samples but the procedure must be modified because it is necessary to destroy the nonconducting membrane filter. Place the sample in an aluminum dish (an aluminum bottle cap will serve) or a stainless-steel planchet, saturate the filter with ethyl alcohol, and ignite. After the membrane filter has burned, direct the flame of a meker burner down on the sample to assist in more complete ignition. Not all of the carbon is consumed in this short burning period and the bottom of the dish remains black. This step takes approximately 5 min so it is necessary to correct for the decay during this period by extrapolating the counting data, if this is required.

In the event that immediate beta activity measurements of fission products are desired, count the sample for both alpha and beta activity and make a correction for the contribution from a natural activity. For the latter, assume that the beta contribution is equal to 1.5 times that of the alpha activity. The alpha, it must be remembered, is also counted at the beta plateau.

Allow the sample to stand for 2 days and then count in an internal proportional counter. This period of waiting is necessary for a shorter period is not sufficient to permit the decay of the natural radioactive products of radon and thoron.

d. Ashless Filters

In Chapter 5 of Jacobs (9), the use of Schleicher and Schuell acid-washed FF2W filter papers, commonly called fast-flow filter papers, for sampling for suspended particulate matter was discussed in detail. Such papers can also be used for determination of radioactivity as detailed in this chapter in Section C-2.

The Institute of Paper Chemistry (34) has developed an air filter impregnated with an organic liquid for the collection of radioactive particles in the upper atmosphere. The IPC 1478 filter paper, which is impregnated with dibutoxy ethyl phthalate, is reported to trap particles as small as 0.003-μ average diameter and to be applicable to many industrial air pollution problems (35).

E. Identification

The identification of a particular radioisotope is based on chemical separation techniques that may include separation of a daughter activity, or on radiation characteristics such as the half-life or type of radiation (alpha, beta, or gamma), or on energy. Usually a combination of chemical and physical procedures is more suitable than either approach alone. In many instances, determination of radiation characteristics may not be practical because the radionuclides being determined or identified are present in extremely low concentration.

At low concentration levels, it is generally necessary to concentrate the active material from relatively large samples. At still smaller concentrations, and in instances in which large samples are not available, specialized types of counting equipment must be used. With these types the background count may be lowered sufficiently by use of heavy shielding and other devices so that it does not interfere in the analysis.

The preliminary sample preparation is a major problem with many kinds of materials. The analysis of solid samples such as sootfall or the filters or sticky paper requires total dissolution of the sample, which is either wet or dry ashed and then the ash is dissolved.

Because radionuclides are usually present in amounts so small that they cannot be weighed, known quantities of carrier materials are usually added so that the radioisotopes can be manipulated. It is not always necessary for the recovery to be quantitative because the results can be corrected on the basis of the recovery of the carrier. For this reason rapid semiquantitative methods can be utilized. Kahn and Goldin (24) have described a few methods which were developed for the determination of specific radioisotopes at low concentration levels. These methods are sensitive for 30-min counting periods on high efficiency conventional counting equipment in the order of 10 $\mu\mu$c for beta emitters and 1 $\mu\mu$c for alpha emitters. The methods of identification are detailed for rainout or water but with modification can be utilized for the ash from sootfall, sticky paper, and the like.

1. RADIUM-226

Add 200 mg of lead and 5–10 mg of barium to a liter of rainout or the equivalent sample from sootfall as carriers for the radium and add sufficient ammoniacal citrate to prevent precipitation of the carriers before the interchange with radium has occurred. Precipitate the sulfate with sulfuric acid, allow to settle, and collect the precipitates by decanting the supernatant liquid. Wash the precipitates with concentrated nitric acid and then dissolve them in ammoniacal ethylenediaminetetraacetic acid (EDTA). Reprecipitate the barium sulfate, which carries the radium by the addition of excess acetic acid. Wash the precipitate, mount, dry, flame, and weigh.

Determine the radium content by alpha counting. The radium may be checked for radiochemical and isotopic purity by following the growth of radon-222 and its daughters in the precipitate.

2. Strontium and Barium

Add 20 mg each of strontium and barium carriers and carbonate to 4 liters of rainout to precipitate the strontium, barium, and calcium carbonates. Allow to settle, discard the supernatant liquid, transfer to a 50-ml centrifuge tube, redissolve the carbonates in 6N hydrochloric acid and reprecipitate the strontium and barium nitrates (see the method for the determination of strontium-90) in strong nitric acid. The small amount of calcium nitrate that is coprecipitated may be dissolved out by use of anhydrous acetone. After redissolving remove other contaminating active radionuclides by the addition of ferric ion and precipitating the hydroxide. Separate the barium and strontium as in the Goldin method (Section F-1-b of this chapter) by precipitating barium chromate from a buffered solution. Precipitate strontium oxalate, dry, mount, weigh, and count. Additionally purify the barium by precipitation with hydrochloric acid–ether mixture, dry, mount, weigh, and count.

3. Strontium-90

Add 400 mg of strontium nitrate carrier to a liter of rainout or to an equivalent sample preparation. Add sodium carbonate to precipitate the strontium together with the calcium. Collect the precipitate by decanting the supernatant liquid and redissolve in dilute acid. Add barium carrier and precipitate it as chromate from an acetic acid–acetate buffer at pH 5 to remove barium-140, which would subsequently interfere because of its lanthanum-140 daughter. Add ferric ion and precipitate the hydroxides with ammonium hydroxide; this precipitate will include the insoluble rare earth hydroxides. Add rare earth and zirconium carriers and precipitate these with ammonia to insure more complete removal of interfering radionuclides. Precipitate the strontium from the supernatant solution with carbonate and allow to stand overnight or longer if possible for the time required for the ingrowth of yttrium-90. Buffer the solution at pH 5 and extract the yttrium with 2-thenoyltrifluoroacetone (TTA) in monochlorobenzene. Reextract the yttrium-90 from the organic solvent phase with dilute nitric acid and subsequently mount, dry, and count. Determine the yield of strontium by flame photometry.

Determine the strontium-90 by beta-counting the yttrium-90 formed, correcting for the fraction of yttrium which has grown into the strontium sample (see the Goldin method, Section F-1-b of this chapter). Yttrium-90 activity reaches 16% of the strontium-90 activity in 16 hr, 40% in 48 hr, and 84% in 168 hr. The purity of the yttrium-90 may be readily checked by decay measurements.

4. CESIUM

Add 25 mg of cesium chloride and 200 mg of potassium chloride as carriers to a liter of rainout or equivalent sample. Precipitate potassium and cesium as the cobaltinitrites from acetic acid solution. Collect the precipitate by decanting the supernatant solution, wash with acetic acid, and dissolve in $6N$ hydrochloric acid. Add silicotungstic acid to precipitate cesium silicotungstate and thus separate it from the other alkali metals. Add perchloric acid, heat the solution to precipitate the silicon and tungsten oxides, and centrifuge to pack and remove these oxides. Cool the perchloric acid solution and add absolute alcohol to precipitate cesium perchlorate. Collect, wash with alcohol, mount, dry, weigh, and count. Determine the cesium-137 or cesium-134 content by beta- or gamma-counting.

5. IODINE-131

Add sodium iodide as the carrier to the sample to be analyzed. Oxidize with sodium hypochlorite in alkaline solution. Reduce the iodide to elemental iodine and extract with carbon tetrachloride. Reextract the iodine with sodium bisulfite and precipitate as silver or palladium iodide for beta-counting (36).

As an alternative procedure, if a scintillation counter is available, the carbon tetrachloride or sodium bisulfite extract may be gamma-counted. This direct counting will eliminate the troublesome step of handling silver iodide which tends to form colloidal solution.

6. COBALT-60

Add a cobalt carrier to the sample being analyzed and precipitate it as the hydroxide. Dissolve the hydroxide in acetic acid and reprecipitate as potassium cobaltinitrite. Redissolve this precipitate, add a cerium carrier, and precipitate the latter with ammonia to remove contaminating activities. Again precipitate the cobalt as, in this instance, the 1-nitroso-2-naphthol salt, ignite to the oxide, mount, weigh, and beta-count.

7. MANGANESE-54

Add a manganese carrier (26), together with cerium and zirconium holdback carriers, to the dissolved sample and oxidize the mixture with sodium chlorate. Reduce and dissolve the insoluble manganese dioxide with sodium bisulfite and hydrochloric acid, and scavenge the solution with basic ferrous acetate to remove interfering radionuclides. Precipitate the manganese as the ammonium phosphate salt and ignite to form the pyrophosphate which is used to determine the chemical recovery. The resulting precipitate may be gamma-counted with a sodium iodide–thallium activated crystal detector and resubmitted to gamma spectral analysis.

F. Determination of Dangerous Radionuclides

It was noted in the section on radiotoxicity that certain radioisotopes were far more dangerous than others. It is of importance to have methods sufficiently sensitive to measure the amount of such radioisotopes present in fallout, dustfall, and rainout. Methods will consequently be detailed for strontium-90, radium-226, and barium-140.

1. STRONTIUM-90

a. AEC Method

In the method recommended by the Atomic Energy Commission (37), strontium is separated from calcium, other fission products and natural radioactive elements by use of fuming nitric acid, which removes the calcium and most of the other interfering ions because strontium nitrate is insoluble in 80% and higher percentages of nitric acid (38). Radium and lead are removed with barium chromate. Traces of other fission products are scavenged with yttrium hydroxide. After the strontium-90–yttrium-90 equilibrium has been attained, the yttrium-90 is precipitated as the hydroxide and converted to the oxalate for counting.

Preparation of Sample. The method for the preparation of rain-water will be detailed. In general, other waters can be treated in a similar manner, and samples like fallout can be treated similarly, adding the carrier at some appropriate step.

Collect rainwater in stainless-steel pots by exposing the pots for given periods of time, usually 1 month, but when circumstances permit for shorter times. Add 1 ml of nitric acid per liter of the rainwater. Add 1 ml of strontium carrier solution containing 20 mg of strontium per milliliter. Evaporate to approximately 100 ml. Transfer to a 250-ml beaker, using distilled water for the transfer, and police the sides of the stainless-steel collection vessel thoroughly. Wash the collection vessel with nitric acid (1:9). Evaporate carefully to 15–20 ml and transfer to a 40-ml platinum crucible with distilled water. Evaporate to dryness, ignite in a muffle furnace at 500°C, and continue ashing until all of the organic matter has been destroyed. Transfer the residue to a planchet and beta-count for mixed fission products, using 200 mg of potassium carbonate as the standard. Record the total activity in disintegrations per minute per liter, but if the beta activity is not desired, this step can be omitted.

Replace the residue into the platinum crucible, add approximately four times the amount of sodium carbonate, and mix thoroughly. Fuse to obtain a clear melt using a muffle set at 900°C and cool.

Add 25 ml of distilled water to the crucible and a few milliliters of 60% perchloric acid to dissolve the carbonates partially. Transfer the solution and the undissolved residue to a 400-ml beaker and add sufficient 60% perchloric acid to dissolve the carbonates completely. Wash the crucible with 60% perchloric acid and finally with distilled water. Combine all the washings with the test solution. Add 25 ml of 60% perchloric acid to the beaker and evaporate until dense white fumes of perchloric acid are apparent. Add sufficient distilled water to dissolve the perchlorates completely. Heat the solution to 80°C and filter hot through Whatman No. 40 filter paper with the aid of suction. Transfer the silica remaining in the beaker to the filter paper with hot hydrochloric acid (1:9). The solution must be filtered while hot in order to keep the salts in solution. Wash the silica on the filter paper with hot hydrochloric acid (1:9) several times and discard the silica precipitate.

Transfer the filtrate and washings to the original 400-ml beaker. Add 1 ml of calcium carrier solution, containing 200 mg of calcium per milliliter and with continuous magnetic stirring, adjust the pH to 8 with sodium hydroxide pellets. Add 2–3 g of sodium carbonate with stirring. Continue stirring for 15 min more and allow the precipitate to settle. Filter through a 9-cm glass fiber filter with suction. Wash the precipitate with a sodium carbonate solution, prepared by dissolving 10 g of sodium carbonate in 90 ml of water. Dissolve the precipitate on the filter with hot nitric acid (1:9) and collect the solution in a 400-ml beaker. Evaporate until salting out occurs. Add 60 ml of distilled water and then 210 ml of 90% nitric acid in two principal portions, the first sufficient to dissolve completely all the solid matter before reaching the 75% nitric acid concentration and then the remainder. Add the nitric acid slowly in a hood with constant magnetic stirring with a Teflon bar. The first portion of nitric acid can comprise about half the volume to be added. Stir for 30 min.

Procedure. Allow the calcium and strontium nitrates to settle. Filter through a 2.8-cm glass fiber filter with a Fisher Filtrator and a fluoroethene funnel. Be certain to drain the filter thoroughly. Discard the filtrate. Transfer the remaining precipitate in the beaker to the fluoroethene funnel, with the suction off, with water and collect the resulting solution of calcium and strontium nitrates in a 250-ml beaker. Evaporate this slowly to dryness and then dissolve the residue in 23 ml of water. Add 77 ml of fuming 90% nitric acid with stirring and continue stirring for 30 min with the aid of the magnetic stirrer and a Teflon-covered bar. Add the nitric acid gradually and in two portions, the first comprising about 35–40 ml and after solution of the salts is complete add the remainder of the nitric acid.

Allow the strontium nitrate precipitate to settle and filter through a 2.8-cm glass fiber filter with a Fisher Filtrator and a fluoroethene funnel. Remove as much of the nitric acid as possible and discard the filtrate. Place a 40-ml centrifuge tube in position to collect the dissolved precipitate. Dissolve the remaining precipitate in the beaker with water. Transfer to the fluoroethene funnel and collect the solution in the 40-ml centrifuge tube. The volume should be at least 20 ml. Bring the pH up to 8 to check for phosphate ion; if there is no precipitate, adjust the pH to 2; if a precipitate is present, repeat the nitric acid separation.

Add 1 ml of yttrium carrier solution, containing 20 mg of yttrium per milliliter. Heat in a water bath regulated at 90°C. Adjust the pH to 8 with ammonium hydroxide solution. This adjustment is critical for strontium will precipitate incompletely in more basic solutions. The buffering action using the volumes indicated holds only when the yttrium precipitation is made at pH 8.

Cool to room temperature and allow the precipitate to settle. Centrifuge for 5 min, decant, pouring the supernatant liquid into another 40-ml centrifuge tube. Dissolve the precipitate with a minimum volume of hydrochloric acid, dilute to 10 ml, heat in a water bath at 90°C, adjust the pH to 8 with ammonium hydroxide solution, cool to room temperature, and allow the precipitate to settle. Centrifuge for 5 min, decant the supernatant solution, and combine it with the prior supernatant liquid. Discard the precipitate.

Add 1 ml of barium carrier solution, containing 20 mg of barium per milliliter, to the combined test solution. Add 1 ml of acetic acid (360 g/liter) and 2 ml of ammonium acetate solution (463 g/liter). The pH should be 5.5 (use narrow-range pH paper for testing the solution). This adjustment is critical for barium chromate will not precipitate completely in more acid solutions.

Heat in a water bath controlled at 90°C. Add dropwise with stirring 1 ml of sodium chromate solution (48.6 g of anhydrous Na_2CrO_4 per liter). The supernatant solution should have a chromate color. If it does not it is necessary to add more sodium chromate solution for all the barium must be removed. Stir vigorously until precipitation is complete. Allow to cool, centrifuge for 5 min, and decant the supernatant liquid into a 2-oz polyethylene bottle.

Adjust the pH of the solution to 2 and add 1 ml of yttrium carrier solution. Store this solution for 2 weeks.

Transfer the equilibrated solution to a 40-ml centrifuge tube. Heat in a water bath controlled at 90°C. Adjust the pH to 8 with ammonium hydroxide solution, stirring continuously throughout the adjustment. Add 6 drops of 30% hydrogen peroxide solution. Continue heating to remove the hydrogen peroxide. Cool to room temperature before centrifuging. Centrifuge, decant the supernatant liquid into a 150-ml beaker, and record the hour and date.

Add 25 ml of water to the precipitate in the centrifuge tube. Dissolve the precipitate by adding hydrochloric acid dropwise with stirring. Adjust the pH to 8 with ammonium hydroxide solution, stirring continuously. Heat in a water bath regulated to 90°C.

Check to make certain the pH is at 8. Add 6 drops of 30% hydrogen peroxide solution and continue heating to remove the peroxide. Cool to room temperature before centrifuging, centrifuge, and decant the supernatant solution into the same 150-ml beaker holding the first supernatant liquid. Record the date and hour. Reserve the combined supernatant solutions for estimating total radiostrontium.

Add 25 ml of water to the precipitate. Add hydrochloric acid (1:1) dropwise until the precipitate just dissolves. Heat in a water bath regulated at 90°C. Add 15–20 drops of a saturated oxalic acid solution gradually with stirring. Allow the precipitate to digest and then remove from the bath and cool to room temperature. Filter through a 2.8-cm glass fiber filter using suction and a fluoroethene funnel. Dry the precipitate in an oven at 110°C. Mount the precipitate on a plastic disc and cover with Mylar. Beta-count, recording the hour and date. Standardize with yttrium-90 standard.

Chemical Yield. Heat the reserved supernatant solution in the 150-ml beaker to boiling and add 10 ml of a saturated sodium carbonate solution with vigorous stirring. Cool and filter through a weighed 5.5-cm glass fiber filter. Transfer to a tared weighing bottle, dry, and weigh as strontium carbonate to the nearest milligram. The strontium yield is about 85%. The amount of natural strontium present in the original sample must be taken into consideration in calculating the per cent yield.

b. Goldin Method

The principle of this method (39) has been detailed in Section E-3 on identification of radionuclides discussed in this chapter. The preparation of the sample can follow along the lines detailed in the AEC method above.

Concentration. Add 4 ml of $1N$ strontium nitrate solution to the prepared solution, heat to boiling, and precipitate with 5 ml of $3N$ sodium carbonate solution. Allow the precipitate to settle for 0.5–2 hr, decant, and discard the supernatant solution. Transfer the precipitate to a 50-ml centrifuge tube and centrifuge to collect the precipitate.

Barium Removal. Dissolve the precipitate in 2–3 ml of $6N$ hydrochloric acid. Add 1 ml of $0.1N$ barium chloride solution, 15–20 ml of water, and ammonium hydroxide solution to a methyl orange end point. Add 1 ml of $0.5M$ potassium chromate solution, warm in a water bath, and add slowly 5 ml of acetic acid–acetate buffer solution ($2N$ acetic acid and $4N$ ammonium acetate solution). Allow to digest for 5–10 min, add an additional 1 ml of $0.1N$ barium chloride solution, stir well, centrifuge, and pour off the supernatant solution into another centrifuge tube. Discard the barium chromate precipitate. Add $6N$ ammonium hydroxide solution until the test solution is alkaline and reprecipitate the strontium with carbonate. Centrifuge, discard the supernatant solution, wash the precipitate with water containing a drop or two of sodium carbonate solution, and discard the washings. The removal of barium may be omitted at this point if old samples in which it is known that barium-140 is absent are being analyzed.

Removal of Rare Earths. Dissolve the strontium carbonate in 2–3 ml of $6N$ hydrochloric acid, add about 25 ml of water, 1 ml of $0.1N$ ferric chloride solution, heat, and make alkaline with $6N$ ammonium hydroxide. Add an additional 1 ml of $0.1N$ ferric chloride solution. Centrifuge, transfer the supernatant to another centrifuge tube, and discard the precipitate. Add to the supernatant solution 1 ml of $0.02M$ zirconyl chloride solution and 1 ml of rare earth carrier, such as 1 ml of $0.01M$ cerium nitrate solution or $0.01M$ lanthanum nitrate solution. Add $6N$ hydrochloric acid to dissolve any precipitate, warm, and again make alkaline with $6N$ ammonium hydroxide solution. Add 1 ml each of the zirconium and rare earth carrier solutions. Note the time of the precipitation. (This is the start of the ingrowth time for yttrium-90.) Centrifuge, transfer the supernatant solution to another centrifuge tube, and discard the precipitate. Add $3N$ sodium carbonate solution to precipitate the strontium, centrifuge, and discard the supernatant phase. Allow the precipitate to stand overnight. It is preferable to allow the strontium to remain in solid form as strontium carbonate at this point so that the yttrium-90 formed may be trapped in the crystals, thus minimizing absorptive losses to the glassware.

Extraction of Yttrium-90. Dissolve and transfer the strontium carbonate to a separatory funnel, using 2–3 ml of $6N$ hydrochloric acid and 30 ml of water in this manipulative step. Add $6N$ ammonium hydroxide solution dropwise to a methyl orange end point and add 5 ml of the acetate buffer solution ($2N$ acetic acid and $4N$ ammonium acetate solution). Extract the test solution with 5 ml of 5% (w/v) solution of 2-thenoyltrifluoroacetone in monochlorobenzene and transfer the organic solvent layer to another separatory funnel. Repeat the extraction two more times, adding each additional extract to the first. Note the time again, for this is the end of the ingrowth time for yttrium-90 and is the start of the decay time of this radioisotope.

Add sufficient heptane to the organic solvent layer to make the solution lighter than water and wash three times with 5 ml of acetate buffer solution, returning the washes to the original separatory funnel. Extract the organic solvent phase three times with $1N$ nitric acid. Combine the nitric acid extracts, evaporate to dryness in a stainless-steel vessel. Count for yttrium-90. Calculate the strontium-90 content from the growth and decay of yttrium-90.

Calculation. Calculate the strontium-90 activity from the yttrium-90 count (40). This is based on two equations namely, the equation for the ingrowth of yttrium-90 in strontium-90 and the equation for the decay of yttrium-90. The first of these is

$$N_2 = \lambda_1/(\lambda_2 - \lambda_1) \times N_1^0(e^{-\lambda_1 t} - e^{-\lambda_2 t}) + N_2^0 e^{-\lambda_2 t} \qquad (1)$$

in which N = number of atoms, λ = decay constant, t = time, the subscript 2 refers to the daughter, yttrium-90, the subscript 1 refers to the parent, strontium-90, and the superscript 0 refers to zero time.

The second of these equations, that is, the equation for the decay of yttrium-90, is

$$N_2 = N_2^0 e^{-\lambda_2 t} \qquad (2)$$

By making the following assumptions : (a) $\lambda_1 \ll \lambda_2$; (b) over a time, t, of a few days or weeks, $\lambda_1 t \cong 0$; and (c) $N_2^0 = 0$, Eq. 1 can be simplified into

$$N_2 = (\lambda_1/\lambda_2) \times N_1^0(1 - e^{-\lambda_2 t}) \qquad (3)$$

Multiplying Eqs. 3 and 2 throughout by λ_2 gives the activity A_2, since $A = \lambda N$.

$$A_2 = A_1^0(1 - e^{-\lambda_2 t}) \quad \text{(ingrowth)} \qquad (4)$$

$$A_2 = A_2^0 e^{-\lambda_2 t} \quad \text{(decay)} \qquad (5)$$

Goldin (41) gives the following example as an illustration of the above equations in making a calculation.

Data

Time of removal of rate earths	3 P.M. Jan. 3
Time of final TTA extraction	10 A.M. Jan. 6
Time of counting Y-90	1 P.M. Jan. 6
Ingrowth time	67 hr
Decay time	3 hr
Measured counting rate of Y-90	$R = 5.0$ cpm (net)
Efficiency for Y-90 counting	$\eta = 0.75$ (75%)

A: *Calculation of yttrium-90 activity, when counted* (A_2):

$$A_2 = R_2/\eta_2 = 5.0/0.75 = 6.7 \text{ dpm}$$

B: *Calculation of yttrium-90 activity, when extracted* $(A_2{}^0)$:

$$A_2 = A_2{}^0 e^{-\lambda_2 t}$$
$$A_2{}^0 = A_2 e^{\lambda_2 t} = 6.7 e^{0.693(3/64)}$$
$$= 6.7 \times 1.033 = 6.9 \text{ dpm}$$

C: *Calculation of strontium-90 activity:*

$$A_2 = A_1{}^0(1 - e^{-\lambda_2 t})$$
$$6.9 = A_1{}^0(1 - \epsilon^{0.693(67/64)}) = A_1{}^0(1 - 0.484)$$
$$A_1{}^0 = 6.9/0.516 = 13.4 \text{ dpm}$$

and remembering that 1 micromicrocurie is equivalent to 2.22 disintegrations per minute (1 $\mu\mu c$ = 2.22 dpm) then

$$A_1{}^0 = 13.4/2.22 = 6.0 \, \mu\mu c$$

Chemical Yield. *Sample.* Transfer the combined aqueous layers and washes in the original separatory funnel to a 100-ml volumetric flask, dilute to the mark with water, and mix well. Transfer 1 ml with the aid of a pipet to a 50-ml volumetric flask containing 1 ml of 6N hydrochloric acid, dilute to the mark with water, and mix. Determine the strontium content by flame photometry, using the 460.7 mμ line and a hydrogen–oxygen flame. Determine the background reading at 8 mμ above and below 460.7 and subtract from the reading at 460.7 mμ. The exact details of the flame spectrophotometric method depend upon the instrument being used.

Standard. Add 1 ml of 1N strontium nitrate solution with the aid of a pipet to a 1-liter volumetric flask, add 200 ml of the unknown prepared sample or equivalent solution, add 20 ml of 6N hydrochloric acid, dilute to the mark with water, stopper the flask, and mix thoroughly. Determine the strontium content as detailed for the "sample" above.

2. STRONTIUM-90 AND BARIUM-140

Volchok, Kulp, Eckelmann, and Gaetjen (42) developed a method for the determination of strontium-90 and barium-140, attributable to radioactive fallout material. In this method, calcium is used as the carrier for the radionuclides and the sample is prepared in such a manner as to yield a calcium chloride solution carrying the radio-isotopes of strontium and barium. In the instance of samples that are several months old only the strontium-90 will be detected for barium-140 has a half-life of 12.8 days. These investigators stress the need for the elimination of phosphate in this method for the determination of strontium and barium. The activity measurements are made on the daughters of strontium-90 and barium-140, that is, on yttrium-90 and lanthanum-140, respectively, after these daughters are extracted from the test solution.

The principal objective of the manipulative steps in the preparation of the sample in this method is the formation of a test solution which is suitable for the extraction of the daughters, yttrium-90 and lanthanum-140, of strontium-90 and barium-140. A quantitative separation is difficult in solutions containing phosphate ion for the phosphates of the two groups precipitate in a narrow pH range. Thus, the alkaline earth phosphates precipitate at about pH 1.5. The adjustment of the pH in the very low ranges is particularly difficult for the solutions are hot and ammonium hydroxide is used to raise the pH. The concentration of the ammonia will, under such conditions, vary with time and temperature. To avoid this difficulty, it is preferable to remove the phosphate ion completely.

The extraction of the mother test solution for the daughter isotopes is essentially a two-step procedure, designed first to separate the yttrium-90 and the lanthanum-140 quantitatively from the strontium-90 and the barium-140 and second to produce a precipitate of the ytrrium-90 and the lanthanum-140 that is suitable for measurement of radioactivity.

Because the daughter products have far shorter half-lives than the parent compounds—namely, ytrrium-90, 64.24 ± 0.30 hours; lanthanum-140, 40 hours; strontium-90, 19.9 years; and barium-140,

12.8 days—it is far preferable to count the daughters because the decay of the daughter radionuclides can be followed to detect contamination and additional extractions can be made from the mother radioisotopes after a period of only a few days.

Preliminary Treatment. Prepare an ash of the sample as detailed in preceding sections of the chapter. Dissolve the ash containing the strontium and barium in calcium phosphate in an excess of concentrated hydrochloric acid and filter the solution to remove the insoluble matter. Add ammonium hydroxide solution to the clear filtrate and adjust the pH to 1.5. It is essential that this adjustment be made carefully for the reasons noted in the preceding paragraph. Add an excess of ammonium oxalate solution. Filter off the calcium oxalate precipitate, which carries the strontium and barium quantitatively, to separate these from the phosphate. Test for completeness of the removal of the phosphate by ashing the calcium oxalate at 600°C, dissolving the calcium oxide formed in hydrochloric acid, and adjusting the pH to above 3. The formation of a precipitate is indicative of the presence of appreciable quantities of phosphate. If such a precipitate forms, add additional hydrochloric acid to lower the pH to 1.0 and dissolve all of the phosphate. Readjust the pH to 1.5 and repeat the oxalate precipitation. Once the calcium chloride solution finally formed is free of phosphate, the preparation of the mother solution is considered complete and the test solution can be repeatedly extracted to obtain the yttrium-90 and lanthanum-140 without loss of strontium-90 and barium-140.

Chemical Separation. Add about 10 mg of nonradioactive yttrium carrier as a solution to the test solution and mix thoroughly. Adjust the pH to 5 with ammonium hydroxide solution. A white gelatinous precipitate of yttrium hydroxide, with which the yttrium-90, lanthanum-140, and rare earths will coprecipitate, will form. Heat to coagulate. Record the time of precipitation. Filter off the precipitate and reserve the filtrate for additional extraction after the formation of additional daughter radionuclides.

Other long-lived rare-earth fission radionuclides and natural radioisotopes that were coprecipitated with the calcium oxalate are also coprecipitated in this first separation.

The gelatinous character of the yttrium hydroxide precipitate makes it unsuitable for counting. It must be treated in the following manner. Dissolve the precipitate from the filter paper with $6N$

hydrochloric acid, adjust the pH to a point just below precipitation, and add an excess of oxalate. The yttrium oxalate formed has a coarse granular structure that makes it satisfactory for counting. Filter off the precipitate on a stainless-steel funnel with the aid of suction, dry by drawing air through for about 10 min, remove the filter paper from the funnel, mount for counting on a brass disk, cover with Pliofilm or Mylar, and secure with a brass ring.

Chromatographic Separation. If it is desired to separate the strontium-90 and barium-140, a chromatographic technique may be used. Set up a column 2.2 × 20 cm containing 200–400-mesh Dowex-50 cation exchange resin (8% crosslinkage). Add nonradioactive strontium and barium carrier solutions to the prepared calcium chloride test solution. Transfer the test solution to the column and elute with 4N hydrochloric acid at a rate of approximately 0.3 ml/min. Approximately 5.5 hr are required for the collection of the fractions.

Under these conditions calcium, strontium, and yttrium can be separated completely from barium by collecting the first 480 ml as one fraction and collecting a second fraction from 480 to 832 ml. Calcium has a peak at 192 ml, strontium has a peak at 256 ml, and yttrium has a peak at 288 ml, whereas barium has a peak at 672 ml. After the chromatographic separation the radioactive daughters can be extracted as detailed in the chemical separation step.

Volchok, Kulp, Eckelmann, and Gaetjen made their radiometric determination of the final precipitate in a specially designed beta counter (43) that utilized anticoincidence shielding to obtain a low background count.

It was found that 98% of the calcium present as calcium phosphate is recovered as calcium oxalate and that at least 98% of the strontium-90 is recovered.

3. RADIUM-226

The principle of this method (44) was explained in the section on identification in this chapter. It is designed for the determination of radium-266 in water and thus can be applied to rainout also.

Procedure. Add to 1 liter of water or to the equivalent prepared sample 5 ml of 1M citric acid (containing 0.1% phenol to act as a preservative against microbiological growth), 2.5 ml of concentrated ammonium hydroxide solution, 2 ml of 1N lead nitrate solution, and with the aid of a volumetric pipet 1 ml of $0.1N$ barium nitrate solution. Larger volumes of water may be used but in this instance while the volumes of the other reagents are increased the volume of barium nitrate should be kept to 1 ml.

Heat to boiling and add with stirring 10 drops of methyl orange indicator solution. Add with stirring sulfuric acid (1:1) until a pink color is obtained and then 0.25 ml in excess. Digest for 5–10 min, allow to settle for 0.5–2 hr, and decant and discard the supernatant solution. Transfer the precipitate to a 50-ml centrifuge tube. Wash the precipitate with 10 ml of concentrated nitric acid, centrifuge, and discard the washing. Repeat the washing with 10 ml more of concentrated nitric acid.

Dissolve the precipitate in 10 ml of water, 10 ml of $M/4$ solution of the disodium salt of ethylenediaminetetraacetic acid, and 3 ml of $6N$ ammonium hydroxide solution. Warm and add dropwise to the warm solution 2 ml of glacial acetic acid. Digest for 5–10 min, centrifuge, and decant and discard the supernatant solution. The amount of acetic acid added is sufficient to give a 2:1 excess of acetic acid over ammonium hydroxide and to lower the pH to about 4.5. At this pH the barium ethylenediaminetetraacetate is decomposed but the lead complex is not. Note the time at the beginning of the precipitation of the barium sulfate. This is needed for the calculations because from this time on radon and daughters grow into the barium sulfate precipitate.

Wash the reprecipitated barium sulfate with water and transfer to a centrifuge tube adapted for centrifuging precipitates on to planchets. Allow to settle for 5–10 min, centrifuge, dry, flame, weigh, and count.

Calculate the radium-226 activity from the count and from the time of daughter ingrowth. If there is any question as to the isotopic or chemical purity of the radium-226, retain the precipitate for 24–48 hr and recount. Calculate the radium-226 content from the rate of daughter ingrowth.

References

1. Sullivan, W. H., *Chem. Eng. News*, **25**, 1862 (1947).
2. Morgan, K. Z., *Chem. Eng. News*, **25**, 3794 (1947).
3. McMahon, M. M., *N.Y. State Ind. Bull.*, **16**, No. 7 (July 1937).
4. Schwartz, L., F. L. Knowles, R. H. Britten, and L. A. Thomson, *J. Ind. Hyg.*, **15**, 362 (1933).

5. Fairhall, L. T., *Ind. Hyg. Newsletter*, **7**, No. 2, 6 (1947).
6. ICRP Recommendations, *Brit. J. Radiol.*, **28**, Supplement 6 (1955).
7. Adopted at the Clinton National Laboratory.
8. Threshold limit values adopted by American Conference of Governmental Industrial Hygienists, 1948.
9. Jacobs, M. B., *The Chemical Analysis of Air Pollutants*, Interscience, New York, 1960.
10. "Maximum Permissible Body Burdens and Maximum Permissible Concentrations of Radionuclides in Air and in Water for Occupational Exposure," *Natl. Bur. Std. Handbook 69*, June 1959.
11. Morgan, K. Z., *Chem. Eng. News*, **25**, 3794 (1947).
12. Curtiss, L. F., in *Industrial Hygiene and Toxicology*, F. A. Patty, Ed., Interscience, New York, 1948.
13. Holiday, D., *Ind. Hyg. Newsletter*, **7**, No. 8, 8 (1947).
14. *Chem. Eng. News*, **25**, 3100 (1947).
15. Bloomfield, J. J., and F. L. Knowles, *J. Ind. Hyg.*, **15**, 368 (1933).
16. Barker, H. H., *Ind. Eng. Chem.*, **10**, 525 (1918).
17. Roberts, L. D., in *Scott's Standard Methods of Chemical Analysis*, N. H. Furman, Ed., Van Nostrand, New York, 1939.
18. Ives, J. E., F. L. Knowles, and R. H. Britten, *J. Ind. Hyg.*, **15**, 433 (1933).
19. Moore, R. B., S. C. Lind, J. W. Marden, J. P. Bonardi, L. W. Davis, and J. E. Conley, *U.S. Bur. Mines Bull. 212* (1923).
20. Carmichael, H., and P. R. Tunnicliffe, *J. Ind. Hyg. Toxicol.*, **30**, 211 (1948).
21. Korff, M., *Electron and Nuclear Counters*, Van Nostrand, New York, 1947.
22. Curtiss, L. F., in *Industrial Hygiene and Toxicology*, F. A. Patty, Ed., Interscience, New York, 1948.
23. *Anal. Chem.*, **21**, 318–368 (1949).
24. Kahn, B., and A. S. Goldin, "Radiochemical Procedures for the Identification of the More Hazardous Nuclides," presented to the Nuclear Engineering and Science Congress, 1957.
25. Slack, L., and K. Way, *Radiations from Radioactive Atoms in Frequent Use*, Government Printing Office, Washington, D. C., 1959.
26. Shipman, W. H., P. Simone, and H. V. Weiss, *Science*, **126**, 971 (1957).
27. "Measurement of Radioactivity in Water, Bottom Silts, and Biological Materials," Sanitary Engineering Center, U. S. Public Health Service, Cincinnati, Jan. 1957.
28. Setter, L. R., A. S. Goldin, and J. S. Nader, *Anal. Chem.*, **26**, 1304 (1954).
29. Nader, J. S., G. R. Hagee, and L. R. Setter, *Nucleonics*, **12**, No. 6, 29 (1954).
30. Goldin, A. S., J. S. Nader, and L. R. Setter, *J. Am. Water Works Assoc.*, **45**, 73 (1953).
31. Jacobs, M. B., *The Chemical Analysis of Foods and Food Products*, 3rd ed., Van Nostrand, New York, 1958.
32. List, R. J., *Bull. Am. Meteorol. Soc.*, **35**, 315 (1954).
33. Setter, L. R., personal communication, 1958.
34. Institute of Paper Chemistry, Appleton, Wisconsin.
35. *Chem. Eng. News*, **41**, No. 36, 154 (1963).

36. Glendenin, L., and R. Metcalf, in *Radiochemical Studies—The Fission Products*, C. D. Coryell and N. Sugarman, Eds., McGraw-Hill, New York, 1951.
37. Atomic Energy Commission, E-38-01 (1957).
38. Willard, H. H., and E. W. Goodspeed, *Ind. Eng. Chem. Anal. Ed.*, **8**, 414 (1936).
39. Goldin, A. S., "Strontium-90 Determination," Sanitary Engineering Center, U. S. Public Health Service, Cincinnati, 1957.
40. Friedlander, G., and J. W. Kennedy, *Nuclear and Radiochemistry*, Wiley, New York, 1955.
41. Goldin, A. S., personal communication, 1958.
42. Volchok, H. L., J. L. Kulp, W. R. Eckelmann, and J. E. Gaetjen, *Ann. N.Y. Acad. Sci.*, **71**, No. 2, 293 (1957).
43. Bolchok, H. L., and J. L. Kulp, *Nucleonics*, **13**, No. 8, 49 (1956).
44. Goldin, A. S., "Analysis of Water for Dissolved Radium-226," Sanitary Engineering Center, U.S. Public Health Service, Cincinnati, 1957.

General References

"Air Pollution Measurement of the National Air Sampling Network—1953–1957," *Public Health Service Publ. 637* (1958).

Bloomfield, J. J., and W. Blum, "Health Hazards in Chromium Plating," *U.S. Public Health Service Reprint 1245* (1928).

Bloomfield, J. J., and F. L. Knowles, "Health Aspects of Radium Dial Painting, II. Occupational Environment," *J. Ind. Hyg.*, **15**, 368 (1933).

Congressional Joint Committee on Atomic Energy, *Fall-Out from Nuclear Weapon Tests*, Government Printing Office, Washington, D.C., Aug. 24, 1959.

Cook, W. A., "Chemical Procedures in Air Analysis. Methods for the Determination of Poisonous Atmospheric Contaminants," *Am. Public Health Assoc. Yearbook 1935–36*, 80.

Coryell, C. D., and N. Sugarman, Eds., *Radiochemical Studies: The Fission Products*, McGraw-Hill, New York, 1951.

Diehl, H. C., *The Applications of the Dioximes to Analytical Chemistry*, Iowa State College, Ames, 1940.

Dudley, H. C., "Selenium as a Potential Industrial Hazard," *U.S. Public Health Service Reprint 1910* (1938).

Flinn, R. H., P. A. Neal, W. H. Reinhard, J. M. DallaValle, W. B. Fulton, and A. E. Dooley, "Chronic Manganese Poisoning in an Ore-Crushing Mill," *U.S. Public Health Service Bull. 247* (1940).

Furman, N. H., *Scott's Standard Methods of Chemical Analysis*, Van Nostrand, New York, 1939.

General Handbook for Radiation Monitoring, U. S. Atomic Energy Commission LA-1835, 3rd ed. (1958).

Glasstone, S., *Sourcebook of Atomic Energy*, 2nd ed., Van Nostrand, New York, 1958.

Hamilton, A., *Industrial Toxicology*, Harper, New York, 1934.

Hillebrand, W. F., G. E. F. Lundell, H. A. Bright, and J. I. Hoffman, *Applied Inorganic Analysis*, 2nd ed., Wiley, New York, 1953.

Jacobs, M. B., *The Chemical Analysis of Foods and Food Products*, 3rd. ed., Van Nostrand, New York, 1958.

Kahn, B., and A. S. Goldin, "Radiochemical Procedures for the Identification of the More Hazardous Nuclides," presented to the Nuclear Engineering and Science Congress, 1957.

Lanza, A. J., and J. A. Goldberg, *Industrial Hygiene*, Oxford, New York, 1939.

"Measurement of Radioactivity in Water, Bottom Silts, and Biological Materials," Sanitary Engineering Center, U. S. Public Health Service, Cincinnati, Jan. 1957.

Methods Assoc. Official Agr. Chemists, 6th ed., 1945.

Moore, R. B., S. C. Lind, J. W. Marden, J. P. Bonardi, L. W. Davis, and J. E. Conley, "Analytical Methods for Certain Metals, Including Cerium, Thorium, Molybdenum, Tungsten, Radium, Uranium, Vanadium, Titanium and Zirconium," *U.S. Bur. Mines Bull.* 212 (1923).

Natl. Bur. Std. Handbook 69, Washington, D.C., 1959.

Noyes, A. M., A. Tienson, G. W. Daubenspeck, L. Kirschner, and R. Rink, "Industrial Hygiene Survey of Arc Welding Operations," *Illinois State Dept. Labor Tech. Paper 4* (1944).

Patty, F. A., Ed., *Industrial Hygiene and Toxicology*, Interscience, New York, 1962.

Prodinger, W., *Organic Reagents Used in Quantitative Inorganic Analysis*, Elsevier, New York, 1940.

"Radiochemical Determination of Strontium-90," U. S. Atomic Energy Commission, New York Operations Office, E-38-01 (1957).

Schwartz, L., F. L. Knowles, R. H. Britten, and L. A. Thomson, "Health Aspects of Radium Dial Painting, I. Scope and Findings," *J. Ind. Hyg.*, **15**, 362 (1933).

Setter, L. R., G. R. Hagee, and C. P. Straub, "The Analysis of Radioactivity in Surface Waters: Practical Laboratory Methods," *ASTM Bull. 1958*, No. 227, 35.

Standard Methods of Water Analysis, 8th ed., Am. Public Health Assoc., New York, 1936.

Sunderman, D. N., and W. W. Meinke, "Evaluation of Radiochemical Separation Procedures," *Anal. Chem.*, **29**, 1578 (1957).

Underhill, F. P., *Toxicology*, Blakiston, Philadelphia, 1928.

CHAPTER XII

SULFUR COMPOUNDS

The principal mineral acid gases and acids used in industry are compounds of sulfur, phosphorus, chlorine, fluorine, and nitrogen. Some of these acid gases are hazards because of use as such in industry. Others are hazards because they arise or are incidentally or accidentally produced during a step in the manufacture of a product. Examples of the former are the use of hydrofluoric acid in the etching of glass and the use of sulfur dioxide as a fumigant or refrigerant. Instances of the latter are the production of sulfur dioxide during the smelting of ores, the production of nitrous fumes during blasting or welding operations, and the production of hydrogen sulfide during blasting operations in mines having sulfide-bearing rock.

The more usual type of hazard in the use of mineral acids is the one of acid burns resulting from splashing, spilling, spray, or other means of contact. Burns and dermatitis attributable to inorganic acids make up about 3% of the total number of occupational dermatoses reported in the United States. In oil industries where oil is exposed to the action of sulfuric acid and in metal industries where "pickling" is done in open tanks, acid burns are a particular hazard (1).

The more dangerous hazard from these acids is the inhalation of acid fumes and acid gases. Some of these provide a warning by odor, for instance, hydrogen sulfide, but even odor is not reliable for the nose becomes readily fatigued and accustomed to the odor within a short time, thus failing to warn. Others warn by setting up a reflex respiratory action, as in the case of sulfur dioxide, which is a practically irrespirable gas. Nitrogen oxide fumes have little warning effect and do not set up any respiratory reflex. This makes the possibility of breathing lethal amounts probable when gases of this type are inhaled.

A comprehensive bibliography with abstracts of the sulfur oxides and other sulfur compounds has been compiled by Cooper (2).

517

A. Sulfuric Acid

Sulfuric acid is the most widely used chemical compound.   There is probably no manufactured article which does not have some part that has been treated with, or that comes into contact with, sulfuric acid. It was briefly explained that one of the dangers in the use of acid is acid burns.   In the manufacture of sulfuric acid itself other dangers arise.   There are two chief methods for the manufacture of sulfuric acid.   One is known as the contact process, in which sulfur dioxide, very highly purified in order not to injure the catalyst, combines with oxygen in the presence of a catalyst such as finely divided platinum or ferric oxide to form sulfur trioxide, which is subsequently converted to sulfuric acid.   The other method is known as the chamber process, in which process water vapor, sulfur dioxide, nitrous anhydride (N_2O_3), and oxygen react to form sulfuric acid.   Actually, in the gaseous state nitrous anhydride breaks up to form nitric oxide (NO) and nitrogen dioxide–tetroxide complex (NO_2–N_2O_4).   These gases act as the oxygen carrier and the reactants, steam, sulfur dioxide, nitrous anhydride, and oxygen, react to form nitrosylsulfuric acid ($HO \cdot SO_2 \cdot ONO$) which subsequently breaks down to form sulfuric acid and nitrous anhydride again.

When the sludge of the lead chambers, in which this type of acid is made, is cleaned out, there is danger that these nitrous fumes will be released, for some of the nitrosylsulfuric acid crystallizes out on the walls of the chambers.   The detection of such fumes will be discussed under the section on nitrogen acids.

Another danger in the manufacture of sulfuric acid by the chamber process is that due to arsine and hydrogen selenide.   When iron pyrites (ferrous sulfide) are used to generate the sulfur dioxide by roasting, arsine and hydrogen selenide also may be formed because iron pyrites almost invariably contain some arsenic and selenium as much, in some instances, as 1% arsenic or selenium sulfide.   The liberation of these poisonous gases is thus an industrial hazard in this method, for these gases are not easily scrubbed out and must be driven off by heat.

Sulfuric acid is inhaled in the form of droplets; these attack the upper respiratory tract and, if breathed in sufficient quantity, cause death from edema or spasm of the larynx and inflammation of the upper respiratory tract (3).   The threshold limit concentration recommended is 1.0 mg/m³.

1. DETERMINATION

a. Estimation of Sulfuric Acid and Sulfur Trioxide

In order to detect sulfuric acid spray or fumes of sulfur dioxide, the air may be passed through an absorber of the bubbler type or other trapping device containing a known quantity of standard sodium hydroxide solution, generally 0.02N. After sampling has been completed, titrate the excess standard sodium hydroxide with an appropriate normality of standard hydrochloric acid to obtain the acidity. Water may also be used as the absorbing solution. In this instance the pH may be determined or the sample may be titrated with standard alkali solution, using methyl red as indicator.

Sulfate may also be determined by gravimetric procedures.

Procedure. Acidify the solution with hydrochloric acid. Bring the solution to a boil and then precipitate sulfate with 10% barium chloride solution. Digest on a hot plate for an hour or so, or allow to stand overnight in a warm place. Filter on ashless filter paper. Wash well with water. Transfer the filter and precipitate to a tared quartz crucible, dry, char, and ignite. Burn to a white ash in a muffle oven. Cool in a desiccator and weigh. The gain in weight may be considered barium sulfate.

The gravimetric determination of sulfate by use of barium is often beset with errors resulting from the coprecipitation of other materials. The following variation may be used to overcome some of these difficulties or a titrimetric method may be employed. This gravimetric method includes all sulfur compounds that are oxidized by bromine to sulfate.

Ives and his co-workers (4) estimated total sulfur in atmospheric dust by trapping the air containing the contaminants with an impinger.

Procedure. Transfer 50 ml of the impinger solution to a beaker. Add 5 ml of bromine water. Place on a steam bath and drive off the bromine. Evaporate to 10 ml. Add 1 ml of 1N hydrochloric acid. Filter into a 150-ml. beaker. Wash the filter, catching the washings in the 150-ml beaker, until the washings and solution total 75 ml. To the filtrate, add 2 ml of 10% barium chloride solution. Digest the precipitate on the steam bath for 2 hr. Allow to stand overnight. Filter on ashless filter paper, wash with water, and transfer the filter and its contents to a platinum or other crucible. Ignite, cool, and moisten with concentrated sulfuric acid. Drive off the excess sulfuric acid in an air bath. Reignite, allow to cool in a desiccator, and weigh. The additional weight is considered barium sulfate, from which weight the amount of sulfur can be calculated.

b. *Tetrahydroxyquinone Method*

A direct titration method has been developed for sulfates by Schroeder (5). This method is based on the use of the specific indicator, tetrahydroxyquinone, for barium in the titration of sulfate. The tetrahydroxyquinone is used as an internal indicator. Sheen and Kahler (6) recommended the following details.

Reagents. *Standard Barium Chloride Solution.* The strength of this solution may vary from 1 ml (equivalent to 1 mg of sulfate) to 1 ml (equivalent to 50 mg of sulfate). The indicator is composed of disodium tetrahydroxyquinone ground with dried potassium chloride in a 1:300 ratio, and passing a 100-mesh screen. Ethyl alcohol or alcohol denatured by formula No. 30 or No. 3-A of the United States Treasury Department or isopropyl alcohol may be used as the diluent. Phenolphthalein indicator solution is used and also bromocresol green indicator solution if phosphates are present.

Procedure A. Carefully neutralize a 25-ml aliquot of the sample solution containing up to approximately 2000 parts of sulfate per million of solution with approximately 0.02N hydrochloric acid until just acid to phenolphthalein. The temperature of the solution

TABLE XII-1

Tetrahydroxyquinone Required for Various Sulfate Concentrations

Sulfate concentrations, ppm of solution	Quantity of THQ indicator, g	Strength[a] of BaCl₂ solution	NaCl required, g
Up to 100[b]	0.1	1	
100–1,000[b]	0.2	1	
1,000–2,000	0.2	4	
2,000–4,000	0.4	10	2
4,000–10,000	0.4	10	4
10,000–20,000	0.6	50	8
20,000–30,000	0.8	50	8

[a] 1 ml = mg SO₄.

[b] Subtract 0.1 ml as a blank in titration.

should be below 35°C and it is advisable to work between 20 and 25°C. Add either 25 ml of ethyl alcohol or one of the other solvents. Introduce the tetrahydroxyquinone, using 0.1 g of the indicator for sulfate up to 100 ppm and 0.2 g for sulfate up to 2000 ppm. Swirl the flask to dissolve the indicator; the solution will be colored a deep yellow. Titrate with standard barium chloride solution, the strength to be employed depending on the approximate sulfate content of the sample. Add the standard barium chloride solution at a steady dropping rate with constant swirling of the flask, until the yellow color changes to a rose. The rose color is the end point and is due to the appearance of the red barium salt of tetrahydroxyquinone. The rose color should appear throughout the body of the solution and not as spots of color.

Procedure B (sulfate range from 2000 to 30,000 ppm of the sample solution). Add sodium chloride according to Table XII-1. The procedure for neutralization and titration is the same as Procedure A.

Procedure C (with phosphate up to 60 ppm of the sample solution). Carefully neutralize a 25-ml filtered sample with approximately 0.02N hydrochloric acid until just acid, yellow range, to bromocresol green, approximate pH 4. Follow Procedure A or B above; no correction will be required for the phosphate ion present.

c. Visual Thorin Method

Thorin reacts with barium to give a red color. The intensity of the color is dependent on pH, indicator concentration, and the nature of the solvent being more intense in organic media than in water solutions. The color reaction can be utilized to titrate sulfate directly with barium chloride by adding a large volume of organic solvent to the sample and titrating in this mixed medium. The color development is also highly dependent on the nature of the organic solvent; dioxane is superior to either ethyl or methyl alcohol when the end point is detected visually (7). The initial color of thorin in the dioxane–water medium is yellow, and the change in the end point is to pink. The color change is enhanced when the solution is viewed through a pale-blue filter such as a didymium glass filter or glassblowers' goggles.

The optimum pH for the titration is about 2.5, which permits the use of the method for the analysis of many water samples without danger of precipitation of some salts in the organic media. Thorin reacts with many metals, including calcium; therefore, it is necessary to remove all metal ions by cation exchange prior to titration. Phosphate interferes somewhat by coprecipitation; with 100 ppm of sulfate, 10 and 20 ppm of phosphate give a positive error of about 2 and 3%, respectively.

Two strengths of barium chloride and thorin are provided, but there is a rather wide overlap in application. The dilute titrant and indicator are recommended if the sulfate content of the sample is less than 5 mg. The concentrated titrant and indicator give better results in the higher concentration ranges.

Results are accurate and reproducible to ±0.02 mg in the 0–5 mg range and ±1–2% for higher concentrations.

Apparatus and Reagents. *Ion-Exchange Columns* (charged with Amberlite IR-120 and operating on the hydrogen cycle). The column should be at least 10 in. long to assure complete exchange in moderately concentrated water. Highly mineralized water and brine require a longer column. Experience has shown that a strong acid solution (HCl 30% v/v) is required to get uniformly satisfactory regeneration. The frequency of regeneration depends on the mineral content of the samples; with average water, regeneration after 3 or 4 passes is sufficient.

Pale-Blue Filter. A didymium filter or glass-blowers' goggles have been used satisfactorily.

Titration Assembly with a White Porcelain Base and Fluorescent Light.

Buret, 25-ml.

1,4-Dioxane. The grade labeled "purified" is usually satisfactory, but distillation from glass may be required if the blank titration is excessive.

Sodium Hydroxide, 0.05N. Dissolve 2.0 g. of NaOH in water and dilute to approximately 1 liter.

Thorin Indicator, 0.04%. Dissolve 0.20 g of thorin in water and dilute to 500 ml.

Thorin Indicator, 0.1%. Dissolve 0.5 g of thorin in water and dilute to 500 ml.

Barium Chloride, 1.00 ml $\approx$ 1.00 mg $SO_4{}^{2-}$. Dissolve 2.130 g of anhydrous $BaCl_2$, dried overnight in an oven at 180°C, in water and dilute to 1000 ml. This concentration is not strictly stoichiometric but has been determined empirically. Check the titer by titrating standard SO_4^{2-} solutions as directed in the procedure.

Barium Chloride, 1.00 ml $\approx$ 0.50 mg SO_4^{2-}. Dissolve 1.085 g of anhydrous $BaCl_2$, dried overnight in an oven at 180°C, in water, and dilute to 1000 ml.

Sodium Sulfate, 1.00 ml = 1.00 mg SO_4^{2-}. Dissolve 1.4787 g of Na_2SO_4, dried for 2 hr at 180°C, in water, and dilute to 1000 ml.

Procedure. Rinse the ion-exchange column with 20–30 ml of sample and discard the rinse water. (This portion can be checked for calcium if desired.) Pass a sufficient volume of sample through the exchanger to provide 25–30 ml of effluent for the determination. Pipet a volume of effluent containing less than 25 mg of SO_4^{2-} (25.00 ml max) into a 150-ml beaker and adjust the volume to approximately 25 ml. The dissolved-solids content should not exceed 125 mg for the high-range titration or 50 mg for the low range. Adjust the pH to between 2.2 and 5 with $0.05N$ NaOH, if necessary. Add 50 ml of dioxane and 1.0 ml of thorin indicator. Titrate with $BaCl_2$ to the point where the color changes suddenly from yellow to orange when viewed through the filter. On titrating sulfate concentrations of less than 10 ppm, the end point will appear and then fade on stirring. At the true end point the color persists for several minutes.

Calculations. When $BaCl_2$, 1.00 ml $\approx$ 0.50 mg SO_4^{2-}, and 0.04% thorin indicator are used, the titration is not strictly linear below 5 mg SO_4^{2-} and the SO_4^{2-} concentration is determined by reading from a graph prepared by titrating standards. The following titrant volumes have been required.

SO_4^{2-}, mg	ml
0.00	0.05
.25	.55
1.25	2.50
2.50	4.95
5.00	9.90

$$\text{ppm } SO_4^{2-} = \frac{1}{\text{density}} \times \frac{1000}{\text{ml sample}} \times \text{mg } SO_4^{2-}$$

When $BaCl_2$, 1.00 ml $\approx$ 1.00 mg SO_4^{2-}, and 0.1% thorin indicator are used

$$\text{ppm } SO_4^{2-} = \frac{1}{\text{density}} \times \frac{1000}{\text{ml sample}} \times \text{ml } BaCl_2$$

Report sulfate concentrations of <10 ppm to one decimal place, between 10 and 999 ppm to whole numbers, and of >999 ppm to three significant figures only.

d. Spectrophotometric Thorin Method

The spectrophotometric thorin method is useful for waters whose sulfate content does not exceed 200 ppm and for waters with high color that interferes with the visual detection of the end point in the visual thorin method (see p. 521).

The chemistry of the determination is similar to that described in the visual thorin method with the exception that the preferable titration medium consists of 80% ethyl alcohol instead of 66% dioxane. The pH is adjusted to and maintained at 5 by a sodium acetate buffer. The end point of the titration is detected instrumentally. With listed apparatus, results are accurate and reproducible to ± 0.005 mg, which is comparable in terms of parts per million to that for the visual thorin method.

Apparatus and Reagents. *Ion-Exchange Column* (see p. 522).

Absorption Cells, 50-mm. The cement in some cells reacts with thorin to give a red color. Cells should be tested for thorin reaction, and those that give a red color in 10–15 min should be rejected.

Spectrophotometric-Titration Assembly.

Spectrophotometer, Beckman Model B.

    wavelength: 520 mμ

    phototube: blue-sensitive

    initial sensitivity setting: 1

    end point: at 0.20 absorbancy

Buret, 10-ml.

Solvent-Indicator Solution. Dissolve 0.025 g of thorin (the Hach Chemical Co. product has been used satisfactorily) and 0.5 g of anhydrous sodium acetate in 10 ml of water. Add the solution to 1000 ml of 95% ethyl alcohol. Add 12 ml of glacial $HC_2H_3O_2$ (sp gr 1.049) and mix.

Barium Chloride, 1.00m $\backsimeq$ 0.20 mg SO$_4{}^{2-}$. Dissolve 0.434 g of anhydrous BaCl$_2$, dried for 1 hr at 180°C, in water, and dilute to 1000 ml.

Procedure. Rinse the ion-exchange columns with 20–30 ml of sample and discard the rinse (this portion can be checked for the presence of calcium if desired). Pass sufficient sample through the exchanger to provide a 10-ml effluent for the determination. Pipet a volume of sample containing less than 1 mg of SO_4^{2-} and 10 mg of dissolved solids (10.00 ml max) into a 50-mm absorption cell and adjust the volume to 10.0 ml. Add 40 ml of solvent-indicator solution. Start the stirrer and set the absorbancy to 0.100. Titrate with $BaCl_2$, (1.00 ml $\approx$ 0.20 mg SO_4^{2-}) to an absorbancy of 0.20, which is stable for 30 sec. Determine a blank correction by titrating dilution water. The blank is constant throughout the concentration range of the method. A blank of 0.05 ml has been used.

Calculations. Report sulfate concentrations of <10 ppm to one decimal place, of between 10 and 999 ppm to whole numbers, and of >999 to three significant figures only.

$$\text{ppm } SO_4^{2-} = \frac{1}{\text{density}} \times \frac{1000}{\text{ml sample}}$$

$$\times\ 0.2 \times (\text{ml titrant} - \text{ml blank})$$

e. Filter Paper Method

Mader, Hamming, and Bellin (8) devised a method for the determination of small amounts of sulfuric acid mist in air. Specially prepared filter papers are employed for trapping the sulfuric acid aerosol. The acidity can be determined by titration. Sulfur dioxide does not interfere in this method.

Apparatus. The apparatus used to trap the air consists of two pieces of Pyrex tubing, 15-mm inner diameter, the ends of which have been flared to a cross-sectional diameter of 30 mm. The flared ends are ground flat. The two ends are coupled together by means of two perforated metal collars which can be clamped together and pressed tight with the aid of screws and knurled nuts.

Filter Paper Disks. Wash large Whatman No. 4, 18.5-cm filter papers by leaching with successive large quantities of distilled water over a long period of time. Best results are obtained with five 12-hr leachings, using 500 ml of water for each washing. A 19-cm Pyrex crystallizing dish is used for washing. Dry the filter papers in an oven at 100°C. Cut each washed and dried filter paper with the aid of a sharp cutting tool into 1-in. disks and place these into a dry, clean container.

Test the pH of the batch of filter paper disks by placing 2 disks, selected at random, into 20 ml of carbon dioxide-free water of known pH. Macerate the disks thoroughly with the aid of two glass rods in order to form a slurry of paper pulp. Allow to stand for 3 min and determine the pH of the mixture with a pH meter. Determine the uniformity of pH in the filter disks by repeating this test twice more. If the three pH tests indicate a consistency of 0.03 pH unit and a deviation of not more than 0.1 pH unit from that of the water used in the measurement, the filter paper batch may be considered satisfactory for the determination of sulfuric acid mist in the atmosphere.

Procedure. Place two filter paper disks in the paper holder as described above. Draw air through the filters at a rate of 50–60 cfh, recording the pressure drop through the filter and the air temperature. Remove the filter disks after sampling for 1 hr and place in a dry, clean jar.

Macerate the filter paper disks in 20 ml of water. Measure the pH and titrate with 0.002N sodium hydroxide solution. Use a pH meter for determination of the end point which is considered to be that of carbon dioxide-free water, corrected for filter paper batch acidity or alkalinity.

Calculation. Express the titrated acidity as parts per million of sulfuric acid by volume according to the following equation:

$$\text{ppm} = (\text{ml base} \times N \times 0.049 \times 22.41 \times 10^6)/$$
$$(98 \times 28.32 \times \text{cu ft air (STP))}$$

B. Sulfur Dioxide

Sulfur dioxide is one of the more important sulfur acid gases. Its use and production as a by-product in industry is enormous. Of course, its most significant use is in the manufacture of sulfuric acid, but very large quantities are also used in fumigation and bleaching. Very large quantities are produced as by-products in the smelting of sulfur-bearing ores, the manufacture of paper by the sulfite process, and the manufacture of synthetic phenol Its presence in the effluent gas from the combustion of sulfur-bearing fuel makes it one of the more important causes of air pollution.

Sulfur dioxide (sulfurous anhydride, SO_2) is a colorless noninflammable gas with a suffocating odor. It boils at $-10°C$; the liquid form has a specific gravity of 1.5 and its density with respect to air is 2.3. It is soluble in water, with the formation of sulfurous acid.

1. Physiological Response and Toxicity

Sulfur dioxide is an irritant gas (9) that is practically irrespirable to those unaccustomed to it. It readily elicits respiratory reflexes. It affects the upper respiratory tract but with deeper breathing affects the lower system also. Four ppm can readily be detected by odor but as the nose becomes accustomed to it, the amount to produce a reflex respiratory defense response increases. The minimum concentration causing irritation of the eyes is 20 ppm; 8–12 ppm will cause coughing. Jones, Capps, and Katz (10) found it impossible to remain in an atmosphere containing slightly less than 0.02% sulfur dioxide (200 ppm) for more than 1 min, because of eye irritation and the effect on the membranes of the nose, throat, and lungs. Lehmann (11,12) found that 0.05% in an atmosphere (500 ppm) was dangerous to men exposed to it for periods of 30–60 min. This value would indicate that amounts greater than 0.1–0.2% (1000–2000 ppm) might be fatal on continued exposure (13). Fieldner (14), however, states that 0.2% is intolerable but not dangerous. Other authorities give the concentration range which can be tolerated for exposures of 60 min at 50–100 ppm, and the maximum concentration that can be tolerated for several hours without serious disturbances or with but slight symptoms as 10 ppm. The latter concentration is generally accepted as the maximum allowable concentration.

2. Detection and Estimation

The literature on the detection and estimation of sulfur dioxide in air is very large. One of the reasons for the extensive literature is the adverse effect that sulfurous fumes have on human beings and on the surrounding vegetation. Many air-pollution studies have been made in the neighborhood of smelters and in the neighborhood of other industries in which sulfur dioxide occurs in the effluent gas. Another important effect of sulfur dioxide is its corrosive action.

One of the methods used in an early air-pollution study was that of Marston and Wells described by the Selby Smelter Smoke Commission (9). In this method a sample of air was drawn into a partially evacuated 20-liter bottle containing a solution of iodine colored with starch. Absorption of the sulfur dioxide was accomplished by vigorously shaking the bottle. The remaining iodine was titrated with thiosulfate solution (15). This method has been modified by bringing the oxidized sulfur dioxide solution to the same intensity of blue as that of a blank by the addition of standard iodine solution (16,17).

Of the many methods for sulfur dioxide, a review of which has been prepared by Hochheiser (18), to be found in the literature six chemical methods, namely, (1) iodine–thiosulfate, (2) hydrogen peroxide, (3) sulfitomercurate, (4) fuchsin, (5) iodine, and (6) alkali, are most frequently used. A physico-chemical method, namely, that of determining the conductivity of a solution in which the sulfur dioxide has been absorbed, is also widely employed. Each of these methods has its advantages and disadvantages. Where it can be assumed that sulfur dioxide is the major acid contaminant, the hydrogen peroxide and the conductivity methods are the procedures the author prefers. Where sulfur dioxide must be differentiated from other acid gases, the iodine–thiosulfate or iodine methods are useful, provided other reducing substances are not present. In the 1960s, the sulfitomercurate variation of the fuchsin method had a considerable vogue, but there was a great deal of difficulty in obtaining adequate reagents and maintenance of stability of the reagents for adequate performance of the method.

a. Iodine–Thiosulfate Method

In this method, sulfur dioxide is trapped in a standard solution of iodine in potassium iodide solution. The excess iodine is then estimated by titration with standard thiosulfate solution (19).

This method is used by a number of investigators. One variation is an apparatus (15) arranged for the automatic measurement of small concentrations of sulfur dioxide in air.

Sampling. In another variation, three special bubblers are arranged in series (13). The first contains 10 ml of 0.04N iodine in potassium iodide solution, diluted with water to bring the solution to the proper height in the bubbler. The second absorber contains 2 ml of 0.04N sodium thiosulfate solution diluted with water. This absorber is used to catch any vaporized iodine from the first absorber.

Known volumes of these reagents added to the bubblers, of course, will contain known quantities of acid. After sampling is finished, wash the contents of the second sampling bottle into the first absorber if a titration can be performed in it. If not, wash the contents of both absorbers into a Phillips beaker or flask and titrate at room temperature with $0.1N$ sodium hydroxide solution, using bromophenol blue as indicator. The sodium hydroxide must be standardized with this indicator. Bromophenol blue is unaffected by carbon dioxide and also gives a distinct color change in cold hydrogen peroxide solution. One ml of $0.1N$ sodium hydroxide solution is equivalent to 3.2 mg of sulfur dioxide, so that titration of small quantities of sulfur dioxide requiring less than 0.5 ml of sodium hydroxide is not accurate unless weaker standard solutions of the order of $0.05N$, $0.02N$, or $0.01N$ are used (24). A gravimetric determination may be made after titration, the precipitation of barium sulfate being carried out at room temperature. After allowing the precipitate to settle, filter off the supernatant liquid and wash the residual barium sulfate three times by decantation with boiling water. Determine a blank on the reagents both by titration and gravimetrically and correct the results accordingly.

c. Jacobs Variation

The hydrogen peroxide method is particularly useful for field sampling and for automatic sampling as, for instance, with the Wilson automatic impinger (25) because the sulfuric acid formed will not decompose on standing; consequently the sample solution may be titrated long after the sampling period.

Reagents. *Hydrogen Peroxide Absorbing Solution.* Dilute 17 ml of 3% hydrogen peroxide solution to 1 liter with water and adjust the pH to 4 with dilute nitric acid, or if necessary, dilute sodium hydroxide solution.

Sodium Hydroxide Solution, 0.002N. Prepare this solution by dilution of $1N$ sodium hydroxide solution and standardize against $0.002N$ sulfuric acid. Standardize the sulfuric acid by the gravimetric barium sulfate method.

Mixed Indicator Solution. Dissolve 0.6 g of bromocresol green and 0.4 g of methyl red in 1 liter of methyl alcohol.

Procedure. Add 3 drops of mixed indicator solution to 75 ml of absorbing solution in a large impinger and titrate with $0.002N$

sodium hydroxide solution until the red color disappears and a green fluorescence appears. Attach the impinger to its train and pass air through the absorbing solution at a rate of 1 cfm for 30 min. Note the temperature and barometric and vapor pressures. Titrate the absorbing solution at the end of the sampling period with standard sodium hydroxide solution to the reappearance of the green fluorescence and note the volume of sodium hydroxide solution used.

Calculations. Calculate the concentration of sulfur dioxide with the aid of the following formulas:

$$SO_2 \text{ (ppm)} = [(\text{ml NaOH} \times N \times 0.032) (273 + t, °C) (35.4)]/$$
$$(0.00205 \times 273 \times \text{vol air, cu ft})$$

in which the factors 0.00285 represent the weight of 1 ml of sulfur dioxide and 35.4 the number of cubic feet equivalent to 1 million ml. By collecting the factors and substituting, the following somewhat more simplified expression can be used.

$$SO_2 \text{ (ppm)} =$$
$$[\text{ml NaOH} \times 0.002 \times (273 + t, °C) \times 1.45]/(\text{vol. air, cu ft})$$

For routine work, the temperature, pressure, and vapor pressure corrections may be omitted and the following expression may be used:

$$SO_2 \text{ (ppm)} = \text{ml } 0.002N \text{ NaOH} \times 0.027$$

d. Disulfitomercurate Method

West and Gaeke (26) proposed a method in which sulfur dioxide in the atmosphere is removed and concentrated by scrubbing through $0.1M$ sodium tetrachloromercurate(II). Stable, nonvolatile disulfitomercurate(II) is formed. The subsequent determination of the isolated sulfur dioxide is based on the red-violet color produced when pararosaniline hydrochloride–hydrochloric acid mixture (0.01% dye–6% concentrated acid) and formaldehyde (0.2%) are added to the sampling solution. The absorption maximum is at 560 mμ and the color is temperature independent and stable for several hours. The equilibrium effects have been discussed by Huitt and Lodge (27). The method is sensitive, for 0.005–0.2 ppm can be determined with a 38.2-liter air sample scrubbed through 10.0 ml of sampling solution. The reaction involved in the absorption is thought to be an exchange reaction as shown by the equation,

$$(HgCl_4)^{2-} + 2SO_2 + 2H_2O \rightarrow [Hg(SO_3)_2]^{2-} + 4H^+ + 4Cl^-$$

Feigl (28) mentions that disulfitomercurate(II) ion, $[Hg(SO_3)_2]^{2-}$, which is formed when sulfite is added to mercury(II) solutions, is very stable. Even permanganate fails to oxidize the complex except at a very slow rate.

Reagents. *Sodium Tetrachloromercurate(II) Solution, 0.1M.* Dissolve 0.1 mole (27.2 g) reagent grade mercury(II) and 0.2 mole (11.7 g) of reagent grade sodium chloride in water and dilute to 1 liter.

Hydrochloric Acid Bleached Pararosaniline Solution. Mix 4 ml of 0.25% aqueous solution of pararosaniline hydrochloride and 6 ml of concentrated hydrochloric acid and dilute to 100 ml. Only dyes with absorption maxima at 543 or 544 mμ should be employed. Dyes having absorption maxima at 549 or 550 mμ should not be used in this procedure for they do not give correct results (29).

Formaldehyde Solution, 0.2%. Dilute 5 ml of 40% formaldehyde to 1000 ml with water.

Procedure. Pass 38.2 liters (1.35 cu ft) of air through 10.0 ml of sodium tetrachloromercurate(II) solution. The sampling rate may be as high as 0.2 cfm with no loss resulting from decreased efficiency of absorption. To the 10.0-ml sample add 1.0 ml of acidified pararosaniline solution and 1.0 ml formaldehyde solution. Treat **a** blank of 10 ml sodium tetrachloromercurate(II) in the same manner. Allow to stand 20–30 min for full color development. Determine the absorbancy of the test solution compared with the blank at 560 mμ. Read the concentration of sulfur dioxide from a standard curve prepared by using standard solutions of sodium bisulfite in sodium tetrachloromercurate(II) solution. If the sample size is 38.2 liters, then each microgram of sulfur dioxide represents 0.01 ppm of sulfur dioxide in the air.

If sulfides are present, the precipitate formed must be removed by filtration or centrifugation. Nitrites may interfere. Samples may be collected in the field and analyzed within a working day with no loss of sulfur dioxide resulting from either oxidation or volatilization. Other interferences have been discussed, by Zurlo and Griffini (30).

Lodge et al. (31) noted that the addition of sulfamic acid directly to the absorption solution yielded low values. These investigators suggested the addition of the sulfamic acid to the sample during the analysis or the addition of at least 0.2 ml of a 1% o-toluidine solution as suggested by Zurlo and Griffin (30) to prevent any action on the fuchsin–sulfite reagent.

e. Iodine Method

In the iodine method, the sulfur dioxide is trapped in a standard impinger containing a standard solution of sodium hydroxide. This subsequently is acidified and the sulfurous acid liberated is titrated with a standard iodine solution.

Actually, with the iodine method the amount of reducing substances present in the air is determined. It can be shown that for low concentrations, the amount of sulfur dioxide obtained by this method is equivalent to that found by the peroxide method. For higher concentrations of sulfur dioxide in the air, the amounts found with the iodine method are slightly less than those obtained with the peroxide method. This indicates that there are acids present in the air which do not react with iodine.

This method of sampling is not particularly suitable for field work unless a mobile laboratory is available which permits immediate titration of the sample. It has been found, however, that alkaline sulfite solutions in low concentrations do not decompose significantly in 24 hr so that it is possible, though not advisable, to keep such field samples for this period of time.

Reagents. *Sodium Hydroxide Absorbing Solution, 0.1N.* Prepare this solution by dilution of standard 1N sodium hydroxide solution.

Iodine Solution, 0.001N. Dilute sufficient 0.1N iodine solution, prepared by dissolving 20.25 g of potassium iodide and 12.7 g of iodine in a small amount of water and diluting to 1 liter. Standardize the dilute iodine solution against 0.001N sodium thiosulfate solution. Standardize the sodium thiosulfate solution by the customary potassium dichromate titrimetric method.

Starch Solution, 0.5%. Rub 0.5 g of soluble starch to a paste with a little cold water and pour this paste into about 90 ml of boiling water. Dilute to 100 ml.

Procedure. Place 75 ml of sodium hydroxide absorbing solution into a macroimpinger and pass air through the absorbing solution at a rate of 1 cfm for 30 min. Acidify with 3 ml of 6N hydrochloric acid and titrate with 0.001N iodine solution using 1 ml of starch solution as the indicator near the end of the titration. Calculate the parts per million of sulfur dioxide with the aid of the following equation.

SO_2 (ppm) =

$$[ml I_2 \times 0.001 \times (273 + t, °C) \times 1.45]/(vol air, cu ft)$$

Manganous sulfate can catalyze the oxidation of sulfur dioxide to sulfur trioxide. A 0.03% solution may be used in an absorber to trap the sulfur dioxide. The resulting sulfuric acid can be determined by titrating the amount of iodine set free on the addition of potassium iodide and potassium iodate. This method is said to be able to detect as little as 0.1 ppm (32).

f. Fuchsin or Rosaniline Method

In this procedure the sulfur dioxide is again trapped in a standard solution of sodium hydroxide in a macroimpinger. An iodine titration is performed to obtain the range of sulfur dioxide concentration and the trapping solution is then used to develop a color in a decolorized fuchsin–formaldehyde solution.

The fuchsin method (actually the rosaniline method) is relatively specific for sulfur dioxide. The results obtained by use of this method are always slightly less than those obtained by the peroxide or iodine method. This indicates that there are other acids and other reducing substances present in the air in addition to sulfur dioxide. It has been shown by Hochheiser, Braverman, and Jacobs (33) that the three methods, namely, the hydrogen peroxide method, the iodine method, and the fuchsin method, can generally be used interchangeably. The peroxide method can be adopted for routine laboratory work because it is simple in operation, it is a rapid method, the samples taken have good stability, and, finally, the presence of other acids besides sulfur dioxide are also important in an evaluation of pollution of the air.

Reagents. *Stock Solution I.* Add carefully 22 ml of concentrated sulfuric acid to 228 ml of water, mix, and allow to cool. Add 8 ml of a 3% solution of basic fuchsin or rosaniline in ethyl alcohol. Swirl the solution vigorously for 30 min until the initial deep brown color has faded, add an additional 142 ml of water, allow the solution to stand for 3 days, and filter to remove any precipitate which has formed in the interval.

Stock Solution II. Dilute 5 ml of 40% formaldehyde solution to 100 ml with water.

Indicator Solution. Add 1 volume of stock solution II to 10 parts of stock solution I immediately before use.

Sampling Solution. Prepare a 0.1N sodium hydroxide solution in the usual manner.

Standard Bisulfite Solution. Dissolve 8 g of sodium metabisulfite in 500 ml of water. Standardize the solution accurately with the aid of 0.001N iodine solution. Adjust the concentration so that 1 ml equals 10 μg of sulfur dioxide.

Procedure. Pass air through 75 ml of 0.1N sodium hydroxide solution in a macro impinger at the rate of 1 cfm for 30 min. Dilute to a known volume. Transfer an aliquot comprising one-half of the solution to a titrating vessel, acidify, and titrate with 0.001N iodine solution to determine the aliquot necessary for the fuchsin colorimetric method.

Take an aliquot containing from 30 to 60 μg of sulfur dioxide and adjust the alkalinity so that the aliquot contains 25 ml of 0.1N sodium hydroxide solution. Add 4 ml of the indicator solution and dilute to 50 ml in a Nessler tube. Allow to stand for 30 min for color development. Read in a Klett-Summerson colorimeter using the green filter.

$$SO_2 \text{ (ppm)} = [(SO_2) + \text{(aliquot)} \times (273 + t, \text{°C}) \times 382]/$$
$$(273 \times \text{vol air, cu ft} \times 28.32)$$

Standardization. Add 10–60-μg aliquots of sulfur dioxide as metabisulfite solution to 25-ml portions of 0.1N sodium hydroxide solution in 50-ml Nessler tubes. Add 4 ml of indicator reagent to each tube. Dilute the solutions to 50 ml with water and allow to stand for 30 min for full color development. Read the optical densities in a Klett-Summerson colorimeter using the green filter.

g. Alkali Method

Pass the air to be sampled through a fritted bubbler containing 1N sodium hydroxide solution at a rate of 0.5–1 lpm. The amount of sulfur dioxide may then be estimated by one of the methods detailed above.

A simple variation of this method commonly used in the evaluation of the role played by sulfur dioxide in smog formation is to pass the air being sampled through standard sodium hydroxide solution, say 0.01N, and then estimate the excess standard sodium hydroxide solution remaining by titration with standard acid. This method though rapid, has the disadvantage that all acidic components as well as sulfur dioxide are included in the result.

h. Electroconductivity Analyzer

The Davis electroconductivity analyzer operates on the principle of electrical conductance. The basic method of analysis used by this instrument differs very little from the methods of Kohlrausch, Arrhenius, and other pioneer workers in this field. The conductivity of a solution depends on the number of ions in solution. The conductivity of an electrolyte, however, is not measured directly but is estimated from a measurement of the resistance of the solution between two electrodes immersed in it; in this instance, it is accomplished by measuring the resistance of an aqueous sample obtained by passing air through ion-free water and passing this solution over a pair of suitable electrodes. The errors attributable to polarization, that is, the errors attributable to the changes in the composition of the solution adjacent to the electrodes, are eliminated by using alternating current.

Jacobs, Braverman, and Hochheiser (34) adapted the Davis electroconductivity recording and indicating analyzer for the measurement of sulfur dioxide in the outside air in concentrations of the order of 0–0.95 ppm for full-scale reading.

The Davis electroconductivity meter is designed for a continuous system of analysis. This is accomplished by recirculating water from a central supply source. The effluent from the analyzing cell is continuously purged to an ion exchanger where the effluent is deionized. A single pump is used to regulate the flow of the sample and the ion-free water.

Apparatus. The conductivity cell is made of clear, resistant plastic and houses the analyzing and water check electrodes; an ion-exchange unit, a pump, a recorder, and a system for controlling the flow comprise the other units, as shown in Figure XII-1.

The ion-exchange unit of this instrument serves two purposes for it acts both as an ion exchanger for removing ions and as a reser-

voir for holding the water required by the system. The ion-exchange resin is an analytical grade of Amberlite MB-3. This is
a self-indicating mixture of synthetic cation- and anion-exchange
resins. As the useful life of the ion-exchange resin decreases, the
color of the indicator changes from bluish-green to brown. This
change takes place downward from the top to the bottom of the
exchange-resin bed and thus gives warning of the need for changing the resin when it is exhausted.

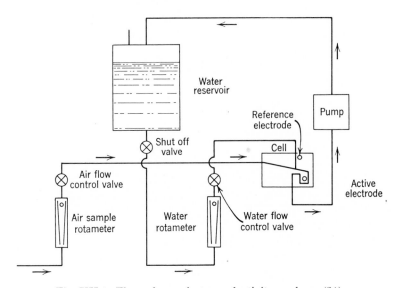

Fig. XII-1. Flow scheme electroconductivity analyzer (34).

The flow of water and air is controlled by a pump which serves two
functions, that of recirculating the water supply and that of drawing
in the air to be sampled and analyzed. In this particular instrument a Gast Model 0406 stainless-steel, oilless rotary vane-type
pump, powered by a $\frac{1}{20}$ hp General Electric 110-V, 60-cycle, split-
phase motor was used.

The recorder was a Brown Electronik circular chart recorder for
one instrument and a 30-day chart was used on another instrument.

Procedure.   The overall flow control for air was from 0 to 7 lpm
while that of the water was from 0 to 20 ml/min. In use, however, the flow rates were adjusted by the use of capillaries to a

constant air flow of 3 lpm and a water flow of 10 ml/min. The instrument is placed in the location it is desired to test and is turned on. To avoid clogging of the air line, it is best to insert an air filter consisting of an adapter tube filled with nonabsorbent cotton. The cotton should be changed from time to time.

Calibration. The instrument is manufactured to the specification desired and a calibration is supplied by the manufacturer. It should be calibrated by passing known concentrations of sulfur dioxide through the cell. If available, a gas chamber should be employed to obtain the sulfur dioxide concentrations desired.

Possibly the most practical method of calibration is to run the electroconductivity analyzer in conjunction with a sequence sampler and calibrate the instrument empirically by adjusting the scale to give the same reading as found by the titrimetric method (see Section B-2-b of this chapter).

Sensitivity. The sensitivity of this instrument is dependent upon the total number and charge of the ions dissolved by the ion-free water from the incoming air stream. By adjustment of the rate of flow of the ion-free water and the air flow, respectively, the concentration of the sample flowing past the electrodes can be controlled. By increasing the rate of flow of air and decreasing the rate of flow of water more ions can be dissolved per unit of water, and therefore apparent sensitivity of the instrument will be increased. The sensitivity of the instrument can also be increased by use of its electrical adjustments. Jacobs and co-workers found that they could adjust the sensitivity so that the instrument would read full scale for 0.5 ppm. In this range as little as 0.001 ppm could then be read.

Interferences. It must be stressed that the electroconductivity method measures not only the conductivity of the ions formed by the solution of sulfur dioxide in the ion-free water supplied to the electrodes but also the conductivity attributable to all of the ions soluble in the water. Since sulfur dioxide is the major ion-forming contaminant in the air of a number of communities, this is not a serious deficiency when such instruments are used in those areas. Indeed, as was shown by Greenburg and Jacobs (35) in the automatic impinger and grab-sample techniques, the results obtained (in New York City) are for total acidity rather than for sulfur dioxide, *per se,* but the total result may adequately be expressed as sulfur dioxide.

C. Hydrogen Sulfide

Hydrogen sulfide is a noxious gas that is extremely poisonous in very small quantities. It is the "stink damp" of miners. It has practically no use in industry but is an industrial hazard in many industries because it is a by-product or because it occurs accidentally. In almost every process where sulfur or sulfur compounds are used it is apt to be present. Burning silk and wool give off hydrogen sulfide and other noxious gases such as hydrogen cyanide, sulfur dioxide, ammonia, and carbon monoxide, some of which have a warning effect. In the Columbus penitentiary fire 320 lives were lost from this cause (36). It is a hazard in the oil-refining industry, especially where high-sulfur petroleum is being refined. Among other industries and places where hydrogen sulfide is a hazard may be mentioned mines, in which hydrogen sulfide is present naturally or in which blasting operations yield this gas, sewers, tanneries or other industries where animal matter is handled, the manufacture of sulfur dyes, the manufacture of artificial silk by the viscose process, and the rubber industry. In the viscose process for the manufacture of artificial silk, cellulose is treated first with sodium hydroxide solution and then with carbon disulfide. These reagents react to form sodium–carbon–sulfur compounds of the type of sodium thiocarbonate, Na_2CS_3, and $NaCS_2$, etc., which decompose in the spinning bath containing warm dilute sulfuric acid into sodium carbonate, Na_2CO_3, and hydrogen sulfide.

1. Physiological Response and Toxicity

In concentrations of 1 in 1000 by volume or higher, hydrogen sulfide (37) will cause immediate unconsciousness and will result in death unless artificial respiration is immediately applied. In such concentrations it is nearly as toxic as hydrogen cyanide and may act with equal rapidity by paralyzing the respiratory center of the brain. Hydrogen sulfide, however, differs from hydrogen cyanide as a poison in that it is not absorbed through the skin. In general its action depends upon its concentration and even a concentration of 0.005% will cause poisoning. Hydrogen sulfide in such low percentage is often found in industry (38). The effects of hydrogen sulfide for weaker concentrations may be summarized as follows:

Concentration in air

Parts by volume	Mg/liter	Effects
1 in 2000	0.76	Very dangerous if inhaled for 15–30 min. Causes severe irritation of the eyes and respiratory tract with risk of pneumonia or serious injury to the lungs, which may readily prove fatal.
1 in 5000	0.304	Dangerous if inhaled for 1 hr. Causes severe irritation of the eyes and respiratory tract. Eyes are affected after 6–8 min.
1 in 10,000	0.152	Symptoms of local irritation of eyes and respiratory tract after 1-hr exposure.

While hydrogen sulfide may be detected by smell, the sense of smell is lost in a 2–15-min exposure to 0.010–0.015% of this gas.

The maximum allowable concentration of hydrogen sulfide for an 8-hr exposure, as recommended by the American Standards Association (39), is 20 ppm of air; this is equivalent to a concentration of 0.028 mg/liter at 25°C and 760 mm Hg.

2. Detection

a. Lead Acetate Test

The atmosphere to be tested may be sampled by means of a hand exhausting pump with a barrel approximately 1.25 in. in bore and a capacity of 126 ml. To the inlet end of the pump is screwed a spigot with an external screw to which a holder containing the test paper may be attached.

Test Papers. These may be made from Whatman No. 1 filter paper, cut into strips 2 × 4 in. The strips are impregnated with lead acetate solution, 10 g of lead acetate dissolved in 100 ml of water plus 5 ml of glacial acetic acid. They are then suspended vertically in an atmosphere free from hydrogen sulfide and left to dry at room temperature. One in. is cut off the top and bottom of each strip and discarded. These papers may be stored in a glass-stoppered, airtight container, in which a drying agent, such as a silica gel capsule, is present.

Method. The lead acetate paper is clamped in a holder of special design (Fig. II-13), which is screwed into the pump. The apparatus having been tested for leaks, a preliminary indication of the atmosphere to be tested is obtained by making 2 slow and steady strokes of the pump, and the paper is then removed from the holder and compared within 10 min with the standard color chart provided by the British Department of Scientific and Industrial Research. A positive test will be obtained if the concentration of the hydrogen sulfide is greater than 1 part in 60,000 (0.025 mg/liter). If no stain has been produced, further tests are made with fresh lead acetate paper, this time increasing the number of strokes to 3 or 5. The concentration is read with the aid of the chart again. The stains obtained should be only on that side of the paper exposed to the gas entering the pump, and the back of the test paper should remain white or nearly so if the stain is very heavy. For sampling the gas from inaccessible places such as acid tanks or sewers the observations of Chapter II, page 71 apply.

It is clear that in the above method a known volume of air is drawn through the test paper. An alternative method of using lead acetate paper is the following (40). The test paper is prepared by dipping filter paper into a solution containing 10 g of lead acetate crystals in 100 ml of 50% glycerol. After removing the excess liquid with blotting paper, the strips of paper are placed in small glass tubes, which are drawn out, evacuated, and sealed. To test a sample of air or gas for hydrogen sulfide, connect the tube to the sample of air or gas by some suitable means, break off the end of the tube, and as a result of the air or gas entering the tube, the paper will react with the hydrogen sulfide in this small volume. By comparing the depth of color produced with that obtained with air or gas containing known volumes of hydrogen sulfide, the approximate hydrogen sulfide concentration can be established. By increasing the size of the ampoule, and by having the ampoules of known volume, this test can easily be applied in the field for the quantitative estimation of hydrogen sulfide.

There are a number of automatic devices in which the quantity of hydrogen sulfide in air may be continuously recorded by impinging the air through a fine jet against a rotating drum on which is a chart of lead acetate paper. One of these devices is so arranged that the stain produced by the hydrogen sulfide causes a change in the optical transparency of a strip of paper that, in turn, interferes with a ray of light directed on a photoelectric cell and causes a bell to ring (41).

b. Impregnated Ceramic Tile Method

Mention should be made of a cumulative method for the determination of hydrogen sulfide devised by Chanin (42). In this method strips of tile about ¾ in. wide are cut from regular, unglazed ceramic tile and a small hole is drilled in one end so that the tile can be suspended.

The tiles are impregnated with lead acetate by soaking them for 2 hr in a solution comprising a mixture of 550 ml of water, 100 ml of glacial acetic acid, 1 lb of lead acetate, and 350 ml of glycerol, the latter component serving as a humectant. The tiles can be stored for about a month but if they darken in the interval, they should be resoaked in the impregnating solution.

Procedure. Expose the tiles in the area to be surveyed for a known period of time. Compare the intensity of darkening with that of standards prepared by exposing tiles to known concentrations of hydrogen sulfide.

3. DETERMINATION

a. Cadmium Sulfide Method

This method (43) is based on the precipitation of cadmium sulfide in weakly acid or in ammoniacal solution from some cadmium salt by the hydrogen sulfide. The amount of the cadmium sulfide precipitate is then estimated iodometrically. The amount of hydrogen sulfide may then be ascertained by calculation.

Procedure. Aspirate a known quantity of air at a known temperature and pressure through two bubblers in series containing water to which has been added 10 ml of ammoniacal cadmium chloride solution, prepared by dissolving 20 g of cadmium chloride in 400 ml of water, adding 250 ml of concentrated ammonia water, sp gr 0.90, and then diluting the whole to 1 liter. After sampling has been completed and the sample has been removed to the place of analysis, remove any sulfur dioxide that may have been trapped along with the hydrogen sulfide by aspirating 10 liters of air through both absorbers. This air may be trapped in turn by one of the procedures described in the section on sulfur dioxide. If any considerable quantity of hydrogen sulfide is present, there will be a distinct yellow precipitate. Transfer the precipitate and solutions from the absorption tubes to a glass-stoppered bottle. Wash the absorbers and add the washings to the bottle. Dissolve the cadmium sulfide by the use of concentrated hydrochloric acid, washing out the absorbers first with the acid before transferring to the bottle. Add the acid slowly and with constant stirring until the solution is virtually colorless and acid to litmus. Titrate at once with $0.04N$ iodine solution, using starch to indicate the end point. If desired, add an excess of iodine and back-titrate with standard thiosulfate solution.

The results of the analysis may be computed to hydrogen sulfide percentages by use of the formula

$$1 \text{ ml } 0.001N \text{ I}_2 \approx 0.112 \text{ ml of H}_2\text{S at STP}$$

Other cadmium solutions, for instance, cadmium acetate (44), may be used as the absorbing solution. The details of the method and the iodometric estimation are practically the same.

An adaptation to this method for field use has been described by Wallach and O'Brien (45).

Another modification of the method is the following (46). Use an apparatus containing three absorbers in series. Each of the absorbers contains 100 ml of cadmium chloride solution (20 g of cadmium chloride, $CdCl_2$, dissolved in 900 ml of water) to which is added 20 ml of $0.5N$ sodium hydroxide solution. Draw air through the train at the rate of 30 lph for about 1 hr.

Transfer the contents of the first two absorbers to a glass-stoppered bottle. Use the contents of the third absorber if the concentration of hydrogen sulfide is high. Rinse the absorbers with water and then with concentrated hydrochloric acid, using 25 ml of the acid for each 100 ml of absorbing solution and rinse collected in the flask. Mix the combined absorbing solution, rinse water, and rinse acid. Rapidly add 25 ml of $0.005N$ iodine solution and titrate the excess iodine with $0.005N$ sodium thiosulfate solution. Use starch solution as indicator near the end point. Continue the titration until no color remains in 5 ml of chloroform when shaken with the solution titrated.

One ml of $0.005N$ iodine solution is equivalent to 0.0846 mg of hydrogen sulfide. This quantity of hydrogen sulfide in 30 liters of air represents 2.0 parts of hydrogen sulfide per million of air at 25°C and 1 atm of pressure.

The method is accurate to about 0.5 ppm for a 30-liter air sample when testing air whose concentration of hydrogen sulfide is within the range of hygienic significance.

b. Methylene Blue Method

Sulfide ion reacts with a mixture of p-aminodimethylaniline, ferric ion, and chloride ion to yield methylene blue. The method is applicable in the presence of zinc and iron. This method was studied by Mecklenburg and Rosenkranzer (47) as early as 1914. Almy (48) and subsequently Sheppard and Hudson (49) devised variations. These methods are also detailed by Jacobs (50).

Pomeroy (51) applied the method to sewage analysis and this work subsequently became the standard colorimetric procedure in the Methods of the American Public Health Association (52).

Later Budd and Bewick (53) absorbed hydrogen sulfide in zinc acetate solution and determined it colorimetrically as methylene blue. Members of the staff of the Los Angeles Air Pollution District (54) applied this variation to air analysis using a midget impinger.

A committee of the American Society for Testing Materials (55) recommended a tentative method for determining sulfides in industrial waste water. Marbach and Doty (56) also trapped hydrogen sulfide in an alkaline suspension of cadmium hydroxide and determined the sulfide colorimetrically as methylene blue but modified the method significantly by protecting the absorbed sulfide from oxidation by air.

The method of choice for the determination of small concentrations of hydrogen sulfide is the Jacobs, Braverman, and Hochheiser variation (57) of the methylene blue method. This variation is suitable for the determination of hydrogen sulfide and other sulfides for the part per billion range. Air is bubbled through an absorption mixture of an alkaline suspension of cadmium hydroxide contained in a macro impinger at rates as high as 1 cfm or in a midget impinger at 0.1 cfm. The concentration of the trapped sulfides is then estimated by the methylene blue method. Procedures for use both in the laboratory and in the field can be devised.

One of the difficulties encountered in the development of this method was the oxidation of the cadmium sulfides formed from the air-borne sulfides by the relatively large volume of air sampled at 1 cfm. The method details how this interference was eliminated.

Reagents (all reagents should be refrigerated for optimum results). *Amine–Sulfuric Acid Stock Solution.* Add 50 ml of concentrated sulfuric acid to 30 ml of water and cool. Add 12 g of N,N-dimethyl-p-phenylenediamine. Stir until solution is complete.

Amine–Sulfuric Acid Test Solution. Dilute 25 ml of stock solution to 1 liter with 1:1 sulfuric acid.

Ferric Chloride Solution. Dissolve 100 g of $FeCl_3 \cdot 6H_2O$ in enough water to make 100 ml of solution.

Absorption Mixture. Dissolve 4.3 g of cadmium sulfate, $CdSO_4 \cdot 8H_2O$, in water. Dissolve 0.3 g of sodium hydroxide in water. Add to the cadmium solution and dilute to one liter. Stir well before using.

Procedure for Low Concentrations of Hydrogen Sulfide (less than 20 ppb). *Colorimetric Variation.* Place 50 ml of absorption mixture in a large impinger and pass air through apparatus for 30 min at the rate of 1 cfm. Add 0.6 ml of amine test solution and 1 drop of ferric chloride solution to the impinger and agitate after each addition. Transfer to a 50-ml volumetric flask, make up to volume, and allow to stand for 30 min. To 45 ml of absorption mixture in a 50-ml volumetric flask, add amine test reagent and ferric chloride solution, agitate after each addition, make up to volume, let stand for 30 min, and use as a reference in setting apparatus to zero. Then read optical density of sample and determine concentration of hydrogen sulfide from the working curve.

Calculation. The following expression may be used to compute the results.

$$H_2S \text{ (ppb)} = (\mu g\ H_2S \times 719)/vol, \text{ liters}$$

Note: This calculation is set empirically at 25°C and 760 mm, using the factor 719 as taken from the Appendix. To correct for other conditions of temperature and pressure use the usual gas law equations.

Spectrophotometric Variation. For use in the spectrophotometer, 25 ml or a one-half aliquot of the final mixture of sample and reference blank is used and the final calculation is multiplied by two.

Note: In both of the above methods, if the concentration of hydrogen sulfide is above the working curve, dilute to the appropriate range, but an analogous dilution must be performed on the reference reagent blank and the apparatus is again set at zero with this solution before measuring the optical density of the diluted sample.

Procedure for Higher Concentrations of Hydrogen Sulfide (20 ppb and above). Under these conditions the midget impinger has been used successfully. Place 10 ml of absorption mixture in midget impinger and aspirate at 0.1 cfm through the mixture for about 15 min. (The midget impinger apparatus is especially useful in field work.) Add 0.6 ml of amine test solution and 1 drop of ferric chloride solution, agitate after each addition, and transfer to a 25-ml volumetric flask for spectrophotometric determination or a 50-ml volumetric flask for colorimetric determination. Dilute to the mark and allow to stand for 30 min. Repeat the same procedure (without aspiration) for the reference reagent blank, set apparatus at zero, and read the optical density of sample. Refer to the working curves for amount of hydrogen sulfide present and calculate as detailed above.

Preparation of Standard Curves. Since two methods of estimating the amount of methylene blue formed were used, two standard curves, namely, a colorimetric one by use of the Klett-Summerson colorimeter and a spectrophotometric one by use of a Coleman spectrophotometer, were prepared.

Colorimetrically by Klett-Summerson Colorimeter. Add 0, 1, 3, 5, 7, and 9 μg of hydrogen sulfide equivalent separately to 50-ml volumetric flasks containing 45 ml of alkaline cadmium hydroxide absorption mixture. Add 0.6 ml of amine test solution and 1 drop of ferric chloride solution and stir after each addition. Dilute each to 50 ml, allow to stand for 30 min, and transfer the first mixture containing no hydrogen sulfide to the colorimeter cell. Insert the red filter, place the cell in position, and adjust the reading to zero. Read the transmission of the five remaining mixtures. Plot optical density vs. concentration in micrograms.

Spectrophotometrically by the Coleman Spectrophotometer. The maximum absorption of the methylene blue as produced in this method, determined in the usual manner, was found to be at 670 mμ.

Add 0, 1, 2, 3, and 4 μg of hydrogen sulfide equivalent separately to 20 ml of absorption mixtures contained in 25-ml volumetric flasks. Add 0.6 ml of amine test solution and 1 drop of ferric chloride solution. Stir after each addition. Dilute to 25 ml and allow to stand 30 min. Set the machine at 670 mμ, place the first mixture containing no hydrogen sulfide in a cuvett, and test in the reference position.

Set the scale at zero. Place the other mixtures in the sample cuvet in increasing order and note the increase in optical density. Plot optical density against concentration of hydrogen sulfide in micrograms.

In place of the usual hydrogen sulfide equivalent sodium sulfide, which requires troublesome protection against oxidation, a solution of allylthiourea may be used. This must be checked by gravimetric determination as silver sulfide after treatment with ammoniacal silver chloride solution.

c. Iodine Method

In the absence of other oxidizing or reducing gases, hydrogen sulfide, as already mentioned, may be estimated iodometrically. The following procedure may be used as a field test. The method is accurate to about 95%.

Procedure. Pass the air being tested through a midget impinger of the fritted-disk type at a measured rate through $0.01N$ iodine in potassium iodide solution until the mixture has been practically decolorized. The amount of hydrogen sulfide present can be calculated from the relationship that

$$1 \text{ ml of } 0.01N \text{ I}_2 \backsimeq 0.1223 \text{ ml H}_2\text{S at } 25°C \text{ and } 760 \text{ mm}$$

hence

$$\frac{\text{ml } 0.01N \text{ I}_2 \times 0.1223 \times 1000}{\text{min sampling time} \times \text{sampling rate (lpm)}} = \text{ppm H}_2\text{S}$$

Consequently, where the rate is 1 lpm the equation reduces to

$$\frac{\text{ml } 0.01N \text{ I}_2 \times 122.3}{\text{min sampling time}} = \text{ppm H}_2\text{S}$$

It may also be estimated by trapping the gas in sulfate-free ammoniacal hydrogen peroxide (58). The ammoniacal hydrogen peroxide oxidizes the hydrogen sulfide to sulfate:

$$\text{H}_2\text{S} + 4\text{H}_2\text{O}_2 \rightarrow \text{H}_2\text{SO}_4 + 4\text{H}_2\text{O}$$

Three per cent sulfate-free hydrogen peroxide is prepared as directed on page 530. To 94 ml of this solution add 6 ml of 25% ammonium hydroxide solution. Fifteen ml of this ammoniacal hydrogen peroxide solution is placed in each absorber and the determination is then made as described for sulfur dioxide.

d. Nitroprusside Method

The sodium nitroprusside test (59,60) is not as sensitive nor as selective as either the lead acetate or the silver cyanide tests for hydrogen sulfide. Of the many variations of this method the following may be used.

Procedure. Aspirate air through a gas-washing bottle containing 25 ml of water to which has been added 2 ml of 1% sodium nitroprusside solution (1 g of $Na_2Fe(CN)_5NO \cdot 2H_2O$ dissolved in water and made up to 100 ml) and a few drops of ammonium chloride solution, until the solution becomes definitely colored. A control solution of 25 ml of water and the same amounts of sodium nitroprusside and ammonium hydroxide is treated dropwise with a solution of arsenious sulfide with the aid of a microburette until the color intensity is the same as that of the unknown. The arsenious sulfide solution is prepared by dissolving 0.0367 g of arsenious sulfide, As_2S_3, in a little ammonium hydroxide and diluting to 100 ml. One ml of this solution is equivalent to 0.1 ml or 0.143 mg of hydrogen sulfide at 0°C and 760 mm Hg. The hydrogen sulfide content may then be calculated according to the formula

$$H_2S = 0.143a/M$$

where a is milliliters of As_2S_3 solution used and M is liters of air passed through the absorber.

D. Oxidizable Sulfur Compounds

While the Titrilog can be used for the determination of sulfur dioxide in air, it can be employed for a broader purpose, namely, that of determining oxidizable sulfur compounds in air. Actually the prototype of the Titrilog was developed by Shaffer, Briglio, and Brockman (61) for the detection of mustard gas and related compounds in the air and thus could serve as a warning device in the case of a poison gas attack with these agents.

The Titrilog is based on an oxidation–reduction reaction, specifically an automatic bromometric titration. It provides a measure of the substances which exert a reducing action on an acid solution of bromine. Oxidizable compounds containing sulfur are titrated with a solution in which bromine is generated electrolytically. Continuous titration is accomplished by applying the principle of the feedback amplifier to control the rate of reaction of reacting bromine upon a set reference level so that it is at all times equal to the rate of

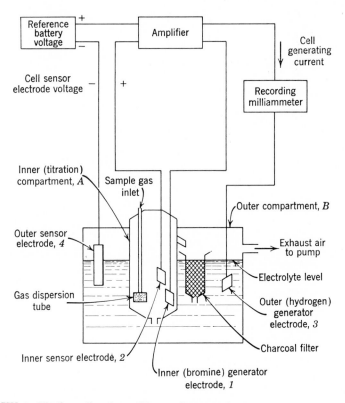

Fig. XII-2. Titrilog cell and amplifier. (Courtesy Consolidated Electrodynamic Corp., Los Angeles, Calif.)

absorption of reactive gas in the titration cell. The Titrilog has been used in industry for the monitoring of sulfur dioxide and hydrogen sulfide gases and has been used in air pollution control work such as described by Thomas (62).

While the instrument, without modification, was not sufficiently sensitive to be used for monitoring the sulfur dioxide concentration in a large urban area, it was adapted by Ettinger, Braverman, and Jacobs (63) for the determination of oxidizable sulfur compounds in incinerator flue gases. The instrument used by these investigators had a threshold sensitivity of 0.1 ppm or 0.005 grain per 100 cu ft, which was adequate for monitoring flue gases.

Operation. The operation of this instrument can be ascertained from Figure XII-2. Titration takes place in inner compartment A. The sample gas is admitted through the disperser. Bromine is generated at electrode 1 while electrode 2 is made of platinum and is responsive to changes in the concentration of bromine. Electrode 3 is a hydrogen electrode and is required to complete the circuit with electrode 4 which is a calomel half-cell reference electrode against which the voltage of electrode 1 is developed. Reference battery voltage is connected to oppose the voltage between the sensor electrode 1 and the reference electrode 4 and is adjusted to a known bromine concentration called the zero adjustment. This is set for a very low bromine concentration. The variation of the bromine concentration gives rise to a net voltage which is applied to the input of the amplifier. The output of the amplifier is applied to the generation of bromine. The chemical cell thus forms the input section of the amplifier feedback loop. The cell also has an activated carbon absorbent unit to take up the reaction products.

The bromine concentration in the cell falls as any reactive gas enters. The sensor voltage changes, giving a high net input to the amplifier which responds by increasing the generating current, thus forming more bromine. The generating current is recorded, the difference between the reaction period and the "zero" level being directly proportional to the concentration of the sulfur compounds.

For the work on incinerator flue gas analysis, it was found by experience that the fluctuations of the instrument could be kept to a minimum if division 10 was used as the zero point on the recorder instrument instead of the designated zero of the chart. The instrument was standardized so that each small division represented 0.2 ppm expressed as sulfur dioxide. The maximum concentration that could be indicated by the device under these conditions was 9 ppm as sulfur dioxide if an undiluted gas was being analyzed. Higher concentrations could be determined by diluting the flue gas being analyzed with air to keep the gas being passed through the instrument within its limits.

E. Carbon Disulfide

Carbon disulfide is a chemical compound which was and is widely used in industry. It was formerly used a great deal in the vulcanization of rubber. It finds use in the manufacture of artificial silk, of textiles, and as a solvent in industry. For instance, it is used to extract the remaining oil from olive marc. Such oil is known as sulfur oil. Carbon disulfide is also used as a disinfectant and fumigant. Dangerous concentrations may also be encountered in works in which coal gas, tar distillation products, and certain chemicals are manufactured.

Carbon disulfide is a colorless, volatile, highly combustible, generally foul-smelling liquid. It boils at 46°C, has a specific gravity of 1.26, a refractive index of 1.629 at 18°C, and a flash point below room temperature. Its lower inflammable limit is 1.25% by volume in air and its upper limit is 50.0% by volume. It ignites spontaneously between 125 and 135°C, so that even contact with a warm steam pipe or an electric light may be sufficient to cause ignition of the vapor. Its inflammability makes it an undesirable material to use in industry.

1. Physiological Response and Toxicity

Carbon disulfide, if inhaled in sufficient quantity, has a narcotic effect. The symptoms of chronic poisoning vary from slight fatigue and giddiness to serious mental derangement, nervous disorders, blindness, and paralysis. In high concentrations, carbon disulfide may cause delirium, coma, and death from respiratory failure.

The effects of the inhalation of various concentrations of carbon disulfide vapor in air may be summarized as follows. Repeated daily exposures to concentrations of the order of 0.1–0.2 mg/liter, that is, 33–66 ppm, produce a general condition of ill health with headache, drowsiness, and hysterical outbursts. An isolated exposure for a few hours to a concentration of 1 mg/liter (333 ppm) will produce severe headache and mental dullness or confusion. Repeated daily exposures to this concentration order result in increasingly severe symptoms with neuritis, distorted vision, and mental disturbance. Exposure to concentrations of the order of 6–10 mg/liter (2000–3333 ppm) for half an hour may result in serious illness and danger of mania and coma (64). The toxic effects of low concentrations of carbon disulfide have been studied by Wiley, Kueper, and von Oettingen (65) and experiences in using this material in industry have been reviewed by Barthélémy (66).

The accepted maximum safe permissible workroom concentration of carbon disulfide vapor in air is 20 ppm, as indicated in Table 5, Appendix.

2. DETECTION AND DETERMINATION

The methods used for the determination of the amount of carbon disulfide in air fall into two main groups. The first is the division in which the sulfur of the compound is oxidized to sulfate, which is subsequently detected and estimated gravimetrically. The second is the division in which the carbon disulfide is condensed with alkali and alcohol and is estimated as the resultant xanthate, or is condensed with diethylamine and a copper salt with the formation of diethyldithiocarbamate. The latter are simpler and more rapid methods. Matuszak (65) reviews some of the methods for the estimation of carbon disulfide.

a. Detection with Diethylamine and Copper Acetate

The British standard method (64) adopted for the detection of carbon disulfide in air depends upon its interaction with diethylamine and copper acetate, with the formation of a colored compound, copper diethyldithiocarbamate. Samples of air to be tested are drawn by means of a hand pump through a bubbler containing the reagents and the mixture is allowed to stand. The color developed is compared with a series of standards and from the number of pump strokes made and the color obtained, the concentration can be estimated by reference to a table. Concentrations down to 0.025 mg/liter can be detected in this manner with 20 strokes, or less, of the pump.

Hydrogen sulfide will also produce a color with this reagent and therefore must be removed by filtering through lead acetate paper.

Apparatus. Sample the atmosphere by means of the hand pump described on page 52, using a nozzle to which a rubber tube can be attached. Draw the sample through the reagent contained in a bubbler consisting of a side arm test tube of approximately 0.75-in. internal diameter and about a 6-in. length. Fit the tube with a rubber

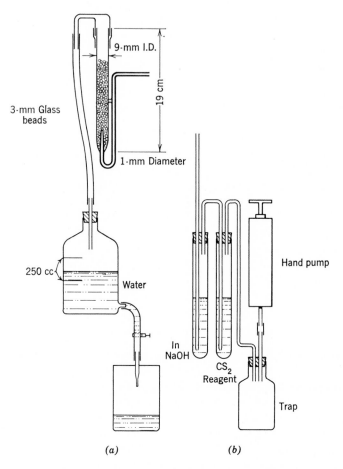

Fig. XII-3. Sampling and analysis of carbon disulfide (68).

stopper through which passes a delivery tube about ⅛-in. bore reaching nearly to the bottom of the tube. The delivery tube must end in a fine jet. The opening of the jet can be adjusted by drawing out the tube and then inserting a gauge wire while the tube is in the flame. The nozzle can be cut at the point desired. A trap must be inserted in the line between the pump and the bubbler in order to prevent any of the reagent from being accidentally drawn into the pump. The apparatus may be mounted as shown in Figure XII-3b.

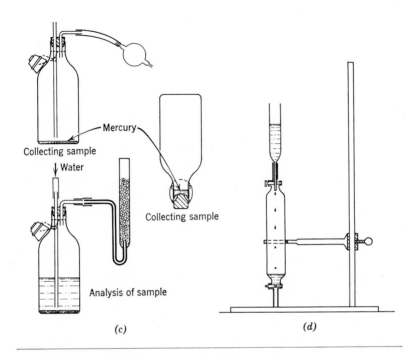

Collecting sample

Mercury

Water

Collecting sample

Analysis of sample

(c)   (d)

Preparation of Reagent. Prepare the reagent by dissolving 2 ml of diethylamine in 100 ml of benzene. Warm 0.1 g of copper acetate with a little absolute alcohol and make up to 100 ml with absolute alcohol. To prepare the mixed reagent used for the test, transfer 10 ml of absolute alcohol to the bubbler, add 2 ml of diethylamine solution and 2 ml of the copper acetate solution, and stir the mixture.

Preparation of Standards. Dissolve 1 ml of reagent carbon disulfide in absolute alcohol in a 100-ml volumetric flask and make up to volume with absolute alcohol. This is a 1% volume solution. Transfer 1 ml of this 1% solution to a 50-ml volumetric flask and make up to volume with absolute alcohol. This yields a 0.02% volume solution.

Transfer the following volumes of 0.02% carbon disulfide solution and make up to 10 ml with absolute alcohol. Add 2 ml of diethylamine reagent, 2 ml of copper acetate solution, mix well, and allow to stand for 15 min for full development of color.

Standard	Volume of 0.02% CS_2 soln., ml
1	0.25
2	0.5
3	1.0
4	2.0

The standards must be prepared in tubes of the same bore as the bubbler. They should be prepared from the 0.02% carbon disulfide solution immediately before the test or at least on the same day. If they are to be kept for some time they must be tightly stoppered and placed in the dark.

Procedure. Before carrying out any test, check the valves of the hand pump, with the bubbler disconnected, by closing the inlet with the finger and drawing out the piston slowly to its full length. On releasing the piston, it should rapidly return to its original position. The washer on the pump piston may shrink in the course of time. This may be remedied by soaking the piston in warm liquid paraffin for a few hours.

Place the reagent in the bubbler as described. If hydrogen sulfide is also present in the atmosphere, fix a dry lead acetate paper (Section C-2-a of this chapter) in a paper holder (Fig. II-13) in such a way that the atmosphere entering the solution passes through the lead acetate paper first. Draw 1, 2, 3, 5, or 20 strokes of the pump very slowly, 10 sec per stroke, in the atmosphere to be tested. Remove the bubbler and allow to stand for 15 min. At the end of this period compare the color, if any is developed, with the prepared standards, holding the test bubbler and the standard tubes side by side and observing by transmitted daylight.

The concentration of carbon disulfide, corresponding to the depth of color produced and the number of strokes, may be obtained from the following table:

Number of strokes	Standard			
	1	2	3	4
1	1/6000	1/3000	1/1500	1/750
2	1/12,000	1/6000	1/3000	1/1500
3	1/18,000	1/9000	1/4500	1/2300
5	1/30,000	1/15,000	1/7500	1/3800
20	1/120,000	1/60,000	1/30,000	1/15,000

To sample and test in inaccessible places, use the methods suggested in Chapter II, page 71.

b. Modified Diethylamine Method

Viles (68) has modified the diethylamine method for the determination of carbon disulfide and has presented alternative methods for sampling.

Preparation of Reagent. Add to 1 liter of 85–100% ethyl alcohol 1 ml of diethylamine, 20 ml of practical triethanolamine, and 0.05 g of copper acetate. Mix thoroughly and allow to stand until all the copper acetate dissolves. If a turbidity develops, allow the mixture to stand 2–3 days to clear. This reagent, if kept well stoppered with a rubber stopper in a glass bottle, is stable. It contains sufficient reagent so that 10 ml of the solution will completely absorb and react with a concentration of 120 ppm of carbon disulfide in 1 liter of air.

Preparation of Standards. A stock standard alcohol solution may be prepared by dissolving a known weight of carbon disulfide in 100 ml of alcohol. Because of the difficulty of accurately weighing out small amounts of carbon disulfide, it is better to prepare the standards from a saturated water solution. This is made by shaking excess liquid carbon disulfide with water in a glass-stoppered bottle. After the droplets of carbon disulfide have settled and the water layer is perfectly clear, pipet exactly 1 ml of this solution into 50–75 ml of alcohol in a 100-ml volumetric flask. Make up to volume with alcohol and mix thoroughly.

The solubility of carbon disulfide in water is 0.22 g per 100 ml at 22°C and 0.195 g at 30°C. It may be assumed, then, that 0.2 g of carbon disulfide per 100 ml is the concentration of the water layer (26–30°C). The resultant alcohol standard solution contains 0.00002 g, or 20 μg, of carbon disulfide per milliliter. Since 0.1 ml can be accurately measured, it is possible to make up standards 2 μg apart. In a 322-ml air volume sample this is equivalent to 2 ppm carbon disulfide.

Color standards can be made up in 4-μg intervals for use in Nessler tubes. Standards ranging from 0 to 50 μg offer best comparisons. If a sample contains more carbon disulfide than the highest color standard, take an aliquot portion of the sample and make it up to 10 ml with additional reagent and then compare with standards. By multiplying the number of micrograms found in the aliquot by the factor, 10/ml of aliquot, the total number of micrograms of carbon disulfide in the sample may be calculated. The standards remain stable, if stoppered, for three days.

Interferences. Hydrogen sulfide interferes and is eliminated by absorption in sodium hydroxide solution in this modification. Dimethyl sulfide, thiophene, and mercaptans do not interfere (69). Thioacetic acid gives reactions similar to carbon disulfide.

Procedure. Viles (68) uses four methods of sampling, as illustrated in Fig. XII-3. The apparatus a is an adaptation of the U.S. Bureau of Mines apparatus for the determination of benzene (70). It consists of a bubbler unit, containing glass beads, which is connected to the air intake of an aspirator.

Place 2–3 ml of the reagent in the trap. Allow water to flow out of the aspirator bottle and regulate the air flow so that a 250-ml air sample is collected in 15–30 min. The volume of air sample is measured by the amount of water displaced.

Empty the contents of the bubbler trap into a beaker and wash the bubbler and the beads with two 3-ml portions of the reagent. Transfer to a tall 50-ml Nessler tube. Make up the volume to 10 ml and allow to stand for 15 min for full development of the color. The test solution should be exposed as little as possible to the contaminated air to prevent any additional absorption of carbon disulfide vapor by the reagent.

A magnesium citrate bottle may be used for sampling by flushing with a rubber-bulb aspirator. Mercury may be used as an internal seal. The air sample is then displaced through the bubbler (as shown in Fig. XII-3c) by water displacement. The analysis is then performed as above.

An evacuated tube of 325-ml capacity may be used to take a sample. The contents are analyzed by setting the tube up vertically and adding 10 ml of the reagent by means of a capillary tube through an open stopcock (Fig. XII-3d). The stopcock is closed, the tube shaken for 0.5–1 hr, and then the contents are transferred to the Nessler tube for comparison with standards.

Viles also uses a hand-pump method, using sodium hydroxide solution to eliminate the interference of hydrogen sulfide (Fig. XII-3b). Place 10 ml of the reagent in the test tube nearest the sampling pump. Before attaching the pump, draw 2 strokes so that the pump is flushed with the atmosphere to be tested. For comparison, two

TABLE XII-2
Concentration of Carbon Disulfide by Diethylamine Method

Number of strokes, 60-ml-capacity pump	Standard 1 22 μg, ppm	Standard 2 45 μg, ppm
1	120	240
2	60	120
3	40	80
4	30	60
6	20	40
8	15	30
12	10	20
24	5	10

standards are kept on the opposite side of the vertical support, one containing 22 μg and the other 45 μg of carbon disulfide. These standards must be kept stoppered to prevent additional absorption of carbon disulfide from the atmosphere.

Draw 6–9 strokes with the pump so that the air bubbles through the solution at a slow rate, 20–30 sec for one pump stroke of 60-ml capacity. Comparisons are made with the standards in order to estimate the concentration of carbon disulfide. Take a second sample so that it matches one of the standards closely. This may be difficult to obtain but between the two samples a fairly accurate estimate of the carbon disulfide concentration can be made. The concentration of the test atmosphere may be obtained from the table above. A sampling bubbler, using a rate of 60 ml/min, may also be employed.

c. Xanthate Method

This method depends upon the fact that when carbon disulfide is drawn through an alcoholic fixed alkali solution, an alkali xanthate is formed.

$$CS_2 + NaOH + C_2H_5OH \rightarrow S{=}C{\Big\langle}{\begin{array}{l} OC_2H_5 \\ SNa \end{array}} + H_2O$$

The xanthate so formed may be estimated as copper xanthate or iodometrically. It is essential for proper estimation that the alcoholic potash or soda used to absorb and react with the carbon disulfide be fresh, that the formation of any appreciable proportion of free xanthic acid be avoided, and that the iodine titration, if one is made, be made as soon as possible after the formation of the xanthate.

Procedure. After passing the air through one or more absorbers, depending on the type governing the completeness of absorption, containing a 5% solution of alkali in ethyl alcohol, transfer the specimen so obtained to a glass-stoppered bottle or flask. Acidify the solution with 1N acetic acid, using phenolphthalein and litmus papers as outside indicators, until the solution is acid to phenolphthalein but alkaline to litmus. Add starch indicator solution and titrate immediately with 0.006862N iodine solution.

$$2S:COC_2H_5 \cdot SK + I_2 \rightarrow 2KI + (S:COC_2H_5 \cdot S)_2$$

With iodine solution of the normality stated, each milligram of carbon disulfide requires about 2 ml of the iodine solution. For less than milligram amounts, a more dilute solution of iodine should be used.

Alternatively, the xanthate may be estimated by adding it slowly with constant stirring to a sufficiently acid mixture of standard iodate containing excess iodine. These reagents will react to liberate iodine, which may then be determined by the usual thiosulfate titration. The exact amount of xanthate, hence of carbon disulfide, can be calculated from the relationship that

$$1 \text{ mole } CS_2 \approxeq 1 \text{ mole } S:COC_2H_5SK \approxeq 1 \text{ mole } I_2$$

By boiling the alcoholic alkali solution with hydrogen peroxide, the xanthate may be oxidized to sulfate, which is ascertained by precipitation as the barium salt.

The xanthate may be precipitated by the addition of copper sulfate solution (71) or by a solution of copper acetate in acetic acid. The cuprous xanthate formed is filtered off, washed, and dissolved in a minimum amount of nitric acid. From this point the copper may be determined iodometrically as described under the estimation of copper (page 445). The copper xanthate may be redissolved after filtration in very dilute nitric acid and may then be estimated colorimetrically as detailed under the xanthate method for copper (page 446).

d. Colorimetric Xanthate Method (46)

Draw air through a train of two absorbers containing 100 ml each of 0.1N potassium hydroxide in absolute ethyl alcohol, at a rate of 30 lph for about 1 hr.

Make up the contents of the two absorbers to 100 ml with alcohol, if necessary. Withdraw a 40-ml aliquot from each and place in separate 50-ml Nessler tubes. Add to each tube 2 drops of phenolphthalein indicator solution, sufficient acetic acid to make the mixture faintly acid, and 4 drops of 0.5% cupric acetate solution. Mix the contents of the tubes and make up to 50-ml volume with alcohol. Simultaneously prepare a series of standards by adding from 0.1 ml to 1.0 ml of a solution of carbon disulfide in alcohol, containing 0.25 mg of carbon disulfide per milliliter, to 40 ml of 0.1N alcoholic potassium hydroxide. Treat each of these tubes similarly with acetic acid and cupric acetate solution. Compare the yellow color of copper ethyl xanthate of the test solutions with the standards having the closest match in color intensity. A colorimeter may be used if available.

One mg of carbon disulfide is equivalent to 10.6 parts of carbon disulfide per million of air if 30 liters of air were sampled. The accuracy of the absorption and estimation is within 0.5 ppm if 30 liters of air containing a concentration of carbon disulfide of hygienic significance is sampled.

F. Mixed Volatile Sulfur Compounds

In many industries volatile sulfur compounds occur together and it is often important to allot to each its proper role as a hazard. For instance, in the manufacture of sulfuric acid by the chamber process sulfur dioxide, sulfur trioxide, and hydrogen sulfide may occur together, not to speak of water vapor, nitric oxide, nitrogen tetroxide, and oxygen. In the artificial-silk industry methyl mercaptan, carbon disulfide, and hydrogen sulfide may happen to be together, as may carbon disulfide and hydrogen sulfide, or carbon disulfide, hydrogen sulfide, and sulfur dioxide. In blasting operations hydrogen sulfide and sulfur dioxide, if formed, are almost always produced together.

The methods for the principal sulfur-bearing air pollutants have been detailed in the previous sections. The major mixture of sulfur bearing components with which air pollution is concerned is that of sulfur dioxide and sulfuric acid mist or sulfur dioxide and sulfur trioxide. In one sense methods have already been detailed for mixtures of these compounds.

For instance, if the iodine method is used for the determination of sulfur dioxide in air, then sulfuric acid mist is not included in the determination as it is on occasion in the peroxide method. In a similar fashion the fuchsin or rosaniline method can be used to distinguish between sulfur dioxide and sulfur trioxide. The Mader method may also be used for this differentiation by passing the air coming from the paper filters through a trapping device arranged for the analysis of sulfur dioxide.

1. Sulfur Dioxide and Sulfur Trioxide

a. Lead Acetate Method

A relatively simple method can be adapted for the differentiation of sulfite from sulfate (72).

Procedure. Pass the air to be tested through a solution of lead acetate in acetic acid. The sulfite is trapped along with the sulfur trioxide as lead sulfite and lead sulfate, respectively. If necessary, use a second trap containing the solution of lead acetate in acetic acid. The lead sulfite is more insoluble than the lead sulfate and forms a turbidity which is stable for sufficient period of time for analysis. Measure the turbidity in a Klett-Summerson photoelectric colorimeter or in a Coleman spectrophotometer at 600 mμ. Carbonates do not interfere if acetic acid is present. Sulfate does not interfere in this method unless its concentration is greater than that of sulfur dioxide. This is a condition which occurs only rarely in air pollution control work.

The trapping solution can be acidified with hydrochloric acid and the sulfite can then be estimated by titration with 0.001N iodine solution. The total sulfate can then be determined by the barium sulfate method and the amount of sulfur trioxide in the mixture can be determined by difference.

b. Flint Method

Flint devised a method by means of which small concentrations of sulfur trioxide or sulfuric acid mist could be determined in the presence of much larger concentrations of sulfur dioxide. It was based on the trapping of both of these pollutants in a mixture containing 80% isopropyl alcohol and 20% water. In such a mixture the oxidation of sulfur dioxide is negligible. The sulfur trioxide can be removed by use of a sintered glass filter and subsequently is estimated as barium sulfate. The sulfur dioxide can be recovered by liberating it by the addition of hydrochloric acid and the use of a stream of nitrogen.

Seidman (73) modified the Flint method (74) so that it could be used for the determination of sulfur oxides in stack gases.

Procedure. Connect three absorbers in series to sample for sulfur trioxide. Fill each with 100 ml of 80% isopropyl alcohol, immerse in an ice-water slurry, and aspirate 1 cu ft in a period of 20 min through the absorbers. Transfer the contents of the absorbers to a 500-ml volumetric flask, rinse each absorber several times with 80% isopropyl alcohol, adding the rinsings to the volumetric flask, make to volume with 80% isopropyl alcohol, and mix. Transfer a 25-ml aliquot with the aid of a pipet to a titration flask, add 25 ml more of 80% isopropyl alcohol and 3 or 4 drops of a 2% solution of thorin in water as indicator. Titrate with $0.01N$ barium chloride solution to a pink end point. It is preferable to complete the titration within 1 hr after sampling to avoid oxidation of the sulfite to sulfate.

Connect two absorbers in series to sample for total oxides. Add 25 ml of 3% hydrogen peroxide solution and 25 ml of $0.2N$ sodium hydroxide solution to each absorber. Draw 1 cu ft of gas through the train in 20 min. Transfer the absorption solutions to a beaker, rinse with water, adding the rinsings to the beaker, and boil for 30 min to remove the peroxide. Acidify with hydrochloric acid and boil for 5 min to remove carbonate. Transfer to a volumetric flask and make up to 500 ml.

Prepare an ion-exchange column 3 × 15 cm with a 10-cm height of Dower 50 or equivalent resin, pass 75 ml of test solution through the column, and discard. Pass an additional portion of the test solution through the column. Transfer 10 ml to a titration vessel, add 40 ml of isopropyl alcohol, add 3–4 drops of 0.2% thorin indicator solution and titrate with $0.01N$ barium chloride solution to a pink end point.

2. HYDROGEN SULFIDE AND SULFUR DIOXIDE

A prior section (page 562) has dealt with the estimation of sulfur trioxide and sulfur dioxide. Methods for the estimation of sulfur dioxide and hydrogen sulfide in the presence of one another have been indicated, on page 530, by a combination of the sulfur dioxide–hydrogen peroxide method and one of the other methods for sulfur dioxide, and on page 543 by the ammoniacal cadmium acetate–hydrogen sulfide method.

Hydrogen sulfide and sulfur dioxide are not compatible in large amounts for they react as follows:

$$SO_2 + 2H_2S \longrightarrow 2H_2O + 3S$$

In limited quantities they do exist together for a short time.

Another method (75,76) is based on the different rates of oxidation of sulfur dioxide and hydrogen sulfide in air with atmospheric oxygen in an ammonium hydroxide solution. The sulfate produced is precipitated with lead nitrate. A known volume of air is passed through an absorber containing 0.2% ammonium hydroxide solution at a temperature of 50°C. The solution is shaken for 30 min. It is then evaporated to half its volume with the addition of water and 1 drop of nitric acid. The residue is dissolved in dilute alcohol and is made up to a definite volume. An aliquot part is treated directly with lead nitrate to determine sulfur dioxide sulfate. Another aliquot is first oxidized with hydrogen peroxide and is then treated with lead nitrate to determine hydrogen sulfide sulfate.

Another method is to trap the air in four absorbers, the first two contain 5% potassium chlorate solution and the second two contain an ammoniacal solution of hydrogen peroxide. The sulfur dioxide is completely oxidized to sulfur trioxide by the potassium chlorate, while only 1–2% of the hydrogen sulfide is oxidized. The remaining hydrogen sulfide is oxidized by the ammoniacal hydrogen peroxide. The sulfate produced in the absorbers is determined and the amount of each gas may then be calculated.

3. CARBON DISULFIDE AND HYDROGEN SULFIDE

Carbon disulfide and hydrogen sulfide often exist together (46, 77,78) during the production of artificial silk by the process that uses carbon disulfide. In the presence of carbon disulfide, the odor of hydrogen sulfide is changed and it requires 0.9 mg/m³ instead of about 0.6 mg/m³ to detect hydrogen sulfide by smell. To estimate these gases in the presence of one another, pass air through five absorbers in series, the first three containing 100 ml each of cadmium chloride solution (20 g of cadmium chloride, $CdCl_2$, dissolved in 900 ml of water) to which is added 20 ml of 0.5N sodium hydroxide solution. The last two bubblers contain 100 ml each of 0.1N potassium hydroxide in absolute ethyl alcohol.

Draw air through the train at the rate of 30 lph for about 1 hr. At the end of the sampling time, draw uncontaminated air through the train for another 5 min to prevent any possible entrainment of carbon disulfide in the first three absorbers.

The hydrogen sulfide is trapped in the first absorbers as cadmium sulfide. The carbon disulfide is trapped in the alcoholic potash. The amount of hydrogen sulfide caught in the first three bubblers may be estimated iodometrically, as detailed on page 534, and the carbon disulfide in the last two absorbers may be estimated by one of the methods detailed for carbon disulfide such as the colorimetric ethyl xanthate method described on page 559.

4. HYDROGEN SULFIDE, SULFUR DIOXIDE, AND SULFUR TRIOXIDE

Hydrogen sulfide can be detected in the presence of other sulfur-bearing compounds (50) because it has a characteristic odor, by means of the silver cyanide detector (79,80) and by the precipitation of various sulfides. The well-known lead acetate test paper (81) and instruments (41,82) using this type of test paper depend on the formation of black lead sulfide. More precise methods depend on the trapping of hydrogen sulfide by the use of various reagents. The most commonly used are solutions of cadmium salts, namely, cadmium chloride (46), cadmium acetate (44), and a complex mixture containing cadmium acetate, uranyl nitrate, and acetic acid (83). A more sensitive reagent has been suggested by Field and Oldach which is prepared from bismuth nitrate and acetic acid. This reagent has been used to determine as little as 7 μg of hydrogen sulfide in a complex gas mixture containing hydrogen, nitrogen, carbon monoxide, methane, ethylene, and carbon dioxide.

Sulfur dioxide may be oxidized to sulfuric acid by hydrogen peroxide. Hydrogen sulfide does not interfere if the solution is acid, but if it is made ammoniacal, then it, too, is oxidized to sulfuric acid. In still another method, the different rates of oxidation of these gases in an ammonium hydroxide solution by atmospheric oxygen is utilized (50).

Sulfur dioxide is completely oxidized to sulfur trioxide by a 5% solution of potassium chlorate while only 1–2% of any hydrogen sulfide is oxidized.   Hence, by use of a series of absorbers, these gases can be differentiated (50).

5. HYDROGEN SULFIDE, SULFUR DIOXIDE, AND CARBON DISULFIDE (84)

These gases may be estimated in the presence of one another by adsorbing the gases in a series of tubes on different adsorbents.   The gases are then liberated individually, reduced, if necessary, to hydrogen sulfide, and estimated iodometrically.

The hydrogen sulfide is trapped by asbestos impregnated with silver chloride.   The adsorbent is prepared by the action of hydrochloric acid on silver oxide, freshly precipitated on asbestos.   The sulfur dioxide is adsorbed on a porous refractory impregnated with manganese dioxide.   This adsorbent is prepared by precipitation from potassium permanganate by alcohol.   The carbon disulfide is adsorbed on porous stone impregnated with an alcoholic solution of sodium hydroxide.   Each adsorbing tube is heated in turn in a current of hydrogen containing a little hydrochloric acid.   The carbon disulfide and sulfur dioxide are thus reduced to hydrogen sulfide. The hydrogen sulfide may then be caught by one of the methods previously detailed and estimated iodometrically or by some other method, if preferred.

6. HYDROGEN SULFIDE, CARBON DISULFIDE, AND METHYL MERCAPTAN

The air in the spinning rooms of rayon factories may sometimes contain hydrogen sulfide, carbon disulfide, and methyl mercaptan together (85).   These gases may be separated by means of solid lead acetate.   Draw the air containing the gases through a series of four wash bottles.   The first two are Jena wash bottles with No. 83 G1 glass filters or equivalent devices and contain 20 ml of $0.5N$ sodium hydroxide solution.   The next two are very small bubblers with gas dispersers and each contains 2 ml of sodium hydroxide in ethyl alcohol.   After sampling is complete, unite the contents of the first two wash bottles, add 4 ml of 25% hydrochloric acid, and connect immediately to an apparatus for detecting mercaptan and sulfide. This apparatus consists of two tubes (20 × 9 cm) connected with a ground joint.   The first tube contains calcium chloride and the second tube contains about 20 g of fine lead acetate. This second tube is connected with a small wash bottle containing 1 ml of isatin–sulfuric acid solution, 10 mg of isatin being dissolved in 100 ml of sulfuric acid and freshly prepared for use. Draw air slowly through the apparatus for 30 min. The hydrogen sulfide is absorbed by the lead salt and the mercaptan colors the isatin reagent a grass green. By the depth of this color the quantity of mercaptan can be estimated colorimetrically within the range of 0.005–0.1 mg with an accuracy of about 0.01 mg. The hydrogen sulfide may be estimated from the depth of color produced in the lead acetate or it may be liberated and estimated as previously described.

Pour the contents of wash bottles 3 and 4 of the first absorption apparatus into a beaker and rinse out the wash bottles first with 2.5 ml of $4N$ acetic acid, then with 10 ml of cupric acetate solution (0.92 mg of cupric acetate in 250 ml of solution). After at least 2 hr, filter off the copper xanthate precipitate in a three G4 glass filtering crucible and wash with not over 25 ml of water. The formation of the yellow precipitate is proof of the presence of carbon disulfide. The quantity may be calculated by determining its copper content iodometrically by one of the methods previously detailed, or as follows.

a. Copper Determination

Place the crucible on a 25-ml suction flask and add 0.5 ml of $4N$ acetic acid and 4 drops of fresh saturated aqueous bromine to the precipitate. Cover with a watch glass. After 5 min connect with suction, add 4 drops more of bromine water, and filter after 5 min. This serves to dissolve the yellow precipitate. Wash the filter until the total volume of the filtrate is 10 ml and mix with 0.5 ml of 5% phenol solution to remove the excess bromine. After 5 min add 2.5 ml of $1N$ potassium iodide solution and titrate the liberated iodine with $0.01N$ sodium thiosulfate solution, 1 ml of which is equivalent to 1.52 of carbon disulfide.

7. SULFUR DIOXIDE, HYDROGEN SULFIDE, CARBON DISULFIDE, AND CARBON OXYSULFIDE

Carbon disulfide and carbon oxysulfide can be determined in the presence of each other (86) by aspirating the gas to be examined through three absorption flasks. The sulfur dioxide and hydrogen sulfide are absorbed in a standard iodine solution, and titrating the test solution with sodium hydroxide solution to methyl orange gives the hydrogen sulfide directly and sulfur dioxide by difference. Carbon oxysulfide can be absorbed in 7.5% calcium chloride containing 1% ammonium hydroxide solution and carbon disulfide in alcoholic potassium hydroxide. The solutions can then be oxidized with hydrogen peroxide or bromine, and the concentration of carbon oxysulfide and carbon disulfide estimated by precipitating the sulfate with barium chloride.

Field and Oldach (83) proposed a method for the determination of such compounds and thiols in the presence of one another in concentrations of the order of a few parts per million. The method is based on the differences in solubility of these gases in an inert solvent such as white oil and subsequent sensitive tests. They used a saturator consisting of a tube 40 ft long with 200 bulb enlargements and reduced the gas after passage through the saturator by passage over alumina at 900°C, thus converting the compounds to hydrogen sulfide. The identification of the sulfur compounds depends on the volume of gas corresponding to each "break" in the curve.

G. Sulfur Monochloride

Sulfur monochloride, S_2Cl_2, sulfur chloride, is a reddish-yellow liquid which boils at 138°C and has a specific gravity of 1.678. It is decomposed by water with the formation of sulfur dioxide, sulfur, and hydrochloric acid. It is soluble in carbon disulfide, ether, benzene, and other organic solvents. It is a solvent for sulfur and fats.

Sulfur monochloride is used in the vulcanization of rubber, in the formulation of printing inks, varnishes, and cements, as a solvent for sulfur, oils, and fats, in the hardening of soft woods, and as an insecticide. It is also used in the chlorination of organic compounds—for instance, in the manufacture of mustard gas.

Sulfur monochloride has a suffocating, nauseating, and pungent odor. It induces lachrymation and is an irritant for the mucous membranes of the nose, throat, and especially the eyes. The compound is highly toxic but because it readily decomposes, as mentioned above, into sulfur dioxide and hydrochloric acid, it may also cause injury because of the presence of these compounds. Since it is often used in combination with other substances such as benzene and carbon disulfide, the hazard resulting from the other components of the mixture may be greater than that attributable to the sulfur monochloride when it is present in low concentration. The recommended maximum allowable concentration is 1 ppm parts of air.

It may be estimated by slowly passing a measured volume of contaminated air through a silver nitrate solution acidified with nitric acid (87). The precipitated silver chloride may be redissolved in ammonia and then reprecipitated with nitric acid. An alternative procedure is to pass the air through a fritted bubbler containing $1N$ sodium hydroxide solution. Chloride may then be estimated by customary methods.

Sulfur chloride may be estimated titrimetrically. Absorb the material in $0.1N$ silver nitrate solution acidified with nitric acid as mentioned. Add a known volume of $0.1N$ sodium chloride solution equivalent to the volume of silver nitrate used. Titrate the excess chloride ion with $0.1N$ silver nitrate solution. Calculate the sulfur chloride from the relationship that

$$2S_2Cl_2 + 2H_2O + 4AgNO_3 \rightarrow 4AgCl + 3S + SO_2 + 4HNO_3$$

H. Thionyl Chloride

Thionyl chloride, sulfurous oxychloride $SOCl_2$, is used industrially in the preparation of chlorinated substances, among which may be mentioned the preparation of mustard gas. It is a colorless, strongly refractive liquid, which fumes on contact with air and has a suffocating odor. It boils at 78–79°C, has a specific gravity of 1.638, and a refractive index of 1.527 at 10°C. It decomposes rapidly in water with the formation of hydrochloric acid and sulfur dioxide. It is soluble in benzene and chloroform but decomposes in acid, alkali, and alcohol.

It is an eye irritant and because of its decomposition into hydrochloric acid and sulfur dioxide exerts the harmful effects of those substances on the human body. Patty (88) suggests a maximum permissible workroom limit of less than 5 ppm.

It may be estimated in a manner similar to that described for sulfur monochloride or by other methods applicable to the determination of chloride ions, as described in Chapter XVI.

I. Sulfuryl Chloride

Sulfuryl chloride, sulfuryl oxychloride, SO_2Cl_2, is used in the preparation of chlorosulfonates—for instance, methyl and ethyl chlorosulfonates. During World War I, it was used in combination with phosgene, chloropicrin, and cyanogen chloride to make the toxic gases visible. It was also used as a smoke agent.

Sulfuryl chloride is a colorless liquid with a pungent odor. It boils at 69°C, has a specific gravity of 1.667, and a refractive index of 1.444 at 20°C. It is decomposed by water with the formation of sulfuric acid and hydrochloric acid, the reaction being very rapid with warm water. It is soluble in acetic acid and benzene and in the war gases mentioned above. Its ability to be used as a smoke depends on its hydrolysis by the water vapor of the air.

Its physiological effect is due no doubt to its hydrolytic products and so it has an irritating effect. The maximum permissible workroom concentration should probably be of the same order as that of thionyl chloride.

It may be estimated by the methods used for the determination of either sulfate or chloride as described in the respective section covering those analytical methods.

J. Carbon Oxysulfide

Carbon oxysulfide, carbonyl sulfide, COS, is a colorless gas with practically no odor when pure. It boils at −48°C and weighs 2.72 g/liter. It forms an explosive mixture with air. It is decomposed by water and bases with the formation of carbon dioxide and hydrogen sulfide.

It is only slightly irritating and works principally on the central nervous system. A concentration of 400 ppm could be borne by mice for 15 min; however, a concentration of 3200 parts of carbon oxysulfide per million parts of air caused serious illness in rabbits after exposures of 60 min and a concentration of 0.6% by volume or 6000 ppm caused death after an exposure of 50 min.

The concentration of carbon oxysulfide can be determined by slowly passing the air containing the gas through a tube having an electrically heated platinum spiral. The gas is decomposed to sulfur and carbon monoxide. The sulfur is oxidized to sulfur dioxide which may subsequently be estimated by absorption by caustic potash.

Preferably pass the gas into a solution of alcoholic potash, in which it decomposes with the formation of potassium carbonate and potassium sulfide, and subsequently estimate the sulfide.

K. Thiocyanates

While few texts on toxicology mention poisoning attributable to thiocyanates, it is known that toxic symptoms occur when thiocyanates are used in the treatment of hypertension. A case of alleged poisoning attributable to potassium thiocyanate was noted in 1945.

1. PYRAZOLONE METHOD

Cyanate ion can be converted to cyanogen chloride with chloramine T, and by the subsequent reaction of this cyanogen chloride with an aqueous pyridine solution containing 0.1% bispyrazolone and 3-methyl-1-phenyl-5-pyrazolone, a dye is formed which is stable for at least 0.5 hr at 25°C and which follows the Beer-Lambert law between the limits of 0.2 and 1.2 μg of cyanate ion (89).

Reagents. Recrystallize commercial 3-methyl-1-phenyl-5-pyrazolone twice from 95% ethyl alcohol to obtain the product melting at 127–128°C.

To prepare bis-(3-methyl-1-phenyl-5-pyrazolone), dissolve 17.4 g (0.1 mole) of recrystallized 1-phenyl-3-methyl-5-pyrazolone in 100 ml of 95% ethyl alcohol and add 25 g (0.25 mole) of freshly distilled phenylhydrazine. Reflux the mixture for 4 hr. Filter the mixture while hot to obtain the insoluble portion, which is the bispyrazolone, and wash the precipitate several times with hot 95% alcohol. The melting point should be higher than 320°C.

Pyridine–Pyrazolone Solution. Mix 500 ml of a saturated water solution of 3-methyl-1-phenyl-5-pyrazolone with 100 ml of pure pyridine in which 0.1 g of the bispyrazolone has been dissolved.

Procedure. Add 0.2 ml of 0.1% ferric chloride solution and 0.2 ml of 1% chloramine T solution to 1 ml of a solution containing up to 2.5 μg of thiocyanate ion. Stopper the tube and shake. After 3 min of contact time, add 6 ml of the pyridine–pyrazolone mixture. Stopper the tube again and mix. After 20 min, take readings in a spectrophotometer set at 630 mμ with the optical density of the reagent blank set at zero. The color is stable for at least 30 min at room temperature.

L. Free Sulfur

It was at one time thought that the free sulfur in the air of Los Angeles was an important contaminant of the air of the area. According to Feigl (90), when free sulfur in solution comes into contact with black thallous sulfide in the pores of filter paper, red-brown thallium polysulfide, $2Tl_2S \cdot Tl_2S_3$, is formed. In place of thallous sulfide, Magill, Roston, and Bremner (91) and also investigators for Stanford Research Institute (92) used thallous acetate paper for greater stability. They collected the sample on thallous acetate paper and measured the volume of air sampled. The test paper was moistened by spraying with pyridine and the test paper plus standard papers were placed in a jar containing hydrogen sulfide for 30 sec, in this manner arranging for the simultaneous development of the sulfide and polysulfide. The papers were then removed and the pyridine permitted to evaporate, after which they were washed successively in $0.5N$ nitric acid to remove thallous sulfide and then with water. The spots produced were compared with the aid of a porcelain plate.

Free sulfur may also be detected by a variation of the mercury test (93). Thus, if gasoline is freed of sulfur by shaking with mercury and this sulfur-free gasoline is used to trap or dissolve any free sulfur trapped from air being sampled, shaking the gasoline test solution with mercury will yield a precipitate of black mercury sulfide. The suspension, itself, is colored grey. The test is one of the more sensitive tests for free sulfur and will detect less than 0.1 ppm.

References

1. Schwartz, L., *U.S. Public Health Service Bull. 249* (1939).
2. Cooper, A. G., *Sulfur Oxides and other Sulfur Compounds*, Public Health Service Publ. 1093, Govt. Printing Office, Washington, D. C. 20402, 1965.
3. Haggard, H. W., *J. Ind. Hyg.*, **5**, 379 (1923–24).
4. Ives, J. E., R. H. Britten, D. W. Armstrong, W. A. Gull, and F. H. Goldman, *U.S. Public Health Service Bull. 224* (1936).
5. Schroeder, W. C., *Ind. Eng. Chem. Anal. Ed.*, **5**, 403 (1933).
6. Sheen, R. T., and H. L. Kahler, *Ind. Eng. Chem. Anal. Ed.*, **8**, 127 (1936).
7. Sorvin, S. B., Yu. M. Redkov, and V. P. Makarova, *Zh. Analit. Khim.*, **17**, No. 1, 43 (1962).
8. Mader, P. P., W. J. Hamming, and A. Bellin, *Anal. Chem.*, **22**, 1181 (1950).
9. Holmes, J. A., E. C. Franklin, and R. A. Gould, *U.S. Bur. Mines Bull. 98* (1915).
10. Jones, G. W., J. H. Capps, and S. H. Katz, *Min. Sci. Press*, **117**, 415 (1918).

11. Lehmann, K. B., in *Kompendium der praktischen Toxikologie*, R. Kobert, Ed., Enke, Stuttgart, 1912.
12. Henderson, Y., and H. W. Haggard, *Noxious Gases*, Reinhold, New York, 1943.
13. Gardner, E. D., S. P. Howell, and G. W. Jones, *U.S. Bur. Mines Bull. 287* (1927).
14. Fieldner, A. C., *U.S. Bur. Mines Inform. Circ. 6099* (1937).
15. Thomas, M. D., and R. J. Cross, *Ind. Eng. Chem.*, **20**, 645 (1928); M. D. Thomas, O. J. Ivie, J. N. Abersold, and R. H. Hendricks, *Ind. Eng. Chem. Anal Ed.*, **15**, 287 (1943).
16. McKay, R. J., and D. E. Ackerman, *Ind. Eng. Chem.*, **20**, 538 (1928).
17. Betz, C. E., J. H. Holden, and J. O. Handy, *Ind. Eng. Chem.*, **25**, 774 (1933).
18. Hochheiser, S., *Methods of Measuring and Monitoring Atmospheric Sulfur Dioxide*, Public Health Service Publ. 999-AP-6, Govt. Printing Office, Washington, D. C. 20402, 1964.
19. Fieldner, A. C., C. G. Oberfell, M. C. Teague, and J. N. Lawrence, *Ind. Eng. Chem.*, **11**, 523 (1919).
20. Griffin, S. W., and W. W. Skinner, *Ind. Eng. Chem.*, **24**, 862 (1932).
21. Monier-Williams, G. W., Ministry of Health, *Reports of Public Health and Medical Subjects*, No. 43, London, 1927.
22. Thomas, M. D., and J. N. Abersold, *Ind. Eng. Chem. Anal. Ed.*, **1**, 14 (1929).
23. Thomas, M. D., *Ind. Eng. Chem. Anal. Ed.*, **4**, 253 (1932).
24. Jacobs, M. B., and L. Greenburg, *Ind. Eng. Chem.*, **48**, 1517 (1956).
25. Jacobs, M. B., *The Chemical Analysis of Air Pollutants*, Interscience, New York, 1960, Chap. 17.
26. West, P. W., and G. C. Gaeke, *Anal. Chem.*, **28**, 1816 (1956).
27. Huitt, H. A., and J. P. Lodge, Jr., *Anal. Chem.*, **36**, 1305 (1964).
28. Feigl, F., *Chemistry of Specific, Selective, and Sensitive Reactions*, Academic Press, New York, 1949.
29. Pate, J., *Anal. Chem.*, **34**, 1661 (1962).
30. Zurlo, N., and A. M. Griffini, *Med. Lavoro (Milan)*, **53**, 330 (1962).
31. Lodge, J. P., J. B. Pate, G. A. Swanson, and B. E. Ammons, *Am. Chem. Soc. Div. Water, Air Waste Chemistry Preprint 4*, No. 2, 107 (1964).
32. Goldberg, Y. D., *J. Appl. Chem. (USSR)*, **7**, 1099 (1934); *Chem. Abstr.*, **29**, 5773 (1935).
33. Hochheiser, S., M. M. Braverman, and M. B. Jacobs, "Comparison of Methods for the Determination of Sulfur Dioxide as an Air Pollutant," Am. Chem. Soc., N. Y. Section Meeting-in-Miniature, Feb. 1955.
34. Jacobs, M. B., M. M. Braverman, and S. Hochheiser, "Ultrasensitive Conductometric Measurement of Sulfur Dioxide in Air," Instrument Society of America Meeting, Paper No. 56-32-3 (Sept. 1956).
35. Greenburg, L., and M. B. Jacobs, *Ind. Eng. Chem.*, **48**, 1517 (1956).
36. Olsen, J. C., G. E. Ferguson, and L. Scheflan, *Ind. Eng. Chem.*, **25**, 599 (1933).
37. *Dept. Sci. Ind. Research Brit. Leaflet 1* (1937); *Analyst*, **62**, 607 (1937).
38. Mitchell, C. W., and S. J. Davenport, *U.S. Public Health Service Reprint 892* (1924).
39. *Am. Standards Z37.2-1941*.

40. Woog, P., R. Sigwalt, and J. de Saint-Mars, *Bull. Soc. Chim. France*, (5)2, 1214 (1935).
41. Roberts, S., and G. Minors, *J. Soc. Chem. Ind.*, **53**, 526T (1934).
42. Chanin, G. J., R. Elwood, and E. H. Chow, *Sewage Ind. Wastes*, **26**, 1217 (1954).
43. Gardner, E. D., S. P. Howell, and G. W. Jones, *U.S. Bur. Mines Bull. 287* (1927).
44. Quitmann, E., *Z. Anal. Chem.*, **109**, 241 (1937).
45. Wallach, A., and E. P. O'Brien, *Proc. Montana Acad. Sci.*, **10**, 39 (1951).
46. Moskowitz, S., J. Siegel, and W. J. Burke, *N.Y. State Ind. Bull.*, **19**, 33 (1940).
47. Mecklenburg, W., and F. Rosenkranzer, *Z. Anorg. Allgem. Chem.*, **86**, 143 (1914).
48. Almy, L. H., *J. Am. Chem. Soc.*, **47**, 1381 (1925).
49. Sheppard, S. E., and J. H. Hudson, *Ind. Eng. Chem. Anal. Ed.*, **3**, 73 (1930).
50. Jacobs, M. B., *The Analytical Chemistry of Industrial Poisons, Hazards and Solvents*, 2nd ed., Interscience, New York, 1949.
51. Pomeroy, R., *Sewage Works J.*, **8**, 572 (1936).
52. *Standard Methods for the Examination of Water and Sewage*, 10th ed., Am. Public Health Assoc., New York, 1955.
53. Budd, M. S., and H. A. Bewick, *Anal. Chem.*, **24**, 1536 (1952).
54. *Test Procedures and Methods in Air Pollution Control*, Air Pollution Control Dist., Co. of Los Angeles, Calif., 1952.
55. ASTM Designation D 1255-55 T.
56. Marbach, E. P., and D. M. Doty, *Abstr. Am. Chem. Soc.*, 128th Meeting (1955).
57. Jacobs, M. B., M. M. Braverman, and S. Hochheiser, *Anal. Chem.*, **29**, 1349 (1957); M. B. Jacobs, in *Atmospheric Chemistry of Chlorine and Sulfur Compounds*, J. P. Lodge, Jr., Ed., American Geophys. Union, Washington, D. C., 1959, p. 24.
58. Zhitkova, A. S., S. I. Kaplun, and J. B. Ficklen, *Poisonous Gases*, Service to Industry, Hartford, 1936.
59. Smirnov, K. A., *Zavodskaya Lab.*, **6**, 240 (1937); *Chem. Abstr.*, **31**, 6135 (1937).
60. Bell, J., and W. K. Hall, *Chem. Ind. (London)*, **1936**, 89.
61. Shaffer, P. A., Jr., A. Briglio, and J. A. Brockman, *Anal. Chem.*, **20**, 1008 (1948).
62. Thomas, F. W., *Air Repair*, **4**, No. 2, 7 (1954).
63. Ettinger, I., M. M. Braverman, and M. B. Jacobs, "The Determination of Oxidizable Sulfur Compounds in Incinerator Flue Gases by Automatic Barometric Titration," Am. Chem. Soc., N. Y. Section, Meeting-in-Miniature, March 1958.
64. *Dept. Sci. Ind. Research Brit. Leaflet 6* (1939).
65. Wiley, F. W., W. C. Kueper, and W. F. von Oettingen, *J. Ind. Hyg. Toxicol.*, **18**, 733 (1936).
66. Barthélémy, H. L., *J. Ind. Hyg. Toxicol.*, **21**, 141 (1939).
67. Matuszak, M. P., *Ind. Eng. Chem. Anal. Ed.*, **4**, 98 (1932).
68. Viles, F. J., *J. Ind. Hyg. Toxicol.*, **22**, 188 (1940).

69. Tischler, N., *Ind. Eng. Chem. Anal. Ed.*, **4**, 146 (1932).
70. Yant, W. P., S. J. Pearce, and H. H. Schrenk, *U.S. Bur. Mines Rept. Invest. 3323* (1936).
71. Huff, W. J., *J. Am. Chem. Soc.*, **48**, 81 (1926).
72. Jacobs, M. B., in *Air Pollution*, L. C. McCabe, Ed., McGraw-Hill, New York, 1952.
73. Seidman, E. B., *Anal. Chem.*, **30**, 1680 (1958).
74. Flint, D., *J. Soc. Chem. Ind.*, **67**, 2 (1948).
75. Gurevich, V. G., and V. P. Vendt, *J. Gen. Chem. USSR*, **6**, 962 (1936); *Chem. Abstr.*, **31**, 629 (1937).
76. Gurevich, V. G., *J. Russ. Phys.-Chem. Soc.*, **62**, 111 (1930); *Chem. Abstr.*, **24**, 5254 (1930).
77. Barthélémy, H. L., *Am. Public Health Assoc. Yearbook 1936–37*, 93; *J. Ind. Hyg. Toxicol.*, **21**, 141 (1939).
78. Frauenhof, H., *Kunstseide*, **17**, 344 (1935).
79. Forbes, J. J., and G. W. Grove, *U.S. Bur. Mines Miners' Circ. 33* (1938).
80. Mine Safety Appliances Co., Pittsburgh, Pa.
81. Liesegang, W., *Gesundh.-Ing.*, **61**, 320 (1938).
82. Jilk, L. T., U.S. Pat. 2,232,622 (1941).
83. Field, E., and C. S. Oldach, *Ind. Eng. Chem. Anal. Ed.*, **18**, 665 (1946).
84. Böeseken, J., and H. D. Muller, *Rec. Trav. Chim.*, **50**, 1117 (1931).
85. Reith, J. F., *Rec. Trav. Chim.*, **53**, 18 (1934).
86. Avdeeva, A. V., *Zavodskaya Lab.*, **7**, 279 (1938); *Chem. Abstr.*, **32**, 8984 (1938).
87. Flury, F., and F. Zernik, *Schaedliche Gase*, Springer, Berlin, 1931.
88. Patty, F. A., Ed., *Industrial Hygiene and Toxicology*, 2nd ed., Vol. II, Interscience, New York, 1962.
89. Epstein, J., *Anal. Chem.*, **19**, 272 (1947).
90. Feigl, F., *Spot Tests*, 3rd ed., Elsevier, New York, 1946.
91. Magill, P. L., M. V. Roston, and R. W. Bremner, *Anal. Chem.*, **21**, 1411 (1949).
92. "The Smog Problem in Los Angeles County—An Interim Report," Stanford Research Institute, Menlo Park, Calif., 1948.
93. Mapstone, G. E., *Ind. Eng. Chem. Anal. Ed.*, **18**, 498 (1946).

CHAPTER XIII

PHOSPHORUS AND PHOSPHORUS COMPOUNDS

The part that phosphorus has played as an industrial hazard is historic. This was undoubtedly due to the notoriety given the cases of industrial poisoning attributable to phosphorus or its compounds as well as to the horrible appearance that the unfortunate victims of this industrial disease assumed. "Phossy jaw" was as much in the public eye not so many years ago as "silicosis" is now.

It was in the manufacture of lucifer matches, matches made with white, i.e., yellow, phosphorus, that these cases first arose. It took more than 50 years to begin to regulate the use of white phosphorus and it was not until the relatively nonpoisonous phosphorus sesquisulfide match was developed that really stringent regulations could be drawn and enforced against the use of white phosphorus as such in matches. Phosphorus sesquisulfide may cause dermatitis in workers allergic to it.

White phosphorus is still a hazard in industry, particularly among workers in fireworks, fertilizers, insecticides, rat pastes, phosphorus-extracting plants, brass foundries, bone-black preparation, substitutes for camphor in celluloid, and in general where phosphorus compounds are used in quantity, including match manufacture (1). The toxicology of chronic phosphorus poisoning has been reviewed in detail by Heimann (2). The maximum allowable concentration of yellow (white) phosphorus is 0.1 mg/m³ of air.

Yellow phosphorus melts at 44.1°C, boils at 280°C, has a specific gravity of 1.8, and a vapor pressure at 25°C of 0.04–0.08 mm Hg. Thus, a cubic meter of air saturated with phosphorus vapor could possibly contain from 240–480 mg of free phosphorus.

Special mention should be made of phosphine (phosphorated hydrogen). This gas is highly poisonous and is closely related to arsine. It is generated in industry under circumstances closely analogous to the generation of arsine.

A. Sampling

Phosphate-bearing dust and phosphorus fumes can be sampled by many of the methods detailed before. The acid fumes may be caught by means of fixed alkali solution. The dusts may be trapped in water, by electrical precipitation, or by filtration. In the latter two methods, after making the cellulosic materials alkaline, the specimen may be ashed, either by the wet method or by ignition. Phosphorus is usually determined and estimated as phosphoric acid expressed as P_2O_5. This may be done gravimetrically as magnesium pyrophosphate, $Mg_2P_2O_7$, titrimetrically, or colorimetrically. In general the ash is dissolved in sulfuric acid or in nitric acid or in both, or the wet ash is used, and a suitable aliquot is taken for the analysis. Phosphorus may also be sampled as detailed below for phosphine.

B. Determination

1. GRAVIMETRIC METHOD

The gravimetric method for phosphorus and phosphates is used for samples containing relatively large amounts or high concentrations of such compounds.

In this method the phosphate is first precipitated as ammonium molybdiphosphate, which is dissolved in ammonium hydroxide and then is precipitated as magnesium ammonium phosphate. This precipitate is then converted to the pyrophosphate by ignition.

Reagents. *Molybdate Solution.* Dissolve 100 g of molybdic acid, MoO_3, in a mixture of 144 ml of ammonium hydroxide and 271 ml of water. Pour this solution slowly and with constant stirring into a mixture of 489 ml of nitric acid and 1148 ml of water. Keep the final mixture in a warm place for several days or until a portion of the reagent heated to 40°C deposits no yellow precipitate of ammonium molybdiphosphate. Decant the solution from any sediment and preserve in glass-stoppered bottles.

Magnesia Mixture. Dissolve 11 g of magnesium oxide in hydrochloric acid (1:4), avoiding an excess of the acid; add a little magnesium oxide in excess; boil a few minutes to precipitate iron, aluminum, and phosphorus pentoxide, and filter. To the filtrate either add 140 g of ammonium chloride and 130.5 ml of ammonium hydroxide and dilute to 1 liter or dissolve 55 g of magnesium chloride, $MgCl_2 \cdot 6H_2O$, in water, add 140 g of ammonium chloride, and dilute to 870 ml. Add ammonium hydroxide to each required portion of the solution just before using, in the proportion of 15 ml to 100 ml of solution.

Magnesium Nitrate Solution. Dissolve 150 g of magnesium oxide in nitric acid (1:1), avoiding an excess of the acid; add a little magnesium oxide in excess, boil, filter from the excess of magnesium oxide, ferric oxide, etc., and dilute to 1 liter.

Procedure. Transfer the solution containing the ash or other solution containing the phosphate to a 250-ml beaker; add ammonium hydroxide in slight excess and barely dissolve the precipitate formed with a few drops of nitric acid, stirring vigorously. If hydrochloric acid or sulfuric acid had been used as a solvent, add about 15 g of crystalline ammonium nitrate or a solution containing that quantity. To the hot solution add 70 ml of the molybdate solution for every decigram of phosphorus pentoxide present. Digest at about 65°C for 1 hr, and determine whether or not the phosphorus pentoxide has been completely precipitated by adding more molybdate solution to the clear supernatant liquid. Filter, and wash with cold water or preferably with a solution of 100 g of ammonium nitrate dissolved in and diluted to 1 liter of water. Dissolve the precipitate on the filter with ammonium hydroxide solution (1:1) and hot water and wash into a beaker to a volume of not more that 100 ml. Neutralize with hydrochloric acid, using litmus paper or bromothymol blue as indicator; cool; and from a buret add slowly, at about 1 drop per second, stirring vigorously, 15 ml of the magnesia mixture for each decigram of phosphorus pentoxide present. After 15 min add 12 ml of ammonium hydroxide. Let stand until the supernatant liquid is clear (about 2 hr), filter, wash the precipitate with ammonium hydroxide (1:9) until the washings are practically free of chlorides, dry, burn at a low heat, and then ignite in an electric furnace at 950–1000°C, cool in a desiccator, and weigh as magnesium pyrophosphate, $Mg_2P_2O_7$. Calculate the result as percentage of phosphorus pentoxide.

2. Titrimetric Method

Add 5–10 ml of nitric acid, depending on the manner of solution, or add the equivalent in ammonium nitrate. Add ammonium hydroxide until the precipitate that forms dissolves slowly on stirring vigorously, dilute to 75–100 ml, and adjust to a temperature of 25–30°C. Add sufficient molybdate solution to insure complete precipitation. Five ml of nitric acid must be added to every 100 ml of molybdate solution, which is then filtered immediately before use. Place the solution in a shaking machine or stirring apparatus and shake for 30 min at room temperature. Decant at once through a filter and wash the precipitate twice by decantation with 25–30 ml portions of water, agitating thoroughly and allowing to settle. Transfer the precipitate to the filter and wash with cold water until the filtrate from two fillings of the filter yields a pink color upon the addition of phenolphthalein and 1 drop of the standard alkali. The standard alkali is prepared by diluting 328.81 ml of $1N$ alkali to liter. One ml of this solution is equivalent to 1 mg of phosphorus pentoxide. Transfer the precipitate and filter to the beaker or precipitating vessel, dissolve the precipitate in a small excess of the standard alkali, add a few drops of phenolphthalein indicator, and titrate with standard acid. The standard acid is prepared to be equal to or one-half of the normality of the standard alkali solution.

3. COLORIMETRIC METHOD

a. Truog Modification (3)

Reagents. *Ammonium Molybdate Solution.* Dissolve 25 g of ammonium molybdate in 200 ml of water heated to 60°C and filter. Cool and dilute with water to 1 liter. This solution then contains 2.5 g of ammonium molybdate per 100 ml.

Sulfuric Acid Solution. Dilute 280 ml of arsenic- and phosphorus-free sulfuric acid to 1 liter with water. This is approximately a $10N$ sulfuric acid solution.

Stannous Chloride Solution. Place 25 g of stannous chloride, $SnCl_2 \cdot H_2O$, in a solution of 100 ml of hydrochloric acid diluted to 500 ml with water. Let stand in a warm room until dissolved; then dilute to 1 liter with water. Filter if necessary. This reagent may be stored in a bottle with a side opening near the bottom and equipped with a stopcock for delivering the solution in drops. The solution may be protected from the air by floating a layer of white mineral oil about 5 mm thick on the surface.

Standard Phosphate Solution. Dissolve 0.2195 g of recrystallized potassium dihydrogen phosphate, KH_2PO_4, in water and dilute to 1 liter. This solution contains 50 parts of phosphorus per million of solution and is too concentrated to use directly. A second stock solution may be made by taking 50 ml of the first stock solution and diluting to 500 ml. The standard solution for color comparison is made by diluting 5 ml of the second stock solution to 91 ml with water; 4 ml each of the ammonium molybdate solution and sulfuric acid solution are added and mixed thoroughly by swirling in a 150-ml flask. Six drops of the stannous chloride solution are added and the solution is shaken again. The solution is diluted to 100 ml and again mixed by swirling in the flask. The standard phosphate solution is ready for use but it is necessary to add a drop of stannous chloride solution every 10–12 min to obtain the full color. One ml of this standard phosphate solution contains 0.00025 mg of phosphorus per milliliter.

Procedure. Dissolve the ash in 1 ml of $10N$ sulfuric acid. Add sufficient water to insure complete solution and transfer to a small beaker. If the specimen is in solution, evaporate to a small volume, add the same amount of acid, and transfer, if desired, to a small beaker. Neutralize with ammonia water using phenolphthalein as indicator. Transfer to a 100-ml volumetric flask and make to volume.

Transfer by means of a pipet an appropriate aliquot to a 100-ml volumetric flask with a mark at 91 ml, and dilute to that volume with water. Add 4 ml each of the ammonium molybdate and $10N$ sulfuric acid solutions, swirling after each addition. Add 6 drops of stannous chloride solution, shake, and make up to volume. Compare in a colorimeter within 10 min with a standard prepared as directed above. Comparison may also be made in Nessler tubes by using varying proportions of the standard phosphorus solution. Computation of the amount of phosphorus present may be made by use of the relationship that 1 ml of the final prepared standard phosphate solution contains 0.00025 mg of phosphorus per milliliter.

b. Microcolorimetric Method

Phosphorus in the form of phosphate reacts with ammonium molybdate to form a complex molybdiphosphate. This complex is reduced to form a molybdenum blue by the use of solutions of hydroquinone and sodium sulfite (4,5).

Reagents. *Ammonium Molybdate Solution.* Dissolve 25 g of ammonium molybdate in 300 ml of water. Add slowly 75 ml of concentrated sulfuric acid to water, make up to 200 ml with water, and add to the ammonium molybdate solution.

Hydroquinone Solution. Dissolve 0.5 g of hydroquinone in 100 ml of water and add 1 drop of sulfuric acid to retard oxidation.

Sodium Sulfite Solution. Dissolve 200 g of sodium sulfite, Na_2SO_3, in water, make up to 1 liter, and filter. Keep this solution well stoppered or prepare a fresh equivalent each time it is to be used.

Standards. *Potassium Dihydrogen Phosphate Solution.* Dissolve 0.4394 g of pure, dry potassium dihydrogen phosphate, KH_2PO_4, in water and make up to 1 liter. Dilute 50 ml of this solution to 100 ml. Each milliliter of the latter solution is equivalent to 0.05 mg of phosphorus.

Procedure. Convert the phosphorus and phosphorus compounds to phosphate as detailed above. Transfer to a volumetric flask and make to volume. Transfer a 5-ml aliquot to a 10-ml volumetric flask. Add 1 ml of the ammonium molybdate solution, rotate the flask to mix, and allow to stand a few moments. Add 1 ml of the hydroquinone solution, again rotate the flask; add 1 ml of the sodium sulfite solution and mix. Make to volume with water. Stopper the flask and shake thoroughly. Allow to stand 30 min for development of the blue color and compare immediately thereafter in a colorimeter with 2 ml of the standard potassium dihydrogen phosphate solution treated at the same time with the same reagents as the test solution and in the same way. With either the test solution or the standard set at 25.0 mm, readings within 10 mm, that is, with a range of 20 mm, are accurate. If concentrations of the test solution are outside this range, larger or smaller aliquots of the sample solution should be used.

c. Ferrous Sulfate Modification

Instead of the use of hydroquinone solution and sodium sulfite as the reducing agent, Sumner (6) suggested the use of ferrous sulfate which has the advantage of being able to be used in a weak acid solution and has greater specificity. The use of this reagent was additionally developed by Rockstein and Herron (7) and independently by Taussky and Shorr (8) who further simplified the method by use of a combined ferrous sulfate ammonium molybdate reagent made up just prior to use. Transfer 10 ml of ammonium molybdate stock solution, made up by dissolving 50 g of ammonium molybdate, $(NH_4)_6Mo_7O_{24}·4H_2O$, in 400 ml of $10N$ sulfuric acid which is then made up quantitatively to 500 ml in a volumetric flask, to a 100-ml amber volumetric flask and dilute to about 70 ml. Add 5 g of FeSO$_4$·7H$_2$O, make up to volume, and shake until all the ferrous sulfate crystals are dissolved. The method is sensitive from 2 to 40 μg. Properly treated and diluted samples are pipetted directly into colorimeter tubes and followed by the addition of the ferrous sulfate–molybdate reagent. The intensity of the blue color which develops is determined in a Klett-Summerson photoelectric colorimeter with a No. 66 filter against a potassium acid phosphate standard.

4. Determination of Phosphate in Air Samples

Phosphorus in the form of phosphate reacts with ammonium molybdate to form a complex molybdiphosphate (phosphomolybdate) which is subsequently reduced to form a molybdenum blue.

Reagents. *Ammonium Molybdate Solution.* Dissolve 25 g of ammonium molybdate tetrahydrate, (NH$_4$)$_6$Mo$_7$O$_{24}$·4H$_2$O, in distilled water and dilute to 1 liter.

Sulfuric Acid, 11.3N. Add cautiously 320 ml of concentrated sulfuric acid, arsenic and phosphorus free, to 500 ml of distilled water in a beaker, mix, allow to cool, and transfer to a 1-liter volumetric flask. Dilute almost to volume and allow to cool again to room temperature. Make to volume with distilled water. This solution is approximately 11.3N.

Ferrous Sulfate Solution. Add 6.0 g of ferrous sulfate heptahydrate, FeSO$_4$·7H$_2$O, in some water containing 1 ml of 11.3N sulfuric acid to a 50-ml volumetric flask. Dissolve the ferrous sulfate and dilute to the mark with distilled water. This solution must be prepared fresh for each series of determinations.

Procedure. Transfer the test solution from the titration tube to a 50-ml volumetric flask (or other appropriate volumetric flask) and make to volume with distilled water. Mix thoroughly and take a 10-ml aliquot and place in a glass-stoppered 25-ml cylinder. Add 1 ml of 11.3N sulfuric acid, stopper, mix, and allow to cool. Add 4 ml of ammonium molybdate solution, restopper, and mix. Add 1 ml of ferrous sulfate solution, restopper, mix, and allow to stand for at least 5 min for color development. Read the absorption in a spectrophotometer at 720 mμ and obtain the phosphate concentration from a standard curve.

Calculation. Multiply the micrograms of phosphorus (phosphate) obtained from the graph by 5 to obtain the total amount of phosphorus (phosphate) in the original test sample, if a 50-ml volumetric flask and a 10-ml aliquot were used, or use an appropriate factor if another volume and aliquot were used. Divide the result by the number of liters sampled to obtain the amount of phosphorus (phosphate) in 1 liter and multiply by 1000 to obtain the amount in 1 m³. This result, of course, is not corrected for pressure and temperature. To convert phosphorus to phosphate multiply by 3.

Standard Curve. Dissolve 0.4394 g of anhydrous, recrystallized, reagent grade potassium dihydrogen phosphate, KH_2PO_4, in distilled water and dilute to 1 liter. This standard stock solution contains 0.1 mg of phosphorus per milliliter. Transfer 5 ml of this solution with a pipet to a 100-ml volumetric flask and complete to volume with distilled water. Each milliliter of this solution contains 5 μg of phosphorus. Transfer with volumetric pipets 0, 0.5, 1.0, 2.0, 3.0, 4.0, and 5.0 ml of the diluted standard to 25-ml glass-stoppered cylinders, and dilute to 10 ml with distilled water. Each standard contains, respectively, 0, 2.5, 5, 10, 15, 20, and 25 μg of phosphorus. Proceed with the method as detailed in the procedure. The method should be applicable in the range of 0–35 μg. Each microgram of phosphorus is equivalent to 3 μg of phosphate.

C. Phosphine

Phosphine is an industrial hazard in a number of industries, among which may be mentioned the manufacture of acetylene, where calcium phosphide is an impurity in the calcium carbide, phosphorus extraction, the manufacture of phosphorus sesquisulfide, and operations with phosphorus-bearing ferrosilicon.

Phosphine, PH_3, is a colorless gas of nauseating odor. It acts on the central nervous system and the blood (9). The symptoms exhibited by phosphine poisoning are an oppressed feeling in the chest, headache, vertigo, general debility, loss of appetite, and great thirst. A concentration of 2.8 mg/liter, equivalent to 2000 ppm, is lethal to men in a few minutes. Concentrations of 0.56–0.84 mg/liter, that is, 400–600 ppm, are dangerous to life after exposures for 30–60 min. The maximum concentration tolerated for exposures of 60 min is in the range 0.14–0.26 mg/liter or 100–190 ppm. The maximum concentration that can be tolerated without symptoms for several hours is 0.01 mg/liter, or 7 ppm (10). The minimum warning concentration is 0.002–0.004 mg/liter, that is, 1.4–2.8 ppm. The maximum allowable concentration (11) is considered to be of the same order as arsine, namely, 0.05 ppm.

1. DETECTION AND DETERMINATION

Phosphine may be detected by the brown to black color imparted to filter paper wet with silver nitrate solution by this substance. It may be estimated by trapping the gas in bromine water or sodium hypochlorite solution in a fritted bubbler and after the elimination of the bromine, determination as phosphate as detailed above.

Phosphine may be determined rapidly in gases by use of the reaction

$$PH_3 + 3HgCl_2 \rightarrow P(HgCl)_3 + 3HCl$$

In this reaction, the quantity of acid liberated is proportional to the volume of phosphine present. A 100-ml sample of the gas is measured into a flask over water. An open tube containing an excess of solid mercuric chloride is introduced into the flask and the mixture is shaken. The precipitate is filtered off and washed. The combined filtrate and washings are titrated with sodium hydroxide using methyl orange as indicator. The number of milliliters of $0.1N$ alkali multiplied by 0.784 gives the volume of phosphine at 15°C and 760 mm Hg. For percentages below 0.5% a colorimetric determination may be made by suspending the $P(HgCl)_3$ precipitate, whose color varies from yellow to brown. This color is matched against a freshly prepared standard obtained with a gaseous mixture of known phosphine content (12).

Phosphine, and phosphorus as well, may be sampled by drawing the air to be analyzed through three scrubbers in series each of which contains 10 ml of $0.01N$ potassium permanganate solution and 1 ml of 5% sulfuric acid to convert the phosphorus to phosphoric acid (13). The absorbing solution may then be combined, the excess permanganate is decolorized by heating with $0.01N$ oxalic acid and the colorimetric procedures detailed above applied.

An alternative method for the determination of phosphine is to trap it in 10% silver nitrate solution and proceed with the Rushing method for elemental phosphorus (Section F) starting in the Procedure after the addition of silver nitrate solution to the xylene trapping solution and its subsequent separation (p. 587).

D. Phosphorus Trichloride

Phosphorus trichloride is used in the manufacture of phosphorus oxychloride, phosphorus pentachloride, and as a chlorinating agent for the manufacture of chlorinated organic compounds. It is used as a solvent for phosphorus.

Phosphorus trichloride, PCl_3, is a colorless liquid with a sharp smell and it fumes on exposure to air because of decomposition to phosphorus acid and hydrochloric acid. It boils at 76°C and has a specific gravity $d_{21} = 1.574$. It dissolves in water with the formation of the aforementioned compounds. It is also decomposed by alcohol. It is soluble in benzene, chloroform, ether, and carbon disulfide.

It enters the body as a vapor through the respiratory tract, which it attacks. It causes a sensation of suffocation, difficulty in breathing, lachrymation, bronchitis, edema, and inflammation of the lungs with frothy bloodstained expectoration. A concentration of 600 ppm is lethal in a few minutes. Concentrations of 50–80 ppm are harmful after exposures of 30–60 min. Two to 4 ppm can be borne for exposures of 60 min without serious symptoms. A concentration of 0.7 ppm is the maximum that can be tolerated for exposures of several hours (10). The maximum allowable concentration is considered to be 0.5 ppm (11).

It may be estimated by trapping in 20% sodium hydroxide solution with subsequent determination of the liberated chloride.

Phosphorus pentachloride, PCl_5, and phosphorus oxychloride, $POCl_3$, which are also poisonous and have similar physiological effects may be estimated in an analogous manner. The maximum allowable concentration for phosphorus pentachloride is 1 mg/m³ of air (11).

E. Phosphorus Pentasulfide

Phosphorus pentasulfide is used in the manufacture of safety matches, for the introduction of sulfur into organic compounds, and for the manufacture of ignition materials. Phosphorus pentasulfide, P_2S_5, also known as phosphoric sulfide and phosphorus persulfide, occurs in light-yellow crystalline masses, which have a peculiar odor.

It melts at about 280°C and boils at 523°C in an inert atmosphere. It is soluble in carbon disulfide and in aqueous alkali solutions.

The maximum allowable concentration recommended for this compound is 1 mg of phosphorus pentasulfide per cubic meter of air.

Phosphorus pentasulfide decomposes in water, forming hydrogen sulfide and phosphoric acid. Methods for the determination of these substances have been previously detailed.

F. Elemental Phosphorus

Rushing (14) has stressed that in the manufacture of elemental phosphorus it is possible that solid fragments of elemental phosphorus may be ejected and that free phosphorus can exist in air as a vapor because there are lower and upper limits on the ratios in which oxygen and phosphorus react. Therefore, it cannot be assumed that all of the free phosphorus reacts to form phosphorus oxides and suboxides.

He has devised a method for the determination of free phosphorus and phosphorus vapor in air that depends on trapping the elemental phosphorus and phosphorus compounds in xylene, separating the phosphorus compounds from the free phosphorus by dissolving the former in water and separating the phases, converting the free phosphorus to silver phosphide, oxidizing the phosphide to phosphate, and estimating the phosphate by the molybdenum blue method. Phosphine is not readily absorbed by xylene.

Reagents. *Ammonium Molybdate Solution.* Weigh out 8.33 g of ammonium molybdate tetrahydrate and dissolve in water. Transfer to a 1-liter flask and dilute to volume with water.

Ferrous Sulfate Solution. Add 6.0 g of ferrous sulfate heptahydrate and 1 ml of 11.3N sulfuric acid to a 50-ml volumetric flask. Dilute to the mark with distilled water. Prepare immediately before using.

Silver Nitrate Solution. Dissolve 10 g of silver nitrate in water and dilute to a liter.

Standard Solution. Prepare a standard solution of phosphate from KH_2PO_4 dried at 110°C (1 μg P $\backsimeq$ 4.3936 mg KH_2PO_4). Prepare dilute solutions which contain the desired amounts of phosphorus in 1 ml of solution.

Sampling. Sample the air by drawing it at a rate of 1 cfm for 15 min through a macro impinger containing 100 ml of xylene. Attach a small circle of Whatman No. 41 filter paper in a convenient holder on the exit side of the impinger to catch any fume which passes through the xylene. Transfer the xylene to a glass-stoppered bottle and add the filter paper. As soon as is feasible (within a few hours) after taking the sample, proceed with the removal of phosphorus oxides. This must be done in an environment which is free of phosphorus compounds.

Procedure. Transfer the xylene to a separatory funnel and shake vigorously with 25 ml of oxidant-free distilled water for 1 min. Allow the layers to separate and draw off the aqueous layer. Repeat the step of washing the xylene using about 15 ml of oxidant-free distilled water to make certain that all of the phosphorus pentoxide present is removed. Add 10 ml of 1% silver nitrate solution and shake vigorously for 2 min. Elemental phosphorus will react to give a black precipitate or darkening in the silver nitrate layer at this point. A few micrograms of phosphorus will produce a noticeable darkening. (The sample can be stored indefinitely after this treatment.)

Add 10 ml of concentrated nitric acid with swirling and shake immediately for 2 min. Exercise care at this point because there is some reaction between the nitric acid and xylene. Allow the layers to separate and draw off the aqueous layer into a 100-ml beaker. Repeat the extraction of the xylene with 10 ml of nitric acid (1:1) and add to the same beaker. Repeat the extraction with another 10-ml portion of nitric acid (1:1) and add to the beaker. The phosphorus originally present as elemental phosphorus will now be in the beaker. Discard the xylene layer.

Evaporate the contents of the beaker to dryness on a steam bath. Add 2 ml of nitric acid and 50 ml of water, precipitate the silver as silver chloride by adding 10 ml of hydrochloric acid (1:3), filter, wash with 1% hydrochloric acid, and catch the washings in the same beaker. Evaporate the filtrate to dryness on a steam bath, add into the beaker 5 ml of concentrated nitric acid, and heat long enough to eliminate the chloride. Transfer the test solution to a platinum dish, evaporate to dryness on a steam bath, add a 1-drop excess of 5% sodium carbonate solution, as evidenced by no further liberation of carbon dioxide, and again evaporate to dryness. Remove all organic matter by gentle ignition. Avoid overheating because a small amount of silver will be present and may alloy with the dish.

Add 2 ml of nitric acid, evaporate to dryness, and add 5 ml of 11.3N

sulfuric acid. Evaporate to incipient fumes, cool, add 2 drops of saturated ammonium oxalate solution, and again evaporate to incipient fumes to remove any residual nitric acid. Transfer to a 10-ml volumetric flask and dilute to 10 ml with water. Transfer a 1-ml aliquot of the sample to a colorimeter tube or cuvette, add 1 ml of 11.3N sulfuric acid and 12 ml of ammonium molybdate reagent with the aid of volumetric pipets. Cool to room temperature. (The solution must be clear.) Add 1 ml of ferrous sulfate solution and read samples in a spectrophotometer at 720 mμ after about 1 min. Colors do not change noticeably within 2 hr.

Standards should be prepared from the standard solution in the range 0–35 μg of phosphorus. The colorimetric portion of the procedure should be carried out with each standard.

This colorimetric phosphate determination is a variation of the method of Rockstein and Herron (7).

Investigation of Variables in Method. The following variables which were of interest in connection with the method were investigated:

(*1*) The effect of the concentration of the silver nitrate solution.

(*2*) Various solutions other than silver nitrate for extracting the phosphorus from the xylene.

(*3*) The efficiency of collection of phosphorus in xylene.

(*4*) The recovery of the phosphorus from the xylene.

(*5*) The absorption of phosphine by xylene.

An obvious omission is an investigation of the possible oxidation of the phosphorus by air during sampling.

References

1. Ward, E. F., *U.S. Bur. Labor Statistics Bull. 405* (1926); *J. Ind. Hyg.*, **10**, (1928).
2. Heimann, H., *N.Y. State Ind. Bull.*, **26**, No. 4, 17 (1947); **26**, No. 5, 22 (1947).
3. Truog, E., and A. H. Meyer, *Ind. Eng. Chem. Anal. Ed.*, **1**, 136 (1929).
4. Briggs, A. P., *J. Biol. Chem.*, **59**, 255 (1924).
5. *Methods Assoc. Official Agr. Chemists*, 4th ed., 1935.
6. Sumner, J. B., *Science*, **100**, 413 (1944).
7. Rockstein, M., and P. W. Herron, *Anal. Chem.*, **23**, 1500 (1951).
8. Taussky, H. H., and E. Shorr, *J. Urol.*, **69**, 454 (1953); *J. Biol. Chem.*, **202**, 675 (1953).
9. Flury, F., and F. Zernck, *Schaedliche Gase*, Springer, Berlin, 1931.

10. Sayers, R. R., in *International Critical Tables*, Vol. II, McGraw-Hill, New York, 1927.
11. *Ind. Hyg. Newsletter*, **7**, No. 8, 15 (1947).
12. Wilmet, M., *Compt. Rend.*, **185**, 206 (1927); *Analyst*, **52**, 558 (1927).
13. Muller, W., *Arch. Hyg. Bact.*, **129**, 286 (1943).
14. Rushing, D. E., *A Tentative Method for the Determination of Elemental Phosphorus in Air*, Public Health Service, U.S. Dept. Health, Education, and Welfare, Colorado River Basin Water Quality Control Project Lab., Salt Lake City, Utah.

CHAPTER XIV

NITROGEN COMPOUNDS

A. Nitrogen Oxides

Industrial poisoning from the oxygen compounds of nitrogen is a hazard in many industries. Among the industries where this hazard is particularly present are the manufacture of sulfuric acid by the chamber process, which was discussed in a prior section, the manufacture of nitric acid and nitrates such as ammonium nitrate, the manufacture of dyes and explosives, the production of pyroxylin-type plastics, the formulation of nitrocellulose paints, lacquers, and artificial cloths, the manufacture of fertilizer and cyanamide, and photographic-film works. These gases are also a hazard in certain operations, for example, blasting, welding, electroplating, metal cleaning, and in fires. In the Cleveland Hospital fire, in which many lives were lost, the lethal agent was mainly nitrogen oxides from burning film (1). Nitrogen oxides are also produced in carbon-arc combustions. The concentration of these oxides expressed as nitric oxide varies from 200 to 1500 ppm, depending on the type of arc and the power consumption (2).

1. Physiological Response

The fumes of the nitrogen oxides are extremely dangerous because of their insidious character. The bad feature of this type of poisoning is that little warning is given to the worker for the oxides of nitrogen fail to set up defense respiratory reflexes. Thus, a worker may inhale quantities of these gases that will affect him seriously and even cause death, without knowing it. Cases have been recorded where the workman felt entirely well throughout the working day after the inhalation of these fumes, only to die the following day because of pulmonary edema. Symptoms after exposure are restlessness, with a dry cough and shortness of breath. These symptoms increase and are accompanied by a frothy sputum tinged with blood. Death may follow from pulmonary edema, even after several days.

As little as 0.01% (100 ppm) may cause illness if breathed for a short time and 0.07%, or 700 ppm is fatal if breathed for 30 min or even a lesser time (3,4). The maximum allowable concentration for an exposure of several hours' duration is of the order of 10 ppm (5). The generally accepted maximum allowable concentration (6) for daily 8-hr exposures is 25 parts of nitrogen oxides, other than nitrous oxide, per million parts of air. When the nitrogen oxides are calculated as NO_2, this concentration is equivalent to 0.047 mg/liter at 25°C and 760 mm Hg.

2. CHEMICAL RELATIONSHIP OF THE NITROGEN OXIDES

Nitrogen forms a series of oxides, most of which may occur in industry. They are:

Nitrous oxide, N_2O	Anhydride of hyponitrous acid, $H_2N_2O_2$
Nitric oxide, NO	Anhydride of nitrohydroxylamic acid, $HON:NO_2H$
Nitrous anhydride, or nitrogen trioxide, N_2O_3	Anhydride of nitrous acid, HNO_2
Nitrogen tetroxide, or dioxide, $NO_2 \rightleftharpoons N_2O_4$	Yields both nitrous and nitric acids
Nitric anhydride, or nitrogen pentoxide, N_2O_5	Anhydride of nitric acid, HNO_3

Only the first four are gases, and of these only the NO_2 form of tetroxide is colored the familiar brown-red, the other gases, including the N_2O_4 form of nitrogen tetroxide, being colorless or practically colorless. There is another oxide of nitrogen, namely, nitrogen hexoxide, NO_3 or N_2O_6, about which little is known and which in all probability is seldom encountered in industry.

The relationships of nitric oxide, NO, nitrous anhydride, N_2O_3, and nitrogen tetroxide, N_2O_4, are so very close that they seldom occur separately in industry. Thus nitric oxide reacts readily with oxygen to form nitrogen tetroxide:

$$2NO + O_2 \rightleftharpoons 2NO_2 \rightleftharpoons N_2O_4$$
$$\text{brown} \quad \text{faint yellow}$$

Nitrous anhydride in the gaseous state is almost completely dissociated into nitric oxide and nitrogen tetroxide:

$$N_2O_3 \rightarrow NO + NO_2$$

Nitrogen tetroxide dissolves in *cold* water to form both nitric and nitrous acids:

$$2NO_2 + H_2O \rightarrow HNO_3 + HNO_2$$

If the water is not cold, the nitrous acid decomposes to form nitric acid and nitric oxide:

$$3NO_2 + H_2O \rightarrow 2HNO_3 + NO$$

Nitrogen pentoxide, or nitric anhydride, is a white solid that has to be prepared by special methods. It decomposes readily, forming nitrogen tetroxide:

$$2N_2O_5 \rightarrow 4NO_2 + O_2$$

3. Detection and Determination

Because of these relationships and reactions, the mixture of nitric oxide, nitrous anhydride, and nitrogen tetroxide, which appears as reddish-brown fumes, is preferably estimated as nitrate (7). In the specific instance of arc welding, the nitric oxide (NO) content is probably only one-fifth of the total calculated as nitrate.

Samples of nitrogen oxides may be taken in special glass vacuum-tube collectors of approximately 250–300-ml capacity. These tubes should be rinsed with water several times before the absorbing solution is added, to free the tubes of nitrogen oxides that may have collected on the walls during their manufacture. The tubes are prepared beforehand as follows: Place 10 ml of $0.1N$ sulfuric acid and 3 drops of a 3% solution of hydrogen peroxide into the bottle through the 6-mm shell-tubing neck on each bottle. Connect the tube to a high-vacuum pump and evacuate until the solution in the collector begins to boil. Seal the tube with an alcohol hand torch. Make a file mark on the neck of the collector near the end and break the tube at this point in the place where the sample is to be collected. After the tip is broken, the surrounding air rushes in until it reaches the pressure of the surrounding atmosphere. The tips of the collectors then may be sealed with a rubber policeman or with a short piece of pure gum-rubber tubing having a stub of solid glass rod in the end.

Sampling of the oxides of nitrogen may also be accomplished by absorption of the fumes in sodium hydroxide solution, oxidation with hydrogen peroxide to insure that all of the oxides are in the nitrate form, and subsequent determination of the nitrate by the phenoldisulfonic acid method.

An alternative method of sampling is to pass 10 liters of the air to be sampled by aspiration over a period of 1 hr through 40 ml of absorbing solution consisting of 35 ml of 5% potassium hydroxide solution and 5 ml of 3% hydrogen peroxide solution (8). This absorbing solution is then analyzed by the phenoldisulfonic acid method.

It is customary to sample in the manner described, particularly in mine work, but it should be noted that in Goldman's (9) opinion it is preferable to add the trapping reagent after sampling and not to evacuate the flask with the hydrogen peroxide in it because the vapor pressure attributable to the decomposition of the hydrogen peroxide and the absorption liquid may be appreciable and vary.

Immerse the samples obtained as described above in a brine bath and freeze the absorbing solution (10). Keep the samples in the low-temperature bath for at least 2 hr to insure complete oxidation of the oxides. After the gases are completely oxidized, wash the outside of each tube thoroughly and dry. Then open the tube and wash the contents into a 150-ml beaker. Make slightly alkaline with 1N sodium hydroxide solution, cover the beaker with a watch glass supported on glass hooks, and evaporate nearly to dryness on an electric hot plate. To prevent baking, drive off the last traces of moisture by placing the beaker in a constant-temperature oven thermostatically controlled at 85°C. As soon as dryness is attained, cool the beaker in a cold water bath and proceed with the method as detailed below, beginning with, "Add 1 ml of the phenoldisulfonic acid solution . . ."

a. Phenoldisulfonic Acid Method

The following method (11–13) is based on the nitration of phenoldisulfonic acid by any nitrate present in the sample with the formation of a colored nitrophenoldisulfonic acid compound. Any nitrite present is oxidized to nitrate and thus reacts the same way. Nitric oxide is also oxidized to nitrate in this method.

Reagents. *Phenoldisulfonic Acid Solution.* Dissolve 25 g of pure phenol in 150 ml of concentrated sulfuric acid on a steam bath, cool, and add 75 ml of fuming sulfuric acid (15% SO_3). Heat to 100°C for 2 hr. Do not expose to light.

Standard Comparison Solution: Stock Nitrate Solution. Dissolve 0.4025 g of recrystallized and dried potassium nitrate in water and dilute to 1 liter.

Standard Nitrate Solution. Dilute 10 ml of the stock nitrate solution to 1 liter with water. One ml of this solution is equivalent to 0.001 ml of nitrogen dioxide at 25°C and 740 mm Hg. Transfer aliquot portions to 150-ml beakers; thus, 1 ml of standard nitrate solution would be equivalent to 5 ppm on the basis of a 200-ml sample. Add 10 ml of 0.1N sulfuric acid, 3 drops of hydrogen peroxide, and sufficient 1N potassium hydroxide solution to make the mixture alkaline. Dilute to 110 ml, evaporate to dryness, and proceed with the method as detailed.

Procedure. Transfer the sample solution to a beaker. Heat, if not collected by the vacuum-tube method, for a few minutes with a few drops of nitrate-free hydrogen peroxide, or oxidize any nitrite present with dilute potassium permanganate solution, adding the permanganate until a faint pink coloration persists. Evaporate. Transfer to a 100-ml volumetric flask. If the chloride content exceeds 3 mg, add to the cold solution sufficient silver sulfate solution, prepared by dissolving 4.397 g of Ag_2SO_4, nitrate free, in 1 liter of water (1 ml of this solution is equivalent to 1 mg of chloride ion) to precipitate all but about 0.1 mg of chloride. Add 5 ml of alumina cream. Make up to the mark with water, shake thoroughly, and filter through a folded filter, returning the filtrate to the filter until it runs through clear. Evaporate 25 ml or other suitable aliquot of the filtrate to dryness.

Add 1 ml of the phenoldisulfonic acid solution. Mix quickly and thoroughly by means of a glass rod. Add 1 ml of water and 3–4 drops of sulfuric acid. Heat on a steam bath for 2–3 min, being careful not to char the material. Then add about 25 ml of water and an excess of ammonium hydroxide (1:1), about 20 ml. Transfer to a 100-ml volumetric flask, add 1–2 ml of alumina cream if not perfectly clear, dilute to volume with water, and filter. Fill a 50-ml Nessler tube to the mark with the filtrate and determine the quantity of sodium nitrate present in the sample by comparison with the standard comparison tubes prepared as directed above. If the solution is too dark for comparison with the standards, dilute with water and correct the result accordingly.

b. Nitrogen Oxides as Nitrite

The determination of nitrogen dioxide or nitrogen tetroxide (in aqueous solution, nitrite ion) by formation of a dye by use of diazotization and coupling (or for that matter determination of the other two reactants in this reaction) is a well-known method commonly known as the Griess-Ilosvay method which was originally devised by Griess (14) in 1879. This method depends, as is well known, on four components, namely, the substance which can be diazotized, nitrite ion, a proper acidity, and a coupling agent.

Among the principal variations of this method are those of Griess who used sulfuric acid, sulfanilic acid, and α-naphthylamine and of Ilosvay (15) who modified the method in 1889 by the substitution of dilute acetic acid as the acid component. Subsequently, the method was modified by others, such as Lunge and Lwoff (16) who used glacial acetic acid and Tschirikow (17) in 1891 who used hydrochloric acid. An advance was made by Germuth (18) in 1929 substituting dimethyl-α-naphthylamine for α-naphthylamine.

A significant development in this field was the introduction of N-(1-naphthyl)ethylenediamine dihydrochloride by Bratton and Marshall (19) in 1939. The definitive work on the use of this reagent was done by these investigators in their search for a stable coupling agent for determination of sulfanilamide and its analogues. Since Bratton and Marshall were interested in the determination of the product to be diazotized, namely, the sulfa drug, they used excess quantities of nitrite ion for the diazotization. In order to avoid the effect of excess nitrite on the color of the dye produced, Bratton and Marshall used sulfamic acid to destroy excess nitrite (a suggestion of Lubs) and this step was published by Marshall and Litchfield (20) in 1938. In 1941, Shinn (21) adapted the use of N-(1-naphthyl)-ethylenediamine dihydrochloride and sulfanilamide for the determination of nitrite in water spectrophotometrically and stated that the method could be used for foods, sewage, and the like. Shinn retained the use of ammonium sulfamate even though she recognized that the use of sulfamate was not pertinent to the nitrite determination.

In 1941 Jacobs (22) adapted the variation using sulfanilamide and the Bratton and Marshall coupling agent for the determination of nitrite in meats, specifically cured meats, and other foods, and in December of that year for the determination of chloropicrin and nitrile in air. He discarded the use of sulfamate since no excess nitrite was present. This was consequently the first use of these reagents for the determination of nitrogen dioxide, i.e., nitrite, in air.

In this test any chloropicrin in the air is passed into a solution of sodium ethylate by which it is decomposed with the formation of nitrite and chloride, the nitrite being determined by the use of either sulfanilic acid and α-naphthylamine hydrochloride in the presence of acetic acid or hydrochloric acid or sulfanilamide and N-(1-naphthyl)-ethylenediamine hydrochloride in the presence of acetic acid. Of course, the sulfanilamide can replace the sulfanilic acid or vice versa. In 1945 Jacobs and Brodey (23) presented a paper at a meeting of the Metropolitan New York Section, American Industrial Hygiene Association, on a rapid method for the determination of nitrogen dioxide–nitrogen tetroxide mixtures within an atmosphere. The details of this method were published in the second edition of *The Analytical Chemistry of Industrial Poisons, Hazards, and Solvents* in 1949 (24) and comprise the use of a mixed solid reagent containing sulfanilamide, N-(1-naphthyl)ethylenediamine, and tartaric acid. Dyer (25) in 1945 published a method using sulfanilamide and the ethylenediamine coupling reagent for the determination of nitrite in fish, measuring the transmission at 5400 Å.

Patty and Petty (26) in 1943 used a syringe for the sampling of air for the determination of nitrogen dioxide by the Griess-Ilosvay method and Jacobs and Brodey introduced the use of the newer reagents and an automatic stop for the sampling procedure, continuing to use a syringe. Probably the first published method for the use of the combined Griess-Ilosvay reagents as both absorbent and reactants for the determination of nitrogen dioxide in air was the British method (24,27) published in 1939. Saltzman (28) used a combination of sulfanilic acid, N-(1-naphthyl)ethylenediamine hydrochloride, and acetic acid as a reagent for nitrogen dioxide in air sampling with a fritted bubbler. This combination of reagents was subsequently used in instruments for the continuous sampling and determination of nitrogen dioxide in air by Thomas and co-workers (29). Katz and co-workers (30) and Cholak and co-workers (31) used this combination of reagents with sequence samplers.

c. Nitrite by the Griess-Ilosvay Reaction

The nitrite present in the absorbing solution may be estimated by using it to diazotize some added sulfanilic acid. In this instance, of course, hydrogen peroxide must not be used. The diazotized sulfanilic acid is then coupled with α-naphthylamine hydrochloride.

The official British (27) test is performed by passing the gas or atmosphere to be tested directly through the Griess-Ilosvay reagent.

Reagents. *Sulfanilic Acid Solution.* Dissolve 1 g of sulfanilic acid in hot water, cool, and dilute to 100 ml.

α-Naphthylamine Hydrochloride Solution. Boil 0.5 g of the salt with 100 ml of water, kept at constant volume for 10 min.

Standard Nitrite Solution. Dissolve 1.1 g of silver nitrite in nitrite-free water, precipitate the silver with sodium chloride solution, dilute to 1 liter, mix, allow to settle. Dilute 100 ml of the supernatant liquid to 1 liter and then 10 ml of this solution to 1 liter, using in each case nitrite-free water. One ml of the final dilution is equivalent to 0.0001 mg of nitrogen as nitrite.

Procedure (32–34). Transfer the solution containing the nitrite to a suitable volumetric flask. Almost neutralize with sulfuric acid. Add 5 ml of alumina cream and swirl. Make to volume with water, mix, and filter. These steps may be omitted if a clear test solution is used. Place 100 ml of the suitable aliquot in a 100-ml Nessler tube and treat with 1 or 2 drops of hydrochloric acid. Add 1 ml of the sulfanilic acid solution, 1 ml of the α-naphthylamine hydrochloride solution, and mix thoroughly. Set aside for 30 min with other Nessler tubes containing known quantities of the standard nitrite solution made up to 100 ml with nitrite-free water and treated with hydrochloric acid, sulfanilic acid, and the α-naphthylamine hydrochloride solutions in the same manner as the sample. Determine the quantity of the nitrite by comparison with the depth of pink color in the known and unknown solutions. If the color of the sample is deeper than that of the highest standard, repeat the test on a diluted sample.

Permanent standards may be prepared by matching the nitrite standards with dilutions of a solution of fuchsin, 0.1 g of basic fuchsin in 1 liter of water.

Because of the instability of the α-naphthylamine complex, Germuth (18) recommends that dimethyl-α-naphthylamine, $C_{10}H_7N(CH_3)_2$, be substituted for the α-naphthylamine. A solution of 5.25 g of dimethyl-α-naphthylamine dissolved in 1 liter of $4N$ acetic acid in 95% methanol insures the most satisfactory results in the colorimetric estimation of nitrites. Such a solution is stable and is used in exactly the same manner as the α-naphthylamine hydrochloride as directed above. However, the method using N-(1-naphthyl)ethylenediamine, detailed below, is preferred.

British Modification (27)

It is well to note that although the official British test is termed the detection of "nitrous fumes," it actually only detects the vapors of nitrous acid and its anhydride, nitrogen trioxide, N_2O_3. For the distinction between these terms see page 591.

The hand pump apparatus used in this test is described on page 52 and in the section on carbon disulfide, page 553.

Reagents. *Sulfanilic Acid.* Dissolve 0.5 g of sulfanilic acid with slight warming in 150 ml of a solution of 70 ml of glacial acetic acid in 500 ml of water.

α-Naphthylamine. Boil 0.1 g of α-naphthylamine for a few minutes with 20 ml of water and pour the mixture into 150 ml of a solution of 70 ml of glacial acetic acid in 500 ml of water.

Immediately before the test is made, place 5 ml of each of these reagent solutions in the bubbler trap and mix.

Preparation of Standard Color. Solution A. Weigh accurately 0.1 g of dimethylaminazobenzene, dissolve in acetone, and make up the solution to 100 ml with acetone in a volumetric flask.

Solution B. Pipet 5 ml of solution A into a 250-ml volumetric flask and make to volume with acetone. Keep well stoppered and in the dark.

When required prepare the standard color from solution B as follows: Transfer 1 ml of solution B by means of a pipet to a tube of equal bore as that of the test bubbler. Make up the volume to 10 ml with 7% hydrochloric acid. Keep the standard well stoppered or sealed and in the dark when not in use.

Procedure. On entering the atmosphere to be tested, draw the pumping strokes very slowly, using approximately 10 sec per stroke. Continue pumping, counting the number of strokes made, until the depth of color developed is a little weaker than that of the standard color. Remove the test bubbler and after 2 min, to allow for the full development of color, compare with the standard tube, the two tubes being observed side by side by transversely transmitted daylight.

If the depth of color is the same in both tubes, the concentration of nitrite present is obtained from the table given below. If the test color is less than the standard, replace the test bubbler and draw further strokes of the pump until exact equivalence is reached on standing 2 min. If the test color is deeper, repeat the test with fresh reagent using fewer strokes.

Concentration	No. of strokes
Above 1/8000	Less than 1
1/8000–1/13,000	1–2
1/13,000–1/20,000	2
1/20,000–1/27,000	3
1/27,000–1/35,000	4
1/35,000–1/45,000	5
1/45,000–1/55,000	6
1/55,000–1/65,000	7
1/65,000–1/75,000	8
1/75,000–1/85,000	9
1/85,000–1/100,000	10

Under certain conditions a cloudiness may be produced in the test solution. This does not interfere with the comparison with the standard color.

d. Jacobs and Brodey Method

Jacobs and Brodey (23) devised a rapid method by which nitrogen dioxide–nitrogen tetroxide may be detected and estimated within the atmosphere in which firemen and others are working. In this method, the Bratton and Marshall (19) reagents and a modification of the Patty and Petty (26,35) apparatus are employed. Permanent color standards have been developed for use with the Patty and Petty method.

Apparatus. The apparatus is a simple standard 50-ml glass syringe which is placed in a holder (as shown in Fig. XIV-1) so that it can be operated in the dark. By removing the rubber retaining policemen, the plunger of the syringe falls to the stop, drawing in 50 ml of air.

Reagents. *Nitrite Reagent Powder.* Because of the necessity of having a reagent ready for use at moment's notice and the well-known instability of most of the liquid nitrite reagents commonly used, a powder reagent was prepared. This reagent has the following composition:

N-(1-naphthyl)ethylenediamine dihydrochloride (coupling reagent)	1.0 g
Sulfanilamide (p-aminobenzenesulfonamide)	4.0 g
Tartaric acid	95.0 g
Total	100.0 g

The substance should be in a fine powder and should be mixed dry.

Reagent powders containing 100 mg of the mixed powder may be weighed out in papers and stored. Each powder is thus equivalent to 1 mg of coupling reagent, 4 mg of sulfanilamide, and 95 mg of acid. The powders are stable for more than 1 year if kept dry and in the dark.

Reagent Solution. Dissolve 1 powder in 10 ml of water. This is sufficient for one test. This solution is relatively stable. Solutions

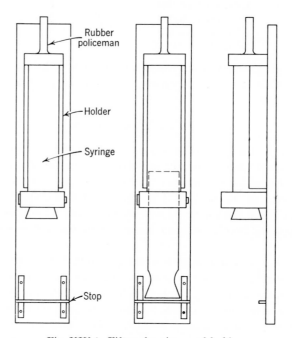

Fig. XIV-1. Fifty-ml syringe and holder.

of the mixed reagent have been kept for more than 1 month with no precautions other than being in a glass-stoppered bottle. At the end of this period the color produced with standard nitrite solution was the same as that produced with freshly prepared reagent. Even though the reagent may become slightly colored on standing for longer than 1 month, there is little effect on its reactivity.

Standards. *Solution A: Stock Solution.* Dissolve 0.402 g of reagent grade sodium nitrite in 1 liter of water.

Solution B. Dilute 5 ml of solution A to 250 ml with water.

Solution C. Add 5 ml of solution B to 80 ml mixed reagent as noted below and dilute with this reagent to 100 ml.

Mixed Reagent. The mixed reagent consists of powders previously prepared dissolved in water. To make up 80 ml of mixed reagent, weigh out 800 mg of powder reagent, dissolved in water, and dilute to 80 ml with water.

Procedure. Hold the syringe stoppered tip down and remove the plunger. Place 10 ml of mixed reagent in the syringe. Reinsert the plunger and reset in an upright position. Expel the air in the barrel by raising the plunger, taking care not to force out the reagent and recap with the policeman. Remove the policeman and allow the plunger to fall. If the syringe is to be connected to a sampling line, which has been properly purged, hold the plunger, remove the policeman, attach the sampling line, and allow the plunger to fall. A 50-ml air sample is drawn into the syringe. Stopper, shake, return to a safe atmosphere, and after 5 min compare the color produced with standards.

The shade of color produced by the nitrite obtained from fire and other air samples and that of the standards, made from sodium nitrite, are not the same. Consequently, photoelectric methods cannot be employed and the concentration should be estimated by visual comparison of the color produced.

e. Jacobs and Hochheiser Method

The following method (36) may be used for the determination of nitrogen dioxide in air in the presence of much higher concentrations of sulfur dioxide, either as a single sample or on an hourly basis with the aid of an automatic 24-hr sampler. Air is aspirated through a fritted-glass bubbler containing $0.1N$ alkali solution. The sulfur dioxide present is also absorbed but is oxidized to sulfate with hydrogen peroxide so that it does not interfere with the reaction. The absorbed nitrogen dioxide is determined colorimetrically as the azo dye by using it to diazotize sulfanilamide in phosphoric acid and then coupling with N-(1-naphthyl)ethylenediamine dihydrochloride. Nitrogen dioxide in the order of parts per hundred million in air can be determined by this method.

Apparatus. *Automatic Air Sampler.* Replace the modified Greenburg-Smith impinger of a Wilson automatic impinger sampler (see Chapter II, Section F-1, Fig. II-27) by a bubbler of equivalent dimensions equipped with a coarse fritted-glass dispenser. Katz and co-workers (30) used a similar apparatus with a medium porosity absorption disperser tube. Insert a filter paper trap in the sampling line to retain particulate matter and a flowmeter capable of registering 1.3 lpm.

Reagents. *Absorbing Reagent: Sodium Hydroxide Solution.* Add 2 ml of butyl alcohol per liter of 0.1N sodium hydroxide solution to increase foaming and to assist in trapping the nitrogen dioxide.

N-(1-Naphthyl)ethylenediamine Dihydrochloride Solution. Prepare a solution containing 1 mg of the coupling agent per milliliter.

Diazotizing Reagent. Dissolve 20 g of sulfanilamide in 1 liter of water containing 50 ml of phosphoric acid.

Standard Sodium Nitrite Solution (1 ml = 10 μg NO_2). Dissolve 150 mg sodium nitrite, $NaNO_2$, in 1 liter of water. Dilute 10 ml of this solution to 100 ml.

Procedure. Aspirate air at 1.3 lpm through 30–35 ml of absorbing reagent in a fritted bubbler or through the automatic air sampler apparatus. Twenty-four 40-min samples are obtained in the latter manner. Transfer the samples to 50-ml Nessler tubes. Add 1 drop of 1% hydrogen peroxide solution and mix to oxidize the dissolved sulfur dioxide to sulfate. Add 10 ml of diazotizing reagent and then 1 ml of N-(1-naphthyl)ethylenediamine dihydrochloride reagent. Dilute to 50 ml and mix. Allow to stand for 30 min and determine the optical densities in a Coleman spectrophotometer at 550 mμ, using a reagent blank as the reference and matched cuvettes 20 $\times$ 40 mm.

If the three-way stopcock of the Wilson automatic impinger is replaced by solenoid valves, twenty-four 57-min samples can be collected. The sampling rate can be reduced to 1 lpm to give about the same volume of air sampled and thus keep the calculation nearly the same.

Calibration. Add 0.2, 0.4, 0.6, 0.8, and 1.0 ml of standard sodium nitrite solution to 35 ml of absorbing reagent contained in 50-ml Nessler tubes. Add 1 drop of hydrogen peroxide solution, 10 ml of diazotizing reagent, 1 ml of coupling reagent, and dilute to 50 ml. Read in the spectrophotometer at 550 mμ, using the reagent blank as reference. The maximum absorption was determined in the usual manner by Jacobs and Hochheiser and was found to be 550 mμ.

Calculations. Quantities of NO_2 can be expressed as parts per hundred million of the air sample (pphm). For a 52-liter air sample at 760 mm Hg and 25°C, 1 μg of NO_2 is equivalent to 1 pphm of NO_2.

Effect of Sulfur Dioxide. It was determined that 1 ppm of sulfur dioxide in a 52-liter air sample having a concentration of 5 pphm of nitrogen dioxide caused a 50% reduction in color after one-half hour. It was necessary to find an oxidant of the proper potential that would oxidize sulfur dioxide to sulfate and not affect the nitrite. One drop of a 1% hydrogen peroxide solution satisfied this condition and did not interfere with the intensity of the color produced when color intensities were determined after 30 min.

Absorption Efficiency. To evaluate the empirical absorption efficiency of the 0.1N sodium hydroxide solution, air (1.3 lpm) was aspirated through the fritted-glass bubblers in series containing 35 ml of absorbing reagent. The absorption efficiency is better than 90% with the dispersers Jacobs and Hochheiser used. To ensure this absorption efficiency in air that is relatively acid, it is necessary that 0.1N sodium hydroxide solution be used. For a 52-liter air sample 35 ml of an 0.1N sodium hydroxide solution satisfies this requirement. It was also established that the nitrite formed is stable in the absorbing reagent for 48 hr. It must be stressed, however, that the absorption efficiency is also dependent upon the dimensions and the porosity of the frit of the absorbers, as previously noted by Saltzman (28).

Color Production. A rapid and quantitative method of dye production is necessary. It was found by Jacobs and Hochheiser that a pH of less than 2 is required for maximum color production. Because a final volume of 50 ml is desirable and since 35 ml of absorbing reagent is used, the proper pH is not obtainable with acetic acid. Hydrochloric acid does not give sufficiently rapid color development. It was found that phosphoric acid gives both rapid and maximum color development. The diazotizing and the coupling reagents are more stable when stored separately.

This method for the determination of nitrogen dioxide, as virtually all methods for the determination of nitrogen oxides in air, is an empirical one because of the dismutation of the nitrogen dioxide–nitrogen tetroxide mixture and because of the need for standardization of the absorbers. The quantitative aspects of the dismutation of nitrogen dioxide–nitrogen tetroxide when absorbed in aqueous solution are not entirely known. Patty and Petty (26) found that the apparent average recovery of nitrite from nitrogen dioxide–

nitrogen tetroxide mixtures (i.e., on the assumption that 1 mole of NO_2 gas yields 1 mole of NO_2^- ion) was $57 \pm 2.6\%$. Their maximum recovery was 65% and their minimum recovery was 52%. Others on this basis reported nitrite recovery of the order of 72% (28). Thus, the actual amount of nitrogen dioxide in the air is probably greater than the results, i.e., the uncorrected results, obtained by this method, since only approximately 60–70% of the nitrogen dioxide–nitrogen tetroxide that is converted to nitrite is measured. Possibly more accurate results can be obtained by use of methods in which all of the nitrogen oxides are converted to nitrate but such methods are far more tedious.

f. Automatic Estimation

A number of instruments have been proposed for the determination and the recording of concentrations of nitrogen dioxide in air. The devices of Thomas and co-workers (29) and of Cholak and co-workers (31) depend, in general, on the use of an absorption reagent which is prepared by dissolving 5 g of sulfanilic acid in somewhat less than a liter of water containing 140 ml of glacial acetic acid, adding 20 ml of 0.1% solution of N-(1-naphthyl)ethylenediamine dihydrochloride, and diluting to 1 liter. Then the difference in light absorption is determined at a given wavelength between a portion of the absorbing solution alone and a portion that had passed through a scrubbing tower. Cholak used a recirculating type of scrubber tower that permitted a rate of sampling of 850 ml of air per minute and determined the light absorption at 550 mμ. Thomas sampled at a rate of 250 ml/min and used a nonrecirculating type of absorption tower. In both devices the difference in light absorption was recorded.

Moore, Cole, and Katz (30) and also Jacobs and Hochheiser (36) used sequence samplers and the reagent in the preceding paragraph for the monitoring of nitrogen dioxide in air. Because of the difficulties involved in the use of sulfanilic acid reagent for the direct absorption of nitrogen dioxide, Jacobs and Hochheiser (36) abandoned its use and substituted an absorbing reagent comprising $0.1N$ sodium hydroxide solution containing 2 ml of butyl alcohol per liter. Air was aspirated through a bubbler equipped with a gas disperser of coarse fritted glass in a Wilson sequence sampler at a rate of 1.3 lpm through 30–35 ml of absorbing reagent. The analysis was then carried out as detailed above.

Adley and Skillern (37) used both the mixed reagent given in the preceding paragraph and a reagent, consisting of 0.1 g of N-(1-naphthyl)ethylenediamine dihydrochloride, 0.4 g of sulfanilamide, and 9.5 g of tartaric acid dissolved in 1 liter of water, first developed by Jacobs (24) for the monitoring of nitrogen dioxide with the aid of a portable multirange monitor. The Jacobs reagent was used for environmental sampling where a quick initial response was wanted.

g. Xylenol Method

In this method (38) nitrogen oxide vapors are sampled by use of an evacuated flask containing sulfuric acid. The nitrous acid in the mixture of nitric and nitrous acids produced is oxidized to nitric acid by the use of potassium permanganate. The total nitric acid is then used to nitrate m-xylenol to 4-hydroxy-1,3-dimethyl-5-nitrobenzene. The latter is steam distilled and estimated colorimetrically.

Sampling. Sample air by means of an evacuated Shepherd bottle (Fig. II-3) containing 5 ml of sulfuric acid (5:3) and prolong the sampling period to 1 min by use of a capillary tube side arm so that the operator can move about and obtain a more representative sample. Close the cap and set the flask aside for 2 hr to effect solution of the nitrogen oxides.

Procedure. Add a single drop, 0.05 ml, of 2% potassium permanganate solution to the flask and mix thoroughly. Add 0.2 ml of a 1% solution of m-xylenol in propylene glycol. Allow to stand for 10 min. Add 100 ml of water, some boiling chips or glass beads, and connect the flask to a distillation apparatus (Fig. XIV-2). Bring the solution to the boiling point; then reduce the size of the flame to about 2 cm so that the distillate comes over at the rate of about 1 ml/min. Trap the distillate in a water-cooled 25-ml graduated cylinder containing 1 ml of 2% sodium hydroxide solution.

Compare the color of the distillate with solutions obtained by the distillation of appropriate quantities of potassium nitrate. One mg of potassium nitrate is equivalent to 0.455 mg of nitrogen oxides expressed in terms of nitrogen dioxide, NO_2.

The quantity of m-xylenol mentioned in the method is adequate for 0.5 mg of nitrogen oxides. Sampling vessels of 500-ml capacities will provide for concentrations of nitrogen dioxide up to 500 ppm. The

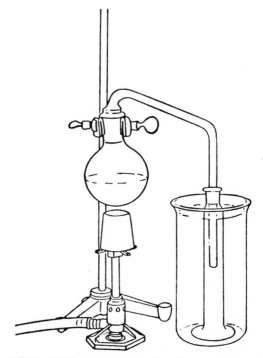

Fig. XIV-2. Distillation apparatus for the *m*-xylenol method.

method is adequate for concentrations of 2 ppm, equivalent to 5 μg of potassium nitrate in the standard.

h. *Nitrosyl Ferrous Sulfate Method*

Kothny and Mueller (39) developed a method for the determination of higher concentrations of nitrogen oxides of the order of greater than 100 ppm. It was based on the well-known so-called brown ring test for nitrate and nitrite. This test was developed by Desbassinde Richemont in 1835.

$$FeSO_4 + NO \rightarrow FeSO_4 \cdot NO$$

$$3FeSO_4 + NO_2 + H_2SO_4 \rightarrow FeSO_4 \cdot NO + Fe_2(SO_4)_3 + H_2O$$

$FeSO_4 \cdot NO$ is dark green with absorption maxima at 445 and 580 mμ. The response to nitric oxide and nitrogen dioxide or tetroxide is the same. Since ferric sulfate, $Fe_2(SO_4)_3$, is brown, it is necessary to add sodium fluoride to form a complex sodium ferrifluoride, which is colorless, and thus eliminate this interference.

$$Fe_2(SO_4)_3 + 12NaF \rightarrow 2Na_3FeF_6 + 3Na_2SO_4$$

Reagents. *Absorbing Solution.* Prepare a 25% solution of ferrous sulfate by dissolving 125 g of reagent grade $FeSO_4 \cdot 7H_2O$ in water and diluting to 500 ml. Dissolve 6 g of NaF in water and dilute to 200 ml. Mix together 400 ml of 25% ferrous sulfate solution, 150 ml of 3% sodium fluoride solution, and 4 ml of concentrated sulfuric acid and dilute to 1 liter with water. This yields a 10% solution of ferrous sulfate hydrate, a 0.75% solution of sodium fluoride, and a 0.7% solution of sulfuric acid (w/v).

Sampling. Set up a train consisting of a glass intake tube, a tube bubbler (which is preferable to a fritted bubbler for this determination), an appropriate flowmeter or rotameter, a valve or bleed, and a pump. Draw air at a rate of 0.5 lpm through 10 ml of the absorbent in the bubbler for 5 min.

Procedure. Transfer the absorbing solution to a 0.5-in. or 1-in. cell or cuvette and read the absorbance at 455 mμ within a total elapsed sampling and procedure time of 5–15 min. Obtain the concentration from a standard curve prepared from a standard solution of sodiuim nitrite.

i. Nitric Oxide

Nitric oxide, NO, may at times be the predominant nitrogen oxide in the atmosphere being tested. In general, the method of analysis comprises making two determinations of nitrogen dioxide in one of which the air stream is exposed to an oxidizing agent to oxidize the nitric oxide to nitrogen dioxide and in the other the nitric oxide is not oxidized. The difference in the two determinations may be calculated to nitric oxide. Thomas and co-workers (29) used ozone, potassium permanganate, and chlorine dioxide to oxidize the nitric oxide.

The Jacobs and Hochheiser method (see Section A-3-e of this chapter), used for single samples, can be adapted to the estimation of nitric oxide in air.

Procedure. Set up two trains as detailed in the method. Place a large fritted bubbler containing sufficient acid solution of permanganate (prepared by dissolving 25 g of $KMnO_4$ in a liter of 2.5%

H$_2$SO$_4$) to cover the frit or use a Milligan gas washing bottle packed with glass beads containing the oxidizing solution in front of the bubbler containing the sodium hydroxide absorbing solution in one train.   In this manner the incoming air stream of one sample will be washed by the permanganate solution.   Continue with the method as detailed.   The difference in the two determinations may be calculated as nitric oxide.

j. Nitrous Oxide

It is seldom necessary to estimate the amount of nitrous oxide, N$_2$O, as such in air.   Since, however, it is a frequently used anesthetic, it is useful to have such methods.

Determination.   Absorption methods such as are used in ordinary gas analysis are not entirely suitable for nitrous oxide determinations, for there is no known substance (40) which will absorb this gas without appreciably absorbing other gases.   It is appreciably soluble in the aqueous solvents used for other gases so that when it is present, it causes errors in the determination of these other gases if they are estimated by gasometric absorption methods and subsequent decreases in volume.   If it is presumed to be the only contaminant present in otherwise normal air, it may be separated from the other components of air by first absorbing any carbon dioxide and water present by passing the gas through solid alkali or other solid alkaline absorbent and then condensing the nitrous oxide by passing it through a U tube immersed in liquid air.

Nitrous oxide is best estimated by absorbing interfering gases with dry absorbents and then reducing, oxidizing, or decomposing the nitrous oxide itself.   The water vapor and carbon dioxide in air may be removed as explained, the nitrous oxide may be condensed by liquid air, or the oxygen may be removed as well as the carbon dioxide and water vapor by passing the gas through yellow phosphorus and fused potassium hydroxide (41).   The nitrous oxide may then be estimated by passing it over a heated copper gauze previously reduced by a current of hydrogen (42).   A current of hydrogen is now passed over the gauze again.   The cupric oxide formed by the reaction between the nitrous oxide and the reduced copper is reduced with the formation of water.   The amount of water formed is collected in a calcium chloride drying tube and is estimated gravimetrically.

Nitrous oxide may be reduced by combustion with hydrogen with a consequent contraction of 1 volume per volume of nitrous oxide (43). Thus

$$N_2O + H_2 \rightarrow N_2 + H_2O$$
(1 vol) (1 vol) (1 vol) (vol negligible)

A measured volume of pure hydrogen is added to the nitrous oxide, which has been freed from oxygen, carbon dioxide, and water. This mixture is passed over a combustion coil in a gas chamber. After completion of the combustion the coil may be removed, the water vapor formed absorbed by fused potassium hydroxide, and the volume of the remaining gases measured. The decrease in volume is a direct measure of the nitrous oxide present in the original sample.

Nitrous oxide may also be estimated by reduction with carbon monoxide:

$$N_2O + CO \rightarrow CO_2 + N_2$$

While there is no volume change, the carbon dioxide may be absorbed by a dry absorbent as described and the total reduction in volume is then proportional to the volume of the nitrous oxide.

It may also be estimated by thermal decomposition by passing the gas through a heated platinum capillary (44). The gas decomposes as follows:

$$2N_2O \rightarrow 2N_2 + O_2$$
(2 vol)   (3 vol)

There is thus an increase in volume that is equivalent to one-half the volume of nitrous oxide present.

B. Ammonia

Ammonia is an industrial hazard in numerous industries, especially where it is used as a refrigerant and may be present in dangerous concentrations if a break should occur in the refrigerating system. Among the workers who are exposed to this hazard may be mentioned coke-oven workers, textile workers, calcium carbide makers, dye makers, tannery workers, and those employed in the munitions, explosives, glue, lacquer, fertilizer, artificial ice, artificial silk, and many other industries.

Anhydrous ammonia, NH_3, is a colorless gas with a pungent odor. It boils at $-33.4°C$, has a specific gravity of 0.597 referred to air, and can be easily liquefied. It is extremely soluble in water, with the formation of ammonium hydroxide, a colorless liquid with a pungent odor. Strong ammonia water contains 28–29% ammonia and has a specific gravity $d_{25}^{25} = 0.90$.

1. Physiological Response

Ammonia acts principally on the upper respiratory tract where it exerts an alkaline, caustic action. It elicits immediate violent respiratory reflexes such as coughing and arrest of respiration. It affects the conjunctiva and cornea immediately. Inhalation causes acute inflammation of the respiratory organs, cough, edema of the lungs, chronic bronchial catarrh, secretion of saliva, and retention of urine (45).

Concentrations of the order of 0.5–1.0% by volume are lethal to men for exposures of a few minutes. Concentrations of 0.25–0.45% are dangerous for exposures of 30–60 min. The maximum concentration of ammonia that can be tolerated for 60 min is 0.03% and the maximum concentration that can be tolerated for several hours without serious disturbances is 0.01%. The least detectable odor is about 53 parts of ammonia per million of air. The smallest concentration which will cause immediate irritation of the eyes is 698 ppm and the least concentration causing coughing is 1720 ppm or 0.17% (46,47). The generally accepted maximum allowable concentration is 100 ppm of air.

2. Detection and Determination

Ammonia has adequate warning properties and, since its odor is detectable in concentrations below that causing injury, its odor can be used as a means for detection. A concentration of 0.07 mg/liter, equivalent to 100 ppm, will affect phenolphthalein paper immediately and litmus paper in 1 sec. Concentrations of 10 ppm will take 5 and 6.5 sec, respectively, to affect these test papers (48).

a. Estimation by Titration

The concentration of ammonia in air may be obtained by passing a known volume of the air through two efficient bubblers in series containing known volumes of standardized 0.02N sulfuric acid. After sampling is complete, combine the solution in the two bubblers by transfer to a titration flask and wash the bubblers well, adding the washings to the flask, or if the bubblers are of an appropriate type the titration can be made directly in the trapping device. Titrate the excess acid with 0.02N sodium hydroxide solution using methyl red indicator, 1 g of the dye dissolved in a mixture of 50 ml of 95% alcohol plus 50 ml of water. One ml of 0.02N sulfuric acid is equivalent to 0.00034 g of ammonia. When other alkaline substances are present, it is best to distil the ammonia in the usual way.

A simple variation of the titration method (49) of estimating ammonia in air is based on the computation explained in Chapter III. Air is drawn through a bubbler containing 0.01N sulfuric acid with some methyl red as the indicator. This method can be used as a field test.

Procedure. Draw air at a known rate through the acid until the indicator changes at its customary pH. The amount of acid used in the bubbler is governed by the concentration of ammonia expected.

One ml of 0.01N sulfuric acid is equivalent to 0.00017 mg or 0.2445 ml of ammonia gas at 25°C and 760 mm Hg. Hence

$$\frac{0.2445 \times 1000 \times \text{ml } 0.01N \text{ H}_2\text{SO}_4}{\text{rate of sampling} \times \text{min}} = \text{ppm NH}_3$$

in which the rate of sampling is expressed in liters per minute and 1000 is a factor converting the milliliters of ammonia per liter of air, i.e., parts per thousand, to parts per million.

When a midget impinger is used, at its standard sampling rate of 2.83 lpm (0.1 cu ft/min) and 1 ml of 0.01N sulfuric acid is placed in the bubbler, then the equation becomes

$$\frac{86}{\text{min sampling time}} = \text{ppm NH}_3$$

b. Nessler's Method

Preparation of Folin's Nessler Reagent (50). Nessler's solution is an alkaline solution of the double iodide of mercury and potassium (HgI$_2$·2KI). Transfer 30 g of potassium iodide and 22.5 g of iodine to a 200-ml flask; add 20 ml of water and, after solution is complete, an excess of metallic mercury, i.e., approximately 30 g. Shake the flask continuously and vigorously until the dissolved iodine has nearly all disappeared, which takes about 7–15 min. The solution becomes hot. When the red iodine solution has begun to become visibly pale, though still red, cool in running water and continue shaking until the reddish color of the iodine has been replaced by the greenish color of the double iodide. The whole operation generally takes 15 min. Test a portion of the solution with starch solution. Unless the starch test is positive, the solution may contain mercurous compounds. Decant the solution, washing the mercury and flask with water. Dilute the solution and washings to 200 ml and mix well. If the cooling was begun in time, the resulting reagent is clear enough for immediate dilution with 10% alkali and water and the finished solution can be used at once for nesslerization.

From this stock solution of potassium mercuric iodide prepare the final Nessler's solution as follows: To 975 ml of an accurately prepared 10% sodium hydroxide solution add the 200 ml of the double iodide solution. Mix thoroughly and allow to clear by standing.

The 10% sodium hydroxide solution should be made from a 1:1 solution of sodium hydroxide and water that has been allowed to stand until the carbonate has settled, the clear solution being decanted and used. This solution should be standardized to an accuracy of at least 5% by titration and subsequent adjustment by the addition of more water or alkali as the case may be. The alkalinity of Nessler's reagent is important and should be checked against $1N$ hydrochloric acid. Twenty ml of $1N$ hydrochloric acid should require 11–11.5 ml of Nessler's solution.

Procedure 1. Trap the ammonia in the air in a bubbler containing $0.02N$ sulfuric acid. Transfer to a volumetric flask and make to volume. Transfer from 1 to 5 ml of this solution, according to the nitrogen content, to a 50-ml volumetric flask, dilute to 35 ml, add 6 ml of the Folin-Nessler reagent prepared as directed, and make to volume. Read in a colorimeter against a standard prepared by diluting 10 ml of ammonium sulfate solution containing 0.4716 g/liter to 100 ml. Pipet 20 ml of this solution into a 50-ml volumetric flask, dilute to 35 ml, add the same quantity of Folin-Nessler reagent as above, and make to volume. Each milliliter of the standard solution now contains 0.004 mg of nitrogen. If the nitrogen content of the unknown is much higher than the standard, less than 4 ml of the unknown is nesslerized, and conversely, if the nitrogen content is much lower than the standard, more than 4 ml is nesslerized.

This method is capable of estimating relatively low concentrations of ammonia with a high degree of accuracy.

Procedure 2. Place 50 ml of absorbing solution, prepared by adding 1 ml of concentrated sulfuric acid to 10 liters of water, into a macro impinger. Connect the impinger to the sampling train and sample at a rate of 1 cfm for 30 min. Transfer the contents of the impinger to a 50-ml volumetric flask or to a 50-ml glass-stoppered Nessler tube. The actual volume of the sample will be about 46 ml as a result of loss of water attributable to evaporation during the sampling. Add 46 ml of absorbing solution to a second Nessler tube as the blank. Add 4 ml of Nessler reagent to each tube or flask, mix thoroughly, and read exactly 10 min later in a Klett-Summerson photoelectric colorimeter using the No. 54 filter (green). Use the 50-ml glass cells for the reading and use the reagent blank as the reference.

If a cloudy solution forms after the addition of the Nessler reagent, add drop by drop with constant shaking a solution of alkaline Rochelle salts, prepared by dissolving 10 g of Rochelle salts (potassium tartrate, $KNaC_4H_4O_6 \cdot 4H_2O$) in 200 ml of $0.01N$ sodium hydroxide solution, until the cloudiness disappears.

Calibration Curve. Prepare a standard solution using ammonium chloride so that each milliliter contains 1 μg of ammonia, NH_3. Transfer to a series of large impingers 0, 5, 10, 15, 20, 25, and 30 ml of the standard solution and make up the volume to 50 ml. Proceed with the method as detailed above to obtain the calibration curve.

C. Ammonium Salts

It may at times be necessary for the industrial hygienist to ascertain the amount of ammonium salts such as ammonium chloride, ammonium sulfate, ammonium nitrate, or ammonium picrate present as a fume or dust in the atmosphere. These instances arise particularly in plants where explosives are manufactured.

a. Ammonium Chloride

In the case of ammonium chloride it is customary to trap the compound using a midget impinger with water as the collection medium.   The concentration of ammonia may then be determined on an aliquot by the Nessler method detailed above.

If desired to eliminate interferences transfer the sample solution or an aliquot to a kjeldahl flask or a similar device, make distinctly alkaline with sodium hydroxide solution, and distil, trapping the distillate in standard acid.   Titrate the excess acid with standard alkali, using sodium alizarinesulfonate as indicator.   The Winkler modification may also be used by trapping the ammonia in boric acid solution, keeping the latter cool in order to avoid loss of volatile ammonium borate, and titrating the ammonia directly with standard acid, using methyl red as indicator.

b. Ammonium Sulfate

Ammonium sulfate may be sampled and estimated in an analogous manner to ammonium chloride.

c. Ammonium Nitrate

Ammonium nitrate is a common ingredient of high explosives and propellent powders.   It is usually estimated in dusts by determining the ammonia content of the sample by nesslerization, as described. When the dust also contains nitrotoluene derivatives, it is necessary to make a distillation in the presence of alkali as explained above to obtain a solution clear enough for the Nessler method.   Ammonium nitrate may also be estimated by the xylenol method (38).

Procedure.   Sample the air at a rate of 3 lpm with a midget impinger containing 10 ml of water, sampling a minimum of 30 liters of air.   Transfer a 5-ml aliquot to a 250-ml flask, add 0.3 ml of 1% m-xylenol dissolved in one of the glycol solvents, cool, and add 8.5 ml of concentrated sulfuric acid slowly and with constant cooling to avoid a temperature of 35°C or above.   Allow the reaction to proceed for 10 min at room temperature, dilute with 100 ml of water, and distil the nitroxylenol formed into a cylinder containing 1 ml of 2% sodium hydroxide solution, as described for the estimation of nitrogen oxide vapors (page 605).

Compare the yellow color of the sample with a standard made by the distillation of 500 μg of potassium nitrate dissolved in 5 ml of water.   One mg of potassium nitrate is equivalent to 0.792 mg of ammonium nitrate.   The 3 mg of m-xylenol added as reagent is adequate for the analysis of aliquots containing not more than 1.5 mg of ammonium nitrate. The lower limit of sensitivity is 4 μg of ammonium nitrate.

d. Ammonium Picrate

Ammonium picrate may be sampled by use of the midget impinger with water as the collection medium. Liberate the ammonia by the addition of alkali, distil, and estimate either titrimetrically or colorimetrically with Nessler reagent. Picric acid may be determined as described on page 728 of the second edition of Jacobs, *The Analytical Chemistry of Industrial Poisons, Hazards, and Solvents* (24).

Since ammonium picrate is a colored compound, its concentration in air may be determined by absorption in water and direct comparison with standards for there is a distinct difference in color between 10 μg in 10 ml of water and 20 μg in the same volume of water. Collect a sample until there is a measurable color, noting the volume of air sampled, and compare with standards.

D. Hydrazine

It is very likely that hydrazine will find increasing use in industry and as a propellent fuel. Hydrazine, N_2H_4, is a colorless liquid, melting at 1.4°C and boiling at 113.5°C. It is readily soluble in water and alcohol. Hydrazine forms a hydrate and also forms a series of salts with sulfuric and hydrochloric acids and with other acids. Hydrazine and its salts are poisonous. No maximum working concentrations have been established for these compounds.

The concentration of hydrazine or the hydrate in air may be estimated by trapping the compounds in water and then titrating with $0.01N$ iodine in potassium iodide solution in the presence of sodium bicarbonate:

$$N_2H_4 + 2I_2 \rightarrow N_2 + 4HI$$

or by titration with standard potassium permanganate solution in the presence of sulfuric acid.

$$N_2H_4 + 2O \rightarrow N_2 + 2H_2O$$

The salts may be determined by the latter method.

E. Nitrogen Trichloride

Nitrogen trichloride, NCl_3, nitrogen chloride, is used as a fumigant for citrus fruit and was used for the bleaching of flour but this use was prohibited after August, 1949 (51). It is a yellowish, oily, explosive liquid boiling below 71°C. It is soluble in benzene, carbon disulfide, carbon tetrachloride, and chloroform but it is insoluble in water.

It is an irritant but is considered less irritating than chlorine. It appears to cause epileptiform seizures in dogs eating a ration containing this bleaching agent. No working standards have been evolved.

Nitrogen trichloride decomposes in hot water and it reacts with ammonia with the formation of ammonium chloride:

$$NCl_3 + 4NH_3 \rightarrow N_2 + 3NH_4Cl$$

hence, it may be estimated by a determination of the chloride ion as detailed in Chapter XVI.

F. Nitrosyl Chloride

Nitrosyl chloride, $NOCl$, is an industrial hazard where aqua regia is used for it is evolved along with chlorine. It is also used as a flour bleach and maturation agent. It is a yellowish gas boiling at $-5.5°C$ and has a suffocating odor. No criteria have been established for allowable concentrations in the working room atmosphere.

It is readily decomposed by water and alkalies:

$$NOCl + 2KOH \rightarrow KNO_2 + KCl + H_2O$$

hence, it can be estimated as the nitrite by the methods detailed above or as the chloride by the methods detailed in Chapter XVI.

References

1. Olsen, J. C., A. S. Brunjes, and V. J. Sabetta, *Ind. Eng. Chem.*, **22**, 860 (1930).
2. Coltman, R. W., *J. Ind. Hyg. Toxicol.*, **20**, 289 (1938).
3. Gardner, E. D., S. P. Howell, and G. W. Jones, *U.S. Bur. Mines Bull. 287* (1927).
4. *Fed. Board Vocational Education Bull. 39* (1931).
5. *Dept. Sci. Ind. Res. Brit. Leaflet 5* (1939).
6. *Am. Standards* Z37.13-1944.
7. McCord, C. P., G. C. Harrold, and S. F. Meek, *J. Ind. Hyg. Toxicol.*, **23**, 200 (1941).
8. MacQuiddy, E. L., J. P. Tollman, L. W. LaTowsky, and M. Mayliss, *J. Ind. Hyg. Toxicol.*, **20**, 312 (1938).

9. Goldman, F. H., and M. B. Jacobs, *Chemical Methods in Industrial Hygiene*, Interscience, New York, 1953, p. 67.

10. Perrott, G. St. J., L. W. Babcock, C. D. Bitting, and G. W. Jones, *U.S. Bur. Mines Tech. Paper 482* (1930).

11. Beatty, R. L., L. B. Berger, and H. H. Schrenk, *U.S. Bur. Mines Rept. Invest. 3687* (1943).

12. Piccard, J., E. G. Peterson, and C. D. Bitting, *Ind. Eng. Chem. Anal. Ed.*, **2**, 3 (1930).

13. Harrold, G. C., S. F. Meek, and C. P. McCord, *J. Ind. Hyg. Toxicol.*, **22**, 347 (1940).

14. Griess, P., *Chem. Ber.*, **12**, 427 (1879).

15. Ilosvay, M. L., *Bull. Soc. Chim. France*, (3)**2**, 317 (1889).

16. Lunge, G., and A. Lwoff, *Bull. Soc. Chim. France*, **1894**, 345.

17. Tschirikow, A. D., *Pharm. Z. Russland*, **30**, 802 (1891).

18. Germuth, F. G., *Ind. Eng. Chem. Anal. Ed.*, **1**, 28 (1929).

19. Bratton, A. C., and E. K. Marshall. *J. Biol. Chem.*, **128**, 537 (1939).

20. Marshall, E. K., and J. T. Litchfield, *Science*, **88**, 85 (1938).

21. Shinn, M. B., *Ind. Eng. Chem. Anal. Ed.*, **13**, 33 (1941).

22. Jacobs, M. B., *War Gases—Their Identification and Decontamination*, Interscience, New York, 1942.

23. Jacobs, M. B., and M. Brodey, "Rapid Method for Nitrogen Dioxide–Nitrogen Tetroxide in Atmosphere," presented at meeting Metropolitan N.Y. Sect. Am. Ind. Hyg. Assoc., May 1945.

24. Jacobs, M. B., *The Analytical Chemistry of Industrial Poisons, Hazards, and Solvents*, 2nd ed., Interscience, New York, 1949.

25. Dyer, W. J., *J. Fisheries Res. Board Can.*, **6**, 414 (1945).

26. Patty, F. A., and G. M. Petty, *J. Ind. Hyg. Toxicol.*, **25**, 361 (1943).

27. *Dept. Sci. Ind. Res. Brit. Leaflet 5* (1939).

28. Saltzman, B. E., *Anal. Chem.*, **26**, 1949 (1954).

29. Thomas, M. D., J. A. MacLeod, R. C. Robbin, R. C. Goettelman, R. W. Eldridge, and L. H. Rogers, *Anal. Chem.*, **28**, 1810 (1956).

30. Moore, G. E., A. F. W. Cole, and M. Katz, *J. Air Pollution Control Assoc.*, **7**, No. 1, 25 (1957).

31. Cholak, J., L. J. Schafer, D. Yeager, and W. J. Younker, *A.M.A. Arch. Ind. Health*, **15**, 198 (1957).

32. *Methods Assoc. Official Agr. Chemists*, 10th ed., 1965.

33. *Standard Methods of Water Analysis*, 8th ed., Am. Pub. Health Assoc., 1936.

34. Weston, R. S., *J. Am. Chem. Soc.*, **27**, 281 (1905).

35. Averell, P. R., W. F. Hart, N. T. Woodbury, and W. R. Bradley, *Anal. Chem.*, **19**, 1040 (1947).

36. Jacobs, M. B., and S. Hochheiser, *Anal. Chem.*, **30**, No. 3, 426 (1958).

37. Adley, F. E., and C. P. Skillern, *Am. Ind. Hyg. Assoc. J.*, **19**, 233 (1958).

38. Yagoda, H., and F. H. Goldman, *J. Ind. Hyg. Toxicol.*, **25**, 440 (1943).

39. Kothny, E. L., and P. K. Mueller, 7th Conference on Methods in Air Pollution Studies, Calif. State Dept. Public Health, Jan. 1965.

40. Ambler, G., and H. R. Lunge, *Technical Gas Analysis*, Van Nostrand, New York, 1934.

41. Blacet, F. E., and P. A. Leighton, *Ind. Eng. Chem. Anal. Ed.*, **3**, 266 (1931).
42. Baskerville, C., and R. Stevenson, *Ind. Eng. Chem.*, **3**, 579 (1911).
43. Blacet, F. E., and D. H. Volman, *Ind. Eng. Chem. Anal. Ed.*, **9**, 44 (1937).
44. Menzel, H., and W. Kretzschmar, *Angew. Chem.*, **42**, 148 (1929).
45. Sayers, R. R., in *International Critical Tables*, Vol. II, McGraw-Hill, New York, 1927.
46. Fieldner, A. C., S. H. Katz, and S. P. Kinney, *U.S. Bur. Mines Tech. Paper 248* (1921).
47. Sayers, R. R., J. M. DallaValle, and W. P. Yant, *Ind. Eng. Chem.*, **26**, 1251 (1934).
48. Smolczyk, E., *Gasmaske*, **2**, 27 (1930).
49. Patty, F. A., Ed., *Industrial Hygiene and Toxicology*, 2nd ed., Vol. II, Interscience, New York, 1962.
50. Jacobs, M. B., *The Chemical Analysis of Foods and Food Products*, Van Nostrand, New York, 1945.
51. U.S. Food Drug Admin., S.R.A.F.D.C.2, rev. 1, 1949.

CHAPTER XV

OXYGEN AND OZONE

A. Oxygen

Oxygen, O_2, is necessary for life, but nevertheless it is in certain instances an industrial hazard, particularly if it is compressed. In this state it is an explosion hazard. Compressed oxygen is a very dangerous substance. It readily forms explosive mixtures with oils. Fieldner (1) states that an oxygen cylinder containing no more than a film of oil on its inner surface is just as truly an explosive as nitroglycerin. Instances of accidental explosions of oxygen cylinders or attached equipment are too numerous to mention. Even ordinary compressed air is subject to explosion hazard with oil, if the heat of compression is not removed by suitable coolers or if the oil has a low flash point.

Another danger is the accidental mixture of a combustible gas with compressed oxygen. Fieldner (1) cites the example of reversing the polarity of the generator in the manufacture of oxygen by the electrolytic process, with the consequent result of hydrogen going into the oxygen collecting chamber.

It should be noted by the industrial toxicologist that there can be instances of oxygen poisoning. Thus, newborn infants are especially susceptible. Administration of oxygen for long periods for resuscitation may cause a proliferation of the retinal vessels into the vitreous humor with excess formation of fibrous tissue, a condition known as retrolental fibroplasia, and even blindness (2). Inhalation of oxygen at pressure over 3 atm for periods greater than 30 min may cause oxygen poisoning (3).

Zacharias (4) has pointed out that use of oxygen in the treatment of infants at concentrations of less than 40%, which was considered safe, should be reconsidered for it may not be harmless.

1. DETERMINATION

The industrial hygiene chemist may be interested in the analysis of an atmosphere for the presence and amount of oxygen for two reasons:

first, to ascertain whether or not an oxygen-deficient atmosphere exists and second, to ascertain whether or not oxygen is a component of a gaseous mixture or is in solution.   Atmospheres containing concentrations of oxygen below 16% may be detected by the use of a flame safety lamp (ref. 22, p. 501) which is extinguished in atmospheres containing less than 16.5% oxygen.

Oxygen as a gross component of an atmosphere may be estimated volumetrically by absorption in a gas pipet by potassium pyrogallate solution, sodium hyposulfite ($Na_2S_2O_4$), solid phosphorus, or ammoniacal copper (small, thin copper coils immersed in a mixture of equal volumes of saturated ammonium carbonate solution and ammonia, sp gr 0.96) and then noting the difference in volume produced before and after the absorption of the oxygen.   For details the reader is referred to standard texts on gas analysis.

Oxygen may be estimated conveniently by absorption in a dilute alkaline mixture of sodium anthraquinone-β-sulfonate and sodium hyposulfite (5).

Oxygen dissolved in water may be estimated colorimetrically with 2,4-diaminophenol dihydrochloride, which yields a color formed by a mixture of red, proportional to the oxygen content, and yellow, not proportional to the oxygen content (6).

Instrumental methods for the determination of the oxygen content of the air are available commercially.

B. Ozone

Ozone is prepared on a technical scale by the exposure of air or oxygen to brush discharges.   It is used industrially for bleaching oils, fats, waxes, flour, and starch, for the sterilization of drinking water, and for the purification of air.

Ozone is a powerful oxidizing agent and hence is a powerful poison.

The toxicology of ozone has been considered in depth by Stokinger (7).   It acts locally as an irritant to the eyes and mucous membranes. The route of entry is through the lungs by inhalation.   Severe exposure results in pulmonary edema and hemorrhage.   Exposure to a lesser degree produces headache, shortness of breath, uneasy listlessness, and drowsiness or languor.   Ozone also causes extrapulmonary effects such as deoxygenation of oxyhemoglobin.   Stokinger (7) states that three long-term effects from repeated exposure to ozone have been recognized, namely, chronic pulmonary effects, aging, and lung-tumor acceleration.

The threshold limit value for ozone is 0.1 ppm. It is to be noted, however, that levels of oxidant in Los Angeles smog of which ozone is a major component have been reported to have reached a level of 1 ppm.

1. DETECTION

Ozone will liberate iodine from starch–iodide paper. This test is also given by other oxidizing agents such as hydrogen peroxide, chlorine, nitrogen peroxide, etc. If, however, potassium iodide-impregnated litmus paper is used instead, the presence of ozone may be differentiated from other oxidizing agents, with the exception of hydrogen peroxide, by the formation of a blue color, as can be seen from the reaction

$$O_3 + 2KI + H_2O \rightarrow O_2 + 2KOH + I_2$$

The potassium hydroxide formed changes the color of the litmus paper.

Ephraim (8) notes that among the methods for its detection are the potassium iodide–starch paper, which is affected by most oxidizing agents which also turn it blue; the guaiac test, which is also a general test for oxidants; and the test with thallous hydroxide paper, which is turned brown because of the formation of Tl_2O_3 by ozone and oxidants.

Another reaction that can be used to differentiate the ozone from other oxidants is the "tetrabase" reaction (9). Diaminotetramethyl-diphenylmethane, $(CH_3)_2N \cdot C_6H_4 \cdot CH_2 \cdot C_6H_4 \cdot N(CH_3)_2$, gives distinctive colors with various oxidants, namely, violet with ozone, blue with chlorine or bromine, and straw yellow with nitrogen dioxide. It gives no color with hydrogen peroxide.

Dye methods utilizing leucofluorescein and indigosulfonates are also nonspecific or lack sensitivity. The formation of silver oxide also falls into this category. The principal instrumental methods used are variations of the buffered neutral potassium iodide method or the alkaline potassium iodide method to which a photometric system is applied.

There has been considerable interest in methods for the determination of ozone, in particular, and oxidants, in general, in the atmosphere for monitoring air pollution, as there is considerable data to indicate that there is a high degree of correlation between high ozone concentration and (1) decrease in visibility, (2) plant damage, and (3) eye irritation in the Los Angeles area. The major oxidant in Los Angeles air is believed to be ozone (10). These methods can be used for industrial hygiene work.

2. DETERMINATION

No really satisfactory method for the determination of ozone itself in air was available in 1965. One of the difficulties stems from the fact that there is no satisfactory method of preparing standard curves from ozone. The principal methods used in the early 1960s were the alkaline iodide methods, mainly variations of the Smith and Diamond (11) method, and the neutral iodide method. Other methods that found some utilization were (a) a titrimetric variation of the iodide method, (b) the phenolphthalin method, (c) the ferrous thiocyanate method, (d) the nitrogen oxide equivalent method, (e) the ozonolysis method, and (f) rubber cracking. The lack of specificity and unsuitability of methods (b), (d), and (f), as well as the use of leuco dyes and other methods, has been briefly discussed by Bravo and Lodge (12). My preference is my modification of the sulfamic acid variation of the alkaline iodide method.

a. Alkaline Iodide Method

Acetic Acid Variation

This method is based on the absorption of oxidant, presumably ozone, from the air, in an alkaline solution of potassium iodide. The absorption solution is oxidized with hydrogen peroxide to avoid interference of sulfur dioxide and the pH is adjusted to avoid the interference of nitrogen dioxide. On acidification, iodine is liberated from the hypoiodite formed on absorption of the oxidant and the amount of triiodide subsequently produced is determined with the aid of a spectrophotometer by measuring the absorption of light at 352 mμ. This method is a variation of the Smith and Diamond procedure (11,13).

The reaction mechanism of the reaction between ozone and iodide ion is not entirely clear. Smith stated that:

Studies indicate that using the alkaline iodide method of sampling and analysis, ozone reacts quantitatively with potassium iodide according to the following net reaction:

$$KI + 3O_3 \rightarrow KIO_3 + 3O_2$$

The reported reaction

$$KI + O_3 \rightarrow KIO_3$$

does not take place; because the reagent is alkaline, the reaction

$$4O_3 + 10HI \rightarrow H_2O_2 + 5I_2 + 4H_2O + 3O_2$$

does not occur either. This latter reaction, the so-called peroxide side reaction, is believed to be one of the reasons, however, that acid, and even neutral potassium iodide solutions to a lesser degree, yield consistently higher results than does the alkaline reagent. Upon acidifying the alkaline reagent, each mole of potassium iodate releases 6 atoms of iodine, so the net result is the same as though the reaction

$$2KI + H_2O + O_3 \rightarrow I_2 + 2KOH + O_2$$

had occurred. It is thus seen that each mole of ozone produces 2 atoms of iodine.

It is more likely that hypoiodite rather than iodate is formed in the alkaline absorbing solution so that the reaction probably is

$$KI + O_3 \rightarrow KOI + O_2$$

This reaction is possibly the result of two reactions:

$$2KI + H_2O + O_3 \rightarrow I_2 + 2KOH + O_2$$

and

$$\frac{I_2 + 2KOH \rightarrow KOI + KI + H_2O}{KI + O_3 \rightarrow KOI + O_2}$$

Sampling. There is a marked difference of opinion as to whether or not glass affects the decomposition of ozone or oxidant prior to sampling. It is preferable therefore to use Tygon tubing as the probes and impingers rather than fritted bubblers as the sampling vessels. Contact with rubber, cork, etc. should be avoided.

Reagent. *Alkaline Iodide Absorption Solution.* Dissolve 10 g of potassium iodide and 4 g of sodium hydroxide in water and make up to 1 liter with water. This solution is approximately 1% with respect to potassium iodide and 0.1N with respect to sodium hydroxide.

Procedure. Pass air through 30 ml of absorbing solution diluted to 75 ml in each of two macro impingers in series at a rate of 1 cfm for 0.5 hr. The second impinger serves as a blank of the air washed free of oxidant.   Transfer the contents of each impinger to 100-ml beakers and add 1 drop of 1% hydrogen peroxide solution, prepared by dilution of 30% hydrogen peroxide, to oxidize to sulfate the sulfite formed from the sulfur dioxide absorbed.   Boil the solution in each beaker down to 40 ml to decompose the excess hydrogen peroxide, cool, and transfer to 50-ml Nessler glass-stoppered tubes.   Add 3N acetic acid (1:5) to get a pH of 3.8 (about 10 ml), mix, and transfer some of the test solution to a test-tube cuvette of a Coleman spectrophotometer or equivalent instrument set at 352 mµ with water as the zero reference.   The optical density of the test is considered to be the optical density of the test solution minus the optical density of the blank.

When a Beckman model DU spectrophotometer is used, 1-cm Corex cells are suitable.   The blue-sensitive phototube should be used with an ultraviolet filter and a tungsten light source.   Greater sensitivity can be obtained by using the absorption peak at 289 mµ but in this instance quartz cells and an ultraviolet source are necessary.

Calibration Curve.   Prepare a potassium iodate solution so that 1 ml is equivalent to 1.5 µg of potassium iodate which is equivalent to 1 µg of ozone.

Without adding peroxide, boiling, or passing air through the solution, add aliquots of iodate solution equivalent to 1–15 µg of ozone in a series to 50-ml, glass-stoppered Nessler tubes containing 30 ml each of absorbing solution.   Add sufficient water to bring each volume up to 40 ml.   Then add successively for each standard, just before reading, 3N acetic acid (1:5), stopper, mix, and read in the spectrophotometer at 352 mµ with water as the zero reference.

Calculations.   The concentration of oxidants in parts per billion are

Oxidants, as O_3 (ppb) =

$$(mg\ O_3 \times 509 \times 1000)/(vol\ of\ air\ (cf) \times 28.32)$$

In preparing the standards from iodate, it must be remembered that

$$KIO_3 + 5KI + 6HCl \rightarrow 6KCl + 3H_2O + 3I_2$$

$$I\ ^1/_6KIO_3\ \ ^6/_6KI$$

and that

$$O_3 + 2KI + H_2O \rightarrow O_2 + 2KOH + I_2$$

Hence

$$O_3 \quad I_2 \quad \text{and} \quad I_2 \quad {}^2/_6 KIO_3$$

and therefore

$$O_3 \quad {}^1/_3 KIO_3$$

Other useful relationships are (1) 1 μg of O_3 yields 5.29 μg of I_2 and (2) 1 ppb of O_3 (by volume, at 25°C and 760 mm Hg) equals 1.96 μg of O_3 per cubic meter.

Interferences. The Smith and Diamond method is designed to avoid the interferences of the neutral iodide method and the Thorp method (14) attributable to nitrogen oxides and sulfur dioxide which are among the more important of the common air contaminants.

Oxides of nitrogen do not oxidize iodide ion appreciably in alkaline solution, because of the very low hydrogen ion concentration, but the resulting nitrite ion would release iodine if the solution were made strongly acid. Adjusting the pH of the reaction mixture to 3.8 prevents this reaction from occurring at an appreciable rate and thus interference by nitrite is eliminated. Hypoiodite and iodate will react with iodide to form iodine at this pH within the time required for the addition of the reagents and the reading in the spectrophotometer.

For 30 ml of 0.1N alkaline iodide solution, about 10 ml of 3N acetic acid are required to bring the solution to a pH of 3.8. Where the nitrogen dioxide is of the order of 5 pphm or less, it does not appear necessary to correct for nitrogen dioxide interference and consequently the method detailed above, using 1 ml of sulfuric acid (1:2), is adequate.

The sulfur dioxide in the air being sampled forms sodium sulfite, which would reduce some of the iodine formed to iodide after acidification if it were not destroyed. Sulfite does not reduce hypoiodite and iodate in alkaline solution; consequently, it can be oxidized to sulfate by hydrogen peroxide and thus be removed as an interference.

Cholak and co-workers (15,16) suggested that their work on the ozone concentration of various cities indicated that while the stoichiometry of the reactions

$$2KI + H_2O + O_3 \rightarrow O_2 + 2KOH + I_2$$

and

$$SO_2 + 2H_2O + I_2 \rightarrow H_2SO_4 + 2HI$$

the reduction, as indicated by recorders using neutral buffered potassium iodide, of 1 pphm of ozone required 3 pphm of sulfur dioxide. It is difficult to apply such a correction factor in an area with high sulfur dioxide concentrations in the absence of an absolute method for the determination of ozone.

Hydrogen peroxide, would, if present in the air being sampled, oxidize iodide ion to iodine when the test solution is acidified but boiling the alkaline test solution is sufficient to decompose it. Hydrogen peroxide does not oxidize iodide ion in alkaline solution.

Because there is no method available for the direct preparation of known concentrations of micro amounts of ozone, the absolute accuracy of the alkaline iodide method, or for that matter any ozone method, cannot be established. The precision appears adequate.

Sulfamic Acid Variation

In the Smith and Diamond method, the interference of nitrogen dioxide is eliminated by the adjustment of the pH. A more certain means of eliminating this interference is to use sulfamic acid which reacts with the nitrous acid formed to yield nitrogen.

Procedure. Aspirate air through two fritted, rod-form, coarse-porosity bubblers in series containing 50 ml of 1% potassium iodide in 0.01N sodium hydroxide solution at 3 lpm for 1 hr. Take 25 ml of the absorption solution, add 1 ml of a saturated aqueous solution of sulfamic acid, wait 2–5 min, transfer to an oblong cuvette and read at 352 mμ in a Coleman spectrophotometer or equivalent device.

McQuain and co-workers (17), sampling aloft with a helicopter, used another variation of this method. Place 10 ml of neutral 1% potassium iodide solution in a buffer solution 0.1M K$_2$HPO$_4$·7H$_2$O and 0.1M KH$_2$PO$_4$ to keep the pH at 7 in a midget impinger and sample for 10 min at 0.1 cfm. Add 2 ml of phosphoric acid saturated with sulfamic acid. Stopper and allow to stand for 10 min in a water bath at 72°F. Transfer to a Corex or silica cuvette and read the absorbance at 352 mμ. Obtain the concentration of oxidant from a standard curve.

b. Modified Smith and Diamond Method

The principle of the modified Smith and Diamond method, which is being considered as a tentative method of the ASTM, is the same as that of the preceding method, namely, the liberation of iodine from an alkaline iodide solution by ozone or oxidant. The absorbing reagent used is the same as that of the preceding method.

Procedure. Bubble the air being tested through the absorbing solution at a rate of 5 lpm. Transfer the absorbing solution or a 15-ml aliquot to a small beaker, add 2 drops of 1% hydrogen peroxide solution, prepared from 30% hydrogen peroxide solution as required, and bring the mixture to a boil to expel excess peroxide. Cool, transfer the test solution to a 25-ml, glass-stoppered graduated cylinder, and add sufficient 3N acetic acid (1:5) to obtain a pH of 3.8. Adjust the final volume to 25 ml.

Approximately 2 min after the addition of the acid, read the optical density of the solution at 352 mμ. Use water as a reference and determine the blank for the reagents used. A standard curve may be prepared by making appropriate additions of a standard solution of potassium iodate to the absorbing solution and treating the standards so prepared in exactly the same manner as the test solution. One μg of iodine is equivalent to 0.19 μg of ozone.

c. Titrimetric Method

In general, titration of the iodine produced in the reaction between ozone or oxidants in the air and iodide with standard thiosulfate solution is not of sufficient sensitivity, but it should prove of value for higher concentrations of ozone. Thus, according to Thorp (14), the greatest sensitivity that can be obtained with this method is the detection of 0.0013 mg of ozone per milliliter of 2N potassium iodide solution.

Thorp increased the sensitivity of the potassium iodide method by the addition of a buffer solution consisting of 5 g of aluminum chloride, $AlCl_3 \cdot 6H_2O$, and 1 g of ammonium chloride made up to 1 liter. Five ml of this solution is added to each 100 ml of potassium iodide test solution before the titration is made. The solution should not be acidified during the titration. The use of aluminum chloride as outlined gives a minimum sensitivity of 0.62 μg of ozone per milliliter of potassium iodide solution. The iodide solution treated in this manner will have a stability of over 3 hr, which gives sufficient time for the manual type of analysis.   Exclusion of light from the solution will increase the stability, as will the use of dark-colored glass bottles.

Ehmert (18) used a well-known technique of including an excess of standard sodium thiosulfate solution in his iodide-absorbing solution and then back-titrating with standard solution to determine

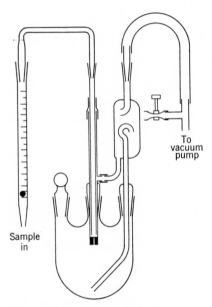

Fig. XV-1. Assembly of glassware for sampling ozone.   After Wadelin (19) and Crabtree and Kemp (20).

that excess.   Wadelin (19) adopted the Ehmert technique but employed an amperometric method for titration.

Apparatus.   The sampling arrangement of Crabtree and Kemp (20) was used with a round-bottomed flask (Fig. XV-1).   It has a special spray jet.   In addition to a rotameter capable of measuring a flow rate of 7 lpm and a pump capable of drawing 5 liters of air per minute, a calomel reference electrode, Beckman No. 1170, a platinum thimble indicator electrode, Beckman No. 1271, a galvanometer with a sensitivity of at least 0.05 μA/mm, and a magnetic stirrer were employed. It is important that the platinum electrode have a surface area of at least 1.5 cm². If a small area such as a short platinum wire is used, the instrument will lack sensitivity.

Reagents. *Buffer Solution.* Dissolve 1.8 g of disodium hydrogen phosphate and 1.7 g of potassium dihydrogen phosphate in water and dilute to 1 liter.

Iodate Standard Solution. Dissolve 0.0357 g of potassium iodate in water in a 1-liter volumetric flask and make up to the mark with water. This is a 0.0010N solution.

Standard Thiosulfate Solution. Dissolve 0.25 g of sodium thiosulfate, $Na_2S_2O_3 \cdot 10H_2O$, and 0.1 g of sodium carbonate in water in a 1-liter volumetric flask and make to volume with water.

Procedure. Place 70 ml of buffer solution, 1 g of potassium iodide, 5 ml of standard sodium thiosulfate solution measured with the aid of a pipet, and 10 ml of 2N sulfuric acid into a beaker. After a few moments of mixing the galvanometer will settle down to a steady reading. The speed of stirring should be constant during a titration but need not be duplicated from one titration to another. Titrate with potassium iodate standard solution until a permanent galvanometer deflection of 5 mm is obtained. This is considered the end point. Repeat the titration and obtain the average value. As the standard sodium thiosulfate changes in strength, it is necessary to obtain the value of the blank every day.

Place 70 ml of the buffer solution, 1 g of potassium iodide, and 5 ml of standard sodium thiosulfate solution into the sampling flask. Draw about 125 liters of sample through the absorbing solution in the flask at a rate of about 5 lpm, adjust the rate with a pinch clamp or other suitable device, and record the exact flow rate and time. Empty the test solution into a beaker, add 10 ml of 2N sulfuric acid, and titrate as detailed above.

Precautions. It is necessary to keep the flow rate high enough to have the flask filled with a fine mist during sampling. The sample must be large enough so that the sample titration and the blanks will differ by at least 1 ml. If the sampling is continued for such a long time or the ozone concentration is high enough to exhaust the thiosulfate concentration, the determinations must be repeated so that the thiosulfate will not be exhausted.

Calculations. From the reaction of ozone and iodide, it is known that 1 mole of ozone forms 2 equivalents of iodine, hence

$$Z = [(A - B) \times N \times 11.21 \times 760 \times T \times 10^6]/$$
$$(F \times t \times p \times 273)$$

in which Z is oxidant concentration, ppb; A is milliliters of potassium iodate solution required for blank; B is milliliters of potassium iodate solution required for sample; N is the normality of potassium iodate solution; T is temperature, $°K$; F is the flow rate, lpm; t is sampling time, minutes; and p is the barometric pressure, mm Hg.

d. Phenolphthalin Method

In 1923, Katz and Longfellow (21) employed a wet test paper containing phenolphthalin, $(C_6H_4OH)_2CHC_6H_4COOH$, as a test for hydrocyanic acid. In 1940 this test was adapted by the Medical Division of Merck and Co., Rahway, N. J., as a test for cyanide (ref. 22, p. 450). It was pointed out that chlorine, bromine, iodine, phenol, and high concentrations of hydrogen sulfide interfere. This test depends on an oxidation–reduction reaction in which phenolphthalin is oxidized to phenolphthalein in the presence of copper sulfate. It is clear that this is a general reaction for oxidizing substances, even one as weak as hydrogen cyanide. Phenolphthalin is easily affected by reducing agents such as sulfur dioxide.

This test was adapted by Haagen-Smit and Fox (23) as a method for the determination of oxidants in air. Hydrogen peroxide was used to obtain the calibration curve. With this oxidizing agent, the intensity of colors produced are higher than colors that would be produced by an equivalent amount of ozone by a factor of 2 or 3. In addition, since the final color produced is readily reduced by sulfur dioxide, the method is of little value in regions, principally urban areas, where the sulfur dioxide concentration is high. It must also be remembered that nitrogen dioxide, peroxides, organic peroxides, and other oxidants also affect this reagent. For these reasons, this method has only very limited value and results obtained by its use must be interpreted with caution. The method has been described in detail by Jacobs (24).

e. Ozonolysis

A specific method for the determination of ozone and thus a method capable of distinguishing between ozone and other oxidants is the method of Bravo and Lodge (12) which depends on the ozonolysis of 4,4'-dimethoxystilbene with the subsequent breaking of the ethylene linkage and the production of anisaldehyde. Color reactions can then be used to determine the anisaldehyde (25).

Reagents. Prepare the sampling reagent by dissolving 5 mg of 4,4'-dimethoxystilbene in 100 ml of *sym*-tetrachloroethane. Make the coupling reagent by preparing a 5% solution of fluoranthene in chloroform. Filter the *sym*-tetrachloroethane through a short

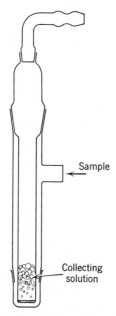

Sample

Collecting solution

Fig. XV-2. Special inverted bubbler (26).

column of sodium carbonate. The mixed reagents are stable for about 1 week.

Apparatus. Sample with a modification of the "inverted bubbler," described by Ehmert (26). This is shown in Fig. XV-2.

Sampling and Analysis. Transfer 3 ml of the sampling solution with the aid of a pipet into the lower cups of two of the special bubblers. Connect the two bubblers in series, and draw air through them at a rate between 0.10 and 0.15 lpm for a period from 15 min to 1 hr, depending upon the expected ozone concentration. At the end of the sampling period, transfer 1 ml of the reagent from each flask to a 10-ml volumetric flask. To each add 1 ml of the chloroform solution of fluoranthene and 0.8 ml of trifluoroacetic anhydride. Agitate this mixture strongly and then allow to stand for 5 min. Then dilute to 10 ml with trifluoroacetic acid.

If ozone is present, the resulting solution in the first bubbler should be blue in color. Determine the absorption at a wavelength of 610 mμ against a reagent blank. If any visible color appears in the sample from the second bubbler, it should also be measured and the total ozone determined. In general the collection efficiency of the first bubbler is near 98%, so the second solution can be discarded.

Calculation. Compute the ozone concentration from a curve constructed by carrying known solutions of anisaldehyde through the analytical procedure.

f. Ferrous Thiocyanate Method

According to Todd (27) this method is more sensitive to hydrocarbon peroxides, particularly ozonated hexane, than ozone. The original method can be improved by using a paper filter to eliminate ferric salts and oxidizing particulate matter which would give erroneous results. The use of two impingers in series gives a constant air blank.

Absorbing Solution. Dissolve 2.5 g of potassium thiocyanate, KCNS, 5 ml of 6N sulfuric acid, and 0.5 g of ferrous ammonium sulfate in water and dilute to 1 liter. Prepare this solution daily.

Standard Curve. Add known amounts of hydrogen peroxide in microgram quantities, from 1 to 10 μg, to portions of the absorbing solution in 50-ml volumetric flasks, mix, and dilute to volume with the absorbing solution. Determine the optical density using a Klett colorimeter and its blue filter.

Procedure. Filter the air to be sampled through No. 4 Whatman filter paper held in a filter holder and then bubble the air through two impingers in series containing 50 ml of the absorbing solution at a rate of 0.8–1.0 cfm for 1 hr. Obtain the net optical density (the optical density of the test solution minus the air blank) by use of a Klett colorimeter.

The results for oxidants by this method are lower than with the iodide method, indicating that ozone apparently does not affect this reagent.

g. Neutral Iodide Method

This method depends on the liberation of iodine from iodide by ozone in a neutral phosphate-buffered 0.1% solution of potassium iodide. It has the same advantages and disadvantages of other iodide methods for ozone. The method has been discussed in detail by Saltzman and Gilbert (28).

h. Nitrogen Oxide Equivalent Method

Saltzman and Gilbert (29) developed a method for the determination of ozone by the addition of nitric oxide to the atmosphere being sampled and subsequently estimating the nitrogen dioxide produced by a variation of the diazotization methods detailed in Section A-3 Chapter XIV. The method is impractical as a field method and is not an easy laboratory method either.

References

1. Fieldner, A. C., U.S. Bur. Mines Circ. 6009 (1937).
2. Bell, G. H., J. N. Davidson, and H. Scarborough, Textbook of Physiology and Biochemistry, Livingston, Edinburgh, 1961.
3. Comroe, J. H., R. D. Dripps, P. R. Dumke, and M. Deming J. Am. Med. Assoc., 128, 710 (1945).
4. Zacharias, L., J. Pediatrics, 64, 156 (1964).
5. Fieser, L. F., J. Am. Chem. Soc., 46, 2639 (1924).
6. Gilcreas, F. W., J. Am. Water Works Assoc., 27, 1166 (1935).
7. Stokinger, H. E., Arch. Environ. Health, 10, 719 (1965).
8. Ephraim, F., Inorganic Chemistry, 3rd ed., Nordeman, New York, 1939.
9. Arnold, C., and C. Mentzel, Chem. Ber., 35, 1324 (1902).
10. The Smog Problem in Los Angeles, Stanford Research Institute, Stanford, Calif., 1954.
11. Smith, R. G., and P. Diamond, Am. Ind. Hyg. Assoc. J., 13, 235 (1952).
12. Bravo, H. A., and J. P. Lodge, Jr., Anal. Chem., 36, 671 (1964).
13. Smith, R. G., Determination of Ozone in Air, Bur. Ind. Hyg., Detroit Dept. Health, 1953.
14. Thorp, C. E., Ind. Eng. Chem. Anal. Ed., 12, 209 (1940).
15. Cholak, J., L. J. Schafer, and D. W. Yeager, J. Air Pollution Control Assoc., 5, No. 4, 227 (1956).
16. Cholak, J., L. J. Schafer, W. J. Younker, and D. Yeager, A.M.A. Arch. Ind. Health, 11, 280 (1955).
17. McQuain, R. H., J. M. Leavitt, R. C. Wanta, and W. W. Frisbie, Meeting Air Pollution Control Assoc., Philadelphia, May 1958.
18. Ehmert, A., J. Atmospheric Terrestr. Phys., 2, 189 (1952).
19. Wadelin, C. W., Anal. Chem., 29, 441 (1957).

20. Crabtree, J., and A. R. Kemp, *Ind. Eng. Chem. Anal. Ed.*, **18,** 769 (1946).
21. Katz, S. H., and E. S. Longfellow, *J. Ind. Hyg.*, **5,** 97 (1923–4).
22. Jacobs, M. B., *The Analytical Chemistry of Industrial Poisons, Hazards, and Solvents*, 2nd ed., Interscience, New York, 1949.
23. McCabe, L. C., *Ind. Eng. Chem.*, **45,** No. 9, 111A (1953).
24. Jacobs, M. B., *The Chemical Analysis of Air Pollutants*, Interscience, New York, 1960.
25. Sawicki, E., T. Stanley, and T. Hauser, *Chemist-Analyst*, **47,** 31 (1958).
26. Ehmert, A., *Meteorol. Rundschau*, **4,** 65 (1954).
27. Todd, G. W., *Anal. Chem.*, **27,** 1490 (1955).
28. Saltzman, B. E., and N. Gilbert, *Anal. Chem.*, **31,** 1914 (1959).
29. Saltzman, B. E., and N. Gilbert, *Am. Ind. Hyg. Assoc. J.*, **20,** 379 (1959).

CHAPTER XVI

COMMON POISONOUS COMPOUNDS OF THE HALOGENS

A. Chlorine

1. Chlorine Gas

Chlorine gas is used in a number of industries. It is particularly hazardous where chlorine is manufactured by the electrolytic method. Chlorine is an industrial hazard among dye workers, laundry workers, employees detinning tinplate scrap, bleachers, chloride of lime makers, and in the manufacture of poison war gases such as phosgene. It is also a danger in instances where it is used as a water purifier.

Chlorine is a heavy greenish yellow gas which has a characteristic choking and pungent odor with an irritating effect on the nose and throat. It boils at $-33.6°C$, melts at $-102°C$, has a density of 2.5 referred to air, and can be easily liquefied as its critical temperature is 146°C. Its specific gravity is 1.41. Its vapor pressure at 20°C is 6.57 atm, at 30°C it is 8.75 atm, and at 40°C it is 11.5 atm. It has a high coefficient of expansion and its solubility in water at 20°C is 215 volumes in 100 volumes.

a. Physiological Response and Toxicity

Chlorine is a strong lung irritant. It was the first chemical war gas used in World War I. A concentration of 2.5 mg/liter breathed for 30–60 min will cause death. Inhalation of chlorine elicits respiratory reflexes and causes coughing, smarting of the eyes, a general feeling of discomfort in the chest, a hoarse cough, nausea, and vomiting. The face may become red and bloated because of venous congestion, or gray in color, showing failing circulation. Inhalation of chlorine affects both the lower and upper respiratory tracts and produces inflammation of the entire respiratory tract and edema of the lung after severe exposure (1). The most pronounced symptoms (2) are suffocation, constriction in the chest, and tightness in the throat.

Concentrations of 0.10% are lethal for most animals in a few minutes. Exposure to a concentration range of 0.004–0.006% for 30–60 min will have fatal or serious consequences. The maximum concentration to which animals can be exposed for a period of 60 min without serious disturbances is 0.0004% and the maximum concentration to which they may be exposed for several hours without serious disturbance or with but slight symptoms is 0.0001% volume.

The least detectable odor of chlorine is 3.5 ppm (3). It has adequate warning properties, provided one can get away from its vapors. The recommended maximum allowable concentrations are in the range of 1–2 ppm.

b. Detection and Determination

Iodide–Thiosulfate Method

A simple method for the detection and determination of chlorine in air is to pass the air through two bubblers in series, the first containing a 4% potassium iodide solution and the second containing a 2% potassium iodide solution. The incoming chlorine reacts with potassium iodide liberating iodine. Most of this is fixed by the potassium iodide with the formation of triiodide but any iodine carried out in effluent air is trapped by the second bubbler. The solutions are combined and the free iodine is titrated with 0.1286N sodium thiosulfate solution. One ml of this solution is equivalent to 1000 ppm of chlorine by volume at 25°C and 760 mm Hg for a 1-min sample of 1571 ml (4).

o-Tolidine Method

This is a colorimetric method (5) which depends on the production of a yellow color by the reaction between chlorine and o-tolidine. It is subject to disturbing influences of small amounts of iron, manganic manganese, and nitrite nitrogen. If these interferences are present, it is better to use the iodide–thiosulfate method. If the chlorine is trapped in a series of bubblers containing water, proceed with the following method. Porter (6) recommends passing a measured volume of air through 10 ml of o-tolidine reagent, prepared by dissolving 1 g of o-tolidine in 100 ml of concentrated hydrochloric acid and diluting to 1 liter. After sampling, the color produced is compared in a Nessler tube with the permanent standards as described in the method.

Reagents. *o-Tolidine Solution.* Weigh out 1 g of *o*-tolidine (melting point, 129°C), transfer to a 6-in. mortar and add 5 ml of hydrochloric acid (1:4). Grind the material to a thin paste and add 150–200 ml of water. The *o*-tolidine should go into solution immediately. Transfer to a 1-liter cylinder and make up to 505 ml. Make up to the 1000-ml mark by adding hydrochloric acid (1:4). The reagent should be stored in amber bottles and should not be used after 6 months.

Copper Sulfate Solution. Dissolve 1.5 g of copper sulfate, $CuSO_4 \cdot 5H_2O$, and 1 ml of concentrated sulfuric acid in water; make up to 100 ml.

Potassium Dichromate Solution. Dissolve 0.25 g of potassium dichromate, $K_2Cr_2O_7$, and 1 ml of concentrated sulfuric acid in distilled water and make up to 1 liter.

Permanent Standards. Table XVI-1 lists the volumes of copper sulfate solution and potassium dichromate solution to be used to give standards corresponding to the chlorine contents listed. The color comparisons must be made in 100-ml Nessler tubes having the graduation mark at 300 mm from the bottom. If the Nessler tubes do not have the graduation mark at 300 mm, the standards used must be checked against known concentrations of chlorine. The variation in the 300-mm mark must not be more than ±6 mm. The standard

TABLE XVI-1
Permanent Chlorine Standards

Chlorine, mg/100 ml	Copper sulfate solution, ml	Potassium dichromate solution, ml
0.001	0.0	0.8
0.003	0.0	3.2
0.005	0.4	5.5
0.008	1.5	8.2
0.01	1.8	10.0
0.025	1.9	25.0
0.05	2.0	45.0
0.07	2.0	58.0
0.08	2.0	63.0
0.1	2.0	72.0

comparison tubes should be protected from dust and evaporation by sealing on micro cover glasses with collodion, Canada balsam, or other appropriate transparent sealing material.

Procedure. If the temperature of the bubbler sample solution is less than 20°C, bring a suitable volume to above that temperature but not above 40°C by warming in a flask in hot water. Place 100 ml of the sample or take an aliquot and dilute to 100 ml in a 300-mm 100-ml Nessler tube. Add 1 ml of the *o*-tolidine reagent, mix, and place in the dark to allow the color to develop. The sample must be placed in the dark and at no time may it be exposed to direct sunlight before the reading. The period allowed for color development should be not less than 5 min nor more than 15 min, except when it is definitely shown that the maximum color development occurs and fading begins in less than 5 min. Compare the color developed with that of the standards under a daylight lamp or against a white background with "north" daylight. Comparisons must not be made in sunlight; they must be made by sighting from above through the liquid.

For greater quantities of chlorine, permanent standards may be made according to Table XVI-2. The copper solution used is the same. The potassium dichromate solution contains, however, 10 times as much of the salt, i.e., 2.5 g of potassium dichromate and 1 ml of concentrated sulfuric acid are dissolved in water and made up to 1 liter. When the standards are made according to Table XVI-2 and 300-mm 100-ml Nessler tubes are used, the tubes must be filled

TABLE XVI-2
Permanent Chlorine Standards

Chlorine, mg/100 ml	Copper sulfate solution, ml	Potassium dichromate solution, ml
0.1	8	9
0.2	8	16
0.3	8	22
0.4	8	28
0.5	8	33
0.6	8	38
0.7	8	44
0.8	8	50
0.9	8	57
1.0	8	66

only to a height of 240 mm in order to give the proper comparison. These comparisons must be made by viewing from above.

Modified o-Tolidine Method

The official British (7) method is a modification of the o-tolidine method. The concentration of chlorine in an atmosphere is estimated by passing the air to be tested directly through the o-tolidine reagent. The hand pump apparatus and bubbler used are similar to that described for carbon disulfide (p. 553–554).

Preparation of Reagent. Dissolve 1 g of pure o-tolidine (melting point, 129–131°C) in 100 ml of concentrated hydrochloric acid and make up to 1 liter with water. The reagent will generally not deteriorate for 6 months.

Preparation of Standard Colors. Weigh out 1 g of potassium dichromate, $K_2Cr_2O_7$, dissolve in water, and transfer to a 1-liter volumetric flask. Make up to volume with water. This yields a 0.1% solution. Make a series of standards by diluting the following quantities of the 0.1% solution to 10 ml with water, in tubes of exactly the same bore as the bubbler.

Standard	Vol (ml) of 0.1% $K_2Cr_2O_7$ soln diluted to 10 ml
1	5
2	3
3	2
4	1

The standards must be well sealed or stoppered and kept in the dark. Under these conditions no change should occur in 6 months.

Procedure. Place 10 ml of the o-tolidine reagent into the side arm bubbler and connect to the hand pump through a trap as previously described. The delivery tube should be approximately central and must not touch the side of the bubbler.

On entering the atmosphere to be tested, draw the strokes with the pump very slowly, using approximately 10 sec per stroke. Continue pumping until the depth of color developed, if any, is approximately equal to that of one of the standards. Remove the bubbler and compare immediately with the standard tube, the two tubes being observed side by side by transversely transmitted daylight.

If the depth of color is the same in both tubes, the concentration of chlorine present, corresponding to the standard used for comparison and the number of strokes made, may be obtained from the following table:

No. of strokes	Standard			
	1	2	3	4
2	1:16,000	1:27,000	1:40,000	1:80,000
5	1:40,000	1:67,000	1:100,000	1:200,000
10	1:80,000	1:130,000	1:200,000	1:400,000
20	1:160,000	1:260,000	1:400,000	1:800,000
25	1:200,000	1:330,000	1:500,000	1:1,000,000

Sodium Hydroxide Modification

The o-tolidine method is less efficient with higher concentrations of chlorine particularly when only one bubbler is used. Wallach and McQuary (8) found that by use of a fritted-glass bubbler or a midget impinger tube containing sodium hydroxide solutions ranging from 0.0125 to 0.1N, 99.9% efficiency in trapping chlorine could be obtained.

Procedure. Pass air through a midget impinger tube containing 10 ml of 0.1N sodium hydroxide solution at 0.1 cfm. Sample 3.44 liters of air at 25°C and 760 mm Hg in 1 min and 13 sec to give a direct reading in parts per million.

Proceed with the method detailed above for the determination of chlorine by the o-tolidine method but add 0.1 ml (2 drops) of 5N sulfuric acid after the addition of the o-tolidine to neutralize the excess alkalinity. Light transmission can be measured at 445 mμ, if desired.

2. Hydrochloric Acid and Chlorides

Hydrochloric acid, commercial muriatic acid, is used in many industries. The principal hazardous effects of this substance in industry are burns and dermatitis, although its importance as a respiratory irritant should not be overlooked. Hydrogen chloride, the gas from which the acid is formed, is a colorless, pungent, and poisonous substance, which is very soluble in water. It fumes very strongly in air and is extremely corrosive, for the fume is actually composed of minute droplets of hydrochloric acid. It is a gaseous by-product in a number of industries and, if not properly eliminated from the effluent gas, it may be a source of air pollution. Among the industries in which it is a hazard are the manufacture of hydrochloric acid, chlorine, and chlorine compounds and the use of the acid by etchers, engravers, metal picklers, acid dippers, and electroplaters. It is also a hazard where zinc chloride is used because of the hydrolysis of that compound with the formation of hydrochloric acid.

a. Physiological Response and Toxicity

Hydrogen chloride gas attacks the upper respiratory tract. The acid formed neutralizes the alkali of the tissues and causes death as a result of edema or spasm of the larynx and inflammation of the upper respiratory system. Concentrations of 0.13–0.2% are lethal for human beings in exposures lasting a few minutes. Concentrations in the range of 0.1–0.13% are dangerous if breathed for 30–60 min. The maximum concentration tolerated for exposures of 60 min is in the range 0.005–0.01% and the maximum tolerated for several hours of exposure is 0.001–0.005% (3,9,10). The effect of inhalation of hydrogen chloride on animals was studied by Machle and co-workers (11). The maximum concentration permissible for working conditions is 10 ppm, according to Matt (12). The maximum allowable concentration adopted by the Conference of Governmental Hygienists in 1948 was 5 ppm.

b. Detection and Determination

Hydrochloric acid and hydrogen chloride as well as other chlorides may be detected in air simply by trapping the fumes or dust in a standard solution of sodium hydroxide in an impinger or efficient gas-washing bottle. This absorbing solution may then be transferred to a flask and the excess sodium hydroxide determined by titration with standard sulfuric acid, in so far as the acidity is concerned. The amount of chloride may be estimated preferably by the Fajans method or by the Volhard method detailed below. Sodium carbonate solution is also used as the absorbing agent.

A refinement of the method of trapping the hydrochloric acid fumes is to draw 20–50 liters of air through a solution of glycerol–potassium carbonate–water in the ration of 1:1:1 in a gas-washing bottle (13). The chloride concentration may then be determined by the Volhard method.

Fajans Method

The use of dyes which are absorbed near the end point of a titration has been investigated by Fajans (14) and by Kolthoff (15). Dichlorofluorescein is adequate for dilute chloride solutions and concentrations of the order of $0.0005N$ in chloride ion may be titrated with an accuracy of 1–2%.

Indicator Solution. Prepare a 0.1% solution of the dye in 60–70% alcohol or a 0.1% solution of the sodium salt of the dye in water. About 2.5 ml of $0.1N$ sodium hydroxide solution are required to neutralize 100 mg of the indicator.

Procedure. Add 2–4 drops of indicator solution to 50 ml of the test solution. As the end point is reached, the silver chloride flocculates. Near the end point the solution turns brown; when the end point is reached, the color changes sharply to orange. A slight excess of silver nitrate produces a rose or red color.

Volhard Method

The thiocyanate method for the determination of chloride in which the silver chloride precipitate is removed by filtration before back-titrating may be improved by eliminating the filtration. This may be done by the use of nitrobenzene (16), which inhibits the darkening of silver chloride in the light and improves the end point. This immiscible liquid draws the silver chloride to the interface and thus removes it from the aqueous solution, the nitrobenzene forming an insoluble layer over the precipitate.

Titrations may be made in 250-ml glass-stoppered bottles. Twenty-five to 50 ml of the sample solution containing from 0.048 to 0.26 g of sodium chloride, free from the usual interfering ions, is acidified with 8–10 drops of nitric acid and 1 ml of nitrobenzene is added for each 0.05 g of chloride. Standard silver nitrate is added until an excess of 1–4 ml of $0.1N$ solution is present. The bottle is then tightly stoppered and shaken vigorously until the silver chloride settles out in large spongy flakes. Usually 30–40 sec of agitation is required. A perfectly clear supernatant solution is not necessary. Fine droplets of nitrobenzene are left in suspension. However, nearly all the nitrobenzene is so closely attached to the silver chloride that there is little evidence of a separate phase.

One ml of ferric alum indicator, prepared by adding concentrated freshly boiled nitric acid to a saturated solution of ferric alum until the solution becomes greenish yellow, is added and the titration completed with 0.05N potassium thiocyanate solution. The ferric alum acts as an effective flocculating agent and coagulates any suspended matter that is present. Standard potassium thiocyanate solution is added slowly with gentle swirling until a pink color is produced. Usually a false end point appears one drop before the true end point. It fades in about 30 sec and may be due to the desorption of the last traces of silver nitrate from the precipitate. The next drop of thiocyanate produces a decided color change which persists for 10–15 min. Titration should be made at temperatures below 25°C as is customary in other titrations with thiocyanate. If nitric acid and subsequent boiling was used in the preparation of the sample, the addition of a saturated solution of hydrazine sulfate just prior to the addition of the ferric alum indicator removes any nitrous acid formed.

Diphenylcarbazide and Diphenylcarbazone Indicator for Chloride

Diphenylcarbazone was suggested as a specific indicator for the titration of chloride and bromide ions by silver ion by Chirnoaga (17). Others (18,19), have suggested the use of both diphenylcarbazide and diphenylcarbazone with mercuric nitrate as the titrating agent. The method depends upon the formation, from mercuric ion and the indicator, of a deep blue-violet complex, after the chloride ions have combined to form slightly ionized mercuric chloride. Diphenylcarbazide is an acid–base indicator, changing from a light yellow in acid solution to a deep orange in alkaline solution, in the pH range of 6.6–7.4. It is probable that the alkaline form of the indicator forms the deep blue-violet complex with the mercuric ion.

Reagents. *Diphenylcarbazide.* Prepare a saturated solution of diphenylcarbazide in 95% alcohol. This solution gradually turns red after standing for several days and may be used as the indicator. No apparent difference results if a fresh solution of diphenylcarbazide or diphenylcarbazone solution in alcohol is used.

Mercuric Oxide. Dissolve mercuric oxide in nitric acid (1:1) and filter. Add 8N sodium hydroxide to the filtrate until precipitation is complete. Filter the precipitate and wash free from alkali. The yellow mercuric oxide may be dried over phosphorus pentoxide for 10 days, during which period it should be powdered.

Mercuric Nitrate Solutions. Weigh out accurately the required amount of mercuric oxide necessary to make 0.1N and 0.025N solutions of mercuric nitrate and suspend in water. Add the calculated equivalent amount of nitric acid. To the well-stirred mixture add nitric acid dropwise until complete solution takes place. Make up to volume. The solution should be no more than $0.01N$ with respect to nitric acid.

Determination. With $0.1N$ mercuric nitrate solution the following procedure should be followed: The final volume of the solution in which the determination for chloride is to be made should be about 80–100 ml. If the chloride solution to be titrated is acid, it should first be neutralized with $0.1N$ sodium hydroxide solution. If the acid titer is also required, 5 drops of diphenylcarbazide are added and the solution is titrated with the standard sodium hydroxide solution to an orange color. Four ml of $0.2N$ nitric acid are added and the solution is then titrated with $0.1N$ mercuric nitrate solution. About 5 drops before the end point, a pink-violet color begins to develop. At the end point, 1 drop changes the color from a light violet to a deep blue-violet.

If the chloride solution is dilute and requires $0.025N$ mercuric nitrate solution, additional precautions need be observed. The final volume should be 65 ± 10 ml. If the chloride solution to be titrated is acid, 2 drops of 0.2% bromophenol blue are added, and the solution is titrated with standard sodium hydroxide solution to the full blue color. Four ml of $0.2N$ nitric acid are added, then 5 drops of the diphenylcarbazide indicator, and the solution is titrated with $0.025N$ mercuric nitrate solution to a definite pink color, which can be reproduced to ± 0.02 ml, with the aid of a daylight lamp. The yellow color imparted by the bromophenol blue in no way interferes with the mercuric nitrate end point, and to make conditions uniform for all titrations 2 drops of bromophenol blue should be added whenever $0.025N$ mercuric nitrate solution is used.

A blank correction should be determined with the 2 drops of bromophenol blue, 4 ml of $0.2N$ nitric acid, and with the nitric acid equivalent to the amount of acid in the mercuric nitrate solution used in the titration.

Turbidimetric Method

In air pollution control work, the turbidimetric method for the determination of chloride is often preferred, for very small amounts of chloride can be estimated. The air can be sampled with the aid of a macro impinger.

Procedure. To an aliquot of not more than 25 ml in a 50-ml volumetric flask or Nessler tube add 20 ml of nitric acid (1:1) and 5 ml of $0.1N$ silver nitrate solution. Mix, dilute to the mark, and read immediately in a Klett-Summerson colorimeter, using filter No. 42. Read the milligrams of chloride from a standard curve prepared by using the above method on known concentrations of sodium chloride. If a nephelometer is available, it is preferable to use such an instrument (see below).

Nephelometric Method

Procedure. Place 55 ml of chloride-free water into a macro impinger and sample at 1 cfm for 70 min, giving a sample volume of 2 m^3. Filter the absorbing solution through Whatman No. 42 filter paper and use the filtrate adjusted to 45 ml as the reference for the nephelometric setting on a Coleman spectrophotometer. Switch the nephelometric position to 560 mμ, with the galvanometer knobs fully clockwise, and set the zero percentage transmission with the BLK knob.

Add 5 ml of $0.01N$ silver nitrate in nitric acid (1:5) to the 45 ml of filtrate. Age for exactly 5 min and read the percentage transmission of the sample.

Compare with a standard curve obtained by treating known amounts of chloride in microgram quantities in the same way to obtain the amount of chloride in the sample. Compute the air concentration from the expression

$$NaCl = \mu g/2\ m^3$$

3. CHLORINE DIOXIDE

Chlorine dioxide, ClO_2, is a dark-yellow, heavy gas, which can easily be liquefied to a red liquid boiling at 10°C. Both forms are explosive. Chlorine dioxide probably exists as such when dissolved in water but slowly hydrolyzes in water and reacts more rapidly with bases to give a mixture of equivalent amounts of chlorite and chlorate. This is analogous to the formation of nitrite and nitrate from nitrogen dioxide. Chlorine dioxide is used for water purification and for bleaching fats.

To sample chlorine dioxide use a bubbler containing 5% potassium iodide solution, drawing the air through at the customary rate of

0.5–1 lpm.   The amount of chlorine dioxide may then be determined iodometrically.   To obtain the stoichiometrical relationships, it is best to standardize the standard thiosulfate solution against a weighed amount of the chlorine dioxide used at the plant.

4. Chlorates

Chlorates are used industrially in several industries such as dyeing and printing for the oxidation of colors, in the manufacture of matches, and in explosives and fireworks.

They may be sampled by use of an impinger containing water or sodium hydroxide solution.   The amount of chlorate may then be estimated by a variation (20) of the ferrous sulfate–potassium dichromate or potassium permanganate method.   The former has been modified to estimate small amounts of the order of milligram quantities in caustic soda solution.   This can be modified for use in air analyses.

Procedure 1.   Transfer a 25-ml aliquot to a flask.   Add 20 ml of phosphoric acid (1:1) and swirl.   Add 25 ml of $0.1N$ ferrous ammonium sulfate or ferrous sulfate in $4N$ sulfuric acid and 25 ml of $12N$ sulfuric acid.   Allow to stand for 10 min or longer, add approximately 0.5 ml of $0.01M$ diphenylamine sulfonic acid, and titrate the excess ferrous sulfate with $0.1N$ potassium dichromate solution.   The end point should be taken when the maximum purple color develops.

The ferrous sulfate should be standardized each time it is used and the same amount of other reagents should be used in the standardization.

Procedure 2.   To determine microgram quantities of chlorates, the following modification of the iodometric method (21) may be employed.   Samples may be obtained as above but they should not be stored in rubber-stoppered bottles.   No-Sol-Vit screw-cap bottles are recommended.   Transfer an aliquot portion of the sample solution to the reaction flask of the apparatus shown in Figure XVI-1, add 1 ml of potassium iodide solution containing 50 g of KI per liter and add sufficient water so that the total volume will be 100 ml after the addition of the acid, as mentioned below.   Add one or two glass beads to prevent bumping and connect the distillation flask to the dropping funnel.   Place 50 ml of the 5% potassium iodide solution and 5 ml of 1% starch indicator solution into the receiving flask, with the receiver supported on a wooden block so as to make a liquid seal at

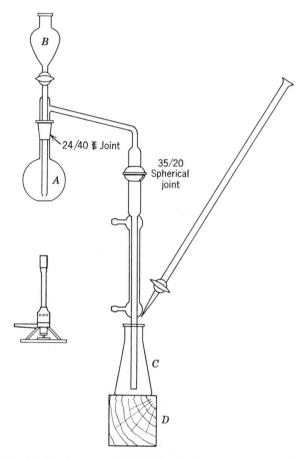

Fig. XVI-1. Distillation apparatus for determination of chlorates iodometrically: (*A*) reaction flask, 250 ml; (*B*) dropping funnel; (*C*) receiver, 250 ml; (*D*) wooden block.

the outlet of the condenser. Place sufficient concentrated hydrochloric acid in the dropping funnel to provide a 5-ml excess and allow it to run into the distillation flask. Close the stopcock and light the burner. Adjust the flame so that the solution boils vigorously. Titrate the iodine as it is liberated with $0.01N$ sodium thiosulfate solution. Continue boiling until no more iodine is liberated during a 2-min interval.

Prepare a reagent blank by introducing 100 ml of water, 1 ml of 5% potassium iodide solution, and one or two glass beads into the distilling flask. Acidify with 5 ml of concentrated hydrochloric acid and distil into a mixture of 50 ml of 5% potassium iodide solution and 5 ml of starch solution as before. The distillation should be continued until half of the water distils over. After each analysis the distillation flask should be rinsed with water, the ground-glass surfaces should be wiped, and fresh lubricant should be applied.

Iron and manganese introduce errors which should be corrected for when necessary. An empirical factor of 1.04 should be used to correct for an average recovery of 96%.

5. Phosgene

Phosgene, carbonyl chloride, $COCl_2$ is a colorless gas with an odor like that of musty hay. During World War I, it was used as a poison war gas and was the agent that caused more casualties than any other chemical-warfare agent. Its interest as an industrial hazard lies not only in its production as a chemical intermediate but also in the fact that phosgene is formed by the thermal decomposition of chlorinated hydrocarbons (22). Thus, it may arise in the use of carbon tetrachloride and similar types of chlorinated hydrocarbon fire extinguishers. It has been shown that carbon tetrachloride (23–27), trichloroethylene, and other chlorinated hydrocarbons yield measurable quantities of phosgene when in contact with a flame or hot surface. The concentrations of toxic gases that arise, however, are dangerous, principally in enclosed spaces like small rooms and closets and where no easy exit exists (28).

Phosgene may be encountered in dangerous concentrations in works manufacturing organic chemical and pharmaceutical products and, in particular, dyestuffs. It is of course, an industrial hazard where it is being manufactured for industrial or war use.

At low temperatures phosgene is a liquid. It boils at 8.2°C, freezes at −118°C, has a specific gravity of 1.38, and a density with respect to air of 3.41; hence, it is a comparatively heavy gas. It does not expand as readily as liquid chlorine. It has a low specific heat and a low heat of vaporization. It dissolves readily in many organic solvents and is, itself, a solvent for many organic chemicals. It is hydrolyzed by water with the formation of hydrochloric acid.

a. Physiological Response and Toxicity

The importance of phosgene as an industrial hazard is its toxicity. It is over ten times as toxic as chlorine, for a concentration of 0.50 mg/liter is lethal for an exposure of 10 min. Serious symptoms may not develop until several hours after exposure, for the immediate symptoms produced by even a fatal dose may be relatively mild since phosgene elicits no marked respiratory reflexes; thus, a person who appears to be but slightly gassed immediately following exposure may become a serious casualty several hours later. Phosgene is a lung irritant and causes severe damage to the alveoli of the lungs. This is followed by pulmonary edema, resulting in asphyxiation. Inhalation of this gas produces catching of the breath, choking, immediate coughing, tightness of the chest, slight lachrymation, difficulty and pain in breathing, and cyanosis. Its effects are probably due to hydrolysis and the formation of hydrochloric acid inside the body. It is considered in this section because of the similarity of its reactions with chlorine and hydrochloric acid. The most pronounced symptoms of phosgene poisoning are coughing with bloody sputum and weakness, which may last for months (2).

An atmosphere containing 1 part by volume of the gas in 6000 may cause lung injuries in 2 min, even 1 part in 30,000 is very dangerous, and as little as 1 part in 200,000 is probably fatal for exposures of 30 min. The maximum permissible concentration for a prolonged exposure period is about 1 ppm, i.e., 0.004 mg/liter (27).

The least detectable odor of phosgene is 5.6 ppm, the least concentration that affects the throat is 3.1 ppm, the least concentration causing irritation of the eyes is 4.0 ppm, and the least concentration causing coughing is 4.8 ppm (29). A concentration of 0.02–0.05% is lethal to most animals in a few minutes. A concentration of 0.0025% is dangerous for exposures of 30–60 min. The maximum concentration to which animals can be exposed for several hours without serious symptoms is 0.0001%, or 1 ppm (3). This is the generally accepted maximum allowable concentration.

b. Detection and Determination

Harrison's Reagent

The yellow or orange stain produced by phosgene on test paper containing diphenylamine and p-dimethylaminobenzaldehyde has been adopted as the standard test for the detection of phosgene in Britain (27). The test, which is capable of detecting about 1 part of phosgene in 1,000,000 of air, is made quantitative by drawing known volumes of the atmosphere to be tested through a definite area of the test paper by means of a hand pump of specified capacity, as described on page 52, and noting the number of strokes required to produce stains of certain intensity. The concentration is then obtained by reference to standard stains on a color chart. The stains produced by phosgene are transient, and the test papers are sensitive to chlorine and hydrogen chloride. To remove traces of these gases, the atmosphere to be tested is drawn through a guard tube containing pumice impregnated with sodium thiosulfate before it comes in contact with the test paper.

Patty (30) states that this phosgene test paper method is more reliable and satisfactory than any other published method for the estimation of phosgene in concentrations of 0.5–2 ppm. When the paper is suspended in the atmosphere, 0.5 ppm phosgene produces a light lemon yellow color in 4–5 min and a dark yellow in 10–15 min. Higher concentrations produce proportionately greater color changes up to a dark orange shade, which occurs in about 8 min for 2 ppm, and in 15 min with 1 ppm.

Reagent. Dissolve 5 g of p-dimethylaminobenzaldehyde and 5 g of *colorless* diphenylamine each in 50 ml of carbon tetrachloride and mix. Dip filter papers immediately into this solution and dry. Store the papers in tightly sealed brown bottles.

Procedure. The dry paper when exposed to phosgene changes from colorless to yellow.

Dimethylaminobenzaldehyde Test

It has been found that a mixture of p-dimethylaminobenzaldehyde and N-ethyl-N-2-hydroxyethylaniline gives a color change with phosgene from white to bright blue that is not affected by any reasonable concentration of mineral-acid vapor (31).

Preparation of Test Paper. Prepare the test paper by dipping Whatman No. 1 filter paper into a solution of 1.68 g of N-ethyl-N-2-hydroxyethylaniline (crystallizing point 37.2°C), 0.75 g of p-dimethylaminobenzaldehyde, and 2.5 ml of diethyl phthalate in 25 ml of ethyl alcohol. Acetone or chloroform may also be used as the solvent. Permit the solvent to evaporate completely for the wet paper is insensitive to phosgene. Prepare the papers as required. The reagent solution is stable for a number of months if kept in the dark.

Procedure. Place the test paper in a suitable holder through which known quantities of air can be drawn and draw air through the test paper. When 500 ml of air containing 1 μg/liter of phosgene is drawn through a disk with a diameter of 0.1 in., an identifiable blue color will be produced. When 75 ml of air containing a concentration of 5 μg of phosgene per liter of air is drawn through such a test paper, a good blue color is obtained.

Nitroso Reagents

Reagent. Prepare two solutions and retain in separate bottles: (A) dissolve 0.25 g of 1,2,4-nitrosodiethylaminophenol in 50 ml of benzene; (B) dissolve 0.20 g of *m*-diethylaminophenol in 50 ml of benzene. The 1,2,4-nitrosodiethylaminophenol generally cannot be purchased from the usual supply houses but can be readily prepared by the following procedure: Dissolve 0.50 g of *m*-diethylaminophenol (from the Eastman Kodak Co.) in 15 ml of water containing 1 ml of concentrated hydrochloric acid and cool to 0°C. Dissolve a 0.22-g portion of sodium nitrite in 5 ml of water and add to the phenol solution in small portions. The additions are made below the surface of the liquid, and the temperature is maintained at 0°C at all times. This addition requires about 20 min. Make the mixture nearly neutral by the addition of a solution of 2 g of sodium acetate in 5 ml of water and then extract with 50 ml of benzene. Filter the separated benzene layer through a dry filter paper and it is ready for immediate use as reagent A.

Procedure. Mix equal parts of solutions A and B and apply to a piece of filter paper. Exposure of this paper to phosgene changes the color from brown to green. A colored "Michler's" ketone is probably formed. Its sensitivity is 0.0008 mg/liter, or 0.2 ppm. This reaction is considered specific for phosgene. The nitroso solution is somewhat unstable and must be renewed every 3–4 months.

Estimation as Chloride

During World War I a method for the detection and estimation of phosgene was developed. It depends upon the absorption of the phosgene in a standard solution of alcoholic soda and the subsequent titration of excess alkali or estimation of the chloride content by some appropriate method.

$$COCl_2 + 2NaOH \rightarrow 2NaCl + CO_2 + H_2O$$

One can see that chlorides from other sources such as from chlorine or from hydrochloric acid must be absent for this method to be applicable (25).

The gas samples to be tested may be freed from interferences by the use of zinc and mercuric sulfide rather than using silver nitrate and antimony trisulfide. The principal objection to the latter reagents is that the nitric acid formed in the removal of hydrochloric acid by the silver nitrate reacts with the antimony trisulfide to give hydrogen sulfide, which will interfere with the estimation of the phosgene. This may be obviated by passing the gas to be tested first over the antimony trisulfide and then over the silver nitrate, for any hydrogen sulfide formed by the reaction between the hydrochloric acid and the antimony trisulfide is removed, as is any free chlorine, by the silver nitrate (32).

The gas, free from interferences, is passed through two gas-washing bottles containing 50 ml of alcoholic sodium hydroxide solution, prepared by dissolving 40 g of sodium hydroxide in 125 ml of water and adding this solution to 875 ml of 95% alcohol. After sampling is complete, neutralize with approximately $1N$ nitric acid using phenolphthalein as indicator and determine the chloride ion concentration by titration with $0.1286N$ silver nitrate solution using sodium chromate solution as the indicator. One ml of $0.1286N$ silver nitrate solution is equivalent to 1000 ppm of phosgene (by volume at 25°C and 760 mm Hg) for a 1-min sample of 1571 ml (4).

Standard sulfuric acid may be used to neutralize the alkali if the remaining alkali is to be estimated. This method can be improved by acidifying the absorbing solution with nitric acid and expelling the carbon dioxide by boiling before neutralizing with more alkali and titrating. It can also be improved by eliminating the use of alcohol, for aqueous sodium hydroxide absorbs phosgene effectively, is more stable, and absorbs less chlorinated hydrocarbons (32).

Phosgene may also be absorbed in silver nitrate solution to which ammonia has been added in excess of that required to dissolve the precipitate first formed (25). With this reagent the phosgene decomposes, forming a soluble silver ammonium chloride. On acidifying with nitric acid, the silver chloride is precipitated and may be filtered off and weighed, or the excess silver may be determined by titration.   Both chlorine and hydrochloric acid interfere.

Iodide–Acetone Method

Phosgene may be estimated by use of its reaction with iodide in acetone (33).

$$COCl_2 + 2NaI \rightarrow 2NaCl + I_2 + CO$$

Any substance capable of liberating iodine from iodide interferes in this reaction.

Procedure.   Absorb the phosgene, freed from acid gases by one of the devices indicated above or as described in the following method, in a saturated solution of potassium iodide in acetone.   The amount of solution to be used should contain sufficient potassium iodide so as to have a concentration several times as much as the amount of iodine that will be liberated.   Add an excess of iodate and then a measured excess of $0.01N$ sodium thiosulfate solution.   Allow to stand for $\frac{1}{2}$ hr or more.   Make sure that the solution contains more water than acetone, add several drops of starch indicator, and then titrate back with $0.01N$ iodine solution to a distinct coloration.   Finally discharge the iodine–starch color with standard thiosulfate solution.   The total thiosulfate solution used, minus the exact equivalent of the added iodine solution, represents the amount of phosgene.   Since excess iodate is present, $0.01N$ hydrochloric acid may be used instead of the standard iodine solution.

Aniline Method

Phosgene may be estimated by a characteristic reaction with aniline, which gives quantitative results for small quantities of this gas in air (25).   Absorb the phosgene in a saturated aqueous solution of aniline.   Such a solution contains about 26 g of aniline per liter of water.   In this reaction diphenylurea is formed when excess aniline is present, according to the following equation:

$$4C_6H_5NH_2 + COCl_2 \rightarrow CO(NHC_6H_5)_2 + 2C_6H_5NH_2 \cdot HCl$$

The diphenylurea is only slightly soluble in water as well as in a saturated aqueous solution of aniline, and may be filtered off, washed with cold water, dried at 70–80°C and weighed.   Hydrochloric acid interferes by conversion of the aniline into aniline hydrochloric and chlorine by oxidizing the aniline to insoluble compounds.

Procedure. Pass air through a purifying tube, a 5-cm glass U tube with arms 22 and 30 cm long. The short arm of the purifying tube contains 6 cm of absorbent cotton at the top where the gas enters and, below the cotton, 12 cm of 10–12-mesh calcium chloride, previously neutralized with hydrogen chloride gas. A small amount of cotton is placed in the connection between the two arms of the U tube. The long section of the purifying tube contains 10 cm of amalgamated mossy tin at the bottom, then 3 cm of mossy tin, and at the top, 15 cm of closely packed mossy zinc.

Each sample is then led through two simple absorption tubes of the petticoat (hoopskirt or inverted thistle tube) bubbler type in series, each of which contains 25 ml of the phosgene absorbent. The purifying train and connections to the absorption bottles should be purged with the test atmosphere before sampling.

In preparing the absorption solution an excess of aniline is kept in a bottle of water for 1 week with occasional shaking, then phosgene is passed through the solution until a permanent precipitate of diphenylurea is formed and the mixture is kept ready for use. Diphenylurea can be bought commercially and the saturated solution may be prepared without the aniline–phosgene reaction.

When a determination is made, some of the solution is filtered several times through a Gooch crucible and 25-ml portions are placed in each of the bubblers. After the measured volume of sample is passed through the bubblers, they are allowed to stand 2 hr and the aniline reagent is then filtered through a tared prepared Gooch crucible. Any precipitate which adheres to the sides of the absorption flasks is dissolved in warm alcohol and evaporated almost to dryness in a small beaker on a steam bath. Several milliliters of water are added and the evaporation is continued until there is no longer an odor of alcohol. This additional precipitate is then washed, with thorough policing, into the prepared Gooch crucible and the entire precipitate is washed thoroughly with a solution of $1N$ hydrochloric acid saturated with pure diphenylurea. The precipitate is then aerated several minutes and finally dried at 70–80°C to constant weight.

The diphenylurea is extracted from the Gooch crucible by washing with several portions of boiling ethyl alcohol and the crucible is again dried at the same temperature to constant weight. The alcoholic extract is then dried in a tared weighing bottle, first to dryness at room temperature and then to constant weight at 70–80°C. These final weights may be used in calculating the phosgene content of the air sampled.

At a room temperature of 23°C and a barometric pressure of 740 mm Hg, 1 mg of diphenylurea is equivalent to 0.1175 ml of phosgene. This value may be calculated in parts of phosgene per million parts of air by volume as follows (26):

$$1 \text{ mg of diphenylurea} = \frac{0.1175 \times 1000}{\text{liters of sample}} \text{ ppm}$$

B. Bromine

The use of bromine and bromides in industry is increasing with the development of cheaper methods of production. Among the workers exposed to the hazard of these chemicals may be mentioned photographic-film makers, tetraethyllead gasoline workers, and those employed in the manufacture of war gases of the tear-gas type like bromobenzylcyanide and bromoacetone. Other industries are those engaged in the manufacture of brominated dyes and colors, brominated drugs, and other organic chemicals. Bromine is used in the manufacture of refrigerants, fumigants, and germicides; it also is used in the extraction of gold and as a depolarizer in batteries.

Bromine is a dark red, almost black, heavy liquid. Its vapor is also dark red in color. It boils at 58.7°C but vaporizes readily at room temperature. It has a specific gravity of 3.12 at 15/15°C and its density with respect to air is 5.5. It is soluble in water, 1 ml of bromine dissolving in about 30 ml of water. It is readily soluble in alcohol, ether, chloroform, benzene, and many other organic solvents.

1. PHYSIOLOGICAL RESPONSE

The fumes of bromine are highly irritating to the eyes and the respiratory tract, both upper and lower sections. It has an oxidizing action and elicits respiratory reflexes. Inhalation causes inflammation of the entire respiratory system with edema of the lungs after severe exposure (1).

The least detectable odor of bromine is of the order of 3.5 ppm; the least concentration causing irritation of the throat is 15.1 ppm and 30.2 ppm will cause coughing (29).   A concentration of 1000 ppm will be lethal for men for exposures of a few minutes.   Concentrations in the range of 40–60 ppm are dangerous to life after exposures of from 30 to 60 min.   The maximum concentration that can be tolerated for an exposure of 60 min is 4 ppm and the maximum that can be tolerated for several hours without serious symptoms is 1.0 ppm.   The latter concentration is the generally accepted maximum allowable concentration.

2. Detection and Determination

A simple method for the detection and estimation of bromine and inorganic bromides in air is to pass the air through a gas washing bottle containing a cold solution of potassium hydroxide:

$$Br_2 + 2KOH \rightarrow KBr + KBrO + H_2O$$

Add some hydrogen peroxide to react with the hypobromite,

$$KBrO + H_2O_2 \rightarrow KBr + H_2O + O_2$$

and then estimate the bromide as silver bromide.   The Kolthoff and Yutzy method (34), in which the bromide is oxidized to bromate and subsequently estimated iodometrically, is described in the following section.

Bromine vapor can be caught completely (35) using a single sintered-glass bubbler containing 3% potassium iodide solution when sampled at a rate of 0.5 lpm.   The liberated iodine can be determined by titration with $0.01N$ thiosulfate using starch as indicator.

a. Kolthoff-Yutzy Method

Wash the hydrolyzed sample into a 250-ml flask and add 0.5 ml of saturated sodium chloride solution and approximately 0.5 g of sodium bicarbonate.   Evaporate over a flame or on a hot plate in a well-ventilated hood to remove the dense fumes of ethanolamine. Reduce the volume to not less than 10 ml, then continue the evaporation to dryness while blowing steam through the flask.   The steam displaces the air and sweeps out the vapors.   Swirl the flask constantly to prevent bumping and drive off all the ethanolamine on the sides of the flask.   Allow the flask to cool with the steam off, and then pass steam in again to dissolve the salts without the aid of external heat.   Rinse the steam tube with water and bring the volume of the solution to 50 ml.

Add to the solution 2.5 ml more of saturated sodium chloride solution, about 1 g of sodium acid phosphate ($NaH_2PO_4 \cdot H_2O$ crystals), and 2 ml of $1N$ sodium hypochlorite solution in $0.1N$ sodium hydroxide solution.   Heat the mixture to boiling.   After a minute or so, add 2 ml of sodium formate solution (50 g of sodium formate, HCOONa, dissolved in water and diluted to 100 ml), and continue boiling for 2 min more.   Cool the solution, dilute to 75 ml and add 1 drop of sodium molybdate solution (1 g of sodium molybdate, Na_2MoO_4, dissolved in water and diluted to 100 ml).   Add 0.5 g of potassium iodide and 10 ml of $6N$ sulfuric acid and titrate immediately with standard $0.01N$ sodium thiosulfate solution, adding 1% starch solution just before the end point.   A blank on an equivalent amount of ethanolamine with all other reagents should be carried through the entire procedure and subtracted from the test result.   One ml of $0.010N$ thiosulfate solution is equivalent to 0.1583 mg of methyl bromide.

C. Iodine and Iodides

Although iodine is an essential nutrient since it is required by the body to form the thyroid hormones thyroxine and triiodothyronine, it can be an industrial poison in several industries such as in the manufacture of iodine itself, iodides, iodoform, and other iodine-bearing pharmaceuticals.   Industrial poisoning attributable to iodine is rare.

1. Physiological Response

Iodine vapor is a pulmonary irritant and, since it sublimes even at $0°C$ and yields an appreciable vapor pressure at ambient temperatures, it does present an industrial hazard.   Iodine vapor is lachrymatory and industrial exposure has produced pulmonary edema, eye irritation, rhinitis, chronic pharyngitis (36), and catarrhal inflammation of the mouth.   Chronic ingestion of iodides produces nervousness and irritability.   Iodine possibly exerts its toxic action by oxidation of enzyme functional groups such as their —SH and —SS—.   Excess amounts of iodine and iodides inhibit formation of thyrotropic stimulating hormone (TSH).

2. Detection and Determination

Iodine itself yields a characteristic violet vapor not given by any other substance and it has a characteristic odor. Iodine reacts with starch to give blue or black colors, depending on the concentration. Degraded starch produces a red color with iodine.

Iodine is readily soluble in various solvents, forming violet solutions in chloroform and carbon tetrachloride, brown solutions in water, ethyl alcohol, and ether, and red solutions in benzene. The colors formed in carbon tetrachloride and chloroform, as well as the starch reaction, are relatively very sensitive tests. Iodine absorbs strongly at 352 mμ and thus aqueous solutions can be used to estimate it.

Iodides can be detected by oxidation of the iodide to free iodine with subsequent tests for the iodine. The liberation of iodine from iodides can be done by use of chlorine water, bromine, iodate, nitrous acid, and dichromate or by metals such as $As(V)$, $Sb(V)$, $Cu(II)$, $Tl(III)$, and $Cr(IV)$.

Iodine and iodides may be trapped by use of fritted-glass bubblers and subsequent determination can be done titrimetrically with standard sodium thiosulfate solution and starch as the indicator.

A colorimetric method for iodine was developed by Berezina (37). The iodine is absorbed in a 1% potassium iodide solution and is read at 440 mμ. The zero is set with the same potassium iodide solution that is used for absorbtion to eliminate interference of free iodine present in the potassium iodide. Petri-type absorbers are used with a train of 3 and the concentration is read from a standard curve.

D. Fluorine and Fluorides

1. Fluorine

Relatively little use of gaseous and liquid fluorine was made prior to World War II. After this war, there was a great expansion in the use and consequently the manufacture of fluorine-bearing organic compounds and also of inorganic compounds such as boron trifluoride and uranium hexafluoride. All of these new developments involved the manufacture of free fluorine on a large scale. Although elemental fluorine is a very reactive substance and never occurs as a free element in nature, it can be handled safely and relatively easily. The chemistry of fluorine has been considered in a symposium (38).

a. Physiological Response

Fluorine is a pulmonary irritant and can cause pulmonary edema. It can cause severe chemical and thermal burns. Exposure to high concentrations is usually fatal, respiratory damage and pulmonary edema being the cause of death. Prolonged exposure to as little as 5–10 ppm causes irritation of the eyes and nasal and buccal mucosa. On the skin, direct exposure to pure fluorine can cause severe burns in 0.2 sec, and an exposure for as long as 0.6 sec can result in thermal flash burns comparable with those produced by an oxyacetylene flame.

2. HYDROFLUORIC ACID

The use of this acid directly and its occurrence as a by-product in industry is increasing and consequently the dangers associated with its use are more prevalent. This acid is used in the etching of glass and in the production of clouded glass, as in opalescent electric light bulbs. The use of hydrofluoric acid for clouding of glass is diminishing and is being replaced by sand blasting. Industries using this acid are silicate extraction, phosphorus extraction, and gold refining. It is a particular hazard in the electrolytic production of aluminum. In this instance hydrogen fluoride occurs as a by-product during the electrolysis of bauxite, a hydrated alumina, $Al_2O_3 \cdot 2H_2O$, in molten cryolite, Na_3AlF_6, a double fluoride of aluminium and sodium (also written in symbols as $3NaF \cdot AlF_3$).

Hydrogen fluoride is a colorless liquid boiling at 19.4°C. It is very soluble in water and fumes very strongly in moist air, being similar to hydrogen chloride in this respect. The water solution yields hydrofluoric acid. At low temperatures the vapor of hydrogen fluoride is dimeric and corresponds to the formula H_2F_2.

a. Physiological Response

Hydrofluoric acid is violently corrosive. It attacks the skin vigorously, yielding slowly healing sores. Inhalation of the vapor causes a sense of constricted breathing, coughing, and irritation of the throat. The vapor causes ulceration of the mucous membranes and may cause chemical pneumonia. It may attack the eyes, causing conjunctivitis.

The effect of hydrogen fluoride on guinea pigs and rabbits was studied by Machle (39) and co-workers. The recommended maximum allowable concentration for this compound ranges from 1.5 to 3.0 ppm.

b. Detection and Determination

Hydrofluoric acid vapor may be caught in gas-washing bottles, preferably coated with paraffin, containing sodium hydroxide solution, or it may be sampled as detailed under the section on fluorides. Various tests have been devised for the detection of hydrogen fluoride. Some of these are discussed on page 662.

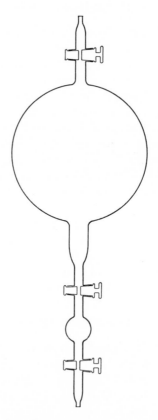

Fig. XVI-2. Sampling apparatus for hydrogen fluoride.

Direct Titration. Machle (39) and his co-workers estimated the amount of hydrogen fluoride in air by direct titration with standard nitric acid solution.

They used a special two-bulb three-stopcock sampling apparatus (Fig. XVI-2). The small bulb contained sufficient standard sodium hydroxide solution to absorb five times the amount of hydrogen fluoride expected. The large bulb is evacuated to 1 mm. The sample is taken so that it is drawn through the small bulb and the sodium hydroxide reagent and is sprayed against the sides of the large bulb by the force of the incoming mixture, thus protecting the glass against etching. The volume of the sample is obtained by calculation from the pressure after evacuation, the pressure after sampling, and the barometric pressure, as previously explained.

The bulb is shaken well to complete absorption and about 80% of the sodium hydroxide solution is titrated with standard nitric acid solution using 2 ml of 0.04% phenol red solution as indicator. The solutions are titrated at the boiling point to a clear yellow end point.

A like amount of sodium hydroxide solution used to fill the small bulb is titrated in an identical manner. The difference between the two titrations, after correcting for the aliquot of test solution used, represents a decreased total alkalinity attributable to the absorption of hydrogen fluoride. The results, corrected to 760 mm Hg and 25°C, are expressed in terms of milligrams per liter as follows:

$$\frac{\text{mg } H_2F_2 \text{ equivalent to decrease in fixed alkali}}{\text{liters of sample corrected to } 25°C \text{ and } 760 \text{ mm}} = \text{mg } H_2F_2/\text{liter at } 25°C \text{ and } 760 \text{ mm Hg}$$

For conversion to parts per million, multiply milliliters by 1.223.

3. FLUORIDES

The two principal fluorides used in industry are cryolite, a sodium aluminum fluoride, $3NaF \cdot AlF_3$, and fluorspar or fluorite, a calcium fluoride, CaF_2. Cryolite is used widely as an agricultural insecticide.

Fluorides are used in aluminum and magnesium foundries, in the welding of aluminum and of alloy steels, in glass manufacture, and in alkylation plants, as well as in other industries. Fluorides may occur in industrial processes as dusts, fumes, and vapors. Dusts are adequately sampled by the use of the midget impinger, fumes by use of the electrostatic precipitator, and vapors by employing a fritted bubbler.

The maximum allowable concentration is considered to be 2.5 mg/m³ of air. Harrold (40), however, considers this value too high, for such concentrations are said to have caused dermatitis. He recommends a value of 1.0 mg/m³ (10 mg per 10 m³) as the proper maximum allowable concentration.

a. Detection

Various test papers have been suggested for the detection of fluorides in air. One of these, devised by Harrold (41), employs a pump. The test paper is immersed in an activating solution, is inserted in the holder of the pump, and the number of strokes necessary to produce a detectable color change is noted. The fluoride concentration may be read from a chart.

A qualitative test (42) has been devised which depends on the insolubility of thorium fluoride and the intense red color of the lake of alizarinsulfonate adsorbed on thorium hydroxide. If fluorine is absent, the lake forms and a red color is observed. If fluorine is present, thorium fluoride is formed and no color is detected. The test has been adapted for the detection of fluorine in organic fluorides.

b. Determination

Distillation Method

The determination of fluorine as developed by Willard and Winter (43) is based on the isolation of fluorine accurately and expeditiously from interfering materials by distillation as hydrofluosilicic acid, which may be subsequently estimated colorimetrically by the bleaching of a zirconium–alizarin lake or by titration with thorium or cerous nitrate. If ashing has to be performed in order to free trapped fluorine dust of organic material, the fluorine will be lost in the ashing or will not be completely volatilized when the ash is distilled with sulfuric acid. A 5% magnesium acetate solution (44) should be used to moisten the material to be ashed. Dry the material in an oven for at least 24 hr and ash in a muffle at dull redness. Brush the ash into the distillation flask.

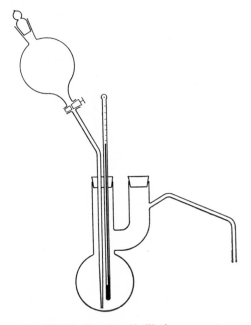

Fig. XVI-3. Fluorine distillation apparatus.

Apparatus. The distillation apparatus (Fig. XVI-3) consists of a Claissen flask with necks 10 cm long instead of the usual length, connected with an upright condenser. The side arm that connects the flask with the condenser is bent upward for about 4 cm and then downward at two points in order to fit the vertical condenser. Preferably the side arm should fit the condenser by a ground-glass joint. More elaborate trapping devices are inadvisable because the possible adsorption on the glass of fluorine causes fluorine deficiencies. The straight neck of the distilling flask carries a rubber stopper fitted with a thermometer and a dropping funnel whose stem has been drawn to a capillary. Both the thermometer and the dropping funnel extend to within 5 mm of the flask bottom.

Distillation Procedure. Evaporate the trapping solution to 50 ml, if the volume is greater than that, and transfer to the distilling apparatus, or wash the ashing crucible or dish several times with water and a small amount of sulfuric acid, after having brushed the ash into the distillation flask. Connect the apparatus as directed above.

Remove the stopper and add concentrated sulfuric acid until the effervescence ceases or until the mixture is distinctly acid and then add approximately 12 ml more of sulfuric acid. Sufficient water should be added so that the mixture will begin to boil at 110°C. Replace the stopper, boil, and distil, allowing the temperature to rise to 135–140°C, and collect the distillate in a 100-ml volumetric flask. When the temperature of the liquid being distilled reaches 135°C, sufficient water is slowly dropped from the funnel to compensate for the water distilling out; in this manner the temperature is maintained at 135°C. The distillation requires constant supervision. After the 100-ml flask is filled (distillate 1), collect another 50 ml (distillate 2) to be certain that all the fluorine has been volatilized.

It has been shown that phosphates interfere in the determination of fluorine by distillation as hydrofluosilicic acid (45), for it is at times possible that the phosphates are reduced to a form which is readily carried over in the distillate. In such an instance, a double Willard-Winter distillation of the fluorine from the ash should be made. The first distillation should be made with sulfuric acid to eliminate hazard, especially when carbonaceous matter is present, and the second may be made with perchloric acid at 135°C. This procedure yields a distillate free from sulfate and phosphate. Great care should be exercised in all distillations and operations using perchloric acid because of danger from explosion.

Eriochrome Cyanine R Method

Dust samples. The fluoride can be isolated from the dust or particulate matter recovered from the air passing through a filter by the following modification of the Willard-Winter distillation procedure (43).

Reagents. *Calcium Hydroxide Suspension.* Dissolve 25.0 g of calcium metal turnings in 1 liter of water or add 47.0 g of fluoride-free calcium hydroxide, $Ca(OH)_2$, to 1 liter of water.

Silver Perchlorate. Powdered material, obtainable from A. D. Mackay Inc., 198 Broadway, New York, N. Y., or G. Frederick Smith Chemical Company, 867 McKinley Avenue, Columbus, Ohio.

Standard Sodium Fluoride Solution. Dissolve 0.221 g of reagent grade sodium fluoride, NaF, in water and dilute to 1 liter. Dilute 50 ml of this stock solution to 1 liter with water. One ml of this final solution is equivalent to 0.05 mg F⁻. Store the fluoride solutions in Pyrex or polyethylene bottles.

Eriochrome Cyanine R (C.I. No. 722). Dissolve 1.80 g of eriochrome cyanine R and 1.83 g of reagent grade sodium arsenite, $NaAsO_2$, in 1 liter of water containing 5 ml of hydrochloric acid. Eriochrome cyanine R (Na salt), may be obtained from Geigy Company, Inc., 89 Barclay St., New York, N. Y., and Hartman-Leddon Company, 5817 Market St., Philadelphia, Pa. Use the commercial product in the reagents described.

Zirconyl Salt–Acid Solution. Dissolve 0.265 g of purified zirconyl chloride octahydrate, $ZrOCl_2 \cdot 8H_2O$, or 0.220 g of purified zirconyl nitrate dihydrate, $ZrO(NO_3)_2 \cdot 2H_2O$, in about 100 ml of water. Add 700 ml of concentrated hydrochloric acid and dilute to 1 liter with water.

Reference Solution. Add 10.0 ml of eriochrome cyanine R reagent solution to 103 ml of water and then add 7.0 ml of concentrated hydrochloric acid. Use this solution to set the reference point of the spectrophotometer.

Preparation of Standard Curve. Prepare fluoride standards in the range 0.00–100 μg in 50 ml by diluting appropriate quantities of standard sodium fluoride solution to 50 ml with water. Adjust the standards to the temperature at which subsequent analyses of the unknown solutions are to be made.

Add 5.00 ml of eriochrome cyanine R solution and 5.00 ml of zirconyl chloride–acid solution to each standard and mix well. Set the spectrophotometer to zero absorbance (100% transmittance) with the reference solution and the wavelength set at 530 mμ. Transfer a portion of each standard to a 1-cm cuvette and read the absorbance (or transmittance). Plot the curve showing the relationship of absorbance (or transmittance) to the fluoride ion concentration. Whenever a new solution of any of the reagents used in the evaluation of fluoride ion is made a new standard curve must be prepared.

Ashing. Place a sample of suitable estimated concentration, collected as described in Chapter V, Section C, in a platinum dish and cover with 10 ml of the calcium hydroxide suspension. Evaporate to dryness on a steam bath, heat for 0.5 hr in an oven at 150°C, and ignite in a muffle furnace at 550°C as measured with a pyrometer for 5–6 hr. Break up the ash in the dish by stirring with a glass rod flattened at one end and mix in 1 g of powdered silver perchlorate.

Distillation. Transfer the ash–silver perchlorate mixture to the distillation apparatus (Fig. XVI-4) (set up in a hood), with the aid of water and a few drops of 60% perchloric acid. Add to the distillation flask 10 ml of 60% perchloric acid, two or three small pieces (approximately ¼ in. thick) of pure silica and 2 small glass beads. Steam distil at a temperature of 135°C, controlling the temperature by regulating the amount of heat applied beneath the flask and the amount of steam permitted to flow through the flask. Collect approximately 190 ml of distillate and make up to 200 ml with water.

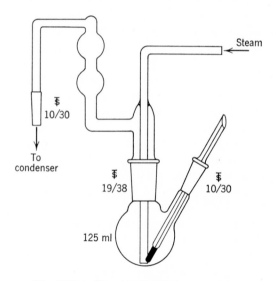

Fig. XVI-4. Fluoride distillation apparatus.

Colorimetric Procedure. Use a 50-ml portion of the fluoride solution obtained in the distillation procedure for the colorimetric determination (46). Adjust the temperature to that used in preparing the standard curve. Add 5.0 ml of zirconyl chloride–acid solution and mix well. Transfer to the spectrophotometer cuvette and read the absorbance or transmittance at 530 mμ, after first setting the instrument to read zero absorbance (or 100% transmittance) with the reference solution.

Determine the amount of fluoride in a blank, carrying out the procedure as described on unexposed collection material.

Subtract the blank value from the sample value and calculate the amount of fluoride in the sampled air, expressing the results as micrograms of fluoride ion per cubic meter of air.

Impinger and Bubbler Samples. Because the amount of fluorides is so very low, it is necessary to sample large volumes of air and/or for long periods of time. Suspended particulate matter samples have been discussed in detail. To get sufficient sample to analyze from impinger and bubbler samples, it is necessary to use automatic sequence samples and then concentrate the sample.

Procedure. Collect 24 1-hr samples with a sequence sampler using 0.1N sodium hydroxide solution as the collection medium. Transfer all of the samples to a 2-liter beaker and evaporate carefully on a hot plate, transferring first to a smaller beaker, washing the larger beaker, adding the washings to the smaller beaker, and continuing the evaporation to a small volume. Transfer to a platinum crucible, wash the beaker, add the washings to the platinum crucible, evaporate to a small volume, add 10 ml of calcium hydroxide suspension, and proceed with the method as detailed above.

It is necessary to run a blank on all the reagents and the water used.

Colorimetric Method

Dissolve 0.87 g of zirconium nitrate, $Zr(NO_3)_4 \cdot 5H_2O$, in 100 ml of water and 0.17 g of sodium alizarinate in 100 ml of water. Mix equal parts of the two solutions and dilute the mixture (1:4) with water.

Make up a series of standards in Nessler tubes or test tubes of about 80-ml capacity by placing 0.02, 0.04, 0.06, 0.09, and 1.20 mg of fluorine in each tube, respectively, prepared from 0.02N lithium fluoride solution, containing 0.5188 g/liter of lithium fluoride, or from specially purified 0.02N sodium fluoride (made from sodium carbonate and hydrofluoric acid) solution, containing 0.840 g/liter. Add water to make about 50 ml and 10 ml of hydrochloric acid (1:1), mix thoroughly, add 2 ml of the dye solution, and bring all the tubes to the same level with water. Again mix thoroughly, place the tubes in a steam bath for 30 min, and cool. For unknowns take aliquots of the distillates whose fluorine contents fall within the above range of standards. The fluorine is determined from the nearest standard (47).

The fading of the zirconium–alizarin lake is a measure of the amount of fluorine present (48). If quantities of fluorine fall below the range given, less dye should be used and if quantities above the range are to be determined, more dye should be used.

The individual tubes show a fading in color which increases as the fluorine content increases; hence, a comparison of the fading caused by an aliquot of the unknown with the standards prepared gives the measure of the fluorine content of the sample.

Titrimetric Method

Cerous Nitrate Modification (49). Several drops of 0.04% phenol red solution are added to the distillate obtained as detailed in the foregoing and the liquid is neutralized with dilute sodium hydroxide solution, avoiding a large excess. The alkaline solution is boiled and repeatedly brought back to the apparent neutral point with $0.02N$ or $0.01N$ perchloric acid. During this neutralization, the volume is reduced to 5–10 ml. When the faint pink color is no longer restored by boiling (carbonate free), the solution is cooled, transferred quantitatively to a 50-ml beaker, and concentrated from about 25 ml down to 2–3 ml with the aid of a hot plate. Two drops of a saturated alcoholic solution of methyl red and 10 drops of 0.04% bromocresol green solution are added. The bromocresol green is weighed out exactly and neutralized with standard sodium hydroxide to yield the monosodium salt. This prevents the alteration of the neutrality of the solution when the indicator is added. The liquid is titrated at 80°C to the maximum red color with cerous nitrate solution, 1 ml of which is equivalent to 0.5 mg of fluorine. When the amount of fluorine is less than 0.2 mg, 0.01–$0.02N$ thorium nitrate solution may be substituted for the cerous nitrate.

Thorium Nitrate Modification (50). The thorium nitrate solution may be standardized by titration against known volumes of $0.02N$ fluoride solution. Transfer a known aliquot of standard $0.02N$ fluoride solution to a flask, add water to bring the volume to 20 ml, and then add an equal volume of ethyl alcohol. Add 6 drops of alizarin red indicator (prepared by dissolving 1 g of sodium alizarin-sulfonate in 100 ml of ethyl alcohol, filtering off the residue, and making up the filtrate to 250 ml with alcohol) and then only enough dilute hydrochloric acid to destroy the color. Avoid excess acid. Titrate with the thorium nitrate solution over a white surface in a good light to a faint permanent reappearance of color. Titrate slowly near the end point. Run a blank titration on the indicator by determining the volume of standard 0.02N fluoride solution necessary to cause disappearance of color in a slightly acid water–alcohol solution of 6 drops of the indicator and compare this with the volume of standard thorium nitrate necessary to discharge the color. Calculate the strength of the thorium nitrate solution by use of the following equation:

$$1.0 \text{ ml Th(NO}_3)_4 = \frac{\text{ml of } 0.02N \text{ F}^- \text{ soln}}{\text{ml of Th(NO}_3)_4 \text{ soln}} \times 0.38 = A \text{ mg of F}^-$$

The unknown distillates may be titrated in a similar manner by making alkaline, neutralizing, and concentrating as described above. Add 6 drops of indicator, dilute acid until the color of the indicator just disappears, and then add an equal volume of alcohol. The solution should be only faintly acid. If no fluorides are present, the color will not be discharged. Titrate at once, if fluorides are present, with the standardized thorium nitrate solution to the faint reappearance of the pink color.

Williams Modification

The thorium nitrate titration of fluorides has been simplified by Williams (51) by using a single titration against a permanent color standard. It is suitable for microgram quantities. Higher concentrations may be estimated by the Matuszak and Brown variation (52).

Reagents. *Acidified Standard Thorium Nitrate Solution.* Stock Solution. Dissolve 1.27 g of thorium nitrate, Th(NO$_3$)$_4 \cdot$4H$_2$O, and 72 ml of 1N hydrochloric acid in water and make up to 100 ml.

Dilute Solution. Dilute 5 ml of the stock solution to 500 ml with fluorine-free water. One ml of the dilute solution is equivalent to 5 μg of fluoride.

Acid Indicator Solution. Dissolve 0.020 g of sodium alizarin monosulfonate (alizarin S) in water, add 100 ml of the dilute acidified thorium nitrate solution and 14.3 ml of 1N hydrochloric acid, and make up to 200 ml. Two ml of this solution added to 50 ml of fluorine-free water and 10 ml of 2N sodium chloride solution in a Nessler tube should give the correct end-point color; if not, impurities in the salt or other chemicals may be responsible and the proportion of the dilute standard thorium nitrate solution used should be modified accordingly. The color should be judged when making the acid-indicator solution, for it is likely to alter on standing.

2,5-Dinitrophenol Indicator Solution. Prepare a 0.05% aqueous solution.

Color Standards. *Temporary.* Dilute an aliquot of a standard fluoride solution (made from sodium fluoride prepared from the purest sodium carbonate and hydrofluoric acid) containing 100 μg of fluorine to 50 ml with water. Add 10 ml of 2N sodium chloride solution, 2 ml of the acid indicator solution, 20 ml of the dilute standard thorium nitrate solution, and mix. This color is stable for several hours.

Permanent. Mix 3 ml of 10% hydrochloric acid with 50 ml of a solution containing 1% of cobalt chloride, $CoCl_2$, add 30 ml of 0.1% potassium chromate solution, and dilute to 100 ml. Dilute 3 ml of this stock mixture with water to a volume approximately equal to the anticipated volume of the test solution when titrated. The color should be identical with that of the temporary standard. If it is not, possibly because of differences in the thorium nitrate used, the proportions of the components should be adjusted until a match is obtained. Alternatively, alizarin S may be used as a color standard in a buffered solution of suitable pH.

Procedure. Add 3 drops of 2,5-dinitrophenol indicator solution to an appropriate aliquot of the distillate or fluoride solution in a Nessler tube and add 0.05N sodium hydroxide solution until the solution when mixed assumes a faint yellow color. Then add 1 drop or sufficient 0.01N hydrochloric acid solution to just discharge the color. It is useful to have a Nessler tube containing water for comparison, for the color becomes very pale near the end point. If the presence of free halogen is suspected, add 1 ml of 1% hydroxylamine hydrochloride solution just before the neutralization.

Transfer accurately 50 ml of the neutralized solution, containing between 0.5 and about 150 μg of fluorine, to another Nessler tube, add 10 ml of 2N sodium chloride solution and 2 ml of the acid indicator solution, and mix. Titrate with the dilute standard thorium nitrate solution until the color exactly matches that of the standard color solutions. For a 5-g sample, 1 ml of dilute thorium nitrate solution is equivalent to 1 ppm, subject to correction blanks.

Fluorometric Method

Powell and Saylor (53) developed a method which depends upon the fact that the intensity of fluorescence of the compounds formed on reaction of aluminum chloride with the dihydroxyazo dyes, eriochrome red B and superchrome garnet Y, is decreased on the addition of fluoride. The method is deemed adequate in the range of 0.2–100 μg of fluoride. Powell and Saylor used a Lumetron fluorometer with 25-ml rectangular cells. A Corning 5860 primary filter was used for the isolation of the excitation band and a Corning 3389 secondary filter for the fluorescence band.

Preparation of Standard Dye. To prepare 1 liter of eriochrome red B standard solution, mix 60 ml of $2M$ acetic acid, 40 ml of $2M$ sodium acetate solution, 40 ml of aluminum chloride solution containing 50 μg of aluminum per milliliter, and 440 ml of 95% ethyl alcohol in a 1-liter volumetric flask. Add 60 ml of a 1% solution of the dye in 95% alcohol, which is prepared from the dye as received by dissolving and filtering, and make up to 1 liter with water. Eriochrome red B [Color Index No. 652 (old system)] can be obtained from Geigy and Company or from E. I. du Pont de Nemours & Company.

To prepare the superchrome garnet Y standard solution, mix 50 ml each of $2M$ acetic acid and $2M$ sodium acetate solution, 40 ml of aluminum chloride solution containing 50 μg of aluminum per milliliter, 48 ml of a 0.1% aqueous solution of the National Aniline dye or 33.2 ml of a 0.1% solution of the Du Pont dye, and sufficient water to make 1 liter.

Allow both types of standard solution to stand for 1 day at room temperature before use. The solutions are stable for about 2 weeks. Aging effects are avoided by using the same dye solution for preparation of the standard curve and for the test solution.

Procedure. Remove interfering ions by a Willard-Winter distillation as previously detailed. Adjust the pH to between 4 and 5 with $0.05N$ sodium hydroxide using a pH meter, make up exactly to volume, and mix well. Take an aliquot of 35 ml or less, containing an amount of fluoride in the range of the standards, and place in a 50-ml volumetric flask. Prepare four or five standards in the range 0–50 μg of fluoride. Add 12.5 ml of standard solution at about the same time to the standards and sample, make up to volume, and mix. At about the same time dilute 12.5 ml of the blank solution, which contains all reagents except aluminum chloride and fluoride ion, to 50 ml, and mix.

Let all solutions stand for 1 hr at room temperature if superchrome garnet Y is used and 3 hr if eriochrome red B is used. Rinse the 25-ml fluorometer cell with the solution containing no fluoride, fill the cell, wipe with tissue paper, and set the instrument so that this solution reads 100. In a similar manner use the blank solution to set the instrument on zero. Read the intensity of fluorescence for the sample and standards, plot a calibration curve, and determine the fluoride content of the sample from the curve.

Ion-Exchange Method

Among the difficulties encountered in determining fluoride in air as well as in other materials is the problem of eliminating interfering ions. This is generally done by a Willard-Winter distillation. Nielsen and Dangerfield (54) adopting a system proposed by Attebury and Boyd (55), used ion-exchange resin Duolite A41 in the hydroxyl form for the determination of atmospheric fluoride. Nielsen (56) found that anion-exchange resin Dowex 1-X8 permitted better isolation of fluoride and used this resin in combination with the spectrophotometric procedure of Megregian (46) to estimate fluoride in the range of 1–10 µg.

Reagents. *Dye Reagent.* Dissolve 1.000 g of eriochrome cyanine R (Geigy) in water and dilute to 1 liter.

Zirconyl Nitrate Solution. Dissolve 0.175 g of zirconyl nitrate dihydrate, $ZrONO_3 \cdot 2H_2O$, in water, make up to 500 ml and add 500 ml of concentrated hydrochloric acid and mix.

Reference Solution. Add 10 ml of the dye reagent and 5 ml of concentrated hydrochloric acid to 105 ml of water and mix. Use this solution to set the zero point on the spectrophotometer.

Preparation of Ion-Exchange Columns. Use straight borosilicate glass tubes, 9-mm i.d. and approximately 12 in. long. Cover a 00, one-hole, rubber stopper containing a piece of 5- or 6-mm glass tubing 4 or 5 cm long with a circular piece of nylon cloth slightly larger than the smaller diameter of the stopper. A small wad of glass wool may also be used. Insert this into the column. Do not permit any portion of the cloth to extend beyond the end of the tube.

Suspend some 200–400-mesh Dowex 1-X8 ion-exchange resin in water and allow it to settle. Decant the fines. Add sufficient resin slurry to the tube to make a column when settled 2 cm in height. Permit the water to drain off and insert a small plug of glass wool to prevent distortion of the surface when solutions are added.

Convert the resin to the acetate form by dripping 25 ml of 1M sodium acetate solution into the column at a rate of 4–12 drops per minute. A small amount of chloride remaining in the resin will not affect the results. The resin will swell to about 2.5 cm when converted to the acetate form.

Nielsen suggests that the solutions and samples be added to the columns by means of pipets, the suction ends of which are equipped with short lengths of gum rubber tubing and screw clamps. Support each pipet above a column and allow the solution added to drip onto the resin. Insert a piece of 26-gauge Nichrome wire to control the flow rate.

Remove the excess acetate solution by filling the tube with water and allow it to run through at an unrestricted rate.

Procedure. Add the sample to the column from a pipet at a rate of 6–12 drops per minute. Use an aliquot containing from 6 to 8 μ g of fluoride.

Elute the fluoride stepwise from the resin with solutions containing increasing concentrations of sodium acetate. Run 10 ml of 0.1M sodium acetate solution through the column at a rate of about 6–8 drops per minute. Repeat with 10 ml of 0.2M sodium acetate solution and then with 0.3M sodium acetate solution. Collect the eluate from each elution in a separate test tube.

Add 0.5 ml of dye solution and 0.5 ml of zirconyl nitrate solution to 5-ml aliquots of the fractions collected. Mix thoroughly and allow to stand for 10 min. Transfer to 10-mm matched cuvettes. Read the absorbance in a Beckman Model DU or B or equivalent spectrophotometer at 527 mμ, using the reference solution for setting the zero. Compute the fluoride concentration by comparison with a standard curve.

Preparation of Standard Curve. Determine the absorbance of known concentrations of fluoride ion in the microgram range making up to volume in each instance with 0.2M sodium acetate solution and the concentrations of reagents noted in the procedure. One to 5 μg per 5 ml at intervals of 1 μg are convenient standards. Plot the absorbance against micrograms of fluoride.

Notes. If the sample contains less than 6–8 μg of fluoride, usually all will be eluted in the second fraction. If very small amounts of fluoride are expected, collect the 0.2M sodium acetate eluate in two 5-ml fractions. This will assist in obtaining greater precision, for with proper adjustment of resin height and rate of flow, all of the fluoride will appear in the first 5-ml fractions. Both fractions of the eluate should, however, be tested for fluoride.

The 0.3M sodium acetate solution regenerates the resin adequately when distillates are analyzed. If the sample contains phosphate, chloride, or sulfate, the resin should be cleaned with 25 ml of 1M sodium acetate solution followed by water to remove excess acetate.

It is best to include a few control standards with each group of samples analyzed to make certain that they fall within the expected error limits of the curve. The method has a precision of about 5%.

References

1. Haggard, H. W., *J. Ind. Hyg.*, **5**, 397 (1923–24).
2. Berghoff, R. S., *Arch. Internal Med.*, **24**, 678 (1919).
3. Sayers, R. R., J. M. DallaValle, and W. P. Yant, *Ind. Eng. Chem.*, **26**, 1251 (1934).
4. Fieldner, A. C., C. G. Oberfell, M. C. Teague, and J. N. Lawrence, *Ind. Eng. Chem.*, **11**, 523 (1919).
5. *Standard Methods of Water Analysis*, 8th ed., Am. Public Health Assoc., New York, 1936.
6. Porter, L. E., *Ind. Eng. Chem.*, **18**, 730 (1926).
7. *Dept. Sci. Ind. Research Brit. Leaflet 10* (1939).
8. Wallach, A., and W. A. McQuary, *Ind. Hyg. Quarterly*, **9**, 64 (1948).
9. Lehmann, K. B., as quoted by F. Flury and F. Zernik, *Schaedliche Gase*, Springer, Berlin, 1931.
10. Henderson, Y., and H. W. Haggard, *Noxious Gases*, Reinhold, New York, 1943.
11. Machle, W., K. V. Kitzmiller, E. W. Scott, and J. F. Freon, *J. Ind. Hyg. Toxicol.*, **24**, 222 (1942).
12. Flury, F., and F. Zernik, *Schaedliche Gase*, Springer, Berlin, 1931.
13. Heller, A., *Gesundh. Ing.*, **55**, 261 (1932).
14. Fajans, K., and H. Wolff, *Z. Anorg. Allgem. Chem.*, **137**, 221 (1924).
15. Kolthoff, I. M., and V. A. Stenger, *Volumetric Analysis. Titration Methods*, Interscience, New York, 1947.
16. Caldwell, J. R., and H. V. Moyer, *Ind. Eng. Chem. Anal. Ed.*, **7**, 38 (1935).
17. Chirnoaga, E., *Z. Anal. Chem.*, **101**, 31 (1935).
18. Dubsky, J. V., and J. Trtilek, *Mikrochemie*, **12**, 315 (1933).
19. Roberts, I., *Ind. Eng. Chem. Anal. Ed.*, **8**, 365 (1937).
20. Williams, D., *Ind. Eng. Chem. Anal. Ed.*, **17**, 533 (1945).

21. Williams, D., and C. C. Meeker, *Ind. Eng. Chem. Anal. Ed.*, **17**, 535 (1945).
22. Fieldner, A. C., and S. H. Katz, *U.S. Bur. Mines Rept. Invest. 2262* (1921).
23. Biesalski, E., *Angew. Chem.*, **37**, 314 (1924); *Chem. Abstr.*, **18**, 2480 (1924).
24. Stuber, E., *Arch. Gewerbepath. Gewerbehyg.*, **2**, 398 (1931).
25. Olsen, J. C., G. E. Fergusen, V. Sabetta, and L. Scheflan, *Ind. Eng. Chem. Anal. Ed.*, **3**, 189 (1931).
26. Yant, W. P., J. C. Olsen, H. H. Storch, J. B. Littlefield, and L. Scheflan, *Ind. Eng. Chem. Anal. Ed.*, **8**, 20 (1936).
27. *Dept. Sci. Ind. Research Brit. Leaflet 8* (1939); *Analyst*, **65**, 290 (1940).
28. Nuckolls, A. H., *Natl. Board Fire Underwriters Misc. Hazard 2375* (1933).
29. Fieldner, A. C., S. H. Katz, and S. P. Kinney, *U.S. Bur. Mines Tech. Paper 248* (1921).
30. Patty, F. A., *Am. J. Public Health*, **30**, 1191 (1940).
31. Liddel, H. F., *Analyst*, **82**, 375 (1957).
32. Matuszak, M. P., *Ind. Eng. Chem. Anal. Ed.*, **6**, 374 (1934).
33. Matuszak, M. P., *Ind. Eng. Chem. Anal. Ed.*, **6**, 457 (1934).
34. Kolthoff, I. M., and H. C. Yutzy, *Ind. Eng. Chem. Anal. Ed.*, **9**, 75 (1937).
35. Goldman, F. H., and J. M. DallaValle, *U.S. Public Health Rept.*, **54**, 1728 (1939).
36. Luckhardt, A. B., F. C. Koch, W. F. Schroeder, and A. H. Weiland, *J. Pharmacol. Exp. Therap.*, **15**, 1 (1920).
37. Berezina, T. A., *Gigiena i Sanit.*, **22**, No. 12, 88 (1957); Office of Technical Services, B. S. Levine, Translator, USSR Literature on Air Pollution and Related Occupational Diseases, Vol. 1, 60-21049, 1960, p. 184.
38. "Symposium on Fluorine Chemistry," *Ind. Eng. Chem.*, **39**, 236 (1947).
39. Machle, W., F. Thamann, K. Kitzmiller, and J. Cholak, *J. Ind. Hyg.*, **16**, 129 (1934).
40. Harrold, G. C., personal communication, 1948.
41. Production Equipment Co., Detroit 2, Mich.
42. Bennett, E. L., C. W. Gould, Jr., and E. H. Swift, *Anal. Chem.*, **19**, 1035 (1947).
43. Willard, H. H., and O. B. Winter, *Ind. Eng. Chem. Anal. Ed.*, **5**, 7 (1933).
44. Winter, O. B., *J. Assoc. Official Agr. Chemists*, **19**, 362 (1936).
45. Churchill, H. V., R. W. Bridges, and R. J. Rowley, *Ind. Eng. Chem. Anal. Ed.*, **9**, 222 (1937).
46. Megregian, S., *Anal. Chem.*, **26**, 1161 (1954).
47. Allen, N., and N. H. Furman, *J. Am. Chem. Soc.*, **54**, 4625 (1932).
48. Smith, O. M., and H. A. Dutcher, *Ind. Eng. Chem. Anal. Ed.*, **6**, 61 (1934).
49. Scott, E. W., and A. L. Henne, *Ind. Eng. Chem. Anal. Ed.*, **7**, 299 (1935).
50. Boruff, C. S., and G. B. Abbot, *Ind. Eng. Chem. Anal. Ed.*, **5**, 236 (1933).
51. Williams, H. A., *Analyst*, **71**, 175 (1947).
52. Matuszak, M. P., and D. R. Brown, *Ind. Eng. Chem. Anal. Ed.*, **17**, 100 (1945).
53. Powell, W. A., and J. H. Saylor, *Anal. Chem.*, **25**, 960 (1953).
54. Nielsen, J. P., and A. D. Dangerfield, *A.M.A. Arch. Ind. Health*, **11**, 61 (1955).
55. Attebury, R. W., and G. E. Boyd, *J. Am. Chem. Soc.*, **72**, 4805 (1950).
56. Neilsen, J. P., *Anal. Chem.*, **30**, 1009 (1958).

CHAPTER XVII

CARBON MONOXIDE, CARBON DIOXIDE, CYANIDES, AND NITRILES

The gases containing carbon are the most numerous of industrial hazards. We have already had occasion to discuss phosgene, or carbonyl chloride, carbon disulfide, nickel carbonyl, iron carbonyl, etc., because of their relationship to other gases and elements. In this chapter, other carbon compounds, namely, carbon monoxide, carbon dioxide, cyanogen, and hydrogen cyanide, will be discussed.

A. Carbon Monoxide

The carbon compound which is the most important industrial hazard is carbon monoxide. Indeed, it has been said that carbon monoxide is now, and has been since the first discovery of fire, the most widespread poison connected with human life and activity (1–3). Only the means by which a person is poisoned by this substance has changed.

1. Industrial and Nonindustrial Hazard

This gas is met in any industry in which there is the possibility of incomplete combustion of carbon compounds or carbonaceous material. Not only is carbon monoxide an important industrial poison but it is also the greatest single nonindustrial hazard because it is a component of nearly all types of illuminating and heating gas, it is a component of the exhaust gases of automobiles, and it is a probable component of the flue gas produced by whatever form of heat is used in the home—wood, coal, illuminating gas, or oil.

For these reasons carbon monoxide is a hazard in the home, in the private garage, and in the street, as well as in the public garage and in the shop.

Dublin and Vane (4) list over 100 industries in which carbon monoxide poisoning is a hazard. A comprehensive review of the hazards and mechanism of action of carbon monoxide is given by von Oettingen

TABLE XVII-1
Carbon Monoxide Content (6,7)

Type and source	CO by volume, %
Mine explosion, immediately after dust explosion (exptl.)	8.0
Mine explosion, 1 day after explosion in coal mine	1.0
Mine fire	1.0
Blasting with 40% gelatin dynamite, 7 min after shooting 100 sticks	1.2
Blasting, products of combustion	
Black blasting powder	10.8
40% Nitroglycerin dynamite	28.0
40% Ammonia dynamite	5.0
TNT	60.0
Blast-furnace stack gas	28.0
Bessemer-furnace gas	25.0
Crucible furnace; gas fuel melting Al–Cu–Sn alloy	5.5
Arc furnace melting aluminum	32.2
Cupola gas	17.0
Coke-oven gas	6.0
Coal gas	16.0
Carbureted water gas	30.0
Blau gas (cracked heavy oils)	40.0
Producer gas from coke	25.0
Distillation coal oil mixtures	7.4
Producer gas from oil	5.0
Fuel gas	30.0
Gas range burning natural gas	0.2
Room heater burning natural gas	0.5
Automobile exhaust gas (average of tests of 101 cars of all types)	7.0
City fire (black smoke from burning buildings)	0.1
Insulation burning in electric arc	0.5
Furnace gas of small-house heating and hot-water system	1.0
Railroad-locomotive stack gas	2.0

(5).   Table XVII-1 lists the approximate amount of carbon monoxide in gases which may be present at several common sources of poisoning by this substance.

Carbon monoxide is a colorless and odorless gas.   It is combustible and is lighter than air, having a specific gravity of 0.967.   It used to be termed "white damp" by miners but that is an inappropriate term.

Air containing 12.5–74% carbon monoxide will explode if ignited (8,9). Therefore, 12.5% and 74% are known as the upper and lower explosive limits.

2. Physiological Response and Toxicity

Carbon monoxide in excess of 0.01% will produce symptoms of poisoning if breathed for a sufficiently long time. As little as 0.02% will produce slight symptoms in several hours. Four parts in 10,000, which is equivalent to 0.04%, will produce headache and discomfort within 2–3 hr. With moderate exercise 0.12% will produce slight palpitation of the heart in 30 min, a tendency to stagger in $1\frac{1}{2}$ hr, and confusion of mind, headache, and nausea in 2 hr. A concentration of 0.20–0.25% will usually produce unconsciousness in about 30 min. Its effects in high concentrations may be so sudden that a man has little or no warning before he collapses (10). These symptoms are summarized in Table XVII-2.

TABLE XVII-2
Carbon Monoxide Poisoning (3,11)

Effect	CO, %
Allowable for an exposure of several hours	0.01
Can be inhaled for 1 hr without appreciable effect	0.04–0.05
Causing a just appreciable effect after 1-hr exposure	0.06–0.07
Causing unpleasant but not dangerous symptoms after 1-hr exposure	0.1–0.12
Dangerous for exposure of 1 hr	0.15–0.20
Fatal in exposure of less than 1 hr	0.4 and above

Carbon monoxide is really an asphyxiant and not a poison because it produces its harmful effect by combining with the hemoglobin of the red cells to form a relatively stable compound, carbon monoxide hemoglobin, usually abbreviated HbCO, preventing this combined hemoglobin from taking up oxygen to form oxyhemoglobin, abbreviated HbO_2, and thus depriving the body of its oxygen. The affinity of carbon monoxide for hemoglobin is about 300 times that of oxygen. Hence, if only a small amount of carbon monoxide is present in the air taken into the lungs, the carbon monoxide will be absorbed in preference to the oxygen by the blood. Since carbon monoxide is not definitely a poison, it does not have much effect on the body. However, carbon monoxide asphyxia, and probably other types of asphyxia, produces degenerative changes in nerve cells and throughout the entire brain (12).

The percentage of hemoglobin of the blood combined with carbon monoxide instead of with oxygen is termed "percentage of blood saturation." Symptoms of poisoning more or less parallel the blood saturation. The first decided symptoms during rest make their appearance when 20–30% of the hemoglobin is combined with carbon monoxide. Unconsciousness takes place at about 50% saturation and death may occur at a saturation between 65 and 80%. Table XVII-3 summarizes the symptoms at various stages of blood saturation.

The symptoms decrease in number with the rate of saturation. If exposed to high concentrations, the victim may experience but few symptoms. The rate at which a man is overcome and the sequence in which the symptoms appear depend on several factors: the concentration of gas, the extent to which he is exerting himself, the state of his health and individual predisposition, and the temperature, humidity, and air movement to which he is exposed. Exercise, high temperature, and humidity, with little or no air movement, tend

TABLE XVII-3

Symptoms of Carbon Monoxide Poisoning (6,13)

Blood saturation, %	Symptoms
0.0–10	None
10–20	Tightness across forehead, possibly headache
20–30	Headache, throbbing in temples
30–40	Severe headache, weakness, dizziness, dimness of vision, nausea and vomiting, and collapse
40–50	Same as previous item with more possibility of collapse and syncope, increased pulse and respiration
50–60	Syncope, increased respiration and pulse, coma with intermittent convulsions
60–70	Coma with intermittent convulsions, depressed heart action and respiration, possibly death
70–80	Weak pulse and slowed respiration, respiratory failure, and death

to increase respiration and heart rate and consequently result in more rapid absorption of carbon monoxide. The symptoms of chronic carbon monoxide poisoning are a tired feeling, headache, nausea, palpitation of the heart, and sometimes mental dullness (10).

The above discussion shows that though carbon monoxide is not as poisonous a chemical as many others encountered in industry, it is still one of the most serious hazards. Four parts of carbon monoxide in 10,000 parts of air (400 ppm) is considered the maximum concentration to which a person may be exposed for 1 hr without noticeable effects; or, if the concentration is increased from zero uniformly for 1 hr, the maximum concentration tolerable is 6 parts per 10,000 (600 ppm), averaging 3 parts per 10,000 (300 ppm) per hour (14–16). The generally accepted maximum allowable concentration for daily 8-hr exposures is 100 ppm (17).

Large numbers of people die from carbon monoxide poisoning every year. In 1946 in New York City there were 268 suicide deaths and 281 accidental deaths from carbon monoxide poisoning alone. Of the latter, 254 were attributable to the accidental absorption of manufactured (illuminating) gas.

3. Classification of Methods for Detection and Determination of Carbon Monoxide

The methods for the detection and estimation of carbon monoxide in air are numerous. They may be placed into the following groups.

1. *Use of canaries and Japanese waltzing mice.*

These small animals are more rapidly affected by carbon monoxide than are human beings.

2. *Absorption methods* (18).

(a) Ammoniacal or acid cuprous chloride.

(b) Cuprous sulfate–β-naphthol.

(c) Iodine pentoxide in oleum (19).

Absorption methods are used for the relatively high percentages of carbon monoxide found in fuel gas, flue gas, etc., or in badly contaminated atmospheres. A known volume of the gas examined is shaken with one of the absorbents in a volumetric gas-analysis apparatus and the resulting decrease in volume is measured. Absorption methods are generally not practical when used for estimation of carbon monoxide present in less than 0.2% quantity. Since this percentage is far above the toxic limits of carbon monoxide, absorption methods are of limited value from the standpoint of health and safety.

3.   *Reduction methods.*

(*a*) Reduction of palladious chloride.

(*b*) Reduction of ammoniacal silver nitrate.

These solutions react with carbon monoxide yielding, respectively, metallic palladium and silver.

4.   *Oxidation methods.*

(*a*) Hoolamite method.

This method depends upon the oxidation of carbon monoxide by an activated iodine pentoxide indicator.   The amount of carbon monoxide present is shown by a color change produced by the coliberation of iodine from the iodine pentoxide.

(*b*) Iodine pentoxide method.

A known volume of air is passed through a tube containing iodine pentoxide at a temperature of 150°C.   The liberated iodine is then trapped in potassium iodide solution and estimated by titration or the amount of carbon dioxide formed is ascertained.

(*c*) Red mercuric oxide method (20).

The amount of carbon monoxide in air may be determined with the aid of the reaction.

$$CO + HgO \rightarrow Hg + CO_2$$
$$\text{gas} \quad \underset{\text{red}}{\text{solid}} \quad \text{gas} \quad \text{gas}$$

The sample of air is passed through a reaction tube containing granular red mercuric oxide held at a temperature of 175–200°C.   The loss in weight of the reaction tube is a measure of the quantity of carbon monoxide present.

5.   *Combustion methods.*

(*a*) Platinum wire.

Any carbon monoxide present in a sample is burned on the surface of an electrically heated platinum wire.   The heat developed by the exothermic reaction of forming carbon dioxide is then measured by some electrical device such as a Wheatstone bridge (19).

(*b*) Hopcalite method.

Hopcalite is a catalyst which has the property of enabling carbon monoxide to be burned to carbon dioxide at ordinary temperatures.

With a special apparatus the concentration of carbon monoxide may be read directly from the dial of a milliammeter registering the heat evolved and calibrated to read parts per million of carbon monoxide.

 6. *Colorimetric methods.*

  (*a*) Chemical.

These methods may also be considered as part of category *3* reduction methods above.

   (*1*) NBS indicating gel.

Purified silica gel impregnated with ammonium molybdate, and a sulfuric acid solution of palladium or palladium oxide, forming a yellow silicomolybdate, is reduced to a molybdenum blue by carbon monoxide, the reaction being catalyzed by the palladium.

   (*2*) Palladium chloride–phosphomolybidic acid–acetone reagent.

In this method too, developed by the U. S. Bureau of Mines, a molybdenum blue is formed, the depth of color being proportional to the amount of carbon monoxide drawn through the test solution.

  (*b*) Biochemical.

Carbon monoxide forms carboxyhemoglobin, a characteristically colored compound with the hemoglobin of blood. When diluted, normal blood has a yellow color but when blood containing carbon monoxide is diluted, it has a pink color. These methods are based on estimating the amount of carbon monoxide by the amount of color attributable to carboxyhemoglobin.

   (*1*) Pyrotannic acid method.

Treatment of a diluted blood sample with tannic and pyrogallic acids yields a gray-brown suspension with normal blood and a light carmine suspension with blood containing carboxyhemoglobin (10,21,22).

   (*2*) Haldane carmine method (23).

This method depends on the ratio between the amount of carmine (a dye solution) which must be added to diluted blood to yield the same color as blood completely saturated with carbon monoxide and the amount of carmine solution added to diluted normal blood to give it the color of the blood with the unknown content of carbon monoxide. The ratio of these additions gives a measure of the blood saturation.

 7. *Physicochemical methods.*

The method of choice for the monitoring of carbon monoxide is the employment of a nondispersive, infrared, recording spectrometer.

8. Blood methods.

Such methods are described briefly in Chapter XIX.

4. DETECTION

a. Canaries and Japanese Waltzing Mice

Small birds such as canaries may be used to detect carbon monoxide. Generally they will exhibit signs of distress and fall from their perch before sufficient carbon monoxide is present to affect a man. It has been shown that a man may feel only a slight headache at the end of 20 min in an atmosphere containing 0.25% carbon monoxide, while canaries will show signs of distress in 1 min and fall from their perch within 3 min (24).

The U. S. Bureau of Mines (25) has shown that Japanese waltzing mice are as equally susceptible to carbon monoxide as canaries. They are black and white in color, with an average body length of 72 mm, tail length 52 mm, and weight 17 g. They appear to be unable to orient themselves in a horizontal plane. As a result they run erratically, sometimes in circles and sometimes in wide, narrow, or figure-eight forms, repeated many times in rapid succession. At other times they pivot on one foot and make many gyroscopic circles without stopping. They are totally deaf, this condition being probably due to the same morphological or physiological cause as that of the peculiar running movement. The effect of a small fraction of 1% carbon monoxide on the mice is to quiet their movements immediately. Waltzing mice are more sensitive to lower percentages of carbon monoxide than canaries, for waltzing mice exposed to 0.10–0.12% carbon monoxide gave positive indication of carbon monoxide poisoning after 5–10 min, whereas canaries failed to give such indication after 75–131 min.

These small animals are comparatively widely used as carbon monoxide detectors, especially in coal mines. Although Japanese waltzing mice appear to be slightly more sensitive to atmospheres deficient in oxygen and to the presence of carbon monoxide than canaries and the latter are more sensitive than man, the margin of time between serious response in man and observable response in these animals is not wide enough in most instances for either canaries or waltzing mice to be of really practical use for avoiding harmful exposure of man (25).

b. Palladious Chloride Detector

There are many variations of this detector. One of the simplest is an ampoule type of carbon monoxide detector. It was devised primarily for examining the air of manholes and sewers for possible dangerous contamination with carbon monoxide before workmen enter these places. It may also be used for examination of atmospheres that are known to be contaminated with carbon monoxide, such as the air in garages, tunnels, mines, around blast furnaces, gas plants, and even in the home. The NBS carbon monoxide indicating tubes described in Chapter XVIII, Section D are better.

Ampoules

The detector consists of an absorbent-cotton-covered, easily crushed, glass ampoule, which is filled with a palladious chloride solution that changes color when exposed to carbon monoxide and a color chart. The procedure is to crush the ampoule, which in turn wets the absorbent cotton covering with palladium chloride solution. When it is exposed to the air being tested and carbon monoxide is present, it will react with the palladious chloride and change the color of the ampoule from the brownish-yellow stain of the solution to varying degrees of yellowish black to black, depending on the concentration of carbon monoxide.

The chemical reaction involved, as was explained above, is a reduction of the palladious chloride by carbon monoxide to form a finely divided black precipitate of metallic palladium while the carbon monoxide is oxidized to carbon dioxide. The finely divided precipitate of metallic palladium, which in appearance is much like carbon black, is deposited in the cotton fiber. The detector gives semiquantitative indications of carbon monoxide in a concentration range of 2–10 parts per 10,000 parts of air by volume when the temperature of the air is above 10°C, or 50°F. The sensitivity of the detector decreases with low air temperatures and a longer period of exposure than the prescribed 10 min are required to give a satisfactory indication of the amount of carbon monoxide present; 20–30 min are required for temperatures between 50 and 32°F.

It has been shown (26) that gasoline vapor, ethylene, hydrogen, and hydrogen sulfide produced a change in the color of the ampoules similar to that caused by carbon monoxide (6,27). Concentrations of these gases which produced the change, however, were also dangerous due to the hazard of either poisoning or explosion.

Test Papers (28)

Another variation of this method is a device which consists essentially of a sheet of dry paper impregnated with a 2% solution of palladious chloride and a sheet of plain paper held together between two plates of glass. The device is suspended in the suspected atmosphere for a definite time and in the presence of carbon monoxide the sensitized paper uniformly turns gray. Illuminating gas acts in the same manner. Hydrogen sulfide produces a blackish-brown coloration, but only along the edges of the paper. The test can be made roughly quantitative by making the unsensitized paper into a series of panels of colors corresponding to increasing carbon monoxide contents and cutting a circle out of each panel, through which the sensitized paper can be observed, so that the color produced on the sensitized paper can be compared directly with those of the various panels.

Still other variations of this test designed to increase its accuracy are described by Winkler (29).

British Method

The official British (30) method for the detection of carbon monoxide by means of palladious chloride uses the following procedure:

Apparatus. The atmosphere being tested is sampled by means of the apparatus shown in Fig. XVII-1. A 5-liter aspirator A is fitted with a device to control the rate of flow. The air sample is drawn through a test paper clamped in a holder (Fig. II-13), the holder being screwed into the stopper of the aspirator. A glass extension tube D fits into the lower part of the stopper and extends almost to the bottom of the aspirator; its lower end must always be below the surface of the water. In this way a constant head of water is maintained and the flow from the aspirator remains constant. The depth from the lower end X of the glass tube to the end of the outlet tube Y should be at least 18 in. A drying tube, approximately 6 in. × 1-in. bore, filled with activated charcoal, 12–18 mesh, fits by means of a rubber stopper into the inlet of the paper holder, so that its lower end is as far as possible above the test paper. Small pieces of fine wire gauze keep the charcoal in position, and the tube is closed at the top by a bored rubber stopper. Care must be taken to free the drying tube and activated charcoal from charcoal fines. The charcoal must be renewed after about 250 tests.

Preparation of Test Papers. Prepare the palladium chloride solution as follows: Boil 0.1 g of pure palladious chloride for a few minutes in 20 ml of water.   Filter the mixture, cool the filtrate, and make up to exactly 20 ml with water.   Add 20 ml of acetone and stir the mixture.   Keep the solution in well-stoppered hard-glass bottles that have been thoroughly washed, first with acid and then with water.

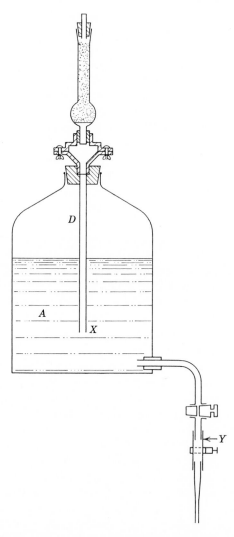

Fig. XVII-1. Apparatus for the detection of carbon monoxide.

Normally, no deterioration should take place. If, however, at any time the solution becomes cloudy, with the formation of an orange deposit, a fresh reagent solution must be prepared.

Prepare the test papers from Postlip No. 633 extra-thick white filter paper (18 × 24, 60 lb) or equivalent filter paper, cut into strips 2 in. wide. Immerse the strips in the palladious chloride reagent solution for 1 min. Allow to drain for a few seconds and then remove the superfluous liquid by pressing *very lightly* between filter paper. Cut off 1 in. at the top and bottom of each strip and cut the remainder into 3-in. lengths. The papers must be prepared immediately before use.

Procedure.   Fill the aspirator with water and adjust so that it will give a flow of 50 ml/min. This rate need not be exact but should be within the range of 45–55 ml/min. Insert the test paper prepared as directed above into the holder and clamp firmly by tightening the wing nuts.

To obtain an approximate estimate of the carbon monoxide concentration, open the tap of the aspirator and start a stop watch. After the first 2 min stop the flow and examine the test paper. If only a slight stain is obtained, continue the test, examining the test paper every 5 min, until a stain is obtained slightly deeper than the first standard stain but lighter than the second standard stain.   The total sampling time from the beginning of the test is noted and the corresponding concentration is obtained from a chart accompanying the standard stains.

5. Determination

The sampling methods detailed in Chapter II are, in general, suitable for sampling atmospheres for the estimation of carbon monoxide. Particular attention is called to the continuous sampling device of Goldman and Mathis (31) described in Chapter II for this purpose.

a. Iodine Pentoxide Method

The iodine pentoxide method (32–35) depends on the release of iodine from iodine pentoxide by the reducing action of carbon monoxide. It is generally used as a reference method, for it is accurate for all concentrations of carbon monoxide. It is necessary, however, to take special precautions for concentrations above 0.3% (36).

The gas sample is first passed through a U-tube containing small pieces of potash, then over pumice impregnated with sulfuric acid, and finally through a U-tube containing iodine pentoxide immersed in an oil bath at 150°C. An absorption tube containing 10 ml of sodium hydroxide solution is used for absorbing the carbon dioxide formed and the iodine liberated.

In the American Gas Association Laboratories iodine pentoxide method (37) the concentration of carbon monoxide in a flue gas is determined by passing a known volume of the flue gas sample through a chromic acid wash trap which removes interfering components, such as unsaturated hydrocarbons, aldehydes, and some water vapor; acid spray and some carbon dioxide are removed by potassium hydroxide pellets at the inlet of a Y-tube and the gas being tested is passed through a phosphorus pentoxide trap for the removal of traces of water vapor; the dry gas is passed through a U-tube containing iodine pentoxide, where, if carbon monoxide is present, free iodine is liberated by the following reaction:

$$5CO + I_2O_5 \rightarrow 5CO_2 + I_2$$

The iodine liberated in the reaction is absorbed in a potassium iodide solution in a Gomberg trap. The apparatus is purged with water-pumped nitrogen after which the solution containing the iodine is transferred to another vessel and titrated with standard sodium thiosulfate solution. The amount of iodine formed is calculated as carbon monoxide. In flue gas analysis this may be reported on an air-free basis.

Apparatus. The AGA iodine pentoxide apparatus is designed somewhat differently but in general follows the equipment described in the literature such as the setup of Teague (38). The major improvement in the design of the AGA units is the use of $\mathbb{T}$ glass joints by which the sections of the apparatus are joined together. Another important improvement is the redesign of some of the sections for greater strength and thus for greater freedom from breakage and by use of heat resistant glass. A third change is in the design of the chromic acid wash trap permitting the chromic acid to be changed more readily. The apparatus is shown in Fig. XVII-2.

Sample Bottle. The sample to be analyzed can be drawn into a known-volume sample container *1* by water displacement in the sheet metal reservoir *2*. The sample bottle should have a volume of

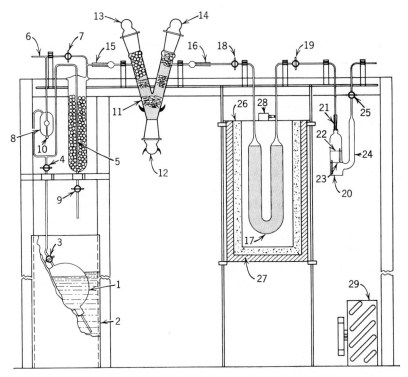

Fig. XVII-2. Diagrammatic sketch of AGA iodine pentoxide apparatus.

approximately 500 ml but the exact volume must be accurately determined before use for tests.   An inverted separatory funnel, the volume of which has been accurately measured, serves adequately as the known-volume container.   The stopcock *3* on the sample bottle is attached to the iodine pentoxide apparatus gas sample inlet cock *4* by means of a short piece of rubber hose.

Chromic Acid Wash Tower.   The chromic acid wash trap consists of the gas sample inlet stopcock *4* through which the sample is drawn into the perforated tube *5* in the wash tower by vacuum at the outlet of the iodine pentoxide apparatus, the nitrogen inlet *6*, and a stopcock *7* which permits the nitrogen to pass through the mercury trap *8* and into the tower through the perforated tube *5*. The mercury trap serves to prevent the flow of the sample from bypassing the chromic acid tower and to collect any overflow of chromic acid if the pressure is reversed.   Stopcock *7* is kept in the closed position while the iodine pentoxide apparatus is being operated and is opened when the apparatus is not in operation to balance the pressure on both sides of the chromic acid tower. The tower is filled partially with small glass rings to break up the bubbles of gas issuing from the perforated tube *5*.

This unit is prepared for use by filling the chromic acid tower with chromic acid to a level approximately 1.5 in. below the top of the tower by means of a separatory funnel used as a leveling bottle attached to stopcock *9* at the bottom of the tower. Spent chromic acid may be drained by gravity through stopcock *9*. A few drops of mercury sufficient to cover the top of the tube in the trap at *10* can be drawn by vacuum through the nitrogen inlet.

Drying Tube. The Y-tube *11* contains alternate layers of phosphorus pentoxide and glass wool with a layer of potassium hydroxide pellets at the inlet side of the Y. The bottom glass ℥ 24/40 plug *12* is dipped into hot paraffin and sealed in place. Additional sealing may be insured by use of springs or rubber bands attached to the main body of the Y-tube. A glass wool pack is shoved through one of the upright legs of the Y, filling the bottom leg. A layer of approximately 1–1.5 in. of phosphorus pentoxide is then poured into each of the two upper legs, followed by a small amount of glass wool to separate it from the second layer of phosphorus pentoxide, etc. The layer of potassium hydroxide pellets is added last at the inlet side. The ℥ 24/40 plugs *13* and *14* are then sealed into place with paraffin.

Because the phosphorus pentoxide is very hydroscopic, speed in preparing the tube is essential. One leg of the Y-tube should be filled at a time. The tube and the bottle containing the desiccant should be kept covered as much as possible. Potassium hydroxide pellets in addition to being hydroscopic also absorb carbon dioxide. The alkali should therefore be handled carefully and as quickly as possible to avoid unnecessary contamination.

To clean the Y-tube remove it from the train, remove the glass plugs *12*, *13*, and *14*, and push out the contents of each leg into a convenient vessel. The Y-tube can then be washed and dried thoroughly before it is refilled.

Iodine Pentoxide Tube. The U-tube *17* for the iodine pentoxide should be made by a glass blower. The contents consist of alternate

0.5-in. layers of iodine pentoxide and glass wool. Iodic acid anhydride (Merck C.P.) is recommended by the AGA Laboratories.

To prepare the iodine pentoxide tube for gas analysis, it must be thoroughly purged from free iodine. This is accomplished by placing the tube in the train and heating at a temperature of 420°F while drawing nitrogen through at the same rate as for a typical analysis for a period of 2 or 3 days. After this time has elapsed, the temperature is reduced to 302°F and the purging is continued for 2 days. No trace of free iodine should be indicated when starch solution is added to the potassium iodide solution taken from the Gomberg trap as detailed in the procedure for the blank determination. If free iodine is found, the temperature should be increased and the apparatus purged for another day until no iodine is detected as above.

Stopcocks *18* and *19* should be lubricated before the above treatment with a small amount of silicone lubricant. If necessary to lubricate these stopcocks again, they should be lubricated very quickly to avoid exposing the iodine pentoxide to the moisture of the air. The lubrication should be followed by making a blank determination to check for any possible contamination.

Gomberg Trap. The Gomberg trap or bulb is a multicompartment glass vessel that should be made by a glass blower. It is made ready for use by pouring into the female tapered joint *21* a sufficient volume of 10% potassium iodide solution to cover each plate *22* and *23* in the Gomberg trap without leaving any excess that may be drawn up into the outlet leg *24* under vacuum. This is approximately 5 ml. To transfer this solution from the Gomberg bulb, air is blown through the glass tube *24* while the bulb is inclined to the left to drain the bottom segment first, inclined to the right to drain the center section, and then inverted to drain the top segment by gravity. It is the customary practice to rinse the trap once with approximately 10 ml of water before refilling it with potassium iodide solution for a subsequent determination, adding the rinse water to the solution that was transferred.

Before attaching the Gomberg trap to the iodine pentoxide train, the female taper glass joint *21* is wiped with a tapered filter paper plug to prevent any free iodine from being adsorbed on the male end of the taper glass joint where it may escape analysis. It is essential not to lubricate this joint with stopcock grease. The Gomberg trap is attached to stopcock *25* by means of a smaller rubber tube. The stopcock is connected in turn to the vacuum pump.

Framework. The framework of the iodine pentoxide apparatus is preferably made of 1-in. stainless-steel angle iron and is 31 in. wide × 24 in. high. The glass tubing supports are of ⅜-in. wide brass bars ⅛-in. thick chromium plated, slotted to permit vertical position adjustment.

Iodine Pentoxide Heater. The electric resistance furnace *26* enclosing the iodine pentoxide tube is made of stainless steel and contains a Hoskins muffle furnace refractory *27* (5985A-FD202) around which is wrapped 66 ft of coiled 20-gauge Hoskins Chromel A resistance wire, having a resistance of 42 Ω. It is insulated from the box with asbestos fiber insulation. The temperature is controlled with a Cenco DeKhotinsky single pole, single throw thermoregulator *28* (type G24675) wired in series with the heating element. A 5-in. adjustable rheostat *29*, 50 Ω and 2.5 A, is wired in series to control the voltage across the heating element. In preheating the furnace, the rheostat is turned wide open for rapid heating and after the required temperature is attained, the rheostat is turned down so that the fluctuation controlled by the thermostat is at a minimum.

Preliminary Adjustment. Before the iodine pentoxide apparatus can be used, the furnace must be set at a temperature above the sublimation temperature of iodine. It is the practice of the AGA Laboratories to have the heater turned on approximately 1–1½ hr before the apparatus is actually used. The temperature of approximately 302°F is maintained automatically by means of the rheostat and thermostat.

Nitrogen Purge. Turn on the vacuum pump. Check the water level in the nitrogen pressure relief device, adding water, and set it to provide a pressure of approximately 1 in. Remove any excess water that may be accumulated in water trap. Turn on the nitrogen cylinder two-stage regulator valve, adjusting it so that provision is made for a slight excess of nitrogen to escape from the relief device.

Reagents. *Iodine Pentoxide.* As mentioned, the AGA Laboratories recommend the use of iodic acid anhydride (Merck C.P.) for their variation of the iodine pentoxide method. One lb will be adequate for three U-tubes.

Chromic Acid. Prepare this reagent by saturating concentrated sulfuric acid with potassium dichromate. Dissolve 70 g of finely ground potassium dichromate in 1 liter of concentrated sulfuric acid while heating cautiously in a hood. Cool and decant. Permit this solution to stand for 2 weeks and then decant the supernatant reagent again. The length of time this reagent can serve depends upon the number of samples analyzed.

Potassium Iodide Solution. AGA Laboratories recommends that this solution be prepared freshly at least once every day. Prepare a solution containing 10 wt % potassium iodide and 90 wt % water. Boil and cool the water before weighing. Keep the reagent in a dark-colored bottle. Test the reagent for the presence of free iodine by use of starch and reject any solution that gives a positive test.

Starch Indicator Solution. AGA Laboratories prefer powdered potato starch. Prepare this solution daily. Suspend 2 or 3 g of starch in a few milliliters of water and after the paste is made, add it to 200 ml of water brought just to the boiling point. Cool the prepared starch solution to room temperature.

Potassium Dichromate Solution (0.001N). Grind about 0.5 g of reagent grade potassium dichromate to a powder. Spread it into a thin layer on a watch glass and dry it in an oven at 120–150°C for 2–4 hr. Cool in a desiccator. Weigh out 0.4904 g and transfer to a 1-liter volumetric flask quantitatively. Add water, shake to dissolve, make to volume with water, stopper, and mix thoroughly.

If the amount of potassium dichromate transferred is determined by the difference of two weighings, calculate the normality from the following equation

$$N \ K_2Cr_2O_7 = \text{wt } K_2Cr_2O_7/49.04$$

where 49.04 is the equivalent weight of potassium dichromate.

This is a 0.01N solution of potassium dichromate. To prepare the 0.001N solution, transfer 10 ml of the 0.01N solution with the aid of a volumetric pipet to a 100-ml volumetric flask. Dilute to the mark with water, stopper, and mix thoroughly to obtain the 0.001N solution.

Iodine Solution (0.001N). Exercise care in the preparation of this reagent because iodine is volatile. Place about 2 g of potassium iodide and 1 ml. of water into a weighing bottle and weigh. Add approximately 0.127 g of iodine to the concentrated potassium iodide solution and reweigh. The difference in weight is the weight of the iodine. Stopper the weighing bottle, shake to make certain that all of the iodine is dissolved, and transfer quantitatively to a 1-liter volumetric flask. Wash the weighing bottle thoroughly, adding the washings to the volumetric flask. Make to volume with water, stopper, and mix thoroughly.

Compute the normality from the equation

$$N \; I_2 = \text{wt } I_2 / 126.9$$

where 126.9 is the equivalent weight of iodine. If exactly 0.1269 g of iodine was weighed out and transferred, the solution is 0.001N.

Sodium Thiosulfate Solution (0.001N). Clean a 1-liter glass-stoppered bottle with cleaning solution and rinse thoroughly. Boil 1 liter of water and, while still hot, transfer to the cleaned bottle, stopper, and allow to cool. Weigh out 24.8 g of reagent grade sodium thiosulfate and 2–3 g of borax crystals. Add each of these to the cooled water and shake the bottle until the salts are dissolved. This is an approximately 0.1N solution. Store this solution for 4–6 weeks in order to permit it to come to equilibrium. Transfer 10 ml of the equilibrated solution to a 1-liter volumetric flask and dilute to the mark with water. Stopper and mix thoroughly. Standardize this solution as detailed below at least once a week or as often as experience indicates.

Sodium thiosulfate solutions are not stable for they are affected by oxygen, carbon dioxide, and microorganisms. For this reason it is essential to use boiled water in its preparation and to include a preservative. AGA recommends borax. Other preservatives that have been suggested are sodium furoate and sodium carbonate. Evidence of decomposition is the appearance of a cloudy solution attributable to the precipitation of colloidal sulfur.

Standardization with Potassium Dichromate. Dissolve 0.5 g of potassium iodide (iodate free) and 1 g of sodium bicarbonate in 30 ml of cooled freshly boiled water in a 125-ml glass-stoppered erlenmeyer flask. Then add concentrated hydrochloric acid slowly, swirling the flask, until no more carbon dioxide is generated and add about 1 ml more of acid.

Add 20 ml of 0.001N potassium dichromate solution with the aid of a volumetric pipet and swirl the mixture very gently. Wash the sides of the flask with a few milliliters of water and allow this rinse to form a layer above the acid dichromate solution without mixing. Stopper the flask and allow to stand for about 10 min.

Mix thoroughly by swirling, remove the stopper, and run in the $0.001N$ sodium thiosulfate solution to be standardized from a volumetric buret until the solution becomes light yellow. Add a few drops of starch indicator solution and continue the titration until the bright blue color has disappeared and only the pale green color of the chromic chloride remains. Add the last few drops very cautiously; stopper the flask, shake, remove the stopper, and wash down the sides with a little water.

Compute the exact normality of the sodium thiosulfate solution by use of the following equation:

$$N \ Na_2S_2O_3 = (ml \ K_2Cr_2O_7 \times N \ K_2Cr_2O_7)/ml \ Na_2S_2O_3$$

Perform the titration in duplicate; such duplicate determinations should agree within a reading of 0.002 ml.

It is well to remember that errors may be introduced by: (1) oxidation of the iodide ion by air and ozone; (2) the incomplete reduction of the dichromate ion by iodide ion if the acid concentration is not sufficiently great; (3) the loss of iodine vapor by too vigorous stirring of the reaction mixture while the flask is not stoppered; (4) the addition of starch too soon; and (5) the presence of iodate in the potassium iodide. The first four causes of error can be controlled by proper manipulative technique. The error attributable to iodate must be avoided by using iodate-free iodide. To test for iodate, dissolve 0.5 g of potassium iodide in 10 ml of water, add 1 ml of $6N$ sulfuric acid and 2 ml of starch indicator solution. Immediate appearance of a blue color indicates the presence of iodate. A blue color formed on standing may be disregarded for this may be due to air oxidation.

Standardization with Iodine. An alternative method of standardizing sodium thiosulfate solution and the method preferred by the AGA Laboratories is the one employing standard iodine solution.

Place 10 ml of standard $0.001N$ iodine solution in a 125-ml erlenmeyer flask with the aid of a volumetric pipet. Titrate with the $0.001N$ sodium thiosulfate solution to be standardized until the yellow color of the iodine solution is very faint. Add a few drops of starch indicator solution, mix by swirling, and continue the titration adding the sodium thiosulfate solution drop by drop until the blue color is discharged. Compute the normality of the sodium thiosulfate solution in the manner indicated above.

Blank Determination. Close stopcocks *25* and *19*. Detach the Gomberg trap from the apparatus, rinse with water, and fill with 5 ml of fresh 10% potassium iodide solution. Dry tapered joint *21* with a tapered plug of filter paper and reconnect the bulb to the apparatus.

Open stopcocks *25* and *19* and permit nitrogen to purge the iodine pentoxide apparatus for 30 min. Close stopcocks *25* and *19*. Remove the Gomberg bulb. Drain the potassium iodide solution into a small erlenmeyer flask in the manner detailed. Rinse the trap twice with about 10 ml of water and add the rinsings to the erlenmeyer flask. Titrate the mixture with standard sodium thiosulfate solution. The amount of free iodine found is considered the blank for the apparatus and should be subtracted from subsequent determinations in calculating the carbon monoxide concentrations in the test samples.

In AGA Laboratories practice, when more than 1 ml of standard sodium thiosulfate solution is used for the blank, the apparatus should be checked. The chromic acid should be brown in color not green. The Y-tube of phosphorus pentoxide should appear dry. If the condition of these sections of the apparatus is satisfactory, the source of nitrogen should be checked, and finally it should be determined whether or not the iodine pentoxide tube should be replaced.

After the blank determination, refill the Gomberg trap with potassium iodide solution and attach it to the apparatus which is now ready for the sample determination.

Procedure. Transfer the sample of flue gas or other sample such as incinerator gas to the known-volume container from the aspirator bottle or other original sampling vessel, and allow it to stand until it reaches the temperature of the water in the reservoir *2*. Connect the sample bottle to the sample inlet stopcock *4*.

Open stopcocks *25* and *19* and open stopcocks *3* and *4*, permitting the gas sample to pass through the chromic acid tower. The sample of gas in the sample bottle is displaced by the water in the reservoir. This takes approximately 7–10 min. Raise the water level to stopcock *4* by pinching off the nitrogen supply tubing ahead of the glass tubing *6*. Turn off stopcocks *3* and *4* and permit the nitrogen to pass through the mercury trap *8* and through the rest of the system as a purge for approximately 20–23 min, making a total of 30 min.   At the end of this period, turn off stopcocks *25* and *19*, disconnect the Gomberg trap, transfer its contents as detailed above to a titration vessel, and titrate the free iodine formed with standard thiosulfate solution.   Refill the Gomberg bulb with another 5-ml portion of potassium iodide solution, connect it again to the apparatus, and proceed with the next sample.

It is usual to pass the entire volume of the gas sample through the iodine pentoxide apparatus except when it is thought that the carbon monoxide concentration exceeds 0.1 vol %.   In such an instance, only a small portion of the sample may be passed through the apparatus at a time.   This practice will avoid the release of excessive amounts of free iodine.   If this precaution is not observed, iodine crystals may deposit in the glass capillary tubing leading to the Gomberg trap.   Such deposits would make it impossible to perform a proper analysis and thus impossible to calculate the concentration of the carbon monoxide accurately.   In addition it would make it very difficult to clean the apparatus.   The difference in the volume of gas analyzed from that in the sample container is estimated by measuring the amount of water remaining in the known-volume gas sample container.   When high concentrations of carbon monoxide are found— that is, concentrations greater than 0.1%—it is necessary to run another blank determination to find out if all the free iodine has been purged from the apparatus.

Calculation.   If carbon monoxide is present in the sample being analyzed, then iodine is evolved and titrated in accordance with the following equations:

$$I_2O_5 + 5CO \rightarrow I_2 + 5CO_2$$

and

$$I_2 + 2Na_2S_2O_3 \rightarrow 2NaI + Na_2S_4O_6$$

The equations show that 5 gram-molecular weights of carbon monoxide are equivalent to 1 gram-molecular weight of iodine or to 2 gram-molecular weights of sodium thiosulfate, expressed numerically as

$$140 \text{ g CO} \backsimeq 253.8 \text{ g } I_2 \backsimeq 496.4 \text{ g } Na_2S_2O_3 \cdot 5H_2O$$

Since a normal solution of iodine contains 0.127 g of iodine per milliliter, then the equivalent weight of sodium thiosulfate is 0.248 g and the equivalent weight of carbon monoxide is 0.07 g.

Furthermore, since 1 ml of carbon monoxide at 0°C and 760 mm Hg equals its molecular weight, 28, divided by the standard molecular volume 22,400 ml, that is, 0.00125 mg, then 0.07 g of carbon monoxide has a volume of 56.0 ml at 0°C and 760 mm Hg (dry).

To convert to standard conditions at 60°F and 30 in. Hg, that is, 15.6°C and 760 mm Hg, and to correct for the fact that the sample of carbon monoxide is saturated with water vapor, the combined gas law has to be applied as detailed in Chapter III, Section C-3. Thus

$$V_1(760 - 13.29)/288.6 = (56.0 \times 760)/273$$

in which the number 13.29 is the vapor pressure of water at 15.6°C

$$V_1 = (56.0 \times 760 \times 288.6)/(746.71 \times 273)$$
$$= 60.2 \text{ ml at } 15.6°C \text{ and } 760 \text{ mm Hg (saturated)}$$

Hence, at standard conditions, 1 ml of $1N$ sodium thiosulfate solution containing 0.248 g equals 60.2 ml or 0.07 g of carbon monoxide. Therefore, 60.2 multiplied by the volume of sodium thiosulfate solution used to titrate the iodine liberated in the analysis of a sample multiplied by the normality of the sodium thiosulfate solution is equivalent to the volume of carbon monoxide in the sample analyzed at standard conditions (60°F and 30 in. Hg). This may be expressed on a percentage basis by the following equation:

CO (%) =

[(ml $Na_2S_2O_3$ × thio factor)/(vol of gas sample × CF)] × 100

where milliliters of $Na_2S_2O_3$ is equal to the volume of standard $Na_2S_2O_3$ solution required to titrate the liberated iodine, thio factor is the product of 60.2 and the normality of the standardized $Na_2S_2O_3$ solution, and CF is the pressure–temperature correction for converting the volume of sample to standard conditions.

b. Hopcalite Method

Hopcalite is a general name for catalysts of a certain group that are capable of converting carbon monoxide to carbon dioxide at ordinary temperatures while leaving hydrogen unaffected (39,40). Hopcalite I was the name used to designate the mixture:

Compound	%
Manganese dioxide, MnO_2	50
Cupric oxide, CuO	30
Cobaltic oxide, Co_2O_3	15
Silver oxide, Ag_2O	5

The physical characteristics of the catalyst have a great deal to do with its efficiency.

A cheaper and very likely more widely used type of Hopcalite catalyst is composed of manganese dioxide, 60%, and cupric oxide, 40% (8–14-mesh granules) (41).

This catalyst is used in two ways as may be noted from the equation:

$$2CO + O_2 \rightarrow 2CO_2 + (67,960 \text{ gram-calories per gram-molecule of CO})$$

In other words, either the heat produced in the reaction may be measured by some electrical device or the carbon dioxide produced may be estimated by one of the methods detailed in a subsequent section.

Automatic Devices.   A number of continuous carbon monoxide recorders for small concentrations in air have been described (15,42–44). As mentioned previously, the major automatic continuous carbon monoxide recorders are monodispersive infrared recording spectrometers. For many years some of the following types were widely used and are still in use. In some devices the oxidation of the carbon monoxide as it comes in contact with the granular Hopcalite catalyst results in a temperature rise in the air stream within the catalyst cell, which is transmitted to a recording potentiometer through a series of differential thermocouples. The cell potential is directly proportional to the carbon monoxide concentration in the absence of readily oxidizable or inhibiting impurities that affect the catalyst.

To remove moisture and other condensable components the air sample is passed through a train of concentrated sulfuric acid, soda lime and charcoal, and calcium chloride, before passing through the Hopcalite catalyst. In practice the use of sulfuric acid as an air drier is objectionable because of its corrosive nature and the difficulties of frequent renewal and disposal. Frevert and Francis (44) developed a modified form of analyzer, in which the acid train, whose chief function is the removal of moisture, is replaced by duplicate adsorbers using either silica gel or activated alumina. Alumina of 1.2–2.4-mm size is probably adequate.

One variation of this method is the portable MSA carbon monoxide indicator. This device (45) comes in several models. In one of these a small pump draws the sample continuously into the instrument. The sample first passes through a flowmeter, consisting of an orifice and a differential pressure gauge. The latter is used to maintain a constant flow by having a constant differential on the flowmeter through adjustment of a volume control valve. The sample passes through a dehydrating canister, which removes any moisture, and from the canister it enters the cell containing the Hopcalite, after which it passes out of the exhaust valve of the pump. In the Hopcalite cell any carbon monoxide present in the air stream is oxidized to carbon dioxide. The heat liberated by this reaction is directly proportional to the amount of carbon monoxide present and is measured by a series of thermocouples in series with the indicating meter. The meter is calibrated to read directly in percentage of carbon monoxide and has a scale range of 0–0.15% carbon monoxide graduated in hundredths of a per cent. It can be read directly to 0.005% and estimated to 0.001%, or 10 ppm. The sensitivity of this carbon monoxide indicator is reduced when operated in temperatures below freezing (Fig. XVII-3).

The small amount of Hopcalite in the cell should be renewed after

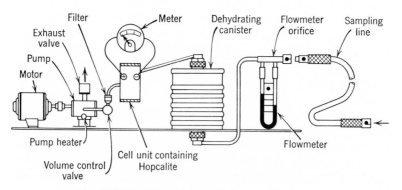

Fig. XVII-3. Hopcalite carbon monoxide indicator.

8 hr of actual service.   The canister for removing moisture should be replaced after 20 hr of service.

In another model, a hand-operated pump, analogous to that described for the midget impinger is used to draw the air sample through the Hopcalite.

Such indicators must be set to zero by passing carbon monoxide-free air through them.   The motor-driven device requires 15–30 min for adjustment, while the hand-driven model is equilibrated for 2 min before adjusting the meter needle.   To overcome this difficulty and the errors involved attributable to deflections caused by change in temperature when the instrument is moved or because of needle drift, Setterlind (46) mounted an additional canister of the universal type plus a three-way stopcock on the device.   The additional canister removes carbon monoxide by means of the Hopcalite it contains, providing a carbon monoxide-free air stream.

The air inlet is connected to the common branch of the stopcock, and the top of the canister to one of the others by means of tubing.

In use the instrument is taken directly to the point of testing, the flap on the bottom of the universal canister is opened, the valve is turned to let the air pass through the canister, the motor is started, and the air flow is adjusted.   After the device has warmed up, the needle is adjusted to zero and the amount of drifting observed. If the drift does not exceed 1 division in 3 min, the instrument is ready to use.   The needle is then adjusted accurately to zero and the stopcock is turned to a position letting the air directly into the indicator.   If carbon monoxide is present, the indicator will start registering within 10–30 sec, depending upon whether or not an extension hose is being employed.   A maximum should be reached in about 1 min and the reading recorded.   The valve may now be moved to the purge position, the indicator taken to the next test position, and the operation repeated.

If the response to carbon monoxide is sluggish, after the instrument has been serviced, the lag is probably attributable to dirt accumulating in the orifice of the flowmeter.   Periodic cleaning of the orifice and the three-way stopcock is essential.

c. Infrared Monitor

The main type of instrument used for the monitoring of carbon monoxide in the concentrations of the order or magnitude found in

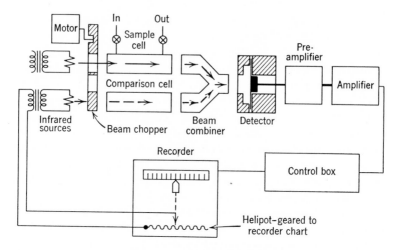

Fig. XVII-4. Basic infrared analyzer system MSA Lira.   (Courtesy Mine Safety
Appliances Co., Pittsburgh, Pa.)

outside air is a pressurized, nondispersive, infrared spectrometer
equipped with a 40-in. cell.   The instrument has been described in
detail by Waters and Hartz (47).   An outline of the system is shown
in Fig. XVII-4.

Jacobs, Braverman, and Hochheiser (48) adapted the Mine Safety
Appliances Company Lira infrared analyzer for the determination of
carbon monoxide in the range of 0–20 ppm.   Initially the instrument was run with a compressor at 10 atm but subsequently this
was reduced to 2 atm without decrease in sensitivity.

The Mine Safety Appliances Company Lira infrared analyzer is
a selective, nondispersion-type, infrared analyzer comprising a
source of radiation, a beam chopper, sample and comparison cells,
a beam combiner, a detector, preamplifier, amplifier, control box,
and recorder.

Two equivalent infrared sources equipped with calcium fluoride
windows are activated and the beam chopper, consisting of a re-
ciprocating metal slide, alternately blocks the rays.   One ray travels
through the comparison cell while the other travels through the
sample cell, both of which are equipped with quartz windows.   The
emergent rays go into the beam combiner which contains a filter
gas of 50% carbon dioxide and 50% isobutane.   The emergent rays

impinge on the detector cell which contains a detector gas of 4% carbon monoxide in argon and a membrane. The detector gas absorbs the radiation and its temperature and pressure increase. The expansion of the detector gas causes the membrane of the condenser of a microphone to move. This movement when converted and amplified produces an output signal. The amplifier is actuated only by variations in the ray intensity. When the beams are equal, the absorption is equal and the amplifier output is zero.

When the air to be analyzed is passed through the sample cell, it absorbs radiation. The amount of radiation reaching the detector is reduced. The beams become unequal and the detector gas will flicker, causing expansions and contractions. These cause the membrane to move and this movement varies the condenser microphone capacity generating an electric signal which is proportional to the difference in the radiation of the beams. The electrical signal is amplified by an ac amplifier and is then conducted to a synchronous rectifier which generates a dc signal, the polarity of which is dependent upon which beam is stronger. An increase in the sample absorption causes the electronic recorder to drive upscale. This causes a reduction in the voltage applied to the comparison beam radiation source. The reduction in the radiation causes the beams to be balanced again. The position of the recorder is thus a measure of the absorption of the sample and consequently is a measure of its concentration.

Prepurified nitrogen gas is used to set the zero and a known concentration of carbon monoxide in nitrogen gas can be used to set the span of the instrument. Jacobs, Braverman, and Hochheiser calibrated the instrument so that the relative humidity was approximately 100% all the time by having the incoming air stream pass through a trap containing water. By setting the zero at this relative humidity, the error attributable to water vapor in the incoming air stream was very nearly eliminated.

d. Palladious Chloride Method

By means of the following method the amount of carbon monoxide in air can be ascertained quantitatively from the reduced palladious chloride (49). A definite volume of palladious chloride solution is exposed to the air containing carbon monoxide and after the reaction is complete, the excess chloride is separated from the metallic palladium by filtration and this excess palladious chloride is estimated colorimetrically. The reactions that occur are probably the following (50):

$$PdCl_2 + CO \rightarrow Pd + COCl_2$$
$$COCl_2 + H_2O \rightarrow CO_2 + 2HCl$$

The addition of potassium iodide, in excess of that required to precipitate the palladious chloride as palladious iodide, dissolves the latter salt to yield a red solution, which, in the presence of a protective colloid such as gum ghatti or gum arabic, remains perfectly clear for at least 24 hr.

Reagents. *Gum Ghatti Solution.* Add 5 g of gum ghatti to 500 ml of water and allow to stand for 24–48 hr with occasional shaking. After filtration, a clear solution results. It becomes slightly turbid on standing and must be refiltered from time to time.

Palladious Chloride Solution. Dry 500 mg of palladious chloride at 100°C for 1 hr. Place the dried salt in a beaker and cover with 150 ml of water, add 2.5 ml of concentrated hydrochloric acid, and heat the mixture until complete solution of the palladium chloride results. After cooling, transfer this solution to a 500-ml volumetric flask and make up to volume. Analyze the resulting solution by the standard gravimetric method, which consists of the precipitation of palladium in acid solution as the salt of dimethylglyoxime (51,52) to obtain the palladious chloride content. If large volumes of this solution are made, it is advisable to store it in a number of well-stoppered, small bottles rather than in one large bottle, to minimize the deterioration due to exposure to air and dust when aliquots are removed for use.

Apparatus. The apparatus (Fig. XVII-5) required for this determination consists of a 500-ml round-bottomed, short-necked Pyrex flask, *A*, fitted through a one-hole rubber stopper with a two-way stopcock, *B*. The volume of the flask with the stopcock in position must be determined, and for convenience in calculation it is desirable that any flasks used be of approximately the same volume, around 500 ml. One of the upper outlets of the stopcock is fitted with a small reservoir, which has a capacity of approximately 7 ml, *C*. The second upper outlet of the stopcock is a tube extending upward for 2–3 cm and is then bent at right angles away from the reservoir for another 2–3 cm, *D*. The lower outlet of the stopcock is cut off at approximately 4.5

cm and protrudes through the lower surface of the stopper far enough, about 0.5–1.0 cm to ensure the passage of the palladium chloride solution into the flask without contact with the stopper.   The inside diameter of the tube should be less than 1.5 mm.

Attach the flask to a vacuum pump connected with a manometer, evacuate to less than 1 mm of pressure, and close the stopcock.

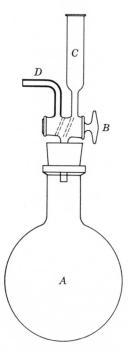

Fig. XVII-5. Apparatus for the determination of carbon monoxide by palladious chloride.

There should be no appreciable change in the pressure within the flask at the end of 24 hr, provided the stopcock is properly ground and greased and all rubber connections are tightly fitted.   Stopcocks that do not meet these requirements should not be used.   Lubricants which contain ingredients that react with palladium chloride must not be used (53).   Flasks prepared as described may be used to obtain the samples by opening the stopcocks of evacuated flasks and then closing the stopcocks again after equilibrium has been established.   Other vacuum sampling devices of known volume may also be used.

Procedure.   Connect the side tube of a flask containing the sample to be analyzed to the side tube of another evacuated flask of approximately equal volume by means of pressure tubing.   Turn the stopcocks of both flasks so that the contents of the flasks are brought into equilibrium.   Place 3 ml of the palladious chloride solution and 0.2 ml of 10% aluminum sulfate solution into the reservoir and transfer quantitatively to the flask by means of three 1-ml washings of water.   Take care at all times to prevent the access of air to the flask.   Shake the flask at intervals for the next 2 hr, particularly during the period when the major part of the metallic palladium is forming, to prevent the formation of a layer of metallic palladium on the surface of the liquid which will prevent the free access of the carbon monoxide to the palladium chloride.   The presence of aluminum sulfate facilitates the flocculation of the colloidal palladium. After the period of shaking, allow the flask to stand overnight, or for at least 4 hr.

Separate the excess of palladium chloride quantitatively from the metallic palladium by filtration through quantitative filter paper into a 50-ml volumetric flask.   The volume of liquid in the 50-ml flask, after the apparatus and the filter paper have been thoroughly washed, should be 25–30 ml.   The filtrate should be perfectly clear.   Add 2 ml of gum ghatti solution and mix.   Add 5 ml of freshly prepared 15% potassium iodide solution and swirl.   Since it has been found that small amounts of palladium chloride are adsorbed by the filter paper, remove these last traces by washing the filter twice with 2-ml portions of 15% potassium iodide solution and once with a 1-ml portion. Each washing with potassium iodide solution is followed by small volumes of water.   Filter these washings directly into the colored solution already in the volumetric flask and make to volume with water.   Add a trace of caprylic alcohol to the flask to minimize the foaming attributable to the gum ghatti solution.

Prepare the standard for the colorimetric comparison by the addition of 2 ml of the palladious chloride solution, 25 ml of water, 2 ml of gum ghatti solution, and 10 ml of 15% freshly prepared potassium iodide solution to a 50-ml volumetric flask.   Add the potassium iodide solution while swirling and make up to volume.   The color produced by the addition of potassium iodide reaches maximum intensity in a few minutes and remains constant for at least 24 hr.   The standard color is set at 20 mm when matched in a colorimeter.

Sample Calculation.   Assume the volume of the sampling flask and the flask with which it is to be equilibrated is 530 ml.   The sample of air is taken at 23°C and 744 mm Hg.   From the colorimetric determination of the excess palladious chloride it is calculated that 1.582 mg of palladious chloride had been reduced by carbon monoxide. This reduction is due to the carbon monoxide in 265 ml of air, since the flasks to which the palladious chloride solution was added were at a pressure of half that at which the sample was taken, approximately 0.5 atm.   One mg of palladious chloride is reduced by 0.1261 ml of carbon monoxide at 0°C and 760 mm Hg.   Therefore

$$1.582 \times 0.1261 \times \frac{760}{744} \times \frac{296}{273} + \frac{10,000}{265}$$

$$= 8.34 \text{ parts of carbon monoxide per 10,000 parts of air}$$

In general the factors $(0.1261 \times 760 \times 10,000)/273$ will appear in all calculations.   They are equivalent to the factor 3510.4.   Hence, the simplified equation for all calculations is

$$3510.4 \times (T/PV) \times \text{mg PdCl}_2 \text{ reduced}$$

$$= \text{parts of CO per 10,000 parts air}$$

where T is the absolute temperature at which the sample was taken, P is the barometric pressure in millimeters at which the sample was taken, and V is the volume of air taken for analysis.   In the above example the latter is 265 ml.

Because there is a loss of palladious chloride, which is greater in the presence of larger amounts of metallic palladium, Christman and co-workers (49) recommend the following corrections in order to avoid high results for carbon monoxide.

PdCl₂ reduced, mg	Subtract from calculated CO values
0.5	0.19
1.0	0.28
1.5	0.33
2.0	0.38

If the air under examination contains unsaturated hydrocarbons or hydrogen sulfide in amounts which would yield high results for carbon monoxide, these interfering substances may be effectively removed by successive passage of the gas through a scrubber solution of bromine water and a 33% potassium hydroxide solution. The bromine solution is prepared by adding one volume of water to two volumes of saturated bromine water. To every 100 ml of this mixture, add 5 g of potassium bromide. Sintered-glass aeration tubes are to be preferred to insure efficient washing.

Prior to taking a sample for analysis, the gas under examination must be forced through the scrubber solutions until the gas above these solutions has been replaced. The gas is then drawn through the scrubber solutions into the analysis flask at a slow rate to ensure complete absorption of the interfering substances. The rate of passage must be slow to permit the complete removal of bromine vapor by the alkali. After the air has stopped bubbling through the absorbent solutions, an aspirator bulb is attached and air is forced through the solutions and into the analysis flask until a slight positive pressure within the flask is obtained. The flask is then disconnected from the scrubber system and the stopcock opened momentarily to allow the flask to come to atmospheric pressure.

Where a pump is not available that will evacuate the flasks to 1 mm Hg, sampling may be performed by the vacuum bottle method, as described in Chapter II. If interferences are not present, sampling by liquid displacement may also be made.

This quantitative method is useful as a laboratory method but cannot be used to detect carbon monoxide in the field.

e. Phosphomolybdate Method

In this method (54) a measured volume of air sample is brought into contact with an acid solution containing palladium chloride, phosphomolybdic acid, and acetone. The sample is equilibrated with the solution by rotation in a bath at 60°C, during which operation reactions take place that result eventually in the production of molybdenum blue by reduction of the phosphomolybdic acid. The intensity of the molybdenum blue produced is proportional to the concentration of carbon monoxide in the air sample and may be expressed in terms of carbon monoxide by a colorimetric comparison with standards representing known concentrations of carbon monoxide. The color comparisons may be made conveniently with a photoelectric colorimeter.

The method is sensitive to approximately 0.001 vol % carbon monoxide and the range is 0–0.06%. The accuracy of the method decreases with increasing concentration of carbon monoxide: at 0.06% the accuracy is about ±0.005% carbon monoxide. Concentrations somewhat higher than 0.06% may also be determined but with decrease of accuracy. The range may be extended without significant sacrifice in accuracy by dilution of the original air sample with known proportions of carbon monoxide-free air.

As the method is based upon a reduction reaction, it is not specific for carbon monoxide and other gases that exert a reducing effect will interfere with the determination of carbon monoxide. Therefore, the method is applied most satisfactorily to samples known not to contain interfering gases, or to samples from which interfering gases may be removed before the determination of carbon monoxide. The effects on the method of gases other than carbon monoxide are discussed below.

Reagents. *Palladium Chloride Solution.* Weigh 0.5 g of chemically pure palladious chloride in a beaker. Add 2 ml of concentrated hydrochloric acid and approximately 100 ml of water. Cover the beaker with a watchglass and heat until the salt is dissolved. Transfer the solution to a 250-ml volumetric flask, add 3.5 ml of concentrated hydrochloric acid, and, after cooling, dilute with water to the indicated flask volume.

Phosphomolybdic Acid Solution. Dissolve 5 g of chemically pure phosphomolybdic acid, $20MoO_3 \cdot 2H_3PO_4 \cdot 48H_2O$, in water and dilute to 100 ml.

Acetone. Use reagent grade acetone. Considerable variation may be observed in the suitability of different lots of acetone obtained from different manufacturers, although lots may meet the specifications of the American Chemical Society for reagent grade material. Some lots of acetone are suitable for use as received, while others may cause color production in the reagent without contact with carbon monoxide. Unsuitable acetones can be made fit for use in this method by refluxing for 1 hr with potassium permanganate or by contact with permanganate at room temperature for 48 hr. After this treatment the acetone is dried over anhydrous potassium carbonate and distilled.

Mixed Carbon Monoxide Reagent. Mix equal volumes of the solutions of palladium chloride, phosphomolybdic acid, and 3N sulfuric

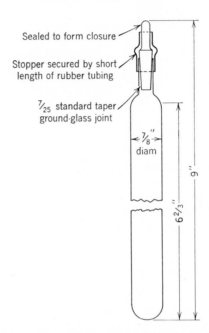

Sealed to form closure

Stopper secured by short
length of rubber tubing

$7/25$ standard taper
ground-glass joint

$7/8''$ diam

$9''$

$6\,2/3''$

Fig. XVII-6. Special test tube for phosphomolybdate method in which reactions
are carried on and comparisons of color are made (54).

acid.   Age the mixed reagent for 48 hr at room temperature before
use or hasten the aging process by maintaining the reagent at 60°C
for 4 hr.   The reagent tends to darken on standing at room temperature, but this does not interfere with the final results as long as the
colorimeter may be adjusted with a reagent blank to compensate for
the darkening of the reagent.   Change in color may be prevented by
storing the reagent in a refrigerator.

Collection of Sample.   Collect the air samples in or transfer them to
special 50-ml glass-stoppered tubes (Fig. XVII-6).   These are
optically matched test tubes modified by sealing to them ⚶ 7/25
ground-glass joints, the male portion of which is sealed to form
a closure.   The volume of the tube is approximately 50 ml.   Calibrate each tube and etch its volume on the upper portion of the tube.
By using optically matched tubes the reaction between sample and
reagents and the color comparison may be carried out in the same
tube.   Introduce the sample into the tube by water displacement.

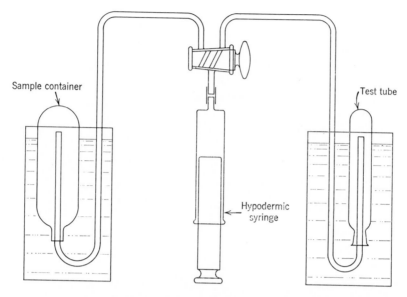

Fig. XVII-7. Diagrammatic sketch of apparatus for transferring air sample from sampler container to test tube for phosphomolybdate method (54).

It has been found advisable to fill the tubes with distilled water when not in use and to use only distilled water in washing the tubes. Care must be exercised also to prevent introduction of droplets of mercury or other extraneous material into the tubes.   When it is desired to transfer the sample from some other type of container, the apparatus shown in Fig. XVII-7 may be used.   When the carbon monoxide content of the sample is expected to exceed the maximum of the normal range of the method (0.06%), dilute the sample by introducing a measured volume into the tube by the use of a hypodermic syringe fitted with a U-shaped needle and then displace the remaining water in the tube with carbon monoxide-free air.   Drain excess water from the interior surfaces of the tube by removing the stopper momentarily and inverting the tube upon a towel.

   Procedure.   Add 3 ml of the carbon monoxide reagent, then 3 ml of the acetone reagent, and insert the stopper.   Carry out this step rapidly to minimize the possibility of dilution of the tube contents with air.   Fasten the stopper in place with a short length of rubber tubing (Fig. XVII-6).   When a number of samples are to be analyzed,

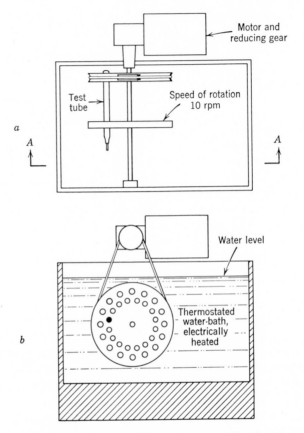

Fig. XVII-8. Diagrammatic sketch of apparatus for equilibrating air sample and reagent at constant temperature (54): (a) from top; (b) from side at cross section A-A.

it has been found convenient to add the carbon monoxide reagent to all the tubes first, and then the acetone.

With each sample or group of samples analyzed a blank determination is made with carbon monoxide-free air. Note that the air must be carbon monoxide free; trace amounts of carbon monoxide from laboratory burners or other sources may affect the results. The analysis of a blank sample is important in obtaining satisfactory results and should always be made with the same lot of reagents that has been used with the samples under analysis.

Equilibrate the samples and the blank by rotation for 60 min in a water bath at 60°C with the aid of a device similar to that shown in Fig. XVII-8. The water bath temperature should be controlled to ±1°C. The time of equilibration should be exact also, as color intensity increases at a lesser rate on further heating. The color developed in 60 min at 60°C was found to remain essentially constant for 24 hr after the tubes are cooled to room temperature.

Clean the exterior of each tube after equilibration by immersion to the neck in chromic acid cleaning solution. Wash, dry, and cool the tubes.

Color Comparison. Measure the color intensity of the molybdenum blue, using a filter having a transmission band of 635–720 mμ. In making color comparisons, insert the tube containing the blank determination with carbon monoxide-free air in the instrument and adjust the galvanometer to read 100% transmission. If the galvanometer scale consists of 100 equal divisions, the galvanometer readings obtained with samples or standards containing carbon monoxide may be taken directly as percentage transmission compared with the blank.

f. Pyrotannic Acid Method

The pyrotannic acid method is adapted to rapid and accurate determination of small amounts of carbon monoxide in air. It will not indicate more than 0.2%. Therefore, if more than this amount is present, other means of estimation should be employed for quantitative results, such as the NBS indicator, the MSA indicator, the Hoolamite detector, iodine pentoxide method, and volumetric methods. In the range of low percentages, from 0.01% to approximately 0.2%, the pyrotannic acid method is very accurate, and for this reason was formerly used in preference to other methods or apparatus by the gas laboratory of the U. S. Bureau of Mines experiment station at Pittsburgh for determining or confirming the presence of low percentages of carbon monoxide in samples of mine air, especially mine fire atmospheres. The presence of carbon monoxide, even in minute quantity, behind fire seals is always a strong indication that the fire is still burning, or at least has been burning too recently for the area to be opened with safety. It is in work such as this that the pyrotannic acid method can be used to its greatest value in the mining industry (10).

The method (21,22) is based on the fact that a light brownish-gray suspension is formed in a few minutes when normal blood diluted with water is treated with a solution of pyrogallic and tannic acids, whereas light carmine suspensions are formed with blood having carbon monoxide in combination with hemoglobin. When compared with color standards of known concentration, the intensity of the carmine-colored suspension gives the saturation of the hemoglobin being tested. The standards used with the apparatus can be made from human or animal blood, such as guinea pig, cattle, etc. Although they are reliable for a limited time, standards prepared from blood deteriorate and are not accurate over long periods. Permanent standards may be prepared from artists' oil-color pigments, which are ready to use at all times and change color relatively little. Permanent standards are furnished with purchased equipment.

The pyrotannic acid method is adaptable for the determination of carbon monoxide in both blood and air. The procedure for the determination of carbon monoxide in air differs slightly from that for determining blood saturation. The two methods are usually called "determination of blood saturation," as in the case of a person poisoned with carbon monoxide, and "determination of percentage of carbon monoxide in air," as in the investigation of contaminated atmospheres.

Apparatus. A set of color standards to represent the color of blood having varying amounts of carboxyhemoglobin. The standards are contained in small, clear test tubes $\frac{5}{16}$ in. in diameter and 2 ml in volume. These are arranged in a suitable rack with spaces between for interposing tubes of similar size that contain the prepared blood samples for analysis.

Small test tubes, $\frac{5}{16}$ in. in diameter and 2 ml in volume, in which to prepare specimens for analysis.

A dilution pipet, which consists of a pipet with a capillary stem that holds 0.1 ml and a bulb above that has a total volume of 2 ml, thus making a dilution of 1:20, which is the most suitable blood concentration for this test.

A spring hemospast or blood lancet for making a small wound in the finger or other convenient place from which blood may be obtained.

A small watch glass or spot plate for catching the blood as it flows from the wound. The blood may be drawn up directly from the bead over the wound, but the spot plate will be found convenient where two or more specimens are desired from the same wound.

A mixture or equal parts of pyrogallic and tannic acids, either solid or in solution. Usually it is in powdered form and is kept in a small bottle with a measuring spoon holding approximately 0.04 g, which is found to be most suitable for 2 ml of a 1:20 blood solution. If less blood solution is used, the amount of acids used must be correspondingly decreased.

Air-sample bottles of 250-ml capacity, fitted with rubber stoppers.

A rubber aspirator bulb with an attached scrubber tube containing soda lime for removing gases that might have an interfering effect.

Procedure.   Obtain samples of air by inserting the glass tube on the end of the soda lime scrubber into the sample bottle and aspirate the air through the sample bottle long enough to purge it of its original contents; this requires at least 25 squeezes. Expel the last bulbful of air through the sample bottle while the glass tube is being removed. Insert the rubber stopper quickly and tightly. If regular sample bottles and aspirator bulbs are not available, the samples may be collected in any ordinary bottle having a capacity of about 250 ml by the liquid-displacement method, in which the bottle is filled with water and the bottle is then emptied at the sampling place. The walls should be well drained, as an excess of water will interfere with the accuracy of the result.

Take the collected samples to the place where the analysis is to be made, preferably away from the place where the samples were obtained.

The blood to be used in making the analysis may be taken from a stock solution of relatively fresh human or animal blood or from a person who has not been exposed to carbon monoxide. Make a small puncture wound, approximately 2 mm deep, with the hemospast in the tip of the finger of the person whose blood is to be used. Catch several drops of blood on the spot plate or draw the blood directly into the pipet. If the blood does not flow freely, wrap the finger with rubber hose, beginning at the base and progressing toward the tip; massaging the finger also aids the flow. When the blood has been produced, draw it quickly into the stem of the pipet to the 0.1-ml mark. Hold the pipet horizontal and remove any blood on the exterior of the tip. Raise the tip slightly and permit a little of the blood to flow into the diluting bulb. Insert the pipet quickly into a bottle of water and by using suction at the same time fill to the 2-ml mark to give the proper dilution.

Transfer the 2 ml of blood solution to the sample bottle, being careful to allow as little air to escape from the bottle as possible. It is best first to discharge the solution from the pipet into one of the small test tubes and to pour from this tube into the sample bottle. After the blood solution has been added to the bottle, replace the stopper tightly, hold the bottle horizontal, and rotate constantly for 15–20 min avoiding violent shaking and agitation. After the 15–20 min, when equilibrating has been finished, pour the blood solution back into the same test tube used for the transfer, add approximately 0.04 g of the pyrogallic–tannic acid mixture, and invert the tube gently several times to insure thorough mixing with the reagents.

Place the tube in a rack and allow to stand 15 min at room temperature. If particles of the solid acids settle out, invert the tube several times more. At the end of the 15-min period compare the sample with the standards by interposing

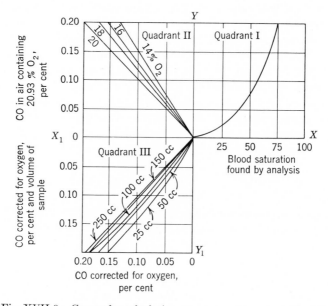

Fig. XVII-9. Curves for calculating per cent carbon monoxide (10).

it between them until the standard is found which most nearly matches the unknown. If carbon monoxide is indicated, the sample should be allowed to stand 15 min longer and another reading made. The latter reading should be taken as the more accurate.

The equilibrating should be done in a rather dimly lit place. When the sample bottle is rotated, as much of the surface of the bottle as possible should be covered with blood solution. Every now and then the solution should be thrown centrifugally from the sides to the bottom of the bottle by a quick swirling motion, which allows a new surface to form and aids in reaching equilibrium of the gases in the air above the blood and the blood solution. When a large number of samples have to be analyzed a motor-driven equilibrator will save time. On this machine or similar types, sample bottles are held at a 60° angle from a revolving vertical disk, the speed of revolution being such as to allow the solution to flow over the inner surface of the bottles.

To transpose the amount of blood saturation obtained in the sample bottle to the percentage of carbon monoxide in the air, several formulas are used, as described by Sayers and his co-workers (21,22). To simplify the operation of making computations and applying all the corrections for the calculation of the carbon monoxide content in the air, the graphs of Fig. XVII-9 may be used. These graphically represent the calculations and corrections from which the carbon monoxide content in air can be determined from the blood saturation. The original papers of Forbes and Grove (10) should be consulted.

The pyrotannic acid method is a quick, efficient, and accurate means for ascertaining the amount of carbon monoxide in air. It will indicate low percentages of carbon monoxide. Its deficiency lies in the inability to calculate the amount of carbon monoxide directly and the difficulty, at times, of obtaining normal blood.

B. Carbon Dioxide

1. Increasing Industrial Use and Dangers

Carbon dioxide is able to paralyze the respiratory center. Because of this action it is an industrial hazard. It is heavier than air (sp gr 1.529) and thus may collect in manholes, mine floors, ship holds, wells, brewery vats and similar vats, garbage dumps, etc. Furthermore, because of its heaviness, it does not tend to diffuse away readily. It is the product of complete combustion of carbonaceous material and occurs where fires are present or where explosions have occurred. Where persons are working in a confined space, the amount of carbon dioxide formed by the breathing of these workers may assume dangerous proportions.

The dangers associated with carbon dioxide are increasing with increasing use of this substance. It is now used extensively in a solid form, known as dry ice, as a refrigerant. In the liquid state it is employed for charging water and in a special Bureau of Mines permissive cartridge for the blasting of coal (55).

In 1936 in Brooklyn, several persons were asphyxiated while working in the hold of a ship in which solid carbon dioxide was the refrigerant (56). This instance shows that wherever solid carbon dioxide is used in poorly ventilated quarters it is a serious hazard.

There have been serious airplane accidents because of its use as a fire extinguisher.

Blackdamp is the term applied to atmospheres depleted of oxygen containing relatively large proportions of carbon dioxide. Haldane (57) defines blackdamp as an accumulation of carbon dioxide and nitrogen in proportions larger than that found in pure air. This term is often used in miners' terminology.

2. PHYSIOLOGICAL RESPONSE

Carbon dioxide is a noncombustible, colorless, odorless, slightly acid gas. It is the regulator of the breathing function. An increase in the amounts of carbon dioxide breathed results in an increased rate of breathing. High concentrations, however, paralyze the respiratory center, resulting in asphyxiation and death. Its concentration in some atmospheres is sufficient to cause symptoms in man, or even unconsciousness and death (10,24,58). One-half of 1 vol % carbon dioxide in normal air causes a slight and unnoticeable increase in the ventilation of the lungs, that is, a man exposed to 0.5% carbon dioxide will breathe a little deeper and a little faster than when in pure air. If there is 2% carbon dioxide in the air, the lung ventilation will be increased about 50%; if there is 3% the lung ventilation will be increased about 100%; 5% causes about a 300% increase in the lung ventilation and breathing is laborious; 10% can be endured for only a few minutes. With 12–15% the person soon becomes unconscious, and death may take place after exposure for several hours to 25%. The generally recommended maximum allowable concentration is 5000 ppm.

It is particularly regrettable that many working in the fields of industrial hygiene and air pollution are under the mistaken notion, fostered even by some who deem themselves toxicologists, that carbon dioxide is harmless and innocuous. This is repeated over and over again in phrases implying that the products of complete combustion are harmless. This notion is, of course, false, for carbon dioxide, in contrast to carbon monoxide which is a chemical asphyxiant, is a true poison. It is one that exerts its baneful effects at relatively high concentrations, but one that is nevertheless a serious poison responsible for many deaths. Indeed, one of the aspects of carbon monoxide toxicity little appreciated is that when carbon dioxide is also present, the consequent increase in respiration rate caused by the carbon dioxide causes a subsequent faster depletion of oxygen transport by tying up the hemoglobin faster as carboxyhemoglobin.

3. Classification of Methods for Determination of Carbon Dioxide

The volume and amount of carbon dioxide present in an atmosphere may be ascertained by a number of methods. These have been classified by Martin and Green (59) as follows:

1. *Gravimetric methods.*

(a) Carbon dioxide absorbed in strong alkaline solutions or solid absorbents, such as soda lime and Ascarite (sodium hydroxide dispersed on asbestos fibers), and the increase in weight of absorbent determined.

(b) Absorbed in dilute solution of sodium or potassium hydroxide and weighed as barium carbonate.

(c) Absorbed in a strong solution of barium hydroxide and the resulting carbonate either weighed directly or converted to the corresponding sulfate.

2. *Titrimetric methods.*

(a) Carbon dioxide absorbed in a dilute standard solution of sodium or potassium hydroxide and the carbonate determined by double titration, using phenolphthalein and methyl orange or other suitable indicators.

(b) Absorbed in a standard solution of barium hydroxide and the carbonate determined by a single titration.

(c) Absorbed in a dilute standard solution of sodium or potassium hydroxide, an excess of neutral barium chloride added, and the excess of alkali titrated.

(d) Absorbed in a strong solution of barium hydroxide and the resulting carbonate filtered, washed, dissolved in a standard acid solution, and titrated.

3. *Volumetric methods.*

(a) By volumetric gas apparatus. Either the carbon dioxide is absorbed directly in strong alkali in gasometric apparatus and the decrease in the volume of the gas mixture is measured at atmospheric pressure or it is absorbed in strong alkali, the carbon dioxide liberated in an acid solution in a gas apparatus, and its volume measured at atmospheric pressure.

(b) By manometric gas apparatus. The carbon dioxide is absorbed in strong alkali and liberated in the manometric apparatus by excess acid. The volume of the gas then is increased to a fixed value and its pressure measured manometrically.

4. *Electrometric methods.*

(a) Electrolytic resistance method. The carbon dioxide is absorbed in a standard solution of alkali, preferably barium hydroxide, and the decrease in its electrolytic conductivity measured.

(b) Thermal conductivity method. The concentration of carbon dioxide in a gas mixture is indicated by its thermal conductivity, which is determined by measuring the electrical resistance of a wire heated by a constant electric current and surrounded by the gases under study.

5. *Colorimetric method.*

Carbon dioxide is absorbed in a solution of the sodium salt of phenolphthalein and its concentration is indicated by the diminution in color intensity. Trace amounts (60) may be estimated by this method.

6. *Physicochemical method.*

This is probably the method of choice for determination of higher concentrations of carbon dioxide, such as is found in exhaust gases. It involves the use of a nondispersive infrared recording spectrometer.

4. Determination

Of the various methods mentioned, the volumetric methods and the titrimetric methods for the estimation of carbon dioxide are those most frequently used.

a. Volumetric Estimation

The volume of carbon dioxide present in an atmosphere may be ascertained very simply by volumetric methods. There are numerous volumetric methods, nearly all of which depend on the principle outlined above. A sample of the gas is collected by one of the devices detailed in Chapter II. The volume of this sample is measured and then the sample is passed through an adequate portion of some absorbing agent, such as potassium hydroxide solution (300 g of KOH in 1000 ml of water) or sodium hydroxide solution (200 g of NaOH in 1000 ml of water), contained in a volumetric apparatus. The volume of gas remaining is now measured at atmospheric pressure and the percentage of carbon dioxide may be calculated from the contraction in volume.   Among the variations of this method may be mentioned those which use the Haldane apparatus (61) and the Orsat apparatus (18).

b.   *Titrimetric Estimation with Barium Hydroxide*

The carbon dioxide in an atmosphere may be estimated very simply by the following titrimetric method.   Pass a known volume of the air to be examined through an efficient absorber, which can subsequently be utilized for the titration, containing a known volume of standard dilute barium hydroxide solution.   A $0.10N$ barium hydroxide solution containing barium chloride works well, for the mass-action effect of the barium chloride reduces the solubility and hydrolysis of the barium carbonate (62).   After sampling is complete, connect the absorber, if possible, to a source of carbon dioxide-free air which will act as a stirring device and which will provide a carbon dioxide-free atmosphere above the liquid being titrated and so exclude the carbon dioxide of the surrounding atmosphere from interfering.   Titrate the excess barium hydroxide without prior filtration with $0.0454N$ oxalic acid, using phenolphthalein or preferably thymolphthalein as the indicator.   The same strength hydrochloric acid may also be used but oxalic acid is to be preferred because this acid has little effect on the barium carbonate (63).   One ml of $0.0454N$ acid is equivalent to 1 mg of carbon dioxide (59,64).

C. Cyanides and Nitriles

1. Hydrocyanic Acid and Cyanides

Hydrocyanic acid, hydrogen cyanide, HCN, or, as it is often called, prussic acid, is a colorless gas with a penetrating odor resembling that of bitter almonds.   It is highly toxic, acting directly on the nervous system.   It can be absorbed through the skin so that masks are protective only for a short time.

Liquid hydrocyanic acid, known to the fumigation trade as liquid gas, or liquid cyanide, is a colorless fluid.   It is exceedingly volatile in warm dry air, for it has a boiling point of 26°C.   It is lighter than water, having a specific gravity of 0.699.   Large concentrations of the gas in air provide an inflammable mixture so that care must be taken not to ignite such mixtures.

Hydrocyanic acid is used extensively as a fumigant, particularly in the fumigation of ships and of citrus trees.   In the case of ships its main purpose is to rid the ship and cargo of rodents and vermin such as cockroaches. In the case of citrus trees, tent-field fumigation is practiced to control red scale. It is finding a growing use in the fumigation field, and naturally there is an increased hazard, when destroying insect pests of plants and insect pests of man such as the louse, bedbug, flea, and mosquito, by both outdoor and building fumigation.

Hydrogen cyanide is not a bactericide or germicide and therefore has no effect on the bubonic plague bacillus or other bacteria. It protects by killing the pests that harbor the bacteria.

Apart from its principal use in the fumigation of ships, buildings, citrus trees, etc., hydrogen cyanide is used as a reagent in industry and is encountered in concentrations that may be dangerous in certain industrial processes, as for instance in blast furnaces, dyestuff works, gas works, coke ovens, tanneries, fertilizer plants, and gold mining and gilding.

Cyanides such as potassium, sodium, and calcium cyanide find use in various industries such as the extraction of noble metals and the manufacture of organic chemicals, fertilizer, rodenticides, and explosives, and in such industrial processes as case-hardening, electroplating, metal polishing, photography, etc.

a. Toxicity and Physiological Response

Hydrogen cyanide acts by stopping the oxidation of protoplasm in the tissue cells. With high concentrations the symptoms appear rapidly, namely, giddiness, headache, unconsciousness, and convulsions, with cessation of respiration as a result of paralysis of the respiratory center in the brain. With weaker concentrations there may be the following symptoms: irritation of the throat, palpitation, difficulty in breathing, watering of the eyes, salivation, headache,

TABLE XVII-4
Effects of Hydrocyanic Acid Vapor (65,66)

Parts/volume, approx.	Mg/liter, approx	Effects
1:50,000	0.025	Slight symptoms after several hours
1:10,000	0.12	Very dangerous within 1 hr
1:500	2.5	Fatal

weakness of the arms and legs, giddiness—followed by collapse and convulsions. It is not a respiratory irritant.

Table XVII-4 shows the effects produced by different concentrations of hydrocyanic acid vapor.

The generally accepted maximum allowable concentration of hydrogen cyanide is 10 ppm. Repeated exposure to small concentrations of cyanides over long periods causes symptoms such as weakness, nausea, muscle cramps and paralysis of legs and arms, loss of appetite, and psychoses. The recommended maximum allowable concentration of cyanides is 5 mg/m^3 of air, calculated as CN.

b. Forms Used in Fumigation

Hydrocyanic acid (67) may be generated at the point or in the place to be fumigated by the reaction between sodium cyanide, sulfuric acid, and water or by the reaction between sodium cyanide, sodium chlorate, hydrochloric acid, and water, in which instance cyanogen chloride is also generated.   While these extremely hazardous methods are still used, the following methods have found increasing use.

(1) Liquid hydrogen cyanide containing either 20% cyanogen chloride or 5–10% chloropicrin, trichloronitromethane, both of which are lachrymators and therefore act as warning agents, is spread over and into the area to be fumigated by means of spray guns or jets.

(2) Zyklon consists of an earthy substance like Fuller's earth or kieselguhr impregnated with hydrocyanic acid. This is packed in strong tin containers, which are opened in or near the place to be fumigated and the contents are spread by knocking holes in each end of the can with a special hammer and sprinkling the contents on the floor of the hold or spreading the contents in a thin layer on canvas or paper on the floor of a compartment. The hydrocyanic acid evaporates into the surrounding air. Zyklon may also be scattered by means of a pump.

(3) Another "solid type" of cyanide product is "HCN Discoids," which consist of highly porous and absorptive wood-pulp disks 3⅝ in. in diameter and 3⁄32 in. thick. They absorb two and a half times their weight of liquid hydrogen cyanide. They come in cans holding about 64 discoids, which contain about 1 lb of liquid hydrogen cyanide and contain in addition about 5% chloropicrin, which serves as the warning gas. The cans are opened by a special type of can opener and from the open can the discoids are shaken out on the

hold or floor. In the superstructure compartments it is necessary to scatter the discoids on paper, otherwise slight staining of floor coverings may result. The hydrocyanic acid evaporates rapidly from the discoids as in the case of Zyklon.

(4) Still another means of obtaining hydrogen cyanide is from a mixture of calcium cyanide and inert ingredients supplied in metal containers, called Cyanogas (68). When treated with water or acids or exposed to moist air, hydrocyanic acid is liberated.

c. Detection

Of the many methods for the detection and determination of hydrocyanic acid and cyanides, the pyridine–pyrazolone test, the ferrocyanide test, the thiocyanate method, the benzidine–copper acetate test, the methyl orange–mercuric chloride test, the silver nitrate test, and the picric acid test will be described. Animals like rats and mice are also used. If an animal of this type remains unaffected for 10 min, a fumigated place may be considered safe. The Prussian blue and thiocyanate reactions, which are specific for hydrogen cyanide, are not sufficiently sensitive. The picrate test is neither specific nor sufficiently sensitive. The silver nitrate test is affected by acid and alkaline gases but it is sensitive.

Practical tests for hydrogen cyanide are especially important for use in vessel and other types of fumigation, first, for determining when a vessel or building is safe for habitation by its crew and by workers after the fumigation has been completed, and second, to establish the earliest moment when it is safe for a fumigating crew to enter a hold, compartment, vessel, or building for the purpose of further ventilation or to search for rats. Where the air workers breathe is to be tested for cyanide, sampling must be done at a point closely adjacent to the workers for the test to be of value and if there is any chance of the hydrogen cyanide concentration rising, sampling and testing should be performed at frequent intervals during the work.

Benzidine–Copper Acetate Test (69)

The benzidine–copper acetate test is one of the more widely used tests for the detection of hydrogen cyanide in atmospheres. It depends upon the production of a blue color with moist, freshly prepared benzidine and copper acetate test paper in the presence of hydrogen cyanide. This color is produced in periods varying from 3 to 30 sec, depending upon the concentration of hydrogen cyanide.

Reagents. *Copper Acetate Solution.* Dissolve 2.86 g of cupric acetate, $Cu(C_2H_3O_2)_2 \cdot H_2O$, in water and dilute to 1 liter.

Benzidine Acetate Solution. Dilute 475 ml of saturated benzidine acetate solution with 525 ml of water.

Procedure (70). Mix equal parts of the cupric acetate solution and the benzidine acetate solution just before using. Dip slips of filter paper into the mixed reagent and take into the compartment to be tested in closed tubes or vials. Open the tubes and note the time to the second. Upon exposure in an atmosphere of hydrocyanic acid, the test paper will show a color varying from a very faint to an intense blue, indicating from 20 to 80 mg of hydrocyanic acid per cubic meter.

The benzidine–copper acetate test requires that the test papers be read for a change in color after an exposure of 7–10 sec, which necessitates entering the compartment, hold, or building, if no auxiliary equipment is used, before making the test. This may be a dangerous procedure. An error of 3 sec in reading the time factor might mean an error of 30% or more in the accuracy of the test. The results must be read while the color is rapidly changing and the operator is in the presence of the cyanide. The color changes in widely varying concentrations of hydrocyanic acid are so slight that it requires considerable laboratory experience with known concentrations of hydrogen cyanide in order to make accurate determinations.

British Modification

The official British modification of the benzidine–copper acetate test is the following:

Reagents. *Benzidine Acetate Solution.* Heat 2–3 g of pure benzidine acetate in 100 ml of water for 10–15 min at 80°C with constant stirring. When cold, filter the mixture by suction. The filtrate will contain about 1% benzidine acetate.

Copper Acetate Solution. Dissolve 3 g of cupric acetate, $Cu(C_2H_3O_2)_2 \cdot H_2O$, in 100 ml of water.

Immediately before the test is made, mix 25 ml of the benzidine acetate solution with 2 ml of the copper acetate solution and stir well. The mixed reagent will not keep more than 15 min.

The test papers may be prepared from extra-thick white filter paper cut into strips 2 in. wide. Immerse them in the mixed reagent for 1 min, drain, and allow to dry in a warm atmosphere. Cut off 1 in. at the top and bottom of the strip and discard. Cut the remainder of the strip into 3-in. lengths. The papers must be used immediately.

Procedure.   Place a prepared test paper into a holder and attach to a hand exhausting pump which has a barrel of approximately 1.25-in. bore and a capacity of 125 ml.   Make a preliminary test of the atmosphere by making 8 slow and steady strokes with the pump. Remove the paper and compare with the stains on standard charts (65).   In this way an estimate may be made of any concentration between 1 part in 10,000 and 1 part in 20,000 of air by volume, the latter being the maximum that can be inhaled for 1 hr without serious disturbance.   If the stain indicates a concentration greater than 1 part in 20,000, a fresh paper is placed in the holder and further tests are made with 1, 2, 3, or 5 strokes of the pump; if a concentration of less than 1 in 100,000 is indicated, a rough estimate of the concentration may be obtained by repeating the test with a greater number of strokes of the pump, until a stain equal to one of the standards is obtained.   Comparison of the stains should be made in diffused daylight or with the use of a daylight lamp.

Methyl Orange–Mercuric Chloride Test (70)

This test depends on the change in color produced in a methyl orange–mercuric chloride test paper by hydrocyanic acid.   The color changes from orange to pink.   These test papers may be prepared in advance at a convenient place and will keep under proper conditions of humidity for as long as 30 days.

Reagents.   *Mercuric Chloride Solution.*   Dissolve 1.25 g of mercuric chloride in 250 ml of water.

Methyl Orange Solution.   Dissolve 0.60 g of methyl orange in 250 ml of water.

Mix 10 ml of mercuric chloride solution with 5 ml of methyl orange solution and add 1 ml of glycerol.   Immerse strips of Whatman No. 40 filter paper into the mixed reagent and hang them up to dry in air which is free from any trace of acid.   When dry, cut the filter paper into strips $\frac{1}{4}$-in. wide and preserve in glass tubes protected from the light.

Procedure.   Attach the test paper by means of a clip or other holding device to some type of line such as a fishing line and reel.   Lower the test paper into the place to be tested.   Withdraw at the end of 2 min.   A definite pink color at the end of a 2-min exposure indicates a dangerous concentration of hydrogen cyanide gas in the air unless the humidity is great enough to accelerate the reaction.   The test can also be made by carrying a small vial into the place to be tested and noting

the change in color at the end of a known period of time.   The use of
a line eliminates the need of masking, which is, of course, required
when entering an unknown concentration of hydrocyanic acid.   It
is best to have two vials, one containing a strip of unaffected test
paper, and the other containing a strip of paper with the pink danger
color.   Table XVII-5 shows the relationship of hydrogen cyanide
concentration, color of test paper, and time of test.

Simultaneous Test

Katz and Longfellow (71) describe a series of three tests for the
simultaneous testing of hydrogen cyanide.   They use a dry picric

TABLE XVII-5
Methyl Orange–Mercuric Chloride Test (70)

HCN per 1000 cu ft, g	Proportion of standard[a]	Duration of test, min				
		0.5	1	1.5	2	3
6.7	1:10	Slight pink at edge	Faint pink	Definite pink	Red	Red
3.35	1:20	No change	Slight pink at edge	Faint pink	Definite pink	Red
1.675	1:40	No change	No change	Br. orange	Faint pink	Faint pink
0.8375	1:80	No change	No change	No change	Slight pink	Very faint pink
0.4187	1:160	No change	No change	No change	No change	No change
0.2093	1:320	No change	No change	No change	No change	No change

[a] The word standard indicates 2 oz of HCN per 1000 ft of air space.

acid test paper, which changes color from yellow to tan to brown; a
wet guaiacum–copper test paper, which changes color from white to
blue; and a wet phenolphthalein–copper test paper, which changes
color from pink to bluish-pink, depending upon the hydrocyanic acid
concentration.   They estimate the quantity of hydrogen cyanide
from the range of color with the aid of a color chart and the time
required to yield the color.
   The picrate papers may be prepared by dipping filter paper strips,
2 × ¾ in. into a solution containing 1 g of picric acid and 10 g
of sodium carbonate dissolved in 100 ml of water, and then drying

the papers in room air. The papers may be prepared as much as 1 week in advance. The test paper is used dry and in the presence of hydrogen cyanide it changes color from yellow to tan to brown within a time period of 5 min, depending upon the hydrocyanic acid concentration.

The phenolphthalein ($C_{20}H_{16}O_4$) papers are prepared in the atmosphere to be tested by dipping a copper sulfate paper into a phenolphthalein solution. To prepare this solution, dissolve 20 g of sodium hydroxide in 100 ml of water; stir in 0.5 g of phenolphthalein dissolved in 30 ml of alcohol; transfer to a 12-in. evaporating dish to prevent loss of froth; add 25 g of 30–60-mesh aluminum powder; heat, and add water as required to continue the reaction; after 20 min to 1 hr, when the solution is colorless, filter with suction, dilute to 250 ml, and preserve. The solution may develop a light pink color but this will not appear on the test papers. When used in the atmosphere to be tested the solution should be restoppered immediately. The test paper is used wet and changes color from white to pink to bluish-pink with the formation of phenolphthalein.

Guaiacum papers must be prepared in the atmosphere to be tested by dipping filter-paper strips of the aforementioned size previously wetted with a solution of copper sulfate (50 mg in 100 ml of water) into tincture of guaiacum (4 g of guaiacum in 100 ml of alcohol).

In making the simultaneous test with the three papers, the picrate paper is suspended first; while observing the picrate paper, the phenolphthalein paper is prepared and suspended; and while observing both of these tests, the guaiacum paper is prepared and suspended. The quantity of hydrogen cyanide is estimated from the times and color changes of the three test papers. These papers are affected by oxidizing agents and reducing agents in general and by chlorine, nitrogen peroxide, smoke, ammonia, and formaldehyde in particular. Changes are inhibited by sulfur dioxide.

Phenolphthalein Field Method

This method (72) is designed for the spot sampling of hydrogen cyanide in air and is based on the reaction devised by Katz and Longfellow as described on page 727.

Reagents. *Stock Solution* (Solution A). Dissolve 0.166 g of phenolphthalein, $(C_6H_4OH)_2CHC_6H_4COOH$, in 75 ml of ethyl alcohol. Dissolve 0.33 g of copper sulfate, $CuSO_4 \cdot 5H_2O$, in 100 ml of water. Transfer both solutions to a 200-ml volumetric flask and make to volume with water. This reagent will remain stable for at least a week if kept in a refrigerator.

Buffer Solution (Solution B). Dissolve 2.5 g of trisodium phosphate, $Na_3PO_4 \cdot 12H_2O$, in water and dilute to 1 liter.

Test Reagent. Dissolve 2 ml of solution A in 98 ml of solution B. The test reagent is stable for 8–24 hr after which time it may develop a slight color but this does not interfere with the sensitivity of the test.

Standard. Dilute 10 ml of the test reagent to 50 ml with solution B and add a small grain of sodium cyanide. The color developed is equivalent to that given by sampling the following volumes of air containing the designated concentrations of hydrogen cyanide.

Air sampled, ml	Concentration HCN, ppm	Time effect
2000	10	
1000	20	
500	40	
250	80	Maximum for 30 min
125	160	Dangerous for 30 min
75	320	Fatal in 5 min

Procedure. Place 10 ml of test reagent in a midget impinger tube and aspirate a known volume of air through it until the color matches the standard. Obtain the concentration of hydrogen cyanide from the volume of air sampled and the above table.

Chlorine, bromine, iodine, phenol, and high concentrations of hydrogen sulfide interfere with the test. If the air being sampled has a high acid concentration, the pH of the reagent should be checked after 1 liter of air has been sampled. This should be done by adding 1 drop of phenolphthalein indicator solution. The test reagent should turn red.

d. Determination

Pyridine–Pyrazolone Method

By converting cyanide to cyanogen chloride with Chloramine T and by the subsequent reaction of this cyanogen chloride with an aqueous pyridine solution containing 0.1% bis-pyrazolone and 3-methyl-1-phenyl-5-pyrazolone, a dye is formed which is stable for at least ½ hr at 25°C and follows the Beer-Lambert law between the limits of 0.2 and 1.2 μg of cyanide ion (73,74).

Reagents. Recrystallize commercial 3-methyl-1-phenyl-5-pyrazolone twice from 95% ethyl alcohol to obtain the product melting at 127–128°C.

To prepare bis(3-methyl-1-phenyl-5-pyrazolone), dissolve 17.4 g (0.1 mole) of recrystallized 1-phenyl-3-methyl-5-pyrazolone in 100 ml of 95% alcohol and add 25 g (0.25 mole) of freshly distilled phenylhydrazine. Reflux the mixture for 4 hr. Filter the mixture while hot to obtain the insoluble portion, which is the bis-pyrazolone, and wash the precipitate several times with hot 95% ethyl alcohol. The melting point should be higher than 320°C.

Pyridine–Pyrazolone Solution. Mix 500 ml of a saturated water solution of 3-methyl-1-phenyl-5-pyrazolone with 100 ml of pure pyridine in which 0.1 g of the bis-pyrazolone has been dissolved.

Standard Cyanide Solutions. Dissolve 95% sodium cyanide in water and analyze by the Liebig method (see page 733). Adjust the concentration of the solution to exactly 10 μg of cyanide ion per milliliter and use this as a stock solution. Withdraw 2-, 4-, 6-, 8-, 10-, and 12-ml aliquots of the stock solution and dilute to 100 ml with water. These solutions contain 0.2, 0.4, 0.6, 0.8, 1.0, and 1.2 μg of cyanide per milliliter, respectively.

Procedure. Place 1 ml of the unknown solution containing up to 1.2 μg of cyanide ion into a test tube and add 0.2 ml of 1% aqueous solution of Chloramine T. Stopper the tube immediately and shake. After 1 min add 6 ml of the pyridine–pyrazolone reagent, stopper the tube, and again mix. After 20 min compare the optical density at 630 mμ with that of a blank and standards in a 1–1.5-cm cell. A Coleman Universal spectrophotometer No. 11 with PC No. 4 filter is adequate. The standards can be used to set up a calibration curve and the concentration of the unknown can be obtained from that curve. The color is stable for at least 30 min after maximum development at room temperature.

Prussian Blue Test

This test is one of those most characteristic for hydrocyanic acid and cyanogen. However, unless special precautions are taken, it is not sufficiently sensitive. It cannot be easily used in the field as a test and therefore has its main use as a laboratory test.

In making the test, an alkaline solution of cyanide is warmed with a few drops of a solution of ferrous sulfate. This converts the cyanide to ferrocyanide:

$$2KCN + FeSO_4 \rightarrow K_2SO_4 + Fe(CN)_2$$

$$Fe(CN)_2 + 4KCN \rightarrow K_4Fe(CN)_6$$

Ferrocyanide may in turn be detected by acidification and the subsequent addition of dilute ferric chloride solution, yielding a blue precipitate of ferric ferrocyanide:

$$3K_4Fe(CN)_6 + 4FeCl_3 \rightarrow 12KCl + Fe_4[Fe(CN)_6]_3$$

It should be noted that the Prussian blue reaction is a time reaction and that excess ferric ion hinders the formation of the blue pigment.

Procedure. Pass the gas to be tested through a series of two or three gas bubblers containing a few milliliters of 0.5% potassium hydroxide solution to which a few drops of freshly prepared ferrous sulfate solution has been added. If the gas has been sampled in a gas collector, shake the gas in the collector with a few milliliters of the dilute alkali containing the ferrous sulfate. After sampling is complete—if necessary, sampling 100 liters of air—or sufficient time has elapsed to permit the hydrogen cyanide to be absorbed by the alkali, transfer the alkali solution to a beaker and heat to boiling, or allow to stand for at least 2 hr. This insures complete conversion to ferrocyanide. Cool, if necessary, filter off excess ferrous hydroxide, acidify slightly with hydrochloric acid, and add 1 drop of ferric chloride solution. In the presence of hydrogen cyanide, a blue color is formed.

Quantitative estimation may be made colorimetrically. Prepare a standard solution of potassium cyanide, 1 ml of which is equivalent to 0.1 mg of hydrogen cyanide. Dissolve 0.2411 g of potassium cyanide in 1 liter of water. Dilute 100 ml of this solution to 1 liter. One ml of this solution contains 0.01 mg of hydrogen cyanide. Prepare a series of control tubes containing from 0.02 to 0.1 mg of hydrogen cyanide. Treat them exactly the same way the unknown is treated. Make the comparison after diluting to the same volume after 3–4 hr. A water blank should be run also.

An alternative color standard may be prepared by titrating an equal volume of water, slightly acidified, containing an equivalent quantity of ferric chloride, with potassium ferrocyanide solution, 3.1 g/liter, until a match is obtained. One ml of this solution is equivalent to 1 ml of hydrogen cyanide or cyanogen at STP (75).

For very small quantities of hydrocyanic acid, of the order of 0.00002 g/ml, it is convenient to use the following procedure (76). Add to the trapping solution or other test solution 2 drops of 10%

caustic soda, and evaporate nearly to dryness. Cool, add 1 drop of 2% freshly dissolved ferrous sulfate, and leave in the cold for 10–15 min. Add 2–3 drops of concentrated hydrochloric acid, warm gently, and cool. If cyanide is present, the liquid will show a blue color with careful dilution.

Test Paper Method

Gettler and Goldbaum (77) found that the sensitivity of the Prussian blue test could be enhanced by leading the hydrocyanic acid through an impregnated piece of filter paper held in a glass test paper holder equipped with ground flanges.

To prepare the test paper, dissolve 5 g of hydrated ferrous sulfate in 50 ml of water and filter to remove any insoluble residue. Immerse a single sheet of Whatman No. 50, smooth-glazed, acid- and alkali-treated filter paper into the ferrous sulfate solution by suspending it from a clamp and allow to dry in the air. Dip the dried ferrous sulfate impregnated filter paper into a 20% solution of sodium hydroxide and again allow to dry in the air. Cut circular pieces of paper having the same diameter as the ground-glass flanges of the holder. The papers are stable for several weeks if stored in a dark, cool place.

Procedure. Pass the air being tested through the test paper held by the test paper holder by aspiration or suction. Place the samples (2 g) being tested for cyanides in a 50-ml aeration tube, add 3 ml of water, and acidify with dilute sulfuric acid. Connect one end of the aeration tube with one end of the holder and place the aeration tube itself in a beaker containing water at 90°C, the surface of the water in the beaker being no higher than that of the liquid in the tube. Apply suction at the maximum rate for 5 min. Remove the test paper from the holder and place it in a dilute solution of hydrochloric acid (1:4) to dissolve any iron hydroxides which may mask the color. Wash the test paper with water and dry. A blue stain indicates the presence of cyanide, the intensity being proportional to the amount of cyanide present.

Thiocyanate Method

This method (78) depends upon the conversion of cyanide to cyanate by boiling an alkaline solution of cyanide with ammonium polysulfide until the solution is colorless or down to dryness.

$$KCN + (NH_4)_2S_2 \rightarrow (NH_4)_2S + KCNS$$

The subsequent addition of acid and ferric ion will produce the red color of ferric thiocyanate, a soluble nonionized substance.

In order to eliminate the interference of alkali and acid, the cyanate may be extracted from the dry residue obtained by evaporation of the test solution, with 3 successive portions of acetone (79). The combined acetone layer is evaporated and the residue is dissolved in water and transferred to a Nessler tube. Then 2 ml of 0.5% ferric chloride solution are added and the color produced is matched against standards treated the same way.

Procedure (80). Pass a known volume of the air to be tested through a series of absorption bubblers containing about 15 ml of 0.5% alkali solution, at the rate of about 1 cfh. Transfer the contents of the collectors to a volumetric flask and make to volume. Transfer an aliquot portion to a porcelain evaporating dish with the aid of a pipet. Add 1 ml of ammonium polysulfide solution, and evaporate slowly to dryness. Dissolve the residue in a small volume of water, add 3 ml of a 10% solution of cadmium nitrate solution, and filter into a Nessler tube. Add 2 ml of 0.5N sulfuric acid. Prepare a series of standards containing from 0.003 to 0.02 mg of hydrogen cyanide by transferring suitable aliquots of a standard potassium cyanide solution to porcelain evaporating dishes. Add 10 ml of 0.5% potassium hydroxide solution to each dish. Evaporate to dryness and then proceed as detailed for the unknown. Adjust the level in all the tubes to the same height. Add 2 ml of 10% ferric chloride solution. Compare the color produced at the expiration of ½ hr.

Silver Nitrate Method (81)

The well-known Liebig method for determining hydrocyanic acid in air consists in absorbing it in dilute sodium hydroxide solution and titrating with standard silver nitrate solution. The reaction may be expressed by the equation

$$2NaCN + AgNO_3 \rightarrow NaAg(CN)_2 + NaNO_3$$

Absorb the hydrocyanic acid in 100 ml of 2% sodium hydroxide solution, add 5 ml of 2% potassium iodide solution, and titrate with standard silver nitrate solution containing approximately 3 g of silver nitrate per liter. The volume of the gas sampled should be adjusted to provide enough hydrocyanic acid, when it is present, for a satisfactory titration and should be bubbled through the trapping liquid at the rate of about 1 lpm.

In this method of analysis the addition of potassium iodide increases the sharpness and reliability of the end point, which is indicated by the first permanent turbidity of the solution. The end point is somewhat difficult to see unless the illumination is favorable. Daylight is more satisfactory than ordinary artificial light. The end point is sharp when the titration is performed in semidarkness with a condensed beam of light passing through the solution in a generally horizontal direction. Satisfactory results may be obtained by the use of a focusing flashlight or the more powerful beam from a microscope illuminator. With such illumination a slight excess of silver nitrate produces a distinct Tyndall effect.

The end point of this titration may be obtained with greater accuracy by means of a photronic photoelectric turbidimeter, which works on the principle of determining the beginning and the degree of turbidity (82).

Bicarbonate–Iodine Method (83,84)

Hydrocyanic acid in sodium carbonate solution absorbs iodine with the formation of cyanogen iodide:

$$NaCN + I_2 \rightarrow NaI + CNI$$

Upon acidification of this mixture, iodine is released. No other gas behaves this way.

Cupples (81) modifies this method by absorbing the hydrocyanic acid in a 2% solution of sodium carbonate and subsequently titrating with standard iodine solution. The iodine solution must be added slowly, with very efficient stirring for the results to be consistent and in agreement with those of the silver nitrate method. Unless precautions are taken, it is comparatively easy to incur errors of 5–10%.

Satisfactory analyses may be made by absorbing the hydrocyanic acid in about 100 ml of 2% sodium carbonate solution, adding 10 ml of 10% potassium iodide solution and 5 ml of 2% starch solution, then titrating with standard iodine solution with efficient stirring.

Ammonia Method (85)

Small amounts of hydrocyanic acid may be determined quantitatively by use of a general characteristic reaction of *alkyl nitriles*, that is, the hydrolysis of these nitriles with either acid or alkali to form the alkyl acids or their salts and ammonia or its salts. Hydrocyanic acid follows this reaction for it is the nitrile of formic acid:

$$HCN + HCl + 2H_2O \rightarrow HCOOH + NH_4Cl$$

$$HCN + KOH + 2H_2O \rightarrow HCOOK + NH_4OH$$

The hydrolysis must be carried out in a closed system; otherwise the hydrocyanic acid would be volatilized with acid hydrolysis and the resultant ammonia with alkaline hydrolysis.

Apparatus.   For analytical purposes it is best to hydrolyze by autoclaving in a glass autoclave at 140–150°C for 30 min in an acid solution.   The Leiboff (86) urea apparatus is suitable.   The Leiboff autoclave is a resistant glass ampoule of about 35-ml capacity with an inner-seal ground-glass rod so that the autoclave may be sealed and suspended from the glass rod at the same time.   With care, satisfactory results can be obtained with medicinal ampoules if made of resistant glass.

Procedure.   Transfer the test solution, which consists of the hydrocyanic acid trapped in 0.1N sodium hydroxide solution, to a volumetric flask.   Make to volume.   Transfer a 25-ml aliquot with the aid of a pipet to the autoclave or ampoule and add 5 ml of concentrated hydrochloric acid.   Seal the ampoule, if used.   Heat slowly in an oil bath and maintain the temperature between 140 and 150°C for 30 min.   Cool, break the ampoule, if used, and transfer with the aid of water to a 50-ml beaker.   Evaporate slowly, almost to dryness, on a hot plate.   This is done to remove excess acid.   Dilute with water, transfer to a Nessler tube, and add 5 ml of Nessler's reagent (page 611).   Compare the resulting color as directed in the method for ammonia (page 612).   When an ampoule is used instead of the autoclave, cool the ampoule in an ice bath before the addition of hydrochloric acid and seal it immediately.

2. CYANOGEN

Cyanogen, (CN)₂, may occur in coal gas and is often associated with hydrogen cyanide.   Its degree of hazard is relatively the same as hydrogen cyanide.   It is so closely allied to that compound, both in its physiological and chemical action, that they are generally estimated together as hydrocyanic acid.

Cyanogen may be differentiated from and estimated in the presence of hydrocyanic acid by means of silver nitrate solution acidified with about 2 drops of dilute nitric acid for each 10 ml of $0.1N$ silver nitrate solution. This solution will absorb only the hydrocyanic acid and will not absorb the cyanogen. Since the cyanogen is not absorbed, it will pass out with the effluent gas and thus may be estimated by one of the other methods previously detailed for hydrocyanic acid such as the ferrocyanide method or the thiocyanate method. The hydrogen cyanide trapped by the silver nitrate solution may be estimated in the usual way.

3. Cyanogen Chloride and Cyanogen Bromide

Cyanogen chloride, CNCl, is a colorless, highly volatile liquid. It boils at 12.5°C, solidifies at −6.5°C, and has a specific gravity of 1.2 and a vapor density of 2.1. One volume of water will dissolve 25 volumes of cyanogen chloride at 20°C. It is soluble in organic solvents like ether and alcohol but decomposes rather readily in alcohol. Cyanogen chloride polymerizes into cyanuryl chloride, $(CNCl)_3$, which is physiologically inactive. This cyanogen compound is used industrially as a fumigant, as a warning agent in other fumigants, and in the manufacture of organic chemicals. During World War I it was used alone and in combination with arsenious chloride.

Cyanogen chloride, in addition to being a systemic poison, is a lachrymator and is used as a warning agent in commercial fumigation with hydrogen cyanide. Concentrations of the order of 0.0025 mg/liter of air induce copious watering of the eyes. A concentration of 0.5 mg/liter is intolerable and exposure to a concentration of 0.4 mg/liter for 10 min is probably a lethal exposure.

Cyanogen bromide, CNBr, is a solid which forms transparent crystals melting at 52°C. It has a sharp penetrating odor, boils at about 61°C, and has a specific gravity of 1.9 and a vapor density of 3.6. It is not readily soluble in water but dissolves more readily in alcohol and the usual organic solvents. This compound is used industrially in the synthesis of organic chemicals. In World War I it was used in mixtures with bromoacetone dissolved in benzene. This mixture was known as Campiellite by the French.

It is fairly strong lachrymator and irritant as well as systemic poison; 0.006 mg/liter will affect the conjunctiva and the mucous membranes of the respiratory tract. The limit of intolerance is 0.085 mg/liter, although some authorities give a lower concentration as the intolerable limit. It can cause death.

Sodium Sulfide Test Paper

Aspirate the air to be tested through a paper soaked in a saturated sodium sulfide solution and used moist.

$$CNBr + Na_2S \rightarrow NaCNS + NaBr$$

Add 1 drop of concentrated hydrochloric acid, followed by a few drops of 1% ferric chloride solution.   A red color due to ferric thiocyanate indicates the presence of a hydrogen halide.

Since both cyanogen chloride and bromide are very volatile, it is best to carry out this test on the original sample rather than by absorbing the gases on activated charcoal or silica granules before applying the test.

Cyanogen bromide reacts with hydrogen sulfide, hydrogen iodide, and sulfur dioxide to yield hydrogen cyanide.   This may be detected as explained.   Cyanogen chloride undergoes a similar reaction with hydrogen iodide but its reaction with hydrogen sulfide is more complex, since thiocyanic acid is also formed.   Cyanogen bromide will give the Prussian blue reaction but cyanogen chloride must be converted to hydrogen cyanide before this test can be applied.   If sodium hydroxide solution is added to a sample and it is boiled, the cyanogen halides yield ammonia.

Cyanogen chloride can be detected and estimated by the pyridine–pyrazolone method detailed in Section C-1-d of this chapter.

4. Calcium Cyanamide

Calcium cyanamide, $NC \cdot NCa$, also known as "Nitrolime" and "cyanamide" (cyanamide is actually $NC \cdot NH_2$), is made by heating calcium carbide, CaC_2, in an atmosphere of nitrogen at 1000°C.

$$CaC_2 + N_2 \rightarrow CaCN_2 + C$$

It is being manufactured in large quantities for use as a fertilizer and also for the production of ammonia and explosives.   It is a hazard in the industries mentioned above.

a. Physiological Response

Calcium cyanamide powder is caustic.   It may cause severe abscesses and cellulitis on sweating skins.   Deep-seated ulcers may occur in the mucous membranes of the nose, mouth, and throat. The symptoms exhibited in poisoning by this substance are transitory redness of the face, irritation of the nose, throat, and skin, flushing of the skin, headache, marked congestive hyperemia of the face and upper third of the body, accelerated and deepened respiration, rapid pulse, vasodilation with lowered blood pressure, and a feeling of giddiness. These symptoms are intensified in workers who have consumed alcohol. The duration as well as the severity of the poisoning are proportional to the amount and time of exposure to the substance and the condition of the subject. Attacks, according to McNally (87), last from ½ to 2 hr.

b. Detection and Determination

The amount of calcium cyanamide dust in a working atmosphere can be determined by an appropriate method described in Chapter V, such as filtration or electrostatic precipitation. The simplest method of detection is to trap the dust in water, heat, and test for ammonia. The simplest method of determination is to trap the dust in a sulfuric acid solution and then run nitrogen according to the Kjeldahl-Gunning-Arnold method for protein (88).

Calcium cyanamide is hydrolyzed with *hot* water forming ammonia:

$$CaCN_2 + 3H_2O \rightarrow CaCO_3 + 2NH_3$$

Hence, it can be estimated by direct nesslerization after distillation as described for ammonium chloride (page 613). It is well to bear in mind that small amounts of complex organic compounds may be formed during the hydrolysis.

References

1. Lewin, L., *Die Kohlenoxydvergiftung*, Stilke, Berlin, 1920.
2. Forbes, H. S., *J. Ind. Hyg.*, **3**, 11 (1921).
3. Frederick, R. C., *Analyst*, **56**, 561 (1931).
4. Dublin, L. I., and R. J. Vane, *U.S. Dept. Labor Div. Labor Standards Bull. 41* (1941).
5. von Oettingen, W. F., *U.S. Public Health Service Bull. 290* (1944).
6. Sayers, R. R., and S. J. Davenport, *U.S. Public Health Service Bull. 195* (1937).
7. Sayers, R. R., and W. P. Yant, *U.S. Bur. Mines Rept. Invest. 2476* (1923).
8. Coward, H. F., and G. W. Jones, *U.S. Bur. Mines Bull. 279* (1928).
9. Jones, G. W., *U.S. Bur. Mines, Tech. Paper 450* (1929).
10. Forbes, J. J., and G. W. Grove, *U.S. Bur. Mines Miners' Circ. 33* (1938).
11. Henderson, Y., and H. W. Haggard, *Noxious Gases*, Reinhold, New York 1927.

12. Yant, W. P., J. Chornyak, H. H. Schrenk, F. A. Patty, and R. R. Sayers, *U.S. Public Health Service Bull. 211* (1934).

13. Sayers, R. R., and W. P. Yant, *U.S. Bur. Mines Tech. Paper 373* (1925).

14. Henderson, Y., H. W. Haggard, M. C. Teague, A. L. Prince, and R. M. Wunderlich, *J. Ind. Hyg.*, **3**, 72, 137 (1921).

15. Katz, S. H., D. A. Reynolds, H. W. Frevert, and J. J. Bloomfield, *U.S. Bur. Mines Tech. Paper 355* (1926).

16. Fieldner, A. C., Y. Henderson, H. W. Haggard, A. L. Prince, and M. C. Teague, *U.S. Bur. Mines Monograph 1* (1927).

17. *Ind. Hyg. Newsletter*, **7**, No. 8, 19 (1947).

18. Yant, W. P., and L. B. Berger, *U.S. Bur. Mines Miners' Circ. 34* (1936).

19. Lunge, G., and H. R. Ambler, *Technical Gas Analysis*, Van Nostrand, New York, 1934.

20. McCullough, J. D., R. A. Crance, and A. O. Beckman, *Anal. Chem.*, **19**, 999 (1947).

21. Sayers, R. R., and W. P. Yant, *U.S. Public Health Service Reprint 790* (1922).

22. Sayers, R. R., W. P. Yant, and G. W. Jones, *U.S. Public Health Service Reprint 872* (1924).

23. Douglas, C. G., and J. S. Haldane, *J. Physiol.*, **44**, 305 (1912).

24. *Fed. Bd. Vocational Education Bull. 39*, Coal-Mine Gases (1931).

25. Yant, W. P., F. A. Patty, H. H. Schrenk, and L. B. Berger, *U.S. Bur. Mines Rept. Invest. 3040* (1930).

26. Berger, L. B., and W. P. Yant, *U.S. Bur. Mines Repr. Invest. 3030* (1930).

27. U.S. Pat. 1,644,014.

28. Chaignon, E., *Compt. Rend. Congr. Intern. Chim. Ind. 15th*, **1936**, 261; *Chem. Abstr.*, **30**, 5464 (1936).

29. Winkler, L. W., *Z. Anal. Chem.*, **102**, 99 (1935), *Chem. Abstr.*, **29**, 3626, 7222 (1935).

30. *Dept. Sci. Ind. Research Brit. Leaflet 7* (1939).

31. Goldman, D. E., and J. A. Mathis, *Naval Med. Res. Inst., Research Project X-417, Rept. 4* (1945).

32. Gautier, A., *Compt. Rend.*, **126**, 793, 931 (1898).

32a. Niclaux, M., *Compt. Rend.*, **126**, 746 (1898); 154, 1166 (1912).

33. Kinnicutt, L. P., and G. R. Sanford, *J. Am. Chem. Soc.*, **22**, 14 (1900).

34. Pire, L. R., *Anales Real Soc. Espan. Fis. Quim.*, **27**, 192 (1929).

35. Lunge, G., and C. A. Keane, *Technical Methods of Chemical Analysis*, Van Nostrand, New York, 1924.

36. Goldman, F. H., A. A. Coleman, H. B. Elkins, H. H. Schrenk, and C. A. Smucker, *Am. Public Health Assoc. Yearbook 1940–41*, 118.

37. American Gas Association Laboratories, Cleveland, Ohio.

38. Teague, M. C., *Ind. Eng. Chem.*, **12**, 964 (1920); *U.S. Bur. Mines Monograph 1*, 51 (1927).

39. Lamb, A. B., W. C. Bray, and J. C. W. Fraser, *Ind. Eng. Chem.*, **13**, 213 (1920).

40. Fraser, J. C. W., and C. C. Scalione, U.S. Pat. 1,345,323 (1920).

41. Lamb, A. B., C. C. Scalione, and G. Edgar, *J. Am. Chem. Soc.*, **44**, 738 (1922).

42. Fieldner, A. C., S. H. Katz, and E. G. Meiter, *Eng. News-Record*, **95**, 423 (1925).
43. Katz, S. H., and H. W. Frevert, *Ind. Eng. Chem.*, **20**, 564 (1928).
44. Frevert, H. W., and E. H. Francis, *Ind. Eng. Chem. Anal. Ed.*, **6**, 226 (1934).
45. Mine Safety Appliances Co., Pittsburgh, Pa.
46. Setterlind, A. N., *Ind. Hyg. Newsletter*, **7**, No. 4, 8 (1947).
47. Waters, J. L., and N. W. Hartz, "An Improved Lift-Type Infrared Gas and Liquid Analyzer," Industrial Soc. of America Meeting, Houston (1951).
48. Jacobs, M. B., M. M. Braverman, and S. Hochheiser, "Variation of Carbon Monoxide Concentration in New York City Atmosphere," Am. Chem. Soc. N.Y. Section Meeting-in-Miniature, March 1958.
49. Christman, A. A., W. D. Block, and J. Schultz, *Ind. Eng. Chem. Anal. Ed.*, **9**, 153 (1937).
50. Winkler, L. W., *Z. Anal. Chem.*, **97**, 18 (1934).
51. Hillebrand, W. F., G. E. Lundell, H. A. Bright, and J. I. Hoffman, *Applied Inorganic Analysis*, 2nd ed., Wiley, 1953.
52. Diehl, H. C., *Applications of the Dioximes to Analytical Chemistry*, Iowa State College, Ames, 1940.
53. Lubriseal (Arthur H. Thomas Co.) is satisfactory.
54. Polis, R. D., L. B. Berger, and H. H. Schrenk, *U.S. Bur. Mines Rept. Invest. 3785* (1944).
55. Tiffany, J. E., *U.S. Bur. Mines Rept. Invest 2920* (1929).
56. Gonzales, J. A., M. Vance, and M. Helpern, *Legal Medicine and Toxicology*, Appleton-Century, New York, 1937.
57. Haldane, J. S., *Trans. Inst. Mining Engrs. (London)*, **8**, 567 (1894–95).
58. Sayers, R. R., *U.S. Bur. Mines Tech. Paper 334* (1923).
59. Martin, W., and J. R. Green, *Ind. Eng. Chem. Anal. Ed.*, **5**, 114 (1933).
60. Spector, N. A., and B. F. Dodge, *Anal. Chem.*, **19**, 55 (1947).
61. Berger, L. B., and H. H. Schrenk, *U.S. Bur. Mines Inform. Circ. 7017* (1938).
62. Mack, W. B., *Plant Physiol.*, **5**, 1 (1930).
63. Sutton, F., *Volumetric Analysis*, 11th ed., Blakiston, Philadelphia, 1924.
64. Fieldner, A. C., C. G. Oberfell, M. C. Teague, and J. N. Lawrence, *Ind. Eng. Chem.*, **11**, 523 (1919).
65. *Dept. Sci. Ind. Research Brit. Leaflet 2* (1938).
66. *Analyst*, **63**, 658 (1938).
67. Williams, C. L., B. E. Holesendorf, and J. R. Ridlon, *U.S. Public Health Service Reprint 1518* (**1932**).
68. Underwriters Laboratories, Ind., *List of Inspected Appliances*, December 1938.
69. Sieverts, A., and A. Hermsdorf, *Angew. Chem.*, **34**, 3 (1921).
70. Sherrard, G. C., *U.S. Public Health Service Reprint 1224* (1928).
71. Katz, S. H., and E. S. Longfellow, *J. Ind. Hyg.*, **5**, 97 (1923–24).
72. Medical Division, Merck & Co., Ind., Rahway, N. J.
73. Nicholson, R. I., *Analyst*, **66**, 189 (1941).
74. Epstein, J., *Anal. Chem.*, **19**, 272 (1947).
75. Lunge, G., and H. R. Ambler, *Technical Gas Analysis*, Van Nostrand, New York, 1934.

76. Lander, G. D., and A. E. Walden, *Analyst*, **36**, 266 (1911).
77. Gettler, A. O., and L. Goldbaum, *Anal. Chem.*, **19**, 270 (1947).
78. Francis, C. K., and W. B. Connell, *J. Am. Chem. Soc.*, **35**, 1624 (1913).
79. Johnson, M. O., *J. Am. Chem. Soc.*, **38**, 1230 (1916).
80. Zhitkova, A. S., S. I. Kaplun, and J. B. Ficklen, *Poisonous Gases*, Service to Industry, Hartford, 1936.
81. Cupples, H. L., *Ind. Eng. Chem. Anal. Ed.*, **5**, 50 (1933).
82. Bartholomew, E. T., and E. C. Raby, *Ind. Eng. Chem. Anal. Ed.*, **7**, 68 (1935).
83. Seil, G. E., *Ind. Eng. Chem.*, **18**, 142 (1926).
84. Lunge, G., and H. R. Ambler, *Technical Gas Analysis*, Van Nostrand, New York, 1934.
85. Gales, N., and A. Pensa, *Ind. Eng. Chem. Anal. Ed.*, **5**, 80 (1933).
86. Leiboff, S. B., and B. S. Kahn, *J. Biol. Chem.*, **83**, 347 (1929).
87. McNally, B. D., *Toxicology, Industrial Medicine*, Chicago, 1937.
88. Jacobs, M. B., *The Chemical Analysis of Foods and Food Products*, Van Nostrand, New York, 1945.

CHAPTER XVIII

DETECTOR TUBES

Although the use of detector tubes for checking the atmosphere to which workers are exposed has been widely expanded over the past 15 years, it would be a mistake to think that this is really a new method. Actually one of the first detector tubes, developed by U.S. Bureau of Mines personnel for the detection of hydrogen sulfide, was produced in 1935 (1). The U.S. Bureau of Mines personnel also developed the Hoolamite detector tube for carbon monoxide and a tube for organic halide gases as early as 1943. Actually the precursors of the modern tubes for the detection and estimation of industrial poisons were those tubes developed by the Chemical Warfare Service of the U.S. Army before and during World War II for the detection of war gases. This work resulted in the development of the M-4 and M-9 kits used in World War II. Some of these tests were tube tests in which the war gas agent was adsorbed on silica gel and then drops of reagents were added. Some of the tests in the unclassified literature were described in U.S. Office of Civilian Defense Publication 2219, *Identification of Chemical Warfare Agents*. Jacobs described and discussed a number of such tests, and Fig. 3 on page 72 of his book, *War Gases—Their Identification and Decontamination* (2), shows an absorption tube with a reagent and a pump to draw in the air to be tested.

A major step in the development of detector tubes was the preliminary work at the Royal Aircraft Establishment, Farnborough, England, and the subsequent work of the U.S. National Bureau of Standards, as explained in Section D-1 of this chapter.

It is beyond the scope of this chapter to detail methods for the manufacture and use of all tubes that can be used for industrial hygiene purposes, but a representative number will be described. Tubes for inorganic elements and compounds such as ammonia, arsine, bromine, carbon dioxide, carbon monoxide, chlorine, chlorine dioxide, chromic acid mist, hydrazine, hydrocyanic acid, hydrogen fluoride, hydrogen sulfide, lead dust and fume, mercury, nitrogen

742

dioxide, and sulfur dioxide are commercially available (3). Table XVIII-1 (4) summarizes some of the detector tubes available and their characteristics.

A. Evaluation

In evaluating the use of detector tubes as contrasted with more precise methods of analysis, one must take into consideration the general objectives of the analytical chemistry of industrial toxicology. These are the prevention, control, and regulation of industrial poisoning. Prevention, protection, control, and regulation depend upon chemical analyses preformed to give the following:

(1) The concentration of a poisonous or noxious substance in the working atmosphere and therefore the exposure level.

(2) The amount of poisonous or harmful material absorbed by the worker.

(3) The efficiency of control devices.

(4) The adequacy of placement of control devices.

It is clear that detector tubes can be used in some measure for the first, third, and fourth types of chemical analysis, but not for the second.

Detector tubes have an important role to play in industrial toxicology. They have, however, important limitations. In the brochures of various tube manufacturers, it can be seen that the sensitivity of some tubes is not great enough to detect the maximum allowable concentration of a given pollutant. This in itself does not mean that the detector tube has no value, but in such instances it is essential to employ from time to time those wet test or instrumental methods that are sensitive enough. It is also best to check air analyses by different methods to make certain that the detector tubes or, for that matter, the wet test methods are giving corrrect values.

1. INTERPRETATION

One of the chief advantages claimed for detector tube testing is that "untrained" personnel can be used to perform the tests. Caution should be observed in accepting this claim since interpretation of the results is not as simple as the testing procedure (5). The author has seen experienced chemists differ when reading the color results of carbon monoxide detector tube tests. If trained personnel can

Gases and vapors[a]	Minimum scale	Full scale	Detecting limit	Feeding time, min
Acetone	0.25%	5.0%	50 ppm	3
Acetylene	20 ppm	1300 ppm	10 ppm	3
Acrylonitrile				
low	10 ppm	500 ppm	5 ppm	3
high	0.10%	3.5%	10 ppm	3
Ammonia				
low	30 ppm	800 ppm	5 ppm	3
high	1.0%	25%	500 ppm	3
Arsine	5 ppm	160 ppm	1 ppm	3
Benzene	10 ppm	310 ppm	1 ppm	3
Bromine	10 ppm	300 ppm	0.1 ppm	3
Carbon dioxide				
low	300 ppm	8000 ppm	50 ppm	5
high	0.10%	2.6%	100 ppm	5
Carbon disulfide				
low	10 ppm	200 ppm	5 ppm	5
high	20 ppm	500 ppm	10 ppm	3
Carbon monoxide				
A	0.01%	0.1%	10 ppm	0.5
B	0.01%	0.1%	10 ppm	0.5
C	0.01%	0.1%	10 ppm	0.5
Chlorine	1 ppm	100 ppm	0.1 ppm	3
Chlorine dioxide	10 ppm	500 ppm	0.3 ppm	3
Cyclohexane	0.01%	0.6%	0.3 ppm	3
Diethyl ether	0.04%	1.4%	1 ppm	3
Dimethyl ether	0.01%	1.2%	4 ppm	3
Ethyl acetate	0.10%	5.0%	100 ppm	3
Ethyl alcohol				
low	0.01%	0.11%	20 ppm	0.5
high	0.10%	5.0%	20 ppm	3
Ethylene	0.1 ppm	100 ppm	0.1 ppm	3 × 5 times
Ethylene oxide	0.10%	3.5%	10 ppm	3
Hexane (n)	0.01%	0.6%	0.1 ppm	3
Hydrogen cyanide				
low	5 ppm	100 ppm	5 ppm	3
high	0.01%	3.0%	10 ppm	3
Hydrogen sulfide				
low	1 ppm	160 ppm	0.5 ppm	3
high	100 ppm	1700 ppm	10 ppm	3
high	50 ppm	1600 ppm	2 ppm	3

XVIII-1
Tubes (4)

Measuring method	Original color	Changed color	Remarks
Length	Yellowish orange	Blue	
Length	Pale yellow	Brownish blue	
Length	Orange	Blackish green	Without an orifice plate
Length	Orange	Blackish green	
Length	Pink	Yellow	
Length	Pink	Purplish blue	
Length	White	Brownish black	
Length	White	Reddish orange	
Length	Grayish white	Orange	
Length	Blue purple	Pale pink	
Length	Blue purple	Pale pink	
Length	Blue purple	White	Hydrogen sulfide can
Length	Blue purple	White	be measured simultaneously
Colorimetric	Pale yellow	Green-blue	
Colorimetric	Pale yellow	Green-blue	In presence of ethylene
Colorimetric	Pale yellow	Green-blue	In presence of ethylene and nitrogen dioxide
Length	Grayish white	Orange	
Length	Grayish white	Orange	
Length	Orange	Blackish green	
Length	Orange	Blackish green	
Length	Orange	Blackish green	
Length	Orange	Blackish green	
Colorimetric	Yellow orange	Blue green	Without an orifice plate
Length	Yellow orange	Blue green	
Colorimetric	Pale yellow	Dark blue	
Length	Yellow orange	Dark yellow green	
Length	Orange	Blackish green	
Length	Yellow	Reddish brown	
Length	Yellow	Reddish brown	
Length	White	Brown	
Length	White	Black	
Length	Pale yellow	Blackish blue	In presence of sulfur dioxide

(continued)

TABLE XVIII-1

Gases and vapors[a]	Minimum scale	Full scale	Detecting limit	Feeding time, min
Mercury	0.1 mg/m³	12.0 mg/m³	0.02 mg/m³	1 × 5 times
Methyl alcohol				
low	10 ppm	1000 ppm	10 ppm	0.5 × 5 times
high	0.1%	6.0%	20 ppm	3
Nickel carbonyl	20 ppm	700 ppm	10 ppm	3
Nitrogen dioxide	1 ppm	5000 ppm	0.05 ppm	3
Perchloroethylene	10 ppm	400 ppm	1 ppm	3
Phosphine				
low	5 ppm	90 ppm	1 ppm	3
high	20 ppm	900 ppm	5 ppm	3
Sulfur dioxide				
low	5 ppm	300 ppm	1 ppm	3
high	0.1%	4.0%	100 ppm	3
Toluene	10 ppm	1500 ppm	1 ppm	3
Trichloroethylene	10 ppm	400 ppm	1 ppm	3
Vinyl chloride	0.05%	1.0%	20 ppm	3

[a] Volume of sample gas = 100 ml.

have such differences of opinion, untrained personnel will differ or be prone to misread results much more readily.

2. INTERFERENCE

In general the customary methods of analysis are designed to avoid or eliminate the interference of conflicting substances, thus making the method "specific." Often this is difficult to do with wet test and instrumental methods. It is even more difficult to achieve at times with detector tubes (5). Consequently, one must be particularly aware of the conditions under which the tube tests are performed.

3. ECONOMIC ASPECTS

It is necessary at times to estimate the actual costs of using detector tubes as compared with more precise methods. It is clear, of course, that if the cost of a laboratory is included, then detector kits are far more inexpensive. If a laboratory is available, however, then even if one includes the cost of special equipment, it may well be that

(continued)

Measuring method	Original color	Changed color	Remarks
Length	Yellowish gray	Pale orange	Operate five times without an orifice plate
Colorimetric	Yellow orange	Blue	
Length	Yellow orange	Blue	
Length	Pale yellow	Blue purple	
Length	Grayish white	Orange	
Length	White	Reddish orange	
Length	Pale blue	Dull yellow	
Length	Pale blue	Reddish purple	
Length	Blue purple	White	
Length	Yellow	Blue	
Length	White	Reddish brown	
Length	White	Reddish orange	
Length	Orange	Blackish green	

the ultimate total cost of using detector tubes will be higher than use of a more precise instrumental method.

Thus, once a monitoring instrument is set up in proper working condition, the amount of labor expense is very small since all that is required is a renewal of ink, replacement of charts, reading of the charts, and a check of the instrument regularly to see that it is operating properly. Assume that the cost of the device is $3000. For this amount of money, information can be obtained on a minute by minute basis, 24 hr a day, 7 days a week, 365 days a year. Use of detector tubes, for example, even once an hour only 8 hr a day means a charge of $4 per day or a charge of nearly $1000 a year for the tubes alone, not counting labor costs. It is clear that if regular and periodic testing is performed, precise instrumental methods, in the long run, may be cheaper as well as better than the use of detector tubes.

4. EASE OF DETERMINATION

It is often assumed that detector tubes are always simpler to use than other methods. This is not necessarily true. Thus, methods have been developed for testing sulfur dioxide which employ sequence

TABLE XVIII-2
Results of Tests on Specific Gases (5)

Gas (TLV)	Tube[a]	Response
Arsine (0.05 ppm)	A	Indication is by abrupt color change from yellow to pale gray, difficult to see. Tubes read high (safe side) by factor of 2.5. One run at 0.072 ppm resulted in estimates ranging from 0.31 to 1.1 ppm with mean of 0.45 ppm (factor = 6.25). To users inexperienced with this tube errors on unsafe side may occur.
	B	High-range phosphine tube responded to arsine. Length-of-stain tube, color change from light blue to brown, easy to see. Potentially capable of calibration and use as arsine detector.
	C	Arsine tube unavailable at time of test, but same tube used for stibine.
Carbon monoxide (100 ppm)	A	Length-of-stain tube, color change from white to blue diffiult to evaluate as 2 separate shades developed. Results of estimates erratic at concentrations ranging from 2.5 to 230 ppm.
	B	Color-change tube, yellow to green to blue. Color judgment varies with observer. Gave good results at 25 and 230 ppm, showed ability to detect CO at 2.5 ppm. Not affected by 200 ppm CH_4 or 7 ppm NO_2. Use of temperature correction chart supplied led to some error.
	C	Color-change tube, from yellow to green to blue, same as D. This tube was not tested.
	D	National Bureau of Standards color-change tube. Change from yellow to green to blue. Color judgment varies with observer. Response at 25 and 230 ppm good. Ability to estimate concentration of 2.5 ppm. At 100 ppm some differences between observers' interpretation of colors noted. No interference with 200 ppm CH_4. Serious interference with 7 ppm NO_2.
	E	National Bureau of Standards color-change tube, same as D.
	F	Length-of-stain tube, color change from yellow to dark brown, very easy to see. Good response at 2.5, 25, and 230 ppm. No interference with 200 ppm CH_4 or 7 ppm NO_2.
NO_2 (5 ppm)	A	Length-of-stain tube, color change from white to orange, read with some difficulty. Read high by a factor of 2–4 at 5 and 77 ppm. Some response shown at 0.1 ppm. Error here is on safe side. No interference from standard mixture.

(continued)

TABLE XVIII-2 (*continued*)

Gas (TLV)	Tube[a]	Response
	B	Length-of-stain tube, color change from white to brown, fairly easy to read. Very erratic results from tubes on hand. At 4.9 ppm, of 17 tubes taken at random, 8 were poorly packed; remainder estimated range 0.5–10 ppm with mean of 2.4 ppm(unsafe error). At 77 ppm, response ranged from 30 to 500 ppm. Manufacturer indicates improved tube now available.
Stibine (0.1 ppm)	A	Color-change tube, abrupt change from yellow to gray. Immediate color change hard to see. Uses arsine tube, no stibine calibration supplied. At 0.08 ppm mean response was 0.04 ppm with range of 0.02–0.06, based on arsine calibration scale. At 0.64 ppm mean estimate was 1.1 ppm. Tube responded at 0.006 ppm. Negligible effect with standard interferences. Incorrect instructions were packed with tubes used.
	B	No response with phosphine tube.
	C	Color-change tube, abrupt change from yellow to gray. Ease in seeing color depends upon relative concentration. Tube performed as claimed by manufacturer. Not affected by standard interferences.
Phosgene (1 ppm)	A	Length-of-stain tube, color change from blue to green. Leading edge of stain sharp. Very easy to see. Tube response excellent, with scale factor of approximately 2 (safe side). Bleaching of color noted after 4–8 hr. Tube could then be reused once. Questionable effect from standard interferences, causing tube to respond closer to manufacturer's rating.
Chlorine (1 ppm)	A	Length-of-stain tube, color change from white to orange, fairly easy to read. Correction factors of two batches at 1.1 ppm were 4 and 2.5. Analysis of variance showed significant differences between lots. Tests run 6 months later showed scale factors of 1.8. At 11 ppm, scale factor was approximately 2. All errors were on safe side. Many tubes in early lots were poorly packed.
	B	Length-of-stain tube, color change from white to brown, easy to read. Mixed response; one batch gave no readings; one batch showed mean concentration of 1.2 ppm (range 1–1.75 ppm) when exposed to 1.1 ppm.

(*continued*)

TABLE XVIII-2 (*continued*)

Gas (TLV)	Tube[a]	Response
Chlorine dioxide (1 ppm)	A	Length-of-scale tube, same as for chlorine tube A. At 1 ppm, estimations ranged from 1.7 to 2.5 ppm. At 0.14 ppm estimates ranged from 0.25 to 0.29 ppm. Scale factor of 2 appeared to be consistent.
Chlorine dioxide (1 ppm)	B	Length-of-stain tube same as for type B chlorine and NO₂, but different calibration curve. At 1 ppm estimates ranged from 1.75 to 2.0 ppm. At 0.14 ppm estimates ranged from 0.1 to 0.2 ppm. Scale factor and response appeared to be consistent.
Mercury vapor (0.5 mg/m³)	A	No response at TLV values. Tube indicated presence of Hg vapor when placed in flask containing the metal.

[a] Descriptions of tube types are as follows:

A: A kit. A bellows device with a nominal capacity of 100 ml is used as a pump. Flow rate through the sampling tube depends on the packing. Outside diameter approximately 7.5 mm; length approximately 75 mm. In most cases the calibration is marked directly on the tube.

B: A kit. The pump is a cylinder of 100-ml nominal capacity fitted with a hand-honed piston. A critical flow orifice is placed between the sampling tube and the pump. Approximate diameter, 4 mm; approximate length, 85 mm. Calibration chart is supplied.

C: A kit. Two models, with or without furnace for combustion of halogenated hydrocarbons to halide, available. The pump is a squeeze bulb of 50-ml nominal capacity with a check valve. Flow rate depends on tube packing. Diameter, approximately 5 mm; length, approximately 45 mm. Manufacturers' calibrations are semiquantitative. Tubes indicate concentrations at the threshold limit value, approximately one-half threshold limit value or less, and approximately twice the threshold limit value or greater.

D: A complete unit. The pumps are usually squeeze bulb devices of 50-ml nominal capacity. Flow rate controlled by adjustable needle valve. Tube diameters and lengths vary with type.

E: Carbon monoxide detecting tube only. Developed by National Bureau of Standards. A squeeze bulb pump with adjustable needle valve is used.

F: Carbon monoxide detector only. Estimate of concentration is made by measuring the length of the developed stain. The pump is a spring-loaded diaphragm of 16-ml nominal capacity.

G: Single tube for determination of tri- and perchloroethylene and gasoline vapors. The pump is a squeeze bulb of approximately 50-ml capacity. No flow regulating device is used.

samplers that require only the replenishment of a reservoir, the removal of 24 test tubes, and replacement of 24 other test tubes; then one can obtain the result either by a very simple titration or the rise of a conductivity meter. Here less labor is required than detector tube tests, the results are more accurate, the costs are less, and 24 samples per day can be obtained.

B. Accuracy

The Occupational Health Program of the U. S. Public Health Service made a study of the accuracy and reliability of some of the detector tubes commercially available. Kusnetz and co-workers (5) point out that gas-detecting tubes are, in general, semiquantitative devices useful largely for screening or preliminary survey work. Even at this level their use and interpretation of the results obtained should be by qualified industrial hygienists. The accuracy of the devices is enhanced by careful calibration of the tubes and auxiliary equipment.

Detector tubes indicate the presence of contaminants in the air either by changes in color or color intensity or by the length of a stain apparent in the tube. In tubes dependent on change of color or color intensity, the contaminant is only slightly sorbed, the composition of the gas is almost the same in the exit stream as in the entering mixture, and a uniform color is developed throughout the tube. If temperature, flow rate, and sample volume are constant, tints related to concentration of the contaminant are developed.

In those tubes which indicate concentration by length of stain, complete sorption of the contaminant is assumed. The accuracy of the result (4) depends upon the particle size of the detecting reagent, the volume of the sample gas, the feeding speed, the diameter of the detector tube, and the temperature.

Seven types of commercial detector tubes were tested (5). Those described as kits consist of a single aspirator device with a variety of tubes for different contaminants. Others contain a special pump and tubes for a specific gas or vapor. A summary of results using these devices on a variety of gases is given in Table XVIII-2.

C. Calibration

The theoretical aspects of the calibration of detector tubes has been discussed at length by Kusnetz and co-workers (5) and by Kitagawa

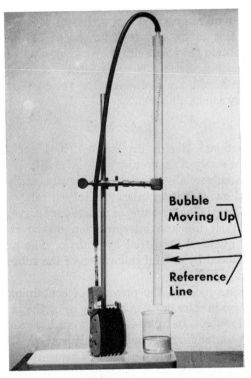

Fig. XVIII-1. Field calibration assembly showing the plastic bubble meter attached to one type of sampler.

(4).   In addition Kusnetz (6) has designed a device for calibration suitable for field use.   This consists of a buret with a capacity of approximately 125 ml which was constructed from ¾-in. i.d. thin-wall (¹⁄₁₆-in.) plastic tubing.   The capacity of the buret between 90 and 100 ml was marked off in 1-ml divisions by using a volumetric pipet and filling the buret with successive known quantities of water.   A nipple was sealed to the top of the plastic tube to facilitate the attachment of rubber tubing.   The device (Fig. XVIII-1) was then ready for use in calibrating the pumps used with detector tubes.

   Procedure.   Make a solution of synthetic detergent and permit the foam to subside.   Pour the solution into the buret very carefully to avoid raising additional foam.   Then empty the buret so that its inside walls are coated with a thin film of the detergent solution.   Place the open end of the buret in contact with the surface of the detergent solution for a moment in such a manner that a detergent film adheres to the mouth of the buret when withdrawn. When suction is applied through the rubber tube attached to the nipple on the buret, the detergent bubble can be pulled up through the length of the buret.

Friction between the detergent bubble and the wall of the buret is negligible; for example, 0.02 in. of water pressure would move the bubble. In the calibration procedure, start the bubble at the reference point, draw air through the sampling tube with the particular aspirating device under test, and note the total volume after the bubble has come to equilibrium.

D. Carbon Monoxide Detectors

1. NBS INDICATOR

The National Bureau of Standards carbon monoxide indicator (7) is based on preliminary work done by the Royal Aircraft Establishment, Farnborough, England. The discovery by the National Bureau of Standards investigators of the necessity for the elimination of all traces of chlorides and organic matter in the indicating gel was the basis of a significant advance in the development of detector methods for carbon monoxide.

When highly purified silica gel, impregnated with ammonium molybdate and a solution of palladium or palladium oxide digested in sulfuric acid, is exposed to carbon monoxide, a molybdenum blue is formed, the depth of color varying from faint green to blue in proportion to the amount of carbon monoxide.

Preparation of the Indicating and Guard Gels. As mentioned, traces of chlorides or organic matter will spoil the indicating gel; therefore, all glassware must be carefully cleaned, preferably with fuming sulfuric acid.

Purification of the Silica Gel. Use Davison Chemical Corporation (Baltimore, Md.) No. 697535-600-C silica gel for the preparation of the indicating gel and their No. 69520-650 for the guard gel. These should be free from bits of wood, paper, or other foreign matter. The gels must be purified by oxidation with nitric acid as follows:

Place approximately 3.2 lb of gel into a 4-liter Pyrex serum bottle, cover 2 in. with nitric acid (sp gr 1.42), and immerse the bottle to its upper shoulder in a steam bath. Digest for 1 week, during which time the level of the acid should be maintained, and keep a free flow of steam stirring through the bath. A ⚡ 45/50 male grinding should be drawn into a retort-shaped delivery tube and inserted in the corresponding grinding of the bottle neck to discharge condensate into a beaker, or a reflux condenser can be used.

Remove the acid by means of an immersion filter attached to a trap and suction. A satisfactory filter is made from a 25-mm porcelain plate with 1-mm holes, sealed loosely into a 18 × 22-mm Pyrex tube. Smaller holes tend to plug. In removing acid or water from the gel, try to avoid producing a water hammer with the suction.

Wash the gel with distilled water according to the following schedule, and replace in the steam bath after each complete washing:

Time after removal of acid, days	Complete changes of water, with removal of water between each change
0	12
1	7
2	5
3	3
4	2

The pH of the wash water after a final 4-day leaching in the steam bath should be 5.0 or greater for the No. 697535-600-C gel, and 4.9 or greater for the No. 69520-650 gel. Continue washing if necessary to achieve this condition. When the proper pH is reached, remove water thoroughly with the immersion filter, place the bottle in an electric oven at 100°C until the gel appears dry, and then heat 3 days at 320°C. In the same oven place a tube containing the guard gel. This tube is made from a ⚡ 45/50 male grinding extended 5 cm at the small end and then closed except for 20 1-mm holes. The large end is rounded and drawn down to a 1-cm ringed neck, which may be grasped with crucible tongs. The whole tube is filled with the guard gel previously prepared. After 3 days, remove the bottle of activated gel and immediately insert the guard tube. When the gel is cool, it is ready for use.

Guard Gel. The No. 69520-650 gel needs no further treatment other than the purification given above. It is the guard gel used to protect the indicating gel in the final indicating tube. It must be kept dry and free from organic vapors and must therefore be stored in ⨍ 45 bottles equipped with guard tubes, which are themselves filled with guard gel.

Indicating Gel. After purification and activation, the No. 697-535-600-C gel is converted into indicating gel by impregnating with a palladium and molybdenum solution, followed by drying in two successive states.

Reagents. *Palladium Sulfate Solution.* Heat about 14 g of finely divided palladium metal at 600°C overnight in a furnace to convert as much as possible to palladium oxide, PdO. Transfer this to a 500-ml Pyrex boiling flask having a thermometer well and a ⨍ joint, add 175 ml of concentrated sulfuric acid, connect a reflux condenser, and heat to boiling (about 300°C) until all of the palladium and its oxide appear to have been converted to sulfate. At this point, a dark-brown, shiny, crystalline precipitate will be formed. Continue heating, and add water slowly and cautiously, not more than 1 ml at a time, through the top of the condenser. If sulfur dioxide is evolved, as evidenced by its odor, stop adding water and heat at the then existing temperature until no more sulfur dioxide is evolved. Then slowly continue the addition of water, stopping the refluxing if necessary, until all of the crystalline precipitate has dissolved and the boiling temperature is 200°C. Cool the solution, filter through a porous porcelain or glass filtering crucible of fine porosity, and dilute to 500 ml in a volumetric flask.

Dilute a 5-ml aliquot of this solution to 250 ml and determine the palladium content by precipitation with dimethylglyoxime (8) and the sulfuric acid content by titrating the filtrate and washings from the palladium precipitation with standard alkali, using methyl red as the indicator. Calculate the amount of additional sulfuric acid needed and the volume to which the solution must be diluted to give a final solution containing 0.013 g of palladium and 0.33 g of sulfuric acid per milliliter.

Molybdenum Solution. Dissolve 50 g of reagent grade ammonium molybdate in 1 liter of water.

Impregnating the Gel. Mix 750 ml of water, 450 ml of ammonium molybdate solution, and 100 ml of palladium sulfate solution in a clean 4-liter Pyrex serum bottle. Slowly add to this 2 liters of the purified, freshly activated silica gel, rotating the bottle so that the gel is always submerged. The bright yellow silicomolybdate complex forms immediately. Allow to stand 2 hr or overnight.

Initial Drying. Heat the bottle of impregnated gel to 60°C in a water bath, reduce the pressure in the bottle to about 4 cm Hg, and evaporate off the excess water. During this process remove the bottle from the water bath every minute or two and tap it firmly on a sponge rubber pad in such a way that the solid which tends to coat out on the walls of the bottle is continually moistened and taken up by the gel. When the gel is surface dry, continue to heat and evacuate, rotating the bottle vigorously in the water bath every 2 or 3 min. At first, when a fresh portion of the surface-dry gel comes in contact with the hot wall of the bottle, the evolution of water vapor is evidenced by the quivering and dancing of the gel. When this finally ceases, the initial drying is completed. The gel has now turned from pale to bright yellow. The time required for this process is about 6 hr.

To reduce the pressure in the bottle for the above process, first connect it to an adapter made from a ⊤ 45/50 male grinding drawn out to a 10-mm tube pointing downward. This grinding should fit the corresponding female one in the neck of the bottle well enough so that when water is used as a lubricant no excessive leakage occurs at 4 cm Hg absolute. About two-thirds of the bottles and grindings taken from the stock should meet this requirement. Never lubricate this grinding with anything but water. It will operate dry satisfactorily during the last stages of drying. Connect the adapter to a 2-liter filter flask, and this in turn to an efficient water aspirator. A mercury manometer may be teed into the line to indicate proper operation of the aspirator. A 25-lb lard can can serve as the water bath, and a rubber tube tied between its handles keeps the bottle submerged to the proper level between the periodic shakings.

Final Drying. Transfer equal portions of the partially dried indicating gel to fourteen 500-ml round-bottom boiling flasks having necks 35 cm long and with a 2.5-cm bore, which terminate in a ⊤ 24/40 grinding. This transfer is facilitated by an adapter made from a ⊤ 45/50 male grinding, drawn down and curved like a spout. Connect these flasks to a manifold having a series of ⊤ 24/40 female grindings sealed as tees to a horizontal tube, which in turn connects through a trap immersed in liquid air to a McLeod gauge, a mercury-vapor pump, and a mechanical backing pump. The cold trap should accommodate about 50 g of ice without plugging. (Apiezon L may be used to lubricate ⊤ joints and stopcocks in this vacuum system, but the pumps must be started immediately after the flasks are connected and some positive flow from the gel to the trap and pump must be maintained hereafter.)   Evacuate the system until the pressure has dropped to approximately 0.028 mm Hg.   This will probably vary some with each apparatus.   The time required is about 20 hr.

Shut off the pump, gauge, and trap, and slowly open the flasks to the atmosphere through a large drier containing alternate layers of silica gel, Hopcalite, and silica gel.   When atmospheric pressure is reached, remove the flasks, very carefully remove grease from the male grindings, using only a dry, clean cloth, and transfer the dried gel back into the serum bottle, closing this with a dry ⨎ 45 stopper. Determine the water content of the gel as detailed below.

Determination of Water Content, Optimum Water Content, and Blending.   Make an empirical test as follows: Weigh out 1–2 g of the gel in a conical glass-stoppered weighing bottle, place this in a small Pyrex vacuum desiccator containing purified and activated silica gel, and put this in turn in a vacuum electric oven at 105°C for 16 hr while continuously evacuating.   Admit air to the cooling desiccator through a drying tube, and weigh the cooled bottle to determine the loss in weight.   It is recognized that this test is not a true determination of water, since all of the water is not driven off, and some of the acid probably is.   However, it is sufficient for controlling the preparation of the gel.

The sensitivity of the gel is a function of its residual water content, and while gels are sensitive over a fairly wide range—about 2–20 mg/g—the optimum lies between 8 and 14 mg/g.   For immediate use in laboratory-type tubes (see below) against dry silica gel, reduce the water to 10 or 12 mg/g.   For field use after storage for 1 month or longer in sealed tubes against dry gel reduce the water to 15 or 18 mg/g.

If the drying process yields gels with less water than corresponds to the optimum, blend these with gels containing more water than the optimum.   Blend by mixing *thoroughly* in 6- or 9-liter serum bottles in the proper proportion by weight (or volume) to produce the desired total water content per gram.   The water content of the wet gel should not exceed 100 mg/g; and the dry gel should contain no less than 4 mg/g.   Allow a 1-month storage to secure equilibrium.

Blending is not necessary if a product of uniform calibration is not required.   Thus, in the laboratory determinations may be made with color standards prepared from indicating tubes, and the same gel used for the unknowns. But matching to a definitely set series of colors in the field requires a gel of uniform sensitivity.

Preparation of the Indicating Tubes. *Laboratory Tubes.* These are for immediate use for accurate determinations. They are capable of yielding values within 0.0002 vol % in the range 0–0.01% carbon monoxide. These tubes cannot be stored longer than 8 hr. The indicating gel need not be adjusted to a standard sensitivity as long as one lot of gel is used to make the color standards and tests of the unknowns.

Use 7-mm clear Pyrex glass tubing without noticeable color. Cut into 15-cm lengths and fire polish. Clean with fuming sulfuric acid, or by heating at 550°C for 1 hr, or select freshly drawn tubing which has been carefully protected from dirt. Plug a 000 cork in one end, insert loosely a small pad of absorbent cotton, and then fill alternately and in order with 4 cm of guard gel, 15 mm of indicating gel, and 3 cm of guard gel. Insert a second cotton pad and tamp loosely to hold the gel in place, then close with a second 000 cork.

Glass-stoppered pear-shaped separatory funnels with dry ⨝ 4 stopcocks make convenient gel venders. A system of dosing stopcocks may be made from ⨝ 19/22 male joints sealed to ⨝ 4 stopcocks. The ⨝ 19/22 joint plugs into a ⨝ 19 reagent bottle which holds the gel. Two stopcocks can be spaced to form a pocket of the proper size for a dose of guard gel. A solid ⨝ 4 stopper can be drilled with a pocket of proper size to hold a dose of the indicating gel.

The day's supply of laboratory tubes may be stored in a desiccator over guard gel.

NBS Indicating Tubes for Field Use. These tubes are used for the rapid determination of any physiologically significant amount of carbon monoxide. The colors developed are matched against painted chips, and the indicating gel must accordingly be adjusted to a standard sensitivity.

Use the same size tube, but for convenience cut 23-cm lengths. Clean and fire polish as above. Draw down one end of the tube to a tip 1 cm long and 1–1.5 mm o.d. The length from the rounded shoulder to the end of this tip should be nearly 15 mm. Heat in an electric oven to expel any condensed water.

Insert a rectangular piece of 1 × 0.007-in. Fiberglas tape No. ECC1B, cut 1 × 7/16 in., which was previously cleaned by heating in an electric furnace to 550°C for 2 hr. Tamp this firmly into the sealed end with a clean 4.5-mm steel drill rod.

Fill the tubes with alternate layers of guard and indicating gel as follows: 4.5 cm of guard gel, 14 mm of indicating gel, and 2.5 cm of guard gel. Insert a second Fiberglas plug and tamp firmly against the gel. Tap down the gel thoroughly by vibrating the tube held vertically. Tamp down the glass plug a second time. Seal off the tube 2 cm or more away from the gel, drawing into a second tip like the first.

In handling large batches of tubes, large desiccators containing a layer of guard gel offer satisfactory temporary storage. However, the tube should be sealed within 1 hr after filling. The room where this work is done should be free from carbon monoxide, organic vapors, reducing or oxidizing gases such as ethylene, acetylene, and hydrogen sulfide, or ozone, and nitrogen peroxide. The humidity should not be excessive, and air conditioning is helpful.

If a glass-sealing machine is used, proper mechanical adjustment will always keep the tip of the flame away from an open end of the tube. In sealing off by hand this must carefully be avoided for the carbon monoxide generated in the partial combustion caused by contact of flame with cold glass will usually ruin the indicating tube.

If the indicating tube is properly prepared, it should remain useful for several years.

a. Colorimetric Determination

As has been stated, the color response of the indicating gel is a function of time times concentration at any constant rate of flow, and most of the analytical methods used or proposed have taken advantage of this fact. A fairly close estimation of the concentration of carbon monoxide in an unknown may be made by simply measuring the time (at constant flow) necessary to produce a standard color. A more accurate determination can be made by matching an unknown with a set of standard colors produced by exposing the tubes themselves to known concentrations.

Interfering substances can be strong reducing or oxidizing gases or vapors which are present in amounts sufficiently large to escape the inlet guard gel. The field tubes were made to remove any interfering substances ordinarily present in any of the atmospheres associated with military equipment or installations, and are probably good for any ordinary industrial or household use. However, this should be checked in special cases. The indicating gel has so little sensitivity toward hydrogen that its presence in large amounts does not interfere with determinations of carbon monoxide.

It is possible to modify the indicating tube so that it will serve to detect and estimate the presence of other reducing or oxidizing gases. Hopcalite can serve to remove any carbon monoxide present, and an anhydrous calcium sulfate can be substituted for the guarding silica gel. This combination will detect many organic vapors or unsaturated gases. The oxidation of a previously reduced tube is also possible.

Laboratory Method

Air to be tested is passed through a NBS indicating tube (laboratory type) at 90 ml/min for a definite period. The color obtained is compared with freshly prepared standards of carbon monoxide. In the range 0–0.01 vol %, carbon monoxide can be determined with a reproducibility of 0.0002% and a probable accuracy of 0.001% or better. Above 0.01% the sample may be diluted with a known proportion of carbon monoxide-free air if sufficient differentiation of the darker colors proves difficult.

Apparatus. One calibrated flowmeter registering 90 ml/min; two or three additional flowmeters for diluting the sample in known proportions with carbon monoxide-free air; one stop watch; standard mixtures of carbon monoxide in air under pressure; and laboratory-type indicating tubes.

Procedure. Pass sample to be tested through a freshly prepared indicating tube at a measured rate of 90 ml/min. Note time in seconds required to match approximately the color developed by exposure to 0.005% carbon monoxide for 50 sec, an easy color to match. The composition of the unknown can now be approximately computed.

Example. Unknown developed the "0.005% 50-sec color" in 95 sec. Concentration of unknown was therefore $50/95 \times 0.005 = 0.0026$ (approximately).

Now prepare a set of color standards from freshly filled indicating tubes and the 0.005% standard mixture, using the knowledge derived above in order to bracket the unknown with lighter and darker colors, and taking the nearest 10-sec interval as the exposure time for the unknown. To continue the example given above: Exposure time for the unknown is conveniently selected as 100 sec. Since it is approximately 0.0025%, to bracket it would require exposure of 0.005% for 50 sec as a base time, with greater and lesser exposures. With

0.005% for 50 sec as a base, each 1-sec difference should correspond to 0.0001% carbon monoxide. If tubes were then exposed to this concentration for 46, 48, 50, 52, and 54 sec, this standard set would represent 0.0046, 0.0048, 0.0050, 0.0052, and 0.0054%, respectively, on the 50-sec base, but one-half these amounts on the 100-sec base: 0.0023, 0.0024, 0.0025, 0.0026, and 0.0027%. The unknown, exposed for 100 sec, is now compared with this standard set. Suppose its color lies between the 52- and 54-sec tube, or between 0.0026 and 0.0027%. It would be reported as 0.00265% ± 0.00005. During the determination of the order of the color intensity of these tubes, the identifying labels should be obscured. If the observer then arranges the color *standards* in their proper order, he has proved his analysis. Often differences in color are not apparent at first glance but resolve upon close comparison. North or sky light or a daylight fluorescent lamp is recommended for this work.

In actual practice, if the accuracy indicated above is to be realized, the standard color tubes should have been prepared from a mixture containing 0.0025% carbon monoxide in air. The color developed is practically, but not *exactly*, determined by concentration of carbon monoxide times duration of exposure. If an exposed tube is immediately flushed with carbon monoxide-free air, thus removing unreacted residual carbon monoxide, the expressed relation is more nearly exact. If a 0.005% standard is used to make color tubes for determinations in the range 0–0.01%, a reproducibility of 0.0002% and an accuracy of 0.0001% or better are easily achieved, however.

As the concentration of carbon monoxide increases, the colors developed become darker and more difficult to match. Reduction of the exposure time with some loss in reproducibility and accuracy will serve for a while; above 0.02% dilution is comforting, and with increasing concentrations, is finally necessary.

Field Method

A 2-oz aspirator bulb equipped with a rate-controlling valve is adequate. It is cheap, readily available, and apparently can be used successfully by anyone. The tubes and an aspirator bulb equipped with a color chart are commercially available.

b. Quantitative Method for Low Concentrations

The NBS indicator tube method was originally designed for relatively higher concentrations of carbon monoxide, that is, for 10 ppm and above. It can, however, be readily adapted for the analysis of carbon monoxide in the range of 1–2 ppm by substituting a small vacuum pump for the customary aspirator bulb.

Procedure. Break the tips of an NBS carbon monoxide indicator tube and insert the tube with the unfilled end in the sampling line directed toward the pump, that is, place the tube so that the incoming air stream has to pass through the longer section of silica gel. Draw air at a rate of approximately 100 ml/min through the tube with the aid of the small pump. Note the time that the pump is started and observe the indicator gel carefully until the color matches the first green of the comparison color chart provided with the tubes. Note the time again.

Calculations. Calculate the concentration of carbon monoxide in the air sample from the time of sampling, the volume of air drawn through the tube, and the color change. When 5 squeezes of the aspirator bulb yield a color change that matches the first green, the corresponding carbon monoxide concentration is 0.001%. This relationship can be used to calculate the concentration when sampling with a pump, for

$$0.001\% \times 10,000 = 10 \text{ ppm CO}$$

Assume the measured volume of the aspirator bulb for 5 squeezes is 240 ml. Then from the above relationship

$$\text{CO (ppm)} = 10 \times 240/\text{vol of sample, ml}$$
$$= 2.4/\text{vol of sample, liters}$$

when expressed in liters. Since at a rate of 100 ml/min it requires, with the procedure detailed, 10 min to draw 1 liter and 1 min to draw 0.1 liter, it can be shown that the carbon monoxide concentration can be calculated by the expression

$$\text{CO (ppm)} = 24/\text{time, min}$$

The indicator tube method is not a very accurate method and therefore does not warrant correction for temperature and pressure, for these would not be significant. Its precision is sufficiently adequate for using the method routinely.

Calibration. The NBS indicator tube method can be calibrated by use of tanks of compressed nitrogen containing known concentrations of carbon monoxide. For example, assume that a tank of carbon monoxide in nitrogen, in which the concentration of carbon monoxide is 10 ppm, is available. Assume further that this tank is connected to a train and an indicator tube and the gas mixture is drawn through the tube at a rate of 100 ml/min. The time for the production of the first green color is found to be 2 min and 30 sec. Then the actual concentration found by substitution in the above equation is

$$CO \text{ (ppm)} = 24/\text{time, min} = 24/52 = 9.6 \text{ ppm}$$

a value which checks the delivered value within the experimental error of the method.

2. Hoolamite Detector

Hoolamite, $I_2O_5 + H_2SO_4 + SO_3$, activated iodine pentoxide, named after Hoover and Lamb (9) who patented the formula, is a mixture of iodine pentoxide and fuming sulfuric acid on granular pumice stone. When carbon monoxide comes in contact with this reagent, iodine is liberated, changing the originally white granules to bluish green of increasing depths, then violet brown, and finally black, depending upon the concentration of carbon monoxide. The chemical reaction that liberates the iodine is

$$I_2O_5 + 5CO \rightarrow 5CO_2 + I_2$$

Hoolamite averages approximately 12.29% iodine pentoxide, 51.89% sulfuric acid (47% sulfur trioxide, SO_3), and 35.82% pumice granules. As moisture causes deterioration of Hoolamite, it is marketed in small glass ampoules tapered at both ends and hermetically sealed.

The Hoolamite indicator for carbon monoxide was used by engineers of the U. S. Bureau of Mines and others engaged in rescue and recovery operations, such as men engaged in fighting mine fires or performing mine rescue work. This detector largely replaced the use of canaries and mice, as it required less care and attention under most conditions and is more accurate (10).

The complete indicator comprises a metal barrel filled with activated charcoal, through which air is drawn by means of a rubber aspirator. The inlet end of the barrel has a corrugated tip, to which an extension sampling line may be attached. The air is then discharged by the aspirator through a small glass tube containing

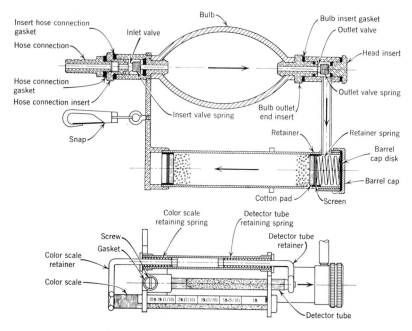

Fig. XVIII-2. Cross section of carbon monoxide detector (arrows show course of air sample). (Courtesy Mine Safety Appliances Co.)

Hoolamite. A comparison color tube having 5 permanent colors in pumice stone, graduated from 0.10 to 1.0% carbon monoxide, is placed alongside the Hoolamite tube. The scale and tube are kept in position by holders firmly attached to the metal barrel.

Another type of this detector (Fig. XVIII-2) consists of a short metal barrel having a corrugated tip containing the inlet opening and valve, a rubber aspirator, another short barrel containing the outlet valve, a metal tube connecting the outlet valve barrel to a larger barrel containing activated charcoal, a Hoolamite tube, a color tube, a tube holder, and a metal strip connecting the charcoal barrel and the inlet valve barrel. Air entering the rubber bulb by way of the inlet opening and valve is discharged when the bulb is depressed through the outlet valve, through the small metal tube, and through the activated charcoal into the Hoolamite tube. A comparison color tube for the aforementioned percentages of carbon monoxide is held in place by placing one end of the tube in a small depression on the tube holder and by slipping a spring fastener over the other end.   The Hoolamite tube is held in place in a similar manner, except that the bottom end of the tube is inserted into an opening having a rubber tube that serves as a gasket.   The tip of the inlet valve is also equipped with a corrugated tip to which an extension sampling line may be attached.   The location of the valves and the ease with which they may be removed and cleaned or repaired makes this type of detector preferable to the former type.

Before either type of Hoolamite detector is taken into an atmosphere to be inspected, the aspirator bulb should be carefully tested to see (1) if it works, that it does not leak, and has the proper resilience; (2) that the valves of the detector are tight and function properly; (3) that the color tube is held securely in place; and (4) that the activated charcoal is in good condition.   If the material in the Hoolamite tube becomes discolored when squeezed 20 times in pure air, the charcoal container should be refilled with fresh activated charcoal.   When reassembling the instrument, care should be taken to replace the spring that holds the charcoal in place correctly, otherwise air channels through the charcoal might result.

Procedure.   If no extension sampling line is used, the operator of the detector should be protected by a suitable respiratory apparatus when working in an atmosphere liable to contain carbon monoxide.

Squeeze the bulb once or twice to remove any moisture and to fill the instrument with air identical with that to be tested.   Break both tips of a Hoolamite tube and insert it firmly in the instrument with the shoulder securely seated in the rubber connecting joint.   Squeeze the bulb 10 times in succession, collapsing it completely each time.   This will force about 350 ml of air through the impregnated pumice.   A slight amount of smoke or fume should issue from the Hoolamite tube when the bulb is squeezed.   Although this smoke is harmful if breathed directly, under ordinary conditions it will be diluted so quickly by the surrounding air that no symptoms other than coughing are likely to be noted if no respirator is worn.   Observation of the smoke, however, is often advantageous because it indicates the direction and velocity of the ventilating current in the surrounding atmosphere.

After squeezing the aspirator the full number of times, compare the resulting color, if any, with the permanent colors in the color tube and note the corresponding percentage of carbon monoxide.   At low concentrations of carbon monoxide the color in the Hoolamite tube fades rapidly; hence, the comparison with the color tube should be made at once. If no color comparable with those in the color tube results from 10 squeezes, repeat the test, using some multiple of 10, and make the corresponding correction in the percentage indicated by the color obtained. For instance, if a color corresponding to that for 0.1% is obtained with 20 successive squeezes, the amount of carbon monoxide in the air samples is about 0.05% or, if a color corresponding to that for 1.0% is obtained with 5 squeezes, approximately 2% carbon monoxide is indicated in the air being sampled. As stated, the operators should use a respiratory device capable of protection against carbon monoxide while working in an atmosphere suspected of containing that poison.

Remove the Hoolamite tube from the instrument promptly, as it should not be left in place longer than the time necessary to make the test. If the color in the tube does not fade or if a yellow discoloration appears, the tube should be discarded. As the iodine pentoxide mixture is highly acid, a discarded tube should not be thrown where it can do any damage. If the tube is to be used again, the tips should be covered with rubber caps, like those used for serum ampoules, to prevent the deterioration of the contents through entrance of moisture.

If an extension line is attached to the corrugated tip of the barrel and the other end of the sampling line is connected with a pipe leading through a stopping of a sealed area in a mine, or extends to an inaccessible place, the percentage of carbon monoxide in the air of the immediate region behind the seal or in the inaccessible place may be ascertained, provided the pipe in the stopping is not intaking or the stopping is not leaking. Furthermore, the line to the inaccessible place must be properly purged first with the air or atmosphere sampled before it is connected to the corrugated tip. Determinations of this sort are particularly useful when fighting mine fires.

The detector does not indicate a deficiency of oxygen or the presence of other gases such as carbon dioxide or hydrogen sulfide in the atmosphere being tested, nor does it automatically give warning of the presence of carbon monoxide. The operator may actually be in an atmosphere containing this gas while using the instrument without knowledge of its presence. Hence, in these respects, the detector is inferior to canaries or Japanese waltzing mice. However, when in good condition and used in the manner described above, the detector affords a reasonably accurate quantitative means of determining carbon monoxide.

Although the iodine pentoxide indicator is used more or less generally, it should not be forgotten that the canary is exposed continuously to indicate the presence of carbon monoxide, whereas when using the iodine pentoxide indicator frequent determinations are necessary. Furthermore, persons with poor eyesight or color blindness may be unable to read the scale and make the necessary color comparisons; persons so affected should not use this device. On the other hand, canaries and Japanese waltzing mice have the disadvantages previously detailed (see Section A-4-a, Chapter XVII).

Acetylene, alcohol, ammonia, benzine, ether, ethylene, gasoline, hydrogen sulfide, hydrogen chloride, and natural gas containing some higher hydrocarbons color the Hoolamite when no absorbent such as activated charcoal is interposed between the Hoolamite tube and the source of the gas tested, but with activated charcoal placed in the barrel of the detector no color is visible. Carbon dioxide, carbon tetrachloride, chlorine, hydrogen, methane, nitrogen peroxide, phosgene, and sulfur dioxide have no effect on the Hoolamite tubes.

E. Hydrogen Sulfide

1. Silver Cyanide Detector

The U. S. Bureau of Mines has developed a detector that provides a simple and fairly accurate means of detecting hydrogen sulfide (10). It is rapid in giving results and accurate enough to indicate concentrations of hydrogen sulfide ranging from those that are harmless or but slightly harmful to those immediately dangerous to life. It will indicate hydrogen sulfide in the range of 0.0025–0.05%.

The complete detector (Fig. XVIII-3) consists of a small-inlet metal barrel corrugated on the end to permit a rubber tube to be attached, to which is attached a rubber aspirator bulb, a movable scale, and a tube containing the white granular reagent.

The reagent used in the hydrogen sulfide detector tubes consists of silver cyanide, $Ag(CN)_3$, on activated alumina, Al_2O_3 (1). The activated alumina serves as a carrier for the silver cyanide in a manner analogous to the pumice used in the Hoolamite carbon monoxide tube,

Fig. XVIII-3. Hydrogen sulfide detector. (Courtesy Mine Safety Appliances Co.)

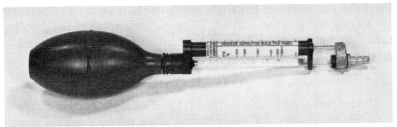

Fig. XVIII-4. Hydrogen sulfide detector tube in place with aspirator. (Courtesy Mine Safety Appliances Co.)

as explained on page 763. The chemical action which proceeds is given by the following reaction formula:

$$2AgCN + H_2S \rightarrow Ag_2S + 2HCN$$

The reaction of the silver cyanide in the presence of hydrogen sulfide turns the white granules to a dark gray because of the formation of black silver sulfide. This reaction begins at the end of the tube where the sample enters.

When the detector is used in the presence of hydrogen sulfide, hydrogen cyanide is liberated. This is an equally deadly gas. However, no anxiety should be felt regarding the use of the detector, even in still air, for the amount of hydrogen cyanide liberated is so small that the amount that can be formed by an entire tube is harmless, even if the user inhaled the entire amount.

Assuming that the person using the detector is protected by suitable respiratory apparatus when working in an atmosphere liable to contain hydrogen sulfide, the detector should be used as follows.

Break the tips of a detector tube and insert the red end—which is the end that should always be placed in the detector so that it will be nearest the aspirator bulb—through the tube guide at the top of the detector and place it in the opening directly above the aspirator bulb (Fig. XVIII-4). Place the retaining head containing the inlet opening over the upper end of the detector tube. Slight pressure against the retaining head will insure a snug fit of the tube in the rubber seat. Loosen the thumb nut on the back of the detector and adjust the sliding scale until the zero is directly opposite the beginning of the chemical granules; then tighten the thumb nut and squeeze the aspirator bulb 10 times, allowing it to expand completely each time. This will draw approximately 750 ml of air through the chemical in the tube.

Read the percentage of hydrogen sulfide on the scale midway between the longest and shortest ends of the gray discoloration of the detector tube. Temperature and storage have little effect on the tubes or the reaction. The commonly occurring gases do not interfere.

F. Nitrogen Dioxide Detector Tube

The reagent used in this method (11) for nitrogen dioxide–nitrogen tetroxide is prepared by impregnating silica gel with sulfanilic acid and N-(1-naphthyl)ethylenediamine dihydrochloride. When this reagent is packed into a glass tube, and air containing small amounts of nitrogen dioxide is drawn through the tube, the nitrogen dioxide in the air is adsorbed on the reagent where a diazotizing and coupling reaction takes place to form a red stain. By standardizing the reagent preparation, the cross-sectional area of the reagent column, the volume of air sampled, and the sampling rate, it is possible to utilize the length of stain formed on the reagent column to estimate the concentration of nitrogen dioxide in the air sampled.

Reagent Preparation. Wet 100 g of 28–35-mesh silica gel uniformly with a freshly prepared solution of 1% sulfanilic acid and 0.08% N-(1-naphthyl)ethylenediamine dihydrochloride. Add the solution slowly with constant stirring until the silica gel appears to be thoroughly moistened. Forty to 80 ml of the solution is required per 100 g of the silica gel.

Place the reagent gel in a desiccator containing calcium chloride desiccant. In a period of 24–48 hr the product should appear dry, granular, "free running" like sugar, and preferably white. Transfer it to a tightly stoppered, dark-colored bottle for protection from light, water vapor, and nitrogen dioxide. Reagent gel prepared in this manner and kept in a refrigerator will remain stable for 3 months and may possibly be stored for a considerably longer period of time without deterioration.

Preparation of Indicator Tubes. Prepare indicator tubes from glass tubes 12 cm long and 3.0 mm i.d. Push a piece of glass cloth about 1 cm square about 3 cm into the end of one of the tubes as a porous plug. Pour silica gel reagent into the opposite end of the tube to a point about 3 cm from the top. This will provide a column of silica gel approximately 6 cm in length. Push another plug of glass cloth down into the top of the tube to hold the silica gel reagent in position.

Following this, hold the tube vertically and tap gently against a

table top.   This will pack and level the surface of the reagent.   Push
the upper glass plug firmly down against the level surface of the
reagent.   Invert the tube and complete a similar cycle of tapping,
packing, leveling, and pushing the porous plug firmly into place.

Careful and uniform packing produce a face (where the plug and
reagent meet) that is planar and perpendicular to the tube axis.
This is important because such packing is an aid in obtaining a stain
that is of equal length on the various sides of the column; this type of
stain is desired because it can be measured with greater accuracy.

Sampling tubes are easily filled by means of a small bottle fitted
with a rubber stopper through which a small hole has been bored.
Silica gel reagent in the bottle can easily be poured directly into a
sample tube placed in the hole.

Pumping and Metering Apparatus.   Sampling can be accomplished
with any source of vacuum and a small flowmeter suitable for metering
air through the sampling tubes.   For field sampling, a rubber aspirator
bulb fitted with a rapid air release valve and a capillary to regulate the
rate of inward airflow can be used.   For this work short pieces of glass
and rubber tubing can be used to connect a glass T with a 50-ml
laboratory-type rubber aspirator bulb.   A pinch clamp on a piece of
rubber tubing fitted on the side arm of the T provides a quick air release valve.   The remaining open end of the T can be connected with
a capillary by a short length of rubber tubing.   The open end of
the capillary was also fitted with a short length of rubber tubing for
connection with successive sampling tubes.

Procedure.   Sampling with this apparatus is accomplished by expelling the air from the bulb through the sidearm valve, closing the
pinch clamp, and allowing the bulb to expand and consequently to draw
a 50-ml air sample inward through a sampling tube and the capillary.
Sampling from a tank is accomplished by connecting the open end of
the sampling tube to the tank with a short piece of rubber tubing.

The capillary chosen should have a high resistance as compared
with the sampling tubes and thus serve to maintain a constant rate of
flow, regardless of any possible small changes in resistance of sampling
tubes.   When the bulb and capillary are used, the time for the bulb to
expand completely should be fixed at 34 ± 3 sec or at an approximate
average rate of 90 ml/min.

In practice, 4 bulb volumes or 200 ml of air were drawn through the
sampling tube for each sample.   This volume and sampling rate

were chosen arbitrarily on an empirical basis for the range of concentration (1–50 ppm) of nitrogen dioxide under consideration; calibration can, of course, be made for other rates and sample volumes.

Tubes are calibrated and calibration curves prepared by drawing the chosen volume (200 ml) of gas containing known nitrogen dioxide concentrations through the tube, measuring the stain length, and plotting the stain length as a function of the logarithm of the nitrogen dioxide concentration. Determinations of unknown concentrations are made by drawing the same quantity of air as in the calibration sample through the sampling tube with the pumping device. The length of the stain is measured and the nitrogen dioxide concentration is obtained from the calibration curve.

References

1. Littlefield, J. B., W. P. Yant, and L. B. Berger, *U.S. Bur. Mines Rept. Invest. 3276* (1935).
2. Jacobs, M. B., *War Gases—Their Detection and Decontamination*, Interscience, New York, 1942.
3. *Air Sampling Instruments*, 1st ed., American Conference of Governmental Industrial Hygienists, 1014 Broadway, Cincinnati, 1960.
4. Kitagawa, T., "The Rapid Measurement of Toxic Gases and Vapors, 13th Intern. Congr. Occupational Health," New York City, July 25–29, 1960.
5. Kusnetz, H. L., B. E. Saltzman, and M. E. Lanier, *Am. Ind. Hyg. Assoc. J.*, **21**, No. 5, 361 (1960).
6. Kusnetz, H. L., *Am. Ind. Hyg. Assoc. J.*, **21**, No. 4, 340 (1960).
7. Shepherd, M., *Anal. Chem.*, **19**, 77 (1947).
8. Gildchrist, R., and E. Wickers, *J. Am. Chem. Soc.*, **57**, 2565 (1935).
9. Lamb, A. B., and C. R. Hoover, U.S. Pat. 1,321,062 (1919).
10. Forbes, J. J., and G. W. Grove, *U.S. Bur. Mines Miners' Circ. 33* (1938).
11. Kinosian, J. R., and B. R. Hubbard, *Am. Ind. Hyg. Assoc. J.*, **19**, 453 (Dec. 1958).

CHAPTER XIX

CLINICAL CHEMISTRY AND INDUSTRIAL TOXICOLOGY

The combined talents of several professional diciplines are required for the promotion of a comprehensive industrial toxicology or occupational health program. A continuous appraisal of the health of workers is the function of the physician and his associates. The industrial hygienist is concerned with workers' environment and its effect on health. The function of clinical chemistry in industrial toxicology is to exercise needed analytical control over the chemical determinations performed on samples of environmental and clinical studies.

A. General Methods

1. TOTAL PROTEIN

The concentration of total protein in various body fluids is frequently an excellent indication of functional disturbance. The Kjeldahl method is most commonly used where samples of sufficient quantity can be obtained. Conditions required for complete recovery of nitrogen by modifications of this method have been reviewed in considerable detail, particularly for proteinaceous material, by Kirk (1,2). Where only small samples are available, a microkjeldahl method is necessary.

a. Microkjeldahl Method

In this method, which is a modification of the Pregl-Parnas-Wagner method, protein and other forms of organic nitrogen are converted to ammonia and fixed as ammonium sulfate by digestion with sulfuric acid. Potassium sulfate is used to raise the temperature of the digestion mixture, and copper sulfate is used as the catalyst. The ammonia formed is liberated by the addition of sodium hydroxide solution, is steam distilled, trapped in standard hydrochloric acid solution,

773

and the excess hydrochloric acid is estimated titrimetrically with standard sodium hydroxide solution, or the ammonia is trapped in boric acid solution and the amount is determined by direct titration with standard hydrochloric acid.

The apparatus is that of Parnas and Wagner (3) or the modification of this apparatus described by Shepard and Jacobs (4).

Preparation of Reagent. Dissolve 6 g of recrystallized copper sulfate, $CuSO_4 \cdot 5H_2O$ and 105 g of potassium sulfate, K_2SO_4, in 600 ml of water by bringing the mixture to boiling. Cool approximately to room temperature and cautiously add 150 ml of concentrated sulfuric acid. Cool again to room temperature, transfer to a graduated cylinder, and make up to a total volume of 900 ml.

The results obtained with this reagent will be detailed and discussed below.

Procedure. Dilute an aliquot portion of the material being analyzed, if necessary, to a known volume in a volumetric flask, so that the amount of nitrogen will be of the order of 0.5 mg/ml. Transfer 1 ml of this solution to a microkjeldahl digestion flask. With the aid of a buret, or similar device, add 1 ml of concentrated sulfuric acid and 1 ml of a 4% copper sulfate solution, prepared by dissolving 4 g of $CuSO_4 \cdot 5H_2O$ in water and diluting to 100 ml. Add 0.7 g of potassium sulfate, mix, and digest in a digestion oven. Raise the heat slowly, boil vigorously, and after the material has been digested, as evidenced by a clear, straw yellow or light green color, reduce and cut off the heat. This process generally takes about 20 min. If the mixture does not clear in this time, reduce the heat, carefully add 2–3 drops of 30% hydrogen peroxide solution, and then continue heating for 5–10 min. Allow to cool, add 4 ml of water, and stir to dissolve the salts.

Add 7.0 ml of $0.01N$ hydrochloric acid, accurately measured, to a 25-ml flask and add a trace of methyl red indicator solution. Allow the water in the steam generator to boil gently, remove the clamp from the line leading from the steam generator to the vapor vessel, and open the pinch clamp or stopcock at the bottom of the steam vessel so that the steam can escape. Transfer the digest from the microkjeldahl digestion flask to the distillation tube through the small funnel. Wash out the microkjeldahl digestion flask with two 2-ml portions of distilled water and add these washings to the distillation tube. Place the receiving flask under the condenser so that the tip of the silver tube condenser is below the standard acid. With the aid of a pipet, add 7 ml of 30% sodium hydroxide solution to the mixture in the distillation tube through the small funnel.

Close the stopcocks or pinch clamps of the small funnel, the vapor vessel, and the steam escape, if one is used, thus compelling the steam to pass through the distillation tube. Distil for exactly 3 min. Lower the receiving flask so that the tip of the condenser is about 1 cm above the surface of the distillate. Continue the distillation 1 min more. Rinse the tip of the condenser tube with a few drops of water. Add another trace of methyl red indicator solution, if necessary. Titrate with standard $0.01N$ sodium hydroxide solution. One ml of standard hydrochloric acid $(0.01N)$ is equivalent to 0.14 mg of nitrogen. Run a blank and subtract the blank from the volume of standard hydrochloric acid used.

Instead of using a known volume of standard hydrochloric acid, trap the ammonia being distilled in 10 ml of cold 2% boric acid solution (5,6). Proceed with the method as detailed, except titrate the boric acid solution directly with $0.01N$ hydrochloric acid. Run a blank and subtract this from the volume of standard hydrochloric acid used.

Procedure with Single Reagent. The method as detailed above, and the washing procedure and apparatus described in the paper of Shepard and Jacobs (4) was followed and used, with the exception that 6, 7, 8, and 9 ml of the prepared digestion reagent were used in place of the 1 ml of sulfuric acid and the weighed amounts of potassium sulfate and copper sulfate.

Because of the increase in volume of the material being digested, attributable to the volume of reagent added, it is necessary to heat the mixture cautiously to prevent excessive frothing while the water is being driven off. Small sections of melting-point tubes or glass beads may be used to avoid bumping and decrease frothing, but care should be exercised not to permit them to get into the distillation tube.

2. NONPROTEIN NITROGEN

Nonprotein nitrogen may also be determined (7) by the microkjeldahl method. However, for determination in any body fluid of various substances, such as creatinine, creatine, urea, uric acid, etc., and drugs, such as isoniazids and the sulfas, it is necessary to prepare a protein-free filtrate.   The principal method used for this purpose is that of Folin and Wu (8), and, of the various modifications, that of Haden (9) is probably the most common, and that of Van Slyke and Hawkins (10) is noteworthy.   Other methods of deproteinization that have been proposed are discussed by Hiller and Van Slyke (11) and by Horvath (12).

a. Preparation of Protein-Free Filtrate

Reagents.   Dissolve in some water 10 g of reagent grade, carbonate-free sodium tungstate, $Na_2WO_4 \cdot 2H_2O$, and dilute to 100 ml.

Sulfuric Acid, 0.67N.   Tare a 50-ml beaker and weigh into it 35 g of concentrated sulfuric acid (sp gr 1.84).   Place about 500 ml of distilled water into a 1-liter volumetric flask and then pour in the sulfuric acid carefully while swirling the flask.   Cool, dilute to volume, and check the normality against a standard sodium hydroxide solution.   Adjust the concentration to the proper normality, if necessary.

Procedure.   Transfer 1 ml of blood, plasma, or serum to a 16 × 50-mm test tube.   Add 7 ml of water and mix; add 1.0 ml of 10% sodium tungstate solution and mix; add 1.0 ml of 0.67N sulfuric acid and mix.   Then place the tube in a water bath at 80–85°C for 1 min to coagulate the precipitate.   Remove the tube from the hot bath, chill in a cold water bath, dry the outside of the tube, and filter the contents through a 9-cm, extremely retentive, hardened filter paper. The filtrate may then be used for the analysis desired.

To obtain a greater volume of blood filtrate, follow the above procedure substituting "volumes" for "milliliters."

At times 0.5 ml of each reagent (i.e., 10% sodium tungstate solution and 0.67N sulfuric acid) may give adequate results, but in such instances the 1 ml of blood must be diluted with 8 ml of water. This procedure was compared with the original Folin and Wu method, the trichloroacetic acid method, and the hexametaphosphoric acid method (13).   In the trichloroacetic acid method, 1 ml of this acid was used in a total volume of 10 ml, and in the hexametaphosphoric acid method, 1 ml of 10% sodium hexametaphosphate solution and 1 ml of 1.8N sulfuric acid were used in a total volume of 10 ml.   The last two protein precipitants were handled in a manner similar to that detailed for tungstic acid.   Greatest clarity was achieved with the hexametaphosphoric acid as shown by turbidity measurements with a photoelectric colorimeter. However, this protein precipitant cannot be used when it acts as a sequestering agent, e.g., in the determination of isoniazids by the ferricyanide method (14).

3. CREATINE AND CREATININE

In aqueous solutions creatine and creatinine exist in an equilibrium

which is catalyzed toward the right by hydrogen ions and in both directions by hydroxyl ions (15–19). It is therefore best to use fresh samples for the determination of these substances. Taussky (19) found that storage, even when thymol crystals were used as a preservative and the samples were refrigerated, resulted in unpredictable variations in content of creatine, creatinine, and even in the sum of both.

Taussky-Jaffe Method (19)

The Jaffe reaction for creatine and creatinine depends on the color produced by alkaline picrates. Many substances, however, interfere with this reaction and procedures to eliminate them have been detailed by Taussky (19,20). Ether extraction has been found to be satisfactory for treatment of urine samples while for plasma the ether extraction must follow treatment with iodine. In addition, a strongly acid medium is necessary for precipitation of serum proteins in order to obtain 100% recoveries of creatine and creatinine in the filtrate. To complete the conversion of creatine to creatinine, the pH of the filtrate must be raised to 2.0–2.5, which can be done conveniently by the use of granulated zinc and picric acid (19).

Reagents. *Creatinine Stock Solution.* Creatinine is dried at 105°C to constant weight and 0.6666 g of this material is dissolved and diluted to 1 liter with $0.1N$ hydrochloric acid. This solution contains 666 μg of creatinine per milliliter.

Creatine Stock Solution. Creatine monohydrate is dried until the weight is constant. Either 0.8799 g of creatine monohydrate or

0.7733 g of anhydrous creatine is dissolved and diluted to 1 liter with water. The solution is not stable. Either solution contains 666 μg in terms of creatinine per milliliter.

Picric Acid, 0.04N. Prepare a saturated solution of picric acid at about 80°C by dissolving 16 g of the acid in 1 liter of water. When cooled to room temperature, the excess picric acid crystallizes out. About 690 ml of the saturated solution are diluted to 1 liter and titrated with 0.1N NaOH with phenolphthalein as the indicator.

Sodium Hydroxide, 0.75N. Dilute 42 ml of NaOH (1:1 by weight) to 1 liter and titrate against 1.0N HCl with a mixture of bromocresol green and methyl red as indicator.

Ether (anhydrous). Use analytical reagent low in peroxide and containing a very small amount of sodium diethyldithiocarbamate to improve stability. Peroxides cause a fading effect on the final color of the Jaffe reaction and must be tested for with ferrous sulfate or potassium iodide. Absence of peroxide is indicated by retention of the green color of the ferrous sulfate or continued colorlessness of the iodide for a few minutes.

Procedure. For preformed creatinine adjust the pH of the sample to 5.5 with concentrated HCl or 5N NaOH and dilute 1 or 2 ml to 100. Six ml of the adjusted, diluted sample are pipetted into 60-ml glass-stoppered Pyrex bottles. Add about 8 ml of ether, stopper, and shake for about 30 sec. Release stoppers and allow separation of the phases, which takes place in a few minutes with an emulsion interphase. Pipet 4 ml of the clear lower phase into colorimeter tubes, add 1 ml of 0.75N NaOH, shake, and read after 20 min in a Klett-Summerson colorimeter with filter No. 54 or in a spectrophotometer with light of 510-mμ wavelength.

For creatinine plus creatine, the 6-ml sample is pipetted into heavy-walled 12-ml Pyrex centrifuge tubes graduated with a complete ring at 5 and 8 ml. Add 1 ml of 0.04N picric acid, shake, and place into a constant-level boiling water bath. When the sample volume is between 5 and 3 ml (about 1¼ hr), cool, add 1 ml of 0.04N picric acid, and adjust volume to 8 ml. Transfer to 60-ml glass-stoppered bottles by pouring once back and forth. There is no necessity for a quantitative transfer. Complete the determination as for preformed creatine.

Prepare a standard curve from appropriate dilutions of the stock solutions of creatine and creatinine. It is best to run a blank and one standard with each series of determinations.

Calculation.

$$\frac{\mu\text{g found (from calibration curve)}}{30 \text{ (for } 1:100)} \times (V/24\,\text{hr})$$

    = mg total preformed creatinine or total creatinine per 24 hr

For creatine expressed as creatinine, subtract milligrams of preformed creatinine from milligrams of total creatinine; milligrams of true creatine are obtained by multiplying by 1.159.

Modifications in the method and calculation are necessary for determinations in serum or in samples containing phenolsulfophthalein or bromosulfophthalein, and these modifications are detailed by Taussky (19).

B. Methods for Specific Metals

1. Lead

Interest in the absorption and excretion of lead has remained at high level for many years. Recently additional interest has been displayed because of many instances of lead poisoning in children (21).

The literature concerning the determination of lead in biological materials has been covered in the booklet *Methods for Determining Lead in Air and in Biological Materials* (22), by Sandell (23), and by Jacobs (24) and need not be repeated here. One must, however, mention the rapid methods of Woessner and Cholak (25), of Amdur (26), and of Bessman and Layne (27). In general these methods are either spectrographic, polarographic, or dithizone methods, the latter being used in several variations, namely, mixed-color, titrimetric, or one-color procedures. The one-color method of Fischer and Leopoldi (28) was modified by Harrold, Meek, and Holden (29) and subsequently by others.

a. Determination in Urine

Jacobs-Herndon Method

This (30) is a modification of the one-color method for lead substituting alpha naphtholphthalein for phenol red as indicator, using a single Mojonnier extraction tube instead of multiple separatory funnels, adding fixed amounts of dithizone extraction solution, and using filter paper instead of cotton to get a final clear solution for reading in the spectrophotometer. Some of the reagents employed are those suggested by Horwitt and Cowgill (31) and by Moskowitz and Burke (32).

Apparatus. A Bausch and Lomb Spectronic 340 was used as the spectrophotometer. Readings were made using 1-in. diameter cuvettes.

Fig. XIX-1. Glass-stoppered Mojonnier extraction tube.

The Mojonnier extraction flask (Fig. XIX–1) used was their G3A model which has a capacity of 104.5 ml in the top chamber and 21.5 ml in the bottom chamber and is stoppered with a No. 16 pennyhead standard taper glass stopper.

All glassware is washed with dilute nitric acid.

Reagents. *Dithizone Solution.* Dissolve 50 mg of pure diphenyl-thiocarbazone in reagent grade chloroform and make up to 500 ml with chloroform.

Ammoniacal Sodium Citrate Solution. Dissolve 100 g of reagent grade sodium citrate in distilled water and dilute to 500 ml. Add 150 ml of ammonium hydroxide solution (1:1). Mix thoroughly.

Potassium Cyanide Solution, 10%. Dissolve 20 g of reagent grade KCN in distilled water in a 200-ml volumetric flask and make up to volume with water. Transfer to a reagent bottle and keep in the dark, storing it, for instance, in a full metal cabinet. If it becomes discolored, discard it and make a fresh solution.

Hydrochloric Acid (1:1). Dilute highest purity hydrochloric acid with an equal volume of distilled water.

Hydroxylamine Hydrochloride, 20%. Dissolve 40 g of hydroxylamine hydrochloride, $NH_2OH \cdot HCl$, in distilled water and dilute to 200 ml in a volumetric flask. This solution can be purified by shaking out with dithizone extraction solution as detailed by Sandell (23) and by Jacobs and co-workers (33).

Ammonium Hydroxide Solution (1:1). Dilute one volume of concentrated ammonium hydroxide solution, sp gr 0.90, with an equal volume of distilled water.

Dithizone Extractive Solution. Transfer 5 ml of 10% potassium cyanide solution and 15 ml of concentrated ammonium hydroxide solution to a 500-ml volumetric flask and dilute to the mark with distilled water.

Indicator Solution. Weigh out 100 mg of α-naphtholphthalein (National Aniline No. 249) and transfer to a 20-ml beaker. Add 10 ml of distilled water and stir to wet the indicator. Add 4 ml of 0.01N sodium hydroxide solution. The indicator dissolves to form a deep blue solution. Transfer to a 250-ml volumetric flask, wash the beaker thoroughly with water, and transfer the washings to volumetric flask. Add an additional 6 ml of 0.01N sodium hydroxide solution, make to the mark with distilled water, stopper, and mix thoroughly. This is a 0.04% solution of α-naphtholphthalein. It is virtually colorless in acid solution and changes to a green to blue green at pH 8.

Standard Solutions. *Stock Standard Lead Solution.* Weigh out accurately 1.598 g of recrystallized lead nitrate, $Pb(NO_3)_2$, transfer to a 1-liter volumetric flask. Dissolve in 0.1% nitric acid and make to the mark with this acid. One ml of this solution contains 1 mg of lead.

Standard Working Lead Solutions. Transfer 1 ml of this stock standard solution to a 100-ml volumetric flask and dilute to volume with distilled water. This solution contains 10 $\mu g/ml$. Transfer 10 ml of this dilution to a 100-ml volumetric flask and dilute to volume. This final dilution contains 1 $\mu g/ml$.

Standard Curve. Transfer with the aid of pipets 0, 0.25, 0.5, 1.0, 2.0, 4.0, 6.0, 10.0, and 15.0 ml of the 1-$\mu g/ml$ working standard solution to 100-ml volumetric flasks. These volumes are equivalent to 0,

0.25, 0.5, 1.0, 2.0, 4.0, 6.0, 10.0, and 15.0 μg of lead, respectively. Add 15 ml of hydrochloric acid and continue with the method as detailed in the procedure but omit the heating steps. Place the final chloroform solution in 1-in. tube cuvettes and read in the Bausch and Lomb spectrophotometer at 525 mμ. Plot the micrograms of lead against the transmission.

Procedure. Transfer 50 ml of urine to a Coors porcelain casserole, size 180-3A, and evaporate cautiously on a hot plate in a hood to dryness, using low heat at first. After the urine has been evaporated, continue heating on the hot plate at high heat until the material chars. Transfer the casserole to a muffle furnace that has been adjusted to 550°C and heat at that temperature for 10 min. Remove the casserole from the furnace and allow to cool. Add 2 ml of concentrated nitric acid and replace it on the hot plate in the hood and drive off the nitrogen oxides. Replace in the muffle furnace at 550°C and again heat for 10 min. Do not permit the temperature to rise above this. Remove from the muffle furnace, allow to cool, add 15 ml of hydrochloric acid to the casserole, washing the sides with the acid, heat on the hot plate, and transfer to a 100-ml volumetric flask. Add 10 ml of distilled water to the casserole, washing the sides of the dish with the water, heat on the hot plate, and transfer to the 100-ml volumetric flask. Repeat this step using 15 ml of ammoniacal sodium citrate solution. Repeat the washing again with 10 ml of water and add the washing to the volumetric flask.

Allow the flask to cool to room temperature and add 1 ml of 20% hydroxylamine hydrochloride solution and 0.5 ml of α-naphtholphthalein indicator solution. Add sufficient ammonium hydroxide solution (1:1) to turn the indicator blue. Add 5 ml of 10% potassium cyanide solution and make to volume.

Place 10 ml of chloroform solution in a Mojonnier tube and transfer the contents of the volumetric flask to the tube. Add 0.2 ml of the dithizone solution, stopper the flask, and shake thoroughly, holding the stopper firmly. Set upright and release the stopper cautiously. Add additional volumes of dithizone solution 0.1 ml at a time, shaking after each addition until the chloroform layer turns purple. Allow to stand until the phases separate. Pour off the supernatant solution to the constriction and discard. Add an additional 10 ml of chloroform and discard most of the remainder of the aqueous layer.

Add 10 ml of potassium cyanide–ammonium hydroxide extractive solution, stopper the tube, shake, and allow to separate. Pour off the supernatant as before. Repeat by adding an additional 10 ml of this extractive solution. (If care is exercised in addition of the dithizone solution so that not too large an excess is added, only two washings with the cyanide–ammonia extractive solution are required.) Add sufficient chloroform to raise the level of the chloroform layer to just above the middle of the constriction so that the water layer can be poured off completely.

Wet a 9- or 11-cm Whatman No. 41H filter paper with chloroform and filter the chloroform layer into a 1-in. cuvette. Read the absorption at 525 mμ. Obtain the concentration from the standard curve and compute the concentration on the basis of micrograms per liter.

Elimination of Bismuth. In order to eliminate interference of bismuth, the method of Bambach and Burkey, Chapter VIII, Section D-4-d may be followed or the Jacobs and Herndon method may be varied by use of a modification suggested by Dick, Ellis, and Steel (34).

Proceed with the method detailed above to the step in which the ash is dissolved in ammonium citrate solution. Transfer the contents to a separatory funnel. Add a drop of methyl orange indicator solution (0.1% in lead-free water) and add 5N ammonium hydroxide solution until a yellow color is produced. Adjust the pH to 3.0–3.4 by adding 0.5N nitric acid until a peach color is obtained. Add 5 ml of chloroform and 5 drops of a solution of 15 mg of dithizone in 20 ml of chloroform. Shake the funnel for 30 sec and allow the chloroform layer to separate. The color of the chloroform layer should be green. If it is orange, indicating the presence of bismuth, add more dithizone solution dropwise, shaking after each addition, until the chloroform layer is green. Allow to stand until the layers separate cleanly and then draw off and discard the chloroform phase. Return the aqueous layer to the volumetric flask, add the α-naphtholphthalein indicator, and proceed with the method.

b. Determination in Blood

Berman (35) has modified the Hammond (36) technique for the determination of lead in blood so that it can serve as a routine procedure. Blood proteins are removed by means of precipitation with trichloracetic acid and centrifugation. The lead in the supernatant liquid is converted to lead citrate and cyanide by an alkaline citrate–cyanide reagent which also provides a pH of 11, optimal for extraction by a solution of dithizone in chloroform.

Reagents. *Trichloracetic Acid.* Five per cent solution in distilled water.

Alkaline Citrate–Cyanide Reagent. Dissolve 100 g of sodium carbonate, 150 g of sodium citrate, 20 g of potassium cyanide, and 20 g of sodium hydroxide in distilled water and make up to 1 liter.

Dithizone. Three different strength solutions of dithizone are required: solution A, 8 mg of diphenylthiocarbazone per liter of chloroform; solution B, 16 mg of diphenylthiocarbazone per liter of chloroform; solution C, 32 mg of diphenylthiocarbazone per liter of chloroform.

All chemicals are reagent grade.

Procedure. Set up each sample in quadruplicate. Add 10 ml of 5% trichloracetic acid to 1 ml of whole blood in a test tube. Stir and allow to stand for 1 hr, stirring occasionally. Centrifuge for 5 min. Set two tubes aside. Decant the supernatant liquid of the other two tubes into 60-ml cylindrical separatory funnels. Add 10 ml of 5% trichloracetic acid to the sediment in the tubes, stir, centrifuge again for 5 min, and decant the supernatant liquid into its corresponding separatory funnel. Add 5 ml of the alkaline citrate–cyanide reagent and 10 ml of dithizone (8-mg strength) to the combined supernatants, shake mechanically for 10 min, and remove the chloroform layer into optically matched round-bottomed centrifuge tubes. Centrifuge for 5 min and read the optical densities in a spectrophotometer at 520 mμ.

If values calculate at 80 μg per 100 ml or more, repeat the procedure using 10 ml of dithizone (16-mg strength) and 10 ml of dithizone (32-mg strength), respectively, on each of the two samples previously set aside. The increased concentrations of dithizone are necessary to maintain a linear increase in optical density with higher concentrations of lead. Sixteen mg of dithizone are satisfactory up to 120 μg of lead, and 32 mg up to 240 μg.

c. Determination of Coproporphyrin (37)

Coproporphyrin (CP), coproporphyrinogen (CPG), and protoporphyrin (PP) can be extracted with ether. CPG is oxidized with iodine to CP after which this and the native CP are returned to the aqueous phase by extraction with 0.1N hydrochloric acid. At this concentration of the acid, most of the PP, if any, remains in the organic phase.

The light absorption of the aqueous phase is determined at 380 and 430 mμ and at the "Soret maximum," that is, about 402 mμ. The calculation was made by use of the formula given by Rimington and Sveinsson (38), and the corrected extinction constant and correction divisor recommended by With (39).

Reagents. *Glacial Acetic Acid.*

Ether.

Stock Iodine Solution. Dissolve 1 g of iodine in 100 ml of ethyl alcohol (96%). A working solution of 1:200 aqueous dilution of this stock solution is used in the test.

Hydrochloric Acid, 0.1N.

Procedure. When possible the sample should be fresh. If this is not possible, the sample should be kept in the dark at 4°C with a pH of 6.5–8.5.

Adjust 15 ml of the sample to pH 3–4 in a separatory funnel with about 1 ml of glacial acetic acid. Shake twice for 3 min with 30 ml of ether each time and combine the ether layers. Wash twice with about 15 ml of water for each washing, and a third time with 10 ml of a fresh 1:200 aqueous dilution of 1% iodine in alcohol.

Coproporphyrin is extracted repeatedly from the ether with 1-ml portions of 0.1N hydrochloric acid until the aqueous phase is no longer fluorescent under ultraviolet light. This usually requires 6–10 ml of the hydrochloric acid. Collect the extracts in a graduated cylinder and note the volume. Centrifuge if turbid and read the extinction of the combined extracts at 380 and 430 mμ and at the "Soret maximum," about 402 mμ in a 1-cm cuvette against a blank of 0.1N hydrochloric acid.

Calculation.

$$\frac{100 \times V_0 \times [2E_{\max} - (E_{380} + E_{430})]}{15 \times k \times d} = \mu\text{g of CP per 100-ml sample}$$

where V_0 = volume of combined extracts of hydrochloric acid, in milliliters; $E_{\max}$, E_{380}, and E_{430} = extinction at the "Soret maximum," 380, and 430 mμ; k = correction divisor for CP = 1.835; and d = $E_{1\text{cm}}^{10-4\%}$ = extinction constant for CP, i.e., the extinction of a solution containing 1 μg of pure CP per milliliter of 0.10–0.15N hydrochloric acid, read at the "Soret maximum" in a 1-cm cuvette. This constant is 0.667.

The analysis gives only an approximate value for the CP + CPG content. Thus

$$5.45 \times V_0 \times [2E_{max} - (E_{380} + E_{430})] = \mu g \text{ of CP} + \text{CPG per 100 ml}$$

d. Determination of δ-Aminolevulinic Acid (40)

A method for determination of δ-aminolevulinic acid and porphobilinogen, another heme precursor in lead workers, using anion- and cation-exchange resins has been developed by Mauzerall and Granick (41). PBG (porphobilinogen) is retained in the acetate form by the anion exchanger Dowex 2 while ALA (δ-aminolevulinic acid) is retained in the hydrogen form by cation exchanger Dowex 50. The presence of PBG and ALA can be demonstrated, after elution from the Dowex resins, by means of colored complexes formed with DMAB (p-dimethylaminobenzaldehyde). PBG forms the complex directly, but ALA must be converted quantitatively to the 3-acetyl-2-methylpyrrole-4-(3′)-propionic acid by heating with acetylacetone. The colored complexes are formed in acid solution and are spectrophotometrically read.

Reagents. *Dowex 2, × 8, 200–400* mesh. Place the ion exchanger in water and allow it to sediment. Draw off the water. Repeat the washing until the supernatant liquid is clear. Convert to the acetate form by washing with 3M sodium acetate on a column until the eluate is chloride free (as tested with silver nitrate), and then wash with water until the washings are neutral (as tested with litmus paper). Store in about twice its volume of water in a covered vessel. The exchanger will keep for at least 3–4 months at room temperature.

Dowex 50, × 8, 200–400 mesh. Separate off the finest particles by repeated suspension and sedimentation in water. Convert to the sodium form by storing it for about 20 hr in twice its volume of 2N sodium hydroxide. Wash with water until the washings are neutral. Reconvert to the acid form by treating alternately with about 1 volume of 4N hydrochloric acid and 6 volumes of 2N hydrochloric acid. Store the exchanger in twice its volume of 1N hydrochloric acid in a covered vessel. It will then keep for at least 3–4 months at room temperature.

Acetic Acid, 1N and 2N.

Sodium Acetate, 0.5*M*.

Acetate Buffer, pH 4.6.   Dilute 57 ml of glacial acetic acid and 136 g of sodium acetate trihydrate to 1000 ml with water.

Acetylacetone.

Ehrlich's Reagent I.   Add 2 g of *p*-dimethylaminobenzaldehyde to 100 ml of 6*N* hydrochloric acid.

Ehrlich's Reagent II.   Dissolve 1 g of *p*-dimethylaminobenzaldehyde in about 30 ml of glacial acetic acid and 8 ml of 70% perchloric acid in a 50-ml volumetric flask.   Dilute the solution to the 50-ml mark with glacial acetic acid (stable only for about 6 hr).

Procedure.   If an analysis for PBG is to be made, the sample should be fresh or have been stored at pH 7–8 (alkalinized with sodium carbonate) at +4°C.   If only ALA is to be determined, the sample may be kept for about 20 days at the same temperature at pH 4–6.

Place a cotton wool plug in the bottom of a chromatographic column about 1 × 10 cm.   Pack the ion exchanger by sedimentation to a height of 2–3 cm and place a filter paper on top.   Wash the Dowex 2 column with about 5 ml of water and the Dowex 50 column with about 25 ml of water before use.

Place exactly 1 ml of sample on the Dowex 2 column.   After it has passed through into a test tube at a flow rate of about 6 drops per min, wash twice, each time with 2 ml of water.   Add the washings to the test tube and transfer quantitatively to a Dowex 50 column. Remove the urea from the ion exchanger by washing with about 30 ml of water.   (If the eluate contains urea, a bright lemon-yellow color will develop on mixture with an equal volume of Ehrlich's reagent I.) Then wash with 3 ml of 0.5*M* sodium acetate.   Drain thoroughly. Place a 10-ml volumetric flask under the column and pass 7 ml more of 0.5*M* sodium acetate through it.   Add 0.2 ml of acetylacetone directly to the flask and shake.   Dilute with acetate buffer, pH 4.6, to the mark, transfer the entire mixture to a 15-ml glass-stoppered test tube, and heat for 10 min in boiling water and then cool to room temperature.   Remove 2 ml of this mixture and add to it 2 ml of Ehrlich's reagent II.   If the test is positive, a pink to cherry-red color will develop.   Read the extinction after exactly 15 min in a spectrophotometer with a 1-cm cuvette at 553 mμ.   A blank of 7 ml of 0.5*M* sodium acetate treated in the same manner as the sample should be used.

If a determination of PBG is to be made, elute this material from the Dowex 2 column with 2 ml of $1N$ acetic acid and, after this, with 2 ml of $0.2N$ acetic acid. Collect the combined eluates in a 10-ml volumetric flask and dilute to the mark with water. Remove a 2-ml aliquot of this mixture and add 2 ml of Ehrlich's reagent I. If the result is positive, a pink to cherry-red color develops rapidly. The extinction is read after exactly 5 min in a spectrophotometer with a 1-cm cuvette at 555 mμ. The blank for this determination consists of an equal volume of Ehrlich's reagent I and water.

Calculation. *ALA*. To known volumes of normal human urine add known amounts of ALA in the form of ALA·HCl. Analyze the samples according to the method given. Correct for the original ALA content of the urine and plot a standard curve. Calculate from the curve, provided $E \leqslant 1.2000$

$$4.74 \times E = \text{mg of ALA per 100 ml of urine}$$

PBG. PBG of reliable purity was not available. Therefore, the apparent molar extinction coefficient of 3.6×10^4 given by Mauzerall and Granick (41) was taken for the calculation. The standard curve given for determination of PBG by this method was also used.

Beer's law is obeyed when the extinction $E \leqslant 0.200$. Thus, when $E \leqslant 0.200$

$$12.6 \times E = \text{mg of PBG per 100 ml of urine}$$

but when $E > 0.200$, the concentration can be obtained directly from the graph in milligrams per 100 ml of urine.

2. MERCURY

The methods for the determination of mercury in biologic materials usually require three types of manipulation: first, destruction of organic matter generally by wet ashing; second, the isolation of the mercury; and third, the estimation of the isolated mercury. Representative of the first group of manipulative steps are the methods of Cholak and Hubbard (42), Barrett (43,44), Vesterberg and Sjöholm (45), Miller and Swanberg (46), and Monkman, Maffett, and Doherty (47).

Cholak and Hubbard (42) used a method in which the organic matter was destroyed by boiling with a mixture of sulfuric and nitric acids, followed by a second boiling with potassium permanganate.

Barrett (44), employing a combination of the Cholak and Hubbard method and that of Laug and Nelson (48), digested the biologic material with sulfuric and nitric acids, and with permanganate, using a reflux condenser to minimize losses of mercury during the heating step.   Such losses were stressed by Simonsen (49).

Vesterberg and Sjöholm (45) wet-ashed the sample with an acid solution of chlorine after separation of the mercury as the sulfide with cadmium sulfide as the collector.   Then a second wet combustion with chlorate, hydrochloric acid, and chlorine was performed.

Polley and Miller (50) used sulfuric acid and hydrogen peroxide, destroying excess peroxide with permanganate and the permanganate with hydroxylamine hydrochloride.   Gettler and Lehman (51) used potassium permanganate with sulfuric and nitric acids, and Johansson and Urnell (52) also used sulfuric acid and permanganate but destroyed the excess permanganate and manganese dioxide with peroxide and oxalic acid instead of the customary hydroxylamine hydrochloride.

Elkins (53) suggests the use of hydrochloric acid and potassium chlorate.   Other variations are those of Milton and Hoskins (54) and Maren (55).

Monkman, Maffet, and Doherty (47) employed cold digestion with solid potassium permanganate and concentrated sulfuric acid and permitted the mixture to stand overnight.   Miller and Swanberg (46) also used cold digestion with hydrogen peroxide and a catalyst of ferric chloride and potassium chromium sulfate.

Campbell and Head (56) have critically reviewed a number of these types of wet digestion and recommend the use of potassium permanganate and sulfuric acid for the determination of mercury in urine.

Most methods utilize dithizone to isolate the mercury from the digestion mixture after adjustment to a pH of about 1 to avoid interference of other metals in the extraction.   Hubbard (57) and Cholak and Hubbard (42), however, used di-β-naphthylthiocarbazone for this purpose.   Campbell and Head (56) following the technique of Vašák and Šedivec (58) employed the disodium salt of ethylenediaminetetraacetic acid to chelate interfering substances before the dithizone extraction.

Ballard and Thornton (59) separated the mercury by filtration through a bed of asbestos fiber impregnated with cadmium sulfide, modifying the method of Clarke and Hermance (60) who used filter paper impregnated with cadmium sulfide. Monkman et al. (47) modified this manipulative step additionally by impregnating glass filter pads.

Kozelka (61) separated the mercury after a digestion with sulfuric acid, copper sulfate and ammonium sulfate by distillation with chlorine. Barrett (44) as well as Laug and Nelson (48) used a second extraction with potassium bromide to free the mercury from interferences and Winkler (62) employed sodium thiosulfate. Storlazzi and Elkins (63), using a procedure modified after the method of Stock and Lux (64), separated the mercury by electrolysis.

In the third group of manipulative steps, namely, those for estimating the isolated mercury, representative variations are the colorimetric or spectrophotometric determination usually of a solution of mercury dithizonate at 490 mμ as done by Barrett (44) by Campbell (56), and Johansson and Urnell (52); colorimetric determination of the di-β-naphthylthiocarbazone complex (42,56); colorimetric estimation of cuprous mercuric iodide as done by Gettler and coworkers (65,66); titrimetric estimation as in the methods of Locket (67) and of Noble and Noble (68); microscopic estimation as detailed in the method of Storlazzi and Elkins (63); and estimation by ultraviolet photometry based on the method of Woodson (69) by Ballard et al. (59,70,71), Monkman et al. (47), and Lindström (72).

a. Determination in Blood

Ultraviolet Photometric Method (73)

The photometric method (33,74,75) consists of combining cold incomplete digestion of the biologic material, extraction with dithizone, decomposition of the mercury dithizone complex by heating to produce mercury vapor, and subsequent estimation of the mercury by ultraviolet photometry. It is a simple and relatively rapid method capable of determining mercury concentrations of the order of nanograms, that is, 10^{-9} g of mercury in 1 ml of blood or an equivalent amount of other biologic material.

Apparatus. The combustion-ultraviolet photometric equipment (76) consists of a heating chamber connected to a U-tube containing nonabsorbent cotton connected in turn to a cold trap, a rotameter, an additional cold trap, a modified Beckman mercury vapor meter Model

23, a water trap, and a water aspirator pump. The mercury vapor meter is modified by replacing the grille with a cylindrical optical cell, 23 cm long and 4 cm in diameter, with removable silica end windows and inlet and outlet ports for the air stream drawn by the aspirator pump. The rotameter is a calibrated Fischer and Porter Flowrator equipped with both glass and stainless-steel floats or an equivalent Gilmont rotameter can be used. The water trap prevents any backflow of water from the aspirator pump to the optical cell. The cold traps bring the temperature of the air stream down to room temperature.

The heating unit comprises a thermostatically controlled furnace consisting of a specially built 1-in. diameter, 8-in. long, S-hinged multiple-unit organic combustion furnace mounted on a pyramidal stand. The furnace is equipped with a thermocouple connected to an R7161B Versa-Tronik indicating and controlling potentiometer. The furnace is also connected to a rheostat which with the potentiometer are wired to an Allen Bradley Series K starter.

The glassware used includes 125-ml glass-stoppered erlenmeyer flasks, 125-ml separatory funnels, pipets, 25-ml glass-stoppered graduated cylinders, and 25×200-mm Pyrex ignition tubes. For each run the glassware is cleaned with cleaning solution, then washed with copious amounts of hot water, cold tap water, and distilled water, and air or oven dried.

Reagents. *Dithizone Extraction Solution.* Weigh out accurately 6 mg of purified diphenylthiocarbazone, transfer to a 1-liter volumetric flask, dissolve in chloroform, and make to volume with that solvent.

Potassium Permanganate Solution, 6%. Dissolve 60 g of highest purity, reagent grade potassium permanganate in distilled water with the aid of heat, transfer to a 1-liter volumetric flask, allow to cool, and make to volume with distilled water.

Sulfuric Acid. Use concentrated reagent grade sulfuric acid. Follow the customary procedure in preparing $0.25N$ sulfuric acid.

Hydroxylamine Hydrochloride Solution, 20%. Dissolve 200 g of reagent grade $NH_2OH \cdot HCl$ in 500 ml of distilled water. Transfer to a separatory funnel and shake out with several 5-ml portions of the dithizone extraction solution. Draw off the chloroform layers and discard. Transfer the hydroxylamine hydrochloride to a 1-liter volumetric flask and make to volume with distilled water.

Standard Solutions.   *Standard Stock Mercury Solution.*   Weigh out exactly 0.1354 g of reagent grade mercuric chloride and dissolve in 0.25N sulfuric acid.   Transfer to a 100-ml volumetric flask and dilute to the mark with 0.25N sulfuric acid.   This solution contains 1000 μg of mercury per milliliter.

Standard Working Mercury Solution.   With a volumetric pipet transfer 1 ml of the stock standard mercury solution to a 100-ml volumetric flask.   Dilute to volume with distilled water.   Stopper, invert, and shake well.   This solution contains 10 μg of mercury per milliliter.

With another volumetric pipet, transfer 1 ml of the 10 μg/ml mercury solution to a 100-ml volumetric flask and dilute to the mark with distilled water.   Stopper, invert, and shake well.   This working standard solution contains 0.1 μg/ml.   These solutions must be prepared fresh as required.

Preparation of Standard Curve.   Place 250 ml of 0.25N sulfuric acid in a separatory funnel with a dry stem.   Add 1 ml of the 10 μg/ml working mercury standard solution, stopper, and mix.   Extract with 5 ml of the dithizone extraction solution, shaking the separatory funnel for 1 min, and allow the phases to separate.   Swirl the contents of the funnel to make certain that all the chloroform solution is brought into the bottom phase.   Release the pressure caused by the chloroform vapor through the mouth of the funnel, not through the stopcock.   Transfer the clear extract to a dry 100-ml glass-stoppered volumetric flask, being careful not to draw any of the aqueous layer into the flask.   Repeat the extraction twice with two more 5-ml portions of the dithizone extraction solution, and then extract once more with 5 ml of chloroform.   Transfer each extract in turn to the 100-ml volumetric flask as before, and complete to the mark with chloroform.   Stopper and mix thoroughly.   Each milliliter of this solution contains 0.1 μg of mercury as mercury dithizonate.   With pipets, transfer 0.2 ml of dithizone solution to each of two 25 × 200-mm Pyrex ignition tubes.   These serve as blanks.   With volumetric pipets, transfer 0.1, 0.2, 0.3, and 0.4 ml of the chloroform–dithizone solution containing 0.1 μg of mercury as dithizonate in duplicate to separate ignition tubes.   The respective tubes will contain 0, 0.01, 0.02, 0.03, and 0.04, μg of mercury in duplicate.   Place the tubes in a beaker of hot water (70–80°C), and evaporate off the chloroform completely.   Continue as detailed in the procedure.

Plot the maximum arbitrary scale reading, in milligrams per cubic meter multiplied by 1000, against micrograms of mercury in the standards.

Procedure.   Transfer 0.5 ml of blood to a 125-ml glass-stoppered erlenmeyer flask.   Place in a shallow pan containing water and ice and cautiously add 2 ml of concentrated sulfuric acid.   Remove from the ice bath and warm (not over 50°C) on a hot plate until solution is complete.   Avoid charring.   Replace in the ice bath and add 10 ml of 6% potassium permanganate solution.

Warm on a hot plate, set at low heat (do not boil), remove from the hot plate, swirl, and allow to stand for 15 min.   Repeat the warming on the hot plate, removing, swirling, and cooling two more times. Allow to stand until the supernatant solution is clear or for a total elapsed time of 1 hr.   Add 20 ml of water.   Dissolve the precipitate with 0.5 ml of 20% hydroxylamine hydrochloride solution.   Swirl to assist in dissolving the precipitate.   Stopper the flask, shake, cautiously release the pressure, and allow to stand for 10 min.   Add 20% hydroxylamine hydrochloride solution drop by drop if more is required to dissolve the precipitate.

Transfer the solution to a dry 125-ml separatory funnel with a dry stem.   Wash the erlenmeyer flask with three 10-ml portions of distilled water, add the washings to the separatory funnel, and mix. Add 5 ml of the dithizone extraction solution.   Stopper the separatory funnel and shake vigorously for 1 min.   Release the pressure through the mouth.   Swirl to bring down any chloroform droplets and allow to stand until the phases separate completely.   Draw off the chloroform layer into a glass-stoppered, 25-ml graduated cylinder, being careful not to draw off any of the aqueous layer.   Repeat the extraction with 5 ml more of dithizone extraction solution and then wash with 3 ml of pure chloroform.   Add the chloroform wash to the graduated cylinder.   Add sufficient chloroform directly to the cylinder to make the total volume 15 ml.

Transfer, with the aid of a pipet and a safety pipetter, 1 ml of the chloroform solution of mercury dithizonate to a Pyrex ignition tube 25 × 200 mm and place in a hot water bath.   Evaporate off the chloroform completely at 70–80°C.

While the chloroform is being evaporated, check the apparatus, turn on the Beckman mercury vapor meter, turn on the aspirator pump so that the air flow is about 3300 ml/min, and allow the instrument to come to equilibrium.   Check the span of the instrument. After all the chloroform has evaporated, dry the outside of the tube and insert the ignition tube into the heating unit, placing it so that the flame will heat the bottom end of the tube.   Light a match, insert it into the lighting opening, turn on the gas, allow it to ignite, remove the match, and start a stop watch.   Record the starting time, in seconds, of the movement of the meter needle, the maximum deflection of the meter needle, the meter readings at 10-sec intervals, if possible, and the time of return of the meter needle to zero.   Obtain the concentration from the standard curve.

In the case of a 0.5-ml blood sample, multiply the reading from the standard curve by 3000 to express the concentration of mercury in micrograms per 100 ml; for a 1-ml urine sample multiply by 15,000 to express the results in micrograms per liter.

Jacobs Ultramicromethod

Most of the methods presently used for the determination of mercury in blood require at least 10 ml of blood and preference is expressed for 20 ml.   The requirement of only 1 ml in the method presented here is a marked advantage.   Since only 1 ml of a total volume of 15 ml of chloroform solution is used for the photometric step, even smaller volumes of blood can be analyzed by a simple modification of the method in which smaller volumes of reagents and a smaller final volume are employed.

The isolation of mercury by means of extraction with dithizone serves not only to separate it from other metals but also serves to free it from most other materials so that in the heating step no interferences such as those elaborated by Lindström (72) are encountered. Furthermore, since a type of destructive distillation is used, no products of combustion such as those produced in the flame combustion variation of Lindström are introduced into the photometer cell.

A cold digestion similar to that of Monkman et al. (47) was followed with two variations.   First, a solution of potassium permanganate was used instead of solid permanganate.   This circumvented the need to raise the temperature to dissolve the crystals or pellets and, in addition, the reaction time was reduced because the permanganate was able to react immediately.   Second, no attempt was made to destroy the organic matter completely.   It was shown by Jacobs (77,78) years ago that it was not necessary to destroy all the organic

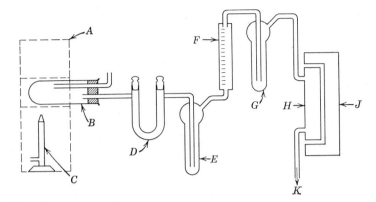

Fig. XIX-2. Diagrammatic sketch of the apparatus for the microdetermination of mercury: (A) wire enclosure of heating chamber; (B) ignition tube; (C) bunsen burner; (D) U-tube containing absorbent cotton; (E) cold trap; (F) rotameter; (G) cold trap; (H) optical cell; (J) mercury vapor meter; (K) to water aspirator pump.

matter to determine the amount of arsenic in milk. Noble and Noble (68) also do not destroy the organic matter completely in their method for the determination of mercury in urine. McBryde and Williams (79) eliminated the digestion for urine samples completely, filtering them directly through cadmium sulfide-impregnated pads. It is unlikely that such a variation would work with blood. Weiner and Müller (80) have stressed the need for adequate digestion in order to avoid the interference of sulfhydryl groups.

The avoidance of high temperature in the digestion (not over 50–60°C) and the elimination of the use of nitric acid are advantageous; indeed, the elimination of the need of relatively large amounts of sulfuric acid, nitric acid, and potassium permanganate is a great advantage but, in addition, the elimination of nitric acid avoids subsequent oxidation of dithizone.

The convention of taking the maximum deflection of the meter pointer as representative of the concentration of mercury follows the variation of Yamaguchi (81) and is somewhat similar to the convention adopted by Lindström (72) in taking a reading at exactly 45 sec. A reading of the maximum meter deflection to obtain the concentration of mercury serves very well for the standard curve and for concentrations less than 0.02 μg. There is greater variation for concentrations above 0.02 μg in both the standard and blood determinations.

Apparatus. The apparatus, Figure XIX-2, comprises a heating chamber, connected to a U-tube containing absorbent cotton and followed by a cold trap, a rotameter, an additional trap, a modified Kruger mercury vapor meter Model 23 (see Fig. IX-1) and a water aspirator pump. The mercury vapor meter was modified by altering the grille so that it could be removed easily and be replaced by an optical cell. This cell is a cylinder 23 cm in length and 4 cm in diameter. It has removable silica end windows, and is fitted with inlet and outlet ports for the air stream drawn by the aspirator pump. Gilbert proposed the use of such a cell in 1957. A calibrated Fischer and Porter rotameter equipped with both glass and steel floats was used to measure the air flow.

The heating chamber consists of a Bunsen burner mounted in a Nichrome wire cage $3\frac{3}{4} \times 3\frac{3}{4} \times 12$ in. Two cylindrical openings having a diameter of 1 in. capable of snugly accepting a 25×200-mm Pyrex ignition tube are cut in opposite faces of the unit about $6\frac{1}{2}$ in. from the bottom and about 2 in. above the top of the burner. A 25-mm diameter wire cylinder fits between the two openings, and the ignition tube passes through this cylinder.

Procedure. Reagents standard solutions, and the standard curve are prepared as described in the previous section, pages 791–793.

Transfer 1 ml of blood with the aid of a pipet to a 125-ml glass-stoppered erlenmeyer flask. Dilute with 20 ml of water. Add 10 ml of 6% potassium permanganate solution and add cautiously 2 ml of concentrated sulfuric acid and swirl. Warm on a hot plate set at low heat (do not boil), remove from hot plate, swirl, and allow to stand for 15 min. Repeat the warming on the hot plate, removing, swirling, and cooling two more times. Allow to stand until the supernatant solution is clear or for a total elapsed time of 1 hr. Dissolve the precipitate with 0.5 ml of 20% hydroxylamine hydrochloride solution. Swirl to assist in dissolving the precipitate. Stopper the flask, shake, cautiously release the pressure, and allow to stand for 10 min. Add 20% hydroxylamine hydrochloride solution drop by drop if more is required to dissolve the precipitate.

Transfer the solution to a dry 125-ml separatory funnel with a dry stem. Wash the erlenmeyer flask with three 10-ml portions of distilled water, add the washings to the separatory funnel, and mix

Add 5 ml of the dithizone extraction solution.   Stopper the separatory funnel and shake vigorously for 1 min.   Release the pressure through the mouth.   Swirl to bring down any chloroform droplets and allow to stand until the phases separate completely.   Draw off the chloroform layer into a glass-stoppered, 25-ml graduated cylinder, being careful not to draw off any of the aqueous layer.   Repeat the extraction with 5 ml more of dithizone extraction solution and then wash with 3 ml of pure chloroform.   Add the chloroform wash to the graduated cylinder.   Add sufficient chloroform directly to the cylinder to make the total volume 15 ml.

Transfer with the aid of a pipet and a safety pipetter, 1 ml of the chloroform solution of mercury dithizonate to a Pyrex ignition tube 25 × 200 mm and place in a hot water bath.   Evaporate off the chloroform completely at 70–80°C.

While the chloroform is being evaporated, check the apparatus, turn on the Kruger mercury vapor meter, turn on the aspirator pump so that the air flow is about 3300 ml/min, and allow the instrument to come to equilibrium.   Check the span of the instrument.   After all the chloroform has evaporated, dry the outside of the tube and insert the ignition tube into the heating unit placing it so that the flame will heat the bottom end of the tube.   Light a match, insert it into the lighting opening, turn on the gas, allow it to ignite, remove the match, and start a stop watch.   Record the starting time, in seconds, of the movement of the meter needle, the maximum deflection of the meter needle, the meter readings at 10-sec intervals, if possible, and the time of return of the meter needle to zero.   Obtain the concentration from the standard curve.

Multiply this reading by 15 to obtain the concentration in micrograms of mercury in 1 ml of blood and subsequently by 100 to express the result in micrograms per 100 ml of blood.

b. Determination in Urine

Ultraviolet Photometric Method

This may be run according to the procedure described in Section B-2-a of this chapter, pp. 790–794, except that 1 ml of urine is used as a sample instead of 0.5 ml of blood.

Jacobs-Singerman Method

A simplified variation of the dithizone method for the determination of mercury in urine has been developed (82). This involves cold digestion with sulfuric acid and potassium permanganate, extraction of the mercury present with a carbon tetrachloride solution of dithizone employing a Mojonnier tube to eliminate the use of multiple separatory funnels, separation and reextraction of the mercury if necessary to avoid copper interference, and finally determination of the mercury concentration by reading the absorption of light by the mercury dithizonate at 490 mμ. Normally analysis is performed on 25–50 ml of urine. With these volumes, the method is sufficiently sensitive to enable one to determine 0.02 μg of mercury per milliliter. For moderate concentrations of mercury in urine, 5-ml aliquots can be used, and for high concentrations, as little as a 1-ml specimen will be adequate.

Apparatus. Bausch & Lomb Spectronic 340 colorimeter. Mojonnier tubes (Fig. XIX-1) (5,83) glass-stoppered, No. G3, and separatory funnels.

Reagents. *Concentrated Sulfuric Acid.*

Potassium Permanganate Solution, 6%. Dissolve 60 g of reagent grade potassium permanganate in distilled water with the aid of heat and dilute to 1 liter with distilled water when cool.

Hydroxylamine Hydrochloride Solution, 20%. Dissolve 100 g of reagent grade hydroxylamine hydrochloride, NH$_2$OH·HCl, in 300–350 ml of distilled water and make up to 500 ml with water. Purify by shaking this solution with 15 ml of dithizone stock solution. Allow the layers to separate and discard the carbon tetrachloride layer.

Dithizone Stock Solution. Weigh out accurately 50 mg of purified diphenylthiocarbazone and dissolve in reagent grade carbon tetrachloride. Transfer to a 1-liter volumetric flask and make up to volume with carbon tetrachloride.

Dithizone Working Solution. Dilute 20 ml of dithizone stock solution to 100 ml with carbon tetrachloride.

Ammonium Hydroxide Solution, 1:1. Dilute 500 ml of concentrated ammonium hydroxide solution with distilled water to make 1 liter.

Standard Solutions. *Standard Stock Mercury Solution.* Weigh out exactly 0.1354 g of mercuric chloride, reagent grade, and dissolve in 0.25N sulfuric acid.   Transfer to a 100-ml volumetric flask and dilute to the mark with 0.25N sulfuric acid.   This solution contains 1 mg of mercury per milliliter.

Standard Working Mercury Solution.   Transfer 1 ml of the stock standard mercury solution to a 100-ml volumetric flask and dilute to the mark with distilled water.   This solution contains 10 μg of mercury per milliliter and must be prepared fresh as required.

Preparation of Standard Curve.   Place the following amounts of standard working mercury solution in 250-ml glass-stoppered erlenmeyer flasks, each of which contains 50 ml of distilled water: 0.0, 0.05, 0.1, 0.2, 0.4, 0.6, 1.0, and 1.5 ml corresponding to 0.0, 0.5, 1, 2, 4, 6, 10, and 15 μg of mercury.   Place the erlenmeyer flasks in an ice bath and cautiously add 10 ml of concentrated sulfuric acid, drop by drop.   Allow to cool and then add 50 ml of 6% potassium permanganate solution, very slowly and with swirling.   Allow to stand overnight or for at least 2 hr.   Add 10 ml of 20% hydroxylamine hydrochloride solution dropwise, swirling to dissolve any precipitate. Stopper the flask, shake gently, release the pressure, and allow to stand loosely stoppered for 1 hr.

Transfer the solutions to dry 250-ml separatory funnels, washing the erlenmeyer flasks with three 5-ml portions of distilled water. Add the washings to the separatory funnels and mix.   Add 20 ml of the working dithizone solution and shake vigorously for 1 min.   Release the pressure through the mouth of the separatory funnel, swirl to bring down any carbon tetrachloride droplets, and allow to stand until the phases separate.   Draw off the carbon tetrachloride layers into dry 125-ml separatory funnels, add 25 ml of 1:1 ammonium hydroxide solution and shake 6 times; release the gas, shake 6 times, release the gas, shake 6 times more, and again release the gas.   Transfer the carbon tetrachloride layers quantitatively to 125-ml separatory funnels and repeat the washing with additional 25-ml portions of 1:1 ammonium hydroxide solution.

Filter the carbon tetrachloride layers through Whatman No. 42 filter papers into 1-in. diameter Bausch & Lomb colorimeter tubes and read the percentage transmission at 490 mμ exactly 45 min after adding the ammonium hydroxide solution for the first washing. Space the additions of the ammoniacal wash solution so that each standard can be read 45 min later.

If Mojonnier tubes are used for the method instead of separatory funnels, run the calibration curve with only 25 ml of distilled water in each erlenmeyer flask and half the volume of the reagents detailed in the procedure for the digestion.

Procedure. *A. Separatory Funnel Variation.* *(1) Digestion.* Transfer 50 ml of urine specimen to a 250-ml glass-stoppered erlenmeyer flask; place the flask in an ice bath and cautiously add 10 ml of concentrated sulfuric acid, drop by drop. When cool, add 50 ml of 6% potassium permanganate solution, again drop by drop while gently swirling, still keeping the flask in the ice bath.

Stopper the flask loosely and allow to stand overnight. A rapid digestion may be performed by warming the mixture on a hot plate at low heat (not higher than 50°C), removing the flask from the hot plate, swirling, and allowing to stand for 15–20 min. Repeat the warming step 2 more times. Allow to stand for a total elapsed time of 3 hr.

Dissolve the precipitate with 10 ml of 20% hydroxylamine hydrochloride solution, adding this reagent cautiously drop by drop with constant swirling. Stopper the flask, shake gently but thoroughly, release the pressure, and allow to stand loosely stoppered for 2 hr.

(2) Extraction. Transfer the digested sample to a 250-ml separatory funnel, wash the erlenmeyer flask with three 5-ml portions of distilled water, add the washings to the separatory funnel, and mix. Extract with 20 ml of working dithizone solution, shake vigorously for 1 min, release the pressure through the mouth of the funnel, swirl to bring down any carbon tetrachloride droplets, and allow to stand until the phases separate. Swirl again, if necessary, to shake down any carbon tetrachloride droplets and then transfer the dithizone layer to another separatory funnel; add 25 ml of 1:1 ammonium hydroxide solution and shake 6 times, release the gas, shake 6 times, release the gas, shake 6 times more, and release the gas again. Allow to stand for the phases to separate. Transfer the carbon tetrachloride layer quantitatively to a third separatory funnel and wash again in the same manner with 25 ml of 1:1 ammonium hydroxide solution. It is generally unnecessary to perform a third washing.

(3) Reading. Filter the carbon tetrachloride layer through a Whatman No. 42 filter paper into a 1-in. colorimeter tube and read the percentage transmission at 490 mμ with a Bausch & Lomb Spectronic colorimeter or an equivalent instrument. Obtain the concentration

of mercury from the standard curve; if a 50-ml test sample was used, multiply by 20 to express the results in micrograms of mercury per liter of urine.

The reading must be performed exactly 45 min after adding the ammonium hydroxide solution for the first washing in order to obtain uniform results. A blank should be run through the entire procedure in both variations.

B. Mojonnier Tube Variation. (*1*) *Digestion.* Follow the procedure detailed in the Separatory Funnel Variation on a 25-ml urine test sample. Add, however, only 5 ml of sulfuric acid, 25 ml of potassium permanganate solution, and subsequently 5 ml of hydroxylamine hydrochloride solution. Use an ice bath during the additions and observe all the precautions noted. Adhere to the same time schedule.

(*2*) *Extraction.* Transfer the digested sample to a Mojonnier tube equipped with a glass stopper. Wash the erlenmeyer flask with three 5-ml portions of distilled water and add the washings to the Mojonnier tube. Add 20 ml of working dithizone solution and shake vigorously for 1 min. Carefully loosen the stopper to release the pressure and add 2.5 ml more of carbon tetrachloride in order to bring the level of the carbon tetrachloride solution to the top of the constricted part of the tube. Draw off the aqueous layer as completely as possible, add 25 ml of 1:1 ammonium hydroxide solution, shake 6 times, release the gas pressure, and continue the washing as detailed in the preceding variation.

(*3*) *Reading.* Draw off the aqueous layer as completely as possible, being careful, however, not to pour off any of the lower phase. Filter the carbon tetrachloride layer through Whatman No. 42 paper into a 1-in. colorimeter tube and read 45 min after the addition of the first wash solution as detailed above.

C. Copper-Elimination Variation. If the determination yields results that are considered "normal" for mercury content of urine, it is unnecessary to resort to a copper-elimination step. If, however, the mercury results are high, it is best to repeat the determination with a copper-elimination step.

After digestion, transfer the sample to a 250-ml separatory funnel, wash the erlenmeyer flask with three 5-ml portions of distilled water, and add the washings to the separatory funnel. Shake with two 5-ml portions of dithizone solution. Separate the carbon tetrachloride layers, transfer to another separatory funnel, and add 45 ml of distilled water, 2 ml of 1:1 sulfuric acid, and 4 ml of 1.5% sodium thiosulfate solution. Shake vigorously for 1 min, discard the carbon tetrachloride layer after the phases have separated, and eliminate any trace of dithizone by shaking twice with 2-ml portions of carbon tetrachloride.

Add 5 ml of 6% potassium permanganate solution to the aqueous layer, allow to stand for at least 30 min, and decolorize with 4 ml of 20% hydroxylamine hydrochloride solution. After waiting an additional 30 min, transfer the solution to a Mojonnier tube, wash the separatory funnel with three 5-ml portions of distilled water, and add the washings to the test solution. Extract with 20 ml of dithizone working solution and continue with the procedure as detailed in Mojonnier Tube Variation.

3. ARSENIC

a. Determination in Urine

Jacobs Molybdenum Blue Method

The modified method consists of ashing the biologic sample by a wet test technique, generating and liberating the arsenic in the sample as arsine, trapping the arsine in hypobromite solution, developing the molybdenum blue color, and reading the absorption in the near infrared.

Apparatus. The apparatus consists of the Gutzeit generator described in detail by Jacobs (5,24). This is a 60-ml glass bottle with a mouth wide enough to accept a No. 5½ or 6 one-hole rubber stopper equipped with an adapter (actually the trap of a Folin ammonia generator), containing 3-mm diameter glass beads wetted with lead acetate solution to absorb any hydrogen sulfide formed. This adapter is connected in turn to a 3-mm i.d. tube bent to form a right angle and this is attached to a special vapor trap used as the absorber. It has a closely wound but independent glass spiral around the inlet tube which assists the absorption. This makes a very efficient absorber for arsine.

The author also used a 12/30 ⸫ outer joint to hold a dental cotton roll wet with lead acetate solution as the absorbent for any hydrogen sulfide elaborated with the arsine.

Reagents. *Ammonium Oxalate Solution.* Prepare an aqueous saturated solution of ammonium oxalate, $(NH_4)_2C_2O_4 \cdot H_2O$.

Potassium Iodide Solution. Dissolve 15 g of potassium iodide in water and complete to a volume of 100 ml.

Stannous Chloride Solution. Dissolve 40 g of arsenic-free stannous chloride, $SnCl_2 \cdot 2H_2O$, in concentrated hydrochloric acid and complete to 100 ml with this reagent.

Lead Acetate Solution. Dissolve 10 g of lead acetate, $Pb(OOCCH_3)_2 \cdot 3H_2O$, in water and complete to a volume of 100 ml.

Sodium Hypobromite Solution. Add 3 volumes of half-saturated bromine water to 1 volume of $0.5N$ sodium hydroxide solution. This reagent must be made up immediately prior to use.

Ammonium Molybdate Solution. Dissolve 25 g of ammonium molybdate, $(NH_4)_6Mo_7O_{24} \cdot 4H_2O$ in 300 ml of water. Dilute 75 ml of concentrated sulfuric acid to 200 ml with water by adding the acid carefully to the water, and add the diluted acid to the ammonium molybdate solution.

Hydrazine Sulfate Solution. Prepare a half-saturated solution of hydrazine sulfate, $N_2H_4 \cdot H_2SO_4$, by diluting a saturated solution of hydrazine sulfate in water with an equal volume of water.

It is to be understood that all these reagents must be as free of arsenic as possible. It is best to purchase reagents specially prepared for arsenic determinations.

Procedure. Place the sample, for instance, 50 ml of urine, into a 300-ml kjeldahl flask and add 20 ml of nitric acid and 5 ml of sulfuric acid. Heat until dense fumes of sulfur trioxide are produced. If necessary, add small amounts of nitric acid to clear the residue. When the digestion is complete, add 5 ml of a saturated solution of ammonium oxalate and again heat until fumes are given off. Cool and transfer to a Gutzeit generator bottle. Wash the kjeldahl flask five times with 5-ml portions of water and add these washings to the generator. This makes a total volume of about 30 ml. Add 5 ml of 15% potassium iodide solution, 4 drops of the stannous chloride solution, and allow to stand for 20 min so that reduction of the arsenic will be complete. Add a piece of $1/4$-in. zinc rod, about 1 in. in length that has been activated and connect the rest of the Gutzeit molybdenum blue apparatus, that is, the hydrogen sulfide absorber and the tube leading to the arsine absorber. Add 3 ml of sodium hypobromite solution to the absorber tube and after connecting the apparatus, put the generator in an ice bath. Allow the generation to proceed for 1 hr. Transfer the sodium hypobromite solution to a 1-in. Bausch & Lomb colorimeter tube. Wash the absorber five times with 2 ml of water and add these washings to the colorimeter tube. Add 10 ml of $1N$ sulfuric acid, 1 ml of ammonium molybdate solution, and 1 ml of half-saturated hydrazine sulfate solution. Mix after the addition of each reagent. Allow to stand for 30 min and read in a Bausch & Lomb colorimeter at 830 mμ.

4. Thallium

a. Determination in Urine

Jacobs Triphenylmethane Dye Method (84)

Thallium in small and minute concentrations has been determined colorimetrically by means of dithizone, p-phenetidine, aminopyrine, and more recently by use of triphenylmethane dyes. Other methods for this range of thallium concentrations involve polarographic, chromatographic, radioactivity, fluorimetric with Rhodamine B, and complexon procedures.

It would be out of place here to review the literature of the analytical chemistry of thallium in depth but it is of interest, since there is no general review of the literature of the method using methyl violet and triphenylmethane dyes in general, to mention that since the introduction of the method by Gurev (85) and Shemeleva and Petrashen (86) in 1955, over 16 references (87–103) to the use of the variations of this method have appeared. Those of Reis (100), Gorzelewska (92), and Campbell et al. (88) are concerned with variations used for the determination of thallium in urine. Other methods recently employed for the detection and estimation of thallium in urine are those of Rappaport and Eichhorn (104) using Rhodamine B, Kliffmuller (105) using (1) the fluorescence method of Feigl et al. (106) and (2) the paper chromatographic method of Diller (107), Jamrog and Piotrowski (108) using dithizone, and Stavinoha and Nash (109) using flame spectrophotometry. The toxicology of thallium has recently been reviewed by Truhaut (110).

In the method described, the thallium is freed from organic matter by means of wet ashing, is oxidized to the thallic state, and is sub-

Procedure.   Place a portion of the ashed sample containing less than 10 μg of cadmium in a separatory funnel.   If more than 0.5 ml of acid is present, add thymol blue as indicator and titrate to a yellow color with NaOH.   Adjust the volume to 25 ml and add the reagents in the order given, mixing between each addition: 1 ml of sodium potassium tartrate, 5 ml of 40% sodium hydroxide–1% potassium cyanide, 1 ml of hydroxylamine hydrochloride, and 15 ml of extraction dithizone.   Now shake for 1 min and drain the chloroform layer into a second funnel containing 25 ml of cold tartaric acid.   Add 10 ml more of chloroform to the first funnel.   Shake and combine chloroform layers.   The aqueous layers must be kept rigorously separated; gas should be vented through the stopper rather than through the stopcock in all operations.   The extractions should be performed without delay after the addition of the dithizone in order to keep the contact time of the chloroform and strong alkali to a minimum.   If the amounts of lead and zinc in the sample are large, small amounts may be extracted in this step and give the misleading impression that the extraction of cadmium is not complete.   If the orange color of excess dithizone is not present in the aqueous layer, too large a portion of sample was taken.

The second funnel should be shaken for 2 min and the chloroform layer discarded.   If more than 10 μg of cadmium is present, the aqueous layer should be aliquoted at this point and the aliquot made up to 25 ml with additional tartaric acid.   The quantity of cadmium may be estimated by the difference in the intensity of the pink color of the first extract and the pink color of the chloroform wash extract.   The cadmium is largely present in the first extract, interfering metals giving about the same color in both extracts.   The pink color of the cadmium dithizonate changes immediately to green when shaken with tartaric acid, while the colors of most interfering substances, except lead, do not change.   Add 5 ml more of chloroform, shake 1 min, and discard the chloroform layer in as close a separation as possible, evaporating the last drops from the surface by gentle blowing of air.   Add 0.25 ml of hydroxylamine hydrochloride, exactly 15 ml of standard dithizone, and 5 ml of 40% sodium hydroxide–0.05% potassium cyanide.   Shake for 1 min.   Insert a dry pledget of cotton in the stem of the funnel and filter the chloroform layer into a dry photometer tube.   If water droplets appear in the light path, the chloroform should be carefully transferred to another tube.   The tubes should be stoppered to prevent evaporation and kept out of sunlight. Read the optical density of the pink color at 518 mμ. A tube of distilled water should be used as reference.

A blank containing all reagents should be run through the entire procedure.

Standards may be prepared by placing graduated amounts of cadmium up to 10 μg in a series of separatory funnels, adding tartaric acid to make 25 ml in each and following the regular procedure, beginning with the wash with 5 ml of chloroform.

6. SELENIUM

Because of its increasing use in the electronics field, selenium is a growing industrial hazard. Identification of selenium in the urine is conclusive evidence of intoxification by this substance.

a. Determination in Urine

3,3'-Diaminobenzidine Method (23,113)

This method is sufficiently sensitive to determine the low concentrations of selenium likely to be found in biologic materials.

Apparatus.   Spectrophotometer and pH meter.

Reagents.   *3,3'-Diaminobenzidine Hydrochloride*, 0.5% solution in distilled water.   Store in the refrigerator.

Standard Selenium Solution.   Prepare a 1-mg/ml stock solution by dissolving 1.6337 g of selenous acid (H_2SeO_3) in 1 liter of distilled water.   Standardize gravimetrically.   A working solution may be prepared by diluting the stock solution to 1 μg/ml.

Formic Acid.   2.5M solution in distilled water.

Ethylenediaminetetraacetic Acid (EDTA).   0.1M solution in distilled water.

Procedure.   Place an aliquot containing not more than 50 μg of selenium in a 100-ml beaker.   Wet-ash the sample.   Dilute to 50 ml with water after adding 2 ml of 2.5M formic acid.   Adjust the pH to 2–3.   Add 2 ml of 0.5% diaminobenzidine solution and allow to stand for 30–50 min. Adjust the pH to 6–7 with ammonium hydroxide.   Transfer to a 125-ml separatory funnel, add exactly 10 ml of toluene, and shake vigorously for 30 sec.   Centrifuge the toluene portion.   Separate and determine the absorbance at 420 mμ, using a reagent blank.

Standard Curve. A standard curve may be prepared by running 1–50-μg portions of the standard selenium solution through the above procedure. The results should be plotted as micrograms of selenium versus optical density.

Rapid Test (114)

Procedure. To 25 ml of urine in a beaker add 10 ml of a mixture of HNO_3, $HClO_4$, and H_2SO_4 (8:4:1). Cover with a watch glass and digest to white fumes of $HClO_4$. The solution is normally pale yellow at this point.

Cool the digest and add 30 ml of water. Filter with gentle suction through a Millipore (AA) filter supported by a strong filter paper such as the nutrient pad (Type A10) supplied with Millipores. Both filter media are clamped between the two sections of a Chromaflex column, 12 mm i.d. (Kontes Glass Co.). Filtration is necessary to remove silica and adventitious dust.

Bring the filtrate to boiling and add 20 ml of concentrated HCl which has been saturated with SO_2. Heat in a boiling water bath for 30 min, cool in running water for 30 min, and filter on a new Millipore in the same manner as described above. Compare the selenium stain with standards concurrently run on selenium-free urine to which known amounts of selenium (1–6 μg) have been added or with colored artificial standards.

7. Tellurium

a. Determination in Urine

Sodium Diethyldithiocarbamate Method (23)

The cupferron solution is used to eliminate the following impurities: bismuth, copper, iron, molybdenum, antimony, tin, titanium, and vanadium. The volume used in the extraction process must, therefore, be adjusted according to the concentration of the impurities.

Apparatus. Spectrophotometer and pH meter.

Reagents. *Hydrochloric Acid*, concentrated.

Tartaric Acid. Reagent grade.

Sodium Hydroxide.

Cupferron (nitrosophenyl hydroxylamine, $NH_4 \cdot NO \cdot NPh$). Prepare a 2% solution fresh.

Buffer, pH 8.6.   Dissolve 5 g of boric acid, 1 g of ethylenediamine-tetraacetic acid, and 1 g of potassium dihydrogen phosphate (KH_2PO_4) in about 50 ml of distilled water and adjust to a pH of 8.6 with sodium hydroxide solution.   Dilute to 100 ml with distilled water.

Potassium Cyanide.   Reagent grade.

Sodium Diethyldithiocarbamate.   Make up 0.5 g of sodium diethyldithiocarbamate to 100 ml with distilled water.

Procedure.   Prepare a $4N$ hydrochloric acid solution in urine, filter off insoluble matter, and evaporate to dryness.   Dissolve the residue in $2N$ hydrochloric acid, add 20 mg of tartaric acid, and dilute to 20 ml with water.   Adjust the ph to 1–2 with sodium hydroxide solution.   If the solution is not clear at this point, filter again and then cool to 15–20°C.   Transfer to a separatory funnel and shake with cupferron solution (the volume of the cupferron to be used depends upon the concentration of impurities).   Extract with chloroform until the extract is colorless, and then two times more to remove residual cupferron.   Add 5 ml of buffer and 50 mg of potassium cyanide.   Adjust to a pH of 8.5–8.7.   Add 1 ml of sodium diethyldithiocarbamate solution.   Extract three times with carbon tetrachloride, using 10, 10, and then 5 ml and shaking for 2 min after each addition.   Filter the extracts through dry filter paper and dilute with carbon tetrachloride to 25 ml.   Read the yellow color at 428 mμ, using pure carbon tetrachloride as a reference and a reagent blank as zero.

The concentration is obtained from a standard curve prepared from known concentrations of pure tellurium of 10–150 μg run through the procedure with the exception of the cupferron treatment.

Rapid Method (114)

Procedure.   Perform the entire procedure given under Selenium, Rapid Method, p. 811.   After the selenium has been filtered out, evaporate the filtrate to H_2SO_4 fumes.   Cool and wash into a 25-ml volumetric flask or cylinder with small portions of water, not exceeding a total volume of about 20 ml.   Add 5 ml of $SnCl_2$ solution (30 g of $SnCl_2$, 350 ml of concentrated HCl, 100 ml of water), filter at once through a Millipore as in the selenium procedure, and compare the tellurium stain with standards made up as in the selenium procedure.

Short Version.   Selenium, which would interfere in the estimation of tellurium, may be removed and the selenium part of the procedure eliminated by adding 1 ml of concentrated HBr and about 10 ml of water to the solution obtained after wet ashing, and boiling again to $HClO_4$ fumes with no watch glass on the beaker. Selenium will be quantitatively volatilized. Then proceed with the filtration for silica and finally with the precipitation and filtration of tellurium.

8. COBALT

Methods for the colorimetric microdetermination of cobalt in biologic material have been reviewed by Saltzman and Keenan (115). Among the color reagents, the most promising and the one which has found most extensive use is Nitroso-R salt. The cobalt–Nitroso-R salt complex may be formed is a hot acetate medium as by the procedure given by McNaught (116,117) or in a citrate–phosphate–borate buffer according to the procedure described by Marston and Dewey (118). However, for the trace quantities encountered in general biological material, it is necessary to concentrate the cobalt and to free it from excess salts and particularly from iron. Cobalt is extractable with sodium diethyldithiocarbamate under the same conditions described for manganese and nickel by Cholak and Hubbard (119) and by Bode (120), while iron may be removed almost completely by the use of cupferron. The color of the cobalt complex developed in a hot acetate medium is then read spectrophotometrically at 550 mμ after boiling the final solution with nitric acid to destroy interfering colors formed by the presence of traces of iron, nickel, and copper.

a. Determination in Urine and Blood

Nitroso-R Salt Method (121)

Reagents. *Ammonium Citrate Solution.* Dissolve 400 g of citric acid in 500 ml of water. Neutralize with phenol red as an indicator and dilute to 1 liter with water. Treat the cooled solution first with dithizone in chloroform, 40 mg/liter, and finally with 20 ml of 10% aqueous diethyldithiocarbamate. Follow by repeated extractions with 10-ml portions of chloroform to remove metals present, particularly cobalt. Discard the chloroform.

Acetate Buffer Solution. Dissolve 247 g of ammonium acetate, $NH_4C_2H_3O_2$, 109 g of sodium acetate, $NaC_2H_3O_2 \cdot 3H_2O$, and 6 g of glacial acetic acid in water. Transfer to a 1-liter volumetric flask and dilute with water to the mark. The pH of this solution will be approximately 6.75. For removal of trace metals, particularly cobalt, purify the solution exactly as the ammonium citrate solution was purified.

Sodium Diethyldithiocarbamate Solution, aqueous. Dissolve 66 g of reagent grade sodium diethyldithiocarbamate, $(C_2H_5)_2NCSSNa \cdot 3H_2O$, in water. Filter through a fluted filter paper to remove insoluble matter and finally dilute to 500 ml. Treat this filtered solution with 10 ml of redistilled chloroform to remove any cobalt that may be present (122). Store in a polyethylene container.

Ammonium Hydroxide Solution. Reagent grade, sp gr 0.90.

Chloroform. Add 1% absolute alcohol by volume as a preservative.

Standard Cobalt Solution. Dissolve 0.1 g of cobalt metal in hydrochloric acid (1:9). Dilute with 1:9 hydrochloric acid to a 100-ml volume so that 1 ml = 1 mg of Co. This stock solution can be diluted additionally as required for use in preparing standards used to develop the working graphs.

Cupferron Solution, aqueous. Dissolve cupferron in triple-distilled water to make a 6% aqueous solution. Store in the refrigerator.

Preparation of Samples. *Biological Material.* Urine, blood, and tissue samples may be prepared for analysis by either dry- or wet-ashing procedures. Place 100 ml or less of urine or 20 or more g of blood or tissue in a 150-ml silica dish. In the case of urine, add 10–20 ml of nitric acid and evaporate to dryness. Blood and tissue samples are merely dried in the dish. Ash the dried material in a muffle furnace maintained at 500°C. Ashing should be completed in 1–2 hr. If the ash is not carbon free, treat it with a few milliliters of nitric acid, evaporate to dryness, and replace in the furnace. Repeat the acid and ashing treatments until carbon-free ash is obtained. Dissolve the ash of urine in 2–3 ml of nitric acid and about 20–30 ml of water. (Dissolve the ashes of blood and tissues in a mixture of hydrochloric acid–nitric acid and water.) Transfer the solution to a 50- or 100-ml graduated cylinder and make up to the mark with water.

The wet-ashing method entails the customary sulfuric–nitric–perchloric acid mixture. The digestion is made in open 600-ml Griffin beakers. This step involves the addition of 20 ml of concentrated reagent grade sulfuric acid (sp gr 1.84), plus 20 ml of concentrated reagent grade nitric acid (sp gr 1.42). The sample is partially digested on a hot plate until oxidation produces a dark brown color. Then add 10 ml more of nitric acid, followed by 5 ml of reagent grade perchloric acid (70–72%). Continue the digestion until all traces of organic matter have disappeared and heavy dense fumes of sulfur trioxide appear, following the removal of perchloric acid. Remove the sulfuric acid by fuming to disappearance of sulfur trioxide fumes.

Procedure. When dealing with blood samples it is necessary to remove iron as completely as possible prior to the extraction of cobalt. Free the solution of the ashed blood, contained in a 250-ml Pyrex beaker, from sulfuric acid by fuming until free from sulfur trioxide.

Add 5 ml of concentrated hydrochloric acid and take the sample to dryness on the hot plate. Remove the sample from the hot plate, allow to cool, rinse down the sides of the beaker with water, add 4 ml of concentrated hydrochloric acid, heat gently to dissolve salts, and transfer the solution to a 125-ml Squibb-type separatory funnel. Adjust the volume to 20 ml with water.

Add 25 ml of 6% aqueous cupferron solution and mix well by shaking for 1 min. Add 10 ml of chloroform, shake well for 30 sec, and discard the chloroform fraction. Repeat this operation until no more iron is removed, as is evidenced by the color of the chloroform. Finally, return the iron-free aqueous fraction to the original beaker, rinse the inside of the separatory funnel with about 10 ml of water, and add this washing to the sample contained in the beaker. Copper is also partially removed by the cupferron treatment.

Add 5 ml of concentrated nitric acid and evaporate to dryness on the hot plate. Add a second 5-ml portion of nitric acid and again evaporate to dryness. Rinse down the sides of the beaker with water and add another 1 ml of nitric acid. Add 95 ml of distilled water. (It may be necessary to warm the solution to dissolve salts.) Add 4 drops of 0.1% aqueous chlorphenol red, 20 ml of ammonium citrate solution, and 10 ml of the buffer solution, followed by ammonium hydroxide, until a pH of 6.5 is reached. The indicator changes to red.

Transfer the solution to a 500-ml Squibb-type separatory funnel and dilute to approximately 400 ml with distilled water. Add 20 ml of the sodium diethyldithiocarbamate solution. Mix and then add 10 ml of chloroform. Shake vigorously for 2 min and transfer the chloroform layer to a 125-ml separatory funnel. Repeat the extraction with 10-ml portions of chloroform two more times, collecting all of the chloroform layers in the 125-ml separatory funnel.

Add 50 ml of water to the chloroform solution. Shake and remove the chloroform layer to a 50-ml conical centrifuge tube. Treat the water layer with 10 ml of chloroform and add the chloroform to the centrifuge tube. Evaporate the contents of the centrifuge tube to dryness in a glycerine bath. Add 1 ml of nitric acid and heat in a glycerine bath to get a clear solution.

CAUTION: For the extraction of cobalt, it has been found imperative to avoid the use of stopcock grease commonly used for separatory funnel stopcocks. Therefore, Squibb pear-shaped funnels equipped with Teflon plug stopcocks are used. *This is important.* If stopcock grease enters the chloroform used for extracting the cobalt, subsequent oxidation of the residue is incomplete.

The sample is next transferred totally to a clean 125-ml Phillips beaker, which contains a few small pieces of clean silicon carbide bumping stones. The contents of the beaker are evaporated at low heat almost to dryness. If necessary, repeat the addition of 1 ml of nitric acid and the evaporation to dryness until a carbon-free residue is obtained. Cool, add 5 ml of distilled water, 0.25 ml of 1:1 hydrochloric acid and 0.25 ml of 1:10 nitric acid, and bring to a boil to dissolve any solid material. Cool again, add exactly 0.5 ml of Nitroso-R salt (0.2% aqueous) and 1 g of hydrated sodium acetate; then boil for 1 min.

Cool to room temperature in the dark and after 5 min transfer the sample to a 10-ml glass-stoppered cylinder and dilute to the mark.

Transfer to an appropriate cell and measure the transmittance at 550 mμ in a suitable spectrophotometer, reading against distilled water as the solvent. Read the cobalt values in micrograms from standard graphs, depending on the expected concentration. A 100-mm length cell is used for the 0–5 μg range and a 25-mm length cell for the 0–25-μg range.

Preparation of Standard Graphs. The graphs are prepared by adding appropriate amounts of the standard cobalt solution to 20-g portions of whole blood and going through the entire procedure. A straight-line relationship is obtained. Cobalt cannot be detected in 20–40-g samples of normal blood and, therefore, it is believed that a true zero point is obtained.

9. ANTIMONY

a. Determination in Urine

Rhodamine B Method

In this method (24) all the antimony in the intermediate or unreactive state is either oxidized to the pentavalent state by use of perchloric acid at the end of the digestion or is reduced to trivalent antimony by sulfur dioxide, following the destruction of organic matter by the acid digestion, and is subsequently oxidized to the pentavalent state by ceric sulfate in the presence of hydrochloric acid. A lake is prepared using Rhodamine B; this lake is extracted by a suitable solvent and the color is estimated colorimetrically or photometrically. If perchloric acid is used in the digestion (123), it is not necessary to use the sulfur dioxide reduction or the ceric sulfate oxidation.

Reagents. *Nitric Acid*, concentrated, reagent grade.

Sulfuric Acid, concentrated, reagent grade.

Perchloric Acid, 60%, reagent grade.

Hydrochloric Acid, 6N, reagent grade.

Phosphoric Acid, 3N. Prepared by diluting 70 ml of concentrated, reagent grade acid to 1 liter.

Rhodamine B, 0.02%. Dissolve 0.20 g of Rhodamine B in water and dilute to 1 liter.

Preparation of Sample. Transfer 25 ml of urine or 10 ml of blood to a 125-ml kjeldahl flask and add 5 ml of concentrated nitric acid and 5 ml of concentrated sulfuric acid. Boil until heavy white fumes appear. If organic matter remains, as shown by a black residue or solution, cool, add 2-ml portions of concentrated nitric acid and boil repeatedly until organic matter is gone.

Benzene Extraction. Add 2 drops of 60% perchloric acid to the water-white acid digest and heat until fumes of sulfur trioxide are evolved. If charring or yellowing occurs, it is necessary to add additional perchloric acid, but not over a total of 0.5 ml when 10 ml of 18N sulfuric acid are used initially. Cool, add 3 ml of water, and heat until fumes are evolved. Cool and place in a cold-water bath. Add 5 ml of 6N hydrochloric acid.

Add 8 ml of 3N phosphoric acid and 5 ml of 0.02% Rhodamine B solution. Shake the flask and cool again if necessary. The benzene extraction must now be performed without delay. Transfer to a separatory funnel. Rinse the digestion flask with 10 ml of benzene and transfer the benzene to the separatory funnel. Shake 150–200 times, draw off the lower aqueous layer, and transfer the benzene phase to a tube. Allow to stand and settle. The color is stable at this point. Transfer 6–8 ml to a cuvette and read at 565 mμ or use a green filter.

Isopropyl Ether Extraction. After the addition of the hydrochloric acid, add 13 ml of water and transfer to a separatory funnel. Add 15 ml of isopropyl ether to the digestion flask, rinse, and transfer to the separatory funnel. Shake about 100 times and discard the aqueous layer. Add 5 ml of 0.02% Rhodamine B solution. Shake again 150 times and, after settling, discard the aqueous layer. Transfer the ether layer to a tube. Read immediately at 545 mμ or use a green filter.

Standard Solutions. Weigh accurately 0.1000 g of chemically pure antimony and add 25 ml of concentrated sulfuric acid. Heat until the metal dissolves. Cool and dilute to 1 liter. The solution is stable and contains 100 μg/ml of antimony. It can be further diluted to give working standards.

In preparing a standard curve, add known amounts of antimony up to 40 μg to 5 ml of sulfuric acid. Make an acid digestion with nitric acid. Treat with perchloric acid as detailed and then proceed with the remainder of the analysis.

10. URANIUM

a. Determination in Urine

Fluorophotometric Determination (124–128)

This method is based on the intense yellow-green fluorescence produced by traces of uranium fused in sodium fluoride. The principal line is at 555 mμ. The method is sensitive to 10^{-10} to 5×10^{-11} g per 0.25 g of sodium fluoride.

Reagents. *Sulfuric Acid*, 96%, sp gr 1.84.

Hydrochloric Acid, 36%, sp gr 1.19.

Nitric Acid, 69%, sp gr 1.42.

Sodium fluoride, NaF—AR powder. The sodium fluoride must be specially pure. Uranium content must not exceed 5 parts per 10^{10} and the uranium content of different lots may vary widely. The sodium fluoride is tested by running blanks on each lot. Standards are also run on each lot to check the fluorescent response to uranium.

Lithium Fuoride Flux, 2%. Place 350 g of sodium fluoride in a 1-qt Twin-Shell blender and add 7 g of lithium fluoride (LiF—AR). Seal the shell and mix for 8 hr. Intimate mixing is critical.

Nitric Acid, 2N. Add 128.2 ml of concentrated nitric acid to 500 ml of distilled water in a 1-liter volumetric flask. Make up to volume with distilled water and mix.

Stock Uranium Standard. Place 2.11 g of uranyl nitrate [UO_2-$(NO_3)_2 \cdot 6H_2O$—AR] in a 1-liter volumetric flask and make up to volume with 2N nitric acid. This solution contains 1 mg of uranium per milliliter. If precise standardization is desired, the uranium in an aliquot of the solution may be converted to uranium oxide (U_3O_8) and weighed.

Intermediate Standard. Dilute 10 ml of stock uranium standard to 1000 ml with 2N nitric acid. The solution contains 10^{-5} g of uranium per milliliter.

Standard I. Dilute 10 ml of the intermediate standard to 100 ml with 2N nitric acid. The solution contains 10^{-6} g of uranium per milliliter.

Standard II. Dilute 10 ml of standard I to 100 ml with 2N nitric acid. The solution contains 10^{-7} g of uranium per milliliter.

Apparatus. *Platinum Dishes.*

Micropipets. Transfer-type ("capillary") pipets in 10, 25, 50, 75, and 100-μliter sizes. These pipets are boiled twice in concentrated nitric acid, rinsed thoroughly in distilled water, boiled in distilled water, and dried in an oven.

Spot Plates. Use porcelain spot plates to hold and carry the platinum dishes.

Infrared Lamp, 250 W. General Electric reflector infrared Pyrex heat lamp. Use to dry the platinum dishes and samples.

Fusion Rack. Place the rack in a spot free from drafts and air currents and support it so that the dishes are $\frac{1}{4}$ in. above the top of the burner. Care must be taken to have the rack and dishes level to ensure good mixing of the flux and urine salts.

Sodium Fluoride Dispenser. The dispenser is made from an 8-cm length of a 10-ml graduated pipet and a 10.5-cm length of glass rod that slides easily but not loosely inside the tube.

Fisher Blast Burner (Fisher blast burner, high-temperature, for cylinder gas with a 2-in. head). The intensity of the flame is adjusted until the flux (mp 1150°C) melts in approximately 1 min or less (1000–2000°C). High oxygen concentration in the flame should be avoided. Excessive oxygen causes a chemical reaction between the flux and platinum which stains the dish bottom brown, and sometimes gives the disk a yellow, orange, or brown color.

Didymium Glasses. Didymium glass glassblowers goggles. These should be used to observe the molten flux.

Platinum Evaporating Dish. With lip, 4-in. diameter. Use to clean the platinum dishes.

Fluorophotometer. The current generated in the photocell is measured with a simple direct-current slide-back-type voltmeter constructed using electrometer tube techniques. The obvious advantage of this type of voltmeter is that any nonlinearity of the electronic circuit is cancelled out. In operation, galvanometer deflection is kept at zero by manipulation of the helipot vernier from which voltage readings are taken.

Precautions. The uranium procedure is empirical and for reproducible and reliable results strict attention must be paid to each detail. The samples, blanks and standards must be treated identically.

Cleanliness. The most scrupulous attention to cleanliness is necessary for analyses at high sensitivities. All equipment and samples should be protected from atmospheric dust. The dishes should never be touched with fingers from the time of final rinsing until after the dishes are removed from the instrument. Use platinum-tipped forceps to handle the dishes.

Interference. When large amounts of heavy metals are present, as small an aliquot as the uranium concentration will permit is used in order to reduce damage to the platinum dishes.

High Blanks. High readings for blanks may result from any of the following ten sources:

(1) Dark current or zero drift in the fluorophotometer.

(2) Fluorescence of fluorophotometer parts.

(3) Light leakage in the fluorophotometer.

(4) Fluorescence of dust particles or grease on dishes or disks after fusion.

(5) Uranium introduced by touching dishes or fusion material.

(6) Uranium introduced by splattering during evaporation.

(7) Uranium introduced as dust from the atmosphere.

(8) Uranium present in the original fusion material.

(9) Uranium introduced from the platinum dishes.

(10) "Blank rise" from standing in air (due to absorption of moisture).

Procedure.   Add approximately 1 ml of concentrated hydrochloric acid for every 100 ml of urine.   Uranium is not coprecipitated in urines acidified with hydrochloric acid.

The ultraviolet light source of the fluorophotometer and the galvanometer must warm for a minimum of 30 min before reading samples.   If the light should go off for any reason, even momentarily, it must be turned off and allowed to cool for at least 30 min before being turned on again.   Set the vernier knob and the sensitivity scale knob at zero.   After the lamp has warmed sufficiently, the galvanometer should be at zero, the ampere scale should read 1, and the milliampere scale should read 0.5.

Clean the dishes by heating in concentrated sulfuric acid in a platinum evaporating dish until all flux from past determinations dissolves.   Flood under tap water, rinse twice with concentrated nitric acid, boil in concentrated nitric acid, and store in concentrated nitric acid.   Before use, the acid in which the dishes have been stored should be brought to a boil.   Then they should be rinsed and boiled twice in fresh distilled water.

Place the clean platinum dishes on the back of a porcelain spot plate and add 0.10 ml of urine.   (Samples should be run in triplicate.)   Dry completely under the infrared lamp and place in the fusion rack.   Ignite over the Fisher blast burner until all visible material becomes clear, molten, or volatilized.   Pour a small amount of sodium fluoride flux powder into a petri dish.   Hold the flux dispenser like a hypodermic syringe and press some of the powder into the tube.   Hold a spatula flat against the end of the tube and push the plunger down to compress the powder into a firm tablet.   With the aid of the spatula, adjust the amount of powder to give a tablet volume of about 0.25 ml (approximately 0.25 g).   Extrude the tablet directly onto the cooled platinum dish.   Fuse the dishes with the Fisher burner, moving the burner slightly to spread the flux evenly over the bottom of the dish.   Timing of the fusion should begin when the last bit of sodium fluoride melts and should continue for 1 min.   During fusion, center the flame under the center of the dish and wear didymium glasses.   Cool the dishes without disturbing on the fusion rack for about 5 min. The fused disk should be white and crystalline. Read the fluorescence of the disks in the fluorophotometer approximately 30 min after fusing.

Prepare the blanks by placing 3 clean dishes on the fusion rack and running through the entire procedure. Place these blanks in the carrier and read first. The readings should not differ by more than 2–3 vernier units. Select the best of the blanks and place it in the first position in the carrier. Read the blank before each set of samples.

Turn the sensitivity scale selector to the correct scale. Push the slide carrier in until the first dish is positioned under the lamp. Bring the galvanometer back to zero with the vernier knob. Take the vernier reading. The grams of uranium per sample are determined from the appropriate standard curve (made with the sensitivity scale used for reading the samples) after the vernier reading of the blank has been subtracted from the average vernier reading of the sample.

Calculations.

$$\frac{g \text{ U in sample} \times 10^6 \,\mu g/g \times 1000 \text{ ml/liter}}{\text{ml of sample aliquot}}$$

$$= \mu g \text{ of uranium per liter of urine}$$

$$\frac{g \text{ U per sample} \times 10^9}{0.1 \text{ ml of urine}} = \mu g \text{ of uranium per liter of urine}$$

Preparation of Standard Curves. Prepare two standard curves (3 points) and read daily. In addition, make complete curves (5 points) when dark current or zero drift is noted in the fluorophotometer, a new lamp is installed, a new lot of sodium fluoride is used, or whenever there is a change in procedure of instrument behavior. Each standard is done in triplicate and three blank dishes are prepared as described above. In routine work only 0.025, 0.075, and 0.10 standards are done daily. The complete curve is run monthly.

Standard Curve I. Pipet 0.01, 0.025, 0.050, 0.075, and 0.10 ml of standard I in triplicate onto the platinum dishes. This gives standards containing 10^{-8}, 2.5×10^{-8}, 5.0×10^{-8}, 7.5×10^{-8}, and 10^{-7} g of uranium per dish. Read this set of standards with sensitivity scale 2.

Standard Curve II. Pipet 0.01, 0.025, 0.050, 0.075, and 0.10 ml of standard II in triplicate onto the platinum dishes. This gives standards containing 10^{-9}, 2.5×10^{-9}, 5.0×10^{-9}, 7.5×10^{-9}, and 10^{-8} g of uranium per dish. Read this set of standards with sensitivity scale 3.

The fluorescence of the disks is read and the standard curves are plotted with grams of uranium per dish versus the average vernier readings for the standards minus the vernier reading for the blank.

Alpha Activity (125,129,130)

Wet-ash the urine for the determination of uranium and extract with di-*n*-butyl orthophosphoric acid in carbon tetrachloride. Evaporate the phosphoric acid on platinum plates, fuse, and alpha-count with a low-background proportional counter. The method has an accuracy of $84 \pm 14\%$ with 1–10 disintegrations/min/liter of enriched uranium. With higher concentrations, the recovery approximates 100%.

Reagents. *Nitric Acid*, 70%, sp gr 1.42.

1N. Dilute 64 ml of concentrated nitric acid to 1 liter with distilled water.

20%. Dilute 200 ml of concentrated nitric acid to 1 liter with distilled water.

Uranium Spike Solution. The spike solution is a solution of uranium-235 or enriched uranium in 1N nitric acid. It contains approximately 10 disintegrations/min/liter. Plate four 1-ml aliquots of the spike solution directly on 1-in. square platinum planchets. Dry the planchets under an infrared lamp and flame to red heat over a bunsen burner. Count the planchets in an electronic counter for 30 min. Count each planchet twice. The average of the 8 counts is used as the concentration of the spike solution in disintegrations per minute.

Di-n-butyl Orthophosphoric Acid (DBP). Place 200 ml of DBP, 800 ml of carbon tetrachloride, and 500 ml of distilled water in a 2-liter separatory funnel. Shake for 15 min and allow to separate. Drain the organic layer into a 1-liter storage bottle. This gives a solution which is 0.3–0.4N in DBP. The monobutyl phosphoric acid is extracted into the water phase by this method and is discarded.

Carbon Tetrachloride, reagent grade.

Procedure. Samples should not be more than 1 or 2 days old. Add 5% by volume of nitric acid. Record the original sample volume and the volume after the addition of the acid. Mix and allow to stand for several hours. Place a 105-ml aliquot of the urine in a round-bottomed 500-ml flask, add 25 ml of concentrated nitric acid, place on a Hotcone heater, and evaporate to dryness. Cool, add 10 ml of concentrated nitric acid, and evaporate to dryness again. If the residue retains any color, repeat the addition of nitric acid and heating until the salts are white. Cool and dissolve the residue in 5–10 ml of 20% nitric acid by warming gently. Transfer quantitatively to 40-ml centrifuge cones, washing with distilled water to give a total volume of 30 ml. Cool and mix by swirling. Add 1 ml of the DBP solution and stir mechanically for 10 min with an electrically driven glass stirrer. The tip of the glass rod should be just above the carbon tetrachloride layer. Allow to separate, remove the DBP layer with a 0.5-ml glass transfer pipet with a syringe, and place on a platinum counting planchet. Evaporate the carbon tetrachloride slowly under an infrared lamp. Any aqueous solution transferred to the planchet will cause spattering and recovery loss. The planchets are made from 2 mil platinum foil cut in $1\frac{1}{8}$-in. squares. The squares are shaped into flat-bottomed cups on a $\frac{1}{2}$-in. square die. Add 0.5 ml of DBP solution to the centrifuge cones and stir again for 10 min. Remove carbon tetrachloride phase and evaporate as above. Repeat a third time so that a total of 2 ml of DBP is used. Add 1 ml of carbon tetrachloride and wash by stirring for 10 min. Remove the carbon tetrachloride with the same pipet and add to the combined extracts. When the planchet is dry, lower the infrared lamp to 4 in. above the planchet and heat several hours or overnight until the residue is charred and dry. Then place the planchet on a holder and keep at the top of the oxidizing flame of a Fisher burner until it has stopped boiling. Lower to the reducing flame and heat until the black residue disappears. Remove immediately; excessive heating causes a loss of uranium. Flatten the plate carefully to give a smooth surface for counting. Count in a low background proportional counter for 30 min.

A blank consisting of 100 ml of pooled urine from persons unexposed to uranium and a spike consisting of another 100-ml portion of pooled urine to which 1 ml of uranium spike solution has been added should be run through the entire procedure with each group of urine samples.

Calculation.

$$100 \times \frac{\text{counts/min}}{\% \text{ efficiency of counter}} \times \frac{1000 \text{ ml}}{\text{ml aliquot}}$$

$$= \text{d/min found per liter of urine}$$

$$\frac{\text{d/min/liter found in spike} - \text{d/min/liter found in blank}}{\text{d/min of uranium added to spike}}$$

$$= \text{recovery factor}$$

$$\text{d/min/liter found in sample} \times \text{recovery factor}$$
$$= \text{d/min/liter per urine sample}$$

where d = disintegrations.

11. Tritium

a. Determination in Urine

The method (125,131–135) consists of dropping urine onto metallic calcium so that hydrogen and tritium are evolved.   The beta activity is counted with a scaling circuit having an input sensitivity of 0.25 V and inert hydrogen is counted simultaneously to determine the environmental background.   The background count is subtracted from the sample count to obtain the true sample count.   The method has an efficiency of approximately 40% and a precision of ±5% in the range of 1–250 μcuries of tritium per liter.   Samples with higher concentrations may be determined with appropriate dilutions.   The tolerance for tritium in urine used at the Los Alamos Scientific Laboratory is 85 μcuries per liter.   The biological half-life of tritium is about 10 days.   This may be decreased by increasing the fluid intake of the individual.

Reagents.   *Metallic Calcium*, No. 10 mesh.   The calcium used is specially purified and is sold by the New England Lime Co., Adams, Mass.

Ethylene.   99.5%, commercial grade.

Argon.   Commercial grade.

Drierite.   Indicating, anhydrous calcium sulfate, 8 mesh.

Apiezon M Stopcock Grease.

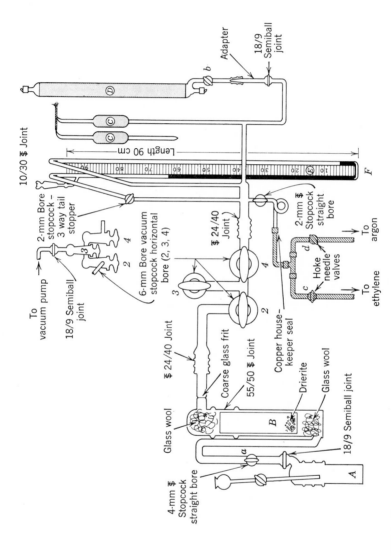

Fig. XIX-3. Vacuum line: *A*, generator; *B*, drying trap; *C*, Pirani tubes; *D*, counting tube; *E*, manometer; *F*, constriction in manometer (133).

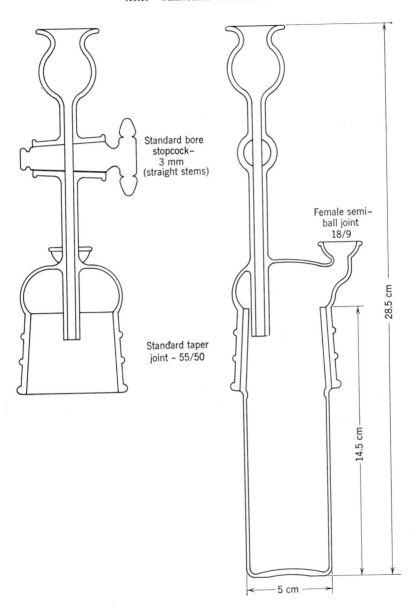

Standard bore
stopcock–
3 mm
(straight stems)

Female semi-
ball joint
18/9

28.5 cm

Standard taper
joint – 55/50

14.5 cm

←— 5 cm —→

Fig. XIX-4. Complete generator flask (133 .

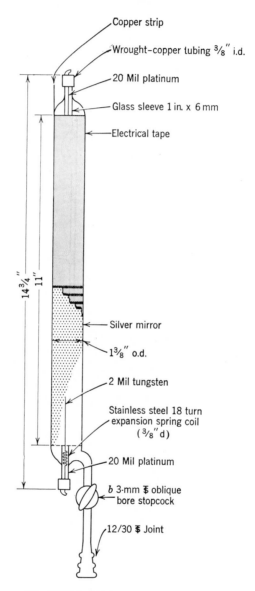

Fig. XIX-5. Tritium counting tube (133).

Dow-Corning High-Vacuum Grease.

Dow-Corning Antifoam A.

Tritium Standard. The stock standard is water containing tritium oxide obtained from the Chemistry and Metallurgy Division, Los Alamos Scientific Laboratory. The standard contains 85 μcuries of tritium per liter as of November 1957.

Preparation of Apparatus. *Vacuum Line* (Fig. XIX-3). Grease the stopcocks and joints on the vacuum line (manifold) periodically with Dow-Corning high vacuum grease. Stopcock *6* to the gas lines is left open except when isolating leaks in the system.

Procedure. Place about 2 g of metallic calcium in the bottom of a glass generator (Fig. XIX-4). The lower part of the bottom of the generator should be smeared with a ring of Dow-Corning Antifoam A before the top of the generator is fitted to the bottom and sealed with Apiezon M stopcock grease. Fill the drying column with Drierite. Fit the generator to the vacuum line, sealing the joint with Apiezon M grease. Open stopcock *a* between the generator and the vacuum line. Place the glass counting tube (Fig. XIX-5) on the right side of the manifold. Leave stopcock *b* closed. Open the valves on the ethylene and on the argon cylinders. The pressure should be between 1 and 2 psi. Start the vacuum pump (⅓ horsepower) and allow it to run for 15 min until the system is evacuated. Close stopcock *4*. Open needle valve *c* and let ethylene flow into the system until a pressure of 5 cm Hg is obtained. Open needle valve *d* and let argon flow into the system until 5 cm Hg is obtained. These two operations flush the gas lines. Open stopcock *4* and stopcock *b* (on the tube) and continue pumping the system. Pump for about 5 min or longer and check the pressure with the Pirani gauge. The system should be pumped until the pressure is about 0.05 mm Hg.

Counters. The Geiger-Müller tubes are counted with a decimal scaler (Los Alamos Scientific Laboratory Model 700) having a 10-μsec resolving time. The scaler has a six-place mechanical register that will handle 72,000 counts per min with a counting loss of less than 1%. Two scalers are used—one to count the background Geiger-Müller tube and one to count the sample Geiger-Müller tube. The scalers are equipped with a control panel and a Graylab universal timer so that they can be operated simultaneously for a preset time.

Turn on the master switch on both scalers and let the instruments warm for 30 min. Turn on the ac switch on the control panel. Fill the background Geiger-Müller tube with inert hydrogen by running a sample of distilled water through the entire procedure. The high voltage must always be turned off when inserting or removing tubes in the lead pig in order to avoid shock. Place the background tube in the lead pig (Fig. XIX-6) with the anode (center wire) in contact with the high voltage lead from the background scaler to the copper foil cathode (the silver tube lining). The scale selector switch on the scalers should be set for 100×.

Calibration of the Manometer. Evacuate the right side of the manifold with the counting tube in place and open. Note the level of the mercury in the manometer when the system is evacuated. With needle valve *c*, add ethylene until the pressure in the system is 15 cm Hg. The pressure in the system is measured by the difference in level between the mercury in the arms of the manometer. Close stopcock *b*. Add ethylene until the pressure is approximately 19 cm Hg. Open stopcock *b* to allow the pressure to equalize in the tube and the system. The pressure should now be about 17 cm Hg. Repeat until a manometer reading is obtained which allows the pressure in the tube to increase by exactly 2 cm Hg. Note this reading. Fill the system (and the tube) with ethylene until the pressure is at 17 cm Hg. Close stopcock *b*. Add ethylene until the pressure is approximately 27 cm Hg. Open stopcock *b* and allow the pressure in the system to equalize. The pressure should now be about 22 cm Hg. Repeat the last two steps until a manometer reading is obtained which allows the pressure in the tube to increase by exactly 5 cm Hg. Note this reading. The manometer settings thus obtained can be used until the volume of the system is changed.

Preparation of Counting Tubes. The counting tubes are made with a 200-ml volume, according to specifications at Los Alamos Scientific Laboratory, of lime glass with a 2-mil stainless steel center wire. The center wire has a hook at each end. On one end it is fastened to a small stainless steel spring. At each end of the tube is a 20-mil platinum lead (fused with the glass) which extends at least 1 in. beyond the end of the tube and approximately 1 in. inside the tube. The inner ends of the leads are hooked.

Hook one lead to the stainless steel spring and the other to the center wire. Secure the metal-to-metal connections with silver solder. Coat the outside of the tube with a silver mirror which serves as the cathode.

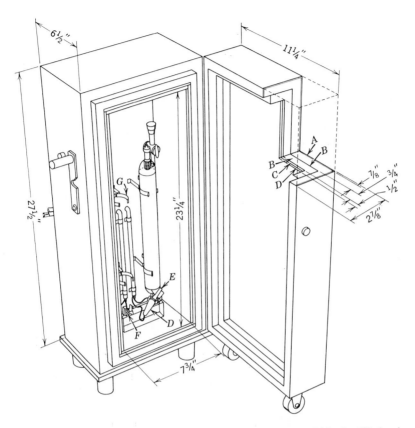

Fig. XIX-6. Lead counting shield: (*A*) sheet metal cover; (*B*) lead; (*C*) aluminum; (*D*) Lucite; (*E*) ground connection; (*F*) high-voltage connection; (*G*) friction clip (133).

Drill a small hole in the end of a wrought copper tube cap ($\frac{3}{8}$-in.
i.d.).   Fill the cap partially with Armstrong's cement and place over
the end of the glass tube with the center wire through the hole.
When the cement is thoroughly set and the cap firmly fixed on the
tube, clip off the protruding wire and seal it to the cap with a drop of
solder.   Clean the tube by rinsing with 15 ml of 1% nitric acid,
rinsing 5 or 6 times with distilled water, and washing with a weak
solution of Alconox.   Remove the detergent by thorough rinsing
with distilled water and then twice with ethyl alcohol.   Dry the tube

by evacuating for several hours. Wash and polish the outside of the tube and then silver with Brashear's Silvering Solution (134). The tube should be silvered to the shoulder and the ends covered by masking tape and paraffin to keep them from being silvered. Each tube should have two coats of silver. After the tubes have been plated and the paraffin cleaned off, place a strip of copper foil (20 mil, $3\frac{1}{4}$ in. $\times$ $3\frac{1}{2}$ in.) in contact with the silver mirror; $2\frac{1}{2}$ in. of the strip should be in contact with the mirror. Fasten the strip in place with electrical tape and wrap the entire mirror tightly with electrical tape to protect the plate. One in. of the copper strip extends beyond the wrapping and serves as a lead to which the ground lead from the scaler is clipped. Number each tube with a distinctive number.

Counting Tube Backgrounds. Fill each tube with inert hydrogen generated from distilled water by following the steps under Procedure (p. 833). Count as described under Counting the Sample. Obtain a sufficient number of counting rates so that the tube backgrounds do not differ by more than the standard deviation. The differences between the counts per minute of the background tube and the counts per minute of the new tube is known as the tube background (expressed in counts per minute). The background tube should be chosen so that its counting rate is lower than that of the sample tubes. The tube background changes with use. It should be rechecked every week or two or after being filled with samples with extremely high tritium concentrations. If the tube background is more than 30 counts/min, the tube should be recleaned until the background drops to 30 counts/min or less.

Tube Standardization Factor. The tube standardization factor gives the number of counts per minute for each microcurie of tritium in 1 liter of tritium standard. The factor is expressed in terms of counts per minute per microcurie per liter of tritium. Fill each tube with tritium generated from the working tritium standard (tritium = 85 μg/liter) following the regular procedure. Count and calculate the tube standardization factor.

$$\frac{\text{average net counts/min, tube background}}{85\,\mu\text{curie/liter}}$$

$$= \text{tube standardization factor, counts/min/}\mu\text{curies/liter}$$

Procedure. Fill the thistle tube on the generator (Fig. XIX-4) with 10–15 ml of the urine sample. As little as 5 ml may be used if extreme care is exercised. Close stopcock 3 (Fig. XIX-3) to the vacuum pump. Drop the urine slowly on the calcium until a pressure of 16–17 cm Hg is attained. Close stopcock 2 to close the left side of the manifold and immediately remove the generator from the manifold to release the pressure on the left side of the system. With stopcock 3 (this stopcock is ground for microcontrol) bleed off the gas in excess of 15 cm Hg pressure. The tube is now filled with hydrogen–tritium gas at a pressure of 15 cm Hg. Close stopcock b on the tube. Open stopcock 3 to the vacuum pump and evacuate the right side of the manifold to a pressure of 0.05 mm Hg. Check with the Pirani gauge. Close stopcock 4. (Leave stopcock 3 open.) Using needle valve c (to the ethylene cylinder), let ethylene flow into the system to such a pressure that opening stopcock b will give a final pressure of 17 cm Hg. Ethylene is added to the tube filling as a quenching agent. Open stopcock b on the tube momentarily; the pressure of the entire system and the tube will fall to 17 cm Hg. Open stopcock 4 and evacuate the right side of the manifold. When the manifold is evacuated, close valve 4 and using needle valve d (to the argon cylinder), let argon flow into the system to such pressure that opening stopcock b will give a final pressure of 22 cm Hg in the tube. Argon increases the specific ionization and lowers the starting potential of the counting tube. Open stopcock b on the tube momentarily; the pressure of the entire system and the tube will equalize at a pressure of 22 cm Hg. Remove the tube from the vacuum line, place in the lead pig, and count as described below. Place a freshly charged generator on the manifold. Open stopcock 2. Stopcock a is open. Place a counting tube on the right side of the manifold, open stopcocks b and 4, and evacuate the manifold while counting the filled tube. Wash the used generator by taking apart and flooding the bottom with water. Rinse out the spent calcium. Soak both parts of the generator for several hours in kerosene to remove the Apiezon M grease. Wash the generators with Alconox and water (with scrubbing). Rinse well and dry in an oven. The generators must be thoroughly dry before use to prevent reaction with the calcium metal.

Counting the Sample. The tritium beta activity is counted in this procedure at a controlled voltage exactly 50 V above the starting potential.   It has been found that this voltage is on the flat portion of the plateau curve.

Place the Geiger-Müller tube, filled with gas from the sample, in the lead pig with the anode in contact with the high-voltage lead from the sample scaler.   Clip the ground lead from the sample scaler to the cathode.   Turn on the high voltage on the background and sample scalers.   Set the universal timer for 30 sec.   Turn on the count switch on the control panel.   Turn the high-voltage adjustment up slowly on both scalers until the counter just starts to count.   Note the reading on the voltage scale and check the point several times by approaching it from both sides.   Set the high-voltage adjustment at the point where the scaler just starts to count.   Add 50 V to both counters with the preset addition switches on the scalers.   Reset the interpolation lights with the reset button on the control panel and reset the registers on both scalers to zero.   Set the timer for 2 min. Turn on the count switch on the control panel.   Count the sample and the background tubes for 2 min and record each count.   The count is obtained by multiplying the figure on the register by 100 and adding to this the count on the interpolation lights.   Count the sample until the observed single counts, obtained by subtracting the background count from the sample count and dividing this net count by the number of minutes counted, do not differ by more than one standard deviation from the average net count.   When the count is completed, turn the voltage down with the high voltage off on the sample scaler.   Remove and evacuate the Geiger-Müller tube.   The tubes should not be allowed to stand with a filling in them.

Calculation.   Results are reported in microcuries per liter.

$$\frac{\text{average net sample count per minute } - \text{ GM tube background}}{\text{tube standardization factor}}$$

$$= \mu\text{curies of tritium/liter}$$

The procedure for obtaining the Geiger-Müller tube background and the tube standardization factor are described above under Preparation of Apparatus (p. 832).

12. PLUTONIUM

a. Determination in Urine

The analytical procedure for separating plutonium from uranium, actinium and its daughters, americium, curium, and thorium has been described (125).   The extracted plutonium is oxidized to plutonium-(VI) and electrodeposited on a stainless steel disk.   The disks may be counted electronically or exposed to nuclear-track alpha plates and the number of tracks from the alpha particles counted visually with a microscope.

Analytical Procedure

Reagents.   *n-Octyl Alcohol* (primary).   Commercial grade.

Nitric Acid, concentrated, 70%, sp gr 1.42.

2N.   Dilute 128 ml of concentrated nitric acid to 1 liter with distilled water.

1N.   Dilute 64 ml of concentrated nitric acid to 1 liter with distilled water.

Boiling Chips.   Carborundum abrasive grains, 20 mesh.

Hydroxylamine Hydrochloride.   Reagent grade.

Lanthanum Nitrate Solution.   Place 10 g of lanthanum nitrate, $La(NO_3)_3 \cdot 6H_2O$ reagent grade, in a 400-ml beaker and dissolve in 200 ml of distilled water.   Add 50 ml of ammonium hydroxide (25%). Transfer the solution to four 90-ml centrifuge tubes.   Rinse the beaker with distilled water and add the washings to the tubes to give equal volumes.   Centrifuge at 2000 rpm for 5 min.   Discard the supernatant fluid.   Add concentrated nitric acid, with stirring, to tube *1* until the precipitate is just dissolved.   Transfer the clear solution to tube *2*.   Rinse tube *1* with 2–3 ml of concentrated nitric acid and add to tube *2*.   Stir and add concentrated nitric acid, if necessary, until the precipitate is just dissolved.   Transfer the solution to tubes *3* and *4* in the same manner.   Transfer the combined solutions in tube *4* to four clean 90-ml centrifuge tubes.   Divide the solution to give equal volumes.   Add 10 ml of ammonium hydroxide to each tube and stir.   Centrifuge at 2000 rpm for 5 min and discard the supernatant fluid.   Repeat the nitric acid and ammonium hydroxide treatment.   Add concentrated nitric acid with stirring to tube *1* until the precipitate is just dissolved.   Transfer the clear solution to tube *2*. Rinse tube *1* with 2–3 ml of concentrated acid and add to tube *2*. Stir and add concentrated nitric acid, if necessary, until the precipitate just dissolves. Transfer to tubes *3* and *4* in the same manner. Transfer the clear solution to a 250-ml graduated cylinder. Rinse the centrifuge tubes with 2–3 ml of distilled water and add to the solution in the cylinder. Add distilled water to the solution to give a total volume of 160 ml. Stir and transfer to a glass-stoppered bottle. This gives a solution containing 20 mg of La^{3+} per milliliter.

Concentrated Hydrofluoric Acid. HF 48%, 27N.

Aluminum Nitrate Solution. Dissolve 740 g of aluminum nitrate, $[Al(NO_3)_3 \cdot 9H_2O]$, reagent grade, in 1 liter of distilled water containing 20 ml of concentrated nitric acid.

Sodium Nitrite Solution, 2N. Dissolve 1.40 g of sodium nitrite, $NaNO_2$, reagent grade, in 10 ml of distilled water. Prepare fresh daily.

TTA Solution. Dissolve 50 g of 2-thenoyltrifluoroacetone (TTA), $C_8H_5O_2SF_3$, 4,4,4-trifluoro-1-(2-thienyl)-1,3-butanedione, in toluene ($CH_3C_6H_5$, reagent grade) in a 1-liter volumetric flask and make up to volume with toluene. Store in a brown glass bottle in the dark.

Hydrochloric Acid, 8N. Add 688 ml of concentrated hydrochloric acid, HCl 36%, sp gr 1.19, to 100–200 ml of distilled water in a 1-liter volumetric flask. Mix, cool, dilute to 1 liter with distilled water, and mix.

Potassium Hydroxide. 12N. Dissolve 390 g of potassium hydroxide (KOH 86%—AR) in distilled water, with stirring, and dilute to 500 ml.

2N. Dissolve 130 g of potassium hydroxide in distilled water and dilute to 1 liter.

Phenolphthalein Indicator. Dissolve 0.1 g of phenolphthalein in 60 ml of alcohol (C_2H_5OH, 95%) and dilute to 100 ml with distilled water.

Sodium Hypochlorite. Commercial sodium hypochlorite, NaOCl, 5–6% available chlorine.

Plutonium Spike Solution. Dilute a plutonium solution of known concentration to 1 liter with 1N nitric acid to give approximately 5 disintegrations/min/ml.

Procedure. Two morning and two evening voidings of urine are collected in 3-pint glass bottles. The total sample is mixed in a 2-liter beaker. For routine analysis the minimum sample volume accepted is 700 ml. Measure and record the sample volume and specific gravity. Add about 1 ml of octyl alcohol. Then put about 50 ml of concentrated nitric acid in each sample bottle, rinse, and add the combined 150 ml to the urine in the beaker. Evaporate to dryness on a hot plate using high heat until the volume has been reduced to 100 ml, and use low heat thereafter. Oxidize to a white ash by repeated evaporation with 5–10 ml of concentrated nitric acid, covering the beaker with a Speedyvap. Allow to cool for several minutes, and add 50 ml of 2N nitric acid, washing down the beaker and Speedyvap. Replace the Speedyvap and bring the solution to a boil for about 1 min. Remove from hot plate and transfer the solution to a 90-ml centrifuge tube, washing the beaker with small volumes of 2N nitric acid and adding the washings to the centrifuge tube. Any undissolved salts should be washed into the tube and the final volume should be approximately 75 ml. (If necessary, this solution may be allowed to stand for a week or more.) Let the solutions cool for 30 min or more and add 0.5 g of hydroxylamine hydrochloride to each tube to reduce the plutonium to the trivalent state for coprecipitation with lanthanum fluoride. Stir until dissolved. Add 1 ml of lanthanum nitrate solution (20 mg of La^{3+} per milliliter) to each tube and transfer the solutions from the Pyrex tube to new 100-ml Lusteroid centrifuge tubes. Rinse the Pyrex tubes with several small amounts of distilled water and add to the solution in the Lusteroid tubes. Add exactly 5 ml of 27N hydrofluoric acid, stir with a glass stirring rod, and allow the samples to stand for 5 min. Rinse the rods into the sample each time they are removed. Centrifuge at 2000 rpm for 5 min. Pour off and discard the supernatant fluid as completely as possible. Slurry the precipitate with 2 ml of 8N nitric acid, add 6–8 ml of distilled water, and stir vigorously. Add 2N nitric acid in 10-ml portions until the volume is 75 ml, stirring well after each addition. Add 5 ml of 27N hydrofluoric acid, stir, and allow the samples to stand for 5 min. Centrifuge and discard the supernatant fluid. Dissolve the precipitate in 40 ml of aluminum nitrate solution by first slurrying with 1–2 ml of the solution to break up the gelatinous lumps. Add the remainder of the aluminum nitrate solution in 10-ml portions with vigorous stirring until all the lanthanum fluoride precipitate is in solution. Add 0.25 ml of freshly prepared 2N sodium nitrite solution to the samples. The sodium nitrite oxidizes the trivalent plutonium to the tetravalent state so that it can be extracted with TTA. Note the time of addition of the sodium nitrite. Transfer the solution to a 125-ml Squibb separatory funnel. Wash the Lusteroid tubes with 10 ml of distilled water and add to the solution in the funnel. Shake the funnels for a few seconds to mix thoroughly. Discard the Lusteroid tubes. Exactly 15 min after addition of the sodium nitrite solution, add 10 ml of TTA solution, shaking for 30 min with an automatic wrist-action shaker. Allow to separate and discard the aqueous phase. Wash first with 20 and then with 10 ml of distilled water, shaking for 10 min and discarding the washings. Add 10 ml of $8N$ hydrochloric acid, shake for 20 min, and collect the acid layer in a 20-ml low-form beaker. Wash with 5 ml of $8N$ hydrochloric acid, shaking for 5 min and adding the washing to the acid phase in the beaker. Evaporate without boiling until 1–2 ml remain. (The sample should not be permitted to go to dryness, but if this should happen, add 2–3 ml of $8N$ hydrochloric acid and boil for a few seconds.) Neutralize with $12N$ potassium hydroxide, using phenolphthalein as an indicator or watching for a color change from yellow to brown. Care must be taken not to exceed the end point since plutonium(IV) will precipitate from alkaline solution. Add 2 ml of sodium hypochlorite and 5 ml of $2N$ potassium hydroxide. The sodium hypochlorite oxidizes plutonium(IV) to plutonium(VI) to form the plutonyl ion for electrodeposition. (The samples may be permitted to stand overnight before electrodeposition, if necessary, but if so, merely bring to a boil and cover. Do not evaporate.) Evaporate the solutions carefully until the volume is reduced by half and transfer the samples carefully to the electrodeposition cells with distilled water to give a total volume of 10 ml.

Electrodeposition

Apparatus. *Stainless Steel Disks.* Diameter $\frac{1}{2}$-in., 5 mil of 18-8 stainless steel, Type 347, No. 4 finish.

Platinum Disks. Platinum sheet, 10-mil, wrinkle free, 6 × 12 in., approximately 255 g per sheet.

Disk Holder. White cardboard, $2^{13}\!/_{16}$ × $4\frac{1}{4}$ in. with an 8-disk capacity and disk-holder envelope from Grigsley Bros., Portland, Oregon.

Reagents. *Electrolyte Solution.* Dissolve 200 g of citric acid,

$H_3C_6H_5O_7 \cdot H_2O$, reagent grade, in 200 ml of distilled water and add 57.5 ml of concentrated sulfuric acid slowly with stirring.

Alcohol, 1:1. Combine 50 ml of ethyl alcohol (95%) and 50 ml of distilled water.

Procedure for Electropolishing Disks. Fill a 75 × 150-mm Pyrex crystallizing dish about two-thirds full with electrolyte and heat to a constant temperature between 90 and 105°C. Place a platinum wire mesh screen in the solution and attach the cathode clip (negative terminal) from the power supply to the screen. Clip the disk to be polished to the anode lead (positive terminal) and submerge it. Polish for 20 sec at 8–10 V and 3–5 A. Rinse the polished disks thoroughly in distilled water to remove all traces of electrolyte solution and store in 1:1 alcohol.

Procedure for Electrodepositing.

$$PuO_2^{2+} + 2H_2O + 2e^- \rightarrow Pu^{4+} + 4OH^-$$

$$4OH^- + Pu^{4+} \rightarrow Pu(OH)_4 \cdot nH_2O$$

$$Pu(OH)_4 \cdot nH_2O \xrightarrow{\Delta} PuO_2 + (n - 2)H_2O$$

The electrodeposition cells should be assembled before use. Remove the polished plates from the alcohol solution and wipe dry with Kleenex. (Stainless steel disks are used routinely; platinum disks are used for samples which are to be pulse-height analyzed. The platinum plates are rinsed in acetone and wiped dry before use to remove any traces of grease.) Place the shim plate in the depression in the cell cap, place a clean, dry disk on top, and screw the Lucite barrel in position. Fill the cell with approximately 5 ml of distilled water and let stand until use. Check the water-filled cells carefully for leaks before using. Empty the cells and transfer the sample solution to the cell with distilled water so that the final volume is approximately 10 ml. The electrodeposition is usually started in the morning in order to have 5 hr of plating time during the working day. Clamp the cell in position on the electrodeposition apparatus and attach the cathode clip to the cell cap. Turn the power on and adjust the voltage to 10 V. Adjust all ammeters to read 200 mA. Electroplate for 5 hr. Then remove each cell without turning off the current. Discard the caustic solution and rinse the cell thoroughly with distilled water. When all the cells are off the instrument, turn down the voltage on the electrodeposition apparatus and turn off the power. Disassemble the electroplating cell and remove the plated disk by inserting a stainless steel wire through the hole in the cell cap. Remove the disk with forceps, rinse with distilled water, drain in air or on low heat on a hot plate, and place in position in the disk holder. The holder slots should be numbered with the laboratory sample numbers. Flame each disk to cherry red, identify, and store in a disk holder.

The disks may be counted electronically or exposed to nuclear-track alpha plates and the tracks counted by microscope according to standard procedures (125).

13. Carbon Monoxide

a. Determination in Blood

Pyrotannic Acid Method.

This method is described in detail on pages 713–717, Chapter XVII.

Spectrophotometric Method (136)

Methods for the determination of carbon monoxide in blood based on spectroscopic analysis (137,138) are accurate only when high concentrations of carbon monoxide are present. The two most accurate methods in current use are the manometric method of Van Slyke and Salvesen (139) and the volumetric method of Scholander and Roughton (140). Considerable skill and practice are needed, however, to obtain accurate results. These methods have certain disadvantages in that the carbon monoxide is determined after absorption of other blood gases, and corrections have to be made for dissolved nitrogen.

Apparatus. *Infrared Analyzer.* Dispersion of the infrared spectrum is not required in this apparatus, the principles of which were first described by Pfund (141). The analyzer used is similar to that of Luft (142) in which the portion of the spectrum that is examined is determined by a radiation detector limited in its response by being filled with a pure sample of the gas to be estimated.

Blood Gas Extraction Apparatus. P in Fig. XIX-7 is a 1000-ml flask equipped with a two-way tap T_1 and a tight-fitting rubber bung. By means of taps T_2 and T_3 the flask can be evacuated using a high-vacuum pump. Q is a cut-down boiling tube of approximately 35-ml capacity connected to flask P by means of a three-way tap, T_2. S is a 5-ml pipet, the tip of which reaches the bottom of the boiling tube Q, and the upper end of which is fitted with the two-way tap T_4. U is a phosphorus pentoxide drying tube 10 cm long. R is a reservoir filled with water and connected to P by rubber tubing. V is the infrared analyzer.

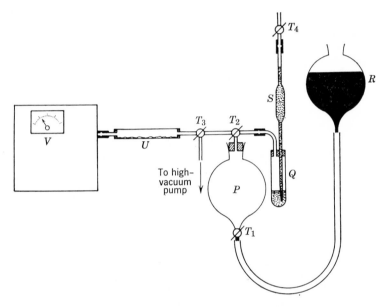

Fig. XIX–7.   Blood gas extraction apparatus: P, 1000-ml flask connected to R, a water reservoir, by a length of rubber tubing; Q, boiling tube; S, 5-ml pipet; T_{1-4}, taps; U, phosphorus pentoxide drying tube connected to V, the infrared analyzer, by a short piece of rubber tubing.

Reagents.   *Acid–Potassium Ferricyanide–Saponin Reagent.*   Make up as follows:

Solution 1	
Potassium ferricyanide	25 g
Saponin	5 g
Water	to 100 ml
Solution 2	
Lactic acid	4.8 ml
Water	to 100 ml

Procedure. Pass a stream of dry oxygen or carbon monoxide-free air through the analyzer and adjust to zero. Then pass a calibration mixture of 0.04% carbon monoxide in air and adjust the analyzer to read 0.04%. Flush the analyzer through again with dry oxygen or air and check the zero. Remove the pipet S (Fig. XIX-7) from the boiling tube and fill it with 5 ml of the blood under examination. Close tap T_4. Place 5 ml of solution 1 and 5 ml of solution 2 in the boiling tube, together with a few drops of octyl alcohol to prevent frothing. Fix the pipet, in its bung, firmly into the boiling tube. Connect flask P to the high-vacuum pump. When evacuation is complete, turn tap T_3 to a neutral position, and turn tap T_2 slowly to bring P and Q into communication. This results in the blood in the pipet being drawn into the boiling tube. In the presence of the acid ferricyanide under vacuum, the blood gases are liberated. Now very gently turn tap T_4 and allow carbon monoxide-free air to bubble through. When all bubbling has ceased (about 20 min) turn tap T_2 to a neutral position. Any carbon monoxide in the blood will now be in flask P. Now raise reservoir R. After setting taps T_2 and T_3, the gas is displaced by water and passed through the analyzer via the phosphorus pentoxide drying tube. Note the steady analyzer reading.

Calculation.

$$X \frac{V(P_a - P_w) \times 273}{v \times 760 \times T} = \text{Volume of CO per 100 ml blood at NTP}$$

where X is the analyzer reading, P_a is atmospheric pressure in mm Hg. T is atmospheric temperature in degrees absolute, P_w is the saturated vapor pressure of water (blood) at temperature T, V is the volume of flask P in milliliters and v is volume of blood in milliliters.

References

1. Kirk, P. L., "Chemical Determinations of Proteins," in *Advances in Protein Chemistry*, Vol. III, Academic Press, New York, 1947.
2. Kirk, P. L., *Anal. Chem.*, **22**, 354 (1950).
3. Parnas, J. K., and R. Wagner, *Biochem. Z.*, **125**, 253 (1921).
4. Shepard, D. L., and M. B. Jacobs, *J. Am. Pharm. Assoc.*, **40**, 154 (1951).
5. Jacobs, M. B., *Chemical Analysis of Foods and Food Products*, 2nd ed., Van Nostrand, New York, 1950.
6. Wagner, E. C., *Ind. Eng. Chem. Anal. Ed.*, **12**, 771 (1940).
7. Jacobs, M. B., *Chemist Analyst*, **42**, No. 3, 69 (1953).

8. Folin, O., and H. Wu, *J. Biol. Chem.*, **38**, 81 (1949).

9. Haden, R. L., *J. Biol. Chem.*, **56**, 469 (1923).

10. Van Slyke, D. D., and J. A. Hawkins, *J. Biol. Chem.*, **79**, 739 (1928).

11. Hiller, A., and D. D. Van Slyke, *J. Biol. Chem.*, **53**, 253 (1922).

12. Horvath, A. A., *Ind. Eng. Chem. Anal. Ed.*, **18**, 229 (1946).

13. Jacobs, M. B., and R. J. Gillis, *J. Am. Pharm. Assoc. Sci. Ed.*, **40**, 488 (1951).

14. Jacobs, M. B., *Science*, **118**, No. 3057, 142 (1953).

15. Edgar, G., and H. E. Shiver, *J. Am. Chem. Soc.*, **47**, 1179 (1925).

16. Edgar, G., and R. A. Wakefield, *J. Am. Chem. Soc.*, **45**, 2242 (1923).

17. Hahn, A., and G. Barkan, *Z. Biol.*, **72**, 25, 305 (1920).

18. Gaede, K., and R. Gruttner, *Naturwissenschaften*, **39**, 63 (1952).

19. Taussky, H. H., *Clin. Chim Acta*, **1**, 210 (1956).

20. Taussky, H. H., *J. Biol. Chem.*, **208**, 853 (1954).

21. Kaplan, E., and R. S. Shaull, *Am. J. Public Health*, **51**, 65 (1961).

22. *Methods for Determining Lead in Air and Biological Materials*, 2nd ed., Am. Public Health Assoc., New York, 1955.

23. Sandell, E. B., *Colorimetric Determination of Traces of Metals*, 2nd ed., Interscience, New York, 1950.

24. Jacobs, M. B., *The Analytical Chemistry of Industrial Poisons, Hazards, and Solvents*, 2nd ed., Interscience, New York, 1949.

25. Woessner, W. W., and J. Cholak, *A.M.A. Arch. Ind. Hyg.*, **7**, 249 (1953).

26. Amdur, M. O., *A.M.A. Arch. Ind. Hyg.*, **7**, 277 (1953).

27. Bessman, S. P., and E. C. Layne, Jr., *J. Lab. Clin. Med.*, **45**, 159 (1955).

28. Fischer, H., and G. Leopoldi, *Angew. Chem.*, **47**, 90 (1934).

29. Harrold, G. C., S. F. Meek, and F. R. Holden, *J. Ind. Hyg. Toxicol.*, **18**, 724 (1936).

30. Jacobs, M. B., and J. Herndon, *Am. Ind. Hyg. Assoc. J.*, **22**, 372 (1961).

31. Horwitt, M. K., and G. R. Cowgill, *J. Biol. Chem.*, **119**, 553 (1937).

32. Moskowitz, S., and W. J. Burke, *J. Ind. Hyg. Toxicol.*, **20**, 457 (1938).

33. Jacobs, M. B., S. Yamaguchi, L. J. Goldwater, and H. Gilbert, *J. Am. Ind. Hyg. Assoc.*, **21**, 475 (1960).

34. Dick, J. M., R. W. Ellis, and J. Steel, *Brit. J. Ind. Med.*, **18**, 283 (1961).

35. Berman, E., *Am. J. Clin. Path.*, **36**, 549 (1961).

36. Hammond, P. B., H. N. Wright, and M. H. Roepke, *Univ. Minn. Agric. Exper. Sta. Bull. No. 221*, (1956).

37. Haeger-Aronsen, B., *Scand. J. Clin. Lab. Invest.*, **12**, Supplement 47, 37 (1960).

38. Rimington, C., and S. L. Sveinsson, *Scand. J. Clin. Lab. Invest.*, **2**, 209 (1950).

39. With, T. K., *Biochem. J.*, **60**, 703 (1955).

40. Haeger-Aronsen, B., *Scand. J. Clin. Lab. Invest.*, **12**, Supplement 47, 52 (1960).

41. Mauzerall, D., and S. Granick, *J. Biol. Chem.*, **219**, 435 (1956).

42. Cholak, J., and D. M. Hubbard, *Ind. Eng. Chem. Anal. Ed.*, **18**, 149 (1946).

43. Barrett, F. R., *Med. J. Australia*, **42**, 411 (1955).

44. Barrett, F. R., *Analyst*, **81**, 294 (1956).

45. Vesterberg, R., and O. Sjöholm, *Arkiv Kemi, Mineral. Geol.*, **22A**, No. 22 (1946).

46. Miller, V. L., and F. Swanberg, Jr., *Anal. Chem.*, **29**, 391 (1957).

47. Monkman, J. L., P. A. Maffett, and T. F. Doherty, *Am. Ind. Hyg. Assoc. Quart.*, **17**, 418 (1956).

48. Laug, E. P., and K. W. Nelson, *J. Assoc. Offic. Agr. Chemists*, **25**, 399 (1942).

49. Simonsen, D. G., *Am. J. Clin. Pathol.*, **23**, 789 (1953).

50. Polley, D., and V. L. Miller, *Anal. Chem.*, **27**, 1162 (1955).

51. Gettler, A. O., and R. A. Lehman, *Am. J. Clin. Pathol.*, **8**, 161 (1938).

52. Johansson, A., and H. Urnell, *Acta Chem. Scand.*, **9**, 583 (1955).

53. Elkins, H. B., *The Chemistry of Industrial Toxicology*, 2nd ed., Wiley, New York, 1959.

54. Milton, R. F., and J. L. Hoskins, *Analyst*, **72**, 6 (1947).

55. Maren, T. H., *J. Lab. Clin. Med.*, **28**, 1511 (1943).

56. Campbell, E. E., and B. M. Head, *Am. Ind. Hyg. Assoc. Quart.*, **16**, 275 (1955).

57. Hubbard, D. M., *Ind. Eng. Chem. Anal. Ed.*, **12**, 768 (1940).

58. Vašák, V., and V. Šedivec, *Collection Czech. Chem. Commun.*, **15**, 1076 (1951).

59. Ballard, A. E., and C. W. D. Thornton, *Ind. Eng. Chem. Anal. Ed.*, **13**, 893 (1941).

60. Clarke, B. L., and H. W. Hermance, *Ind. Eng. Chem. Anal. Ed.*, **10**, 591 (1938).

61. Kozelka, F. L., *Ind. Eng. Chem. Anal. Ed.*, **19**, 494 (1947).

62. Winkler, W. O., *J. Assoc. Offic. Agr. Chemists*, **21**, 220 (1938).

63. Storlazzi, E., and H. B. Elkins, *J. Ind. Hyg. Toxicol.*, **23**, 459 (1941).

64. Stock, A., and H. Lux, *Angew. Chem.*, **44**, 200 (1931).

65. Gettler, A. O., *Am. J. Clin. Pathol. (Tech. Supplement)*, **7**, 13 (1937).

66. Gettler, A. O., and S. Kaye, *J. Lab. Clin. Med.*, **35**, 146 (1950).

67. Locket, S., *Clinical Toxicology*, Mosby, St. Louis, 1957.

68. Noble, S., and D. Noble, *Clin. Chem.*, **4**, 150 (1958).

69. Woodson, T. T., *Rev. Sci. Instr.*, **10**, 308 (1939); U.S. Pat. 2,227,117 (Dec. 31 1940).

70. Ballard, A. E., D. W. Stewart, W. O. Kamm, and C. W. Zuehlke, *Anal. Chem.*, **26**, 921 (1954).

71. Zuehlke, C. W., and A. E. Ballard, *Anal. Chem.*, **22**, 953 (1950).

72. Lindström, O., *Anal. Chem.*, **31**, 461 (1959).

73. Jacobs, M. B., "The Determination of Microquantities of Mercury, Lead, and Arsenic in Biological Materials," School of Public Health and Administrative Medicine, Columbia University, New York, May 1965.

74. Jacobs, M. B., and L. J. Goldwater, *Food Technol.*, **15**, 357 (1961).

75. Jacobs, M. B., "Microdetermination of Mercury in Tissue," Am. Ind. Hyg. Conference, May 1965.

76. Jacobs, M. B., L. J. Goldwater, and H. Gilbert, *Am. Ind. Hyg. Assoc. J.*, **22**, 276 (1961).

77. Jacobs, M. B., *Technical Manual for Gas Reconnaissance Officers*, Dept. of Health, City of New York, 1943.

78. Jacobs, M. B., and J. Nagler, *Ind. Eng. Chem. Anal. Ed.*, **14**, 442 (1943).

79. McBryde, W. T., and F. Williams, *U.S. At. Energy Comm. Rept. Y-1178*, Nov. 20, 1957.

80. Weiner, I. M., and O. H. Müller, *Anal. Chem.*, **27**, 149 (1955).

81. Yamaguchi, S., *M.D.J.* (Philippines), **8**, 558 (1959).

82. Jacobs, M. B., and A. Singerman, *J. Lab. Clin. Med.*, **59**, 871 (1962).

83. Mojonnier, T., and H. C. Troy, Technical Control of Dairy Products, Chicago, 1925, Mojonnier Bros.

84. Jacobs, M. B., *Am. Ind. Hyg. Assoc. J.*, **23**, 411 (1962).

85. Gurev, S. D., *Sbornik Nauch. Trudy Gosudarst. Nauch. Issledovatel. Inst.*, *Tsvetnykh Metal*, **1955**, No. 10, 371; *Referat. Zhur. Khim*, **1956**, Abstr. No. 4155; *Chem. Abstr.*, **52**, 970d (1958); *Anal. Abstr.*, **3**, 3301 (1956).

86. Shemeleva, G. C., and V. I. Petrashen, *Trudy Novocherkassk, Politekh. Inst.*, **31**, 87 (1955); *Referat-Zhur. Khim.*, **1957**, Abstr. No. 27164; *Chem. Abstr.*, **53**, 8937d (1959).

87. Blyum, I. A., and I. A. Ulyanova, *Zavodskaya Lab.*, **23**, 283 (1957); *Chem. Abstr.*, **52**, 970c (1958).

88. Campbell, E. E., M. F. Milligan, and J. A. Lindsey, *Am. Ind. Hyg. Assoc. J.*, **20**, 23 (1959).

89. Efremov, G. V., and Chzhi-Gu Syui, *Vestnik Leningr. Univ.*, **1958**, No. 15, *Ser. Fiz. i Khim.*, (3), 156; *Anal. Abstr.*, **6**, 2509 (1959).

90. Efremov, G. V., and A. M. Blokhim, *Vestnik Univ.*, **14**, No. 22, *Ser. Fiz. i Khim.*, No. 4, 148 (1959); *Chem. Abstr.*, **54**, 8462h (1960).

91. Efremov, G. V., and V. A. Galibin, *Uchenye Zapiski Leningrad. Gosudarst. Univ.*, Im A. A. Zhdanova, No. 211, *Ser. Khim. Nauk*, No. 15, 83 (1957); *Anal. Abstr.*, **5**, 2558 (1958); *Chem. Abstr.*, **52**, 1849c (1958).

92. Gorzelewska, K., *Med. Weterynar.* (Poland), **14**, 553 (1958); *Chem. Abstr.*, **53**, 15189b (1959).

93. Gurev, S. D., and E. P. Shkrobot, *Sbornik Nauch. Trudy Gosudarst. Nauch. Inst.*, *Tsvetnykh Metal.*, **1956**, (12), 79; *Referat-Zhur. Khim.*, **1957**, Abstr. No. 34, 700; *Anal. Abstr.*, **5**, 418 (1958).

94. Korenman, I. M., V. G. Potemkina, and L. S. Federova, *Zh. Anal. Khim.*, **11**, (3), 307 (1956); *Anal. Abstr.*, **4**, 1162 (1957).

95. Kovarik, M., and M. Moucka, *Anal. Chim. Acta*, **16**, 249 (1957).

96. Lapin, L. N., and V. O. Gein, *Trudy Komiss, Anal. Khim. Akad. Nauk SSSR*, **7**, (10), 217 (1956); *Referat-Zhur. Khim.*, **1957**, Abstr. No. 11, 982; *Anal. Abstr.*, **4**, 3630 (1957).

97. Milaev, S. M., *Sbornik Nauch. Trudy Vsesoyuz. Nauch.-Issledovatel. Gorno-Met. Inst. Tsetnoi Met.*, **1958**, No. 3, 258; *Referat-Zhur. Khim.*, **159**, Abstr. No. 34604; *Chem. Abstr.*, **53**, 19700e (1959).

98. Minczewski, J., E. Wieteska, and Z. Marczenko, *Chem. Anal. Warsaw*, **6**, (4), 515 (1961); *Anal. Abstr.*, **9**, No. 4, 1402 (1962).

99. Radu, A., *Rev. Chim. Bucharest*, **9**, (6), 326 (1958); *Anal. Abstr.*, **6**, 1227 (1959).

100. Reis, N. V., *Laboratornoe Delo*, **3**, No. 6, 12 (1957); *Anal. Abstr.*, **5**, 4229 (1958); *Chem. Abstr.*, **53**, 6336g (1959).

101. Shemeleva, G. C., *Trudy Komiss. Anal. Khim., Akad. Nauk SSSR*, **8**, (11),

135 (1958); *Referat-Zhur. Khim.*, **1958** (23), Abstr. No. 77,239; *Anal. Abstr.*, **6**, 2072 (1959).

102. Shemeleva, G. C., and V. I. Petrashen, *Trudy Novocherkass K. Politekh. Inst.*, **41**, 35 (1956); *Referat-Zhur. Met.*, **1957**, Abstr. No. 9236; *Referat-Zhur., Khim.*, **1957**, Abstr. No. 19,562; *Anal. Abstr.*, **4**, 3600 (1957); *Chem. Abstr.*, **52**, 11658d (1958); *Chem. Abstr.*, **53**, 5017c (1959).

103. Voskresenskaya, N. T., *Zh. Anal. Khim.*, **11**, (5), 585 (1956); *Anal. Abstr.*, **4**, 2131 (1957).

104. Rappaport, F., and F. Eichhorn, *Clin. Chim. Acta*, **2**, 16 (1957)

105. Kliffmuller, R., *Z. Anal. Chem.*, **157**, (2), 81 (1957).

106. Feigl, F., V. Gentil, and D. Goldstein, *Anal. Chim. Acta*, **9**, 393 (1953).

107. Diller, H., and O. Rex, *Z. Anal. Chem.*, **137**, 241 (1952).

108. Jamrog, D., and J. Piotrowski, *Med. Pracy*, **9**, 299 (1958); *Chem. Abstr.*, **53**, 3352b (1959).

109. Stavinoha, W. B., and J. B. Nash, *Anal. Chem.*, **32**, 1696 (1960).

110. Truhaut, R., *J. Occupational Med.*, **2**, 334 (1960).

111. Saltzman, B. E., *Anal. Chem.*, **25**, 493 (1953).

112. Saltzman, B. E., *Anal. Chem.*, **24**, 1016 (1952).

113. Kellcher, W. J., and M. J. Johnson, *Anal. Chem.*, **33**, 1429 (1961); T. Chang, *Anal. Chem.*, **28**, 1738 (1956).

114. Nelson, K. W., and D. M. Swingle, "Rapid Estimation of Selenium and Tellurium in Urine," Am. Ind. Hyg. Conf., April 29, 1964, Philadelphia, Pa.

115. Saltzman, B. E., and R. G. Keenan, *Methods of Biochemical Analysis*, Vol. V, p. 181, Interscience Publishers, New York, 1957.

116. McNaught, K. J., *Analyst*, **67**, 97 (1942).

117. McNaught, K. J., *New Zealand J. Sci. Technol.*, **30A**, 109 (1949).

118. Marston, H. R., and D. W. Dewey, *Australian J. Exptl. Biol. Med. Sci.*, **18**, 343 (1940).

119. Cholak, J., and D. M. Hubbard, *Am. Ind. Hyg. Assoc. J.*, **21**, No. 5, 356 (1960).

120. Bode, H., *Z. Anal. Chem.*, **144**, 165 (1955).

121. Hubbard, D. M., F. M. Creech, and J. Cholak, "Determination of Cobalt in Air and Biological Material," Kettering Laboratory, Dept. Preventive Medicine and Industrial Health, College of Medicine, Cincinnati, Ohio; R. S. Young, E. T. Pinkney, and R. Dick, *Ind. Eng. Chem. Anal. Ed.*, **17**, 474 (1946); A. J. Hall and R. Young, *Anal. Chem.*, **22**, 497 (1950).

122. Ellis, G. H., and J. F. Thompson, *Ind. Eng. Chem. Anal. Ed.*, **17**, 254 (1945).

123. Freedman, L. D., *Anal. Chem.*, **19**, 502 (1947).

124. "Fluorimetric Determination of Uranium in Urine," I. B. Whitney, Ed., Manual of Standard Procedures, Analytical Branch, HASL N.Y., At. Energy Comm. N.Y. Operations Office Document NYO—4700, 1957.

125. "Methods of Radiochemical Analysis," *World Health Organization Technical Report Series No. 173*, Palais des Nations, Geneva, 1959; also issued as *FAO Atomic Energy Series No. 10* (1959).

126. Price, G. R., R. J. Ferretti, and S. Schwartz, *Anal. Chem.*, **25**, 322 (1953).

127. Centanni, F. A., A. M. Ross, and M. A. DeSesa, *Anal. Chem.*, **28**, 1651 (1956).

128. Milligan, M. F., and R. J. Watts, *Nucleonics*, **13**, No. 6, 83 (1955).
129. Campbell, E. E., B. M. Head, and M. F. Milligan, "An Extraction Method for the Determination of Uranium Alpha Activity in Urine," Los Alamos Sci. Lab. Rept. LASL-1920, June 1955.
130. Steward, D. D., and W. C. Bentley, Argonne National Laboratory Report ANL-5155, Nov. 1953.
131. Healy, J. W., "Urine Analysis for Tritium Oxide," Hanford Works Reports HW-13949 July 29, 1949; HW-17257, March 20, 1950; HW-18038, June 9, 1950.
132. Maze, R., *J. Phys. Radium*, **7**, 164 (1946).
133. McClelland, J., and M. F. Milligan, "Determination of Tritium in Urine and Water," Los Alamos Sci. Lab. Rept. LA-1645, Apr. 1954.
134. Strong, J., *Procedures in Experimental Physics*, Prentice-Hall, New York, 1938, pp. 152–157.
135. Wolfgang, R. L., and W. F. Libby, *Phys. Rev.*, **85**, 437 (1952).
136. Lawther, P. J., and G. H. Apthorp, *Brit. J. Ind. Med.*, **12**, 326 (1955).
137. Hartridge, H., *J. Physiol. London*, **57**, 47 (1922).
138. Klendshoj, N. C., M. Feldstein, and A. L. Sprague, *J. Biol. Chem.*, **183**, 297 (1950).
139. Van Slyke, D. D., and H. A. Salvesen, *J. Biol. Chem.*, **40**, 103 (1919).
140. Scholander, P. F., and F. J. W. Roughton, *J. Biol. Chem.*, **148**, 551 (1943).
141. Pfund, A. H., *Science*, **90**, 326 (1939).
142. Luft, K. F., *Z. Tech. Phys.*, **24**, 97 (1943).

APPENDIX

Introduction

In order to be able to evaluate and interpret the results obtained with the methods of analysis detailed in this text it is necessary to have comparison data. For this reason a series of tables of analytical data is included here. These data comprise information relating to suspended particulate matter in the air, gaseous contaminants, and motor-vehicle exhaust-gas composition. For particulate matter and gaseous contaminants, both recent analytical data and some data about 10 years old are included because the change with time is interesting in the study of air pollution. A table containing factors for gases and vapors for conversion of concentrations expressed in milligrams per liter to parts per million is included. In addition, tables describing normal blood and urine values and the variations in those values caused by occupational poisons are included.

TABLE 1. Conversion Table for Gases and Vapors[a] (milligrams per liter to parts per million and vice versa, at 25°C and 760 mm Hg)

Molecular weight	1 mg/liter ppm	1 ppm mg/liter	Molecular weight	1 mg/liter ppm	1 ppm mg/liter	Molecular weight	1 mg/liter ppm	1 ppm mg/liter
1	24,450	0.0000409	51	479	0.002086	101	242.1	0.00413
2	12,230	0.0000818	52	470	0.002127	102	239.7	0.00417
3	8,150	0.0001227	53	461	0.002168	103	237.4	0.00421
4	6,113	0.0001636	54	453	0.002209	104	235.1	0.00425
5	4,890	0.0002045	55	445	0.002250	105	232.9	0.00429
6	4,075	0.0002454	56	437	0.002290	106	230.7	0.00434
7	3,493	0.0002863	57	429	0.002331	107	228.5	0.00438
8	3,056	0.000327	58	422	0.002372	108	226.4	0.00442
9	2,717	0.000368	59	414	0.002413	109	224.3	0.00446
10	2,445	0.000409	60	408	0.002554	110	222.3	0.00450
11	2,223	0.000450	61	401	0.002495	111	220.3	0.00454
12	2,038	0.000491	62	394	0.00254	112	218.3	0.00458
13	1,881	0.000532	63	388	0.00258	113	216.4	0.00462
14	1,746	0.000573	64	382	0.00262	114	214.5	0.00466
15	1,630	0.000614	65	376	0.00266	115	212.6	0.00470
16	1,528	0.000654	66	370	0.00270	116	210.8	0.00474
17	1,438	0.000695	67	365	0.00274	117	209.0	0.00479
18	1,358	0.000736	68	360	0.00278	118	207.2	0.00483
19	1,287	0.000777	69	354	0.00282	119	205.5	0.00487
20	1,223	0.000818	70	349	0.00286	120	203.8	0.00491
21	1,164	0.000859	71	344	0.00290	121	202.1	0.00495
22	1,111	0.000900	72	340	0.00294	122	200.4	0.00499
23	1,063	0.000941	73	335	0.00299	123	198.8	0.00503
24	1,019	0.000982	74	330	0.00303	124	197.2	0.00507
25	978	0.001022	75	326	0.00307	125	195.6	0.00511
26	940	0.001063	76	322	0.00311	126	194.0	0.00515
27	906	0.001104	77	318	0.00315	127	192.5	0.00519
28	873	0.001145	78	313	0.00319	128	191.0	0.00524
29	843	0.001186	79	309	0.00323	129	189.5	0.00528
30	815	0.001227	80	306	0.00327	130	188.1	0.00532
31	789	0.001268	81	302	0.00331	131	186.6	0.00536
32	764	0.001309	82	298	0.00335	132	185.2	0.00540
33	741	0.001350	83	295	0.00339	133	183.8	0.00544
34	719	0.001391	84	291	0.00344	134	182.5	0.00548
35	699	0.001432	85	288	0.00348	135	181.1	0.00552
36	679	0.001472	86	284	0.00352	136	179.8	0.00556
37	661	0.001513	87	281	0.00356	137	178.5	0.00560
38	643	0.001554	88	278	0.00360	138	177.2	0.00564
39	627	0.001595	89	275	0.00364	139	175.9	0.00569
40	611	0.001636	90	272	0.00368	140	174.6	0.00573
41	596	0.001677	91	269	0.00372	141	173.4	0.00577
42	582	0.001718	92	266	0.00376	142	172.2	0.00581
43	569	0.001759	93	263	0.00380	143	171.0	0.00585
44	556	0.001800	94	260	0.00384	144	169.8	0.00589
45	543	0.001840	95	257	0.00389	145	168.6	0.00593
46	532	0.001881	96	255	0.00393	146	167.5	0.00597
47	520	0.001922	97	252	0.00397	147	166.3	0.00601
48	509	0.001963	98	249.5	0.00401	148	165.2	0.00605
49	499	0.002004	99	247.0	0.00405	149	164.1	0.00609
50	489	0.002045	100	244.5	0.00409	150	163.0	0.00613

(continued)

TABLE 1 (*continued*)

Molecular weight	1 mg/liter ppm	1 ppm mg/liter	Molecular weight	1 mg/liter ppm	1 ppm mg/liter	Molecular weight	1 mg/liter ppm	1 ppm mg/liter
151	161.9	0.00618	201	121.6	0.00822	251	97.4	0.01027
152	160.9	0.00622	202	121.0	0.00826	252	97.0	0.01031
153	159.8	0.00626	203	120.4	0.00830	253	96.6	0.01035
154	158.8	0.00630	204	119.9	0.00834	254	96.3	0.01039
155	157.7	0.00634	205	119.3	0.00838	255	95.9	0.01043
156	156.7	0.00638	206	118.7	0.00843	256	95.5	0.01047
157	155.7	0.00642	207	118.1	0.00847	257	95.1	0.01051
158	154.7	0.00646	208	117.5	0.00851	258	94.8	0.01055
159	153.7	0.00650	209	117.0	0.00855	259	94.4	0.01059
160	152.8	0.00654	210	116.4	0.00859	260	94.0	0.01063
161	151.9	0.00658	211	115.9	0.00863	261	93.7	0.01067
162	150.9	0.00663	212	115.3	0.00867	262	93.3	0.01072
163	150.0	0.00667	213	114.8	0.00871	263	93.0	0.01076
164	149.1	0.00671	214	114.3	0.00875	264	92.6	0.01080
165	148.2	0.00675	215	113.7	0.00879	265	92.3	0.01084
166	147.3	0.00679	216	113.2	0.00883	266	91.9	0.01088
167	146.4	0.00683	217	112.7	0.00888	267	91.6	0.01092
168	145.5	0.00687	218	112.2	0.00892	268	91.2	0.01096
169	144.7	0.00691	219	111.6	0.00896	269	90.9	0.01100
170	143.8	0.00695	220	111.1	0.00900	270	90.6	0.01104
171	143.0	0.00699	221	110.6	0.00904	271	90.2	0.01108
172	142.2	0.00703	222	110.1	0.00908	272	89.9	0.01112
173	141.3	0.00708	223	109.6	0.00912	273	89.6	0.01117
174	140.5	0.00712	224	109.2	0.00916	274	89.2	0.01121
175	139.7	0.00716	225	108.7	0.00920	275	88.9	0.01125
176	138.9	0.00720	226	108.2	0.00924	276	88.6	0.01129
177	138.1	0.00724	227	107.7	0.00928	277	88.3	0.01133
178	137.4	0.00728	228	107.2	0.00933	278	87.9	0.01137
179	136.6	0.00732	229	106.8	0.00937	279	87.6	0.01141
180	135.8	0.00736	230	106.3	0.00941	280	87.3	0.01145
181	135.1	0.00740	231	105.8	0.00945	281	87.0	0.01149
182	134.3	0.00744	232	105.4	0.00949	282	86.7	0.01153
183	133.6	0.00748	233	104.9	0.00953	283	86.4	0.00157
184	132.9	0.00753	234	104.5	0.00957	284	86.1	0.01162
185	132.2	0.00757	235	104.0	0.00961	285	85.8	0.01166
186	131.5	0.00761	236	103.6	0.00965	286	85.5	0.01170
187	130.7	0.00765	237	103.2	0.00969	287	85.2	0.01174
188	130.1	0.00769	238	102.7	0.00973	288	84.9	0.01178
189	129.4	0.00773	239	102.3	0.00978	289	84.6	0.01182
190	128.7	0.00777	240	101.9	0.00982	290	84.3	0.01186
191	128.0	0.00781	241	101.5	0.00986	291	84.0	0.01190
192	127.3	0.00785	242	101.0	0.00990	292	83.7	0.01194
193	126.7	0.00789	243	100.6	0.00994	293	83.4	0.01198
194	126.0	0.00793	244	100.2	0.00998	294	83.2	0.01202
195	125.4	0.00798	245	99.8	0.01002	295	82.9	0.01207
196	124.7	0.00802	246	99.4	0.01006	296	82.6	0.01211
197	124.1	0.00806	247	99.0	0.01010	297	82.3	0.01215
198	123.5	0.00810	248	98.6	0.01014	298	82.0	0.01219
199	122.9	0.00814	249	98.2	0.01018	299	81.8	0.01223
200	122.3	0.00818	250	97.8	0.01022	300	81.5	0.01227

[a] A. C. Fieldner, S. H. Katz, and S. P. Kinney, "Gas Masks for Gases Met in Fighting Fires," *U.S. Bur. Mines Tech. Paper 248* (1921).

TABLE 2
Limits of Inflammability and Explosive Range[a,b]

Substance	Lower limit, % by vol	Upper limit, % by vol	Range
Acetaldehyde, CH_2CHO	4.0	57.0	53
Acetic acid, CH_3COOH	4.0		
Acetone, CH_3COCH_3	3.0	11	8.0
Acetylene, C_2H_2	2.5	80.0	77.5
Allyl alcohol, $CH_2:CHCH_2OH$	2.4		
Ammonia, NH_3	16.0	27.0	11.0
Amyl acetate, $CH_3COOC_5H_{11}$	1.1		
Amyl alcohol, $C_5H_{11}OH$	1.2		
Amyl chloride, $C_5H_{11}Cl$	1.4		
Amylene, C_5H_{10}	1.6		
Benzene, C_6H_6	1.4	6.8	5.4
Benzine	1.1		
Blast-furnace gas	36	65	29
Butane, C_4H_{10}	1.85	8.4	6.55
Butyl acetate, $CH_3COOC_4H_9$	1.7		
Butyl alcohol, C_4H_9OH	1.7		
Butylene, $C_2H_5CH:CH_2$	1.7	9.0	7.3
Butyl methyl ketone, $CH_3COC_4H_9$	1.2	8.0	6.8
Carbon disulfide, CS_2	1.25	44.0	42.75
Carbon monoxide, CO	12.5	74.0	61.5
Carbon oxysulfide, COS	11.9	28.5	16.6
Coal gas	6	33	27
Cyanogen, $(CN)_2$	6.6	42.6	35.0
Cyclohexane, C_6H_{12}	1.3	8.4	7.1
Cyclopropane, C_3H_6	2.4	10.3	7.9
Decane, $C_{10}H_{22}$	0.7		
Dichloroethylene, $C_2H_2Cl_2$	9.7	12.8	3.1
Dioxane, $C_4H_8O_2$	2.0	22.3	20.3
Ethane, C_2H_6	3.2	12.5	9.3
Ethyl acetate, $CH_3COOC_2H_5$	2.2	11.4	9.2
Ethyl alcohol, C_2H_5OH	4.3	19.0[c]	13.7
Ethyl bromide, C_2H_5Br	6.7	11.3	4.6
Ethyl chloride, C_2H_5Cl	4.0	14.8	10.8
Ethyl ether, $(C_2H_5)_2O$	1.9	48	46.1
Ethylene, C_2H_4	3.0	29	26.0
1,2-Dichloroethane (ethylene dichloride), $ClCH_2CH_2Cl$	6.2	15.9[d]	9.7
Ethylene oxide, $(CH_2)_2O$	3.0	80.0	77.0
Ethyl formate, $HCOOC_2H_5$	3.5	16.4	12.9
Ethyl methyl ether, $CH_3OC_2H_5$	2.0	10.1	8.1
Ethyl methyl ketone, $CH_3COC_2H_5$	1.8	10.0	8.2

(continued)

TABLE 2 *(continued)*

Substance	Lower limit, % bs vol	Upper limit, % by vol	Range
Ethyl nitrite, C_2H_5ONO	*3.0*		
Ethyl selenide, $(C_2H_5)_2Se$	*2.5*		
Gasoline	1.4	6.0	4.6
Heptane, $CH_3(CH_2)_5CH_3$	1.0	*6.0*	5.0
Hexane, $CH_3(CH_2)_4CH_3$	1.2	6.9	5.7
Hydrogen, H_2	4.1	74	70.1
Hydrogen cyanide, HCN	5.6	*40.0*	34.4
Hydrogen sulfide, H_2S	*4.3*	*45.5*	41.2
Illuminating gas (manufactured gas)	5–7	21–31	
Isoamyl alcohol, $C_5H_{11}OH$	*1.2*		
Isobutane, $(CH_3)_3CH$	1.8	8.4	6.6
Isobutyl alcohol, $(CH_3)_2CHCH_2OH$	*1.8*		
Isopentane, C_5H_{12}	*1.3*		
Isopropyl acetate, $CH_3COOCH(CH_3)_2$	*1.8*	*7.8*[d]	6.0
Isopropyl alcohol, C_3H_7OH	*2.6*		
Lead tetramethyl, $Pb(CH_3)_4$	*1.8*		
Methane, CH_4	*5.0*	*15.0*	10.0
Methyl acetate, CH_3COOCH_3	*3.1*	*15.6*	12.5
Methyl alcohol, CH_3OH	6.7	36.5	29.8
Methyl bromide, CH_3Br	13.5	14.5	1.0
Methyl chloride, CH_3Cl	*8.2*	*18.7*	10.5
Methylcyclohexane, $CH_3C_6H_{11}$	1.2		
Methyl formate, $HCOOCH_3$	5.0	22.7	17.7
Methyl propyl ketone, $CH_3COC_3H_7$	1.5	8.2	6.7
Natural gas	4.8	13.5	
Nonane, C_9H_{20}	*0.83*		
Octane, C_8H_{18}	0.95		
Pentane, $CH_3(CH_2)_3CH_3$	1.4	7.8	6.4
Propane, C_2H_3	2.4	9.5	7.1
Propyl acetate, $CH_3COOC_3H_7$	2.0	*8.0*	
Propyl alcohol, C_3H_7OH	*2.5*		
Propylene, $CH_2{:}CHCH_3$	*2.0*	*11.1*	9.1
Propylene dichloride, $CH_2ClCHClCH_3$	*3.4*	*14.5*[d]	
Propylene oxide, C_3H_6O	2.1	21.5	19.4
Pyridine, C_5H_5N	*1.8*	*12.4*	10.6
Sewage tank gases	5.3–8.3	16.0–19.3	
Tin tetramethyl, $Sn(CH_3)_4$	*1.9*		

(continued

TABLE 2 (*continued*)

Substance	Lower limit, % by vol	Upper limit, % by vol	Range
Toluene, $C_6H_5CH_3$	*1.3*	6.8	*5.5*
Turpentine	0.8		
Vinyl chloride, $CH_2:CHCl$	4.0	21.7	17.7
Vinyl ether, $(CH_2:CH)_2O$	*1.7*	*27*	25.3
Water gas	6–9	55–70	
o-Xylene, $C_6H_4(CH_3)_2$	*1.0*	6.0	*5.0*

[a] At atmospheric pressure and ordinary temperature in air.

[b] Values in italics obtained in closed apparatus.

[c] At 60°C.

[d] At 100°C.

This table was compiled by the author from the following references:

B. Lewis and G. von Elbe, *Combustion Flames and Explosions of Gases*, Cambridge, 1938.

W. A. Bone and D. T. A. Townend, *Flame and Combustion in Gases*, New York, 1927.

A. H. Nuckolls, *Natl. Bd. Fire Underwriters, Misc. Hazard 2375* (1933).

A. C. Fieldner, *U. S. Bur. Mines Circ. 6009* (1937).

G. W. Jones and W. P. Yant, *U.S. Bur. Mines Tech. Paper 352* (1924).

J. J. Forbes and G. W. Grove, *U.S. Bur. Mines Miners' Circ. 33* (1938).

A. H. Nuckolls, *Natl. Bd. Fire Underwriters Misc. Hazard 1130* (1923).

M. J. Burgess and R. V. Wheeler, *J. Chem. Soc.*, **99**, 2013 (1911).

G. A. Burrell and G. G. Oberfell, *U.S. Bur. Mines Tech. Paper 119* (1915).

H. F. Coward and G. W. Jones, *U.S. Bur. Mines Bull. 279*, rev. (1931); rev. (1939).

G. W. Jones, *U.S. Bur. Mines Tech. Paper 450* (1929).

G. W. Jones, *Ind. Eng. Chem.*, **20**, 367 (1937).

TABLE 3. Threshold Limit Values for 1964*

There were in 1958 no standards or maximum allowable concentrations of pollutants in outside air in the United States. It is impractical to apply a factor to the industrial hygiene maximum allowable concentrations or threshold limits which apply to an 8-hr working day in a 5-day working week, in a working atmosphere, to a 24-hr living day in a 7-day living week.

The threshold limit values refer to air-borne concentrations of substances and represent conditions under which it is believed that nearly all workers may be repeatedly exposed, day after day, without adverse effect. Because of wide variation in individual susceptibility, exposure of an occasional individual at or even below the threshold limit may not prevent discomfort, aggravation of a preexisting condition, or occupational illness.

Threshold limits should be used as guides in the control of health hazards and should not be regarded as fine lines between safe and dangerous concentrations. Exceptions are the substances given in appendix A and certain of the substances given a C listing. The values not given a C listing refer to time-weighted average concentrations for a normal workday. The amount by which these concentrations may be exceeded for short periods without injury to health depends upon a number of factors such as the nature of the contaminant, whether very high concentrations even for short periods produce acute poisoning, whether the effects are cumulative, the frequency with which high concentrations occur, and the duration

of such periods. All must be taken into consideration in arriving at a decision as to whether a hazardous situation exists. Enlightened industrial hygiene practice inclines toward controlling exposures below the limit rather than maintenance at the limit.

Threshold limits are based on the best available information from industrial experience, from experimental human and animal studies, and, when possible, from a combination of the three. The basis on which the values are established may differ from substance to substance; protection against impairment of health may be the guiding factor for some, whereas reasonable freedom from irritation, narcosis, nuisance, or other forms of stress may dominate the basis for others. The Committee holds to the opinion that limits based on *physical* irritation should be considered no less binding than those based on physical impairment; growing bodies of evidence indicate that physical irritation may promote and accelerate physical impairment. On what basis a limit is developed is given separately for each listed substance in *Documentation of Threshold Limit Values*, a publication of the Threshold Limits Committee of the American Conference of Governmental Industrial Hygienists.

Ceiling Versus Time-Weighted Average Limits. Although the time-weighted average concentration provides the most satisfactory, practical way of monitoring air-borne agents for compliance with the limits, there are certain substances for which it is inappropriate. In the latter group are substances

* "Threshold Limit Values for 1964," adopted at the 26th Annual Meeting of the American Conference of Governmental Industrial Hygienists, Philadelphia, April, 1964, *Arch. Environ. Health*, **9**, 545 (1964).

which are predominantly fast acting and whose threshold limit is more appropriately based on this particular response. Substances with this type of response are best controlled by a ceiling, C, limit that should not be exceeded. It is implicit in these definitions that the manner of sampling to determine compliance with the limits for each group must differ; a single grab sample, that is applicable to a C limit, is not appropriate to the time-weighted limit; here, a sufficient number of samples are needed to permit a time-weighted average concentration throughout a complete cycle of operations or throughout the work shift.

Whereas the ceiling limit places a definite boundary which concentrations should not be permitted to exceed, the time-weighted average limit requires an explicit limit to the excursions that are permissible above the listed value. The magnitude of these excursions may be pegged to the magnitude of the threshold limit by an appropriate factor shown in appendix C. It should be noted that the same factors are used by the Committee in making a judgment whether to include or exclude a substance for a C listing.

"*Skin" Notation.* Listed substances followed by the designation *skin* refer to the potential contribution to the overall exposure by the cutaneous route including mucous membrane and eye. This attention-calling designation is intended to suggest appropriate measures for the prevention of cutaneous absorption so that the threshold limit is not invalidated.

Mixtures. Special consideration should be given also to the application of these values in assessing the health hazards which may be associated with exposure to mixtures of two or more substances. A brief discussion of basic considerations involved in developing threshold limit values for mixtures, and methods for their development, amplified by specific examples are given in appendix B.

"*Inert" or Nuisance Particulates.* A number of dusts or particulates that occur in the working environment ordinarily produce no specific effects upon prolonged inhalation. Some insoluble substances are classed as inert (e.g., iron and steel dusts, cement, bentonite, silicon carbide, titanium dioxide, cellulose); others may be soluble (starch, soluble oils, calcium carbonate) but are of such a low order of activity that in concentrations ordinarily encountered they do not cause physiologic impairment; others may be rapidly eliminated or destroyed by the body (vegetable oils, glycerine, sucrose). In the case of the insoluble substances, there may be some accumulation in the respiratory passages. In the case of the soluble substances, this accumulation will ordinarily be temporary but may interfer to some extent with respiratory processes. Hence, it is desirable to control the concentrations of such particulates in the air breathed by an individual, in keeping with good industrial hygiene practice.

A threshold limit of 15 mg/m³ or 50 million particles per cubic foot (mppcf), whichever is less, is recommended for substances in these categories and for which no specific threshold limits have been assigned.

This limit, for a normal workday, does not apply to brief exposures at higher concentrations. Neither does it apply to those substances which may cause physiologic impairment at lower concentrations but for which a threshold limit has not yet been adopted.

Recommended Threshold Limit Values in Alphabetic Order

Substance	ppm[a]	mg/m³[b]	Substance	ppm[a]	mg/m³[b]
Acetaldehyde	200	360	ANTU (α-naphthylthiourea)	—	0.3
Acetic acid	10	25	Arsenic and compounds (as As)	—	0.5
Acetic anhydride	5	20	Arsine	0.05	0.2
Acetone	1000	2400	Barium (soluble compounds)	—	0.5
Acetonitrile	40	70	C Benzene (benzol)—Skin	25	80
Acetylene tetrabromide	1	14	Benzidine	—	A[c]
Acrolein	0.1	0.25	Benzyl chloride	1	5
Acrylonitrile—Skin	20	45	Beryllium	—	0.002
Aldrin (1,2,3,4,10,10-hexachloro-1,4,4a,5,8,8a-hexahydro-1,4,5,8-dimethanonaphthalene)—Skin	—	0.25	Boron oxide	—	15
Allyl alcohol—Skin	2	5	C Boron trifluoride	1	3
Allyl chloride	1	3	Bromine	0.1	0.7
C Allyl glycidyl ether (AGE)	10	45	Butadiene (1,3-butadiene)	1000	2200
Allyl propyl disulfide	2	12	2-Butanone (methyl ethyl ketone)	200	590
Ammonia	50	35	2-Butoxyethanol (Butyl Cellosolve)—Skin	50	240
Ammonium sulfamate (ammate)	—	15	Butyl acetate (n-butyl acetate)	200	950
Amyl acetate	100	525	Butyl alcohol	100	300
Amyl alcohol (isoamyl alcohol)	100	360	tert-Butyl alcohol	100	300
Aniline—Skin	5	19	C Butylamine	5	15
Antimony and compounds (as Sb)	—	0.5	C tert-Butyl chromate (as CrO₃)—Skin	—	0.1

(continued)

Recommended Threshold Limit Values (*continued*)

Substance	ppm[a]	mg/m³[b]	Substance	ppm[a]	mg/m³[b]
n-Butyl glycidyl ether (BGE)	50	270	Decaborane—Skin	0.05	0.3
Butyl mercaptan	10	35	Diacetone alcohol (4-hydroxy-4-methyl-2-pentanone)	50	240
p-tert-Butyltoluene	10	60	Diborane	0.1	0.1
Cadmium oxide fume	—	0.1	1,2-Dibromomethane (ethylene dibromide)	25	190
Calcium arsenate	—	1	C o-Dichlorobenzene	50	300
Camphor	—	2	p-Dichlorobenzene	75	450
Carbon dioxide	5000	9000	Dichlorodifluoromethane	1000	4950
Carbon disulfide—Skin	20	60	1,1-Dichloroethane	100	400
Carbon monoxide	100	110	1,2-Dichloroethane (ethylene dichloride)	50	200
Carbon tetrachloride—Skin	10	65	1,2-Dichloroethylene	200	790
Chlordane (1,2,4,5,6,7,8,8-octachloro-3a,4,7,7a-tetrahydro-4,7-methanoindane)		0.5	C Dichloroethyl ether	15	90
Chlorinated camphene, 60%	—	0.5	Dichloromonofluoromethane	1000	4200
Chlorinated diphenyl oxide	—	0.5	C 1,1-Dichloro-1-nitroethane	10	60
Chlorine	1	3	Dichlorotetrafluoroethane	1000	7000
Chlorine dioxide	0.1	0.3	Dieldrin (1,2,3,4,10,10-hexachloro-6,7-epoxy-1,4,4a,5,6,7,8,8a-octahydro-1,4,5,8-dimethanonaphthalene)—Skin	—	0.25
C Chlorine trifluoride	0.1	0.4			
C Chloroacetaldehyde	1	3			
Chlorobenzene (monochlorobenzene)	75	350			
Chlorobromomethane	200	1050			

Substance		
Chlorodiphenyl (42% chlorine)—Skin	—	1
Chlorodiphenyl (54% chlorine)—Skin	—	0.5
C Chloroform (trichloromethane)	50	240
1-Chloro-1-nitropropane	20	100
Chloropicrin	0.1	0.7
Chloroprene (2-chloro-1,-3-butadiene)	25	90
Chromic acid and chromates (as CrO₃)	—	0.1
Cobalt	—	0.5
Crag herbicide (sodium 2-[2,4-dichlorophenoxyl] ethanol hydrogen sulfate)	—	15
Cresol (all isomers)—Skin	5	22
Cyanide (as CN)—Skin	—	5
Cyclohexane	400	1400
Cyclohexanol	50	200
Cyclohexanone	50	200
Cyclohexene	400	1350
2,4-D (2,4-dichlorophenoxyacetic acid)	—	10
DDT (2,2-bis [p-chlorophenyl]-1,1,1,-trichloroethane—Skin	—	1
DDVP (O,O-dimethyl-2,2-dichlorovinyl phosphate)	—	1
Diethylamine	25	75
Difluorodibromomethane	100	860
C Diglycidyl ether (DGE)	0.5	2.8
Diisobutyl ketone	50	290
Dimethylacetamide—Skin	10	35
Dimethylaniline (N-dimethylaniline)—Skin	5	25
Dimethylformamide Skin⁴	10	30
1,1-Dimethylhydrazine—Skin	0.5	1
Dimethylsulfate—Skin	1	5
Dinitrobenzene—Skin	—	1
Dinitrotoluene—Skin	—	1.5
Dinitro-o-cresol—Skin	—	0.2
Dioxane (diethylene dioxide)	100	360
Dipropylene glycol methyl ether—Skin	100	600
Endrin (1,2,3,4,10,10-hexachloro-6,7-epoxy-1,4,4a,5,6,7,8,8a-octahydro-1,4-endo-5,8-dimethanonaphthalene)—Skin	—	0.1
EPN (O-ethyl-O-p-nitrophenyl-thionobenzenephosphonate)—Skin	—	0.5
Ethyl acetate	400	1400

(continued)

Recommended Threshold Limit Values (*continued*)

Substance	ppm[a]	mg/m[3b]	Substance	ppm[a]	mg/m[3b]
Ethyl acrylate—Skin	25	100	Isophorone	25	140
Ethyl alcohol (ethanol)	1000	1900	Isopropylamine	5	12
Ethylamine	25	45	Isopropyl glycidyl ether (IGE)	50	240
C Ethylbenzene	200	870	Ketene	0.5	0.9
Ethyl bromide	200	890	Lead	—	0.2
Ethyl chloride	1000	2600	Lead arsenate	—	0.15
Ethyl ether	400	1200	Lindane (hexachlorocyclohexane, γ-isomer)	—	0.5
Ethyl formate	100	300	Lithium hydride	—	0.025
C Ethyl mercaptan	20	52	Magnesium oxide fume	—	15
Ethyl silicate	100	850	Malathion(O,O-dimethyl dithiophosphate of diethyl mercapto-succinate)—Skin	—	15
Ethylene chlorohydrin—Skin	5	16	C Manganese	—	5
Ethylenediamine	10	30	Mercury—Skin	—	0.1
C Ethylene glycol dinitrate—Skin	0.2	1.2	Mercury (organic compounds)—Skin	—	0.01
Ethylene imine—Skin	5	9	Mesityl oxide	25	100
Ethylene oxide	50	90	Methoxychlor (2,2-di-p-methoxyphenyl-1,1,1-trichloroethane)	—	15
2-Ethoxyethanol (Cellosolve)—Skin	200	740	Methyl acetate	200	610
2-Ethoxyethylacetate (Cellosolve acetate)—Skin	100	540	Methyl acetylene	1000	1650
Ferbam (ferric dimethyl dithiocarbamate)	—	15			
Ferrovanadium dust	—	1			
Fluoride (as F)	—	2.5			

Substance	ppm	mg/m³
Fluorine	0.1	0.2
Fluorotrichloromethane	1000	5600
C Formaldehyde	5	6
Furfural	5	20
Furfuryl alcohol	50	200
Gasoline	500	2000
Glycidol (2,3-epoxy-1-propanol)	50	150
Heptachlor(1,4,5,6,7,8,8a-heptachloro-3a,4,7,7a-tetrahydro-4,7-methanoindane)	—	0.5
Heptane (n-heptane)	500	2000
Hexane (n-hexane)	500	1800
Hexanone (methyl butyl ketone)	100	410
sec-Hexyl acetate	50	295
Hexone (methyl isobutyl ketone)	100	410
Hydrazine—Skin	1	1.3
Hydrogen bromide	3	10
Hydrogen chloride	5	7
C Hydrogen cyanide—Skin	10	11
Hydrogen fluoride	3	2
Hydrogen peroxide, 90%	1	1.4
Hydrogen selenide	0.05	0.2
Hydrogen sulfide[d]	10	15
Hydroquinone	—	2
C Iodine	0.1	1
Iron oxide fume	—	15
Methyl acrylate—Skin	10	35
Methylal (dimethoxymethane)	1000	3100
Methyl alcohol (methanol)	200	260
C Methyl bromide—Skin	20	80
Methyl Cellosolve (2-methoxyethanol)—Skin	25	80
Methyl Cellosolve Acetate (ethylene glycol monomethylether acetate)—Skin	25	120
C Methyl chloride	100	210
Methyl chloroform (1,1,1-trichloroethane)	350	1900
Methylcyclohexane	500	2000
Methylcyclohexanol	100	470
Methylcyclohexanone	100	460
Methyl formate	100	250
Methyl isobutyl carbinol (methyl amyl alcohol)	25	100
Methyl mercaptan[d]	10	30
C α-Methyl styrene	100	480
Methylene chloride (dichloromethane)	500	1750
Monomethyl aniline—Skin	2	9
Molybdenum (soluble compounds)	—	5
(insoluble compounds)	—	15

(continued)

Recommended Threshold Limit Values (*continued*)

Substance	ppm[a]	mg/m³[b]	Substance	ppm[a]	mg/m³[b]
Naphtha (coal tar)	200	800	Propyl alcohol (isopropyl alcohol)	400	980
Naphtha (petroleum)	500	2000	Propyl ether (isopropyl ether)	500	2100
β-Naphthylamine	—	A2ᶜ	n-Propyl nitrate	25	110
Nickel carbonyl	0.001	0.007	Propylene dichloride (1,2-dichloropropane)	75	350
Nicotine—Skin	—	0.5	Propylene imine—Skin	25	60
Nitric acidᵈ	2	5	Propylene oxide	100	240
p-Nitroaniline—Skin	1	6	Pyrethrum	5	5
Nitrobenzene—Skin	1	5	Pyridine	5	15
Nitroethane	100	310	Quinone	0.1	0.4
C Nitrogen dioxide	5	9	Rotenone (commercial)	—	5
C Nitroglycerin + EGDN—Skin	0.2	2	Selenium compounds (as Se)ᵈ	—	0.2
Nitromethane	100	250	Sodium fluoroacetate (1080)—Skin	—	0.05
1-Nitropropane	25	90	Sodium hydroxide	—	2
2-Nitropropane	25	90	Stibine	0.1	0.5
N-Nitrosodimethylamine (dimethylnitrosamine)—skin	A3ᶜ	—	Stoddard solvent	500	2900
Nitrotoluene—Skin	5	30	Strychnine	—	0.15
Octane	500	2350	C Styrene monomer (phenylethylene)	100	420
Oil mist (mineral)	—	5	Sulfur dioxide	5	13
Osmium tetroxide	—	0.002	Sulfur hexafluoride	1000	6000
Ozone	0.1	0.2	Sulfuric acid	—	1
Parathion (O,O-diethyl O-[p-nitrophenyl] thiophosphate)—Skin	—	0.1			

Substance			Substance		
Pentaborane	0.005	0.01	Sulfur monochloride	1	6
Pentachloronaphthalene—Skin	—	0.5	Sulfur pentafluoride	0.025	0.25
Pentachlorophenol—Skin	—	0.5	Sulfuryl fluoride	5	20
Pentane	1000	2950	2,4,5 T (2,4,5-trichloro-phenoxyacetic acid)	—	10
Pentanone (methyl propyl ketone)	200	700	TEDP (tetraethyl dithiono-pyrophosphate)—Skin	—	0.2
Perchloroethylene (tetrachloroethylene)	100	670	Teflon decomposition products	—	A4
Perchloromethyl mercaptan	0.1	0.8	TEPP (tetraethyl pyro-phosphate)—Skin	—	0.05
Perchloryl fluoride	3	13.5	Tellurium	—	0.1
Phenol—Skin	5	19	1,1,2,2-Tetrachloroethane—Skin	5	35
Phenyl glycidyl ether (PGE)	50	310	Tetrahydrofuran	200	590
Phenylhydrazine—Skin	5	22	Tetranitromethane	1	8
Phosdrin (2-carbomethoxy-1-methylvinyldimethyl phosphate)—Skin		0.1	Tetryl (2,4,6-trinitrophenyl-methylnitramine)—Skin	—	1.5
Phosgene (carbonyl chloride)[a]	0.1	0.4	Thallium (soluble compounds)—Skin	—	0.1
Phosphine	0.3	0.4	Thiram [bis(dimethylthio-carbamoyl) disulfide]	—	5
Phosphoric acid	—	1	Titanium dioxide	—	15
Phosphorus (yellow)	—	0.1	Toluene (toluol)	200	750
Phosphorus pentachloride	—	1	o-Toluidine—Skin	5	22
Phosphorus pentasulfide	—	1	C Tolylene-2,4-diisocyanate	0.02	0.14
Phosphorus trichloride	0.5	3	Trichloroethylene	100	520
Picric acid—Skin	—	0.1	Trichloronaphthalene—Skin	—	5
Platinum (soluble salts)	—	0.002			
Propyl acetate	200	840			

(continued)

Recommended Threshold Limit Values (*continued*)

Substance	ppm[a]	mg/m[3b]	Substance	ppm[a]	mg/m[3b]
1,2,3-Trichloropropane	50	300	C Vanadium (V$_2$O$_5$ dust)	—	0.5
1,1,2-Trichloro 1,2,2-trifluoroethane	1000	7600	C Vanadium (V$_2$O$_5$ fume)	—	0.1
Triethylamine	25	100	C Vinyl chloride (chloroethylene)	500	1300
Trifluoromono-bromomethane	1000	6100	Vinyl toluene	100	480
Trinitrotoluene—Skin	—	1.5	Warfarin (3-[α-acetonylbenzyl]-4-hydroxycoumarin)	—	0.1
Triorthocresyl phosphate	—	0.1	C Xylene (xylol)	200	870
Triphenyl phosphate	—	3	Xylidine—Skin	5	25
Turpentine	100	560	Yttrium[d]	—	1
Uranium			Zinc oxide fume	—	5
(soluble compounds)	—	0.05	Zirconium compounds		
(insoluble compounds)	—	0.25	(as Zr)	—	5

[a] Parts of vapor or gas per million parts of air by volume at 25°C and 760 mm Hg pressure.

[b] Approximate milligrams per cubic meter of air.

[c] A numbers, see appendix A, p. 869.

[d] 1964 revision, see tentative values, p. 868.

Radioactivity: For permissible concentrations of radioisotopes in air, see US Department of Commerce, National Bureau of Standards, Handbook 69, "Maximum Permissible Body Burdens and Maximum Permissible Concentrations of Radionuclides in Air and in Water for Occupational Exposure," June 5, 1959. Also, see U.S. Department of Commerce, National Bureau of Standards, Handbook 59, "Permissible Dose from External Sources of Ionizing Radiation," Sept. 24, 1954, and addendum of April 15, 1958.

Mineral Dust

Substance	mppcf[a,b]	Substance	mppcf[a,b]
Silica, crystalline		Silicates (less than 1% crystalline silica)	
Quartz, threshold limit calculated from the formula	$250 / \% \ SiO_2 + 5$	Asbestos	5
	$250 / \% \ SiO_2 + 5$	Mica	20
Cristobalite		Soapstone	20
Silica, amorphous, including natural diatomaceous earth	20	Talc	20
		Portland cement	50
		"Inert" or nuisance particulates	50 (or 15 mg/m³ whichever is the smaller)

[a] Millions of particles per cubic foot of air, based on impinger samples counted by light-field techniques.

[b] Conversion factors:

mppcf × 35.3 = million particles per cubic meter
= particles per cc

[c] The percentage of crystalline silica in the formula is the amount determined from air-borne samples, except in those instances in which other methods have been shown to be applicable.

Tentative Threshold Limit Values

Substance	ppm[a]	mg/m³[b]	Substance	ppm[a]	mg/m³[b]
Anisidine (o,p-isomers)	—	0.5	Methyl mercaptan[c]	10	20
Benzoyl	—	5	Methyl methacrylate	100	410
Calcium oxide	—	5	C Methylene-bis-phenylisocyanate	0.02	0.2
Carbaryl (Sevin) (1-naphthyl-N-methyl-carbamate)	—	5	Mineral wood, fibrous glass	—	2
Copper fume	—	0.1	Monomethylhydrazine—Skin	0.2	0.35
Dusts and mists	—	1.0	Morpholine—Skin	20	70
Cotton dust (raw)	—	1	Naphthalene	10	50
Cyclopentadiene	75	200	Nickel, metal, and soluble compounds	—	1
Demeton (Systox)	—	0.1	Nitric acid[c]	2	5
1,3-Dichloro-5,5-dimethylhydantoin	—	0.2	p-Nitrochlorobenzene	—	1
Dimethyl 1,2-dibromo-2,2-dichloroethyl phosphate (Dibrom)	—	3	Nitrogen trifluoride	10	29
Dimethylamine	10	18	C Oxygen difluoride	0.05	0.1
Dimethylformamide—Skin[c]	10	30	p-Phenylenediamine—Skin	—	0.1
Di-sec-octylphthalate (di-2-ethylhexyl-phthalate)	—	5	Phosgene (carbonylchloride)[c]	0.1	0.4
Epichlorhydrin	5	19	Phthalic anhydride	2	12
Ethanolamine	3	6	Propane	1000	1800
Graphite	—	15 mppcf	β-Propiolactone	—	A5
Hafnium	—	0.5	Selenium compounds[c] (as Se)	—	0.2
			Silver, metal and soluble compounds[c]	—	0.01

	ppm[a]	mg/m³[b]
Hexachloroethane—Skin	1	9.7
Hydrogen sulfide	10	15
LPG (low pressure gas) (liquid petroleum gas)	1000	—
Maleic anhydride	—	8
Methane	1000	—
Methyl acetylene-propadiene mixture, (MAPP)	1000	—
Methylamine	25	31
Tantalum	—	5
1,1,1,2-Tetrachloro-2,2-difluoroethane[c]	500	4170
1,1,2,2-Tetrachloro-1,2-difluoroethane	500	4170
Tetraethyllead—Skin	—	0.075
Tin (inorganic compounds)	—	2
(organic compounds as Sn)—Skin[c]	—	0.1
Yttrium[c]	—	1

[a] Parts of vapor or gas per million parts of air by volume at 25°C and 760 mm Hg pressure.

[b] Approximate milligrams per cubic meter of air.

[c] 1964 revisions.

Table 3, Appendix A

A1, Benzidine. Because of high incidence of bladder tumors in man, any exposure, including skin, is extremely hazardous.

A2, β-Naphthylamine. Because of the extremely high incidence of bladder tumors in workers handling this compound, and the inability to control exposures, β-naphthylamine has been prohibited from manufacture, use, and other activities that involve human contact by the state of Pennsylvania.

A3, N-Nitrosodimethylamine. Because of extremely high toxicity and presumed carcinogenic potential of this compound, contact by any route should not be permitted.

A4, Teflon (R) decomposition products. At least one identified component of Teflon decomposition products is extremely toxic, but, in the absence of more complete toxicity information and suitable analytic methods, a definite threshold limit value is not recommended at this time; but air concentrations should be minimal.

A5, β-Propiolactone. Because of high acute toxicity and demonstrated skin tumor production in animals, contact by any route should be avoided.

Table 3, Appendix B. Threshold Limit Values of Mixtures

When two or more hazardous substances are present, their combined effect, rather than that of either individually, should be given primary consideration. *In the absence of information to the contrary, the effects of the different hazards should be considered as additive.* That is, if the sum of the following fractions

$$\frac{C_1}{T_1} + \frac{C_2}{T_2} + \frac{C_n}{T_n}$$

exceeds unity, then the threshold limit of the mixture should be considered as being exceeded. C_1 indicates the observed atmospheric concentration, and T_1 the corresponding threshold limit (see Example A, *a*).

Exceptions to the above rule may be made when there is good reason to believe that the chief effects of the different harmful substances are not in fact additive, but independent as when purely local effects on different organs of the body are produced by the various components of the mixture. In such cases, the threshold limit ordinarily is exceeded only when at least one member of the series

$$\frac{C_1}{T_1} \text{ or } \frac{C_2}{T_2} \text{ etc.}$$

itself has a value exceeding unity (see Example A, *b*).

Air contains 5 ppm of carbon tetrachloride (TLV, 10), 20 ppm of ethylene dichloride (TLV, 50), and 10 ppm of ethylene dibromide (TLV, 1).

$$\frac{5}{10} + \frac{20}{50} + \frac{10}{25} = \frac{65}{50} = 1.3$$

Threshold limit is exceeded.

(*b*) Independent Effects.   Air contains 0.15 mg/m³ of lead (TLV, 0.2) and 0.7 mg/m³ of sulfuric acid (TLV, 1).

$$\frac{0.15}{0.20} = 0.75, \quad \frac{0.7}{1} = 0.7$$

Threshold limit is not exceeded.

B. Special case when source of contaminant is a mixture and atmospheric composition is assumed similar to that of original material, i.e., vapor pressure of each component is the same at the observed temperature.

(*a*) Additive Effects, Approximate Solution.   A Mixture of equal parts of (*1*) trichloroethylene (TLV, 100) and (*2*) methyl chloroform (TLV, 350).   (Solution applicable to "spot" solvent mixture usages, where all or nearly all solvent evaporates.)

$$\frac{C_1}{100} + \frac{C_2}{350} = \frac{C_m}{T_m}$$

Antagonistic action or potentiation may occur with some combinations of atmospheric contaminants. Such cases at present must be determined individually. Potentiating or antagonistic agents are not necessarily harmful by themselves. Potentiating effects of exposure to such agents by routes other than that of inhalation is also possible, e.g., imbibed alcohol and inhaled narcotic (trichlorethylene). Potentiation is characteristically exhibited at high concentrations, less probably at low.

When a given operation or process characteristically emits a number of harmful dusts, fumes, vapors, or gases, it will frequently be only feasible to attempt to evaluate the hazard by measurement of a single substance. In such cases, the threshold limit used for this substance should be reduced by a *suitable* factor, the magnitude of which will depend on the number, toxicity, and relative quantity of the other contaminants ordinarily present.

Examples of processes which are typically associated with two or more harmful atmospheric contaminants are welding, automobile repair, blasting, painting, lacquering, certain foundry operations, diesel exhausts, etc.

Examples. A. General case where air is analyzed for each component.

(a) Additive Effects:

$$\frac{C_1}{T_1} + \frac{C_2}{T_2} + \frac{C_3}{T_3} \cdots \frac{C_n}{T_n} = 1$$

$$C_1 = C_2 = {}^1\!/_2 C_m$$

$$\frac{C_1}{100} + \frac{C_1}{350} = \frac{2C_1}{T_m}$$

$$\frac{7C_1}{700} + \frac{700}{2C_1} = \frac{2C_1}{T_m}$$

$$T_m = 700 \times {}^2/_9 = 155 \text{ ppm}$$

(b) General Solution for Mixtures of N Components with Additive Effects and Different Vapor Pressures.

$$\frac{C_1}{T_1} + \frac{C_2}{T_2} + \cdots + \frac{C_n}{T_n} = 1 \tag{1}$$

$$C_1 + C_2 + \cdots + C_n = T \tag{2}$$

$$\frac{C_1}{T} + \frac{C_2}{T} + \cdots + \frac{C_n}{T} = 1 \tag{2a}$$

By the law of partial pressures

$$C_1 = ap_1 \tag{3}$$

and by Raoult's law

$$p_1 = F_1 p_1^0 \tag{4}$$

Combine (3) and (4) to obtain

$$C_1 = aF_1 p_1^0 \tag{5}$$

Combining (1), (2a), and (5), we obtain

$$\frac{F_1 p_1^0}{T_1} + \frac{F_2 p_2^0}{T_2} + \cdots + \frac{F_n p_n^0}{T_n} =$$

$$\frac{F_1 p_1^0}{T_1} + \frac{F_2 p_2^0}{T_2} + \cdots + \frac{F_n p_n^0}{T_n} \qquad (6)$$

and solving for T

$$T = \frac{F_1 p_1^0 + F_2 p_2^0 + \cdots + F_n p_n^0}{\dfrac{F_1 p_1^0}{T_1} + \dfrac{F_2 p_2^0}{T_2} + \cdots + \dfrac{F_n p_n^0}{T_n}} = \frac{\sum\limits_{i=1}^{i=n} F_1 p_1^0}{\sum\limits_{i=1}^{i=n} \dfrac{F_n p_n^0}{T_n}} \qquad (6a)$$

$$T = \sum_{i=1}^{n} \frac{F_1 p_1^0}{T_1} \qquad (6b)$$

where

T = threshold limit value in ppm
C = vapor concentration in ppm
p = vapor pressure of component in solution
p^0 = vapor pressure of pure component
F = mole fraction of component in solution
a = a constant of proportionality. Subscripts $1, 2, \ldots n$, relate to the above quantities to components $1, 2, \ldots n$, respectively. Subscript i refers to an arbitrary component from 1 to n. Absence of subscript relates the quantity to the mixture.

$$C_m = 3C_1$$

$$\frac{C_1}{0.1} + \frac{2C_1}{0.5} = \frac{3C_1}{T_m}$$

$$\frac{7C_1}{0.5} = \frac{3C_1}{T_m}$$

$$T_m = \frac{1.5}{7} = 0.21 \text{ mg/m}^3$$

D. TLV for Mixtures of Mineral Dusts. For mixtures of biologically active mineral dusts, the general formula for mixtures may be used. With the exception of asbestos, pure minerals are assigned TLVs of 2.5, 20, or 50.

For a mixture containing 80% talc and 20% quartz, the TLV for 100% of the mixture C is given by

$$\frac{C}{\text{TLV}} = \frac{0.8}{20} + \frac{0.2}{2.5}$$

$$TLV = \frac{20}{2.4} = 8.4 \text{ mppcf}$$

Essentially, the same result will be obtained if the limit of the more (most) toxic component is used, provided the effects are additive. In the above example, the limit for 20% quartz is 10 mppcf.

Solution to be applied when there is a reservoir of the solvent mixture whose composition does not change appreciably by evaporation.

C. A mixture of one part of (1) parathion (TLV, 0.1) and two parts of (2) EPN (TLV, 0.5).

$$\frac{C_1}{0.1} + \frac{C_2}{0.5} = \frac{C_m}{T_m} \qquad C_2 = 2C_1$$

For another mixture of 25% quartz, 25% amorphous silica, and 50% talc:

$$\frac{0.25}{2.5} + \frac{0.25}{20} + \frac{0.5}{20} = 7.3 \text{ mppcf}$$

The limit for 25% quartz approximates 8 mppcf.

Exact Arithmetic Solution of Specific Mixture

	Mol. wt.	Density, g/ml	T	p^0 [a]	Mole fraction, half/half soln by vol
Trichloroethylene (1)	131.4	1.46	100	73	0.527
Methyl chloroform (2)	133.42	1.33	350	125	0.473

$F_1 p_1^0 = (0.527)(73) = 38.2$

$F_2 p_2^0 = (0.473)(125) = 59.2$

$$T = \frac{38.2 + 59.2}{(38.2/100)(59.2/350)} = \frac{(97.4)(350)}{133.8 + 59.2} = \frac{(97.4)(350)}{93.0} = 177$$

$T = 177$ ppm (note differences in TLV when account is taken of vapor pressure and mole fraction in comparison with Example B (a), p. 871, where such account is not taken).

[a] At 25°C and in mm Hg.

Table 3, Appendix C. Bases for Assigning Limiting "C" Values

By definition in the introduction to Threshold Limit Values, a listed value bearing a C designation refers to "ceiling" value that should not be exceeded; all values should fluctuate below the listed value. In general, the bases for assigning or not assigning a C value rest on whether excursions of concentration above a proposed limit for periods up to 15 min may result in (a) intolerable irritation, (b) chronic, or irreversible tissue change, or (c) narcosis of sufficient degree to increase accident proneness, impair self-rescue or materially reduce work efficiency.

In order for the Committee to decide whether a substance is a candidate for a C listing, some guidelines must be formulated on the permissive fluctuation above the limit in terms of the seriousness of the response in the categories (a), (b), (c), given above. For this, the factors given in the table below have been used by the Committee. For both technical and prac-

tical reasons, the factors have been pegged to the concentration in an inverse manner. It will be noted that as the magnitude of the TLV increases, a correspondingly decreased range of fluctuation is permitted; not to decrease the factor for TLV of increasing magnitude would permit exposures to large absolute quantities, an undesirable condition, a condition that is minimized at low TLV. Moreover, larger factors at the lower TLV are consistent with the difficulties in analyzing and controlling trace quantities.

As stated in the introduction, the same factors may be used as guides for reasonable excursions above the limit for substances to which the time-weighted average applies. The time-weighted average implies that each excursion above the limit is compensated by a comparable excursion below the limit.

Bases for Assigning Limiting C Values

TLV range ppm or mg/m³ᵃ	Test TLV factor	Examples
0 to 1	3	Toluene diisocyanate (TLV, 0.02 ppm) if permitted to rise above 0.06 ppm may result in sensitization in a single subsequent exposure. C listing recommended on category (*b*).
1+ to 10	2	Manganese (TLV, 5 mg/m) contains little or no safety factor. All values should fluctuate below 5 mg/cu m. C listing recommended on category (*b*).
10+ to 100	1.5	Methyl styrene (TLV, 100) if encountered at levels of 150 ppm will prove intensely irritating. C listing recommended on category (*a*).
100+ to 1000	1.25	Methyl chloroform (TLV, 350 ppm) at 438 ppm for periods not exceeding 15 minutes is not expected to result in untoward effects relating to category (*c*). No C listing recommended.

ᵃ Whichever unit is applicable.

TABLE 4

Probable Safe Concentration Limits of Exposure for Gases

Substance	1 Govt. hygienists[a]		2 A.S.A.	3 Calif.	4 Conn.	5 Cook	6 Mass.	7 Matt.	8 N.Y.	9 Oregon	10 U.S.S.R.	11 Utah	12 Wis.
	ppm	mg/m³	ppm	ppm	ppm	ppm	ppm	ppm	ppm	ppm	ppm	ppm	ppm
Ammonia	50	35	—	100	—	100	100	100–200	100	100	40	100	100
Arsine	0.05	0.2	—	1	—	1	0.05	—	1	0.5	1	1	1
Bromine	0.1	0.7	—	1	—	1	—	0.15–0.3	1	—	—	1	1
1,3-Butadiene	1000	2200	—	5,000	—	5000							
Carbon dioxide	5000	9000	—	5,000	—	5000	—	—	5000	5000	—	5550	
Carbon monoxide	100	110	100	100	100	100	100	—	100	100	8–16	100	100
Chlorine	1	3	—	1	1	5	1	1–2	1	1	0.35–0.6	1	1
Cyanogen	—	—		20									
				(0.043 mg/liter)									
Cyclopropane	400	687											
Dichlorodifluoromethane	1000	4950	—	—		100,000							
Dichloromono-fluoromethane	1000	4200	—	—		5000							
Dichlorotetra-fluoroethane	1000	7000	—	—		10,000							
Formaldehyde	5	6	10	10	10	10	5	—	5	10	—	20	20
Hydrogen chloride	5	7	—	10	10	10	10	10	10	10	—	10	10
Hydrogen cyanide	10	11	—	20	20	20	20	—	20	20	—	20	20
Hydrogen fluoride	3	2	—	3	3	3	1.5	—	3	3	—	3	3
Hydrogen selenide	0.05	0.2	—	0.1	—	0.1							
Hydrogen sulfide	10	15	20	20	20	20	20	—	20	20	2–10	20	20

Nitrogen oxides (other than nitrous oxide) (calculated as NO_2)	5	9	25	25	25	25	10	40	—	10–40	10
Ozone	0.1	0.2	—	1	—	1	1	1	0.5	1	1
Phosphine	0.3	0.4	—	1	—	1	1	1	1	2	2
Stibine	0.1	0.5	—	10	—	10	1				
Sulfur dioxide	5	13	—	10	10	10	10	10	10	3–13	10

[a] Values in Column 1 are from 1964, *Arch. Environ. Health*, **9**, 545 (1964). Other values are from 1947–1948.

References:

1. Committee on Threshold Limits, American Conference of Governmental Hygienists, *Ind. Hyg. Newsletter*, **7**, No. 8, 15 (1947); revision adopted April, 1948.
2. American Standards Association, *Am. Standards* through 1948.
3. State of California, Div. Ind. Safety, Dept. Ind. Relations, "Dusts, Fumes, Mists, Vapors, and Gases," 1948.
4. State of Connecticut, Dept. Health, Sanitary Code, *Regulation 280*, 1948.
5. W. A. Cook, "Maximum Allowable Concentrations of Industrial Atmospheric Contaminants," *Ind. Med.*, **14**, 936 (1945).
6. Massachusetts Dept. Labor Industries, Div. Occupational Hyg., "Maximum Allowable Concentrations," 1948.
7. E. Matt, Dissertation (Wuertzburg, 1889), as quoted by F. Flury and F. Zernik, *Schaedliche Gase*, Springer, Berlin, 1931.
8. New York State, Dept. Labor, Div. Ind. Hyg. These values are not official; they are used by the Div. Ind. Hyg. as a guide.
9. Oregon State Board of Health, "Rules and Regulations for the Prevention and Control of Occupational Diseases," 1945.
10. A. S. Zhitkova, S. I. Kaplun, and J. B. Ficklen, *Poisonous Gases*, Service to Industry, Hartford, 1936.
11. Utah Dept. Health, Ind. Hyg. Div., "Useful Criteria in the Identification of Certain Occupational Health Hazards," 1945.
12. Industrial Commission of Wisconsin, "General Orders on Dusts, Fumes, Vapors, and Gases," 1947.

TABLE 5

Probable Safe Concentration Limits of Exposure for Vapors

Substance	1 Govt. hygienists[a] ppm	mg/m³	2 A.S.A. ppm	3 Calif., ppm	4 Conn., ppm	5 Cook, ppm	6 Mass., ppm	7 N.Y., ppm	8 Oregon, ppm	9 Utah, ppm	10 Wis., ppm
Acetaldehyde	200	360	—	200	—	200	—	—	—	—	
Acetic acid	10	25	—	10	—	10	—	10			
Acetic anhydride	5	20									
Acetone	1000	2400	—	1000	—	500	500	1000	500	200	
Acrolein	0.1	0.25	—	0.5	—	0.5	—	—	1	3.3	
Acrylonitrile	20	45	—	20	—	20	—	20	20		
Allyl alcohol	2	5	—	15					20		
Allyl chloride	1	3	—	(0.035 mg/liter) 50							
Amyl acetate	100	525	—	(0.156 mg/liter) 200	—	200	200	400	400	400	400
Aniline	5	19	—	5	—	5	5	5	5	5–7	5
Benzene (benzol)	25	80	100	100	100	100	35	50	75	75–100	75
Benzine	—	—	—	(4.0 mg/liter) 1000	—	500	—	1000	—	1000	
n-Butyl acetate	200	950	—	200	—	200	200	400	—	—	400
n-Butyl alcohol (butanol)	100	300	—	100	—	50	50	200	—	100	
Butyl methyl ketone (methyl butyl ketone)	100	409	—	200	—	200					
Carbon disulfide	20	60	20	20	20	20	20	20	20	20	15
Carbon tetrachloride	10	65	—	100	100	100	50	75	50	100	100
2-Chlorobutadiene (chloroprene)	25	90	—	25	—	25	—	—	—	83	

Chloroform	50	240	—	100	—	100	—	100	
1-Chloro-1-nitropropane	20	100	—	20					
Cresols and cresylic acid	5	22	—	5 (0.022 mg/liter)					
Cyclohexane	400	1400	—	400					
Cyclohexanol	50	200	—	100					
Cyclohexanone	50	200	—	100					
Cyclohexene	400	1350	—	400					
o-Dichlorobenzene	50	300	—	75	75	75	75	—	75
1,1-Dichloroethane (ethylidene dichloride)	100	400	—	100					
1,2-Dichloroethane (ethylene dichloride)	50	200	—	100	75	100	100	100	100
1,2-Dichloroethylene	200	790	—	100					
Dichloroethyl ether	15	90	—	15	15	15	—	15	15
Dichloromethane (methylene chloride)	500	1750	—	500		500			
1,1-Dichloro-1-nitroethane	10	60	—	10					
1,2-Dichloropropane (propylene dichloride)	75	350	—						
Diethylene glycol monoethyl ether (Carbitol)	—	—	—	50 (0.274 mg/liter)					
Dimethylaniline	5	25	—	5	—	5	5		
Dioxane	100	360	—	500					
Ethyl acetate	400	1400	—	400	400				
Ethyl alcohol	1000	1900	—	1000		1000			
Ethylbenzene	200	870	—	200					
Ethyl bromide	200	890	—	400			—	1700	

(continued)

TABLE 5 (continued)

Substance	1 Govt. hygienists[a] ppm	mg/m³	2 A.S.A. ppm	3 Calif., ppm	4 Conn., ppm	5 Cook, ppm	6 Mass., ppm	7 N.Y., ppm	8 Oregon, ppm	9 Utah, ppm	10 Wis., ppm
Ethyl chloride	1000	2600	—	1000	—	5000	—	—	—	20,000	
Ethylene chlorohydrin	5	16	—	10	—	10					
Ethylene glycol mono-butyl ether (butyl Cellosolve)	50	240	—	200	—	200					
Ethylene glycol mono-ethyl ether (Cellosolve)	200	740	—	200	—	200	—		—	500	
Ethylene glycol mono-ethyl ether acetate (Cellosolve acetate)	100	540	—	200	—	100					
Ethylene glycol mono-methyl ether (methyl Cellosolve)	25	80	—	100	—	100	—	—	—	<25	
Ethylene glycol mono-methyl ether acetate (methyl Cellosolve acetate)	25	120	—	100		100					
Ethylene oxide	50	90	—	100	—	100					
Ethyl ether	400	1200	—	1000	—	500	400	400	400	<250	400
Ethyl formate	100	300	—	200	—	200					
Ethyl methacrylate	—		—	400 (1.864 mg/liter)							
Ethyl methyl ketone (2-butanone)	200	590	—	200	—	200	300			400	400

	1	2	3	4	5	6	7	8	9	10
Ethyl silicate	100	850	—	100	100	1000	100	500	1000	1000
Gasoline	500	2000	—	1000	500	500	—	—	1000	1000
Heptane	500	2000	—	500	500	500	—	—	—	—
Hexane	500	1800	—	1000	1000	200	—	—	55.6	—
Isoamyl alcohol	100	360	—	100	100	100	—	—	—	—
Isobutyl methyl ketone (methyl isobutyl ketone)	100	409	—	200	200	100	—	—	—	—
Isophorone	25	140	—	25	25	25	—	—	—	—
Isopropyl alcohol	400	980	—	400	400	400	—	—	—	—
Isopropyl ether	500	2100	—	500	500	500	—	—	—	—
Mesityl oxide	25	100	—	50	50	50	—	—	—	—
Methyl acetate	200	610	—	100	100	100	—	—	—	—
Methyl alcohol (methanol)	200	260	200	200	200	200	100	100	100–200	200
Methyl bromide	20	80	—	20	20	—	35	35	50	—
Methyl chloride	100	210	—	200	200	—	100	100	500	—
Methylcyclohexane	500	2000	—	1000	1000	1000	—	—	—	—
Methylcyclohexanol	100	470	—	100	100	100	—	—	—	—
Methylcyclohexanone	100	460	—	100	100	100	—	—	—	—
Methyl formate	100	250	—	400	400	400	—	—	—	—
Methyl methacrylate	100	410	(2.045 mg/liter)	500	—	—	—	—	—	—
Methyl propyl ketone (pentanone)	200	700	—	400	400	400	—	—	—	—
Methyl sulfate	1	5	—	1	1	1	—	—	—	—
Monochlorobenzene	75	350	—	75	75	75	75	75	75	75
Mononitrotoluene	5	30	—	5	5	5	—	5	—	75
Naphtha (coal tar, solvent)	200	800	—	100–200	100–200	200	—	200	—	—

(continued)

TABLE 5 (continued)

	1 Govt. hygienists[a]		2 A.S.A.,	3 Calif.,	4 Conn.,	5 Cook,	6 Mass.,	7 N.Y.,	8 Oregon,	9 Utah,	10 Wis.,
Substance	ppm	mg/m³	ppm	ppm	ppm	ppm	ppm	ppm	ppm	ppm	ppm
Naphtha (petroleum)	500	2000	—	500	—	500	—	—	500	5000	
Nickel carbonyl	0.001	0.007									5
Nitrobenzene	1	5		5		5	5	5	5	1–5	
Nitroethane	100	310		200		200					
Nitroglycerin	0.2	2		0.5		0.5					
Nitromethane	100	250		200		200					
2-Nitropropane	25	90									
Octane	500	2350		500		500					
Pentane	1000	2950		5000		5000					
Phenol	5	19		5	(0.019 mg/liter)						
Phosgene	0.1	0.4		1	1	1		1	1	1	1
Phosphorus trichloride	0.5	3		0.5		0.5	—	—	—	0.7	
Propyl acetate	200	840		200		200					
Stoddard solvent	500	2900		500		500		750			
Styrene monomer	100	420	400	400	400	400	400	400	400		
Sulfur monochloride	1	6		1		1					
1,1,2,2-Tetrachloroethane	5	35		10		10	5	10	10	10	10
Tetrachloroethylene	100	679		200		200	200	200	200	200	200
Toluene (toluol)	200	750	200	200	200	200	200	200	200	200	200
Toluidine	5	22		5		5					
Trichloroethane	—	—		50	(0.272 mg/liter)						
Trichloroethylene	100	520	200	200		200	200	200	200	200	200

Trichloromonofluoro-methane	1000	5620	—	—	—	10,000	200	200	200
Turpentine	100	560	—	100	700	200	200	—	500
Vinyl chloride	500	1300	—	1000	1000	—	200	—	200
Xylene (xylol)	200	870	200	200	200	200	200	200	200

[a] Values in Column 1 are from 1964, *Arch. Environ. Health*, **9**, 545 (1964). Other values are from 1947–1948.

References:

1. Committee on Threshold Limits, American Conference of Governmental Industrial Hygienists, *Ind. Hyg. Newsletter*, **7**, No. 8, 15 (1947); revision adopted April, 1948.
2. American Standards Association, *Am. Standards*, through 1948.
3. State of California, Div. Ind. Safety, Dept. Ind. Relations, "Dusts, Fumes, Mists, Vapors, and Gases," 1948.
4. State of Connecticut, Dept. Health Sanitary Code, *Regulation 280*, 1948.
5. W. A. Cook, "Maximum Allowable Concentrations of Industrial Atmospheric Contaminants," *Ind. Med.* **14**, 936 (1945).
6. Massachusetts Dept. Labor Industries, Div. Occupational Hyg., "Maximum Allowable Concentrations," 1948.
7. New York State, Dept. Labor, Div. Ind. Hyg. These values are not official; they are used by the Div. Ind. Hyg. as a guide.
8. Oregon State Board of Health, "Rules and Regulations for the Prevention and Control of Occupational Diseases," 1945.
9. Utah Dept. Health, Ind. Hyg. Div., "Useful Criteria in the Identification of Certain Occupational Health Hazards," 1945.
10. Industrial Commission of Wisconsin, "General Orders on Dusts, Fumes, Vapors, and Gases," 1947.

TABLE 6

Probable Safe Concentration Limits of Exposure for Toxic Dusts, Fumes, and Mists (mg/m³)

Substance	1 Govt. hygienists	2 A.S.A.	3 Calif.	4 Conn.	5 Cook	6 Mass.	7 N.Y.	8 Oregon	9 Utah	10 Wis.
Antimony	0.5									
Arsenic (except volatile hydrides)	0.5	0.15	3.0	—	0.15	0.15	0.15	0.15	0.5	
Barium	0.5									
Barium peroxide as Ba	—	—	0.5		0.5		0.5			
Cadmium	0.1	0.1	0.1	0.1	0.5		0.5	0.1	0.1	0.1
Chlorides	—		15.0		0.1	0.1	0.1			0.1
Chlorinated diphenyl oxide	0.5		1.0							
Chlorodiphenyl	1	—	1	—	1	1-5	1	—	—	1.0
Chloronaphthalenes	0.5	—	—	—	—	1-5	—	—	—	1-5
Chromic acid and chromates as CrO_3	0.1	0.1	0.1	0.1	0.1	0.1	0.1	0.1	0.1	0.1
Cyanide as CN	5									
Dinitrotoluene	1.5	—	1.5	—	1.5	—	1.5	—		
Fluorides	2.5	—	2.0	—	—	1	—	2		
Hexachloronaphthalene	—		0.5							
Hydrochloric acid mist	7		2.0							
Iodine	1.0		1		1		1	0.5-1.0		
Iron oxide fume	15		10.0		30		30			
Lead	0.2	0.15	0.15	0.15	0.15	0.15	0.15	0.15	0.15	0.15
Magnesium oxide fume	15	—	0.15	—	15	—	—	—	15	
Manganese	5	6	6	6	6	6	6	6	5-50	
Mercury	0.1	0.1	0.1	0.1	0.1	0.1	0.1	0.1	0.1	0.1
Metal fumes (total)	—	—	30							

Nitric acid	5	—	2.0	0.5		0.5	0.5	0.5
Pentachloronaphthalene	0.5	—	1.0					
Pentachlorophenol	0.5	—						
Phosphorus (yellow or white)	0.1							
Phosphorus pentachloride	1							
Phosphorus pentasulfide	1							
Selenium compounds as selenium (except volatile selenides)	0.2							
Sulfuric acid	1.0	—	5	5		5	—	2
Tellurium	0.1	—	0.01	—		—		
Tetrachloronaphthalene	—	—	1.0					
Tetryl	1.5	—	1.5	1.5				
Trichloronaphthalene	5	—	5.0	5		5	5	5
Trinitrotoluene	1.5	—	1.5	1.5				
Zinc oxide	5	—	15	15	15	15	15	15

References:

1. Committee on Threshold Limits, American Conference of Governmental Industrial Hygienists, *Arch. Environ. Health*, **9**, 545 (1964).
2. American Standards Association, *Am. Standards* through 1948.
3. State of California, Div. Ind. Safety, Dept. Ind. Relations, "Dusts, Fumes, Mists, Vapors, and Gases," 1948.
4. State of Connecticut, Dept. Health Sanitary Code, *Regulation 280*, 1948.
5. W. A. Cook, "Maximum Allowable Concentrations of Industrial Atmospheric Contaminants," *Ind. Med.*, **14**, 936 (1945).
6. Massachusetts Dept. Labor Industries, Div. Occupational Hyg., "Maximum Allowable Concentrations," 1948.
7. New York State, Dept. Labor, Div. Ind. Hyg.   These values are not official; they are used by the Div. Ind. Hyg., as a guide.
8. Oregon State Board of Health, "Rules and Regulations for the Prevention and Control of Occupational Diseases," 1945.
9. Utah Dept. Health, Ind. Hyg. Div., "Useful Criteria in the Identification of Certain Occupational Health Hazards," 1945.
10. Industrial Commission of Wisconsin, "General Orders on Dusts, Fumes, Vapors, and Gases," 1947.

TABLE 7

Probable Safe Limits of Exposure for Certain Industrial Dusts

Dust or locality	Safe limit, MPPCF[a]	Free silica, %	Size, μ	Refer-ence
Alundum	50			8
Anthracite coal	50	3		1
Anthracite mines (haulage way)	10–15	13		1
Anthracite mines (rock workers)	5–10	35		1
Asbestos (textile)	5			2
Asbestos	5		0.5–10	3, 8, 9
Asbestos	10		0.5–10	4
Australia	14	10–17		5
Carborundum	50			8
Cement	15			3
Dusts (other than silica or those of toxic nature)	50	<5	0.5–5	4, 8
Dust, total	50	<5	0.5–10	3, 8
Dust, foundry	25			9
Gold mines (Ontario)	8.5	About 35 in rock		5
Granite	15			9
Granite (Barre)	10–20	35		6
Mica	50	<5		8
Organic	50		0.5–5	3
Portland cement	50			8
Pottery	4			3
Sandstone (Australia)	6	90		5
Silica	50	<5		8
Silica	10	25–35	0.5–5	3
Silica	5	over 75	0.5–10	3, 8
Silverware	12			7
Slate	15			3
Slate	50	<5		8
Soapstone	50	<5		8
South Africa	4.5	80		5
Talc	15			3
Talc	20			8

[a] Million particles per cubic foot.

References:

1. J. J. Bloomfield, J. M. DallaValle, R. R. Jones, W. C. Dreessen, D. K. Brundage, and R. H. Britten, *U.S. Public Health Service Bull. 221* (1935).

2. W. C. Dreessen, J. M. DallaValle, T. I. Edwards, J. W. Miller, R. R. Sayers, A. F. Easom, and M. F. Trice, *U.S. Public Health Service Bull. 241* (1938).

3. State of California, Div. Ind. Safety, Dept. Ind. Relations, "Dusts, Fumes, Mists, Vapors, and Gases," 1948.

4. C. O. Sappington, *Medicolegal Phases of Occupational Diseases*, Industrial Health, Chicago, 1939.

5. U.S. Dept. Labor, *Div. Labor Standards Bull. 13* (1927).

6. A. E. Russell, R. H. Britten, L. R. Thompson, and J. J. Bloomfield, *U.S. Public Health Service Bull. 187* (1929).

7. J. C. Goddard, *U.S. Public Health Service Bull. 208* (1933).

8. Committee on Threshold Limits, American Conference of Governmental Hygienists, *Ind. Hyg. Newsletter*, **7**, No. 8, 15 (1947); revision adopted 1948.

9. *Massachusetts Dept. Labor Industries, Div. Occupational Hyg.*, "Maximum Allowable Concentrations," 1948.

TABLE 8

Concentrations of Common Air Pollutants in the Average
Urban Area Circa 1954[a] (ppm except as indicated)
(Courtesy Dr. Eugene Sawicki)

Contaminant	Concentration range	Average
Sootfall (dustfall)	5–100[b]	20[b]
Suspended particulate matter	0.1–3.0[c]	0.3[c]
Carbon dioxide	300–1000	300
Carbon monoxide	1.0–200	2.0
Oxides of nitrogen (NO_2)	0.01–1.0	0.10
Sulfur dioxide	0.01–3.0	0.10
Aldehydes (acrolein)	0.01–1.00	0.10
Chlorides	0.00–0.3	0.05
Ozone (oxidants)	0.0–0.80	0.03
Ammonia	0.00–0.21	0.02
Fluorides	0.00–0.08	0.002

[a] After J. Cholak, *A.M.A. Arch. Ind. Hyg. Occupational Med.*, **10**, 203 (1954).

[b] Tons per square mile per month.

[c] Milligrams per cubic meter.

TABLE 9

Sulfur Dioxide, Qualifying Stations (1963)[a]

(ppm in 24-hr samples)

(Courtesy Dr. Eugene Sawicki)

Station	No. of samples	Min	Max	Av.
Hartford, Connecticut	26	0.01	0.09	0.03
New Haven, Connecticut	23	0.01	0.13	0.04
Boston, Massachusetts	22	0.01	0.10	0.03
Providence, Rhode Island	22	—[b]	0.11	0.05
Wilmington, Delaware	26	0.01	0.13	0.05
Newark. New Jersey	25	0.01	0.32	0.08
New York City, New York	25	0.04	0.38	0.15
Buffalo, New York	19	—[b]	0.05	0.02
Philadelphia, Pennsylvania	25	0.02	0.27	0.10
Pittsburgh, Pennsylvania	25	0.01	0.12	0.04
Washington, D.C.	24	—[b]	0.08	0.03
Baltimore, Maryland	24	—[b]	0.09	0.04
Charleston, West Virginia	23	—[b]	0.04	0.01
Chattanooga, Tennessee	25	—[b]	0.07	0.01
Nashville, Tennessee	24	—[b]	0.05	0.01
Chicago, Illinois	24	0.01	0.30	0.11
Indianapolis, Indiana	26	—[b]	0.05	0.02
Detroit, Michigan	26	—[b]	0.07	0.02
Cincinnati, Ohio	25	—[b]	0.06	0.02
Youngstown, Ohio	26	0.01	0.10	0.04
Cleveland, Ohio	23	—[b]	0.10	0.04
Dayton, Ohio	24	—[b]	0.04	0.01
Milwaukee, Wisconsin	22	—[b]	0.03	0.01
Des Moines, Iowa	24	—[b]	0.03	0.01
Wichita, Kansas	25	—[b]	0.01	0.02
Minneapolis, Minnesota	24	—[b]	0.09	—[b]
St. Louis, Missouri	26	—[b]	0.10	0.02
Denver, Colorado	23	—[b]	0.02	0.01
Salt Lake City, Utah	22	—[b]	0.04	0.01
Portland, Oregon	24	—[b]	0.06	0.02
Seattle, Washington	26	—[b]	0.07	0.02

[a] Air Pollution Measurements of the National Air Sampling Network, *Analysis of Suspended Particulates*, 1963, U.S. Department of Health, Education, and Welfare, Public Health Service, Division of Air Pollution, Cincinnati, Ohio, 1965, p. 72.

[b] Denotes value less than 0.01 ppm.

TABLE 10
Oxidant Concentrations Circa 1956[a] (pphm)
(Courtesy Dr. Eugene Sawicki)

City or area	Range	Average
Los Angeles, California	100	
College, Alaska	0.6–45	5.9
Charleston, West Virginia	1.2–11.8	4.9
Ann Arbor, Michigan	2.7–7.4	4.7
Washington, D.C.	0.3–7.8	3.9
Whiting-Hammon, Indiana	0.0–10.0	3.7
Cincinnati, Ohio	0.2–8.0	3.3
St. Louis, Missouri	0.2–8.0	2.7
London, England	0.0–6.0	
Detroit, Michigan	0.8–5.5	2.6
Philadelphia, Pennsylvania	0.0–5.0	1.5
Akron, Ohio	0.2–3.2	1.1
Elizabeth, New Jersey	0.9–2.8	0.9
Europe	0.4–2.8	

[a] After data in *The Smog Problem in Los Angeles County*, Stanford Research Inst., Menlo Park, Calif., and J. Cholak, L. J. Schafer, and D. W. Yeager, *J. Air Pollution Control Assoc.*, **5**, No. 4, 2 (1956).

TABLE 11

Concentrations of Sulfur Dioxide (ppm) in the Atmosphere
of a Number of Communities[a,b]
(Courtesy Dr. Eugene Sawicki)

Community	Number of samples	Range	Average or mean
Chicago (1937)			
Railroad station	32	Trace–2.54	0.67
Manufacturing area	99	0.17–3.16	0.50
Commercial area	89	Trace–3.16	0.41
Pittsburgh (1931–32)			
Industrial area	607	0.00–2.5	0.30
St. Louis (1937)			
Cold months	663	0.0?–1.86[c]	0.25[c]
Chicago (1937)			
Residential area	32	Trace–0.47	0.16
Donora (1949)	529	0.00–0.50	0.15
St. Louis (1937)			
Warm months	673	0.0?–0.756[c]	0.127[c]
Baltimore (1950)			
Industrial area	79	0.01–0.46	0.074
Cincinnati (1947–51)			
Industrial and commercial areas	227	0.00–0.46	0.064
All areas	298	0.00–0.46	0.061
Residential area	71	0.00–0.27	0.044
Cleveland (1949–50)			
Industrial area	290	0.0–0.489[c]	0.042[c]
St. Louis (1950)			
Cold months	243	0.0–0.51[c]	0.041[c]
Los Angeles (1949–50) (5,6,7)	?	Trace–0.60	?
Cincinnati (1947–51)			
Rural area	69	0.00–0.31	0.037
Salt Lake City (1919–20)	27	?	0.036
Yonkers (1936–37)	?	0.0–0.75	0.032
St. Louis (1937)			
Warm months	294	0.0–0.24[c]	0.03[c]
Charleston (1950–51)	143	0.001–0.18	0.023
Baltimore (1950)			
Rural area	12	0.00–0.11	0.023
Manhattan (July, 1955)	—	0.10–0.34	0.17
Staten Island (July, 1955)	—	0.02–0.60	0.27

[a] After J. Cholak, *2nd Natl. Air Pollution Symposium* (*Los Angeles*), *1952*, 6.

[b] After L. Greenburg and M. B. Jacobs, *Ind. Eng. Chem.*, **48**, 1517 (1956).

[c] Sulfur dioxide values as such.

TABLE 12
Suspended Particulates, Urban (1963)[a]
(Courtesy Dr. Eugene Sawicki)

Location: region, state, or station	Years	Number of samples	Micrograms per cubic meter		
			Min	Max	Arith mean
Alabama					
Birmingham	63	26	49	505	149
Huntsville	63	25	31	166	80
Montgomery	63	26	29	163	84
Alaska					
Anchorage	63)	26	5	234	71
Arizona					
Phoenix	63	25	93	377	201
Tucson	63	25	49	219	118
California					
Berkeley	63	23	22	194	75
Glendale	63	26	38	284	116
Long Beach	63	25	37	557	133
Los Angeles	63	26	40	251	127
Oakland	63	25	32	197	88
San Bernardino	63	23	52	316	173
San Diego	63	25	35	282	87
San Francisco	63	26	29	158	72
San Jose	63	26	32	287	101
Santa Barbara	63	25	23	162	75
Stockton	63	26	27	172	76
Colorado					
Denver	63	26	86	673	191
Pueblo	63	25	67	222	121
Connecticut					
Hartford	63	25	45	185	103
New Haven	63	25	38	167	85
Norwich	63	26	31	171	71
Waterbury	63	25	26	165	71
Delaware					
Wilmington	63	25	68	621	168
District of Columbia					
Washington	63	25	63	231	116
Florida					
Miami	63	25	24	154	62
Orlando	63	22	40	136	76
St. Petersburg	63	25	28	78	50
Tampa	63	23	45	184	102

(continued)

TABLE 12 (*continued*)

Location: region, state, or station	Years	Number of samples	Microgams per cubic meter		
			Min	Max	Arith mean
Georgia					
Atlanta	63	26	33	186	104
Augusta	63	25	45	144	71
Savannah	63	26	16	145	80
Hawaii					
Honolulu	63	26	24	88	42
Idaho					
Boise	63	23	26	167	77
Illinois					
Chicago	63	24	67	257	144
East St. Louis	63	23	69	550	210
Joliet	63	26	35	480	136
North Chicago	63	23	20	539	114
Indiana					
East Chicago	63	21	42	409	191
Hammond	63	26	30	581	186
Indianapolis	63	23	93	367	174
Muncie	63	25	34	195	99
South Bend	63	26	52	236	126
Terre Haute	63	23	41	219	137
Iowa					
Cedar Rapids	63	26	39	319	137
Davenport	63	25	47	270	114
Des Moines	63	25	40	351	127
Kansas					
Topeka	63	26	32	379	93
Wichita	63	26	35	400	102
Louisiana					
New Orleans	63	26	49	187	96
Maine					
Portland	63	25	34	118	69
Maryland					
Baltimore	63	26	43	292	137
Cumberland	63	26	58	220	120
Fort Howard	63	25	28	191	75
Hagerstown	63	24	51	135	97
Riviera Beach	63	24	35	179	89
Rockville	63	25	32	89	61

(*continued*)

TABLE 12 (*continued*)

Location: region, state, or station	Years	Number of samples	Micrograms per cubic meter		
			Min	Max	Arith mean
Massachusetts					
Boston	63	22	42	180	114
Lowell	63	26	30	213	75
Worcester	63	26	32	161	74
Michigan					
Dearborn	63	26	37	409	127
Detroit	63	26	52	404	131
Flint	63	23	26	504	105
Grand Rapids	63	24	44	588	177
Jackson	63	26	28	330	87
Muskegon	63	26	23	287	103
Minnesota					
Duluth	63	25	16	128	64
Minneapolis	63	26	24	166	77
St. Paul	63	26	32	277	117
Mississippi					
Jackson	63	23	29	148	85
Missouri					
Kansas City	63	24	64	465	160
St. Louis	63	25	42	180	118
Montana					
Helena	63	26	15	98	47
Nebraska					
Omaha	63	25	26	326	109
Nevada					
Las Vegas	63	24	43	553	171
Reno	63	24	33	224	107
New Jersey					
Atlantic City	63	25	31	142	79
Bayonne	63	24	45	163	94
Hamilton	63	23	52	171	95
Jersey City	63	25	60	189	124
Newark	63	26	41	246	110
Paterson	63	26	43	200	91
New Mexico					
Albuquerque	63	25	39	421	160
New York					
Albany	63	26	28	216	86
Binghamton	63	23	42	290	103

(*continued*)

TABLE 12 (*continued*)

Location: region, state, or station	Years	Number of samples	Micrograms per cubic meter		
			Min	Max	Arith mean
Buffalo	63	26	37	254	115
Massena	63	26	18	129	47
Mt. Vernon	63	26	47	262	106
New Rochelle	63	26	28	165	69
New York	63	25	75	431	215
Niagara Falls	63	26	30	359	140
Rochester	63	25	47	219	94
Schenectady	63	26	37	275	99
Syracuse	63	26	48	269	123
Troy	63	21	16	129	74
Utica	63	26	43	228	101
North Carolina					
Charlotte	63	26	36	246	112
Durham	63	26	31	172	106
Gastonia	63	26	20	113	58
Greensboro	63	26	28	123	68
Raleigh	63	24	16	121	58
Wilmington	63	26	28	109	58
North Dakota					
Bismarck	63	26	15	679	108
Ohio					
Akron	63	25	37	288	132
Canton	63	26	59	289	155
Cincinnati	63	26	69	204	121
Cleveland	63	24	72	344	156
Columbus	63	26	37	227	112
Dayton	63	26	48	198	114
Hamilton	63	26	35	222	106
Toledo	63	26	45	412	114
Youngstown	63	26	82	397	161
Oklahoma					
Tulsa	63	25	27	108	65
Oregon					
Eugene	63	21	17	400	105
Medford	63	24	40	374	99
Portland	63	24	26	166	87
Pennsylvania					
Allentown	63	26	43	176	106
Altoona	63	22	49	254	110

(*continued*)

TABLE 12 (*continued*)

Location: region, state, or station	Years	Number of samples	Microgand per cubic meter Min	Max	Arith mean
Bethlehem	63	26	27	188	118
Erie	63	25	59	214	100
Johnstown	63	23	59	485	171
Philadelphia	63	25	73	308	156
Pittsburgh	63	25	53	402	185
Scranton	63	26	57	413	177
York	63	26	40	274	143
Rhode Island					
East Providence	63	25	31	112	66
Providence	63	21	23	422	129
South Carolina					
Charleston	63	25	22	131	69
Columbia	63	23	21	141	68
South Dakota					
Sioux Falls	63	23	17	387	71
Tennessee					
Chattanooga	63	25	73	328	189
Knoxville	63	25	52	314	124
Memphis	63	23	59	229	133
Nashville	63	26	58	285	133
Texas					
Abilene	63	25	42	231	102
Amarillo	63	25	16	710	86
Austin	63	26	39	227	122
Corpus Christi	63	23	40	174	83
Dallas	63	23	30	324	88
El Paso	63	26	51	294	136
Ft. Worth	63	24	41	184	93
Galveston	63	23	25	297	87
Houston	63	22	37	199	100
Lubbock	63	26	47	270	134
Odessa	63	26	18	185	107
San Angelo	63	26	21	259	93
San Antonio	63	24	41	144	77
Tyler	63	26	32	128	61
Waco	63	25	46	216	94
Wichita Falls	63	25	50	342	140
Utah					
Salt Lake City	63	25	51	293	123

(*continued*)

TABLE 12 (*continued*)

Location: region, state, or station	Year	Number of samples	Micrograms per cubic meter		
			Min	Max	Arith mean
Vermont					
Burlington	63	21	18	87	55
Virginia					
Hampton	63	26	22	110	59
Norfolk	63	25	47	301	119
Portsmouth	63	25	30	167	85
Richmond	63	25	53	138	83
Roanoke	63	22	51	260	106
Washington					
Bellingham	63	25	21	151	77
Clarkston	63	26	55	396	168
Everett	63	26	33	256	90
Seattle	63	26	29	129	63
Spokane	63	24	34	191	93
Tacoma	63	26	35	251	81
Vancouver	63	26	27	587	102
West Virginia					
Charleston	63	26	42	459	192
Wisconsin					
Kenosha	63	25	27	420	107
Madison	63	26	20	230	85
Milwaukee	63	26	41	297	129

[a] Air Pollution Measurements of the National Air Sampling Network, *Analysis of Suspended Particulates*, 1963, U.S. Dept. Health, Education, and Welfare, Public Health Service, Division of Air Pollution, Cincinnati, Ohio, 1965, pp. 22–27.

TABLE 13

Composition of Exhaust Gases from Diesel, Gasoline, and Propane-
Powered Motor Coaches[a]

(Courtesy Dr. Eugene Sawicki)

A. Observed Concentrations of Exhaust Gas Constituents

Driving Condition	Carbon monoxide, vol. %	Oxides of nitrogen, ppm	Formalde-hyde, ppm	Hydro-carbons, ppm
Idle				
Diesel	0.0	59	9	390
Gasoline	11.7	33	30	4,830
Propane	5.1	47	30	2,410
Acceleration				
Diesel	0.05	849	17	210
Gasoline	3.0	1347	16	960
Propane	3.5	1290	18	390
Cruise				
Diesel	0.0	237	11	90
Gasoline	3.4	653	7	320
Propane	1.75	2052	23	330
Deceleration				
Diesel	0.0	30	29	330
Gasoline	5.5	18	286	16,750
Propane	4.2	56	172	19,030

B. Total Hourly Emission Based on the Chicago Transit Driving Pattern

Type of coach	Carbon monoxide, SCFH	Oxides of nitrogen, SCFH	Formalde-hyde, SCFH	Hydro-carbons, lb/hr
Diesel	2	5.4	0.24	0.47
Gasoline	194	3.8	0.17	1.24
Propane	96	4.9	0.11	0.57

[a] After F. G. Rounds and H. W. Pearsall, "Diesel Exhaust Odor," SAE National Diesel Engine Meeting, Chicago, Nov. 1956, and M. A. Elliott, G. J. Nebel and F. G. Rounds, "The Composition of Exhaust Gases from Diesel, Gasoline, and Propane Powered Motor Coaches," Air Pollution Control Assoc. Meeting, Detroit, May 1955.

TABLE 14. Value of the Gas Constant, R, for Various Units

Units of pressure	Units of volume	R per gram molecule
Atmospheres	volume at 0°C	0.003662
Atmospheres	cm³	82.057
Atmospheres	liters	0.082054
Atmospheres	m³	8.2057×10^{-5}
Dynes/cm³ (barye)	cm³	8.3144×10^{7}
kg/m² $(g = 908.6)$	cm³	8.48×10^{5}
		R per lb molecule °F
lb/in.²	in.³	18,510
lb/in.²	ft³	10.73
Atmospheres	in.³	1260
Atmospheres	ft³	0.7302

TABLE 15. Normal Urine Values

Test	Range of normal values	Significance
Color	Pale straw to deep amber	Low specific gravity usually associated with pale color, high specific gravity with a deeper color.
Turbidity	Usually clear, if specimen is freshly voided.	Turbidity not necessarily an indication of abnormal status.
Acidity	pH 4.8–7.5	Fresh urine is usually slightly acid. On standing, urine may become alkaline due to decomposition with formation of ammonia.
Specific gravity	1.001–1.030	Specific gravity depends on fluid intake. In certain kidney diseases it may become fixed at 1.010.
Sugar (glucose or reducing bodies)	None	A meal high in carbohydrate may give transient sugar in urine. Its presence does not necessarily mean diabetes.
Albumin (protein)	None	Albumin in the urine usually denotes the presence of kidney disease. Occasionally albumin appears in the urine of normal persons following long standing (postural albuminuria).
Casts	0–9000 in 12 hr	In routine examinations of
Red blood cells	0–15,000,000 in 12 hr	urine a few casts and blood
Leukocytes and epithelial cells	32,000–4,000,000 in 42 hr	cells may be found in normal specimens.

TABLE 16

Abnormal Values in Urine Caused by Occupational Poisons

Substance	Findings	Significance
Aniline dye inter-mediates	Dark color, blood cells	Suggests presence of cancer of bladder
Arsenic	Albumin, blood cells	Due to damage to the kidneys
Benzol	Red blood cells	Severe poisoning with bleeding into urinary tract
Cadmium	Dark color, red blood cells	Due to kidney irration
Carbon disulfide	Albumin	Kidney damage
Carbon tetrachloride	Albumin, casts, blood cells, impaired function	Due to kidney damage
Cobalt		Questionable
Chlorobenzenes	Albumin, red blood cells, dark color	Kidney damage
Cresol	Albumin, red blood cells	Due to kidney irritation
DDT	Albumin	Kidney degeneration
Dichloroethyl ether		Kidney damage produced in experimental animals
Dioxan	Red blood cells, disturbed function	Hemorrhagic nephritis
Dimethyl sulfate		Kidney damage produced in experimental animals
Ethylene chlorhydrin		Kidney damage produced in experimental animals
Ethylene dichloride		Kidney damage produced in experimental animals
Glycols	Red blood cells, impaired function	Has occurred following ingestion
Lead	Increases phorphyrins, albumin	Questionable
Mercury	Albumin, impaired function	Due to kidney injury
Methyl bromide	Albumin	Kidney damage
Methyl chloride	Albumin	Kidney damage
Methyl formate		Kidney injury has been produced in experimental animals
Naphthols	Albumin, blood cells	Due to irritation of kidneys
Naphthylamines		See Aniline dye intermediates
Nitrobenzol	Albumin, blood cells	Kidney irritation
Oxalic acid	Albumin	Occurs in severe poisoning

(continued)

TABLE 16 (*continued*)

Substance	Findings	Significance
Petroleum hydrocarbons		Kidney damage reported in very severe cases of acute poisoning
Phenols	Albumin, blood cells	Kidney irritation
Phenyl hydrazine		Kidney damage in experimental animals
Tetrachlorethane	Albumin, casts	Due to kidney damage
Thallium		Kidney damage following accidental ingestion
Trinitrophenol		Kidney damage from ingestion
Trinitrotoluol (TNT)	Dark color, albumin, casts, blood cells	Dark color caused by excretion products
Turpentine	Blood cells	Kidney irritation
Uranium	Albumin	Kidney damage
Vanadium	Albumin, blood cells	Kidney damage
Phosphorus		Kidney damage in severe cases

TABLE 17
Normal Blood Values

Test	Normal range	Comments
Red blood cells		
Males	4.5–6.0 million/mm³	
Females	4.0–5.0 million/mm³	
Hemoglobin		Values given in per cent are
Males	14–18 g/100 cm³	meaningless unless the gravi-
Females	12–16 g/100 cm³	metric equivalent of 100%
		is stated.
White blood cells		Total white cell counts fluc-
Total	5000–10,000/mm³	tuate widely from hour to
Differential		hour. Differentia. counts
Band forms	0–5%	remain fairly static.
Segmented	35–70%	
Lymphocytes	20–60%	
Monocytes	2–10%	
Eosinophiles	0–5%	
Basophiles	0–2%	
Platelets	200,000–350,000/mm³	Count varies with method.
Reticulocytes	0.1–0.5%	High values indicate active
		blood regeneration.
Erythrocyte sedi-	Wintrobe method	Values differ in males and
mentation rate	Males 0–9 mm in 1 hr	females.
(ESR)	Females 0–20 mm in	
	1 hr	
	Westergren method	
	Less than 20 mm in	
	1 hr	
Hematocrit	40–48% cell volume	Affected by dehydration.
Mean corpuscular	80–94 μ³	Average size of red blood cells.
volume (MCV)		
Mean corpuscular	27–32 μμg	Average hemoglobin content
hemoglobin (MCH)		per cell.
Mean corpuscular	32–38%	Average concentration of
hemoglobin concen-		hemoglobin in red blood
tion (HCC)		cells.
Red cell fragility	Hemolysis starts in	
	solution of 0.42%	
	NaCl, complete in	
	0.32% NaCl.	
Bleeding time	Less than 3 min	Capillary bleeding
Coagulation time	6–10 min	Venous blood
Appearance of red	Uniform size and	Parasites such as those of
blood cells	staining, appear	malaria may be found in
	circular.	stained blood smears.

(continued)

TABLE 17 (*continued*)

Test	Normal range	Comments
Blood urea	20–35 mg per 100 cm³	Elevated in kidney disease.
Urea nitrogen	9–17 mg per 100 cm³	
Nonprotein nitrogen, (NPN)	15–40 mg per 100 cm³ blood	Elevated in kidney disease.
Total protein (LF)[a]	6.0–8.0 g per 100 cm³	
Serum albumin (LF)[a]	4.0–5.0 mg per 100 cm³	
Serum globulin (LF)[a]	2.0–3.5 mg per 100 cm³	
Albumin–globulin ratio (A/G) (LF)[a]	1.5:1 to 3:1	
Uric acid	2–4 mg per 100 cm³ of blood	
Chlorides		
Total cholesterol (LF)[a]	150–230 mg per 100 cm³	Increased in biliary obstruction, decreased in diseases of liver.
Cholesterol esters (LF)[a]	65–75% on total cholesterol	Decreased in liver disease.
Serum bilirubin (LF)[a]	0.4–1.5 mg per 100 cm³ of serum	Elevated in biliary obstruct.
Alkaline phosphatase (LF)[a]	3.0–4.5 Bodansky units per 100 cm³ of serum	High values in biliary obstruction. Little change in intrinsic liver disease.
Acid phosphatase	0.5–2.0 Gutman units per 100 cm³ of serum	Not related to liver disease.
Blood sugar	90–120 mg per 100 cm³ of blood	
Icterus index (LF)[a]	2–8 units	Frequently used as a measure of jaundice, but unreliable because of interfering substances.
Calcium	8.5–11.5 mg per 100 cm³ of serum	
Chlorides	570–620 mg per 100 cm³ of plasma	
Creatinine	1–2 mg per 100 cm³ of blood	
Oxygen capacity	18–24 cm³ per 100 cm³ of blood	
Potassium	16–22 mg per 100 cm³ of serum	
Sodium	315–30 mg per 100 cm³ of serum	
Phosphorus	3–4 mg per 100 cm³ of serum	Inorganic phosphates.

[a] Tests marked (LF) are used in liver function studies.

TABLE 18. Abnormalities in Blood produced by Occupational Poisons

Substance	Findings	Comments
Acrylonitrile	Anemia, leucocytosis	Reported but not definitely established.
Aniline	Anemia, stippled red cells, leukocytosis	Findings differ in acute and chronic exposure.
Antimony	Leukopenia	Effects may resemble those of arsenic.
Arsenic	Anemia, leukopenia	Industrial poisoning may be caused by arsine.
Benzene	Decrease in all formed elements	Death may result from depression of the bone marrow.
Carbon disulfide	Anemia, leukocytosis, immature WBC	Conflicting reports in medical literature
Carbon tetrachloride	Anemia, leukopenia	Questionable
Cobalt	Increased RBC	Animal experiments only
DDT	Anemia, leukepenia	Rarely occurs.
Ethyl silicate	Anemia, leukocytosis	Animal experiments only
Ethylene glycol monomethyl ether	Decrease in all formed elements, increased % age of immature WBCs	Based on human observations
Ethylene oxide		Questionable
Lead	Mild anemia, stippling of RBC	Well established
Manganese	Leukopenia	Questionable
Mercury	High hemoglobin	Reported but unconfirmed
Methyl chloride	Decrease in formed elements	Animal experiments
Nitrobenzenes (nitro phenols)	Reduced RBC with signs of regeneration	Due to blood destruction
Nitrous fumes	Decreased WBC	Reported but unconfirmed
Phenylhydrazine	Anemia with signs of regeneration	Due to blood destruction
Radium	Decrease in all formed elements	Well established in humans
Selenium	Anemia	Animal experiments
Tetrachlorethane	Signs of blood destruction	Not fully established in
Thallium	Increased WBC and eosinophiles	Reported but unconfirmed
Thorium	Decrease in all formed elements	Due to radioactivity
Toluene	Anemia, leukopenia	Mild when compared with benzene
Toluidine	Anemia	Questionable
Trichlorethylene	Anemia	Reported but unconfirmed
Trinitrotoluene	Anemia, leukopenia	Well established
Uranium	Anemia, leukopenia	Due to radioactivity
Vanadium	Anemia	Questionable
Xylene	Anemia, leukopenia	Questionable

AUTHOR INDEX

Numbers in parentheses are reference numbers and indicate that an author's work is referred to although his name is not mentioned in the text. Numbers in *italics* show the pages on which the complete references are listed.

SUBJECT INDEX

A

Abnormal blood values, from occupational poisons, 903

Abnormal urine values, from occupational poisons, 899–900

Absorbers, absorbents, and adsorbents, 132–163

Absorbers, classification of, 155, 158
efficiency of, 133–136
percentage efficiency of, 133
sequence type, 67
tests for efficiency of, 135

Absorbing devices, for determining gases, 156, 157

Absorption, 162, 163
of radiation, 483

Absorption and adsorption, sampling by, 81, 82

Absorption methods, of dust sampling, 179–183

Absorptions, calculations of efficiency, 134

ACGIH (American Conference of Governmental Industrial Hygienists) method, 235–238

Acid digestion, 370, 371

Adsorbents, efficiency of, 158, 159

Adsorption, activated, 160
factors governing, 158

Adsorption tubes, standard method of filling, 162

Adsorption value, 160, 161

AEC method, for strontium-90, 502–506

Aerosols, 168

Aerosol spectrometer, 257

Air-borne contaminants, action of, 21, 22

Air flow. *See also* Gas flow.
comparison of devices used for, 117

Air flowmeters. *See also* Gas flowmeter.
characteristics of, 91, 116

Airfoil pitometer, 103

Air measurement devices. *See also under* Gas.
calibration of, 118–120

Air pollutants in urban areas, 887

Air pollution, 27

Air sampling, basic methods for, 37–39

Air speed nozzle, 103

Air velocity. *See also* Gas velocity.
characteristics of instruments for, 106

Air volume, determination of, with pitot tube, 101

ALA. *See* δ-Aminolevulinic acid.

Alkalies, 458, 459

Alkali method, for sulfur dioxide, 536, 537

Alkaline iodide method, for ozone, 622–626
acetic acid variation of, 622–626
sulfamic acid variation of, 626

Alpha activity, calculation of, 485
and determination of uranium in urine, 823–825

δ-Aminolevulinic acid (ALA), determination of, 786–788

Ammonia, 609–613
detection and determination of, 610–613
estimation of, by titration, 610, 611
by Nessler's method, 611–613
physiological response to, 610

Ammonia method, for hydrocyanic acid, 734, 735

Ammonium chloride, 613, 614

Ammonium nitrate, 614, 615

Ammonium picrate, 615

Sulfuric acid, 518–526
  determination of, 519–526
  estimation of, 519, 520
  filter paper method for, 525, 526
  spectrophotometric thorin method
    for, 524, 525
  tetrahydroxyquinone method for,
    520, 521
  visual thorin method for, 521–524
Sulfur monochloride, 568, 569
Sulfurous anhydride. *See* Sulfur
  dioxide.
Sulfurous oxychloride. *See* Thionyl
  chloride.
Sulfur trioxide, estimation of, 519,
  520
Sulfur trioxide and sulfur dioxide,
  Flint method for, 562, 563
  lead acetate method for, 562
Sulfur trioxide, sulfur dioxide, and
  hydrogen sulfide, determination
  of, 565, 566
Sulfuryl chloride, 570
Sulfuryl oxychloride. *See* Sulfuryl
  chloride.
Surface catalysis, 160
Suspended particulate matter, in
  urban air, 891–896
  radioactivity in, 492–498
Swinging vane aneometer, 94–97

T

Talvitie method, Landry's modification of, 288–295
Tape samplers, for mercury, 358
Taussky-Jaffe method, for creatine
  and creatinine, 777–779
Tellurium, 431, 432
  detection of, 431, 432
  determination of, 431, 432
    in urine, 811, 812
      short method for, 812, 813
    sodium diethyldithiocarbamate
      method for, 811, 812
Temperature variation, instruments for,
  103–105

Test paper method, for hydrogen
  cyanide, 732
Tetrahydroxyflavanol. *See* Morin.
Tetrahydroxyquinone field test, for
  lead, 315, 316
Tetrahydroxyquinone method, for
  sulfuric acid, 520, 521
Thallium, 433–438
  detection of, 433–438
  determination of, 433–438
    in urine, 804–807
  extraction–titration method for,
    433–436
  Jacobs triphenylmethane dye method
    for, 436–438, 804–807
  separation of, from cadmium, 416
  titrimetric method for, 435, 436
Thermal precipitation, of dust, 186,
  187
Thermocouple anemometer, 104
Thermometer anemometer, 103, 104
Thermopile anemometer, 104
Thief, 85, 86
Thiocyanate method, for cyanide, 732,
  733
Thiocyanates, 571
  pyrazolone method for, 571
Thioglycolic acid method, for tin,
  449
Thionyl chloride, 569
Thomas electric gas meters, 105
Thorin method, spectrophotometric,
  for sulfuric acid, 524, 525
  visual, for sulfuric acid, 521–524
Threshold limit values, 24–26, 857–
  875
  bases for limiting "C" values, 874–
  875
  for mineral dusts, 867
  of mixtures, 870–873
  recommended values for, 859–866
  tentative values for, 868–869
Tin, 447
  determination of, 447–449
  sulfide method for, 448, 449
  thioglycolic acid method for, 449